A GLOSSARY

OF

BOTANIC TERMS

" Indocti discant, et ament meminisse periti."

HÉNAULT, after POPE.

A GLOSSARY OF BOTANIC TERMS

WITH THEIR DERIVATION
AND ACCENT

BY

BENJAMIN DAYDON JACKSON

KNIGHT OF THE POLAR STAR, HON. PH.D. (UPSALA)
EMERITUS SECRETARY OF THE LINNEAN SOCIETY OF LONDON

Fourth Edition

GERALD DUCKWORTH & CO. LTD.
3, HENRIETTA STREET, LONDON, W.C.2

HAFNER PUBLISHING CO. INC.
NEW YORK

First Edition, May 1900

Second Edition, September 1905

Third Edition, July 1916

Fourth Edition, January 1928

Reprinted June 1949, January 1953, February 1960,

January 1965, September 1971

ISBN 0 7156 0144 X

PRINTED BY UNWIN BROTHERS LIMITED
THE GRESHAM PRESS, OLD WOKING, SURREY, ENGLAND
A MEMBER OF THE STAPLES PRINTING GROUP

CONTENTS

"Every other authour may aspire to praise, the lexi-
cographer can only hope to escape reproach."
                                   DR. SAMUEL JOHNSON.

PREFACE

THE task of selecting the terms to be included in any branch of science offers many difficulties : in the case of botany, it is closely linked on with zoology and general biology, with geology as regards fossil plants, with pharmacy, chemistry, and the cultivation of plants in the garden or the field. How far it is advisable to include terms from those overlapping sciences which lie on the borderland is a question on which no two people might think alike. I have given every word an independent examination, so as to take in all, in fact, which might be fairly expected, and yet to exclude technical terms which really belong to another science. Words in common use frequently have technical meanings, and must be included; other technical words are foreign to botany, and must be excluded. Thus " entire " must be defined in its botanic sense, and such purely geologic terms as Triassic and Pleistocene must be passed by. The total number of rare alkaloids and similar bodies recorded in pharmacologic and chemical works, if included, would have extended this Glossary to an inconvenient size; I have therefore only enumerated those best known or of more frequent mention in literature, or interesting for special reasons. Many words only to be found in dictionaries have been passed by; each dictionary I have consulted contains words apparently peculiar to it, and some have been suspected of being purposely coined to round off a set of terms.

The foundations of the list here presented are A. Gray's " Botanical Text-Book," Lindley's " Glossary," and Henslow's " Dictionary," as set forth in the Bibliography. To these terms have been added others extant in the various modern text-books and current literature, noted in the course of reading, or found by special search. The abstracts published in the " Journal of the Royal Microscopical Society " afforded many English equivalents of foreign terms. In drawing up definitions, the terms used to denote colour were found to be so discordant that I was compelled to make a special study of that department, and the result will be found in the " Journal of Botany," xxxvii. (1899), 97–105.

I have carefully considered the criticisms of this work which have come under my notice, and have adopted all those suggestions which could be taken up, so far as they did not contradict the plan on which this volume was drawn; some criticisms were mutually destructive, others were due to insufficient knowledge of the original definitions on the part of the critic, whilst others advocated radical changes, which would have made this, not my book, but some other person's product. I have tried to furnish the terms in use in various periods, so that a paper or book of any period can be read, and its special expressions understood; to cut down the volume would have been therefore unwise, and the attempt would have failed to gain the approval of competent judges, as no two teachers would have agreed upon the exclusion of given terms. In more than one case, an obsolete term has been lately revived.

In issuing a new edition of this book, I should have much preferred to blend old and new into one alphabet; but the increased cost of type-setting has made that impracticable from the publishing point of view, and has necessitated a reprint of the pages here numbered 1 to 414, by photo-zincography.

The total numbers included in this Glossary now amount to nearly 25,000, and if the various meanings were added, they would amount to about 1400 more. The derivations have been carefully checked, but as this book has no pretension to be a philological work, the history of the word is not attempted; thus in " etiolate " I have contented myself with giving the proximate derivation, whilst the great Oxford dictionary cites a host of intermediate forms deduced from *stipella*. The meaning appended to the roots is naturally a rough one, for to render adequately all that may be conveyed by many of the roots is manifestly impossible when a single word must serve. The accent has been added in accordance with the best discoverable usage; where pronunciation varies, I have tried to follow the best usage; in some words such as "medullary" I have given the accent as it is always spoken, though all the dictionaries, except Henslow's, accent it as "med'ullary." When words have become thoroughly anglicised, it would have been mere pedantry to accent them otherwise; we say or'ator, not as in Latin, *ora'tor.* The accent does not imply syllabic division, but when the accent immediately follows a vowel, that vowel is long; if one or more consonants intervene, then the vowel is short; thus *ca'nus*, *cas'sus*, as though they were printed *cā-nus*, *căs-sus*; in a few instances the pronunciation is also given when the word would otherwise be doubtful as to sound.

It has been my duty to condense the definitions, often a difficult matter when a longer explanation would have been easier to draw up. I trust that I have in each case succeeded in setting out the main or central meaning, but many writers have their own modified or restricted meaning of even well-known terms. To still further economise space, words drawn from the same leading word have been grouped into paragraphs, thus obviating the necessity of repeating the leading word with its meaning many times over, and only requiring the additional root to be given; occasionally this has led to the intentional neglect of strict alphabetic sequence. The names of groups of plants have given much trouble; whilst all proposed terms manifestly could not be included, many have become so often quoted as to demand recognition; as a rule I have not admitted groups of even ordinal value, still less of lower rank. Compound terms have been left out when intermediate between the meaning of the primitives; those included seem to require mention on special grounds.

The number of recently-coined terms in ecology and genetics will be noted; I have not included many compound terms, such as "Carex-Sieversia-Polygonum-Coryphium," or its vernacular equivalent, "The Sedge-smartweed-Alpine meadow formation."

Authors' names in parentheses, following definitions, are those who have been taken as authority for such definition, and when the actual language is used, it is indicated by quotation marks; the authority sometimes coincides with the inventor of the term. As instances I may mention the use of "creek," "blow-out,"

" sand-bar " in the American usage of those terms. Substantives in the headings have been shown by the use of a capital letter, adjectives and other parts of speech by a small letter; exceptions being adjectives drawn from a proper name as " Darwinian," and those which form part of such terms as " Conjoint Bundle." Greek is quoted in the original characters, Latin in italic, or where otherwise it would be doubtful, it is indicated; this is further explained on the page facing page 1 of the Glossary; the use of small capitals refers the reader to the word so printed for a definition of the term, or to a correlative term.

The Appendixes hardly need any detailed explanation; it will be seen that the Bibliography is a selected list of works chiefly in alphabetic form, arranged chronologically. General dictionaries, and large works in which technical terms form only a small proportion of the whole, have been omitted.

The pleasant duty now remains of acknowledging most gratefully the invaluable help I have received from a host of friends during the progress of the work. I must name as principal helpers, the following; the star prefixed shows help extended to this edition. Mr. L. A. BOODLE, F.L.S., Mr. N. E. BROWN, A.L.S., Mr. I. H. BURKILL, M.A., Sir FRANCIS DARWIN, F.R.S., Prof. J. B. FARMER, F.R.S., *Dr. R. R. GATES, F.L.S., Prof. M. M. HARTOG, F.L.S., Mr. G. E. MASSEE, A.L.S., Dr. C. E. MOSS, F.L.S., Prof. H. H. W. PEARSON, F.R.S., Mr. R. A. ROLFE, A.L.S., Mr. E. S. SALMON, F.L.S., Dr. D. H. SCOTT, F.R.S., Mr. A. G. TANSLEY, F.R.S., Prof. J. W. H. TRAIL, F.R.S., Dr. HAROLD WAGER, F.R.S., Mr. W. C. WORSDELL, F.L.S., and Mr. C. H. WRIGHT, A.L.S.; their help remains embodied in the text, though six of the helpers have passed away. To all, my indebtedness is great, the value of this Glossary being largely due to their ready aid.

In every volume of similar character to this which I have had to consult, I have found errors, sometimes numerous, occasionally serious. This much larger volume offers a greater chance of error, but I trust that comparatively few errors will be found.

B. DAYDON JACKSON.

CLAPHAM : *August*, 1927.

PUBLISHER'S NOTE

At the time of his death, Dr. Daydon Jackson
was completing the revision of the proofs of
this, the fourth edition of his book.

EXPLANATION

Headings in black type; substantives are shown by the use of an initial capital letter; adjectives and adverbs by the use of a small initial letter (exceptions are explained in the Preface); the sign ~ is used to avoid repetition of the heading; ‡ was used by Lindley to denote a word which is obsolete or improperly formed, and is used here for undoubtedly obsolete terms.

Latin words are shown by being in *Italic* where practicable, elsewhere by the abbreviation Lat. appended; other languages are indicated by Fr. for French, Ger. or Germ. for German, Ital. for Italian.

Cross-references in SMALL CAPITALS are employed to spare repeated definitions; they are usually preceded by the sign of equality, =. When variants do not differ save by the termination, that only is given, but if the accent varies, they are spelled out in full. A few well-known abbreviations are also employed, such as dissyll. for dissyllable, pr. for pronounced, and the like.

A GLOSSARY
OF BOTANIC TERMS

a, privative ; in Greek compounds = without, as apetalous, without petals ; modified into **an-** for euphony.

ab (Lat.), from ; as abnormal, a deviation from rule.

abax'ial (*ab, axis,* an axle) ; (1) applied to an embryo which is out of the axis of the seed by one-sided thickness of the albumen ; (2) the side of a lateral organ away from the axis.

abbre'viated, *abbrevia'tus,* shortened, as when one part is shorter than another ; **Abbrevia'tion,** a selection of those most frequently used will be found in the Appendix.

aber'rant, *aber'rans* (*aberro,* I go astray), differing from usual structure, departing from the type. **Aberra'tion,** non-typical structure.

abiet'ic (*Abies,* a fir-tree), used of certain coniferous products which are not exclusively from *Abies ;* ∼ **Anhy'dride,** the resin in turpentine ; ∼ **Ac'id,** a compound of the last with water, forming a large proportion of the constituents of frankincense ; **abiet'iform Hairs** (*forma,* a form), having a uniseriate main axis, with whorls of ray-cells (Solereder) ; **Ab'ietin,** resin from *Abies pectinata,* DC., and **Ab'ietite,** a sugar from the leaves of the same species ; **abieti'neous, abieti'nean,** allied to or resembling *Abies ;* **abieti'nus** (Lat., made of fir), applied to cryptogams which (1) grow on firs, or (2) resemble a fir-tree in habit, as *Alsia abietina,* Sulliv.

Abiogen'esis (α, not ; βίος, life ; γένεσις, beginning), spontaneous generation ; the assumed origin of living organisms from non-living matter.

Abjec'tion (*abjectio,* a throwing away), casting off spores from a sporophore.

abjoint' (*ab* + joint ; a hybrid word), to delimit by septa or joints.

Abjunc'tion (*abjunctus,* unyoked), cutting off spores on portions of growing hyphae by septa.

Ablacta'tion (*ablacto,* I wean), an inarching.

Ablaquea'tion, *Ablaquea'tio,* loosening the soil round trees.

Ab'last (α, not ; βλαστὸς, a bud or shoot), the entire suppression of an organ, as distinct from ABORTION, in which it remains rudimentary or partially developed (Eichler) ; **ablast'ic,** applied to parts of a flower or other organ which have not been developed ; **ablas'tous,** without germ or bud.

Abnoda'tion (*abnodo,* to clear of knots), cutting away knots from trees.

abnorm'al, *abnorma'lis* (*abnormis,* irregular), deviating from rule, as when stamens are opposite the petals instead of being alternate.

aborig'inal (*ab,* from ; *origo,* a source), indigenous ; not introduced.

Abor'tion (*abortio,* a miscarriage), non-formation or incompletion of a part ; **abort'ive,** *aborti'vus,* imperfectly developed, as abortive stamens when filaments only ; *abort'iens,* becoming abortive.

abra'ded, *abra'sus,* rubbed or scraped off.

abrupt', *abrup'tus,* suddenly ending as though broken off ; **abrupt'ly-acu'minate,** having a point arising from a broad extremity ; ∼ **pin'nate,** a pinnate leaf ending with a pair of leaflets.

Ab'sciss-lay'er, a layer of separation, especially with reference to the phenomena of defoliation.

1

Abscis′sion (*abscissus*, cut off), detachment of spores from a sporophore by the disappearance of a connecting zone.

absinth′ic, referring to *Artemisia Absinthium*, Linn. ; **Absinth′in**, a bitter principle obtained from the same.

ab′solute (*absolu′tus*, perfect, complete), actual, the opposite of relative. The absolute direction of an embryo may be inverted, but erect relatively to the carpel.

Absorp′tion (*absorp′tio*, a swallowing), the act of imbibing liquids or gases.

Abstric′tion (*ab*, from, *strictus*, drawn together), a term which covers both Abjunction and Abscission.

abys′sal (ἄβυσσος, bottomless), applied to organisms existing in the depths of the ocean (Warming).

acalyca′lis (*a*, not ; κάλυξ, a cup) ; (1) having no calyx ; (2) having no adhesion to the calyx ; **acal′ycine**, **acalyc′inous**, *acalyci′nus*, *acal′ycis*, destitute of calyx.

acana′ceous (ἄκανος, a thistle-head ; + ACEOUS), used of prickly plants, such as thistles.

Acanth′a, Acan′thon (ἄκανθα, a thorn), a spine or prickle ; **acantha′ceous** (+ ACEOUS), (1) armed with prickles ; (2) belonging to the natural order Acantha′ceae, the typical genus being *Acanth′us*, Tourn. ; **acanth′ine**, pertaining to that genus ; **acanthocarp′ous** (καρπὸς, fruit), having spiny fruit ; **acanthocla′dous** (κλάδος, a branch), *acanthocla′dus*, with spiny branches ; **acanthoph′orous**, (φέρω, I bear), *acanthoph′orus*, spine-bearing ; **acanthop′odous** (ποῦς, ποδὸς, a foot), having petiole or peduncle furnished with spines or prickles ; **Acanth′ospheres** (σφαῖρα, a sphere), ciliated bodies in the cells of *Nitella*, termed "Stachelkügeln" by the Germans.

Ac′aro-doma′tia (*Acarus*, the typical genus of mites ; δωμάτιον, a little house), formations on plants adapted to shelter *Acari* when they are of service to the host.

Acaroph′ily (φιλέω, I love), mutual advantages between plants and mites ; adj., **acaroph′ilous** ; **acarophyt′ic** (φύτον, a plant), harbouring mites ; **Acarophyt′ism** is the condition itself.

acarpotrop′ic (+ CARPOTROPIC), not throwing off its fruits.

acarp′ous (*a*, not ; καρπὸς, fruit), destitute of fruit.

acaulesc′ent, *acaulesc′ens*, becoming stemless ; **acaul′ine**, **acaul′ose**, **acaul′ous**, *acaul′is*, stemless or seemingly so ; **Acaulo′sia**, abnormal deficiency of stem.

accessor′ial, *accessor′ius*, specially applied to those branches of *Pithophora* arising from near the base of the mother-cell (Wittrock).

Acces′sory (*Accessio*), an addition or appendage ; ∼ **Buds**, those additional to the axillary and normal buds, and frequently assuming their function ; ∼ **Branches**, those which spring from the foregoing ; ∼ **Cell**, the sister-cell of a guard-cell of a stoma ; ∼ **Fruits**, parts which are conspicuous but form no part of the pistil, as the enlarged torus of the strawberry ; a pseudo-carp ; ∼ **Gonid′ia**, formations occurring in Mucorini besides the typical gonidia ; ∼ **Indu′sium**, when the margin of a fern-frond is inflexed over the sorus.

accident′al = ADVENTITIOUS.

acci′sus (Lat.) denotes an end having an acute sinus between two rounded angles.

Acclima′tion (*ac* = *ad*, to, *clima*, climate), used by L. H. Bailey for the natural process of becoming inured to a climate at first harmful ; **Acclimatiza′tion**, is preferred for scientific use, especially when denoting human action in inuring plants to a strange climate.

Accommoda′tion (*accommodatio*, an adjustment), Adaptation.

accresc′ent, *accresc′ens*, increasing in size with age, as the calyx of some plants after flowering.

accrete′ (*accre′tus*, grown together),

agglutinate, naturally grafted.
Accre'tion, *Accre'tio,* (1) growing to
one another ; (2) increase by addition of particles to the outside.

accumb'ent, *accumb'ens,* lying against
another body ; ~ **Cotyle'dons,** those
having their edges against the
radicle, thus o = .

accu'ment (Heinig) = ACCUMBENT.

acellera'tus (Lat.), somewhat acerose.

Acen'ium = ACHENE.

aceph'alous, *aceph'alus* (a, without ;
κεφαλὴ, a head), headless ; used for
an ovary which is not terminated
by the stigma, as in Labiatae.

a'cer, used by some authors instead
of the generally adopted **a'cris,**
(1) sharp, pointed ; (2) acrid, as
in *Ranunculus acris,* Linn.

acera'ceous, relating to the genus
Acer, or its allies ; **acer'ic,** pr.
a-ser'-ik, pertaining to the genus
Acer, the Maple or Sycamore.

a'cerose, a'cerous, *acero'sus* (*acer,*
sharp), needle-shaped, like the
leaves of *Pinus ;* **Acero'sae,** a term
proposed by A. Braun for the
Coniferae.

acer'vate (*acervus,* a heap), heaped
up ; **Acer'vulus** (Lat., a little heap),
pl. **Acer'vuli,** small clusters, as of
Fungi appearing on bark or leaves.

acetab'uliform, *acetabuliform'is* (*Ace-
tabulum,* a cup or vinegar-cruet ;
forma, shape), saucer-shaped, used
of the fructification of some Lichens ;
acetab'ulous, *acetabu'leus, acetabu-
lo'sus* are variations in form of the
word ; **Acetab'ulum** (Lat.), the receptacle of some Fungi.

aceta'rious (*acetaria,* vegetables with
vinegar), relating to salad herbs ;
Ac'etary, Grew's term for salading.

ace'tic, pertaining to vinegar, *ace-
tum ;* ~ **Fermenta'tion,** oxidation
of alcoholic liquids, caused by
the Fungus popularly known as
" Mother of Vinegar," *Bacterium
xylinum,* A. J. Brown ; **ac'etose,**
aceto'sus, sour, acid.

a'ceus, a Latin suffix of resemblance,
as *folia'ceus,* leaf-like ; in English it
becomes **-aceous.**

Achae'na, Achae'nium, = ACHENE.

Achae'nocarp (a, not ; χαίνω, I gape ;
καρπὸς, fruit), or **Ache'nocarp,** any
dry indehiscent fruit.

Achascophy'tum (a, privative ; χάσκω,
I open ; φυτὸν, a plant), a plant with
indehiscent fruit.

acheil'ary (a, without ; χεῖλος, a
lip), wanting a lip, as some
Orchids.

Achene, pr. a-kēn', *Ache'nium* (a, not;
χαίνω, I gape), a small, hard, dry,
indehiscent fruit, strictly of one
free carpel as in the buttercup ;
occasionally consisting of more than
one carpel as in Composites, in the
latter case with adnate calyx. Also
spelt **Akene', Ake'nium,** etc.; **Ache-
no'dium,** a double achene, as the
cremocarp of Umbelliferae.

achlamyd'eous, *achlamyd'eus* (a, without ; χλαμὺς, a cloak), destitute of
perianth, as in willows.

achlorophylla'ceous (a = without, +
CHLOROPHYLLACEOUS), destitute of
chlorophyll.

achromat'ic (a, without ; χρῶμα,
colour) ; (1) without colour, ach-
roous ; (2) not readily taking colour ;
~ **Spindle,** the thread-like protoplasmic figures between the poles
in karyokinesis ; **Achro'matin,**
Flemming's term for the basic
substance of the nucleus, less susceptible of staining than the chromosomes ; the Nuclein of Strasburger ; **achromat'ophile** (φιλέω, I
love), applied to a structure which
does not take staining.

achro'mus, ach'roos (ἄχροος, to be
without colour, pale), colourless ;
hyaline ; **Achro'ocyst** (κύστις, a
cavity), Arbaumont's term for cells
of the terminal meristem, which
have clear contents : *cf.* CYANOCYST ;
Achroodex'trin (+ Dextrin), one of
the group of dextrins not coloured
by iodine : *cf.* ERYTHRODEXTRIN,
AMYLODEXTRIN.

Achyrophy'tum (ἄχυρον, chaff ; φυτὸν,
a plant), a plant with glumaceous
flowers, as grasses.

Acic'ula, (*acus,* a needle), the bristle-like continuation of the rhachilla of a grass; **Acic′ulae**, tooth-like processes of the hymenium of certain Hymenomycetous Fungi; **acic′ular**, *acicula′ris*, (1) slender or needle-shaped, (2) a phase of *Bacterium Termo*, Cohn, when it becomes needle-shaped; ~ **Crystals**, needle-shaped crystals; ~ **Fi′bres**, fibrous cells or raphidines, occurring in Acanthaceae; **acic′ulate**, *acicula′tus*, *aciculi′nus*, superficially marked as if scratched with a pin; **acicu′liform** (*forma*, shape), needle-like.

acido′tus (ἀκιδωτὸς, pointed), when branches or organs end in a spine or hard point.

A′cies (Lat., edge), the edge or angle of certain stems.

ac′iform (*acus*, a needle; *forma*, shape) = ACICULAR.

acina′ceous (*acinus*, a grape seed + ACEOUS), full of kernels.

acinac′ifolius (*acinaces*, a scimitar; *folium*, a leaf), a fleshy leaf, curved like a scimitar; **acinac′iform**, *acinaciform′is*, scimitar-shaped.

acina′rius (*acinus*, a grape-seed), when a stem is covered with vesicles resembling grape-seeds; **Ac′ine**, **Ac′inus**, a single member of such fruits, as the raspberry; a drupel; formerly used for a bunch of fruit, as of grapes; **Acinoden′drus** (δένδρον, a tree), a plant whose fruit is in bunches; **ac′inose**, *acino′sus*, like grapes, or of granular bodies resembling them.

aciphyl′lus (ἀκὴ, a point; φύλλον, a leaf), a linear and pointed leaf.

Acla′dium (α, without; κλάδος, a branch), in *Hieracium*, the peduncle of the terminal flower-head; **Aclythrophy′tum** (κλεῖθρον (?), a door, φυτὸν, a plant), plants whose seeds are supposed to be naked, without a pericarp; **acond′ylose**, **acond′ylous** (κόνδυλος, a knuckle or finger-joint), said of plants which have no joints or nodes.

Aconi′tin, the alkaloid derived from monkshood, *Aconitum Napellus*, Linn.

Ac′orin, a glucoside from *Acorus Calamus*, Linn., which is used in perfumery.

A′corn, the fruit of the oak.

Ac′ospores, -*ae* (ἀκὴ, point, + SPORE), plants having awned seeds, as grasses (Clements).

Acotyle′don (α, without; κοτυληδὼν, used for seed-lobe), a plant destitute of cotyledons or seed-lobes; Cryptogams and such plants as *Cuscuta*; adj. **acotyle′donous**, *a-cotyledo′neus*.

acqui′red (*acquiro*, I acquire), used of those characters which arise in the life-time of the organism as the result of the environment, in distinction to hereditary characters.

acramphib′ryous (ἄκρος, apex; ἀμφὶ, on both sides; βρύω, to bud), plants producing lateral as well as apical buds; **Acramphib′rya**, a division proposed by Endlicher to embrace Dicotyledons and Gymnosperms; **Acran′dry** (ἀνὴρ, ἀνδρὸς, a man), when antheridia occupy the apex of a shoot in Bryophytes; adj. **acran′-drous**; **Acran′thi**, pl. (ἄνθος, a flower), employed by W. Wilson to denote terminal inflorescences in Mosses.

acris, *cf.* ACER.

Acroblaste′sis (ἄκρος, apex; βλαστὸς, a bud), when the germ-tube of Lichens proceeds from an end of the spore; **acroblas′tic**, Celakovsky's term for the branch of an inflorescence which arises from a terminal bud; **Acrob′rya** (βρύω, to bud), plants growing at the point only, as all Acrogens having a distinct axis; adj. **acrob′ryous**; **acrocarp′ous** (καρπὸς, fruit), terminal fruited; a main division of Mosses; **Acrocecid′ium** (+ CECIDIUM), a deformity of the terminal bud, due to gall-insects; **Acrochlamyd′eae** (χλαμὺς, a tunic), a term proposed by Hoeck for all haplostemonous Gamopetalae exclusive of Cucurbitaceae, but inclusive of Umbelliferae; a group considered by him to stand at the head of Dicotyledons ; **Acroconid′-ium** (+ CONIDIUM), used of those conidia which successively mature and break away from the apex of the conidiophore (A. Fischer) ; **acrod′-romous** (δρόμος, a course), venation-strands uniting at the apex of the leaf, as in *Plantago ;* acrofu′gal (*fugio,* a flight), basipetal ; **Ac′rogam** (γάμος, marriage), the same as chal-azogamic ; **acrog′amous** (γάμος, marriage), plants producing the egg-apparatus at the summit of the embryo-sac, as in most Angiosperms (Van Tieghem) ; **Acrog′amy,** may be double, as when the pollen-tube and egg-apparatus are both apical ; or partly basigamic, either of male (pollen-tube) or female (egg-apparatus) (*cf.* BASIGAMOUS) ; **acrog′-enous,** (γένος, race), (1) used of plants growing at the apex, such as **Ac′rogens,** Ferns ; (2) produced at the end of a filament, as some fungus spores ; **Acrogen′esis** (γένεσις, origin), terminal fructification ; **Acro-gonid′ium** (γόνος, offspring, εἶδος, form), a gonidium formed at the apex of a gonidiophore ; **acrog′ynous** (γυνή, a woman), having the stem terminated by female organs, as archegonia ; **acrogyra′tus** (*gyratus,* turned round), having an elastic ring at the point (Lindley) as in *Schizaea.*

Acro′nus (perhaps from ἄκρον, the highest point), Necker's term for an ovary without a basal disk.

acronych′ius (ἄκρος, apex ; ὄνυξ, a claw), curved like the claw of an animal ; **acrop′etal** (*peto,* I seek), produced in a succession towards the apex, as applied to development of organs ; the antithesis of basipetal ; **acroph′-ilus** (φιλέω, I love), dwelling in the alpine region ; **Acrophy′ta** (φυτόν, a plant), alpine plants ; **Acrophyti′a,** alpine plant formations (Clements) ; **Acrosarc′um** (σάρξ, σαρκός, flesh), Des-vaux's term for a berry from an ovary with adnate calyx, as the currant ; **acroscop′ic** (σκοπέω, I see), looking towards the summit ; the reverse of

basiscopic ; **Acrosperm′eae** (σπέρμα, a seed), **Ac′rosperms,** those Angio-sperms which are presumed to have begun with simple porogamous mode of impregnation ; *cf.* PLEUROSPERM ; **Ac′rospire** (σπεῖρα, a coil), Grew's name for the first sprout of a germi-nating seed, the extruded radicle ; **acrospi′red,** germinated, as in malt-ing ; **Ac′rospore** (σπορά, a seed), a spore formed at the summit of a sporophore or filament ; **acrothe′cal** (θήκη, a case), applied to virescent anthers when the polliniferous por-tion is confined to the apex, the lower portion becoming leaf-like (Celakovsky) ; **Acrot′onous** (τόνος, a cord), the tissue of the pollen-sac in Orchids prolonged to the upper end of the anther ; **Acrot′ropism** (τροπή, a turning), the continued direction of a root so long as its apex is uninjured.

Ac′rose = FRUCTOSE.

Ac′tad (ἀκτή, rocky coast ; ἄδης, patro-nymic suffix), a plant of a rocky shore (Clements).

Actinench′yma (ἀκτίς, a ray ; ἔγχυμα, an infusion), cellular tissue formed in a star-shaped manner, as seen in a cross-section of *Juncus ;* **actin′ic,** used of certain rays of the spectrum, which have a powerful effect on growth ; **Act′inism,** the chemical action of sunlight ; **Act′inocarp,** a fruit which is **actinocarp′ic** (καρπός, fruit), having the carpels or pla-centas radiating like the spokes of a wheel ; **actinod′romous** (δρόμος, a course), when veins are palmately or radially arranged, as in *Acer ;* **Actinomor′phy** (μορφή, a change), an ACTINOMORPHIC arrangement ; **actinomorph′ic, -ous,** having flowers of a regular or star pattern, capable of bisection in two or more planes into similar halves ; **Actinomyco′sis,** a disease in the jaw-bone of man and animals attributed to a Fungus, *Nocardia Actinomycosis,* Trev. ; **Act′inostele** (+ STELE), the stele of most roots and certain stems, con-sisting of alternating or radial groups of xylem and phloem within a pericycle (Brebner) ; **actinost'omous** (στόμα, a mouth), radiate structure round the ostioles of Lichens and other Cryptogams.

Actinoph'ryds (*Actinophrys*, Ehrenb., a genus of Rhizopods), Gobi's term for globes with radially-arranged pseudopodia in *Pseudospora*, a parasite on *Vaucheria*.

Acti'um, pl. **Acti'a** (ἀκτή, rocky coast), a rocky seashore plant formation ; **actoph'ilus** (φιλέω, I love), growing on the seashore ; **Actophy'ta**, plants of the rocky shore (Clements).

ac'tive, in a growing condition ; not dormant.

acu'leate, *aculea'tus* (*aculeus*, a sting or prickle), armed with prickles, as the stem of a rose ; **acu'leiform**, *aculeiform'is* (*forma*, shape), prickle-shaped ; **acu'leolate**, *aculeola'tus*, somewhat prickly ; **aculeo'sus**, decidedly prickly ; **Acu'leus** (Lat.), a sharp epidermal emergence, a prickle ; pl. **Acu'lei** ; **Acu'leolus**, a diminutive of the last.

Acu'men (Lat., a point), a tapering point; **acu'minate**, *acumina'tus*, having a gradually diminishing point ; **acuminifo'lius** (*folium*, a leaf), with acuminate leaves ; **acu'minose**, *acumino'sus*, approaching acuminate; **acumin'ulate**, having a small terminal point.

acutang'ular, *acutang'ulus*, (Lat.), when stems are sharply angular ; **acutate'** (*acu'tus*, sharp), slightly sharpened, as at the apex ; **acu'te**, *acu'tus*, distinctly and sharply pointed, but not drawn out ; **acutiflor'us** (Lat., *flos*, *floris*, a flower), with acute perianth segments ; **acutifo'lius** (Lat., *folium*, a leaf), with pointed leaves ; **acutilo'bus** (Lat., *lobus*, a lobe), composed of lobes which are acute ; **acutius'culus** (Lat.), somewhat acute.

acyanophor'ic (α, not; κύανος, dark blue; φορός, bearing), applied to plants which do not produce cyanogen ; **acyc'lic** (κύκλος, a circle), used of flowers whose parts are arranged spirally, not in whorls.

ad (-αδης, patronymic suffix) used by Clements as an addition meaning ECAD.

Adapta'tion (*adaptatus*, fitted), the means by which an organism adapts itself to changed surroundings ; ~ **Direct'or**, employed to denote an advantageous change by reaction to a stimulus (Lotsy) ; *cf.* BIAIOMETA-MORPHOSIS ; **adapt'able**, "able to originate Ecads" (Clements); **adapt'ive** modifications are those which obviously fit an organism to exist in given environments, and perhaps produced by the latter ; ~ **Par'a-sites**, saprophilous fungi become parasitic ; ~ **Ra'ces**, morphologically identical, but differing physiologically ; *cf.* BIOLOGIC RACES.

adax'ial (*ad*, to ; *axis*, an axle), the side or face next the axis, ventral.

adducent'ia Va'sa (*ad*, to ; *duco*, I lead), the spirals in tracheids, which spirals were formerly supposed to be vessels ; **Adducto'res**, Hedwig's term for archegonia.

Adelogam'icae, (ἄδηλος, unknown ; γάμος, marriage), Radlkofer's term for Fungi and Lichens ; **adelosiphon'ic** (σίφων, a tube), applied to a DICTYOSTELE when complex, and ceasing to be tubular (Brebner).

Adelph'ia (ἀδελφός, a brother) ; (1) a fraternity ; a collection of stamens by their filaments into one bundle ; pl. **Adelph'iae**, two or more similar bundles ; (2) used by Galton for fraternities in variation ; **adelph'ic**, *adelph'icus;* **adelph'ous**, *adelph'us*, having brotherhoods of stamens ; **Adelphog'amy** (γάμος, marriage), fertilization between neighbouring plants of the same species ; **Adelph-oph'agy** (φάγος, a glutton), the union of two gametes of the same sex (Giard) ; **Adelphotax'y** (τάξις, order), used by Hartog to express the mutual attraction of spores of *Achyla* and of Pedastreae after extrusion.

Ade'lome (possibly from ἄδηλος, concealed) = ALBURNUM (Lindley).

Aden (ἀδήν, a gland), a gland or

tubercle : **aden′iform** (*forma*, shape), a hybrid term for gland-shaped ; **adenoca′lyx** (καλὺξ, a cup), where the calyx is studded with glandular spots ; **Ade′nocyst** (κύστις, a cavity), the membrane of a cell or cells surrounding a gland (Vuillemin) ; **ad′enoid** (εἶδος, like), gland-like ; ~ **Or′gan**, Williamson's term for the ligule of *Lepidodendron ;* **Adenopet′aly** (πέταλον, a flower leaf), a term proposed by C. Morren for the transformation of nectaries into petals, or similar structures ; **Ade′nophore** (φορέω, I bear), a stalk supporting a gland ; **adenoph′orous**, bearing glands ; **adenophyl′lous** (φύλλον, a leaf), glandular leaved ; **adenop′odous**, *aden′opus* (πούς, ποδὸς, a foot), with the petiole or peduncle glandular ; **adenoste′mon** (στήμον, a stamen), having glands on the stamens ; **ad′enose, ad′enous**, glandular.

Ades′my (a, without ; δεσμὸς, a bond), Morren's term for congenital separation of parts normally united.

Adflux′ion (*ad*, to ; *fluxio*, a flowing), the attraction by which sap is drawn towards the leaves.

adglu′tinate, *adglutina′tus* (*ad*, to ; *glutino*, I glue), grown together, accrete.

adhe′rent, *adhe′rens* (*adhaereo*, I stick to), the union of parts usually separate ; ~ **Verna′tion**, when the bases of Fern-fronds are continuous with the caudex ; **Adhe′rence, Adhe′sion**, the state of union with some other organ or part ; Goebel restricts it to union of dissimilar parts ; *cf.* COHESION.

Adichog′amy (a, without + DICHOGAMY), both sexes developed at the same time (Knuth).

Adipocel′luloses (*adeps, adipis*, fat, + Cellulose), a group of bodies which constitute the cuticular tissues of leaves and fruits ; *cf.* CELLULOSE.

adisca′lis (a, without ; δίσκος, a quoit), destitute of a disk.

Adjust′ment (*ad,*to;*justus*, right, just), used for the functional response to a stimulus.

adli′gans (*ad*, to ; *ligo*, I tie), holding fast or binding, as the aërial hold-fasts of ivy ; **ad′ligant, al′ligant** (Heinig) ; *cf.* ADLIGANS.

Adminic′ulum (Lat., a prop) = FULCRUM.

admoti′vus (*ad*, to ; *moveo*, I move), when in germination the albumen remains attached to the sheath of the cotyledon.

adnas′cent, *adnas′cens* (*adnascor*, to grow to), growing to or upon something else ; **Adnas′cens** ; (1) a young bulb, as a "clove" of garlic ; (2) a sucker of some Monocotyledons.

ad′nate, *adnatus* (*adnascor*, I grow to), attached the whole length, ~ **Anth′ers** have the lobes attached their entire length to the filament ; **Adna′tion**, the state in question.

adnexed′ (*adnexo*, I tie), used of the lamellae of some Agarics, which reach the stem, but are not adnate to it.

ad′pressed, *adpress′us* = APPRESSED.

adscend′ent = ASCENDENT.

adsurg′ent, *adsurg′ens* = ASSURGENT.

adunc′ate,adunc′ous (*aduncus*,hooked), bent or crooked as a hook.

adust′us (Lat., swarthy), soot-coloured, fuliginous.

adventit′ious, *adventit′ius* (*ad*, to ; *venio*, I come), applied to plants lately introduced ; ~ **Buds**, those produced abnormally, as from the stem instead of the axils of the leaves ; ~ **Roots**, those which do not arise from the radicle or its subdivisions, but from another part ; **advent′ive** = ADVENTITIOUS.

ad′verse (*ad*, to ; *verso*, I turn) ; (1) opposite ; (2) facing the main axis or other object ; **adversifo′liate**, *adversifo′lius* (*folium*, a leaf), having opposite leaves ; **advers′us** (Lat.), opposite.

Adynaman′dry (ἀδυναμία, weakness ; ἀνήρ, ἀνδρὸς, a man), Delpino's term for self-sterility ; that is, when a flower does not set seed from its own pollen.

aec′ial, aecid′ial, relating to or resembling the form-genus *Aecidium ;* ~

Form, a fungus in that stage of development ; **Aecid′iolum**, in Uredineae, a small form and usually a later development of the *Aecidium*-stage ; a spermogonium.

Aecid′iospore (*Aecidium*, infra ; σπορὰ, a seed), a spore formed in the following : **Aecid′ium** (probably from οἰκίδιον, a little house), a sporocarp consisting of a cup-shaped envelope, its interior surface consisting of a hymenium, from whose basidia the aecidiospores are successively thrown off ; the name was propounded by Persoon as a genus of Fungi, but it is now regarded as only a form-genus of Uredineae.

Ae′ciospore (+ SPORE) = AECIDIOSPORE ; **Æ′cium**, Arthur's term for AECIDIUM.

Aecol′ogy = ECOLOGY or OECOLOGY.

Aegagropi′lae, pl. (αἴγαγρος, a wild goat ; πῖλος, felt), Lagerheim's term for those marine Algae which are more or less spherical, and freely driven about in the sea.

aeloph′ilous (ἄελλα, storm-wind; φιλέω, I love), applied to plants disseminated by wind.

aeo′lian (αἰόλος, shifting), used of sandy soils liable to rapid removal by wind (Clements).

ae′neus (Lat., bronze), used for brass-coloured ; sometimes for verdigris.

aequa′lis, ae′quans (Lat.), equal or equalling ; similar in size, uniform ; **aequilat′eral**, *aequilatera′lis*, equal-sided, of equal length ; **aequali-flor′us** (Lat.), with flowers alike in form and character ; **aequimag′nus** ‡ (Lat.), equal sized ; **aequinoc′tial**, *aequinoctia′lis*, pertaining to the equinox ; used of flowers, which open or close at stated hours ; **aequivalv′is** (Lat.), having valves of flowers or fruit of similar size ; **aequive′nius** (Lat.), all the veins are equal distinctness.

aë′rating (*aër*, air) **Roots**, peculiar roots rising out of the mud, covered with a loose, corky tissue, and having large intercellular spaces ; **Aërench′yma** (ἔγχυμα, that poured

out), Schenk's term for a tissue of thin-walled cells, and large intercellular spaces, found in the stems of some marsh-plants, serving for aëration or floating tissue : adj.

aërenchy′matous ; aë′rial, *aë′rius*, used for plants (or parts of plants) living above the surface of the ground or water ; ~ **Plants**, epiphytes as, *Tillandsia* and many tropical orchids ; ~ **Roots**, those which vegetate altogether above the ground.

ae′reus (Lat.), copper-coloured or bronzed.

A′ërobe (βίος, life), a suggested abbreviation of AEROBIUM ; **aëro′bic**, pertaining to such organisms ; ~ **Energe′sis**, the disruptive process by which energy is released (Barnes) ; *cf.* RESPIRATION ; **Aërobi′ont**, a plant dependent upon free oxygen for its respiration ; **aërobiot′ic**, needing air for existence ; **Aërobio′sis**, life in atmospheric air ; **Aërob′ium**, an organism which thrives only in the presence of air or free oxygen ; applied to certain bacteria ; **Aëro-car′py** (καρπὸς, fruit) producing fruit above ground ; *cf.* AMPHICARPY, GEOCARPY ; **Aë′rocyst** (κύστις, a bag or pouch), the air-bladders of such algae as *Fucus vesiculosus*, Linn. ; **A′ërogams** (γάμος, marriage), phanerogams ; **Aëroidot′ropism** (τροπὴ, a turning) = AEROTROPISM ; **Aëromorpho′sis** (μόρφωσις, a shaping), changes in water plants induced by growth in air (Herbst) ; **aëroph′ilous** (φιλέω, I love), (1) Beyerinck's term for essentially aërobiotic organisms ; *cf.* MICROAËROPHILOUS ; (2) Areschoug's term for renovation buds produced above ground ; *cf.* PHOTOPHILOUS ; ~ **Shoot**, the growth from such ; **Aë′ropyle** (πύλη, a gate), a pore at the base of the pod in certain Leguminosae, as *Faba vulgaris* (A. H. Church) ; **Aë′rophyte** (φυτὸν, a plant), air-plant, epiphyte ; **Aërotax′is** (τάξις, arrangement), used by Hartog to express positive stimulus by oxygen to the irritability of zoospores, adj. **aërotact′ic** ; **Aërot′ropism**

($τροπή$, a turning), the influence of gases on growth and curvature; it is a form of CHEMOTROPISM; adj. **aërotrop′ic.**

aeru′ginose, aerug′inous, *aerugin′eus, aerugino′sus,* (*aerugo,* the rust of brass), the blue-green colour of verdigris.

Aesc′ulin, an alkaloid from the horse-chestnut; *Aesculus Hippocastanum,* Linn.

Aestatifrutice′ta, pl. (*aestas,* the hot season; *fruticetum,* a thicket), deciduous bush formation; **Aestatisil′vae,** pl. (*silva,* a wood), deciduous forests.

Aesthe′sia ($α'ίσθησις$, perception by sense), Czapek's expression to denote the capacity of an organ to respond to definite physical stimuli; **Aesthe′sis,** the apparent perception on the part of a root (Czapek).

aes′tival, *aestiva′lis,* belonging or peculiar to summer; **Aestiva′ria,** the summer quarters of plants in botanic gardens.

Aestiva′tion, *Aestiva′tio,* the manner in which the parts of a flower are folded up before expansion.

Aestuar′ium (Lat., a tidal estuary), applied to a flat shore which is flooded with sea-water at spring-tides (Warming).

Aete′rio = ETAERIO.

Aetha′lium ($α'ίθαλος$, soot), a compound sporiferous body, formed from a combination of plasmodia in Myxogastres; *Ae. septicum,* Fr., is known as "Flowers of Tan"; **aetha′lioid** ($ε'ίδος$, form), like the last

aëthe′os ($ἀήθης$, unusual), in compounds = unusual; **aëtheogam′ic, aëtheog′amous** ($γάμος$, marriage), synonymous with cryptogamic.

aethe′reus (Lat.), aërial.

aetiog′enous ($α'ίτιον$, cause; $γενὸς$, offspring), caused externally; *cf.* AITIO-; **Aetiol′ogy** ($λόγος$, discourse), the doctrine of the cause of disease, as of Vegetable Galls; also spelled **Aitiology** and **Etiology.**

Affin′ity (*affin′itas,* near alliance), the closeness of relation between plants as shown by similarity of important organs.

affix′ed (*affix′us,* fastened to), fixed upon.

afo′liate ($α$, without; *folium,* a leaf), leafless; a hybrid word for APHYLLOUS.

Aft′er-ri′pening, applied to the period of dormancy in many seeds before germination, as those of *Crataegus.*

Ag′ad ($ἀγὴ$, beach), a beach plant; **Agi′um,** an association of beach plants (Clements).

Ag′amae ($α$, without; $γάμος$, marriage) = Cryptogamae; **Agamandroe′cism** (+ ANDROECIUM), in Compositae, having male and neuter flowers in the same individual; **agam′ic, ag′amous,** Necker's term for cryptogamous; **Agamob′ium** ($βίος$, life), Harvey Gibson's term for the asexual generation in organisms showing alternation of generations; the sporophyte; **Agamogen′esis** ($γένεσις$, origin), asexual reproduction by buds, gemmae, etc.; **Agamogynae′cism** (+ GYNAECEUM), in Compositae, having female and neuter flowers in the same individual; **Agamo-gynomonoe′cism,** the presence of neuter, female, and perfect flowers in the same individual; **Agamo-hermaph′roditism** (+ HERMAPHRODITE), with hermaphrodite and neuter flowers in the same plant; **Agamonoe′cia** (+ MONOECIA), used by Engler and Prantl for those plants which have hermaphrodite and barren flowers in the same inflorescence, as *Viburnum Opulus,* Linn.; **Agamonoe′cism,** the condition named; **Agamophy′ta** ($φυτὸν$, a plant), C. MacMillan's term for protophytes; **Agam′ospore** ($σπορὰ$, a seed), a spore or gonidium produced asexually; **agamotrop′ic** ($τροπή$, a turn), applied to flowers which remain open without closing.

A′gar, a gelatinous product from Agar-agar, or Agal-agal, which consists of various marine Algae from tropical Asia; also called "Ceylon Moss" and "Bengal Isinglass."

Agar′ic Acid (*Agaricus*, Tourn., a genus of Fungi), found in *Polyporus officinalis*, Fr. ; **agaricic′ola** (*colo*, I inhabit), applied to a parasite on Hymenomycetous Fungi ; J. S. Henslow prints it as **agaric′olus.**

agen′ius ‡ (*a*, without ; γένος, sex, race) = neuter ; **a′genus**, used of cellular Cryptogams, "which are enlarged by the addition of new parts."

ageotrop′ic (+ GEOTROPIC), negatively geotropic.

Agged′ula (derived by Necker from ἀγγείδιον, a little vessel), the sporangium of Mosses, and of *Puccinia.*

Ag′geres (Lat.), banks or rockwork in botanic gardens.

agglom′erate, agglom′erated, *agglomera′tus* (Lat., crowded together), collected into a head, as the flowers of Scabious.

agglu′tinate (*agglutino*, I glue), glued together, as the pollen-masses of Asclepiads or Orchids ; accrete.

ag′gregate, ag′gregated, *aggrega′tus* (Lat., assembled), collected together, as the flowers of *Cuscuta ;* ∼ **Flowers**, those gathered into a head, as *Dipsacus*, but not as in Compositae, which are capitulate ; ∼ **Fruits**, collection of separate carpels produced by one flower, the product of a polycarpellary apocarpous gynaeceum ; ∼ **Spe′cies**, a super-species, which may be compounded of more than one true species ; **Aggrega′tion**, (1) condensation of cell-contents under some stimulus ; (2) the coming together of plants into groups (Clements).

Ag′rad (ἀγρὸς, a field), a cultivated plant (Clements).

agrar′ian (*agrar′ius*, pertaining to the field). H. C. Watson's term for the cultivable portion of Great Britain; ∼ **Region**, divided into three ∼ **Zones**, the super-, mid-, and inferagrarian zones.

agrest′al (*agrestis*, belonging to the field) ; (1) Watson's term for plants growing in arable ground ; (2) rural generally.

Agric′ola (Lat., a rustic), a native or country dweller.

agricult′ural Bot′any (*agricultura*, husbandry), that part of economic botany which relates to farm plants ; **agricult′ural Spe′cies**, so-called, are constant forms or varieties of cultivated plants, as maize, wheat, etc.

Agri′um (ἀγρὸς, a field), "a culture formation" ; **Agroc′olus** (Clements) = AGRICOLA, a native of the fields ; **agroph′ilus**, "dwelling in grain fields " ; **Agrophy′ta**, " culture plants " (Clements).

Agropyre′tum, a formation of *Agropyrum* grasses.

Agrostog′raphy(ἄγρωστις,grass; γραφὴ, writing), the description of grasses ; **Agrostol′ogist**, an expert or writer on grasses ; **Agrostol′ogy** (λόγος, discourse), the botany of grasses.

agyna′rius ‡ (*a*, without ; γυνὴ, a woman) ; **agyn′icus** ; (1) said of stamens which are free from the ovary ; (2) pistils wanting, destitute of pistils ; **ag′ynous**, monstrous flowers with pistils missing.

aheliotrop′ic (*a*, not : ἥλιος, the sun ; τρυπὴ, a turn), neutral to light, neither attracted to nor repelled by it ; more correctly APHELIOTROPIC.

aianth′ous (ἀεί, ever ; ἄνθος, a flower), (1) constantly flowering ; (2) everlasting flowers, as *Helichrysum.*

Aigiali′um (αἰγιαλὸς, seashore), a beach-plant formation ; **aigialoph′ilus** (φιλέω, I love), beach-loving ; **Aigialophy′ta** (φυτὸν, a plant), beach or strand plants (Clements).

Ai′gret (Fr., Aigrette, tuft of feathers), the pappus of Compositae ; Englished by T. Martyn as **E′gret.**

aima, in Greek compounds = blood-coloured ; properly **hæma** (from αἷμα, blood).

aiophyl′lus (αἰὼν, eternity ; φύλλον, a leaf), evergreen.

Aiphyll′ium (ἀείφυλλος, evergreen), an evergreen forest formation ; **aiphylloph′ilus** (φιλέω, I love), growing in such forests ; **Aiphyllophy′ta** (φυτὸν, a plant), plants forming evergreen forests; **Aiphyti'a**, ultimate or fixed formations (Clements).

Air-Blad'ders, intercellular spaces in some Algae, serving as floats; ~ **Cav'ity** = ~ -CHAMBERS (2); ~ -**Cells**, ~ -**Chambers**, (1) intercellular spaces occurring in aquatic plants, usually prismatic in form, (2) the intercellular space beneath a stoma; ~ **Passage**, = ~ -CHAMBER; ~ -**Plants**, epiphytes, as Bromeliads and some Orchids; ~ **Pores**, (1) = STOMATA, (2) Pneumathodes of Hepaticae, ~ **Roots** = PNEUMATOPHORES; ~ **Sacs**, cavities in the pollen-grains of *Pinus*; ~ **Vessels**, term formerly applied to empty tracheids, etc.

Aithali'um (ἀειθαλής, an evergreen thicket), a formation of evergreen thickets; **aithaloph'ilus** (φιλέω, I love), plants delighting in such habitats; **Aithalophy'ta** (φυτόν, a plant), plants composing such formations (Clements).

aitiogen'ic, aitiog'enous (αἴτιος, causing; γένος, offspring), due to external causes; **Aitiomorpho'sis** (μόρφωσίς, change), change in shape caused by external factors (Pfeffer), adj. **aitiomorph'ous**; **aitionast'ic** (ναστός, pressed close), bent from some external cause **Aitionas'ty**, the condition itself; **aitionom'ic, aition'omous** (νόμος, law), due to external circumstances, as growth-curvature; **Aition'omy** is the condition; **Aitiot'ropism** (τροπή, a turning), movement depending upon outside causes; adj. **aitiotrop'ic**; **aitog'enous** = AITIOGENOUS.

akar'yote (α, without; κάρυον, a nut), the chromidial condition after the close of the vegetative phase in Plasmodiophoraceae, when the nucleus has disappeared.

Akene', Ake'nium, = ACHENE, ACHENIUM.

Akine'sis (α, without; κίνησις, movement), increase without the phenomena of karyokinesis; **A'kinetes**, in green Algae, single cells whose walls thicken and separate off from the thallus, corresponding to the

chlamydospores of Fungi; immotile reproductive cells, formed without true cell-formation, or rejuvenescence.

Akla'dium = ACLADIUM.

A'la (Lat., wing), (1) formerly an axil, but now obsolete in that sense; (2) a lateral petal of a papilionaceous flower; (3) a membranous expansion of any kind, as in the seed of Bignoniaceae; (4) employed by Wm. Smith for the marginal processes in *Surirella;* (5) the outer segment of the coronal lobes in some Asclepiads; (6) in Mosses, the **a'lar** cells are those at the basal angle of a leaf.

Alabas'trum (Lat., bud), a flower-bud.

a'lar, *ala'ris* (*ala*, wing), (1) formerly used for AXILLARIS; (2) ~ **Cells**, *cf.* ALA (6).

alate', *ala'tus* (Lat., winged), furnished with an expansion, as a stem or petiole; **alatepinna'tus**, when the common petiole of a pinnate leaf is marginally winged.

alba'tus (Lat.), whitened; **Albe'do** (Lat.), whiteness; **Albefac'tion** (*facio*, I make), blanching; **albes'cent**, *albes'cens*, becoming white; **al'bicant**, *al'bicans*, tending to white: **Albica'tion**, becoming blanched or variegated with white; **albid'ulus**, **al'bidus, albin'eus** (Lat.), whitish; **Al'binism**, a disease from absence of normal colouring, producing an **Albi'no**: *albi'nus*, **al'bulus** (Lat.), somewhat white.

Al'bumen (Lat., white of an egg), the nutritive material stored within the seed, and in many cases surrounding the embryo. (NOTE. Not to be confounded with animal Albumen.) Restricted by Van Tieghem to the result of the development of the TROPHIME, the central nucleus of the embryo-sac; **Al'bumin**, in plants, the proteids which readily coagulate from their aqueous solutions by the action of heat or acids; **Albu'minates**, nitrogenous substances insoluble in water, soluble in dilute acids or alkalies, *e. g.* gluten of wheat ; **Albu'minoids** (εἶδος, resemblance), nitrogenous organic substances, proteids ; **albu'minose, albu'minous,** *albumino'sus,* containing albumen, a term restricted to seeds ; **Albumo'ses,** similar to albuminates, but soluble in water ; common constituents of aleuron.

Albur'nitas (*alburnum,* sap-wood), a disease in trees, a tendency to remain soft like the recent wood ; **albur'nous,** relating to the sap-wood ; **Albur'num,** the outermost and youngest portion of the wood, still permeable by fluids.

al'bus (Lat.), dead white, without lustre.

Alcaliot'ropism (alkali, Fr. ; τροπή, a turning), chemotropism induced by alkalies (Massart).

Alchemille'tum, an association of *Alchemilla* plants.

Alcohol'ase, the same enzyme as ZYMASE.

alcohol'ic Fermenta'tion, *see* FERMENTATION.

Al'der-Will'ow association, a wood usually showing a dominance of alder, with a mixture of willows, and sometimes of ash and oak.

alector'ioid (*Alectoria,* Ach., εἶδος, resemblance), filamentous, as the thallus of the genus after which it is named.

alepido'tus, ‡ (α, not; λεπιδωτὸς, scaly), destitute of scurf or scales.

Ale'tophytes (ἀλήτης, vagrant ; φύτον, a plant), ruderal or wayside plants (Clements).

Aleu'ron, or **Aleu'rone** (ἄλευρον, wheaten flour), proteid granules of globulins and peptones, present in seeds, ~ **Lay'er,** a special peripheric layer in most seeds, especially in grasses ; adj., **aleuron'ic.**

Alex'ine (ἀλέξω, I ward off), a substance hypothetically assumed to be formed by plants for protection against bacteria ; antitoxine.

Al'gae (*alga,* seaweed), chlorophyll-containing Thallophytes, which usually grow immersed in water, fresh or marine ; known popularly as

" Seaweeds," or "Waterweeds" ; **al'gal,** relating to Algae ; ~ **-Layer,** the green band of gonidia in the thallus of heteromerous lichens, also styled ~ **-Zone** ; **algi'nus** ‡ resembling a thread-like Alga ; **Al'gist** = **Algol'ogist,** a student of Algae ; **al'goid** (εἶδος, resemblance), like an Alga ; **Al'go-li'chenes,** Lindsay's term for certain transitional forms between Algae and Lichens ; **al'gous** = ALGAL ; **Algol'ogy,** (λόγος, discourse), the science of Algae ; **Algs,** F. von Mueller's word for Algae.

A'lien, used by H. C. Watson for introduced plants which have become naturalised in Britain.

alif'erous (*ala,* a wing ; *fero,* I bear), having wings ; **al'iform** (*forma,* shape), wing-shaped ; **alig'erous** (*gero,* I bear) = ALIFEROUS (Crozier).

alig'ular (*a,* from ; *ligula,* strap), Russow's term for that leaf-face in *Selaginella* which is turned away from the ligule and stem.

Alimo'nia ‡ (Lat., nourishment) = ascending sap.

Al'iquote (*aliquot,* some, in numbers), the constant of temperatures for a given event in the life-cycle of an organism ; the sum-temperature of the event divided by the total sum-temperature of the year (Linsser).

-alis, Latin termination indicative of belonging to ; thus *radic-alis,* belonging to the root, *radix.*

alisma'ceous (*Alisma,* Dill., + CEOUS), belonging to the order Alismaceae, of which the genus named is the type.

Aliz'arine (Fr., Alizari, madder-root), the colouring matter of the root of madder, *Rubia tinctoria,* Linn.

Alkachlor'ophyll (Alkali + CHLOROPHYLL), a presumed constituent of chlorophyll, produced by the action of an alkali ; **alkales'cent,** of the nature of an alkali ; **Alk'aloids** (εἶδος, resemblance), general term for the organic bases in many plants, markedly medicinal or poisonous, as Morphia, Strychnia.

allagophyll'ous (ἀλλαγή, a change ;

φύλλον, a leaf), alternate-leaved ;
allagoste′mon, allagostem′onous,
when stamens are attached alternately to the petals and the torus.
allanto′dioid, applied to ferns which
resemble the genus *Allantodia,* R.
Br., in habit or fructification.
allant′oid (ἀλλᾶς, a sausage ; εἶδος,
form), sausage-shaped ; **Allanto-
spor′ae** (+ SPORA), Traverso's term
for cylindrical spores somewhat
lunate.
allassoton′ic (ἀλλάσσω, I vary ; τόνος,
turgescence), movements of mature
organs, caused by augmentation of
turgor with diminution of volume.
Allautogam′ia (ἄλλος, other ; αὐτὸς,
self ; γάμος, marriage), unusual
method of pollination (Clements).
Allegog′amy = ALLOG′AMY.
Alle′lomorph (ἀλλήλως, mutually ;
μορφή, shape), applied to "unit-
characters existing in antagonistic
pairs " (Bateson) ; *cf.* HYPALLELO-
MORPH ; adj. **allelomor′phic** ; **Alle-
lomor′phism,** the condition in
question ; **Allelosit′ism** (σῖτος, food),
Norman's term for SYNTROPHY ;
All′esy or **Alle′sis,** employed by
Massart for the power of an organ
to show interference.
allia′ceous, *-ceus* (*allium,* garlic, +
ACEUS), having the smell of garlic
or onions ; **allia′rius** (Lat.) is a
synonym.
Alli′ance, a group of Families now
usually styled COHORT.
Alliga′tor (*alligo,* I bind) = FULCRUM.
Allochlor′ophyll (ἄλλος, another, +
CHLOROPHYLL), a second green substance accompanying chlorophyll
(Schunck and Marchlewski) ; **allo-
ch′rous** (χρόα, complexion), changing
from one colour to another ; **Allo-
car′py** (καρπὸς, fruit), fruiting from
cross-fertilized flowers ; **Allog′amy**
(γάμος, marriage), cross-fertilization :
sub-divided into GEITONOGAMY, from
another flower on the same plant,
and KENOGAMY, from another plant
of the same species ; adj. **allog′am-
ous** ; **All′ogene** (γένος, descent), the
recessive element of a couplet or

pair of Allelomorphs ; *cf.* PROTO-
GENE (Pearson); **Allomet′ron** (μέτρον,
a measure), a quantitative change,
the genesis of new proportions in
an existing character (H. F. Osborn).
Allöol′ysis (ἀλλοῖος, different ; λύσις,
loosing), applied to the mode in
which natural diastase acts on the
endosperm of the date, and the
changes thereby caused.
Al′losperm (ἄλλος, another ; σπέρμα, a
seed), an embryo arising through
ALLOGAMY (MacMillan) ; **Al′lospore**
(+ SPORA), a spore which gives rise
ultimately to a gametophyte (Radlkofer) ; **Allot′rophy** (τροφή, nourishment), (1) when plants are not in a
condition to assimilate CO_2 (Pfeffer);
(2) the condition of flowers of low
adaptation to insect-visitors (Loew) ;
allot′ropous (τροπή, a turn), Mac-
Leod's term for plants having stores
of honey open to all insect-visitors ;
Allot′ropy, otherwise turned or
formed ; adj. **allotrop′ic** ; **allotyp′ic,**
proposed by Strasburger in place of
atypic mitosis ; heterotypic followed
by homotypic nuclear division :
Allozy′gote (+ ZYGOTE), a homozygote displaying recessive characters
exclusively (K. Pearson).
Allu′ring Glands of *Nepenthes,* glands
in the pitchers which tempt insects
down the tube (Macfarlane).
Alne′tum, an association of alder
plants, *Alnus.*
alpes′trine, *alpes′tris,* strictly appli-
cable to plants growing above the
limit of forest growth, on the Alps,
but practically synonymous with
Alpine ; **alpes′ter** (Lat.) is used by
some botanists for the more usual
form.
alphitomor′phous (ἄλφιτον, pearl
barley ; μορφή, form), like barley-
meal ; applied to certain fungi.
alp′igene (*alpig′ena,* bred in the Alps)
= ALPINE.
alp′ine, *alpi′nus,* properly denoting
plants belonging to the Alps (*alpes,*
mountains), but frequently used in
a wider sense, embracing alpestrine,
as well as the higher situated plants ;

~**Regions**, defined thus by Schimper: **ba′sal**~, hygrophilous warmthloving plants of the foothills; **mon′tane**~, the same as the last, but able to endure cooler temperature; **alp′ine**~, restricted to actual alpine plants.

Al′sad (ἄλσος, a grove, + AD), a grove plant; **Alsi′um**, a grove formation; **alsoph′ilus** (φιλέω, I love), groveloving plants; **Alsophy′ta** (φυτὸν, a plant), grove plants (Clements); **alsoc′olus** (Clements) = **alsoc′ola**, dwelling in groves.

alsina′ceous (*Alsine*, Tourn., +CEOUS), (1) used of a petal having a short, but distinct claw; (2) belonging to, or resembling the group of plants of which *Alsine* is the typical genus.

alterna′rioid (εῖδος, likeness), resembling the genus *Alternaria;* **Alterna′riose**, a disease caused by the same fungus genus.

alter′nate, *alter′nus; alterna′tus*, *alter′nans*, (1) placed on opposite sides of the stem on a different line; (2) when between other bodies of the same or different whorls, as in Umbelliferae, where the stamens are alternate with the petals, that is, between them; **Alterna′tion**, *Alternatio*, (1) interchange, by turns; (2) the heterogeneous arrangement of plant groups and formations (Clements); ~ of **Genera′tions** the reproduction by organisms which do not precisely resemble the parent, but the grand-parent, applied especially to the regular succession of sexual and asexual phases, as in Ferns, etc.

alter′native, *alternati′vus*, in aestivation when the perianth segments are in two rows, and the inner so covered by the outer, that each exterior member overlaps the half of two interior members.

alternipet′alous (*alternus*, every other; πέταλον, a flower leaf), applied to stamens alternating with the petals; **alternisep′alous** (+ SEPALUM), used of petals alternating with the sepals.

alternipin′nate, or **altern′ately-pin′-**nate, when the leaflets of a pinnate leaf are not exactly opposite each other.

Al′theine, a principle from the marshmallow, *Althaea*, Tourn., analogous to Asparagin.

Alt′itude, *Altitu′do* (Lat., height), used to specify the height above the sea of the vegetation in question.

Altoherbipra′ta, pl. (*altus*, high; *herba*, a plant; *pratum*, a meadow), a division of TERRIPRATA characterised by the dominance of tall-growing herbs.

Alu′mina Bod′ies, substances found in the mesophyll and cortex of *Symplocos* (Radlkofer).

aluta′ceous, *aluta′ceus* (*aluta*, soft leather + CEOUS), (1) the colour of buff leather, or light tan; (2) leathery in texture, coriaceous.

Al′var, applied to peculiar dwarfed growth, resembling steppe vegetation, in Öland, etc. (Sernander).

Alve′ola (*alveolus*, a hollow vessel), pl. **Alveolae**; (1) cavities on the surface, as the pits on the receptacle of many Compositae, honeycombed; (2) the pores of such Fungi as *Polyporus;* (3) the perithecia of certain other Fungi; adj. **al′veolar;** ~ **Theory**, applied to Bütschli's theory of protoplasm as a foam-like substance; **Alveolarplas′ma** (πλάσμα, modelled), term used by Strasburger in place of TROPHOPLASM, granular protoplasm; **al′veolate**, *alveola′tus*, *alveola′ris*, marked as though honeycombed; **Alve′oli**, the pit-like markings on the valves of many Diatomaceae; **Alveoliza′tion**, the process of becoming granular or honeycombed; **alve′olized**, the process named.

Amadou′ (Fr.), (1) the substance of certain Fungi used as tinder, as *Polyporus fomentarius*, Fr.; (2) as a styptic when from the pubescence of the Phanerogam *Melastoma hirta*, Linn.

Amalthe′a ‡ (ἅμα, together; ἀλθέω, I increase), used by Desvaux for an aggregation of dry fruits within a calyx which does not become fleshy, as *Alchemilla*, and *Sanguisorba*.

Aman′itin (from *Amanita*, Dill.), (1) the red pigment of the pileus of the Fly-Agaric, (2) the poisonous alkaloid from the same, also written **Aman′itine**.

Amath′ad (ἄμαθος, sandy soil + AD), a sand-hill plant ; **Amathi′um**, a sand-hill formation ; **amathoc′olus** (*i.e.* = **amathoc′ola**), a sandy dwelling plant (Clements) ; **amathoph′ilus** (φιλέω, I love), dwelling on sand-hills or sandy plains ; **Amathophy′ta** (φυτὸν, a plant), sand-plain plants.

Am′ber, the English name of SUCCINITE.

ambig′enus (*ambo*, both ; *genus*, offspring), applied to a perianth whose exterior is calycine, and interior corolline, as *Nymphaea*.

ambiguiflor′us (*ambiguus*, doubtful ; *flos, floris*, flower), applied by Cassini to flowers of an indeterminate form ; **ambig′uous**, (1) said of an organ when its origin is uncertain, thus the dissepiments of an orange may belong to the axis or the paries ; (2) of a plant when its position is doubtful.

ambip′arous, *-rus*, (*ambo*, both ; *pario*, I bring forth), producing two kinds, as when a bud contains both flowers and leaves, as the Horse-chestnut ; **ambisporang′iate** (+ SPORANGIUM), hermaphrodite flowers, otherwise macro- and micro-sporangiate, that is, bearing ovules and pollen-sacs ; *cf.* AMPHISPORANGIATE.

Amb′itus (Lat., a going round), the outline of a figure, as of a leaf.

ambleocar′pus (ἀμβλόομαι, to be abortive ; καρπὸς, fruit), when most of the ovules abort, a few only becoming perfect seeds.

Ambro′sia (ἀμβρόσια, divine food), the mycelial or oidial stage of a Fungus, probably of some Ascomycete, found in the burrows of some beetles in fruit-trees, and

believed to be used as food ; **ambros′iacus**, possessing a strong scent of *Ambrosia* ; fragrant.

Ambula′crum (Lat.), a walk laid out in a botanic garden.

ame′liorating (Fr., *amélioration*, an improvement) ~ **Plants**, those bacteria which cause nodules on the roots of Leguminosae.

Am′ent, *Ament′um* (Lat., a strap), a catkin, a spike of flowers usually bracteate, and frequently deciduous ; **amenta′ceous**, *-ceus* (+ CEUS), **ament′iform** (*forma*, shape), **amentif′erous** (*fero*, I bear), catkin-bearing ; catkin-like ; **Amentiflo′rae** (*flos, floris*, a flower), wind-fertilized, catkin-bearing plants, as the hazel or willow (Delpino).

Ament′ula (diminutive), the so-called catkins of the male inflorescence in *Sphagnum*.

ameris′tic (a, not ; μερίστος, divisible) ~ **Ferns**, are those whose prothalli being insufficiently provided with nutriment are destitute of meristem, and produce antheridia only.

Am′erosporae (a, without ; μέρος, a part, + SPORA), applied to pluricellular spores, subdivided into ALLANTOSPORAE, HYALOSPORAE, PHAEOSPORAE (Traverso).

ametab′olous, *ametab′olus* (a, without ; μεταβολή, change), used of species of *Equisetum* where fertile shoots die away after dispersal of the spores (Goebel).

amethyst′eus, amethyst′inus (Lat.), the colour of amethyst, violet.

ametoe′cious (a, not ; μετὰ, with, after ; οἶκος, house), a parasite which does not change its host ; the reverse of METOECIOUS.

amicron′ic (a, not ; μικρὸς, small), applied to particles beyond the powers of the microscope.

Am′idases (+ AMIDE), enzymes occurring in the mycelium of *Aspergillus*, which split off ammonia from urea, etc., but are not proteolytic (Shibata) ; and diffuse into the air, such as the hawthorn and elder.

Am′ides (Am[-monia] + ide), certain

substances occurring in plants, soluble in water, diffusible, crystallizable, not coagulating on boiling ; those of common occurrence are Asparagin, Leucin, and Tyrosin ; **Amid′ulin**, soluble starch, existing in small quantity in ordinary starch-grains ; **Ami′doplast** (πλαστὸς, modelled), an error for AMYLOPLAST ; **am′inoid** (εἶδος, resemblance), used by Kerner for those scents which have an amine as their foundation.

Amito′sis (α, without ; μίτος, a web), defined as degenerate mitosis, when nuclear division takes place directly without the phenomena of karyokinesis ; adj. **amito′tic**.

Am′me (Ger., nurse), cf. TROPHO-.

Ammoch′thad (ἄμμος, sand ; ὄχθη, bank + AD), a sand-bank plant ; **Ammochthi′um**, a sand-bank formation ; **ammochthoph′ilus** (φιλέω, I love), plant dwelling on sandbanks ; **Ammochthophy′ta** (φυτὸν, a plant), plants of sand-banks (Clements) ; **Am′modytes** (δύω, I sink in), living in sandy places ; **ammoph′ilous**, -lus (φιλὲω, I love), sandloving.

Ammo′nia (Ammon, the Libyan Jupiter; first found near his temple), a pungent gas; the so-called volatile alkali ; **Ammonifica′tion** (facio, I make), the production of ammonia by certain bacteria ; **Ammo′nobacte′ria** (+ BACTERIUM), organisms capable of producing ammonia from nitrogen compounds (Lipman).

Ammophile′tum, an association of *Ammophila arundinacea*, on sanddunes.

Am′nion, Am′nios (ἀμνίος, foetal membrane), a viscous fluid which surrounds certain ovules in an early stage ; **amniot′ic Sac** = EMBRYO-SAC.

amoe′boid (ἀμοιβαῖος, interchanging), applied to the jelly-like plasmodium of Myxogastres when in motion, resembling an *Amoe′ba*, a proteanshaped rhizopod ; **Amoeboid′eae**, used by Gobi for the lowest forms of plant-life which are destitute of chlorophyll ; **Amoe′bulae**, the separa-

tion of plasma round each nucleus in *Sorosphaera* (Schwartz).

amorph′ous, *amorph′us* (α, without ; μορφὴ, form), shapeless, the form not regular or definite ; **Amorph′ophyte** (φυτὸν, a plant), a plant with anomalous flowers.

Am′pelid, (ἄμπελος, a vine ; εἶδος, like), used by J. Smith for any climbing plant ; **Ampelog′raphist** (γράφω, I write), a writer on vines.

Amphanth′ium ‡ (ἀμφί, around ; ἄνθος, flower), the dilated receptacle of an inflorescence, as in *Dorstenia ;* clinanthium ; **Am′phiaster** (ἀστὴρ, a star), the combined nuclear-spindle and cytasters ; also for the combined cytasters only (Crozier) ; **amphib′ious** (βίος, life), growing on dry land or in water equally well ; ~ **Alterna′tion**, the adaptation of organism, originally of aquatic habit, to subaërial conditions ; **Amphib′rya** (βρύω, to sprout), Endlicher's name for Monocotyledons ; **amphib′ryous**, -yus, growing by increase over the whole surface ; **amphicarp′ic, -pous,** -pus (καρπὸς, fruit), possessing two kinds of fruit, differing in character or time of ripening ; **Amphicarp′ium**, an archegonium persisting as a fruit-envelope, after fertilization ; **amphicarpog′enous** (γενος, offspring), producing fruit above ground, which is subsequently buried beneath ; cf. HYPOCARPOGENOUS ; **Am′phichrome** (χρῶμα, colour), used for plants which abnormally produce flowers of two different colours on the same stock (Lindman) ; cf. POLYCHROME, HETEROCHROME, METACHROME ; **Amphichro′matism**, the condition named ; **amphicoe′lous** (κοῖλος, hollow), concave on both sides (Heinig) ; **Amphicotyle′don** (κοτυληδών, a hollow), De Vries's term for cotyledons united so as to form a cup ; **Amphicot′yly**, cf. AMPHISYNCOTYLY ; **amphicri′bral** (*cribrum*, a sieve), applied to a hadrocentric bundle (Haberlandt).

amphige′al (ἀμφὶ, around ; γῆ, the earth), applied to a plant which bears dimorphic flowers, the upper from the stem, the lower from the root or root-stock, as *Kraschenini-kowia;* **amphigae′us, amphige′an** (1) plants which are natives of both Old and New worlds ; (2) used of flowers which arise from the rootstock ; **Amphig′amae** (γάμος, marriage), plants whose fructification is unknown, possibly of both sexes ; **amphigam′eous, amphig′amous,** supposed to be destitute of sexual organs, or where their presence has not yet been ascertained ; it has been applied to Cryptogams ; **Amphigast′er,** proposed alteration of the following : **Amphigast′ria** (γαστήρ, belly), stipular organs in Hepaticæ, which clasp the stem ; **amphig′enous** (γένος, offspring), growing all round an object ; used of Fungi when the hymenium is not restricted to any particular surface ; ~ **Castra′tion,** the action of *Ustilago antherarum,* DC., when it mingles the characters of both sexes by developing in each some of the characters of the other ; **Amphigen′esis** (γένεσις, beginning), Haeckel's term for sexual reproduction ; **Amphig′ony** (γόνος, offspring), sexual reproduction (Haeckel) ; **Amphigon′ium,** Kerner's term for ARCHEGONIUM; **Amphile′psis** (λῆψις, a receiving), the ordinary result of fertilization ; *cf.* MONOLEPSIS (Bateson) ; **Amphimix′is** (μῖξις, a mingling) : (1) sexual reproduction (Weismann), (2) the union of parental characters in the embryo (Sargent) ; **Amphinu′cleus** (+ NUCLEUS), Goldschmidt's term for the nucleus when it possesses both generative and somatic functions ; **amphiphlo′ic,** applied to the central cylinder of stems, with phloem on both sides of the xylem ; *cf.* ECTOPHLOIC (Jeffrey) ; ~ **Pro′tostele** (or ~ **Hap′lostele**), a stele in which the solid central xylem is traversed by a continuous internal strand of phloem, connecting with the external phloem at the nodes (Chandler) ; ~ **Phyllosi′phony,** when the tubular central

cylinder exists with foliar gaps, and without external phloem ; **Am′phiphyte** (φυτὸν, a plant), a plant on boundary zone of wet land, amphibious in life and hydrophytic in adaptation (Schröber) ; **Amphipy′renin** (πυρὴν, stone of fruit), the membrane of the pyrenin, the body of the nucleus ; **Amphisarc′a** (σάρξ, σαρκὸς, flesh), an indehiscent multilocular fruit, dry without, pulpy within, as a melon ; **Amphisor′us** (+ SORUS), a group or patch of AMPHISPORES (Arthur and Holway) ; **Amphisper′mium** (σπέρμα, a seed), a fruit which is **amphisper′mous,** when the pericarp closely invests the seed and assumes its shape; **amphispor′al, amphispor′ic** (+ SPORE), relating to an **Am′phispore,** Carleton's name for MESOSPORE ; **amphisporan′giate,** an emendation of AMBISPORANGIATE (Arber and Parkin) ; **Amphisporangia′tae,** plants possessing micro- and megaspores, *i.e.* stamens and pistils ; **amphistomat′ic, amphistom′atous** (+ STOMA), with stomata on both upper and lower leaf-surfaces ; **Amphisyncot′yly** (+ COTYLEDON), having cotyledons coalescent in the form of a funnel or trumpet (De Vries) ; shortened to **Amphicot′yly ; Amphithe′cium** (θήκη, a case), peripheral layer of cells surrounding the endothecium in the early stage of the development of the moss-capsule ; adj. **amphithe′cial; amphit′ropal,** or more correctly **amphit′ropous** -*pus* (τρόπος, turn), said of the ovule when it is curved so that both ends are brought near to each other ; **amphitroph′ic,** relating to AMPHITROPHY ; **Amphit′rophy,** Wiesner's term for growth when greatest in the shoots and buds on the sides of the mother shoot; **amphiva′sal** (*vasa,* vessels), used of a leptocentric bundle (Haberlandt).

Am′phora (Lat., a wine jar), the lower part of a pyxis, as in Henbane.

amplect′ant, *amplect′ans, amplecti′vus amplex′ans* (Lat.), embracing ; **amplex′us,** in Vernation, when two

sides of one leaf overlap the two
sides of the one above it ; **amplex'-
icaul**, *amplexicau'lis* (*caulis*, stem),
stem-clasping, when the petiole-
leaf, or stipule, is dilated at the
base, and embraces the stem.

am'pliate, *amplia'tus* (Lat.), enlarged ;
ampliatiflor'us ‡ (*flos*, flower), used
for Composites having the ray-
florets enlarged, as in the Cornflower.

Amplifica'tion (*amplificatio*, an enlarg-
ing), term used for all changes
leading to increased formal or structural complexity of the plant (Bower).

Ampul'la (Lat., a bottle), the flasks
found on aquatics such as *Utricularia;* **ampulla'ceous**, *-ceus*, **ampul'liform**, *ampullifor'mis*, swollen
out in flask-shape, as the corolla in
some Heaths.

Amyg'dala (*amygdalum*, a kernel), an
almond ; **amygd'aliform** (*forma*,
shape), almond-shaped ; **Amyg'da-
lin**, a glucoside found in the fruit of
many Rosaceae ; **amyg'daline**, pertaining to or resembling an almond.

amyla'ceous (ἄμυλον, fine flour +
ACEOUS), starchy ; **Am'ylase**, an enzyme, the same as DIASTASE ; **amylif'e-
rous** (φέρω, I bear), starch-bearing ;
Am'ylin, a product of the action
of diastase on starch ; **Am'ylites**,
skeletons of starch-granules composed of amylodextrin (Belzung) ;
Amylobacte'ria (βακτήριον, a little
rod), microbes producing butyric
fermentation, ascribed to the action
of *Bacillus Amylobacter*, Van Tiegh. ;
Amylocel'lulose (+ CELLULOSE), a
supposed constituent of starch-
granules ; **amyloclas'tic** (κλαστὸς,
broken in pieces), the breaking down
of starch by an enzyme ; **Amylo-
dex'trin** (+ DEXTRIN), an intermediate in converting starch into
dextrin ; *cf.* ACHROODEXTRIN ; **Amy-
loer'ythrin** (ἐρυθρὸς, red), a carbohydrate resembling starch occurring
in rice and millet ; **Amylogen'esis**
(γένεσις, beginning), the formation
of starch ; **amylogen'ic** (γένος, offspring), producing starch ; **~ Bodies**,

LEUCOPLASTIDS ; **Amylohy'drolist**
(ὕδωρ, water ; λύσις, a loosing),
an enzyme which transforms starch
by hydrolysis ; **Amylohydrol'ysis**,
the act in question ; **am'yloid** (εἶδος,
resemblance), analogous to starch ;
Amyloleu'cites (λευκὸς, white), plastids producing starch-granules ;
Amylol'ysis (λύσις, a loosing), transformation of starch into other bodies,
as sugar ; **amylolyt'ic En'zyme**, an
unorganised ferment, which breaks
up the starch cell-contents into
dextrin and sugar ; **Amy'lome**, a
term applied to xylemparenchyma,
when it contains starch ; **Amy'lon**,
Amy'lum,in composition = STARCH ;
Amylopec'tin (+ PECTIN), a mucilaginous constituent of starch
(Maguenne and Roux) ; **Amy'lum-
Bod'y**, a rounded body in a chlorophyll band or plate, which is a
centre of starch formation ; **~
Cen'tres**, Strasburger's term for
PYRENOIDS ; **~ Grains**, or **~ Gran'-
ules**, the laminated bodies which
are formed of starch as reserve
material in plant cells ; **~ Star**, a
tuber-like organ in *Chara stelligera*,
Bauer, which is closely packed with
starch, it consists of an isolated
subterranean node ; **Amyloph'ylly**
(φύλλον, a leaf), the production of starch-leaves ; **Amy'loplast**
(πλαστὸς, moulded) = LEUCOPLAS-
TID, a colourless granule of
protoplasm, which generates a
starch - granule ; **amyloplast'ic**,
starch-forming ; **Am'yloses** (Amyl,
a chemical term + ose), a group of
substances of which cellulose and
starch are the commonest ; **Amyl-
osyn'thesis** (σύνθεσις, composition),
the formation of starch (Hick).

Anab'iont (βίος, life), perennials,
flowering and fruiting many times
(A. Braun).

Anabio'sis (ἀναβιόω, I revive), the condition of latent life, which may occur
through loss of moisture (Areger).

An'abix, pl. **Anab'ices**, those vegetative parts of Cryptogams which
perish below, but vegetate above,

as *Lycopodium*, Lichens, and Hepatics.

anabol'ic (ἀνὰ, up ; βολὴ, a throw, stroke) ; adj. of **Anab'olism**, constructive metabolism of the protoplasm, the building up of more complex from simpler substances ; "Baustoffwechsel" of the Germans ; **Anab'olite**, any product of constructive metabolism in the plant ; *cf* KATABOLITE.

Anacamp'yla ‡ (κάμπυλος, bent), lacerations of the epidermal layer as in some Agarics.

anacanth'ous (αν, without ; ἄκανθα, a thorn), without thorns or spines.

anacardia'ceous, resembling *Anacardium*, Linn., as to arrangement of fruit, etc.

Anachore'sis (ἀναχώρησις, a going back), retrograde metamorphosis of an organ or whorl.

Anaclinot'ropism (ἀνὰ, up ; κλίνη, a bed ; τροπὴ, a turning), positive clinotropism, that is, having the direction of growth oblique or horizontal.

anacrog'ynous (αν, not ; ἄκρος, apex ; γυνὴ, woman), said of Hepatics in which archegonia do not arise at the extremity of the shoot, which continues to grow ; *cf.* ACROGYNOUS.

anad'romous (ἀνὰ, up ; δρόμος, a course), in venation, that in which the first set of nerves in each segment of the frond is given off on the upper side of the midrib towards the apex, as in *Aspidium*, *Asplenium*, etc.

anaëret'icus (αν, without ; αἱρετικὸς, power of choosing), applied by C. Schimper to an abnormal arrangement of the leaves in single rows on the axis, as happens in torsion, etc. ; **Anaëro'be**, **Anaërob'ium**, pl. **Anaërob'ia** (ἀὴρ, air ; βίος, life), an organism able to live in the absence of free oxygen, as many bacteria ; **fac'ultative ~**, organisms which can live as Anaërobes ; **ob'ligate ~**, those which can exist or thrive only in the absence of free oxygen ; **anaërob'ian, -b'ious, -bic, anaërobiot'ic**, adj. ; **Anaërobi'ont** (α, without ; ἀὴρ, air ; βίος, life), a plant independent of free oxygen for respiration ; **Anaërobio'sis**, the state of living without oxygen ; **anaërob'ic Energe'sis**, the disruptive process without air, by which energy is released (Barnes) ; **Anaë'rophyte** (φυτὸν, plant), a plant which does not need a direct supply of air.

Anal'ogy (ἀναλογία, proportion), (1) resemblance in certain points, as in form not function, or function not form, as the tendrils of the Pea, *Smilax*, or Vine ; (2) "that resemblance of structures which depends upon similarity of function " (Darwin) ; **anal'ogous**, resembling, but not homologous ; **An'alogues**, structures corresponding to previous definition.

Anal'ysis (ἀνάλυσις, releasing), (1) the examination of a plant to determine its affinities and position ; (2) the details of the flower, etc., on a botanic drawing.

anametad'romous (ἀνὰ, up, + METADROMOUS), in the venation of Ferns, when the weaker pinnules are anadromous, and the stronger are catadromous ; **Anamor'phose** (Goebel), **Anamorph'ism** (Crozier), = **Anamorph'osism**, **Anamorpho'sis** (μόρφωσις, a shaping), (1) a gradual change of form in a group of plants in geologic time ; (2) a similar change in a group now existing ; (3) a striking change in form, the result of changed conditions of growth (Crozier).

anandrar'ious, -rius, anan'drous (αν, not ; ἀνὴρ, ἀνδρὸς, a man), having no stamens, but with floral envelopes and pistils ; **ananth'erous**, **Ananthe'rum** (ἀνθηρὸς, flowering), applied to filaments destitute of anthers.

ananth'ous, -thus (ἄνθος, a flower), wanting the flower ; **An'aphase**, **Anaph'asis** (φάσις, appearance), the formation of daughter-nuclei in karyokinesis, following the METAPHASIS ; **An'aphyte** (φυτὸν, plant), the potential independence of every branch or shoot ; **Anaphyto′sis**, the building up of plant structure by ANAPHYTES.

An′aplast (πλαστὸς, moulded), A. Meyer's term for LEUCOPLASTID ; **Ana-sar′ca** (σάρξ, σαρκὸς, flesh), dropsy in plants.

anaschis′tic (ἀνὰ, up ; σχιστὸς, cleft), used of chromosomes which split longitudinally ; *cf.* DIASCHISTIC (Farmer) ; **Anasor′ium** (σωρὸς, a heap), the building up of nutritive material in the protoplasm, but not an integral part of it (Hartog) ; **anastat′ic** (στάσις, a standing), reviving, as certain plants after desiccation.

Anast′ates, pl. (ἀνάστατος, removed), the products of anabolic or ascending conversion of food-material into protoplasm (Parker).

Anastomo′sis (ἀναστομόω, I form a mouth), (1) union of one vein with another, the connection forming a reticulation ; (2) Vuillemin's term for conjugation in *Mucor*, two equal gametes conjugate and are cut off from the parent hypha by a septum.

Anataximorph′osis (ἀνὰ, up ; τάξις, order ; μορφὴ, change), Gubler's term for teratologic changes which are in conformity with the normal order ; **Anat′omy** (τομὸς, cutting) in botany, the study of structure ; **anat′ropal**, more correctly **anat′ropous**, *anat′-ropus* (τροπὴ, a turn), the ovule reversed, with micropyle close to the side of the hilum, and the chalaza at the opposite end ; **an-atyp′ic** (τύπος, a type), applied to an anomaly which conforms to the general law of the organism ; **Ana-ty′pose**, an anomaly of the kind specified (Gubler).

An′bury, Am′berry, a disease caused by *Plasmodiophora Brassicae*, Woron., in Crucifers, the root becoming clubbed.

Anc′ad (ἄγκος, mountain glen, + AD), a cañon plant.

an′ceps (Lat., two-headed), **ancip′ital, ancip′itous**, two-edged, flattened or compressed, as the stem of *Sisymbrium anceps*, Cav.

anchor′aeform (*anchora*, an anchor ; *forma*, shape), with two limbs, as in the petals of *Ankyropetalum*, Fenzl ; **Anc′hor-hairs**, hairs having recurved barbs, distinctive of the Loasaceae ; **Anc′horing Disk**, a growth from rhizoids in *Lejeunia* ; ~ **Or′gan**, the ends of tendrils with flattened disks for clinging ; ~ **Root**, holdfasts such as those of *Hedera*, for support, not nourishment (Goebel).

Anchu′sin, the colouring matter of *Anchusa tinctoria*, Linn., now referred to the genus *Alkanna*.

ancis′trus (ἀγκίστριον, a small hook), barbed.

Anci′um, pl. **Anci′a** (ἄγκος, a hollow, as a glen), a cañon forest formation ; **ancoph′ilus** (φιλέω, I love), haunting cañons ; **Ancophy′ta** (φυτὸν, a plant), plants of cañons ; **an-coc′olus**, *i. e.* ancoc′ola, living in cañons (Clements).

ander, -dra, -dro, -drum (ἀνὴρ, ἀνδρὸς, a man), in Greek compounds = the male sex ; **An′drochore** (χωρέω, I spread abroad), a plant dispersed by human agency ; **Androclin′ium** (κλινὴ, bed), the bed of the anther in Orchids, an excavation on the top of the column, usually written CLINANDRIUM.

Androconid′ium (+ CONIDIUM), term propounded by Cohn for a spermatium of assumed male function ; **An′drocyte** (κύτος, hollow vessel), the cell which afterwards develops into the antherozoid (Allen) ; **andro-dioe′cious** (δὶς twice ; οἶκος, house), used of a species with two forms, one male only, the other hermaphrodite ; **Androdioec′ism**, the condition itself ; **androdynam′ic**, = ANDRODY-NAMOUS ; **andrody′namous** (δύναμις, power), of Dicotyledons in which the stamens are highly developed ; **An-droe′cium** (οἶκος, house), the male system of a flower, the stamens collectively ; **androe′cial**, relating to an androecium ; **Androgametan′-gium** (γαμέτης, a spouse ; ἀγγεῖον, a vessel), = ANTHERIDIUM, the organ in which the male sexual cells are formed ; **Androgam'etes,** zoosperms, male sexual cells ; **Androgam'etophore** (φορὸς, carrying), male sexual form of a plant, as in *Equisetum;* **Androg'amy** (γάμος, marriage), employed by Dangeard for the impregnation of a male gamete by a female ; it may be, (*a*) **cytoplas'mic** ~, the cytoplasm of the female gamete acting, or (*b*) **nu'clear** ~, when the nucleus of the female effects the impregnation; **Androgen'esis** (γένεσις, beginning), the growth of an individual from a male cell ; *cf.* PARTHENOGENESIS ; **androg'enous** (γένος, offspring), male-bearing ; ~ **Castra'tion,** the action of *Ustilago antherarum,* DC., when inciting production of male organs ; **An'drogone** (γόνος, offspring), any cell within an antheridium other than the androcyte or androcyte-mother-cell (Allen) ; **Androgonid'ium** (+ Gonidium) = ANDROSPORE; **androg'ynal, androg'ynous** - *nus* (γυνή, woman), (1) hermaphrodite, having male and female flowers on the same inflorescence, as in many species of *Carex;* (2) occasionally used for MONOECIOUS ; **androgyna'ris** (Lat.), of double flowers in which both stamens and pistils have become petaloid; **androgyn'icus‡**(Lat.), belonging to, or of an hermaphrodite flower;**androgyniflor'us‡** (*flos, floris,* a flower), a hybrid term for when the head of a composite bears hermaphrodite flowers ; **Androg'ynism,** a change from dioecious to monoecious.

Andromedotox'in, a glucoside occurring in *Andromeda* and other Ericaceae.

andromonoe'cious (ἀνὴρ,ἀνδρὸς, a man ; μόνος, alone ; οἶκος, house), having perfect and male flowers, but no female flowers; **Andromonoec'ism,** the state described ; **Andromorpho'sis** (μόρφωσις, a change), the alterations caused by the excitation of the pollen tubes (Schröter) ; **andropet'alous,** *andropetala'rius* (πέταλον, a

flower leaf), flowers double, the stamens petaloid, the pistils unchanged ; **An'drophore, Androph'orum** (φορὸς, carrying), (1) a support of a column of stamens, as in Malvaceae ; (2) a stalk supporting an androecium ; **An'drophyll** (φύλλον, a leaf), a male sporophyll, a stamen ; **An'drophyte** (φυτὸν, a plant), a male plant in the sexual generation.

Androsac'ile (+ILE), a "Society" of *Androsace* (Clements).

Androsporan'gium (ἀνὴρ, ανδρὸς, a man, σπορὰ, a seed ; ἀγγεῖον, a vessel) ; a microsporangium, a sporangium containing **An'drospores,** (1) swarmspores of Oedogoniae, which give rise to Dwarf-males destined to produce spermatozoids, (2) (A. W. Bennett) = MICROSPORE ; **an'drous,** staminate, male.

Anelectrot'onus (ἀνὰ, up ; ἤλεκτρον, amber ; τόνος, stress), the diminished excitation produced on the vital movements of plants by a constant current of electricity from the anode.

An'emad (ἄνεμος, wind, + AD), a "blow-out" plant ; **Anemi'um** (+ IUM), a "blow-out" formation ; **Anemo'chore** (χωρέω, I spread abroad), a plant distributed by wind (Clements) ; **Anemocho'ry, anemochor'ous** (χωρίς, asunder), applied by Sernander to plants which retain their seeds through the winter, and then disseminate them by the instrumentality of the wind ; **Anemodi'um,** suggested by Clements for plants of "blow-outs," hollows in dunes excavated by wind ; **anemodoph'ilus** (φιλέω, I love), plants dwelling in "blow-outs" ; **Anemodophy'ta** (φυτὸν, a plant), "blow-out" plants ; **Anemoëntomoph'ily,** (+ENTOMOPHILY), employed of a polymorphic species which in some individuals is adapted for wind-fertilization, and in others for insect-fertilization (Knuth).

Anem'onin, an acrid substance from several species of *Anemone,* Tourn.

anemoph'ilous (ἄνεμος, wind ; φιλέω, I love), applied to flowers which are wind-fertilized, the pollen being conveyed by the air ; **Anemoph'ilae,** wind-fertilized plants ; **Anemoph'ily,** the condition described ; **Anemo'sis,** wind-shake, a disease of timber-trees.

Anemog'amae (γάμος, marriage), wind-fertilized plants ; also as **Anemoph'ilae** (φιλέω, I love) ; **an'emophile,** delighting in wind, growing in breezy places ; **ane'mophobe,** shunning wind ; **Ane'mophyte,** Hansgirg's term for a wind-fertilized plant.

anfract'uose, *anfractuo'sus,* **anfrac'tous,** *anfrac'tus* (Lat., a curving), sinuous, as the anthers of gourds ; also spirally twisted.

angianth'eous, employed by A. Gray as pertaining to *Angianthus,* a genus of Inuloid Compositae.

Angiench'yma (ἀγγεῖον, a vessel ; ἔγχυμα, an infusion), vascular tissue of any kind ; **angiocar'pic, angiocarp'ous,** *-pus* (καρπὸς, fruit), (1) having the fruit invested by some covering which masks it, as in the Cupuliferae ; (2) with spores enclosed in some kind of receptacle ; a closed apothecium in Lichens ; **Angiocy'cads,** proposed by F. W. Oliver for fossil cycads, having an hermaphrodite flower ; **Angiog'amae,** Ardissone's group for Angiosperms and Gymnosperms ; **Ang'iclum,** the spore-case of certain Fungi (Lindley) ; **angiomonosperm'ous** (μονός, one ; σπέρμα, seed), having only one seed in the carpel ; **Angiosperm'ae, An'giosperms,** plants having their seeds enclosed in an ovary ; **angiosperm'al, angiosperm'ous,** belonging to the plants classed as Angiosperms ; **~type of Stomata,** characterized by the development of the inner and outer borders of their cuticle, the outer border usually considerably thickened ; **angios'porous,** used of Cryptogams producing spores in a closed receptacle ; **Angiosp'orae,** plants so characterized.

An'gle, *An'gulus* (Lat., a corner), in botany not limited to the inclina-tion of two lines, but often refers to the meeting of two planes to form an edge, as in angular stems ; **~ of Deviation,** that which a branch or similar organ makes with its axis ; **of Diver'gence,** the degree of difference in the position of two adjacent leaves or organs on the same or different planes, as in ⅖ phyllotaxis, it is 144° ; **ide'al ~,** Schimper's term for a theoretic angle for a "central station of rest" in phyllotaxis, as 130° 30′ 27″ ·936 ; **ang'ular,** *angular'is angula'tus, angulo'sus,* used when an organ shows a determinate number of angles, as the quadrangular stems of Labiatae ; **~ Divergence,** in phyllotaxis, is given under **Angle** of divergence ; **ang'ulate,** *angula'tus,* more or less angular ; **angulinerv'ed,** *angulinerv'ius* ‡ (*nervus,* a nerve), when veins form an angle with the midrib, as in most Dicotyledons ; **angulodent'ate** (*dens, dentis,* a tooth), having angular teeth (Crozier).

anguillulaeform'is (Lat., shaped like a small eel), applied by Koerber to Lichen-spores which are worm-like in shape.

angustifo'liate, -lious, *-lius* (*angustus,* narrow ; *folium,* a leaf), narrow leaved ; **angustisept'al,** *angustiseptatus* (*septum,* a division), having a narrow-partitioned fruit, as the silicle of *Thlaspi ;* **Angustisep'tae,** plants so characterized.

Anhalo'nine, a poisonous alkaloid from *Anhalonium Lewinii,* Hennings ; it resembles Strychnine.

An'ilophyll, a product from Chlorophyll after treatment with Aniline, whence the name.

An'ime, a transparent resin from *Hymenaea Courbaril,* Linn.

anisa'tus, partaking of the scent of Anise, *Pimpinella Anisum,* Linn.

anisob'rious, *anisob'rius* ‡ (ἄνισος, unequal ; βρύω, I swell), a name given to Endogens, from one side being supposed to possess greater developing force than the other, hence only one cotyledon is formed ;

anisocotyle'donous (+Cotyledon), unequal development of the cotyledons ; **Anisocot'yly**, the condition in question (K. Fritsch) ; **anisody'namous**, -*mus* (δύναμις, power) = anisobrious ; **anisogametan'gous Copula'tion** (+ Gametangium), when gametes are sexually diverse, as Oogonia and Antheridia, *e. g.* in Ascomycetes (Hartmann) ; **Anisogam'etes** (γαμέτης, a spouse), sexual cells, showing a difference between male and female ; **Anisog'amy** (γάμος, marriage), the union of two gametes differing chiefly in size ; the smaller (micro-) gamete is male, the larger (mega-) gamete is female (Hartog) ; **anisog'onous** (γόνος, offspring), applied to hybrids which do not equally combine the characters of their parents ; *cf.* isogonous ; **anisog'ynous** (γυνὴ, woman), with fewer carpels than sepals ; **Anisoholog'amy** (+ Hologamy), union of gametes somewhat differing in size, with slight sexual difference (Hartmann) ; **anisom'erous**, *anisomer'icus* (μέρος, a part), where the parts of a flower are not all regular, unsymmetrical ; **Anisomerog'amy** (+ Merogamy) or Oogamy, the union of macro- and microgametes, eggs and spermatozoa, as *Volvox*, many Algae and Fungi(Hartmann); **Anisomor'phy** (μορφὴ, shape), change in form of an organ caused by its position in relation to the horizon of the motheraxis ; **anisopet'alous**, -*lus*, (πέταλον, a flower leaf), having unequal-sized petals ; **anisophyll'ous** (φύλλον, a leaf), when the two leaves of a pair are diverse in shape or size ; **An'isophylly**, (1) used by Krasser for the different forms of leaf structure due to difference of position, as in aquatic plants, the submerged or floatingleaves ; (2) the occurrence of leaves varying in form or size on shoots which are obliquely inclined to the light ; it may be (*a*) **habitual** ~, so fixed as to be capable of being artificially propagated ; (*b*) **common** ~, throughout the whole shoot; or

(*c*) **lateral** ~, where only the sidebranches display the inequality (Wiesner) ; **Anisophy'tes** (φυτὸν, a plant), formerly used for Muscineae ; **an'isoschist** (σχιστὸς, cleft), used of gametes which are unequal, some being degraded or aborted (Hartog) ; **anisosep'alous**, -*lus* (+ Sepalum, calyx-leaf), the sepals unequal ; **anisosta'menous** (Crozier), **anisoste'monous**, -*nus* (στήμων, a thread) = having stamens of different size : **anisostemopet'alus** = anisostemonous ; **anisotrop'ic**, **anisot'ropous** (τροπὴ, a turn), endowed with different kinds of irritability ; **Anisot'ropism**, **Anisot'ropy**, the quality itself, as shown in leaves and roots which respectively seek and shun light.

Anla'ge (Ger.), has been variously rendered as Rudiment, Inception, Primordium, Fundament.

annex'ed, *annex'us* (Lat., fastened to), = adnate.

annot'inous, -*nus* (Lat., a year old), applied to branches of last year's growth.

an'nual, *annua'lis*, *an'nuus* (Lat., lasting a year), within one year ; (1) used of plants which perish within that period ; (2) of the rings in wood which denote the year's growth ; **Annual Ring**, the marks seen on cross-section of wood which show the respective increment during each year ; ~ **Shoot**, = ramus annotinus.

ann'ular, *annular'is*, *annular'ius* (*annulus*, a ring), used of any organs disposed in a circle ; ~ **Duct**, ~ **Vessel**, one in which the secondary thickening has taken place in the form of rings ; **an'nulate**, *annula'tus*, *annuliform'is* (*forma*, shape), ring-shaped ; **Annula'tion**, a ring or belt (Crozier) ; **annulat'iform**, ring-like, as the apex of the thecae of *Schizœa*.

An'nulus (Lat., a ring) ; (1) in Ferns, the elastic organ which partially invests the theca, and at maturity bursts it ; (2) in Fungi, a portion of the ruptured marginal veil, forming a frill upon the stipe after the expansion of the pileus ; (3) in Mosses, the ring of cells between the base of the peristome or orifice of the capsule and the operculum ; (4) in Diatoms, used by W. Smith for a compressed rim of silex within the frustules of such genera as *Rhabdonema*, Kütz.; (5) in Equisetaceae, the imperfectly developed foliar sheath below the fruit spike ; (6) the fleshy rim of the corolla in Asclepiads, as the genus *Stapelia;* ~ in'ferus, ~ mo'bilis, as defined in 1 ; ~ su'perus, = ARMILLA.

anod'al, anod'ic (ἀνά, up ; ὁδὸς, a way), in the upward direction following the genetic spiral.

an'oderm (ἀν, without ; δέρμα skin), destitute of covering membrane or cuticle.

anom'alous *·lus* (α, not ; ὁμαλός, equal), unlike its allies in certain points, contrary to rule ; **anomaloe'- cious** ‡ (οἶκος, a house), = polygamous ; **Anom'aly,** variation from normal character.

Anomod'romy (ἄνομος, without law ; δρόμος, a course), venation which cannot be assigned to any special order (Prantl).

Anophy'ta, An'ophytes (ἀνὰ, upward ; φυτὸν, plant), = BRYOPHYTA.

An'sae (*ansa*, a handle), the partial leaf stalks of a compound leaf ; **an'- sulate,** coiled at the apex and then bent over in a loop, as the shoots in some Cucurbitaceae (Crozier).

Ant-ep'iphytes (+ EPIPHYTE), certain plants cultivated by ants (Ule) ; ~ -guards, (1) ants attracted by nectaries on involucral bracts ; (2) some Compositae which guard the flowers from predatory beetles (Kerner) ; ~ -plants, plants utilized by ants for habitation ; see MYRMECOPHILOUS plants.

antagonist'ic (ἀνταγωνιστὴς, adversary) **Symbio'sis,** where the symbionts are not mutually helpful or neutral, but hurtful, at least on the part of one.

Ante-cau'lome (*ante*, before, + CAU-

LOME), Potonié's term for the theoretic plant possessing an axis ; **An'te- chamber,** the space immediately below the guard-cells of a stoma ; **antedimor'phic** (+ DIMORPHIC), the condition of a species previous to its attaining Dimorphism, as *Viola*, supposed to be at one time trimorphic (S. Moore) ; **An'teform** (*forma*, shape), an original form which has died out, but has given rise to modified offspring (Kuntze) ; **antemarg'- inal** (*margo*, edge), used of sori which are a little within the margin ; **ante- me'dius** ‡ (*medius*, middle), standing before the middle of another body, opposite.

Anten'na (Lat., sail- yard), Darwin's term for the slender process of the rostellum in *Catasetum*, borrowed from entomology ; **antennaeform'is** ‡ (*forma*, shape), used of the fruit of *Ammi majus*, Linn., the two styles suggesting the antennae of insects.

Ante-phyll'ome (*ante*, before, + PHYLLOME), the theoretic leaf ; *cf.* POST- PHYLLOME (Potonié) ; **anteplacen'tal** (+ PLACENTA), in front of the placentae ; *cf.* INTERPLACENTAL ; **Anteposit'ion** (*pono, positum*, placed) = SUPERPOSITION.

ante'rior (Lat., that before), (1) of time, previous ; (2) of place, position in front, or turned away from the axis.

an'tero-poste'rior (Lat., later), median.

Ante-spor'ophyll (*ante*, before, + SPOROPHYLL), the primitive structure of the spore-bearing organ (Potonié) ; **Ante-troph'ophyll** (+ TROPHOPHYLL) the ancestral form of the leaf (Potonié) ; **Ante-trophospor'ophyll,** the ancestral leaf-like organ, possessing the function of leaf and sporophyll (Potonié).

Anthe'la (ἀνθήλιον, a little flower), the panicle of *Juncus*, where the lateral axes exceed the main axis.

Anthe'lia or **Anthelie'tum,** an arctic alpine association with *Anthelia* as a constituent ; SNOW-FLUSH vegetation.

Anth'emy, Anthe'mia (*ἀνθέμον*, flower-pattern ?), a flower-cluster of any kind.

An'ther, Anthe'ra (*ἀνθηρὸς*, flowering), (1) that portion of a stamen which contains the pollen, usually bilocular, and sessile, or attached to a filament ; (2) an old term in Fungi, for the Antheridium ; (3) also used by Linnaeus for the seta and capsule of Mosses, as in *Bryum* ; ~ **Cap**, ~ **Case**, in Orchids, the outer deciduous case or bag, which is virtually the anther minus the pollinia ; ~ **Dust** = POLLEN ; ~ **like**, ~ **shaped**, recalling the form of a stag's horns, as certain trichomes ; ~ **Lobes**, the cells which contain the pollen ; ~ **Wings**, the horny, lateral expansions of the anther-lobes in Asclepiadeae : **Antheran'gium** (*ἀγγεῖον*, a vessel), the sporocarp of *Dioonites* containing both macro- and microspores (Wittrock) ; **An'therid, Antherid'ium** (*εἶδος*, resemblance) ; (1) the male sexual organ in Cryptogams, the analogue of the anther in Phanerogams ; (2) in Hymenomycetes, an old term for CYSTIDIUM ; **Antheridan'gia** (*ἀγγεῖον*, a vessel), microspores of *Marsilea* and allied plants ; **antherid'ial, antherid'ic**, pertaining to antheridia ; ~ **Cell**, the product of a prothallial cell, which divides into the GENERATIVE CELL, and the STALK-CELL ; **Antherid'iophore** (*φορὸς*, bearing), a unisexual gametophore, bearing antheridia only, a specialized branch in *Sphagnum* and Hepaticae ; **antherif'erous**, *-rus* (*fero*, I bear), anther-bearing ; **an'-therless**, destitute of anthers, female or neuter flowers ; **An'therocyst** (*ἄνθος*, a flower, *κύστις*, a bladder), (1) Caruel's term for ANTHERIDIUM, (2) restricted by Vuillemin to a unicellular structure developing antherozoids ; **antherog'enous**, *-nus* (*γένος*, offspring), applied to double flowers arising from the transformation of anthers (De Candolle) ; **an'theroid** (*εἶδος*, like), anther-like ; **Antheroma'nia** (*mania*, madness), an inordinate development of anthers ; **An'therophore** (*φορὸς*, bearing), a cylindrical or flattened axis in *Ephedra* bearing the anthers.

Antherophyl'ly (*ἀνθηρὸς*, flowering ; *φύλλον*, a leaf), the virescence and phyllomorphy of anthers ; **Antherosporan'gium** (*σπορὰ*, a seed ; *ἀγγεῖον*, a vessel), a synonym for MICROSPORANGIUM ; **Antherozo'a, Antherozo'ids** (*ζῶον*, an animal ; *εἶδος*, resemblance), male motile cells provided with cilia, produced in antheridia.

Anthe'sis (*ἄνθησις*, flowering), the expansion of the flower, the time when fertilization takes place.

Anthesmol'ysis ‡ (ANTHESMUS ; *λύσις*, a loosing), the metamorphosis of inflorescence (Lindley) ; **Anthesmotax'is** (*τάξις*, order), the arrangement of the different parts of the flower (F. N. Williams) ; **Anthes'mus** ‡, an inflorescence ; **Anthobiol'ogy** (+ BIOLOGY), Hansgirg's term for the life-history of the flower ; **An'thocarp, *Anthocarp'ium***, a fruit formed by the union of the floral organs or part of them, with the fruit itself, as in Nyctagineae ; **anthocarp'ous**, *-pus* (*καρπὸς*, fruit), applied to fruits with accessories, sometimes termed pseudocarps, as the Strawberry and Pineapple.

anthoc'erotoid (*εἶδος*, resemblance), resembling the hepatic genus *Anthoceros*.

Anthochlor'in (*ἄνθος*, a flower ; *χλωρὸς*, pale green), the yellow colouring of flowers ; xanthein ; **Anthoclin'ium** (*κλίνη*, a bed), the receptacle of a Composite ; **Anthocy'anin** (*κύανος*, dark blue), the blue, sometimes red, colouring of flowers.

Antho'dium (*ἄνθωδης*, flower-like), the capitulum of the Compositae, by some restricted to the involucrum.

Anthoe'cium (*ἄνθος*, a flower ; *οἶκος*, a house), the spikelet of such grasses as *Panicum ;* **Anthoëcol'ogist** (*οἶκος*, house ; *λόγος*, discourse), a student of plant-life in its environment

Anthog′amae (γάμος, marriage), Trevisan's term to include Bryophytes and Characeae ; **an′thoid** (εἶδος, resemblance), flower-like, as the male inflorescence of *Polytrichum;* **Antholeu′cin** (λευκός, clear), the so-called colouring matter of white flowers ; **An′tholite** (λίθος, a stone), a fossil plant which has the appearance of a flower ; **Anthol′ysis** (λύσις, a loosing), the retrograde metamorphosis of a flower ; **Anthophae′in** (φαιὸς, dusky), (1) the brown colouring matter of flowers ; (2) the colouring of the black spots on the corolla of *Vicia Faba* (Moebius) ; **anthoph′ilous** (φιλέω, I love), applied to plants with flower-visiting insects which aid cross-fertilization ; **Anthoph′ilus**, a florist, a cultivator of garden flowers ; **An′thophore, Anthoph′orum,** -*us* (φορέω, I bear), a short stalk which sometimes occurs between the calyx and petals, supporting the interior organs, as in *Silene;* **anthoph′orous,** -*rus*, bearing flowers, floriferous ; **An′thophyta** (φυτὸν, plant), R. Brown's term for Phanerogams ; **An′thophyte** (φυτὸν, a plant), a flowering plant, a Phanerogam ; **Anthopto′sis** (πτῶσις, a falling), the fall of flowers.

An′thos, *An′thus* (ἄνθος, a flower), used in Greek compounds ; **An′thosperm** (σπέρμα, a seed), "a little coloured concretion scattered in the tissues of certain Fucoids" (Lindley) ; **Anthosper′mae** (σπέρμα, a seed), a division of plants intermediate between Angiospermae and Gymnospermae (Williams) ; **Anthostrob′ilus** (στρόβιλος, a fir-cone), the theoretic type of an Angiospermous flower (Arber and Parkin) ; **anthostrob′iloid** (εἶδος, resemblance), the adjective of the preceding ; **Anthotax′is, Anthotax′y** (τάξις, order), the arrangement of the flower ; **anthotrop′ic** (τροπὴ, a turning), employed by Hansgirg for any curvature of the peduncle during flowering ; **Anthot′ropism,** any movement of the flower and its parts (Clements) ; **Anthoxan′thin**

(ξανθὸς, yellow), (1) the colouring-matter of yellow flowers ; (2) used by Frank as a synonym of CAROTIN ; **Anthozy′mase** (+ ZYMASE), an enzyme found by Béchamp in the petals of flowers.

anthrac′inus (Lat.), coal-black.

Anthrac′nose (ἄνθραξ, coal ; νόσος, disease), the "Bird's-Eye Rot" of the Vine, caused by *Phoma ampelinum*, Berk. et Curt.

An′thrax, disease in animals due to *Bacillus Anthracis*, Cohn.

Anth′rochore, an abbreviation of the following; **Anthro′pochore** (ἄνθρωπος, man ; χωρὶς, asunder); **anthropoch′orous,** following man, used by Rikli to denote plants which are introduced involuntarily by the agency of man ; **Anthro′pophile** (φιλέω, I love), a plant which follows cultivation ; **Anthro′pophyte** (φύτον, a plant), a plant introduced by cultivation ; *cf.* HEMEROPHYTE.

Anthu′rus ‡ (ἄνθος, flower ; οὐρὰ, tail), a cluster of flowers at the end of a long stalk ; **An′thus,** of old authors= COROLLA.

anti-, in composition=against.

An′tiarine, the active poisonous principle of the upas tree, *Antiaris toxicaria*, Lesch.

Antibi′onts (ἀντὶ, against ; βίος, life), antipathetic organisms ; **Antibio′sis,** antipathy, a term proposed by Vuillemin.

anti′cal, anti′cous, *anti′cus* (Lat., foremost), the fore-part : (1) that most remote or turned away from the axis ; (2) Spruce uses antical to denote the upper (dorsal) face of a stem in Hepaticae ; (3) occasionally employed for introrse, as applied to anthers.

Anti-cen′tral (ἀντὶ, against), employed by Praeger for plants whose distribution tends towards the coasts, avoiding the centre of the island ; **Antichem′ism** (+ CHEM), Cope's term to denote the protoplasm-producing energy, as antagonizing chemical force.

Anticipa′tory Inher′itance, suggested

by Boulger for what has since been called Precocity.

anticli′nal (ἀντὶ, against ; κλίνεω, I incline), perpendicular to the surface ; ~ **Cells**, "parent"-cells which persist in their primitive state without producing antipodal cells or vesicles ; Vesque further subdivides them into (a) inert, (b) active or albuminigenous, (c) cotyloid ; ~ **Planes**, ~ **Walls**, those which cut the surface or the periclinal walls at right angles ; **An′ticlines**, anticlinal walls or planes ; **anticlinan′thous** (ἄνθος, flower), the inferior scaly parts of some Composite flowers ; **anticryptogam′ic** (+CRYPTOGAMIC), used of mixtures for destroying fungi; **Antidimor′phism** (+ DIMORPHISM), varied shape of an organ in the same plant, as distinct from variation in two distinct individuals (Lindman) ; **antid′romal, antid′romous** (δρόμος, a course), the direction of a lateral spiral being different to that of the main stem ; ~ **Torsion**, a twist against the direction of twining ; **Antid′romy**, diverse twining ; used also when different individuals of the same species display right- and left-hand torsion ; **Antifer′ment** (+FERMENT), bodies which inhibit the action of enzymes ; **Antihet′erophylly** + (HETEROPHYLLY) = ANTIDIMORPHISM ; **Antikin′ase** (+ KINASE = ANTIFERMENT ; **Antily′sin** (λύσις, a loosing), any substance which inhibits catalytic action ; **antimycot′ic** (μύκης, μύκητος, fungus), fungicidal ; **antipathet′ic** (παθητικὸς, suffering), applied to plants which do not easily unite by grafting (Crozier) ; **Antip′athy**, the quality shown by antipathetic plants ; **antipedunc′ular** (pedunculus, a stalk), placed opposite a peduncle ; **antipet′alous** (πέταλον, a flower leaf), opposite or superposed to a petal, not alternate ; the same as OPPOSITIPETALOUS; **An′tiphyte** (φυτὸν, plant), in alternation of generations, that generation which produces reproductive cells asexually, the antithetic

generation (Celakovsky) ; adj. **antiphyt′ic** ; **antip′odal** (ποῦς, ποδὸς, foot) ~ **Cells**, three cells at the base of the embryo sac, formed by division of the primary nucleus, when surrounded by protoplasm and finally cell walls ; **antisep′alous** (+ SEPALUM), opposite to or upon a sepal, that is, not alternate with it ; a shorter word for OPPOSITISEPALOUS ; **antisep′tic** (σηπτικὸς, putrefying), preventing putrefaction.

Antisperm′y (ἀντὶ, against ; σπέρμα, a seed), Delpino's term for the coalescence of the fertile divisions of the phyllome into a single fertile body opposed and superposed to the sterile division, in Phanerogams ; in Pteridophytes he terms this phenomenon **Antisporan′gism** (σπορὰ, seed ; ἀγγεῖον, vessel).

antithet′ic (ἀντίθεσις, opposition), in alternation of generations opposed to homologous, implying that the two generations are different in origin.

Antitox′in (ἀντι, against + TOXIN), a substance secreted by the plant to protect itself against harmful bacteria ; adj. **antitox′ic** ; **antit′ropal, antit′ropous**, -*pus* (τροπὴ, a turn), a synonym of Orthotropal as applied to ovules ; **antitrop′ic** (τροπὴ, a turning), (1) suggested by A. Gray for twining against the sun, that is, sinistrorse ; (2) relating to **Antit′ropy** ; Lopriore's term for roots which branch in opposite directions from the main axis ; **antiulto′nian** (+ ULTONIAN), used by Praeger for plants whose distribution is least in the province of Ulster ; **antizy′mic, antizymot′ic** (ζύμη, yeast), preventing fermentation.

an′trorse, *antror′sus* (*antero-*, before ; *versus*, turned backwards), directed upwards, opposed to RETRORSE.

Ant′rum ‡ (Lat., a cave) = POMUM.

anu′cleate (*a*, without, + NUCLEUS), non-nucleate.

-a′num, Clements's suffix to denote "LAYER."

ap-, apo-, prefix of negation (Rothert);

Apaërotax′is ($ἀὴϵ$, air ; $τάξις$, order), used by Rothert for negative stimulus by oxygen, in the case of anaërobic organisms.

apag′ynus ‡ ($ἄπαξ$, once; $γυνὴ$, woman), monocarpic.

Apan′dry ($ἀπο$, without ; $ἀνὴρ$, $ἀνδρὸς$, man) ; (1) M'Nab's term for fusion of the antheridium with the oogonium ; also applied to the pollen-tube ; (2) the loss of function in the male organs ; adj. **apan′drous.**

aparaph′ysate (a, without ; $παρὰ$, near ; $φύομαι$, I am born), destitute of paraphyses ; **aperisperm′ic,** *aperisperma′tus* (+ PERISPERM), exalbuminous.

apertiflo′rous (*flos, floris,* a flower), Boulger's term for CHASMOGAMIC.

Aper′tio (Lat., unfolding)= ANTHESIS.

Apertu′ra (Lat., opening), (1) formerly used of the dehiscence of anthers ; (2) the ostiole of certain Fungi ; **apert′us** (Lat., opened), exposed, naked.

Apet′alae (a, without ; $πέταλον$, a flower leaf), plants wanting petals or corolla ; **apet′alous,** *-lus,* **apet′alose,** without petals, or with a single perianth, as in *Clematis,* where the coloured sepals simulate petals ; **Apet′alousness,** being without petals; **Apet′aly,** the condition of wanting petals ; *cf.* APETALOUSNESS.

A′pex ‡ pl. **A′pices** (Lat., summit), (1) an old name for Anther ; (2) the ostiole of Fungi (Lindley) ; (3) the growing point of a stem or root ; (4) the tip of an organ ; **Floral ∼ =** MAMELON.

Aphan′eri, pl. (a, not ; $φανερὸς$, manifest), organisms which are not visible without the aids of re-agents (Maggi).

Aphan′isis ($ἀφάνισις$, disappearance), suppression of parts.

Aphanocy′clae ($ἀφανὴς$, unseen; $κύκλος$, a circle), Sachs's name for certain plants where the whorls are not very manifest, as Nymphaeaceae.

Aphaptot′ropism (+ HAPTOTROPISM), not influenced by touching stems or other surfaces (G. Henslow).

Apheliot′ropism ($ἀπο$, from ; $ἥλιος$, the sun ; $τροπὴ$, a turning), turning away from the light, negative heliotropism, as in roots ; adj. **apheliotrop′ic.**

Aphleb′ia (a, without ; $φλὲψ$, $φλεβὸς$, vein), used generically by C. Presl, but descriptively by Solms-Laubach for anomalous pinnae on the rhachis of certain fossil ferns, and the existing *Hemitelia capensis,* R. Br. ∼ **Traces,** pinna traces in *Diplolabis* derived from aphlebiae ; **apho′tic, aphotis′tic** ($φῶτιστής$, one who gives light), growing practically without light, as abyssal organisms may do ; *cf.* APHOTISTES ; **Aphotis′tes** ‡, a plant growing in the absence of light, as a Truffle.

aphotomet′ric (a, not ; $φῶς$, $φωτὸς$, light ; $μέτρον$, measure), applied by Strasburger to phototactic zoospores, which constantly turn the same extremity to the light ; opposed to PHOTOMETRIC ; **Aphototax′is** (+ PHOTOTAXIS), the condition of organisms which are unaffected by the stimulus of light ; adj. **aphototac′tic** **Aphotot′ropism** (+ PHOTOTROPISM), turning away from light.

Aph′rostase ‡ ($ἀφρὸς$, froth ; $στάσις$, standing), cellular tissue.

Aph′thae ($ἄφθαι$, ulcerations in the mouth), the disease known as Thrush, ascribed to *Saccharomyces albicans,* Reess ; **Aphthaphy′te** ($φυτὸν$, plant), the Fungi mentioned above as causing the disease.

Aphydrotax′is ($ἀπο$, from ; $ὕδωρ$, water $τάξις$, order), repulsion from water.

Aphyll′ae (a, without ; $φύλλον$, leaf) (1) Lindley's term for THALLOPHYTES ; (2) plants having only rudimentary leaves or none (Schimper) **aphyll′ous,** *-lus,* **aphyll′ose,** wanting leaves ; **aphyllop′odous** ($πούς$, $ποδὸς$ a foot), the stem of *Hieracium* when leafy, and without a basal rosette of leaves ; **Aph′ylly,** suppression of leaves.

a′pical, *apica′lis* (*apex, apicis,* summit), at the point of any structure ∼ **Axis,** in Diatoms, the line through the centre of the pervalvar axis is the direction of the raphe, at equal distances from homologous points of the girdle band surfaces, and through the apices ; ~ **Cell**, the single cell in many plants which is the origin of all longitudinal growth ; ~ **Cone** = PUNCTUM VEGE-TATIONIS ; ~ **Growth**, extension in the length of the axis ; ~ **Plane**, in Diatoms, the plane at right angles to the valvar plane, which passes through the pervalvar and apical axes ; *cf.* PERVALVAR ~ ; TRANS-APICAL ~ ; ~ **Pores**, special hyd-athodes and monocotyledons (Haber-landt) ; **apicicircinna'tus** ‡ (*circin-natus*, turned round), ending in a circinnate manner ; **apicil'lary**, *apicilla'ris*, inserted on, or per-taining to the summit, as in the dehiscence of the capsule of *Cerastium* ; **apic'ifixed** (*fixus*, fastened), descriptive of a suspended anther (Groom).

Apic'ula, *Apic'ulum* (Lat., a little point), a sharp and short, but not stiff point, in which a leaf may end ; **apic'ulate**, *apicula'tus*, fur-nished with an apicula.

Apig'enin, a glucoside found in many Umbelliferae, especially *Apium*.

A'pilary (*a*, without ; πῖλος, hat), sup-pression of the upper lip in such flowers as *Calceolaria;* **Aplano-gametan'gium** (ἀγγεῖον, a vessel), the organ which gives rise to aplano-gametes ; **Aplanogam'etes** (ἀπλανής, not wandering ; γαμέτης, a spouse), a non-ciliated gamete, which may or may not be set free ; **Aplan'ospores** (σπορὰ, a seed), non-motile cells which are detached for propagation, formed asexually by true cell-forma-tion and rejuvenescence ; **aplasmo-dioph'orus** (*a*, without ; πλάσμα, moulded ; εῖδος, resemblance ; φορὸς, bearing), used of Myxogastres which do not produce plasmodia ; **aplas'tic** (πλαστὸς, moulded), not convertible into organic tissues ; **aplolepid'eous** (λεπὶς, a scale), applied to those Mosses having a single row of teeth or scales in the peristome ; **Aploperi-**

st'omi (ἀπλόος, simple ; περὶ, around ; στόμα, mouth), Mosses having a single row of teeth in the peristome, or none ; adj. **aploperistom'atous**.

apobat'ic (ἀποβαίνω, I depart), re-pulsive ; *cf.* STROPHIC.

Ap'oblast (ἀπο, up ; βλαστὸς, a germ), a barren shoot, as from pollard willows ; adj. **apoblas'tic** ; **Ap'ocarp**, *Apocarp'ium* (καρπὸς, fruit), a fruit which is **apocarp'ous**, *-pus*, that is, when the carpels of a Gynaecium are separate ; **Apocar'py** is the con-dition ; **Apochemotax'is** (+ CHEMO-TAXIS), negative attraction due to chemical influence ; repulsion ; adj. **apochemotac'tic**.

apocyna'ceous, **apocyn'eous**, relating to or resembling the genus *Apocy-num* or its allies.

apocyt'ial (κύτος, a hollow), of the nature of an **Apocyt'ium** or **Ap'ocyte**, an habitually plurinucleate mass of protoplasm, cell-division remaining in abeyance ; multinucleate and unicellular ; **Apoc'yty**, Vuillemin's term for non-cellular tissue in Fungi and Algae, the cells being reduced to several nuclei within the cell-wall.

apod'ial (*a*, without ; ποῦς, ποδὸς, foot), destitute of a PODIUM or foot-stalk ; **apodog'ynus** ‡ (γυνὴ, woman), applied to a disk which is not ad-herent to the ovary.

Apoëm'bryony (ἀπο, from ; ἔμβρυον, an embryo), the embryo-stage sup-pressed, the oosphere giving rise immediately to the vascular mem-bers ; **Apogalvanotax'is** (+ GAL-VANOTAXIS), negative GALVANO-TROPISM ; **apogam'ic**, apogamous.

Apog'amy (γάμος, marriage), (1) ab-normal budding and production of a bion by a prothallus without sexual intervention ; (2) indepen-dently framed by Romanes to ex-press "indiscriminate isolation" ; **meiot'ic** ~, apogamy after meiosis ; when the sporophyte originates from the oosphore or from gametophytic tissue ; **dip'loid** ~ = EUAPOGAMY ; **hap'loid** ~ = MEIOTIC APOGAMY ;

ob'ligate ~ = PARTHENAPOGAMY : somat'ic ~ = EUAPOGAMY ; gen'erative ~ = MEIOTIC APOGAMY ; adj. apog'amous ; Apog'eny (γένος, offspring), loss of power for sexual reproduction, the function of both male and female organs being destroyed.

apogeoesthet'ic (ἀπο, from ; αἰσθητικὸς, perceptible), when the young hypocotyl bends upwards (Czapek) ; Apoge'otaxis (γῆ, the earth ; τάξις, order), negative GEOTAXIS ; Apogeot'ropism (γῆ, the earth ; τροπὴ, a turn), growing away from the earth, as normal stems ; apogeotrop'ic, negatively geotropic ; Apogesta'tion (gestatio, a bearing), defined by A. S. Wilson as "the gestation of the germ of one plant in the tissue of a wholly different plant away from the generating system" ; Apog'yny (γυνὴ, woman), loss of reproductive power in the female organ.

apo'lar (α, privative ; πόλος, a pivot), applied by Bertrand and Cornaille, to indeterminate fibrovascular masses without tracheae, in Ferns.

apomic'tic, relating to Apomix'is (ἀπο, from ; μῖξις, intercourse) = APOGAMY ; apopet'alous (πέταλον, a flower leaf), having free petals ; polypetalous ; apophyll'ous (φύλλον, leaf), applied to parts of a single perianth whorl when free ; Apophototax'is (+ PHOTOTAXIS), the action of light causing no definite arrangement of organisms or chlorophyll granules ; adj. apophototac'tic ; Apoph'ysis (φύω, I grow), (1) the swelling below the capsule of *Splachnum* and other Mosses ; (2) also in the cone scale of *Pinus Pinaster*, Soland. ; apoph'ysate, possessing such an enlargement ; Ap'ophytes, pl. (φύτον, a plant), (1) Boulger's term for Lichens ; (2) Rikli's term for autochthonous plants which follow cultivation ; adj. apophyt'ial, -ic ; Apoplas'tidy (πλαστὸς, formed), modifications of the same species ; apoplasmo'dial (+ PLASMODIUM)), and apoplastog'amous (+ PLASTOGAMY), said of

the Acrasieae, as differing from the Myxogastres by the non-fusion of their cytoplastic elements (Hartog) ; apora'chial (+ RHACHIS), directed away from the rhachis (Davie) ; Aporog'amy (+ POROGAMY), when the pollen-tube does not pass through the micropyle ; adj. aporog'amous ; ap'oschist (σχιστὸς, split), used of a gamete in which cell-division does not occur, but the cell directly assumes the behaviour of a gamete (Hartog) ; aposep'alous (*sepalum*, calyx-leaf), having free sepals ; Aposmotax'is (+ OSMOTAXIS), the repulsive influence of certain solutions on organisms ; Ap'osperms (σπέρμα, a seed), plants defined by MacMillan as integrated separately from the placenta ; *cf.* SYNSPERMS ; Aposp'ory (σπορὰ, seed), suppression of spore-formation, the prothallus developing direct from the asexual generation ; direct ~, is normal but prolonged ; induced ~, where the prothalli produce buds forthwith (Lang) ; adj. aposp'orous ; Apost'asis (στάσις, standing), the monstrous disunion of parts normally united ; Apostax'is (στάζω, I drip) the abnormal loss of nutritive or secreted fluids by bleeding, gumming, etc. ; Apost'-rophe (στροφὴ, turning), the position assumed by the chloroplastids during intense light, along the sides of the cell-walls, instead of the outer surface ; negative ~, is caused by weak light, as at night, and positive ~, by strong light ; apostroph'ic, relating to APOSTROPHE ; ~ In'terval, the space on the PHOTRUM capable of apostrophizing chlorophyll granules (S. Moore) ; also termed Apostro-ph'ion ; Apostrophiza'tion, the act of chlorophyll granules in taking up the position of APOSTROPHE ; Apotaximorpho'sis (τάξις, order ; μόρφωσις, a shaping), Gubler's term for any teratologic change which seems antagonistic to the normal laws governing the organism ; Ap'o-thece = Apothe'cium (θήκη, a case), (1) an organ of fructification peculiar to lichens, and usually cup-shaped "Shields"; (2) bowl-shaped fructifications in Pezizaceae ; **Apothermotax'is** (+ THERMOTAXIS), insensibility to the influence of temperature ; **Apothigmotax'is** (+ THIGMOTAXIS), irritability induced by contact with a solid body (Rothert); **apotrop'ic**, used of the ascending axis (White); **Apot'ropism** = APOGEOTROPISM; **apot'ropous** (τροπὴ, a turning), used of an anatropous ovule with the raphe ventral ; **apotyp'ic** (τύπος, a type), an anomalous departure from the general law of development ; **Ap'otype**, a supplementary type, aiding the completion of descriptions ; *cf.* HYPOTYPE ; **Apoty'pose**, an abnormality in development (Gubler).

Appen'dage, Appen'dix (Lat., an addition), (1) a part added to another, as leaves are appendages to the stem; (2) a name given to processes of any kind, especially those of the perithecia of fungi ; (3) in the plural the term **Appen'dices** was formerly applied to suckers, such as the offsets of the pineapple.

appen'dent, *appen'dens* (*appendo*, I hang by), when the hilum is directed towards the upper part of the seed, which is sessile, or nearly so, on the placenta, as in stonefruits.

appendic'ulate, *appendicula'tus* (*appendicula*, a small appendage), (1) furnished with appendages ; (2) the pileus of an agaric, when portions of the secondary veil remain attached to the margin of the pileus ; **appendic'ular Ridges**, on guard-cells of certain Rhizophoreae, dividing the front cavity into two compartments ; **appen'dicled**, having small appendages.

Appendic'ulum ‡, diminutive of APPENDIX.

appense' (*appen'sus*, weighed), being hung up as a hat is upon a peg, an approach to pendulous (Lindley in Loudon, Encyc. Pl. 1095).

ap'planate, *applana'tus* (*ad*, to ; *plan-*

atus, made flat), flattened out or horizontally expanded.

Ap'ple, a fleshy, inferior, plurilocular, two to five-seeded fruit, technically styled a Pome.

applica'tus (Lat., *applicati'vus*, close to, or attached), applied face to face, without folding.

ap'posite, *appos'itus* (Lat., applied to), when similar parts are placed close to or side by side ; **apposifo'liar** (*folium*, leaf), an error for oppositifolious ; **Apposit'ion**, side by side or close to ; ~ **Theory**, of the growth of the cell-wall, as due to repeated disposition of layers of substance on the internal surface of the original cell-wall.

appress'ed, *appress'us*, (*ad*, to ; *pressus*, kept under), lying flat for the whole length of the organ ; **Appres'sors**, organs of attachment of germinating filaments of parasite to host ; **Appressor'ia**, pl., Frank's term for the exterior organs of attachment of parasitic Fungi, as distinct from the HAUSTORIA or absorbing organs.

approx'imate, *approxima'tus* (*ad*, to ; *proximo*, I approach), drawn close together, but not united.

Aprica'rium (*apricus*, lying open), the summer habitation of plants in botanic gardens, for exposure to sun and air ; **apri'cus** (Lat.), living in open sunny places.

ap'terous, *-rus* (*a*, without ; πτερὸν, a wing), wingless, used of petioles, seeds, and the like ; **apyre'nus** (πυρὴν, seed), applied to fruit which is seedless, as cultivated varieties of the pineapple, orange, or grape.

Aquar'ium (Lat., relating to water), a tank for aquatics in botanic gardens.

aquat'ic, *aquat'icus* (*aqua*, water), living in water ; *aquat'ilis*, has been defined as living under water ; the first category would include *Lemna* and *Typha*, the second, *Ceratophyllum, Chara*, etc.

aq'ueous *aq'ueus*, *aquo'sus* (Lat., watery), (1) indicates some colourless structure, hyaline ; (2) having much water in the tissues ; **aq'ueous Tissue**, consists of one or more layers

of thin-walled parenchymatous cells,
destitute of chloroplastids, with much
watery sap, without interspaces, and
acting as water-reservoirs ; **aquif′er-
ous** (*fero*, I bear) **Tissue,** is a synonym.
Aquilo′nary   Pe′riod (*aquilonaris*,
northern) = XEROTHERM.
Aquipra′ta (*aqua* water ; *pratum*, a
meadow), pl. plant-communities and
herbs, grasses, and bryophytes, where
influenced by ground-water.
Ar′abin, a substance derived from Gum
Arabic, deflecting the polarized beam
to the left ; **Ar′abinose,** a glucose
obtained from it, also from cherry-
gum; **Arabinox′ylan,** a hemicellulose,
found in the bran of wheat and rye.
ara′ceous, relating to the order
Araceae.
arach′noid, *arach′noideus* (ἀράχνη,
spider, or spider's web ; εἶδος, resemblance), like a cobweb, from an
entanglement of fine whitish hairs.
aralia′ceous, resembling the genus
Aralia, or the order of which it is
the type.
ara′neous ‡, *araneo′sus* ‡, **ara′neose**
(*aranea*, a spider), have the same
meaning as arachnoid.
Araro′ba, a powdery excretion in cavities of the Brazilian tree, *Andira
Araroba*, Aguiar.
Ar′bor (Lat., tree), a woody perennial
plant, having a bole from which
the branches spring ; **arbor′eous,**
arbor′eus, tree-like ; **arbores′cent,**
arbores′cens (+ ESCENS), attaining
the size or character of a tree ;
Ar′boret, a small tree or shrub ;
Arbore′tum, a place assigned for
the culture of trees, usually in
systematic order ; also the title of
a book devoted to trees ; **arboric′ol-
ine, arboric′olous** (+ suffix *-cola*,
inhabitant), dwelling on trees, as
the habitat of Fungi or epiphytes ;
ar′boroid (εἶδος, resemblance), a
hybrid word for dendroid, tree-
like.
Arbus′cula (Lat.), a small shrub with
the aspect of a tree, as some heaths ;
Ar′buscle is an old term for the
same ; **Arbus′culus** (Lat.), a small

tree ; **arbus′cular,** *arbuscula′ris*,
shrubby, and branched like a tree.
arbus′tive, *arbusti′vus* (Lat., planted
with trees), coppiced.
Arbus′tum (Lat.), (1) a shrub, a
branched woody perennial plant, but
wanting a distinct bole ; (2) applied
to an account of the woody plants of
a country ; a Sylva.
Ar′butin, a glucoside occurring in many
plants, especially Ericaceae ; it derives its name from *Arbutus*.
Arces′thide, Arces′thida (ἀρκευθίς, ίδος,
juniper berry) = GALBULUS.
Archae′ophytes (φυτόν, a plant), Rikli's
term for weeds introduced into cultivated ground in prehistoric time.
archa′ic (ἀρχαϊκός, antiquated), used
with reference to a type of a former
age, as *Casuarina*.
Archebio′sis (ἀρχή, beginning ; βίος,
life), origin of life ; **Arch′egone** =
ARCHEGONIUM ; **archego′nial** (γονή,
race), applied by Tschirch to stomata,
whose outer walls of the guard cells
are thickened, inner walls only a thin
lamella, the guard cells separated in
their central part but not at the
poles, as in Gymnosperms ; **archego′-
niate,** possessing archegonia ; **Arche-
gonia′tae,** plants producing archegonia, applied to Bryophytes and
Pteridophytes ; **Archego′niophores**
(φορέω, I bear), the supports of
archegonia in certain ferns, outgrowths of the prothalli, also
specialized branches on *Sphagnum*
with the same function ; **Archego′-
nium,** the female sexual organ in
Cryptogams, containing the oosphere,
which after fertilization develops
within the venter ; **Archene′ma**
(νῆμα, a thread), term proposed by
C. MacMillan for gametophytic structures in Thallophytes ; **Arch′esperm**
(σπέρμα, a seed), (1) the fertilized
contents of an archegonium (Bennett
and Murray) ; (2) also employed by
MacMillan, for plants with obligatory and **archesper′mic** seeds, with
monomorphous embryos ; **Arch′-
espore, Archespor′ium** (σπορά, a
seed), the cell or cells from which

the spores are ultimately derived as in the pollen-sac, or its homologue ; **archespor'ial**, belonging to the same ; **~ Cells**, the original cells in spore-formation ; **~ Pad**, Bower's term for a mass of cells developing beneath the sporogenous tissue in certain Pteridophytes; **Arch'etype** (τύπος, a type), an original simple type ; restricted to a series of forms from the simplest to complicated, with common type of structure and phylogenetic connections.

Archianth'emum (ἀρχι, prefix for chief or primitive ; ἄνθεμον, a flower), C. Schimper's term for a well-developed flower at the apex of a botryoid inflorescence, where it is normally absent (Penzig).

Arch'icarp (ἀρχή, beginning ; καρπός, fruit), in ascomycetous Fungi, the beginning of a fructification, the cell or group of cells fertilized by a sexual act ; **Archichlamyd'eae** (χλαμύς, -υδος, a mantle), Engler's term to include the Polypetalae and Incompletae of Phanerogams ; **Age of ~** , the Middle Tertiary Period is so termed by MacMillan ; **Archicleistog'amy** (+ CLEISTOGAMY), the condition of permanently closed flowers, whose organs are considerably smaller than those of normal flowers (Loew); **archigon'ic** (γόνος, offspring), arising by spontaneous generation (Haeckel) ; **Archigymnosper'mae** (+ GYMNOSPERM), Jeffrey's term for the ferns and the lower Gymnosperms ; **Archimyce'tes** (μύκης, a mushroom), unicellular Fungi, parasitic on Diatoms (Marpmann).

arch'ing, curved like a bow.

Arch'isperm (ἀρχή, beginning ; σπέρμα, seed), (1) another name for Gymnosperms, from their presumed antiquity ; (2) Boulger's term for structures formed before fertilization, or at an early stage in the macrospore ; **Arch'isphere** (σφαῖρα, a sphere), the contents of an archegonium previous to fertilization.

Archistrep'tes (ἀρχι, chief ; στρεπτὸς

twisted), the principal spirals formed in phyllotaxis.

Archocleistog'amy (ἀρχὸς, chief ; + CLEISTOGAMY), when the flowers remain closed at the time when the sexual organs ripen (Knuth) ; *cf.* ARCHICLEISTOGAMY ; **Arch'oplasm** (πλάσμα, moulded), Boveri's term for KINOPLASM ; adj. **archoplas'mic** ; **~ Sphere** = ACHROMATIC SPINDLE.

arct'ic, a term applied by H. C. Watson to a British region, comprising three zones, styled **super-**, **mid-**, and **infer-arctic** zones, relating to plants growing above the limits of cultivation.

arctogae'al (γαῖα, the earth), in plant-distribution refers to Huxley's term **Arctogae'a**, which includes Europe, Asia, Africa, and North America as far as Mexico.

arc'uate, *arcua'tus* (Lat.), bent like a bow, curved ; **arcua'to-areola'tus**, divided into spaces by curves ; **~ -contort'us**, forming a depressed spiral, as in some legumes.

Ardell'a (ἄρδω, I sprinkle), small apothecia of certain lichens, as *Arthonia*, seemingly dusty ; **Ardi'um** or **Ardi'on** (ἄρδω, I irrigate), a formation of plants due to irrigation (Clements).

ardos'iacus (Mod. Lat., from Fr. ardoise, slate), slate-grey ; **arde'siacus**, slate-coloured (Clements).

-are, suffix denoting a community (Clements).

A'rea (Lat., a space), (1) a bed in botanic gardens ; (2) in Diatoms, the surface of a valve when circular and destitute of a stauros ; (3) ‡ the receptacle of certain Fungi (Lindley) ; (4) A. Braun's term for the space round the sporangium in *Isoëtes ;* **~ of Infec'tion**, the part open to attack, as the stomata, epidermis or wound.

arena'ceous, **arena'rious**, *arena'rius*, *areno'sus* (arena, sand), growing in sandy places.

Arenariet'um, a formation in which *Arenaria* is dominant or exclusive (Clements) ; **Arena'rion**, a family of *Arenaria* (Clements).

arenic'olous (*arena*, sand ; *colo*, I inhabit), growing in sand or sandy places ; **Arenoph'ilae** (φιλέω, I love), sand-loving plants.

Are'ola (Lat., diminutive of AREA), (1) a space marked out on a surface ; (2) a small cell or cavity ; (3) a tessellation in the thallus of some Lichens ; (4) a lumen in the sporangium of *Achlya* due to the influx of water (Harper) ; **are'olar, are'olate,** *areola'-tus*, marked with areolae, divided into distinct spaces ; **Areola'-tion**, in Mosses, the arrangement of the cells.

arg'entate, *argent'eus* (Lat., silvery), silvery as to tint and lustre ; **argenta'tus** (Lat.), silvered.

argilla'ceous, *-ceus* (Lat.), clayey, growing in clay, or clay-coloured ; **argil'licole** (+ *colo*, I inhabit), dwelling on clay ; **argillo'sus** (Lat.), living in clayey places.

Ar'ginin (deriv. ?), a proteid peculiar to the Coniferae, occurring in their seeds and etiolated seedlings.

arg'os, in Greek compounds = white ; in Latin, *candidus*.

Argotax'is (ἀργὸs, passive ; τάξιs, order), passive movements due to surface-tension (Pfeffer).

argute', *argu'tus* (Lat.), sharp, as *argute'-serra'tus*, sharply-serrate.

arg'yros, in Greek compounds = silvery ; Lat., *argenteus*.

arhi'zal, *arhi'zus* = ARRHI'ZAL, etc.

Ar'icine, an alkaloid from cinchona bark, obtained from Arica, in Chili.

arieti'nous (*arieti'nus*, pertaining to a ram), like a ram's head (Heinig).

A'ril, Arill'us (Fr., arille), (1) an expansion of the funicle, arising from the placenta, and enveloping the seed ; mace is the aril of the nutmeg ; (2) used by J. E. Smith for the utricle of *Carex* ; **ar'illate,** *arilla'tus*, possessed of an aril ; **arilliform'is** ‡ (*forma*, shape), bag-shaped ; **A'ril-lode, Arillo'dium,** a false aril, a coat of the seed, and not arising from the placenta ; **aril'loid** (εἶδοs, resemblance), like an aril.

ari'nus (ἄρρην, male), Necker's suffix

to words enumerating stamens, instead of the Linnean -androus.

Aris'ta (Lat.), an awn, the beard of corn ; **arist'ate,** *arista'tus*, awned ; **aris'tulate,** *aristula'tus*, bearing a small awn.

aristolochia'ceous, resembling the genus *Aristolochia*, Tourn.

aristosty'lous (ἀριστερὸs, left ; στῦλοs, a pillar), applied to a flower with an exserted style bent towards the left.

Arm-pal'isade (+ PALISADE), cells having protrusions which amalgamate with each other in the palisade-tissue ; ~ -por'tion, of two-armed hairs ; ~ -tis'sue, elements having the shape of the letter **H** (Haberlandt).

Ar'ma (Lat.), **Ar'mature**, any kind of defence, as prickles or thorns ; **armed**, bearing thorns or similar defences.

armenia'ceous, *armen'iacus*, (1) apricot-coloured, a dull orange, named from *Prunus Armeniaca*, Linn. ; (2) a native of Armenia.

Armill'a (Lat., bracelet), the frill of the stipe of Agarics left attached on the expansion of the pileus ; at first it forms a covering of the hymenium ; **ar'millate**, consisting of rings or circles ; **ar'millary**, like a bracelet (Heinig).

Arnat'to, also written **Arnotto** and **Annotto**, the red colouring matter from the pulp of the fruit of *Bixa Orellana*, Linn.

aroid'eous, relating to the family Aroideae.

Aro'ma (Lat., spice), the perfume of a plant ; **aromat'ic,** *-cus*, possessing a spicy smell or taste.

arrect', *arrect'us* (Lat., set upright), stiffly erect.

Arrest' (*arrestare*, Late Lat., to stop), employed by Goebel to include ABORTION and SUPPRESSION ; **sporal** ~ , see SPORAL ARREST.

arrhi'zal, arrhi'zous, *arrhizus* (α, without ; ρίζα, a root), rootless, wanting true roots ; **Arrhizoblas'tus** ‡ (βλαστὸs, a germ), an embryo which has no radicle.

Ar′row-head′ed, ~ **shaped**, barbed like an arrow, sagittate.

arth′onoid, artho′nioid, of the form or consistence of the apothecia in the genus *Arthonia*, Ach. (The generic name is falsely derived from an imaginary ἄρθω ; it should be *Ardonia* from ἄρδω).

arthrodes′moid, resembling in form the Desmid genus *Arthrodesmus* (Archer).

arthrog′enous (ἄρθρον, a joint; γένος, offspring), when portions separate from the cell, and gradually develop into distinct individuals (Massee) ; *e. g.* ~ **Spores**, in Bacteria when portions separate from the cell and develop into spores ; **Arth′rospore** (σπορὰ, a seed), one of spores like a chain of beads, formed by fission ; **arthrospor′ic, arthrosp′orous**, applied to Schizomycetes, in those species which have no endogenous spore-formation ; **Arthrosterig′mata** (στήριγμα, -ατος, a prop), jointed sterigmata in some Lichens, made up of rows of cells from which spores are abstricted.

Art′icle, *Artic′ulus* (Lat.), a joint ; **artic′ulated**, *articula′tus*, (1) jointed, separating freely by a clean scar, as in leaf-fall ; (2) used by Bentham and Hooker for the jointed pod of *Desmodium* ; **Articula′tion**, (1) a joint, popularly applied to the nodes of grasses ; (2) the basal portion of the sensitive bristle in *Dionaea ;* **Artic′uli**, the segments of coralline Algae, usually incrusted with lime.

Art′ifact (*ars*, art ; *factus*, made), a substance not naturally existing, but resulting from laboratory treatment ; **artific′ial**, *artificia′lis* (Lat., according to rules of art), applied to any scheme of classification which is based on one set of characters, as opposed to a natural scheme, which takes all characters into account.

artiphyll′ous, *-lus* (ἄρτιος, complete ; φύλλον, leaf), used of nodes which bear manifest buds.

Ar′tolin (ἄρτος, a loaf), the proteid of wheat-gluten.

arun′coid (εἶδος, like), resembling *Spiraea Aruncus.*

arundina′ceous, *arundina′ceus*, reed-like, having a culm like tall grasses ; **arundin′eous**, reedy, abounding in reeds.

arven′sis, (*arva*, arable land), applied to plants of cultivated land, especially of ploughed fields.

Asafoet′ida (*aza*, Persian for mastic ; *foetidus*, stinking), a gum-resin of a persistent alliaceous odour and taste, yielded by *Ferula Narthex*, Boiss., and other allied Umbelliferae.

As′arin, the bitter principle of Asarabacca, *Asarum europaeum*, Linn. ; **As′arine**, a crystallized substance resembling camphor.

Ascell′us, (1) diminutive of Ascus ; (2) the spores of certain Fungi (Lindley).

ascend′ent, *-ens*, **ascend′ing**, (1) directed upwards, as the stem ; the ascending axis is oblique at first, then erect ; (2) opposed to descending.

-ascens, a suffix denoting a tendency towards something, as *ciner-ascens*, becoming ash-coloured, *cinereus.*

ascidia′tus (Lat.), furnished with ASCIDIA ; **Ascid′ium** (ἀσκίδιον, a little pitcher), pl. **Ascid′ia**, (1) the pitcher of *Nepenthes*, etc., the metamorphosed lamina of the leaf, becomes tubular, usually with a lid, which is a development of the apical portion of the leaf ; (2) the asci of certain Fungi ; **ascid′iform** (*forma*, shape), pitcher-shaped.

ascif′erous (*ascus*, Mod. Lat., a wineskin ; *fero*, I bear), bearing asci ; **ascig′erous** (*gero*, I produce) = ASCIFEROUS.

asciifor′mis (*ascia*, a hatchet ; *formis*, shape), used by Masters for hatchet-shaped ; dolabriform.

asclepiad′eous, like the genus *Asclepias* or its allies, as to structure ; **Asclepiadol′ogy** (λόγος, discourse), the science, or a treating of the order of Asclepiadeae (Schlechter).

As′cocarp (ἀσκὸς, a wine-skin ; καρπὸς, fruit), the sporocarp of Ascomycetes producing asci and ascospores ; **its**

three kinds are termed APOTHECIUM, PERITHECIUM and CLEISTOCARP ; **As′cocyst** (κύστις, a cavity), a large hyaline empty cell with a thick wall, by some authors termed a paraphysis, occurring in *Myrionema* and allied genera (Sauvageau) ; **ascogen′ic, ascog′enous** (γένος, offspring), producing asci, asciferous ; **ascogo′nial**, relates to an **As′cogone,** or **Ascogo′nium** (γονὴ, race), (1) a synonym of ARCHICARP ; (2) a portion of an Archicarp, the contents taking part in forming ascogenous hyphae = reproductive cells containing female nuclei (V. Blackman) ; **Ascoli′chenes,** Lichens producing asci ; **Asc′oma,** Wallroth's term for Receptacle and Hymenium of Fungi ; **Ascomyce′tes** (μύκης, fungus), Sachs's name for a large group of Fungi, forming ascospores and stylospores.

Ascop′ora, an error (?) for the next.

Asc′ophore, (ἀσκὸς, a bag ; φορέω, I carry), the ascus-bearing hyphae within an ascocarp ; **ascoph′orous** ascus-bearing ; **Ascoph′yses** (φύω, I make grow), the hyphae which constitute the ascogenous cushion in *Chaetomium ;* **As′cospore** (σπορὰ, a seed), a spore produced by an ascus, sometimes termed sporidium or sporule ; **As′cus,**pl. **As′ci** (pr. as′si), a large cell, usually the swollen end of a hyphal branch, in the ascocarp of which normally eight spores are developed ; ~**Appara′tus,** a portion of the sporocarp, comprising the asci and the ascogenous cells ; ~ **suffulto′rius,** Corda's term for BASIDIUM.

ascy′phous (α, without ; σκύφος, a beaker), without SCYPHI ; **asep′tate** (*septum,* an enclosure), without partitions or cross-divisions ; **asep′-tic** (σηπτικός, putrefying), not liable to become rotten ; **asex′ual** (*sexualis,* pertaining to sex), destitute of male or female organs ; neuter ; ~ **Genera′tion,** in alternation, that generation which produces spores asexually, but is itself the product

of a sexual act ; thus, in Ferns, the full-grown form is the asexual form or sporophyte, the prothallus the sexual form or gametophyte.

Ash, the mineral residue of plants after complete combustion.

Ash-Oak′wood association, woodland having a quantity of ash-trees with oak usually co-dominant ; **Ash′wood** association, the ash dominant, characteristic of limestone hills in Yorkshire and Derbyshire.

Asim′ina = ASSIMINUM.

Asiphon′ogam (α, privative + SIPHONOGAM), a plant fertilized by antherozoids ; a cryptogam ; **asomat′ic** (σῶμα, body), having only embryonal parts (Pfeffer) ; **Asomat′ophyte** (φύτον, a plant), plants without permanent tissues.

Aspar′agi (ἀσπάραγος, *asparagus*), formerly used for TURIONES or suckers, young shoots emerging from the rootstock under ground, and at first bearing scales only, as in *Asparagus ;* **Aspar′agin,** a commonly occurring amide, which was first obtained from *Asparagus officinalis,* Linn., hence its name ; **asparag′inous,** applied to plants whose young shoots are eaten as asparagus.

As′pect (*aspectus,* sight, view), "the seasonal impress of a formation, *e. g.* the spring aspect" (Clements).

as′per (Lat., rough), **as′perate, as′-perous,** rough with hairs or points.

aspergill′iform, *aspergilliform′is* (*aspergillum,* Mod. Lat., holy-water brush ; *forma,* shape), tufted, brush-shaped as the stigmas of grasses.

Aspergill′in, pigment of the spores of *Aspergillus niger,* Van Tiegh., now known as *Sterigmatocystis nigra,* Sacc.

asperifo′liate, asperifo′lius (*asper,* rough ; *folium,* leaf), rough-leaved, as *Borrago officinalis,* Linn. ; **As′per′ity** (*asperitas*), roughness.

asperm′ous (α, without ; σπέρμα, seed), seedless.

as′perous (*asper,* rough), scabrous, harsh to the touch ; **asper′ulous,** slightly rough with little points (Braithwaite).

Åsphyx′ia (ἀσφυξία, without a pulse), in plants, insensibility brought on by suspension of respiration due to absence of oxygen (Dutrochet).

Aspide′tum Ganong's term for a bog-marsh plant-association of *Carex* and *Aspidium*, whence the name.

Aspidia′ria, formerly the name of a genus of fossils, now applied to a lepidodendroid stem when the cortex has been stripped off (Scott).

Aspidosper′motype, a wind-dispersed seed resembling the seed of *Aspidosperma*, circular in shape, with the weight of the seed in the centre (Dingler).

asple′nioid, (εἶδος, resemblance), like the Fern genus, *Asplenium*.

Asporomyce′tes (α, without ; σπορὰ, a seed ; μύκης, fungus), Marchand's name for Fungi imperfecti.

Assimila′tion, *Assimila′tio* (*assimulo*, I make like), the process by which extraneous matter, crude food, is converted into plant substance ; constructive metabolism ; used especially for the formation of organic substance from carbon dioxide and water by green plants in sunlight ; **Assimila′ta**, pl., the first-formed products ; **assim′ilative**, conducing to Assimilation ; ~ **Fil′aments**, sterile hairs which grow intermixed with the sporangia of such Algae as *Ectocarpus*.

Assim′inum (Fr., Assiminier, a name of *Asimina triloba*, Dun.), Desvaux's name for Syncarpium.

Association (Plant) ; term proposed to supersede Plant Formation or Plant Society ; Dan. Plantesamfund, Ger. Pflanzenverein ; **Chief** ~ , = stable association ; **Closed** ~ , the ground fully covered by plants ; **Interme′diate** ~ , more or less covered ; **Mixed** ~ , several species competing for dominance ; **O′pen** ~ , partly covered with vegetation ; **Pas′sage** ~ , leading from one to another ; **Progres′sive** ~ , open and intermediate, tending towards stable ; **Pure** ~ , a single species dominant ; **Retrogres′sive** ~ , a decaying stable-association ;

Stable ~ , in a state of equilibrium, but may degenerate ; **Subor′dinate** ~ , a progressive or retrogressive association ; **Sub′stitute** ~ , a secondary formation (W. G. Smith) ; **Transit′ional** ~ , in course of development ; **Unsta′ble** ~ , leading to an intermediate association.

Assumen′ta (pl. of *assumentum*, a patch), the valves of a siliqua.

assur′gent, *assur′gens* (*ad*, to ; *surgo*, I rise), rising upward ; ascending.

Astath′e ‡ (ἀσταθής, unstable), " a substance supposed by Hartig to lie between the outer and inner lining of a cell " (Lindley) ; secondary membrane (von Mohl).

Aste′ly (α, without ; στήλη, pillar), destitute of a stele, or axial cylinder of tissue ; *cf.* Schizostely ; adj. **aste′lic**.

As′ter (ἀστήρ, a star), a stage in nuclear division ; the chromatin forms rods over a great part of the fusiform nucleus, its poles being occupied by fine achromatic filaments ; *cf.* Dyaster.

astera′ceous, allied to the group of Compositae of which the genus *Aster* is the type.

aster′iate (Heinig) = Asteroid.

Asterid′ia, pl. (ἀστήρ, a star, ιδιον = diminutive), spinous or . stellate bodies occurring in the cells of Conjugatae, possibly some parasitic form (Archer) ; **Asterosphae′ria**, pl. (σφαῖρα, a sphere), a synonym of the same.

As′terile (*Aster*, Tourn., + ILE), Clements's term for a " Society " of *Aster ;* **ast′eroid** (εἶδος, resemblance), (1) star-shaped ; (2) like the genus, *Aster*, Tourn.

ast′ichous, *as′tichus* ‡ (α, without ; στίχος, row, line), not arranged in rows.

Astig′matae (α, without, + Stigma), Van Tieghem's name for the Archegoniatae ; *cf.* Stigmatae ; **Astigmat′icae**, Knuth's term for wind-fertilized plants which do not possess stigmas, such as Gymno-

sperms; **astip'ulate** (α, without, +
STIPULA) = EXSTIPULATE ; **astom'-
atal** (+ STOMA), wanting stomata ;
ast'omous, *ast'omus* (στόμα, mouth),
not having an orifice.

astrag'aloid (ἀστράγαλος, a knuckle-
bone; εἶδος, resemblance), (1) dice-
shaped (Heinig) ; (2) having affinity
with the genus *Astragalus*.

as'tral (+ ASTER), relating to the
ASTER in cytology.

Astrocen'ters (ἀστήρ, a star ; κέντρον,
point, centre), C. MacMillan's term
for the bodies variously known as At-
traction-spheres, Directive-spheres,
Tinoleucites, etc. ; **Astroscle'reids**
(σκληρὸς, hard), thick-walled star-
shaped cells occurring in the leaves
of *Camellia*, and frequently in bark
amongst the surrounding parenchymatous cells (Tschirch); **Ast'rospheres**
(σφαῖρα, a sphere), Strasburger's term
for ASTROCENTERS.

As'trophe, or **As'trophy** (α, not ; στροφή,
a turning), negative EPISTROPHE
(S. Moore) ; **Asymblas'ty** (α, not ;
σὺν, with ; βλαστὸς, shoot), the
various periods of germination of the
seeds of the same plant (Haberlandt) ;
asymmet'ric, asymmet'rical (σύμμετρος, symmetric), (1) irregular in
outline or shape ; (2) used of a flower
which cannot be divided in any vertical plane into two similar halves ;
(3) dissimilarity of the number of the
members in calyx, corolla or genitalia;
Asym'metry (+SYMMETRY), term extended by Goebel to express the
dissimilarity of lateral halves and
leaflets, irrespective of the entire
leaf ; **asyngam'ic** (γάμος, marriage),
used of plants prevented from intercrossing by their flowering at different times ; **Asyn'gamy** (γάμος,
marriage), the natural prevention of
cross-pollination by the respective
plants or species flowering at different times (Kerner) ; **asynthet'ic**
(σύνθετος, compounded) **Gonid'ia**,
free Lichen gonidia, occurring on the
outside of the thallus (Koerber).

atactodes'mic (ἄτακτος, out of order ;
δεσμή, bundle), applied to the vas-

cular system of Monocotyledons
(Brebner) ; **Atact'ostele** (+STELE),
Brebner's term for the monostele of
Monocotyledons, having scattered
vascular bundles imbedded in conjunctive ground-tissue ; also in Dicotyledons when the meristeles are not
in a single ring ; adj. **atactoste'lic** ;
Atactoste'ly, the condition described.

At'avism (*atavus*, an ancestor), ancestral resemblance, reversion to an
older type ; **At'avist**, applied to a
plant showing that tendency ; **ata-
vist'ic**, reverting to an older type of
structure.

ataxinom'ic (α, not ; τάξις, order ; νόμος
law), used for teratologic, abnormal
structures not represented among
plants in a normal condition, as
Fasciation, Chloranthy, etc.

ataxonom'ic (α, not, + TAXONOMIC),
any part of botany which is
not concerned with systematic
work.

ateg'minous, (α, without ; *tegmen*,
covering), used of naked ovules
(Goebel) ; **Ateg'miny**, is the state.

a'ter (Lat.), pure, lustreless black ; in
composition, atro-.

athal'amous (α, without ; θάλαμος,
bride-chamber), said of Lichens
without apothecia on their thallus.

athall'ine (α, without ; θαλλὸς, young
shoot), without thallus.

Ath'era, (ἀθήρ, -έρος, beard of corn),
in Greek compounds=awn or stiff
bristle.

Atlant'ic Type of Distribution, H. C.
Watson's term for British plants
which occur most frequently towards
the west of Great Britain.

At'mograph (ἀτμὸς, vapour ; γράφω, I
write), an instrument for measuring
the amount of water evaporated.

At'om (α, not ; τέμνω, I cut), defined by
Nägeli as the ultimate particle of a
chemical element ; in botanic par-
lance it means the smallest divisible
portion of any substance.

at'omate (+ATOM), " sprinkled with
atoms " (Stevenson).

Atomogyn'ia (ἀτομὸς, cannot be cut ;
γυνή, woman), the elder Richard's

name for the ANGIOSPERMIA of Linnaeus.

Atracten'chyma ‡ (ἄτρακτος, a spindle; ἔγχυμα, that poured in), prosenchyma, a tissue of fusiform cells.

atramenta'rius (*atramentum*, inky fluid), inky ; black.

atrate', **atra'tous**, *atra'tus*, (garbed in black) ; defined by Heinig as "turning black " ; blackened, as in some species of *Carex*, the apex of the glumes being darkened ; **atric'olor** (*color*, colour), inky-black.

Atriplice'tum, an association of species of *Atriplex*, with *Suaeda* and similar plants (Warming).

at'ropal, preferably **at'ropous** (α, not ; τροπή, a turn), a synonym of ORTHOTROPOUS ; applied to the ovule.

atroph'ic (α, without ; τροφὴ, nourishment) = APLASTIC ; **At'rophy** (τροφὴ, nourishment), wasting away, abortion or degeneration of organs ; **At'rophytes** (φυτὸν, a plant), those Fungi which cause atrophy of important organs of the host-plant.

At'ropine, a poisonous alkaloid obtained from *Atropa Belladonna*, Linn.

atro-purpu'reus (Lat.), black-purple, the colour of Sweet Scabious, *Scabiosa atropurpurea*, Linn. ; ~ **-violaceus** (Lat.), very dark violet ; ~ **-virens**, ~ **-viridis** (Lat.), dark or blackish green ; **a'trous**, dead black (Heinig).

Attach'ment-disc, the holdfast or basal hapteron of an Alga.

atten'uate, *attenua'tus* (Lat., thinned), narrowed, tapered.

Attire', Grew's term for stamens and pistils.

Attrac'tion-spheres, the same as **Attrac'tive-spheres**, CENTROSPHERES, or Tinoleucites ; ~ **Glands** of *Nepenthes*, situated within the ascidia, to·tempt insects farther down the tube (Macfarlane).

-a'tus, a suffix indicating the presence of an organ, thus : foli-atus, having leaves.

atyp'ic (α, not ; τύπος, a type), (1) not typical, departing from the type ; (2) ALLOTYPIC MITOSIS.

auc'tus (Lat., increased) ; (1) enlarged after flowering, accrescent ; (2) augmented by an addition.

aucupa'rious (*aucupari*, to catch birds), "attracting birds " (Heinig), employed in bird-snaring.

Augment-Cells, a modification of an auxospore in Diatoms, after division becoming transformed into daughter-cells, and the starting-points of new generations ; **Augmenta'tion**, increase beyond the normal number of parts.

aulacocar'pous (αὔλαξ, a furrow ; καρπός, fruit), with furrowed fruit, sulcate (Heinig).

Aulae'um ‡ (Lat., a curtain), used occasionally for COROLLA by Linnaeus.

Au'lax-galls, galls which resemble stone-fruits produced by gall-wasps of the genus *Aulax*, especially on Labiatae (Kerner).

Aulog'amae (αὐλὸς, a tube ; γάμος, marriage), employed by Ardissone for Muscineae.

Aul'ophyte (αὐλή, abode ; φυτὸν, a plant), one plant living in the cavity of another for shelter only, not parasitic ; the German is "Raumparasit."

aurantia'ceous *auran'tiacus*, *auran'tius* (Lat.), (1) orange-coloured ; (2) like the Orange, *Citrus Aurantium*, or the order to which it belongs.

Auran'tium (Lat., an orange), a succulent superior fruit with a rough rind, such as the Orange.

aura'tus (Lat., gilt), metallic yellow, shot with gold ; **Au'rea** (*aureus*, golden), a plant deficient in chlorophyll ; **au'reus** (Lat., golden), glowing yellow, not metallic.

Aur'icle, *Auric'ula* (Lat., ear-lap), (1) a small lobe or ear, an appendage to the leaf, as in Sage, or the Orange ; (2) the lobule, or minor lobe of the leaf of Hepaticae, often balloon-shaped ; (3) formerly and erroneously used for AMPHIGASTRIA ; (4) a small lobe or special patch of cells at the basal angle of the leaf in Mosses ; **auric'ular**, *auricula'ris*, auricled ; ~ **Cells**, the cells in the leaf described above (4), also termed alar cells.

auric′ulate, *auricula′tus,* eared, auricled.

aur′iform (*auris,* the ear; *formis,* shape), ear-shaped.

Auri′go (*aurugo,* jaundice), a leaf disease shown by the yellow colour usually due to intumescence-formation (Sorauer).

auror′eus (Lat.), the colour of dawn, rosy or golden.

austere′ (*auste′rus,* harsh), astringent to the taste, as a sloe.

austra′lis (Lat., southern), occasionally applied to plants which are natives of warmer countries, even if not from the southern hemisphere.

Autaesthe′sia (αὐτὸς, self + AESTHESIA), sensibility to some internal stimulus; **Autallogam′ia** (ἄλλος, other; γάμος, marriage), normal pollination (Clements); **Aut′ecology** (+ ECOLOGY), the relation of individual plants to their habitats (Schröter); **Autem′-bryosperm** (ἔμβρυον, a foetus; σπέρμα, a seed), MacMillan's term for PARTHENOSPERMS with the endosperm the result of fecundation from effective pollen arising in the same flower; **Auten′dosperm** (+ ENDOSPERM); the embryo being the result of fecundation, the effective pollen arising from the same flower as the seed (MacMillan); **Auto′allog′amy** (+ ALLOGAMY), the condition of a species when some individuals are adapted for self-fertilization and others for cross-fertilization, as in *Viola tricolor,* Linn. (Engler and Prantl); **Aut′oblast** (βλαστὸς, a bud), a free and independent "Bioblast" (Schlater); **Autob′olites** (βολὶς, a missile, + ite), the products of division of the living protoplasm (Beyerinck); **Autocarp′-ius** ‡ (καρπὸς, fruit), (1) a superior fruit, not adherent to the pericarp; (2) see AUTOCARPY; adj. **autocarp′-ian, autocarp′ic,** *autocarpia′nus;* **Autocarp′y,** the fruiting of a self-fertilized flower, the product of autogamy; adj. **autocarp′ous; autocarpotrop′ic** (+ CARPOTROPIC),

automatic separation of fruit; **Auto-catal′ysis** (+ CATALYSIS), self-fermentation (Johannsen); adj. **auto-catalyt′ic; Aut′ochore** (χωρέω, I spread abroad), motile plants or those with motile spores (Clements); **autochor′ic** (χωρὶς, separate), applied to plants distributed by means of their own movements (Kirchner); **Autocho′ry,** the state itself.

Autoch′thon (αὐτόχθων, indigenous), an aboriginal form; a native plant, not an introduction; adj. **autoch′-thonal, autoch′thonous;** ~ **The′ory,** the theory that each species originated where now found (L. H. Bailey).

Autodeple′tion (αὐτὸς, self; *depleo,* I empty out), self-digestion by the endosperm of grasses and palms.

Autodifferentia′tio (*differencia,* a difference), inherent power to vary.

Autodiges′tion (*digestio,* digestion), the endosperm digesting reserve material; **autoe′cious** (οἶκος, a house), applied to a parasite which runs its whole course on a single host of a particular species; this state of things is **Autoe′cism**; **Autoeu′forms** (εὖ, well; *formis,* shape), Arthur's term for those species of *Puccinia* which produce every kind of spore on the same host; **Autofecunda′tion** (+ FECUNDATION), self-fertilization; **autogam′ic,** auto-gamous, self-fertilized; **autog′amous** (γάμος, marriage), self-fertilization; **Autog′amy,** (1) when a flower is fertilized by its own pollen; (2) self-fertilization by a single cell = AUTO-MIXIS; **Autogen′esis** (γένεσις, beginning), a synonym of SPONTANEOUS GENERATION; **autogenet′ic,** self-derived; ~ **Fertiliza′tion** = self-pollination; **autogen′ic** (γένος, race, descent), self-derived; **autog′enous** (γένος, race), self-derived, used of diseases, etc., which have their origin within the organism; **autog′enus,** term proposed in place of monotypic, to show that the genus contains but a single species (Crozier).

autoi′cous, used for Bryophytes, when the male and female inflorescences are on the same plant; the following modifications occur ; **cla′do-** ~ (κλάδος, a branch), the male inflorescence on a proper branch ; **go′nio-** ~ (γόνος, offspring), the male inflorescence bud-like and axillary on a female branch ; **rhiz-** ~ (ρίζα, a root), the male branch very short, cohering to the female by a rhizoid ; **Autol′ysis** (λύσις, a loosing), chemical changes in dead cells in which microbial decomposition is excluded ; adj. **autolyt′ic.**

automat′ic (αὐτόματος, self-moving), spontaneous movement of certain parts, as the leaflets of *Desmodium gyrans*, DC.

Automix′is (αὐτός, self ; μῖξις, a mixing) ; self-fertilization (Hartmann) ; **Automorpho′sis** (+ MORPHOSIS) = MUTATION ; **autonas′tic** (ναστὸς, pressed close), relating to **Autonas′-tism,** curvature of an organ not attributable to any outside force.

autonom′ic, auton′omous (αὐτόνομος, independent), used of plants which are perfect and complete in themselves, and not simply phases of other forms.

autonyctitrop′ic (αὐτὸς, self ; νὺξ, νυκτὸς, night ; τροπὴ, a turn), spontaneously assuming the position usual during the night ; **autopelag′ic** (πέλαγος, the sea), applied to plankton which lives continuously on the surface (Forel) ; **Autoph′agy** (φάγω, I eat), employed by Dangeard to express complete fusion of gametes ; **recip′rocal** ~, or **sex′ual** ~, sexuality in primitive forms of Algae,—further differentiated into, PROTOGAMY, HOLOGAMY, and MEROGAMY ; **Autophyllog′eny** (φύλλον, a leaf ; γένος, offspring), the production of a leaf upon the blade of another ; **Aut′ophyte** (φυτὸν, plant), a plant not dependent on humus, as opposed to SAPROPHYTE ; adj. **autophyt′ic** ; **Aut′oplast** (πλαστὸς, moulded), (1) a synonym of chlorophyll granule ; (2) occasionally employed for PLASTID ; **autopot′amic** (ποταμὸς, a river), applied to Algae which have become adapted to living in streams ; a modi-

fied form of tychopotamic plankton (Zimmer) ; **Autop′sia** (ὄψις, sight), actual inspection of the plant or phenomenon in question ; **Aut′osperm** (σπέρμα, a seed), a plant whose embryo arises through autogamy (MacMillan) ; **autosymbion′tic** (+ SYMBIONT), used of cephalodia having similar commensals (Bitter) ; **autotem′nous** (τέμνω, I cut), capable of spontaneous division, as cells in growing tissue ; **autotroph′ic** (τροφὴ, food), (1) applied to plants which can collect their own nutriment, non-parasitic ; (2) digesting reserves of food-material (Keeble and Gamble) ; **Autot′ropism,** the same as RECTIPETALITY, the tendency of an organ to grow in a straight line ; **autox′-enous** (ξένος, a host or guest) = AUTOECIOUS ; **Autox′eny,** the autoecious condition ; **Autox′idators** (ὀξὺς, sharp), cell-substances, which at a low temperature and with absorption of molecular oxygen, can be oxidized by decomposing water ; **Autoxida′tion,** the phenomenon in question ; **autoxidi′zable,** the property of readily undergoing this transformation.

autum′nal *autumna′lis* (Lat.), belonging to autumn ; flowering at that season ; ~ **Wood,** wood formed at the close of the growing season and notable for its smaller cells ; ~ **Xan′-thophyll** (+ XANTHOPHYLL), the autumnal colouring-matter of leaves (Tswett).

Auxan′agram, another spelling of AUXANAGRAMME.

Auxan′agrammes, pl. (αὐξάνω, I increase ; ἀνὰ, up ; γράμμα, an outline), bacterian fields of increase, marked by greater development within the diffusion area of the nutrient substance (Beyerinck) ; **Auxanom′eter** (μέτρον, measure), apparatus for measuring increase of growth in plants.

Auxe′sis (αὔξησις, growth), (1) dilatation or increase in the valves of Diatoms, etc. ; (2) new formation of organs (Czapek) ; (3) predominance of leaves, hairs, etc., on a particular side (Pfeffer).

Auxil'iaries, used by S. Moore for SYNERGIDAE.

Auxil'iary (*auxiliaris*, helpful) **Cell,** a cell borne by a specialized branch in certain Algae, which unites with the conjugating tube emitted by the fertilized trichophore, and then gives rise to filaments bearing the spores (Osterhout) ; ~ **Nu'cleus,** the nucleus of the auxiliary cell in *Drudesnaya purpurifera,* J. Ag., which does not fuse with the nucleus of the sporogenous cell when the cytoplasm does (Oltmanns) ; ~ **Ve'sicles** = SYNERGIDAE.

Aux'oblast, (αὔξη, increase ; βλαστὸς, shoot), employed by Kirchner for any shoot which can serve for vegetative reproduction ; **Auxo'sis,** used when the general growth of an organ has suffered a change (Massart) ; **Aux'ospore** (σπορὰ, seed), in Diatoms, the spore formed by the union of two frustules, or the excessive growth of a single frustule, whence arises a new bion, larger than the parents ; **auxoton'ic** (τόνος, strain), applied to the movements incident to increase of growing organs, as heliotropism, nutation, etc.

avella'neus (Clements), **avellan'icus** (*avellana,* a filbert), drab, the colour of the fresh shell of the Hazel-nut, *Corylus Avellana,* Linn.

avena'ceous, *-ceus* (*avena,* oats), relating to oats ; **Av'enine,** a substance derived from oats.

ave'nius (*a,* without ; *vena,* vein), veinless, or seemingly so.

Averrunca'tion (*averrunco,* I remove), (1) pruning ; (2) uprooting.

averse', *aver'sus* (Lat.), turned back or away from.

Av'oform (*avus,* a grandfather, + FORM), the still existing stem-form of RAMIFORM and PRAEFORM (Kuntze).

awl-shaped, narrow and tapering to a point ; subulate.

Awn, a bristle-like appendage, especially occurring on the glumes of grasses ; ~ of *Chaetoceras,* a diatomaceous genus, having prolongations of the frustules, recalling the awns of grasses ; **awned,** having awns ; bearded.

axe-shaped, dolabriform, as the leaves of some species of *Mesembryanthemum.*

ax'ial (*axis,* an axle), relating to the morphological axis, as distinct from its appendages ; ~ **Row,** the two or more first-formed cells in the embryosac (Wiegand) ; ~ **Shoot,** a cylindrical appendage in the axil between stem and leaf in *Zygopteris* ; it is a prolongation of the ~ **Strand,** itself the stele of the main stem (Scott) ; ~ **Wood,** the normal central cylinder of xylem ; **axif'erous** (*fero,* I bear), bearing an axis, but without leaves or other appendages.

Ax'il, **Axill'a** (Lat., arm-pit), the angle formed between the axis and any organ which arises from it, especially of a leaf.

ax'ile (*axis,* an axle), belonging to the axis without reference to its morphological nature, as axile placentation.

axill'ant (*axilla,* arm-pit), subtending an angle ; **axill'ary,** *axilla'ris,* growing in an axil ; **axilla'tus,** having axils.

Ax'is (Lat., an axle), an imaginary line, round which the organs are developed ; ~ **of Inflores'cence,** that part of the stem or branch upon which the flowers are borne ; **access'ory** ~, an axis of secondary rank ; **a'pical** ~ of Diatoms, is that line which passes through the centre of the pervalvar axis in the direction of the raphe and at equal distances from homologous points of the girdle-band surfaces ; **Append'ages** of the ~, such organs as leaves, flowers, etc. ; **ascend'ing** ~, = the stem ; **descend'-ing** ~, = the root ; **pervalv'ar** ~, the main longitudinal axis of Diatoms ; **transa'pical** ~, the axis which passes at right angles to the apical axis of Diatoms, and through the centre of the pervalvar axis ; **trans-**

vers′al ~, the axis which lies in the transversal plane of Diatoms, cutting the pervalvar axis.

Axog′amy(ἄξων, axis; γάμος, marriage), plants bearing sexual organs on the leafy stem; adj. axogam′ic; Axophy′ta (φυτὸν, a plant = CORMOPHYTA; plants having an axis, that is, stem and root; axosperm′ous (σπέρμα, seed), with axile placentation of ovules.

azo′nal (a, not; ζώνη, girdle), C. MacMillan's term for Plant-associations which show no well-marked radial symmetry; Azote′ (ἄζωτος, ungirt), Lavoisier's name for nitrogen, still used in French works; azo′tised, compounded with nitrogen; Azo′tobacte′ria (+ BACTERIA), applied to bacteria capable of changing elementary into combined nitrogen (Lipman); Azotifica′tion, the process itself.

az′ure, azu′reus (late Lat., sky-blue), blue as the sky.

Azy′gosperm (a, not; ζυγὸς, a yoke; σπέρμα, seed), a synonym of Azy′-gospore (σπορὰ, seed), the growth of a gamete direct without conjugation, a parthenogenetic spore; pl. Azy′gospores, — ae (+ SPORE), the spores of Phycomycetes (Saccardo); az′ygous, unpaired, as a leaflet which is not matched on the opposite side of the rhachis.

Bac′ca (Lat.), a berry, a succulent fruit with seeds immersed in the pulp, as the Gooseberry; ~ cortica′ta, berry with a rind; the term has been applied to the ovary; ~ sicc′a,‡ succulent while unripe, dry when mature; ~ spu′ria,‡ any fleshy fruit which is not a true berry, as raspberry and strawberry; bac′cate, bacca′tus, berried; "semina baccata," seeds having a pulpy skin, as in Cycas; Baccaular′is, Baccaular′ius,‡ (deriv. ?), Desvaux's name for CARCERULE; Baccau′sus = ETAERIO; Bacce′tum, Dumortier's term for SYNCARP; baccif′erous, bac′cifer, (fero, I

bear), berry-bearing, the fruit a berry, usually applied when the normal fruit of the genus is otherwise; bac′ciform, bacciform′is (forma, shape), like a berry in shape.

Bacill′us, pl. Bacill′i (bacillum, a staff), (1) ‡ young bulb; (2) the frustules of certain Diatomaceae, as Bacillaria; (3) rod-shaped BACTERIA; bac′illar, bacilla′ris, bacil′liform (forma, shape), rod- or club-shaped.

Back, that side which is turned from the part or substratum to which an organ is attached; the dorsal surface; Back-cav′ity, the inner cavity of a stoma; in Germ. "Hinterhof."

Bacte′rium, pl. Bacte′ria (βακτήριον, a small staff), Cohn's name for low forms of organic life, multiplying by fission, Schizomycetes; see also, AMMONO-, AZOTO-, FERRI-, PROTEO-, SULPHO- BACTERIA, with their reduction forms having DE- prefixed (Lipman); bacteria′ceous, relating to bacteria; bacterici′dal (-cida = killer), germicidal, destructive of bacteria; Bacte′rio-pur′purin, the purple colouring-matter of some bacteria; Bacte′rioblast (βλαστὸς, a bud), applied by Winkler to gelatinous bodies, homogeneous at first, then in succession finely-, and coarsely-granular, at last becoming detached bacteria; bac′teroid (εἶδος, resemblance), resembling bacteria; ~ Tissue, applied to the root-tubercles of various plants; Bac′-teroids or Bacter′ioids, organisms found in nitrifying tubercles on the roots of plants, especially Leguminosae, attributed to the action of bacteria; Bacteriol′ogist (λόγος, discourse), a person versed in the knowledge of bacteria; Bacteriol′-ogy (λόγος, discourse), the science of the life-history of bacteria; Bacterio′sis, disease due to the attack of bacteria; Bacteriotox′in (+ TOXIN), any substance poisonous or harmful to bacteria.

baculif′erous (baculum, a staff; fero,

I bear), bearing canes or reeds ; **bacu'liform**, *baculiform'is* (*forma*, shape), stick-shaped, rod-like, as the ascospores of certain Lichens.

bad'ious, *bad'ius* (Lat.), dark reddish-brown ; chestnut-brown.

baeomy'cetoid (*Baeomyces*, εἶδος, resemblance), like the genus of Lichens named.

Balanoph'orin, a waxy substance which occurs in quantity in the stems of certain species of *Langsdorffia*, a genus of Balanophoreae, whence the name.

Balaus'ta (βαλαύστιον, pomegranate flower), the fruit of *Punica Granatum*, Linn., with firm rind, berried within, crowned with the lobes of an adnate calyx.

bald, destitute of pubescence or downy appendages.

Bale ‡ (Fr., Bâle, chaff), cited by S. F. Gray for the outer glume of grasses.

Ball'ing, in nuclear development, the fusion of nuclei into one nucleus.

ballis'tic, or **balis'tic** (*ballista*, a catapult) **Fruits**, used by Kerner to describe those fruits which discharge their seeds elastically ; catapult-fruits.

Balm (βάλσαμον, balsam), pr. Bahm, a thick, usually resinous exudation of reputed medical efficacy ; **Bal'sam**, pr. Bawls'm ; a similar exudation, generally of resin mixed with volatile oil ; **balsam'ic**, having the qualities of balsam ; **balsam'ifer**, (Lat.) **balsamif'erous**, (*fero*, I bear), producing balsam.

Balus'tra, "sometimes applied to fruits like the pomegranate" (Crozier) ; *cf.* BALAUSTA.

Bamb'oo, the name applied to the culm of arborescent grasses, notably species of *Bambusa* ; **Bambuse'tum**, a tropical bamboo forest association.

Band, (1) space between two ridges in the fruit of Umbellifers ; (2) a stripe generally ; (3) certain marks in the fruit of *Zostera minor*, termed by Reichenbach PROCESSUS ; ~ **shaped**, used of long narrow leaves, linear ;

band'ed, marked with stripes of colour.

Ban'ner, the standard of a papilionaceous flower.

Barb, hooked hairs, frequently doubly-hooked.

Barba (Lat.), a beard; **bar'bate**, *barba'tus*, bearded, having long weak hairs in tufts ; **Barbell'ae** ‡, the short stiff straight hairs of Composite pappus ; adj. **barbell'ate** ; **Barbell'ulae**, ‡ similar structures in the pappus of *Aster* ; adj. **barbell'ulate**, *barbellula'tus* ; **Barb'ule**, *Barb'ula*, (1) the inner row of teeth in the peristome of such Mosses as *Tortula* ; (2) a small barb (Crozier).

Barill'a (Spanish), the crude soda obtained from *Salsola* and allied genera.

Bark, (1) the outer integuments of the wood and exterior to it ; all tissues outside the cambium ; (2) frequently restricted to the periderm and tissues external to it ; ~ **bared**, stripped of the bark ; ~ **bound**, having the bark too tense, thus impeding growth ; ~ **galled**, having the bark injured ; ~ **parench'yma**, the same as cortex-parenchyma.

Barm, the floating yeast used in bread-making, the "Oberhefe" of the Germans ; **barm'y**, containing yeast.

barred, crossed by lines approximately parallel.

bar'ren, unproductive, infertile ; applied to the male inflorescence of certain Mosses ; ~ **Flow'er**, the male or staminate flower ; ~ **Ground**, in North America, is mainly TUNDRA (Warming).

Bar'riers, Clements's term for the limiting forces which hinder dispersion ; these may be **biological** ~, due to the habit of the plant or its rivals, or **physical** ~, such as mountains, deserts, seas, etc.

Bars, the persistent portions in a scalariform perforation ; see also SANIO'S BARS.

Barymorpho'sis (βαρὺς, heavy ; μόρφωσις, shape), Sachs's term for the changes produced in organisms in consequence of gravitation.

ba′sal (*basis*, foundation), at the base of an organ or part ; ~ **Cell**, the first cell of an angiospermous embryo which becomes attached to the wall of the embryo-sac ; ~ **Growth**, increase near the base, as distinguished from apical growth ; ~ **nerved**, *basiner′vis*, with nerves from the base of the leaf ; ~ **Placen′ta**, the placenta at the base of the ovary ; ~ **Wall**, the division of the oospore in Archegoniatae into an anterior and a posterior half ; **Base**, the extremity of attachment, by which nutrition takes place ; **Basichro′matin** (+ CHROMATIN), chromatin in the usual sense ; that portion of the nuclear network stained by basic tar-colours.

Bas′id = **Basid′ium**, pl. **Basid′ia** (*basidium*, a little pedestal), (1) the spore-mother-cells of Hymenomycetous and Gasteromycetous Fungi, having little points from which spores are thrown off ; (2) employed by Thaxter for the swollen attachment of the conidium to the conidiophore in *Basidiobolus*, Eidam ; (3) by older authors employed for the central FERTILE CELLS of Uredineae.

basid′ial, relating to a BASIDIUM ; ~ **Lay′er**, the structure in Agarics which produces or bears the basidia. **basidiogenet′ic** (γένος, race, descent), produced upon a basidium ; **Basidiogonid′ium** (γονή, race, offspring), proposed emendation of "basidiospore" ; **Basidioli′chenes** Lichen-forming Basidiomycetes ; **Basidiomyce′tes** (μύκης, μύκητος, fungus), Fungi producing spores on basidia ; **Basid′iophore** (φορέω, I carry), a sporophore bearing a basidium ; **Basidiorhi′zae** (ῥίζα, a root), Vuillemin's name for BASIDIOMYCETES ; **Basid′iospore** (σπορά, a seed), a spore produced by a basidium ; **basidiosp′orous**, producing such spores.

basifix′ed, *basifix′us* (*basis*, foundation; *fixus*, fast), attached by the base ; **basif′ugal** (*fugo*, I put to flight),

developing from the base upwards ; **basigam′ic**, **basig′amous** (γάμος, marriage), when the normal position of egg-apparatus and antipodals is reversed ; the oosphere and synergidae being at the lower end of the mother-cell of the endosperm (embryo-sac) ; Van Tieghem contemplates the possible occurrence of double **Basig′amy** ; **Basigyn′ium** (γυνή, a woman), a thecaphore, the stalk of an ovary above the stamens and petals ; **bas′ilar**, *basila′ris*, basal.

basila′tus ‡ arising from a broad base as certain hairs.

Ba′sin, the connection between the pouch of certain secretory cells and the cell-wall in Magnoliaceae and a few other families (Solereder) ; ~ **shaped** dished or hollowed out.

basiner′ved, (*basis*, foundation ; *nervus*, a nerve), veined from the base.

basip′etal (*peto*, I seek), growth in the direction of the base.

Bas′iplast, adj. **basiplas′tic** (πλαστός, moulded), Prantl's term for those leaves whose permanent tissue appears first at the apex, the lower portion continuing longer as meristem.

Ba′sis (Lat.), the base ; **basiscop′ic** (σκοπέω, I look), looking towards the base, the reverse of acroscopic ; **basisolu′tus**, ‡ (*solutus*, unbound), used of such leaves as those of *Sedum* which are prolonged downwards beyond their true origin ; **basithe′cal** (θήκη, a box), applied to virescent anthers, the upper portion leafy, the pollen-bearing portion extending toward the base (Celakovsky) ; **Basit′onus** (τόνος, a cord), the prolongation of the tissue of the pollen-sac to the lower end of the anther in Ophrydineae ; **bas′ophil** (φιλέω, I love), readily taking stain from basic substances.

Bass, the inner fibrous bark of the lime, used by cultivators for temporary ties ; the liber.

Bass′orin, a product of Bassora Gum, Tragacanth, etc., which does **not**

dissolve like Gum Arabic, but swells up when placed in water, and forms a pasty mass; **bassorinog'enous** (γένος, offspring), producing BASSORIN; ~ **Lay'er**, the tissue concerned in the production of this substance.

Bast, (1) the same as BASS; (2) phloëm; (3) fibrous tissues serving for mechanical support; ~ **Cells**, the components of the bark; ~ **Collench'yma**, tissue with the walls of the sides thickened on all sides (C. Mueller); ~ **Fi'bres**, = liber-fibres; ~ **Group**, the phloëm elements and individual vascular bundles; ~ **Sheath**, layer of thin-walled cells surrounding the fibro-vascular cylinder next within the cortex; the periphloëm; ~ **Tis'sue**, phloëm; ~ **Ves'sel**, sieve-tube; ~ **Wedg'es**, groups of phloëm, wider in section outwards; — **Hard** ~, liber-fibres; **Soft** ~, the sieve-tubes, with the thin-walled part of the phloëm.

Bastardem'bryosperm (σπέρμα, a seed), C. MacMillan's term for any plant with parthenogenetic embryo, the effective pollen derived from another plant or variety; **Bastarden'dosperm**, a similar plant with parthenogenetic endosperm, the effective pollen arising from another individual or variety; **Bastard'ocarpy** (καρπὸς, fruit), the production of fruits by hybrids.

Bast-i'slands, another name for PHLOËM-ISLANDS; ~ **Nerves**, libriform cells in the leaf of *Najas graminea*, Delile; ~ **Parench'yma**, phloëm parenchyma; ~ **Rays** = MEDULLARY RAYS.

Bath'mism (βαθμὶς, a step or degree), Cope's term to denote the force or energy of growth.

bathyb'ic (βαθὺς, deep or high; βίος, life), applied to the deepest plankton (Forel); **bathylimnet'ic** (λίμνη, a lake), used of plants sometimes rooted, sometimes floating, with a tendency towards deep water (Kirchner); **bathymet'rical** (μέτρον, measure), used of the distribution of plants on the sea-bottom; and the depths at which they grow; **bathy-pelag'ic** (+ PELAGIC); plankton companies which daily descend from the surface (Forel); **bathyph'ilus** (φιλέω, I love), dwelling in lowlands; **Bathyphy'ta**, the plants of a lowland association (Clements); **Bathyphyti'um** (φυτόν, a plant), a lowland plant formation.

Batol'ogist (βάτος, a bramble; λόγος, discourse), a student of brambles, the species and forms of *Rubus*; **Batol'ogy**, the study of brambles; **batolog'ical**, adj. of BATOLOGY.

Batrachie'tum, an association of water-crowfoot; of any form of the *Batrachium* section of *Ranunculus*.

bay, dun-colour; an equivalent of BADIOUS.

Bays, applied to recessed or undulating cell-walls (Solereder).

Beak, a pointed projection; **beaked**, used of fruits which end in a long point.

Beard, synonymous with AWN; **beard'ed**, (1) awned, as bearded wheat; (2) having tufts of hairs, as on the lip of *Pentstemon barbatus*, Roth; **beard'letted**, having small awns.

Bear'ers, used by Blair for flower-buds.

Bebeer'in, a tonic alkaloid from the Greenheart, *Nectandra Rodiaei*, Hook., native name, *Bebeeru*.

Bedeguar', a fibrous gall produced on a rose-bush by the puncture of a species of *Cynips*.

Bee-bread, the pollen of flowers, collected by bees as food for the young larvae; ~ **-flow'ers**, those flowers which afford honey to an insect having a proboscis of 7 mm. (·275 in.) in length.

Beech'wood Association, natural beech-woods found on the chalk, *Fage'tum sylvat'icae calcareum*.

Beglei'ter (Ger., companion) **Cells**, small groups of thin-walled cells associated with DEUTER CELLS, and probably serving as conductors of water (Limpricht); *cf.* COMPANION CELLS (Salmon).

bell-shaped, tubular and inflated, as the corolla of Campanulaceae.

bell'ying, swelling on one side, as in the corolla of many Labiatae.

Belt Tran'sect, a strip of a few inches or feet in width, with its constituent plants recorded (Clements).

Belt's Corpus'cles, Schimper's expression for the FOOD-BODIES of certain species of *Acacia* used by ants as food ; **Belt'ian Bod'ies** are the same.

bennettit'ean, resembling the fossil genus *Bennettites.*

Benth'on, or **Benth'os** (βένθος, depth, bottom), the vegetation at the bottom of the sea, lakes, or streams ; the fixed growth as distinct from the plankton or floating growth ; Forel distinguishes **necton'ic** ~, organisms which float freely ; **ses'sile** ~, those which remain attached, and **vag'il** ~, wandering organisms ; **Ben'thophyte** (φυτὸν, a plant), a plant whose habitat is at the bottom.

Benzoin', a fragrant resinous exudation from *Styrax Benzoin,* Dryand. ; called also Gum Benjamin.

ben'zoloid, used for a group of scents derived from aromatic bodies, as eugenol or oil of cloves, and in the flowers of Heliotrope, Lilac, etc. (Kerner).

Ber'berine, a yellow bitter principle from the root of *Berberis vulgaris,* Linn.

Berge'ria, formerly considered a genus of fossils, now applied to a lepidodendroid stem when the epidermis has been stripped off (Scott).

ber'ried, baccate, possessing berries.

Ber'ry, a pulpy fruit, with immersed seeds ; *cf.* BACCA ; ~ **-cone,** a cone whose scales have become fleshy and fused, as in *Juniperus.*

Bes'imen, ‡ pl. **Besim'ina** (βιώσιμος, having the power of living), Necker's name for a spore.

Be'tain, an amide-like substance from *Beta,* the beet.

Bet'ulase, the same enzyme as GAULTHERASE, but obtained from the bark of *Betula lenta,* Linn. ; **Betule'-** tum, a plant association of birch trees (Clements) ; pl. **Betule'ta cladino'sa,** an association of birch with the lichen *Cladina;* ~ **hylocomio'sa,** birch and *Hylocomium* moss association.

Between Races, intermediates between a species and a variety of it.

bi-, bis-, in compound words meaning "twice."

Biachae'nium (*bi* + ACHAENIUM), Beck's term for a SCHIZOCARP, of two carpels, as in *Galium;* **biacu'minate,** *biacumina'tus* (+acuminate), having two diverging points, as the hairs of Malpighiaceae, attached by the centre.

Biaiometamorpho'sis (βίαιος, forced, + METAMORPHOSIS), Lotsy's term for a disadvantageous change, in response to stimulus : **Biaiomor'phose, Biaiomorpho'sis,** the form so produced.

Bianc'oni's Plate, a plexus of sclerenchymatous fibres near the vascular bundles towards the concave or sensitive face of tendrils ; so termed by Borzi after the discoverer.

biang'ulate (*bi,* twice ; *angulus,* a corner), having two corners or angles ; **biartic'ulate,** *biarticula'tus* (*articulus,* a joint), two-jointed.

Biastrep'sis (βιάω, I force ; στρέψις the act of turning), (1) C. Schimper's term for TORSION ; (2) the transition from decussate to spiral phyllotaxis (De Vries).

biator'ine, resembling the Lichen genus *Biatora.*

biauric'ulate (*bi,* twice; *auricula,* the ear lobe), with two auricles or ear-like appendages ; **biauri'tus** (Lat.) is substantially the same ; **biax'ial** (+ AXIS), used of a spore germinating at both ends (S. Moore) ; **Bibac'ca** (+ BACCA), a double berry as in some species of *Lonicera;* **bibract'eate,** *bibractea'tus* (*bractea,* a thin plate), having two bracts ; **bibract'eolate,** with two bracteoles ; **bicalc'arate** (*calcar,* a spur), having two spurs ; **bicall'ose** *bicallo'sus* (*callus,* hardened skin), with two callosities ; **bicap'sular** (*capsula*, a box), (1) with two capsules ; (2) having a capsule which is bilocular ; **bicar'inate**, *bicarina'tus* (*carina*, a keel), with two keels ;· **Bicar'pals**, proposed by Bessey for the **Bicarpella'tae** of Bentham and Hooker, a series of gamopetalous Phanerogams (*cf*. Gen. Pl. ii. pp. vi.–vii.) ; the latter term also used by Boulger to embrace the majority of Gamopetalae with Umbelliferae ; **bicar'pellary** (+ *carpellum*), of two carpels or pistils ; **bicarpell'ate**, having a two-celled fruit ; **bicel'lular**, of two cells ; **biceph'alous** (κεφαλή, head) ; **bi'ceps**(Lat.),two-headed ; **bichron'ic** (χρόνος, time), applied to an equation, in which the mutations multiplied by the intervals of time, equal the biologic time (De Vries) ; **bicil'-iate**, *bicilia'tus* (*cilium*, an eyelash), with two cilia, as many zoospores ; **bicip'ital**, with two heads or two supports ; **bicollat'eral** (*con*, + *latus, lateris*, side), applied to a vascular bundle with two groups of phloëm lying upon opposite sides of the xylem ; **Bicollateral'ity**, is the state just described.

bic'olor (Lat.), two-coloured, particoloured.

biconcen'tric (*bi, con* + *cen'rum*, a point), Poulsen's term for the fibrovascular bundles in Eriocauleae ; round the axial hadrome bundle is a layer of leptome, which is again enclosed by a hadrome layer ; **bicon'jugate**, *biconjuga'tus* (*conjugatus*, joined), twice-conjugate, that is, when each of two secondary petioles bears a pair of leaflets ; **biconjuga'to-pinna'tus**, similar to the last, but each petiole pinnate.

Bicor'nes (*bicornis*, two-horned), the heaths, from their horned anthers ; **bicor'nis** (Lat.) **bicorn'ute**, *bicornu'tus*, two-horned, as the siliqua of *Matthiola bicornis*, DC. ; **bicotyle'-donary**, having two seed-lobes, more correctly called DICOTYLEDONOUS.

bicre'nate (*bi*, twice ; *crena*, a notch), (1) having two crenatures or rounded

teeth (Crozier) ; (2) doubly crenate ; **bicru'ris** (Lat.), two-legged, as the pollen-masses of Asclepiads ; **bicusp'id** (*cuspis*, spear-point) ; **bicusp'idate**, having two sharp points ; **bident'ate**, *bidenta'tus* (*dens, dentis*, a tooth), (1) having two teeth ; (2) doubly dentate, as when the marginal teeth are also toothed ; **bidigita'tus** (Lat.) = BICONJUGATE.

biddulph'ioid (εἶδος, like), resembling the genus of Diatoms, *Biddulphia*.

Biden'ton (*Bidens* + ON) Clements's term for a " family " of *Bidens*.

bid'uous, *bid'uus* (*biduum*, two days long), lasting for two days.

Bienn'ial (*biennium*, a period of two years), a plant which requires two years to complete its life-cycle, growing one year, and flowering and fruiting the second ; signs ⊘ or ⊙ ; **bien'nial**, *bien'nis*=monocarpic.

Biere'mus (*bi*, twice, *eremus*, a hermit), a two-celled fruit, the cells so far apart as to seem separate, as in *Cerinthe;* **bifa'cial** (*facies*, an appearance), (1) when the leaf has spongy tissue on the lower face, and compact tissue on the upper sides ; opposed to centric ; (2) having the opposite sides alike ; (3) dorsiventral ; **bifa'riam** (Lat., in two parts), arranged in two rows ; ~ **imbrica'-tus**, imbricated in two rows ; **bifa'rious**, *bifa'rius*, distichous.

Bi'fer (*bi*, twice ; *fero*, I bear), a plant which ripens fruit twice a year (Crozier) ; **bif'erous**, *biferus*, double bearing, producing two crops in one season ; **bi'fid**, *bif'idus* (*findo, fidi*, to cleave), twice-cleft, divided halfway into two ; **bif'idate** = BIFID (Crozier) ; **bifist'ular** (*fistula*, a pipe), with two tubular openings (Crozier) ; **biflor'ate** (Crozier), **biflor'ous**, *-rus* (*flos, floris*, a flower), having two flowers ; **bifo'liate**, *bifolia'tus* (*folium*, a leaf), two-leaved ; **bifo'liolate**, *bifoliola'tus*, having two leaflets ; ~ **Leaf**, binate ; **bifollic'-ular**, possessing a **Bifollic'ulus** (*folliculus*, a small sack) ; a double follicle, as in Asclepiads.

48

bifo′rate, *bifora′tus* (*biforis*, having two doors), with two perforations; **Bif′orine,** an oblong cell, opening at each end, containing raphides; **bifo′rous** = biforate.

biform′is (Lat.), two formed; in two shapes.

bi′frons (Lat.), (1) having two faces or aspects; (2) growing on both surfaces of a leaf; amphigenous.

bifurc′ate, *bifurca′tus* (*bifurcus*, two-pronged or forked), twice forked; **Bifurca′tion,** division into two branches.

bigem′inate, *bigemina′tus* (*geminus*, a twin) = BICONJUGATE; **bigem′inus,** in two pairs, as in the placentae of many plants.

Bi′gener (Lat., a hybrid), mule plants obtained by crossing species of different genera, usually spoken of as a **bigener′ic Cross.**

bigland′ular (*bi*, two; *glandula*, a gland), with two glands; **biglu′mis** (*gluma*, a husk), consisting of two glumes, the components of the perianth of grasses.

bignonia′ceous, resembling or allied to the genus *Bignonia*.

bihila′tus ‡ (*bi*, + HILUM), having two scars, as in certain pollen; **bi′jugate,** *bijuga′tus*, **bi′jugous** (*jugum*, a yoke), (1) applied to a pinnate leaf, with two pairs of leaflets; (2) [**bi′jugate**], type of phyllotaxis in which the parastichy ratios are divisible by 2; **bila′biate,** *bilabia′tus* (*labium*, lip), divided into two lips, as are many gamopetalous corollas, etc.; **bilam′ellar,** **bilam′ellate,** *bilamella′tus* (*lamella*, a thin plate), consisting of two plates, as some placentae; **bilat′eral,** *bilatera′lis* (*latus*, side), arranged on opposite sides, as the leaves of the yew; **Bilat′eralism** (*latus, lateris*, a side), having similar or bilateral symmetry; taken by L. H. Bailey as the type of animal evolution; **Bilateral′ity,** means the same.

Bil′berry Moor Associations, *Vaccinieta Myrtilli*, especially abundant in the Pennines.

bilo′bate, *biloba′tus*, **bilo′bed** (λοβὸς,

the ear-flap), divided into two lobes, as most anthers, or the leaves of *Bauhinia*; **bilocell′ate** (*locellus*, a small compartment), made up of two locelli; **biloc′ular,** *bilocular′is* (*loculus*, a compartment), two-celled; **Bilomen′tum** (+ LOMENTUM), a double lomentum as in some species of *Raphanus* (Beck); **bimac′ulate** (*macula*, a spot), with two spots.

bimes′tris (Lat.), of two months' duration.

bi′mus (Lat.), lasting for two years.

bi′nary, *bina′rius*, (*bini*, by twos), consisting of two members; **bi′nate,** *bina′tus* (Lat.), (1) where a leaf is composed of two leaflets at the end of a common petiole; (2) a simple leaf nearly divided into two; **bina′tim** (Lat.), in pairs; **bina′to-pinna′tus** ‡ = BIPINNATE.

biner′vate (*bi*, two; *nervus*, a nerve), with two nerves, especially if prominent; **binervula′tus** ‡ (Lat.), having two vascular strands.

bi′ni (Lat.), two together, twin; as **biniflor′us,** bearing flowers on pairs.

bino′dal, *bino′dis* (*bi*, two; *nodus*, a knot), consisting of two nodes.

bino′mial (*bi*, two; *nomen*, a name), in botanic nomenclature, the use of a generic and specific name to connote a given organism; used also for NEWTONIAN CURVE.

bi′nous, *bi′nus* (Lat.), in pairs; *cf.* BINI.

binu′clear, **binu′cleate** (*bi*, two; *nucleus*, a kernel), having two nuclei; **binu′cleolate,** *binucleola′tus* (Lat.), with two nucleoli.

Bi′oblast (βίος, life; βλαστὸς, a shoot), term proposed by Schlater for the unit of life, comprising autoblasts, or free-existing bioblasts, and cytoblasts or colonies of such bioblasts as have lost their independent existence; *cf.* BIOPHOR.

bioc′ellate (*bi*, two; *ocellus*, a little eye), marked with two eye-spots.

Biochem′ist (βίος, life), an expert in the chemistry of living organisms; **Biochem′istry,** the branch of

chemistry concerned with biology ;
Bi′ochore (χωρὶς, asunder), a plant-
climate boundary ; **biochron′ic**
(χρόνος, time), the period during
which mutations have been possible
(De Vries) ; **Biocoeno′sis** (κοῖνος, in
common), the conjoint life of certain
plants with animals ; **biodynam′ic**
(δύναμις, force), vital power or force ;
subst. **Biodynam′ics** ; **Biogen′esis**
(γένεσις, beginning), the doctrine of
life from life, the production of
organisms from others already in
existence ; in opposition to Spontaneous Generation ; **biog′enous**
(γένος, race), growing on living
organisms ; **Biog′eny**, the evolution
of living forms, including ONTOGENY
and PHYLOGENY ; **biogeograph′ic**
(+ GEOGRAPHIC) concerned with the
distribution of living forms over
the world ; **biolog′ical** (**Races**, or)
Spe′cies, those species which differ
only by their physiological behaviour,
being morphologically identical :
Biol′ogy (λόγος, discourse), the
science which investigates vital
phenomena, both of plant and
animal ; as limited by Delpino =
ERGOLOGY) ; **biolyt′ic** (λύω, I break
down),destructive of life ; **Biom′etry**,
(μέτρον, a measure), the application
of statistical methods to biological
data ; adj. **biomet′rical** ; **Biomol′ecule**
(+ MOLECULE), a living molecule ;
adj. **bimolec′ular** ; **Biomon′ad**, a
symbiotic system of biomores ; when
very complex it constitutes a cell ;
Bi′omore an aggregation of biomole-
cules, living particles (these three
terms are due to Giglio-Tos) ; **Bi′on**,
an individual, morphologically
and physiologically independent ;
Bionom′ics (νόμος, a law), Geddes's
term to express Phytobiology, the
ecology of plants ; in German,
Pflanzenbiologie ; **Bion′omy** (νόμος,
usage, law), the principles of plant
economy, or ecology (Pfeffer) ;
Bioph′agism (φάγω, I eat), the
absorption and digestion of the
matter of living organisms (Boulger) ;
bioph′agous (φάγος, a glutton), feed-

ing on living organisms, truly parasitic ; **bioph′ilous** (φιλέω, I love),
used of Fungi which are parasitic on
leaves or stems of living plants ;
Bi′ophor (φορέω, I carry), G. C.
Bourne's name for the cell, as the
vital unit ; **Bi′ophores** (φορέω, I bear),
hypothetical units which are grouped
into determinants (Weismann) ;
Biophys′ics (φυσικὸς, inborn) =
BIODYNAMICS ; **Bi′ophyte** (φυτὸν, a
plant), a biophagous plant ; **Bi′o-**
plasm (πλάσμα, moulded), Beale's
name for PROTOPLASM ; **bioplasmat′ic**,
relating to BIOPLASM ; **Bioplas′son**
(πλάσσω, I mould), Elsberg's emendation of BIOPLASM ; **Bi′os**, a substance so termed by Wildiers, as
indispensable to the development
of fermentation.

Bio′sis (βιώσις, the act of living), the
state of vital activity ; life (Escombe) ; **Bio′ta**, pl. (living things) ;
biology (Grinnell) ; **biot′ic**, vital ;
~ **Fac′tors**, the relation of plants
to each other from an ecologic stand-
point ; ~ **Succes′sion**, a sequence of
living forms.

Bi′otype (βίος, life ; τύπος, a type), an
elementary stable form (Johannsen);
biova′rial (+ OVARY), derived from
the ovaries of the same plant
(Pearson).

bipal′eolate, *bipaleola′tus* (*bi*, + PALE-
OLA), consisting of two paleae, or
small scales in grasses ; **bipal′mate.**
bipalma′tus (*palma*, the palm of the
hand), twice palmate, palmately
compound ; **bip′arous** (*pario*, I
bring forth), bearing two ; ~ **Cyme**,
Bravais's expression for a normal
dichotomous inflorescence ; **bipart′-**
ible, *bipartib′ilis*, **bipar′tile** (*part′-*
ilis, divisible), capable of ready
division into two similar parts ;
bipart′ite, *biparti′tus* (Lat.), divided
nearly to the base into two portions ;
Bipartit′ion, the act of dividing into
two ; **bipect′inate** (*pecten*, a comb),
toothed like a comb on two sides ;
bipelt′ate (*pelta*, a shield), having
two shield-shaped parts (Crozier) ;
biperenn′ial (*perennis*, perpetual),

used of a part that lives two years,
but reproduces itself indefinitely
(Crozier) ; **bipet′alous** (πέταλον, a
flower leaf), Blair's term for two-
petalled flowers, as *Circaea ;* **bipen-
taphyll′us** (πέντη, five ; φύλλον,
leaf), having from two to five leaflets.
bi′pes (Lat., two-footed) = BICRURIS.

bipin′nate *bipinna′tus* (*pinnatus*, feathered), when both primary and
secondary divisions of a leaf are
pinnate ; **bipinnat′ifid**, *bipinnatif′i-
dus*, when the divisions of a pinnatifid leaf are themselves pinnatifid ;
bipinnatipart′ed = bipinnatifid ; **bi-
pinnat′isect**, *bipinnatisect′us* (*sectus*, cut) = bipinnate ; **bi′plicate**,
biplica′tus (*plico*, I fold), doubly
folded in a transverse manner, as
some cotyledons ; **bipo′lar** (*polus*,
the end of an axis), having two
poles, the usual number in nuclear
division ; ~ **Expan′sion**, growth at
both extremities, root and shoot ;
Bipolar′ity, (1) the condition of
possessing two poles ; (2) in distribution when the same species is
found towards the north and south
poles, but is wanting in intermediate regions ; **bipolymor′ious** ‡ (πολὺς,
many ; μόριον, a small portion), consisting of two or many parts ; **bipo′-
rose**, *biporo′sus* (*porus*, channel),
opening by two pores as the anthers
in *Erica ;* **biprophylla′tus** (+ PRO-
PHYLLA), Buchenau's term for
possessing two prophylla (Vorblätter); **bipunc′tate** (*punctum*, a
point), having two spots ; **bira′-
diate**, *biradia′tus* (*radius*, the spoke
of a wheel), of two rays, as in certain
umbels.

Birch′wood Association, characteristic
of the Highland valleys above the
limit of the oak.

biri′mose, *birimo′sus* (*bi*, two ; *rima*,
a chink), opening by two slits as most
anthers ; **bisac′cate** (*saccus*, a bag),
having two pouches.

biscoctiform′is (*bis*, twice ; *coctus*,
cooked ; *forma*, shape), biscuit-
shaped, applied by Koerber to some
Lichen-spores.

biscuit-shaped, when used in transla-
tions from the German, means
oblong, and slightly constricted in
the middle.

bisep′tate, *bisepta′tus* (*bi*, two; *septum*,
a wall), having two partitions ;
bise′rial, *biseria′lis*, **bise′riate**,
biseria′tus (*series*, a succession),
arranged in two rows as on a flat
surface ; **biser′rate**, *biserra′tus* (*serra*,
a saw), twice serrate, as when the
serratures are themselves serrate ;
bise′tose, **bise′tous** (*seta*, a bristle),
with two bristles ; **bisex′ual**, *bisex-
ua′lis* (*sexus*, sex), having both stamens and pistils, possessing perfect,
that is, hermaphrodite flowers ; ~
Hered′ity, transmission of qualities
of both parents ; **bispathel′lulate**,
bispathellula′tus ‡ (+ SPATHELLA),
consisting of two glumes (Lindley) ;
bispi′nose (*spino′sus*, thorny), having
two spines ; **bispi′rous** (σπεῖρα, a
twist), term used by Spruce for
elaters having two spirals; *cf.* DIS-
PIROUS ; **bisporang′iate** (+ SPOR-
ANGIUM), (1) used when a plant
possesses two sporangia in place
of one ; (2) AMPHISPORANGIATE ;
Bi′spore (σπορὰ, seed), (1) " a two-
spored tetraspore " (Crozier) ; (2) an
ascus with two cells, in place of the
normal eight ; **biste′lic** (στήλη, a
pillar), having two steles ; **bistip′-
ulate** (+ STIPULA), with two stipules ; **bistip′ular**, bistipulate ; **bis-
tra′tose** (*stratum*, a layer), cells
disposed in two strata or layers ;
bistri′ate (*striatus*, striped), marked
with two parallel lines or striae ;
bisulc′ate *bisulca′tus* (*sulcus*, a
groove), two-grooved ; **bisymmet′ric**
(σύμμετρος, commensurate), bilateral
symmetric, each side alike ; **Biteg-
mina′tae** (*tegmen*, a cover), Van
Tieghem used this for Phanerogams
whose seeds have double integuments ; **biteg′minous**, used of ovules
possessing double integuments ; the
condition is **Biteg′miny** (Balfour) ;
bitern′ate, *biterna′tus* (*ternus*, by
threes), compound ternate, as in a
leaf.

bit′ten, abruptly ended, of roots or leaves, praemorse.

Bitt′er Orange Spot, on leaves and fruit, due to *Colletotrichum gloeosporoides.*

Bitt′er Pit, an abnormal spotting of the fruit of the apple, ascribed to peculiar external conditions (Pole Evans).

bityp′ic (*bi*, two ; τύπος, a type), applied to those genera which consist of two widely separated species ; **biv′alent** (*valens*, strong), having hypothetically two chromosomes in each of the apparent chromosomes, in nuclear reduction divisions ; **bi′valve,** *bival′vis* (*valvae*, leaves of a door), having two valves, as some capsules ; **Bi′valve,** "a capsule of two valves" (Crozier) ; **bival′ved,** (1) used of Diatoms, as possessing two valves ; (2) the indusia of certain ferns, as *Dicksonia ;* **bival′vular** = BIVALVE ; **bivasc′ular** (*vasculum*, a vessel), with two vessels ; **bivert′ed** (*verto*, I turn), O. Müller's term for an inverted diagonal symmetry in diatoms ; **bivit′tate** (*vittae*, fillets), having two partitions which appear as bands or fillets.

Bix′in, the colouring-matter of *Bixa Orellana.*

Bizzari′a (Ital., extravagant whim), a hybrid between the orange and the citron which has the character of both in juxtaposition, but without blending (Heinig).

Black Blight, *Capnodium citricolum* on *Citrus* leaves ; ~ **Earth,** rich in mineral salts, found in Asiatic steppes and in North America (Warming) ; ~ **Knot,** a devastating disease on plum and cherry trees, caused by *Plowrightia morbosa ;* ~ **Leg,** a bacterial disease of potatoes due to *Bacillus phytophthorus ;* ~ **Root Rot,** due to *Thielavia basicola,* Zopf ; ~ **Rot,** diseases from *Guignardia Bidwellii* and *Pseudomonas campestris ;* ~ **Rust,** *Puccinia graminis,* a universally distributed rust attacking cereals ; ~ **Scab,** of potatoes, caused by a *Synchitrium.*

Blad′der, (1) Grew's term for a cell ; (2) a hollow membranous appendage on the roots of *Utricularia,* which entraps water insects ; (3) similar growths in the frond of some Algae, serving as floats ; (4) an inflated membranous pericarp, as in *Physalis ;* ~ **Plums,** an abortion of the fruit of plums, the stone being wanting, and a thin bladder representing the rest of the fruit ; **blad′dery,** thin and inflated.

Blade, the limb or expanded portion of a leaf.

blanched, (1) the whitened appearance of leaf or stem from the want of iron ; (2) artificially produced by exclusion of light, the green chlorophyll pigment not being developed in either case.

Blaste′ma (βλάστημα, a sprout), (1) originally the axis of an embryo, the radicle and plumule, excluding the cotyledons ; (2) ‡ the Lichen-thallus ; **blaste′mal,** (1) rudimentary ; (2) asexual (White) ; **blastemat′icus,** thalloid ; **Blaste′sis,** the reproduction of the thallus of Lichens by gonidia (Minks).

Blastid′ia (βλαστὸς, shoot), Schleiden's term for secondary cells generated in the interior of another cell ; daughter-cells ; **Blast′idules,** M‘Nab's expression for all reproductive bodies which are not spores, but produced asexually, as gemmae, propagula, etc. ; **blastocarp′ous** (καρπὸς, fruit), applied to those fruits which germinate within the pericarp ; **Blast′ochore** (χωρὶς, separate), plants distributed by offshoots (Clements) ; **Blastocol′la** (κόλλα, glue), the balsam which is produced on buds by glandular hairs (Hanstein) ; **Blastogen′esis** (γένεσις, beginning), M‘Nab used this for all methods of asexual reproduction which are not due to Sporogenesis ; **blastogen′ic** (γένος, offspring), employed by Weismann for those characters which have originated from changes in the germ (L. H. Bailey) ; **Blastograph′ia** (γράφω, I

write), the study of buds (Du Petit
Thouars) ; **Blastoma'nia** (*μανιά*,
madness), the production of an
abnormal number of leaf-shoots (A.
Braun) ; **Blastomyce'tes** (*μύκης*,
fungus), a synonym of Saccharo-
mycetes, the yeast Fungus, etc. ; adj.
blastomyce'toid (*εἶδος*, resemblance);
Blast'ophore, *Blastoph'orus* ‡ (*φορέω*,
I carry), the vitellus, the sac of the
amnios in a thickened scale, forming
a case in which the embryo lies;
Blast'us ‡, the plumule.
Blaze-currents, ~ -**reaction**, electric
response in definite direction in
plants (Waller).
Blea, pr. blee ; the liber or inner
bark.
Bleb, Hill's term for a pith-cell.
blech'noid, resembling the Fern genus
Blechnum.
Bleed'ing, applied to an extravasation
of sap, such as occurs in vines if
injured in spring during leaf expansion ; ~ **Pres'sure**, exsudation
pressure, the internal force needed to
cause an abnormal flow.
Blend'ing, a hybrid formed by the
crossing of races (Heinig) ; Ger.,
Blendling.
Blendl'ing, a hybrid between races,
not species.
Bleph'arae, pl. (*βλέφαρον*, an eyelash),
the teeth belonging to the peristome
of a Moss ; **Bleph'aroplast** (*πλαστός*,
moulded), the specialized protoplasm which gives rise to the motile
cilia of the antherozoids as in *Zamia*
and *Cycas;* **Blepharoplast'oids** (*εἶδος*,
resemblance), the two bodies appearing between the 2- and 4-celled
stage at each pole of the two
spindles, in nuclear division, disappearing into the cytoplasm before
the rise of the blepharoplasts themselves (Shaw).
Blet, a soft spot on fruit ; **Blet'ting,**
the change in consistence without
putrefaction, of certain fruits, as the
medlar.
Blight, popularly applied to an epidemic, either of minute Fungi, or of
aphides.

Blind, a cultivator's expression for
abortion, as when a flower-bud is
said to go blind, that is, does not
develop.
Blister Blight, of the tea plant due
to *Exobasidium vexans ;* ~ **Rust,**
due to *Peridermium Strobi.*
Bloom, (1) synonymous with BLOSSOM ;
(2) the white waxy or pruinose
covering on many fruits and leaves.
Blos'som, the flower, especially of fruit
trees ; ~ **Bud,** = Flower-bud.
blotch'ed, colour irregularly disposed
in patches.
Blow-off Lay'er, an epidermal layer of
presumably mucilage-cells, forming
the outermost investment of the
testa of palaeozoic seeds (Oliver and
Salisbury).
blunt, ending in a rounded form,
neither tapering to a point, nor
abruptly cut off.
boat-shaped, having the figure of a
boat, with or without a keel.
Bod'y-cell, the cell which divides to
form the male cells in certain
Conifers (Nichols).
Bog-moss Association, *Sphagnum* dominant in moorland vegetation ; ~
Xerophytes (+ XEROPHYTE), plants
presenting the appearance of xerophytes though growing in water
(Clements).
bola'ris (Mod. Lat.), dark red, brick-
coloured ; from the earth, Armenian
Bole.
Bole, the main trunk of a tree, with a
distinct stem.
bole'tic, obtained from the genus
Boletus, as boletic acid ; **Bole'tol,**
Bertrand's name for the blue colouring-matter in certain Fungi, as
Boletus.
Boll, pr. boal, the fruit capsule or
pericarp, especially of the cotton
plant ; **Bo'lling,** pr. boal'ing, =
POLLARD ; **bolled,** pr. boald, come
into fruit, as flax when the capsule
is formed.
Bol'ochore (*βολή*, a throw ; *χωρέω*, I
spread abroad), a plant distributed
by propulsion (Clements).
bomby'cinus, (Lat.), silky, feeling as

smooth as silk ; **bom'bysine** (Heinig)
= BOMBYCINUS.

bo'ny, of a close and hard texture, as
the stones of plums, etc.

boragina'ceous, belonging to or resembling the genus *Borago* or its
allies ; **bor'agoid**, or **bor'ragoid**, from
the genus *Borago*, applied to a form
of inflorescence which finds its fullest
development in *Anchusa*, an extreme
case of extra-axillary inflorescence
(K. Schumann).

bord'ered, having a margin distinct in
colour or texture from the rest ;
~ **Pit**, a pit in which the margin
projects over the thin closing membrane, as in coniferous wood ; ~
Pore, is the same thing.

Bo'rer, (1) the penetrating root of a
parasite (De Bary) ; (2) an insect
tunnelling into the wood of trees
during its larval stage.

bor'ragoid = BORAGOID.

Boss, a protuberance ; **bossed**, with a
rounded surface having a projection
in its centre.

bost'rychoid (βόστρυξ, a ringlet ; εἶδος,
resemblance), having the form of a
BOSTRYX ; ~ **Cyme**, a sympodial
branch-system in which the right-
or left-hand branch is always the
most vigorous ; a helicoid cyme ;
~ **Dichot'omy**, a dichotomy or
repeated forking of an inflorescence, within the previous definition ; **Bost'ryx**, a uniparous, helicoid
cyme.

botan'ic (βοτάνη, a herb), pertaining to
the knowledge of plants ; ~ **Gar'den**,
a garden especially devoted to the
culture of plants for scientific ends ;
Bot'anist, a student of plant life, in
any of its departments ; **bot'anize**,
(1) to seek for plants in their places
of growth ; (2) to study actual
plants ; **Botanol'ogy** (λόγος, discourse) = BOTANY ; **Bot'any**, (1) the
study of the vegetable kingdom in
all its divisions ; its classification,
morphology, physiology, and eco-
imnocs ; (2) also used for a text-
book or local-flora.

Bothrench'yma (βόθρος, a pit ; ἔγχυμα,

that poured in), tissue composed of
dotted or pitted ducts or cells.

Bot'rus (Crozier) = BOTRYS.

bot'ry-cy'mose (βότρυς, a bunch of
grapes ; κῦμα, a wave), racemes or
any botryose clusters cymosely
aggregated ; **bot'ryoid**, **botryoid'al**
(εἶδος, resemblance), like a cluster
of grapes ; **bot'ryose**, *botryo'sus*
racemose ; **Bot'rys**, a raceme.

Bottom-yeast, or Low-yeast, the yeast
which forms at the bottom of the
vats ; in German, "Unterhefe."

bot'uliform, *botuliform'is* (*botulus*, a
sausage ; *forma*, shape), sausage-
shaped, allantoid.

Boui'llon (Fr.), meat-broth, used for
cultures.

Bound'ary Cell, Ger., Grenzzelle =
HETEROCYST.

bour'geon (Fr., in English pr. bur'jun),
to bud or sprout.

Brach'eid, Tschirch's suggested abbreviation of his own term
BRACHYSCLEREID.

brachia'lis (*brachium*, the fore-arm),
a cubit long, roughly about 18
inches ; **bra'chiate**, *brachia'tus*,
when branches spread and widely
diverge.

brachy (βραχύς) = short, used in Greek
compounds.

brachybiostigmat'ic (βραχύς, short ;
βίος, life ; στίγμα, a spot), a term
proposed by Delpino to express
stigmas which are short-lived,
withering before their proper anthers
ripen ; protogynous ; **Brach'yblast**
(βλαστὸς, a bud), Hartig's term for
a spur, or short branch ; also spelled
Brach'yoblast ; **brachychi'mous**
(χεῖμα, winter), exposed to short
winters (Drude) ; **brachyclad'ous**,
-dus (κλάδος, a branch), applied by
Russow to those species of *Sphagnum*
which bear short branches ; **brachy-
dod'romous** (δρόμος, a course), with
looped veins (Kerner), *cf.* BROCHI-
DODROMUS ; **Brach'yforms** (+ *forma*,
shape), Arthur's term for *Brachy-
puccinia*, the ascidia being wanting,
but spermagonia, uredospores and
teleutospores occur on the same

54

host ; **Brachymeio'sis** (+ Meiosis), abnormal nuclear division in which half the heterotype number of chromosomes are present, sometimes without their visible union (Fraser and Brooks) ; adj. **brachymeiot'ic** ; **brachyphyll'ous** (φύλλον, a leaf), short-leaved ; **brachyp'odous** (πούς, ποδὸς, a foot), having a short stalk or foot ; **Brachyscle'reids** (σκληρὸς, hard), stone-cells, the sclereids in barks and fruits (Tschirch) ; **brachy-sty'lous** (+ Style), a synonym of microstylous ; **brachytheroxero-chi'mous** (ξηρὸς, dry), adapted to short summers and dry winters (Drude) ; **brachyther'ous** (θέρος, summer), exposed to short summers; **Brachytme'ma** (τμῆμα, section), a disc-shaped cell, which by its rupture sets free a gemma in Bryophytes (Correns) ; **brachyxerochi'mous**, inured to short, dry winters (Drude).

Brack'et-cells, secretory cells in *Lonchocarpus* with papillose epithelium ; ~ **-epithe'lium**, leaf epithelium showing finger-like differentiation of the component cells ; ~ **-hairs**, bent or hooked at the apex ; ~ **-shaped**, a term used by Boodle and Fritsch, for a body curved like a parenthesis.

Bract, *Bract'ea* (Lat., a thin plate of metal), the modified leaves intermediate between the calyx and the normal leaves ; ~ **-cell**, used for certain cells on the branchlets of *Chara ;* ~ **-scale**, in Coniferae, a scale of the cone above which lies the seed-bearing scale ; **bract'eal**, of the nature of a bract ; **bract'eate**, *bractea'tus*, provided with bracts ; **bracteif'erous** (*fero*, I bear), bearing bracts ; *bractea'nus* ‡, formed of bracts ; **Bracteo'dy** (εἶδος, resemblance), the change of foliar organs into bracts (Worsdell) ; **Bract'eole**, *Bracte'ola*, (1) a bractlet, or small bract ; (2) a prophyll ; (3) a postical bract of Hepaticae (Spruce) ; **Bract'eole-succulents**, such plants as lose their leaves by drying up, but the bracteoles round the flowers become enlarged and succulent, e. g.

Salsola ; **bract'eolate**, *bracteola'tus*, having bract!ets ; **Bracteoma'nia** (*mania*, madness), excessive development of bracts ; **bract'eose**, *bracteo'sus*, having conspicuous or numerous bracts ; **bract'less**, wanting bracts ; **Bract'let**, a bract of the last grade, as one inserted on a pedicel or ultimate flower-stalk, instead of subtending it.

brad'yschist (βραδὺς, slow ; σχιστὸς, split), when in a brood mother-cell successive nuclear divisions are completed before cell-division (Hartog).

Bran, the husks or outer coats of ground corn, separated from the flour by bolting ; **bran-like**, scurfy in appearance.

Branch, a division of the stem, or axis of growth ; **Branch'ery**, Grew's term for the ramifications in the pulp of fruits ; **Branch'ing, Interc'alary**, in Hepaticae where branching arises below the apical cell ; **Ter'minal** ~, the branching arising from a division of the apical cell (Leitgeb) ; **branch'-less**, bare of branches ; **Branch'let**, a twig or small branch, the ultimate division of a branch.

Brand, disease caused by minute Fungi on leaves, as *Ustilago*, etc.; **Brand'-spore** = Uredospore.

Bras'ilin, the colouring - matter of Brazil wood, *Caesalpinia brasiliensis*, Linn.

brassica'ceous (*Brassica* + aceous), resembling the genus *Brassica*, or belonging to it.

Braun's Series, the same as Fibonacci Series.

break, (1) to put out new leaves ; (2) to show a variation, as in florist's flowers ; **Break-back**, reversion to an earlier type ; **Break'ing**, a popular expression for a sudden profusion of algal life in certain lakes or meres.

Brea'thing-pores = Stomata.

Breed = Race ; **Cross-breed** = Hybrid.

bre'vi-ramo'sus (*brevis*, short ; *ramosus*, branched), short-branched.

brick-colour, usually implies a dull-red ; latericious, testaceous ; ~**like,**

resembling courses of brickwork, as tissue of rectangular cells.

Bridge, a narrow band of tissue connecting larger masses of the same (Kearney) ; **bridg'ing,** applied to certain species which act as intermediate hosts of Fungi, thus breaking down immunity, *e. g.* ~ **Spe'cies,** as in *Bromus.*

Bri'dles, (1) strings of protoplasm which often connect the nucleus with the layer of protoplasm next the cell-wall ; (2) strands of cells connecting other tissues.

Bris'tle, a stiff hair, or any slender body which may be likened to a hog's bristle ; ~ **like,** resembling bristles ; ~ **point'ed,** ending in a stiff short hair ; **bris'tly,** beset with bristles.

Brit'ish, used by H. C. Watson to express the distribution of those plants which are found throughout the island of Great Britain.

brochidod'romus (βρόχos, a noose ; εἶδos, like ; δρόμos, a course), Ettingshausen's term for loop-veined.

Bro'mare (+ -ARE), Clements's term for a "community" of *Bromus.*

Bro'melin, a proteolytic enzyme occurring abundantly in the juice of the pineapple, which is a member of the Bromeliaceae, whence the name.

Bronte'sis (βροντὴ, thunder), injury to plants by electric shock.

Brood-bod'ies, gemmae on leaves of Mosses, becoming detached and growing into protonemal filaments ; ~ **Buds,** (1) a synonym of Soredium in Lichens ; (2) the same as Bulbil in Archegoniatae ; ~ **Cell,** asexually produced propagative cell of a gonidium ; ~ **Gem'ma,** a pluricellular propagative body produced asexually and passing gradually into a brood-cell on one side, and a bulbil on the other.

Broti'um, or **Broti'on** (βρoτὸs, mortal), a succession of plants due to human agency ; **Brot'ochores,** *-ae* (χωρίς, separate), dispersion by man (Clements).

Brown Rot, of cacao pods, attributed to *Diplodia cacaoicola,* P. Henn. ; ~ of potatoes, due to *Stysanus Stemonilis,* Corda.

Brown'ian Move'ment, motion shown by minute particles when suspended in a liquid.

Bru'cine, a poisonous alkaloid from *Strychnos Nux-vomica,* Linn., formerly supposed to be from *Brucea ferruginea,* L'Hérit.

Bruguiere'tum (+ ETUM), an association of *Bruguiera,* a mangrove formation.

bruma'lis (Lat.), pertaining to the winter solstice ; flourishing in midwinter.

Brunissure' (Fr.), injury caused to vines by *Plasmodiophora Vitis,* Viala.

brun'neolus (Mod. Lat.), brownish.

brun'neus or **brun'eus** (Mod. Lat.), brown in colour.

Brush, applied to the young fruit of the hop, when the stigmas are protruding ; ~ **Form,** of stigmas of some papilionaceous flowers, as of *Phaseolus, Vicia, Lathyrus,* etc. ; ~ **-shaped,** aspergilliform.

Bry'ogams, Bryogam'ia (βρύον, a moss; γάμos, marriage), term proposed by Caruel for the Bryophytes ; **Bryol'-ogy** (λόγos, discourse), the science of Mosses, or Bryophytes generally ; **Bryo'ma,** the vegetative substance of Mosses.

Bry'onine, a poisonous principle extracted from the roots of *Bryonia alba,* Linn.

Bry'ophytes (βρύον, a moss ; φυτὸν, a plant), moss-like plants, the true Mosses and the Hepaticae or Liverworts ; **bryophyt'ic,** pertaining to BRYOPHYTES.

Bucc'ae ‡ (Lat., cheeks), the lateral sepals or wings of the flower of aconite.

buck'ler-shaped, resembling a round buckler with a raised rim.

Buck'mast, the fruit of the beech tree.

Bud, the nascent state of a flower or branch ; ~ **Cones,** of the carob, *Ceratonia Siliqua,* Linn., arrested or abortive inflorescences ; ~ **-corm,**

the root-system of most herbaceous plants (J. Smith) ; ~ -gall, Kerner's term for a gall which involves several or all the members of a shoot, and may be leafless or leafy ; ~ Glue = BLASTOCOLLA ; ~ Rot, a disease of palms caused by *Pythium palmivorum;* ~ Ru'diment, in *Chara,* a cell cut off from a pro-embryonic branch as the primordium of the young plant; ~ Scales, the coverings of a bud; ~ Sport = BUD-VARIATION ; ~ Varia'tion, changes of colour or form in plants arising from a flower or leaf bud.—Adventit'ious ~, a bud arising out of the normal course or locality; Brood ~ = BROOD-BUDS; Flow'er ~, the inflorescence before expansion, or a unit thereof; Leaf ~, an undeveloped leaf; Bud'dage, propagation by buds (L. H. Bailey); Bud'ding, (1) propagation of a garden form by inserting a bud or "eye" on another stock ; (2) used also for expansion of the buds; Bud'let, "a little bud attached to a larger one" (Crozier)

Bulb, *Bul'bus* (Lat.), a modified bud, usually underground; (1) na'ked ~, *bulbus squamosus,* having scaly modifications of the leaves, as in the lily; (2) tunica'ted ~, whose outer scales are thin and membranous, as the onion or hyacinth; (3) the so-called sol'id ~, is a CORM; (4) the swollen base of the stipe of the sporophore in Hymenomycetes ; ~ Scale, one of the components of a bulb; Plu'mule ~, bulb produced direct from the seed; Run'ner ~, bulb arising from a stolon (Blodgett).

bulba'ceous, *-ceus,* (1) bulbous ; (2), having bulbs.

Bul'biceps, (*bulbus,* a bulb ; *caput,* a head), a stem bulbous at base; bulbif'erous, *-rus* (*fero,* I bear), bulb-bearing, as when bulbils are amongst the florets of an inflorescence, or axils of the leaves ; Bul'bil, *Bulbill'us;* Bulb'let, *Bulb'ulus,* (1) a small bulb, usually axillary, as in *Lilium bulbiferum;* (2), Bulbil is also applied, (*a*) in some

fungi to small pluricellular bodies incapable of germination; (*b*) deciduous leaf-buds capable of developing into a new bion or brood-bud, in Archegoniatae ; Bulbo'dium ‡ = CORM.

bulb'ose, *bulbo'sus,* bulb'ous, having bulbs or the structure of a bulb; bulb'ous Hairs, *bulbo'si pi'li,* hairs with an inflated base ; Bulbotu'ber, Gawler's name for CORM; Bul'bule = BULBIL (Crozier).

Bul'garine, Zopf's term for an orange pigment produced by *Bulgaria polymorpha,* Wett.

Bulk'head, transverse divisions and air-chambers in stem of *Scirpus* (Plowman).

bul'late, *bulla'tus* (*bulla,* a bubble), blistered or puckered, as the leaf of the primrose ; Bullescen'tia (+ ESCENS), the state of being blistered, as the Savoy Cabbage; bul'liform (*forma,* shape), used of some large thin-walled cells, occurring on the epidermis of certain grasses (Duval-Jouve).

Bul'lions, a local name for COAL-BALLS.

bunched, gibbous.

Bun'dle, a strand of specialized tissue, variously modified ; ~ -ends, the peripheral ends of bundles when spread out in the leaves or periphery of the stem; ~ Flange, communications between the unbranched leaf-bundles of Gymnosperms and the surrounding tissues ; ~ Sheath, the enveloping cylinder of closely united parenchyma; ~ -trunks, those bundles which pass through the stem, root, leaf-stalk, and thick nerves of the leaf; they may be complete or incomplete ; — Bicollat'eral ~, when a second bast-strand exists on the inner, medullary, side of the wood of the conjoint-bundle; Caul'ine ~, confined to the stem; Closed ~, destitute of cambium, the procambium having become permanent tissue ; Collat'eral ~, when the wood and bast lie side by side; Com'mon ~, that is, to stem and leaf, becoming a leaf-

trace; **Concen'tric** ~, when either
the wood, or the bast-system surrounds the other; **Conjoint'** ~, consisting of both wood and bast;
Cort'ical ~, peculiar to the cortical
region; **Medul'lary** ~, the vascular
bundles occurring in the pith, when
there is a well-defined exterior ring;
O'pen ~, when the bundle possesses
a portion of cambium; **Ra'dial** ~,
having the strands of wood and bast
alternately as in roots; **Phlo'ëm** ~,
the bast portion; **Vasc'ular** ~, the
entire strand, consisting of liber or
bast portion (phloëm) and tracheal
or wood portion (xylem) in various degrees; **Xy'lem** ~, the wood
portion.

Bunt, a common disease of the wheat
plant, from *Tilletia Tritici*, Winter.

Bur or **Burr**, (1) a prickly-headed
fruit; applied to the chestnut, *Arc-
tium*, and the like; (2) the female
inflorescence of the hop, when the
stigmas forming the **Brush** are
visible; **bur'ry**, resembling a bur.

Bur'gundy Pitch, a resin from species
of *Abies*.

Burr, a woody outgrowth from the
bark of certain trees; *cf.* **Gnaur**.

Bur'sa (Lat., a purse), ‡ the antheridium of *Chara;* **Bur'sicule, Bursic'ula** (Lat., a small purse), the
pouch-like expansion of the stigma
into which the caudicle of some
Orchids is inserted; **bursic'ulate,**
bursicula'tus, purse-like.

Bush, a low shrub, branching from the
ground.

Bush'land, shrubs and small trees constituting a formation (Warming);
arctic ~, with *Betula nana;* **subal'-
pine** ~, Rhododendrons, *Vaccinium*,
etc.; **Bush-swamp**, made up of
woody plants as alder and willow
with marsh plants; **Bush-wood**, of
taller, lignified plants, but falling
short of **Forest**.

But'terfly Flowers, Lepidopterid
flowers, usually red, whose honey-
store can only be reached by a long
proboscis (Knuth); ~ **like**, ~ **shaped**,
= **papilionaceous**.

But'tons, (1) an old term for **Buds**,
(2) J. E. Smith's name for **Tricae**.

But'tress, the knee-like growths of
trunk or roots in certain trees.

Butyr'ic Fer'ment, caused by *Bacillus
Amylobacter*, Van Tiegh.; *see* **Fermentation**.

bux'eous, *bux'eus* (*Buxus*, the Box-
tree), (1) the colour of box-wood,
(2) pertaining to that tree; **Bux'ine**,
an alkaloid from *Buxus sempervirens*, Linn.

Bynedes'tin (βύνη, malt, + **Edestin**),
a globulin found in malt with
By'nin, a proteid which replaces
Hordeïn when barley is malted.

byssa'ceous, *-ceus* (*byssus*, fine flax),
composed of fine threads.

bys'sine, **bys'soid** (εἶδος, resemblance),
the same as **byssaceous**.

Bys'sus, the stipe of certain Fungi.

Caa Ting'a, Brazilian forests, which
are deciduous during the hot and
dry season (Warming).

caca'inus, chocolate brown; from the
name of *Theobroma Cacao*, Linn.

Cach'rys ‡ (Lat.), the cone of a pine-
tree.

Cac'onym (κακὸs, bad; ὄνομα, a name),
a name rejected for linguistic reasons
(O. F. Cook).

cact'al (*Cactus*, a genus of succulents),
cacta'ceous (+ **aceous**), cactus-like,
or pertaining to the order Cactaceae;
cac'tiform (*forma,* shape), applied to
succulent stems like those of cacti,
and of *Euphorbia*.

Cacu'men ‡ (Lat.), the apex of an
organ.

ca'dens (Lat., falling), when the funiculus passes over the top of the
seed, as in Plumbagineae; **cadu'cous,**
cadu'cus, dropping off early, as the
sepals of a poppy on expansion.

Cae'cum (Lat., blind), a prolongation
of the embryo in *Casuarina* and
certain Amentiferae.

Caeno'bio = **Coenobio**.

Caenody'namism (καινὸs, recent;
δύναμις, power), Giard's term for
the replacement of complex functions by simpler; adj. **caenody-**

nam'ic; Caenogen'esis (καινὸς, new; γένεσις, beginning), the acquisition of characters of a recent date from readjustment to the environment (spelled also in various ways); *cf.* PALINGENESIS; adj. **caenogenet'ic; Caenomorph'ism** (μορφή, shape), simple modifications from complex, in living organisms (Giard).

Caeo'ma (καίω, I burn), term derived from the genus *Caeoma*, Link, a form of uredineous fungi having the spores in chains, and destitute of peridium; ~ **Cush'ions**, or ~ **Disks**, enlargements of the tips of twigs, due to the attack of forms of *Caeoma*, Link, believed to be a stage of *Melampsora;* **Caeo'mospores**—*ae* (+ SPORE), spore of Uredineae in the Caeoma stage.

caerulesc'ent (*caeruleus*, sky-blue + escens), verging towards blue; **caeru'leus**, sky-blue.

caesalpina'ceous, or **caesalpin'eous**, pertaining to the tribe of Leguminosae named after the genus *Caesalpinia*.

cae'sian, resembling the Dew-berry, *Rubus caesius* (Rogers).

cae'sious, cae'sius (Lat., grey of the eyes), light grey in tint; **caesiel'lus** is a diminutive.

caespitell'ose (*caespes*, or *cespes*, a sod), somewhat tufted; **cae'spitose**, *caespito'sus*, growing in tufts like grass; **caespit'ulose**, somewhat crowded in tuft-like patches.

Caespit'ulus (late Lat., a little sod), employed of Hymenomycetes for a Fungus tuft.

Caeto'nium, Lindley's spelling of COETONIUM.

Caff'eine, an alkaloid from coffee berries, *Coffea arabica*, Linn.

Cakile'tum (+ ETUM) an association of *Cakile maritima*, Linn.

Calamagrostide'tum (+ETUM), an association of *Calamagrostis*.

Calama'riae (*calamus*, a reed), (1) a term of vague application, which has been used for plants resembling grasses, chiefly sedges, but even including *Isoëtes, Juncus, Typha*, etc.; (2) restricted to fossil plants, Equisetineae; **calama'rian**, sedge-like; calamitean; **calamif'erous** (*fero*, I bear), having a hollow, reed-like stem; (2) producing reeds; **Cal'amite**, a fossil type, resembling recent *Equiseta* on a gigantic scale; **calami'tean**, resembling the last; **calam'itoid** (εἶδος, resemblance) = CALAMITEAN; **Cal'amus**, a fistular stem without an articulation.

cala'thial, relating to the heads of Compositae.

Cal'athide, *Cal'athida, Calath'ium Calathid'ium* (κάλαθος, a wicker basket), the head of a Composite; preferably restricted to the involucre of the same; **calathidiflor'us ‡** (*flos, floris*, a flower), having a Calathidium or Capitulum; **Calathidiph'orum** (φορέω, I bear), the stalk of a Capitulum; **cal'athiform**, *calathiform'is*, cup-shaped, almost hemispherical; **Cal'athis**, see CALATHIDE; **Calathoclad'ium** (κλάδος, a branch), in *Hieracium* and its allies, the upper part of the stem bearing flower-heads as distinct from the unbranched part or CLADOPHORE (F. N. Williams).

Calc'ar (Lat.), a spur; **calc'arate**, *calcara'tus*, furnished with a spur; **calcariform'is** (*forma*, shape), spurshaped.

Calca'rion (*calcarius*, pertaining to lime, + ON), a plant formation of calcareous soils (Moss); **calc'areous**, *-eus*, (1) chalk-white, as to colour; (2) growing in chalky or limestone places; (3) having the substance of chalk, as the chalk-glands of certain saxifrages.

cal'ceiform, *calceiform'is;* **cal'ceolate**, *calceola'tus* (*calceolus*, a slipper; *forma*, shape), shaped like a shoe.

cal'ceus (Lat. from *calx*, chalk), chalkwhite; **cal'cicole, calcic'olous** (*colo*, I inhabit), dwelling on chalky soil; **Calcifica'tion** (+ *facio*, I make), deposition within cells of carbonate of lime, in hairs, or cell-contents; **cal'cified**, the process completed;

59

calc'iform (*forma*, shape), "powdery, like chalk or lime," (Crozier); **Calciph'ilae** (φιλέω, I love), plants addicted to calcareous soils; **calciph'ilous**, chalk-loving; **calcif'ugal** (*fugo*, I flee), shunning chalk, as heather; **Calciph'obae** (φόβος, fear), plants avoiding chalk or limestone; **calciph'obous** (φοβέω, I fear), chalk-hating, plants shunning chalk or limestone; **calciv'orous** (*voro*, I devour), applied to Lichens which eat into their limestone matrix; **Cal'cosaxic'olae** (*saxum*, a rock, + COLA), plants of rocky limestone, as some Lichens.

Calc'ulary (*calculus*, a pebble), Grew's term for the sclerogenous tissue of a pear.

Calda'rium (Lat., warm bath-room) in botanic gardens signifies an intermediate or warm greenhouse.

Calenda'rium (Lat., an account-book), **~ Flor'ae**, an arrangement of plants according to their period of flowering.

Calend'ulin, a mucilaginous substance from the marigold, *Calendula officinalis*, Linn.

calicalis = CALYCALIS.

calica'tus = CALYCATUS.

calicina'ris, **calicina'rius** = CALYCINARIS, etc.

calicinia'nus = CALYCINIANUS.

calic'ular, *calicula'ris* = CALYCULAR, etc.

calic'ulate = CALYCULATE.

Caliol'ogy (καλία, a cabin; λόγος, discourse), juvenescence; the dynamics of the young cell (J. C. Arthur).

Ca'lix = CALYX.

call'ose, *callo'sus* (*callus*, hard skin), (1) bearing callosities; (2) hard and thick in texture; **Call'ose**, Mangin's term for a presumed essential constituent of the cell-wall; **Callos'ity**, a leathery or hard thickening of part of an organ; **callo'so-serra'tus** when the serratures are callosities.

Callune'tum, Warming's term for a plant-association consisting of heather, *Calluna*.

Call'us (Lat., hard skin); (1) an abnormally thickened part, as the base of a cutting; (2) a special deposit on sieve-plates; (3) a synonym of VERRUCA; (4) the hymenium of certain Fungi; (5) an extension of the flowering-glume below its point of insertion, and grown to the axis or rhachilla of the spikelet; **Callusheteroplas'y** (+ HETEROPLASY), the cell-structures or tissues which arise as the result of a wound; **Callushomöoplas'y** (+ Ho MÖOPLASY), increase of normal tissue due to an injury; **Callusmetaplas'y** (+ METAPLASY) when through injury to an organ, the contents of cells change, but not the cell-wall; **~ Cush'ions**, hemispherical pads covering the pits on the side of sieve-tubes; **~ Rods**, thread-like portions crossing the walls of sieve-tubes.

Calopo'dium ‡ (καλὸς, fair; ποὺς, ποδὸς, foot), Rumph's term for SPATHE.

caloritrop'ic (*calor*, heat; τροπὴ, a turn); Klercher's term for thermotropic; **Calorit'ropism**, curvature produced by conducted heat (Klercker), THERMOTROPISM.

Cal'pa (κάλπη, an urn), Necker's term for the capsule of *Fontinalis*.

cal'vous, *cal'vus* (Lat., bald), naked, as an achene without pappus.

Calyb'io (καλύβιον, a cottage), Mirbel's name for a hard, one-celled, inferior, dry fruit, such as the acorn, or hazel-nut; **Calyb'ium** ‡ is a synonym.

calyc'alis, of or belonging to the calyx (κάλυξ, a cup); **Cal'ycals**, proposed by Bessey for Calyciflorae; **calycanth'emous** (ἄνθος, a flower), (1) having the sepals converted wholly or partially into petals; (2) the corolla and stamens inserted in the calyx; **Calycanth'emy**, a monstrosity of the calyx imitating an exterior corolla; **calyca'tus** (Lat.), furnished with a calyx; **Calyc'ia**, a stipitate and boat-shaped apothecium; **Calyciflor'ae** (*flos, floris*, a flower), plants having their petals and stamens adnate to the calyx; adj., **calyci-flor'al**, **calyciflor'ous**; **calyc'iform** (*forma*, shape), cup-shaped, applied to an indusium; **Cal'ycin**, a bitter, yellow, crystallizable substance from *Calicium chrysocephalum*, Ach., and other Lichens; **calycina'lis** (Lat.), **cal'ycine**, *calyci'nus*, (1) belonging to the calyx; (2) of the nature of a calyx; (3) denoting a calyx of unusual size; **calycinia'nus** ‡, **calycina'ris** ‡ polyphylly of the calyx; **calycina'rius**, formed from the calyx; **Cal'ycle**, *Calyc'ulus*, the epicalyx, or involucre simulating an additional calyx, a whorl of bracts outside the true calyx; **cal'y-cled**, provided with a ring of bracts like an additional calyx; **cal'y-coid**, *calycoid'eus* (εἶδος, resemblance), resembling a calyx; **Caly-coste'mon** (στήμων, a filament), a stamen seated on the calyx; **calyc'ulate**, *calycula'tus*, bearing bracts which imitate an external calyx; **Calyphy'omy** (φύομαι, I spring from), adhesion of the sepals to the petals.

Calyp'tra (καλύπτρα, a veil) or **Calyp'-ter**, (1) the hood or cap of a Moss in fruit when it crowns the capsule, formed from the archegonial wall; (2) applied to any cap-like covering of a flower or fruit, as the extinguisher-shaped calyx of *Eschscholtzia*, or the lid which falls off on expansion of some Myrtaceae, as *Eucalyptus;* (3) Gomont's term for a thick membrane shutting off the apical cell of a trichome in Oscillarieae; (4) a term proposed by Van Tieghem and Douliot for that portion of the root-cap in lateral roots which belongs strictly to the root-system; (5) Tournefort's word for CARUNCLE; ~ **thalamog'ena** (+ THALAMUS, γένος, race, descent), a structure of the capsule and stalk in some Hepaticae acting as covering for the young sporogonium; **calyp'trate**, *calyptra'-tus*, bearing a calyptra; **calyp'tri-form**, *calyptriform'is* (*forma*,

shape), shaped like an extinguisher; **calyptrimorph'ous** (μορφή, shape), a synonym of the last; **Calyp'trogen** (γένος, offspring), (1) the layer of cells from which the root-cap takes its origin, (2) the layer of tissue covering the young embryo, as in Ferns; **calyptrogen'ic**, producing a cap or calyptra.

Ca'lyx (κάλυξ, a cup), the outermost of the floral envelopes; ~ **ad-he'rens**, when not separable from the ovary; ~ **calycula'tus**, when surrounded by a ring of bracts; ~ **commu'nis**, the involucre of Composites; ~ **infe'rior**, ~ **li'ber**, when free from the ovary; ~ **supe'-rior**, when adherent to the ovary; ~ **Tube**, (1) a tubular form of the calyx, due to the union of the sepals; (2) ‡ the receptacle of certain Fungi; (3) the "perianth" of Hepaticae, that is, the COLESULA (Hooker and Taylor).

Cam'ara (καμάρα, a vault), occasionally used for the cells of a fruit; **Camer'ula**, a diminutive of the foregoing; **cama'rius**, resembling a simple carpel, as the berry-like fruit of *Actaea*.

camb'ial (*cambio*, I change), relating to CAMBIUM; **camb'iform** (*forma*, shape), resembling cambium; **Camb'ium** (Mediaeval Lat., = exchange), a layer of nascent tissue between the wood and bast, adding elements to both; formerly considered as a mere viscous mass; ~ **Fi'bres**, the immediate derivatives of the cambium; partly formed woody fibres (Sanio); ~ **Lay'er**, the formative tissue during active growth; ~ **Ring**, the complete system of the cambium, separating the wood from the bast in the shoot; — **fascic'ular** ~, that which belongs to the vascular bundles; **interfascic'ular** ~, that which is formed between the vascular bundles, and the primary medullary rays; **cambiogenet'ic** (+ CAMBIUM, γένος, offspring), giving rise to cambium (De Bary).

cameli'nus (Lat.), camel - coloured,
tawny.

Camni'um (κάμνω, I cultivate), a
succession due to cultivation
(Clements).

campana'ceus (*campana*, a bell); cam-
pan'iform, *campaniform'is;* cam-
pan'ulate. *campanula'tus,* bell-
shaped, applied to a corolla;
Crozier adds campanil'iform.

campes'ter (Lat.), *campes'tris,* growing
in fields; the second form is that
usually found in botanic works;
adj. campes'tral.

Camph'or, a solid essential oil from
Cinnamomum Camphora, T. Nees
et Eberm., and other trees; camphora'ceous (+ ACEOUS), camphor'ic,
pertaining to, or of the nature of,
camphor.

Camp'o, Brazilian savannahs, low open
woods with ground vegetation.

camptod'romus (κάμπτω, I bend; δρόμος,
course), venation in which the
secondary veins curve towards the
margins, but do not form loops;
camptot'ropal (τροπὴ, a turn), an
orthotropal ovule, but curved like a
horse-shoe; Camptot'ropism, (τροπὴ,
a turn), the tendency to resume the
natural position if forced out of it.

campulit'ropal (καμπύλος, curved;
τροπὴ, a turn); campulit'ropous, *see*
CAMPYLITROPAL, etc.; Campylid'-
ium, described by Mueller-Arg. as
an accessory fruit in certain lichens;
now known to be a Fungus, *Cyphella
aeruginascens,* Karst.; campylod'-
romous, *-mus* (δρόμος, a course),
venation with its primary veins
curved in a more or less bowed
form towards the leaf apex; cam-
pylosper'mous, *-mus* (σπέρμα, seed),
having the albumen curved at the
margin so as to form a longitudinal
furrow; campylot'ropal, campylot'-
ropic, campylot'ropous (τροπὴ, a
turn), applied to an ovule, one side
of which has grown faster than the
other so as to bring its true apex
(micropyle) near the hilum; Campylot'ropism, the state of being bent
back.

Can'ada Bal'sam, an oleo-resin obtained from *Abies balsamea,* Mill.,
much used in the preparation of
microscopical specimens.

Canal', *cana'lis* (Lat., pipe or channel),
an internal channel; ~ Cells, an
axial row of cells in the neck of the
archegonium, ultimately forming a
canal by disappearance of the septa,
which becomes the way of access for
antherozoids; ~ Ra'phe, modification of the raphe in Diatoms, with
longitudinal fissure, as in *Surirella;*
canalic'ulate, *canalicula'tus,* chan-
nelled, with a longitudinal groove;
Canalic'ulus (Lat., a small channel),
a diminutive of CANAL; *see* GUM-
CANAL, SORUS-CANAL.

can'cellate, *cancella'tus* (Lat., latticed),
as in *Clathrus,* and *Ouvirandra.*

Candela'bra Hairs, stellate hairs in
two or more tiers.

can'dicant, *cand'icans* (Lat.), white,
clear, and shining.

cand'idus (Lat.), white, and shining;
brilliant.

Cane, the stem of reeds, large grasses,
and small palms; Cane-sugar, a
sucrose, the crystallized product of
Sugar-cane, *Sorghum,* Beetroot, etc.;
~ Und'ershrubs, plants having
lignified but commonly monocarpic
shoots, as various species of *Rubus;*
—Sugar-cane, *Saccharum officinarum,* Linn.: its chief Fungus-dis-
eases are Cane Freckle, ~ Rust,
causes uncertain; ~ Soot, by *Macrosporium graminum,* Cooke; ~
Spume, by *Strumella Sacchari,*
Peck.

canella'ceous, (1) pertaining to the
order of which *Canella,* P. Br., is
the type; (2) resembling cinnamon,
Ital., Canella, in taste or shape.

canes'cent, *canes'cens* (Lat.), growing grey or hoary; Canes'cence,
hoariness.

Cank'er (*cancer,* an ulcer), a disease in
deciduous-leaved trees, ascribed to
Nectria ditissima, Tul., shown by
malformed rind, with swollen
cushion-like margin, and depressed
centre.

canna'ceous, relating to the genus
Canna or its allies.

Can'opy (Mediaeval Lat., *canopium*,
tent), (1) a characteristic membrane
within the testa surrounding the
free part of the nucellus in *Lagenostoma* (Williamson); (2) the high,
leafy covering in woodlands, the
uppermost layer in forests; ~ **Trees**,
those having well-branched crowns
and abundant leafage (Warming).

Cantharoph'ilae (κάνθαρος, a beetle;
φιλέω, I love), plants which are
fertilized by beetles, having showy
colours, and abundance of pollen;
adj. **cantharoph'ilous**.

ca'nus (Lat.), hoary, grey.

Caoutch'ouc, (S. American), pr. koot'-
shook, a substance occurring in
the milky latex of many plants; it
is allied to the Hydrocarbons; ~
Bod'ies, small particles in the latex.

Cap, (1) Grew's term for the husk of
a nut; (2) the pileus of Hymenomycetous fungi; (3) the calyptra
of Mosses; (4) the short, upper
division of the dividing cell in
Oedogonium; ~ **Cells**, the upper
sister-cells of the embryo-sac in the
ovule which are compressed as the
embryo-sac develops and for a time
figure as a cap on its apex; ~ **Fungi**,
pileate Fungi, as the mushroom;
Cellulose ~, formation by protoplasm of cells of certain trichomes.

capilla'ceous, -*ceus*, **cap'illary**, *capilla'ris* (*capillus*, a hair), slender,
comparable with a hair; *capilla'tus*,
hairy; **capilla'tae Radi'ces**, roots
with evident root-hairs; **Capil'-
lament**, *Capillament'um*, the filament of an anther; **capillamento'sus**
(Lat.), comose; **Capillit'ium**, sterile,
thread-like tubes or fibres growing
amongst the spores in a sporogenous
body, frequently forming a net,
especially in Myxogastres; adj.
capillit'ial; **Capill'us**, the width of
a hair, taken as $\frac{1}{12}$th of a line or
about ·17 mm.

Cap'italist, a term applied to plants
which have a large reserve of
material, and are insect-fertilized.

cap'itate, *capita'tus* (Lat., having a
head), (1) pin-headed, as the stigma
of a primrose; (2) growing in heads,
as the flowers of Composites;
capitell'ate,*capitella'tus*, diminutive
of CAPITATE; **Capitell'um**, the capsule of Mosses; **capitiform'is**, ‡
(*forma*, shape), shaped like a head,
somewhat globose; **capit'ular** =
CAPITELLATE (Crozier); **capit'uliform**, shaped somewhat like a head;
Capit'ulum (Lat., a little head), (1)
a close head of sessile flowers; (2)
a term vaguely applied to the
pileus, etc. of Fungi; (3) a rounded
cell borne upon each of the manu-
bria in the antheridium of *Chara;*
head-cell.

capno'des, **capnoi'des** (καπνώδης,
smoky), smoke-coloured.

cappari'nus (Mod. Lat., from *Capparis*,
the caper-bush), brownish-green.

cap'reolate, *capreola'tus* (*capreolus*, a
tendril), having tendrils.

Caprifica'tion, *Caprifica'tio* (Lat.), (1)
the fertilization of the fig by
insects, branches of the wild fig
being placed among the cultivated
kind; the subsequent fertilization
is attributed to the punctures of an
hymenopterous insect; (2) fecundation by artificial means; **Caprifi'cus**,
(Lat.), the wild or "male" fig, the
uncultivated form.

Capsell'a (κάψα, a box), Link's term for
ACHENE.

Cap'sicin, an acrid alkaloid principle
found in some species of *Capsicum*.

Capsoma'nia (κάψα, a box; μανία,
madness), a multiplication of pistils.

Cap'sule, *Cap'sula*, (1) a dry, dehiscent
seed-vessel; (2) the theca of Mosses;
(3) ‡ the perithecium or receptacle
of Fungi; **cap'sular**, *capsula'ris*,
possessing a fruit of the kind just
mentioned; **cap'sulate**, enclosed in
a capsule; **capsulife'rous**, -*rus*,
(*fero*, I bear), bearing capsules.

Cap'ut, (Lat., the head), the peridium
of some Fungi; ~ **Flor'um** ‡ = CAPIT-
ULUM; ~ **Radi'cis**, the crown of the
root; the obsolete stem or bud of
herbaceous plants.

Carbohy'drates, (Carbon + Hydrate), non-volatile solids, as arabic acid, cellulose, dextrin, starch, sugar ; the non-saccharine members may be turned into sugars by boiling in dilute acids, usually into glucose (dextrose).

Car'bon Diox'ide = CO_2 ; **carbona'ceous** (+ ACEOUS), (1) consisting chiefly of substances in which carbon predominates ; (2) resembling charcoal, in colour or substance ; **carb'onised,** turned into nearly pure carbon by slow combustion, as charcoal.

Carbozy'mase ($\zeta\acute{\upsilon}\mu\eta$, leaven), an enzyme occurring in yeast.

Car'cerule, *Carceru'lus* (*carcer*, prison), (1) Desvaux's name for a dry, indehiscent, many-celled, superior fruit, such as that of the lime-tree ; (2) it has also been employed for the sporangia of some Fungi ; **carcer'ular,** *carcerula'ris*, having a carcerule fruit.

Carcino'des ($\kappa\alpha\rho\kappa\iota\nu\hat{\omega}\delta\eta\varsigma$, cancerous disease) and **Carcino'ma** ($\kappa\alpha\rho\kappa\acute{\iota}\nu\omega\mu\alpha$, cancerous ulcer), have been used to denote CANKER and kindred diseases.

Carcith'ium ‡ or **Carcyth'ium** ‡ ($\kappa\alpha\rho$-$\kappa\iota\nu o\hat{\upsilon}\sigma\theta\alpha\iota$, to become entangled, as roots), Necker's word for MYCELIUM ; **Carcy'tes,** ‡ = MYCELIUM.

card'inal (*cardinalis*, principal), applied by Malinvaud to those species which cannot be reduced ; **Card'inal-grade,** points of temperature, (*a*) lowest, (*b*) optimal, and (*c*) highest, at which vital functions can be performed (Kirchner).

Carene' (Fr.,Carène) = CARINA, keel ; has been used for the keel or midrib in the leaves of grasses.

Carice'tum, a plant-association of *Carex* (Warming).

Caricog'raphy (*Carex, Caricis,* $\gamma\rho\acute{\alpha}\phi\eta$, writing), a treatise on Cyperaceae, sedges, from the genus *Carex,* the largest in the order : **Caricol'ogist** ($\lambda\acute{o}\gamma o\varsigma$, discourse), a writer on sedges.

Car'ies (Lat., rottenness), putridity, decay.

Cari'na, (Lat., keel) ; (1) the two anterior petals of a papilionaceous flower, or similar organ ; (2) the keel of the glume of grasses ; (3) the principal nerve of a sepal ; **cari'nal,** relating to the keel in aestivation when the carina includes the other parts of the flower ; ∼ **Canal',** in *Equisetum,* a water canal on the inner side of the xylem, opposite a ridge on the surface of the stem ; **carina'lis,** that side of the fruit of Umbelliferae which represents the carina, or principal nerve of the adherent calyx ; **car'inate,** *carina'tus,* keeled ; **carina'to-plica'tus,** plaited so that each fold resembles a keel, as the peristome of some Mosses.

Cariop'side, Cariop'sis ($\kappa\acute{\alpha}\rho\upsilon o\nu$, a nut ; $\acute{o}\psi\iota\varsigma$, resemblance), a one-celled, one-seeded, superior fruit, with pericarp united to the seed ; the fruit of cereals; **cariopsid'eous,** having a cariopsis as fruit, also spelled CARYOPSIS.

car'iose, *cario'sus,* **car'ious,** decayed ; **cario'so-can'cellate,** used of Lichens becoming latticed by decay.

Car'mine (Mediaeval Lat., *carmesinus*), the purest red pigment obtainable, without admixture of blue or yellow.

carna'tion, (*carnatio,* fleshiness), flesh-coloured. [Wheat-ear Carnation is a monstrous state of that flower with multiplied bracts.]

carn'eous, *carneus* (Lat., of flesh), flesh-coloured ; **Carniv'orism,** the condition of insectivorous plants (Baillon); **Carniv'orophyte** ($\phi\upsilon\tau\grave{o}\nu$, a plant), a carnivorous or flesh-digesting plant ; **carniv'orous** (*voro,* I devour), flesh-eating; applied to those plants which digest insects ; **Carno'sitas** (Lat.), fleshiness ; **carn'ose, carn'ous,** *carno'sus* (Lat.), fleshy, pulpy ; **Ca'ro** (Lat., flesh), (1) the fleshy parts of fruits ; (2) the tissue of some Fungi.

Caro'tin, (1) the red colouring-matter of chromoplasts ; name from *Daucus Carota,* Linn.; pl. **Caro'tins** ; (2) a group of red and yellow colouring-matters (Czapek); also styled **Caro'-tinoids** ($\epsilon\hat{\iota}\delta o\varsigma$, resemblance) (Tswett).

Car'oubin, a carbohydrate first observed in the Carob; **Caroub'inase,** a hydrolytic enzyme formed during germination in seeds of *Ceratonia Siliqua,* Linn.; French, Caroube.

Carpade'lium ‡ **Carpade'lus** ‡ (καρπὸς, fruit; ἄδηλος, not manifest) = CREMOCARP.

Carp, a suggested abbreviation of **Carp'el,** *Carpel'lum* (καρπὸς, fruit), a simple pistil, or element of a compound pistil, answering to a single leaf; a female sporophyll; **carpel'-lary,** *carpella'ris, carp'icus,* relating to a carpel; ~ **Disk,** Williamson's term for the ovuliferous expansion in *Williamsonia;* **carpel'late,** possessing carpels; **Carpel'lody** (εἶδος, resemblance), the change of a floral leaf into a carpel (Worsdell); **Carpellotax'y** (τάξις, order), the arrangement of carpels in the fruit.

Car'phospore (κάρφος, a scale), a plant whose seeds are disseminated by means of a scaly or chaffy pappus (Clements).

Carp'id, *Carpid'ium* (καρπὸς, fruit) = diminutive of CARPEL; **Carp'ium,** (1) the oogonium modified by fertilization, which remains as an envelope around the embryo; (2) ‡ = CARPEL; **Carpoas'ci** (ἀσκὸς, a wine-skin), the more complex Ascomycetous Fungi; all, except the Exoascaceae (Kerner); **Carpoceph'-alum** (κεφαλή, a head), the sporogonial receptacle of the Marchantieae (Campbell); **Carpoclo'nium** (κλωνίον, a young shoot), "a free case or receptacle of spores found in certain Algals" (Lindley); **Carpoderm'is** (δέρμα, skin), Bischoff's emendation of PERICARP; **Carpo'des,** *Carpo'dium,* pl. *Carpo'dia,* abortive carpels, as in *Typha;* **Carp'ogam** (γάμος, marriage), the female organ in a procarp, producing a cystocarp; **Carpog'amy,** the process itself; **carpogen'ic, carpog'enous** (γένος, race), producing fruit; in Florideae, applied to special cells of the carpogonium; **Carp'ogone, Carpogon'ium** (γονή, offspring), (1) part of a procarp of

carpogenous cells resulting in a sporocarp after fertilization; (2) in Ascomycetes = ARCHICARP; **carpogon'ial,** relating to a carpogonium; **Carpogonid'ium** (+ GONIDIUM), suggested by Svedelius as an emendation of CARPOSPORE; **Carpog'raphy** (γράφω, I write), description of fruits; **Carp'olite, Carp'olith** (λίθος, stone), a fossilized fruit, or cast, found in the coal measures, probably of gymnospermous origin; **Carpol'ogist,** *Carpol'ogus* (λόγος, discourse), a specialist in fruits; **Carpol'ogy,** classification of fruits; **Carpo'ma** ‡ "a collection of spermangia" (Lindley), *i. e.* a compound sporocarp; **Carpoma'nia** (μανία, frenzy), a disease of grittiness in fruit; **Carpoma'ny,** pistillody, or substitution of pistils for stamens; **Carpomorph'a** ‡ (μορφή, shape), apothecia of Lichens, resembling true fruits.

Car'pon (καρπὸς, fruit), in Greek compounds = fruit; **Carp'ophore,** *Carpophor'ium* (φορέω, I carry); (1) the stalk of a sporocarp; (2) that part of the receptacle which is prolonged between the carpels as a central axis, as in *Ceramium;* (3) used by Fayod as inclusive of stipe, pileus and lamellae of Fungi; **Carp'ophyll,** *Carpophyl'lum* (φύλλον, leaf), synonym of CARPEL; **Carp'ophytes** (φυτὸν, a plant), Phanerogams; adj. **carpophyt'ic;** ~ **Fun'gi,** Clements's term for Fungi which produce Conidia; **Carpopod'ium** (*podium,* an elevation), fruit-stalk; **Carpopto'sis** (πτῶσις, falling), abnormal falling of the fruit; **Carposo'ma** (σῶμα, body), the fruit-body of Fungi; **Carp'osperm** (σπέρμα, seed), the impregnated oosphere of Algae; **Carp'osphere** (σφαῖρα, a sphere), the oosphere of Algae before impregnation (Bennett and Murray); **Carposporan'gia** (σπορὰ, a seed; ἀγγεῖον, a vessel), differentiated sporangia in the cystocarp of Rhodophyceae; **Carpospo'reae,** one of Cohn's, also Sachs's, main divisions of Thallophytes, of plants which produce spore-fruit as the result of fertilization ; **Carp′ospore** (σπορά, a seed) ; (1) a spore ; (2) a spherical uninuclear spore formed in a sporocarp, arising from the swollen tips of branched filaments resulting from the fertilization of the carpogonium ; (3) used by Clements for a plant possessing chaffy pappus ; adj. **carpospor′ic** ; **Carp′ostome**, *Carpostom′ium* (στόμα, the mouth), the opening in the cystocarp of some Algae ; **Carp′ostrotes**, *-ae* (στρωτός, spread), plants whose distribution is effected by fruits (Clements) ; **Carpot′ropism** (τροπή, a turning), the movements of fruits before or after pollination ; adj. **carpotrop′ic** ; **Carpozy′gote** (+ ZYGOTE) = ZYGOSPORE.

Carr, an association of scattered trees and shrubs progressing from fen to scrub (Tansley) ; **Fen ~**, ultimate stage of fen formation ; **Swamp ~**, occurs on edge of water as a Swampwood.

Car′ragheen Moss, chiefly of *Chondrus crispus*, Ag.

Carth′amine, red colouring-matter from flowers of *Carthamus tinctorius*, Linn.

cartilag′inous, *cartilagin′eus* (Lat., gristly), hard and tough, as the skin of an apple-pip.

Carunc′le, *Carunc′ula* (Lat., a little piece of flesh), a wart or protuberance near the hilum of a seed ; **carunc′ulate**, *caruncula′tus*, possessing a caruncle ; **caruncula′ris** = CARUNCULATE.

Caryog′amy (κάρυον, a nut ; γάμος, marriage), the fusion of male and female nuclei ; adj. **caryogam′ic** ; **Caryokine′sis** or **Caryocine′sis** (Crozier) = KARYOKINESIS ; nuclear division ; **caryolcg′ic** (λόγος, discourse), relating to the nucleus ; **caryolyt′ic** (λυτικὸς, able to loose), relating to nuclear dissolution ; **Caryomi′tome** (+ MITOM), the chromatin portion of the nucleus.

caryophylla′ceous, *-ceus*, relating to the Caryophyllaceae ; **caryophyll′eous**, **-lous**, used of a corolla having petals with a long claw as in *Dianthus Caryophyllus*, Linn., whence the name ; **caryophylla′tus**, = the same.

Car′yoplasm (κάρυον, a nut = nucleus ; πλάσμα, moulded), Vuillemin's term for the plasma of the nucleus ; **caryopsid′eus** (Mod. Lat.), like a CARIOPSIS ; **Caryop′sis** (ὄψις, resemblance) = CARIOPSIS ; **Caryorhex′y** (ῥῆξις, a breaking), the loss or dissolution of a nucleus ; **Car′yosomes** (σῶμα, the body), the constituents of the nucleus (Vuillemin).

cascarill′us (Lat.), the colour of the inner bark of *Cascarilla* (Heyne).

Cas′ein, see PLANT-CASEIN.

Caspa′rian Dots, markings on the cell-walls of the endodermis of *Dianthera;* they are named after R. Caspary.

Casque = GALEA.

cassid′eous, *-eus* (*cassis*, a helmet), helmet-shaped, as the upper sepal in *Aconitum*.

cas′sus (Lat., empty), empty, as an anther destitute of pollen.

casta′neus (Lat.), chestnut-coloured.

cast′ing, prematurely shedding leaves, or fruit.

cas′trate, *castra′tus* (Lat., gelded), said of a defective part, as a filament without an anther ; **Castra′tion**, in botany, (1) removal of anthers for artificial crossing ; (2) the action of *Ustilago*, etc., on *Lychnis* and allied genera ; divided into **amphig′enous ~**, transformation in either stamens or pistils ; **androg′enous ~**, production of anthers ; **thelyg′ynous ~**, production of pistils in male-host.

Casts, fossils showing the impressions of the structures whence their forms are derived ; **medul′lary ~**, impressions of the internal cavities of *Calamites*, etc.

Cas′ual (*casualis*, fortuitous), H. C. Watson's term for an occasional weed of cultivation, which is not naturalized.

catabol′ic, (κατὰ, down ; βόλος, a throw), adj. of **Catab′olism**, destructive metabolism of the protoplasm, or the formation of simpler substances from more complex, accom-

panied by a conversion of potential
into kinetic energy; also spelt
KATABOLISM; **Catab'olites**, the products of CATABOLISM; *cf.* HETERO-
BOLITES, SCHIZOBOLITES; **cata-
clad'ous**, *-dus* (κλάδος, a branch), deflexed; applied to certain species of
Sphagnum; **Catacle'sium** ‡ (κλῆσις,
a shutting up) = DICLESIUM; **Cata-
coroll'a** (*corolla*, a little garland), a
second corolla formed exterior to
the true one; resembling a hose-in-
hose flower; **catad'romous** (δρόμος,
course), Luerssen's term when the
first set of nerves in each segment
of a Fern frond is given off on the
basal side of the mid-rib, as in
Osmunda; **Catagen'esis** (γένεσις, a
beginning), retrogressive evolution,
by loss of attributes or simplification of structure; **catagenet'ic**,
relating to CATAGENESIS.

Cat'alase (deriv. from the next), an
enzyme in fresh tobacco leaves
(Loew). **Catal'ysis** (κατά, down;
λύσις, a loosing), chemical changes
effected by a substance which does
not itself undergo change; ferment
action; **catalyt'ic**, modification of
chemical force which causes catalysis; **catametad'romous** (+ META-
DROMOUS) in Ferns, when they are
sometimes catadromous and sometimes metadromous, which may occur
in the same species; **catapet'alous**,
-us, (πέταλον, a flower-leaf), where
petals are united only by cohesion
with united stamen, as in *Malva;*
Cat'aphyll, Cataphyl'la, pl. (φύλλον,
leaf), the early leaf-forms of a plant
or shoot, as cotyledons, bud-scales,
rhizome-scales, etc. ; in German,
Niederblätter; **cataphyl'lary**, of the
nature of the foregoing; ~ **Leaves**
= CATAPHYLLS.

Cat'apult Fruit; those fruits dispersing seeds or fruit-segments by the
elasticity of their peduncles.

Cat'echin, a crystallizable constituent
of catechu; **Cat'echu**, pr. Cat'eshoo,
cutch, the heart-wood of *Acacia
Catechu*, Willd., powerfully astringent from its rich tannin-contents.

cate'nate (*catena*, a chain), the co-
herency of Diatom frustules in a
connected chain; **cate'nulate**, *ca-
tenula'tus*, formed of parts united or
linked as in a chain.

Cath'edrus (καθέδρα, a chair), a part
growing between the angles of a
stem.

Cath'ion (κατά, down + ION), an ion
charged with electricity which mi-
grates toward the cathode or negative
pole (J. F. Smith); in physics the
word is usually spelled "Cation";
cathod'al, cathod'ic (ὁδός, a way) =
KATHODIC.

Cat'kin, (1) a deciduous spike, consisting of unisexual apetalous flowers;
an amentum; (2) improperly used
by J. E. Smith for the spikelet of
Carex; (3) the male flowers of
Cycads and Conifers are erroneously
styled catkins; **Cat'ulus** (Lat.,
puppy), ‡ a synonym of CATKIN.

Cau'da (Lat.), a tail, any tail-like
appendage; **cau'date**, *caudatus*,
tailed.

Cau'dex (Lat.), the axis of a plant,
consisting of stem and root; ~ **de-
scen'dens**, the root; ~ **Radi'cis**, the
root-tip; ~ **re'pens** ‡ = RHIZOME;
caud'ici-contin'uus ‡ continuous
with the stem, used of those leaves
which have no articulation with the
stem; **caudic'iform** (*forma*, shape),
like a caudex in form; **Cau'dicle**,
Caudic'ula, the cartilaginous strap
which connects certain pollen-masses
to the stigma, as in Orchids.

caulesc'ent, *-ens* (*caulis*, a stalk), becoming stalked, where the stalk is
clearly apparent; **Caul'icle, Caul'icule**, *Caulic'ulus*, a diminutive stalk;
(1) a small stem produced on the
neck of a root without the previous production of a leaf; (2) the
initial space between the radicle and
the cotyledons of an embryo, now
termed the hypocotyl; (3) the stipe
of certain Fungi; **caulic'olous** (*colo*,
I dwell), applied to Fungi which
live on stems; **Caulid'ium**, term
proposed by Bower to express the
leaf in the oophore generation; its

analogue in the sporophore generation is CAULOME; **caulif'erous** (*fero*,
I bear), bearing a stalk; **caul'iform**
(*forma*, shape), having the shape of
a stalk; **Cauliflo'ry**, the production
of flowers from the old wood (C.
Schimper); **Caul'iflower** (+Flower),
hypertrophy of the flower-stalk,
accompanied by defective flowers;
caulig'enous (γένος, race), arising
from a stem; **caulig'erous** (*gero*, I
bear), borne on a stem; **caul'inar**,
caulina'ris, **caul'inary**, *caulina'rius;*
caul'ine, *cauli'nus*, belonging to the
stem or arising from it; ~ **Bun'dles**,
vascular bundles growing acropetally
with the stem, having no direct
communication with the bundles
which pass into the leaves.

Caul'is (Lat.), a stem; the ascending
axis, restricted to the above-ground
portion in its normal state; ~ **deli-
quesc'ens**, ‡ a stem which branches
irregularly; ~ **excur'rens**, a stem
shooting straight upwards, having
side branches, as in *Abies;* **Caulo-
ca'lyx** (κάλυξ, a cup), the PSEUDO-
PERIANTH of Hepaticae; **caulo-
carp'ic**, **caulocarp'ous**, *caulocarp'eus*,
-p'icus (καυλὸs, stem; καρπὸs, fruit),
bearing fruit repeatedly, as trees
and shrubs; **Caul'ode** (εἶδος, resemblance), a portion of a Thallophyte
which simulates a stem; **caul'oid**
(εἶδος, resemblance), emulating a
stem, as in *Pithophora* (Wittrock);
Caulo'ma, ‡ (1) the stem of a palm;
(2) the stem-like portion of such
Algae as *Fuci;* **Caul'ome**, the stem
as an abstract entity; the leaf-
developing axis; Bower suggests its
restriction to the sporophore generation only; **Caul'omer** (μέρος, a part),
a secondary axis in a sympodium;
Caulotax'is (τάξις, arrangement), the
order of branches upon a stem.

caust'icus (Lat., burning), biting in
taste, as Cayenne Pepper.

caverna'rius (*caverna*, a cave), growing in caves; **Cavern'uli**, the pores
of such Fungi as *Polyporus.*

Cav'itus ‡ (*cavus*, hollow) and **Cav'us**
are given by Lindley as respectively

the perithecium and peridium of
some Fungi; also **Cav'us sup'erus**,
defined by him as the hymenium of
certain Fungi.

Cecidiol'ogy (κηκὶs, a gall; λόγος, discourse), the science of galls and
their origin; **Cecidi'um**, the galls
produced by Fungi or insects, the
consequence of infection being an
abnormal growth.

Cell, *Cel'lula* (Lat., a small apartment),
(1) an independent unit of proto-
plasm, strictly with a single nucleus,
contained in a chamber of cellulose,
etc., which originally was recognized
and called cell, now CELL-WALL;
(2) the cavity of an anther, otherwise anther-lobe; (3) the cavity of
an ovary or pericarp, containing the
ovules or seeds; ~ **Bun'dles**, a band
or bundle of similar cells, as the
bast fibre in dicotyledons; ~ **Cap**,
an appearance in *Oedogonium*, due
to intercalary surface-growth; ~
Ker'nel = NUCLEUS; ~ **Con'tents**, of
two kinds, living or protoplasmic,
and non-living, such as starch, fats,
proteids, crystals, cell-sap, and
the substances dissolved in it; ~
Divis'ion, in free cell-division,
several daughter-cells are formed
in the cavity of the mother-cell;
in ordinary cell-division, as a rule
only two daughter-cells are formed,
usually followed by a subsequent
further division of each; ~ **Fam'ily**,
a group of cells of common origin, a
colony or coenobium; ~ **Fi'bres**,
the achromatic filaments which form
the nuclear spindle in nuclear-division; ~ **Forma'tion**, the construction
of a new cell by reorganization of
the protoplasmic energid, with or
without division of the cytoplasm;
~ **Fu'sions**, cells united by absorption or perforation of transverse
walls as Sieve-vessels; ~ **Groups**,
associations of similar cells, as the
sclerenchyma in the pulp of the
pear, or in cork; ~ **Mas'ses**, when
cells are united in all directions
of space, not having necessarily
any definite form; ~ **Multiplica'-**

tion takes place by the formation of two or more protoplasmic bodies out of one; ~ **Nu'cleus**, an organized structure within the cell, the active agent in division, usually spherical in form, and of higher refractive power than the rest of the cell-contents; ~ **Plate**, formed by the thickening of threads of kinoplasm, marking out the future septa; ~ **Rows**, have the cells in contact by their ends, thus making a filament; ~ **Sap**, a watery solution of various substances, salts, sugars, alkaloids, and the like; ~ **Sur'faces**, where the cells form a single layer, as in some Algae; ~ **Tis'sue**, distinguished from vascular tissue by being made up of cells only; ~ **Wall**, a closed membrane, formed of cellulose, and a small proportion of mineral substances, originated by the layer of protoplasm which lines it, frequently thickened by secondary deposits; **Hinge** ~ = HINGE-CELL; **Primord'ial** ~, a cell previous to the creation of a cell-wall; **Stalk** ~ = STALK-CELL.

Cel'la (Lat., storeroom), (1) Scopoli's name for the fruit of *Couroupita*, Aubl.; (2) ‡ a form of perithecium in Fungi (Lindley); **Cel'lase**, an enzyme which reduces CELLOSE; **cellif'erous** (*fero*, I bear), bearing or producing cells; **Cellobi'ose** formerly **Cel'lose**, a sugar stated to have nearly the same composition as CELLULOSE; **Cel'lul** (*cellula*, a cell), Blair's term for anther; **cel'lular**, *cellula'ris*, consisting of cells, spongy: ~ **Bark**, ~ **Envel'ope**, the middle layer of the bark, mesophloeum; ~ **Plants**, plants which do not possess vascular tissue; nonvascular Cryptogams; ~ **Spore** = SPORIDESM; **Cellula'res**; (1) plants which are built up of cells only, as those last mentioned; (2) the term has been applied to all plants built up of cells, in opposition to non-cellular or unicellular; **Cel'lule**, *Cel'lula*, diminutive of cell; **Cel'lules**, pl.,

used by J. E. Smith for CISTULAE; **cellulif'erous** (*fero*, I bear), bearing or producing cellules; **Cel'lulin**, Pringsheim's term for a modification of cellulose; ~ **Grains**, bodies found in vegetative hyphae; **Cellulo'sae**, Corda's name for SPORIDESM; **Cel'lulose**, (1) a carbohydrate, the chief organic base of the cell-wall; (2) Diatom valves composed of cellules are termed cellulose, a synonym of CELLULAR; (3) an enzyme occurring in *Polyporus* and *Merulius* which attacks woody tissues; **Cel'luloses**, a generic term for the carbohydrate group above mentioned; divided by chemists into sub-groups, as **Adipocel'luloses**. (*adeps, adipis*, fat), consisting of cuticular tissues of leaves and fruits and of cork; **Hemicel'luloses**, all carbohydrates in the cell-wall which are not coloured blue by chlor-zinc-iodide, such as reserve-cellulose, etc.; **Lignocel'luloses**, lignin combined with cellulose, as in Jute fibre; **Metacel'luloses**, in Fungi and Lichens; the fungine of Braconnot; **Paracel'luloses**, the cellular tissue and epidermal cells of leaves; **Pectocel'luloses**, composed of pectic acids and cellulose, such as the purified bast of Russian flax.—Other modifications are named but not characterized by Messrs. Cross and Bevan in their work "Cellulose," 1895, as **Cuto-, Hydra-, Hydro-, Muco-, Nitro-, Pseudo-celluloses. Fung'us-cel'lulose** = CHITIN; **Reserve'** ~, cellulose which is stored up as a food-supply; **cellulo'sic**, composed of CELLULOSE; **Cellulo'side**, a mixture of cellulose and pectose, composing the primitive cell-wall (Green); **cellulo'so-plic'ate**, folded so as to form small cells (Phillips).

Cement'-disk, the retinaculum in Orchids.

Cementa'tion, union of the membranes of hyphae by a slip of cementing substance, concrescence; in German, Verklebung.

Cenanth'y (κενός, empty; ἄνθος, a

flower); suppression of the stamens and pistils, leaving the perianth empty; adj. **cenan'thous.**

ceno'biar, *cenobio'neus cenobiona'ris, Ceno'bium ;* = COENOBIAR, etc.

cenogenet'ic (καινὸς, recent; γενέτηρ, a parent),· secondary (Crozier); *cf.* CAENOGENETIC.

Cen'ser-ac'tion, used for such capsules as partially open by valves, the seeds being gradually shaken out by the wind, as in *Papaver* and *Cerastium* (Kerner); **Cen'ser-holes,** apertures in the capsule, as in *Campanula.*

centifo'lious (*centum,* a hundred ; *folium,* a leaf), literally having a hundred leaves ; actually, more than can be readily counted ; **Cent'imetre,** *Centime'trum,* 0·3937 of an English inch, roughly, two-fifths.

cen'tonate (*cento,* patchwork), used by F. N. Williams for the blotched leaves of *Hieracium.*

cen'tral (*centrum,* the middle), (1) relating to the centre of a body ; (2) applied by Praeger to those plants which are distributed centrally, and die out towards the extremities of a country or island ; ~ **Cell,** in the archegonium, that in the venter from which the oosphere, and ventral canal-cell arise ; ~ **Cord,** a series of cells in the leaves and other parts of Mosses, which simulates a vessel; ~ **Cyl'inder,** in stems and roots the portion within the endodermis ; **Cen'trarch** (ἀρχή, beginning), solid xylem, protoxylem elements being in the centre (Lang) ; **Centraxo'nia** (ἄξων, an axle) = SYNGRAMME ; ~ **Cent're,** in Diatoms, the middle point of the pervalvar axis ; **cent'ric,** in the middle ; **centrif'ugal** (*fugo,* I flee), tending outwards or developing from the centre outwards ; **Cen'triole,** Boveri's term for CENTROSOME ; **centrip'etal** (*peto,* I seek), developing towards the centre from without ; **Centrogen'esis** (γένεσις, beginning), the rotate or peripheral type of form assumed by plants (L. H. Bailey);

adj. **controgen'ic** ; *cf.* DIPLEUROGENESIS.

Cent'ron (κέντρον, a sharp point), in compounds = Spur.

Centronu'cleus (*centrum,* the middle + NUCLEUS), a nucleus whose centrosomes are active during division and intranuclear (Olive) ; **Cent'rosome** (σῶμα, body), minute bodies believed to have directive influence in nuclear division ; the central particle of the centrosphere; **Cent'rospheres** (σφαῖρα, a sphere), two small colourless bodies near the nucleus, imbedded in the cytoplasm, having a centrosome in each.

Cen'trospores, *-ae* (κέντρον, a spur + SPORE), plants having spurred fruits (Clements).

Centrostig'ma (*centrum,* the middle ; στίγμα, a point) = SYNSTIGMA ; **centroxyl'ic** (ξύλον, wood), referring to **Centrox'yly,** centrifugal primary woody structure (Van Tieghem) : **Cent'rum** (Lat.), the centre of a solid body.

Cent'ury (*centuria,* a hundred), in sets of dried plants, each hundred is styled a century.

cepa'ceous, *-ceus* (*cepa,* an onion), having the taste or smell of garlic; alliaceous.

Cephalanth'ium ‡ (κεφαλή, a head ; ἄνθος, a flower), the capitulum or head of Composites; anthodium ; **Cepha'lium,** a woody enlargement at the apex of the stem in some Cacteae, from which the flowers appear ; **Cephaliza'tion,** the simplification of floral elements ; **ceph'alodine,** forming a head (Leighton) ; **Cephalo'dium,** (1) a knob-like shield, as in the genus *Scyphophorus ;* (2) the capitulum of Composites ; (3) peculiarly shaped, branched or convex outgrowth of a Lichenthallus, in which algal cells are situated ; (4) a synonym of TUBERCULUM ; **ceph'aloid, cephaloid'eous,** *-deus* (εἶδος, resemblance), capitate ; **Cephalo'nion** Gall, a sac-like gall, joined to the leaf by a narrow neck (Kerner) ; **Cephaloph'orum** (φορέω,

I carry), (1) the receptacle, or (2), the stipe of some Fungi.

cera′ceous, *-eus* (*cereus*, Lat.), waxy, (1) in appearance, or (2) colour, that of unbleached wax.

Ceramid′ium (κεράμιον, a jar), synonym of CYSTOCARP.

Cer′asin, a gummy exudation from plum and cheery trees, swelling in water but not dissolving ; the name is from *Prunus Cerasus*, Linn.

Ceratench′yma (κέρας, a horn; ἔγχυμα, poured in), the tissue of effete sieve-tubes which becomes horny in texture ; **Cera′tium**, a long, slender, one-celled, two-valved, superior fruit, as in *Hypecoum*, " capsula siliquiformis " ; **Ceratoma′nia** (μανία, frenzy), monstrous production of horn-like or hooded structures in the flower.

Cer′atrin, the bitter principle of " Iceland Moss," *Cetraria islandica*, Linn.

Cercid′ium (κερκίδιον, a small comb), the mycelium of some Fungi.

ce′real, *cerea′lis* (*Ceres*, goddess of agriculture), applied to any Gramineae whose seeds serve as food ; **Cerea′lia**, corn-plants generally ; **Ce′-reum**, **Ce′rium**, **Ce′rio** = CARIOPSIS.

cer′ebriform (*cerebrum*, the brain ; *forma*, shape), having an irregular brain-like appearance, as the kernel of a walnut.

cerif′erous (*cera*, wax ; *fero*, I bear), wax-producing ; **ceri′nus** (Lat.), the colour of yellow wax.

Ce′rin, **Ce′rine** (*cera*, wax), a substance stated to be a constituent of cork.

cern′uous, *cernuus* (Lat.), nodding, applied to such flowers as *Narcissus*, or Coltsfoot when in fruit.

cerussa′tus (Lat.), white as though painted with white lead.

cerv′ine, *cervi′nus*, *cervic′olor* (*cervus*, a stag), dark tawny colour.

Cerv′ix (Lat., the neck) = RHIZOME.

ce′sious (*caesius*, the grey of the eye), blue-grey, usually spelled CAESIOUS.

cespitit′ious (*caespiticius*, made of turf), pr. cespitish′us ; **cesp′itose**, pertaining to turf, or growing in tufts ; **cespit′ulose**, somewhat tufted ; *cf.* CAESPES.

Cet′rarin, a principle from several species of the genus *Cetraria*.

Chae′ta (χαίτη, a bristle), the slender sporophore of Mosses, the seta ; **Chaetoplank′ton** (+ PLANKTON), plankton composed of Diatoms with awn-like processes, as *Chaetoceras* (Cleve).

Chaff, (1) small membranous scales, degenerate bracts, in many Compositae ; (2) the outer envelopes of cereal grains ; **chaff′y**, paleaceous.

Chain-gem′ma (*gemma*, a bud), in Fungi, having the form of a septate confervoid filament, the segments of which are capable of growth ; termed also SPROUT-GEMMA.

Chala′za (χάλαζα, small tubercle), that part of the ovule or seed where the nucellus joins the integuments ; it is the base of the nucellus and is always opposite the upper end of the cotyledons ; **chala′zal**, pertaining to the CHALAZA ; **chala′zian**, or **chalazi′nus**, like a CHALAZA, or pertaining thereto ; **Chala′zogams** (γάμος, marriage), plants which are fertilized through the chalaza, and not the foramen, as *Casuarina*, and many Cupuliferae ; *cf.* POROGAMS ; **Chalazog′amy**, fertilization by the chalaza ; adj. **chalazogam′ic.**

Chal′icad (χάλιξ, gravel + AD), a gravel slide plant ; **Chalico′dium**, " a gravel slide formation " ; **chalicodoph′ilus** (φιλέω, I love), " dwelling in gravel slides " ; **Chalicodophy′ta** (φυτὸν, a plant), " gravel slide plants " (Clements) ; **Chalicophy′ta** (φυτὸν, a plant), gravel plants ; **Chalicophy′tia**, gravel plant formations (Clements).

Chalk-glands, multicellular glands which deposit calcareous matter, as in some Saxifrages, the secretion escaping through a special channel, the water-pore ; ~ **White**, pure white, cretaceous.

chalyb′eus (*chalybeius*, of steel), steel-grey, or lead-coloured.

Cha′maephytes (χαμαὶ, on the ground ;

φύτον, a plant), plants whose resting-buds are but slightly above the ground (Raunkiær); adj. **chamaephyt'ic.**

Cham'ber-flu'id, the Kammerflüssigkeit of Crato, comprising cell-sap and enchylema between lamellae of protoplasm.

Cham'bered-fi'bres, fibres which have become septate and seemingly multicellular, as in the secondary wood of Dicotyledons; ~ **O'vary,** when the margins of the carpels project into the interior to form incomplete longitudinal dissepiments, the ovary remaining unilocular.

Cha'nar Steppe, regions in Argentine predominating in *Gourlica decorticans* and other Leguminosae and Composites (Grisebach).

chan'nelled, hollowed out like a gutter, as in many leaf-stalks.

Chap'let, a series of objects arranged like beads on a string, as the spores of *Cystopus* (Crozier).

Chap'paral (Span.), dry shrubby regions, the plants usually leafless in summer.

Charace'tum, an association of plants of the genus *Chara* ; **Char'acine,** a species of camphor from terrestrial Algae, as *Palmella, Oscillaria,* etc. ; it smells like *Chara,* hence the name ; **characi'nus ‡** *Chara*-like, composed of a single, or a few parallel tubes.

Char'acter (Lat., a mark), the technical difference whereby allied forms are distinguished, as ordinal, generic, specific, and so on.

Chart Quad'rats, metre-squares of vegetation, each plant being accurately plotted on the chart (Clements).

charta'ceous, *-ceus* (*charta,* paper + aceous), papery.

chasmanthe'ric, chasmanth'erous (χάσμα, a chasm ; ἀνθηρὸς, flowering), in cleistogamic flowers, when the anthers open, and liberate their pollen ; **Chasmanthe'ry,** partial cleistogamy, when the stamens are exserted from the otherwise closed flowers (Knuth) ; **Chasmocho'mophyte** (χῶμα, an aggregation ; φύτον, a

plant), a plant of a rock-crevice ; **Chas'mocleistog'amy** (+ CLEISTOGAMY), the condition of possessing both cleistogamic and chasmogamic flowers (Delpino) ; adj. **chasmocleistog'amous ; Chas'mo-dichog'amy** (+ DICHOGAMY), when cleistogamic flowers are accompanied by others which are chasmogamic (Delpino) ; **chasmogam'ic, chasmog'amous** (γάμος, marriage), pollination effected during expansion of the floral envelope ; **Chasmog'amy,** the opening of the perianth at the time of flowering, as opposed to cleistogamic ; **Chasmopet'aly** (*petalum,* a flower-leaf), persistent opening of the floral envelopes : *cf.* CLEISTOPETALY ; **Chas'mophyte** (φυτὸν, a plant), a plant which grows in rock-crevices (A. F. W. Schimper).

Check, an experiment or observation for confirmation; frequently the word " Control " is used for this.

cheilod'romous (χεῖλος, lip ; δρόμος, a course) = CRASPEDODROMOUS ; **Cheiloma'nia** (μανία, frenzy), Morren's term for the doubling of the lip in Orchids, as in *Orchis Morio,* Linn.

cheiroste'monous (χείρ, hand ; στήμων, thread), (1) with five stamens united at the base (Heinig) ; (2) relating to the genus *Cheirostemon.*

che'late (χηλή, a hoof or claw), " with two cleft claws : " *cf.* BIFURCATE (Heinig).

Chemaux'ism (*chem* + αὔξη, growth), incitement to growth by certain reagents or other compounds ; **Chemiotax'is** = CHEMOTAXIS ; **Che'moaesthe'sia** (αἴσθησις, perception by sense) ; term employed by Czapek to express the capacity of a plant-organ to respond to chemical stimuli ; **Chemokine'sis** (κίνησις, motion), the action of zoopores induced by chemical attraction ; **Chemol'ysis** (λύσις, a loosing), chemical solution or analysis ; **Chemomorpho'sis** (μόρφωσις, a shaping), an alteration in shape caused by some compound, as galls by insect puncture ; **chemonas'tic** (ναστὸς, pressed close), cur-

vature due to chemical stimuli;
Chemosyn'thesis (σύνθεσις, composition), the composition of carbohydrates by chemical forces (Macdougal); **Chemotax'is** (τάξις, order), the attraction of bacteria, antherozoids, etc., by certain substances; sometimes spelled **Chemiotax'is**; adj. **chemotact'ic**; **neg'ative Chemotax'is**, repulsion instead of attraction, = APOCHEMOTAXIS; **Chemot'ropism** (τροπή, a turning), the condition of CHEMOTAXIS (Miyoshi); **Chemozo'ophobe** (ζῷον, an animal; φόβεω, I fear), a plant which defends itself against insect- or animal-attack by tannin, raphides, etc.; adj. **chemozooph'obous**.

Chera'dad (χέραδος, silt, + AD), a wet sandbar plant; **Cheradi'um**, a sandbar formation; **cheradoph'ilus** (φιλέω, I love), dwelling on sandbars; **Cheradoph'ytae** (φυτὸν, a plant), sandbar plants (Clements).

chermesi'nus (Lat., dyed with Chermes), crimson.

Cher'sad (χέρσος, dry land + AD), a plant of a dry waste; **Chersi'um**, a dry waste formation; **chersoph'-ilous** (φιλέω, I love), dwelling in dry wastes; **Cher'sophytes** (φυτὸν, a plant), dry waste plants (Clements).

Chila'rium (χειλάριον, a lip), the boundary of a small pit in the testa of *Phaseolus*, of two movable valves, which by hygrometric movements cause the rupture of the testa; **chi'-lary Lay'er**, the investment of the seed which contains the chilarium.

chi'lding, proliferous.

Chimæ'ra (Lat., a monster), the product from a bud with mechanical coalescence of two parent-forms (Winkler); **pericli'nal ~**, = GRAFT-HYBRID, as *Cytisus Adami* (Keeble and Armstrong).

Chimio'sis (χεῦμα, that poured; μείωσις, reduction), the alteration in time of action of digestive fluid in a carnivorous plant (Massart).

Chimiot'ropism = CHEMOTROPISM.

Chim'ney, applied to protrusion of epidermal cells round the guard-cells of a stoma, producing a long respiratory cavity.

chimonochlo'rous (χειμὼν, winter; χλωρὸς, pale green), applied to plants whose thin herbaceous leaves persist through the winter (F. Ludwig); **chimonoph'ilous** (φιλέω, I love), the chief development taking place in the winter season (F. Ludwig); **chimopelag'ic** (πέλαγος, the sea), Forel's term for plankton found on the surface only in winter.

Chi'na (Ital.), (1) a synonym for QUININE; (2) the bark of *Cinchona*, supplying valuable febrifuges and tonics.

Chi'na-grass, the fibre from *Boehmeria nivea*, Gaudich.; it was formerly confounded with RAMIE; *cf.* Kew Bulletin, 1898, p. 209.

Chinin' = QUININE.

Chio'nad (χιὼν, snow + AD), a snow-plant; **Chioni'um** a snow-plant formation (Clements); **chionoph'ilous** (φιλέω, I love), F. Ludwig's term for the winter-leaves of *Helleborus foetidus*, Linn.; **chionoph'obous** (φόβος, fear, dismay), the same author's word for the summer-leaves of the same plant; **Chio'nophobe**, a plant shunning snow; **Chionophy'ta** (φυτὸν, a plant), snow-plants; **Chionophyti'um**, a snow-plant association (Clements).

Chi'ronym (χείρ, hand; ὄνομα, a name), a manuscript name; **Chi'rotype** (τύπος, a type), the specimen on which a manuscript name is based.

Chiropteroph'ilae (Chiropteron = bat, φιλέω, I love), plants which are fertilized by bats; adj. **chiropteroph'ilous**.

Chi'tin (χιτὼν, coat of mail), a substance allied to horn, which forms the protective covering of many insects such as beetles, identified as being of the same composition as Fungus-cellulose.

Chive, (1) an old word for ANTHER; (2) sometimes confined to the FILAMENT; (3) an offset of a bulbous plant.

Chlamyd'ia, (1) bud-scales; (2) floral envelopes.

Chlamydogonid'ium (χλαμὺς, χλαμύδος, a cloak ; γονὴ, race, offspring), unicellular gemmae of certain Fungi, which are relatively large and thick-walled, and adapted for a period of quiescence before vegetating ; **Chlam'ydospore**, a spore having a very thick membrane.

chlamydomon'ad, applied to the type of Alga represented by *Chlamydomonas* (F. Blackman) ; **chlamydomon'adine**, the phase of algal growth resembling that genus ; **Chlamydomone'tum**, an association of *Chlamydomonas* and Diatomaceae lying loose on the sand and not cemented together (Warming).

Chle'dad (χλῆδος, rubbish + AD), a ruderal plant ; **Chledi'um**, a waste formation ; **chledoc'olus**, *i.e.* **chledoc'ola**, inhabiting wastes ; **chledoph'ilus** (φιλέω, I love), dwelling in waste places ; **Chledophy'ta** (φυτὸν, a plant), plants of waste places (Clements).

Chloram'ylite (χλωρὸς, grass green ; ἄμυλον, fine flour), Belzung's term for chlorophyll granules derived from the transformation of starch ; **chloranth'ous** (ἄνθος, a flower), with green, usually inconspicuous flowers ; **Chlor'anthy** (ἄνθος, a flower), the change of all or most parts of the flower into leaf-like organs ; frondescence ; **chloras'cens**, green, inclining to yellow ; **Chlorench'yma** (ἔγχυμα, an infusion), assimilating tissues : **Chlor'in**, used by Kraus to denote the green constituent of chlorophyll ; **Chlori'na**, a plant deficient in chlorophyll, xanthein and carotin ; **chlori'nus**, yellowish-green ; **Chlor'is**, used as the title of a work on the plants of a district ; analogous to Flora ; **Chlor'ites**, Arbaumont's term for chlorophyllous plastids, further specialized as ENDOCHLORITES and GYMNOCHLORITES ; **chloroch'rous** (χρόα, complexion), having a green skin ; **Chlorocypera'ceae**, those Cyperaceae which have little sclerenchyma in the cortex, but much assimilatory tissue and numerous

stomata (Plowman) ; **Chlor'ocyst** (κύστις, a cell) a chlorophyll cell ; **Chlorofu'cine** (φῦκος, *fucus*, seaweed), a chlorophyll of a clear yellowish-green colour (Sorby) ; **Chloroglob'in** (*globus*, a ball), the green colouring-matter of chlorophyll, which has been separated from it in the form of minute globules (Tswett) ; **Chlorogonid'ium** (γονὴ, offspring), the green gonidia of Lichens, as distinguished from the chrysogonidia ; **chlorogon'imus** (γόνιμος, productive), applied to the gonidial layer in Lichens ; **Chloroleu'cite** (λευκός, pale), Van Tieghem's term for chlorophyll granule, by Belzung restricted to those which are formed from protoplasm, albuminous ; syn. CHLOROPLASTID (A. Schimper), AUTOPLAST (A. Meyer) : **chlorophae'us** (φαιὸς, dun-coloured), yellow-green as the colouring-matter of Algae ; **Chlor'ophore** (φόρεω), I carry), Schmitz's term for chlorophyll granule ; a chloroleucite ; **Chlor'ophyll** (φύλλον, leaf), the green colouring-matter of plants ; ~ **Bod'y**, ~ **Cor'puscle**, ~ **Grain**, ~ **Gran'ule**, a proteid or plastid in the cells of plants, usually of a green colour ; *cf.* CHLOROLEUCITE, etc. ; ~ **Ve'sicles**, chlorophyll granules ; **chlorophy'ceous**, resembling or relating to the Chlorophyceae, or green Algae ; **chlorophylla'ceous** (+ ACEOUS), applied to cells which contain chlorophyll, in contra-distinction to those which do not, and are consequently colourless ; **Chlorophyl'lan**, a synonym of HYPOCHLORIN ; **chlorophyllig'erous** (*gero*, I bear), bearing chlorophyll, or containing it, etc. ; **Chloroph'ylline**, the green principle of chlorophyll ; **Chloroph'yllins**, Tswett's name for those constituents of chlorophyll which are fluorescent ; *cf.* METACHLOROPHYLLINS, XANTHOPHYLLINS ; **chlorophyl'lose**, containing chlorophyll ; ~ **Cells**, those small cells in leaves of *Sphagnum* and other Mosses which contain chlorophyll ; **Chlor'oplast**, **Chloro-**

plast′id (πλαστὸς, moulded), the
plastids or granules of protoplasm
which are of a green colour ; **Chloro-
plast′in,** Schwarz's term for a proteid
constituting the ground substance of
the chlorophyll granule ; **Chlororu′fin**
(*rufus,* reddish), a reduced chlorophyll, the red pigment of Chlorophyceae, so named by Rostafinski ;
Chloro′sis, a disease, shown by loss
of colour ; **chlorosperm′ous** (σπέρμα,
a seed), belonging to those Algae
having green spores ; **chlorot′ic,**
chlorot′icus, greenish in colour :
Chlorovaporiza′tion (*vaporatio,* a
reeking), a function analogous to
transpiration, but proceeding only
from the chloroleucites under certain
lights (Van Tieghem).

Chomap′ophyte (χῶμα, accumulation ;
ἀπὸ, form ; φύτον, a plant), ruderal
plants (Simmons) ; **Cho′mophyte,** a
plant growing on ledges or in
fissures (Öttli).

Chon′driokonts, pl., (χόνδρος, grain ;
κοντὸς, a pole) = MITOCHONDRIA, or
CHROMIDIA ; **Chon′driom,** the entire
number of chondriosomes in a cell ;
Chon′driomes, pl., a collective term
for CHONDRIOSOMES ; **Chon′driomites**
(μίτος, a web), also **Chon′driosomes**
(σῶμα, a body), the same as CHON′-
DRIOKONTS ; **chon′droid** (εἶδος,
resemblance) applied to a Lichen
medulla with the hyphae forming
a solid axis ; **Chon′drome,** granular
masses in the fluid cell-contents
(Schneider) ; *cf.* LINOME.

Chord′a (Lat., a cord) **pistilla′ris,** the
line of tissue between the stigma
and the cavity of the ovary ; **chor-
da′ceous** ‡ (+ ACEOUS), having the
figure of a rope.

chordorrhi′zal (χορδὴ, catgut ; ῥίζα, a
root), where the rootstock produces
numerous flowering-stems one before the other from its sides (Syme),
as in *Carex chordorrhiza,* Linn. f.

-chore (χωρέω, I spread abroad), a
combining term to denote agent of
migration (Clements).

Chor′ion (χωρίον, a caul), (1) Malpighi's term for the pulpy matter

which fills the young ovule, and is
absorbed during development ; (2)
‡ a carpel ; **Choriona′rius,** ‡ =
ETAERIO.

Choripet′alae (χωρὶς, separate ; πέταλον,
a flower-leaf), (1) proposed by
Bessey for Polypetalae ; (2) by
W. R. M‘Nab for Polypetalae and
Incompletae ; **choripet′alous,** *-us*
(πέταλον, a flower leaf), having
petals separate, polypetalous ; **chori-
phel′loid** (φελλὸς, cork bark), applied to the separated suberized cells
and lenticels (Klebahn) ; **choriphyl′-
lous** (φύλλον, a leaf), having separate
leaves, used of the floral members ;
chorisep′alous, *-us* (+ SEPAL), with
separate sepals, polysepalous ; **Cho′-
risis,** the separation of a leaf or
phylloid member into more than one,
dédoublement, doubling ; **collat′eral**
~, when the plane of separation
is antero-posterior ; **par′allel** ~,
the plane of separation lateral ;
chorisolepid′eus ‡ (λεπὶς, λεπίδος, a
scale), when the scales of the involucre of Composites are distinct
from each other ; **cho′ristate,** unlined (Lindley) ; *cf.* CHORISIS ; **chori-
stophyl′lous,** *-us* (φύλλον, a leaf),
separate leaved ; **Choriza′tion** =
CHORISIS.

Chortonom′ia ‡ (χόρτος, green herbage ;
νόμος, law). "The art of making
an herbarium."

Chre′sard (χρῆσις, use), the available
water of the soil, the physiological
water-content (Clements).

chromat′ic (χρῶμα, colour), relating to
colour ; ~ **Sphere,** the coalescence
of the chromosomes after anaphasis ;
the nuclear membrane is formed
round it (B. M. Davis) ; ~ **Thread,**
the filiform body in nuclear division,
which breaks up into CHROMOSOMES ;
Chromatid′ium, ‡ the colouring-
matter of plants ; **Chro′matin**
(Flemming), that portion of the
nucleus which readily takes artificial staining, termed Nuclein by
Strasburger ; **chromatin′ic,** relating
to CHROMATIN ; **Chromatol′ogy**
(λόγος, discourse), used by Sorby to

express the science of vegetable colouring-matters ; **Chromatol′ysis** (λύσις, a loosing), (1) Cavara's term for the condensation of nuclear chromatin in a homogeneous mass, which afterwards subdivides ; (2) the solution of chromatin (Němec); **Chro′matomere** (μέρος, a part) = CHROMOSOME ; **chromat′ophile** (φιλέω, I love), readily receptive of stain ; easily colourable ; **Chromat′o-phore** (φορέω, I carry), a collective term for the various plastids, chloro-, chromo-, leuco-plastids ; **Chro′matoplasm** (πλάσμα, moulded), the protoplasm of the colouring and allied substances (Strasburger); **Chromid′ium,** (1) the gonidium of a Lichen, (2) pl. **Chromid′ia,** Hertwig's term for discrete chromatin granules derived from the nucleus (Wager) ; **gen′erative** ~, those which replace the nucleus or can be reformed into nuclei ; **veg′etative** ~, those extruded for metabolism, or accumulated in nuclear-like structures ; adj. **chromid′ial ; Chromidiocen′trum** (*centrum,* a centre), chromidia when grouped into a well-defined mass in the cell (Wager); **Chromidiog′amy** (γάμος, marriage), fusion of chromidia (Wager) ; **Chromid′iosome** (σῶμα, a body), Minchin's term for CHROMIDIUM ; **Chromid′iosphere** (σφαῖρα, a sphere), the same as CHROMIDIO-CENTRUM ; **Chro′mism,** an abnormal colouring as of leaves ; **Chro′moblast,** an error of some writers for CHROMO-PLAST ; **Chro′mogen** (γένος, offspring), applied to sundry colourless substances in plants, which by artificial oxidation or fermentation produce a colouring-matter ; Indican is an example ; **chromogen′ic, chromog′enous** (γένος, offspring), colour-producing, as some bacteria ; **Chromoleu′cite** (λευκὸς, white), Van Tieghem's name for protoplasmic colour granules ; **Chro′momeres** (μέρος, a part), granules susceptible of staining darkly in chromosomes ; adj. **chromomer′ic ; chromop′arous** (*pario,* I produce), colour-producing, applied to bacteria

(C. Jones) ; **chromoph′ilous** (φιλέω, I love), employed for those nuclei which readily take up staining ; **chromoph′orous** (φορέω, I carry), used of protoplasm which is itself coloured (C. Jones); **Chro′mophyll** (φύλλον, a leaf), any substance which colours plant-cells ; **Chro′mo-plast** (A. Meyer), **Chromoplast′id** (A. Schimper) (πλάστος, moulded), are synonyms for granules containing other colouring than chlorophyll; **Chro′mosomes** (σῶμα, a body), fibrillar bodies of definite number formed during nuclear division, dividing by fission into new groups, and contributing to form the daughter nuclei ; adj. **chromoso′mal ; Dau′ghter** ~, secondary or derived chromosomes ; **Chro′mospire** (+ SPIREM), the folds of the spirem in nuclear division (Dangeard) ; **Chro′mula,** colouring-matter of the plant, other than chlorophyll ; applied especially to petals ; **Chro′mule,** Sorby's term for any colouring-matter in plants.

Chron′ispore (χρόνος, time ; σπορὰ, a seed), a resting-spore ; **Chronisporan′-gium**(ἀγγεῖον, a vessel), the sac which produces chronispores (Vuillemin) ; **Chronizo′ospore** (ζωὸς, living ; σπορὰ, a seed), a microzoogonidium produced by *Hydrodictyon,* which rests for some weeks before germinating ; also called **Chron′ispore** (Pringsheim); **Chronot′ropism** (τροπὴ, a turning), changes due to age, as the position of leaves.

chroococ′coid, resembling *Chroococcus ;* **chroococca′ceous,** allied to the same genus.

chroole′poid, (1) like the genus *Chro-olepis ;* (2) consisting of yellow scales.

chrysaloi′deus(χρυσαλλὶς, a pupa ; εἶδος resemblance), rolled up and folded up at the same time ; wrapped up as an insect pupa or chrysalis.

chrysan′thine (χρύσος, gold ; ἄνθος, a flower), yellow flowered ; **chry-sell′us,** somewhat golden-hued ; **chry′seus,** yellow as gold ; **chrysi′-tes** (χρυσίτης, like gold), gold-coloured ; **Chrysochlor′ophyll** (+

CHLOROPHYLL), according to Gaidukov, a constituent of CHRYSOCHROME; **Chry'sochrome** (χρῶμα, colour), Klebs's term for a characteristic pigment found in *Chromulina Rosanoffi;* **chrysoch'rous** (χρὼs, skin), having a yellow skin; **Chrysogonid'ium** (γονὴ, offspring), a yellow gonidium of Lichens; **chrysogon'imus** (γόνιμοs, productive), the layer of yellow gonidia in some Lichens; **Chry'sophan** (φαίνω, I show) occurs in *Physcia parietina,* De Not., etc., as gold-coloured crystals; also known as **chrysophan'ic Ac'id**; **Chry'sophyll** (φύλλον, a leaf), a yellow colouring-matter from leaves; **chrysophyl'lous**, having CHRYSOPHYLL; **Chrysorham'nin**, a yellow substance from unripe buckthorn berries, *Rhamnus catharticus,* Linn.; **Chrysotan'nin** (+ TANNIN), a group of colouring-matters in plants, when oxidized giving rise to brown tints in autumn foliage; **Chrysoxanth'ophyll** (+ XANTHOPHYLL), said to be a constituent of CHRYSOCHROME (Gaidukov).

Chylocau'la, pl. (χυλὸs, juice; καυλὸs, a stem), plants with succulent stems, as Cacti (A. F. W. Schimper); adj. **chylocau'lous**; **Chylocau'ly**, the condition; **Chylophyl'lae**, pl.(φύλλον, a leaf), plants with succulent leaves (A. F. W. Schimper); adj. **chylophyl'lous**; **Chylophyl'ly**, the condition.

chymif'erus (*chymus,* juice; *fero,* I bear), **chymif'era Va'sa,** ‡ Hedwig's term for an imaginary "sap-thread" rolled round a tube to form a tracheid or spiral vessel.

Chytridio'sis, a disease due to *Cladochytrium viticolum,* Prunet.

Cic'atrice, *Cicatric'ula, Cica'trix* (Lat., a scar), the mark left by the separation of one part from another, as by the leaf from the stem; **cicatrisa'tus, cic'atricose,** *cicatrico'sus* scarred or scarry; **cicatric'ial**, relating to a CICATRIX.

Cicin'nus (κίκιννοs, a ringlet) = CINCINNUS.

Ciench'yma (possibly, κίω, I go; ἔγχυμα, an infusion), a system of intercellular spaces (Köhler, fide Crozier).

Cil'ia, pl. of **Cil'ium** (Lat., an eyelash), (1) Vibratile whip-like processes of protoplasm by which zoospores and similar bodies move; (2) the hair-like processes in the endostome in Mosses; (3) the marginal hairs of *Luzula;* **cilia'ris** (Lat.), like an eyelash, or short hair; **cil'iate,** *cilia'tus,* fringed with hairs; **cilia'to-denta'tus,** the teeth finely serrate, as if fringed; **cil'iiform** (*forma,* shape), resembling cilia; **cil'iograde** (*gradus,* a step), moving by means of cilia (Crozier); **Cil'iola**, secondary or diminutive cilium.

cimici'nus (*cimex,* a bug), smelling of bugs, as Coriander.

Cincho'na (genus), compounds, *see* CHINA, QUININE, etc.; **cinchona'ceous** (+ ACEOUS), relating to Cinchona plants; **Cin'chonine**, one of the alkaloids found in the bark of *Cinchona;* **cinchon'ic**, relating to the same genus.

cin'cinnal, *cincinna'lis* (Lat., curled), applied to curled inflorescences, as ~ **Cyme**, a cyme in which the successive flowers are on alternate sides of the pseudaxis; ~ **Dichot'omy**, a cyme in which alternate branches develop; **Cincin'nus** (Lat., a curl), applied to a uniparous scorpioid cyme; the erroneous form CICINNUS is found in some writers.

cinc'tus (Lat., girded), used of albumen when surrounded by an annular embryo.

Cinench'yma (κινέω, I move; ἔγχυμα, an infusion), laticiferous tissue; **cinenchym'atous**, possessing latex vessels.

cinera'ceous, *-eus* (Lat.), somewhat ashy in tint.

cineras'cens (*cinis, cineris,* ashes), turning ashy grey; **ciner'eous,** *-eus* (Lat., ashy), the grey of wood ashes; **cineric'ius, cinerit'ious,** *-ius* = CINEREOUS.

Cingu'lum (Lat., a girdle), (1) the neck of a plant, that which is

between stem and root, the collum;
(2) the connecting zone, girdle, or
hoop of Diatom frustules.

Cin'nabar ($\kappa\iota\nu\nu\acute{\alpha}\beta\alpha\rho\iota$, a red pigment),
(1) Dragon's blood, a resinous gum
from *Daemonorops Draco*, Blume,
and other plants; (2) also the colour
obtained from it, vermilion; **cin'na-
barine**, scarlet-coloured; **cinnabari'-
nus**, scarlet.

cin'namic, or **cinnamo'mic**, pertaining
to cinnamon; **cinnamo'meus** (Lat.),
cinnamon colour, a light yellowish
brown.

Ci'on, an old form of SCION.

Cionosper'meae ($\kappa\acute{\iota}\omega\nu$, a column; $\sigma\tau\acute{\epsilon}\rho\mu\alpha$,
a seed), plants whose ovules develop
on a central, more or less columnar
placenta, as Olacineae and Santalaceae.

cir'ca, in Latin compounds = round
about.

cir'cinal, *circina'lis* (*circino*, I make
round), involute from the tip into
a coil; **cir'cinnate**, *circinna'tus*,
coiled into a ring or partially so;
sometimes spelled **cir'cinate**.

Cir'cle, Migra'tion (*migratio*, change
of habitation), movement of migration of plants from a parent
individual or group (Clements).

Circula'tion (*circulatio*, a revolution),
the streaming motion of protoplasm
in cells; *cf.* ROTATION.

circumax'ile, *circumax'ilis* (*circum*,
round; *axis*, an axle), surrounding a
central axis which separates when
the fruit splits open; **circumcinc'tus**
(Lat.), girded round; **Circumciss'ion**
(*circumcissus*, cut around), (1) Blair's
term for ringing fruit trees; (2) cut
round, as the apothecia of some
Lichens; **circumferen'tial** (Lat., *cir-
cumferentia*), relating to the circumference; **circumflor'al** (*flos, floris*, a
flower), applied to nectaries on the
outer side of a flower, as in EU-
PHORBIA; **Circumlat'eralism** (*latus,
lateris*, a side), the tendency in plant
phylogeny to develop a circular
arrangement of parts (L. H. Bailey);
circummedul'lary (*medulla*, the
spinal marrow), a proposed emenda-

tion of "perimedullary"; **circum-
nu'tate** (*nuto*, I nod), the movements
of the growing points of plants
round the axis; **Circumnuta'tion**, the
phenomenon of the apical portions
of stem, tendril, root, turning to
various quarters of the compass;
circumpo'lar, round the pole, as of
arctic or antarctic plants confined
to high northern and southern
latitudes; **Circumposit'io** (*positus*,
placed), a layer, or branch laid into
the earth to root, whilst still connected with the parent stock; **circumsciss'ile**, *circumsciss'ilis*, *circumsciss'us* (*scindo, scissus*, to split),
dehiscing as if cut circularly around,
as in the capsule of *Anagallis;* **Cir-
cumscrip'tion** (*scribo, scriptum*, to
write), (1) the outline of any organ;
(2) the definition of a form or group
of forms, as of species, genera,
orders; **circumse'piens** (*sepio*, I
enclose), surrounding, as a protection; *circumsepien'tia fo'lia*, is used
by de Candolle for leaves which surround the stem, as if to protect the
young growth.

Circumvalla'tion(*circumvallatus,*walled
round), a method of layering, by
ringing the stem and surrounding it
with soil kept moist, while the stem
continues erect.

cir'rhate, *cirra'tus, cirrha'tus, cirrh-
a'lis* (*cirrus*, a tendril), tendrilled,
or assuming the functions of a tendril; **cirrhif'erous** (*fero*, I bear),
producing tendrils; **cirrh'iform**,
cirrhiform'is (*forma*, shape), apparently a tendril; **cirrhig'erous** (*gero*,
I bear), cirrhiferous (Crozier); **Cir-
rho'sitas**, the state of possessing
tendrils; **cirrh'ose, cirrh'ous**, *cirrh-
o'sus*, (1) tendrilled, (2), with a wavy
hair-point (Braithwaite); **Cirrh'us**,
since Linnaeus, used for a tendril,
a filiform organ of attachment,
modified from a leaf, stipule, or
aborted branch. — The foregoing
are frequently spelled **cirrif'erous**,
cirr'iform, **cirr'ose**, **Cirr'us**, etc.
(from *cirrus*, a curl).

Cistel'la, Cis'tula (Lat., a little chest),

used for the apothecia of Lichens, which, globular at first, burst at maturity.

Cis´tern-ep´iphyte (+ EPIPHYTE), employed by A. F. W. Schimper for that class of epiphyte in which the roots are mere supports or altogether suppressed, and the entire nourishment takes place by the leaves.

Cist´olith = CYSTOLITH.

Cist´ome, *Cisto´ma* (Mod. Lat. contracted from *Cistostoma*) (κίστη, a box; στόμα, a mouth), a membranous sac which was supposed to pass beneath the stomatic guard-cells; but the cells at the bottom of the stomatic cavity are destitute of cuticle.

Cistoph´orum (φορέω, I carry), "the stipe of certain Fungals" (Lindley).

Cistula = CISTELLA.

Cis´tus-Ma´qui, (Maqui, Corsican for thicket), a mass of mostly evergreen vegetation in the Mediterranean region largely composed of *Cistus* spp.

citrel´lus (from *Citrus*, Linn.), somewhat yellow; **cit´reus**, lemon-yellow; **citrinel´lus**, yellowish; **cit´ric Ac´id** is abundant in lemon juice; **cit´rine**, **citri´nus**, lemon-yellow.

cladautoi´cous (κλάδος, a branch; αὐτος, self; οἶκος, a house), having the male inflorescence of a Moss on a proper branch; **Claden´chyma** ‡ (ἔγχυμα, an infusion), branched parenchyma.

cladino´sus, Nilsson's term for those heaths which have a substratum of *Cladina* lichen.

cladocarp´ous (κλάδος, a branch; καρπός, fruit), having a fruit terminating a lateral shoot in Mosses; **Clad´ode**, a branch of a single internode simulating a leaf; **Clado´dium**, a flat expansion of the stem; **Clado-dystroph´ia** (δυς,bad; τροφή, nourishment), the perishing of branches; **Cladoma´nia** (μανία, madness), an extraordinary exuberance of branches (Penzig); **Clad´ophore** (φορέω, I bear), the portion of the stem in *Hieracium* giving rise to the branches of the

inflorescence; **Clad´ophyll**, *Cladophyl´la* (φύλλον, a leaf), (1) a branch assuming the form and function of a leaf, a cladode; (2) **Cladophyl´lum**, a cone-scale (Archangeli); **Cladopto´-sis** (πτῶσις, a fall), abnormal casting off of branches; **Cladosele´reids** (σκληρὸς, hard; εἶδος, resemblance), stellate bodies containing calcium oxalate in leaves and floral envelopes of *Euryale ferox*, Salisb.; **cladosipho´nic** (σίφων, a tube), having a tubular stele interrupted at the insertion of branches (Jeffrey).

cladospor´oid, L. Planchon has employed this to express likeness to *Cladosporium*, Link.

cladoste´monus (κλάδος, a branch; στήμων, a stamen), Hayne's term for semi-connate filaments in willows (Wimmer); **Cladostro´ma** ‡ (στρῶμα, something spread), a receptacle or growing-point covered with carpels, each of which has a free placenta.

Clamp-cells, (1) small semicircular hollow protuberances, laterally attached to the walls of two adjoining hyphal-cells, and stretching over the septum between them; (2) "the nipple-like cells by which an epiphytic root adheres to its support" (Heinig); ~ **Connec´tions**, are the same.

Clap´per, the water-sac, or lobule of Hepaticae.

Clasileu´cite (κλάσις a fracture + LEUCITE), that part of the protoplasm differentiated in nuclear division to form the spindle and centrosomes or spheres when present (Dangeard).

Clasp´ers, Grew's term for tendrils.

Class, *Clas´sis* (Lat., a fleet), (1) a primary group of Orders, Dicotyledons for example; (2) ~ of **Var´iates**, a group all of which show a particular value falling between certain limits (Lock); **Classifica´tion**, arrangement under respective groups; taxonomy, from Class to Variety, or Form.

clathrar´ian, the characteristic markings of the fossil *Clathraria*, now referred to *Sigillaria*.

clath′rate, *clathra′tus* (Lat., latticed), latticed, or pierced with apertures ; ~ **Cell** = Sieve-tube ; **Clath′rus** (Lat., a lattice), a membrane pierced with holes and forming a sort of grating ; **Clath′rophores** (φορέω, I bear). D. Don's term for the glands in the pitchers of *nepenthes*.

Claus′ilus (*clausus*, shut), Richard's term for his macropodal embryo, when its radicle is united by its edges, and entirely encloses the rest (Lindley).

cla′vate, *clava′tus* (*clava*, a club), club-shaped, thickened towards the apex ; **clav′ellate**, *clavella′tus*, diminutive of the foregoing ; **Clav′icle**, *Clavic′ula* (Lat., vine-tendril), tendril, cirrhus ; **clavic′ulate**, *clavicula′tus*, furnished with tendrils or hooks ; **clav′iform**, *claviform′is* (*forma*, shape), club-shaped ; **clavillo′sus** (Lat.), clubbed, or markedly club-shaped ; **Clav′ule**, *Clav′ula*, the club-shaped sporophore in certain Fungi, as *Clavaria;* **Cla′vus**, the disease of Ergot in grasses, the young grain being malformed and club-shaped, from the attack of *Claviceps purpurea*, Tul.

Claw, the narrowed base of the petals in such plants as *Dianthus* ; ~ **Hook**, the petiole of a well-developed leaf which is transformed into a hook after the fall of the lamina (Goebel).

Cleat (pr. Cleet) of Diatoms, a small outgrowth of silica from the secondary hoops of certain Diatoms (Palmer and Keeley).

Clea′vage [disyll.], (1) sporangial division by which sporangiospores and conidia are formed ; either (*a*) progressive, or (*b*) complete (Harper) ; (2) in xylem by cell-division in wood-parenchyma, pith and medullary rays, resulting in formation of separate strands, sometimes followed by growth of meristem (Solereder).

Cleft, cut half-way down ; ~ **-graft′ing**, insertion of a scion in a cleft made in a stock ; **Clefts**, used by Sir W. J. Hooker for LIRELLAE.

Cleistanthe′ry (κλειστὸς, shut; ἀνθηρὸς,

flowery), the anthers of a partially cleistogamous flower remaining inside and not exserted (Knuth) ; **Cleis′tocarp** (καρπὸς, fruit), an ascocarp, which is completely closed, the spores escaping by rupture, a cleistothecium ; adj. **cleistocarp′ic, cleistocarp′ous**, applied to those Mosses whose capsules do not open by a lid ; **cleistogam′ic, cleistog′amous** (γάμος, marriage), with close fertilization, it taking place within the unopened flowers ; **Cleistog′amy**, the condition described ; **Cleis′togene** (γένος, offspring), a plant which bears cleistogamous flowers (Crozier) ; **Cleistog′eny**, the bearing cleistogamic flowers ; adj. **cleistog′enous;—Pseu′do** ~ ; Hansgirg's term for an intermediate condition, the flowers being normal, but not opening, and pollination taking place within the closed perianth ; **Cleistopet′aly** (πέταλον, a leaf), permanently closing of the floral envelopes, thus ensuring CLEISTOGAMY ; **Cleistothe′cium** (θήκη, a case), an ascocarp which remains closed till decay or rupture sets free the ascospores, a cleistocarp.

Clepsy′droid (κλεψίδρα, a water-clock ; εἶδος, resemblance) **Trace**, a band of centrifugal xylem separating into halves, each having parenchyma and dying-out remains of centripetal xylem (Lang).

Clest′ines (deriv. ?), large parenchymatous cells in which raphides are frequently deposited.

Climacorhi′zae (κλῖμαξ, a ladder ; ῥίζα, a root), Van Tieghem's term for Gymnosperms and all Dicotyledons except the Nymphaeaceae, their root-hairs having an epidermal origin ; **climacorhi′zal**, relating to the CLIMACORHIZAE.

climat′ic (κλῖμα, a climate), relating to climate ; ~ **Fac′tors**, the elements resulting in a stable plant formation due to climate.

cli′max (*climax*, from κλῖμαξ, a ladder) **Leaves**, the most developed and complete leaves of a given plant ; ~ **Vegeta′tion** growth of mature age.

cli′mbing, ascending by using other objects as supports.

Clinand′rium (κλίνη, a bed; ἀνήρ, ἀνδρὸς, a man), the anther-bed in Orchids, that part of the column in which the anther is concealed; Clinanth′ium (ἄνθος, a flower), the receptacle in Compositae; Clinid′-ium, the stalk supporting a stylo-spore.

Cli′nism (κλίνω, I bend), inclination of the axis due to each unit bending, the axis making an angle to its original direction.

Cli′nium (κλίνη, a bed), (1) the recep-tacle of a Composite flower; (2) the sporophore of some Fungi; Cli′node, a term proposed by Léveillé for the conidiophores of certain Fungi, as the Uredineae, etc.; cf. STERIGMA; clinomorpho′us (μορφή, shape), when asymmetric organs are without defi-nite relation to the horizon (Wies-ner); Clinosporang′ium (σπορὰ, a seed; ἀγγεῖον, a vessel), a synonym of PYCNIDIUM; Cli′nospore = STYLO-SPORE; Cli′nostat = KLINOSTAT; clinotrop′ic (τροπὴ, turning), used of an obliquely placed organ, which shows no vertical plane of symmetry (Wiesner); Clinot′ropism, the con-dition in question.

Clip, the seizing mechanism in the flowers of Ascepiads; Ger., Klemm-körper.

Cli′tochores, -ae (κλιτὺς, a slope; χωρὶς, asunder), plants which are dis-tributed by falling or sliding (Clements).

clock′wise, in the same direction as the hands of a clock; dextrorse.

Clona′rium ‡ (κλὼν, a little branch), the ripe, spiral-coated nucule of Chara; Clone, Webber's term for a bud individual.

Close Fertiliza′tion, fecundation by its own pollen.

closed, used of those fibro-vascular bundles in which all the pro-cam-bium cells become permanent tissue; ~ Bun′dles, as described, so that in-crease is prevented; ~ Fertiliza′tion = CLOSE FERTILIZATION; ~ Forma′-tions, when the component plants are so crowded that invasion by other species is very difficult (Clements); ~ Flow′ers are cleisto-gamic Flowers; ~ Nu′cleus, that of the higher plants.

Clo′sing Mem′brane, the original un-thickened cell-wall at the centre of a pit.

Clo′ster, Clo′strum (κλωσστήρ, a spin-dle), elongated cells, pointed at each end, frequent in wood.

cloud′ed, when colours are unequally blended.

Clove, a gardener's name for a young bulb developed by the side of the mother-bulb, as in garlic.

Club, a pluricellular hair, one of the elements of the pulp of the orange or lemon fruit (Crozier); club-shaped, gradually thickened upward from a slender base, clavate; Club-root, malformation in Crucifers caused by Plasmodiophora Brassicae, Woron.; Clubb′ing is a synonym.

Clusi′um, -on (κλύζω, I dash against), an association of plants growing in flooded places (Clements); also spelled Clysi′um.

Clus′ter, (1) old name for raceme, as used by John Hill; (2) ‡ = VASCULAR BUNDLE; ~ Cups = AECIDIUM; ~ Crys′tals, groups of single crystals; clus′tered, compactly gathered to-gether, as the flower of Cuscuta; ~ -gall, a gall with stunted axis and densely crowded leaf-like append-ages (Kerner).

clyp′eate, clypea′tus (clypeus, a round shield), buckler or shield-shaped; clypeastriform′is (forma, shape), clypeola′ris, clyp′eiform, clypei-form′is, all denote shield-shaped; clyp′eolar, clyp′eolate, somewhat shield-shaped; Clyp′eus, a covering of the perithecia formed of myce-lium, as in Clypeosphaeria (Traverso).

Clysi′um, cf. CLUSIUM.

Cnice′tum, an association of road-side weeds and Cnicus, whence the name.

coacerv′ate, coacerva′tus (Lat., heaped up), clustered.

coad′nate, *coadna′tus (coaduna′tus,* gathered into one); (1) an equivalent of ADNATE; (2) cohering; (3) connate.

coadni′tus, cited by Lindley as equal to COADNATUS.

coaeta′neous *(coaetaneo,* to be of the same age), existing or appearing at the same time.

Coag′ulase *(coagulum,* I cause to curdle), an enzyme which can precipitate starch in solution (Butler).

Coal-balls, calcareous masses in coal-seams containing fragments of fossil plants.

Coales′cence *(coalesco,* to grow together), the act of growing together; ~**of Cells,** the absorption or disappearance of partitioning cell-walls, as in the formation of vessels; **coales′cent,** *coalesc′ens,* union by growth.

Coalit′io *(coalitus,* fellowship), the growth together of parts, as the coalescence of petals causes that condition; adj. **coal′itus.**

coarc′tate, *coarcta′tus* (Lat., pressed together), crowded together; **Coarc′-ture,** *Coarctu′ra,* Grew's term for the neck or collum, the junction of root and stem at the level of the ground.

Coat, the successive layers of a bulb; **coat′ed,** occurring in layers, usually of varying consistence, as the bark of a tree, the rind of fruits, etc.; ~ **Bulb,** a tunicated bulb.

coax′ial *(co* for *con,* with, and *axis,* an axle), parallel with the axis, or having a common axis.

Cob, the spike of maize.

cobalti′nus (Mod. Lat.), the colour of cobalt, a light blue, azure.

cob′webbed, cob′webby, entangled with fine filaments, arachnoid.

Coca′ine, an alkaloid from the leaves of *Erythroxylum Coca,* Lam.

Coc′ci, pl. of COCCUS.

Coccid′ium † (κόκκος, a kernel or berry) =CYSTOCARP; **coccif′erous** *(fero,* I bear), bearing berries.

cocciform′is *(coccum,* kermes; *forma,* shape), used by Koerber to denote Lichen spores shaped like the kermes, or insect which affords the scarlet dye from *Quercus coccifera,* Linn.; **coccinell′us,** light scarlet in colour; **coccin′eus,** scarlet, with a tendency towards carmine.

coccochromat′ic (κόκκος, a berry; χρῶμα, colour), colour distributed in granular patches, as in some Diatoms, *cf.* PLACOCHROMATIC.

Cocco′des, spherical granulations resembling pills; **Coc′cogone,** *Cocco-go′nium* (γονή, offspring), a propagative cell of the nature of a sporangium in Cyanophyceae; **coc′coid** (εἶδος, resemblance), applied to amorphous colonies of propagative cells in *Nostoc* (Sauvageau); ~ **State,** the unicellular state of Algae (F. F. Blackman); **Coc′colith** (λίθος, stone), constituent plates of COCCO-SPHERES.

Coccolo′ba Associa′tion, an association in which the shrub *Coccoloba uvifera* is predominant.

Coc′cosphere (κόκκος, a berry; σφαῖρα, a sphere), spherical masses of protoplasmic origin, bearing coccoliths on their external surface, *Coccosphaera leptopora,* G. Murr. & Blackm. **Coc′cule,** *Coc′culum,* a portion of a divided COCCUS; **Coc′cus,** *Coc′cum,* (1) part of a schizocarp or lobed fruit; (2) also applied to the rounded bacteria.

Coch′lea *(cochlea,* a snail or spoon), a closely coiled legume; **coch′lear,** *cochlea′ris;* (1) spoon-shaped; (2) used of a form of imbricate aestivation with one piece exterior; **coch-lear′iform,** *cochleariform′is,* spoon shaped; **coch′leate,** *cochlea′tus,* shell-shape, in the manner of a snail-shell; **Cochlidiosperm′ata** (σπέρμα, seed), seeds convex on one side, concave on the other, from unequal growth or anomalous structure.

cocks′combed, fasciated (Crozier).

Cod = a seed pod; **cod′like,** follicular; **Cod′ware,** an old word for pulse.

Co′deine (κώδεια, a poppy-head), an alkaloid in the opium poppy.

odiophyl′lus (κώδου, a fleece ; φύλλον, a leaf), when a leaf is covered with a woolly pubescence.

o-dom′inant (+ DOMINANT), dominant in common with another species, neither preponderating.

oelen′terate (κοῖλος, hollow ; ἔντερον, a bowel), used by Boulger for the carnivorous habit of *Nepenthes* and *Cephalotus* ; **Coe′loblast** (βλαστὸς, a bud), employed by Sachs for noncellular Algae and Fungi ; *cf.* APOCYTIUM ; **Coelone′mata**, pl. of **Coelone′ma**, Myxogastres having a hollow capillitium ; *cf.* STEREONE-MATA.

oelo′ma, pl. **Coelo′mata** (κοίλωμα, a hollow), Kuetzing's term for the body of *Vaucheria*, etc. ; an unseptate coenocyte.

oelosperm′ae (κοῖλος, hollow ; σπέρμα, a seed), plants whose seeds have albumen curved at the ends ; **coelosperm′ous**, *coelosperm′us*, hollow-seeded ; used for the seed-like carpels of Umbelliferae, with ventral face incurved at the top and bottom, as in coriander ; **Coenanth′ium** (ἄνθος, a flower) = CLINANTHIUM.

oe′nobe = COENOBIUM.

oeno′bium (κοινόβιον, a cloister) ; (1) the same as CARCERULE ; (2) a colony of independent organisms united by a common investment, as *Volvox*, *Pandorina*, etc. ; (3) fruits such as those of Labiates, consisting of distinct lobes but not terminated with a stigma ; sometimes spelled CENOBIUM, etc. ; adj. **coeno′biar**, *coenobia′ris*, *coenobio′neus* ; **coeno′-bioid** (εἶδος, resemblance), like a coenobium.

oenocar′pium (κοινὸς, in common ; καρπὸς, a fruit), the collective fruit of an entire inflorescence, as a fig or pine-apple.

oenocen′trum (καινὸς, new, + CEN-TRUM), a dense, deeply stainable mass of granules, probably of the nature of CHROMIDIA, found by Wager in the oosphere of *Albugo*, and since in other Fungi ; present before fertilization and disappearing later ; presumably nutritive, and possibly concerned in producing oily reserves in the oosphere.

Coenoclad′ia (κοινὸς, in common ; κλάδος, a branch), natural grafting, where branches have grown together ; **Coen′ocyte** (κύτος, a vessel), an aggregation of protoplasmic units (energids) enclosed in a common wall, as in *Vaucheria ;* **coenocyt′ic**, of the nature of a coenocyte, non-cellular or multinucleate ; **Coen′ogamete** (+ GAMETE), a multinucleate mass of protoplasm, whose individual nuclei are sexual elements (Stevens) ; **Coenogen′esis** (γένεσις, beginning), development by adjustment to the environment ; *cf.* PALINGENESIS : —it is also spelled **Caen-**, **Cain-**, **Cen-**, **Kenogenesis ; Coenomonoe′cia** (+ MONOECIA), polygamous plants, the same individual having male, and female flowers, as well as the normal hermaphrodite flowers ; the condition is **Coenomonoe′cism** (Kirchner) ; **coenop′odus** = COINOPODUS ; **coeno′-pterid** (πτέρις, a fern), resembling or allied to the Coenopterideae, Seward's name for Palaeozoic ferns previously termed Botryopterideae ; **Coe′nosphere**, Dangeard's term for COENO-CENTRUM.

coerules′cens, *coeru′leus* = CAERULES-CENS, CAERULEUS.

coesius = CAESIUS.

coëta′neous, *coaeta′neus*, of the same age, existing at the same time ; also spelled COAETANEOUS.

Coeto′nium (κοιτὼν, a bed-chamber), the outer glumes of a multifloral spikelet in grasses (Trinius).

coffea′tus (Mod. Lat.), the colour of roasted coffee-berries, *Coffea arabica*, Linn.

cogener′ic, preferably CONGENERIC.

cohe′rent, *cohe′rens*, **cohe′ring**(*cohaereo*, I cleave to) ; (1) the act of **Cohe′-sion**, the incorporation of one part with another, as the petals to form a tubular corolla ; (2) adherent.

Co'hort, *Co'hors* (Lat., a band of soldiers), a group of orders, forming an Alliance.

coinop'odus ‡ (κοινόπους, with common foot), terminating downwards in a cone, as most embryos ; Lindley also spells it **coenop'odus.**

Colch'icine, an alkaloid yielded by *Colchicum autumnale,* Linn.

Co'leïn, the red colouring-matter of *Coleus Verschaffeltii,* Lem.

Colench'yma = COLLENCHYMA.

Col'eogen (κολεὸς, a sheath ; γεννάω, I bring forth), a ring-shaped group of cells, surrounding the mestome of *Dicksonia,* etc. (Haberlandt) ; **Coleophyl'lum** (φύλλον, a leaf), the first leaf in germination of monocotyledons, which sheathes the succeeding leaves.

coleop'teroid (Coleopteron, εἶδος, resemblance), resembling a beetle or tick, as the seeds of many Euphorbiaceae (S. Moore).

Coleop'tilum (κολεὸς, a sheath ; πτίλον, a feather) = COLEOPHYLLUM ; **Coleorhi'za** (ῥίζα, a root), the sheath of a monocotyledonous embryo, when pierced by the true radicle ; adj. **coleorhiza'tus** ; **Col'esule,** *Coles'ula;* a membranous bag-like organ enclosing the sporangium of Hepaticae, the perichaetial sheath, usually termed the Vaginule.

collap'sing, used by Babington for the form compared to a painter's pencil, assumed by the submerged leaves of some aquatic plants when taken out of the water ; **Collap'sion,** *Collap'sio* (Lat., falling together), the act of closing or falling together.

Col'lar, *Col'lum* (Lat., neck) ; (1) the "neck" of a plant, the imaginary boundary between the above- and underground portion of the axis ; (2) the annulus in Agarics ; (3) an encircling outgrowth at the base of the ovule in *Ginkgo* (Potter).

Colla're ‡ (Lat., a collar) = LIGULE.

collat'eral (*col'latero,* to admit on both sides), standing side by side ; ~ **Bun'dles,** those having a single

strand of bast and wood, side by side, and usually in the same radius ; BICOLLATERAL BUNDLES are a vari ation on this type, having two o one element to one of the other ~ **Cho'risis,** *see* CHORISIS.

collect'ing (*collect'io,* a gathering to gether) **Cells,** are roundish cells at the base of palisade tissue, destitute of chlorophyll and densely filled with protoplasm ; in German "Sam menzellen" ; ~ **Hairs,** hairs on the styles of some Compositae serving to collect the pollen on its discharge from the anthers ; **collect'ive Fruits** the aggregation of the fruits o several flowers into one mass, such as the mulberry ; ~ **Spe'cies,** super-species, an assemblage of sub species ; **Collect'ors,** *Collector'es,* the hairs of certain styles, as in *Cam panula,* which collect or brush ou the pollen from the anthers ; *cf* COLLECTING HAIRS.

Collench'yma (κόλλα, glue ; ἔχγυμα an infusion) ; (1) parenchymatou cells with cellulose walls usually elongated, forming strands of grea strength under the epidermis, thick ening in angles, etc. ; (2) the cel lular matter in which the pollen is formed, usually absorbed, bu remaining and assuming a definit form in some plants, as in Orchids or delicate threads, as in *Oenothera* (Lindley) ; — **Bast** ~, thickenin chiefly involving the whole wall **Cart'ilage** ~, walls thickened al round with sharply differentiate inner lamella ; **Met'a-** ~, caused b slow death of the cell, and metamor phosis of the cell-wall ; **Plate** ~ a form which resembles the tru hard bast ; **Rift** ~, portion of wal bordering on an intercellular spac alone thickened ; **collenchymat'ic collenchym'atous,** relating to Col LENCHYMA.

Col'let = COLLAR.

Colle'ter (κολλητὸς, glued), mucila ginous hairs on the buds of man phanerogams which secrete gum.

collic'ulose, *colliculo'sus* (*colliculus,*

little hill), covered with little round elevations or hillocks.

collif'erous (*collum*, a collar), bearing a collar, as the stipe of an Agaric ; **Colliform'e** (*forma*, shape), an ostiole, the orifice being lengthened into a neck.

colliga'tus (Lat., fastened together), collected (S. F. Gray).

colli'nus (Lat., appertaining to a hill), growing on low hills.

colliques'cent (*colliquescere*, to become liquid), becoming fluid, dissolving in moisture.

Col'loids (κόλλα, glue ; εἶδος, resemblance), substances of a gelatinous character ; opposed to crystalloid ; adj. **colloid'al.**

Col'lum (Lat., neck) ; (1) the collar or neck of a plant, see COLLAR ; (2) the lengthened orifice of the ostiole of Lichens.

colo'nial (*colonia*, a band of settlers), in cell-division, every cell dependent on the other cells of the organism at large (Hartog) ; **Col'onist,** H. C. Watson's term for weeds of the cultivated land and about houses, seldom found elsewhere ; **Col'ony** : see COENOBIUM. **Ener'gid ~ , Pro'-toplast ~ ,** a temporary union of Meriplasts, the individuality of the Protoplasts not being disturbed (Pirotta).

colorif'ic (*color*, colour ; *facio*, I make), applied to those Lichens which yield a dye.

Col'our, col'oured, possessing any tint but green, technically white is regarded as a colour, green is not ; **col'ourless,** (1) pale, and hyaline ; (2) in Lichens, not brown.

Colpench'yma (κόλπος, bosom ; ἔγχυμα, an infusion), cellular tissue with sinuous cell-walls.

col'ubrine (*colubrinus*, like a serpent), snake-like in appearance (Heinig).

Co'lum ‡ (Lat., a strainer) = PLACENTA.

columbi'nus (Lat.), dove-coloured ; sometimes used for the tint of a blue pigeon.

Col'umel (*columella*, a small pillar), **Jaccard's** term for lignified tissue

formed in place of the fertilized archegonium, bearing at its extremity the privileged embryo, the only one which develops, as in *Ephedra helvetica*, C. A. Mey. ; **Columel'la ;** (1) a persistent central axis round which the carpels of some fruits are arranged as in *Geranium ;* (2) the axis of the capsule in Mosses ; (3) the receptacle bearing the sporangia of *Trichomanes,* and other Ferns; (4) the central portion of the anther in Solanaceae (Halsted) ; (5) a sterile axial body within the sporangium of Fungi ; **columel'liform** (*forma*, shape), shaped like a small pillar or column.

Col'umn, *Colum'na* (Lat., a pillar) ; (1) the combination of stamens and styles into a solid central body, as in Orchids ; (2) the lower, twisted portion of the awn of grasses, not always present (Trimen); **colum'nar,** *columna'ris*, having the form of a column, as the stamens of *Malva ;* ~ **Crys'tals** = STYLOIDS.

com, in Latin composition, a modification of *con*, with.

Co'ma (Lat., the hair); (1) the hairs at the end of some seeds ; (2) the tuft at the summit of the inflorescence, as in the pineapple; (3) the entire head of a tree ; **co'mal Tuft,** a tuft of leaves at the tip of a branch ; **co'mate,** *coma'tus,* tufted.

combina'te-veno'sus ‡ (Lat.), joined veins, when in a leaf the lateral veins unite before reaching the margin.

combi'ned Hy'brids, hybrids having the strain of more than two species, as one arising from a simple hybrid + another hybrid or species.

comb-shaped, pectinate.

Com'bus, used by S. F. Gray for CORMUS, for which it is probably a misprint.

Com'ites (pl. of *comes*, a companion), Hegelmaier's term for certain cells occurring in the embryo-sac of *Lupinus.*

commen'sal (*com* = *con*, with ; *mensa*, a table), used of two organisms living in mutual beneficent relations, as in the dual-lichen theory, where the Fungus stimulates the host-Alga to greater energy of function; **Com′men′salism,** the state in question.

Com′missure, *Commissu′ra* (Lat., a joint or seam), the face by which two carpels adhere, as in Umbelliferae; adj. **commissu′ral;** ∼ **Col′umn,** the central vascular strand in ferns; ∼ **Strand,** the same structure; ∼ **Sieve-tubes,** structures which unite the different kinds of Sieve-tubes with each other (A. Fischer).

com′mon (Lat., *commu′nis*), general or principal, as opposed to partial; ∼ **Bud,** containing both leaves and flowers, or more than one flower; ∼ **Bun′dles,** those which are common both to stem and leaf, being continuous from one to the other; ∼ **Ca′lyx ‡** = Involucre; ∼ **Involu′cre,** that belonging to the main inflorescence, as of the general umbel; ∼ **Name,** one in popular use for a plant, exclusive of the scientific name; ∼ **Ped′uncle,** the main stalk, when it supports several subordinate ones, or pedicels; ∼ **Per′ianth,** occasionally used for the involucre, as in Compositae; ∼ **Pet′iole,** the first and principal leaf-stalk in compound leaves, the secondary petioles being termed "partial"; ∼ **Recept′-acle,** that which supports more than one organ; ∼ **Um′bel** = COMPOUND UMBEL.

commu′nis (Lat.), growing in society; not common, which is rendered by *vulgaris;* **Commu′nity,** Clements's term for growths intermediate between SOCIETY and FAMILY; he uses -ARE to denote it.

co′mose, *como′sus* (Lat., with much hair), tufted, comate.

Com′ospores (κόμη, the hair, + SPORE), seeds maned or comate (Clements).

compact′, *compact′us* (Lat.), closely joined or pressed together.

Compa′go, pl. **Compa′gines** (Lat., a connection), used by Wallroth in speaking of the Lichen-thallus when more or less brittle or readily parting into layers; **compagina′tus**

(Lat.), packed closely one over another.

Compan′ion-Cells, (1) in Phanerogams, cells which are associated with sieve-tubes and are of common origin, filled with granular proteid contents, and possessing strongly marked nuclei; (2) Salmon's term for Begleiter-Zellen, *cf.* BEGLEITER-CELLS; ∼ **Hy′phae** (ὑφή, a web), the tip of the trichogyne of *Polystigma* passing through a stoma into the air is accompanied by slender mycelial hyphae, which form a tuft, the so-called companion hyphae (De Bary).

Com′pass-plants, those which place their leaves so that their surfaces face east and west, the edges north and south, such as *Silphium laciniatum,* Linn.

Compensa′tion (*compensatio,* weighing together) **of Growth,** used when the development of a primordium of an organ is suppressed, or its growth limited by another organ (Goebel).

Competit′ion (*competitor,* a rival), the relation between plants occupying the same area, and dependent upon the same physical factors (Clements); **Compet′itive Society,** applied to two or more species whose roots occupy the same level in the soil (Adamson).

comp′ital (*compita′lis,* pertaining to cross roads) in venation when the veinlets angularly intersect; also when the sori are on the point of junction.

com′planate, *complana′tus* (Lat., levelled), flattened, compressed.

complement′ary (*complementum,* that which completes), when plants reciprocally help, as Mosses protect soils and profit by shade and trees above them; ∼ **Cells,** the components of lenticel tissue arising from the phellogen; ∼ **chromat′ic Adapta′tion,** the power of Algae to make effective use of the light which reaches them, complementary to their own coloration (Engelmann); ∼ **Soci′ety,** two or more species which root at different levels in the soil to each other (Adamson); **sea'sonal ~ ~**, when different plants use the same ground at different seasons.

complete', *comple'tus* (Lat., filled), having all the parts belonging to it or the type.

Com'plex (Lat.), interwoven fibres, or group of complicated parts (Crozier); **complex'us** (Lat., embraced), in vernation when a leaf is folded over another at the sides and apex; ~ **cellulo'sus** (Lat.) = cellular tissue; ~ **membrana'ceus** (Lat.), elementary membrane, ground-tissue; ~ **tubula'ris** (Lat.), woody tissue, xylem; ~**utricula'ris** (Lat.), angular cellular tissue; ~ **vascula'ris** (Lat.), spiral vessels, sometimes used for small vessels showing secondary deposits; **complexi'vus** =COMPLEXUS.

com'plicate, *complica'tus* (*complico*, I fold together), folded upon itself.

Composit'ion, *composit'io* (Lat., putting together), the combination of parts to form the whole, as of subordinate parts to form an organ, or elements to form a substance.

com'pound, similar parts aggregated into a common whole; ~ **Cor'ymb**, one having more than one flower to each branch; ~ **Dicha'sium**, that in which the primary axis divides into secondary dichasia; ~ **Flow'er**, an accumulation of florets as in the Compositae, ANTHODIUM; ~ **Fruit**, where many distinct carpels are associated, as in the mulberry; ~ **Fun'gus-body,** growth-form in which the thallus is constituted by the coherence of separate hyphal ramifications; ~ **Hairs**, branched or ramified hairs; ~ **Inflores'cence**, where an inflorescence is itself composed of secondary ones; ~ **Leaf**, one divided into separate blades; ~ **O'vary**, an ovary having more than one carpel; ~ **Pis'til**, two or more carpels coalescent into one body; ~ **Raceme'** = PANICLE; ~ **Spike**, occurring frequently on grasses, when the inflorescence is made up of spikes; ~ **Spore** = SPORIDESM;

~ **Spor'ophore,** formed by cohesion of the ramifications of separate hyphal branches, Ger., Fruchtkörper; ~ **Stem,** one that is branched; ~ **Um'bel,** an association of simple umbels, each ray being itself an umbel.

compress'ed, *compress'us* (Lat., pressed together), flattened, complanate; **compressis'simus** (Lat.), excessively flattened.

con (Lat., with), modified by euphony frequently into **co** and **com**—meaning "with" in Latin compounds.

concat'enate, *concatena'tus* (Lat., linked together), joined as links in a chain, as when strings of spores, or frustules of Diatoms are linked together.

Concaulesc'ence (*con*, with; *caulis*, stem), the coalescence of axes.

con'cave, *conca'vus* (Lat., hollowed out), hollow, as the inside of a saucer.

con'centrate (*còn*, with; *centrum*, centre), to bring to a common centre; **concen'tric**, having a common centre; ~ **Bun'dles**, where one element is wholly surrounded by the others, as the xylem by the phloëm; ~ **Cells**, in Cyanophyceae, destitute of nucleus, and yielding on slight pressure, the cell-walls curved inwards (Kohl); ~ **Vasc'ular-bun'dle** is the same as ~ BUNDLE; **Concentra'tion**, applied to the growth of Primordia with the bulk remaining constant (Church).

Concep'tacle, *Concepta'culum* (Lat., a receptacle), (1) originally used by Linnaeus to express FOLLICLE; (2) afterwards for the fruit of Asclepiads and Apocyneae; (3) a hollow case covering the sexual organs in some Algae; (4) the peridium of Fungi; (5) the capsule of Mosses; (6) by Medicus, following Jung, used for pericarp; (7) a general expression for a superficial cavity opening outwards, within which reproductive cells are produced.

conch'iform, *conchiform'is* (*concha*, a shell; *forma*, shape), shaped like the shell of a bivalve.

concin'nus (Lat.), neat, elegant.

concolor'ous, *con'color* (Lat., of one colour), uniform in tint.

concom'itant (*concom'itans*, attending), used of vascular bundles which run side by side without being separated by other bundles.

Concresc'ence (*concresco*, to grow together); (1) growing into union; coalescent; (2) a synonym of CEMENTATION; adj. **concres'cent**; **concrete'**, *concre'tus*, growing together.

Condensa'tion (*condensatio*, making dense) = CONCENTRATION; **condens'ing Len'ses**, epidermal papillae acting so as to focus the available light on the chloroplasts in the palisade-cells (Haberlandt).

Conduct'ing Bun'dles, strands of elongated cells in leaves and even the stems of Mosses, simulating a vascular bundle; also used for VASCULAR BUNDLES; ~ **Cells**, long narrow cells, associated with sieve-tubes, but having imperforate walls; ~ **Sheath**, elongated parenchymatous cells in the inner cortex of the stem, continued into the leaves as an investiture of the vascular bundle; ~ **Sur'face**, in the pitchers of *Nepenthes*, upon which insects have no foothold, but fall downwards; ~ **Tis'sue**, a loose tissue of the style through which the pollen-tubes can readily make their way; **Conduct'ive Tis'sue** is the same.

condu'plicans (Lat., doubling), doubling up, as *conduplicant'ia Fo'lia*, the leaflets of a compound leaf which apply themselves to each other's surfaces; **condu'plicate**, *conduplicati'rus*, folded together lengthwise; **Conduplica'tion**, in æstivation when the sides of an organ are applied to each other by their faces.

Con'dyle, Condyl'ium (κόνδυλος, a knuckle), (1) the antheridium of *Chara*, (2) the swelling which terminates the rhizoplast of *Polytoma* (Dangeard).

Cone, *Co'nus* (Lat.), the fruit of the pine or fir-tree with scales forming a STROBILE; ~ **Gen'us**, a fossil

genus only known by its cones; ~ **of Growth,** the apical growing portion of the stem.

Co'nein = *Conia.*

Cone'let (disyll.), the diminutive of CONE, applied to a cone of the first year (Mohr).

Conench'yma (κώνος, a cone; ἔγχυμα, an infusion), conical cells which constitute hairs (Lindley).

conferru'minate, *conferrumina'tus* (Lat., cemented), adherent by adjacent faces, as the cotyledons of Horse Chestnut.

confert'ed, *confert'us* (Lat., brought together), closely packed or crowded.

conferva'ceous, confer'void, composed of threads, resembling the genus *Conferva.*

con'fluent, *con'fluens* (Lat., flowing into), blended into one, passing by degrees one into the other; ~ **Fruit,** a compound fruit, such as the mulberry or pineapple.

conformed' (disyll.), *conform'is* (Lat., shaped), (1) similar in form; (2) closely fitting, as a seed-coat to the nucellus.

Con'gener (Lat., of the same race), another plant of the same genus; **congener'ic,** belonging to the same genus; **Congener'ity,** the condition of belonging to the same genus.

congen'ital (*congenitus*, born together), grown to anything; strictly, of the same origin.

congest'ed, *congest'us* (Lat., brought together), crowded.

conglo'bate, *congloba'tus* (Lat., made like a ball), collected into a ball.

conglom'erate, *conglomera'tus* (Lat., rolled together), clustered.

Conglu'tin (*conglutinatus*, cemented together), a constituent of plant-casein, usually with legumin; **conglu'tinate,** *conglutina'tus*, as though glued together.

con'gregate (*congrego*, to assemble), collected into close proximity.

Coni'a (κώνειον, hemlock), the active principle of *Conium maculatum*, Linn., a poisonous alkaloid.

con'ical, *con'icus* (Lat., cone-shaped),

having the figure of a cone, as the carrot.

conid'ian (κόνις, dust), referring to conidia; **conid'ioid** (εἶδος, resemblance), like conidia in form or function (W. G. Smith); **conidiif'erous** (φορέω, I carry), bearing CONIDIA; **Conid'iophore**, *Conidioph'ora* = GONIDIOPHORE; the organ which produces CONIDIA in the Hyphomycetes and Phycomycetes (Saccardo); **Conid'iospore** (σπορὰ, a seed) = CONIDIUM; **Conid'ium** (pl. Conidia)=GONIDIA; **Con'ids**, simplification proposed by Bennett and Murray for CONIDIA.

Conif'erin (*conus*, a cone; *fero*, I bear), a glucoside derived from coniferous wood; **conif'erous**, producing or bearing cones, as many Gymnosperms; **co'niform** (*forma*, shape) = CONICAL; **Conifrutice'ta**, pl. (+ FRUTICETUM), forests composed of or dominated by coniferous shrubs.

Coni'in, **Cone'in**, the same as CONIA.

Coniligno'sa, pl. (*conus*, a cone; *lignosus*, woody), dominated by trees and shrubs with typical needle-like foliage.

Coniocyst', **Coniocyst'a** (κόνις, dust; κύστις, a bag), a closed sporangium resembling a tubercle, containing a mass of spores; **Coniothe'ca** ‡ (θήκη, case), the loculus of an anther.

Conisil'vae, pl. *conus*, a cone (+ SILVA), coniferous forests.

Con'joint Bun'dle, a vascular bundle when it is composed of wood and bast elements.

con'jugate, *conjuga'tus* (Lat., united), coupled; as a pinnate leaf, of two leaflets; ~ **Spi'rals**, whorled leaves so arranged as to give two or more genetic spirals running parallel with each other; **Conjuga'ting Tubes**, long processes emitted by the fertilized trichophore in certain Algae, which unite with the auxiliary cells (Osterhout); **Conjuga'tion**, (1) the fusion of sexual elements, the union of two gametes to form a zygote, used especially when the two gametes are similar, as in some Algae and Fungi; (2) the temporary and incomplete fusion of two individuals (Hartmann); ~ **Canal'**, an open tube formed between the conjugation cells (gametes) of certain Algae (F. Blackman and Tansley); ~ **Tubes** = CONJUGATING TUBES, various kinds of, as **cross** ~, when some cells in a given algal filament are active, and others passive; **lat'eral** ~, when it takes place cell by cell; **scala'riform** ~, when the entire filament is concerned; ~ **-Cell**=GAMETE; **conjuga'-to-palm'ate**, when a leaf divides into two arms, each of which is palmate.

conjunc'tive (*conjunctivus*, joined), serving to unite; ~ **Symbio'sis**, applied by Frank to those cases in which the symbionts are so intimately blended as to form apparently a single body; ~ **Threads**=SPINDLE Fibres; ~ **Tis'sue**, the fundamental tissue or ground tissue interior to the stele; **Conjunctor'ium** ‡, the operculum of a Moss.

conna'cian, used by Praeger for plants chiefly growing in Connaught.

connas'cent (*con*, with; *nascor*, to be born), produced at the same time (Crozier).

con'nate, *conna'tus* (Lat., born at the same time), united, congenitally or subsequently; **con'nate-perfo'liate**, united at the base in pairs around the supporting axis.

Connect'ing (*connectus*, fastened together) **Cell** = HETEROCYST; ~ **Tis'sue**, a special colourless tissue adjoining the veins of some leaves (Soleneder); ~ **Zone**, the "hoop" or girdle connecting the valves of a Diatom frustule; **Connect'ive**, *Connecti'vum*, the portion of a stamen distinct from the filament which connects the two lobes of an anther; **connectiva'lis**, having to do with the connective.

conni'vent, *conni'vens* (Lat., winking), coming into contact or converging.

Connu'bium (Lat., wedlock), the stage of protoplasmic coalescence in the conjugation of filamentous Algae.

Conocarp′ium (κῶνος, a cone ; καρπὸς fruit), an aggregate fruit consisting of many fruits on a conical receptacle, as the strawberry ; **co′noid** (εἶδος, resemblance), cone-like ; **conoid′al**, *conoida′lis*, resembling a conical figure, but not truly one, as the calyx of *Silene conoidea*, Linn.

conop′eus (κώνωψ, κώνωπος, a gnat), a correction of *conopseus*, gnat-like, as in *Habenaria conopsea* ; *cf.* Gras, in Bull. Soc. Bot. Fr. ix. (1862), pp. 333–334.

Conophor′ium (κωνοφόρος, cone-bearing), a coniferous forest ; **conophoroph′ilous** (φιλέω, I love), dwelling in coniferous forests ; **Conophorophy′ta** (φυτὸν, a plant), coniferous forest plants (Clements).

Conopod′ium (κῶνος, a cone ; ποῦς, ποδός, a foot), a conical floral receptacle.

Conostro′ma ‡ (στρῶμα, spread out), Endlicher's term for a growing point, constituting a free central placenta.

Conserv′ative Or′gans (*conservatio*, a keeping), those which are employed in nutrition, as root, stem, leaves.

consim′ilar (*consimilis*, entirely alike), applied to the valves of a Diatom, when both sides are alike ; **Consimil′itude**, resemblance of the two valves, unequal but similar, of the EPITHECA and HYPOTHECA.

Consocia′tion (*consociatio*, union), a group formed by **Consoc′ies** (Lat.), used by Clements in the sense of ASSOCIATION ; **Consocie′tum** (+ ETUM), an association.

consol′idated (*consolido*, I make firm) ; (1) when unlike parts are coherent ; (2) Crozier adds, having a small surface in proportion to bulk, as many Cacti.

Con′sortism (*consors*, sharing property), Reinke's term for SYMBIOSIS.

Consor′tium (Lat., fellowship), (1) the relations of Lichen life (Reinke) ; (2) the intimate association or felting of certain algal vegetation (F. E. Fritsch).

con′stant (*constans*, steadfast), in the same condition, or always present.

Constella′tion (Lat., *constellatio*, a starcluster), employed by Pfeffer for the aggregate of conditions regulating the vital mechanism, *e. g.* of the protoplast.

con′stipate (*constipatio*, crowding together), crowded or massed together.

constrict′ed (*constrictus*, compressed), drawn together, contracted.

Constric′tion (*constrictio*, binding together), the narrowest portion of Diatoms and Desmids seen from the side.

Construct′ive Metab′olism = ASSIMILATION.

consu′tus (Lat., stitched together), when parts are united by a membrane of threads.

Contabesc′ence (*contabesco*, to waste away), the abortive condition of stamens and pollen.

con′tact (*contactus*, touching) **Cy′cles**, individual members of a phyllotactic system overlapping to form continuous investments of the axis (Church) ; ∼ **Lines** = PARASTICHIES ; ∼ **Parastich′ies** is a synonym ; ∼ **Pres′sures**, those between growing primordia in a CONCENTRATION system.

conta′gious (*contagio*, touch), used of diseases when communicable by touch ; *cf.* INFECTIOUS.

contemato′sus ‡ (deriv. ?) covered by an armature between bristly and aculeate (Lindley).

conter′minous (*conterminus*, neighbouring), of equal boundaries.

Con′text (*contextus*, woven together) employed by Murrill for the flesh of Fungi ; **contex′tus** = TISSUE.

contig′uous, *contig′uus* (Lat., adjoining), when neighbouring parts are in contact, as most cotyledons.

contin′gent (*contingens*, touching) **Symbio′sis**, see SYMBIOSIS ; in Ger. Raumparasitismus.

contin′uous (*continuus*, running on), the reverse of interrupted ; also used for ASEPTATE ; **Continu′ity**, uninterrupted connection.

contort'ed, *contor'tus* (Lat.), twisted or bent ; in aestivation the same as CONVOLUTE ; **Contor'tion,** a twisting ; **Contortoplank'ton** (+ PLANKTON), a neritic floating mass of Diatoms, especially of *Chaetoceras debile* and *C. contortum,* whence the name ; **contortu'plicate** (*plicatus,* woven), (1) twisted and plaited or folded ; (2) twisted back upon itself.

contra-, in Latin compounds=against ; ~ **clock'wise,** against the motion of the hands of a clock ; sinistrorse.

contract'ed, *contract'us* (Lat.), narrowed or shortened ; spreading but slightly ; **contract'ile,** capable of actively shrinking in volume and expanding again, used of protoplasm ; ~ **Vac'uoles,** small cavities in protoplasm, which increase and decrease in size rhythmically ; **Contractil'ity,** the capacity of altering spontaneously in volume.

con'trary, *contra'rius* (Lat.), in an opposite direction, as a silicle compressed contrary to the dissepiment.

Control', frequently used in the sense of the English word Check, as ~ Experiments, to check the original observation.

Co'nus (Lat.) = CONE, STROBILE.

Convar'iants, pl. (*con* = with ; *vario,* I alter), individuals of equal age or the same generation, who are liable to vary ; *cf.* DEVARIANTS ; **converg'ent** (*vergens,* bending), applied to veins which run from the base to the apex of the leaf in a curved manner ; **converg'iner'vis, -vius, convergen'tinervo'sus** (Lat.), simple veins diverging from the midrib and converging towards the margin.

con'vex, *convex'us* (Lat., arched), having a more or less rounded surface ; **convexiusc'ulus,** somewhat convex.

con'volute, *convolu'tus* (Lat., rolled round), **convolu'tive,** *convoluti'vus :* (1) when one part is wholly rolled up in another, as the petals of the Wallflower ; (2) in a spathe when the margins mutually envelope each other.

convolvula'ceous, denoting affinity with the genus *Convolvulus.*

co-ovar'ial, derived from cells of the same ovary (K. Pearson).

co'pious (*copiosus,* plentiful), abundant; abbreviated cop.³ cop.² cop.¹ to show decreasing frequency (Warming).

cop'pery, brownish red, with a metallic lustre ; cupreous.

Cop'pice, a small wood which is regularly cut at stated intervals, the new growth arising from the stools ; **Copse** is practically the same ; **cop'picing,** in forestry, cropping the plantation by cutting the underwood every few years.

coproph'ilous (κόπρος, ordure ; φιλέω, I love), applied to Fungi whose habitat is the dung of animals ; **Cop'rophyte** (φυτον, plant) = SAPROPHYTE.

Cop'ulae (pl. of *copula,* a thong or band), intermediate bands of cell-wall in Diatoms, as in *Terpsinoë,* etc.

Copula'tion (*copulatio,* coupling), (1) used for CONJUGATION, the union of sexual cells ; (2) the entire blending of two individual nuclei (Hartmann) ; **cop'ulative** ‡, used of dissepiments not readily separating from the axis or walls of the pericarp.

Coque (Fr., shell), used by S. F. Gray for COCCUS.

Cor Se'minis ‡ (Lat.) = Embryo.

corac'inus (Lat., raven-black), glossy black.

cor'acoid (κόραξ, a raven ; εἶδος, resemblance), " shaped like a crow's beak " (Crozier).

Cor'al Spot, a fungus disease caused by the wound parasite *Nectria cinnabarina,* Fr.

coralliform'is (*corallum,* coral ; *forma,* shape), coral-like in form ; **cor'alline,** *coralli'nus* (Lat., coral red), resembling coral in appearance ; **cor'alloid,** *coralloi'des* (εἶδος, resemblance), coral-like, as the roots of *Neottia Nidus-avis,* Rich., and also certain Lichens.

Cor'cle (Crozier) ; **Cor'cule,** *Cor'culum*

(Lat., a little heart) = (1) embryo ; (2) plumule, or plumule and radicle.

Cord, a synonym of STRAND ; **umbili'-cal** ~ = FUNICULUS.

cordai'tean, resembling the genus of fossils, *Cordaites.*

cor'date, *corda'tus* (Lat.), heart-shaped, applied to leaves having the petiole at the broader and notched end ; **cor'diform,** *cordiform'is* (Lat.) ; shaped like a heart.

cord'shape = FUNILIFORM.

Core, (1) the seeds and integuments of a pome, such as an apple ; Grew spells it "Coar" ; (2) an axial strand of parenchyma in the haustorium of certain parasites (De Bary) ; **core'less** [disyll.], without core (Bailey).

core'mial (κόρημα, a broom), like the genus *Coremium,* Link ; **core'mioid** (εἶδος, resemblance), applied to a fasciated form, as of *Penicillium,* etc. ; **Core'mium** = SYNNEMA.

Cor'eses (κόρις, a bug), "dark red, broad, discoid bodies, found beneath the epicarp of grapes" (Lindley).

coria'ceous, *coria'ceus* (*corium,* leather), leathery.

Cork, protective tissue replacing the epidermis in older superficial parts of plants ; the outer cells contain air, and are elastic and spongy in texture, but impervious to liquids ; ~ **Camb'ium** = PHELLOGEN ; ~ **Cor'tex,** the corky layers of the bark ; ~ **Mer'istem** = PHELLOGEN ; ~ **Pore'cork,** suberised portion of lenticels, with intercellular spaces between the cork-cells (Klebahn) ; ~ **Warts,** local formations of cork on leaves (Solereder) ; **cork'y,** of the texture or quality of cork ; ~ **Envel'ope,** ~ **Lay'er,** the bast layer beneath the epidermis which gives rise to cork ; ~ **Scab,** a potato disease due to the Myxomycete *Spongospora Solani.*

Corm, *Corm'us* (κορμὸς, a trunk), a bulb-like fleshy stem or base of stem, a "solid" bulb ; **cormo'des** (εἶδος, resemblance), possessing an axis (A. Braun) ; **Cormog'amae** (γάμος, marriage), Ardissone's division for Char-

aceae and Muscineae ; **cormog'enous** (γένος, offspring), having a stem or corm ; **cormophylla'ceous** (φύλλον, a leaf, + ACEOUS), used by E. Newman for those Ferns whose fronds are attached to the caudex ; **Corm'ophyte** (φυτὸν, plant), Endlicher's term for plants possessing axis and foliage, that is, Phanerogams and vascular Cryptogams ; adj. **cormophyt'ic ;** ~ **Associa'tion,** dominated by cormophytes (F. E. Fritsch).

Corn, cereals generally ; in the United States it is confined to maize.

corna'ceous, (1) allied to the cornel tree, *Cornus ;* (2) "of a horn-like consistence" (Vasey).

cor'neous, *cor'neus* (Lat.), horny, with a horny texture.

Cor'net (*cornu,* a horn), a hollow horn-like growth ; ~ **-shape,** cuculliform, hooded ; **cornic'ulate,** *cornicula'tus* (Lat.), furnished with a little horn or horns ; **corniculif'erous,** *-rus* (*fero,* I bear), bearing horns or protuberances ; **cor'niform** (*forma,* shape), shaped like a horn.

Cor'nine, a bitter principle in the bark of *Cornus sanguinea,* Linn.

Cor'nu (Lat., a horn), (1) a horn-like process ; (2) occasionally used for Calcar or Spur ; **cor'nute,** *cornu'tus,* horned or spurred ; ~ **Leaves,** a sudden projection of the midrib forming a spine-like outgrowth, often in a different plane ; **Cornu'tin,** a poisonous body derived from ergot, the "spur" of rye and other grasses.

Cor'ol (Crozier) = COROLLA.

Corol'la (Lat., a little crown) ; (1) the interior perianth, composed of petals, free or united ; (2) ‡ the annulus of Fungi ; (3) employed by Sir J. E. Smith for the utricle of *Carex ;* **corolla'ceous** (+ ACEOUS) corolla-like, petaloid ; **cor'ollate,** *corolla'tus,* **corolla'ris,** possessing a corolla ; **Cor'ollet,** a floret of a Composite ; **corollif'erous,** *-rus* (*fero,* I bear), corolla-bearing ; **corolliflor'al** (*flos, floris,* a flower), **corolliflor'ous,** *-rus,* having the calyx, petals and ovary inserted separately on the disk, the stamens on the corolla; **cor'olline,** *corolli'nus*, (1) seated on a corolla, (2) corolla-like, petaloid, (3) belonging to a corolla; **Cor'ollule**, *Corollu'la ;* (1) a diminutive corolla; (2) floret of a head, as in Compositae.

Coro'na (Lat., a crown); (1) a coronet, any body which intervenes between the corolla and stamens; (2) ‡ the "eye" of apples or pears, the remains of the calyx limb; (3) ‡ the ray of the capitula in Compositae; (4) a whorl of ligules or petals, united or free; (5) a synonym of CUCULLUS; (6) used by J. Hill for the pericycle, or "circle of propagation"; (7) the ring of primary wood in the medullary sheath; (8) the MEDULLARY CROWN, or ∼ SHEATH; ∼ **stipula'ris**, the circle of stipulodes in *Chara* (Migula); ∼ **Se'minis** = PAPPUS; ∼ **stamin'ea** = Orbiculus, a coronet formed from the transformation of stamens; **cor'onal**, appertaining to a corona, as ∼ **Ves'sels**, those of the corona; **coro'nans** (Lat.), crowning, seated on the apex; **cor'onate**, *corona'tus* (Lat.), crowned, having a corona; ∼ **Papil'lae**, growths with an appearance of crown-like cells at their apex (Solereder); **Cor'onet** = CORONA; **coro'niform**, *coroniform'is* (*forma*, shape), shaped like a crown or coronet; **Coro'nule**, *Coron'ula ;* (1) a diminutive of corona, a floret; (2) = PAPPUS; (3) the small calyx-like body which crowns the nucule of *Chara ;* (4) in Diatoms, a set of spines which terminate the frustules.

coronopifo'lioid (εἶδος, resemblance), recalling the foliage of *Plantago coronopifolia*, Brot., now merged in *P. macrorhiza*, Poir.

Cor'pora (pl. of *corpus*, a body) **carno'sa** (Lat., fleshy), the sporangia of certain Fungi; **Cor'pus**, the mass or substance of anything; ∼ **lig'neum,** ∼ **ligno'sum**, the mass of the woody tissue of a plant; ∼ **medulla're**, the mass of the cellular tissue in the pith.

Corpus'cle (*corpusculum*, a small body), a small mass or body; **Corpusc'ula**, sing. **Corpusc'ulum**; (1) sporangia of some Fungi; (2) archegonium, or the central cell of the same in Coniferae; (3) the connections between the arms of the pollen-masses in Asclepiads; (4) = EGG, OOSPHERES; ∼ **vermiform'ia**, spiral vessels in a contracted, strangled condition.

correla'ted (*con* = with, *relatus*, returned); ∼ **Variabil'ity**, having reciprocal variation; **Correla'tion**, the reciprocal influence of one organ upon another.

cor'rugate, *corruga'tus ;* **corrugati'vus** (Lat.), wrinkled.

Cor'sican Moss, dried Algae.

Cor'tex (Lat.), (1) the bark or rind; the ground tissue between the stele and epidermis; (2) the peridium of Fungi; **cor'tical**, *cortica'lis*, relating to the cortex; ∼ **Intru'sion** (*intrusus*, thrust in), applied to growth of external tissues into stelar or vascular structures (Lang); ∼ **Lay'er,** ∼ **Integ'ument**, the investing layers of the bast system; *see also* ENDO-, EXO-, MEDIO-CORTEX; ∼ **Pore** = LENTICEL; ∼ **Rays** = medullary rays in the phloëm; ∼ **Sheath**, Naegeli's term for the whole of the primary bast bundles; ∼ **Stra'tum**, the superficial layer of the Lichen-thallus; **cor'ticate**, *cortica'tus* (Lat.), covered with bark, or with an accessory bark-like covering; **cortica'ting**, constituting cortex, as ∼ **Cells**, those which make up the cortex; **Cortica'tion**, the formation of cortex; **corticif'erous** (*fero*, I bear), producing bark; **cortic'iform** (*forma*, shape), like bark; **cor'ticole, cortic'olous** (*colo*, I inhabit), living on bark, as some Lichens and Fungi; **cor'ticose, cor'ticous**, barky, full of bark.

Corti'na (Late Lat., a curtain), the filamentous annuli of some Agarics; **cor'tinate**, *cortina'rius* (Lat.), having a web-like texture.

corvi'nus (Late Lat., pertaining to the raven), raven-black.

Coryd'alin, an alkaloid present in the

root of *Corydalis tuberosa*, DC.; **coryd'aline**, *corydalin'eus*, resembling the genus *Corydalis*.

Cor'ymb, *Corym'bus* (Lat., a cluster of flowers), a flat-topped or merely convex and open flower-cluster of the indeterminate or centripetal order; the term formerly included most cymes; **cor'ymbate, corymb'-iated,** having corymbs or growing in corymbs; **corymbif'erous,** *-rus (fero,* I bear), bearing corymbs; **corym'-biform** (*forma*, shape); **cor'ymbose,** *corymbo'sus*, **corym'bous,** arranged in corymbs; **corymb'ulose, -lous,** in small corymbs.

Corynid'ia (κορύνη, a club), "Processes sunk into the margin of the germinating leaf of Ferns, and containing spiral threads" (Lindley) [= Antheridia?].

Coryphi'um, pl. **Coryphi'a** (κορυφή, summit), alpine plant formations; **coryphoph'ilus** (φιλέω, I love), growing in alpine places; **Coryphophy'ta** (φυτὸν, a plant), alpine plants (Clements).

Coryphyl'ly (κορυφή, the crown of the head; φύλλον, a leaf), a monstrosity in which the axis ends in a leaf, sometimes coloured.

Cosmaesthe'sia (κόσμος, the world, + AESTHESIA), sensibility to external stimuli; **Cosmop'olite** (πόλις, a city), a plant of well-nigh universal distribution; **cosmopol'itan,** distributed throughout the world.

Cos'ta (Lat.), a rib, when single, a midrib or middle-nerve; **cos'tal-nerved,** nerves springing from the midrib; **cos'taeform** (*forma*, shape), applied by J. Smith for primary veins in ferns when parallel to each other and very evident; **cos'tate,** *costa'tus* (Lat.), ribbed, having one or more primary longitudinal veins; **costa'to-veno'sus,** when the parallel side veins of a feather-veined leaf are much stouter than those which intervene; **costel'late,** having small ribs; **Cost'ulae,** used by J. Smith for the primary veins of Fern-segments.

Cot'ton, the hairs of the seeds of species of *Gossypium;* **Cot'ton-grass Associa'tion,** an association in which *Eriophorum* is dominant; **cot'tony,** pubescence of long soft hair.

cot'ylar (κότυλη, a hollow vessel), cotyledonary.

Cotyle'don (κοτυληδών, a hollow), applied first by Linnaeus to the seed-lobes, the first leaves of the embryo, one in monocotyledons, two or more in dicotyledons, rarely a whorl borne by the radicle or caudicle; ~ **-trace,** the common bundle in the stem proper to the cotyledon; its leaf-trace; **cotyledona'ris,** union or close approximation of the seed-lobes; **Cotyle'donoid** (εἶδος, resemblance), a germinating thread of a Moss, a protonema; **cotyle'donous,** *cotyledo'neus,* possessing seed-lobes.

cotyl'iform, *cotyliform'is* (κότυλη, a hollow; *forma*, shape), dish-shaped or wheel-shaped, with an erect or ascending border; **Cot'yloid Cell,** a single huge cell in *Avicennia officinalis*, acting as a haustorical organ; its branches ramify throughout the nucellus and finally invade the placenta (Haberlandt); possibly a sister-cell of the embryo-sac (Treub); **cotyloi'deus** (Mod. Lat.), = COTYLIFORM; **Cotylvar'iants,** pl. (*varians*, varying), variation in the number of cotyledons (De Vries).

Coum'arin, the fragrant principle of the Tonquin bean, *Dipteryx odorata*, Sw.

coun'ter (*contra*, against) **clock-wise,** sinistrose, turning the reverse way of clock-hands.

Cou'ple-cell, Hartog's term for ZYGOTE.

Coup'let, the result of **Coup'ling;** union due to affinity in the same individual between allelomorphs which belong to distinct pairs; also termed **Game'tic Coupling.**

Cour'baril, a resin from *Hymenaea Courbaril*, Linn.

Cov'er = OPERCULUM.

Cov'er-cell, of Hepaticae, the apical cells of the neck of a young archegonium (Campbell); **cov'er-like** =

OPERCULARIS; **cov′ering** = VEXIL-
LARIS; ~ **-Plate**, in Ferns, see STEG-
MATA of Mettenius.

cowled = CUCULLATE (Crozier).

Crab, a disease of the larch, due to the
mycelium of *Peziza Willkommii*,
Hartig.

Crad′ina (κράδος, the wild fig-tree), a
proteolytic enzyme existing in the
juice of the common fig-tree, *Ficus
Carica*, Linn.

cra′dling = INVOLVENTIA (folia).

Cram′pon (Fr.), hooks or adventitious
roots, which act as supports as in
ivy.

craspedod′romous, -*mus* (κράσπεδον, a
border; δρόμος, a course), when the
lateral veins of a leaf run from midrib to margin without dividing.

Crassinucella′tae (*crassus*, thick, +
NUCELLUS), Van Tieghem's term
for plants whose nucelli remain of
considerable bulk up to the time
of the formation of the embryo;
cf. TENUINUCELLATAE.

crass′us (Lat.), thick.

Crate′ra (κρατήρ, a cup), a cup-shaped
receptacle; **Crate′ria**, pl., ascidia
which are derived from the surface
of a leaf (C. Schimper); **crate′riform,**
crateriform′is (*forma*, shape), goblet
or cup-shaped, hemispheric or shallow in contour.

cratic′ular (*craticula*, a small grid-
iron), a resting condition of
Diatomaceae, in which a pair of
new valves are formed within the
original valves.

Cra′zy-weeds, the same as LOCO-
WEEDS, chiefly species of *Astragalus*
and *Lupinus* which produce "Loco"
disease in animals which have eaten
them.

cream-colour, white with a slight inclination to yellow.

Creat′ospores, -*ae* (κρέας, flesh,
+ SPORE), "nut-fruited" plants
(Clements).

creep′ing, running along or under the
ground and rooting at intervals;
restricted by Syme to those cases
where there is only one, or rarely
two, flowering stems from each

branch of the rhizome; ~ **Stem,**
often means RHIZOME.

cre′meus (Mod. Lat., creamy) =
CREAM-COLOUR.

Crem′nad (κρημνός, a cliff), a cliff
plant; **Cremni′on,** a suggested
emendation of **Cremni′um,** a cliff
plant association; **cremnoph′ilus,**
(φιλέω, I love), cliff-dwelling;
Cremnophy′ta (φυτόν, a plant), cliff
plants (Clements).

Crem′ocarp, *Cremocarp′ium* (κρεμάω, I
hang; καρπός, fruit), a dry and
seed-like fruit, composed of two
one-seeded carpels invested by an
epigynous calyx, separating when
ripe into mericarps.

cremoric′olor (*cremeus, color,* colour)
= CREAM-COLOUR.

Cre′na (Mod. Lat., a notch), a rounded
tooth or notch; **cre′nate,** *crena′tus,*
scalloped, toothed with crenatures;
Cre′nature, *Crenatu′ra,* a rounded
notch on the margin of a leaf;
Cren′el,   **Cren′elling** = CRENA;
cren′elled,   *crenula′ris,* margined
with crenatures; **cren′ellate,** *crenel-
la′tus,* **cren′ulate,** *crenula′tus,* crenate, but the toothings themselves
small; **Cren′ule,** a diminutive Crena.

Cre′nad (κρήνη, a spring or source), a
spring-loving plant; **Creni′um,** a
spring formation; **crenoph′ilus**
(φιλέω, I love), spring-loving; **Cre-
nophy′ta** (φυτόν, a plant), plants of
springs (Clements).

creoph′agous (κρέας, flesh; φάγω, I
eat), a synonym of carnivorous, as
applied to plants.

cres′cent-shaped, approaching the
figure of a crescent, as the leaves of
certain species of *Passiflora*.

Cres′cograph (*cresco*, I grow; γραφὴ,
writing), employed by Bose for an
instrument to measure growth.

Crest, (1) an elevation or ridge upon
the summit of an organ; (2) an
outgrowth of the funiculus in seeds,
a sort of axil; **crest′ed,** possessing
any elevated line or ridge on the
surface such as may be compared
with the crest of a helmet.

creta′ceous, -*ceus* (*creta,* chalk), (1)

chalky, as the chalk-glands found in Saxifrages; (2) chalk-white, dead-white.

Crev′ice-plant = CHASMOPHYTE; crev′-iced = RIMOSE.

cri′brate (cribrum, a sieve), usually written CRIBROSE; cri′briform, cri-briform′is (forma, shape), sieve-like, pierced with many holes; ~ Cells = SIEVE-CELLS; ~ Tis′sue, containing sieve-cells and tubes; cri′brile, (Kearney), cri′brose, cribro′sus, pierced like a sieve; ~ Cells = SIEVE-TUBES.

crinif′erous (crinis, hair; fero, I bear), used by J. Smith for hirsute; cri′nite, crini′tus, bearded with long and weak hairs.

crin′oid (κρίνον, a lily; εἶδος, resemblance), lily-like (Crozier).

Crin′ula (crinis, hair) = ELATER; Cri′nus, a stiff hair on any part.

crisp, crisp′us (Lat.), curled; crispa′-bilis, capable of curling up; crisp′-ate, crisped, crispa′tus, crispati′vus, curled; Crisp′ature, Crispatu′ra, (1) when the edge is excessively and irregularly divided and twisted; (2) or the leaf much puckered and crumpled, but not so much as bullate; crispes′cens, able to curl up; crispiflor′al (flos, floris, a flower), having curled flowers; crispifo′li-ous (folium, a leaf), with curled leaves.

Cris′ta (Lat.), a crest or terminal tuft; crist′aeform (forma, shape), used by J. Smith for crested appendices in Ferns, as in Actinostachys, Wall.; cris′tate, crista′tus, crested; in Ferns, having a tasselled margin to the fronds.

Crist′arc (Fr., cristarque, from cristal and arque), Van Tieghem's term for a layer of cortical tissue, whose arc-shaped cells contain macled crystals and are strengthened by sclerogen; occurring in Ochnaceae.

Critench′yma (κριτὸς, chosen; ἔγχυμα, an infusion), the tissue of bundle-sheaths, open or closed envelopes which accompany fibro-vascular bundles; crit′ical, used of plants which need great discrimination in classifying.

Crithme′tum (+ ETUM), an association of Samphire, Crithmum maritimum.

croca′tus, cro′ceous, croc′eus (Lat.), saffron-yellow; a deep yellow tint from the stigmas of Crocus sativus, Linn.; Cro′cin, the colouring-matter of the foregoing.

Cro′mules (G. T. Moore) = CHRO-MULES.

Crop-hairs, trichomes occurring in Cordia, unicellular and usually knobbed at the extremity (Mez), resembling a bird's crop in shape.

crook′ed, curved.

Cross, term implying a hybrid of any description; ~ armed, brachiate (Crozier); ~ Breeds, the progeny of interbred varieties; ~ -conjuga′tion, see CONJUGATION, CROSS; ~ Fertili-za′tion, fecundation by pollen from another flower of another individual; ~ Pollina′tion, dusting the stigma of one flower with pollen from another; ~ Septa′tion, division by transverse septa; ~ Type, in nuclear division, the formation of tetrads.

Crossed-pits, cells in sclerenchyma, with the slits on opposite walls at right angles to each other.

crowd′ed, closely pressed together or thickly set.

Crown, see CORONA; also (1) in Characeae, the apex of the nucule; (2) in Diatomaceae, a series of teeth connecting the frustules into filaments, as in Stephanopyxis; ~ of the Root, the point where root and stem meet; ~ -gall, disease of the root-crown of fruit-trees, ascribed to a Myxogaster, Dendrophagus (Tou-mey); ~ -rust, of cereals due to Puccinia coronata; crowned, coro-na′tus, furnished with a coronet; crown′ing, coro′nans, borne on the summit of an organ.

Cro′zier, "anything with a coiled end, as the young leaves of most Ferns" (Crozier).

cru′ciate, crucia′tus (Lat.), cross-shaped, used especially of the flowers of Cruciferae; ~ Tetragon-

id'ia, those gonidia formed by two divisions at right angles to each other; **Cru'cifer** (Lat. cross-bearing), a plant with four petals and tetradynamous stamens; **crucif'erous**, cross-bearing, used of the corolla of Crucifers, which have four petals; **cru'ciform**, *cruciform'is* (Lat.), cross-shaped.

cruenta'tus (Lat. stained with blood), dyed or blotched with red.

cruent'us (Lat. gory), dark purplish red, the colour of gore.

crum'pled = CORRUGATE; ~ **Aestiva'-tion**, when folded in bud irregularly, as in the poppy.

Cru'ra (pl. of *crus*, a leg), divisions of the teeth of the peristome in Mosses.

cru'ral, *crura'lis* (Lat. pertaining to the legs), "somewhat leg-shaped; used mainly in composition" (Crozier).

Crust, *Crust'a* (Lat. rind or shell), the hard and brittle part of certain Lichens; **crusta'ceous**, *-eus*, of brittle texture, some Lichens are thus termed; **crust'ose** = CRUSTACEOUS; **crustuli'nus**, toast-colour, darker and warmer in tint than a cracknel biscuit.

Cry'mad ($\kappa\rho\upsilon\mu\grave{o}s$, cold), a polar plant, **Crymi'um**, a "polar barrens" formation; **crymoph'ilus** ($\phi\iota\lambda\acute{\epsilon}\omega$, I love), dwelling in polar regions; **Cry'mophyte** ($\phi\upsilon\tau\grave{o}\nu$, a plant), a polar plant (Clements); adj. **crymophyt'ic**.

Cry'ophite ($\kappa\rho\acute{\upsilon}os$, frost, $\phi\upsilon\tau\grave{o}\nu$, a plant), a glacial association of microphytes periodically exposed to ice-cold water (Warming); **cryoscop'ic** ($\sigma\kappa o\pi\acute{\epsilon}\omega$, I see), observation of low temperatures as a method; **Cryos'copy**, the study described; **Cryot'ropism** ($\tau\rho o\pi\grave{\eta}$, a turning), movements influenced by cold or frost.

Crypt (*crypta*, a vault), used by G. Henslow for the front cavity of a stoma; **Cryp'ta**, applied to sunken glands, receptacles for secretions of plants in dotted leaves.

cryptan'thous ($\kappa\rho\upsilon\pi\tau\grave{o}s$, hidden, $\check{\alpha}\nu\theta os$, a flower), an emendation of cleistanthous; the stamens remaining enclosed in the flower (Davis);

Cryptan'thery is the condition; **cryptobio'tic** ($\beta\acute{\iota}os$, life), Kuntze's suggested expression for those lowly organisms which appeared in geologic times, but have left no trace of their existence; **Crypt'oblast** ($\beta\lambda\alpha\sigma\tau\grave{o}s$, a bud) = KRYPTOBLAST; **Cryptocotyle'dons** (+ COTYLEDON), a group to contain syncotyledonous and monocotyledonous plants (Agardh); **cryptocryst'alline** (+ CRYSTAL), of the minute crystals in plant-cells (Kraemer); **Cryptogam'ia** ($\gamma\acute{\alpha}\mu os$, marriage), plants destitute of stamens, pistils, and true seeds, but often reproduced as the result of a sexual act; **cryptogam'ian, cryptogam'ic**, *cryptogam'icus*, **cryptog'amous**, belong to the sub-kingdom just defined; **cryptogam'ic Wood**, the centripetal portion of the xylem in certain fossil Cycadoxyleæ; **Cryptog'amist**, a botanist devoted to the study of flowerless plants; **Cryptog'-amy** (1) the state of concealed fructification; (2) the condition of cryptogamous plants; **Cryptohy'brid** (+ HYBRID), a term for a hybrid which displays unexpected characters; **Cryptone'mata** ($\nu\hat{\eta}\mu\alpha$, a thread), small cellular threads produced in cryptostomata; **Cryp'tomere** ($\mu\acute{\epsilon}\rho os$, a part), applied to plants possessing latent characters; **Cryptom'erism** is the condition; **cryptom'erous**, having latent characters which show in the crossed offspring; **cryptoner'vius** (*nervus*, a nerve), the nervation hidden, as by hairs or texture of the leaf; **Cryp'tophyte** ($\phi\upsilon\tau\grave{o}\nu$, a plant), *Cryptophy'tum*, a cryptogamous plant; **Cryptophyti'um**, an association in which HEMICRYPTOPHYTES and GEOPHYTES together are dominant (Vahl); **Crypt'opore**, adj. **cryptop'-orous**, *-rus* (+ PORE), applied to stomata which are below the plane of the epidermis; *cf.* PHANEROPOROUS; **Cryptostom'ate** ($\sigma\tau\acute{o}\mu\alpha$, a mouth), barren conceptacles in some Algae, containing hairs, or paraphyses.

Crypts, stomatal pits.

Cryst'al (κρύσταλλος, ice), a mineral solid, usually of regular faces or angles, found in the tissues of plants, of very various composition; ~ -cells, cells containing crystals; ~ Dust, exceedingly small crystals in plant-cells (Haberlandt); ~ -conglom'erate, clustered crystals; ~ -hairs, crystal projecting inwards as in some euphorbiaceae; ~ Id'ioblasts, in the epidermis, large or small special cells; ~ Recep'tacles, a term to include all kinds of crystal-containing cells; ~ -sacs, enlarged special cells; ~ -sand = ~ Dust; ~ -scleren'chyma, tissue of cells with thickened walls containing single crystals (Solereder); Crys'tallid, Fischer's emendation of CRYSTALLOID; Cryst'allochores, -ae (χωρίs, separate), plants distributed by the action of glaciers (Clements); Cryst'alloid (εἶδος, resemblance), (1) term applied to protein crystals as being less truly angular than normal crystals, as well as swelling in water; (2) in contradistinction to colloid.

Ctein'ophytes (κτείνω, I kill; φυτὸν, a plant), Fungi whose influence on their hosts is chemical only (Wakker).

cten'oid (κτείs, κτενὸs, a comb, εἶδὸs, resemblance), comb-like, pectinate.

Cu'bebine, the active principle of Piper Cubeba, Linn.

cu'biform (cubus, a die; forma, shape), dice-shaped, cubic; cu'bic, cu'bicus, cu'bical, of a cubic form.

Cu'bit (cubitum, the elbow), a measure, from the elbow to the finger-tips, usually reckoned as equivalent to 18 inches, or 45 cm.; cubita'lis (Lat.), about half-a-yard in length.

Cu'bus (Lat.), a solid figure of six square sides.

cuculla'ris, cu'cullate, cuculla'tus (cucullus, a hood), hooded, or hood-shaped; cucull'iform (forma, shape), hood-like in shape; Cucull'us, a hood.

cucu'miform (cucumis, a cucumber), shaped like a cucumber (Crozier).

cucurbita'ceous (cucurbita, a gourd, + ACEOUS), like a gourd; of gourd-

like growth; cucurbiti'nus has the same meaning.

Cud'bear, the Scotch name for ORCHIL.

Cul-de-sac (Fr.), "a tubular or bag-shaped cavity, closed at one end" (Crozier).

Culm, culm'us (a stalk, especially of grain), the peculiar hollow stem or "straw" of grasses; culm'eus (Lat.), straw-like; culmic'olous (colo, I inhabit), growing on the stalk of grasses; culm'ifer, culmif'erous (fero, I bear), producing culms.

Cul'tiform (cultus, tilled, forma, shape), a cultivated form of a species or variety (Kuntze); Cultohy'bridoform, a cultivated hybrid of mixed parentage (Kuntze).

cult'rate, cultra'tus (Lat. knife-like), the shape of a knife-blade; cult'riform, cultriform'is (culter, a knife; forma, shape), in shape like a knife, or coulter.

Cult'ures, in botany, applied to experimental growth conducted in the laboratory.

cumaphyt'ic (κῦμα, κύματοs, a wave, φυτὸν, a plant), plant-modification due to wave-action (MacMillan); Cumaphy'tism is the condition.

Cu'marin, see COUMARIN.

cu'neal (Crozier), (cuneus, a wedge), cunea'rius ‡ (Lindley), cu'neate, cunea'tus, cu'neiform, cuneiform'is, wedge-shaped, triangular.

cunic'ulate, cunicula'tus (cuniculus, a rabbit), pierced with a long deep passage open at one end, as the peduncle of Tropaeolum.

Cu'nix ‡ (deriv. ?) "The separable place which intervenes between the wood and bark of exogens" (Lindley); the cambium region. Mr. Gepp suggests as a possible derivation, κύων, a dog, ἰξὸs, birdlime, as being viscous but worthless as birdlime.

Cup, (1) an involucre, as of the acorn; (2) the receptacle, or "shield" in some Lichens; (3) used for DISCO-CARP; ~ shaped, formed like a goblet, see CRATERIFORM.

cu'pola-shaped, nearly hemispherical, like an acorn-cup.

cu′preus (*cuprum*, copper), copper-coloured, with its metallic lustre.

cupres′soid (*cupressus*, cypress, εἶδος, resemblance), with foliage like the cypress; appres′sed ~, apically directed and sometimes decurrent; le′pidoid ~ broad and short.

Cu′pule, *Cu′pula* (Lat. a little cup), (1) the cup of such fruits as the acorn, an involucre composed of bracts adherent by their base, and free or not, upwards; (2) a free sheathing structure from the peduncle investing one or more seeds (Oliver and Salisbury); cu′pular-shaped (Lindley) *see* CUPOLA-SHAPED; cu′-pular, cupula′ris, cu′pulate, *cupula′tus*, furnished with, or subtended by a cupule; Cupu′lifer (Lat.), cupu-lif′erous (*fero*, I bear), producing cupules; cu′puliform, *cupuliform′is* (*forma*, shape) cupola-shaped.

Cur′arine, an alkaloid from "Curare," obtained from several species of *Strychnos*.

Cur′cumine, the colouring matter of the roots of Turmeric, *Curcuma longa*, Linn.

Curl, a disease, shown by deformed and curled leaves, ascribed in some cases to *Exoascus deformans*, Fuckel; *see* LEAF CURL; curled, when a leafy organ is folded or crumpled, as Endive.

Cur′tain = CORTINA.

Curv′ature (*curvatura*, a bending), continued flexure or bending from a right line; ~ of Concuss′ion, that produced as the result of a sudden blow; Darwin′ian ~, effects produced on growing organs, as root-tips in consequence of irritation; Sachs′s ~, the difference in growth of the two sides of the root (Wett-stein); curva′tus (Lat.), bent as a bow, or arc of a circle; Curve, the same as curvature; ~ ribbed, ~ veined = CURVINERVED; curved, bent, not rectilinear.

curvembryon′ic (*curvus*, bent, ἔμβρυον, a foetus), used of any curved embryo; all, except the atropous (orthotropous) form; curvicau′date

(*cauda*, a tail), having a curved tail; curvicost′ate (*costa*, a rib), with curved ribs or veins; curviden′tate (*dens*, a tooth), with curved teeth, cur′viform (*forma*, shape)= CURVED; cur′vinerved, *curviner′vius, curvive′-nius* (Lat.), having curved nerves, especially applied to monocotyle-dons; curvip′etal (*peto*, I seek), Vöchting′s term for the causes which tend to curve an organ; Curvipetal′ity is the condition; see AUTOTROPISM; curvise′rial (*series*, a row), (1) in curved or oblique ranks; (2) an orthostichy spiral applied to a cylindric surface (Church).

Cush′ion, (1) the enlargement at or beneath the insertion of many leaves, the pulvinus; (2) the portion of a Fern-prothallus on which archegonia are borne, often perceptibly thicker than the margins; ~ -plants, having the shoot-system much branched, and densely packed to form hemispherical cushions, as *Raoulia, Silene acaulis* and many Mosses; cush′ioned, tufted, as in some Mosses; ~ Fun′gi, Fungi growing in tufts.

Cusp, *Cusp′is* (Lat. a point), a sharp, rigid point; cusp′idate, *cuspida′tus*, tipped with a cusp.

cut, the same as incised, or in a general way as cleft.

Cu′ticle, *Cuti′cula* (Lat. the outer skin), the outermost skin or pellicle, containing the epidermis; *Cuti′cula den′sa, ~ hymeniform′is, ~ primordi-a′lis, ~ pro′pria, ~ regula′ris, ~ subnul′la*, modifications proposed by Fayod, in Ann. Sc. Nat., Bot. Sér. VII. ix. (1889) 243-244; cutic′-ular, pertaining to the CUTICLE; ~ Beads, pearl-like glands, as of *Chenopodium album;* ~ Crown, at the apex of papillae in certain Anon-aceae; ~ Crests, on epidermis and lower side of leaf in certain Mi-moseae; ~ Epithe′lium, formed of cells of the epidermis and primary cortex, with thickened outer walls; ~ Lay′ers, more or less cuticularized and apposed to the cuticle on its inner side; ~ **Pegs**, intrusions of cuticle into epidermal cells; ~ **Ridges**, occurring on the flat epidermis between papillae (Solereder); **Cuticulariza′tion** = CUTINIZATION; **cutic′uloid** (εἶδος, resemblance), a structure resembling skin (G. Murray).

Cu′tin (*cutis*, the skin), the substance, allied to Suberine, which repels liquids from passing the cell-wall; **Cutiniza′tion**, the modification of the cell-wall so as to become impervious to liquids; **Cu′tis**: (1) the skin or epidermis; (2) the peridium of some Fungi; **Cutocel′luloses** (+ Cellulose), modified cellulose, the cuticularized layers of cell-wall, impregnated with cutin; **Cu′tose**, the transparent film covering the aërial organs of plants.

Cut′tage, multiplication by cuttings (L. H. Bailey).

Cut′ting, (1) the severed portion of a plant, used for propagation; (2) the outline of a leaf or frond when incised.

cut-toothed, "deeply and sharply toothed" (Crozier).

cyali′nus ‡ (Mod. Lat.) = CYANOUS.

Cyam′ium ‡ (κύαμος, a bean), "a kind of follicle resembling a legume" (Lindley).

cyanae′us, ‡ *cyan′eus* (κύανος, cornflower), a clear full blue, cornflower-coloured; **cya′neous**, cornflower blue; **cyanel′lus**, almost a skyblue; **cyan′ic**, blue; ~ **Flow′ers**, those whose colouring tends towards blue, in contrast to XANTHIC Flowers; **cyanoch′rous** (χρὼς, χροὸς, the skin), having a blue skin; **Cy′anocyst** (κύστις, a bladder), a cell in which starch and chlorophyll occur, whose contents take a blue stain (Arbaumont); *cf.* ACHROOCYST; **Cyanogen′esis** (γένεσις, origin), the formation of cyanogen in plant-tissues; **cyanoph′ilous** (φιλέω, I love), applied to nuclei which readily take a deep blue stain; **cyanophor′ic** (φορὸς, bearing), used of certain forms which yield cyanogen, as

Lotus corniculatus; **cyanophy′ceous**, resembling or allied to the Cyanophyceae, or Blue-green Algae; **Cyanophy′cin** (φύκος, sea-weed), the blue colouring matter of Algae; **Cy′anophyll** (φύλλον, a leaf) = KYANOPHYLL; **Cy′anoplast** (πλαστὸς, moulded) used of chromatophores, or minute granular pigmentary bodies in Schizophyceae (Hegler); **Cyanoplas′tid** (+ PLASTID) granules of blue colouring matter (Hegler).

cyathea′ceous, allied to the Fern-genus *Cyathea.*

cyath′iform, *cyathiform′is* (κύαθος, a wine-cup; *forma*, shape), shaped like a drinking-cup; **Cyath′ium**, the inflorescence of *Euphorbium*, consisting of involucral bracts, with glands between single stamens each equivalent to a male flower, and a trilocular ovary; **cy′athoid** (εἶδος, resemblance), cup-like; **Cyath′olite** (λίθος, stone) = COCCOLITH; **Cy′athus**, the cup-like body which contains propagula in *Marchantia*, etc.

Cyb′ele (pr. Sib′-e-le), H. C. Watson's name for an estimation of the distribution of plants in a given area, an analogue to Flora; the name is mythological.

cyca′ceous, Hayne's term for "sago-grey"; from *Metroxylon Sagu*, the sago-palm.

cycada′ceous, **cycad′ean**, allied to or resembling *Cycas;* **cycada′lean**, relating to the Cycadales (Wieland); **cycadeoid′ean**, allied to the fossil genus *Cycadeoidea* (Wieland); **cyca-dofilicin′ean**, allied to the Cycadofilicineae, a group of fossil plants partaking of the characters of Cycads and Ferns, such as *Lyginodendron*, Williamson, and *Medullosa*, Cotta (Scott); **Cy′cadophytes** (φύτον, a plant), plants allied to Cycadeae.

Cy′clamine, a principle found in the root of *Cyclamen europaeum*, Linn.

Cy′clarch (κύκλος, a circle; ἀρχὴ, beginning), the first member of a whorl; **Cy′cle**, (1) used for one turn of a helix or spire, in leaf arrangement; (2) for a whorl in floral envelopes;

cy'clic, *cy'clicus*, applied to foliar structures arranged in whorls, coiled into a cycle or relating to a cycle; cy'clical, rolled up circularly, as many embryos; Cyclocho'risis (+ CHORISIS), Fermond's term for the division of an axial organ into a sheaf of secondary axes; cyclodes'-mic (δεσμός, a bond), applied to the vascular system of typical Dicotyledons (Brebner); Cy'clogens (γεννάω, to bring forth), exogenous plants, from their exhibiting concentric circles in the section of their stems; cyclog'enous, having concentric circles in the stem, exogenous; cy-clolyt'ic (λύσις, a loosing) In'terval, the space on the PHOTRUM with all grades of illumination up to direct sunlight, capable of producing cyclosis or rotation of protoplasm in a plant-cell (S. Moore); Cy'clome, a ring-shaped cushion of anthers (M'Nab); Cyclom'eter (μέτρον, a measure), a series of concentric circles traced on a board, for comparison with curved structures; Cyclo'sis, the rotation of protoplasm within the cell, in one or more currents; cyclosperm'ous (σπέρμα, a seed), with the embryo coiled round the central albumen; Cyclu'ra (οὐρά, a tail), the last member of a whorl.

cyg'neous *cyg'neus* (Lat. pertaining to a swan), the seta of Mosses when curved so as to suggest a swan's neck.

cylindra'ceous, *-eus* (κύλινδρος, a cylinder, + ACEOUS), somewhat cylindric; Cylindranth'erae (ἄνθος, a flower), syngenesious, from the stamens forming a tube; Cylindrench'yma (ἔγχυμα, an infusion), tissue made up of cylindric cells; cylind'ric, cylind'rical, elongated, with a circular cross-section; Cylindrobasioste'mon (βάσις, a pedestal; στήμων, a stamen), monadelphous; cylindrogen'ic (γένος, race, offspring), longitudinal expansion of amoeboid organisms (Jensen).

cymaphyt'ic, emended spelling of CUMAPHYTIC.

Cyma'tium (κυμάτιον, a little wave) = APOTHECIUM.

cymb'aeform, more correctly cymb'iform, *cymliform'is* (cymba, a boat; forma, shape), boat-shaped, used for Diatoms, or the keel of Leguminosae.

Cymbel'lae (*cymbula*, a little boat), reproductive locomotive bodies of an elliptic form, found in some Algae.

Cyme, *Cy'ma* (κῦμα, a wave, Lat. the sprout of a cabbage), a flower-cluster of determinate or centrifugal type, especially a broad and flattened one; hel'icoid ~ (*a*) a Bostryx, and (*b*) a Drepanium, the lateral branches of the successive ramifications always occurring on the same side; scorp'ioid ~ (*a*) Cincinnus, and (*b*) Rhipidium, the lateral branches always occurring alternately on opposite sides; Cymelet, pr. sĭm-let, a little cyme; cymif'erous (*fero*, I bear), producing cymes; cy'mo-bot'ryose [or bot'-ryoid], when cymes are arranged in a botryoid manner; cy'moid (εἶδος, resemblance), having the form of a cyme; cy'mose, *cymo'sus*, cy'mous, bearing cymes or relating to cymes; ~ Um'bel, one with centrifugal inflorescence; Cy'mule, a diminutive cyme or portion of one.

Cyn'apine, an alkaloid occurring in *Aethusa Cynapium*, Linn.

Cynarrhod'ion, *-dium, -dum* (κύων, a dog; ῥόδον, a rose), a fruit like that of the dog-rose, fleshy, hollow, and enclosing achenes.

Cy'on, Grew's spelling of Cion = SCION.

cypera'ceous (*Cyperus*, + ACEOUS), relating to sedges, from the typical genus *Cyperus*; Cyperog'rapher (γράφω, I write), a writer on Cyperaceae.

Cyphel'la (κυφός, bent), "collections of gonidia in the form of cups" (Lindley); Cyphel'lae, orbicular fringed spots like dimples, under the thallus of Lichens; cyphel'late, marked with Cyphellae.

cypripe'deous, allied to or resembling *Cypripedium*.

Cyp′sela (κυψέλη, a box), an achene invested by an adnate calyx, as the fruit of Compositae.

Cyriodoch′ae (κύριος, regular, as to time, δοχή, entertainment), employed by Clements to denote regular successions of plants.

Cyr′rhus = Cirrhus, a tendril.

Cyst, *Cyst′is* (κύστις, a cavity), (1) a sac or cavity, usually applied to a structure whose nature is doubtful ; (2) all cells of non-sexual origin in green Algae which reproduce the plant by germination after a resting period as resting spores, hypnospores, chronospores, aplanospores, akinetes (F. Gay) ; **Cyst′a ‡**, Necker's term for a berry with dry, membranous envelope, as in *Passiflora;* **Cysticar′pium** = Cystocarp ; adj. **cysticar′pic** ; **Cyst′id**, a proposed emendation for **Cystid′ium**; (1) large, one-celled, sometimes inflated bodies, projecting beyond the basidia and paraphyses of the hymenium of Agarics, of unknown function ; (2) = Utricle ; **Cyst′oblast** (βλαστός, a shoot), cited by Crozier for Cytoblast ; **Cyst′ocarp** *Cystocarp′ium* (καρπός, fruit), a sporophore in Algae, especially Florideae, a cyst containing sexually produced spores ; **Cyst′olith** (λίθος, stone), mineral concretions, usually of calcium carbonate on a cellulose stalk, occurring chiefly in special cells of the Urticaceae, as in *Ficus elastica*, Roxb. ; adj. **cystolith′ic ;** **Cyst′ophore** (φορέω, I carry), the same as Ascophore ; **Cys′tosphere** (σφαῖρα, a ball), masses of secretion enclosed in a kind of sac or pouch ; **Cyst′osore** *Cystoso′rus* (σωρός, a heap), a group of resting-spores within a cell as in *Woronina ;* **Cyst′ospore** (σπορά, a seed) = Carpospore (Strasburger) ; **Cys′totyle** (τύλη, a lump), mucilaginous concretions resembling Cystoliths, but uncalcified and usually occurring in pairs (Radlkofer) ; **Cyst′ula** = Cistula, Cistella.

Cy′tase (κύτος, a hollow vessel), an enzyme found in germinating seeds which hydrolyses cellulose ; **Cytas′ter** (ἀστήρ, a star), a series of achromatic rays from each pole of the nucleus into the cytoplasm in karyokinesis (Crozier); **Cytench′yma** (ἔγχυμα, an infusion), vacuolar structure in cells, fluid which separates from protoplasm as vacuoles (Crozier) ; **Cy′tioderm** (δέρμα, skin), the cell-wall in Diatomaceae (Crozier) ; **Cytioder′ma**, or **Cy′toderm** (δέρμα, a skin), (1) the cell-wall ; (2) the outer layer of protoplasm next the cell-wall, the primordial utricle ; **Cytioplas′ma** (πλάσμα, moulded), the cell-contents.

Cyt′isine, an alkaloid occurring in the genus *Cytisus.*

Cy′to-anat′omy (κύτος, a hollow vessel + Anatomy), the organisation of the cell (Graf); **Cytoast′er** (+Aster), a star in nuclear division ; *cf.* Dyaster ; **Cy′toblast** (βλαστός, a shoot), (1) Schleiden's name for the cell-nucleus ; (2) a colony of bioblasts which have lost their independent existence ; *cf.* Bioblast ; **Cytoblaste′ma**, the formative material in which cells are produced, and by which they are held in union ; protoplasm ; **Cy′tochem′istry**, the chemistry of the cell (Graf); **Cytocho′rism** (χωρίζω, I separate), division of living cells (Fitting) ; **Cytochyle′ma** (χυλός, juice), the contents of the cell, composed of Plasmochym, and **Cy′tochym** (χύμα, that which is poured), the more watery sap present in the vacuoles of the plant-cell (Strasburger) ; **cytoclas′tic** (κλαστός, broken in pieces), destructive of the cell ; **Cytocoag′ulase** (*coagulo*, I cause to curdle), an enzyme in the cambium region of *Prunus* in autumn, which deposits an insoluble product from gum (Grüss); **Cy′todes**, (1) cells ; (2) nuclear elements in which the caryosomes are not grouped into nuclei (Vuillemin) ; **Cy′toderm** = Cytioderma ; **Cytodier′esis** (διαίρεσις, division), cell-division with nuclear division, and formation of a nuclear-spindle and asters (Crozier); **Cy'to-dynam'ics** (+ DYNAMIC), phenomena of motion, cell-division, maturation, fertilization, death and part pathology (Graf); **Cytog'amy** (γάμος, marriage), the complete fusion of two cells into a seminucleate zygote or oosperm; **Cytogen'esis** (γένεσις, beginning), the origin and development of cells; sometimes written Cytiogenesis; **cytogenet'ic**, pertaining to cell-formation; **cytog'-enous**, producing cells, or cellular tissue; **Cytog'eny** = CYTOGENESIS; **Cytohy'aloplasm** (+ Hyaloplasm), the protoplasm of the cell, apart from any granules or foreign matter; **Cytohy'drolist** (ὕδωρ, water; λύσις, a loosing), an enzyme which attacks and breaks up the cell-wall by hydrolysis; **Cytohydrol'ysis**, the action of an enzyme on the cell-wall, which becomes broken down in consequence; **Cytokine'sis** (κίνησις, motion), cell-division by mitosis; **Cy'tolist** (λύσις, a loosing), an enzyme which dissolves the cell-wall; **Cy'tolite** = CYSTOLITH; **Cy'tolymph** (lympha, spring water), the more fluid contents of a cell; **cytolyt'ic**, of a ferment dissolving cells apart; **Cytol'ogy** (λόγος, discourse), the science of the cell, its life history, nuclear divisions and development; adj. **cytolog'ic, cytolog'ical; Cy'to-mechan'-ics**, physical properties and behaviour to mechanical stimuli (Graf); **Cytomi'crosomes** (μικρὸς, small; σῶμα, a body), the granules or microsomes imbedded in the cell-protoplasm; **Cytomix'is** (μῖξις, a mingling), the extrusion of chromatin from the nucleus of one pollen-mother-cell into the cytoplasm of an adjacent mother-cell (Gates); **Cyto-morphol'ogy** (+ MORPHOLOGY), external form and size of the cell (Graf); **Cyto-physiol'ogy** (+ PHYSIOLOGY); Graf divides this into subheads of CYTO-CHEMISTRY, ~ DYNAMICS, ~ MECHANICS, and ~ STATICS; **Cy'toplasm** (πλάσμα, moulded), the

general protoplasm of the cell (Strasburger); **cytoplas'mic** (πλάσμα, that formed), relating to CYTOPLASM; ~ **Androg'amy**, the male gamete is fertilized by the cytoplasm of the female gamete (Dangeard); ~ **Gynog'amy** the female gamete is impregnated by the cytoplasm of the male gamete (Dangeard); **Cy'toplast** (πλαστὸς, moulded), the cytoplasm as a unit, in contrast to the nucleus; **cytoplas'tic**, relating to the CYTOPLAST; **Cytoplast'in**, a proteid which apparently forms the bulk of the cytoplasm; **Cy'tosarc** (σάρξ, σαρκὸς, flesh), the body of a cell exclusive of the nucleus (Schneider); **Cy'tosomes** (σῶμα, a body), Vuillemin's name for the granules of cell-protoplasm; cytomicrosomes; **Cy'tostat'ics** (στατικὸς, causing to stand), conditions of equilibrium in the cell (Graf); **Cytotax'is** (τάξις, order), the mutual relation of cells or organisms; **neg'ative** ~, the tendency to separate from each other; **pos'itive** ~, the tendency to approach each other; **Cytotox'ins** (τοξικὸς, for the bow, i. e. poison), enzyme-like productions of which little is known; also styled enzymoids; **Cytot'ropism** (τροπὴ, a turning) = CYTOTAXIS.

dacryoi'deus (δάκρυ, a tear; εἶδος, resemblance), used for pear-shaped fruit, oblong and rounded at one end, pointed at the other.

dactyli'nus (δάκτυλος, a finger), divided like fingers; **dac'tyline, dac'tyloid,** (1) finger-like; (2) pertaining to the § *Dactyloides* of the genus *Saxifraga;* **Dactylorhi'za** (ρίζα, root), the forking of roots; **dac'tylose,** *dactylo'sus*, fingered, or finger-shaped.

daeda'leous, *daeda'leus* (Lat. = skilful craft), (1) the apex of a leaf irregularly jagged, though not arcuate; (2) wavy and irregularly plaited as the hymenium of some Agarics; **Daedalench'yma** (ἔγχυμα, an infusion), tissue made up of entangled cells, as in some Fungi.

Dah′line, a substance resembling starch from the tubers of the genus *Dahlia*.

Dam′mar, a transparent resin from *Agathis loranthifolia*, Salisb., formerly named *Dammara orientalis*, Lamb.

Damp′ing, a cultivator's term for premature decay in plants, especially young seedlings, attributed to excess of moisture ; **Damp′ing off**, the collapse of seedlings, ascribed to the attacks of the Fungus *Botrytis vulgaris*, or of *Pythium De-Baryanum*.

Daph′nin, the bitter principle of *Daphne Mezereum*, Linn.

Darwin, *see* KNIGHT-DARWIN Law.

Darwin′ian Curv′ature, the bending induced by the irritation of any foreign substance close to the apex of the root.

dasyclad′ous, *-dus* (δασὺς, thick ; κλάδος, a branch) = COMPACTUS (Russow) ; **dasyphyl′lous**, *-lus* (φύλλον, a leaf), (1) thick-leaved ; (2) leaves thickly set ; (3) with woolly leaves.

date-shaped, resembling a date in form.

Datis′cin, a substance having the appearance of grape-sugar, first obtained from *Datisca cannabina*, Linn. ; it has been used as a yellow dye.

Datu′rine, an alkaloid of *Datura Stramonium*, Linn.

Daugh′ter-cells, young cells derived from the division of an older one, the mother-cell ; ~ **Chro′mosome**, a secondary chromosome, derived from division of the original ; ~ **Skein**, stages in nuclear division when the chromatin is more or less in a reticulate condition ; further distinguished by some observers into "loose" or "close" ; ~ **Spore**, a spore produced immediately from another or upon a promycelium ; ~ **Star**, one of the groups of chromatic filaments at the poles of a dividing nucleus ; the two together with the connecting spindle constitute the "Dyaster" stage.

Day-position, the pose assumed by leaves during the day, in contra-distinction to that taken for the night.

deaf. has been applied to imperfect fruits of *Rumex* ; ~ **-seeds**, imperfect seeds of grasses (Percival).

deal′bate, *dealba′tus* (Lat. whitewashed), whitened ; covered with an opaque white powder.

Deammonifica′tion (*de*, from ; *ammonia*, an alkali ; *facio*, I make) ; a reduction of ammonia by the soil bacteria **Deammonobacte′ria** (Lipman).

Deassimila′tion (*assimilatio*), conversion of food into digested products , the process of plant-katabolism (Quin).

Death-point, the critical point when a spore is rendered permanently incapable of germinating (J. F. Clarke).

Deazotofica′tion (AZOTE ; *facio*, make), the reduction of nitrogenous substances by **Deazotobacte′ria** (Lipman).

Decagyn′ia (δέκα, ten ; γυνὴ, woman), a Linnean artificial order of plants with ten pistils ; **decagyn′ian**, **decag′ynous**, having ten styles or carpels ; **decam′erous**, *decam′erus* (μέρος, a share), in tens ; **decan′der** (Mod. Lat.) = DECANDROUS ; **Decan′dria** (ἀνὴρ, ἀνδρὸς, a man), a Linnean artificial class of plants with ten stamens ; **decan′drian**, **decan′drous** *-rus*, having ten stamens.

decapet′alous, *-lus* (δέκα, ten ; πέταλον, a flower-leaf), with ten petals ; **decaphyl′lous** (φύλλον, a leaf), with ten leaves or segments ; **decari′nus** (ἄρρην, male), Necker's term for ten stamens and one pistil ; **decasep′alous**, *-lus* (+ SEPALUM), with ten sepals ; **decasperm′al** (σπέρμα, a seed), having ten seeds.

decemdent′ate (*decem*, ten ; *dens, dentis*, a tooth), having ten teeth, as the capsule of *Cerastium ;* **decem′fid** (Crozier), **decem′fidus** (*fid*, the root of *fido*, I split), ten cleft decemlocula′ris (*loculus*, a compartment), with ten cells, as an ovary.

decep′tive (*deceptus*, deceived) **Fly-**

plants, applied to *Parnassia* and other flowers which seem to offer much honey, but the apparent glands are dry (Knuth).

Deciduiligno′sa, pl. (*deciduus*, ready to fall ; *lignosus*, woody), associations of trees and shrubs which lose their leaves during unfavourable periods, and usually have protected buds (Rübel); **decid′uous**, *-uus*, falling in season, as petals fall after flowering, or leaves in autumn, evergreens excepted ; **Deciduous′ness**, the quality of falling once a year.

dec′linate, *declina′tus* (Lat. turned aside), bent or curved downward or forward ; **decli′ned**, directed obliquely.

Decoloura′tion, *Decolora′tio* (Lat.), absence of colour ; **decol′orate**, **decolora′tus** (Lat.), discoloured, discharged of colour, colourless.

decom′pound, *decompos′itus* (Lat.), several times divided or compounded.

decort′icated (*decorticatio*, barking), deprived of bark ; **Decortica′tion**, stripping off bark.

decreas′ingly pinn′ate, where the leaflets diminish in size from the base upwards.

decum′bent, *-ens* (Lat. reclining), reclining, but with the summit ascending.

decur′rent, *decur′rens* (Lat.), running down, as when leaves are prolonged beyond their insertion, and thus run down the stem ; **decur′sive**, *decursi′vus* (*decursus*, a descent) = DECURRENT ; **decur′sively pin′nate**, the leaf seemingly pinnate, but the leaflets decurrent along the petiole.

decus′sate, *decussa′tus* (Lat. divided crosswise), in pairs alternately at right angles ; **Decussa′tion**, a crossing by pairs of leaves.

Dédoublement (Fr.), doubling = CHORISIS.

dedu′cens (Lat. leading forth), applied by Macfarlane to the conducting surface in the pitchers of *Nepenthes*.

Deduplica′tion (Fr. déduplication), a synonym of DÉDOUBLEMENT.

Defarina′tion (*de*, from, *farina*, flour), De Vries's term for suppressed or greatly lessened formation of starch.

def′erent (*defero*, 1 bring down), conveying anything downward.

deferred′ Shoots, those produced by buds which have remained long dormant.

Deferrifica′tion (*de*, from, *ferrum*, iron, *facio*, I make), the reduction of iron by **Ferribacte′ria** (Lipman).

def′inite, *defini′tus* (precise, clear), (1) precise ; (2) of a certain number, as of stamens not exceeding twenty ; (3) applied to inflorescence it means cymose ; ~ **Inflores′cence**, where the axis ends in a flower ; **defin′itive Nu′cleus**, a result of the fusion of one nucleus each from the micropylar and chalazal ends of the embryo sac.

defix′ed, *defix′us* (Lat. fastened) = immersed.

deflect′ed, *deflex′us* (Lat. bent aside), bent or turned abruptly downwards ; **deflexed′**, bent outwards, the opposite of inflexed ; **Deflex′ion**, turned downwards.

deflo′rate, *deflora′tus* (Lat.), past the flowering state.

deflow′er, to deprive of flowers.

deflu′ent (Lat. *defluens*), flowing down.

defo′liate, *defolia′tus* (Mod. Lat.), having cast its leaves ; **Defolia′tion**, the act of shedding leaves.

De′form (*deformis*, misshapen), used by O. Kuntze for DEFORMITY ; **Deforma′tion**, a malformation or alteration from the normal state; **deformed′**, disfigured, distorted ; **Deform′ity**, *Deform′itas* (Lat.), an unshapely organism ; a monster.

degen′erate (*degenero*, to become unlike the race), degraded in function or form ; **Degenera′tion**, an alteration for the worse, or less highly developed, as when scales appear instead of leaves.

degerm′ed (*de*, from, *germen*, an embryo), used of a seed deprived of its embryo (Pond).

Degrada′tion (*degradatio*, L. Lat. the act of reducing), (1) less highly differentiated, simpler structures taking the place of more elaborate ; (2) lower in function, retrograde metamorphosis, or a katabolic change, complex substances resolving into simpler ; ~ **Prod'uct**, the result of katabolism, as mucilage.

degress'ive, tending towards degeneration.

dehisce' (*dehisco*, I yawn), to open spontaneously when ripe, as seed capsules, etc. ; **Dehis'cence,** *Dehiscent'ia*, the mode of opening of a fruit capsule or anther by valves, slits or pores ; **dehis'cent,** *dehis'cens*, **dehis'cing,** splitting into definite parts.

Dehydra'tion (*de*, privative ; ὕδωρ, water), depriving of water as a component, as by the use of alcohol, or calcic chloride.

delignify'ing (*lignum*, wood ; *facio*, I make), applied to an enzyme which breaks down the structure of wood, as in *Merulius*.

Deli'la, applied to those colour-forms of *Antirrhinum* with ivory tube and magenta or crimson lips (De Vries).

Delimita'tion (Late Lat. *delimitare*), used for ABJUNCTION ; cutting off by a precise limit ; **delim'ited,** circumscribed.

deliques'cent, *-ens* (Lat. melting away), dissolving or melting away, as (1) when the stem loses itself by repeated branching ; or (2) when certain Agarics become fluid at maturity.

Deliq'uium ‡ (Lat., a defect) = EMARGINATE (Lindley).

Del'phine, an alkaloid present in *Delphinium Staphisagria*, Linn.

del'ta-leaved (δέλτα, the Greek letter Δ), having triangular leaves ; **del'toid,** *deltoi'des*, *-deus* (εἶδος, resemblance), shaped like the Greek Δ ; an equilateral triangle.

demat'ioid (εἶδος, resemblance), like the genus *Dematium*, having a felted layer of hyphae bearing perithecia.

demersed', *demer'sus* (Lat. plunged under), under water, especially of a part constantly submersed.

demis'sus (Lat.), hanging down lowered.

Dena'rii ‡ (Lat.) = ten together (Lindley).

Den'drad (δένδρον, a tree + AD), an orchard plant (Clements) ; **den'driform** (*forma*, shape) = DENDROID **dendrit'ic,** *-icus*, *-ical*, having a branched appearance, as the lirellae of Lichens, etc. ; **Dendrio-thamno'des,** with thallus branched as a bush, as the Reindeer Lichen, *Cladonia rangiferina*, Hoffm. ; **Dendri'tes,** cellulose in crystals ; **Dendri'um,** an "orchard formation" (Clements) ; **dendroph'ilus** (φιλέω, I love), "orchard loving" ; **Dendrophy'ta** (φυτὸν, a plant), "orchard plants" (Clements) ; **den'droid,** *dendroi'des*, *dendroi'deus* (εἶδος, resemblance), tree-like in form, or branching ; **Den'drolite** (λίθος, stone), a fossil tree ; **Dendrol'ogist** (λόγος, discourse), one skilled in the knowledge of trees ; **Dendrol'ogy,** the study of trees.

deni (Lat.), by tens, ten together.

den'igrate, *denigra'tus* (Lat.), blackened.

Denitrifica'tion (*de*, from, *nitron*, nitre, *facio*, I make), the reduction of nitrates by the action of **Denitrobacte'ria** (Lipman).

Den'izen, H. C. Watson's term for plants suspected of foreign origin, though maintaining their place, as *Viola odorata*, Linn.

Dens (Lat.), a tooth ; **den'tate,** *denta'tus* (Lat.), toothed, especially with salient teeth directed forward ; **denta'to-crena'tus** = CRENATODENTATUS ; ~ **-lacinia'tus,** with toothings irregularly extended into long point ; ~ **-serra'tus,** the toothings tapered and pointing forward ; **Dent'icle,** a small tooth (Crozier) ; **dentic'ulate,** *denticula'tus*, minutely toothed ; **Denticula'tions,** small processes or teeth ; **dent'iform** (*forma*, shape), J. Smith's equivalent for toothed ; **den'toid** (εἶδος, form), tooth-shaped.

denu'date, *denuda'tus* (Lat.), stripped,

made bare, or naked; **Denuda′tion,** the act of stripping bare; **denu′ded Quad′rat,** a permanent quadrat, or metre-square of land, from which all the original vegetation has been removed, for the study of invasion (Clements).

deoperc′ulate, *deopercula′tus* (*de* = from, *operculum,* a lid); (1) when the operculum of a Moss does not separate spontaneously from the sporophore; (2) having lost the operculum.

deor′sum (Lat. from *de,* down, *versus* turned towards), downward.

depaup′erate, *depaupera′tus* (Lat.), impoverished as if starved, reduced in function.

depend′, depen′dent, *depen′dens* (Lat.), hanging down.

Deperula′tion (*de,* prefix of separation, + PERULA), the act of throwing off the bud-scales in leafing; **calyp′tral** ∼, thrown off as a cap; **tu′bular** ∼, when remaining as a collar at the base of the shoot (Kirchner).

Depigmenta′tion (*pigmentum,* colouring matter), latency of colour in flowers, etc. (De Vries).

depla′nate, *deplana′tus* (Lat.), flattened or expanded.

Deple′tion (*depletus,* emptied out), enzyme digestion of reserve material in the endosperm (Pond).

Depos′its (*depositus,* laid aside), secondary growths on the cell-wall, more or less covering it, in various forms.

depres′sed, *depres′sus* (Lat.), sunk down, as if flattened from above; **Depres′sio** (Lat.), a pressing or sinking down, a little hollow; ∼ **dorsa′lis,** a depression in the spores of some Agarics extending along the back of the spore; ∼ **hila′ris,** a similar depression, but of less extent, above the hilum (Fayod); **depress′o-trunca′tus** = RETUSE.

Deproteofica′tion (*de,* from, + PROTEID, *facio,* I make), decay and putrefaction due to the action of **Deproteobacte′ria** (Lipman).

deregula′ris ‡ (*de,* opposed; *regularis*

in order), between regular and irregular (Lindley).

Deriv′ative Hy′brids, those sprung from a union of a hybrid, and one of its parent forms or another hybrid.

deri′ved (*derivo,* I turn aside) (disyll.), used by Clements to denote not native.

Der′ma (δέρμα, δέρματος, skin), surface of an organ, bark, or rind; **Dermacalypt′rogen** (καλύπτρα, a veil; γέννaω, I bring forth), Schwendener's term for a common histogen which produces root-cap and root-epidermis in Phanerogams; **derm′al,** relating to the outer covering; ∼ **Tis′sue,** the substance of the epidermis and periderm; **dermati′nus,** applied to those plants such as Lichens, which live on bark or epidermis; **dermat′ioid** (εἶδος, form), skin-like in function or appearance; **Dermatocalypt′rogen** = DERMACALYPTROGEN; **Derm′atocyst,** *Dermatocys′tis* (κύστις, a bag or pouch), inflated hairs on the surface of the sporophore of young Agarics; **Dermat′ogen** (γέννaω, I bring forth), the meristem forming the layer of nascent epidermis; primordial epidermis; **Dermat′ophyte** (φυτὸν, a plant), any Fungus parasitic on the skin of man or other animals (Crozier); **Dermat′osomes** (σῶμα, a body), Wiesner's term for granular bodies in rows, united and surrounded by protoplasm, which form the cell-wall; **Dermoblas′tus** (βλαστὸs, a shoot), "the cotyledon formed by a membrane that bursts irregularly" (S. F. Gray); **Dermocalypt′rogen** = DERMACALYPTROGEN; **Derm′oplast** (πλαστὸs, moulded), Pirotta's term for a MONOPLAST, invested with a membrane; **Dermosym′plast,** the same writer's word for a SYMPLAST as a latex-vessel.

descend′ing, *descen′dens* (Lat.), tending gradually downwards; (1) as the branches of some trees; (2) as the roots; ∼ **Ax′is,** the root system; ∼ **Metamorph′osis,** substitution of organs of a lower grade, as stamens for pistils, petals for stamens, etc. ; ~ **Sap**, formerly applied to the Cambium ; **Descen′sus ‡** = ROOT.

Des′ert, Deser′tum (Lat.), a tract where rain is continuously wanting, and vegetation is most scanty, as the Egypto-Arabian desert; it may be either climatic or edaphic.

Deser′tion of Host = LIPOXENY.

de′sinens (Lat. ceasing), *Desinen′tia*, ending in, the manner in which a lobe terminates.

desmid′ian, allied to the Desmideae ; **Des′midocarp** (καρπὸς, fruit), the special cystocarp of *Balbiania ;* the fertilized trichogynial cell divides transversely, each daughter-cell in turn branching with terminal oospores.

Desmobry′a (δεσμὸς, a bond ; βρύον, a moss), a division of Ferns, where the fronds are adherent to the caudex ; *cf.* EREMOBRYA ; **Desmochon′dria**, pl. (χόνδρος, grain) = MICROSOMES ; **Des′mogen** (γέννάω, I bring forth), distinguished as **pri′-mary ~**, the procambium, or embryonic tissue from which the vascular tissue is afterwards formed ; or **sec′ondary ~**, formed from the cambium, afterwards transferred into permanent vascular strands ; **Desmoplank′ton** (+ PLANKTON), plankton united into bands or ribbons (Forel).

destarch′ed, deprived of starch, as by translocation.

destruct′ive Metab′olism, those changes which take place during the waste of tissues ; ~ **Par′asite**, one which seriously injures or destroys the host.

Desulphofica′tion (*de*, from, *sulfur*, brimstone, *facio*, I make), the reduction of sulphates and sulphites by **Desulphobacte′ria** (Lipman).

detect′us (Lat. laid bare) = naked.

deten′tive (*detento*, I hold back), used of those parts of a Pitcher plant which detain insects (Macfarlane).

Deter′minants, pl. (*determino*, I limit), separate material particles in the germ-cells ; ~ **of Hered′ity**, those

carried by zygotes (Weismann) ; **deter′minate**, *determina′tus* (Lat. bounded), definite ; ~ **Growth**, when the season's growth ends with a bud ; ~ **Inflores′cence**, when it ends with a bud, as in cymes ; **Determina′tion**, *-atio*, the ascertaining the names and systematic position of plants, identification.

deus′tate, deus′tous (*deustus*, burned up), as if scorched (Heinig).

Deu′ter (Gér., an interpreter) **Cells**, a row of large parenchymatous cells, empty or containing starch, which occur in the middle nerve of Mosses (Limpricht) ; *cf.* POINTER-CELLS.

Deuterog′amy (δεύτερος, the second ; γάμος, marriage), peculiar nuclear fusions in certain Cryptogams, superposed upon and subsequent to the sexual act (P. Groom).

deutogen′otypic (+ GENOTYPIC) = ISOGENOTYPIC.

Deuterogonid′ium (+ GONIDIUM), a gonidium in the second generation of a transitorial series (A. Braun ; **Deuteroplas′ma** (πλάσμα, moulded) = PARAPLASM ; sometimes contracted into **Deut′oplasm** ; **Deuterostroph′ies** (στροφή, a twist or turn), spirals of a third degree in the development of leaves ; **Deutoxy′lem** (+ XYLEM), a synonym of META-XYLEM.

Devel′opment, the gradual extension of the parts by which any organ or plant passes from its beginning to its maturity.

Devia′tion, probable, Galton's term for probable variation.

Dew-leaves, leaves which slope upwards, so that dew is collected ; ~ **-rust**, "blotchy discoloration of leaves caused by dew" (Heinig).

dex′trad (*dextra*, the right hand) ; an unusual modification of **dex′tral**, towards or on the right side, as a climbing plant, *cf.* DEXTRORSE ; **Dex′trin**, a substance produced during the transformation of starch into sugar, said to be of two forms :—ACH-ROODEXTRIN and AMYLODEXTRIN ;

Dex′trinase, an enzyme stated to be present in diastase (Wysman); **dex′tro-ro′tatory**, turning towards the right; **dex′trorse**, *dextror′sus* (from *versus*, turned towards), towards the right hand; **dextror′sum volu′bilis** (Lat.), twining towards the right; **Dex′trose**, glucose, or fruit sugar, it turns the plane of polarization to the right; *cf.* LEVULOSE; **Dextrosty′ly** (+ STYLE), the style curves to the right in enantiostylous flowers.

di-, dis-, in Greek compounds = two, or double.

dia-, Greek, for through.

Diablaste′sis (+ BLASTESIS), special growth from the hyphal layer of a Lichen (Minks).

Diache′nium (δι, two, + ACHENIUM), or **Diake′nium** = CREMOCARP.

Diach′yma (διὰ, through : χυμὰ, a libation), Link's term for MESOPHYLL.

diac′mic (δι, two ; ἀκμὴ, a point), employed to denote plankton having two maximum periods ; *cf.* MONACMIC.

Di′ad, a variation in spelling of DYAD, *infra*.

Diadel′phia(δι, two; ἀδελφὸs, a brother), a Linnean class having the stamens in two bundles or brotherhoods ; **diadelph′ian, diadelph′ous, -us, -icus**, with two groups of stamens.

diad′romous (διά, through ; δρόμος, course), applied to a fan-shaped venation, as in *Gingko biloba*, Linn.

diae′cious = DIOECIOUS.

diage′ic (γῆ, earth), plants producing stolons which are below ground ; **diageotrop′ic** (τρόπος, a turn), a modified form of geotropism, the organs placing themselves in a horizontal position, as though opposing forces were neutralised ; **Diageot′ropism**, the state just described; **Diagno′sis** (γνῶσις, wisdom), a brief distinguishing character.

diag′onal (διὰ, across ; γωνία, angle), a mean between two forces, a compromise of position ; ~ **Plane**, in a flower, any vertical plane which is not antero-posterior (front to back)

or lateral (side to side); ~ **Posit′ion**, one intermediate between median and lateral; ~ **Sym′metry**, applied to the valves of Diatoms when their torsion amounts to 180° ; **Di′agram** (γραμμὴ, an outline), see FLORAL DIAGRAM ; **Diaheliot′ropism** (ἥλιος, the sun; τρόπος, a turn), growth more or less horizontal, under the influence of light, as when leaves place themselves at right angles to incident light; adj. **diaheliotrop′ic** ; **Diakine′sis** (κίνησις, energy), the last stage in the heterotype prophase in which the definitive chromosomes have been formed and the nuclear membrane is still intact; adj. **diakinet′ic**.

dialycarp′ic (διαλύω, I disband ; καρπὸς, fruit), having a fruit composed of distinct carpels; **Dialydes′my**(δεσμὸς, a band), the breaking up of a stele, into separate bundles, each with its own endodermis ; **Dialypet′alae** (πέταλον, a flower-leaf), Endlicher's equivalent for the POLYPETALAE of Jussieu; **dialypet′alous**, polypetalous ; **dialyphyll′ous** (φύλλον, a leaf), bearing separate leaves; **dialysep′alous** (+ SEPALUM), bearing separate sepals; **Dial′ysis**, the separation of parts normally in one, especially parts of the same whorl; **dialyste′lic** (+ STELE), having distinct steles; **Dialyste′ly**, a variation of POLYSTELY, in which the separate steles remain for the most part separate during their longitudinal course.

diamesog′amous (διὰ, through ; μέσος, middle ; γάμος, marriage), fertilization by the means of some external agent, as wind or insects; **Diamesog′amy**, the condition just defined.

dian′dreous (δι-, two ; ἀνὴρ, ἀνδρὸς, man ; + EOUS), the condition of Orchids having two perfect stamens (S. Moore); **Dian′dria**, a Linnean class with plants of two stamens ; **dian′drian, dian′drous** (*diander*), possessing two stamens ; **dianth′ic** (ἄνθος, a flower), pollination by a flower of the same plant (K. Pearson).

diaph'anous, -us (διὰ, through; φαίνω, I show), permitting the light to shine through; also written DIA-PHANUS; Diaph'ery (φέρω, I bear), the calycine synthesis of two flowers (Morren); Diaphototax'is (φῶς, light; τάξις, order), the arrangement of *Oscillatoria* threads at right angles to incident light of optimal intensity (Pieper); Diaphotot'ropism (+ PHO-TOTROPISM), the act of self-placing at right angles to incident light; adj. diaphototrop'ic; Di'aphragm (φράσσω, I enclose), a dividing membrane or partition, as (1) the constriction in the neck of the nucule in *Chara*, from the inward projections of the segments; (2) the transverse septa in the stem of *Equisetum* or of grasses; (3) the layer separating the prothallium from the cavity of the macrospore in Vascular Cryptogams; dia-phyl'lous (φύλλον, a leaf) = DIA-LYPHYLLOUS; Diaph'ysis (φύω, to make grow), proliferation of the inflorescence.

di'arch (δι-, two; ἀρχή, beginning), having two protoxylem groups, used of the steles of roots; diari'nus (ἄρρην, male), Necker's term for diandrous.

diaschis'tic (διὰ, through; σχιστὸς, cleft), applied to chromosomes when they divide transversely; cf. ANA-SCHISTIC (Farmer); Dias'pasis (σπάω, I tear), when the daughter-nuclei in amitosis are torn asunder (Wasielewski).

Di'astase (διάστασις, standing apart), an amylolytic enzyme which converts starch into malt-sugar; ~ of Transloca'tion attacks starch grains gradually over their whole surface; it is almost universally distributed in plants; ~ of Secre'tion. acts by corrosion, attacking parts of the starch-grain first; it is formed by the glandular epithelium of the scutellum of grasses; adj. diastat'ic.

Di'aster (δι-, two; ἀστὴρ, a star), see DYASTER.

Diast'ole (διαστολή, separation), the slow dilation of a contractile vesicle cf. SYSTOLE.

Diatherm'ancy (διὰ, through; θερμαίνω, I warm), the relative conductivity of a medium with regard to the transmission of heat (T. W. Engelmann); diathermotrop'ic (+ THERMO-TROPIC) unaffected by or placing itself transversely to the source of heat; Diathermot'ropism, the condition described.

Diatme'sis (τμῆσις, a cut), in Amitosis when the daughter-nuclei become neatly divided (Wasielewski).

diatoma'ceous, resembling or consisting of diatoms whose type is *Diatoma*; Diat'omine, the colouring matter of Diatoms, phycoxanthine; Diat'omist, one devoted to the study of Diatoms; Diat'omphile (φιλέω, I love), an enthusiastic student of Diatoms.

diatrop'ic (διὰ, through; τρόπος, twining), used of organs which place themselves transversely to the operating force; Diat'ropism is the condition; it may be GEOTROPIC or HELIOTROPIC.

dibot'ryal = DIBOTRYOID.

dibot'ryoid (δὶς, double; + BOTRYOID), a compound inflorescence, the branches of the first and succeeding orders being botryoid, such as the compound umbel, panicle, or spike; Dicar'otin (δὶς, twice, + CAROTIN), a lipochrome pigment; dicarp'ellary (καρπὸς, fruit), composed of two carpels or pistil-leaves; Dicar'yocyte (κάρυον, a nut; κύτος, a hollow vessel), a binucleate cell (Moreau); Dicar'yon, the complex of two independent nuclei, united in the same cell (Bonnet); Dicar'yophase (φάσις, a phase), the stage ending in the production of teleutospores (Moreau).

dicha'sial (διχάζω, I disunite), relating to a DICHASIUM; ~ Cymes, cymes whose secondary members are dichasia, such as occur in Euphorbiaceæ; Dicha'sium, a false dichotomy in which two lateral shoots of nearly equal strength arise from the primary axis below the flower which terminates the apex, the process being repeated by each set of branches; a two-parted or two-ranged cyme; **dichast'ic**, spontaneously dividing.

ichlamyd'eous (δίχα, in two; χλαμὺς, χλαμύδος, a cloak), having a double perianth, calyx and corolla; **dichoblas'tic** (βλαστὸς, a shoot), (1) suggested by Celakovsky to replace "dichotomous" when the repeated dichotomy develops into a sympodium; (2) branching intermediate between his acro- and pleuro-blastic conditions, it apparently occurs in the embryo of Pteridophytes; **Dichocarp'ism** (καρπός, fruit), Cooke's term for Fungi producing two distinct forms of fructification; dimorphic as to fruit; **dichody'namous, dichodynam'ic** (δύναμις, power), applied to hybrids in which the characters of both parents are equally represented; **dichog'amous** (γάμος, marriage), hermaphrodite with one sex earlier mature than the other, the stamens and pistils not synchronizing; **Dichog'amy**, insuring cross-fertilization, by the sexes not being developed simultaneously; **Dichog'eny** (γένος, offspring), the condition when of two formative impulses, one is set in motion, and the other inhibited (De Vries); **dichopod'ial** (πόδιον, a small foot), when an axis repeatedly forks, giving rise to an inflorescence termed a **Dichopod'ium** (Pax); **dichot'omal**, (τόμος, a cut), pertaining to a bifurcation, as a ~ **Flow'er**, one seated in the fork of a dichasium; **Dichoto'mia**, forking, as of branches in an inflorescence; dichotomy; ~ **brachia'lis**, in *Cladophora*, the normal forking, the cell-wall remaining unchanged; ~ **conna'ta**, the basal cells of the fork grown together; ~ **matrica'lis**, when the terminal cell forks and the branch and stem are equal in thickness; ~ **spu'ria**, branch and stem of equal size, but the mother cell is bent (Brand); **dichot'-**

omize, to fork or divide in pairs; **dichot'omous**, -us, forked, parted by pairs; ~ **Cyme**, of English authors = DICHASIUM; **Dichot'omy**, the state of being repeatedly forked; — **hel'icoid** ~, in each successive forking, the branch which continues to develop is on the same side as the previous one, the other branch aborts; false ~, = DICHASIUM; **scorp'ioid** ~, the branches develop on each side alternately; **dichotyp'ic** (τύπος, type), the appearance of two or more types on the same plant (Focke); **Dichot'ypy** (τύπος, a type), the occurrence of two different forms of the same stock; **Dicle'sium** (κλῆσις, closing), an achene within a separate and free covering of perianth, as *Mirabilis;* **Di'clinism**, (κλίνη, a bed), the separation of pollen and stigma in space, as dichogamy is in time; **di'clinous**, unisexual, having the stamens in one flower, and the pistils in another; **Di'cliny**, male and female organs separate and in different flowers; **di'coccous**, -us (δίς, two; κόκκος, a kernel), having fruit of two cocci; **dicoe'lous** (κοῖλος, a hollow), with two cavities.

Dicot'ylae, an abbreviation of **Dicotyledoneae; dicot'ylous** = DICOTYLEDONOUS.

Dicotyledo'neae, Dicotyle'dones, Dicotyle'dons (κοτυληδών, cup-shaped hollow, used for seed-lobe), plants of the class denoted by their possession of two cotyledons; **dicotyle'donous**, — *nus*, having a pair of seed-lobes; **Dicot'yls**, an abbreviation for DICOTYLEDONS.

dicrana'ceous, resembling the Moss *Dicranum.*

Dict'ydin, a substance found by Jahn in the Myxomycete *Dictydium umbilicatum*, as granules which resist both acids and alkalis.

dictyodes'mic (δικτύον, a net; δέσμος, a bond), the vascular network in Ferns so termed by Brebner; **dictyod'romous** (δρόμος, a course), with reticulate venation; **Dic'tyogens** (γέννάω, I bring forth), plants having netted veins, proposed by Lindley as intermediate between his ENDOGENS and EXOGENS; **dictyog´enous**, applied to monocotyledons with netted veins; ~ **Lay´er**, a layer of meristem general in monocotyledons, which gives rise to the central "body" and cortex of the young roots (Mangin); **dictyomeriste´lic** (+ MERISTELE), the stem-steles in certain Ferns thus designated by Brebner; **Dictyospo´rae** (+ SPORA), Fungi having muriform spores (Traverso); **Dictyosporan´gium** (+ SPORANGIUM), the sporangium of *Saprolegnia*, with encased spores germinating within the sporangium (Walpole and Huxley); **Dict´yostele** (+ STELE) a stele with large overlapping leaf-gaps; — **dissec´ted** ~, a perforated dictyostele in which the strands of the stelar network are reduced to thin threads (Tansley); **per´forated** ~, a dictyostele in which gaps other than leaf gaps occur; **siphon´ic** ~, when the network of meristeles is simple and tubular (Brebner); adj. **dictyoste´lic**; **Dictyox´ylon** (ξύλον, wood), applied to the cortex of a fossil stem possessing a netted system of hypodermal fibrous strands, as in *Lyginodendron* (Scott).

Dictyu´chus State of Saprolegnieae (Hartog) = DICTYOSPORANGIUM.

dicy´clic (δίς, two; κύκλος, a circle), (1) when a series of organs is in two whorls as a perianth; (2) applied to biennials; **Dicy´cly**, the condition of having two concentric vascular cylinders; **Di´cyme**, a cyme in which the first (or higher) axes again form cymes (Eichler); ~ a two-fifths spiral expressed in terms of two circles, two outside, and three inside (Church); **dicy´mose** (κῦμα, a wave), doubly cymose; **didip´loid** (δι, twice, + DIPLOID), used of a nucleus consisting of the fusion of two diploid nuclei (Němec); *cf.* SYNDIPLOID; **did´romic** (δρόμος, a course), doubly twisted, as the awns in *Danthonia, Stipa*, etc.; **Did´romy**, double torsion; **Didymospo´rae** (+ SPORA), Fungi bearing spores in pairs (Traverso).

did´ymous, *-us* (δίδυμος, twin), (1) found in pairs, as the fruits of Umbelliferae; (2) divided into two lobes; ~ **An´thers**, when the two lobes are almost destitute of connective.

Didyna´mia (δίς, twice; δύναμις, power), a Linnean class marked by didynamous flowers; **didyna´mian, didy´namous**, flower, four-stamened, with stamens in pairs, two long, two short, as in most Labiatae; **Didy´namy**, the condition above defined.

Die-back, of *Salix*, a disease due to *Diplodina salicina*; ~ of *Citrus*, some uncertain condition of health; ~ of *Prunus*, from *Naemospora crocea*.

Dientomoph´ily (+ ENTOMOPHILY), when in a species, some individuals are adapted for insect-fertilization by a different group of visitors from the remaining individuals (Engler and Prantl).

Dieres´ilis, Dieresil´ia (διαιρέω, I divide), Mirbel's name for CARCERULE; adj. **dieresil´ian**.

Diete´siae (δι, two; ἐτήσιος, annual), perennials with short shoots, long shoots being absent or fugacious (Krause).

Differentia´tion, of a Cell-wall, the arising of apparent layers; ~ **of Tis´sues**, their development into permanent tissue and consequent diverse growth.

diff´luent (*diffluens*, dissolving), having the power to dissolve, or readily doing so.

difformed´, *difform´is* (*dis-*, apart; *forma*, shape), of unusual formation or shape; **Difform´itas** (Lat.), an abnormality.

diffract´, *diffrac´tus* (Lat., broken), broken into areolae separated by chinks.

diffuse´, *diffu´sus* (Lat., spread abroad), wide y or loosely spreading; ~ **Col´our**, a colour which has "run" into the surrounding tissues; **Diffu´sion**, (1) term used by Wiesner for the intermingling of different gases under equal pressure, with or without intervening partitions; (2) mixture of fluids, or dispersion of a fluid through a solid or tissue; **stat′ic** ∼, in botany, the absorption of gaseous bodies through stomata and diffusion through tissues; **Diffusiv′ity**, the ratio of such diffusion.

dig′amous, -us (δὶς, twice; γάμος, marriage), having the two sexes in the same cluster; as in Compositae.

dig′enous (δὶς, two; γένος, offspring), containing both sexes, or produced sexually; **digenet′ic**, sexual; **digenodiff′erent** (+ GENODIFFERENT), when in a hybrid, the genotypes of the two genodifferent gametes involved, differ on two points (Johannsen); **Di′gency**, the condition.

Digestive-cells, of the mycorrhiza of *Neottia*: *cf.* HOST-CELLS; ∼ **Glands**, structures in the lower portion of the interior of the pitcher of *Nepenthes* (Macfarlane); ∼ **Pock′et** (or ∼ **Sac**), an investment of the secondary rootlets, which penetrate the tissues of the primary root till they reach the exterior.

Dig′italine, an alkaloid contained in *Digitalis purpurea*, Linn.

digita′lis (*digitus*, a finger), a finger length; **dig′itate**, *digita′tus*, fingered; a compound leaf in which all the leaflets are borne on the apex of the petiole, as in the Horse-Chestnut; ∼ **pin′nate**, when the leaflets of a digitate leaf are pinnate; **digita′tely**, in a digitate manner; **digitaliform′is** (*forma*, shape), shaped like a finger, as the corolla of the Foxglove; **digitinerv′ius** (*nervis*, a nerve), when the secondary nerves of a leaf diverge from the summit of the main petiole, straight ribbed; **Dig′itus**, a measure of about 3 ins. in length, or 8 cm.

dig′onous (δὶς, two; γωνία, an angle), two-angled, as the stems of some cacti (Crozier); **Digyn′ia** (γυνή, a woman), a Linnean class, with a gynaecium of two pistils; **digyn′ian**, **dig′ynous**, with two separated styles or carpels; **dihap′loid** (+ HAPLOID),

the coupling of two haploid nuclei (Bonnet); **Dihap′lophase** (φάσις, an appearance) the condition described.

Di-hybridisa′tion, or **Dihy′bridism** (δὶ, two; + HYBRID) having two pairs of allelomorphs, showing the proportions of 9:3:3:1.

Dikar′yon, *cf.* Dicaryon.

dilac′erate, dilacera′tus (Lat.), torn asunder, lacerated.

Dilamina′tion (*dis*, apart; *lamina*, a thin plate), the separation of a layer from a petal, like or unlike it in form; chorisis.

dila′ted, *dilata′tus* (Lat., widened), expanding into a blade, as though flattened, like the filaments of *Ornithogalum*; **Dilata′tion**, cell-division in the parenchyma of the wood, the pith, and the medullary rays, causing cleavage of the xylem-mass.

dilep′idus ‡ (δὶς, two; λεπὶς, λεπίδος, scale), consisting of two scales.

dilu′tus (Lat. thinned), of a pale tint.

dimer′ic, dim′erous, -rus (δὶς, two; μερὸς, a share), with two members in each part or circle; **Dimer′istele** (+ MERISTELE), two meristeles or vascular bundles (Brebner); adj. **dimeriste′lic**.

dimid′iate, *dimidia′tus* (Lat., halved), (1) halved, as when half an organ is so much smaller than the other, as to seem wanting; (2) used of the calyptra of Mosses when split on one side by the growth of the theca; (3) in Lichens applied to the perithecial wall when it covers only the upper half of the perithecium; **dimidia′tocordatus**, when the larger half of a dimidiate leaf is cordate.

Diminu′tion (*diminutio*, a decrease), simplification of inflorescence in successive branches (Guillard).

Dimonoe′cism (+ MONOECISM), the condition of two out of three kinds of monoecious flowers, having perfect flowers, and (*a*) male, (*b*) female, or (*c*) neuter flowers also (Knuth).

dimorph′ic, dimorph′ous (δὶς, twice; μορφὴ, shape), occurring under two forms; **Dimorph′ism**, the state of presenting two forms, as long or

short-styled flowers in the same
species.
dimo'tus (Lat., separated), somewhat
remote from.
dineur'oid (εἶδος, resemblance), like
the fossil genus *Dineuron*.
Di'odange (+DIODE, ἀγγεῖον, a vessel),
a group of diodes surrounded by one
or more layers of sterile cells (Van
Tieghem) ; **Diodang'ium** (δίοδος, a
passage ; ἀγγεῖον, a vessel), Van
Tieghem's term for a sporangium in
Vascular Cryptogams and Bryophytes ; **Di'ode,** Van Tieghem's term
for a reproductive body peculiar to
vascular plants which develops into
a rudimentary body or prothallium,
the transition between the rudimentary and adult stages ; *cf.*
ISODIODY, HETERODIODY ; **Di'odo-
gone** (γονή, offspring), Van Tieghem's
term for a sporangium which produces diodes in Phanerogams, the
embryo sac and pollen sac ; **Di'odo-
phytes** (φυτόν, a plant), vascular
plants (Van Tieghem).
Dioe'cia (δίς, two ; οἶκος, a house), a
Linnean class of plants with unisexual flowers ; **dioec'ian, dioec'ious,**
unisexual, the male and female
elements in different individuals ;
dioec'io-dimorph'ous, heterogonous ;
dioec'io-polyg'amous, when some
individuals bear unisexual flowers,
and others hermaphrodite ones ;
Dioec'ism, the condition of being
dioecious ; **dioi'cous,** a spelling used
by bryologists for DIOECIOUS, the
male and female organs on separate
plants.
dioph'anus = DIAPHANOUS.
Di'osmose, *Diosmo'sis* (διά, through ;
ὠσμός, a pushing), the transfusion
of liquid through membrane.
dipet'alous, *-us* (δίς, two ; πέταλον,
a flower-leaf), having two petals ;
diphyll'ous, *-us* (φύλλον, a leaf),
having two leaves ; **dipho'tic** (φῶς,
φωτός, light), two surfaces unequally
lighted ; **Dipho'rophyll** (φύλλον, a
leaf), a leaf differentiated into palisade and spongy tissue from unequal
illumination (Clements) ; **diplanet'ic**

(πλάνος, roaming), relating to D
PLANETISM ; **Diplan'etism,** double
swarming ; in certain genera allie
to *Saprolegnia* the zoospores escap
from their sporangium destitute (
cilia, come to rest in a cluster eac
forming a cell-wall, and after som
hours the protoplasmic contents (
each spore escapes, acquires cilia an
active movement ; **Diplecolo'bea**
(πλέκω, I fold ; λοβός, a lobe),
sub-order of Cruciferae, the incurve
cotyledons being twice folded trans
versely ; **Dipleurogen'esis** (πλευρά
the side ; γένεσις, beginning), tern
used by L. H. Bailey for Bilaterality
as the type of animals ; *cf.* CENTRO
GENESIS.
diplo (διπλόος, twofold), in compositio
= duplo ; **Diplobacill'us** (+ BACIL-
LUS), bacilli which are composed
of two cells or adhere in pairs ;
Diplobacte'ria = DIPLOBACILLUS ;
diplocaulesc'ens (*caulescens*, stem-
producing), having axes of the
second order ; **diplochlamyd'eous**
(χλαμύς, a cloak)=DICHLAMYDEOUS,
having a double perianth ; **Diplo-
coc'cus** (+ COCCUS), a coupled
spherule or result of the conjugation
of two cells ; **Dip'locyte** (κύτος, a
hollow vessel), a somatic cell having
the full number of chromosomes
(Benson) ; adj. **diplocyt'ic.**
Dip'loë (διπλόη, doubling), Link's term
for MESOPHYLL.
dip'loid (διπλόος, twofold), applied to
the state of the 2x Generation, the
chromosomes being doubly as many
as in the HAPLOID generation ;
dip'loid Generation, the Sporophyte (Strasburger) ; **Diplogam'ete**
(διπλόος, twofold ; + GAMETE) in
Ascomycetes the double gametes produced in the same cell (Dangeard) ;
Diplogen'esis (γένεσις, a beginning),
doubling of parts normally single ;
Dip'lonasty (ναστός, pressed close),
when organs grow faster on the upper and the under surfaces than on
the sides ; **Diploperisto'mi** (+PERI-
STOMA), with double peristome, applied to Mosses ; **Dip'lophase** (φαίνω,

114

I appear), Vuillemin's term for the diploid generation ; **Dip′lophyll** (φύλλον, a leaf), a leaf having palisade tissue on both surfaces (Clements) ; **diplosporan′giate**, an error for AMBISPORANGIATE ; **Dip′lospore** (+ SPORE), Dangeard's term for TELEUTOSPORE; **diploste′monous** (στήμων, a stamen), with stamens in two whorls, those of the outer whorl alternating with the petals, the inner whorl alternating with the last ; **Diploste′mony**, stamens as just described ; **diplos′tic**, Van Tieghem's term for rootlets when the mother-root has only two xylem bundles ; **Diploteg′ia**, -gis, -gium (τέγος, a covering), a capsule or other dry fruit, invested with an adnate calyx ; an inferior capsule ; **dip′lotene** (ταίνια, a ribbon), the synaptic stage of the nucleus in which the thread is double ; **diplos′tichous** (στίχος, a row), in two series or rows ; **diploxyl′ic** (ξύλον, wood), (1) used of vascular bundles in which the centrifugal part of the wood is secondary ; (2) having two or more vascular bundles in the leaf, e. g. *Pinus longifolia*, Roxb.; **diplox′yloid**, resembling the genus *Diploxylon* (Williamson) ; **diplox′ylous** = DIPLOXYLIC.

Dip′terid (Diptera = flies), or Fly Flowers, chiefly visited by dipterous flies, as *Ruta*, and *Parnassia*.

Dip′tero-cecid′ia (δìs, two ; πτερὸν, a wing ; κηκìs, a gall), galls produced by dipterous flies ; **dip′terous**, -us, two-winged, having two wing-like processes ; **dipyre′nus** (πυρὴν, fruit-stone), containing two stones.

Direct′-Metamorph′osis, the same as PROGRESSIVE METAMORPHOSIS ; ~ **Superposit′ion**, the situation of accessory buds in an axil above the leading bud or that first formed (Crozier); **direc′te-veno′sus**, a feather-veined leaf, where secondary ribs (primary veins) pass direct from mid-rib to margin, DIGITINERVIUS ; **direct′ing Leu′cite**, =TINOLEUCITE ; **Direc′tion Cells**, ~ **Corpus′cles**, syn-

onyms of POLAR CELLS ; **direct′ive Spheres**, = ATTRACTIVE SPHERES ; **Directiv′ity** (*directus*, made straight), the controlling effect of the vital functions (Sir A. H. Church).

Direm′ption, *Direm′ptio* (Lat., a separation), the occasional separation, or displacement of leaves.

dirin′ean, **diri′nold**, resembling the genus *Dirina*.

disappear′ing, branching in extreme.

disartic′ulate (*dis*, apart ; *articulus*, a joint), to separate at a joint, as the leaves in autumn.

Disassimila′tion, the breaking down, the katabolism of plants.

Disc, or **Disk** (*disc′us*, a quoit), (1) development of the torus within the calyx or within the corolla and stamens ; (2) the central part of a capitulum in Compositae as opposed to the Ray ; (3) the face of any organ, in contradistinction to the margin ; (4) certain markings in cell-walls, of circular outline ; bordered pits ; (5) the valves of diatoms when circular ; (6) the base of a pollinium ; (7) the expanded base of the style in Umbelliferae ; (8) in a bulb, the solid base of the stem, around which the scales are arranged ; **adhe′sive ~**, modified tendrils, as in *Vitis heterophylla*, Thunb., *Ercilla*, etc. ; **carpell′ary ~**, expansion of strobilus of fossil cycads bearing ovules (Wieland) ; **stam′inate ~**, the surface bearing the staminate organs in fossil Cycads (Wieland).

disc′al, word used by J. Smith to express " on the surface of the frond, superficial " ; **Dis′cals**, Bessey's proposed abbreviation of Disciflorae, a series of polypetalous Phanerogams.

Discentra′tion (*dis*, apart ; *centrum*, centre), used by C. F. Schimper for (*a*) fasciation of the axis, and (*b*) multiple of a leaf-organ (Penzig).

Dischis′ma (δìs, two ; σχίσμα, separation), the fruit of *Platystemon*, which divides into longitudinal carpels, each of which again divides transversely.

dis′cifer (Lat.), **discife′rous** (*fero*, I

bear), disc-bearing, as the wood of conifers ; **dis'ciform**, *disciform'is* (*forma*, shape), flat and circular, orbicular ; **discig'erous** (*gero*, I bear), disc-bearing ; ~ **Frus'tules**, in Diatoms those having valves more or less circular in outline.

Dis'cocarp (δίσκος, a quoit ; καρπὸς, fruit), an ascocarp in which the hymenium lies exposed while the asci are maturing ; an apothecium ; **Discocarp'ium**, a collection of fruits within a hollow receptacle, as in many Rosaceae ; **disc'oid**, *discoi'deus* (εἶδος, like), with a round thickened lamina, and rounded margins ; ~ **Flow'ers**, those belonging to the disk, usually tubular florets ; ~ **Glands**, stalked glands of Urticaceae with round head of a single layer of cells ; ~ **Mark'ing**, see Disc, (5) **disco'idal**, *discoida'lis*, orbicular ; **Discoli'chenes** (+Lichenes), Wainio's term for **Discomyce'tes**, Fungi with open hymenium, as *Peziza*.

dis'color (Lat. of different colours), used when the two surfaces of a leaf are unlike in colour.

discontin'uous Varia'tion, forms arising at a single step with complete and definite characters of other species.

Discoplank'ton (δίσκος, a quoit, + Plankton), floating diatoms of discoid forms, chiefly of *Coscinodiscus*; **Discopod'ium** (ποῦς, ποδος, a foot), a disc-shaped floral receptacle ; **disc'-ous**, the same as discoid (Crozier).

discrete', *discre'tus* (Lat., parted), separate, not coalescent.

Disc'ulus (dim. of Discus), the adventitious lobule of Hepaticae (Spruce).

Disc'us (Lat. from δίσκος), (1) see Disc ; (2) a flat stroma through which the ostioles of fungi protrude, as in *Valsa*.

disep'alous, *-us* (δὶς, two, + Sepalum), of two sepals.

dishar'mon'ic, used of a flora showing gaps in series and with many monotypic genera.

Disjunc'tion (*disjunctio*, separation), see Dialysis, Fission, Solution, varying degrees of separation in organs ; **Disjunc'tor**, Woronin's

term for a spindle-shaped cellulose connection between the gonidia in certain Fungi ; the developed septum as in *Sclerotinia Vaccinii*, Woron.

disjunc'tive (*disjunctivus*, disjoined **Symbio'sis**, applied by Frank to those cases in which the symbiont do not form an associated organism but are temporarily associated, as in the case of insects and plants.

Disk, see Disc. Disk is the more usual spelling in the case of Compositae, as ~ **Flor'ets**, ~ **Flow'ers**, those occurring on the central portion of the capitulum of compositae, not of the ray (or margin) ~ **shaped** = Discoid.

Disloca'tion (*dis*, apart ; *locus*, a place = Displacement ; **Disloca'tor Cell**, in Gymnosperms, a wall-cell derived from the antheridial mother-cell which sets loose the spermatocyte from its attachment (Goebel); **disoperc'ulate** (*operculum*), a lid), deprived of the cover or lid.

disperm'ous (δὶς, double ; σπέρμα, a seed), two seeded.

Disper'sal, **Dispers'ion** (*dispersus*, scattered), the various ways by which seeds are scattered, by wind, birds, adhesion to animals, etc. ; in Ger. Verbreitungsmittel.

Dispi'rem (δὶς, two, + Spirem) a stage in nuclear division, having two chromatic groups, the achromatic filaments being constricted in the middle, which follows the Dyaster (Rosen).

dispi'rous (δὶς, double ; σπεῖρα, a coil), Spruce's term for the elaters of Hepaticae which have double spirals.

Displa'cement, the abnormal situation of an organ ; diremption.

Disposit'io (Lat , arrangement), the manner in which parts are arranged, as " disp. ⅜ " indicates that phyllotactic system.

dissect'ed, *dissect'us* (Lat., cut up), deeply divided, or cut into many segments.

Dissemina'tion (*disseminatio*, sowing), the contrivances by which ripe seeds are shed by the parent plant ;

(in Ger. Aussaet) ; **Dissem'inule**, a plant in the state of being transported ; a seed fruit modified for migration (Clements).

Dissep'iment, *Dissepiment'um* (Lat., a partition), a partition in an ovary or pericarp, caused by the adhesion of the sides of carpellary leaves ; **spu'rious ~**, a partition not having that origin.

dissil'ient, *dissil'iens* (Lat., flying apart), bursting asunder.

dissim'ilar (*dissimilis*, unlike), when similar organs assume different forms in the same individual, as the anthers of *Cassia*.

Dissocia'tion (*dissociatio*, separation), observed in the fibrovascular system of the Lentibularieae, the wood and bast being mutually independent.

Dis'sophyte (δισσὸς, two-fold ; φυτὸν, a plant), a plant with xerophytic leaves and stems, and mesophytic roots (Clements).

dist'ad = **dis'tal** (*disto*, I stand apart), remote from the place of attachment ; the converse of proximal ; **dist'ant**, *distans*, when similar parts are not closely aggregated, in opposition to approximate.

Disteleol'ogy, defined by Haeckel as purposelessness ; for botanic usage, see DYSTELEOLOGY.

Disten'sion (*distensus*, stretched out), swollen or bulging.

dist'ichous, *-us* (δίστιχος, of two rows), disposed in two vertical ranks, as the florets in many grasses.

dist'inct, *distinct'us* (Lat., separate), separate from, not united.

distrac'tile *distracti'lis* (*distractus*, pulled two ways), borne widely apart, as the anther-lobes in *Salvia*.

Dis'trict, applied as the equivalent of the Ger. Bezirk ; a small region or tract of country.

distromat'ic (δὶs, two, + STROMA), applied to those species of *Porphyra* with the thallus in two layers ; *cf.* MONOSTROMATIC ; **Dis'trophy** (τροφὴ, nourishment), employed for Re for disparity in size of homologous

organs ; **dithe'cal** (θήκη, a case), **dithe'cous**, *dithe'cus*, of two cells, as most anthers ; **Ditopog'amy** (τόπος, place ; γάμος, marriage), Ludwig's term for HETEROSTYLY ; **ditrichot'omous** (τριχῆ, threefold ; τόμη, a cutting), doubly or trebly divided ; **di'triploid** (+ TRIPLOID), the fusion of two triploid nuclei into one (Němec.).

diur'nal, *diur'nus* (Lat., daily), occurring in the day-time, sometimes used for ephemeral ; **~ Sleep**, = PARAHELIOTROPISM.

divar'icate, *divarica'tus* (Lat., spread asunder), extremely divergent.

Diverg'ence (*divergium*, turning in different directions), used when parts gradually separate as they lengthen, as the follicles in *Asclepias* ; **Angle of ~**, the angle between succeeding organs in the same spiral or whorl ; **diver'gent**, *-ens*, **diverg'ing**, separating by degrees) ; **diverginer'vius** (*nervus*, a nerve), with radiating main nerves.

diversiflor'ous, *-rus* (*diversus*, contrary ; *flos*, *floris*, a flower), with flowers of more than one kind ; **diver'sus**, (1) variable (de Candolle) ; (2) different or separate.

Divertic'ulum (Lat., a byeway), in Algae, a protoplasmic protrusion, communicating with the fused procarp cells and the placenta, as in *Gracilaria confervoides*, Grev.

divi'ded, *divi'sus* (parted asunder), used where lobing or segmentation extends to the base ; **divisu'ral** (line), the line down the teeth of the peristome of a Moss by which the teeth split.

Dix'eny (δὶs, two ; ξένos, a host), where an autoecious parasite may infest two species, but does not need a change of host to ensure its development (De Bary) ; **dixyl'ic** (ξύλον, wood), having the xylem in two masses (Brebner).

-doch'e (δοχὴ, succession), used by Clements for " succession."

Dodecagyn'ia (δώδεκα, twelve ; γυνὴ, woman), a Linnean order of plants with twelve pistils ; **dodecag'ynous,** *-nus,* possessing twelve pistils or distinct carpels ; **dodecame'rous,** *-rus* ($\mu\epsilon\rho\grave{o}s$, a share), in twelve parts, as in a cycle ; **dodecan'der,** dodecandrous ; **Dodecan'dria** ($\grave{a}\nu\grave{\eta}\rho$, $\grave{a}\nu\delta\rho\grave{o}s$, a man), a Linnean class of plants with twelve stamens ; **dodecan'drian, dodecan'-drous,** *-drus,* of twelve stamens, normally (occasionally extended to nineteen) ; **dodecapet'alous** ($\pi\acute{\epsilon}\tau\alpha\lambda o\nu$, a flower-leaf), with twelve petals, or less than twenty ; **dodecari'nus** ($\check{a}\rho\rho\eta\nu$, male), Necker's equivalent for dodecandrous.

Do'drans (Lat., a span), a full span, from thumb tip to extremity of the little finger, about nine inches, or 23 cm. ; **dodranta'lis,** a span long.

dolabra'tus (Lat.), axed, or axe-shaped ; **dolab'riform,** *dolabriform'is* (forma, shaped), hatchet-shaped.

doleiform'is (*dolea,* casks ; *forma,* shape), barrel-shaped.

dolia'rius, dolia'tus (Lat.), circinate.

Dolichone'ma ($\delta o\lambda\acute{\iota}\chi os$, long ; $\nu\hat{\eta}\mu\alpha$, a thread), the stage in nuclear division which immediately precedes synapsis in the formation of the reproductive cells ; **Dolicho'sis,** retardation of growth in length (Czapek) ; **dolichosty'lous** (+ STYLE), in dimorphic or trimorphic species applied to the long-styled form ; **Dolicho'tmema** ($\tau\mu\hat{\eta}\mu\alpha$, free), a filiform cell which ruptures and sets free the gemma of a Moss (Correns).

Doma'tia ($\delta\omega\mu\acute{a}\tau\iota o\nu$, a little house), modified projections for shelter-parasites (Tubeuf).

domestica'ted, thriving under cultivation (Crozier).

dom'inant (*dominans,* prevailing, ruling), (1) in hybrids, the prevalent character, in opposition to RECESSIVE ; (2) chief constituent of a plant-association ; (3) ruling, as the preponderant races and plants at a given period.

Domin'ion, state, condition ; recently used as the equivalent of Goebel's " Staat," as Cell- ~, **Energid-** ~.

Dom'itoform (*domitus,* tamed ; *forma,*

form), a cultivated form, the original being unknown or dissimilar (Kuntze).

dor'mant (*dormiens,* sleeping), applied to parts which are not in active life, as ~ **Buds,** ~ **Eyes,** potential buds which normally do not shoot, until excited to growth by special circumstances ; ~ **State,** the condition of a plant during the winter, or when inactive from any reason.

dor'sal, *dorsa'lis* (*dorsum,* the back), relating to the back, or attached thereto ; the surface turned away from the axis, which in the case of a leaf is the lower surface (NOTE.— This is reversed by some authors) ; ~ **Su'ture,** the suture of a follicle or legume which is exterior to the axis ; the midrib of a carpel ; **dorsicum'bent** (*cumbens,* lying down) = SUPINE (Crozier) ; **dorsif'erous** (*fero,* I bear), borne on the back, as the sori on most Ferns ; **dor'sifixed, dorsifix'us** (*fixus,* fast), fixed on the back or by the back ; **Dorsinas'ty** (*vao\sigma\tau\grave{o}s$, pressed) = EPINASTY ; **dorsivent'ral** (*venter,* the belly), used of an organ which has dorsal and ventral surfaces, as a leaf ; **Dorsiventral'ity,** the condition of possessing upper and lower faces of an organ ; **Dor'sum** (Lat.), (1) the back, or parts of the flower which face the outside ; (2) in Diatoms, in forms which are more or less lunately curved, the convex side of the girdle.

Dots (1) receptacles of oil in the leaves ; (2) pits in the cell-wall ; **dotted,** punctured with dots ; ~ **Ducts,** vessels with pit-like markings on the walls ; ~ **Tis'sue** = BOTHRENCHYMA.

dothidia'ceous, like the genus *Dothidia.*

doub'le, *du'plex* (1) twice ; (2) used of flowers when the petals are monstrously increased at the expense of other organs, especially the stamens ; ~ **bear'ing,** producing a crop twice in the same season ; ~ **Fert'iliza-tion,** in Angiosperms, when one male cell from the pollen-tube fuses with the egg nucleus, the other with the upper polar nucleus, and this last with the lower polar nucleus ; also termed TRIPLE FUSION ; ~ **Fructifica'tion**, dimorphism in fruit, applied to certain Algae ; ~ **Nee'dle**, in *Sciadopitys*, a dwarf branch without bud-scales, the two leaves being fused together at the edges into one needle ; ~ **Recip'rocal Cross**, the offspring of two reciprocal crosses, as $(b \times m) \times (m \times b)$ resulting in the usual suppressing of the characters of the middle parent, m : ~ **Rosette'**, = DYASTER ; **Doub'ling**, the same as CHORISIS ; **doub'ly**, something repeated, as ~ **toothed**, the teeth themselves being toothed.

Down (1) soft pubescence ; (2) the pappus of such plants as thistles ; **down'y**, pubescent, with fine soft hairs.

Dra'canth (*draganthum*, Mid. Lat.), a synonym of Gum Tragacanth.

Draco'nine, a red resinous substance from "Dragon's Blood," produced by *Daemonorops Draco,* Blume, and *Dracaena Draco*, Linn.

Draining-point, of a leaf ; *cf.* DRIP-POINT.

drawn, applied to attenuated shoots, diminished and etiolated, often increased in length.

drep'aniform (δρέπανον), a sickle ; *forma*, shape), falcate (Crozier) ; **Drepa'nium**, a sickle-shaped cyme ; **drepanoclad'ous** (κλάδος, a branch), having sickle-shaped branches (Russow).

Dri'mad (δριμύς, pungent, + AD), a plant of an alkaline formation ; **Drimi'um**, an alkali plain or salt basin formation ; **drimyph'ilus** (φιλέω, I love), salt-loving, halophilous ; **Drimyphy'ta** (φυτόν, a plant), salt-plants (Clements).

Dri'odad (δρίος, a thicket, + AD), a plant of a dry thicket ; **Driodi'um**, a dry thicket formation (Clements).

Drip-point, **Drip-tip**, the acuminate apex of a leaf, from whose point water soon drips ; Germ. Träufelspitze.

Dromot'ropism (δρόμος, a course ; τροπή, a turning), the irritability of climbing plants which results in their spiral growth (MacMillan) ; adj. **dromotrop'ic**.

droop'ing, inclining downwards, cernuous, but not quite pendent.

Drop-dis'ease, a disease of lettuce ascribed to *Botrytis vulgaris* and *Sclerotinia Libertiana*.

Drop'per, the young bulb of a tulip, not of flowering size.

Drop'ping-point = DRIP-POINT.

Drought (pr. drowt), want of rain hindering plant-growth ; **phys'ical** ~, when the soil contains very little free water ; **physiolog'ical** ~, when the soil contains a considerable amount of water, which, by reason of the character of the soil or weak osmotic force of the roots, cannot be used by the plant (Warming).

drupa'ceous(*drupa*,an olive,+ACEOUS), resembling a DRUPE, possessing its character, or producing similar fruit ; **Drupe**, *Dru'pa*, a stone-fruit such as a plum ; the pericarp fleshy or leathery, containing a stone with a kernel ; **false** ~, a nut-like fruit where the lower persistent part of the perianth becomes fleshy, as in *Neea ;* **spu'rious** ~, any fleshy body enclosing a stone ; **Dru'pel**, **Dru'**-**pelet**, *Drupe'ola*, a diminutive drupe, the fruit of the Blackberry is an aggregation of these ; **Drupe'tum**, a cluster of drupes ; **Dru'pose**, a constituent of the stone-cells of the flesh of pears (Cross and Bevan).

dru'sy, a mineralogical term used by G. E. Smith to express the appearance of the stigma of *Orobanche caryophyllea ;* pruinose.

Dry'ads, pl. (δρυάς, a wood-nymph), applied to shade-plants.

Dry-rot, destruction of timber in houses by *Merulius lacrymans*, Fr.

du'bious, *du'bius* (Lat.), doubtful, used for plants whose structure or affinities are uncertain.

Du'ces, pl. (*dux, ducis*, a leader), Lorentz's name for character cells in Mosses ; = DEUTER CELLS.

Duct, *Duct'us* (Lat., led, conducted), an elongated cell or tubular vessel, especially occurring in the fibrovascular portions of plants ; **an'nular** ~, the secondary thickenings occurring more or less in the form of rings ; **closed** ~, long cells, not continuous, but with the intervening septa remaining ; **dott'ted** ~, = BOTHRENCHYMA ; **intercell'ular** ~, passages between the cells ; **retic'ulated** ~, where the markings seem to form a network ; **scalar'iform** ~ with ladder-like markings as in Ferns.

dul'cis (Lat.), sweet. extended to any kind of taste which is not acrid ; **Dul'cite,** a crystalline substance from *Melampyrum,* also found in Madagascar Manna.

du'metose, *dumeto'sus* (*dumetum,* a thicket), bushy, relating to bushes ; **Dume'tum,** a thicket.

dumose' (*dumo'sus,* bushy), full of bushes, of shrubby aspect ; **Du'mus** (Lat.), a bush.

Dune, undulating banks of blown sand, with characteristic vegetation ; *cf.* THINIUM.

duode'ni (Lat.), by twelves, growing by twelves.

du'plex (Lat.), double ; **du'plicate,** *duplica'tus,* double or folded, twin ; ~ **Par'asitism,** self-parasitism, as in the case of mistletoe upon mistletoe ; **Duplica'tion,** doubling, CHORISIS ; **duplica'to-crena'tus,** doubly-crenate ; ~ **denta'tus,** doubly-toothed ; ~ **pinna'tus,** bipinnate ; ~ **serra'tus,** doubly-serrate ; ~ **terna'tus,** biternate ; **duplo** = twice as many ; in Greek compounds it is **diplo.**

Dura'men (Lat., a hardened vine branch), the heartwood of an exogenous stem, which has become hardened by deposits.

Durifrutice'ta (*durus,* hard ; *fruticetum,* a thicket), sclerophyllous scrub formations ; **Duriligno'sa** (*lignosus,* woody), trees and shrubs which have sclerophyllous leaves or green axes which serve as leaves ; **Duripra'ta** (*pratum,* a meadow), where the dominant species are strengthened

by mechanical tissue, largely consisting of grasses and sedges ; **Durisil'vae** (*silva,* a wood), sclerophyllous forest formations, as of *Quercus Ilex* in the Mediterranean region and *Eucalyptus* in Australia.

Dust, Blair's word for Pollen ; **dust'y,** covered with granulations resembling dust ; or powdered, farinose.

dwarf, of small size or height compared with its allies ; ~ **Male,** a short-lived filament of a few cells in Oedogoniaceae, the upper cells being antheridia.

Dy'ad (δυὰς, δυάδος, two), (1) a subdivision of a TETRAD by mitosis, again dividing into single elements (Calkins) ; (2) a bivalent chromosome.

Dyas'ter (δύο, double ; ἀστήρ, a star), the stage of nuclear division when the rays of linin split longitudinally and two stars are formed which move apart, ending with the formation of daughter-skeins ; **dyblas'tus** (βλαστός, a bud), two-celled, applied to Lichen spores ; **Dycle'sium,** or **Dyclo'sium,** see DICLESIUM.

dynam'ic (δύναμις, power), applied to tissue which is capable of strongly swelling on one side ; ~ **Cell,** any thick-walled prosenchymatous element, having its molecules or micellae in transverse rings, which undergoes marked longitudinal contraction in water (Eichholz) ; **Dynam'ia,** used by Linnaeus to express the degree of development of stamens, as Didynamia and Tetradynamia, applied to flowers where respectively two and four stamens have longer filaments than the remaining two ; **dy'namo-stat'ic** (στάσις, a standing) **El'ements,** hygroscopic motor-cells (Eichholz) ; **Dyne,** the unit of force expressed by the weight of one gramme moving one centimetre in one second of time (Errera) [= CGS].

dyploste'monous = DIPLOSTEMONOUS.

Dyploteg'ia = DIPLOTEGIA.

dysanth'ic (ἄνθος, a flower), fertilization by the pollen from a different plant (K. Pearson).

dysgeog′enous (δυσ-, *i. e.* bad ; γῆ, the earth ; γεννάω, I bring forth), employed by Thurmann for those plants growing on soils which do not readily yield detritus ; hard rocks generally, such as granite ; **dyspho′tic. dysphotis′tic** (φῶς, φωτὸς, light), applied by A. F. W. Schimper to the deeper situated BENTHOS ; ∼ **Plants**, are the se which are adapted to a minimum of light ; **dysphototrop′ic** (τροπὴ, a turning), used of leaves adapted to a certain amount of light, but not too intense, as *Lactuca Scariola ;* **Dysteleol′ogy** (τέλος, completion ; λόγος, discourse), frustration of function ; as where an insect obtains honey by puncturing a nectary instead of by the floral opening ; adj., **dysteleolog′ic,** ∼ **cal** ; **Dysteleol′ogist,** an agent which evades the teleologic end, as a bee which obtains honey by means which do not conduce to fertilization ; **dyst′ropous** (τροπὴ, a turning), injurious insect-visiting, so far as the flowers are concerned ; **Dys′tropy,** the condition described.

Dyss′ophytes, *-ae* (δισσὸς, two-fold ; φυτὸν, a plant). Clements's term for plants which are sometimes hydrophytes and sometimes aerophytes ; the author gives the derivation as from " δυσσὸς, double."

e, ex, in Latin compounds, privative, as ecostate, without ribs.

Ear, the spike of corn ; **Ear-coc′kles** of wheat, a disease due to eelworms, *Tylenchus tritici ;* **ear-formed** (Loudon), **eared,** auriculate.

ebe′neous, black as ebony, the heartwood of *Diospyros Ebenum*, Koen.

ebeta′tus = HEBETATUS.

ebori′nus (*eboreus*, made of ivory), ivory-like, or ivory-white.

ebrac′teate, *ebractea′tus* (*e*, priv. ; *bractea,* a biact), without bracts ; **ebrac′teolate,** *ebracteola′tus,* destitute of bracteoles.

eburn′eous, *-eus* (Lat., of ivory), ivory white, white more or less tinged with yellow.

E′cad (οῖκος, a house ; + AD), a habitat form due to origin by adaptation (Clements).

ecalc′arate, *ecalcara′tus* (*e*, priv. ; *calcar,* a spur), spurless ; **ecau′dal** (*cauda*,. a tail), without a tail or similar appendage.

Ecballi′um, or **Ecballi′on** (ἐκβάλλω, I throw out), succession of plants after timber felling (Clements).

Ecblaste′sis (ἐκ, out of ; βλάστη, growth), the appearance of buds within a flower, prolification of the inflorescence.

eccen′tric = EXCENTRIC.

Ec′dysis (ἔκδυσις, a shifting out), exuviation or the physiological mechanism by which Dinoflagellata rid themselves of their carapace (Kofoid).

Ece′sis, or **Oece′sis** (οἴκησις, the act of dwelling), the germination and establishment of invaders.

Ech′ard (ἔχω, I withhold), the non-available water of the soil (Clements).

Echi′nops-fluorescine, Echinops′ein, and **Echinops′ine,** alkaloids found in *Echinops Ritro* (Greshoff).

echlor′ophyllose (*e*, priv.; + CHLOROPHYLL), without chlorophyll ; scarious ; **ech′inate,** *echina′tus* (Lat., prickly), beset with prickles ; **echin′ulate,** *echinulat′us,* having diminutive prickles.

Ech′ma, pl. **Ech′mata** (ἔχμα, a support), the hardened hook-shaped funicle in most Acanthaceae which supports the seed ; *cf.* RETINACULUM (3).

Ecid′ium (Crozier) = AECIDIUM.

ecil′iate (+ CILIUM), without cilia.

Ecogen′esis (οῖκος, a house ; + GENESIS), the origin of ecologic factors ; **ecolog′ic Opt′imum,** when the surroundings offer the most favourable conditions for the life of a given plant ; **Ecol′ogism** = ECOLOGY ; **Ecol′ogist,** or **Oecol′ogist,** a student of the life of the plant in relation to its surroundings ; **Ecol′ogy** (λόγος, a discourse), or **Oecol′ogy,** the study of plant-life in relation to environment ; adj. **ecolog′ical, oecolog′ical ;**

physiograph'ic Ecol'ogy, the distribution of plants according to climate and soil ; **econom'ic** Botany (νομικὸs, resting on laws), applied botany, that branch which takes note of technical application of plants and plant-products ; ~ **Coeffic'ient**, the weight produced by a consumption of 100 parts of the nutrient material (Pfeffer).

Ecopar'asite, or **Oecopar'asite** (οἶκοs, a house ; + PARASITE), a specialized form of a parasitic fungus when growing on one or more host-species to which it is confined under normal circumstances ; cf. XENOPARASITE ; **Ecopar'asitism**, or **Oecopar'asitism**, is the condition in question (Salmon).

ecort'icate, *ecortica'tus* (*e*, priv. ; *cortex*, bark), destitute of bark, or bark-like covering ; **ecos'tate**, *ecosta'tus* (*costa*, a rib), without ribs, nerveless ; **ecrusta'ceous** (*crusta*, rind, + aceous), destitute of thallus, applied to Lichens.

E'cotone (οἶκοs, a house ; τόνος, stress), the stress line or boundaries between plant associations (Clements) ; also spelled **Oe'cotone**.

Ectauxe'sis (ἐκτὸs, outside ; αὔξησιs, growth), the growth of an organ outwards through the substance of the parent shoot (Weisse) ; **ectocy'- clic** (κύκλοs, a circle), used of sieve-tubes which are between the epidermis and the ring of sclerogen (Fischer) ; **Ectogen'esis** (γένεσιs, a beginning), variation induced by external conditions ; **ectogen'ic** (γένος, offspring), capable of living outside of a given body, as certain bacilli ; **Ectopar'asite** (+ PARASITE), a parasite which remains on the exterior of its host, only sending its haustoria within ; opposed to ENDO-PARASITE ; **Ectopep'tase** (πεπτὸs, cooked), an enzyme which peptonizes the more complex of the proteins, and occurring in the excretions of plants, such as the pitcher-liquid of *Nepenthes* (Vines) ; **ectophloeo'des** (φλοιὸs, bark), living on the surface or bark of other plants as some Lichens ; **ectophlo'ic**, the condition of stems when the internal phloem is wanting; cf. AMPHIPHLOIC (Jeffrey); **Ect'oplasm** (πλάσμα, moulded), a delicate, firm, superficial layer of the cytoplasm or general protoplasm of the cell, hyaloplasm.

Ec'topy (ἐκτόπιος, displaced), the abnormal position of an organ.

Ect'ospore (ἐκτὸs, outside ; σπορὰ, seed), a synonym of BASIDIOSPORE ; **Ectospor'ium**, the outer layer of a spore in bacteria (Mühlschegel) ; **ectos'porous**, possessing exogenously formed spores ; **ectothe'cal** (θήκη, a case), in Ascomycetes used for naked-spored ; **ectotroph'ic** (τροφὴ, nourishment), when a fungus clothes a root only externally ; **ectrotrop'ic** (τρόπος, direction), (1) outward curvature ; (2) the course of the pollen-tube in acrogamic fertilization, by the micropyle to the embryo-sac (Pirotta and Longo).

ecy'phellate (*e*, priv. + CYPHELLA), used of Lichens destitute of cyphellae.

edaph'ic (ἔδαφος, the ground), A. F. W. Schimper's term for the influence of the soil on the plants growing upon it ; **Edaph'ophytes** (φυτὸν, a plant), plants which root in the earth, with assimilation organs in the air above it ; normal plants, or EUPHYTES (Schröter).

edent'ate, *edenta'tus* (*dens, dentis*, a tooth), without teeth ; **edent'ulus** (Lat.), toothless.

Ed'estin (ἐδεστὸs, eatable), a globulin constituent of wheat flour, forming about six to seven per cent.

Edge, the margin or outline, as of a leaf ; **edged**, when a patch of colour is rimmed round by another tint.

Edob'oles, *-ae*, pl. (οἶδος, a swelling, βολὴ, a throw), distribution by turgescence of fruits or sporangia (Clements).

Eel-trap Hairs, hairs found in structures which detain insect visitors, as in *Sarracenia* and *Aristolochia Clematitis* (Haberlandt).

effete′, *effe′tus*, *effoe′tus* (Lat., exhausted), past bearing, functionless from age.

effig′urate, *effigura′tus* (*figura*, a figure), (1) when an organ is completed by the full development of its subordinate parts ; (2) of definite outline, opposed to EFFUSE ; **Effigura′tions**, outgrowths of the receptacle or torus, as in *Passiflora*, *Capparis*, etc.

Efflores′ence, *Efflorescen′tia* (*effloresco*, I blossom forth), the season of flowering, anthesis.

Effolia′tion (Lindley) = EXFOLIATION.

effuse, *effu′sus* (Lat., poured out), patulous, expanded ; **Effu′sio**, an expansion ; **Effu′sion**, used by Wiesner for an intermingling of gases under different pressures, the current acting through openings in membranes.

eflagellif′erous (*e*, priv. + FLAGELLUM, *fero*, I bear), destitute of flagella ; **efo′liolate**, *efoliola′tus* (*foliolum*, a small leaf), without leaf-like scales or squamæ ; **efo′liolose** has the same meaning ; **efov′eolate** (*fovea*, a pit), "smooth, without pits or depressions" (Heinig) ;—the form "eforeolate" is a press error ; **eful′crate**, **efulcra′tus** (*fulcrum*, a bed-post), used of buds from which the customary leaf or bract has fallen.

Egg (1), Ovum, ovule ; (2) restricted in meaning as below : ~ **Appara′tus**, the three cells with nuclei at the micropylar end of the embryo sac, two form the synergidæ, and the other forms the oösphere ; ~ **Cell**, the oösphere or gynogamete ; ~ **-sac**, the mesochite and endochite of Fucaceae, the membranes which enclose the egg (Farmer and Williams); ~ **-shaped**, = OVATE ; ~ **Spore** = OÖSPORE.

eglandu′lose, *eglandulo′sus* (*e*, priv., *glandula*, a gland), destitute of glands ; **egran′ulose** (*granula*, a small grain), without granules.

E′gret, Martyn's term for pappus ; Fr. Aigrette.

ehila′tus ‡ (*e*, priv.; + HILUM), imperforate, applied to pollen grains having no perforations.

eis′odal, **eiso′dial** (εἴσοδος, an entry), anterior, as the outer pore of stomates (Tschirch).

Ejacula′tion (*ejaculor*, I shoot forth) = EJECTION.

Ejec′tion (*ejectio*, a casting forth), forcibly throwing out endogenously formed spores from a sporangium.

Elabora′tion (*elaboratio*, persevering labour), used of the changes which take place after the absorption of food material to fit it for the use of the plant.

elaeo′des (ἐλαία, olive), olive colour, brownish green ; **Elaiolen′cites** (λευκὸς, white), Van Tieghem's term for ELAIOPLASTS ; **Elaioplank′ton** (+ PLANKTON), plankton floating by means of fatty matters (Forel) ; **Elai′oplasts** (πλαστὸς, moulded), (1) plastids which are believed to form oil, as leucoplasts form starch ; (2) oil-drops, usually applied to the chromatophores in Diatoms, sometimes free ; they are particularized as LIBROPLASTS, PLACOPLASTS, and SPARSIOPLASTS (Mereschkowsky) ; **Elai′osomes**, pl. (σῶμα, a body), characteristic oily appendages and seeds of myrmecochorous plants, such as arils, crests, etc., offering food-bodies to ants (Sernander) ; **Elai′ospheres** (σφαῖρα, a sphere), bodies in spongy and palisade parenchyma, similar to elaioplasts, probably oil-bodies (Lidforss). The foregoing are also spelled **elaeo-**.

elaphi′nes (ελαφινὴς, a fawn) ; *elaphi′nus* (ἐλαφὸς, a deer), tawny or fulvous.

Elas′tic Lim′it, the extreme load which a vegetable fibre or body can support, without being permanently stretched (Haberlandt).

Ela′ter (ἐλατὴρ, a driver), (1) an elastic spirally twisted filament, occurring amongst the spores in the thecæ of Hepaticæ ; (2) a free capillitium thread in Myxogastres; (3) in *Equisetum*, four clubbed hygroscopic bands attached to the spores, which serve for dispersal.

Elat'erine, the active principle of the fruit of *Elaterium,* Jacq.

Elate'rium (ἐλατήριος, driving away); (1) = COCCUM; (2) the dried juice of the wild cucumber, *Elaterium.*

Elat'erophore (φορέω, I carry), thready organs which bear the elaters in certain Hepaticæ.

ela'tus (Lat., exalted), tall, lofty.

Elcot'ropism (ἕλκω, I drag; τροπή, a turning), compulsory attraction of plants.

Elec'tion (*electio*, a choice), the selection of the fittest, as opposed to the elimination of the unfit.

elec'trinus (ἤλεκτρον, amber), yellowish amber coloured ; **Electrol'ysis** (λύσις, a loosing), analysis by electric force, adj. **electrolyt'ic**; **electrotrop'ic** (τρόπος, direction), actuated by electric force ; **Elect'ropism**, or **Electrot'ropism** (τρόπος, direction), (1) the electric impulse which governs certain plant-functions; (2) the inflection of roots or shoots towards the cathode (Macdougal); **Electro'sis**, reaction from an electrical current (Massart); **Electrotax'is** (τάξις, order), arrangement induced by electric currents, galvanotaxis; **Electrot'onus** (τόνος, stress), a latent period of electric stress (Hoermann); **Elec'tro-vegetom'eter**, an arrangement of insulated wires and points above the plants to be electrified by atmospheric electricity (Berthelon).

Element'ary Or'gans, the constituents of cellular and vascular tissue.

eleutheran'therous (ἐλεύθερος, free, + ANTHER), having the anthers distinct, not united; **eleutheropet'alous** (πέταλον, a flower-leaf), polypetalous, having free petals, choripetalous; **eleutherophyll'ous**, (φύλλον, a leaf), separate leaved ; **eleutherosep'alous** (+ SEPALUM), with distinct sepals; **eleutherotep'alous** (+ TEPAL), having free tepals (Pax).

eleva'ted, applied to a Lichen when raised above the surface of its matrix.

Elf'in-tree ; ~-wood, applied by A. F. W. Schimper, to alpine forest, distorted from mountain climate; Ger., Krummholz.

Elimina'tion (*elimino*, I move out), the destruction of forms from various natural causes (Plate).

Elitric'ulus = ELYTRICULUS.

Ell, a measure variously understood, the English ell being 45 inches, the Flemish ell 54 inches.

Elleb'orin, an acrid resin from *Eranthis hyemalis*, Salisb., formerly considered a species of *Helleborus.*

Ellip'soid (ἔλλειψις, a falling short; εἶδος, like), an elliptic solid; adj. **ellipsoi'dal**, *ellipsoida'lis*; sometimes employed for **ellip'tic, ellip'tical**, *ellip'ticus*, shaped like an ellipse, oblong with regularly rounded ends.

elitt'oral (*e*, from *litoralis* or *littoralis*, pertaining to the shore), employed to denote the coastal region below the sublittoral, and extending as far as the light penetrates (Warming).

eloc'ular, *elocula'ris* (*e*, priv. *loculus*, a cell), unilocular.

elo'dioid (εἶδος, resemblance), like *Elodea ;* applied to a linear leaf (Warming).

Elonga'tion, *Elonga'tio* (*elongo*, I lengthen), remarkable for length in comparison with its breadth ; **elonga'ted** (*elonga'tus*, drawn out in length).

Elu'vium (*eluvio*, a washing away), used by Boulger for sand-blown dunes.

Elyme'tum, an association of *Elymus arenarius.*

Elytric'ulus (ἔλυτρον, a covering), Necker's term for a floret in Compositæ; **ely'triform** *forma*, shape), resembling the wing-case of a beetle (Crozier).

emar'cid, *emar'cidus* (*emarcesco*, I wither), flaccid, withered.

emar'ginate, *emargina'tus* (*emargino*, to deprive of its edge), having a notch cut out, usually at the extremity ; **Emarginatu'ra** (Lat.), the notch at the apex of an emarginate leaf.

Emascula'tion, in plants, the removal

124

of the stamens, before they dehisce, from hermaphrodite flowers previous to artificial hybridization.

embed′ded veins, those surrounded on all sides by assimilatory tissue.

Em′bolus (ἔμβολος, a pump piston), a plug, a process which projects downwards from the upper part of the cavity of the ovary of *Armeria*, and closes the foramen of the ovule.

emboss′ed (dissyl.), umbonate, having a slight central nodule.

embra′cing, clasping by the base, amplectant.

Em′bryo, *Em′bryon* (ἔμβρυον, a foetus), the rudimentary plant formed in a seed or within the archegonium of Cryptogams; ~ **Buds**, "spheroidal solid bodies, of unknown origin, resembling woody nodules formed in the bark of trees, and capable of extending into branches" (Lindley); ~ **Cell** = Oösphere; ~ **-cord**, in *Hydnora*, a single row of flattened cells connecting the embryo with the outer surface of the albumen (Solms-Laubach); — **sec′ondary** ~, = Embryo-sac Tubes; ~ **Nod′ule**, the same as Embryo Buds; ~ **Sac**, the cell in the ovule in which the embryo is formed, also by some termed the macrospore; ~ **Tubes**, tubular upgrowths and compartment walls within which the female nuclei of *Welwitschia* are conducted to the nucellar cone (Pearson); **fixed** ~, a leaf-bud; **Embryoblas′tanon** (βλαστός, a bud), Miquel's term for the suspensor in Cycads; **embryogen′ic** (γεννάω, I bring forth), belonging to the development of the embryo; ~ **Bod′ies**, in Mucorini, naked masses of protoplasm apparently derived from the nuclei, at each end of the zygospore, ultimately fusing together, becoming ~ **Spheres**, then surround themselves with a double cell-wall, and finally become Embryonic Spheres (Léger); **Embryog′eny**, formation of the embryo; **direct** ~, when a spore gives rise to an embryo resembling the adult form; **heteroblast′ic** ~, when the embryo differs widely from the adult form it is not borne direct, but as a lateral outgrowth; **ho′loblastic** ~, in which the whole of the ovum takes part; **ho′moblas′tic** ~, = direct ~; **in′direct** ~ = heteroblastic ~; **meroblast′ic** ~, when only a portion of the ovum takes part in the development; **Embryol′ogy** (λόγος), discourse, study of the embryo; **em′bryonal**, *embryona′lis*, relating to the embryo; ~ **Tubes**, tubular structures which develop in Abietineæ, forming the suspensor; ~ **Ve′sicle**, the oösphere; **em′bryonary Sac** = Embryo Sac; **em′bryonate**, having an embryo (Crozier); **embryon′ic**, rudimentary, in an early stage; ~ **Appen′dage**, the apical portion of the suspensor in grasses (Vines); **Em′bryophore** (φορέω, I carry), in *Equisetum* the homologue of the suspensor of Phanerogams and *Selaginella*, the lower of the two cells first cut off by a septum in the oösphere, then again separated, and this time forming the lower two of the quadrants, one becoming the "foot," the other the first root; **Embryophy′ta** (φυτόν, a plant), plants possessing embryos, divided into ~ **Siphonogam′ia**, having pollen-tubes, practically all flowering plants, and ~ **Zoidiogam′ia**, with ciliated spermatozoids, practically all Cryptogams; **embryophyt′ic**, relating to Embryophyta; ~ **Branches**, in *Chara*, peculiar branches resembling an embryo, which become separate and grow into new plants; ~ **Spheres**, see under Embryogenic Spheres; **Embryote′ga**, **-tegum**, **-tegium**, *-tega* (τέγη), a covering), a callosity in the seed coat of some seeds near the hilum, and detached by the protrusion of the radicle on germination; **Embryotroph′a** (τροφή, nourishment), (1) Perisperm; (2) Amnion (J. S. Henslow).

Emer′gence (*emergo*. I come forth), an outgrowth from the surface, differing from hairs in arising from more than

the superficial cells, and from spines,
in arising from a few layers only ;
prickles, warts, etc. ; **emer′gent,**
emer′gens, used of capsules which
rise slightly above the perichaetium;
emer′sed, *emer′sus,* raised above and
out of the water ; **Emersipra′ta**
(*pratum,* a meadow), marsh plants
which root in water-covered or saturated soil, but have their leafy shoots
erect above the surface.

Em′etin, a supposed alkaloid from
Ipecacuanha and similar emetic
roots.

Emissa′ria, pl. (*emissarium,* an outlet), Moll's term for Hydathodes or
water-glands; **Emissiv′ity, ther′mal,**
the interchange of heat between a
leaf and its surroundings.

Emo′din, a glucoside obtained from
buckthorn and a species of rhubarb,
Rheum Emodi, Wall.

empa′led, Grew's term for hemmed in,
as the flower by the calyx ; **Em-
pa′lement,** = CALYX ; **Empa′lers,**
the calyx segments.

empenna′tus ‡ (Mod. Lat.), pinnate.

emphysemato′sus ‡ (*ἐμφυσάω,* I breathe
upon), bladdery.

Emph′ytism (*ἐμφυὶς,* inhering). W. D.
Cope's term for inherited or simple
type of growth force ; **Emphyto-
gen′esis** (*γένεσις,* beginning), the
origin of inherited growth force
(W. D. Cope).

emphytog′enous (*ἔμφυτος,* innate ;
γενὴν, born), employed by Carrière
to denote graft-hybrids.

Empir′ic Di′agram, a scheme showing
the relative number and position of
parts of a flower as seen by inspection.

emprosthrod′romous (*ἔμπροσθεν,* in
front ; *δρόμος,* a course), used of a
flower when the genetic spiral on its
shortest way from the bract to the
outermost perianth-segment passes
outside the flower, farthest from the
axis.

em′pty, void ; ~ **Glumes,** one or more
glumes subtending a spikelet in
grasses enclosing one or more
flowers.

Emul′sin (*emulsus,* milked), an enzyme
acting upon glucosides, found plentifully in almonds.

En′alid (*ἐνάλιος,* marine), Warming's
term for such plants as *Zostera, Halophila,* and other marine submersed
Phanerograms.

enantioblast′ic, -tous (*ἔναντα,* opposite;
βλαστὸς, a shoot), having the embryo at the end of the seed diametri-
cally opposite the hilum ; **enanti-
osty′lous** (*ἐναντίος,* opposite, +
STYLE), flowers whose styles are
protruded right or left of the axis,
with the stamens opposite ; **Enanti-
osty′ly** is the condition; *cf.* DEXTRO-,
SINISTROSTYLY.

Ena′tion (*enatus,* sprung up), an outgrowth from another organ, as the
corona from the perianth of *Narcissus.*

Enaul′ad (*ἔναυλος,* a water course ; +
AD) "a sanddraw plant" ; **Ena-
uli′um,** a "sanddraw formation"
(Clements) ; **enauloph′ilus** (*φιλέω,* I
love), dwelling in such places ;
Enaulophy′ta (*φυτὸν,* a plant), plants
inhabiting "sanddraws" (Clements).

Encarp′ium (*ἐν,* in ; *καρπὸς,* fruit),
Trattinick's term for sporophore.

Enca′sing, of protoplasm, the formation of cellulose-caps by the protoplasm in the cells of certain trichomes (Haberlandt) ; Ger., Ein-
kapselung.

Enchyle′ma (*ἐγχέω,* I pour in ; *λήμη,*
rheum), the more fluid portion of
the cytoplasm (Hanstein).

Encyoneme′tum (*ἐν,* in; *κίω,* I contain;
νῆμα, νῆματα, a thread), an algal association in Lake Constance of *Spirogyra,* etc. ; **encyst′ed** (*κύστις,* a
bladder), enclosed in a bag, or invested with a coating when in a
non-motile state, as some unicellular plants ; **Encyst′ment,** the condition of being encysted.

end′arch (*ἔνδον,* within ;· *ἀρχὴ,* beginning). applied to a bundle in which
the primary xylem, in most Phanerogams, is wholly centrifugal, cen-
troxylic ; **Endauxe′sis** (*αὔξησις,*
growth), on the inner side of an

organ relatively to the main shoot (Wiesner).

ndecag'ynous, endecagnyn'ian (ἐνδεκάς, eleven ; γυνή, a woman), having eleven pistils ; **endecan'drous** (ἀνήρ, ἀνδρὸς, a man), having eleven stamens ; **endecaphyll'ous** (φύλλον, a leaf), having eleven leaves or leaflets.

nde'mic, ende'micus (ἐν, in ; δῆμος, a country district), confined to a given region, as an island or country ; **Ende'mism**, the condition of endemic plants.

Endhy'menine (ὑμήν, a membrane) = INTINE ; *cf.* EXHYMENINE.

En'distem (ἔνδον, within ; ἵστημι, I stand), young, pith.

ndivia'ceous, light blue, like the flowers of endive, *Cichorium Intybus.*

Endobasid'ium (ἔνδον, within ; *basidium*, a little pedestal), an enclosed basidium, as in Gasteromycetes ; **endobiot'ic** (βιοτὴ, life), living within as a parasite, as *Chrysophlyctis endobiotica*, Rose, in potato tubers ; **En'doblem** (βλῆμα, a coverlet), tissue beneath the dermatogen, of small-celled parenchyma ; **En'docarp** (καρπὸς, fruit), the inner layer of a pericarp ; **endocarp'oid** (εἶδος, resemblance), resembling the Lichen genus *Endocarpon ;* **Endocaryog'amy** = ENDOGAMY ; **endocatad'romous** (+ CATADROMOUS), when Ferns in their nervation have their stronger pinnules catadromous, the weaker ones, anadromous; **En'dochite** (χιτών, a tunic), the innermost membrane of the egg in Fucaceae (Farmer) ; **Endochlor'ites** (+ CHLORITE), chlorophyllous plastids contained in achroocysts (Arbaumont) ; **En'dochro'a** ‡ (χρὼς, skin), a supposed interior layer of the cuticle (Lindley) ; **En'dochrome,** *Endochro'ma* (χρῶμα, colour), the peculiar colouring matter in cells, especially in Algæ ; **-plate,** used of the two bands of colour in the frustule of navicular Diatoms, lying on the connecting band (Pfitzer) ; **En'dochyle** (χυλὸς, juice), a plant which has

its water-tissue within its assimilating tissue (A. F. W. Schimper) ; **endococ'coid**, like the Lichen *Endococcus ;* **Endoconid'ia** (+ CONIDIA), a synonym of ENDOGONIDIA ; **Endocor'tex** (*cortex*, bark), the innermost layer of the cortical region ; **endocri'brose** (+ CRIBROSE), within the sieve-tubes (Buscalioni) ; **En'docyst** (κύστις, a bladder), Cleve's term for a probably sexual organ in the frustules of certain Diatoms ; **Endoderm'is** (δέρμα, skin), the layer of ground-tissue which abuts on the stele, being differentiated as a sheath round it ; adj. **endoderm'al; Endoderm'ogens** (+ ENDODERM, γένος, descent), Van Tieghem's term for Vascular Cryptogams ; **endoderm'oid** (εἶδος, resemblance), like the ENDODERMIS (Rendle) ; **endogam'ic** (γάμος, marriage), crossing between two flowers of the same individual (K. Pearson) ; **Endog'amy,** (1) the condition above described ; (2) an expression for fusion or coalescence of two or more female gametes of the same brood (Hartog) ; adj. **endog'amous; En'dogen** (γένος, race, off-spring), a monocotyledonous plant, supposed to grow by internal accessions ; **endog'enous,** (1) pertaining to an Endogen ; (2) produced within another body, arising from deep-seated tissues ; ~ **Cell-formation,** free cell-formation ; ~ **Spores,** those formed within a cell ; **Endogonid'ium** (+ GONIDIUM), a gonidium formed within a receptacle or gonidangium ; **Endogo'nium,** the contents of the nucule of *Chara ;* **Endohaustor'ium** (+ HAUSTORIUM), a body resembling a young haustorium within a cell of a plant infected by Uredineous Fungi (Eriksson) ; **Endokaryog'amy** (κάρυον, a nut or kernel) = ENDOGAMY ; **endolith'ic** (λίθος, a stone), used of lichens growing below the surface of limestone rock ; **Endomer'istem** (+ MERISTEM), Russow's term employed by Vaizey for that meristem in a Moss which produces the central strand ; **endo-nast'ic** (ναστὸς, close-pressed), applied by Van Tieghem to an anatropous or campulitropous ovule, when the curvature is horizontal towards the edge of the carpel ; **Endo-nucle'olus** (+ NUCLEOLUS), a space inside the nucleolus (Huie) ; **Endo-nu'cleus** (*nucleus*, a small nut), "the nucleolo-nucleus " (Macfarlane) ; **En-dopar'asite** (+ PARASITE), a plant which lives and develops within the tissues of the host ; adj. **endo-parasit'ic** ; **Endoperid'ium** (περίδιον, a little pouch), the inner layer **of** the peridium in Fungi ; **Endo-phloe'um** (φλοιὸς, bark), the inner bark ; **Endophrag'ma** ‡ (φράγμα, a fence), a partition in the frond of some seaweeds ; **endophyl'lous**, *en-dophyl'lus* (φύλλον, a leaf), (1) formed from within a sheathing leaf ; (2) living within the substance of a leaf ; **endophy'tal, endo-phyt'ic**, *-cus* (φυτὸν, a plant), one plant growing inside another plant, whether parasitic or not ; **En'do-phyte,** (1) the woody body or timber of an exogen, including the pith (Lindley) ; (2) a plant which grows in the interior of another living plant ; **Endophy'tism**, the condition last described ; **En'doplasm** (πλάσμα, moulded), the internal granular portion of the protoplasm as distinguished from the outer portion, the ectoplasm, which is free from granules ; **En'doplast** (πγαστὸς, moulded), the protoplasmic contents of a cell (Huxley) ; **Endoplast'id,** a plastid containing one starch granule, simple or compound (Arbaumont) ; **Endopleu'ra** (πλευρὰ, a rib), the inner seed-coat, tegmen ; **Endoprothal'leae,** Van Tieghem's name for Phanerogams ; **endop'tile,** *endop'tilus* (πτίλον, a feather), used of an embryo whose plumule is rolled up in the cotyledon ; **Endorhi'zae** = MONOCOTYLEDONS ; **endorhi'zal, endorhi'zous**, *-us* (ῥίζα, a root), monocotyledonous, for in germination the radicle instead of lengthen-

ing gives rise to secondary rootlets ; **Endosap'rophytism** (+ SAPROPHYT-ISM), Elenkin's term for the Lichen-life, when dead gonidia in a heteromerous Lichen are utilized by the hyphae; **Endosclero'tium** (+ SCLEROTIUM), a persistent tuber-like mycelium of endogenous origin (Fayod) ; **Endos-mom'eter** (μέτρον, a measure, an instrument to show endosmosis.

En'dosmose, *Endosmo'sis* (ὠσμὸς, impulsion), flow of liquid through a membrane into a more viscid fluid ; **En'dosperm,** *Endosperm'um* (σπέρμα, seed), (1) the albumen of a seed in Angiosperms, by recent observers limited to the endosperm deposited within the embryo sac ; (2) in Gymnosperms the prothallium within the embryo sac ; (3) in *Selagi-nella*, tissue formed in the cavity of the macrospore below the prothallium ; **endosperm'ic**, *-icus*, having albumen, or associated with it ; **en-dosphae'rine**, resembling or allied to *Endosphaera*, a genus of Protococ-caceae.

En'dospore, *Endospor'ium* (ἔνδον, within ; σπορὰ, seed), (1) the innermost coat of a spore ; (2) the INTINE of **a** pollen grain ; (3) the interior membrane of the pollen in Angiosperms ; **endosp'orous**, *-us*, having spores formed within; **En'dostere**‡ (στερεὸς, stiff), the timber of an exogen, without the pith (Lindley) ; **En'dos-tome**, *Endost'oma* (στόμα, the mouth), the foramen of the inner coat of an ovule ; **Endotest'a** (+ TESTA), the hard lignified inner integument of the seed of *Cordaicarpus* (Brongniart) ; **Endothe'ca** (θήκη, **a** case), Tulasne's term for endothe-cium ; **Endothe'cium**, (1) Purkinje's name for the inner layer of a pollen grain ; (2) the inner lining of the loculus of an anther ; (3) the inner tissue of the theca in Muscineae ; **Endothe'lium** (θήλη, a nipple), Schwere's name for ENDODERMIS ; **endotherm'ic** (θερμὸς, hot), internal changes of heat within a plant ; **endotroph'ic** (τροφὴ, nourishment), applied to mycorhiza when the fungus attacks the cells of the root itself; **Endot'rophy**, Wiesner's expression for the condition of thickened growth of a shoot in the direction of the parent-shoot; *cf*. EXOTROPHY; **endotrop'ic** (τροπή, a turning), (1) inward curvature; (2) fertilized by pollen from another flower of the same plant (K. Pearson); (3) the path of the pollen-tube in basigamic fertilization; **Endrotryp'sin**, or **Endotryp'tase** (+ TRYPSIN), a proteolytic enzyme in yeast (Vines); **endozo'ic** (ζῶον, an animal), living inside an animal; entozoic (Crozier); **Endozoocho'ry** (χωρέω, I make way), dispersion of plants through the interior of animals.

Eneile'ma (ἐνείλημα, a wrapper), the inner skin of the seed.

Energet'ics (ἐνεργητικὸς, active), the science which treats of the transformation of energy.

Energe'sis (ἐνεργὸς, busy), the disruptive process by which energy is released (Barnes); — **aero'bic** ~, **anaero'bic** ~, **ferment'ative** ~ ; see under RESPIRATION.

En'ergid (ἐνεργέια, action; ἰδης, Greek suffix = paternity), Sachs's term for the nucleus and protoplasm as a vital unit; **En'ergy**, the capacity for doing work, as ~ of actual motion or **kinet'ic** ~ ; or ~ of position or **poten'tial** ~ .

ener'vis, ener'vius (Lat.), destitute of veins or nerves.

Eng'lish Type of Distribution, H. C. Watson's term for those plants whose range in Great Britain is centred in England proper.

Enha'lid Forma'tion, spermophytes and larger Algae growing on loose soil in salt water; *Enhalus* occurs, whence the name.

Enneagyn'ia (ἐννέα, nine; γυνὴ, a woman), a Linnean order of plants with nine pistils; **enneagyn'ian, enneag'ynous**, having nine pistils; **Ennean'dria** (ἀνὴρ, ἀνδρὸς, a man), a Linnean class characterized by

having nine stamens; **ennean'dricus, ennean'drous**, with nine stamens; **enneapet'alous** (πέταλον, a flower-leaf), having nine petals; **enneari'-nus** (ἄρρην, male), Necker's synonym for enneandrous; **enneasep'alous** (+ SEPALUM), with nine sepals (Crozier); **enneasper'mous** (σπέρμα, seed), nine-seeded (Crozier).

Enno'bling, an old term for inarching.

eno'dal, eno'dis (Lat.), without knots or nodes.

en'sate (Crozier), *ensa'tus* (ensis, a sword), sword-shaped; **en'siform**, *ensiform'is* (forma, shape), sword-shaped, as the leaves of *Iris*.

enterophleo'des (ἔντερον, intestine; φλοιὸς, bark), by Wallroth applied to Lichens which need some amount of preparation in the bark, wood, etc., by weathering, before they can thrive.

entire' (1), without toothing or division, with even margin; (2) in Lichens applied to an apothecium in which the perithecium or hypothecium wholly subtends the hymenium, or to the margin of an apothecium when continuous (Leighton).

entocy'clic (ἐντὸς, within; κύκλος, a circle), applied to sieve-tubes on the inner side of the ring of selerenchyma in Cucurbitaceae; **entodis'-calis** (δίσκος, a quoit), inserted within a disc, as in the case of some stamens.

Entomog'amy (ἔντομος = Insect. γάμος, marriage), fertilization of flowers by insects (Kirchner); **entomog'enous** (γεννάω, I bring forth), used of Fungi which are parasitic on insects; **Entomoph'ilae**, plants whose flowers are fecundated by insects, especially Lepidoptera; **entomoph'ilous** (φιλέω, I love), applied to flowers which are fertilized by insects; **Entomoph'ily**, is the condition; **entomophy'tal** (φυτὸν, a plant), entomogenous.

Entopar'asite (ἐντὸς, within; παράσιτος, a parasite), a parasite living entirely within its host (Crozier); **entophy'tal** (φυτὸν, a plant) = endophytal; **En'tophyte**, *Entophy'ta*, a plant which grows within other

129

plants, as some Fungi ; adj. ento-phyt'ic ; **Ent'ospore** (+ SPORA), a primitively interior spore, possessing its own membrane apart from that of the sporophore (Vuillemin) ; **en-tozo'ic** (ζῶον, an animal), growing within animals, endozoic.

En'trance, the outer aperture of a stoma ; in Ger. "Eingang."

enu'cleate (+ NUCLEUS), destitute of a nucleus.

En'velope, a surrounding part ; ~ **Appara'tus**, the sporocarp in Ascomycetes exclusive of the asci, and ascigerous cells ; ~ **Cell**, Archer's equivalent of Cohn's "Hüllzelle" ; the common hyaline envelope of a colony of *Stephanosphaeria pluvialis*, Cohn ; the **Flo'ral En'velopes** are the perianth or its analogues ; **en-vel'oping** = involucrate.

Envi'ronment (Fr., environnement), the aggregate of surrounding conditions.

enzymat'ic (ἐν, in ; ζύμη, yeast), pertaining to a ferment ; **En'zyme**, an unorganised or soluble ferment, as Diastase; **amylolyt'ic** ~, as Diastase, converting starch into sugar ; **fat** ~, converting olein into oleic acid and glycerine ; **glu'coside** ~, as Synaptase or Emulsin ; **hydrolyt'ic** ~, splitting up by hydrolysis ; **in'vert** ~, turning cane-sugar into grape-sugar ; **ox'idising** ~, assisting in the oxidation of various substances ; **proteolyt'ic** ~, decomposing proteids ; **Enzymo'id** (εῖδος, resemblance), a body resembling an enzyme in its action ; CYTOTOXINS ; **Enzymol'ogy** (+ ENZYME, λόγος, discourse), the study of the soluble ferments ; **Enzymol'ysis** (λύσις, a loosing), the action of breaking up a substance by the solvent power of an enzyme ; **Enzymo'sis**, changes induced by the action of an enzyme ; **enzymo'tic**, acting as an enzyme.

eoclad'ous (ἠὼs, dawn = early ; κλάδος, a branch), applied by Prantl to those leaves which in development become branched while in the meristematic state.

Eosin'ophil (eosin, a rose-red dye from coal-tar products ; φιλέω, I love), denotes any substance which becomes coloured by the application of eosin.

Epan'ody (ἐπάνοδος, return to normal), a return to a regular state from an irregular, as a peloria flower.

epan'thous (ἐπί, upon ; ἄνθος, a flower), growing upon flowers, as certain Fungi; **Ep'en** (Crozier) = **Epench'yma** (ἔγχυμα, an infusion), Nägeli's term for fibro-vascular tissue ; **Ephar'-monism, physiolog'ic** (ἁρμονία, concord), Vesque's term, used for the methods by which the plant is adapted to sun and drought ; **Ephar'-mony**, growth form in contradistinction to its systematic form ; adj. **epharmon'ic** (or **epharmon'ical**) ; ~ **Conver'gence**, resemblance of plants which are distant in affinity ; **Epharmo'sis** (ἁρμόζω, I join together), the adaptation of plants under new conditions (Vesque) ; adj. **epharmo'tic**.

ephebogenet'ic (ἔφηβος adult ; γένος, race, descent), matured, applied to development of sperm-cells.

Ephe'mer (ἐφημέριος, short-lived), (1) Rikli's term for introduced plants which are unable to persist, but soon disappear ; (2) flowers which close after a short term of expansion ; **ephem'eral, ephem'erous, -us** (ἡμέρα, day), (1) lasting for a day or less, as the corolla of *Cistus ;* (2) used by Möbius as ~ polycarpic plants, which flower several generations in the same year, as *Stellaria media*, Cyr; **Ephe'merophytes** (φύτον, a plant), casuals.

Ephydrogam'icae, pl. (ἐπί, upon ; ὕδωρ, water ; γάμος, marriage), Knuth's term for plants whose flowers are fertilized on the surface of water, as *Vallisneria ;* **Ephydrog'amy**, the condition described.

Ep'iachene (+ ACHENE), an achene developed from an inferior ovary (Villari) ; **Epiascid'ium** (+ ASCIDIUM), a funnel formed from a leaf, the inner surface corresponding to the upper surface ; *cf.* HYPOAS-

CIDIUM; **epiba'sal** (βάσις, the base), in front of the basal wall, as in the anterior half of a proëmbryo; ~ **Cell**, the upper cell of an oöspore in Bryophytes and Pteridophytes; ~ **Oc'tants**, the subsequent divisions of the ~ CELL; **Ep'iblast**, *Epiblast'us* (βλαστὸς, a shoot), the first and undeveloping leaf of the plumule of grasses, a rudimentary second cotyledon; **Epiblas'tanus** is a synonym; **Epiblaste'ma**, a superficial outgrowth from leaves; **Epiblas'teme**, a tuft of glandular emergences which act as colleters, their cells secreting a viscid substance (Kerner); **Epiblaste'sis**, growth of Lichens from gonidia which develop on the parent Lichen.

Epible'ma (ἐπίβλημα, a cloak), (1) the extremity of the root with its root-hairs (Schleiden), now restricted to the primary integumentary tissue of the root, apart from the root-cap; (2) an epidermis of thickened and flattened cells (Lindley).

epicalyc'ius (ἐπὶ, upon; κάλυξ, a cup) = EPISTAMINEOUS; **Epica'lyx**, an involucre resembling an accessory calyx as in *Malva;* **Ep'icarp** (καρπὸς, fruit), **Epicar'pium**, the external layer of a pericarp; **epicarpan'thous**, *-us* (ἄνθος, a flower), **epicarp'ous**, **epicarp'ius**, *-icus*, superior, applied to a flower or its parts; **Ep'ichil**, **Ep'ichile**, *Epichi'lium* (χεῖλος, a lip), the terminal part of the labellum of an orchid when it is distinct from the basal portion; **Epichro'a** ‡ (χρὼς, skin), a supposed external layer of cuticle; **Ep'icline** (κλίνη, a bed), a nectary when on the receptacle of a flower; **epicli'nal**, *epicli'-nus*, seated upon the torus or receptacle; **Epicop'ula** (+ COPULA) an intermediate band of cell-wall, in the upper or larger valve of Diatoms (O. Müller); **epicor'mic** (κορμὸς, a tree-trunk), (1) applied to preventitious buds which develop on the trunks of trees; (2) used of "branches which develop on the body of a forest tree from which

surrounding trees have been removed" (Crozier); **epicor'olline**, *epicorolla'tus* (+ COROLLA), inserted upon the corolla; **Epicot'yl** (κοτύλη, hollow vessel), the young stem above the cotyledons; adj. **epicot'ylar: epicotyle'donary**, placed above the seed-leaves; **Epicu'tis** (*cutis*, the skin), Fayod's term for the superficial layer of the cuticle in Agarics; **Ep'iderm**, *Epider'mis* (δέρμα, skin); the true cellular skin or covering of a plant below the cuticle; **epider'mal**, relating to the outer covering; ~ **Lay'er**, the outer cortex (Williamson and Scott); ~ **Tis'sue**, the tissue which makes up the epidermis; **epiderm'oid** (εἶδος, like), belonging to or resembling the epiderm; **epidermo'idal Lay'er**, the exoderm of roots; **Epidiphyll'um** (δίς, double; φύλλον, a leaf), Kronfeld's term for a double leaf, when the growth of the lamina has been interrupted at a particular spot; **epi-endoderm'al**, applied to cells with thickening ridges immediately outside the endodermis in the roots of many Cruciferae; **epigae'an**, **epigae'ous**, *epige'us* (γῆ, the earth), (1) growing upon the ground; (2) on land as opposed to water; (3) the above-ground flowers of such genera as have hypogaean flowers also, as *Krascheninikovia;* also occurs as **epige'al**, **epige'an**, **epige'ous**, especially when used of cotyledons which spread above the surface; **epige'ic**, Vahl's term for plants whose stolons are above ground; **epigam'ic** (γάμος, marriage), sex determined during the later stages of development (Correns); **Epigen'esis** (γένεσις, a beginning), the theory that the embryo develops by the differentiation of new organs; opposed to the old theory of "Evolution" or Preformation; adj. **epigenet'ic**; **epig'enous**, *epig'enus* (γένος, race), growing on the surface, as Fungi on leaves; **Epigeot'ropism** (+ GEOTROPISM), growing on the surface of the soil (White); **Ep'igone**, *Epi-*

go'nium (γονὴ, offspring), (1) the cellular layer covering the young sporophore in Hepaticae ; (2) similar tissue in Mosses after formation of the capsule, frequently ruptured, the upper portion carried up as the calyptra, the lower remaining as the vaginule ; (3) the nucleus in *Chara ;* **epigyn'icus**, with the calyx or corolla superior ; **epigynophor'ius** (γυνὴ, a woman ; φορέω, I carry), placed upon a gynophore or stipe of an ovary (Lindley) ; **epig'ynous**, *-us*, on the pistil, apparently above the ovary ; **Epig'yny**, the state of having epigynous flowers ; **epilith'ic** (λίθος, rock), growing on rocks as many Lichens ; **Epimat'ium** (ἱμάτιον, an outer garment), the ovuliferous scale of Coniferae.

epim'enus (ἐπί, upon ; μένω, I remain), Necker's term for the perianth being superior ; **epinast'ic** (ναστὸς, pressed close), (1) in leaves when pressed close to the ground, or away from the axis ; (2) in organs when the ventral surface grows the fastest, as in revolute vernation ; · (3) when ovules are curved in a downward direction (Van Tieghem) ; **Epinas'ty**, De Vries's term for curvature produced by greater growth of the ventral surface ; **Epine'mus** (νῆμα, a thread), the upper part of the filament in Compositae bearing the anther ; **epinyc'tous** (νύξ, νυκτὸς, night), ephemerous, applied to flowers which begin to open in the evening ; **Epiontol'ogy** (+ ONTOLOGY), the developmental history of plant-distribution ; adj. **epiontolog'ic.**

Epipedochor'isis (ἐπίπεδος, level ; + CHORISIS), the division of an axial organ in one plane ; it frequently does not differ from FASCIATION (Penzig).

epipel'tate (ἐπί, upon ; + PELTATE), a phyllome having the base of the limb on the superior face (C. de Candolle) ; **Epiperid'ium** (+ PERIDIUM) = EXOPERIDIUM ; **epiperisperm'icus** (περί, about ; σπέρμα, seed), without perisperm or albumen

(S. F. Gray) ; **epipet'alous**, *-us, epipeta'leus* (πέταλον, a flower-leaf), (1) borne upon the petals ; (2)placed before the petals ; **epipetre'ous** (πέτρα, a rock), growing on rocks, saxicole ; **epiphloe'dic** = EPIPHLOEDAL ; **Epiphlo'ëm** (φλοιός, bark), the outermost or corky bark ; **epiphloe'odal**, existing on the outer bark ; **Ep'iphlosa** = EPIDERM (Lindley) ; **Ep'iphragm**, *Epiphrag'ma* (φράγμα, a fence), (1) a membrane which closes the opening of the theca in Mosses ; (2) a delicate membrane closing the cup-like sporophore in *Nidularia ;* **Ep'iphyll** (φύλλον, a leaf), the upper portion of a leaf, from which the petiole and blade are developed ; **epiphyllosperm'ous** (σπέρμα, seed), bearing seed or the like on leaf-like organs, as the dorsiferous Ferns ; **epiphyll'ous**, *-us*, growing on leaves ; **Epiphyll'ae**, epiphyllous Algae and Lichens.

Epiph'ysis (ἐπιφύω, to grow up), protuberances round the hilum or foramen of some seeds ; strophioles.

Ep'iphyte (ἐπί, upon ; φυτὸν, a plant), a plant which grows on other plants, but not parasitically ; an air-plant ; **epiphyta'ceous** = EPIPHYTIC ; **epiphy'tal, epiphyt'ic**, relating to epiphytes ; **Ep'iphytism**, the condition of epiphytes ; **Epiphy'toid** (εἶδος, like), Johow's term for a phanerogamous para-ite presumably derived from an autophagous epiphyte ; ~ **Par'asites**, as Loranthaceae and Santalaceae ; **epiphyto'tic**, used of wide-spreading disease in plants, as an epidemic (Crozier) ; **Epiplank'ton** (+ PLANKTON), (1) the upper portion of pelagic plankton ; (2) floating organisms attached to pelagic organisms (Forel) ; **Ep'iplasm** (πλάσμα, moulded), protoplasm rich in glycogen, which remains in the ascus after the formation of ascospores ; glycogen-mass ; **Epipleu'ra** (πλευρά, a rib), the outer half of the diatomgirdle, belonging to the epitheca ; **Epipod'ium** (πούς, ποδὸς, a foot), (1) the apical portion of a developing phyllopodium or longitudinal axis of a leaf ; (2) ‡ a form of disk consisting of glands upon the stipe of an ovary ; (3) ‡ the stalk of the disk itself (Lindley) ; **epipol′yarch** (πολὺς, many ; ἀρχὴ, beginning), the division of the median protoxylem in a triarch stele (Prantl) ; **epipro′-teoid** (+ PROTEOID), applied to plants whose leaves have sclerogamous cells on the upper surface (Vesque) ; **epip′terous**, *epip′terus* (πτερὸν, a wing), winged, especially at the summit.

Epirrheol′ogy (ἐπιρρέω, I overflow ; λόγος, discourse), the effects of external agents on living plants.

epirhi′zous, *-zus* (ἐπὶ, upon ; ῥίζα, a root), growing on roots, as certain parasites ; **episep′alous** (+ SEPALUM) (1) on the sepals : (2) standing before the sepals ; **Ep′isperm** (σπέρμα, seed), the coat or outer covering of the seed, spermoderm, perisperm ; **episperm′icus**, exalbuminous ; **Episporang′ium** (σπορὰ, seed ; ἀγγεῖον, a vessel), the indusium of Ferns ; **Ep′ispore**, *Epispor′ium*, an external coat or perinium formed from the periplasm round the oöspore in some Fungi and the spores of certain of the higher Cryptogams ; **epispor′ic**, connected with the outer coat of a spore ; **epistamina′lis** (+ STAMEN), on the stamens, as hairs ; **epistat′ic** (στατικὸς, causing to stand), applied to a unit-character becoming invisible but not inactive (Shull) ; **Epist′asis** is the condition ; **epistom′eous** (στόμα, a mouth), "spigot-shaped" (Heinig).

Epist′rophe (ἐπιστροφὴ, turning about), the arrangement of chlorophyll granules on the upper and lower faces of the cells in diffused light ; *cf.* APOSTROPHE ; adj. **epistroph′ic** ; ~ **Int′erval**, or **Epistroph′ion**, S. Moore's term for that range of intensity of sunlight needed to produce Epistrophe ; **Epistrophiza′tion**, the condition described ; **Epist′rophy**, Morren's term for the reversion

of a monstrous form to the normal condition : epanody.

epitact′ic (ἐπίτακτος, commanded), placed behind another ; *cf.* PANTOTACTIC ; PARATACTIC.

Epit′eospores, — *ae*, (ἐπὶ, upon ; + SPORA), spores in a sorus surrounded by prominent paraphyses, as in the genus *Epitea*, Fries, whence the term ; **epitet′rarch** (+ TETRARCH), when in a triarch stele, the third (median) protoxylem group is divided (Prantl) ; **epithall′ine** (θαλλὸς, a young shoot), growing on the thallus; **Epithall′us**, the cortical layer of Lichens, by Zukal employed for all modifications of the cortical hyphae at the margin or apex of the thallus, which serve as protection to the gonidia ; **Epithe′ca** (θήκη, a case). the outer and larger half-frustule of Diatoms ; adj. **epithe′cal** ; **Epithe′cium**, the surface of the fructifying disc in Lichens ; **Epithe′lium** (θήλη, a nipple), (1) any distinct layer of one or more cells in thickness which bounds an internal cavity ; (2) ‡ = EPIDERMIS.

Ep′ithem, or **Epithe′ma**, pl. **Epithe′-mata** (ἐπίθημα, a cover), masses of tissue in the mesophyll of leaves, serving as internal hydathodes, the cells being usually devoid of chlorophyll, as in *Crassula*.

epitri′arch (ἐπὶ, upon, + TRIARCH), when in a triarch stele, the third (median) protoxylem group is uppermost, *i.e.* ventral (Prantl); **epitroph′ic** (τροφὴ, nourishment), having relation to EPITROPHY (Wiesner) ; **Epit′-rophy**, the condition when the growth of the cortex on wood is greater on the upper side of the organ ; or having buds or shoots on the upper side (Wiesner) ; **epitrop′ic** (τρόπος, direction), below the axis ; **epicotyl-ary** ; **Epit′ropism** = GEOTROPISM ; **epit′ropous** (τροπὴ, a turn), denotes an anatropous ovule with its raphe averse when ascending, adverse when suspended ; **Epival′va**, **Ep′i-valve** (*valva*, a valve), the valve belonging to the epitheca of a

Diatom; **epixylo'neus** (ξύλον, wood) ; **epix'ylous** (Crozier), growing on wood, as *Hypoxylon ;* **epizoa'rius** (ζῶον, an animal), growing on dead animals ; **epizo'ic, epizo'us,** (1) growing on living animals, parasitic or not ; (2) the dispersal of fruits by their adhesion to passing animals (Sernander) ; **Epizoocho'ry** (ζῶον, an animal ; χωρέω, I wander), dispersal of plants by animals carrying them on their fur (Sernander).

eplica'tus (*e*, priv. ; *plicatus*, folded), not plaited or folded.

Epoik'ophytes (ἐποικέω, I settle as colonist ; φύτον, a plant), fairly naturalized plants, but almost entirely confined to roadsides or paths, as *Lepidium ruderale* (Rikli).

eprophylla'tus (*e*, priv. ; + Prophylla), without prophylla, bracteoles ;—in Ger. Vorblätter ; **epru'inose** (*pruinosus*, frosty), without surface farina.

e'qual (*aequalis*), (1) alike as to length or number ; (2) in Mosses when the capsule is symmetrical ; ~ **si'ded,** equal, when applied to the two sides of an organ ; **e'qually-pin'nate =** abruptly pinnate, having no terminal leaflet ; **e'quans** (Lat.), equalling.

Equator'ial Plane, the line which passes through the mother-star of the nucleus, the plane of cell-division; ~ **Plate**. the nuclear disc of Strasburger, the grouping of chromosomes at the middle of the spindle in nuclear division.

equilat'eral, *equilatera'lis* (*aequilateralis*), equal-sided.

equinoct'ial, *equinoctia'lis* (*aequinoctialis*, pertaining to the equinox), used of plants whose flowers expand and close at particular hours of the day.

equiseta'ceous = Equisetic ; **Equisete'tum,** Warming's term for a plant-association of *Equisetum ;* **equise'tic,** pertaining to the genus *Equisetum ;* **equise'tiform,** resembling the same genus as to form.

e'quitant, *e'quitans* (Lat. riding), folded over, as if astride ; **equitati'vus** (Lat.) ‡ = equitant.

equivalv'ular (*aeque*, equally ; *valva*, leaf of a door), having the valves of a fruit equal in size.

Equiv'ocal (*aequivocus*, ambiguous) **Genera'tion,** spontaneous generation.

eradic'ulose (*e*, priv. ; *radicula*, a small root), without rootlets or rhizoids ; **eramo'sus** (*ramus*, a branch), unbranched.

erect', *erect'us* (Lat.), upright, perpendicular to the ground or its attachment ; **erec'to-pat'ent** (*patens*, lying open), between spreading and erect.

Eremacau'sis (ἠρέμα, gently ; καῦσις, burning), slow combustion or oxidation, such as long preserved seeds show, as if charred.

Ere'mad (ἐρημία, a desert ; + AD), a desert plant ; **Eremi'on, Eremi'um** (+ ION) = a desert formation ; **eremoc'ola,** desert dwelling ; **eremoph'ilus** (φιλέω, I love), desert loving ; **Eremophy'ta** (φυτόν, a plant), desert plants (Clements).

Ere'moblast (ἐρῆμος, solitary ; βλαστὸς, a shoot), cells which, united at first, afterwards separate themselves ; **Eremobry'a** (βρύω, I grow), a division of Ferns having articulated fronds, and not adherent to the stem or rhizome ; **Ere'mus** ‡ a carpel apart from its sister carpels.

Erep'sin, a fibrin-digesting enzyme ; **Erep'tases,** peptolyzing enzymes (Vines).

Ergasiap'ophytes (ἐργασία, labour ; + Apophytes), colonists of cultivated fields (Simmons) ; **Ergasiali'pophytes** (λιπαρέω, I persist), relics of cultivation (Nägeli and Thellung) ; **Ergasiophy'gophytes** (φυγὴ, flight), fugitives from cultivation ; **Ergas'iophytes,** foreign cultivated plants, which have reached their habitats by the conscious action of man (Woodhead) ; **Ergas'iphytes,** foreign cultivated plants (Simmons).

Ergastoplas'ma (πλάσμα, moulded), applied to protoplasmic filaments observed in the embryo-sac of certain Liliaceae whose origin and formation are still uncertain (Bonnet) ; adj. **ergastoplasmat'ic.**

Erge'sis (ἔργω, I work), the ability of an organ to exhibit reaction (Massart).

Ergogen'esis (ἔργον, work ; γένεσις, beginning), the exhibition of growth-energy (J. A. Ryder) ; **Ergol'ogy** (λόγος, discourse), proposed by Lindman for Delpino's "Biology."

ergoplas'tic Nu'cleus, Schwarz's term for the vegetative nucleus.

Er'got (Fr.), also pr. Er'got ; *Claviceps purpurea,* Tul., causing "Spur." in grasses ; **Ergost'erin, Ergot'ic Acid, Er'gotin,** substances occurring in the sporophore of the Ergot Fungus ; **er'gotised,** infected with Ergot ; **Er'gotism,** the effect produced by eating bread which is ergotized.

erianth'ous, *-us* (ἔριον, wool ; ἄνθος, a flower), woolly-flowered.

erica'ceous, heath-like, or allied to the genus *Erica.*

eri'cetal (*ericetum,* Mod. Lat., a heath), H. C. Watson's term for plants which grow upon moors, such as heather, *Erica;* **erice'tinous,** *ericeti'nus* (Mod. Lat.), (1) growing on heaths ; (2) heath-like, in form or habit : **Erice'tum,** (1) an account or monograph of heaths ; (2) a heath plant-association ; pl. **Erice'ta,** employed by Nilsson, as ~ **cladino'sa,** ~ **hylocomio'sa,** ~ **polytricho'sa,** ~ **pu'ra,** ~ **sphagno'sa,** according to the substratum of Lichen or Moss (Heinig) ; **Ericifrutice'ta,** pl. (*fruticetum,* a thicket), heath communities ; **Ericiligno'sa** pl. (*lignosus,* woody) community of heath characterized by rolled-up leaves ; **Eri'ci-ma'qui** (+ MAQUI), preponderance of arboreal heaths with *Ulex* and *Sarothamnus,* as in the "Landes" of France ; **erico'id** (εἶδος, like), used of leaves which are like those of heaths.

e'rigens (*erigo,* I raise), used of a branch, horizontal at first, rising at the point.

eri'nous (*er, eris,* a hedgehog), "prickly, rough with sharp points" (Heinig).

Eriophore'tum (+ ETUM), a plant formation of cotton grass, *Eriophorum.*

erioph'orous (ἔριον, wool ; φορέω, I carry), wool-bearing, densely cottony; **eriophyll'ous,** *-us* (φύλλον, a leaf), woolly leaved.

Eris'ma (ἔρεισμα, a buttress), Necker's term for the rhachis in grasses.

ermin'eus (Mod. Lat.), the colour of the fur of ermine, white, broken with yellow.

ero'ded, ero'se, *ero'sus* (Lat. gnawed), as though bitten or gnawed.

erost'rate, *erostra'tus, erost'ris* (Lat.), beakless.

Er'ror, probable, see DEVIATION.

Ersatzfas'ern, Sanio = SUBSTITUTE FIBRES, intermediate in form between woody fibres and parenchyma.

erubesc'ens (Lat. blushing), blush red.

erucaeform'is (*eruca,* a caterpillar ; *forma,* shape), used for such Lichen spores as those of *Graphis,* which are long, septate, blunted at the extremities, and in shape suggest a short caterpillar.

erump'ent, *erump'ens* (Lat. breaking through), prominent as though bursting through the epidermis.

Erys'imin, a glucoside found in *Erysimum.*

Er'ythrism (ἐρυθρὸς, red), a red colour in flowers usually white, the reverse of albinism ; **Erythrobacte'ria** (+ BACTERIA), bacteria of a deep red colour ; in Ger., "Purpurbacterien"; **erythroph'ilous** (φιλέω, I love), used of nuclei which take up red stains in preference to blue ; **Er'ythrophyll** (φύλλον, a leaf), Berzelius's term for the red colouring of leaves ; **Er'ythrophore** (φορέω, I carry), Schmitz's term for a chlorophyll-granule when red, as in certain Algae ; **Erythrost'omum** ‡ (στόμα, the mouth), Desvaux's word for ETAERIO; **Er'ythrozym** (ζύμη, yeast), an enzyme from the root of the madder which acts on glucosides.

Escape', a cultivated plant found growing as though wild, dispersed by some agency.

-escens, a Latin suffix = ish, thus rub-escens = redd-ish.

es'culent (*esculentus*, fit for eating), suitable for human food.

Es'culin = AESCULIN.

esep'tate (*e*, priv.; *septum*, a partition), destitute of septa.

esore'diate, destitute of SOREDIA.

esoter'ic (ἐσώτερος, inner), arising from inside the organism.

Espal'ier, a fruit tree trained lattice-fashion, in one plane, but not attached to a wall; ~ **shape**, stems pressed against the ground (Warming).

espatha'ceus (*e*, priv., + SPATHA, -aceus), wanting a spathe; Lindley gives the form *espatha'tus* ‡.

essen'tial (*essentia*, the being of anything), the necessary constituent of an existing object; ~ **Char'acter**, the distinguishing note by which a form differs from its allies, diagnostic character; ~ **Or'gans**, those which are absolutely necessary, stamens and pistils.

Esthe'sis = AESTHESIS.

esti'val = AESTIVAL; **e'stivate** = AESTIVATE; **Estiva'tion** = AESTIVATION.

estroph'iolate (*estrophiola'tus*, destitute of caruncle, or STROPHIOLE.

Etae'rio, *Etai'rium* (ἑταιρεία, companionship), an aggregate fruit composed of achenes or drupes, as in *Ranunculus*, the Strawberry, and Blackberry; adj. **etairiona'ris**, *etairio'neus*.

Ete'siæ (ἐτήσιος, annual), herbaceous perennials; the root persisting, with the above-ground portion only annual; adj **ete'sial**.

ethnobotan'ic (ἔθνος, a tribe; βοτάνη, a herb), relating to those plants which illustrate or are typical of the customs of a given race or people.

e'tiolative, tending to disease.

e'tiolated, *etiola'tus* (Fr. etiolé, drawn out), lengthened or deprived of colour by absence of light; **Etiola'tion**, the condition of being blanched; **E'tiolin**, the yellow-colouring matter of blanched plants, chlorophyll which has not acquired its green colour (Pringsheim).

etiolog'ical, connected with AETIOLOGY; **E'tiology** = AETIOLOGY.

etrabecula'tus (*e*, priv.; *trabecula*, a little beam), not cross-barred; when the peristome teeth of Mosses want cross-connections.

-e'tum, suffix denoting CONSOCIES (Clements).

eu- (εὖ, well), in Greek compounds = true; often used in sectional names, with a restricted meaning; **euacranth'ic** (ἄκρος, apex; ἄνθος, flower), truly terminal; ~ **Flow'er**, a terminal flower which springs immediately from the apex of a shoot which has produced leaves or other lateral structures; *cf.* PSEUDACRANTHIC; **euanth'ic**, used by Delpino to denote a monothalamic flower, the reverse being PSEUDANTHIC; **Euanthrostrob'ilus** (+ ANTHROSTROBILUS), the theoretic idea of the flowering Angiosperms (Arber and Parkin); **Euapog'amy** (+ APOGAMY), restricted to such cases as have no obvious need for fertilization as in *Athyrium* (Farmer and Digby).

Eucalyptol'ogist, an expert in the polymorphic genus *Eucalyptus* (Maiden).

Eucar'otin (εὖ, well; + CAROTIN), Zopf employs this to denote the yellow carotin as distinct from the red; **eucarp'ic** (καρπὸς, fruit), applied to certain Algae where part only of the body of the plant goes to form the sporangium, in contrast to HOLOCARPIC; **eucar'pous**, (1) = EUCARPIC; (2) of Fungi when producing several successive fructifications from the same thallus; **eucy'clic** (κύκλος, a circle), when flowers are composed of alternate isomerous whorls.

Eudiom'eter (εὐδία, fair weather; μέτρον, measure) an instrument for measuring the quantity of oxygen in a given bulk of fluid; adj. **eudiomet'ric**.

euephem'erous (εὖ, well; + EPHEMEROUS), applied to flowers which open

and close within 24 hours ; **Eu′forms**
(*forma*, a shape) of uredineous Fungi,
whose spores develop on the living
host, but only germinate after the
host's death, usually after a resting
period ; **Eugam′ophyte** (γάμος, marriage ; φυτὸν, a plant), term proposed
by C. MacMillan for such Cryptogams
as *Oedogonium, Marchantia, Sphagnum,* "which support dependent
sporophytes."

Eu′genol, the chief constituent of oil
of cloves, obtained from *Pimenta
acris*, Kostel., and other myrtace-
ous plants, formerly referred to
Eugenia.

eugeog′enous (εὖ, well ; γῆ, the earth ;
γεννάω, I bring forth), Thurmann's
word to indicate rocks readily
yielding detritus and the plants
which grow on it ; **Euisog′amy**
(γάμος, marriage), the union of a
gamete with any other similar gamete
(Hartog) ; **Eugonid′ia**, pl. (+ GONI-
DIA) "bright-green gonidia" (A. L.
Smith) ; **eulimne′tic** (+ LIMNETIC),
plankton exclusively of pools ; **Eu-
meio′sis** (+ MEIOSIS) the opposite
term to PSEUDOMEIOSIS ; a true
meiotic phase ; **eumeriste′lic**, having
reduced EUSTELES, as some species
of *Primula* and *Gunnera* (Brebner) ;
Eunu′cleole (+ NUCLEOLE), used by
Rosen for an erythrophilous nucleus ;
Eunucle′oli (+ NUCLEOLUS), a class
of nucleoli which persist in nuclear
division after the PSEUDONUCLEOLI
have disappeared (Rosen).

Eu′nuchs, pl. (*eunuchare*, to castrate),
Lee's term for flowers destitute of
stamens, as double flowers.

Euparthen′osperm (εὖ, well ; + PAR-
THENOSPERM), C. MacMillan's term
for plants in which both embryo and
endosperm are parthenogenetic.

Eupato′rine, an alkaloid occurring in
Eupatorium cannabinum, Linn. ;
eupelag′ic (+ PELAGIC), applied to
plankton confined to the ocean ;
Euphe′mera (+ EPHEMERA), flowers
which open and close finally within
twenty-four hours.

Euphor′bium, an acrid inspissated

juice or resin from various species
of *Euphorbia*.

eupho′tic (εὖ, well ; φῶς, φωτὸς, light),
applied to hydrophytes which receive
an abundance of light (Warming) ;
euphotomet′ric (μέτρον, a measure),
used of leaves which place themselves
so as to obtain the maximum of
diffused light, as the foliage of
forests (Wiesner) ; **euphototrop′ic**
(τροπή, a turning), Drude's term for
EUPHOTOMETRIC ; **Euphyl′la**, pl.
true leaves ; adj. **euphyl′loid**, *eu-
phylloid′eus ;* **Eu′phylls** (φύλλον, a
leaf), true leaves, foliage leaves ;
euphy′toid (φιτὸν, a plant ; εἶδος,
like) **Par′asites**, are erect land
plants, parasitic in habit (Johow) ;
Euplank′ton (+ PLANKTON), free-
floating organisms (Forel) ; **eupon′tic**,
species which show only a slight
westward range from Pontus, the
N. E. of Asia Minor (Preuss) ; **eupot-
am′ic** (ποταμὸς, a river), applied to
the plankton of running or standing inland waters ; (Zimmer) ; **Eupuc-
cin′ia**, *cf.* EUFORMS ; **eurad′ulan**,
employed by batologists to denote
similarity to *Rubus Radula*.

eurotoph′ilus (εὐρώς, mouldiness ;
φιλέω, I love), dwelling in leaf-
mould ; **Eurotophy′ta** (φυτὸν, a
plant), leaf-mould plants ; **Euro-
tophyti′a**, leaf-mould plant formations (Clements).

eurycho′ric (εὐρὺς, broad ; χωρέω, I
spread), used of plants having a
wide distribution in varying climates
and several plant formations (Drude) ;
Eurycho′ry, is the condition.

euryc′ladous (εὖ, well ; κλάδος, a
branch), employed by Russow for
laxus : **euryhal′ine** (ἅλς, ἁλὸς, salt),
plankton adapted to varying conditions of salinity (Forel) ; **eury-
pho′tic** (φῶς, φωτὸς, light), adapted
to light of varying intensity (Forel) ;
Eu′rytherm (θέρμη, heat, applied to
bacteria capable of enduring great
heat ; adj. **eurytherm′ic** ; **eusigil-
lar′ian**, used of ribbed *Sigillaria*
stems from the Carboniferous Formation ; **eu′schist** (σχιστὸς, split),

when a gamete is formed by successive complete divisions from the parent cell, the gametogonium (Hartog).

Eu′stathe ‡ (εὐσταθής, steadfast), Hartig's term for the outermost layer of a cell.

Eu′stele (εὖ, well ; + STELE), Brebner's term for the monostele of typical dicotyledons, a ring of meristeles, including pericyclic and ground tissue ; the stele of a typical Dicotyledon, with ring of collateral bundles ; adj. **euste′lic** ; the condition is **Euste′ly** ; **eusporang′iate** (σπορὰ, seed ; ἀγγεῖον, a vessel), in Pteridophytes, possessing a sporangium, a **Eusporan′gium**, derived from a group of superficial cells ; **Eusporophy′ta** (φυτὸν, a plant), Cryptogams defined by C. MacMillan as "self-supporting, and do not nurse the gametophytes, e. g. the higher Mosses, the lower Fern-worts and Club-mosses."

Euthal′lophytes, *Euthallophy′ta,* Schroeter's term for THALLOPHYTES exclusive of Myxogastres ; by Wettstein employed in a more restricted sense for Chlorophyceae and Fungi only.

Euthybas′id (εὐθὺς, direct), Van Tieghem's word for those basidia which spring directly from the sporophore ; *cf.* PROBASID ; **Euthymorph′osis** (μόρφωσις, a shaping), the rapid succession of members of different form on the same stem, buds, etc., polymorphism (Caruel).

eu′thyschist (εὐθὺς, immediately ; σχιστὸς. split). in brood-division, when each nuclear division is accompanied by cell division (Hartog).

eutroph′ic (εὖ. well ; τροφὴ, nourishment), applied to plants adapted to live at the expense of nutritive solutions present in the soil ; **eutrop′ic** (τρόπος, direction). (1) A. Gray's word for twining with the sun, that is, left to right, dextrorse ; (2) those flowers which display EUTROPY ; **Eu′tropy,** applied by M'Leod to those flowers to which only a restricted class of specialized insects can gain access ; adj. **eu′tropous.**

evalv′is, evalv′ular (*e*, priv., *valva,* leaf of a door), destitute of valves, not opening by them.

evanes′cent (*evanescens,* vanishing), soon disappearing, lasting only a short time ; **evaniscen ti veno′sus,** when the lateral veins of a leaf do not reach the margin.

Evapora′tion (*evaporatio,* vaporizing), to pass off in vapour ; **Evaporim′eter** (μέτρον, a measure), an instrument to measure the amount of moisture given off by plants.

Evec′tion (*evectus,* carried), when in *Cladophora* the initial cells of the branches arise from the sides of the upper end of the mother-cell; *Evectio dislocans* is an extreme form of this displacement in *C. Nordstedti,* Hauck (Brand).

e′ven, without inequalities of surface ; **E′venness,** absence of elevations or depressions ; **e′ven-pin′nate** = ABRUPTLY-PINNATE (Crozier) ; **ev′ergreen,** bearing green foliage all the year ; **everlast′ing,** used of some flowers which preserve their shape and colour in drying, as species of *Gnaphalium, Helichrysum,* etc.

ever′niaeform (*forma,* shape), like the thallus of *Evernia,* a genus of Lichens ; **Ever′nine,** a principle found in the same genus ; **ever′nioid** (εἶδος, resemblance), like the genus *Evernia* (Leighton).

Ever′sion (*eversio,* an overthrowing), protusions of organs from a cavity, turned backward or outward ; **evert′ed,** turned inside out.

ev′ident (*evidens,* manifest), clearly visible.

evit′tate, *evitta′tus* (*e*, priv. ; *vitta,* a fillet), not having VITTAE, oil-reservoirs in the fruit of Umbelliferae.

e′volute (*evolvo,* I roll forth), unfolded, turned back ; **Evolu′tion,** (1) the act of development ; (2) the theory according to which complex forms are considered to have been evolved from simpler ones ; **sal′tatory ~,** sudden appearance of sports ; mutation.

138

ex, privative prefix in place of e, when a vowel follows.

exalbu'minous, *exalbumino'sus* (*cx*, priv. ; + ALBUMEN), destitute of albumen, used only of seeds when the embryo occupies the whole cavity within the testa ; ex'alate, *exala'tus* (*alatus*, winged), wingless.

exalta'tus (Lat., raised high), lofty, tall.

exan'nulate (*ex*, priv. ; *annulus*, a ring), used of Ferns which do not possess an elastic ring round their sporangia.

Exanth'ema (ἐξ, out of ; ἄνθος, a flower), (1) a blotch on leaves, etc., as though eruptive ; (2) the " Dieback " of *Citrus ;* Exanth'ium ‡ bractlets of the last degree, incapable of forming axillary buds, and immediately external to the flower.

exapophysa'tus (*ex*, priv. ; + APO-PHYSIS), destitute of an apophysis, or swelling below the capsule of a Moss.

ex'arch (ἐξ, out of ; ἀρχή, origin), used of vascular bundles in which the whole primary wood is centripetal ; cf. PERIXYLIC.

exar'eolate, *exareola'tus* (*ex*, priv. ; + AREOLATUS), not spaced out or marked into small areas ; exar'illate (+ ARILLA), without an aril ; exar'istate, *exarista'tvs* (+ ARISTA), destitute of awns.

exas'perate, *exaspera'tus* (Lat., roughened), rough with hard projecting points.

ex'cavate (*excavatus*, hollowed out), as though dug out.

excen'tric, *excen'tricus* (*ex*, out of ; *centrum*, the centre), one-sided, out of the centre, abaxial.

Ex'ciple, Ex'cipule (Crozier), Excip'-ulum, *Excip'ulus* (*excipula*, a basin), wart-like excrescences on the thallus of certain Lichens, which have a narrow opening ; the portion of thallus which forms the rim round the base of apothecia.

Excitabil'ity, *Excitabil'itas* (*excitatus*, roused), the faculty of responding to external stimuli.

Excoe'mum (ἐξ, out ; οἱμάω, I issue), a fringe or tuft of hair at the base of the glumes in some grasses (Richard).

Excoria'tion (*ex*, out of ; *corium*, skin), the falling off of the outer layer of the terminal cells of glandular or capitate hairs, as in *Geranium* (Heinig) ; Excortica'tion (*corticatus*, covered with bark), the stripping of bark.

excres'cent (*excrescens*, growing out), growing in an unnatural way, as a wart or other outgrowth ; Excres'-cence, a gnaur or wart on the stem of a tree ; enation.

Excre'tion (*ex*, out of ; *cretus*, sifted), (1) the action by which any substance is rejected from the organism ; (2) the thing itself excreted, as gum, resin, honey, etc. ; excur'rent, *excur'rens* (Lat., running out), (1) running through to the apex and beyond as a mucro ; (2) where the stem remains central, the other parts being regularly disposed round it ; ~ Vena'tion, in Ferns, when the veinlet is directed outwards.

exendosperm'ous (ἐξ, out ; ἔνδον, within ; σπέρμα, seed), used of seeds which have reserve material stored in the embryo ; exendotrop'ic (+ ENDO-TROPIC), when fertilized from another flower of the same or a different plant (K. Pearson) ; Exendot'ropy, the condition itself.

exe'sus ‡ (Lat., eaten away), applied to a surface irregularly sculptured as though by corrosion.

exfo'liate (*ex*, from : *folium*, a leaf), to come away in scales or flakes, as the bark of the Plane ; Exfolia'tion, peeling off.

exha'lant (*exhalo*, I exhale), breathing out, as exhalan'tia Va'sa ‡ imaginary vessels in the epidermis, actually the sides of confluent cells ; Ex-hala'tion, the function discharged by stomata in passing off vapour ; exhomotrop'ic, (+ HOMOTROPIC), when fertilized from the anthers of the same, or a different plant (K. Pearson) ; Exhomot'ropy, is the condition described ; **Exhy'menine** ($\dot{v}\mu\dot{\eta}\nu$, a membrane) = EXTINE.

exig'uous, *exig'uus* (Lat., scanty), small and narrow, mean.

exi'lis (Lat.), thin, meagre ; lank and straight.

exim'ius (Lat., distinguished), excellent for size, for beauty.

exindu'siate, *exindusia'tus* (*ex*, priv., + INDUSIATE), without an indusium, the membrane which covers the torus in Ferns.

Ex'ine = EXTINE.

Ex'intine (*ex*, out ; + INTINE, the middle coat of a pollen-grain, that which is next the intine.

Ex'istem ($\dot{\epsilon}\xi$, out; $\iota\sigma\tau\dot{o}s$, a web), the "Aussenschicht" of Sanio, consisting of MESISTEM, "thickening ring" and PERISTEM, young cortex ; it is the tissue of protomeristem which is not young pith.

Ex'it, the inner aperture of the slit of a stoma ; in Germ. "Ausgang."

exo, prefix = outward : **Ex'ocarp**, *Exocar'pium* ($\dot{\epsilon}\xi\omega$, outside; $\kappa\alpha\rho\pi\dot{o}s$, fruit), the outer layer of a pericarp ; **Exocaryog'amy** ($\kappa\dot{\alpha}\rho\nu\sigma\nu$, a nut; $\gamma\dot{\alpha}\mu\sigma s$, marriage) = EXOGAMY ; **exocatad'romous** (+ CATADROMOUS), when Ferns in their nervation have their stronger pinnules anadromous, and their weaker catadromous (Prantl) ; **Ex'ochite** ($\chi\iota\tau\dot{\omega}\nu$, a tunic), the outermost membrane of the egg in Fucaceae (Farmer) ; **Exocho'mophyte** ($\chi\dot{\omega}\mu\alpha$, a mound ; $\phi\nu\tau\dot{o}\nu$, a plant), surface-rooting and mat-forming plants. **Exocor'tex** (*cortex*, bark), (1) the outermost portion of the cortex ; (2) in Rhizomorphae specially pervaded by hyphae : (3) a special layer in the roots of saprophytic Orchids ; **Exo'-dermis** ($\delta\dot{\epsilon}\rho\mu\alpha$, skin), the outermost cortical layer of the adult root, answering to the hypoderma of the stem ; **exogam'ic** ($\gamma\dot{\alpha}\mu\sigma s$, marriage), when flowers are crossed from different plants (K. Pearson) ; **Exog'amy** ($\gamma\dot{\alpha}\mu\sigma s$, marriage), (1) the tendency of closely allied gametes to avoid pairing ; (2) the union of two gametes

of distinct broods (Hartog) ; **exog'enous**, *exog'enus* ($\gamma\epsilon\nu\nu\dot{\alpha}\omega$, I bring forth), (1) growing as the wood of Dicotyledons ; (2) arising from superficial tissue ; **Ex'ogens**, *Exog'enae*, plants which increase in growth by the addition of wood on the outside beneath the constantly widening bark ; **exog'ynous**, *exog'ynus* ($\gamma\nu\nu\dot{\eta}$, woman), where the style is exserted beyond the flower ; **exohadromat'ic** (+ HADROME), exterior to the hadrome ; *cf.* PERIHADROMATIC ; **Exoisog'amy** (+ ISOGAMY), when a gamete will pair only with a similar gamete of another brood (Hartog) ; **Exomer'istem** (+ MERISTEM), Russow's term for the meristem which produces all the tissues of a Moss outside the central-strand, namely, cortex and epidermis (Vaizey) ; **exonas'tic** ($\nu\alpha\sigma\tau\dot{o}s$, pressed close), in anatropous or campylotropous ovules when the curvature is horizontal towards the median nerve of the side of the upper face of the carpel (Van Tieghem) ; *cf.* ENDONASTIC ; **Exoneuro'sis**, ($\nu\epsilon\dot{\nu}\rho\sigma\nu$, a nerve), the separation of veins in appendicular organs, and their reappearance as teeth, spines, or bristles, as in the Barberry (Clos) ; **Exoperid'ium** (+ PERIDIUM), the outer layer of the peridium of such Fungi as *Lycoperdon*, which peels or flakes off on maturity ; **exophyl'lous**, -*us* ($\phi\dot{v}\lambda\lambda\sigma\nu$, a leaf), not having a foliaceous sheath, with naked cotyledons ; **Exopleu'ra** ($\pi\lambda\epsilon\nu\rho\dot{\alpha}$, the side) = TESTA (Heinig) ; **Exoprothal'leae**, Van Tieghem's term for vascular Cryptogams ; **exop'tile**, *exop'tilis* ($\pi\tau\dot{\iota}\lambda\sigma\nu$, a wing) = EXOPHYLLOUS, said of an embryo whose plumule is naked upon or between cotyledons and not rolled up in one (Lindley) ; **Exorhi'zae** ($\dot{\rho}\iota\zeta\alpha$, a root), = EXOGENS ; **exorhi'zal**, *exorhiza'lis*, the radicle not sheathed, so the primary root in germination has no covering to pierce ; **Exosclero'tes** ($\sigma\kappa\lambda\eta\rho\dot{o}s$, hard), sclerotia which are external to the surface of Agarics ; **Exos'mose**,

Exosmo'sis (ὠσμὸs, a thrusting), the
passage through a membrane outwards from a thin to a dense fluid ;
Ex'ospore,*Exospor'ium* (σπορὰ, seed),
(1) the outer covering of the spore ;
(2) a thick coat developed from the
periplasm round the oöspore in
Peronosporeae ; (3) the three outer
layers of the spores of *Isoetes* (Fitting) ; **Exosporin'ium**, the outer integument of a pollen-grain, or microspore of flowering plants (Fitting) ;
exos'porous, having scattered spores,
as Fungi ; **Ex'ostome**, *Exost'oma*
(στόμα, a mouth), the foramen of the
outer coat of the ovule ; **Exosto'sis**
(ὀστέον, bone), (1) the nodules on
roots of Leguminosae ; (2) the hard
turgescence of sound wood, showing
as prominent knots ; **Exosty'lus** ‡
(+ STYLUS), Mirbel's word for fruit
as in Labiatae, four seemingly naked
nutlets ; **exoter'ic** (ἐξωτερικὸs, external), arising from outside the
organism, the opposite of ESOTERIC ;
Exotest'a (+ TESTA), the hard outer
layer of a seed-coat (F. W. Oliver) ;
Exothe'cium (θήκη, a case), (1) the
outer case of the anther (Henslow,
Lindley) ; (2) Purkinje's term for
the extine or outer layer of pollen-
grains ; **exotherm'ic** (θερμὸs, hot),
heat derived from outside, and not
as the result of vital action.

exot'ic (ἐξωτικὸs, foreign), not native,
introduced from abroad ; **Exot'ics**
are those plants which are not indigenous ; **Exot'ism**, a shortened
form of **Exot'icism**, the condition
of non-nativity, introduced from
abroad.

exotroph'ic (ἔξω, out of ; τροφή,
nourishment), employed by Wiesner
where an organ or lateral shoot,
as opposed to the mother-shoot,
is most strongly developed ; **Exot'rophy**, development of lateral
shoots instead of the main axis ;
exotrop'ic (τροπὴ, a turning), fertilized from anthers of the same plant
(K. Pearson) ; **Exot'ropism**, the
tendency of lateral roots to grow
away from a main root (Willis) ; **Ex-**

ot'ropy, roots arising from the small
extremities of a flattened secondary
root (Lopriore).

expand'ed, *expan'sus* (Lat. spread
out), diffuse ; **Expan'sion**, the condition of a flower in full perfection ;
~ of protoplasm, the normal condition when it is impermeable
to cell-sap, the opposite of contraction, when it is flaccid and
permeable.

ex'planate, *explana'tus* (Lat., flattened
out), spread out flat.

Explodiflo'rae (*explodo*, I drive off;
flos, floris, a flower), Delpino's term
for wind-fertilized flowers which expel their pollen by explosive action.

expul'sive (*expulsus*, driven out)
Fruits, fruits which forcibly expel
their seeds.

exquisi'tus ‡ (Lat., choice), used of
parts larger or more highly coloured
than usual, as *Bracteae exquisitae ;*
cf. COMA.

exraphid'ian (*ex* = without ; +
RAPHIS), destitute of raphides
(Gulliver).

exscul'ptus (Lat., carved out), showing small depressions as though dug
out, as the seeds of *Anchusa*.

exsert', **exsert'ed**, *exsert'us* (Lat., protruded), protruded beyond, as
stamens beyond the tube of the
corolla.

Exsicca'ta (*exsiccatus*, dry), dried
plants, usually in sets for sale or for
subscribers, frequently with printed
tickets (NOTE. — *Flora exsiccata* is
the full expression).

exstip'ulate, *exstipula'tus* (*ex*, priv. ;
+ STIPULA), wanting stipules.

exsuc'cous, *exsuc'cus* (Lat.), juiceless.

Extensib'ility (*extensus*, spread out),
having the property of stretching.

exten'sus (Lat.), spread out.

extenua'tus (Lat., thinned), a synonym
of VIRGATUS (Henslow).

exte'rior (Lat., outer), outer, in the
flower sometimes = ANTERIOR.

extern'al, *extern'us* (Lat.), outward ;
~ **Sheath**, a modification. of the
bundle-sheath, stated to occur **in**
Ferns (Russow).

Ex′tine (*extimus*, outside ; + ine), the outer coat of a pollen-grain.

ex′tra (Lat.), without, beyond, as **ex′tra-axill′ary**, ~ *axilla′ris*, beyond, or out of the axil ; ~ **-cell′ular**, outside a cell ; ~ **-fascic′ular**, outside the vascular bundles ; ~ **-flor′al**, beyond the flower, as some nectaries ; ~ **-folia′ceous**, away from the leaves, or inserted in a different position from them ; ~ **extramat′rical**, outside of a nidus or matrix ; **Extrameabil′ity** (*meabilis*, penetrable), the capacity of protoplasm to permit substances to pass outwards from its vacuoles.(Janse) ; **extra** (Lat. beyond) **-median**, beyond the middle ; ~ **-nup′tial**, applied to nectaries or honey-glands which are not part of the floral organs ; ~ **-ov′ular** (+ Ovule), exterior to the ovule ; ~ **-prothall′ial** (+ Prothallus) originating outside the prothallium (Bower) ; ~ **-sac′cal**, used of embryos arising outside the cells of the embryo-sac.

extra′rius (Lat.; outward), placed on the outside.

extrasem′inal (*extra*, without), outside the seed, as ~ **Devel′opment**, following the sowing of the seed, as the escape of the embryo, etc.

ex′tra (Lat. beyond) **-ste′lar**, the ground-tissue outside the central cylinder; **extra-trop′ical** (+Tropic), beyond the tropics, to the north or south of them ; **extravagi′nal** (*vagina*, a sheath), beyond or outside the sheath, applied to branches springing from buds, which break through the sheath of the subtending leaf, chiefly in grasses ; **Extravasa′tion** (*vas*, a vessel), unnatural flow of a liquid from a tissue or organ, as the " bleeding " of vines ; **extra-xy′lar**, or **ex′tra-xylem′ic** (+ Xylem), outside the xylem (Roulet).

ex′trorse, *extror′sus* (*exteros*, on the outside; *versus*, towards), directed outward, as the dehiscence of an anther.

ex′tus, a modern term = extra ;

similar in form to *intus*, but not classic Latin.

Exuda′tion (*exudo*, or *exsudo*, I sweat), the transpiration of liquids from hydathodes, etc., as seen on the leaf-tips of Monocotyledons ; ~ **Press′ure**, Pfeffer's term for Root-pressure.

exunguic′ulate (*ex*, priv.; *ungula*, a claw), without a claw (Crozier).

Exn′sion, Berkeley's term for Exudation.

exu′tive (*exutus*, drawn off), applied to seeds wanting the usual integument.

Exu′viae (Lat., stripped off clothing), cast-off parts, as shed scales ; **Exuvia′tion**, the operation of shedding effete material.

Eye, (1) a gardener's name for an undeveloped bud ; (2) the persistent calyx of a pome, *cf.* Crown ; (3) a conspicuous spot in a flower, as a blotch of colour ; (4) = Hilum ; ~ **Spot** (1) a coloured spot in a motile gamete or spore, which is sensitive to light ; (2) markings on the silicious valve of *Coscinodiscus*, consisting of an aperture with a thickened margin in each alveole ; **dor′mant** ~, a bud which is not called into growth.

faba′ceous, *-eus* (*faba*, a bean ; + aceous), like a bean, or having its qualities ; **fabiform′is** (*forma*), applied to Lichen spores which are bean-shaped.

Face, that surface of an organ which is opposed to the back, usually the upper or inner side ; **fa′cial**, applied to a hilum which is on the side and not on the margin of a seed (Heinig).

Fa′cies (Lat., shape), (1) the general aspect of a plant ; (2) suggested for the dominant species of an association, but this usage has been condemned.

factit′ious, *factit′ius* (Lat.), artificial.

Fac′tors, pl. (*factor*, a maker or doer) the elements which in their entirety make up a character or quality.

fac′ultative (*facultas*, capability), occasional, incidental, as opposed to

OBLIGATE ; ~ **An′aërobes**, organisms
which can exist without the presence
of free oxygen or air ; ~ **Par′asites**,
normally saprophytes, but able to
develop as parasites ; ~ **Sap′ro-
phytes**, the converse of the last,
parasites which can run their course
as saprophytes ; ~ **Sym′biont**, an
organism which can either exist and
reach maturity independently or in
symbiosis with another.

fa′ding, withering, without immediately falling away.

Fae′cula, see FECULA.

Fage′tum (*fagus*, a beech-tree), an
association of beeches ; **Fage′ta**,
pl., **asperulo′sa**, beech forests with
ground-vegetation and *Asperula ;* ~
myrtillo′sa, the same with *Vaccinium Myrtillus* in place of *Asperula;* **Fagi′on** (+ION), a formation
of beeches.

Fairy-ring, a circular patch of Agarics
which have grown centrifugally, and
whose influence on the soil is shown
by greener grass after they have
disappeared.

fal′cate, *falca′tus* (Lat.), sickle-shaped ;
falca′rius, **falcator′ius**, are Latin
synonyms ; **fal′ciform**, *falciform′is*
(*falx*, a sickle ;*forma*, shape), sickle-
like.

Fall of the Leaf, defoliation, casting
off the leaves, as done in temperate
climates by deciduous trees in
autumn.

False, *fal′sus* (Lat., untrue), spurious,
having a specious resemblance ;
~ **Ax′is**, a pseudaxis, see SYM-
PODIUM ; ~ **Bark**, a layer on the
outside of endogens of cellular
tissue, into which fibrous tissue
passes obliquely ; ~ **Dichot′omy**, a
dichasium, in which the lateral axes
are two ; ~ **Dissep′iment**, a partition which does not arise from the
edges of carpels, but some form of
cellular tissue ; ~ **Foot**, the base
of the seta in some Bryophytes,
which becomes dilated ; ~ **Fruit**,
a pseudocarp, as a Strawberry ;
~ **Hy′bridism**, Millardet's term
when the hybrid shows the char-

acter of one parent only ; *cf.* MONO-
LEPSIS ; ~ **Indu′sium**, the recurved
margin of some Fern-pinnules, which
serves to protect the sori ; ~ **Par-
ench′yma** = PSEUDOPARENCHYMA ;
~ **Plank′ton**, PLANKTON, at· first
fixed, afterwards broken loose, and
floating (Warming) ; ~ **Raceme′** =
HELICOID CYME ; ~ **Ray**, bands or
aggregations of uniseriate rays in
the wood of certain Cupuliferae
(I. W. Bailey) ; ~ -**stom′ata**
(+ STOMA), pores in the epidermis
of *Equisetum;* ~ **Tis′sue**, hyphal
or mycelial felted tissue ; **falsiner′vis**
(*nervus*, a nerve), when nerves are
formed of cellular tissue, without
fibrovascular bundles, as in Mosses.

Fam′ily, *Famil′ia ;* (1) a group of
genera, formerly styled ORDER ;
(2) "a group of individuals belonging to one species" (Clements) : *i. e.*
the lowest association.

Fan, an equivalent of RHIPIDIUM ;
~ -**nerved**, having the nerves disposed in the fashion of a fan,
radiating from the base ; ~ **shaped**,
flabelliform ; ~**veined**, = ~ NERVED.

farc′tate. *farc′tus* (Lat., stuffed), filled
up, not hollow or tubular.

fa′riam, = in rows, as bi-fariam, in
two rows, etc.

Fari′na (Lat., meal), (1) Blair's term
for pollen ; (2) starch or starchy
matter ; **farina′ceous** (+ ACEOUS), of
the nature of starch, or containing
starch ; **far′inose**, *farino′sus*, (1)
covered with a mealiness ; (2) Mohl's
term for the cellulose of starch.

fa′rious, as bi-, tri-, quadri-**fa′rious**,
in two, three, or four rows.

Fas′cia (Lat., a band), pl. **Fas′ciae**, a
cross-band, as of colour.

fascia′lis. **fasc′iate**, *fascia′tus* (*fascis*,
a bundle), used of the condition of
a stem when several have coalesced ;
Fascia′tion, a band or bundle caused
by a monstrous growth of stems into
one.

fas′ciarius (Lat., band-like), banded,
or band-shaped, narrow and long,
with parallel margins, as in sea-
wrack.

Fas'cicle, *Fascic'ulus* (Lat., a little bundle), a close cluster or bundle of flowers, leaves, stems, or roots ; **fascic'ular**, *fascicula'ris*, **fas'cicled**, *fascicula'tus*, connected or drawn into a fascicle; **fascic'ular Camb'ium**, is that portion which belongs to the vascular bundles ; ~ **Tis'sue**, or ~ **Syst'em**, the fibro-vascular system ; ~ **Xy'lem**, the hadrome, the wood-elements of a bundle ; **fasciola'ris**, **fasciola'tus**, fasciated.

Fasergrübchen (Ger.) = CRYPTO-STOMATA.

fastig'iate, *fastigia'tus* (*fastigium*, a slope, a gable), (1) parallel, clustered and erect, as the branches of *Populus fastigiata*, Linn.; (2) frequently used as if it meant the same as fasciate ; **Fastigia'tion**, when branches become more or less parallel with the main stem.

Fat Bod'ies, pl., fatty oils occurring in plants, often as reserve-material, particularly in seeds ; **Fat En'zyme**, an unorganized ferment which breaks up oils and fats.

Fath'er-plant, in hybrids, the pollen-parent or male element.

Fatigue'-sub'stances, Recnitzer's name for bodies thrown off the plant, which act in a restraining or poisonous way on its own life ; Ger., Ermüdungstoffe.

fatis'cent (*fatisco*, I gape), cracked, or gaping open.

Fau'ces (Lat., the throat), pl., the throat of a gamopetalous corolla ; **Faux**, singular, is an assumed word.

Favel'la (? a diminutive of *favus*, honey-comb), the conceptacle of *Ceramium*, a dense terminal agglomeration of spores within a thin colourless membrane ; **Favellid'ium** (εἰδιον, diminutive) = CYSTOCARP ; **fave'olate**, *faveola'tus* (perhaps from *favus*, honey-comb), honey-combed, alveolate ; **Favil'la**, **Favillid'ium**, Lindley's erroneous spelling of FAVELLA, and FAVELLIDIUM ; **fa'vose**, *favo'sus* (Lat.), honey-combed, as the receptacles of many Compositae ; **favo'so-areola'tus**,

mapped-out into spaces, suggestive of the cavities of honey-comb ; ~ **dehis'cens**, seeming honey-combed after dehiscence, as the anther of *Viscum ;* **favo'sulus**, somewhat honey-combed ; **Fa'vus**, a skin disease caused by *Achorion Schoenleinii*, Remak.

favular'ian, a ribbed surface separated by zigzag furrows in certain genera of fossil Lycopods, derived from the obsolete genus *Favularia*.

feath'er-veined, with secondary veins proceeding from the midrib, penninerved.

feath'ery, plumose, with long hairs which are hairy themselves.

Fe'cula (*faecula*, wine-lees), starch or similar substances ; **fe'culent**, thick with sediment (Crozier).

Fecunda'tion (*fecundo*, to make fruitful) = FERTILIZATION.

Federa'tion, the whole of the plant-associations of the world.

Feed'er, (1) a host-plant ; (2) in *Welwitschia* and other Gnetaceae, an outgrowth of the hypocotyl, serving as a temporary organ of absorption ; (3) used by S. H. Vines for the "foot" of *Selaginella*.

fell'eus (Lat., full of gall), bitter as gall.

Fell-fields, districts of dwarf, scattered plants, chiefly Cryptogams ; **arc'tic** ~, occur round the north pole.

felt'ed matted with intertwined hairs ; ~ **Tis'sue**, hyphal tissue not regularly united, but more or less grown together ; syn. TELA CONTEXTA.

fe'male the fruiting element in plants, the pistil and its analogues, archegonia, oöspheres, etc., shown by ♀.

femin'eus (Lat., womanly), female, as **Flos** ~, a flower which contains pistils but no stamens.

Fen, a moist, level tract, peaty and rich in humus.

Fence, Withering's word for INVOLUCRE.

Fenes'tra (Lat., a window), an opening through a membrane ; **Fenes'trae** (Lat., windows) **apica'les**, and ~ **basa'les**, openings in the outer coat of certain Silicoflagellatae (Lemmermann) ; **fenes'trate**, *fenestra'tus*, *fenestra'lis*, pierced with holes, as the septum in some Cruciferae.

fer, Latin suffix from *fero*, I bear ; occurs in such words as *florifer*, bearing flowers ; sometimes found as -**ferus**, which is very rarely correct.

fe'ral (*fera*, a wild animal), wild, or indigenous ; not cultivated.

Fer'ment (*fermentum*, leaven), a substance which produces or excites chemical changes, but not itself appreciably contributing to the new products. Ferments may be divided into (*a*) organised ~, such as yeast and other Schizomycetes, and (*b*) unorganized ~, or enzymes ; the latter are related to and apparently derived from the proteids ; their composition is not absolutely known, and their names are usually derived from the sources whence they are derived ; diastase, invertase, papain, etc. ; **Fermenta'tion**, the catalytic operation of ferments, particularized as **ace'tic** ~, produced by *Bacterium Aceti*, Lanzi, **alcohol'ic** ~, by yeast, and similar organisms, **butyr'ic** ~, by a *Vibrio*, **lac'tic** ~, by which sugars are turned into acids ; another classification is (1) **diastat'ic** ~, converting starch into sugar ; (2) ferments which decompose glucosides with production of sugar, such as emulsin ; (3) ferments which convert cane-sugar into glucose, as invertase ; (4) and those which convert proteids into peptones, or **pep'tic** ~, such as papain ; **ferment'ative Energe'sis**, the disruptive process by fermentation by which energy is released (Barnes).

Ferrifica'tion (*ferrum*, iron), the action of Ferrobacteria ; **Ferrobacte'ria** (+ BACTERIUM), bacteria which oxidize ferrous to ferric salts ; **ferruginas'cens** (Lat.), becoming rusty ; **ferrugin'eous**, -*eus*, **ferru'ginous**, *ferrugino'sus* (*ferrugo*, rust), rust-coloured ; **Ferru'go** (Lat.), a disease in plants known also as "Rust," due to the *Uredo* stage of various species of *Puccinia*.

fert'ile, *fert'ilis* (Lat.), capable of producing fruit ; ~ **Cells**, binucleate cells forming a basal layer in the aecidium of uredineous Fungi, and giving rise to the aecidiospores ; ~ **Flow'ers**, female flowers, those which possess pistils ; ~ **Sta'mens**, those bearing pollen which fecundates the ovules ; — **self** ~, flowers perfectly fruitful in the absence of insects ; **Fertil'ity**, the state of being fertile ; **Fertiliza'tion**, *Fertilisa'tio*, (1) fusion of two gametes to form a new individual cell (zygote) ; (2) the effect of pollen, deposited on stigmatic surface, resulting in conversion of flower into fruit, and of ovule into seed ; **Close** ~, breeding in-and-in, or successive progeny of closely related parents ; **Cross** ~, progeny by other forms not of close affinity ; *cf.* POLLINATION; **double** ~, one generative nucleus from the pollen-tube fuses with the nucleus of the egg-cell (oosphere), the other with the definite nucleus, itself formed by fusion of the polar nuclei ; **genera'tive** ~, the sexual union of germ plasm of different parentage and diverse potentialities ; **Post-** ~, the stage after fertilization to the ripening of the seed ; **Pre-** ~, the stage of the ovules previous to fertilization ; **reduc'ed** ~, partial fusion of a female cell with a vegetative cell, or the fusion of two female cells ; **vegeta'tive** ~, the stimulus to growth resulting from the fusion of two nuclei or other masses of protoplasm ; — ~ **Tube**, the channel by which gonoplasm passes from the antheridium to the oogonium in Peronosporeae.

ferula'ceous, *ferula'ceus* (Lat.), (1) resembling the genus *Ferula* ; (2) pertaining to reeds or canes, or being formed like them, hollow.

Fervida'rium (*fervidus*, boiling hot), applied in botanic gardens to the Stove.

Festuca're, a community of *Festuca* ; (Clements) ; **Festuce'tum**, an association of the same grass-genus ; **fes'tucine**, straw-coloured, as the dry culm of *Festuca;* **fes'tucous,** formed of straw.

fe'tidus = FOETIDUS.

Fibonac'ci Se'ries, Braun's series of numbers formed thus, 1. 2, 3, 5, 8, 13, 21, 34, 55 . . by successive additions of the last two; they occur in phyllotaxis, and were formulated by Leonardo of Pisa, surnamed Fibonacci.

Fi'bre, *Fi'bra* (Lat.), (1) a fine thread or filament, chambered or woody; (2) the fusiform cells of the inner bark; (3) the ultimate rootlets; **element'ary ~,** the thread in a spiral vessel, secondary deposit in a spiral; **fi'briform** (*forma,* shape), fibre-shaped; **Fi'bril, Fibrill'a,** diminutive of FIBRE; **~ of Nu'cleus** = CHROMOSOME; **fi'brillate,** *fibrillatus,* **fi'brillose, fi'brillous,** *fibrillo'sus,* furnished with fibres, as roots, or having a finely lined appearance; **~ Lay'er,** two outer layers of closely woven hyphae in *Geaster;* **~ Myce'lium** = FIBROUS MYCELIUM; **Fi'brin** (**veg'etable**), occurs in gluten, has no fibrous structure as animal fibrin, but forms when dry a tough, horny mass; **fi'bro-cel'lular,** "composed of spiral cells"; **fibro-va'sal** (Hillhouse) = **~ -vascu'lar,** tissue of mixed vessels and fibres; **~ ~ Bun'dle,** or Vascular Bundle, an association of vessels characteristic of the higher plants, usually consisting of phloëm and xylem elements, often surrounded by a special layer of cells known as the bundle-sheath; **~ Cord,** proposed by Strasburger for the similar structure in monocotyledons; **~ Cyl'inder,** the central cylinder; **~ Sys'tem,** the whole of the fibrous portion of a plant, exclusive of the purely cellular structures; **Fibrole'in,** Fayod's term for a very delicate membrane of the spirals of protoplasm (hyaloplasm); **fi'brous, fi'brose,** *fibro'sus,* having much woody fibre, as the rind of a Coco-nut; **Fi'brous-myce'lium,** when the hyphae form long branching strands; **Fi'brose,** Frémy's term

for the substance of woody fibre, a variety of cellulose; **Fi'brosin,** a reserve substance resembling FIBROSE, found by Zopf in the conidia of certain Fungi, in the form of rounded flattened discs, embedded in the protoplasm; **~ Bod'ies,** the discs described; **Fi'brotype** (*fibra,* a filament; *typus,* a type), Macdougal's expression for the condition of a root of *Cephalanthera* with a reduction and fusion of the stelar compounds, and radially elongated cortex; **fi'bry,** used by Loudon for FIBROUS.

Fi'bula (Lat., a buckle), a cylindrical podetium, terminated by apothecia.

fid'dle-shaped, panduriform.

-fidus, Latin suffix for cleft, as *trifidus,* three-cleft.

Field-stra'tum (*stratum,* a layer), formed by grass and herbs and dwarf shrubs (Warming).

Fig-insect, the fertilizing agent in caprification, *Blastophaga.*

Fi'la (pl. of *filum,* a thread), **adductor'ia,** the abortive "pistillidia" of Mosses; **~ succulent'a,** paraphyses.

Fil'ament, *Filament'um* (*filum,* a thread), (1) the stalk of an anther, the thread-like stem; (2) any thread-like body; **Filament'a ostiola'ria,** delicate colourless threads lining the perithecium round the epithecium of *Verrucaria;* **filament'ous, filament'ose,** *filamento'sus,* formed of filaments or fibres; **~ Fung'us,** growth-form of a branched hypha without union with other hyphae; **~ Myce'lium** = FIBROUS MYCELIUM; **~ Spor'ophore,** a simple sporophore; **~ Thal'lus** = FRUTICOSE THALLUS; **Fi'lar-plas ma** (πλάσμα, moulded), Strasburger's term for KINOPLASM; **fila'rious** (Crozier) = FILAMENTOUS; **fila'tus** (Lat.) = VIRGATUS.

Files, a series of *Navicula*-like frustules as in *Micromega.*

Fil'ial (*filia,* a daughter) **-cell,** Henfrey's term for daughter-cell; **~ Genera'tion,** the first cross-bred generation, denoted by F_1; the second by F_2, etc.

fil′ical (*filix*, a fern), Fern-like, or allied to Ferns; **filicin′ean, filicin′-eous**, relating to the Filicineae, that is, Ferns in the widest sense (Scott); **fil′icoid** (εἶδος, like), Fern-like; **Filicol′ogy** (λόγος, discourse), = PTERIDOLOGY.

fil′iform, *filiform′is* (*filum*, a thread; *forma*, shape), thread-shaped; ~ **Appara′tus**, the upper ends of the synergidae, which pierce through and are prolonged beyond the summit of the embryo-sac; **filipend′ulous,** *-lus* (*pendulus*, hanging down), having tuberous swellings in the middle or end of filiform roots; **Filobacte′ria** (+ BACTERIUM), thread-like bacteria; **fi′lose**, ending in a thread-like process (Crozier).

Fim′bria (Lat., fringe), (1) a fringe; (2) an elastic-toothed membrane beneath the operculum of mosses; **fim′briate**, *fimbria′tus*, with the margin bordered by long slender processes; **fim′bricate** = FIMBRIATE (Crozier); **Fimbril′la**, a diminutive fringe; **fimbril′late**, *fimbrilla′tus*, having fimbrillae; **fimbrillif′erous,** *-rus*, with many little fringes, as the receptacle of the Compositae.

fimeta′rius (*fimetum*, a dung-hill), growing on or amongst dung.

fimic′olous (*fimus*, dung; *colo*, I inhabit), growing on manure-heaps.

Finger-and-toe, a disease in Crucifers caused by *Plasmodiophora Brassicae*, Woron.;—Clubbing or Anbury.

fing′ered, digitate.

Fi′niform (*finis*, a boundary; + FORM), a form whose nearest relations have completely died out (Kuntze).

First′ling-Cell, from the Germ. Erstlingzelle, the first of a new generation from an auxospore in Diatoms.

Fise′tin, the yellow colouring-matter of *Rhus Cotinus*, Linn.

fis′sile, *fis′silis* (Lat.), tending to split, or easily split; **Fis′sion**, splitting; ~ **Fun′gi** = Schizomycetes; **Fissip′arism** (*pario*, I bring

forth), the act of multiplication among the lower forms by breaking up into living portions; **Fissipar′ity** = FISSIPARISM; **fissip′arous**, dividing into two or more divisions by splitting; **fis′sus** (Lat., split), split or divided half-way.

Fis′tula (Lat.), a pipe; ~ **spira′lis** = TRACHEA; **fis′tular, fis′tulose**, *fistulo′sus*, **fis′tulous**, hollow throughout its length as the leaf and stem of an onion.

Fixa′tion of CO_2, respiration of oxygen and retention of carbon dioxide.

flabel′late, *flabella′tus* (*flabellum*, a fan), fan-shaped, dilated in a wedge-shaped, sometimes plaited; **flabel′liform**, *flabelliform′is* (*forma*, shape), shaped as a fan; **flabelliner′ved** (*nervus*, a nerve), radiate-veined.

flac′cid, *flac′cidus* (Lat.), withered and limp, flabby.

Flacherie′ (Fr.), a disease in silkworm caused by *Micrococcus Bombycis*, Cohn.

Flag-appara′tus, Goebel's term for anthers becoming petaloid, as a signal for insect-visitors.

Flagella′ta (*flagellum*, a whip), Algae distinguished by possessing whip-like flagella, by which they are able to progress through the water; **flag′ellate**, *flagella′tus*, provided with whip-like runners; **flagella′ris**, having creeping sarmenta; **flag′ellary**, caused by flagella, as the motion of zoospores (Crozier); **Flagel′lum**, pl. **Flagel′la**, (1) a runner or sarmentum, branchlets in Mosses; (2) the whip-like process of the protoplasm of a swarmspore; (3) similar organs in the cells of some Schizomycetes; **flagel′liform**, *flagelliform′is* (*forma*, shape), (1) resembling a runner, or (2) lash-like, as the cilia of zoospores; **Flagello′sis**, a disease of *Euphorbia* attributed to *Leptomonas Davidi*, a flagellate parasite.

flag′on-shaped (Loudon), used for flask-shaped.

Flake, a nectariferous gland (S. F. Gray); **fla′ky**, lamelliform.

flame-coloured, *flam'meus* (Lat.), fiery red.

Flange, (1) a ring-like projection of the integumental lining of the micropyle of certain fossil seeds ; (2) Bower's term for the apparent margin of the pinnae in *Blechnum*.

Flank-curv'ature, unequal growth of climbers, Ger. " Flanken-Krümmung" ; **Flanks**, the lateral surfaces of a bilateral body.

Flask, the utricle of *Carex;* **flask-shaped**, having the form of a Florence flask, somewhat globular, with a drawn-out neck.

Flats, proposed equivalent for the German " Etagenbildung."

Flat'tening, (1) the fasciation of a stem ; (2) the production of a cladodium.

Flave'do (Lat.), yellowness, a disease in which the green parts have become yellow.

flaves'cent, *flaves'cens* (Lat.), yellowish, becoming yellow ; **fla'vicans**, **fla'vidus** (Lat.), somewhat yellow ; **Fla'vone** (*flavus*, yellow), a natural yellow colouring matter occurring in plants ; **fla'vo-vi'rens** (Lat.), yellowish green ; **fla'vous**, *fla'vus*, nearly pure yellow, a bright clear hue.

Flee'ciness, villosity.

Flesh, the soft parts, as the flesh of apples or pears ; **flesh'y**, succulent.

flexed (*flexus*, bent), used of Diatoms which appear as though bent ; **flex'ible**, *flex'ilis, flexib'ilis*, capable of being bent, but elastic enough to be able to resume its original figure ; **flex'uose**, *flexuo'sus*, **flex-'uous**, bent alternately in opposite directions, zigzag ; **Flex'ure**, the "bend" of Diatoms.

float'ing, borne on the surface of water ; ~ **Tis'sue**, air-containing tissue in the seeds of plants dispersed by water currents (Haberlandt).

Floc'ci, pl. of **Floc'cus** (Lat , a lock of wool), locks of soft hair or wool ; **floc'cose**, *flocco'sus*, bearing flocci, ~ **Myce'lium**, = FIBROUS MYCELIUM ; **floc'culent**, *flocculent'us*, diminutive of FLOCCOSE ; **floc'culose**, like wool (Leighton).

Flo'ra (Lat., goddess of flowers), (1) the aggregate plants of a country or district, (2) a work which contains an enumeration of them ; **Flo'rae Horolo'gium**, a floral clock, certain plants arranged in the order of the hours of opening or closing ; **flo'ral**, *flora'lis*, belong to flowers ; ~ **A'pex** = MAMELON ; ~ **Di'agram**, a drawing to show the relative position and number of the constituent parts ; ~ **En'velopes**, the perianth leaves, calyx and corolla ; ~ **Glume**, the lower glume of the flower in grasses ; flowering glume (Beal) ; ~ **Leaf** = BRACT ; a suggested equivalent for the Ger. "Hochblatt."

Flores'cence, *Florescen'tia*, anthesis, the period of flowering ; **Flo'ret**, a small flower, one of a cluster, as in Compositae.

floribun'dus (*flos, floris*, a flower ; *abundus*, = production of present activity), abounding in flowers ; **Floricul'ture** (*cultura*, cultivation), cultivation of flowers, flower gardening ; **Flor'ie**, Grew's word for perianth ; **flo'rifer** (Lat), **florif'erous**, flower-bearing ; **florif'erae Gem'mae**, flower buds ; **Florifica'tion**, the act or time of flowering ; **flo'riform** (*forma*, shape), shaped like a flower ; **Flo'riglume**, the flowering glume in grasses ; **Flo'rilege** (*lego*, I gather), a treatise on flowers ; **florip'arous**, *-us* (*pario*, I bring forth), (1) producing flowers, (2) a monstrosity producing other flowers instead of fruit ; **Flo'rist**, (1) a cultivator of flowers, especially those variable forms known as florist's flowers, (2) a writer of a Flora, (3) in foreign usage "Florist" means a local botanist ; **Floraëcol'ogy**, used for the ecology of flowers (Lovell) ; **Flo'rula**, (1) a small flora, (2) the botanic account of a small district ; **flo'rulent**, flowery ; **flo'rus**, in composition means flowered, as *uni-florus*, one flowered.

Flos (Lat.), an assemblage of the organs essential for fertilization, as stamens and pistils, with some protecting envelope ; ~ **A′quae,** floating Algae, as *Rivularia fluitans,* Cohn ; ~ **compos′itus** ‡ = CAPITULUM ; ~ **ple′nus,** a double flower, where the stamens or pistils, or both, are converted into petals ; **flos′cular, flos′-culous,** *flosculo′sus* (1) relating to florets or flowers, or presenting many florets ; (2) with tubular florets.

Flos′cule, Flos′culum (Blair), *Flosculus,* a little flower. a floret ; **Sem′i-flos′cule,** a composite floret ; **Floss,** the down in certain Compositae, as Thistle-down : **Flossifica′tion,** flowering, expansion of flowers.

Flou′rish, Blair's word for a disk-floret of Compositae ; **half** ~ the same for ligulate florets.

Flow′er, defined under FLOS ; ~ **Bud,** an unexpanded flower, as distinct from a leaf-bud ; ~ **Head,** a cluster of flowers, as the Capitulum or Head in Compositae ; **Flow′erage,** the state of being in flower ; **Flow′eret,** a small flower, a floret ; **Flow′eriness,** abounding with flowers; **Flow′ering,** the maturity of the floral organs, and expansion of their envelopes ; ~ **Glume,** the lower of the two organs which subtend the flower of Grasses (the upper being the palea) ; ~ **Plants** = PHANEROGAMS ; **flow′erless,** destitute of flowers ; ~ **Plants** = CRYPTOGAMS ; **Flow′erlessness,** absence of flowers ; **flow′ery,** abounding in flowers.

Flow′ers of Tan = *Aethalium septicum,* Fr. ; ~ **of Wine,** growth of *Saccharomyces Mycoderma,* Reess.

flu′itant, *fluitans* (Lat.), floating.

Fluke-cell, resembling the fluke of an anchor ; in shaggy hairs of *Cranocarpus.*

flumina′lis, flumin′eus (*flumen,* a river), applied to plants which grow in running water.

Fluores′cence (from Fluor-spar), the property of diminishing the refrangibility of light ; ~ **of Chlor′ophyll,** the shifting of the spectrum by the colouring matter contained in chlorophyll ; **fluorescigen′ic** (+ FLUORESCENCE ; γένος, offspring), causing fluorescence, as certain bacteria.

Flush, a shallow runnel floored with vegetation result (Crampton) ;— **Snow-** ~ tracks of channels leading from snow-patches ; *cf.* ANTHELIA.

flu′vial, *fluvia′lis,* **fluviat′ic** (Crozier), **flu′viatile,** *fluviat′ilis* (Lat.), applied to plants growing in streams.

Fly-flow′ers, those specially adapted to be fertilized by flies ; **Fly-traps,** contrivances by which insects are caught, as pitchers, tentacles of *Drosera,* etc. ; **Fly-wood,** oakwood destroyed by *Stereum* (Tubeuf).

Fly′ing-hairs, hairs which aid seeds in dispersal ; ~ **Mem′brane,** the expanded structures in winged seeds ; ~ **Tis′sue.** the structure composing the last (Haberlandt).

foemin′eus = FEMINEUS, female.

foeni′nus (*foenum,* hay), "hay-grey" (Hayne).

foe′tidus (Lat., stinking), fetid, smelling strongly and disagreeably ; **Foe′tor** (Lat., a stench), the odour given off by flowers which thereby attract carrion flies.

fo′lded, in vernation when the two halves of a leaf are applied to one another ; ~ **Tis′sue.** endoderm with suberified or liquified membrane, confined to a band on the lateral and transverse faces of the cells, without thickening (Van Tieghem).

Folds of Sa′nio = SANIO'S RIMS.

folia′ceous, *-eus* (*folium,* a leaf; + ACEOUS), having the texture or shape of a leaf, as the branches of *Xylophylla;* ~ **Thal′lus,** a frondose thallus, flat and leaf-like, usually crisped and lobed, which spreads over the surface on which it grows, and can be detached without much injury ; **Folia′ceae,** frondose vascular Cryptogams ; **Fo′liage,** the leafy covering, especially of trees ; ~ **Leaves,** ordinary leaves, as distinguished from those which have undergone metamorphoses as bracts, petals, etc. ; **Fo'lial** = FOLIOLE ; **fo'liar**, *folia'ris*, (1) leafy or leaf-like, (2) inserted on, or forming an appendix to a leaf, epiphyllous ; *cir'rhus folia'ris* = tendril ; ~ **Gap**, a mesh in the vascular bundle cylinder from the margin of which vascular bundles pass into the frond in Ferns ; ~ **Spur**, a dwarf shoot in a pine-tree, which bears a pair of leaves (Hartig) ; ~ **Trace**, = LEAF-TRACE ; the remains of the vascular bundle or bundles which supplied the leaf.

fo'liate, *folia'tus* (Lat.), leaved, clothed with leaves, as **bi-fo'liate**, two-leaved, etc.

Folia'tion, *Folia'tio* (Lat.), vernation ; used by Grew for the act of leafing.

Fo'liature (*foliatura*, foliage), Blair's term for petals.

folif'erous, foliif'erous, -*rus* (*folium*, a leaf ; *fero*, I bear), leaf-bearing ; **foliic'olous** (*colo*, I inhabit), growing on leaves, as some Fungi and Lichens ; **folii'ferae Gem'mae** (Lat.), leaf-buds ; **fo'liiform**, *foliiform'is* (*forma*, shape) = foliaceous ; **foliip'-arous,** -*rus* (*pario*, I bring forth), ·bearing leaves ; **fo'liolar**, relating to a leaflet ; **fo'liolate**, *foliola'tus*, clothed with leaflets ; **bi-, tri-fo'liolate**, two-, three-leafletted ; **folio'-lean**, *foleola'nus*, growing from the end of a leaf.

Fo'liole, *Fol'iola* (dim. of *folium*), (1) a leaflet, the secondary division of a compound leaf ; (2) employed by Spruce for the postical leaves of Hepaticae, those on the ventral or rooting surface ; **fo'liolose**, closely covered with leaflets ; **Fo'liolum**, a small leaf or leaflet ; **fo'liose**, *folio'sus*, (1) closely clothed with leaves ; (2) applied to a Lichen with a leaf-like expansion of the thallus : **fo'lious**, having leaves intermixed with flowers ; **Fo'lium**, (Lat.), a leaf, pl. **Fo'lia.**

Follice'tum (*folliculum*, a small bag), a whorl of follicles ; **Fol'licle**, *Follic'ulus*, (1) a fruit of one carpel, opening by a ventral suture to which the seeds are attached, formerly applied to any capsular fruit ; (2) by Linnaeus used for the bladder of *Utricularia ;* (3) a little bladder on the leaves of some Mosses, as *Pottia cavifolia*, Ehrh. ; **follic'ular**, *follicula'ris*, **folliculiform'is** (*forma*, shape), shaped like a follicle.

fonta'nus, fontina'lis (Lat.), relating to a spring), growing in or near a spring of water.

Food-bodies, small pear-shaped bodies formed on or near the leaves of certain plants, as *Acacia spadicifera*, Cham. & Schlecht., and *Leea aequata*, Linn., which are utilised by ants as food ; Ger. " Ameisenbrödchen."

Foot, (1) as a measure, 12 inches, or 30·5 cm., sign ' ; (2) = PODIUM ; (3) a development from the hypobasal part of the embryo, as an organ of attachment and temporary nutrition ; (4) in Myxogastres, the first development from the plasmodium which leads to the formation of spores, a cell-wall of cellulose, forming an axis (Van Tieghem) ; (5) the base of a hair, often enlarged ; ~ **Cell**, the spore of *Guttulina rosea*, Cienk., arising from a naked cell of protoplasm, from the aggregated plasmodium ; ~ **Em'bryo**, an arrested terminal growth of the embryo of *Cutleria*, thus differing from the protonematoid embryo of the same species ; ~ **Rot**, a disease on species of *Citrus* caused by *Fusarium Limonis*, Briosi ; ~ **Stalk**, a stem specialised as peduncle, petiole, etc.

Fora'men (Lat., a hole), an aperture, especially that in the outer integuments of the ovule; *cf.* MICROPYLE; **foram'inose**, *foramino'sus*, perforated by holes ; **Foramin'ula**, " the ostiolum of certain Fungals " (Lindley) ; **foramin'ulose**, marked with little holes.

Force, any cause which changes the state of a body as to rest or motion ; vital force is kinetic energy.

Forc′ing, the operation by which cultivators produce fruit and vegetables out of season, early or late.

for′cipate, *forcipa′tus* (*forceps*, nippers), forked like pincers.

Fore-leaf, a translation of the Ger. "Vorblatt"; a bracteole or prophyllum.

Fore-run′ner Point, a form of leaf apex which performs all duties of assimilation before the basal portion is mature; Ger. "Vorläuferspitze."

For′est, in a botanic sense, land covered with trees exclusively, or with an undergrowth of shrubs or herbs; many varieties are recognized by ecologists, *e. g.*, **swamp ~**, etc., **forest′ian** (upper), a stage in peat when *Pinus* was dominant; **~** or (lower). *Betula, Corylus* and *Alnus*, the prevalent trees, in the peat-stage.

Fore′wold, the thicket zone bordering a forest (Clements).

forfica′tus, (*forfex*, scissors), scissorlike, resembling shears.

forked, separating into two divisions, more or less apart.

Form (*forma*, shape), a slight variety. or variation, as long and short-styled Forms; nearly thirty special terms are enumerated by O. Kuntze in his "Methodik der Speciesbeschreibung," pp. 15–17; **~ Gen′us**, a genus made up of an assemblage of **~ Spe′cies**, an apparent species which is really a single stage of the life-cycle of a pleomorphous species; **~ Spore**, a body simulating a spore. but without germinating power, or remaining attached to its sporophore; **For′mae oxyda′tae**, (Lat.) crustaceous Lichens which have become rust-coloured from an infiltration of some salt of iron.

Forma′tion, (*formatio*, a shaping), in botany, applied to an assemblage of plants of similar habits and environment, as a forest is a **~** of trees, turf a **~** of grasses; in Ger. "Pflanzenverein"; **closed ~**, when the plants are so crowded that invasion is difficult; **mixed ~**. when a mixture of two or more distinct formations; **o′pen ~**, when the plants and groups are scattered (Clements); **sec′ondary ~**, those which have arisen through human interference (Warming); Dr. Moss's subdivisions are given under ASSOCIATION. NOTE:- *Association* is also used, but both terms are somewhat loosely employed.

form′ative. giving form, plastic; **~ Irritabil′ity**, the capacity of tissues to respond to stimuli and to produce outgrowths (Virchow); **~ Mate′rials**, applied to such as starch, sugar, fats, and albuminoids; **~ Re′gion**, the growing point proper; **~ Stim′ulus**, the capacity of micro-organisms to produce outgrowths of determinate form (Virchow).

formicar′ian (*formica*, an ant), applied by Beccari to those plants possessing saccharine fluids, thus attracting ants.

for′nicate, *fornica′tus* (Lat., arched over), provided with scale-like appendages in the corolla-tube, as in *Myosotis;* **For′nices**, pl. of **For′nix** (Lat.), a little scale.

Fos′sil (*fossus*, dug), the remains of a plant changed to a stony consistence, from various strata; **~ Bot′any**, the department which takes note of fossil plants, palaeobotany.

Fos′sula (Lat., a little ditch), a small groove in some Diatom-valves.

Fost′er-plant = HOST.

Founda′tion, a literal rendering of the Ger. "Anlage."

four-fold, quadruple; **~ Pol′len-Grains**, as in *Oenothera*, which form coherent tetrads.

Fov′ea (Lat., a small pit), a depression or pit, as (1) in the upper surface of the leaf-base in *Isoëtes*, which contains the sporangium; (2) the seat of the pollinium in Orchids; **fov′eate** *fovea′tus*, pitted; **Fov′eola**, (1) a small pit; (2) "the perithecium of certain Fungals" (Lindley); (3) in

Isoëtes, a small depression above the fovea, from which the ligule springs; **fov′eolate**, *foveola′tus*, marked with small pitting.

Fovil′la (*foveo*, I nourish), the contents of the pollen-grain.

Fox′glove-shaped, like the corolla of *Digitalis;* digitaliform.

frac′idus (Lat., mellow), of a pasty texture, between fleshy and pulpy.

Frac′tional (*fractio*, a breaking) **cul′t′ures**, *cf.* SEPARATION CULTURES; **Fractiona′tion**, in biology denoting variation due to the quantitative disintegration of factors (Bateson).

Fragmenta′tion (*fragmentum*, a piece), Van Beneden's term for direct division of the nucleus.

Fran′gulin, a yellow crystalline body from the parenchyma of *Rhamnus Frangula*, Linn.

Fratern′ity (*fraternitas*, a brotherhood), see ADELPHIA.

Fraxine′tum, an association of ash-trees; **Frax′inin**, a principle existing in the bark of the ash, *Fraxinus excelsior*, Linn.

free, not adhering, the reverse of adnate; **Free-cell**, a cell formed by ~ **Cell-forma′tion**, the production of new cells from several nuclei within the mother-cell, as in pollen; endogenous cell-formation.

Fren′ching, a disease caused by *Fusarium vasinfectum*, Atkins., in the leaf of the cotton-plant (Tubeuf).

fre′quent, used of a species often occurring.

Frigida′rium (Lat., the cool room), in botanic gardens applied to the Orangery, or Temperate House with simple exclusion of frost.

Frigofu′ges (*frigidus*, cold; *fugio*, I flee), plants which shun low temperatures; **Frigorideser′ta**, pl. (*frigidus*, cold; + DESERT), cold deserts with vegetation of herbaceous perennials, frequently of tufted growth; they are nearest to the poles of any desert.

Frill = ARMILLA.

Fringe, used by Sir W. J. Hooker for the peristome of Mosses; **fringed**, margined with hair-like appendages; fimbriate.

Frond, *Frons* (Lat., a leaf), (1) the foliage of Ferns and other Cryptogams; (2) the leaves of Palms, according to Linnaeus; ~ **-gen′us**, a genus described solely from fronds, as of Ferns; **frondesce′**, to unfold leaves; **Frondes′cence**, *Frondescen′tia*, (1) vernation; (2) phyllody; (3) by Morren restricted to the formation of leaf-like organs in the place of petals; see also VIRESCENCE; **frondif′erous** (*fero*, I bear), producing fronds; **fron′diform** (*forma*, shape), like the fronds of Ferns; **frondip′arous** (*pario*, I bring forth), (1) bearing fronds; (2) the monstrous production of leaves instead of fruit: **Fron′dlet**, a small frond; **fron′dose**, **fron′dous**, *frondo′sus* (Lat., full of leaves), (1) leafy; (2) frond-like or bearing fronds: ~ **Thal′lus**, foliaceous thallus; **Fron′dula**, **Fron′dules**, used by J. Smith for the main stems of *Selaginella*.

Front, of a Diatom, is that view which has the cingulum facing and the valves fore-shortened in side view.

Front-cav′ity, the outer cavity of a stoma; in Ger. "Vorhof."

Frost-cracks, longitudinal cracks in the bark due to sudden reduction of temperature; **Frost-rib**, callus caused by growth after a rise of temperature of a FROST-CRACK, and consequent closing of the wound; **frost′ed**, with a surface having the appearance of hoar frost.

Fructes′cence, *Fructescen′tia* (*fructus*, fruit), the time of maturity of fruit.

fructif′erous (*fructifer*, fruit-bearing), producing or bearing fruit; **Ca′lyx fruc′tifer**, the fruiting calyx.

Fructif′ication, *Fructifica′tio* (Lat.), (1) fruiting; (2) in Cryptogams, the result of the sexual act; (3) any sporogenous structure or an aggregate of them; **double** ~. dimorphic fructification in Algae.

fructip´arous (*fructus*, fruit; *pario*, I bring forth); **Fruc´tose,** fruit-sugar, or levulose; it exists with other sugars in fruits, honey, and treacle; **Fruc´tus** (Lat.), fruit, the product resulting from fertilization.

frugif´erous (*fruges*, pl. of *frux*, fruits of the earth; *fero*, I bear), produ~ing fruits or crops.

Fruit, (1) strictly, the pericarp and its seeds, the fertilized and developed ovary; (2) widely, the matured pericarp and its contents, with any external part which is an integral portion of it; ~ **-bear´er,** Potter's term for Carpophore; ~ **-bodies,** (1) zygotes which show subdivision into spores; (2) sporophores; ~ **Dots,** the sori of Ferns; ~ **-forms,** forms or means of reproduction of Fungi (Potter); ~ **Galls,** diseased growth caused by *Ustilago Treubii,* Solms; ~ **Stalk,** (1) peduncle; (2) the seta of Mosses; ~ **Su´gar,** = Levulose; ~ **Walls** (or ~ **Coats),** the pericarp; **Spu´rious** ~ = Pseudo-carp.

frumenta´ceous, *frumenta´ceus* (Lat., of corn; **frumenta´rious,** *frumenta´rius* (Lat.), (1) pertaining to grain; (2) producing sufficient starch to warrant culture; **Frumen´tum** (Lat., grain), produce of corn-lands; grain or cereals.

frustra´neous (*frustra,* useless), relating to the Linnean order *Frustranea,* Compositae with the disk flowers hermaphrodite, and those of the ray neuter or imperfect.

Frus´tule, *Frus´tula* (*frustulum,* a small piece), a Diatom cell, consisting of valves, girdle and contents; **Frus´tilla,** an obsolete synonym; **frus´tulose,** consisting of small fragments.

Fru´tex (Lat., a shrub), a woody plant destitute of a trunk; **frutes´cent,** *frutes´cens,* becoming shrubby; **Frut´ical,** a small shrub with a soft-wooded stem, such as shrubby species of *Geranium* (J. Smith); **fru´ticant,** *fru´ticans,* growing into a shrub-like plant; (1) **fru´ticose,**

frutico´sus, shrubby; (2) in *Rubus,* allied or belonging to the super-species *R. fruticosus;* **fru´ticous** is a synonym; ~ **Thal´lus** a Lichen having a shrub-like thallus; **fruti-c´ulose,** somewhat shrubby; **Fruti-c´ulus** (Lat.), a small shrub.

fruticules´cent (*fruticulus,* a small shrub; + escens), applied to a Lichen when somewhat shrubby (Crombie).

Fru´tlet, suggested for low tufted evergreen plants as Saxifrages (J. Smith).

Fru´tose = Fructose, Fruit-sugar.

fuca´ceous (*fu´cus,* from φῦκος, sea-weed; + aceous), relating to the genus *Fucus,* as ~ **Ve´sicles,** the bladders of *F. vesiculosus;* **fu´coid** (εἶδος, like), **fucoi´dal,** resembling seaweed; **Fu´cosan,** Hanstein's name for a granular substance found in the assimilating tissue of Fucoideae, the Phaeophyceae-starch of Schmitz; **Fu´cose** is probably a partial inversion of it; **Fucoxan´thine** (ξανθὸς, yellow) Sorby's name for the colour-ing-matter of the olive-green sea-weeds.

fuga´cious (*fugax,* fleeting), soon perishing.

ful´ciens (*fulcio,* I support), support-ing, used of an organ above another.

Ful´cra (pl. of *fulcrum,* a prop), the appendages of the leaves, as prickles, tendrils, stipules, etc.; **fulcra´ceus,**‡ of or belonging to the fulcra; **ful´-crate,** *ful´cratus,* having fulcra.

fulgin´eus (Lat., sooty), **fulig´inous, fulig´inose,** *fuligino´sus,* sooty, or soot-coloured.

full, used of a double-flower, the stamens and pistils being trans-formed into petals.

fulmin´eus (*fulmen,* lightning), ful-vous, almost brown; used of a species of *Cortinarius* by Fries.

fulvel´lus, fulves´cens, ful´vidus (Lat.), **ful´vid** (Crozier), the diminutive of the next; **ful´vous,** *ful´vus* (Lat.), yellow, tawny.

fuma´goid resembling *Fumago.*

fumaria´ceous, pertaining to *Fumaria,*

or its allies ; **fuma′rioid**, like the genus *Fumaria*.

Fu′marole (It., fumarole, from *fumo*, I give off smoke), a spot in a volcanic region which gives off sulphurous vapour; the surrounding flora is xerophilous (A. F. W. Schimper).

fu′meus (Lat., full of smoke), smoky, or smoke-coloured ; **fu′midus** (Lat.), slightly smoke-coloured; **fumiga′tus** (Lat.), as though smoked, fumed ; **fu′mose**, *fumo′sus*, **fu′mous**, smoke-grey.

funa′lis (Lat., of a rope) = FUNILI-FORM.

Func′tion (*functio*, performance), the peculiar action caused by certain stimuli ; **func′tional Metab′olism**, the kinetic effects of certain chemical changes in the plant.

Fun′dament (*fundamentum*, ground-work), a suggested equivalent of the Ger. "Anlage" (Potter) ; **fundamen′tal**, basic ; ~ **Cells**, parenchyma; ~ **Or′gans**, the nutritive organs essential to plant existence ; ~ **Spi′ral** = genetic spiral ; ~ **Sys′tem** = cellular system ; ~ **Tis′sue**, tissue not belonging to the normal or fasicular system; ground tissue; **fundamenta′lius**, an essential part, as the axis and appendages of a plant ; **Fundamen′tum** = HYPOCOTYL.

Fun′dus (Lat., foundation) = COLLUM.

funga′ceous (*fungus*, a mushroom), F. von Mueller's word for fungoid or fungus-like ; **fun′gal**, relating to Fungi ; **fun′gic**, belonging to mushrooms ; ~ **Ac′id**, a mixture of citric, malic, and phosphoric acids (Cooke) ; **fun′gicidal** (*-cida*, a killer), destructive of Fungi ; **Fungici′de**, an agent or mixture for killing Fungi ; antimycotic ; **fun′giform**, *fungiform′is* (*forma*, shape), **fungil′liform**, *fungilli′form′is*, mushroom - shaped ; **Fungil′lus**, a small parasitic Fungus; **Fung′in**, the "flesh" of mushrooms, Fungus cellulose ; **fungi′nus**, belonging to a Fungus ; **fung′oid** (εἶδος, like), pertaining to a Fungus; ~ **Par′asites**, parasites which are

Fungi ; **Fun′go-li′chens**, Lindsay's term for plants considered to be transitional forms between Fungi and Lichens ; **fung′ose**, *fungo′sus*, **fung′ous**, (1) spongy in texture ; (2) relating to a Fungus ; (3) produced by a Fungus ; **Fungs**, F. von Mueller's word for the plural of **Fun′gus** (Lat., a mushroom), pl. **Fungi**, thallophytes destitute of chlorophyll, parasitic or saprophytic, comprehending forms from the simplest unicellular structure to some of complex character : many are symbiotic ; ~ **Cel′luose**, the substance of the cell-wall in Fungi ; ~ **Gam′boge**, a yellow, resinous colouring matter found in Fungi ; ~ **Traps**, or "catch-crops," quickly growing crops to secure attack from *Plasmodiophora Brassicae*, and removal with the Fungus, leaving the land free for that season for a later crop of Crucifers ; **fung′used**, attacked by a Fungus (Crozier).

Fu′nicle. *Funic′ulus* (*funis*, a rope), (1) the cord or thread which sometimes connects the ovule or seed to the placenta ; (2) in *Nidularia*, a cord of hyphae attaching the peridiolum to the inner surface of the wall of the peridium ; (3) used by W. Griffith for the suspensor of *Gnetum* ; **fu′niform** (*forma*, shape), rope-like ; **funil′iform**, applied to organs tough, cylindrical, and flexible, as the roots of arborescent Monocotyledons.

Fun′nel, in Marsiliaceae, a space below the thick outer coats of the macrospore into which the apical papilla projects (Goebel) ; ~ **Cells**, short and broad cells, shaped as a funnel; **fun′nel-form**, **fun′nel-shaped**, hypocrateriform.

fur′cate, *furca′tus* (Lat.), forked, with terminal lobes which are like prongs; **fur′cellate**, *furcel′latus*, diminutively forked.

furfura′ceous, *-eus* (*furfur*, bran), scurfy, having soft scales.

fur′rowed, sulcate, striate on a large scale.

154

fur′ry, pubescent (Lowe).

fur′vus (Lat., swarthy), black and lustreless.

Fusa′riose, or **Fusario′sis**, disease induced by an attack of the Fungus *Fusarium* (Mortensen).

fusca′tus (Lat.), *fuscel′lus*, **fusces′cent, -ens**, *fuscid′ulus*, somewhat dusky ; **fus′cous,** *fus′cus* (Lat., dark), dusky, too brown for a grey ; the word is akin to *furvus*.

fu′siform, *fusiform′is* (*fusus*, a spindle; *forma*, shape), thick, but tapering towards each end ; **fusi′nus** ‡, a synonym of the last.

Fu′sion (*fusis*, a melting), the complete union of vessels, as in the laticiferous vessels ; **Cell,** a double cell in uredineous Fungi, formed by conjugation of a pair of fertile hyphal cells, their nuclei not fusing (Grove) ; ∼ **Nu′cleus,** in Uredineae immediately after division of the nuclei, each of the Fusion-nuclei gathers round it protoplasm to form a resting spore (Hartog) ; ∼ **Sor′us,** sori run together ; **Trip′le** ∼, Macdougal's term for DOUBLE FERTILIZATION.

fu′soid (*fusus*, a spindle ; εἶδος, like), somewhat fusiform.

Galac′tin (γάλα, milk), (1) a principle in the juice of *Galactodendron ;* (2) a substance in leguminous seeds like Gum Arabic ; **galacti′tes,** white as milk ; **Galac′tose,** a sugar produced from Galactin.

Gal′banum (Lat.), a gum of uncertain origin ; **gal′banus** (Lat.), a colour resembling the same, greenish-yellow.

Gal′bulus (Lat.), the fruit of the cypress, a modified cone, the apex of each carpellary scale being enlarged and somewhat fleshy.

Gal′ea (Lat., a helmet), a petal shaped like a helmet, placed next to the axis, as in *Aconitum ;* **gal′eate,** *galea′tus,* hollow and vaulted, as in many labiate corollas ; **galeiform′is** (*forma,* shape) = galeate.

galeric′ulate (*galericulum,* a cap), covered, as with a hat.

Gall, *Gal′la* (Lat., an oak-apple), a monstrous growth caused by an insect puncture ; ∼ **Flow′ers,** atrophied female flowers of the fig, within whose ovaries the eggs of an insect undergo evolution ; **Gal′lic Ac′id,** an astringent occurring abundantly in oak-galls ; **Gal′lotannin,** a glucoside occurring in oak-bark.

galoch′rous (γάλα, milk ; χρώς, skin), milk white.

Galto′nian Curve, see NEWTONIAN CURVE.

Galvanotax′is (after Galvani, the discoverer of galvanic electricity ; τάξις, order), arrangement induced by galvanic currents ; **neg′ative** ∼, shown by infusoria, Flagellata and Bacteria, collecting round the kathode ; **pos′itive** ∼, the same, collecting round the anode ; **galvano′tropic** (τροπή, a turn), curvature shown when subjected to a galvanic current, usually towards the positive electrode (anode) ; **Galvanot′ropism,** the condition just described ; **neg′ative** ∼, when the curvature is towards the negative electrode (kathode).

Gam′boge, a yellow resinous gum from several species of Guttiferae ; **Fun′gus** ∼, a somewhat similar product found in some Fungi.

Gam′etange, Gametang′ium (γαμέτης, a spouse ; ἀγγεῖον, a vessel), differentiated cavities in the filaments of certain Algae which produce GAMETES ; adj. **gametan′gial ;** ∼ **Copula′tion,** fusion of polynuclear gametangia with reciprocal karyogamy, cell-division ceasing on formation of gametes (Hartmann) ; **Gam′ete,** a unisexual protoplasmic body, incapable of giving rise to another individual until after conjugation with another gamete, and the joint production of a ZYGOTE ; **Game′tocyst** (κύστις, a bag), the envelope enclosing one or more gametes (Vuillemin) ; **Gametogen′esis** (γένναω, I bring forth), the production of gametes ; **gametogen′ic, gametog′enous,** (γένος, race, offspring), giving rise to gametes, sexual cells ; **Gametog'eny**, the production of gametes ; **Gametogon'ium** (γόνος, offspring), the mother-cell of a brood of gametes ; **Gam'etoid** (εἶδος, resemblance), an apocytial structure which unites like a gamete, producing a zygotoid as the result ; **Gam'eto-nu'cleus**, the nucleus of a gamete ; **Gam'etophore** (φορέω, I bear), the portion of an algal filament which produces gametes according to function, further discriminated as ANDROGAMETOPHORE and GYNOGAMETOPHORE ; **Gam'etophyll** (φύλλον, a leaf), a more or less specialized leaf which bears the sexual organs ; **Gam'etophyte** (φυτὸν, a plant), the generation which bears the sexual organs, producing gametes, in turn giving rise to the SPOROPHYTE ; **Gam'etoplasm** (πλάσμα, moulded), the protoplasm of gametes ; **Gametozo'ospore** (+ ZOOSPORE), Pascher's name for the biciliate zoospores of *Ulothrix ;* **gametrop'ic** (τροπὴ, a turning), movements of organs before or after fertilization (Hansgirg).

Gamob'ium (γάμος, marriage; βιος, life), H. Gibson's term for the sexual generation of organisms which show alternation of generations (Parker) ; a gametophyte ; **Gamocen'tres**, pl. (κέντρον, a sharp point, = *centrum*), centres of grouped chromatin granules during synapsis, afterwards becoming the reduced number of bivalent chromosomes (Strasburger); **gamodes'mic** (γάμος, marriage, union ; δεσμὸς, a bond), used of a stele which has its component vascular elements fused together ; **Gamodes'my**, the stelar condition in question ; **Gamoe'cia** (οἶκος, a house), used by Lindberg for the inflorescence of Bryophytes ; **gamogas'trous** (γαστὴρ, the belly), applied to a pistil formed by the more or less complete union of ovaries, the styles and stigmas remaining free ; **Gamogen'esis** (γένεσις, beginning), sexual reproduction ; **gamogen'ic** (γένος,

offspring), developed as the result of a sexual process ; **gam'oid**, sexual, opposed to vegetative reproduction ; **Gamomer'ius** ‡ (μερὸς, a part), a flower whose parts are united by their edges (Lindley) ; **Gamomer'istele** (+ MERISTELE), the lateral fusion of individual bundle sheaths (Jeffrey) ; **gamomeriste'lic** adj. = GAMODESMIC ; **Gam'omites**, pl. (μίτος, a thread or web), the conjugated filaments in karyokinesis (Strasburger) ; **Gamopet'alae** (πέταλον, a flower-leaf), plants having the petals united; adj. **gamopet'alous**, *-lus* ; **gamophyl'lous**, *-lus* (φύλλον, a leaf), with leaves united by their edges ; **Gam'ophyte** (φυτὸν, a plant), proposed by C. MacMillan for "sexual plants ;" **gamosep'alous**, *-lus* (+ SEPALUM), the sepals united into a whole ; **Gam'osomes**, pl. (σῶμα, a body), Strasburger's term for the aggregation of chromatin granules formed from portions of the thread during synapsis ; **Gam'osperms** (σπέρμα, a seed), plants having seeds without parthenogenetic embryos (C. MacMillan) ; **Gam'icae**, Radlkofer's term for Algae ; **Gamospor'ae** (σπορὰ, seed), Cohn's term for those Algae which produce zoogonidia or zygospores, as the Conjugatae, Volvocineae, and Fucoideae *cf.* CARPOSPOREAE ; **Gam'ostele**, (στήλη, a post), a polystele, in which the vascular bundles are not distinct throughout their entire length, but fused together at some portion ; adj. **gamoste'lic** ; **Gamoste'ly**, the state described ; **gamotrop'ic**, (τροπὴ, a turn), the position of flowers when expanded (Hansgirg), *cf.* CARPOTROPIC ; **Gamot'ropism**, (τροπὴ, a turning), C. MacMillan's term for the movement of mutual attraction in similar conjugating gametes.

Gang'lia, pl. of **Gang'lion** (γαγγλίον, a little tumour), (1) used for various enlargements of mycelium, some being rudimentary fructifications (Crozier) ; (2) the origin of the vascular bundles in Dicotyledons ;

ganglion′eous, used by Lindley for hairs which bear branchlets on their articulations.

Gan′grene, *Gangre′na* (γάγγραινα, an eating ulcer), a disease ending in putrid decay.

Gap, see LEAF-GAP.

Garide′ (disyll.), Chodat's term for bushland composed of deciduous shrubs occurring in the Jura and the Rhone Valley.

Garigue′ (disyll.), the French term for vegetation belonging to forest soil, but wanting trees; widespread in the Mediterranean region.

Gas, pl. **Gas′es**, in plants, a continuous system from the stomata and lenticels by the intercellar spaces; **Gas-vac′uoles**, special floating organs in certain Cyanophyceae, as *Anabaina* (Kerner); **Gasoplank′ton** (+ PLANKTON), organisms which float by means of air vacuoles (Forel).

Gasteroli′chenes (γαστήρ, the belly + (LICHEN), defined as Gasteromycetes in symbiosis with Algae; **Gasteromyce′tes** (μύκης, fungus), a division of Fungi which includes *Lycoperdon*, Puff-balls; **Gasterothalam′eae** (θάλαμος, a bed-chamber), referring to those Lichens whose sporangia are always closed or which burst through the cortical layer of the thallus; **gas′tric Bacte′ria**, those which are found in the digestive tract of animals; **Gastronas′ty** (ναστὸς, pressed) = HYPONASTY.

Gattine′ (Fr.), a disease in silkworms caused by parasitic Fungi.

Gaul′therase, an enzyme producing oil of Wintergreen and glucose from **Gaul′therin**, a principle occurring in *Gaultheria*.

Geitonemb′ryosperm (γείτων, a neighbour; ἔμβρυον, foetus; σπέρμα, a seed), a plant with parthenogenetic embryo, fertilized by pollen from a different flower on the same stock; **Geitonen′dosperm** (ἔνδον, within), a plant with parthenogenetic endosperm, fertilized by pollen from a neighbouring flower on the same stock; **Geitonocar′py** (καρπὸς, fruit),

the production of fruit as the outcome of GEITONOGAMY; **Geitonog′amy** (γάμος, marriage), fertilization between neighbouring flowers on the same plant; **Geit′onosperm**, a plant whose embryos arise by geitonogamy, and are not parthenogenetic, three terms due to O. MacMillan.

Gel′atin (*gela′tus*, congealed), in plants confined to albumen-like bodies, which are tough, viscid, and scarcely soluble in water; **Gelat′ina hymene′a**, a gelatinous substance surrounding the asci and paraphyses in some Lichens (Leighton); **Gelatiniza′tion**, used when a membrane breaks down into a jelly-like mass; **gelat′inose**, *gelatino′sus* (*gelatio*, freezing), having the consistence or appearance of jelly; **gelat′inous**, jelly-like; ~ **Felt**; ~ **Tis′sue**, tissue which is slimy from the cell membrane being soft and mucilaginous; **Gel′atoid** (εἶδος, like), suggested for protein-like substances resembling gelatin (Escombe); **Gelifica′tion**, becoming gelatinous; **Gelin′eae**, cells in Algae which secrete vegetable jelly; **Gel′ose**, vegetable jelly from Agar-Agar.

Gem, a leaf-bud, *cf.* GEMMA.

Gem′inate, *gemina′tus* (Lat. doubled), in pairs, binate.

Gem′ini (Lat.), (1) twins, paired; (2) the union of two chromosomes; **Synap′tic ~**, the pairing of somatic chromosomes in prophase of the first or heterotypic meiotic division; **geminiflor′us** (*flos*, *floris*, a flower), bearing two flowers, or two flowers together.

Gem′ma (Lat.), (1) a young bud, either of flower or leaf, as used by Ray; (2) an asexual product of some Cryptogams, as in the Hepaticae, analogous to leaf-buds; ~ **Brood** = BROOD-GEMMA; ~ **Cup** = CYATHUS; **gemma′ceous** (+ ACEOUS), relating to leaf-buds; **Gem′maecorm** (+ CORM), J. Smith's term for a budcorm, applied to herbaceous plants with a root-crown which increases by side-buds; **Gemma′tion**, *Gem-*

ma'tio, (1) budding, vernation ; (2) disposition or phyllotaxis of buds ; (3) budding, as in the multiplication of yeast (Huxley) ; **nu'clear ~**, in *Synchytrium* when the karyosome of the parent nucleus gives off a small karyosome which passes through the nuclear membrane and becomes an independent nucleus, repeated until a definite group of nuclei is formed (Griggs) ; **Gemmid'ium** = TETRASPORE ; **gemmif'erous** (*fero*, I bear), bearing buds ; **gem'miform** (*forma*, shape), budshaped ; **gemmip'arous** (*pario*, I bear), producing buds ; **Gem'mule**, *Gem'mula*, (1) buds of Mosses, and reproductive bodies of Algae ; (2) = PLUMULE ; (3) = OVULE (Endlicher) ; (4) certain primary formative granules in the protoplasm (Naegeli).

Gene (monosyll.), (γένος, race, offspring), Johannsen's term for unitfactors ; allelomorphs.

Geneagen'esis (γενεὰ, stock, race ; γένεσις, beginning) = PARTHENOGENESIS.

Genepist'asis (γένος, offspring ; ἐπίστασις, a halt), graduated evolution, by the persistence of certain individuals at a definite lower grade, the remainder advancing farther in modification (Eimer).

Gen'era, pl. of GENUS.

gen'eral, *genera'lis* (Lat., pertaining to all), opposed to partial, as ~ INVOLUCRE.

Gen'erating (*generatio*, a begetting), producing ; ~ **Spi'ral** = GENETIC SPIRAL ; ~ **Tis'sue** = MERISTEM ; **gen'erative Apog'amy** (+ APOGAMY), the asexual origin of a sporophyte from the vegetative tissues of the gametophyte, when the nucleus of the mother-cell of the sporophyte has only haploid chromosomes (Winkler) ; ~ **Cell**, (1) a gamete or sexual reproductive cell ; (2) the cell in a pollen grain which develops into male gametes ; ~ **Nu'cleus**, the nucleus in a pollen-grain which is actively concerned in fertilization,

see NUCLEUS ; ~ **Parthenogen'esis** (+ PARTHENOGENESIS), the asexual origin of a sporophyte from a germ-cell, when the nucleus of the latter has haploid chromosomes only (Winkler) ; **Genera'tions**, alternation of, see ALTERNATION.

gener'ic, *gener'icus* (*genus*, birth, race), the differences which make the genus as opposed to those which make the order, or species.

Genesiol'ogy (γένεσις, origin ; λόγος, discourse), the doctrine of the transmission of qualities from the parent, both in vegetative and sexual reproduction (Archer) ; **genet'ic**, genealogical, that which comes by inheritance ; ~ **Spi'ral**, a spiral line which passes through the point of insertion of all equivalent lateral members of an axis, in order of age.

Genetic'ian, an expert in **Genet'ics** (γενέτης, an ancestor), the modern science of breeding on Mendelian lines ; heredity and its developments (Bateson).

genic'ulate, *geniculatus* (Lat., with bent knees), abruptly bent so as to resemble the knee-joint ; **Genic'ulum**, (1) a node of a stem (Lindley) ; (2) the junction of the articuli of Coralline Algae, which is destitute of crustation.

Genita'lia, Gen'itals (*genitalis*, pertaining to birth), in plants, the stamens and pistils, or their analogues.

Gennylang'ium (γεννάω, I beget ; ὕλη = MATERIA ; ἄγγειον, a vessel), Radlkofer's term for ANTHER ; **Gennylei'on** (ἤϊα, =food) = ANTHERIDIUM ; **Gennylozo'id** (ζῶον, an animal ; εἶδος, resemblance) = SPERMATOZOON.

Genodiff'erent (γένος, race, offspring ; *differo*, I differ from), a hybrid word used by Johannsen for the gametes forming a monohybrid ; **Genohol'otype** (ὅλος, whole ; τύπος, a type), the one species on which a genus is founded (Schuchert and Buckman) ; **Genolect'otype** (λεκτὸς, chosen), the

one species subsequently selected out
of a series as typical of a genus, there
being no GENOHOLOTYPE (Schuchert
and Buckman); **Gen′oplast** (πλαστὸς,
moulded), H. L. Clark's emendation of Johannsen's GENOTYPE, the
fundamental hereditary combination
of the genes of an organism ; adj.
genoplast′ic ; **Genosyn′type** (σὺν,
with ; τύπος, a type), one of a series
of species upon which a genus is
founded, no one species being the
actual type (Shuchert and Buckman); **Gen′otype**, (1) the type of a
genus, the species upon which the
genus was established ; (2) Johannsen has employed it for a combination of the genes of an organism ;
= BIOTYPE, GENOPLAST ; ∼ **Con-
cep′tion** = HEREDITY ; adj. **geno-
typ′ic, genotyp′ical; Genoty′pist**, a
student of BIOTYPES.

Gens (Lat., a nation), a tribe in
botany.

gentia′neous, resembling or akin to
the genus *Gentiana* ; **Gent′ianose**, a
sugar from *Gentiana lutea*, occurring
with saccharose ; **Gen′tianine**, the
bitter principle of *Gentiana*.

Genuflec′tion (*genu*, the knee ; *flecto*,
I bend), a bend in a conjugating
filament of an Alga ; **gen′uflexed**
(*flexus*, bent), bent, as the valves
of certain Diatoms.

Gen′us (Lat., a race), the smallest
natural group containing distinct
species ; large genera are frequently
for the sake of convenience divided
into sections, but the generic name
is applied to all species ; ∼ **Hy′brid**,
or **gener′ic Hy′brid**, a hybrid between
two genera, a bigener or bigeneric
cross.

Geoaesthe′sia (γῆ, the earth ; αἴσθησις,
perception by sense), the capacity of
a plant to respond to the stimulus
of gravity ; **Geob′ion** (βίος, life),
plant associations of the land, as distinct from water (Forel) ; **Ge′oblast,**
Geoblas′tus (βλαστὸς, a bud), an
embryo whose cotyledons remain
under ground in germination, as the
pea.

geocal′ycal, resembling the Hepatic
genus *Geocalyx*, Nees ; marsupial.

Geocar′py (γῆ, the earth ; καρπὸς, fruit),
the subterraneous ripening of fruits,
which have developed from a flower
above ground ; **geocen′tric** (κέντρον,
a sharp point), used by Wiesner in
opposition to geotropic ; ageotropic ;
Geocrypt′ophyte (+ CRYPTOPHYTE)
= GEOPHYTE ; **Geodiat′ropism** (διὰ,
through ; τροπὴ, a turning) the function by which an organ places itself
at right angles to the force of gravity ;
Geogen′esis (γένεσις, beginning) or
Geog′eny, derived from the ground,
as gravitational movement ; adj.
geogen′ic ; geograph′ic (γραφὴ, writing), descriptive of the earth or **a**
portion thereof ; ∼ **Bot′any**, that
department which takes account of
the ∼ **Distribu′tion** of plants over the
earth's surface ; **Geoheterauxe′cism**
(ἕτερος, other ; αὔξησις, growth),
variation in the relative growth of
opposite sides of an organ due to
gravity, (Pfeffer) ; **geolog′ic** (λόγος,
discourse) **Bot′any** = Palaeobotany or
Fossil Botany ; **geomor′phic** (μορθὴ,
shape), taking its shape from the
earth (=gravity) ; **Geonas′ty** (ναστὸς,
pressed), curved towards the ground
(Pfeffer) ; **geonyctinast′ic** = **geonyc-
titrop′ic** (νὺξ, νυκτὸς, night ; τροπὴ,
a turning), sleep-movements requiring also the stimulus of gravity ;
Geoparallot′ropism (παράλληλος, parallel ; τροπὴ, a turning) when an
organ places itself parallel to the
surface of the earth ; adj. **geoparal-
lelotrop′ic** ; **Geopercep′tion** = GEO-
AESTHESIA ; **Geoph′ilae** (φιλέω, I
love), soil-loving species ; **geoph′il-
ous**, *-us*, (1) earth-loving, used of
such plants as fruit underground ;
(2) land-loving, terrestrial ; ∼ **Fun′-
gi**, those which grow saprophytic-
ally on decaying vegetable matter
on the ground ; **Geoph′ily** is the condition ; **Geophy′ta** (φυτὸν, a plant),
Ge′ophytes, plants which produce
underground buds, with perennial
development there ; **Mat**- ∼ perennial spot-bound plants ; **Rhi′zome** ∼

or **Trav′elling** ~ plants having horizontal hypogeous scaly shoots, giving rise to leaves and flowers (Warming) ; adj. **geophyt′ic; Geophyti′a**, land plant formations (Clements) ; **Geoplagiot′rop′ism** (+ Plagiotropism), having the direction of growth oblique to the ground ; **Geostroph′ism** (+ Strophism) the tendency to twist in response to gravity ; **geotac′tic**, relating to Geotaxis ; it may be **pos′itive** or **neg′ative; Geotax′is** (τάξις, order), movement or arrangement in plants caused by gravity (Czapek) ; **Geotax′y** = preceding ; **Geothermom′eter** (θερμὸς, warm ; μἐτρον, a measure), a thermometer for earth temperatures ; **Ge′otome** (τομή, an edge), an instrument for obtaining samples of soil ; **Geot′onus** (τόνος, stress), the tendency to bring back to a normal condition any organ which has been forced from it (Czapek) ; **Geotort′ism** (*tortus*, twisted), torsion caused by the influence of gravitation (Schwendener and Krabbe) ; **Geot′rophy** (τροφή, food), unilateral inequality in growth due to position with regard to gravity (Wiesner) : **geotrop′ic** (τροπή, a turning), relating to the influence of gravity on growing organs; **Geot′ropism**, the force of gravity as shown by curvature in nascent organs of plants ; **la′teral** ~, curving horizontally, as in twining stems (Macdougal) ; **neg′ative** ~ growing away from the earth, as stems do normally : **pos′itive** ~, growing towards the earth's centre, as roots ; **trans′verse** ~, = Diageotropism; **Geox′yl** (ξύλον, wood), applied by Lindman to any woody plant with numerous stems arising from a subterranean rhizome.

gerania′ceous, resembling or allied to *Geranium*.

Germ (*germen*, a bud), (1) a bud or growing point ; (2) the ovary or young fruit ; (3) a reproductive cell, especially in bacteria ; ~ **Cell**, (1) a female reproductive cell ; (2) a spore of the simplest character, a sporidium

(Brefeld) ; ~ -**disc,** ~ -**fil′ament,** ~ **plants**, stages in the life of Hepaticae. (Goebel) ; ~ **Nu′cleus**, the nucleus resulting from the union of the pronuclei of two gametes in conjugation ; ~ -**plasm**, the assumed original generative substance contained in the body of the parent from which new individuals arise ; *cf.* Soma - plasm (Weismann) ; ~ **Pore**, a pit on the surface of a spore-envelope through which a germ-tube makes its appearance ; ~ **Tube**, a tubular process from a spore developing into a hypha, and then into a mycelium or promycelium.

German′ic, H. C. Watson's term for a type of distribution in Great Britain of those plants whose headquarters are in the eastern portions of the kingdom.

Ger′men (Lat., a bud), (1) Linnaeus's term for the ovary ; (2) formerly used for the capsule of Mosses ; (3) by Pliny and later writers it signified a bud generally ; **Ger′micide** (-*cida*, a killer), an agent which causes the death of bacteria or spores ; *cf.* Sporocide ; **Germicul′ture** (+ Culture), the practice of bacteriology ; **ger′minable** (+ able), capable of germinating ; viable ; **ger′minal**, relating to a bud ; ~ **Appara′tus**, = Egg-apparatus ; ~ **Cor′puscle** = Oösphere ; ~ **Dot**, of Diatoms, the centrosome ; ~ **Lid**, a separable area of a pollen-grain, breaking away to permit a pollen-tube to issue ; ~ **Pro′cess** ‡ a part belonging to or proceeding from an ovary (Lindley) ; ~ **Slit**, a small break in the seed-coat of Scitamineae; ~ **Ve′sicle** = Oösphere ; **Germina′tion**, *Germina′tio*, the first act of growth in a seed ; sprouting ; **germ′inative Nu′cleus** = Nucleus, Generative.

gerontogae′ous, -*aeus* (γἐρων, γἐροντος, an old man ; γῆ, the earth), used of plants which are confined to the Old World.

gib′ber (Lat , hump-backed), **gib′bose, gib′bous**, *gibbero′sus*, more convex in one place than another, a pouch-like enlargment of the base of an organ, as of a calyx ; **Gibbos'ity,** *Gibbos'itas,* a swelling at the base of an organ ; **gibbo'sus** (Lat.) = GIBBEROSUS.

gigan'tic, *gigan'teus* (Lat., pertaining to giants), of unusual height ; **Gigant'ism,** unusual size ; opposed to NANISM.

Gil'iare, (+ -are) a community of *Gilia,* (Clements).

Gills, the plates or lamellae of an Agaric which bear the spores.

gil'vus (Lat.), pale yellow, a term of confused application, sometimes reddish or even greyish.

Ginger-beer "plant," an association of organisms which ferment a sweetened liquid into Ginger-Beer.

gin'glymoid (γιγγλυμὸs, a hinge ; εἶδos, resemblance), like a hinge (Heinig).

ginkgoa'ceous, resembling the Maidenhair tree, *Gingko biloba* ; **ginkgoa'lean,** Wieland's term for the same.

Gir'der-sclerench'yma, strengthening tissue in section recalling a **T** or **H** girder ; ~ **shaped,** an organ so shaped.

Gir'dle, (1) the hoop or cingulum of Diatoms, that portion of the frustule which unites the valves ; (2) also applied to a ring-like branch of the leaf-trace of *Cycas ;* ~ **-band,** the hoop, girdle or cingulum of a Diatom-frustule ; ~ **Canals',** narrow intercellular air-spaces round the palisade cells parallel to the leaf surface (Warming) ; ~ **Struc'ture** vascular bundles surrounded by radially elongated photosynthetic cells (Haberlandt) ; ~ **-view,** the front or back view of a Diatom, in distinction to a lateral view ; **Gird'ling,** in cultivation, ringing.

githagin'eus (Lindley) ; **githagino'sus** (Hayne), defined as greenish red, meaning red or purple streaks on a green ground, as the calyx of *Githago.*

gla'ber (Lat., without hair), **gla'brate,** *glabra'tus,* destitute of pubescence ;

by Bentham extended to mean also destitute of any roughness ; **glabres'cent,** *glabres'cens,* becoming glabrous, or slightly so ; **Gla'brism,** the smoothness of normally hairy parts ; **glabrius'culus** (Lat.), somewhat glabrous ; **gla'brous,** smooth, without pubescence.

gla'cial (*glacies,* ice), employed by C. MacMillan for "distinctively northern plants."

gla'diate, *gladia'tus* (*gladius,* a sword), (1) flat, straight, or slightly curved, with acute apex and approximately parallel edges, ensiform . (2) ancipital.

Gland (*glans, glandis,* an acorn) ; (1) an acorn, or acorn-like fruit ; (2) a definite secreting structure on the surface, embedded, or ending a hair ; any protuberance of the like nature which may not secrete, as the warty swellings at the base of the leaf in the cherry and peach ; (3) in Orchids, see GLANDULA ; ~ of the Torus, see LEPAL (Crozier) ; **allu'ring** or **attract'ive** ~, in *Nepenthes* secreting nectar to attract insects ; **chalk** ~, those which exude salt solutions and give a whitish deposit on drying, as in some species of *Saxifrage ;* **der'mal** ~, external secreting cells or groups of such ; **diges'tive** ~, in the pitcher of *Nepenthes* giving forth a peptic ferment ; **epider'mal** ~, those on the external surface ; **exter'nal** ~, glands not immersed in the tissues ; **intra-mu'ral** ~, tubular curved or sinuate secreting elements in *Psoralea* (Haberlandt) ; **mar'ginal** ~, glands found inside the upper part of the pitchers of carnivorous plants ; **salt** ~, which excrete solutions of hygroscopic salts, are dry in day time and deliquesce at night; **glandif'erous** (*fero.* I bear), bearing or producing glands ; **gland'iform** (*forma,* shape), shaped like a gland ; **Gland'ula, Gland'ule,** a viscid gland in Orchids and Asclepiads, which holds the pollen-masses in their place; the retinaculum; **glandula'ceous,** *-ceus* (+ ACEOUS), the colour of a ripe acorn ; raw sienna yellow ; **glan'du-**

lar, possessing glands; ~ **Disk,** = GLANDULA; ~ **Hair,** an epidermal appendage, the end of which is usually enlarged, and contains a special secretion; ~ **Wood′y Tis′sue,** coniferous pitted tissue; **Glandula′- tion,** -*tio,* the arrangement of the glands on a plant; **glandulif′erous,** -*rus,* gland-bearing; **glan′dulose,** *glandulo′sus,* **gland′ulous,** glandular; **glan′duloso-serra′tus,** having serrations tipped or bordered with glands; **Glans** (Lat.), a fruit one-seeded by abortion, or a few-seeded dry inferior indehiscent pericarp seated within a cupular involucre, as the fruit of the oak, nut, etc.

gla′real (*glarea,* gravel), term employed by H. C. Watson for those plants which grow on dry exposed ground, chiefly gravel or sand; **gla′reose,** *glareo′sus,* frequenting gravel.

Glass′wort Associa′tion, formed of various species of *Salicornia* (Tansley).

Glass′y Fir, an appearance found on sawing fir wood, due to wood-cells being filled with water and then frozen.

glauces′cent, *glauces′cens* (γλαυκός, bluish grey), becoming sea-green; **glauci′nus** (Lat.), bluish sea-green; **Glaucogonid′ium** (+ GONIDIUM), the bluish green gonidium of Lichens (Bornet); **glau′cous,** -*cus* (1), sea-green; (2) covered with a bloom as a plum or cabbage-leaf.

Gle′ba (Lat., a clod), the chambered sporogenous tissue within a sporophore of Phalloideae; **Glebe**=GLEBA; **Gle′bula,** (1) a synonym of GLEBA; (2) the sporangia of certain Fungi, as *Nidularia:* (3) a rounded elevation on the thallus of Lichens; **gle′bulose,** possessing a gleba, or resembling it.

gleiche′nioid, resembling or allied to the fern genus *Gleichenia.*

gleocap′soid (εἶδος, resemblance), like the genus *Gleocapsa.*

Gli′adin (γλία, glue), vegetable glue or gelatin forming part of gluten;

Gli′an, the alcohol-soluble part of gluten.

Gli′ding-growth = SLIDING GROWTH.

glit′tering, lustre from a polished surface which is not uniform.

glo′bate (*globus,* a sphere), globular; **Globes,** Grew's term for pollen-grains; **Glo′bi spermat′ici,** spores of some Fungi (Lindley); **Glo′boids** (εἶδος, like), rounded masses of mineral matter in proteid grains; **glo′bose,** *globo′sus,* nearly spherical; **glob′ular,** *globula′ris,* spheroidal in shape; **Glob′ule,** the spherical antheridium in Characeae; **Glob′ulet** used by Grew for (1) a glandular hair, (2) a pollen-grain; **Glob′ulin,** (1) "round transparent granules in cellular tissue, constituting fecula" (Henslow); (2) the chief ingredient in aleurone or protein granules, occurring amorphous or as crystalloids; (3) in Lichens = Chlorophyll (Olivier); **glob′ulose,** *globulo′sus,* a diminutive of GLOBOSE; **Glob′ulus** (Lat., a little globe), (1) used by Necker for the fruit of Hepaticae; (2) the deciduous shield in some Lichens; soredia.

Glo′chid, Glochid′ium (γλωχίς, an angular end or barb), (1) a barbed hair or bristle; (2) a similar structure on the massulae of certain Cryptogams which act as organs of attachment to a macrospore; **glochid′eous,** -*eus,* **glochid′iate,** *glochidia′tus,* pubescent with barbed bristles; **Glo′chis,** a barb.

Gloeoli′chenes (γλοιός, sticky), Forsell's name for homoeomerous Lichens, as Collemacei, Ascolichens with gonidia belonging to the Chroococcaceae: **Gloe′ophyte** (φυτόν, a plant), Gobi's name for THALLO-PHYTE; **Gloe′ospores,** -*ae* (γλοία, glue; + SPORA), plants having viscid seeds (Clements); **Gloiocar′pus** (καρπός, fruit), a tetraspore (Lindley).

Glome (*glomus,* a ball), a rounded head of flowers; **glom′erate,** *glomera′tus,* agglomerate, collected into heads; **Glom′erule,** *Glomeru′lus,* (1)

a cluster of capitula in a common
involucre, as *Echinops* ; (2) a SORE-
DIUM ; **glomerulif'erous** (*fero*, I
bear), bearing clusters of coral-like
excrescences ; **glomer'ulose**, having
glomerules ; **Glom'us** ‡ = GLOME-
RULE.

Glossol'ogy (γλῶσσα, a tongue ; λόγος,
discourse), the explanation of technical terms ; **Glos'sopode**, **Glossopod'ium** (πούς, ποδὸς, a foot), the
sheathing base of the leaves in
Isoëtes ; adj. **glossopod'ial.**

Glu'case (γλυκὺς, sweet), an enzyme
which hydrolyses maltose ; **Glu'cose**,
(1) a group of carbohydrates, crystallizable and soluble in water, occurring in fruits, as grape-sugar, etc.,
see DEXTROSE, LEVULOSE ; (2) also a
commercial term for syrups made
from starch or grain ; **Glu'coside**
(εἶδος, like), for complex substances
which give rise on decomposition to
Glucose, such as Amygdalin, Coniferin, Salicin ; ~ **En'zyme**, a ferment
such as Synaptase or Emulsin.

Glue, viscid secretion on surface of
some plants ; **Bud** ~ = BLASTOCOLLA.

gluma'ceous (*gluma*, husk of corn ; +
ACEOUS), resembling the glumes of
grasses, as the perianth-segments
of *Juncus* ; **Glume**, *Glu'ma*, the
chaffy two-ranked members of the
inflorescence of grasses and similar
plants ; **bar'ren** ~, **em'pty** ~, glumes
which subtend a spikelet, and do
not include a flower ; **fer'tile** ~, **flo'ral**
~, **flow'ering** ~, the glume in grasses
which includes a flower, the palea ;
fruit'ing ~, the fertile glume at the
time of maturity ; **ster'ile** ~, a
glume which subtends other glumes
or has no flower ; **glu'mal**, characterized by having a glume ; **Glumel'la**, **Glu'melle**, (1) the palea of
grasses ; (2) the lodicule of the same
(Richard) ; **glumellea'nus** ‡ of or belonging to a glumella ; **Glumel'lule**,
Glumellu'la, (1) = palea ; (2) = lodicule ; **glumose'**, *glumo'sus* = GLUMA-
CEOUS ; **glu'mous**, having glumes, as
a flower which has a subtending
glume.

Glu'tamin (*gluten*, glue), an amide
allied to asparagin found with it in
the juice of beets, etc. ; **Glu'ten**, a
tough protein substance occurring in
grain after the removal of the starch ;
~ **Cells**, of the endoderm contain
oil, but no starch ; **Glu'tenin**, a
constituent of wheat gluten ; Gluten-
casein or ZYMOM ; **Glutin'ium**, "the
flesh of certain Fungals" (Lindley) ;
glu'tinous, *glutino'sus*, covered with
a sticky exudation.

Gly'case (γλυκὺς, sweet), an enzyme,
the same as GLUCASE.

Glycerie'tum, an association of *Gly-
ceria*.

Glycerrhiz'in, or **Gly'cion**, a saccharine
matter from the roots of *Glycyrr-
hiza glabra*, Linn., liquorice.

Glycodru'pose (γλυκὺς, sweet ; +
DRUPOSE), a lignocellulose, forming
the hard concretions in the flesh of
pears ; **Gly'cogen** (γεννάω, I bring
forth), a carbohydrate present in
quantity in epiplasm, capable of
being converted into glucose ; ~
Mass, protoplasm permeated with
glycogen, epiplasm ; **Glycolig'nose**
(*lignum*, wood), a presumed glucoside, from pinewood.

glyco'sic, resembling the action of the
enzyme GLUCOSE.

glyphol'ecine (γλύφω, I hollow out ;
λέκος, dish), with wavy longitudinal
canals or grooves (Heinig).

Gnaurs, burrs or knotty excrescences
on tree-trunks or roots, probably
from clusters of adventitious buds.

gnawed, = EROSUS.

Gnesiog'amy (γνήσιος, legitimate ;
γάμος, marriage), fertilization between different individuals of the
same species.

gneta'lean, allied to *Gnetum*.

gnomon'ical, *gnomon'icus* (γνώμων, the
pin of a dial), applied to an appendage when abruptly bent at an
angle to its attachment.

gob'let-shaped = CUP-SHAPED.

Gonang'ium (γόνος, offspring ; ἀγγεῖον,
a vessel), a spherical colony of
Palmella, etc., overgrown with thick-
walled brown Lichen-hyphae ; **Gones,**

163

pl., suggested by Lotsy to cover asexual spores and gametes ; **goneoclin'ic** (κλίνη, a bed), applied to a hybrid which approximates to one parent, and not intermediate.

gongrosi'roid, resembling the genus *Gongrosira*, Kuetz. ; applied to the resting-stage of *Vaucheria.*

gongylo'des (γογγύλος, round), knob-like ; **Gong'ylus** (1) for round corpuscles on certain Algae, which become detached, and germinate as separate ͏individuals ; (2) globular bodies in the thallus of Lichens ; (3) = SPORE, SPORIDIUM, SPEIREMA.

Gonian'gium (γόνος, offspring), term proposed by A. Braun to include cystocarps and the scyphi of Hepaticae ; **goniautoe'cious, goniautoi'cous** (αὐτός, self ; οἶκος, a house), the male inflorescence of a Moss, bud-like and axillary on a female branch ; **Gon'id**, proposed abbreviation of GONIDIUM ; **Gonidan'gium** (εἶδος, like ; ἀγγεῖον, a vessel), in a gametophyte, the organ which produces a sexual spore or gonidium ; **Gonide'ma** (δεῖν, to bind), Minks's term for the entire gonidial layer in Lichens ; **gonid'-ial**, pertaining to gonidia, as ~ **Lay'er**, (1) an aggregation of simple gonidiophores to form a cushion-like layer or crust ; (2) the algal layer in the Lichen-thallus ; **gonid'ic**, possessing gonidia (Lindsay) ; **Gonidim'ium**, a small algal cell occurring in the hymenium of some Pyrenocarpei ; **gonid'ioid** (εἶδος, resemblance), gonidium-like ; **Gonid'-iophore** (φορέω, I carry), a sporophore which bears a gonidium ; **Gonid'iophyll** (φύλλον, a leaf), C. Mac-Millan's term for the sporophyll of *Alaria ;* **Gonid'ium**, (1) in Lichens, an algal cell of the thallus ; (2) the same as Brood-Cell, a propagative cell, asexually produced and separating from the parent.

Gonim'ia, pl. of **Gonim'ium** (γόνιμος, productive), the gonidia in Lichens ; **gonim'ic**, relating to gonidia, as ~ **Lay'er**, the algal layer in the Lichen-thallus ; **Gon'imoblast** (βλαστός, a

shoot), filaments which are often clustered, arising from the fertilized carpogonium of certain Algae ; **Gon'imolobes.** pl. (λοβός, a lobe), the terminal tufts of gonimoblasts ; **Gon'imon**, Wallroth's term for the gonidial layer ; **gon'imous**, relating to gonidia.

Gon'iocyst (γόνος, offspring ; κύστις, a bag), a sporangium (A. Braun) ; **Gonocys'tia** = GONOCYSTS ; **Goniocyt'ium** (κύτος, a hollow) = GONI-DANGIUM ; **Gon'osphere** (σφαῖρα, a sphere), a zoogonidium of Chytridiaceae (Nowakowski) ; **Gon'ocysts** (κύστις, a bag), used by Minks for metamorphosed gonidia extruded on the superficial crust, having a peculiar appearance ; **Gon'o-hyphe'ma** (ὕφα, woven), applied by Minks to the hyphal layer of Lichens ; **Gon'o-meres** (μέρος, a part), the theoretic separate existence of paternal and maternal nuclear parts (Haecker) ; **Gon'ophore**, *Gonoph'orum* (φορέω, I carry), an elongation of the axis, a receptacle bearing stamens and carpels, as in *Capparis ;* **Gon'oplasm** (πλάσμα, moulded), in Peronosporeae, that portion of the protoplasm of the antheridium which passes through the fertilization tube and coalesces with the oösphere ; **Gonotax'is** (τάξις, order), the movement of antherozoids towards the female organ (C. MacMillan) ; adj. **gonotac'tic ; Gonothall'ium** (θαλλός, a twig), the gonidial layer of Lichens (Minks) ; **Gon'otokonts**, pl. (κοντός, a pole), Lotsy's term for the mother-cells which inaugurate reduction phenomena ; **Gonotroph'ium** (τροφή, food) = SOREDIUM ; **Gonot'ropism** (τροπή, a turning), C. MacMillan's term for the motion of antherozoids and pollen-tubes towards the female organ ; the same author also suggests the restriction of this term to pollen-tube growth ; adj. **gonotrop'ic ; Gon'osphere, Gonosphae'rium** (σφαίρα, a sphere), = OÖSPHERE ; **Gonosphaerid'ium**, = GONIDIUM (?)

Gorge, the throat of a flower.

Gos′ling, an old term for catkin, as resembling a soft-feathered young goose.

gos′sypine, *gossypi′nus*, cottony, flocculent, like the hairs on the seeds of *Gossypium*.

Gourd, a fleshy, one-celled, many-seeded fruit, with parietal placentas, as a melon.

grac′ilis (Lat.), slender; Crozier has the needless word "gracile."

Graft, a union of different individuals by apposition, the rooted plant being termed the stock, the portion inserted the scion ; ~ **Hy′brid**, effect produced by one or the other of the united individuals on its grafted fellow ; **Graft′age**, L. H. Bailey's term for multiplication by grafting or the state of being thus increased.

Grain, a general term for cereals, those grasses cultivated for food ; the caryopsis or the fruit of the same ; **grained**, having grain-like tubercles or processes, as in the flowers of *Rumex* (Crozier).

gramina′ceous, gramin′eal (*gramen*, grass), synonyms of **gramin′eous**, *-eus*, **gra′minous**, (1) relating to grass or grain-bearing plants ; (2) grass-coloured ; **graminic′olous** (*colo*, I inhabit), growing on grasses, as some Fungi ; **graminifo′lious**, (*folium*, a leaf), having grass-like leaves ; **Graminol′ogy** (λόγος, discourse) = AGROSTOLOGY (Crozier).

gram′micus (Lat.), (γραμμικὸς, lined), lettered, marked as though inscribed ; **grammopod′ius** ‡ (πούς, ποδὸς, a foot or stem), having a striped stalk.

Gra′na, pl. of **Gra′num** (Lat.), a seed, (1) any small bodies ; (2) the coloured drops in chloroplasts (Strasburger) ; ~ **tetras′ticha**, "the spores of certain Fungals" (Lindley).

granati′nus (Lat.), pale scarlet, the colour of the flower of *Punica Granatum*, Linn., the pomegranate.

grandifo′liate (*grandis*, large ; *folium*, leaf), applied to plants in which the stem is subordinate, the internodes are short, and the leaves the dominant organs, *e. g.* Palms, Water-lilies (Worsdell).

Grand′mother Ax′is, the primary axis of a series of three (Potter) ; ~ **Cell**, the primary cell of a third generation.

Granif′erus (*granifer*, grain-bearing), a synonym of Monocotyledon (J. S. Henslow).

gra′niform (*granum*, a grain ; *forma*, shape), having the shape of grains of corn.

granit′icus (Mod. Lat.), applied to plants growing on granite rocks, as certain Lichens.

Gran′ula, Gran′ule, *Gran′ulum*, pl. **Gran′ula** (*granum*, a grain), (1) any small particles, as pollen, chloroplasts, etc. ; (2) the Naviculae of *Schizonema* (fide Lindley) ; (3) sporangia in Fungi (Lindley) ; (4) by Frommann used for the nucleolus-like structure in the nucleus of the terminal cells of the glandular hairs of *Pelargonium zonale*, Ait. ; (5) a minute particle, the assemblage of such being held to constitute protoplasm (Oltmanns) ; **Gran′ula gon′-ima**, the gonidia in Lichens ; **gran′-ular**, *granula′ris*, (1) composed of grains ; (2) divided into little knots or tubercles, as the roots of *Saxifraga granulata*, Linn. ; **gran′ulate**, *granula′tus*, means the same thing ; **granulif′erous** (*fero*, I bear), granule bearing ; **gran′ulose**, *granulo′sus*, composed of grains ; **Gran′ulose**, used as a substantive by Naegeli for true starch.

Grape-sugar, a sugar found abundantly in the grape, dextrose.

Grascila′tio (Mod. Lat.), used by Desvaux for ETIOLATION.

Grass-green, clear lively green ; in Latin, prasinus, gramineus.

Grass-heath, Tussock-formation ; peculiar to the southern hemisphere ; ~ **Moor**, intermediate between *Scirpus* moors and silicious grass-land, mainly of grass, rushes, and sedges ; **Grass-land**, dominance of grasses, as above the forest belt in alpine regions.

Grav′eolence (*graveolentia*, a rank smell), a smell so strong as to be unpleasant ; **grav′eolent,** *grav′eolens,* strongly scented, of intense and heavy odour.

Gravipercep′tion (*gravis*, heavy ; *perceptio*, receiving), suggested instead of GEOAESTHESIA (F. Darwin).

Gravita′tion (*gravitus*, weight), the act of tending towards a centre, as of the earth ; in botany sometimes confused with Geotropism and Apheliotropism.

greasy, oily to the touch.

greaved (monosyll.) = OCHREATE.

Green-rot, a disease in wood, the tissues becoming verdigris green, ascribed to *Peziza aeru·rinosa,* Pers.

Greffe (Fr.) graft ; ~ **des Charlatans,** a fraudulent apparent graft, the scion being passed through a hole bored in the stock.

gregar′ious (*gregarius*, belonging to a flock), growing in company, associated but not matted ; **sol′itary** ~, a single clump of one species (Warming).

Greg′iform (*grex, gregis,* a flock ; + FORM), a variable or polymorphic FINIFORM (Kuntze).

grey, *gris′eus* (Lat.), cold neutral tint, varied in tone ; ~ **Blight,** a fungus, *Pestalozzia Guepini,* which attacks the tea-plant.

grisel′lus (Lat.), *gris′eolus,* diminutive of foregoing, somewhat greyish.

Grit-cell, a sclerotic cell, as in the flesh of pears.

gromon′ical, an error of Lindley's for gnomonical.

gross′e- (Late Lat.), coarsely.

Grossifica′tion (*grossus*, thick ; *facio,* I make), the swelling of the ovary after impregnation ; **gros′sus** (Lat.), (1) coarse, larger than usual, used adverbially as **gros′se-crena′tus,** ~ **serra′tus,** coarsely crenate or serrate ; (2) **Gros′sus,** an unripe fig (Heinig).

grossula′ceous, gros′sular, relating to the gooseberry, *Ribes Grossularia,* Linn. ; **Gros′suline,** a principle found in certain acid fruits.

Ground Form (Ger. Grund-Form), elementary form, as distinguished from GROWTH FORM ; **Ground Mass,** used of the woody tissues ; ~ **Stra′tum,** from the surface of the soil to about 5 centimetres (two inches); ~ **-tissue,** applied to the pith, cortex, and medullary rays ; ~ **Vegeta′tion,** the plants which cover the soil under trees, etc. ; ~ **Wa′ter,** that collected above the impermeable stratum of soil, and moving in obedience to gravity.

Grow′ing-point, the extremity of the stem, or cone of growth, the seat of the activity of the apical cell, and its divisions.

Growth, increase by new cell-formation or extension of old cells ; ~ **-en′zyme,** a ferment which conduces to growth, by breaking down tissue in advance ; ~ **Form,** a vegetative structure marked by some characteristic feature which does not indicate genetic affinity ; a tree, shrub, sprout-fungus, are growth-forms ; ~ **Ring,** the annual rings of growth in exogens ; ~ **Wa′ter,** the percentage of soil moisture in excess of that present when wilting occurs (Fuller).

Grub′bing, in forestry, the uprooting of trees.

gruina′lis (*grus*, a crane), shaped like the bill of a crane, as the fruit of *Geranium.*

gru′mose, *grumo′sus,* **gru′mous** (*grumus,* a hillock), divided into little clusters of grains.

Grund-Form (Ger.), the original form, sometimes hypothetic, from which other forms have been derived by morphologic variation.

guaiaci′nus, Hayne's term for greenish-brown ; from "Gum guaiacum."

Guar′anine, a bitter principle from Guarana bread, or Brazilian cocoa, isomeric with caffeine.

Guard-cells, Guard′ian-cells, in stomata, two cells which open or close the stoma by their greater or less turgescence.

Guilds, Schimper's term for Saprophytes, Epiphytes, Lianes, **etc.,**

each member group having a close connection with the others.

gu'lar (*gula*, the throat), pertaining to the throat (Crozier).

Gum (*gummi*, gum), a viscid secretion frequently extruded from stems, and hardening in the air ; ~ **Ar'abic**, derived from species of *Acacia* in tropical countries, dissolving easily in water ; ~ **Canals'**, thin-walled sacs in the pith of *Lyginodendron*, now regarded as secretory sacs ; ~ **Cells**, Ger. Kleberzellen, see OIL-CELLS ; ~ **Lac**, excretion by an insect, *Carteria Lacca*, from various trees ; — **Pas'sage**, an intercellular passage containing gum ; ~ **Res'in**, exudation partaking of the nature of gum and resin ; **gummif'erous** (*fero*, I bear), producing gum ; **Gum'ming**, a disease, known also as **Gummo'sis**, producing gum in excess.

Gut'ta-per'cha (*gutta*, a drop), a kind of chaoutchouc, said to be derived from *Dichopsis Gutta*, Benth. and Hook.f. ; **gut'tate** (*gutta'tus*, spotted), as to colour ; **Gutta'tion** the exudation of drops of fluid ; **Gut'tifer** (*fero*, I bear), a plant which produces gum or resin (Crozier) ; adj. **guttif'erous** ; **gut'tulate**, resembling drops of oil or resin ; **Gut'tule**, used for drops of oil or vacuoles contained in the capitate paraphyses of Fungi ; Lat. **Gut'tulae**.

gyalec'tiform (*forma*, shape), urceolate, like the apothecia of the genus *Gyalecta*, now merged in *Lecidea ;* **gyalec'tine**, and **gyalec'toid** (εἶδος, like), are synonyms.

gymnan'thous, *-us* (γυμνὸς, naked ; ἄνθος, a flower), naked-flowered ; **Gymnax'ony** (ἄξων, an axle), Morren's term for the placenta protruding through the ovary ; **gymnoblas'tus** (βλαστὸς, a bud), having the ovary superior ; **gymnocar'pic**, gymnocarpous ; **gymnocar'pous**, **gymnocar'pous**, *-us* (καπρὸς, fruit), (1) naked-fruited ; where the perianth does not adhere to the outer integument ; (2) where the fruit is without pubescence (J. S. Henslow) ; (3)

when the hymenium is exposed during the maturation of the spores ; **Gymnochlor'ites** (+ CHLORITE), chlorophyllous plastids contained in cyanocysts, usually soon becoming detached from the protoplasmic layer of their formation (Arbaumont) ; **Gymnocid'ium** ‡ (ὄγκιδιον, tubercle), Necker's term for the swelling sometimes formed at the base of the capsule in Mosses, the apophysis ; **Gymnocy'cads** naked-flowered Cycads (F. W. Oliver).

Gymnodin'ium Stage, applied to mobile flagellate bodies of certain Peridiniaceae, resembling the genus named.

Gymnog'amae (γυμνὸς, naked ; γάμος, marriage), (1) Ardissone's term for Heterosporous and Isosporous Cryptogams ; **Gym'nogams**, **Gymnog'amae**, (2) Caruel's terms for all plants possessing naked motile male cells ; **Gymnog'amy** (γάμος, marriage), when **cytoplas'mic** ~, the female gamete is impregnated by the cytoplasm of of the male gamete ; when **nu'clear** ~, the female gamete is impregnated by the nucleus of the male gamete (Dangeard) ; **Gym'nogen** (γεννάω, I bring forth), = GYMNOSPERM ; **gymnog'ynous** ‡ (γυνή, a woman), having a naked ovary ; **Gym'noplast** (πλαστὸς, mou ded), a monoplast devoid of covering membrane (Pirotta) ; **Gymnoplast'id**, plastids similar to GYMNOCHLORITES found in the pith of certain shrubs (Arbaumont) ; **gymnop'odal** (πούς, ποδὸς, a foot), applied to peculiar branches of *Chara*, partially or wholly destitute of cortex on the lowest whorl ; **Gymnosper'mae** (σπέρμα, seed), **Gymnosper'mia**, (1) the Linnean order Didynamia, plants having four nutlets. taken for naked fruits, as Labiates ; (2) the modern order of naked-ovuled plants, as Conifers ; **gymnosper'matous** relating to conifers and their allies, recent and fossil ; **Gymnosper'mism**, the real or supposed condition of plants with naked seeds ; **gymnosper'mous**, the ovules developed without the

usual tegumentary pericarp, as in
Coniferae; opposed to angiospermous; **Gymnosper′my**, the state of
bearing really or apparently naked
fruit; **Gym′nospore**, a naked spore,
one not produced in a sporangium;
gymnos′tomous (στόμα, a mouth),
applied to the peristome of Mosses
when destitute of teeth; **Gymno-
sym′plast** (+ SYMPLAST), a plasmodium, a mass of naked protoplasm
(Pirotta); **gymnotetrasper′mus** ‡
(τετρὰς, four; σπέρμα, seed), having
a four-lobed ovary, as in Labiates,
once considered to be naked-seeded;
gymnotre′moid (τρῆμα, a hole; εἶδος,
like), a bare open spot or space
(Leighton).

Gynae′ceum (γυναικεῖον, the women's
house), the pistil or pistils of a
flower; the female portion as a
whole.

gynan′der (γυνή, a woman; ἀνήρ,
ἀνδρὸς, a man) = GYNANDROUS;
Gynan′dria, a Linnean class, with
gynandrous flowers; adj. **gynan′-
drian**; **Gynan′drophore** (φορέω, I
carry), a column bearing stamens
and pistils; **Gynan′drospore** (+
ANDROSPORE), a term applied by
Radlkofer to the majority of Fern
spores; **gynandrosp′orous** (σπορὰ,
seed), used of dioecious forms of
Oedogoniae in which the female
plant produces androspores; **gy-
nan′drous**, when the stamens are
adnate to the pistil, as in Orchids,
etc.; **gynan′therous**, -us(+ANTHER),
used of stamens converted into
pistils; **Gyne′cium** = GYNAECEUM;
Gynix′us, Gyni′zus (ἰξὸς, birdlime),
the stigma in Orchids; **Gyn′obase,**
Gynob′asis (βάσις, a pedestal), an
enlargement of the torus on which
the gynaeceum rests; **gynobas′ic,**
applied to a style which adheres by
its base to a prolongation upwards
of the torus between carpels; **Gyno-
cid′ium,** an error for GYMNOCIDIUM;
Gynodimorph′ism (+ DIMORPHISM),
the occurrence of small female flowers
on a gynodioecious plant; **gynodioe′-
cious,** dioecious, with some flowers

hermaphrodite, others pistillate only,
on separate plants; **Gynodioe′cism**
(+ DIOECISM), the occurrence of
female and hermaphrodite flowers
on a plant separated from its fellows;
gynody′namus (δύναμις, power),
applied to an organism where the
female element is preponderant;
Gynoe′cism, the presence of female
flowers without any male flowers
whatever; **Gynoe′cium** = GYNAE-
CEUM; **Gynogametan′gium** (γαμέτης,
a spouse; ἀγγεῖον, a vessel), an organ
in which female sexual cells are
formed; an archegonium; **Gyno-
gam′etes**, egg-cells (McNab); **Gyno-
gam′etophore** (φορέω, I carry), the
female gametophore; **gynomonoe′-
cious**, monoecious, with female and
hermaphrodite flowers on the same
plant; **Gynomonoe′cism** is the condition; **Gyn′ophore,** *Gynophor′ium*
(φορέω, I carry), the stipe of a pistil;
adj. **gynophora′tus** ‡ **gynophoria′nus**
‡; **Gynophyl′ly** (φύλλον, a leaf),
virescence or phyllomorphy of the
ovary; **Gyn′ophyte** (φυτὸν, a plant),
the female plant in the sexual
generation; **Gyn′ospore** (σπορὰ, a
seed), formerly suggested for macrospore, that is, a MEGASPORE;
Gynosporan′gium (ἀγγεῖον, a vessel),
a sporangium producing the same;
Gynosteg′ium (στέγος, a roof), the
staminal crown in *Asclepias;*
Gynoste′mium (στήμων, a stamen),
the column of an Orchid, the androecium and gynaeceum combined;
Gynoteg′ium (τέγος, a roof), the
sheath or covering of a gynaeceum
of any kind.

gyp′seus (Lat., plastered with lime),
chalk-white, cretaceous.

gypsoph′ilous (γύψος, chalk; φιλέω, I
love), dwelling on limestone; **Gyp-
sophy′ta** (φυτὸν, a plant), chalk
or limestone plants; **Gypso-
phyti′a**, limestone plant formations
(Clements); **Gyp′sum-crystals** occur
in the epidermis of certain species
of *Capparis*, also ~ -spheres.

gy′rate, *gyra′tus* (Lat.), curved into a
circle, or circular; circinate.

Gy'rolith (γύρος, round ; λίθος, stone), the presumed fossil fruits of *Chara ;* **Gyro'ma**, (1) the annulus of Ferns ; (2) the button-like shield of *Gyrophora ;* **gy'rose**, *gyro'sus*, curved backward and forward in turn ; **Gy'rus** (Lat., a circle) = GYROMA.

Hab'it, *Hab'itus* (Lat., appearance), the general appearance of a plant, whether erect, prostrate, climbing, etc. ; **hab'itally**, used in the United States for resembling ; having the habit of another plant.

Hab'itat, *Habita'tio* (Lat., dwelling), (1) the kind of lócality in which a plant grows, as woods, moors, etc. ; (2) the geographic distribution or limits, now termed LOCALITY, or more precisely STATION ; ~ **Form**, the impress given to the plant by the habitat (Clements) ; ~ **Group**, applied to those plants which have common habitats, though not related, as HALOPHYTES, HYDROPHYTES, and the like ; ~ **Ra'ces**, used by Magnus for those heteroecious Uredines, which are adapted to respective species of host (Tubeuf).

hadrocen'tric (+ HADROME ; *centrum*, the middle), **Bun'dle**, having the hadrome in the centre surrounded by the leptome (Haberlandt) ; **Had'romal**, also termed **Had'romase**, an enzyme found in *Merulius lacrymans*, Schum., and other Fungi, which attacks the hadrome and destroys its lignified cell-walls (Czapek).

Had'rome, a shortened form of **Hadromes'tome** (ἁδρὸς, thick, ripe, strong ; μεστὸς, filled), the xylem or woody portion of a vascular bundle ; consisting of the HYDROME and part of the AMYLOME ; together with the LEPTOME it forms the MESTOME.

Hae'matein (αἷμα, αἵματος, blood), the colouring matter of Logwood ; **haemati'nus**, **haem'atites**, **haematit'ic**, *haematit'icus*, **haematochro'os** (χρώς, a tinge), blood-red ; **Haematochro'me** (χρῶμα, colour), Cohn's term for the

pigment of *Haematococcus pluvialis*, etc. ; **Haematox'ylin** (ξύλον, wood), the colouring matter of Logwood, *Haematoxylon campechianum*, Linn. ; **Haemorrha'gia** (ῥαγία, from ῥήγνυμαι, to break forth), a disease in plants when the sap is constantly exuding through an external wound.

Hair, an outgrowth of the epidermis, a single elongated cell, or row of cells ; ~ **Cyst'oliths**, pl., structures resembling cystoliths occurring in trichomes ; ~ **-point'ed**, ending in a fine, weak point ; ~ **-shaped**, filiform, very slender, as the ultimate divisions of the inflorescence of many grasses ; **Hair-breadth** = CAPILLUS ; **Hair'iness**, hirsute, more rigidly hairy than pubescent ; **hair'y**, pubescence when the hairs are separately distinguishable.

hal'berd-, or **hal'bert-shaped**, hastate ; ~ **-headed**, means the same.

Half, (1) a moiety ; one part of that which is divided into two equal portions ; (2) sometimes it means one-sided, dimidiate ; ~ **-anat'ropous**, amphitropous ; ~ **Breed**, the product of a cross-fertilization ; ~ **-cor'date**, heart-shaped on one side, ~ **-cylin'dric**, applied to a stem flattened on one side ; ~ **-equ'itant**, partially equitant ; ~ **-hu'mus Plants**, semi-saprophytes ; ~ **-infe'rior**, used of an ovary when the stamens are perigynous ; ~ **-monopet'alous**, the petals united, but so slightly as to separate easily ; ~ **-moon-shaped**, semilunate, crescent-like ; ~ **-net'ted**, when of several layers, only the outer is netted, as the corm of *Gladiolus communis*, Linn. ; ~ **-race**, a form intermediate between a species and a variety of it, producing but few seedlings of the racial character, the majority reverting to the specific type ; ~ **Sib'ling** (+ SIBLING), a pair of plants from the ovaries of the same parent, or pollen of the same parent (K. Pearson) ; ~ **-stem-clasp'ing**, partly amplexicaul ; ~ **-supe'rior**, the same as half-inferior ; ~ **-terete'**, flat on one side, terete on the other :—**Half-Galtonian-curve**, see NEWTONIAN CURVE.

Halm, see HAULM.

Halobi′on (ἅλς, ἁλός, salt, the sea ; βίος, life), associations of marine plants (Forel) ; **halolimnet′ic** (+ LIMNETIC), belonging to the sea or salt lakes (Forel).

hal′onate, halona′tus (ἅλως, the disc of the sun, halo), when a coloured circle surrounds a spot.

Halodrymi′um (ἅλς, ἁλός, salt, the sea ; δρυμὸς, a coppice), a mangrove formation (Diels) ; **hal′o-ne′reid** (Νηρεῖς, a sea-nymph), pertaining to salt-water.

halo′nial, used of the fertile branches or tubercles of the fossil *Lepidophloios*, formerly considered as belonging to *Halonia*, Lindley et Hutt., non Fries.

haloph′ilous (ἅλς, ἁλός, salt, the sea ; φιλέω, I love), salt-loving ; **Hal′ophobe** (φοβέω, I fear), a plant which shuns salt ; adj. **haloph′obous** ; **Halophy′ta** (φυτὸν, a plant), salt plants ; **Hal′ophyte** (φυτὸν, a plant), a plant which grows within the influence of salt water ; adj. **halophyt′ic** ; **Halophyti′a**, plant associations of salt marshes ; **Halophy′tism**, the condition in question ; **Haloplank′ton** (+PLANKTON), the floating vegetation of salt-water. nerit′ic ∼, confined to the coast ; ocean′ic ∼, or pelag′ic ∼, that of the open sea.

Hal′ospore, an error for HAPLOSPORE.

halved, dimidiate ; **Halves**, *cf.* SEGMENT HALVES.

Hama′da, stony desert tracts in Algeria.

ha′mate, *hama′tus* (Lat. hooked), hooked at the tip ; **ha′mose, ha′-mous**, *hamo′sus*, hooked ; **ham′ulate** ; **ham′ulose**, *hamulo′sus*, beset with small hooks ; **Ha′mulus**, a hooked bristle in the flowers of *Uncinia* ; **Ha′mus**, a hook.

Ham′mock vegetation, a Florida term for CLIMAX Vegetation.

Han′dle, the manubrium of the antheridium of Characeae.

hapaxan′thic, hapaxan′thous (ἅπαξ, once ; ἄνθος, a flower), used of herbs having a single flowering period.

Haplan′the (ἁπλόος, single ; ἄνθη, a blossom), Huxley's term for the hypothetic anemophilous type of the flowers of Gentianaceae ; *cf.* Journ. Linn. Soc., Bot. xxiv. (1887), 112, 122 ; **Haplobacte′ria** (+ BACTERIA), simple bacteria, colonies and cells in aggregation, the product of division as in *Sarcina ;* **Haplobi′ont** (βίος, life ; ὄντα, things existing), a plant which fruits once only : monocarpic ; **haplocaules′cent**, uniaxial ; **haplocau′lous** (καυλὸς, a stem), having a simple unbranched stem ; **haplochlamyd′eous** (χλαμὺς, a mantle), monochlamydeous, having a single perianth ; **Hap′locyte** (κύτος, a hollow vessel), a cell containing nuclei with the reduced number of chromosomes (Benson); adj. **haplocyt′ic** ; **Haplogen′esis** (γένεσις, beginning), the origin of new forms by evolution and development of new characters ; **haplogen′eus** (γεννάω, I bring forth), = HETERONEMEUS ; **Haplogonid′ium** (+ GONIDIUM), a Lichen gonidium occurring singly and resembling *Protococcus ;* **Haplogonim′ia** (+ GONIMIA), gonimia occurring singly ; **Hap′loid** (εἶδος, resemblance), the organism with the single number of chromosomes, the hap′loid, or *x* Generation ; the gametophyte (Strasburger); **haplolepid′eous**, the preferable form of APLOLEPIDEOUS ; **Haplomer′istele** (+ MERISTELE), a simple stele consisting of an axial series of tracheae surrounded by a ring of phloem ; adj. **haplomeriste′lic** (Brebner) ; **Haplomito′sis** (+ MITOSIS), nuclear division in which the spirem does not give rise to the chromosomes but to chromospires (Dangeard) ; **haploperist′omous** (+ PERISTOME), used of Mosses with a peristome of a single row of teeth ; **haplopet′alous**, *-lus* (πέταλον, a flower leaf), with one row of petals ; **Hap′lophase** (φαίνω, I appear), Vuillemin's term for HAPLOID ; **Hap′lospore** (σπορὰ

seed), (1) a simple spore in Lichens ;
(2) an asexual spore (Benson) ; **haplo-
ste′monous** (στήμων, a stamen), with
a single series of stamens in one
whorl ; **Hap′lostele** (στήλη, a pillar),
a simple stele consisting of xylem
surrounded by phloem (Brebner) ;
Hap′lotype (τύπος, a type), used of
a single species in its original place
of publication ; adj. **haplotyp′ic ;
haploxyl′ic** (ξύλον, wood), having a
single vascular bundle in the leaf,
e. g. *Pinus excelsa*, Wall.

Hap′teron, pl. **Hap′tera** (ἅπτω, I fasten
upon), Warming's term for organs
of attachment which do not contain
vascular tissue, as in Podostomaceae ;
Hap′tere, C. MacMillan's term for
HAPTERON, a holdfast ; **hapter′ic**,
of the nature of a holdfast ; **Hapto-
morph′ism**, stimulus by contact ;
Haptotax′is, Haptot′ropism (τρόπος,
direction), the curvature induced in
climbing plants by the stimulus of
a rough surface (Czapek).

hard′y, enduring without protection ;
not injured by the climate.

harmon′ic (ἁρμονία, consonance), applied by Boulger to the development
of large groups characteristic of
continents.

Harmo′sis (ἅρμοσις, an adapting), response to stimulus, both of adjustment and adaptation (Clements).

harpid′ioid, (1) resembling or allied
to the Harpidium section of *Hypnum ;* (2) similarly the Lichen genus
Harpidium.

has′tate, *hasta′tus* (*hasta*, a spear),
halbert-shaped, sagittate, with the
basal lobes turned outward ; **has′ti-
form** (*forma*, shape), spear-shaped,
hastate ; **has′tile**, *hasti′lis* (Lat.,
like the shaft of a spear), used for
hastate.

hatch′et-shaped, dolabriform.

Haulm, Halm, Haum, (1) the culm of
grasses ; (2) the stem of herbaceous
plants.

Haustor′ium (*haustor*, a drawer), (1) a
sucker of parasitic plants ; (2) used
by Komarow for an appendage of perithecia ; (3) a structure arising from

the secondary nucleus of *Lathraea*,
the embryo sac containing two
haustoria, one equatorial, the other
micropylar (Chodat) ; **Haustor′ia**
(pl.) **appendicula′ta**, when they arise
from a protrusion of the hyphae,
appressors ; ~ **exappendicula′ta**,
when they arise directly from the
hyphae without much contortion at
the point of origin ; ~ **lobula′ta**,
lobed appressors.

Haust′rum (Lat. machine for drawing
water), the bulbous nursing foot of
developing plants ; an organ of
attachment and temporary nutrition ; adj. **haust′ral**.

Haut′schicht (Ger.), the layer of cell
protoplasm known as ECTOPLASM.

Head, (1) an inflorescence ; the capitulum of Composites ; (2) formerly
used for the theca of Mosses ; ~ **Cell**,
the capitulum of *Chara ;* **head′ed**,
capitate.

Heart, used by Grew for the centre,
as heart of oak, the duramen ; ~
shaped, cordate ; ~ **Rot**, a disease
of pine-apples of unknown origin ;
~ **Wood**, the innermost and oldest
wood next to the pith, the duramen ;
~ ~ **Rot**, *Polyporus hispidus*, the
cause of this disease on fruit trees ;
it attacks the wood near the pith
and spreads towards the sap-wood.

Heath, an expanse of peaty or sandy
soil, with a predominance of *Calluna ;* ~ **Associa′tion**, a stable principal growth of heather, without
trees ; **Heathland**, a delayed or
abortive stage of Moorland.

Heath′er-moor, *Calluna* is dominant,
often with *Vaccinium Myrtillus.*

Heaut′otype (ἑαυτοῦ, of his own ;
τύπος, a type) applied to a specimen
of a previously described and named
species selected by the author, not
being otherwise recognizable : meant
to supersede AUTOTYPE.

hebecar′pus (ἥβη, puberty ; καρπὸς,
fruit), having the fruit covered with
downy pubescence.

heb′etate, *hebeta′tus* (Lat., blunted),
having a dull or blunt or soft point.

Hecist′otherm = HEKISTOTHERM.

hedera′ceous, *hedera′ceus* (*Hedera,* ivy; + ACEOUS, (1) pertaining to ivy; (2) resembling ivy in habit; **hed′-eral,** composed of ivy; **hederif′erous** (*fero,* I bear), producing ivy; **Hed′erose,** a sugar contained in ivy, *Hedera Helix.*

Hedi′um, or **Hedi′on** (ἕδος, a base), a succession of plants on residuary soils (Clements).

He′gemon ‡ (ἡγεμών, a leader), fibro-vascular tissue.

Hekis′totherm (ἥκιστος, the smallest; θέρμη, heat), a plant which needs but little heat, and can withstand long periods of darkness (Warming); adj. **hekistotherm′ic.**

Hel′ad (ἕλος, a marsh; + AD), a marsh-plant; **Heleoplank′ton,** or **Helei′oplankton** (+ PLANKTON), the float-ing vegetation of marshes, which overpowers the animal plankton; it differs from Potamoplankton by less motion of the water (Zimmer).

Helcot′ropism (ἕλκω, I drag; τροπή, a turning), compulsory attraction of plants; a correction of ELCO-TROPISM.

heliaca′lis (ἡλιακὸς, belonging to the sun), heliacal; spiral.

He′liad (ἥλιος, the sun), a heliophyte or sun-loving plant, adapted to full exposure (Clements); **He′lias,** a "sun form" or heliophyte.

helianth′ine, relating to *Helianthus;* **Helian′thon,** Clements's term for a family of *Helianthus.*

Helichry′sin, the yellow colouring matter of several species of *Heli-chrysum.*

helic′iform (*helix,* a snail; *forma,* shape), coiled like a snail shell.

Hel′icism (ἕλιξ, ἕλικος, twisted), a torsion which shows itself usually at an advanced period of plant-life, as the tendrils and fruit of *Strepto-carpus;* **Hel′icocarp** (καρπὸς, fruit), Nicotra's term for a fruit whose constituent carpels are arranged in a spiral; **helicogy′rate,** *helicogy′ratus* (*gyratus,* turned in a circle), having a ring carried obliquely round, as the annulus in some Ferns; **hel′icoid,**

helicoid′eus (εἶδος, like), coiled into a helix, or like a snail-shell; ~ **Cells,** terminal cells, which are usually branched, of *Pithophora* (Wittrock); ~ **Cyme,** a sympodial inflorescence whose lateral branches are all de-veloped on one side, a bostryx, or drepanium; in some text-books this is erroneously called "scorpioid"; ~ **Cyst′oliths,** twisted cystoliths; ~ **Dichot′omy,** when in two unequal branches, the more vigorous one is uniformly on the same side; ~ **Inflores′cence,** when the flowers are in a single row; ~ **unip′arous Cyme,** a bostryx; **helicoi′dal,** spirally twisted, in the manner of a snail-shell; **Helicomor′phy** (μορφὴ, shape), term covering the young and adult forms of leaf in heteroplastic plants (Diels).

he′lio- (ἥλιος, the sun), Drude's pre-fix to his groups depending upon the sun in summer for the vege-tation period; **helioph′ilous,** *-us* (φιλέω, I love), adapted to full exposure to the sun; **helioph′obic** (φοβέω, I dread), shunning the light), negatively heliotropic; **helioph′obous** (φοβέω, I fear), adapted to a very small amount of light; **He′liophyll** (φύλλον, a leaf), a leaf of a HELIOPHYTE; **He′liophytes,** *-phy′ta* (φυτὸν, a plant), plants adapted to full sunlight; **Heliophyti′a,** forma-tions of such plants (Clements); **Helio′sis,** injury done by sun-burn; **Heliostroph′ism** (+ STROPHISM), a tendency to twist, in response to light (Pfeffer); **Heliotax′is** (τάξις, arrangement), the turning of an organism such as a spore, in relation to light; **Heliotor′tism** (*tortus,* twisted), torsion caused by incidence of light (Schwendener and Krabbe); **heliotrop′ic** (τρόπος, direction), turn-ing towards the light; ~ **An′gle,** the angle of incidence at which light has the most stimulating effect; **Heliot′ropism,** the act of turning towards the sun or source of light; **neg′ative** ~, shunning light; **pos′itive** ~, growing in the direction of

the light ; **trans′verse** ~, = DIA-
HELOTROPISM : **Helioturgot′ropism**
(*turgor*, a swelling ; τροπή, a turning), becoming turgid in response to
light (Pfeffer) ; **helioxeroph′ilous**
(+ XEROPHILOUS), the condition of
plants adapted to strong sunlight
and dryness (Vesque) ; **Helioxero-
ph′yll** (φύλλον, a leaf), the state of
leaves capable of withstanding
drought and strong sunshine (Vesque) ; **heliozo′oid** (ζῶον, an animal ;
εἶδος, like), amoeboid, but having
distinct ray-like pseudopodia.

Heli′um (ἕλος, a marsh), a marsh
formation.

Helkot′ropism (ἕλκω, I drag ; τροπή, a
turning), attraction on plants as of
gravitation ; cf. HELCOTROPISM.

Hel′met, = GALEA ; ~ **shaped** =
galeate.

helminth′oid (ἕλμινς, ἕλμινθος, a worm ;
εἶδος, resemblance), worm-shaped,
vermiform (Heinig).

helminthospor′oid (εἶδος, resemblance),
resembling the genus *Helmintho-
sporium*, Pers.

helo′bious (ἕλος, a marsh ; βίος, life),
living in marshes, paludal.

Helo′dad (ἑλώδης, marshy ; + AD), a
marsh plant ; **Helo′drad**, a plant of
a marsh thicket ; **Helodi′um**, a
swampy open woodland formation ;
Helodri′um (δρίος, a thicket), a
thicket formation : **Helohy′drad**
(ὕλη, forest), a marsh forest plant).

Helohy′lium (ἕλος, marsh ; ὕλη, forest),
a swamp forest formation ; **helo-
hyloph′ilus** (φιλέω, I love), dwelling
in wet forests ; **Helohylophy′ta**
(φυτόν, a plant), wet forest plants
(Clements) ; **Helolochmi′um** (λόχμη,
a thicket), a meadow thicket formation ; **helolochmoph′ilus** (φιλέω, I
love), dwelling in meadow thickets ;
Helolochmophy′ta (φυτόν, a plant),
meadow thicket plants (Clements) ;
heloph′ilus (φιλέω, I love), marsh-
loving ; **Helophyli′um**, a marsh forest
formation (Clements) ; **Hel′ophytes**
(φυτόν, a plant), marsh plants
(Clements) ; **Heloplank′ton** (+
PLANKTON), the floating vegetation

of a marsh ; **Helorgadi′um** (ἕλος,
marsh ; ὀργάς, meadow), swamp formation (Gaong) ; **helorgadoph′ilus**
(φιλέω, I love), dwelling in swampy
woodlands ; **Helorgadophy′ta** (φυτόν,
a plant), plants of that formation
(Clements).

Hel′otism (εἵλως, a serf), Warming's
term for the symbiotic relations of
Algae and Fungi in Lichens.

hel′volus (Lat.), pale ochreous yellow ;
hel′vus (Lat.), light bay, dun-colour.

He′matine = HAEMATIN.

Hemeran′thy (ἡμέρα, day ; ἀνθέω, I
flower), day-flowering ; adj. **heme′-
ranth′ous**.

He′merophytes (ἥμερος, cultivated ;
φυτόν, a plant), plants introduced
by the agency of man ; anthropo-
phytes (Simmons).

hemi- (ἥμι), in composition means half ;
Hemi-albumose′ (+ ALBUMOSES), a
mixture chiefly of proto- and heteroalbumose ; **hemiamphicar′pous** (+
AMPHICARPOUS), having two kinds
of fruit, one of which is both aërial
and subterranean, e. g. *Catananche
lutea* ; **hemianat′ropous** (ἀνά, up ;
τροπή, a turn), half-anatropous, the
ovule being partially bent back, half
the raphe free ; **hemitropous**, amphitropous ; **hemiangiocar′pic**, **he-
miangiocar′pous** (+ ANGIOCARPIC),
when the ascocarp (apothecium) is
closed at first, but opens on
approaching ripeness and discloses
the hymenium of crowded asci ;
Hemiangiasperm′eae (+ANGIOSPER-
MAE), hypothetical direct ancestors
of the Angiosperms (Arber and
Parkin); **Hemiaut′ophyte** (+ AUTO-
PHYTE), chlorphyll-bearing parasites
(Boulger); **Hem′icarp**, *Hemicarp′ium*
καρπός, a fruit), a half-carpel, a
mericarp; **Hemicell′ulose** (+ CELLU-
LOSE), all carbohydrates present in
the cell-wall which are not coloured
blue by chlor-zinc-iodide, such as
pectinaceous substances, reserve
cellulose, etc. (Gilson) ; formerly
termed Pseudo-cellulose ; **hemichi-
monoph′ilous** (χειμών, winter ; φιλέω,
I love), applied by F. Ludwig to

those plants whose above-ground development begins even during the prevalence of frost, as *Ranunculus Ficaria*, Linn.; **hemichlamyd′eous** (χλαμύς, a cloak), half-coated, as ovules when borne on an inverted symphyllodium in Coniferae (Čelakovsky); **Hemicleistog′amy** (+ CLEISTOGAMY), Knuth's term for the condition of plants whose flowers open slightly; adj. **hemicleistogam′ic**; **hemiconcen′tric** (*concentricus*, Late Lat.), having a common centre), incompletely concentric (Solereder); **Hemicrypt′ophytes** (+ CRYPTOPHYTES), perennial plants having their buds at the level of the ground (Raunkiær); **Hemicy′cle** (κύκλος, a circle), a half-circle, or half-coil; **hemicy′clic**, partly in whorls, as the perianth leaves in whorls, and the sporophylls in spirals; **hemicylin′dric** (κύλινδρος, a cylinder), (1) half-terete; (2) a leafy expansion, plane on one side, convex on the other; **Hemidystroph′ia** (δυσ-, bad; τροφή, nourishment), partial nourishment, semistarvation; **hemiendobiot′ic** (+ ENDOBIOTIC), living usually within the host, sometimes outside it; **hemiendophyt′ic** (+ ENDOPHYTIC), used of a fungus parasite sometimes external and sometimes internal (Salmon); **Hemiendozo′a** (ζῶον, an animal), applied to *Torubia*, as though imperfect plants; **Hemiep′iphyte** (ἐπί, upon; φυτόν, a plant), employed by Went for a plant which at first roots in the soil, afterwards developing aërial roots; **Hem′iform** (+ FORM), used of heteroecious Fungi, having uredospores and teleutospores, the latter only germinating after a resting period; **hemigamot′ropous** (γάμος, marriage; τροπή, a turning), used of flowers which open and shut imperfectly; **hemigona′ris** ‡ (γόνος, offspring), employed when a part of both stamens and pistils are changed into petals; **hemigymnocar′pous** (+ GYMNOCARPOUS), used of Fungi which mature their spores

in closed receptacles which open for their dispersal; **Hemigy′rus** ‡ (γῦρος, round) = FOLLICLE; **hemihel′icoid** (+ HELICOID) F. N. Williams's term for Braun's HEMICYCLIC; **hemi′iden′tic**, nearly the same; *e. g.* the red flowers and spots of the leaf-axils in certain races of peas are hemiidentic characters; **Hemimetat′ropy** (μετά, with; τροπή, a turning), in crossing when the interchange between male and female elements from different flowers or plants is only half completed (K. Pearson); adj. **hemimetatrop′ic**; **hemiorthomorph′ic** (ὀρθός, upright; μορφή, shape), symmetric organs which possess an equality in a vertical plane (Wiesner); **Hemiorthot′ropy** (τροπή, a turning), any naturally placed organ displaying vertical symmetry (Wiesner); **Hemipar′asite** (+ PARASITE), (1) plants whose seeds germinate without a host plant, but whose after life is dependent upon a host, as *Bartsia* and *Tozzia*; (2) a facultative saprophyte, a parasite which can exist as a saprophyte; **Hemiparthen′osperm** (+ PARTHENOSPERM), C. MacMillan's term for a plant having either embryo or endosperm parthenogenetic, but not both; **hemipe′lic** (πηλός, clay), rocks which yield a moderate amount of clay detritus, and the plants which affect such localities (Thurmann); **hemipelor′ic** (πελώριος, monstrous), partly peloric flowers in *Linaria*, the flowers being nearly regular (Vernon); **Hemipentacot′yl**, a seedling with partial division of its cotyledons so as to appear as if it had five; **Hem′iphyll** (φύλλον, a leaf), the hypothetic segment of a carpel; **ov′ular** ~, **placen′tal** ~, those which become modified into special parts of the ovary respectively, *cf.* TRIPHYLLOME; **Hemiplank′ton** (+ PLANKTON), the mingled vegetation of shallow and deep water forms in land-locked pools, etc. (A. F. W. Schimper); **hemipsam′mic** (ψάμμος, sand), strata which give a moderately porous detritus, with the plants which prefer such places (Thurmann) ; **Hemipuccin'ia**, a group of *Puccinia*, = HEMIFORM ; **Hemisap'rophyte** (+ SAPROPHYTE), a plant which appropriates humus although capable of self-support, a facultative parasite (Warming) ; **hem'ischist** (σχιστὸς, split), in brood-cell formation when the nucleus only divides, the cytoplasm remaining whole (Hartog) ; **Hemisyncot'yly** (+ SYNCOTYLY), when seedlings have their cotyledons partially fused with one another or some other organ (De Vries) ; **hemisyngyn'icus** (σύν, with ; γυνὴ, γυναικὸς, a woman), half-adherent (Lindley) ; **Hemite'ria** ‡ (τηρέω, I keep), "a monstrosity of elementary organs, or of appendages of the axis" (Lindley) ; **Hemitetracotyle'don** (τετρὰς, four ; + COTYLEDON), De Vries's expression when both cotyledons are divided, or one normal and the other divided ; **hemit'richous** ‡ (θρὶξ, τρικὸς, hair), half covered with hairs ; **Hemitricotyle'don** (τρεῖς, three ; + COTYLEDON), used by De Vries, when one cotyledon is apparently divided into three ; **Hemitricot'yly**, partial division of one cotyledon ; complete fission is TRICOTYLY (De Vries) ; **hemit'ropal, hemit'ropous** (τρόπος, direction), (1) amphitropous, the axis of the ovule being more curved than the anatropous condition ; (2) employed by M'Leod for flowers which are restricted to certain insects for honey-getting ; (3) with flowers of moderate adaptiveness to insect visitors, the mean between ALLOTROPOUS and EUTROPOUS ; (4) also applied to insects which visit the same, as flies, short-tongued bees, and most butterflies (Loew) ; ~ **Herkog'amy** = HERCOGAMY.

Hemp, the fibro-vascular tissue of *Cannabis sativa*, Linn.

Hen-and-chickens, proliferous flowers, the centre flower or head being surrounded by subsidiary flowers.

Henslo'vian Mem'brane, the cuticle ;

so named from Prof. J. S. Henslow's researches on the same.

hepat'ic, hepat'icous, *-cus* (Lat., diseased in the liver), liver-coloured, dark, purplish-red ; **Hepaticol'ogist**, an expert in Hepaticae ; **Hepaticol'ogy** (λόγος, discourse), the study of the Hepaticae or Liverworts.

Hepo'doche (ἔπω, I follow ; δοχὴ, succession), a secondary succession (Clements).

Heptagyn'ia (ἑπτὰ, seven ; γυνὴ, a woman), a Linnean class of plants having seven pistils ; **heptagyn'ian**, possessing seven pistils ; **heptam'erous** (μέρος, a part), having the parts in sevens ; **heptan'der** (ἀνὴρ, ἀνδρὸς, a man), having seven stamens ; **Heptan'dria**, a Linnean order of plants with seven stamens ; **heptan'drian, heptan'drous**, relating to the same, or possessing seven stamens ; **heptapet'alous** (πέταλον, a flower leaf), having seven petals ; **heptaphyl'lous** (φύλλον, a leaf), with seven leaves ; **hep'tarch**, applied to a fibrovascular cylinder or stele with seven rays or bundles ; **heptari'nus** (ἄρρην, male), Necker's term for HEPTANDROUS.

Herb, *Herb'a* (Lat., grass, herbage, plant), a plant with no persistent stem above ground ; **herba'ceous**, *-ceus* (+)ACEOUS, (1) with the texture, colour and properties of a herb ; (2) with annual stems from a perennial root, as an ~ **Peren'nial** ; **Herb'age**, herbs collectively, grass, pasture ; **Herb'al**, (1) an old volume containing descriptions of plants, such as John Gerard's "Herball" ; (2) sometimes = HERBARIUM ; **Herb'alist**, (1) a writer of herbals, one of the old botanists ; (2) a person skilled in the knowledge of herbs ; **Herb'arist**, an old word for botanist ; **Herba'rium**, a collection of dried plants, formerly styled a "*hortus siccus*" ; **Herb'elet, Herb'let**, a small herb ; **he'rbes'cent**, growing into herbs ; **Herb'orist**, a collector of plants for medical use ; **Herboriza'tion**, a botanic excursion for the collection of plants ; **herb'orize**, to botanize.

Hercog'amy (ἔρκος, a fence ; γάμος, marriage), applied to hermaphrodite flowers, when some structural peculiarity prevents self-fertilization ; requiring insect-visitation ; adj. **hercogam'ic, herkogam'ic, hercog'-amous, -mus ; ab'solute** ~, the possibility of self-pollination is always excluded ; **conceal'ed** ~, self-pollination as frequent as insect-pollination ; **contin'gent** ~, accidental and occasional self-pollination is possible ; **half** ~, flowers at first hercogamous, but at a later period self-pollination becomes practicable from growth or change in parts of the flower.

Hered'ity (here'ditas, heirship), possession by inheritance, of certain qualities or structures ; **bisex'ual** ~, **unisex'ual** ~, having the qualities of both, or of one parent only transmitted ; adj. **hered'itary** ; ~ **Symbio'sis**, the presence of Mycobacteria in the tissues, including seeds.

hermaph'rodite, hermaphrodi'tus (Lat. having the characters of both sexes), the stamens and pistils in the same flower.

Her'pes (ἕρπης, a cutaneous eruption) **tonsu'rans** (Lat., shaving), ringworm, a disease of the skin ascribed to Trichophyton tonsurans, Malm.

Herp'ism (ἕρπω, I creep), creeping by means of variously shaped pseudopodia, as in Flagellata ; **Her'poblast** (βλαστὸς, a shoot), Cramer's term for a confervoid prothallium lying flat on its substratum.

Hertzot'ropism (τροπὴ, a turning), movement due to the influence of the Hertzian waves, whence the term (Massart).

Hesperid'ium (from the golden fruit of the garden of the Hesperides), Desvaux's term for a fruit, such as the orange : a superior, polycarpellary, syncarpous berry, pulpy within, and externally covered with a tough rind ; AURANTIUM of de Candolle.

Hetae'rio (ἐταιρεία, a brotherhood); a collection of distinct indehiscent carpels produced by a single flower, dry or fleshy, as in the Strawberry, Buttercup, Raspberry ; usually spelled ETAERIO.

Heterac'my (ἕτερος, other ; ἀκμὴ, apex), = DICOGAMY ; **Heteradel'phy** (ἀδελφὸς, a brother), used of two adherent carpels which develop unequally, one being more or less atrophied (Reymondaud); **heterand'-rous** (ἀνὴρ, ἀνδρὸς, a man), with two sets of stamens ; applied to flowers whose stamens vary in size ; **Heteran'dry**, the condition described ; **Heteranthe'ry**, the condition of having distinct kinds of stamens ; **Heterauxe'sis** (αὔξησὶς, growth), variation in the relative growth of opposite sides of an organ ; **heterax'on** (ἄξων, an axle), applied by O. Mueller to a diatom if the transverse axes are unequal ; **Heteroalbumose'** (+ ALBUMOSE), Kuhne's term for proteid, phytalbumose ; **heteroblas'tic** (βλαστὸς, a shoot), (1) applied to embryogeny which is indirect, the offspring not similar to the parent, but producing the adult form as an outgrowth, as in Chara ; (2) used by Goebel to express the fact that the adult form of a plant is very unlike the young or larval form ; (3) applied by Pfitzer to those Orchids in which the pseudobulbs consist of a single swollen internode ; the condition is **Heteroblas'ty; Heterob'olites** (βολὶs, a missile), a catabolic product with absorption of other bodies (Beyerinck) ; cf. SCHIZOBOLITES ; **heterocar'picus** (fructus), " an inferior fruit " (Lindley) ; **heterocar'pinus** (καρπὸς, fruit), an inferior or partially inferior fruit, as the acorn ; **heterocar'pous, -pus,** producing more than one kind of fruit ; **Heterocar'py,** having two kinds of fruit ; **heteroceph'alus** (κεφαλὴ, the head), bearing two kinds of head or capitulum ; **heterochlamyd'eous, -deus** (χλαμὺς, a mantle), when the calyx and

corolla clearly differ ; **heterocho'ric**
($\chi\omega\rho\acute{\epsilon}\omega$, I spread abroad), used of
a species inhabiting two or more
closely related formations ; **hetero-
chromat'ic**, adj. of HETEROCHRO-
MATISM ; **Heterochro'matism** ($\chi\rho\hat{\omega}\mu\alpha$,
colour), a change in the colouring or
marking of petals ; **Heterochro'mosomes** (+ CHROMOSOMES), aberrant
chromosomes (Gates) ; *cf.* MONO-
SOMES ; **heterochro'mous**, when the
florets of the disc in Compositae
differ in colour from those of the
ray ; **heteroch'ronous** ($\chi\rho\acute{o}\nu\sigma s$, duration of time), in cultures when sow-
ings are made at different times
(Clements) ; **heterocis'mal**, an ill-
contrived version of HETEROECIOUS ;
het'erocline, heterocli'nous, *-nus*,
($\kappa\lambda\acute{\iota}\nu\eta$, a bed), with the male and
female members on separate recep-
tacles.

het'eroclite, *heteroc'litus* ($\dot{\epsilon}\tau\epsilon\rho\acute{o}\kappa\lambda\iota\tau\sigma s$,
varying in declension), anomalous
in formation.

heterocot'ylous ($\dot{\epsilon}\tau\epsilon\rho\sigma s$, other; + COTY-
LEDON), having cotyledons un-
equally developed ; **heterocy'clic**
($\kappa\acute{\nu}\kappa\lambda\sigma s$, a circle), used when the
floral whorls are heteromerous, not
uniform or isomerous ; **Het'erocyst**,
($\kappa\acute{\nu}\sigma\tau\iota s$, a bag), large inert cells
in the filaments of certain Algae,
separating contiguous hormogonia ;
adj. **heterocyst'ous** ; **heterodes'mic**
($\delta\epsilon\sigma\mu\grave{o}s$, a bond), used when the
vascular bundles are partly of
phloem only (Brebner) ; *cf.* HOMO-
DESMIC ; **Heterodichog'amy** ; Engler
and Prantl's synonym for DICHO-
GAMY ; **Heterodi'ode** (+ DIODE),
a term to include MACRODIODE and
MICRODIODE (Van Tieghem) ; **Het-
erodi'ody** ($\delta\iota\acute{o}\delta\sigma s$, a passage), Van
Tieghem's term for the condition of
those DIODES which are differentiated into MACRODIODES, and MICRO-
DIODES ; *cf.* ISODIODY ; **Heterodisty'ly** (+ DI ; *stylus*, a style),
dimorphism, the presence of two
kinds of plant, having either long
or short styles, e.g. *Primula* ; adj.
heterodisty'lous ; **heterod'romous**,

-mus, ($\delta\rho\acute{o}\mu\sigma s$, a course), having
spirals of changing directions, as
in some tendrils, or phyllotaxis ;
Heterod'romy, when two spirals take
different or opposite courses ; **he-
terodynam'ic** ($\delta\acute{\nu}\nu\alpha\mu\iota s$, power), applied to pairs of characters, one
dominant, the other recessive (Correns) ; **heteroe'cious**, forms which
pass through their stages of development on different hosts are
so termed ; metoecious is a synonym ; **Heteroe'cism**, the condition
a heteroecious parasite : **heteroecis'-
mal**, should be HETEROECIOUS ;
Heteroe'cium ($\sigma\hat{\iota}\kappa\sigma s$, a house), a
Fungus which passes its stages on
more than one host plant ; a
metoecious parasite ; **Het'eroecyst**
(Crozier) = HETEROCYST ; **Hetero-
eu'forms** ($\epsilon\mathring{\upsilon}$, well ; + FORM), forms
of *Puccinia*, producing uredospores
and teleutospores on a host other
than that on which they bring
forth spermogonia and aecidia ;
Het'eroforms is a contraction for the
same ; **heterog'amous**, *-mus*, ($\gamma\acute{\alpha}\mu\sigma s$,
marriage), (1) bearing two kinds of
flowers, as in Compositae, the florets
of the ray may be neuter or unisexual, and those of the disk
hermaphrodite ; (2) an abnormal
arrangement of the sexual organs
(Masters) ; **Heterog'amy**, change of
the function of male and female
flowers, or in their arrangement ;
heterogene ($\gamma\acute{\epsilon}\nu\sigma s$, offspring), the
character of offspring when the
parents are hybrids or belong to
different types (Lotsy) ; **heteroge'-
neous** ($\gamma\acute{\epsilon}\nu\sigma s$, race), not uniform in
kind ; **Heterogene'ity**, dissimilarity
of nature ; **heterog'enous Induc'tion**,
used by Noll to denote sensitive
movements in which two different
causes co-operate ; **Heterogen'esis**
($\gamma\acute{\epsilon}\nu\epsilon\sigma\iota s$, beginning), (1) alternation
of generations ; (2) the origin of
organisms from different genera or
orders, or *de novo* (Bastian) ; (3)
origin by sports, or bud variation ;
heterogenet'ic, when applied to
fertilization means cross-pollina-

177

tion ; ~ **Varia′tion** = Mutation; **Heterog′enism** = Heterogenesis ; **Het′erogone** (γονὴ), offspring), a plant whose flowers are dimorphic or trimorphic in the length of the stamens or styles; adj. **heterog′-onous,** *heterogo′neus* : **Heterog′ony,** the same as Heterostyly, *cf.* Homogony ; **Heteroho′motype,** the entire stage of Hetero- and Homotype karyokinesis (Grégoire) ; **heteroi′cous,** a form preferred by some bryologists to the usual spelling heteroecious; **heteroi′deus** ‡ (εἶδος, like), diversified in form (Lindley); **heterokaryot′ic** (κάρυον, a nut), the character of spores in which both male and female nuclei exist (Burgeff; **Heterokaryo′sis** is the condition ; **Heterokine′sis** (κίνησις, motion), heterotypic meiosis (Grégoire); **Heteroli′cheni** (+ Lichen), Lichens in which the gonidia are stratified in the thallus (Jatta) ; **heteromal′lus,** *-lus* (μαλλὸς, a fleece or tuft of wool), spreading in all directions ; **heterom′alous** (Crozier) = the foregoing ; **Heterom′erals,** Bessey's abbreviation for the Heteromerae of Bentham and Hooker, a series of Gamopetalae ; **Heteromer′icarpy** (μέρος, a part ; καρπὸς, fruit), (1) heterocarpy occurring between parts of the same fruit (Delpino) ; (2) Huth's term for a binary fruit, the halves of which differ from each other, as *Turgenia heterocarpa,* DC.; **heteromer′icus,** stratified, as in some Lichens ; **heterom′erous** (1) when the number of the members is not uniform ; (2) in Lichens. the opposite of isomerous ; **heteromor′phic, heteromor′phous** (μορφή, form), (1) variation from normal structure, as deformities, etc. ; (2) having organs differing in length, dimorphic, with long and short styles; trimorphic, with long, short, and medium length, the male organs (stamens) being of corresponding length ; **Heteromesog′amy** (μέσος, intermediate ; γάμος, marriage), when individuals vary in the method of fertilization, as (*a*)

auto-allogamous, (*b*) homodichogamous, and (*c*) dientomophilous; **Heteromorpho′sis** or **Heteromor′phy** = Aitomorphosis in botanic usage; **Heteromorph′ism,** the heteromorphic condition ; **heterone′meus** (νῆμα), a thread), applied to plants which on germination produce thread-like growths, which afterwards give rise to a leafy axis, such as Bryophytes and Pteridophytes ; **Heteropet′alody** (+ Petalody) change from one kind of petal into another; **heteroph′agous** (φάγω, I eat), applied to Fungi which attack plants not congeneric (Eriksson) ; **Heteroph′agy,** used by Dangeard for sexual (protoplasmic) unions which leave a residue ; *cf.* Autophagy ; **heterophyad′ic,** *heterophyad′icus* (φυὴ, growth), used of those species which have fertile stems of different form from the barren stems, as in some *Equiseta ;* **heterophyl′-lous** (φύλλον, a leaf), having leaves of different forms ; **Heterophyl′ly,** used by Krasser, for two different forms of leaves, when caused by difference in organization ; **Het′erophyte,** *Heterophy′tus* (φυτὸν, a plant), (1) Trattinik's name for those plants which bear leaves and flowers on separate stems, as *Curcuma Zedoaria,* Rosc. ; (2) Boulger's term for parasites destitute of chlorophyll ; (3) Warming's term for those plants which are holosaprophytes or parasites, unable to exist independently ; (4) employed for species of wide range of habitats (F. B. H. Brown) ; (5) the dioecious sporophyte ; of heterothallic plants, those with unisexual sporophytes (Blakeslee) ; adj. **heterophy′tic, heterophy′tous ; Heteroplas′tid′s,** those organisms whose differing cells perform different functions ; **Heteroplas′y** (πλὰσσω, I form), applied to all forms, and cells and tissues arising from abnormal growth after a wound ; **heteropo′lar** (πόλος, a pivot), for the axis of Diatomaceae when the extremities differ ; **Heteropro′thally** (+ Prothallus), Van

Tieghem's term for the production of unisexual prothallia ; hetero-rhi′zal (ῥίζα, a root), having roots or similar organs proceeding from any indeterminate portion of a spore in germination or rooting from no fixed point ; ·Heteroschi′zis (σχίζω, I split), the simultaneous fragment-ation of the mother nucleus, giving rise to many (Griggs) ; Heterosepal-o′dy (+ SEPALODY), the change of one sepal into another (Worsdell) ; Heterosper′my (σπέρμα, seed), bear-ing two kinds of seeds, as in Suaeda, some species producing both seeds with endosperm, and other seeds destitute of it ; heterosporan′gic (+ SPORANGE), male and female gametes produced by different sporangia (Blakeslee) ; Het′erospore (+ SPORE), a spore containing male and female energids in variable pro-portion, mixed but not fused (Dan-geard) ; heterospor′ic (+ SPORA), producing spores giving rise to male and female gametophytes ; heteros′-porous (σπορὰ, seed), with spores of two kinds, as in Selaginella ; Het-eros′pory, the condition of produc-ing microspores and macrospores, etc. ; Heterostamino′dy (+ STAM-INODY), the change of a stamen of one type, into that of another (Worsdell) ; het′erostyled, hetero-sty′lous (+ STYLUS) = HETERO-GAMOUS ; Heterosty′lia, heteroga-mous plants ; Heterosty′lism, having flowers differing in the styles, as Compositae when certain florets are unisexual and others hermaphrodite in the same head ; Heterosty′ly = HETEROGAMY ; heterosymbiont′ic (+ SYMBIONT), used of lichens whose algal constituents are diverse in the same example (Bitter) ; het-erotac′tic (τακτικὸς, qualified to ar-range), with more than one system in the same inflorescence ; Hetero-tax′y (τάξις, arrangement), devia-tion, as the production of organs in situations where under normal con-ditions they would not be found ; heterothal′lic (θαλλός, a sprout), em-

ployed by Blakeslee for dioecious, in Mucorineae ; Heterothall′ism is the state ; heterotherm′ic (θερμὸς, hot), applied to porous silicious soil, which absorbs and loses warmth (Krasan) ; heterotop′ic (τόπος, a place), used of plants found on soils apparently very diverse from their normal stations ; Heterotristy′ly, trimorphism, as in Lythrum Sali-caria, Linn. ; heterot′ropal, hetero-t′ropous (τρόπος, direction, (1) in ovules, the same as amphitropous ; (2) employed by Agardh for col-lateral ovules, back to back ; (3) lying parallel with the hilum ; Het′-erotroph (τροφὴ, food), (1) employed by Pfeffer to denote a pure sapro-phyte ; (2) an organ which is de-veloped more on one side than another (Wiesner) ; adj. heterotro-ph′ic, -us ; Heterot′rophy, (1) used by Minks for those Lichens living symbiotically ; (2) by Wiesner for the compound position of a shoot with regard to the horizon and of the mother-shoot ; (3) also applied to nutrition by ingestion, like an animal (Keeble) ; Het′erotype (τύπος, form, type), Flemming's term for a peculiar nuclear division connected with the reduction of the chromo-somes, marked by the early fission of the chromatic thread, a special form of the chromosomes themselves (Farmer) ; adj. heterotyp′ic, which is also employed to denote vegeta-tive division ; heterotyp′ical, de-scribed from more than one species, these differing in structure (Schu-chert) ; heterox′enous (ξένος, a host) = HETEROECIOUS ; Heterozygos′ity, having heterozygotes ; Heterozy′-gote (+ ZYGOTE), a "zygote formed by a pair of opposite allelomorphic gametes" (Bateson).

Hexacoc′cus (ἕξ, six ; κόκκος, a kernel), a fruit of six cells, as in Triglochin : hexacot′ylous, having apparently six cotyledons due to fission of the normal two (de Vries) ; hexacy′clic (κύκλος, a circle), arranged in six whorls ; Hexagoniench′yma (γωνία, angle ; ἔγχυμα, an infusion), cellular tissue which exhibits hexagonal cells in section ; **hexag'onoid** (εἶδος, like), J. Smith's term for hexagonal areolae on Ferns, which are bordered by veins ; **hexag'onus**, six-angled; **Hexagyn'ia** (γυνὴ, a woman), a Linnean order of plants possessing six pistils ; **hexagyn'ian**, plants belonging to that order, or having its character ; **hexag'ynous**, with six pistils ; **hexalep'idus** (λεπὶς, λεπίδος, a scale), six-scaled ; **hexam'erous**, -rus (μέρος, a part), in sixes ; **hexan'der** (ἀνὴρ, ἀνδρὸς, a man), having six stamens ; **Hexan'dria**, a Linnean class characterized by the possession of six stamens ; **hexan'drian**, relating to that class ; **hexan'drous**, with six stamens ; **Hexand'ry**, the state of possessing six stamens ; **hexapet'aloid** (εἶδος, like), having a perianth of six pieces, which resemble petals ; **hexapet'alous** (πέταλον, a flower leaf), with six petals ; **hexaphylet'ic** (φυλὴ, a tribe), applied to those derivative hybrids which are the product of six forms or species, as in some willow-hybrids; **hexaphyl'lous**, -lus (φύλλον, a leaf), six-leaved ; **Hex'apod** (πούς, ποδὸς, a foot), a fathom of six feet, used sometimes as a measure of altitude ; **hexap'terous**, -rus (πτερὸν, a wing), six-winged ; **hexapyre'nus** (πυρὴν, a kernel), having six kernels ; **hex'arch** (ἀρχὴ, beginning), applied to a stele with six strands or origins ; **hexari'nus** (ἄρρην, male), Necker's synonym for hexandrous ; **hexasep'alus**, -lus (+ SEPALUM), with six sepals ; **hexaste'monous**, -nus (στήμων, stamen), hexandrous, six-stamened.

hi'ans (Lat.), gaping, as a ringent corolla.

Hibern'acle, Hiberna'culum (Lat., a winter room), (1) a winter bud ; (2) in botanic gardens, the winter quarters for plants, especially plant houses and frames ; **hiber'nal**, hiberna'lis (Lat.), pertaining to winter ; **Hiberna'tion**, passing the winter in a dormant state.

Hiber'nian, H. C. Watson's term for those plants of the United Kingdom whose headquarters appear to be in Ireland (Hibernia).

hid'den, concealed from view ; ~ **veined**, with veins which are not obvious, as in Pinks and House-leeks, by excess of parenchyma.

hide-bound, a cultivator's expression when the bark does not yield to the growth of the stem.

Hid'roplank'ton (ἱδρὼς, sweat ; + PLANKTON), organisms which float by virtue of some secretion (Forel).

hi'emal, hiema'lis (Lat.), relating to winter; **Hiemisil'vae** (silva, a wood), woods in which the trees shed their leaves in the dry summer season.

Hieraciol'ogist (λόγος, discourse), an expert in the genus Hieracium.

High'land, used by H. C. Watson for a type of distribution in Great Britain, of those plants chiefly found in the Highlands of Scotland.

High-moor, arises in water but emerges from it, and is then dependent upon rain-water ; it is supra-aquatic ; **High-yeast**, barm, the yeast which forms at the surface ; cf. low or bottom yeast.

hi'lar, hila'ris (hilum, a trifle), relating to the hilum ; **Hile** (S. F. Gray) = HILUM ; ~ **bear'ing**, marked with a hilum ; **hilif'erous**, hi'lifer (fero. I bear), having a hilum on the surface ; **Hilof'era**, the second or internal integument of a seed; **Hi'lum**, (1) the scar left on a seed where formerly attached to the funicle or placenta ; (2) the central point in a starch granule which the ring-like markings seem to surround ; (3) ‡ any point of attachment ; (4) ‡ an aperture in pollen grains.

Hinge, (1) the isthmus of Diatoms ; (2) in stomata, delicate lamellae of cellulose, upon which the mobility of the guard-cells usually depends ; they may form an inner or outer hinge ; in German, "Hautgelenk"; (3) a special part of the stem near a node, between two rigid portions, capable of movement (Kohl) ; ~

Cells, cells lying in furrows on the upper face of the leaves of grasses, deeper than epidermal cells and easily folded as the leaf curls ; ~ **Plants,** plants thus susceptible to curvature.

hin′nuleus (Lat., a young stag), a tawny cinnamon colour.

hino′ideus (*h* prefixed ; ἰνοειδής, fibrous), used when veins proceed from the midrib and are parallel and undivided ; **venulo′so-** ~, the same, if connected by cross-veins.

Hip, the fruit of the rose ; technically a cynarrhodium.

hippocre′piform, *hippocrepiform′is* (ἵππος, a horse; κρηπίς, shoe; *forma,* shape), horse-shoe shaped.

hirci′nus (Lat., pertaining to a goat), smelling like a goat; **hirco′sus** ‡ means the same.

hir′sute, *hirsu′tus* (Lat., rough, hairy), hairy, with long, tolerably distinct hairs ; **Hirsu′ties,** the hairiness just described ; **Hirtell′iforms,** in *Rosa,* those forms having hairs on the midrib of the leaf (Almquist) ; named from *R. hirtella* ; **hirtell′ous,** *-lus,* minutely hirsute ; **Hir′tiforms,** in *Rosa,* with lower leaf surface and leaf hairy (Almquist), name from *R. hirta* ; **hir′tose,** used by R. T. Lowe for **hir′tus** (Lat.), hairy, practically the same as hirsute.

his′pid, *his′pidus* (Lat., bristly), beset with rough hairs or bristles ; **hispid′ulous,** *-lus* minutely hispid.

Histiol′ogy (Crozier) = HISTOLOGY.

Histodial′ysis (ἱστός, a web ; διὰ, through ; λύσις, a loosing), the separation of the cells of a tissue from each other (Crozier) ; **Hist′ogen** (γενὸς, offspring), the origin of tissue ; **histogenet′ic, histogen′ic,** tissue-forming ; ~ **Plas′ma,** Weismann's term for tissue-forming protoplasm ; **Histogen′esis** (γένεσις, beginning), or **Histog′eny,** formation or origin of tissue ; **his′toid** (εἶδος, resemblance), arachnoid (Heinig) ; **Histol′ogy** (λόγος, discourse), the science of tissues ; **Histometab′ases,** pl. (μετάβασις, alteration), chemical

changes by which tissues have been fossilized ; **histoph′ilus** (φιλέω, I love), parasitic ; **Histophy′ta** (φυτὸν, a plant), parasites ; **Histophyti′a,** parasitic plant formations (Clements).

hiul′cus, (Lat.), gaping, split.

Hizom′eter (ἵζω, I sink), an instrument for measuring gravitation water (Clements).

hoar′y, canescent, grey from fine pubescence.

Hochblätter (Ger.), bracts.

Hoch-moor (Ger.) moss-moor or Sphagniopratum.

Hof (Ger., a court), (1) the areola of a bordered pit ; (2) Rosen's expression for a clear, granule-free space surrounding the nucleus or nucleolus.

Hol′ard (ὅλος, whole), the total water-content of a soil (Clements).

Hold′fasts, the disc-like attachments of Algae.

holendobiot′ic (ὅλος, whole ; βιωτικὸς, pertaining to life), used of Fungi which produce their spores in other organisms, as *Saprolegnia* ; **Holen′dophytes,** pl. (φυτὸν, a plant), Fungi confined to life within other plants, as Ustilagineae ; **Holendozo′a,** pl. (ξῶον, an animal), Fungi living within animals, as Chytridineae.

holera′ceous (Crozier) = OLERACEOUS.

Holobas′id (ὅλος, whole ; *basidium,* a little pedestal), an undivided basidium in Basidiomycetes (Van Tieghem) ; **holoblas′tic** (βλαστὸς, a bud or shoot), employed when the whole spore is concerned in the embryogeny, *cf.* MEROBLASTIC ; **Hol′ocarp** (καρπὸς, fruit), Nicotra's term for an entire fruit resulting from a number of carpels ; it may be an apocarp, or a syncarp, or an insensible blending of the two forms ; other divisions are actinocarp, and helicocarp, according as it is founded on a whorl or spiral ; and antispermic or pleurospermic according to the position of the placenta ; **holocarp′ic, holocarp′ous,** (1) having the pericarp entire ; (2) in simple

Algae, the whole spore (individual) becomes a sporangium, and invested with a cell-wall; (3) used of Fungi producing fruit once only from the same thallus; *cf.* EUCARPOUS; **holochlamyd'eous** (χλαμύς, a cloak), employed for ovules such as those of *Ginkgo* when the integuments are practically complete (Celakovský); **holocy'clic** (κυκλικὸς, circular), (1) applied to a stem with amplexicaul leaves, regarded as encircling the stem and ending at the node in a leaf (Celakovský); (2) evergreen (Drude); **Holog'amy** (γάμος, marriage), when the nuclei of gametes fuse together (Dangeard); **Hologonid'ium** (γόνος, offspring), employed by Wallroth for the algal gonidia pure and simple, or soredia; **hologymnocarp'ous** (+ GYMNOCARPOUS), permanently gymnocarpous, the fruits being entirely free; **Holopar'asite** (+ PARASITE), a plant entirely dependent upon the host-plant for its existence (Warming); **holophyt'ic**, pertaining to **Holophy'tism** (φυτὸν, a plant), the condition of a plant with its growth maintained entirely by its own organs, without any suspicion of saprophytism or parasitism; **Holoplank'ton** (+ PLANKTON), plankton of the open sea; adj. **holoplankton'-ic**; **Holosap'rophyte** (σαπρὸς, rotten; φυτὸν, a plant), employed by Johow for a true saprophyte, a plant which is dependent upon humus for its existence; **holoseric'eous**, *-ceus*, (*sericeus*, silken), covered with a fine and silky pubescence; **Hol'o-type** (τύπος, a type), the one specimen possessed by the describer of a species, and forming the basis for the original diagnosis.

homalocho'ric (ὁμαλὸς, equal; χωρέω, I spread abroad), refers to a species confined to one formation; **homaloclad'ous**, *-dus* (κλάδος, a branch), Russow's term for straight-branched; **homalot'ropous** (τροπὴ, a turning), applied to organs which grow in a horizontal direction (Noll); **Homa-lot'ropism**, is the condition; = DIATROPISM.

homoblas'tic (ὁμὸς, one and the same; βλαστὸς, a shoot), (1) denotes embryogeny which is direct; (2) used by Goebel to express the fact that the larval and adult forms are practically the same; (3) Pfitzer employs it for those Orchids whose pseudobulbs consist of several internodes, only the terminal one bearing developed leaves; **Homoblas'ty** is the condition; **homocarp'ous**, *-pus* (καρπὸς, fruit), having fruit of one kind only; **homocent'ric** (κέντρον = centre of a circle), concentric (Crozier); **homoceph'alic** (κεφαλὴ, a head), Delpino's term for homogamy when the anthers fertilize the stigma of another flower of the same inflorescence; **homochlamyd'eous** (χλαμὺς, a mantle), the perianth leaves all alike; **Homochro'matism** (χρῶμα, colour), constant as to the colouring of the flower; **homochro'-mous**, uniform in colour; **homocli'nic**, **homocli'nous** (κλίνη, a bed), used by Delpino for that kind of homogamy when the anthers fertilize the stigma of the same complete flower; **homodes'mic** (δεσμὸς, a bond), when the vascular bundles of an atactostele are of the same type (Brebner); **Homodichog'amy** (+ DICHOGAMY), the existence of homogamous and dichogamous individuals in the same species; **homodrom'ic**, **homod'romal**, **homod'romous**, *-mus* (δρόμος, a course), having the spirals all of the same direction; **Homod'romy**, uniformity in direction of spirals; **homodynam'ic** (δύναμις, power), in hybrids in which the parental characters are equally transmitted (Correns); **homody'namous** (δύναμις, strength), equal in strength or vigour.

homoëan'drous (ὅμοιος, like; ἀνήρ, ἀνδρὸς, a man), having only one kind of stamen; **Homoëan'dry**, the condition of having uniform stamens; **Homoeog'amy** (γάμος, marriage), the impregnation of an antipodal cell, instead of the oösphere as in *Balanophora* (Van Tieghem); **Homoeokine′sis** (κίνησις, motion), Grégoire's term for homotypic meiosis; **Homoeoli′chenes** (+ LICHEN) Lichens with gonidia distributed throughout the thallus; **homoeom′erous** (μέρος, a rest, hyphae and gonidia more or less mixed in a lichen thallus; **Ho′moeomorph** (μορφή, shape), similar organisms of different origin due to conditions of the environment, as many species of Cactaceae and Euphorbiaceae; **Homoeomorph′y** is the state; **Hom′eoplasy** (πλάσσω, I form), abnormal growth composed of normal elements; **Homoeo′sis** (ὦσις, = impulse), Bateson's term for metamorphy, a variation by assumption by one member of a meristic series, of the form or character proper to others; **in′ward** ~ outer organs taking on the structure of a whorl internal to itself; **out′ward** ~ assumption of form of outer organs by inner parts, as disc-flowers of Compositae becoming petaloid like those of the ray; **homoët′ic**, metamorphic, *cf.* HOMOEOSIS; **Hom′oetype** = HOMOTYPE; **homoetyp′ic** = HOMOTYPIC.

homog′amous, -mus (ὁμὸς, one and the same, γάμος, marriage), bearing one kind of flower; **Homog′amy**, simultaneous ripeness of pollen and stigmas in a perfect flower; (1) by Delpino divided into HOMOCEPHALIC ~, HOMOCLINIC ~, or MONOECIOUS ~; (2) independently coined by G. J. Romanes to express "discriminate isolation"; **homogen′eal, homogenet′ic, homoge′neous,** (γένος, race, kind), of the same kind or nature, uniform, opposed to heterogeneous; **Homogen′esis, Homog′eny,** the reverse of HETEROGENESIS; the successive generations resembling the parent form; **Hom′ogene,** the condition of offspring whose parents are pure and of the same type (Lotsy); **Hom′ogone** (γόνος, offspring), a plant bearing only one kind of flowers; adj. **homog′onous; Homog′ony,** the

state of uniform respective length of anthers and stigmas in perfect flowers; homostylous; the opposite of Heterogony; **Homoheterosty′ly,** the occurrence of similar and dissimilar styles in the same species (Warming).

homoiochlamyd′eous (ὅμοιος, like; χλαμὺς, a mantle) used by Engler and Prantl when the perianth is uniform; **homoiog′amous** (γάμος, marriage), adj. of the next; **Homoiog′amy,** the fusion of two sexual nuclei of the same kind; **homoiom′erous** (μέρος, a part), used of a Lichen thallus when the gonidia and hyphae are distributed in about equal proportions; Wallroth employed the word *homoeom′eres* from ὁμοιομερής; **Homoi′otherms,** pl. (θέρμος, hot), plants whose vital temperatures are approximately the same as their surroundings.

homokaryot′ic (ὁμὸς, one and the same; κάρυον, a nut), spores which contain nuclei of differing sexuality (Burgeff); **Homokine′sis** (κίνησις, motion), homotypic mitosis (Grégoire); **Homoli′cheni,** a defective term for HOMOEOLICHENES, *i.e.,* Lichens with gonidia distributed generally throughout the thallus (Jatta); **homol′ogous** (λόγος, discourse), of one type, constructed on the same plan though varying in form and function, as leaves and parts which answer morphologically to leaves; ~ Alternation of Generations, differentiation of generations which are fundamentally alike as regards descent, either in form or the character of their reproductive organs; *cf.* ANTITHETIC; **Hom′ologue,** the equivalent of certain organs; **Homol′ogy,** the identity of parts apparently different: **homomal′ious, homomal′alous** (Crozier), *-lus* (μαλλὸς, a lock of wool), recurved, arising from all sides but turned to one direction; **homomer′icus** (μέρος, a part) = HOMOIOMEROUS; **homomor′phous, -phus, homomor′phic** (μορφή, form), uniform in shape; **Homomor′phy,** uniformity, as when the disk and ray florets of Compositae are alike ; either normally or by conversion of the disk florets from tubular into ligulate florets ; **Homone'meae** ($\nu\tilde{\eta}\mu\alpha$, a thread), formerly applied to Algae and Fungi (Henslow) ; **Hom'onym**, **Homon'ymon** ($\delta\nu o\mu\alpha$, a name), (1) botanically, the same specific name in another genus of the same plant, as *Myrtus buxifolia*, Sw., is a Homonym as well as a Synonym of *Eugenia buxifolia*, Willd.; (2) a name rejected because an earlier application of the same name to another genus (O. F. Cooke) ; **Homon'ymy**, the possession of the same specific name under another genus ; **homoö'gonous** ($\gamma\delta\nu o s$, race) = ANISOGONOUS, breeding true; **homoom'erous** = HOMOIOMEROUS ; **Homoöp'lasy** ($\pi\lambda\acute{a}\sigma\omega$, I shape), when an abnormal growth consists of the same elements as the part whence it arises (Küster); **homopet'alous** ($\pi\acute{\epsilon}\tau\alpha\lambda o\nu$, a flower leaf), (1) all petals being alike ; (2) the receptacle of Compositae when the florets are alike, as the Ligulatae; **homophyad'ic**, *homophyad'eus* ($\phi\acute{v}\eta$, growth), applied to those species of *Equisetum*, whose fertile and barren stems are similar in form ; **homophyt'ic**, used of plants having bisexual sporophytes (Blakeslee); **Homoplas'my** ($\pi\lambda\acute{a}\sigma\mu\alpha$, moulded), similar in form but not of similar origin, as *Cacti* and succulent Euphorbias ; **Hom'oplast**, correspondence in external form, but distinct in nature ; adj. **homoplas'tic**; **Homoplas'tids**, pl. organisms derived from similar cells, *cf.* HETEROPLASTIDS ; **Hom'oplasy**, moulded alike but of different origin, analogous, not homologous, *cf.* HOMOPLASMY; **homopo'lar** ($\pi\delta\lambda o s$, a pivot), relating to the same pole; **homopro'teoid** (+ PROTEOID), used of plants whose leaves have sclerotic cells uniformly distributed (Vesque); **Homosporan'gium** (+ SPORANGIUM), a spore-case which develops into a bisexual prothall is, as of a Fern (Worsdell) ; **homosporan'gic**, giving

rise to one sort of spore only (Blakeslee); **homospor'ic** (+ SPORA), derived from one kind only of spore (Blakeslee) ; **homos'porous** ($\sigma\pi o\rho\grave{a}$, seed), (1) similar-seeded, in opposition to HETEROSPOROUS ; (2) neutral-spored; **Homostat'ic** ($\sigma\tau\alpha\tau\grave{o}s$, a standing) **Pe'riod**, that period during which the present vegetation developed after the Pliocene formation (TUZSO) ; **hom'ostyled** (+ STYLE) = HOMOGONOUS ; **Homosty'lia**, homogonous plants ; **Homosty'ly**, (+ STYLE), the same relation of length between all styles and anthers of the same species (Axell); **homotac'tic** ($\tau\alpha\kappa\tau\iota\kappa\grave{o}s$, apt to arrange), when only one system of arrangement prevails in an inflorescence ; **homothal'amus** ($\theta\acute{a}\lambda\alpha\mu o s$, a room, bride-chamber), defined by Lindley as "resembling the thallus, used for Lichens only " ; **homothall'ic** ($\theta\alpha\lambda\lambda\grave{o}s$, a sprout), monoecious, applied to Mucorineae (Blakeslee) ; **Homothalli'um**, Minks's term for the medullary layer of a lichen ; **homother'mic** ($\theta\acute{\epsilon}\rho\mu o s$, hot), applied to firm earth or rocky soil, which absorbs heat and loses it slowly; *cf.* HETEROTHERMIC ; **homot'ropal** ($\tau\rho o\pi\grave{\eta}$, a turning), applied to organs having the same direction as the body to which they belong ; **homot'ropic** ($\tau\rho\acute{o}\pi o s$, direction), fertilized by anthers from the same flower (K. Pearson) ; **homot'ropous**, *-pus* (1) curved or turned in one direction ; (2) used of an anatropous ovule having the radicle next the hilum ; **Homot'ropy** (1) the homotropous condition ; (2) Lopriore's term for secondary rootlets which branch in the same direction from the axis ; it may be **longitu'dinal~**, or **trans'verse~** ; **Hom'otype** ($\tau\acute{v}\pi o s$, form, type), (1) correspondence of parts ; (2) in nuclear division this term is applied to those cases resembling ordinary karyokinesis, save in minor respects, immediately following the HETEROTYPE ; in some cases it occurs in all the stages after the Heterotype, in which the reduced number of chromosomes are retained up to the formation of gametes (Farmer); (3) organs showing no trace of differentiation between one and another in function (K. Pearson); adj. **homotyp'ic**, homologous; **Homotypo'sis**, the principle of the likeness and diversity of homotypes (K. Pearson); **Homot'ypy**, the condition of correspondence of parts which are in series; **Homozygoc'ity, Homozygo'sis**, the condition of producing homozygotes; **Homozy'gote** (+ ZYGOTE), a zygote produced by the union of gametes having similar allelomorphs (Bateson).

Hon'ey, the sweet secretion from glands or nectaries, which acts as an inducement to insect visitors; ~ **Cup**, used by Withering for nectary; ~ **Dew**, a sweet secretion voided by aphides from the juices of their host plants; ~ **Guides**, lines or streaks of honey or colour leading to the nectary; ~ **-leaves**, nectaries such as those of *Aquilegia* (Potter); ~ **Pore**, a supposed pore or gland which secretes honey; ~ **Spot**=~ GUIDES; **Hon'eycomb-cells**, in Diatoms, hexagonal hollows, as in *Triceratium Favus*, Ehrenb.; **hon'eycombed**, alveolate.

Hood, = CUCULLUS; **hood'ed, Hoodshaped** (Crozier) = CUCULLATE.

Hook, a slender process, curved or bent back at the tip; ~ **Cli'mbers**, plants which support themselves by hooks or prickles, as the bramble; **hookedback**, curved in a direction from the apex to the base as the side lobes in a dandelion leaf.

Hoop, the zone or girdle of Diatoms, the connection between the valves of the frustule.

Hop-meal = LUPULIN.

hora'rius, hor'ary (*hora*, an hour), lasting an hour or two, as the expanded petals of *Cistus*.

hordea'ceus (Lat. pertaining to barley), shaped like an ear of barley; **Hor'dein**, a special proteid occurring in barley, *Hordeum vulgare*, Linn.

horizon'tal, *horizontalis* (ὁρίζων, the circular boundary of vision), level; **Horizon'tal Sys'tem**, the cellular, as distinguished from the fibro-vascular system (Crozier).

Hor'mogon (Crozier) = **Hormogone**, *Hormogon'ium* (ὅρμος, necklace; γόνος, offspring), in filamentous Algae, those portions composed of pseudocysts marked off by heterocysts which become detached, and after a short period of spontaneous motion, come to rest and develop into new filaments; **Hormogonim'ium** (+ GONIMIUM), gonimia arranged in necklace fashion; **Hor'mospores** (σπορὰ, seed), a term used by Minks for spores which are similar in origin to stylo- or teleuto-spores of Fungi, colourless, dividing into cells, microgonidia, etc., with deliquescence of the mother-cell, the microgonidia developing into heterocysts.

Horn (1) any appendage shaped like an animal's horn, as the spur in *Linaria*; (2) the antheridium of *Vaucheria*; **Horn'let**, (1) the male organ of *Vaucheria*, a papilla or projection from the filament (Cooke); (2) a little horn (Crozier); **hor'ny**, corneous as to texture.

Horn'bast (Ger.), a tissue of obliterated groups of sieve-tubes, specially thickened and of horny texture (Wigand).

hornot'inus, hor'nus (Lat.), of this year, the present year's growth; *Ra'mi hor'ni*, branches not a twelvemonth old.

horolog'ical (*horologicus*, pertaining to a clock), said of flowers which open and close at stated hours; **Horolo'gium Flo'rae**, a time-table of the opening and closing of certain flowers:—see Linnaeus, Phil. Bot. 274; Kerner, Nat. Hist. Plants, ii. 215–218.

horten'sis (Lat.), pertaining to gardens, or only found there; **Hortula'nus** (Lat.), (1) a gardener; (2) belonging to a garden; **Hort'us** (Lat.), a garden; ~ **sic'cus**, an herbarium; formerly it consisted of volumes

with dried specimens glued down ;
~ vi′vus, also means HERBARIUM.

Hose-in-hose, a duplication of the
corolla, as though a second one
were inserted in the throat of the
first.

hospita′ting (*hospes*, a guest), of plants
which shelter ants, as *Hydnophytum ;*
Hospita′tors, the plants in question
(Beccari).

Host, a plant which nourishes a parasite ; **Host-plant**, the same ; **Host-
cells**, the cells in mycorhiza of
Neottia, associated with the digestive cells (Magnus).

Hosto′rium (*hostio*, I requite, ex
J. S. Henslow) = HAUSTORIUM.

Hov′er-fly flowers, those adapted for
pollination by Syrphidae (Knuth).

Hum′ble-bee flowers, specially adapted
for the visits of species of *Bombus.*

hu′mi (Lat.), in or on the ground.

humic′ular, Beccari's term for SAPRO-
PHYTIC ; **Humifica′tion**, the reduction of dead plant substances to
humus by Fungi (Beyerinck).

hu′mifuse, *humifu′sus* (*humus*, the
ground; *fusus*, spread), spread on
the surface of the ground ; **humi-
stra′tus**, (*stratus*, stretched out),
laid flat on the soil.

hu′milis (Lat.), lowly.

Hu′mor (Lat., moisture) = SAP.

Hu′mulin, the oleoresin of the hop,
Humulus Lupulus, Linn.

Hu′mus (Lat., the ground), decomposing organic matter in the soil ;
~ **Plants** = SAPROPHYTES ; ~ **Soils**,
garden soils enriched with organic
manure.

Husk, the outer covering of certain
fruits or seeds ; **husk′less**, wanting
the usual outer covering, as in
certain forms of barley, walnuts,
etc. ; **hus′ky**, abounding with or
consisting of husks.

hyacin′thine, *hyacin′thus,hyacinth′inus*
(ὑακίνθινος, hyacinth-coloured), (1)
dark purplish blue; (2) hyacinth-
like in habit, a scape bearing spicate
flowers.

hyales′cent (ὑάλινος, ot glass), " somewhat hyaline " (Crozier); **hyalic′olor**

(*color*, colour), wanting in colour ;
hy′aline, *hyali′nus*, colourless or
translucent; ~ **Ar′ea**, the smooth
part of a diatom-valve.

Hyalodict′yae (ὕαλος, crystal; δίκτυον,
a net), Fungi having translucent
muriform or netted spores (Traverso) ;
Hyalodid′ymae, Didymosporae with
clear spores (Traverso); **Hy′alom** =
HYALOPLASMA ; **Hyalophrag′miae**
(φράγμα, a fence), Fungi having
many-septate spores (Traverso) ; **Hy′-
aloplasm, Hyaloplas′ma** (πλάσμα,
moulded), the hyaline matrix or
clear and non-granular portion of
protoplasm ; by some restricted to
the ECTOPLASM ; **Hy′alosomes** (σῶμα,
a body), colourless granules which
do not take up stains : **Hyalospo′rae**
(+ SPORA), having colourless spores
like *Laestadia* (Traverso) ; **Hyalo-
staur′ae** (σταυρὸς, a pole or cross),
Fungi with cruciate spores destitute
of colour (Traverso).

Hyber′nacle, Hyberna′culum=HIBER-
NACULUM.

hyberna′lis = HIBERNALIS.

Hy′brid, Hyb′rida (Lat., a mongrel),
a plant obtained by the pollen of
one species on the stigma of another;
bisex′ual ~, when the offspring
shows the character of the parents
combined in pairs (Clements) ; **de-
riv′ative** ~, when crossed with each
other or a parent ; **doub′le** ~, *cf.*
DIHYBRIDIZATION; **doub′le-recip′ro-
cal** ~, the crossing of reciprocal-
hybrids ; **false** ~, FALSE-HYBRID-
ISM ; **graft** ~, reciprocal influences
of scion and stock on each other ;
heterodynam′ic ~, showing the
characters of male and female parents
in varying degree; **homodynam′ic** ~,
showing equal combination of the
characters of both parents ; **mosa′ic**
~, showing traces of each parent,
as special colour patches; **recip′ro-
cal** ~, obtained from the same
parents, but transposing the male
and female elements ; **sec′ondary** ~,
crossed with a hybrid ; **sesquireci-
p′rocal** ~, when a hybrid is crossed
with one of the parental types ;

twin ~, hybrids identical but from reciprocal sources; **unisex′ual** ~, when a certain character found in one parent does not occur in the other (Clements); **Hybrid′ity,** *Hybrid′itas,* crossed in parentage; **Hybridiza′tion,** (1) the art of obtaining hybrids by artificial crossing; (2) also used for the same operation occurring naturally; **Hyb′ridiform** (+ FORM), a hybrid between FINIFORMS (Kuntze); **Hybridopro′liform** (*proles,* offspring), a fertile hybrid of HYBRIDOFORMS (Kuntze); **Hybridog′amy** (γάμος, marriage), hybrids between different species; **Hybridol′ogy** (λόγος, discourse), the science of hybridizing.

Hy′dathode (ὕδωρ, water; ὁδὸς, a way), Haberlandt's term for water-pore or water-gland, an organ which extrudes water or other liquid; it resembles a stoma with functionless guard-cells; **sub′stitute** ~; *cf.* ŒDEMATA; **Hydatophyti′a,** pl. (φɹτὸν, a plant), submerged formations (Diels); **Hydracel′lulose** (+ Cellulose), see CELLULOSE; **Hy′drad** (+ AD), a hydrophyte (Clements); **Hydral′gae** (+ Algae) = HYDROPHYTES; **hy′drarch** (ἀρχὴ, beginning), applied to successions from ponds or lakes by growth of plants; **Hy′dras,** the "wet form" of a species (Clements).

Hy′drastin, an alkaloid found in *Hydrastis canadensis,* Linn.

Hy′drate (ὕδωρ, water), a compound containing a definite proportion of water in chemical combination; **Hydra′tion,** the act of becoming chemically combined with water; **hy′dric,** pertaining to water; **hydrocar′pic** (καρπὸς, fruit), used of aquatic plants which are fertilized above the water, but withdraw the fertilized flowers below the surface for development, as in *Vallisneria;* **Hydrocar′py,** the condition described; **Hydrocell′ulose,** see CELLULOSE; **Hydroch′arid** Formation, macrophytes such as *Hydrocharis* floating on or in the water; **Macro-**

PLANKTON; PLEUSTON; **Hydrochi′mous** (χειμὼν), winter, used for plants adapted to a rainy winter (Drude); **Hy′drochore** (χωρὶs, asunder), a plant distributed by water (Clements); **hydrocho′ric,** dispersed by water, rivers or floods; **Hydrocleistog′amy** (+CLEISTOGAMY), when flowers do not open in consequence of submersion (Knuth); **Hy′drochrome** (χρῶμα, colour), used by Nadson for the pigments of *Russula* and *Amanita Muscaria,* Fr.; **hydrodynam′ic** (δύναμις, power), used for the action of tides and waves in distribution; **Hy′drogams,** (γάμος, marriage) = CRYPTOGAMS; **Hydrohar′mose** (ἁρμόζω, I join together), response to water stimuli (Clements); **Hy′droid** (εἶδος, like), Potonié's term for a water-conducting strand in aërial stems; a tracheid, *cf.* HYDROME; **hy′droger** (*gero,* I bear), water-bearing, as *hydrog′era Va′sa,* threads in a spiral vessel which were formerly supposed to convey fluid; **hy′drolated,** combined with the elements of water, by **Hydrola′tion; Hydroleu′cite** (+ LEUCITE), Van Tieghem's term for vacuoles in cell-sap, which he further subdivides into tanniferous ~, oxaliferous ~, coloured ~, albuminiferous ~, in accordance with their production of tannin, oxalates, colouring matter. or aleurone; **Hy′drolist,** *cf.* CYTOHYDROLIST, PROTEOHYDROLIST; **hy′drolysed,** (λύσις, a loosing), chemically decomposed by taking up the elements of water; **Hydrol′ysis,** the act of being hydrolysed; **Hy′drolyst** = HYDROLIST; **Hy′drolyte,** the substance which undergoes fermentation (Armstrong); **hydrolyt′ic,** causing hydrolysis; **Hy′drome,** the hydral or water-system of a vascular bundle, *cf.* HADROME; water-conducting tissue in stems, particularized into, ~ -cyl′inder, conducting vascular tissue supplying water; ~ -man′tle, composed of elements identical with the hydroids of the leaf-traces; ~ -sheath, a separation-

layer between HADROME and LEP-
TOME : ~ -stele, = -CYLINDER ; ~
-ste'reome or ~ -strand, a unit of
the water vascular tissues (Tansley
and Chick); **Hydromeg'atherm**,
(μέγα, great ; θέρμη, heat), Warming's
term for a plant which needs much
heat and moisture, as the natives of
most tropical regions ; **Hydromor-
ph'osis, Hydromor'phy** (μόρφωσις, a
shaping), structural peculiarities induced by being submerged (Herbst);
Hydronas'ty (ναστòς, pressed), curva-
tures produced by changes in fluid
relationships in the tissues; adj. **hydronas'tic; Hy'drone**, the simple fundamental molecule of which water is
composed (Armstrong); **Hydroph'ilae**
(φιλέω, I love), (1) water-pollinated
plants ; (2) = CRYPTOGAMS; **hydroph'ilous** (φιλέω, I love), (1) some
aquatic Phanerogams, and many
Cryptogams which need water in
order to be fertilized; (2) dwelling
in wet land or water (Clements) ;
~ **Fun'gi**, refers to those Fungi
which are allied to *Saprolegnia ;*
Hy'drophyll (φύλλον, a leaf), the
leaf of a hydrophyte (Clements).

hydrophylla'ceous, pertaining to *Hy-
drophyllum* or its allies.

Hy'drophytes, Hydrophy'ta (ὕδωρ,
water; φυτòν, a plant), water-plants,
partially or wholly immersed ; **Hy-
drophyti'um**, a plant association of
bog and swamp plants; **hydrophyt'ic**,
relative to Hydrophytes ; **Hydro-
phytol'ogy** (λογός, discourse), a
treatise on water-plants.

hydrop'ic (ύδροπικòς, dropsical), **Cells**,
certain enlarged cells in Cyano-
phyceae (Brand).

Hy'droplast (ὕδωρ, water; πλασòς,
moulded), an apparent vacuole in
which aleurone-grains arise ; **Hydro-
plast'ids**, pl., Van Tieghem's term
for apparent vacuoles in the endosperm of the seed of *Ricinus ;* **Hy-
drople'on** (πλέον, full, = an aggregate
of molecules, but smaller than a
micella), water of crystallization ;
hydrostat'ic (στατικòς, standing),
"completing the succession under

hydrophytic conditions " (Clements);
Hydroste'reids (στερεòς, solid), prosenchymatous thick-walled elements,
with conspicuous pits, but without
spiral thickening on the walls (Haberlandt) ; **Hydroste'reome, transverse**, the transverse parenchyma
of *Podocarpus* and *Cycas* (Bernard) ;
Hydrotax'is (τάξις, order), creeping
from dry to moist situations, as
plasmodia (Verworn); adj. **hydro-
tact'ic**; **Hydrotribi'um** (τριβή,
grinding), "bad lands" formation ;
hydrotriboph'ilus (φιλέω, I love),
dwelling in bad lands ; **Hydrotribo-
phy'ta** (φυτòν, a plant), bad land
plants (Clements); **Hydrot'rophy**
(τροφή, food), unequal growth caused
by unequal supply of moisture on
one side of a part (Wiesner) ; **hydrotrop'ic** (τροπή, a turning), (1) unequal growth due to difference in
the supply of moisture ; (2) applied
to successions which become mesophytic (Clements) ; **Hydrot'ropism**,
the phenomena induced by the
influence of moisture on growing
organs ; **pos'itive ~** , turning towards
the source of moisture ; **neg'ative ~** ,
turning away from moisture.

hy'emal, *hyema'lis* (*hiems*, winter) =
HIEMALIS, pertaining to winter.

hygrochas'tic (ὑγρòς, moist ; χασμάω,
I yawn), applied by Ascherson to
those plants in which the bursting
of the fruit and dispersion of the
spores or seeds is caused by absorption of water, as in *Anastatica
hierochuntica*, Linn. ; **Hygroch'asy**,
the act in question ; **Hy'gro diffu'-
sion**, the taking in of moist air by
diffusion, and its subsequent extrusion from looser tissue of the leaf
(Ohno) ; **Hygrodrimi'um** (δρυμòς, a
coppice), a tropical forest formation
(Diels) ; **hygromet'ric** (μέτρον, a
measure), moving under the influence
of more or less moisture, hygroscopic;
Hygromor'phism (μορφή, shape), (1)
form determined by moist surroundings ; (2) the state of little water
absorption and equally little evaporation (Drude) ; adj. **hygromor'phic;**

hygroph'anous (φαίνω, I appear),
looking watery when moist, and
opaque when dry (Cooke); Hygroph'ilae (φιλέω, I love), moisture-
loving plants; hy'grophile, hy'gro-
ph'ilous, pertaining to Hygrophytes;
Hygrophorbi'um (φορβὴ, pasture),
low moor formation (Diels); hygroph'orous, water-bearing, or saturated
with it; applied by Spruce to certain
Hepaticae; Hy'grophytes (φυτὸν, a
plant), marsh-plants, or plants which
need a large supply of moisture for
their growth; Hygrophyti'a, formations of hygiophytes (Diels);
Hy'groplasm (πλάσμα, moulded),
Nägeli's term for the fluid portion
of protoplasm; cf. STEREOPLASM;
Hygropoi'um (πόα, grass), meadow
formation (Diels); hygroscop'ic
(σκοπέω, I see), susceptible of extending or shrinking on the application or removal of water or vapour;
~ Cells, certain cells in the leaves
of grasses which cause them to alter
in shape in dry weather, known also
as bulliform cells; Hygroscopic'ity,
Hygroscopic'itas, the hygroscopic
property; Hygrosphagni'um (Sphagnum, bog-moss), high moor (Diels).
Hy'lad (ὕλη, forest; + AD), a forest
plant; Hyli'um, a forest formation;
hyloc'ola, dwelling in forests.
hylocomnio'sus, mossy, composed of
Hylocomnium and similar Mosses
as a formation (Nilsson).
Hylo'dad (+ AD), a plant of the following; Hylodi'um (ὕλωδης, wooded),
pl. -ia, dry open woodland formations; hylodoph'ilus (φιλέω, I love),
dwelling in dry woods; Hylo'dophyte
(φυτὸν, a plant), a dry woodland
plant.
Hylog'amy (ὕλη = material; γάμος,
marriage), the fusion of a sexual with
a vegetative nucleus; Hy'loids (εἶδος,
resemblance), crystals in Gouania
leaves suggesting logs of wood as to
shape; hyloph'ilus, dwelling in
forests; Hylophy'ta, pl., forest plants
(Clements); Hy'lophyte (φυτὸν, a
plant), a plant which grows in woods,
usually moist; adj. hylophyt'ic.

Hy'lus, Hy'lum=HILUM.
Hy'men (ὑμὴν, a membrane), a skin
or membrane; hyme'nial (1) pertaining to the HYMENIUM; (2)
relating to the reproductive organs
in certain Cryptogams; ~ Al'ga,
the algal cell in a sporocarp in
Lichens, also termed ~ Gonid'ium;
~ Lay'er = Hyme'nium, an aggregation of spore mother-cells in a
continuous layer on a sporophore,
the sporiferous part of the fructification in Fungi; hymeno'des (εἶδος,
like), having a membranous texture;
Hymenoli'chen (+ Lichen), a term
devised by Mattirolo for a Lichen
which is symbiotically associated
with a hymenomycetous Fungus;
hymenomyce'tous (μύκης, a mushroom), having the hymenium exposed at maturity, the spores borne
on basidia; Hy'menophore, Hymeno-
phor'ium (φορέω, I carry), in Fungi
that part which bears the hymenium, the sporophore; Hy'menopode,
Hymenopod'ium (πούς, ποδὸς, a foot),
Fayod's name for the hypothecium;
hymenopt'erid Flowers, those which
can be pollinated only by Hymenop-
tera, e.g. Leguminosae; Hyme'nulum,
a disc or shield containing asci, but
without an excipulum.
Hyoscy'amin, an alkaloid contained in
henbane, Hyoscyamus niger, Linn.
Hypalle'lomorph, (ὑπὸ, under; +
ALLELOMORPH), the constituents of
compound allelomorphs (Bateson).
Hypan'thium, Hypantho'dium (ἄνθος,
a flower), an enlargement or development of the torus under the calyx;
a syconium.
Hyperanisog'amy (ὑπὲρ, above; ἄνισος,
unequal; γάμος, marriage), the female
gamete, at first active, and much
larger than the male gamete (Hartog);
cf. OÖGAMY; hyperbor'ean, hyperbor'eus (βορέας, the north wind),
northern; Hyperchimae'ra (+ CHI-
MAERA), a graft-hybrid resembling
a true hybrid intermediate between
its parents (Strasburger).
hyperchromat'ic (ὑπὲρ, above; χρωματικὸς, suited for colour), readily

susceptible of taking colour, or intensified colouration; **Hyperd'romy** (δρόμος, a course), when anadromous and catadromous venation occurs on one side of a Fern-frond (Prantl); **hyperhy'dric,** Küster's expression for an outlet or overflow for water in tissues; **hypermetatrop'ic,** defined as when " the ovary of one plant receives pollen from another of a flower of the same or a second plant, while the ovary of the latter flower receives pollen from another associated with the first ovary " (K. Pearson); **Hypermetat'ropy,** the condition in question; **Hy'perplasy** (πλάσσω, I shape), an abnormal growth of tissue due to undue cell-division (Küster); adj. **hyperplast'ic; hyperstomat'ic, hyperstom'atous** (+ STOMA), having the stomata on the upper surface of the leaf; **hypertroph'ic** (τροφή, food), morbidly enlarged; **Hyper'trophy,** an abnormal enlargement of an organ, presumably by excess of nourishment; **Hyper'trophytes** (φυτὸν, a plant), a term employed by Wakker for those parasitic Fungi which cause hypertrophy in the tissues.

Hy'pha (ὑφὴ, a web), pl. **Hy'phae,** element of the thallus in Fungi, a cylindric thread-like branched body developing by apical growth and usually septate; **Sieve ~,** or **Trum'pet ~,** a special form found in Algae, bulging at each septum (F. W. Oliver); **hy'phal,** relating to hyphae; **~ Bod'ies,** short thick hyphae in certain Fungi, which produce fructifying hyphae or conidiophores (Thaxter); **~ Tis'sue,** interwoven hyphae, constituting the tissues of the larger Fungi.

Hyphalmy'ro - plank'ton (ὑφάλμυρος, somewhat salt, + PLANKTON), the floating organisms of brackish water (Zimmermann).

Hyphas'ma (ὕφασμα, a web), the thallus of Agarics.

Hyphe'ma (ὑφή, a web), used by Minks for the hyphal layer in Lichens; **Hyphench'yma** (ἔγχυμα, an infusion),

tissue of felted hyphae; **Hyphid'ium,** a term proposed by Minks for SPERMATIUM; **hyphod'romous, -mus** (δρόμος, a course), used when the veins are sunk in the substance of a leaf, and thus not readily visible; **Hyphomyce'tes** are *Fungi imperfecti;* **hyphomyce'tous** (μύκης, a mushroom), applied to Fungi bearing their spores on simple or branched hyphae; **Hy'phopode,** *Hyphopod'ium* (πούς, ποδὸς, a foot), appendages on the mycelium of *Meliola* which bear the perithecia (Gaillard); **Hyphostro'ma** ‡ (στρῶμα, spread out), the mycelium of Fungi; **Hyphothall'ium** (θαλλὸς, a sprout) = HYPOTHALLUS.

Hyphydrogam'icae (ὑπὸ, under; ὕδωρ, water; γάμος, marriage), plants whose flowers are fertilized under water, as *Naias* (Knuth); **Hyphydrog'amy,** the condition specified.

Hypne'tum, a plant-association composed of Mosses, especially of *Hypnum,* and its allies.

Hyp'nocyst (ὕπνος, sleep; κύστις, a bag or pouch), in Pediastreae, etc., a dormant stage assumed when the conditions for growth are unfavourable; **Hyp'noplasm** (πλάσμα, moulded), the protoplasm of a dormant individual, as of a seed, *cf.* NECROPLASM; **Hyp'noplasy** (πλάσσω, I shape), arrested development due to various inhibiting reactions, which prevent the cells or tissues attaining normal size (Küster); **Hypno'sis,** the state of dormant vitality shown by seeds whilst still retaining their power of germination (Escombe); **Hyp'nosperm** (σπέρμα, a seed), the winter state of the zygosperm of *Hydrodictyon;* **Hyp'nosporange, Hypnosporan'gium** (+ SPORANGE), a product of the modification of the root of *Botrydium,* a sporangium which produces zoospores after a resting period (Rostafiński); **Hyp'nospore,** a resting spore; **Hyp'note,** an organism in a dormant state; **hypnot'ic,** dormant, not dead, as in seeds; **Hypnothal'lus** (θαλλὸς, a young branch), Chodat's term for

growth by cell-division from hypno-
cysts, as in *Monostroma;* **Hypnozy'-
gote** (+ ZYGOTE) a dormant zygote
or union of two sexual cells (Hartog).
Hy'poachene (ὑπό, under; + ACHENE),
an achene from an inferior ovary
(Villari); **Hypoascid'ium** (+ As-
CIDIUM), a funnel-shaped growth,
the inner surface corresponding with
the lower surface of the metamorphosed leaf (C. de Candolle); **hypo-
ba'sal** (βάσις, a pedestal), behind
the basal wall, employed as regards
the posterior half of a proembryo ;
cf. EPIBASAL ; **Hyp'oblast = Hypo-
blas'tus** (βλαστός, a shoot), the
fleshy cotyledon of grasses; **Hypo-
carp'ium** (καρπός, fruit), an enlarged
growth of the peduncle beneath the
fruit, as in *Anacardium;* **hypo-
carpoge'an,** *-geus* (καρπός, fruit; γῆ,
the earth), = HYPOGAEAN ; **hypo-
carpog'enous** (γενος, offspring), the
flowers and fruit produced underground (Pampaloni); *cf.* AMPHICAR-
POGENOUS; **Hy'pochil,** *Hypochi'lium,*
Hypochi'lus (χεῖλος, a lip), the basal
portion of the labellum of Orchids;
Hypochlor'in (χλωρός, light green),
Pringsheim's name for a constituent
of chlorophyll corpuscles, supposed
to be the first visible product of
constructive metabolism ; **Hypochro'-
myl** (χρῶμα, colour) = HYPOCHLO-
RIN ; **Hypocop'ula** (+ COPULA)
the lower or intermediate band of
cell-wall in the lower and smaller
valve of certain Diatoms; **Hypocot'yl**
(+ COTYLEDON), the axis of an
embryo below the cotyledons, but
not passing beyond them ; adj.
hypocot'ylar ; **hypocotyle'donary,**
below the cotyledons and above the
root ; **hypocrate'riform,** *hypocrateriform'is* (κρατήρ, a bowl; *forma,*
shape), salver-shaped, as the corolla
of the Primrose, *Primula vulgaris,*
Huds. ; **hypocraterimor'phous,** *-phus*
(μορφή, shape), salver-shaped ; the
same meaning as in the last, but
derived wholly from the Greek ;
Hyp'oderm=Hypoder'ma, *Hypoder'-
mis* (δέρμα, skin, hide), the inner

layer of the capsules of Mosses ;
hypoder'mal, beneath the epidermis;
~ **Cell,** the apical cell of the nucellus
giving rise to the embryo-sac ; **hypoder'mic Zone,** Bastit's term for structure described by him in the scales
of the rhizome of certain Mosses
distinct from the bundle in the midrib; **hypogae'ous,** *-cus,* **hypoge'al,**
hypoge'an (γῆ, the earth), growing
or remaining below ground, as certain
cotyledons, as in the Pea ; **hypog'-
enous** (γένος, offspring), produced
beneath ; **hypog'ynous,** *-nus* (γυνή,
a woman), free from but inserted
beneath the pistil or gynaecium ;
Hypog'yny, the condition of possessing hypogynous flowers ; **hypolith'ic**
(λίθος, a stone), growing beneath
stones.

hypom'enous, *-us* (ὑπομένω, I stay
behind), free, not adherent, arising
from below an organ without adhesion to it.

Hypomic'lia [*sic,* possibly a misprint
for "Hypomycelia" from ὑπό, under ;
+ MYCELIUM], "the mycelium of
certain Fungals" (Lindley) ; **hyponas'tic** (ναστός, close pressed), (1)
used of a dorsiventral organ in which
the ventral surface grows more
actively than the dorsal, as shown
in flower expansion ; (2) by Van
Tieghem employed for anatropous
or campylotropous ovules when the
curvature is in an upward direction ;
Hyponas'ty, the state in question ;
Hy'ponym (ὄνομα, name), a name to
be rejected for want of an identified
type ; **Hypoög'amy** (ᾠόν, an egg ;
γάμος, marriage), a shortened form
of HYPERANISOGAMY ; **hypopel'tate**
(+ PELTATE), applied to a phyllome
having the base of the limb on the
inferior face ; *cf.* EPIPELTATE (C. de
Candolle) ; **hypophloe'odal, hypophloe'odic** (φλοιός, bark), applied to
Lichens when growing under the
epidermis of the bark ; **Hy'pophyll,**
Hypophyl'lum (φύλλον, a leaf), (1)
an abortive leaf or scale under another
leaf or leaf-like organ, as in *Ruscus* ;
(2) also used for the lower portion

of the leaf from which stipules
develop, adherent to the axis and
ultimately forming the leaf-scar;
hypophyllop′odous (πόνς, a foot),
radical leaves present when flowering, but not numerous; used of
certain *Hieracia; cf.* PHYLLOPO-
DOUS; **hypophyl′lous**, *-lus* (φύλλον,
a leaf), situated under a leaf, or
growing in that position; **Hy′po-
physe, ~ Cell = Hypoph′ysis** (φύω,
I grow), the cell from which
the primary root and root-cap
of the embryo in Angiosperms is
derived; adj. **hypophys′ial; Hy′po-
plasy** (πλάσσω, I mould), defective
development due to insufficient
nourishment, and consequent cessation of growth (Küster); adj. **hypo-
plast′ic; Hypopleu′ra** (πλευρά, a
rib), the inner half-girdle of the
frustule of a Diatom (O. Mueller); **Hypopod′ium** (πούς, ποδός, a
foot), the stalk of a carpel; **hypo-
pro′teoid** (+ PROTEOID), used of
plants having sclerotic cells on
the lower surface of their leaves
(Vesque); **Hypopter′ies** ‡ (πτερὸν,
a feather or wing), a wing growing
from below, as the seed of a Fir-
tree; **hypoptera′tus,** ‡ having wings
produced from below; **Hyposath′ria**
(σαθρὸς, rotten), the state of secondary ripening styled bletting, as in
medlars; **Hy′posperm** (σπέρμα, a
seed), the lower part of an ovule or
seed, below the level where the integument becomes free from the
nucellus (F. W. Oliver); **Hypo-
sporan′gium** (σπορὰ, a seed; ἀγγεῖον,
a vessel), the indusium of Ferns,
when proceeding from below the
sporangia.

Hy′postase (ὑπόστασις, a support), a
disc of lignified tissue at the base of
the ovule in certain orders (Van
Tieghem).

Hypost′asis (ὑπὸ, under; στάσις, a
standing), (1) the suspensor of an
embryo; (2) a unit-factor concealed
or inhibited (Bateson); adj. **hypo-
stat′ic;** *cf.* EPISTASIS; **Hy′postate
= HYPOSPERM; hypostomat′ic,**

hypostom′atous (+ STOMA), with
the stomata on the under surface;
Hypostom′ium, cells forming the
lower portion of the stomium of
the annulus of a rupturing sporangium in the Ferns; **Hypostro′ma**
(στρῶμα, spread-out) (1) = MY-
CELIUM; (2) the stroma at the base
of the fructification only (Traverso);
hypotet′rarch (+ TETRARCH), in a
triarch stele, the division of the
median protoxylem; **hypothal′line**
(θαλλὸs, a young branch), relating
to the hypothallus or resembling
it; **hypothallin′ic,** situated beneath
the thallus of a Lichen; **Hypo-
thal′lium,** Areschoug's term for the
basal rhizoidal layer in calcareous
Algae; **Hypothal′lus,** the marginal
outgrowth of hyphae in crustaceous Lichens; **Hypothe′ca** (θήκη, a
case), the inner half-frustule of a
Diatom (O. Mueller); **hypothe′cal,**
belonging to the hypotheca of a
Diatom; **Hy′pothece = Hypothe′-
cium,** a layer of hyphal-tissue
immediately beneath the hymenium
in certain Cryptogams; **hypotri′arch**
(+ TRIARCH), when in a triarch stele,
the median protoxylem group is
lowermost (Prantl); **Hypot′rophy**
(τροφή, food), Wiesner's term when
the growth of cortex or wood is
greater on the lower side of the
branch; also when buds or stipules
form on the lower side; adj. **hypo-
t′ropous; Hypoval′va** (*valva*, a door),
the valve of the inner "shell" or
hypotheca of a Diatom (O. Mueller);
Hypoxan′thin (ξανθὸs, yellow), a
substance akin to xanthin, which
has been found in germinating seeds.

Hypsi′um, or **Hypsi′on** (ὕψι, high,
aloft), a succession of plants by
elevation (Clements); **Hyp′sophyll**
(φύλλον, a leaf), a bract of the inflorescence, a reduced or modified
leaf towards the upper end of a
shoot; *cf.* CATAPHYLL; Ger. Hochblatt; **hypsophyl′lary,** relating to
bracts; **~ Leaf,** a bract.

hys′ginus (ὕσγινον), a red colour, or
dark reddish pink.

hysteran'thous, *-thus, -this* (ὕστερος, following; ἄνθος, a flower), used of leaves which are produced after the flowers, as in the Almond ; **hysterogenet'ic = hysterogen'ic** (γένος, race, offspring), used of intercellular spaces which are formed in the older tissues ; **hysterolysig'enous** (λύσις, a loosing; γένος, offspring), when a cavity is ultimately formed by the dissolution of cells ; **Hys'terophyme** (φῦμα, a tumour or excrescence), elementary organs which have been mistaken for independent animal or vegetable organisms (H. Karsten) ; **hysterophy'tal** (φυτὸν, a plant), fungoid ; **Hys'terophyte,** a plant which lives upon dead matter ; a saprophyte ; **Hysteroplas'ma** (πλάσμα, moulded), Nägeli's term for the more fluid part of PROTOPLASM ; **Hyst'erostele** (+ STELE), a stele which is supposed to be reduced in structure, as in *Hippuris* and *Potamogeton* (Brebner).

Hystrel'la (ὑστέρη, the matrix), a synonym of CARPEL.

ianth'inus (ἰάνθινος, violet colour), bluish purple, violet.

iced, having a glittering papillose surface, as *Mesembryanthemum crystallinum,* Linn.

Ichneu'mon Flowers, those which are specially visited by Ichneumonidae.

I'cones, pl. *(icon,* εἰκών, a figure), pictorial representations of plants ; botanic figures.

icosahed'ral (εἴκοσι, twenty; ἕδρα, a seat or base), having twenty sides, as the pollen-grains of *Tragopogon ;* **icosan'der, icosan'drous,** *-rus* (ἀνὴρ, ἀνδρὸς, a man), with twenty or more stamens ; **Icosan'dria,** a Linnean class of plants with twenty stamens or more, inserted on the calyx.

I'cotype (ἐικὸς, what is like), types serving for identification, but not previously used in literature.

icter'icus (Lat.), **icteri'nus** (ἰκτερικὸς, jaundiced), the colour of a person suffering from jaundice, impure yellow.

Ic'terus (Lat., a yellow bird), vegetable jaundice ; a form of CHLOROSIS shown by yellowness.

Id (ἴδης, suffix implying paternity), an hereditary unit recognized in granules and chromosomes ; **I'dant,** a serial complex of ids, Weismann's term for CHROMOSOME.

ide'al *(idealis,* existing in idea) **An'gle =** ANGLE, IDEAL.

Identifica'tion, used for Determination (Crozier).

Id'eotype, *cf.* IDIOTYPE.

-i'des, -i'deus (εἶδος, like), a suffix in Greek compounds denoting similar ; *cf.* -O-IDES.

idioandrospor'ous (ἴδιος, peculiar ; + ANDROSPORE), when dwarf-males of Oedogoniaceae are produced from zoospores contained in certain cells of neuter individuals (Wittrock) ; **Id'ioblast** (βλαστὸς, a bud or shoot), (1) a special cell in a tissue which markedly differs from the rest in form, size, or contents, as the "stellate-cells" in *Nymphaea ;* (2) used by Hertwig for PANGEN, a unit of hereditary substance, a biophore ; **ol'eoid** ~, long sinuous sclerenchym cells, occurring in *Olea ;* **prot'eoid** ~, similar cells in *Protea ;* **Idiochro'mosome** (+ CHROMOSOME), special chromosomes believed to convey sex-tendency (Wilson) ; **Idiochromid'ia,** pl. (+ CHROMIDIA), generative chromidia ; **idiog'ynus** ‡ (γυνὴ, a woman), not having a pistil ; **Idiomeres',** pl. (μέρος, a part), structures evolved during the resting stage in nuclear division, and believed to be the sexual elements of the resultant nucleus ; **Idiomorph'osis** (μόρφωσις, a shaping), a special kind of metamorphosis, as the petals of *Camellia,* from bundles of stamens, or petaloid sepals of *Polygala* (Delpino) ; **Id'ioplasm** (πλάσμα, moulded), Nägeli's term for the active organic part of the protoplasm, identified with CHROMATIN ; **Id'ioplast** (πλαστὸς, moulded), employed by F. S. Lloyd for IDIOBLAST; a cell with special contents; **Id'iosome** (σῶμα, a body), a hypothetical ultimate unit of the cell, a biophore; **idiothal'amous,** *idiothal'amus* (θάλαμος, a bedroom), having different coloration from the thallus, a term in lichenology; **Idiot'ery** (τέρας, a monster), Gubler's term for a monstrosity which is peculiar to the individual; *cf.* TAXITERY; **Id'iotype** (τύπος, a type), a specimen identified by the describer, but not from the original locality; **idiotyp'ic,** sexual (Radlkofer); the condition is **Idiot'ypy;** *cf.* ZELOTYPIC.

ig'neus (Lat., fiery), flame-coloured, used for combinations of red and yellow, or brilliant in tone.

ignia'rius (Lat., pertaining to fire), of the consistence of German tinder, derived from puff-balls.

-ile, suffix to denote Society, as Iridile for a society of *Iris* (Clements).

illegit'imate, fertilization in dimorphic or trimorphic flowers so termed, when occurring between parts of diverse length, as long with short, etc.

imberb'is (Lat.), beardless, devoid of hairs.

Imbibit'ion (*imbibo*, I drink in), the act of imbibing; ~ **The'ory,** Sachs's suggestion that water ascends in plants by a chemical process in the cell-walls, and not by actual passage upwards by vessels; ~ **Wa'ter,** the amount which occurs in organic bodies (Warming).

im'bricate, imbrica'ted, *imbrica'tus* (Lat., covered with gutter tiles), (1) overlapping as the tiles on a roof; (2) in aestivation, used of a calyx or corolla where one piece must be wholly internal and one wholly external, or overlapping at the edge only; **imbric'ative** is a synonym.

immarg'inate, *immargina'tus* (*im* = not; *margo, marginis,* a border), not margined or bordered.

immedia'tus (Mid. Lat., not mediate), **proceeding** directly from a part, as **pedic**els of a raceme.

immer'sed, *immer'sus* (Lat., plunged), below the surface; (1) entirely under water; (2) embedded in the substance of the leaf or thallus.

immo'bile, *immo'bilis* (Lat.), immovable, as many anthers; opposed to versatile.

Immotiflor'ae (*immotus,* motionless; *flos, floris,* a flower), Delpino's term for wind-fertilized plants whose flowers are steadily fixed.

immuta'tus (Lat.), unchanged, as the phyllaries of *Hieracium* after flowering.

impa'ri-pin'nate, ~ *-pinna'tus* (*impar,* unequal; + PINNATE), pinnate with an odd terminal leaflet.

imper'fect, *imperfec'tus* (Lat., incomplete), where certain parts usually present are not developed; as a flower may be imperfect, that is, unisexual.

imperf'orate (*in,* into; *per,* through); *fora'tus,* bored), without an opening, closed (Crozier).

implex'us (Lat., an entwining), entangled, interlaced.

implica'tus (Lat.), entangled, woven in.

Impregna'ting Tube, an outgrowth from the antheridium of *Pythium,* which penetrates the periplasm to the surface of the oosphere.

Impregna'tion (*im* = in; *praegnatus,* pregnancy), fertilization, the union of male and female elements; **gen'erative** ~, the fusion of the generative nucleus with the egg; **vegeta'tive** ~, Strasburger's term for the fusion of the polar nuclei, either with each other or with one of the generative nuclei.

impres'sus (Lat., pressed into), marked with slight depressions.

impu'bes, not mature, as *impube'ra Ae'tas,* the period before impregnation.

inadhe'ring (*inadhacrens*, not clinging), free from adjacent parts.

inaequa'lis (Lat.), unequal in size; **inaequimag'nus,** ‡ (*magnus,* large), not the same in size; **inaequilat'eral,** *inaequilatera'lis,* *inaequilat'eris* (*latus, lateris*, a side), unequal sided, as the leaf of *Begonia ;* **inaequiner'-vius** (*nervus*, a nerve), when the veins are of dissimilar size ; **inae'-quivalve, inaequival'vular** (*valva*, a door-leaf), used of the glumes of plants which show inequality in their constituent valves.

inane', *ina'nis* (Lat.), empty, void ; as an anther containing no pollen ; **Inanit'ion**, the condition of green cells induced by want of oxygen and consequent loss of power of assimilation (Pringsheim).

inan'therate (Crozier) = **inanthera'tus**, (*in* = not ; + ANTHER), having no anther ; said of abortive or sterile filaments.

inappendic'ulate, *inappendicula'tus* (*in* = not ; *appendicula*, a small appendage), without appendages ; **inaper'tus** (*apertus*, opened), not opened, contrary to its habit.

Inarch'ing, grafting by approach, the scion remaining partly attached to its parent, until union has taken place.

inartic'ulate, *inarticula'tus* (Lat., indistinct), not jointed, continuous.

incanes'cent, *incanes'cens* (Lat., turning hoary), becoming grey, canescent.

inca'nous (Crozier) = **inca'nus** (Lat.), quite grey, hoary.

incar'nate, *incarna'tus* (Lat., clothed in flesh), flesh-coloured, "carneous."

In'cept, In'ception (*inceptum*, a beginning), suggested rendering of the German "Anlage."

Inch, an English measure, equalling 2.54 cm. ; in Latin, *uncia, uncialis.*

inci'sed, *inci'sus* (Lat., cut into), cut sharply into the margin ; **inci'so-denta'tus**, slashed toothed ; ~ **-serra'tus**, deep-slashed serrations ; **Incis'ion**, *Incis'io*, an indentation on the margin of a foliar organ.

incli'ning, incli'ned (*inclinatus*, bent down), falling away from the horizontal direction.

inclu'ded, *inclu'sus* (Lat., shut in), not protruding beyond the surrounding organ ; **includen'tia Fo'lia**, applied to alternate leaves which in the sleep-position approach buds in their axils, seeming to protect them as in *Sida* (De Candolle).

Incog'nit (*incognitus*, not examined). Used by H. C. Watson for those British plants whose nativity or distribution are matters of doubt.

incomple'te, *incompletus* (Lat., not finished), wanting some essential part ; **Incomple'tae**, usually synonymous with Monochlamydeae, but variously circumscribed by different authors.

incompress'ible (*in* = not ; *compresso*, I press together), "offering resistance to compression" (Drummond).

inconspic'uous, *-cuus* (Lat., not remarkable), not readily seen from small size or lack of colour.

incras'sate, *incrassa'tus* (Lat., thickened), made stout, as the leaves of house-leek.

incre'asing = ACCRESCENT ; **incres'cent** (*incresco*, I grow), growing (Crozier).

Incrusta'tion (*Incrusta'tio*, an encasing), fossils encased in mineral substance, with the actual tissue wanting ; casts which give impressions of markings or cavities, but show no organic structure.

Incrust'ing, *incrusta'tus* (Lat., coated), (1) used of seeds so firm in their pericarp as to seem one with it ; (2) encrusted with earthy matter.

Incuba'tion (*Incubatio*, a brooding), the time from the moment of infection, or sowing of spores, until growth is manifest.

in'cubous, *-bus* (*incubo*, I lie upon), the oblique insertion of distichous leaves, so that the lower overlap the upper on the same side of the stem on the dorsal surface, as in *Bazzania ; cf.* SUCCUBOUS.

incum'bent, *incum'bens* (Lat., leaning on), resting or leaning upon, procumbent ; ~ **An'ther**, one which lies against the inner face of its filament ; ~ **Cotyle'dons**, when the back of one lies against the radicle, shown as ‖ o.

incur'ved, *incur'vus* ; **incur'vate**, *incurva'tus* (*incurvus*, bent), bending from without inwards.

indecid′uous (*in* = not ; *deciduus*, cut or lopped off), evergreen or persistent foliage (Crozier) ; **indef′inite**, *indefini′tus* (Lat., not precise), (1) uncertain or not positive in character ; (2) too many for easy enumeration, as an abundance of stamens, denoted by the sign ∞ ; (3) in an inflorescence, when racemose, the main axis being capable of constant extension ; ~ **Growth**, continuous growth and not the mere extension of a limited organism or bud ; ~ **Inflores′cence**, indeterminate or centrifugal, acropetal of some authors ; **Indehis′cence** (*dehiscens*, gaping), not opening, as of fruits which remain closed at maturity ; **indehis′cent**, *-cens*, not opening by valves or along regular lines.

Indepen′dence, the separation of organs usually entire.

Indeterm′inate, *indetermina′tus*, not terminated absolutely, as an inflorescence in which no flower ends the axis of the flower-cluster.

In′dican, a nitrogenous glucoside, by its decomposition forming INDIGO.

indif′ferent (*indifferens*, without difference), not specialized or differentiated.

In′digene (*indiges*, native), a native plant ; **indig′enous**, *-nus*, original to the country, not introduced.

In′digo, a deep blackish blue obtained from various species of *Indigofera* ; **In′digogene**, white indigo, or colourless indigotine ; **indigot′icus**, indigo blue, atro-cyaneus ; **In′digotine**, pure blue indigo, forming about fourtenths of the commercial indigo ; **Indimul′sin**, an enzyme producing indigo in the leaves of *Indigofera*.

indirec′te veno′sus, Link's term for lateral veins combined within the margins, and emitting other little veins.

Individ′ual, *Individ′uum* (*individ′uus*, inseparable), a unit of the series which constitute species ; **Individ′ualism**, (1) capable of separate existence ; (2) symbiosis in which the total aggregate result is wholly different from any of the symbionts ; **Individua′tion**, a synonym of the last (2).

indivi′sus (Lat.), undivided, entire.

induced′, applied to those movements which are the result of some irritation or stimulus, as pressure, light, heat, etc. ; **Induc′tion**, the production of sensitive movements ; **hetero-g′enous** ~ ,due to two or more causes; **isog′enous** ~ , due to one cause.

Indumen′tum (Lat., a garment), any covering, as hairiness.

indup′licate, *induplica′tus*, **indu′plicative**, with the margins bent inwards, and the external face of these edges, applied to each other, without twisting.

induras′cens (Lat., from *induro*, I harden), hardening by degrees ; **indura′ted**, hardened.

indu′saeform, **indu′siform** (+ INDUSIUM ; *forma*, shape) ; **indu′sial**, having indusia ; ~ **Flaps**, a false indusium in *Woodwardia*; **indu′siate**, *indusia′tus*, possessing an indusium ; **indu′sioid** (εἶδος, like), John Smith's expression for any indusium-like covering in Ferns.

Indu′sium (Lat., a woman's undergarment), (1) an epidermal outgrowth covering the sori in Ferns ; (2) a ring of collecting hairs below the stigma; (3) the annulus of some Fungi (Lindley).

Indu′viae (Lat., clothes), (1) persistent portions of the perianth, or leaves which wither, but do not fall off ; (2) scale-leaves ; **indu′viate**, *induvia′lis*, *induvia′tus*, clothed with withered remnants.

inembryona′tus (*in* = not ; *embryo*, an embryo), having no embryo.

Inench′yma (ἴς, ἰνὸς, muscle-fibres ; ἔγχυμα, an infusion), fibro-cellular tissue, the cells having the appearance of spiral vessels, as in *Sphagnum*.

inerm′, **iner′mous**, *iner′mis* (Lat., unarmed), without spines or prickles.

inexten′sible (*in* = not ; *extensus*, stretched) "offering resistance to stretching" (Drummond).

ineye′, to inoculate, or bud.

infarc'tate (*infarctus*, stuffed into), turgid or solid.

Infec'tion Ar'ea, the portion of the host attacked by a fungus ; ~ **Lay'er,** a patch of hyphae near the base of the scutellum in *Lolium temulentum* (Freeman) ; ~ **Thread,** continuous chains and bacteria passing from cell to cell ; ~ **Tube** = GERM-TUBE ; ~ **Ve'sicle,** the haustorium of an invading fungus ; ~ **Zone,** a series of cells in which the infection threads pass from cell to cell ; **infec'-tious,** communicable by infection, as diseases in plants, etc. ; caused by some organism from outside.

in'fer-agar'ian (*infer*, below) **Zone,** H. C. Watson's term for the lowest portion of the cultivated lands in Great Britain ; ~ **arc'tic Zone,** a similar term for the lowest division of his arctic region in Britain ; **In'ferals,** a division of gamopetalous Dicotyledons proposed for Rubiaceae, Compositae, Companulaceae, etc.

infe'rior (Lat., lower), (1) below some other organ, as an ~ **Ca'lyx** is below the ovary, or an ~ **O'vary** seems to grow below the adnate calyx ; (2) has been used for anterior, or turned away from the axis.

infla'ted, *infla'tus* (Lat., puffed up), bladdery, swollen.

inflec'ted (*inflec'to,* I bend), bent or flexed.

inflex'ed, *inflex'us* (Lat., bent), turned abruptly or bent inward, incurved.

inflex'ible (*in* = not ; *flexibilis,* pliant), "offering resistance to bending" (Drummond).

Inflores'cence, *Inflorescen'tia* (*infloresco,* I begin to bloom), (1), the disposition of the flowers on the floral axis ; (2) less correctly used for the Flower Cluster ; **def'inite** ~, when each axis in turn is terminated with a flower, as in a cyme ; **indef'inite** ~, when the floral axis is capable of continuous extension, as in a raceme.

info'liate (*in,* in ; *folium,* a leaf), to cover with leaves.

infos'sus (Lat., buried), sunk in anything, as the veins in some leaves, but leaving a visible channel.

in'fra-axil'lary, *infra-axilla'ris* (*infra,* below ; + AXILLARIS), below the axil.

infrac'ted, *infrac'tus* (Lat., broken, bent), incurved.

infracuta'neous (*infra,* below ; *cutis,* skin), below the surface, subepidermal ; **infrano'dal** (*nodus,* a knot), below a node ; ~ **Canals',** gaps in the medullary rays of *Calamites,* below the node, leaving prints on the casts (Williamson).

Infructes'cence (*fructus,* fruit, by analogy to inflorescence), (1) the inflorescence in a fruiting stage ; (2) collective fruits.

infruc'tuose (*infructuo'sus,* unfruitful), barren, not bearing fruit.

infundib'ular, *infundibula'ris* (*infundibulum,* a funnel), funnel-shaped ; **infundibu'liform,** *infundibulifor'mis* (*forma,* shape), shaped like a funnel.

infus'cate (*infuscus,* dusky), of a brownish tint.

inhib'ited, (1) used for spores, not killed, but whose germination has been prevented by the use of certain solutions ; (2) hindered.

Inhibit'ion (*inhibitio,* a restraining), modification or restraint in function ; **Inhib'itor,** a restraining or preventing factor.

init'ial (*initialis,* original); ~ **Cells,** cells from which primordial layers or nascent tissues arise ; ~ **Lay'er,** the middle cambium layer ; **Init'ials** the beginnings of tissues, the early stages of cells or tissues, as **Dermat'ogen** ~, or **Per'iblem** ~.

Injec'tion (*injectus,* cast into), the filling of intercellular spaces with water (Crozier).

in'nate, *inna'tus* (Lat., natural), (1) borne on the apex of the support ; in an anther the antithesis of adnate ; (2) imbedded (Leighton).

in'ner, internal, nearer the centre than something else ; ~ **Lam'ina,** the layer of a lignified cell-wall which is next the inside of the cell ; ~ **Perid'ium,** ~ **Tu'nic,** a more or less coloured

membrane which surrounds the hymenium in *Verrucaria* beneath the
perithecium.

in′novans (Lat.), renewing; **innovan′tes
Gem′mae**, the fixed or persistent buds
of Mosses.

Innova′tion, *Innova′tio* (Lat., an alteration), a newly formed shoot in
Mosses, which becomes independent
from the parent stem by dying off
behind ; ∼ **Shoot**, a vigorous shoot
which carries on the further growth
of the plant.

Innucella′tae (*in* = not ; +NUCELLUS),
Van Tieghem's name for phanerogamic plants whose ovules want
nucellus and integuments, such as
the Santalaceae.

Inocula′tion (*inoculatio*, ingrafting),
(1) grafting, more properly budding,
a single bud only being inserted ;
(2) facility for the introduction of
seed to newly established beach
(F. W. Oliver).

inophyl′lous (ἴς, ἰνὸς, a nerve ; φύλλον,
a leaf), with thread-like veins in the
leaf (Heinig). .

in′ops (Lat. destitute), poor, deficient
(Heinig).

inorgan′ic (*in*, not ; +ORGANIC), devoid
of organs ; ∼ **Ash**, the final residuum
after complete combustion ; the
mineral portion of a vegetable tissue ;
∼ **Com′pounds**, those which form
part of animal or plant structure
derived from mineral substances ; ∼
Fer′ments, enzymes, as opposed to
organic ferments, such as bacteria.

inos′culating (*in*, into ; *osculatus*,
kissed), anastomosing ; **Inoscula′-
tion**, budding or grafting.

I′nosite, (ἴς, ἰνὸς, strength, sinew), a
saccharine aromatic principle which
occurs in many seeds and other parts
of plants, especially in climbers;
Inotag′mata, pl. (+ TAGMA), the
hypothetical contractile elements of
protoplasm (T. W. Engelmann).

Inovula′tae (*in*, not; + OVULUM), phanerogamic plants which have no ovules
discernible at the time of fertilization, as the Loranthaceae (Van
Tieghem).

in′quinant (*inquino*, I stain), stained
or staining.

inro′lled, rolled inwards (Boulger).

insculpt′ (*insculptus*, engraved), embedded in rocks, as some Lichens.

In′sect Pollina′tion, the transfer of
pollen from the anther to the stigma
of the same or a different flower by
insect visitors ; entomophily.

insectiv′orous (*insectum*, an insect ;
voro, I devour), used of those plants
which capture insects and absorb
nutriment from them.

Insemina′tae (*in* = not, *semen*, seed),
Van Tieghem's name for those plants
which do not contain seed separable
or distinct at maturity ; in order to
germinate, the fruit must be sown
entire.

Insepara′tion (*inseparatus*, not separated), Masters's term for coalescence;
adj. **insep′arate**.

inser′ted, *inser′tus* (Lat., put into),
joined to or placed on ; **Inser′tion**,
Inser′tio, (1) mode or place where
one body is attached to its support ;
(2) Grew's term for a medullary ray.

Insit′ion (*insitio*, a grafting), the insertion of a scion into a stock,
grafting.

Insola′tion (*insolo*, I expose to the sun),
exposure to the direct rays of the
sun.

inspis′sated (*in*, into ; *spissatus*, thickened), thickened, as juice by evaporation.

instip′ulate (*in* = not ; + STIPULATE),
exstipulate (Crozier).

in′teger (Lat., whole), entire, not lobed
or divided ; **integer′rimus**, an em-
phatic assertion of the entirety of
an organ ; **Integmina′tae** (*in* = not ;
tegmen, a covering), van Tieghem's
name for plants whose nucellus is
devoid of integument; **in′tegra
Ra′dix**, an unbranched root; ∼
Vagi′na, the sheathing petiole which
forms a continuous tube, as in sedges;
integrifo′lious (*folium*, a leaf), with
undivided, or simple leaves.

Integ′ument (*integumentum*, a covering), (1) the covering of an organ or
body ; (2) the envelope of an ovule;

Integumen'ta Flora'lia, the floral envelopes; **integumen'tal Glands**, peltate glands, the integument being raised like a bladder due to the formation of abundant secretion; ~ **Tis'sue**, the epidermis and hypoderm.

in'ter-axill'ary(*inter*, between;+AXILLARIS), between the axils; **interbiomor'ic** (+ BIOMORE), employed to denote the condition of HYALOPLASM.

inter'calary (*intercalaris*, that to be inserted), used of growth, which is not apical but between the apex and the base; ~ **Branch'ing**, intermediate branching short of the apex; ~ **Cell**, a small cell arising from conjugate division, disappearing after the formation of the aecidiospore mother-cell (Grove); ~ **Inflores'cence**, when the main axis continues to grow vegetatively after giving rise to the flowers (Parkin); ~ **veg'etative Zone**, a portion lying between mature tissue, which takes on growth as though a growing point; **inter'calated**, interposed, placed between.

intercarp'ellary (*inter*, between; + CARPEL), between the carpels; **intercell'ular** (+ CELLULAR), between the cells or tissues; ~ **Pas'sage**, a continuous opening between the cells; ~ **Space**, a cavity bounded by the cells of a tissue; ~ **Sub'stance**, material extravasated from within to outside the cell; ~ **Sys'tem**, the intercellular spaces and adjacent tissues (Crozier); **intercos'tal** (*costa*, a rib), between the ribs or nerves of a leaf; **intercotyle'donary** (+ COTYLEDON), between the cotyledons; **Intercros'sing**, cross-fertilization; **Intercu'tis** (*cutis*, the skin), Kroemer's name for the hypoderm of the root; **interfascic'ular** (*fasciculus*, a bundle), between the vascular bundles; ~ **Cam'bium**, that formed between the bundles in the primary medullary rays; ~ **conjunc'tive Tis'sue** = preceding; ~ **Phlo'ëm**, ~ **Xy'lem**, respectively formed from the ~ CAMBIUM; **interfi'lar** (*filum*, a thread), between filaments, as the

resting spore in *Mesocarpus* (Crozier); **interfolia'ceous** (*folium*, a leaf; + ACEOUS) between the leaves of a pair, as the stipules of many Rubiaceae; **interfo'liar**, situated between two opposite leaves; **interfo'liate, interfo'liar** (+ FOLIOLE), between the leaves, or between the leaves and some other structure; **Int'erfoyles**, Grew's name for (1) bracts; (2) scales; (3) stipules.

intergeri'num (Lat., placed between), **Lig'num‡**, the dissepiment of a fruit.

Interkine'sis (*inter*, between; κίνησις, motion), the heterotypic telophase or the period elapsing between the two meiotic divisions; **Interlob'ule** (+ LOBULE), name given by Spruce to a small plane process of a subulate or triangular form, between the lobule and the stem in certain Hepaticae.

interme'diate, *interme'dius* (Lat., that which is between), half-way or between; ~ **Bun'dles**, applied to somewhat later bundles, as the six last in the stem of *Clematis Vitalba*; ~ **Tis'sue**, the ground tissue in exogens, except that of the epidermis and vascular bundles; ~ **Type**, employed by H. C. Watson for those plants whose distribution in Great Britain is of a local or doubtful range; ~ **Zone**, (1) the active zone between the pith and epidermis, containing the vascular bundles in Monocotyledons; (2) used by H. C. Watson as indicating a certain elevation, between the agrarian and arctic zones.

intermicel'lar (*inter*, between; + MICELLA), between the micellae; **intermolec'ular** (+ MOLECULE), between the molecules.

inter'nal (*interne*, inwardly), ~ **Pericy'cle**, Flot's expression for the procambium retained on the inner side of the vascular bundle.

In'ternode, *Interno'dium* (Lat.), the space or portion of stem between two nodes; adj. **interno'dal**.

interpet'iolar, *interpetiola'ris* (*inter*, between; *petiolus*, a little stalk), (1) between the petioles; (2) enclosed

by the expanded base of a petiole ;
(3) also applied to connate stipules
which have coalesced from two opposite leaves ; **interplacen'tal** (+ PLA-
CENTA), between the placentas ;
applied to vascular bundles which
occur in the capsule ; *cf.* ANTE-
PLACENTAL.

interpo'sed (*interpositus*, placed between) **Mem'bers**, those parts which
have arisen in a whorl subsequent to
its earlier members ; **Interposit'ion**,
Interposit'io, formation of new parts
between those already existing in a
whorl ; **interpositi'vus** (Lat.), interposed.

interprotoplas'mic (*inter*, between ; +
PROTOPLASM) **Spa'ces**, gaps in the
reticulum of Myxogastres.

interrup'ted (*interruptus*, broken or
separated), when any symmetrical
arrangement is destroyed by local
causes ; a solution of continuity ; ~
Growth, an alternation of abundant
and scanty development, appearing
as constrictions in an organ, as a
fruit or tap-root ; **interrup'tedly
pin'nate**, (1) a ·pinnate leaf without
a terminal leaflet ; (2) having small
leaflets interposed with those of
larger size.

intersem'inal (*inter*, between ; *semen*,
seed), between or amongst seeds, as
scales on the torus of *Anthemis ;*
interspor'al (σπορὰ, a spore), in a
sporangium, situated between the
spores (Harper) ; **interstam'inal** (+
STAMINAL), placed between two stamens ; **interstam'inate** is a synonym.

Inter'stice (*interstit'ium*, a space between), small air-spaces ; larger are
termed lucunae, still larger, air-
passages ; **interstit'ial Bod'ies**, mucilaginous discs occurring in certain
pollen-grains (Beer) ; ~ **Growth**, the
theory which requires the interpo-
sition of new particles between the
older portions, instead of superficial
additions.

intertrop'ic (*inter*, between ; + TROPIC),
relating to the torrid zone ; within
the tropics ; **intervag'inal** (*vagina*,
a sheath) **Scales**, squamules found

between the leaves of aquatic monocotyledons (Gibson) ; **Interve'nium**
(*vena*, a vein), a portion of parenchyma between the veins of a leaf ;
Interwea'ving (+ weaving), the
union of hyphae by growing amongst
each other, without cohesion ; Ger.
Verflechtung ; **interxy'lary** (+ Xy-
LEM), amongst the xylem elements ;
In'terzones (+ ZONE) Bessey's term
for the portion of a Diatom frustule
which in some cases lies between the
girdle and the valves.

Intex'ine, Intex'tine (*intus*, within ; +
EXTINE), the inner membrane when
two exist in the extine, or outer
covering of a pollen-grain ; **In'tine**,
the innermost coat of a pollen-grain ;
intodisca'lis‡ (*discus*, a disc), inserted within the disc of a flower.

Intor'sio (Lat.), curling or crisping ;
Intor'tion = TORSION ; **intor'tus**
(Lat., twisted), practically a synonym
of contorted ; twisted upon itself.

in'tra-axil'lary (*intra*, within ; +
AXILLARY), within the axil, as
many leaf-buds ; **intracam'bial** (+
CAMBIAL), within the cambium, internal to it ; **intracarp'ellary** (+
CARPEL), within the carpels ; **intra-
cell'ular** (+ CELLULAR), within a
cell ; **intracutic'ular** (+ CUTICLE),
within the cuticle ; applied to parts
or organs whose normal position is
outside ; **intrafascic'ular** (*fasciculus*,
a bundle), within a bundle ; **intra-
fi'lar** (*filum*, a thread), within a
filament ; **intraflo'ral** (+ FLORAL),
within the floral organs, as many
nectaries ; **intrafolia'ceous**, -*ceus*
(*folium*, a leaf ; + ACEOUS), within
or before a leaf, as within the axil ;
intralam'ellar (*lamella*, a small
plate), within plate-like structures,
as the trama of Agarics ; **intramar-
g'inal** (*margo*, a margin), placed
within the margin near the edge ;
intrama'trical (*matrix*, a mould),
inside a matrix or nidus ; **Intra-
meabil'ity** (*meabilis*, penetrable), the
capacity of protoplasm to permit
substances to pass into its vacuoles
(Janse) ; **intramedull'ary** (+ MEDUL-

200

LARY), within the pith (Solereder) ; **intramolec'ular** (+ MOLECULE), within the molecules; **intramu'ral** (*muralis*, pertaining to a wall), between the walls of cells, as ~ **Glands**, used by De Bary for multicellar organs of secretion, whose product appears in the limiting walls; **intranucell'ar** (+ NUCELLUS), within the nucellus ; **intranu'clear** (*nucleus*, a kernel), within the nucleus ; **intraov'ular** (+ OVULE), within an ovule; **intrapal'ear** (+ PALEA), referring to the fertilization of cereals which commonly takes place within the flower, before the exsertion of the anthers ; **intrapet'iolar** (*petiolus*, a small stalk), within the petiole, or between it and the stem, as ~ **Buds**, those which are completely enclosed by the petiole, as in *Platanus;* **intraprothall'oid** (+ PROTHALLUS), in the prothallus or immersed in its tissues ; **intraprotoplas'mic** (+ PROTOPLASM), within the protoplasm ; **intrasac'cal** (+ SAC), employed of embryos arising outside the embryosac.

intrar'ious, *intrar'ius* (L. Lat.), turned inward toward the axis.

intrasem'inal (*intra*, within ; *semen*, a seed), within the seed ; ~ **Devel'opment**, the whole development undergone by the embryo during the conversion of the ovule into the ripe seed; **intrasporang'ial** (+ SPORANGIUM) **Germina'tion**, growth of an embryo within the sporange; **intrastamin'eal** (+ STAMEN), within the stamens, as the disk of Anacardiaceae ; **intraste'lar** (+ STELE), within the stele, as ~ **Tis'sue** = CONJUNCTIVE TISSUE ; **intravag'inal** (*ragina*, a sheath), within the sheath, applied to branches which spring from buds which do not break through the sheath of the subtending leaf (Scribner); **intravalvula'ris** (+ VALVULARIS), within valves, as the dissepiment in many Cruciferae ; **intraxy'lary** (+ XYLEM), within the xylem.

in'tricate, *intrica'tus* (Lat.), entangled.

introcur'ved, *introcur'vus* (Lat.), incurved.

introdu'ced (*introduct'us*, brought within), used of plants which have been brought from another country.

introflex'ed (*intro*, inside; *flexus*, bent), inflexed ; **intromarg'inal** (+ MARGINAL), used of a vein running just within the outer margin of a leaf.

in'trorse, *intror'sus* (Mod. Lat.), turned inward, towards the axis.

introve'nius (*intro*, inside ; *vena*, a vein), hidden veined ; from the abundance of parenchyma, the veins not readily seen ; *cf.* AVENIUS ; **introxy'lic** (ξύλον, wood), within the xylem.

intru'ded, **in'truse**, *intru'sus* (Lat., thrust in), pushed or projecting forward ; **Intru'sion**, **cort'ical**, abnormal growth of cortex in other tissues.

Intumes'cence (*intumescere*, to swell up), any abnormal swelling on the exterior of plants.

Intussuscep'tion (*intus*, within ; *susceptus*, taken up), the theory of growth, which assumes the intercalation of new particles (micellae), between the already existing particles of the cell-wall.

In'ulase (from the genus *Inula*), an enzyme in Compositae which converts Inulin into Levulose ; **Inu'lenin**, a subordinate constituent of Inulin (Tanret) ; **In'ulin**, a body like starch, first found in Compositae, in the form of sphaero-crystals.

inun'cans ‡ (Lat., hooking), the surface covered with glochidia or hooked hairs.

inunda'tal (*inundatus*, overflowed), H. C. Watson's expression for those plants which grow in places liable to be inundated in wet weather, but dry in summer ; **inunda'tus**, flooded, sometimes under water, sometimes dry.

-inus, a Latin suffix, meaning, (1) resemblance ; (2) augmentation.

invag'inated (*in*, into ; *vagina*, a sheath), enclosed in a sheath.

Inva'sion, (*invasus*), an intrusion of an alien plant into regions or stations foreign to it.

inverse' (*inversus*, turned about), inverted ; **Inver'sion,** (1) a change of order or place ; (2) the action of Invertase ; **In'vert-en'zyme, In'vertase,** an unorganized ferment, which transmutes cane-sugar into inverted-sugar ; **inver'ted,** having the apex in an opposite direction to the normal ; **Inver'ted-sugar,** a mixture of fructose and glucose by the action of invertase on cane-sugar ; ~ **Superposit'ion,** the position of accessory buds below the principal bud, or one first formed (Crozier) ; **invor'tens** (Lat.), inverting, becoming reversed, as *inverten'tia Fo'lia,* leaves which in sleep hang downward, but touch by the upper surface, as in *Cassia* ; **In'vertin=** INVERTASE ; this form is chiefly employed by zoologists.

in'visible (*invisib'ilis,* not to be seen), used of any organ which is not sufficiently developed to be seen ; **Invol'ucel,** *Involucel'lum* (Fr., involucelle, from *involucrum,* a wrapper), a secondary partial involucre ; **involucel'late,** *involucella'tus,* provided with a secondary involucre ; **involu'cral,** *involucra'lis,* belonging to an involucre ; **invol'ucrate,** *involucra'tus,* **involu'cred,** having an involucre of some kind ; **Involu'cre,** *Involu'crum,* (1) a ring of bracts, surrounding several flowers or their supports, as in the heads of Compositae, or the umbels of Umbelliferae ; (2) the tissue of the thallus in Anthoceroteae, grown up and overarching the embryo, afterwards pierced by the lengthening sporogonium ; (3) the peridium, volva or annulus in Fungi (Lindley) ; (4) the indusium of Ferns ; **gen'eral** ~, that which is at the base of a compound umbel ; **par'tial** ~, **sec'ondary** ~, that which surrounds a partial umbel ; *Involu'cra lig'nea,* Malpighi's name for the concentric zones of growth in exogens ; **Involu'cret,** an involucel.

in'volute, *involu'tus,* **involuti'vus** (Lat., enwrapped), having the edges of the leaves rolled inwards ; **Involu'tion,** (1) the act of rolling inward ; (2) the return of an organ or tissue to its original state ; ~ **Form,** a swollen bladder-like form of Schizomycetes, supposed to be a diseased condition of the form associated with it ; ~ **Pe'riod,** the resting period ; ~ **Spore,** a resting-spore ; ~ **Stage,** the resting stage.

invol'vens (Lat.), rolling together, as *involven'tia Fo'lia* used by A. P. de Candolle, for trifoliate leaves whose leaflets rise up, unite at the summit . . . so as to form an arch which shelters the flowers, as in *Trifolium incarnatum,* Linn. (Lindley).

io'des (ἰώδης, violet-coloured), *iodi'nus,* violet ; **I'odine,** an elementary body obtained from marine Algae, etc.; **io'nides,** violet-coloured.

I'on (ἰὸν, neut. of ἰὼν, past part. of εἰμί, I go), a physical term, defined by J. F. Clark as the division of a molecule ; adj. **io'nic** ; **Ioniza'tion,** the partitioning of a molecule ; **ioni'zed,** divided into ions.

I'ridile (+ ILE), a society of *Iris* (Clements).

irreg'ular, *irregula'ris* (Late Lat., not according to rule), (1) wanting in regularity of form ; (2) asymmetric, as a flower which cannot be halved in any plane, or one which is capable of bisection in one plane only, zygomorphic ; ~ **Pelor'ia,** a monstrosity by which irregular form has become regular by symmetric development ; **Irregular'ity,** *Irregular'itas,* the state of being unequal in form.

Irritabil'ity (*irritabilis,* easily excited), phenomena induced by stimuli, such as shock, absence or presence of light, warmth, gravity, etc.

is'abelline, *isabelli'nus* (Mod. Lat., refers to Isabella, Queen of Spain), a greyish drab colour, a dirty tawny tint.

isadelph'ous, *-us* (ἴσος, equal to ; ἀδελφὸς, a brother), equal brother-

hood, the number of stamens in the
two phalanges being equal.
I'satin, the colouring principle of
woad, *Isatis tinctoria*, Linn.
isid'ioid, resembling the Lichen genus,
Isidium; **isidiif'erous** (*fero*, I bear),
bearing a thallus like the genus
whence it derives its name.
isid'iose (*ἴσις* = a genus of corals ;
+OSUS) ; **isidio'sus,** having powdery,
coral-like excrescences ; **Isid'ium**
(*εἶδος*, like), the coral-like elevation of
a Lichen thallus with a globule on it.
I'slands, a term applied to isolated
strands of phloëm in the xylem.
i'so- (*ἴσος*, equal to), Drude's prefix
to denote the uniformity as to light,
temperature and rain, of certain
groups of plants ; **isoand'rospore** (+
ANDROSPORE), Janet's term for the
spermatozoids of *Marchantia;* **iso-
bilat'eral** (*bis*, twice ; *latus, lateris*,
a side), capable of being divided
into two similar halves ; **isobria'tus,**
dicotyledonary ; **isob'rious** (*βριάω*, I
strengthen), of equal strength, referring to the embryo of Dicotyledons ;
I'socheim (*χεῖμα*, winter), the isotherm of the coldest months ; **iso-
cho'mous** (*χῶμα*, a mound), applied
to branches springing from the same
stem at the same angle ; **isocot'ylous**
(+ COTYLEDON), having equally
developed cotyledons ; **isochro'mous**
(*χρῶμα*, colour), all of one colour or
hue, uniform in tint ; **isocy'clic**
(*κύκλος*, a circle), eucyclic, a flower
having isomerous whorls ; **isodia-
met'ric** (*διά*, through ; *μέτρον*, a
measure), of equal dimensions ; ~
Cells, those having an equal diameter in each direction ; **Isodi'ode**
(*δίοδος*, a passage), when all the
DIODES produced are alike (Van
Tieghem) ; **Isodi'ody** the condition
of producing Diodes which give
rise to unisexual prothallia (Van
Tieghem) ; **isody'namous** (*δύναμις*,
power), equally developed.
Isoe'toid, applied to a leaf which is
linear, undivided, terete, often
tubular, and sessile, which occurs
in *Isoëtes, Pilularia*, etc. (Warming).

Isogam'ete (*ἴσος*, equal ; *γαμέτης*, a
spouse), gametes or sexual cells of
similar size and appearance, which
conjugate and result in a zygote ;
Isogametang'ium (+GAMETANGIUM)
the organ which produces isogametes ;
isogametan'gial, pertaining to an
isogametangium ; ~ **-copula'tion,**
when the gametangia and nuclei
are alike (Hartmann) ; **isog'amous**
(*γάμος*, marriage), used for those
plants which produce isogametes ;
Isog'amy, the fusion of similar
sexual cells ; **isogenotyp'ic** (+
GENOTYPE), where two or more
generic names have been applied to
the same type species ; **isog'enous**
(*γένος*, race), employed by Johannsen
for individuals which belong to the
same "genotype," *i. e.* = biotype ; ~
Induc'tion, used by Noll to express
sensitive movements arising from a
single cause ; **isog'onous** (*γόνος*, offspring), used of hybrids which combine the parental characters in equal
degree (De Vries) ; *cf.* ANISOGON-
OUS ; **Isogyn'ospore** (+ GYNOSPORE),
Janet's term for the egg of *Marchantia* ; **isog'ynous** (*γυνή*, a woman),
having the pistils similar ; **isogy'rus**
‡ (*γυρός*, round), forming a complete
spire ; **Isoholog'amy** (*ὅλος*, whole ;
γάμος, marriage), when the coalescing individuals are entirely alike
(Hartmann) ; **isolat'eral** (*lateralis*,
pertaining to the side), (1) equal
sided ; (2) employed by Heinricher
for "central" ; ~ **Leaves,** those
which possess palisade tissue on
both surfaces.
Isola'tion (Fr., isolation, insulation,
from *insula*, an island), the prevention of intercrossing between a
separated section of a species or
kind and the rest of that species
or kind (Romanes).
Isomalt'ose (*ἴσος*, equal to; +MALTOSE),
a product of amylodextrin, passing
by fermentation into maltose ; **iso-
mer'ic, isom'erous,** *-us* (*μέρος*, a
part), (1) having the same elements
in the same proportions, but with
different properties ; (2) having

203

members of successive cycles equal in number, as the petals and sepals ; **Isomerog′amy** (μέρος, a part ; γάμος, marriage), the copulation of isogametes, as in many Algae (Hartmann) ; **I′somorph** (μορφή, shape), similar in external form, but not in essential structure ; a mineralogical term; **Isomorph′ism**, the condition described, as exemplified by the outward agreement of purple *Crocus* and *Colchicum ;* **isoph′agous** (φάγω, I eat), applied to Fungi which attack one, or several allied species (Eriksson) ; **isophe′nous** (φαίνω, I appear), used of individuals which belong to the same phenotype (Johannsen) ; **isoph′orous** (φορέω, I carry), transformable into something else (Crozier) ; **isopho′tic** (φῶς, φωτὸς, light), equally illuminated, as leaves which are erect, so that both sides are exposed to the light (Clements) ; **Isopho′tophyll** (φύλλον, a leaf), a leaf in which both halves of the chlorenchym are alike, due to equal illumination (Clements) ; **isophyl′lous**, (1) leaves alike, in shape or size ; (2) bilateral ; **Isophyl′ly**, (1) the condition described ; (2) "bilaterality expressed in the form of two equal sides about an axis of the member in the tangential plane of the system" (Church) ; **Isophytot′-onus** (φυτὸν, a plant ; τόνος, strain), in temperature identical with the plant's requirements (Clements) ; **Isoplan′ogametes** (πλάνος, wandering ; + GAMETE), motile sexual cells of equal size, occurring in Algae ; **isopo′lar** (*polus*, a pole), an axis of Diatom frustules is so termed when its extremities are similar (O. Mueller) ; **Isopro′thally** (+ PROTHALLUS), producing prothallia which are similar in sexual character (Van Tieghem) ; **i′soschist** (σχιστὸς, split), applied to a cell of a brood, all of which are equal in size and function (Hartog) ; **isosmot′ic** (ὠσμὸς, impulse, pushing), passing by osmosis in or out with equal facility ; **I′sospore** (σπορά, seed), a spore produced

by one of the **Isospo′reae**, plants having one kind of spore, as in Ferns, opposed to heterosporous; **isos′porous**, homosporous, or having one kind of spore only ; **Isosp′ory**, the state of producing one sort of spore; **isoste′monous**, *-nus*, having as many stamens as petals, or sepals ; **Isoste′mony**, equality in number of stamens with the segments of the perianth whorls ; **isos′tic**, Van Tieghem's term when the mother root has more than two xylem bundles ; **I′sothere**(θέρος,summer),an isotherm of the hottest months (Boulger) ; **isoton′ic** (τόνος, a strand, a brace) **Concentra′tion**, that degree of different solutions in which they attract water with equal force (De Vries) ; **isos′tomous** (στόμα, a mouth), the calyx and corolla the same size ; **Isot′rophy** (τροφή, food),equalgrowth all round : adj. **isotroph′ic** ; **isosty′-lous** (+ STYLUS), the styles being similar, opposed to heterostylous; **Isot′rophyte** (τροφή, food ; φύτον, a plant), a parasitic Fungus whose influence is only chemical, with but slight changes in the host (Wakker); **isot′ropous** (τρόπος, direction), equal torsion in development, as in valvate and contorted aestivation (K. Schumann) ; **Isot′ropy**, capable of being attracted in any direction ; **I′sotype** (τύπος, a type), forms common to different countries ; **isotyp′ic**, described from more than one species, all of which are congeneric.

Isth′mus (ἰσθμὸς, a neck of land), (1) the narrowed connection between half-cells of Desmids; (2) the girdle of such Diatoms as *Isthmia*.

itera′to-prolif′erous (*iteratus*, repeated ; + PROLIFEROUS), repeatedly bearing prolifications.

Iteol′ogy (ἰτέα, a willow ; λόγος, discourse), the study of the genus *Salix*, willows; adj. **iteolog′ic**.

ithyphyl′lus (ἰθύς, straight ; φύλλον, a leaf), straight and stiff-leaved.

-ium (-εῖον, locative affix), suffix denoting a formation (Clements).

ix′ous (ἰξὸς, bird-lime), sticky, viscous (Heinig).

Jac′ulator (Lat., a darter), a hook-like process on the placenta of certain fruits, which aids in the expulsion of the seeds, as in Acanthaceae (Boulger).

Jag′gery, a coarse dark sugar from the coco-nut and other palms, which produces arrack by fermentation.

Jal′apin, a constituent of the officinal Jalap, a purgative root, derived from *Ipomoea Purga* (Hayne).

Jama′icin, an alkaloid occurring in the cabbage bark-tree, *Andira inermis*, Kunth, a native of the West Indies.

Jamin′s Chain, a chain of air and water in the vessels of plants.

jaspid′eus, or iaspid′eus (Lat., from *iasper*, jasper), a mixture of many colours arranged in small spots.

Je′terus, a mistake of Bischoff, copied by Lindley, for ICTERUS, vegetable jaundice.

Join′ing, used by Babington for the point of union of two different parts ; a node.

Joint, an articulation, as a node in grasses or other plants; joint′ed, articulated, falling apart at the joints.

jonquil′leus (Mod. Lat.), the bright yellow of the Jonquil, *Narcissus odorus*, Linn.

Jord′anism, an excessive multiplication of so-called species, regarded as mere varieties which are tolerably constant under cultivation : the name is derived from Alexis Jordan of Lyons ; *cf.* MICROSPECIES, or elementary species.

Ju′ba (Lat., a mane), a loose panicle, with diliquescent axis ; juba′tus, maned.

ju′gate (*juga′tus*, connected or yoked together), used in composition as conjugate, bijugate, etc.

Ju′gum (Lat., a yoke), pl. Ju′ga ; (1) a pair of leaflets ; (2) the ridges on the fruits of Umbelliferae.

Juice, the liquid contents of any plant-tissue ; ~ Ves′sels, J. Hill′s term for vascular tissue ; juice′less, dry, exsuccous.

jula′ceous, -ceus (*julus*, Mod. Lat., an amentum or spike ; + ACEOUS), bearing catkins, amentaceous ; ju′liform (*forma*, shape), like a catkin ; Ju′lus, an old term for catkin, or spike, such as in *Acorus Calamus*, Linn.

junca′ceous (*juncus*, a rush), rush-like ; Junce′tum, an association of a species of *Juncus ;* junc′oid (εἶδος, resemblance), junc′ous, jun′ceous, rush-like.

Junctu′ra (Lat., a joint), an articulation or note.

Jungerman′nia Form, applied to plants having distichous leaves, usually orbicular and shortly stalked (Warming).

Jun′gle, wild forests and thickets in India, referred by Warming to the savannah type.

juniperi′nus, bluish-brown, like the berries of the juniper (Hayne).

Junquill′o-pam′pa, pampas characterized by *Sporobolus arundinaceus*.

Jute, the fibre of *Corchorus capsularis*, Linn., and *C. olitorius*, Linn.

Juvenes′cence (*juvenesco*, I grow young again) = REJUVENESCENCE.

ju′venile (*juvenilis*, youthful), applied by Goebel to the early forms, as the larval-forms of conifers.

Juxta′position (*juxta*, close to ; *positus*, placed), the relative position in which organs are placed.

K, for many words see also under the letter C.

Kalid′ion, Kalid′ium ; pl. Kalid′ia (καλίδιον, from καλιά, gianary) = CYSTOCARP.

kamptod′rom:ous = CAMPTODROMOUS.

Kar-herb′age (Ger. Karflur), the plants occurring in hollows high amongst mountains ("Kar" is an Austrian geological term for hollows dug out by glaciers).

karpotrop′ic = CARPOTROPIC.

Karyas′ter (κάρυον, a nut; + ASTER), the spindle-figure of the nucleus ; Karyochyle′ma (χυλὸς, juice), pro-

posed by Strasburger for ACHRO-
MATIN ; **Karyoderm′atoplast**, pl.
(δέρμα, δέρματος, the skin; πλαστὸς,
moulded), kinoplasmic asters of
Synchitrium (Kusano); **Karyogam′-
etes** (+ GAMETE), gametonuclei ;
their union is KARYOGAMY ; **Karyo-
g′amy** (γάμος, marriage), the union
of gametonuclei, to form a zygote-
nucleus (Maupas) ; **Kar′yoids** (εἶδος,
like), minute spherical bodies attached to the chlorophyll plate of
Conjugatae and Desmids ; **Karyo-
kine′sis** (κίνησις, motion, I change),
Schleicher's term for the series of
changes undergone by the nucleus
in cell-division; "also spelled Caryo-
cinesis" (Crozier); it is the indirect
division of Flemming ; adj. **karyo-
kinet′ic** ; **Karyol′ogy** (λόγος, discourse), the science of the nucleus
and its development and vital history (Trow); **Kar′yolymph** (+
LYMPH), the nuclear liquid ; **Karyo-
l′ysis** (γύσις, a loosing), the dissolution of the nucleus, in whole or in
part; adj. **karyolyt′ic**; **Karyomito′sis**
(μίτος, a thread or web) = MITOSIS ;
Karyomix′is (μῖξις, intercourse), the
fusion of the two nuclei of a teleutospore (Vuillemin and Maire); **Karyo-
ph′agy** (φάγος, a glutton), the destruction of a nucleus by a special
parasite (Dangeard); **Kar′yoplasm**
(πλάσμα, moulded), the more fluid
protoplasm of the nucleus, between
the nuclear threads ; **Kar′yoplast**,
Strasburger's term for the nucleus
in its entirety ; **Karyorhe′xis** (ῥῆξις,
a breaking), rapid dissolution of a
nucleus (Maire); **Karyoso′ma** (σῶμα,
a body), a close mass of microsomes
in a nucleus ; pl. **Karyoso′mata** ;
Karyosymph′ysis (σύμφυσις, growing
together), nuclear fusion (Hartog).
Kat′ablast (κατὰ, down; βλαστὸς, a
bud), a shoot from an underground
stock.
katabol′ic (καταβάλλω, I cast down),
descending metabolism, the breaking up of compounds into simpler
bodies ; **Katab′olism**, destructive
metabolism ; **Katab′olite**, any pro-

duct of destructive metabolism ; *cf.*
ANABOLITE.
Kataklinot′ropism (κατὰ, down; κλίνω.
I bend), negative klinotropism ;
Kat′alase, see CATALASE ; **Kata-
lysa′tor**, any substance which causes
katalysis (= CATALYSIS); **katalyt′ic**
= CATALYTIC ; **kataphor′ic** (φορέω,
I carry), the power of carrying off
or away; **Kat′astates**, pl. (στατὸς, a
standing), intermediate products of
katabolism, during the breaking
down of protoplasm (Parker); **kata-
ton′ic** (τόνος, a strain), tending to
decrease a stimulus ; **katatrop′ic**
(τροπὴ, a turning), negatively tropic ;
Katelectrot′onus (ἤλεκτρον, amber ;
τόνος, strain), heightened excitation
in plants due to an electric current
(Hörmann).
Katharo′bia (καθαρὸς, clean, pure;
βίος, life), organisms of clean water.
kathod′ic (κάθοδος, a descent), that
half of a leaf which is turned away
from the direction in which the
genetic spiral turns; the opposite of
ANODIC.
Keel, or CARINA, (1) a ridge like the
keel of a boat ; (2) the two anterior
and united petals of a papilionaceous
corolla; ~ -punc′ta, pl., nodulated
thickenings on one margin of the
valves of *Nitzschia* (O'Meara); **keeled**,
carinate.
Kenap′ophytes (κενὸς, empty ; + APO-
PHYTES), plants which colonize
cleared land (Simmons); **Ken-
ench′yma** (ἔγχυμα, an infusion),
permanent tissue which has lost its
living contents, as cork-tissue ; in
Ger., "Leerzellengewebe."
Keramid′ium = CERAMIDIUM, or
Cystocarp.
kermesi′nus (Mod. Lat.), carmine, a
colour from Kermes.
Ker′nel, (1) the nucellus of an ovule, or
of a seed, that is, the whole body
within the coats ; (2) the softer
part of the pyrenocarp within the
outer wall in certain Fungi.
Ke′tones (a variation of "Acetone"),
a class of ethereal oils; camphor is
probably one of this class.

Ket′tle-traps, applied to such flowers as those of *Aristolochia*, which imprison insects until fertilization is effected.

Key, (1) a clavis or short statement of the contrasted characters of a genus or other group; (2) or **Key-fruit,** the SAMARA of sycamore or ash.

kid′ney-form, kid′ney-shaped, oblately cordate; crescent-shaped, with the ends rounded.

Kin′ases, pl., ferments or enzymes.

Kind, genus or species, a sort.

Kine′sis (κίνησις, motion), (1) movement, used by T. W. Engelmann in contradistinction to TAXIS; (2) = KARYOKINESIS; **kinet′ic,** relating to kinesis; ~ **En′ergy,** the energy of actual motion, as opposed to potential energy; **Kine′tosomes,** pl. (σῶμα, a body), small polar plates or bodies of kinoplasm present before mitosis, presumably material for the formation of the spindle-fibres (Allen).

kin′ic (*Kina-Kina*, a name for Cinchona), pertaining to cinchona; ~ **Ac′id,** an organic acid in *Cinchona* barks.

King′dom, one of the highest groups of organic nature; the **Veg′etable** ~ includes all plants.

Ki′noplasm (κινέω, I set in motion; πλάσμα, moulded), that part of cytoplasm involved in spindle formation, as contrasted with TROPHOPLASM; **Ki′nospore** (+ SPORE), a spore resulting from a simple process of division, as motile zoospores, conidia, pycnidospores (Klebs).

Klado′dium = CLADODE.

Kleisanthe′ry = CLEISANTHERY.

kleistogam′ic, kleistog′amous = CLEISTOGAMIC.

Klinogeot′ropism (κλίνω, I bend; γῆ, the earth; τροπή, a turning), the drooping tendency of the free end of a climbing plant whilst mutating (Pfeffer); **Klinomorph′y** (μορφή, a shape), Wiesner's term for the condition of an organ determined by the simultaneous oblique position of the principal and median planes, so that the right and left halves may be distinguished as upper and lower, resulting in a different shape of the two halves; **klinorrhom′bic** (ῥόμβος, a rhomb), a mineralogic term applied by De Bary to oblique rhombic crystals in plants; **Kli′nostat** = CLINOSTAT; **klinotrop′ic** = CLINOTROPIC; **Klinot′ropism** = CLINOTROPISM.

Knaur = GNAUR.

Knee, (1) an abrupt bend in a stem or tree-trunk; (2) an outgrowth of some tree-roots; **-joint′ed,** geniculate; ~ **-pan-shaped,** concavo-convex, patelliform; **kneed,** geniculate.

Knight-Dar′win Law, generally understood as "that no organic being fertilizes itself for an eternity of generations"; preferably "Nature abhors perpetual self-fertilization," *cf.* F. Darwin in *Nature,* lviii., 630–632.

knob-like = GONGYLODES; **knobbed** = TORULOSE; **knob′by** = NODOSE.

Knobs, used by Sir J. E. Smith for CEPHALODIA.

Knor′ria, formerly a genus of fossil plants, now used for lepidodendroid stems when their cortex has been stripped off to a considerable but variable depth (Scott).

Knot, (1) a node in the stem of grasses; (2) a swelling in stems at the attachment of the leaf; (3) various diseases caused by Fungi, as **Black** ~, effected by *Plowrightia morbosa,* Sacc. (Tubeuf); **Knot-phase,** in nuclear-division, is also known as skein-stage, or spirem; **Knot-stage** = SKEIN in nuclear division; **knot′ted, knot′ty,** nodose.

Knur, Knurl, a knob or hard substance = GNAUR.

koele′rian, relating to *Rubus Koeleri* or its close allies.

Koleoch′yma (κολεὸς, a sheath; ἔγχυμα, an infusion) = KRITENCHYMA.

Kol′laplankton (κόλλα, glue; + PLANKTON), used of organisms which float by being encased in gelatinous envelopes (Forel); **Kollen′chym** (ἔγχυμα, an infusion) = HYPNODERM.

Kremast′oplank′ton (κρεμαστὸς, hung up; + PLANKTON), floating organisms supplied with appendages which conduce to that function, as hairs, prickles, etc. (Forel).

Kriten′chyma (κριτὸς, chosen; ἔγχυμα, an infusion), one or more layers of cells which form a sheath for a vascular bundle (Russow).

Kryp′toblast (κρυπτὸς, hidden; βλαστὸς, a bud), a preventitious bud (Hartig).

Kryptocotyle′dons = CRYPTOCOTYLEDONS.

Kun′changraph (Sanscrit, Kunchan, contraction; γραφὴ, writing; pron. Kŏŏnchangraph), apparatus to measure longitudinal contraction (Bose).

Ku′tine = CUTIN.

kyanoph′ilous (κύανος, blue; φιλέω, I love), used of any tissue which readily absorbs blue staining; **Ky′anophyll** (φύλλον, a leaf), nearly pure chlorophyll freed from its associated yellow pigment, xanthophyll (Wiesner); it is bluish-green in colour.

La′bel (*labellum*, a little lip), (1) Grew's term for the pinnule or ultimate segment of a Fern-frond; (2) LABELLUM; **Label′lum**, (1) the third petal of Orchids, usually enlarged, and by torsion of the ovary become anterior, from its normal posterior position; (2) a similar petal in other flowers.

la′biate, *labia′tus* (Lat., lipped), lipped. usually bilabiate; characteristic of the family Labiatae; **labiatiflor′ous**, *-rus*, used of certain Compositae with bilabiate corollas to their florets; **labioscop′ic** (+ LABIUM, σκοπέω, I look), employed by Pfitzer for the condition of certain Orchids when the sepals are combined with an extension of the axis, as in *Drymoda*.

la′bile (*labilis*, slippery), "plastic, easily modified" (Clements); perishable or transient.

la′biose, *labio′sus* (Lat., having large lips), applied to a polypetalous corolla seemingly two-lipped; **La′bium** (Lat., a lip), (1) the lower lip of a

Labiate flower; (2) the lip subtending the ligule in *Isoëtes*.

Laboulbenomyce′tes, Engler's term for Laboulbeniaceae and their allies.

labyrinthifor′mis (*labyrinthus*, a structure with winding passages; *forma*, shape), marked by sinuous lines, *cf.*, DAEDALEUS.

Lac (Ital., *lacca*, a varnish), a resinous exudation from various tropical plants, occurring in commerce in different forms; **Lac′case**, the enzyme which produces LACQUER, from fluid lac; **lac′cate**, as though varnished; **Lac′cine**, a substance found in lac, insoluble in water, alcohol, or ether.

lac′erate, *lac′erus*, Mod. Lat. (*lacer*, mangled); **lacera′ted** *lacera′tus*, torn, or irregularly cleft.

Lach′rima = LACRIMA.

Lacin′ia (Lat., the flap of a garment), a slash or slender lobe; **Lacinia′tion**, fission; **lacin′iate**, *lacinia′tus*, slashed, cut into narrow lobes; **lacin′iform** (*forma*, shaped), fringelike (Crozier); **Lacin′ule**, (1) a diminutive lacina or lobe; (2) the incurved point of the petal in many Umbelliferae; **lacin′ulate, lacin′ulose**, finely laciniate, possessing lacinulae.

Lac′quer, a Japanese varnish; *cf.* LAC and LACCASE.

Lac′rima (Lat., a tear), a drop of gum or resin exuded from a tree; also spelled **Lach′ryma** and **Lach′rima**; **lac′rimiform**, *lacrimiform′is* (*forma*, shape), tear-shaped; sometimes but less correctly spelled **lach′rymaeform**, etc.

Lac′tase (*lac*, milk), Beijerink's name for an enzyme which inverts sugar, but is distinct from Invertase; **Lac′teals, Lac′tifer** (*fero*, I bear); **Lac′tents**, Grew's names for lacticiferous ducts; **lactes′cent**, *lactes′cens*, yielding milky juice; **lac′teus** (Lat.), milky, white as milk; **lactic′olor** (*color*, colour), milk-white; **lacti′ferous**, Grew's word for laticiferous; **Lac′tose**, milk-sugar; the sweet principle of milk, and stated to occur in the fruit of *Achras Sapota*, Linn.

Lactuca′rium, the dried juice of the lettuce, *Lactuca sativa*, Linn., containing an active principle, **Lac′tucine**.

Lacu′na (Lat., a hole or cavity), (1) an air-space in the midst of tissue; (2) a depression on the thallus of a Lichen; (3) applied to the vallecular canals of *Equisetum;* **lacu′nar**, pertaining to or arising from lacunae; ~ **Tis′sue**, thin-walled cells, forming irregular trabeculae radially traversing the intercellular cavity of the stem of *Selaginella;* it may be regarded as the equivalent of the Bundle-Sheath of most other vascular Cryptogams; **lacu′no-rimo′sus**, marked with irregular cracks and excavations; **lacu′no-ru′gose**, ~ *-rugosus*, having irregular wrinkles, as the stone of the peach; **lacu′nose**, *lacuno′sus*, (1) when the surface is covered with depressions; (2) perforated with holes.

lacus′tral (*lacus*, a pond or lake), H. C. Watson's term for plants which are usually floating in water or immersed; **lacus′trine**, *lacus′tris*, belonging to, or inhabiting lakes or ponds; the form *lacus′ter* has been introduced of late years.

laev′igate, *laeviga′tus* (*levigatus*, smooth, slippery), smooth, as if polished.

lae′vis (*levis*, smooth), smooth, in the sense of not being rough.

Lage′nian, pertaining to Leinster, from *Lagenia*, the Latin name of that province.

lage′niform, *lageniform′is* (*lagena*, a flask; *forma*, shape), shaped like a Florence flask.

Lagenost′ome, the free apex of the nucellus in *Lagenostoma*.

lago′pus (λαγώπους, hare's foot), harefooted, densely covered with long hair.

Lair-flo′ra, the flora growing upon ground manured by animals, as sheep or goats (Crampton); ~ -**herb′age**, the plants forming a similar flora.

Lam′el, *Lamel′la* (Lat., a thin plate or scale), a thin plate; pl., **Lamel′lae**, the gills of Agarics; **Lamel′la, mid′-dle**, the membrane or primary septum between any two cells; **lam′ellar**, *lamella′ris*, composed of thin plates; **lam′ellate**, *lamella′tus*, made up of thin plates, as the hymenium of the mushroom; **lamel′liform** (*forma*, shape), in the shape of a plate or scale; **lam′ellose**, *lamello′sus* = LAMELLATE; **Lamel′lulae**, the gills of Fungi.

Lam′ina (Lat., a thin leaf), the limb, blade, or expanded part of a leaf; ~ **prolig′era**, ~ **sporig′era**, the disk or centre of the apothecium of a Lichen; **lamina′ted**, consisting of plates or layers; ~ **Bulb**, a tunicated bulb, as *i*, hyacinth; **lamina′ting**, separating into layers.

Laminarie′tum, an association of the marine algal genus *Laminaria;* **lamina′rioid** (εἶδος, resemblance), resembling or akin to the genus *Laminaria*.

La′na (Lat.), wool, or woolly covering; **la′nate**, *lanatus*, clothed with woolly and intergrown hairs.

lan′ceolate, *lanceola′tus* (Lat., armed with a little lance), (1) narrow, tapering to each end; Linnaeus used it for a leaf having nearly similar extremities, but in modern use the base is usually somewhat broadened, with the greatest breadth at about one-third from the base; (2) the primitive meaning is preserved in *Carduus lanceolatus*, Linn.; ~ -**has′tate**, a hastate leaf with the principal lobe lanceolate; ~ -**sag′ittate**, a sagittate leaf, the middle lobe lanceolate; **lance-o′vate** (Crozier), lanceolate ovate, indicative of a form intermediate between the two named terms; **lance-shaped**, lanceolate.

Landes (Fr.), tracts of "Erica-maquis" in the south of France, but destitute of raw humus (Warming).

la′nose, *lano′sus* (Lat.) woolly, *cf.* LANATE.

lanu′ginose, **lanu′ginous**, *lanugino′sus* (Lat.), woolly or cottony, clothed

with **Lanu'go** (Lat.), woolliness; long
and interwoven hairs.

lapid'eus (Lat., stony), **lapillo'sus**,
stony, as the seeds of "stone
fruits"; **lap'idose**, *lapido'sus*, growing amongst stones.

lappa'ceous, *lappa'ceus* (Lat.), bur-like,
hamate.

lar'val (*larva*, a mask), (1) applied to
the resting stage, as the sclerotium
of ergot; (2) the early form of certain
Conifers, whose perfect and adult
form is very different; **larva'tus**
(Lat.) personate.

lasian'thus (λάσιος, shaggy; ἄνθος, a
flower), woolly-flowered; **lasiocar'-
pous** (καρπὸς, fruit), pubescent-
fruited.

latebro'sus (Lat., full of lurking
places), hidden.

La'tency (*latens*, hidden) of characters,
applied to those which are not observable until brought out in the hybrid
generation by crossing; **la'tent**, dormant; ∼ **Bud**, an adventitious bud;
∼ **Fac'tors**, allelomorphs by themselves invisible, yet when combined
in cross-breeding with certain others,
produce the appearance of new
characters; ∼ **Pe'riod**, (1) resting-
stage; (2) the time required to take
up any stimulus, and respond to it
(Macdougal).

Lat'era, pl. of **Lat'us** (Lat., a side),
the sides; **lat'eral**, *latera'lis*, fixed
on or near the side of an organ; ∼
Bud, adventitious bud; ∼ **Dehis'-
cence**, bursting or opening at the
side; ∼ **Nucle'olus**, ∼ **Nu'cleus**, *cf.*
PARANUCLEUS; ∼ **Plane**, the vertical plane at right angles to the
antero-posterior plane, as of a flower;
∼ **View** of a Diatom frustule, when
the valves are seen in front view, the
girdle being then in side view;
Lateral-geot'ropism(+GEOTROPISM),
the movement of climbing plants
laterally to a support, neither positive nor negative geotropism (Strasburger); **Lateral'ity**, used by Sachs
for SYMMETRY, both radial and
dorsiventral.

lateric'ious or **laterit'ious**, *lateric'ius*,

laterit'ius (Lat., made of bricks),
brick-red.

laterifo'lious (*latus*, *lateris*, a side;
folium, a leaf), growing on the side
of a leaf at the base; **lateriner'vis**,
lateriner'vius (*nervus*, a nerve),
straight-veined, as in grasses; **lateri-
stip'ulus** ‡ (+ STIPULA), having
stipules growing on its sides.

La'tex (Lat., juice), (1) the milky
juice of such plants as spurge or
lettuce; (2) the moisture of the
stigma; (3) the gelatinous matter
surrounding the spores in some
Fungi; ∼ **Cells**, laticiferous coenocytes; ∼ **Gran'ules**, starch or other
granules floating in the latex; ∼
Hairs, hairs continuous with latex-
tubes, easily breaking and then
liberating drops of latex; ∼ **Sacs**,
specialized cells, containing latex; ∼
Tubes, laticiferous vessels; ∼ **Vess'els**,
anastomosing vessels derived from the
original septa becoming absorbed.

laticif'erous (*latex*, *laticis*, juice; *fero*,
I bear), latex-bearing; ∼ **Cells**,
structures which are not cell-fusions;
∼ **Coe'nocytes**, branched cells or
vessels like cells containing latex;
∼ **Tis'sue**, the system of cells or
vessels; ∼ **Ves'sels**, the tubes or
similar structures which have milky
juice, usually branched syncytes,
the walls between adjacent cells
being absorbed; **Latic'ifers**, laticiferous cells or vessels.

latifo'liate, **latifo'lious**, *latifo'lius*
(Lat.), broad-leaved.

latisep'tal (*latus*, broad; *septum* a
hedge), applied to those Crucifers
which have broad septa in their
silicles as Honesty, *Lunaria annua*,
Linn.; **latisep'tate**, *latisep'tus*, with
broad partitions.

lat'ticed, cross-barred; ∼ **Cell** =
SIEVE-TUBE.

Laur'ad (λαύρα, a drain; + AD), a
drain plant; **Lauri'um**, "sewer formation"; **lauroph'ilus** (φιλέω, I love),
"sewer-dwelling"; **Laurophy'ta**
(φύτον, a plant), "sewer plants"
(Clements).

Lauriligno'sa (*laurus*, laurel; *lignosus*,

woody), woods with dominance of evergreen, mostly glabrous bright green leaves; in moist subtropics; Lauri'on, an association of laurels; Laurisil'vae, pl. (*silva*, a wood), the knysna forest of South Africa; Lau'rin, an acrid principle from the berries of *Laurus nobilis* (Linn.).

lav'ender, pale bluish grey; the colour of the flowers of *Lavandula vera*, DC.

lax, *lax'us* (Lat.), loose, distant.

Lay'er, (1) the stroma or receptacle of Fungi; (2) in propagation, a branch caused to root whilst still connected with the parent; (3) different strata of growth, as trees above a lower stratum of shrubs and again of herbaceous plants; ab'sciss ~, usually corky tissue cutting off the leaf from the branch; lig'nified ~, at the base of the leaf before leaf-fall; protec'tive ~, partly suberized; Separa'tion ~, the absciss layer in leaf-fall; Lay'erage, term proposed by L. H. Bailey for propagation by layering, or the state of being so multiplied; Lay'ering, the art of making layers; Lay'ing, a gardener's term for the preceding.

lazuli'nus (Mod. Lat.), ultramarine blue, a pigment obtained from "Lapis Lazuli."

leach'y, losing material by percolation, as rain washing away nutriment through the soil; Leach'ing, is the action itself.

lead-col'oured, dull grey; *cf.* PLUMBEUS.

Lea'der, the primary or terminal shoot of a tree.

Leaf, the principal appendage or lateral organ borne by the stem or axis; it is a sim'ple ~ when undivided, com'pound ~ when divided into distinct parts; ~ Arrang'ement, see PHYLLOTAXIS; ~ Blade = LAMINA; ~ Blis'ter, disease of pear-leaves due to *Taphrina bullata*; ~ Blotch, black patches on sycamore leaves caused by *Rhytisma acerinum*; ~ Bud, a bud which develops into a leafy branch; opposed to a "Flower Bud"; ~ Cast, pine-

leaves diseased by *Lophodermium Pinastri*; ~ Curl, disease due to attack of *Exoascus* on peach leaves; Cy'cle, in phyllotaxis, a spiral which passes through the insertions of intermediate leaves till it attains the next leaf exactly above its starting point; ~ Fall, defoliation; ~ Green = CHLOROPHYLL; ~ Pores = STOMATA; ~ Scar, the mark or cicatrix left by the articulation and fall of a leaf; ~ Scorch, fungus attacks on leaves of various plants, appearing as if scorched; ~ Sheath, the lower part of the petiole which more or less invests the stem; ~ Spot, diseased portions due to fungus attacks on the leaves of many species; ~ Stalk = PETIOLE; ~ Ten'dril, one which is a transformed leaf; ~ Trace, all the common bundles in a stem belonging to one leaf.

Leaf'ing, the unfolding of leaves; Leaf'it, Withering's term for LEAF-LET; leaf'less, wanting leaves; Leaf'let, the blade or separate division of a compound leaf; leaf'like = FOLIACEOUS; leaf'y, full of leaves.

leath'er-yel'low, a vague term for the tint of tan or buff leather; alutaceous.

leath'ery, tough, coriaceous.

Leaves, pl., Pock'et ~ or Man'tle ~, specialized leaves which accumulate humus, as *Asplenium Nidus*, etc.

lecanor'ine, resembling the apothecium of the genus *Lecanora*, which has a paler margin arising from the thallus.

lecid'eiform (*forma*, shape), lecid'eine, like the apothecium of *Lecidea*, which has a margin of the same colour as the disc; lecid'ioid (εἶδος, resemblance), lecideiform.

Le'cithin (λήκυθος, an oil-flask), a type of white, waxy, phosphorus-containing substances, some of which have been separated from the seeds of maize, peas and wheat.

lecot'ropal (λέκος, a dish; τροπή, a turning), shaped like a horse-shoe, as some ovules, *cf.* LYCOTROPOUS.

Lec'totype (λεκτὸς, chosen ; τύπος, a type), a specimen of the original series, chosen after the original description to be the type.

Le'cus (λέχος, a bed) = CORM.

leek-green, vivid green, prasinous.

left, sinistrorse ; see Appendix C.

legit'imate (*legitimus*, allowed by law) **Fertiliz'ation**, in dimorphic or trimorphic plants, fertilization by its own-form pollen, as short-styled flowers by pollen from other shortstamened flowers, etc. (Darwin).

Leg'ume, *Legu'men* (Lat., pulse), the seed-vessel of Leguminosae, onecelled and two-valved, but various in form ; **Legu'min**, an albuminoid from pulse, vegetable casein ; **legu'-minous**, *legumina'ris*, (1) pertaining to a legume ; or (2) to the order Leguminosae.

Leimonap'ophyte (λειμὼν, a meadow; + APOPHYTE), a plant introduced into grassland.

leiodermar'ian, resembling *Leiodermaria* in external markings (Scott).

Lem'ma (λέμμα, a husk), the palea or flowering glume of a grass ; **ster'ile** ~, the third glume.

Lemne'tum, an association of *Lemna*, duckweed.

lem'on-col'oured, pale, pure yellow, citreus.

len'diger (*lens, lendis*, a nit), having the appearance of small insects, as the panicle of *Gastridium lendigerum*, Gaud.

Lens (Lat., a lentil ; gen., *lentis*), the contracted tissue of the free portion of the nucellus frequently attached to the base of the lagenostome (F. W. Oliver); ~ **Cells**, cells of the integument capable of focussing light and other rays ; ~ **shaped**, lentil-like, doubly convex, lenticular ; **conden'sing** ~ or **Len'ses**, epidermal papillae causing photosynthetic activity (Haberlandt).

Len'ticel, *Lenticel'la* (*lens, lentis*, a lentil), lenticular corky spots on young bark, corresponding to epidermal stomata ; syn. **Lent'icelle** (Crozier) ; **lenticella'tus** (Mod. Lat.),

having lenticels ; **Lentic'ulae**, "the spore-cases of certain Fungals" (Lindley) ; **lentic'ular**, *lenticula'ris*, **lentiform'is** (*forma*,* shape), like a doubly convex lens ; **len'tiform** (*forma*, shape), doubly convex, shaped like a lentil-seed.

lentig'inose, **lentig'inous**, *lentigino'sus* (Lat., full of freckles, minutely dotted as though freckled.

leochro'mus (λέων, a lion ; χρῶμα, colour), tawny, the colour of a lion's hide ; **leoni'nus** (Lat., pertaining to a lion), something of the same tint.

Lep'al, *Lep'alum* (Mod. Latin, from λεπὶς, a scale), a nectary originating in a barren transformed stamen (J. S. Henslow).

Lepan'thium (λεπὶς, a scale ; ἄνθος, a flower), "a petal which contains a nectary" (Crozier) ; **Lepic'ena** (κενὸς, empty), the glume in grasses, by Richard used for the lower pair of glumes ; **Lep'ides**, pl., scales, usually attached by their centre.

lepidoden'droid (εἶδος, resemblance), like the fossil genus *Lepidodendron*, a carboniferous Lycopod.

lep'idoid (λεπὶς, a scale ; εἶδος, resemblance), as though scaly, applied to leaves, as in *Thuya ;* **lepidophyl'lous** (φύλλον, a leaf), has the same meaning ; **Lep'idophyte**, *Lepidophy'tae* (φυτὸν, a plant), L. Ward's term for Lepidodendroid fossil plants.

lepidopt'erid, used of flowers adapted for lepidopterous pollination ; **Lepi-dopteroph'ilae** (Lepidopteron, φιλέω, I love), applied to plants which are fertilized by lepidopterous insects.

Lepidosper'mae (λεπὶς, a scale ; σπέρμα, seed), applied to seed-bearing Lycopods (Ward).

lepidos'troboid, recalling the fossil genus *Lepidostrobus* in form or making.

lep'idote, *lepido'tus* (λεπιδώτος, scaly), beset with small scurfy scales.

Lepio'ta (λεπὶς, a scale ; οὖς, ὦτὸς, an ear), "the annulus of certain Fungals" (Lindley) ; but *Lepiota* is a genus of Agarics, having been proposed by Persoon for a section of *Agaricus*; **Le′pis**, a scale.

Lepis′ma (λέπισμα, peeled bark), a membranous scale in some Ranunculaceae, an apparently aborted stamen in *Paeonia papaveracea*, Andrz.; several of them enclose the ovary.

Lep′ra (λέπρα, leprosy), a white mealy matter extruded from the surface of some plants; **lep′rose**, **lep′rous**, *lepro′sus*, scurfy.

lep′rarioid, resembling the old Lichen genus *Lepraria*.

leptocen′tric (+ LEPTOME; *centrum*, the middle), when a vascular bundle has the leptome in the middle, with the hadrome round it (Haberlandt).

leptoclad′ous (λεπτὸς, thin; κλάδος, a branch), slender branched.

leptoder′matous, leptoder′mous (λεπτὸς, thin, delicate; δέρμα, skin), thin-coated, used of moss-capsules when pliable; **Lep′toforms** (*forma*, shape), heteroecious Fungi having teleutospores only, which as soon as they arrive at maturity germinate on living plants.

lepto′gioid (εἶδος, resemblance), like the Lichen genus *Leptogium*.

Leptogonid′ium (λεπτὸς, thin, delicate; + GONIDIUM) = MICROGONIDIUM;

Lept′oid (εἶδος, resemblance), a group of six to eight polygonal cells, resembling sieve-tubes, in the leptome of certain Bryophytes (Tansley and Chick); **Lep′tome**, an abbreviation of **Leptomes′tome** (μεστὸς, filled), Haberlandt's expression for the phloëm-like portion of the vascular bundles in vascular plants; **Lep′tome-mantle**, fusion of several leptoids into a layer; ~ **Strand**, modification of the leptome cylinder; **leptomat′ic**, pertaining to the leptome; **Lep′tomin**, a substance found in the leptome of some plants, especially in the sieve-tubes and laticiferous vessels, the presumed function being to convey oxygen (Raciborski); **Leptone′ma** (νῆμα, thread), the delicate thread formed during the tran-

sition from a reticulum to a spirem in synapsis; **Leptonisa′tion**, the reduction of the nucleus into a finely filamentous condition, from reticulum into spirem; **Leptophlo′ëm** (+ PHLOËM), rudimentary phloëm, for storage or conduction of food material (Vaisey); **leptophyl′lous**, *-lus*, (φύλλον, a leaf), slender-leaved; **Leptopuccin′ia**, a group of the genus *Puccinia*, which produces only teleutospores; **leptosporan′giate** (σπορά, seed; ἀγγεῖον, a small vessel), having leptosporangia; **Leptosporan′gium**, a sporangium derived from one superficial cell, as in the true Ferns, and not from a group of cells as in Ophioglossaceae; **lep′totene** (τένων, a tendon), when the dividing nucleus is extended into a mass of fine filaments; **leptoti′chus** (τεῖχος, a wall), thin-walled, applied only to tissue; **Leptoxy′lem** (+ XYLEM), the water-conducting tissue of the sporophyte of Mosses: functional wood (Vaizey); **lepto-zygotene** (+ ZYGOTENE), a transition stage between the delicate single threads or leptonema of the nucleus and their paired arrangement in the zygonema.

Lepyrophyl′ly (λέπυρον, a scale; φύλλον, a leaf), Morren's term for arrest of the testa in the leaf-stage.

les′keoid, resembling the moss-genus, *Leskea*.

le′thal (*lethalis*, deadly) **Coeffic′ient**; **infe′rior** or **supe′rior**, the lowest or highest temperatures which are fatal to the vital functions of a given organism (O. Jones).

lett′ered, with spots resembling letters; *cf.* GRAMMICUS.

leucan′thous, *-thus* (λευκὸς, white or grey), white-flowered; **Leu′cin** or "Amidocaproic acid" is a white substance, first found in animals, afterwards found in plants; **Leu′-cite**, Van Tieghem's name for LEUCOPLAST; he further modifies the term by prefixing **am′ylo-**, **chlo′ro-chro′mo-**, **ela′io-**, **ox′ali-**, for various modifications; furthermore, **act′ive** ~, or **pas′sive** or **reserve′** ~, accord-

ing to function; **leucophyll′us**
(φύλλον, a leaf), white-leaved;
Leu′cophyll-grain = Leucoplast;
Leu′coplast, Leucoplas′tid (πλαστὸς,
moulded), A. F. W. Schimper's term
for the specialized colourless protoplasmic granule; syn. Anaplast (A.
Meyer), and Leucite (Van Tieghem);
Leucoso′mata, pl. = **Leu′cosomes**
(σῶμα, a body), small spherical
bodies, apparently composed of
albuminoids inclosed in the leucoplasts of Commelynaceae (Zimmermann).

leviga′tus (Lat.), smooth, slippery;
in botanical Latin it is usually
spelled "laevigatus."

le′vis (Lat.), smooth, in the sense of
not rough; from the time of Linnaeus
downward this has been spelled botanically as "laevis."

Le′vulose (*laevus*, on the left side);
Fructose or fruit-sugar; it deflects
polarized light to the left.

Lia′na, Lia′ne (Span. liar, to tie;
pron. lēah-nǎ, lē-ahn), luxuriant
woody climbers in the tropics with
stems of anomalous structure;
lia′noid (εἶδος, like), having a liana-
like habit; **Lia′noid**, Johow's term
for phanerogamous parasites which
proceed from autotrophous climbers.

Lib′er (Lat., inner bark), the inner
bark, which is often fibrous, the
phloëm of the vascular system containing the bast-tissue; ~ **Fi′bres**,
bast-fibres.

li′ber (Lat., free), having no cohesion
with the adjoining parts; **libera′tus**
(Lat.), freed.

liberolig′neous (*liber*, inner bark;
lignum, wood), applied to a conjoint
bundle composed of bast and wood
elements; **Lib′riform** (*forma*, shape),
a tissue composed of Libriform
cells (Tschirch); **lib′riform Cell**, a
narrow, thick-walled cell of woody
tissue resembling bast, wood-fibre
(Crozier); ~ **Fi′bres**, substitute
fibres reduced in form (Germ.,
Ersatzfasern).

Li′broplasts (*liber*, free; πλαστὸς,
moulded), elaeoplasts which are free

on the median line of Diatoms
(Mereschkowsky).

Li′chen (λειχὴν, lichen), a Cryptogam
which forms a thallus that is
either shrubby, leafy, crustaceous or
powdery, generally regarded as a
symbiosis of hyphal filaments with
algal gonidia; ~ **Al′gae**, the gonidia
or green bodies in the thallus; ~
Fun′gi, the filaments of hyphae,
which are usually interwoven with
the gonidia; ~ **Starch** = Lichenin;
~ **Tun′dra**, flat or gently undulating land, chiefly producing Lichens,
especially in the north of Siberia;
lichenic′olous (*colo*, I inhabit), dwelling in or on a Lichen; **Li′chenin**,
the peculiar starch-like body in
Cetraria islandica, Linn., and other
Lichens; **Li′chenism**, the special
symbiosis between Alga and Fungus
occurring in Lichens; **Licheno-
g′rapher, Lichenog′raphist** (γράφω,
I write) = Lichenologist; **Licheno-
g′raphy**, the study of Lichens; adj.
lichenograph′ic; **li′chenoid** (εἶδος,
like), irregularly lobed, as Lichens;
Lichenol′ogist (λόγος, discourse),
a student or writer on Lichens;
Lichenol′ogy (λόγος, discourse), the
science and study of Lichens; **Lich-
noër′ythrine** (ἐρυθρὸς, red), Sorby's
name for the red colouring matter
of Lichens; **Lichnoxan′thine** (ξανθὸς,
yellow), the same observer's term for
the yellow colouring in Lichens.

Lid, (1) the operculum of moss-capsules
(W. J. Hooker); (2) the distal extremity of the ascidium of *Nepenthes*
which forms a lid-like appendage to
the pitcher; (3) the areas of pollen-
grains which are detached to permit
the pollen-tubes to pass; ~ **Cells**,
the terminal cells of the neck of the
archegonium which temporarily close
the canal; the stigmatic cells.

Life, the state in which plants can
grow or perform their functions of
absorption, assimilation, reproduction, etc.; ~ **Cy′cle**, the course of
development from any given stage
to the same again, as from the seed
to the seed once more.

Ligamen'tum ‡ (Lat., a band or bandage) = RAPHE.

Light-absor'ption, the ratio of the whole of daylight to that of the place in which the plant grows (Wiesner); ~ -traps = LENS-CELLS.

lig'neous, lig'nous, *lig'neus* (Lat.), woody.

lignic'olor (*lignum*, wood; *color*, colour), tawny, the colour of freshly cut wood; lig'nicole, lignic'olous (*colo*, to inhabit), applied to plants which live on timber; lignif'erous (*fero*, I bear), used of branches which form wood only but no flowers; Lignifica'tion (*facio*, I make), the hardening or thickening of the cell-wall by secondary deposits; lig'nified, converted into wood; ~ -lay'er, in leaf-fall, the layer of cells immediately above the separation layer; lig'niform (*forma*, shape), like wood; lig'nify, to turn into wood; Lig'nin or Lig'nine, an incrusting or impregnating substance on the cell-wall, producing woody tissue; it is insoluble in water or ether, soluble in alcohol and alkalis, and is the remainder after the cellulose has been removed by chemical means; Lignire'ose (deriv. ?), Payen's term for a constituent of Lignin, only slightly soluble in water; Lig'nite, a fossil or semi-fossil wood substance; jet is an example; Lignocel'lulose (+ CELLULOSE), see CELLULOSE; Lig'none, a substance which differs from Lignin by being insoluble in water, alcohol and ether, but soluble in ammonia, potash, soda (Payen); Lig'nose, a constituent of Lignin, but soluble only in potash and soda solutions (Payen); lig'nose, *ligno'sus*, woody, ligneous; Lig'no-suberization (+ SUBERIZATION); in leaf-fall when the lignification and the protective layer is completed by a layer of suberine, and the disappearance of the protoplasm from the cells (Lee); Ligno'sum, a type of vegetation in which there are several layers, conditioned by the dominant

trees or shrubs; Lig'num, wood, that within the cortex, including both alburnum and duramen.

Lig'ule, *Lig'ula* (Lat., a little tongue), (1) a strap-shaped body, such as the limb of the ray florets in Compositae; (2) a lobe of the outer corona in *Stapelia* (N. E. Brown); (3) the thin, scarious projection from the top of the leaf-sheath in grasses; (4) a narrow membranous, acuminate structure, internal to the leaf-base in *Isoëtes* and *Selaginella;* (5) an appendage to certain petals, as those of *Silene* and *Cuscuta* (A. Gray); (6) the ovuliferous scale in *Araucaria*, united with the bract, and resembling the ligule in *Isoëtes* (Potter); (7) the envelope which protects the young leaf in palms, as *Chamaerops* and *Rhaphis*.

lig'ular, (1) pertaining to a ligule, in its various meanings; (2) Russow's term for that leaf-face of *Selaginella* which is turned towards the ligule; *cf.* ALIGULAR; lig'ulate, *ligula'tus*, furnished with a Ligule; lig'uliform, *liguliform'is* (*forma*, shape), strap-shaped; liguliflor'ate, liguliflor'ous, -*rus* (*flos*, *floris*, a flower), having ligulate florets, as *Hieracium*.

li'lac, pale warm purple, the colour of the flower of *Syringa vulgaris*, Linn.; Li'lacine, a bitter principle from the bark of the same plant; li'lacine (Heinig), lila'ceus (Mod. Lat.), lilaci'nous, -*nus*, lilac in colour.

lilia'ceous, -*ceus* (*lilium*, a lily; + ACEOUS), lily-like.

limaciform'is (*limax*, *limacis*, a slug; *forma*, shape), applied by Koerber to those Lichen spores which are slug-shaped.

Limb, *lim'bus* (Lat., a border or hem), (1) the border or expanded part of a gamopetalous corolla, as distinct from the tube or throat; (2) the lamina of a leaf or of a petal; (3) the margin of the leaf in Mosses when distinct in colour and cell-structure; lim'bate, *limba'tus*, having a margin of the kind stated.

Lime, used to denote calcium carbonate

in plants ; ~ **Gran'ules**,lime-knots in
Myxogastres, concretions occurring
in the capillitium ; ~ **Scales**, the
chalk-glands which excrete lime, as
with certain Saxifrages.

Li'mes (Lat., a cross-path or boundary)
commu'nis‡, the collum or neck of
a plant.

limic'olous (*limicola*, a dweller in
mud), growing in mud, as on the
margins of pools.

lim'itary (*limitaris*, pertaining to a
boundary), placed at the limit, as
a guard; **lim'iting**, restricting ; ~
Cell = HETEROCYST ; ~ **Fac'tor**,
the factor in growth which fails
first ; it may be humidity, or light,
or temperature, etc.

lim'itate (*limitatus*, restricted), limited
or bounded by a distinct line of
hypothallus in Lichens (Leighton).

Lim'nad (λίμνη, a lake ; + AD), a lake
plant (Clements) ; **Limnae'a** Formation, aquatic plants with a loose
substratum of soil; **limnet'ic**, applied
to plants which grow in pools or
their neighbourhood ; **Limni'um**,
lake formation ; **Limno'bion** (βίος,
life), organic associations occurring
in fresh water; *cf.* HALOBION,
GEOBION.

Limno'dad (λιμνώδης, marshy ; + AD),
a plant of a salt marsh ; **Limnodi'um**,
employed by Ganong for wild salt
marsh vegetation ; **limnodoph'ilus**
(φιλέω, I love), marsh-loving ; **Lim-
nodophy'ta** (φυτόν, a plant), marsh
plants (Clements).

Limnone'reid (λίμνη, a lake ; Νηρεΐς, a
sea-nymph), freshwater algal sub-
formation ; **limnoph'ilus** (φιλέω, I
love), pond-loving; **Limnophy'ta**
(φυτόν, a plant), pond plants
(Clements) ; **Limnoplank'ton** (+
PLANKTON), the floating vegetation
of freshwater pools or streams.

Li'namarin (*linum*, flax), a glucoside
in linseed, *Linum ;* the same as
Phaseolunatin ; **Li'nase**, an enzyme
in flax (Armstrong).

Line, *Li'nea* (Lat., a line or thread),
as a measure of length, the twelfth
part of an inch, in millimetres,

2·1167 ; the Paris line is 2·325
mm. ; ~ **Tran'sect**, a record of
the plants occurring along a straight
line (Clements); *Li'nea transversa'lis*,
the ostiolum of some Fungi ; **Lines
of Growth**, the limits of each year's
growth in woody stems ; ~ **of Vegeta'tion**, for any given species, those
obtained by joining all the places in
a given direction where the species
stops ; the resultant lines map out
the distribution of the said species
(Kerner) ; **linea'lis** (Lat., consisting
of lines), measuring about a line ;
lin'ear, *linea'ris*, narrow, several
times longer than wide ; **lin'eate**,
linea'tus, marked with lines; *linea'ta
Va'sa* ‡, vessels transversely marked,
as annulate ducts or tracheids ; **line-
a'tipes** ‡ (*pes*, a foot), having a lined
or striated foot-stalk; **lined** = lineate,
striate; **lin'eolate**, *lineola'tus*, marked
with fine or obscure lines.

linguiform'is (*lingua*, a tongue ; *forma*,
shape), tongue-shaped ; **ling'ulate**,
lingula'tus, also means tongue-
shaped.

Li'nin or **Li'nine** (λίνον, a thread), the
hyaloplasmic filaments of the nucleus
in repose (Schwarz).

Linn'ean Syst'em, the artificial classification devised by Linnaeus, based
upon the number and position of the
stamens and pistils.

Li'nolein (*linum*, flax; *oleum*, oil),
"the glyceride of lineoleic acid
found in linseed oil."

Li'nom = LININ.

linosp'orous (*linea*, a line ; + SPORE),
employed by G. F. Atkinson for
"linear spored."

Liorhi'zae (λεῖος, smooth ; ῥίζα, root),
Van Tieghem's name for Monocotyledons and Nymphaeaceae, the
root-hairs being of exodermic origin ;
liorhi'zal, pertaining to LIORHIZAE.

Lip, (1) one of the two divisions of a
bilabiate corolla or calyx, that is,
a gamopetalous or gamosepalous
organ cleft into an upper (superior
or posterior) and a lower (inferior
or anterior) portion ; (2) the labellum of Orchids ; ~ **Cells**, two narrow,

lignified cells on the sporangia of
some annulate Ferns, distinct from
the annulus, which are the first
to separate on dehiscence; *cf.*
STOMIUM.

Lip′ase (λίπος, grease), a fat-splitting
enzyme occurring in oily seeds;
Lipasei′din, the fat-splitting enzyme
of the cytoplasm in castor-oil seeds,
Ricinus; **Lip′ochrome** (χρῶμα, colour),
the yellow pigment of flowers, so
named by Hansen from its resemblance to an animal pigment;
Lipocy′anin (κύανος, blue), the blue
pigment of some plants; **Lip′oid**
(εἶδος, resemblance), applied to a
series of fatty bodies found in plants
in association with protoplasm; *e.g.*
CYTOLIPOID, TROPHOLIPOID, etc.;
lipolyt′ic (λύσις, a loosing), dissolving fats.

lipox′enous (λείπω, I leave; ξένος, a
host), deserting its host; **Lipox′eny**,
the desertion of a host-plant by a
parasite to complete its development
on reserve materials previously obtained from the host, as in the
falling away of Ergot, the sclerotium
of *Cordyceps purpurea*, Tul.

lipped = LABIATE.

Li′quor (Lat. a liquid) **Am′nios** (*cf.*
AMNIOS), a term borrowed from
zoology for the fluid "contained in
the sac within which the embryo is
engendered" (Lindley).

Lirel′la (dim. of *lira*, a ridge), in
Lichens an oblong apothecium with
a furrow along its middle, as in
Opegrapha; **lirel′late, lirel′line,** lirel-
la-like; **lirel′liform,** *lirelliform′is*
(*forma*, shape), shaped like a lirella.

lisigenet′ic, = LYSIGENETIC.

List-quad′rat, an enumeration of the
plants found in a square space
(Clements).

Lithobib′lion (λίθος, a stone; βιβλίον,
a paper or scroll) = LITHOPHYL;
Lith′ocarp (καρπός, fruit), fossil
fruit; **Lith′ocyst** (κύστις, a bag or
pouch), a crystal cell; **lithoph′ilus**
(φιλέω, I love), rock-loving; **lithoph′-
ilous**, saxicolous, dwelling on rocks;
~ Formation, a formation of aquatic

plants fixed to stones or rocks, as
marine Algae; **Lith′ophyl** (φύλλον,
a leaf), a fossil leaf or leaves;
Lithophy′ta, Lith′ophytes (φυτὸν,
a plant), (1) plants which grow on
stones, but derive their nourishment
from the atmosphere, as saxicolous
Lichens; (2) plants growing amongst
rocks; **Lithophyti′a**, rock plant formations (Clements); **lithosperm′ous**
(σπέρμα, seed), having hard, stony
seeds; **Lithox′yle** (ξύλον, wood),
fossil wood.

Lit′mus, a violet colour derived from
several species of Lichens, such as
Rocella, etc.

lit′oral, *litora′lis* (Lat. pertaining to
the sea-shore), belonging to or growing on the sea-shore (A. Gray adds
"river banks," which strictly speaking is "riparian"); used by H. C.
Watson for plants of the sea-shore;
frequently spelled **lit′toral,***littora′lis.*

Litorideser′ta (*litoreus*, pertaining to
the sea-shore; + DESERTA), strand-
steppes, deserts developed under the
influences of the sea, consisting
chiefly of halophytes and succulents.

litua′tus ‡ (*lituus*, a crooked staff),
forked, with the points turned a
little outward.

litura′tus ‡ (*litura*, a smearing), when
spots are formed by an abrasion of
the surface.

li′vens, liv′id, *li′vidus* (Lat.), pale
lead colour.

liv′er-col′oured = HEPATICOUS.

Liv′erworts, Hepaticae.

Lla′nos (Span.), a special type of
savannah, forming vast plains in
Venezuela, and characterized by
usual absence of trees.

Lobe, Lo′bus (λοβὸς, the lower part of
the ear), any division of an organ
or specially rounded division;
Mid′dle ~, a small conical or tongue-
shaped growth arising from between
the two side-lobes of a Fern-prothallus; **lo′bate,** *loba′tus*, divided
into or bearing lobes; **Lo′belet**, a
small lobe; **Lob′iolus**, a small lobe
into which some Lichen-thalli are
divided; **lobose′**, occasionally used

for LOBED; lob′ulate, *lobula′tus*, having small lobes; Lob′ule, (1) a small lobe, a lobulet; (2) Spruce's word for the minor lobe of the leaf of Hepaticae, the auricle of Nees and others; (3) a tongue-like structure opposite the scutellum in grasses, the epiblast (Van Tieghem); Lob′ulus, a small lobe.

Local′ity (*localitas*, a place), the approximate geographic position of an individual specimen.

locel′late, *locella′tus*, dividing into LOCELLI; Locel′lus (dim. of *loculus*, a little compartment), a secondary compartment, as a primitive pollensac, which, by the destruction of a septum, unites with an adjoining locellus to form an anther-loculus.

Loch′mad (λόχμη, a thicket; + AD), a thicket plant; Lochmi′um, a thicket formation; lochmoc′ola (*colo*, I inhabit), and lochmoph′ilus (φιλέω, I love), dwelling in thickets; Lochmophy′ta (φυτὸν, a plant), thicket plants (Clements).

Lochmo′dium (λοχμώδης, bushy), a dry thicket formation; lochmodoph′ilus (φιλέω, I love), dwelling in dry thickets; Lochmodophy′ta (φυτὸν, a plant), dry thicket plants (Clements).

Lo′co, disease of cattle and sheep from their feeding on Lo′co-plants or ~ -weeds, chiefly species of *Astragalus* and *Lupinus*.

Loc′oform (*locus*, a place; + FORM), a form which differs from its nearest allies by peculiarities derived from the climate or soil (Kuntze); Locogreg′iform (*grex*, *gregis*, a flock), a secondary or tertiary RAMIFORM (Kuntze).

Loc′ulament, *Loculamen′tum* (Lat. a case or box); (1) = LOCULUS of a carpel; (2) "the perithecium of certain Fungals" (Lindley): loc′ular, *locula′ris*, having cavities or Loculi, denoted further by the addition of uni-, bi-, tri-, etc., for one-, two-, three-, etc., celled; locula′tus, divided into cavities; loculici′dal (*caedo*, I cut), the cavity of a pericarp dehiscent by the back, the dorsal

suture; loc′ulose, *loculo′sus*, loc′ulous, divided internally into cells, partitioned; Loc′ulus, (1) the cavity of an ovary or anther; (2) the periderm of certain Fungals (Lindley); (3) a chamber in the apex of the testa of a fossil seed (F. W. Oliver).

Locus′ta (Lat crayfish or locust), the spikelet in grasses.

Lodg′er-arrangements, used by those flowers which detain their insect visitors.

Lod′icule, *Lodicu′la* (Lat. a small coverlet), a small scale outside the stamens in the flower of grasses; glumella.

Loess, drifting dust detained and consolidated by vegetation.

Log′otype (λόγος, word; τύπος, type), a type determined historically from two or more original species; adj. logotyp′ic (O. F. Cook).

Lol′iophyll, Etard's name for chlorophyll from *Lolium* and other grasses.

Lo′ma, a grass-steppe in Peru, the life of plants is during the winter when mists moisten the soil, in summer it is dried up.

lomar′ioid, resembling the Fern genus *Lomaria*.

long′ipes (*longus*, long; *pes*, a foot), long-footed or long-stalked.

lomenta′ceous, -ceus (*lomentum*, bean-meal), bearing or resembling Loments; Lo′ment, *Lomen′tum*, a legume which is contracted between the seeds, falling apart at the constrictions when mature into one-seeded joints.

Long′ipesplankton (+ PLANKTON), a summer boreal association composed of Peridiniaceae, especially of *Ceratium longipes*, whence the name.

longis′simus (Lat.), very long.

Longistamin′eae (*longus*, long; + STAMEN), Delpino's term for flowers with long stamens which are wind-fertilized; adj. longistam′inate.

Longitu′dinal Sys′tem, an old term for fibro-vascular system (Crozier).

longitudinal′iter, longitudina′lis (Lat.), in the direction of the length.

Longitu'do (Lat., length) means, botanically, in the direction of growth.

loose, (1) as applied to inflorescence, lax, as a panicle; (2) hardly coherent, as loose tissue; ~ Smut, a disease of cereals caused by various species of *Ustilago*.

Loph'ad (λοφιά, a crest; + AD), a hill plant; lophios'tomate (στόμα, a mouth), having crested apertures or openings; Lophi'um, a hill or crest formation; lophoph'ilus (φιλέω, I love), hill-dwelling; Lophophy'ta (φυτόν, a plant), hill-plants (Clements); Loph'ospores, -æ (+ SPORE), plants having plumose pappus (Clements); lophot'richous (θρίξ, τριχός, hair), used of those bacteria possessed of a tuft of cilia (Jones).

lor'ate, *lora'tus* (*lorum*, a thong), strap-shaped, ligulate.

Lori'ca (Lat., a leather corslet), (1) the entire silicious covering of the frustule in Diatoms; (2) formerly used for the TESTA; (3) employed by Hance to denote the scales of the fruit of *Calamus*.

lor'icate [clothed in mail], "equally narrow throughout" (Braithwaite), is probably a slip for LORATE.

Lo'rulum (Lat. dim. of *lorum*, a thong), the filamentous and branched thallus of some Lichens.

Lo'tase, an enzyme in *Lotus arabicus*; Lotofla'vin, a yellow colouring matter in the same plant; Lo'tusin, a yellow crystalline glucoside also from it.

low, small as compared to its allies; ~ Moor, a swampy formation developing peat (Warming); ~ Yeast, that which is found at the bottom of a fermenting liquid: Ger. "Unterhefe"; low'ered, used when the lip of a bilabiate corolla is inclined at about a right angle to the tube.

lu'bricous, *lu'bricus* (Lat.), smooth, slippery.

lu'cens, lu'cid, *lu'cidus* (Lat.), shining, referring to the surface.

lumbrica'lis (*lumbricus*, a maw-worm), worm-shaped, as in some Algae;

lum'bricous, shaped like an earth-worm.

Lu'men (Lat., light, opening), the space which is bounded by the walls of an organ, as the central cavity of a cell; Lu'minous Line, in Malpighiaceae, etc., on the testa of the seeds, is due to a modification of the outer layer.

lu'nar (*luna*, the moon), (1) pertaining to the moon; (2) LUNATE; ~ Plants, Grew's term for those which twine "with the moon," against the sun, sinistrorse; lu'nate, *luna'tus*, half-moon shaped; luna'ted, having lunar markings (Crozier); lu'niform (*forma*, shape), crescent-shaped (Crozier); lu'nulate, *lunula'tus*, diminutive of lunate.

Lu'pinine, an alkaloid in the flower-buds of *Lupinus luteus*, Linn.; Lu'pinite, a bitter substance occurring in the leaves of the white lupin, *Lupinus albus*, Linn.

Lu'pulin, (1) a secretion from the glandular hairs of the hop-strobiles, *Humulus Lupulus*, Linn., which gives a bitter taste; (2) see LUPULINIC GLANDS; lu'puline, lupuli'-nous, *lupuli'nus*, resembling a hop-strobile; Lupulin'ic Glands, the resinous glandular bodies within the scales of the female flower of the hop, "also called Lupulin" (Stormonth); Lu'pulite, a lupulinic gland.

lu'rid, *lu'ridus* (Lat., sallow, wan), in botany, dingy brown or yellow; lurid'ic Acid occurs in *Boletus luridus*, Schaeff.

Lu'siform (*lusus*, a game), a new form, due to cultivation, which reproduces itself by vegetable increase only, and not by seed (Kuntze).

Lu'sus (Lat., a game), a sport or variation from seed or bud; ~ Natu'rae a monstrosity.

lu'teo-fus'cus (*luteus*, yellow; *fuscus*, swarthy), blackish-yellow; lu'teolin, a yellow colouring matter found in weld, *Reseda Luteola*, Linn.; lu'teolus (Lat.), yellowish; lutes'cent, *lutes'cens*, becoming yellow; lu'teous, lu'teus (Lat.), a full yellow.

lu′ticole (*lutum*, mud ; *colo*, I inhabit), used of a plant growing in miry places.

Luxu′ria, Luxu′ries (Lat., rankness), exuberant growth ; **Luxu′riant**, *luxu′rians* (Lat.), usually signifies that the organs of nutrition are more developed than those of fructification.

lycoper′dioid (*Lycoperdon*, a genus of Gasteromycetes ; εἶδος, like), resembling a puff-ball.

lycopodia′ceous (+ ACEOUS), resembling the genus *Lycopodium ;* **lycopodin′ean, lycopodi′nous**, resembling in structure *Lycopodium ;* **Lycop′sida, Lycop′sids**, pl. (ὄψις, appearance), a group of cryptogams, consisting of Lycopodiales and Equisetales (Jeffrey) ; adj. **lycop′sid**, sporangiophoric ; the cryptogams specified.

lycot′ropal = lycot′ropous, *-pus* (λύκος, a door-knocker ; τροπή, a twining), when an otherwise orthotropous ovule is bent like a horse-shoe.

Lymph, *Lym′pha* (Lat., spring water), Grew's term for sap ; **Lymph′ae-ducts** = DUCTS ; **lymphat′ic**, clear, pellucid ; ∼ = DUCTS.

lysigenet′ic, lysigen′ic, lysig′enous (λύσις, a loosing ; γένος, offspring), when a cavity is formed by a disorganization or dissolving of cells.

ly′rate, *lyra′tus* (λύρα, a lute or lyre), lyre-shaped, pinnatifid with the terminal lobe large and rounded, the lower lobes small ; **lyra′ti-parti′tus**, ∼ -sec′tus, lyrately pinnate ; **lyreshaped** = LYRATE.

Ly′sin (λύσις, a loosing), a product of the hydrolysis of protamines and other proteids, isolated from sprouting plants ; **Ly′sis**, the metamorphosis of a part.

Mace, the arillus of the nutmeg.

Macera′tion (*Maceratio*, a steeping), steeping, as in the case of barley for malting.

macran′drous (μακρὸς, long ; ἀνὴρ, ἀνδρὸς, a man), having large or long male plants in Algae ; **macran′thus** (ἄνθος, a flower), long flowered.

Mac′ro-, in Greek compounds = long ; frequently but improperly used for **mega-**, or **megalo-**, large.

macroaëroph′ilous (μακρὸς, long ; ἀὴρ, air ; φιλέω, I love), employed by Winogradsky to express the avidity for oxygen shown by *Clostridium ;* **Macroan′drospore** (+ ANDROSPORE), Janet's term for macrospores of *Selaginella* having a male function ; **Macroaplanosporang′ium**(+APLANOSPORE, SPORANGIUM), the sporangium producing macroaplanospores (Thaxter) ; **Macroaplan′ospore** (+APLANOSPORE), aplanospores of large size given off by *Compsopogon* (Thaxter) ; **Macrobiocar′py** (βίος, life ; καρπὸς, fruit), Delpino's expression for the property of certain fruits to retain their seeds during a series of years, as *Callistemon ;* **macrobiostigmat′ic** (βίος, life ; στίγμα, a puncture), Delpino's term for those plants whose stigmas remain capable of fertilization until the anthers are mature ; **Macroblast**(βλαστὸς, a bud), a normal wood bud (Hartig) ; **macroceph′alous**, *-lus* (κεφαλὴ, head), big-headed, dicotyledonous embryos with consolidated cotyledons ; **macroclad′ous** *-dus* (κλαδὸς, a branch), having long branches ; **Macroconid′ium** (+CONIDIUM), a large conidium produced at a different period in the life-cycle to a MICROCONIDIUM ; **Mac′rocyst** (κύστις, a bag or pouch), (1) one of the vesicles which originate the fertile tissue in *Pyronema*, etc. (Tulasne) ; (2) the resting condition of a very young plasmodium, a mass of protoplasm, with nuclei in a double wall (Lister) ; **Macrocy′te**, trisyll. (κύτος, a hollow), the larger form of dimorphic flagellate Algae ; **Macrodi′odange** (+ DIODE ; ἀγγεῖον, a vessel), Van Tieghem's term for MACROSPORANGIUM ; **Macrodi′ode**, the same botanist's word for MACROSPORE ; **Macrogam′ete** (γαμέτης, a spouse)=MEGAGAMETE ; **Macrogonid′ium** (γόνος, offspring ; εἶδος, like), a gonidium of large size in comparison with others produced by the same species ; *cf.* MEGALOGONIDIUM ; **Macrogy′nospore**

(+ Gynospore), Janet's term for gynospores of *Selaginella* having presumably a female function; **Macromicrospor′ophyll** = Carpel.

macromit′reous, resembling the genus *Macromitrium*.

macrophyl′line (μακρὸς, long; φύλλον, a leaf), **macrophyl′lous**, having elongated leaflets or leaves; **Mac′rophyte** (φυτὸν, a plant), employed by Schimper to denote marine Algae of extreme length; **macrophyt′ic**, (1) used by Schimper for the large forms of marine Algae; (2) the non-microscopical plants found in the pleuston or hydrocharid formation (Warming); **Macrophytoplank′ton** (+ Plankton), plants such as *Utricularia;* **Mac′roplast** (πλαστὸς, moulded), Lankester's term for large disc-like plastids in *Bacterium rubescens;* **macrop′odal**, **macrop′odous** (ποῦς, ποδὸς, a foot), used of an embryo with enlarged hypocotyl forming the greater part of its mass; (Crozier adds another meaning, applied to a leaf with a long petiole); **Macroprothall′ium** (+ Prothallium), a prothalloid growth from a microspore of *Selaginella*, etc., having a female function; **Macrop′teres** (πτερὸν, a feather or wing), the wings on the stems of plants with reduced leaves; **Macropyc′nid** (πυκνὸς, dense) = Stylospore; **Macroscle′reids** (σκληρὸς, hard), Tschirch's term for long stone-cells with blunt ends; **macroscop′ic** (σκοπέω, I see), viewed by the naked eye, opposed to microscopic; **Macrospartine′tum**, a salt marsh plant association in which *Spartina* is dominant (Ganong); **macrosporan′giate**, possessing macrosporangia; ~ **Flow′ers**, carpellary flowers, pistillate flowers destitute of stamens; **Macrosporan′gium** (σπορα, seed, ἀγγεῖον, a vessel), (1) a sporangium containing macrospores; (2) the nucellus of the ovule of Phanerogams; **Mac′rospore;** (1) the larger kind of spore in vascular Cryptogams; (2) the embryo-sac in Phanerogams.

macrospor′oid (εἶδος, resemblance), resembling the genus *Macrosporium*, Fries.

Macrospor′ophore (μακρὸς, long) (+ Sporophore), an organ supporting macrospores; **Macrospor′ophyll** (φύλλον, a leaf) = Carpel; **macrosporophyl′lary**, carpellary; **macrosty′lous** (στῦλος, a post), long-styled; **Macrosym′biont** (συμβιόω, I live with), the larger of the associated organisms in symbiosis; **Mac′rotherm** (θέρμη, heat) = Megatherm; **macrothermoph′ilus** (φιλέω, I love), dwelling in the tropics; **Macrothermophy′ta** (φυτὸν, a plant), tropical plants; **Macrothermophyti′a** (Clements). [Note.—These words would have been better coined from **mega-**, instead of **macro-**.]; **Macrozoogonid′ium** (ζῶον, an animal; +Gonidium), in *Ulothrix* the larger kind of zoospore, which germinates independently; *cf.* Microzoogonidium; **Macrozo′ospore**, a large zoospore when compared with others of the same species.

Mac′ula (Lat.), a spot; pl. **Mac′ulae:** (1) areolated pits of Coniferae; (2) also organs on the aërial stem of *Cyathophorum*, large round white dots in two rows, probably water-storing organs; **Macula′tion**, the arrangement of spots on a plant (Crozier); **maculifor′mis** (*formis*, shape), used by Koerber for apothecia which are shaped like irregular spots; **mac′ular, mac′ulate, mac′ulose** (*maculosus*, spotted), blotched or spotted.

madefac′tus (Lat.), moistened, as plants in an herbarium previous to examination.

Madu′ra, the fungus-foot disease supposed to be caused by *Chionyphe Carteri*, Berk.

mag′moid (μάγμα, dregs; εἶδος, like), in Lichens, "like an Alga, consisting of spherical green cellules" (Leighton).

Magnetot′ropism (μάγνης, a magnet; τροπὴ, a turning), a theoretic term for a possible tropic force of a magnet

221

upon responsive particles in a plant (Pfeffer).

Magno-carice′ta, pl. (*magnus*, great), associations of tall-growing species of *Carex*.

Maio′sis =Meiosis ; **maiot′ic** =meiotic.

Ma′jor Quad′rat, Clements's term for a square of four quadrats.

Mak′roflora (+ Flora), applied by Levier and Sommier to the luxuriant vegetation of some of the valleys in the Caucasus.

Malacog′amy (μαλάκια = mollusca ; γάμος, marriage), used in cases of **Malacophilae** (φιλέω, I love), plants which are fertilized by snails or slugs ; adj. **malacoph′ilous**.

mal′acoid (μαλαχὸς, soft ; εἶδος, like)· mucilaginous; **malacophyll′ous** (φύλλον, a leaf), with soft or fleshy leaves.

male, a plant or flower which bears stamens or their analogues ; ~ **Cell**, the smaller of two unequal gametes ; ~ **Flow′ers**, staminate flowers ; ~ **Or′gans**, those structures which, in fertilization, are concerned, as the stamens, antheridia, etc. ; ~ **Pro-thal′lium**, one which bears antheridia only ; ~ **Sys′tem**, all that part of the flower which belongs to the stamen.

ma′lic (*malum*, an apple), pertaining to apples, as ~ **Ac′id**, which is said to be the most frequent of organic acids in cell-sap.

Malicor′ium (Lat.), the rind of the pomegranate.

malig′nant Oedem′a, disease in animals resembling anthrax, and like that, caused by a bacillus.

Mallee′ Scrub, a shrub-steppe largely composed of *Eucalyptus* about the height of a man.

Mal′leolus (Lat., a small hammer), a layer ; a shoot bent into the ground and half-divided at the bend, whence it emits roots.

mallococ′cus, (μαλλός, a lock of wool ; κόκκος, a berry), downy fruited.

Malpighia′œi Pi′li, hairs attached by their middle, frequent in the order Malpighiaceae ; **malpighia′ceous**, re-

lating to Malpighiaceae, as the peculiar hairs of many species ; **Malpig′hian Cells**, those which compose the outer layer of the seed in Malpighiaceae, with a "luminous line" composed of Lignin.

Malt′ase or **Malt′in**, a ferment found in all germinating cereals, and of greater activity than diastase (Dubrunfaut) ; **Malt′ing**, germinating seeds of barley until the radicle (acrospire) is produced, and then checking the further germination by means of heat ; **Maltodex′trin**, a body intermediate in properties between maltose and dextrin ; **Malt′ose**, a sugar formed by the action of diastase on starch.

malva′ceous, resembling or belonging to the order Malvaceae.

Mamelon′ (Fr., nipple), the floral axis (Treub) ; **ov′ular** ~, the papilla which precedes the formation of the nucellus in *Cycas* (Treub).

Mamil′la (Lat., a nipple or teat) = Mammilla.

Mam′miform (*mamma*, a breast; *forma*, shape), breast-shaped, conical with rounded apex.

Mammil′la (Lat.), a nipple or projection ; used for granular prominences on pollen-grains ; **mam′millar**, *mammilla′ris*, **mam′millate**, *mammilla′tus*, having teat-shaped processes ; **mammil′liform** (*forma*, shape), applied to those papillate protuberances on a petal which give it a velvety appearance.

mam′mose (*mammo′sus*, full-breasted), having breast-like protuberances.

man′cus (Lat., maimed), deficient or wanting.

man′icate *manica′tus*, (Lat., long-sleeved), applied to pubescence so dense and interwoven that it may be stripped off, "like a sleeve."

Man′na, the hardened exudation from various trees, as from *Fraxinus Ornus*, Linn. ; **Man′nan**, a hemicellulose ; **Man′nite**, a sweet substance in the sap of the tree mentioned ; **Man′nitose**, sugar from the pith of ash, oak and elder ;

Man'nose, a sugar resulting from the hydrolysis of cellulose ; **Mannocell'-ulose** (+ CELLULOSE), a constituent of gymnosperm wood, which on hydrolysis yields abundant MAN-NOSE (Bertrand).

Manom'eter (μανòς, rare, scanty ; μέτρον, a measure), apparatus to measure the pressure of gas or liquid.

Mantiss'a (Lat., an addition or make-weight), a supplement.

Man'tle, used by Grew for ocrea ; ~ **Cells**, tapetal cells ; ~ -fi'bres, A. A. Lawson's term for the fibres of the nuclear-spindle ; ~ **Lay'er**, a layer of tapetal cells ; ~ **Leaf**, Goebel's term for the prostrate, half-enveloping barren frond, as in *Platycerium alcicorne*, Desv., as distinct from the fertile frond.

Manu'brium (Lat., a handle), a cell which projects inward from the centre of the shields in the globule of *Chara*.

man'y-head'ed, with many distinct buds on the crown of a root.

Ma'qui, a Corsican term for dense thickets of shrubs, mostly evergreen.

marattia'ceous, akin to or resembling the fern genus *Marattia*.

mar'bled, stained with irregular streaks of colour.

marces'cent, *marces'cens* (Lat., withering), withering without falling off ; **mar'cidus** (Lat.), withered, shrunk.

Mar'cor (Lat., decay), welting ; flaccidity caused by want of water.

Margel'la (dim. of *margo*, a border), the elliptic ring round a stoma formed by the guard-cells.

Mar'gin, *Mar'go*, the edge or boundary line of a body ; **mar'ginal**, *margina'lis*, placed upon or attached to the edge ; ~ **Bast**, a strong development of a hypoderm on the edges of the leaves of certain families, as Ilicineae and Myrsineae ; ~ **Glands**, glands on the incurved margin of the pitchers of *Nepenthes ;* ~ **Grow'ing-point**, in a flattened member when the marginal cells remain embryonic and capable of growth ; ~ **Ov'ule**, an ovule borne on the margin of a carpel ; ~ **Pits**, pits which traverse the outer walls of the epidermis in leaves (Solereder) ; ~ **Veil**, a membrane enclosing the hymenium in the young stage of Agarics, the *Velum partiale ;*

Margina'les, leptosporangiate Ferns whose sori arise from the margin of the frond (Bower) ; cf. SUPERFICIALES ; **mar'ginate**, *margina'tus*, *margina'rius*, broad-brimmed, furnished with a margin of distinct character ; **mar'gined**, marginate ; **marginici'dal** (*caedo*, I cut), dehiscent by the disjunction of the united margins of the carpels, a form of septicidal dehiscence ; **Mar'go thallo'des**, the rim of the shield of a Lichen formed by the thallus.

marine', *mari'nus* (Lat., pertaining to the sea), growing within the influence of the sea, or immersed in its waters.

marit'imus (Lat., marine), belonging to the sea, or confined to the seacoast.

Mark'ings, used of various forms of thickening on the cell-wall, as annular, reticulated, spiral, etc.

marmora'tus (Lat., marbled), having veins of colour, as some marbles.

Mar'ram-grass association, formed of *Ammophila*, on sand dunes.

Mar'row, used by Blair for the pith.

Marsh plants = HELOPHYTES.

marsu'pial (μαρσύπιον, a pouch), geocalycal or pouch-fruited, used of certain Hepaticae ; **Marsu'pium**, the fruiting receptacle of the same ; **marsu'pioid**, (εἶδος, resemblance) = MARSUPIAL.

mas, **mas'culus**, **masculi'nus** (Lat.), male ; staminate, or with corresponding structures.

masked, personate.

Mass, (1) usually written MAST ; (2) **Mass**, pl. **Masses**, used by Sir J. E. Smith for SORUS, SORI.

Mas'sa (Lat., a lump), the mass or substance of a body ; ~ **semina'lis**, the flesh of some Fungi (Lindley) ; ~ **sporoph'ora ;** ~ **thecig'era**, the sporangia of some Fungi (Lindley) ; **Mas'ses**, (1) collections of anything in unusual quantity, as pollen-masses ; (2) used by Sir J. E. Smith for SORI.

Mas′sula (Lat., a little lump), (1) the hardened frothy mucilage enclosing a group of microspores in Heterosporous Filicineae ; (2) in Phanerogams, a group of cohering pollen-grains produced by one primary mother-cell, as in Orchideae ; also styled Pollen-mass.

Mast, the fruit of such trees as beech, and other Cupuliferae.

Mas′tic (μαστίχη, gum), a resinous exudation from *Pistacia Lentiscus*, Linn.

mast′igopod (μάστιξ, a whip ; πούς, ποδός, a foot), a stage in the development of Myxogastres, the contents of each spore escape as a zoogonidium enclosing a nucleus and contractile vesicle, with a single cilium ; **Mas′-tigospores**, -*ae* (+ SPORE), plants with flagellate spores (Clements).

mas′toid (μαστός, a breast ; εἶδος, like), nipple-like.

Mat, a closely intertwined vegetation, with roots and rhizomes intermixed ; ~ **Ge′ophytes**, pl. (+ GEOPHYTE), perennial spot-bound plants, mostly monocotyledons.

Math, an old term for crop, as aftermath = second crop.

mato′nioid (εἶδος, resemblance), like the Fern genus *Matonia*.

Ma′trix (Lat., the womb), the body on which a Fungus or Lichen grows ; ~ **Pol′linis**, the cell in which pollen-grains are developed ; the pollen-mother-cell.

matrocli′nous (*mater*, a mother ; κλίνω, I incline), used of hybrids which have the characters of the female parent.

matteuc′cioid (εἶδος, resemblance), akin to or like the Fern genus *Matteuccia*.

Mattul′la, or **Mat′tula** (*matta*, a mat), the fibrous material surrounding the petioles of palms ; cf. MEDULLA (3).

Matura′tion, *Matura′tio* (Lat.), ripening.

matures′cent (*maturescens*, becoming ripe), approaching maturity (Crozier).

matuti′nal, *matutina′lis*, **matuti′nus** (Lat.), pertaining to the morning ; plants flowering early, as *Ipomoea purpurea*, Roth.

max′imal (*maximus*, greatest), employed to denote the utmost which an organism can endure as, the greatest degree of heat.

Mazae′dium (deriv. ?), the fructification of Calicei, the spores free from the asci and forming a powdery mass in nearly closed heads.

Mead′ow, disyll., usually grass-land artificially maintained by mowing and grazing.

meal′y, farinaceous.

mean′driform ‡ (μαίανδρος, a winding river; *forma*, shape), having a winding direction, as the anther-cells of Cucurbitaceae.

Mea′tus (Lat., a passing) **intercel′lularis**, an intercellular passage ; ~ **pneumat′icus**, an air-passage.

Mechanomorph′osis (μηχανή), contrivance ; μόρφωσις, shaping), a word coined by Sachs to express mechanical changes in structure produced in the larger groups by similar external causes, as leaf-like organs in Algae and Phanerogams ; **Mechanot′ropism** (τροπή, a turning), a general term for all orienting movements in response to mechanical agencies.

Me′conine (μήκων, a poppy), an alkaloid contained in opium ; **Meco′nium**, botanically, the juice of *Papaver somniferum*, Linn.

me′dial, **me′dian**, *media′nus* (Lat., in the middle), belonging to the middle ; **me′dian Bract′eole**, one inserted at the middle of the pedicel ; ~ **Chor′isis**, the multiplication of a single organ in the median plane ; ~ **Line**, the central line of a bilateral organ as the midrib of a symmetric leaf ; ~ **Plane**, when used of a flower in the plane of bract and axis ; ~ **Wall**, in Archegoniates, the wall in a plane at right angles to the basal wall dividing the proëmbryo into lateral halves ; ~ **zygo-morph′ous**, capable of division into similar halves by a plane passing through the middle ; *cf*. SAGITTAL SECTION ; **Mediananisophyl′ly** (+ ANISOPHYLLY), the form of leaves on median shoots, as seen when the twigs are normally decussate.

Medica′gophyll (*Medicago*, Tourn. ; + phyll), the characteristic chlorophyll of Lucerne, *Medicago sativa*, Linn.

medifix′us (*medius*, middle ; *fixus*, fastened), fixed by the middle ; **Mediocor′tex** (+CORTEX), the central layer or layers of the bark, usually characterized by inert refractive fungal masses (Groom) ; **Med′ioform** (+ FORM), an intermediate form not due to hybridity (Kuntze) ; **Medioloc′oform** (*locus*, a place), a local MEDIOFORM (Kuntze).

mediterra′neus (Lat., midland), (1) inhabiting spots far from the sea ; (2) occurring in the Mediterranean region.

medival′vis (*medius*, middle ; *valva*, a valve), arising from, or on the middle of the valves.

Medul′la (Lat., pith, marrow) ; (1) the pith ; (2) the central looser portion of the flesh in certain Fungi ; (3) the "Mattulla" of palms (Stormonth) ; ~ **Se′minis‡**, the albumen of seeds ; **medul′lary**, *medulla′ris* (Lat., seated in the marrow), relating to the pith, pithy ; ~ **Bun′dles**, the more lateral vascular bundles of the leaf-trace in Monocotyledons ; ~ **Casts**, impressions of the internal cavity of *Calamites* in solid material ; ~ **conjunc′tive Tis′sue** = PITH ; ~ **Crown,** = ~ SHEATH ; ~ **Phlo′ëm Bun′dles,** independent phloëm bundles developed just within the ring of normal vascular bundles ; ~ **Rays,** plates of parenchyma or cellular tissue radiating from the pith to the cortex ; the "silver-grain" of joiners ; ~ **Sheath,** tracheids forming a circle round the pith, the primary xylem bundles projecting into the pith from the cambium-

ring ; ~ **Spot,** an accumulation of parenchymatous cells in certain woods, as *Alnus* (De Bary) ; ~ **Sys′tem,** sometimes used for the whole ground tissue, but more properly the pith and medullary rays only ; **medull′ated,** possessing pith ; **Medulla′tion** (1) the fact of possessing pith ; (2) the special system of the pith ; (3) the formation of the central tissue of a stele ; **Medul′lin,** the cellulose from pith of the sun-flower and lilac (Braconnot) ; **Medulli′na** (Lat.) = PITH ; **medullo′sus** (Lat., marrowy), having the texture of pith.

megaceph′alus (μέγας, large ; κεφαλή, head), used of large capitula of Compositae ; **Megachlor′oplast** (+ CHLOROPLAST), compound chlorophyll granules in *Tillandsia*, composed of MICROCHLOROPLASTS (Billings) ; **Megaconid′ea,** pl. **Megacon′ids** (κόνις, ashes), Zukal's term for the large conidia borne in pycnidia of certain Ascomycetes ; **Megagam′etes** (γαμέτης, a spouse), the larger motile sexual cells of Algae, presumably female ; adj. **megagam′etal.**

Megalogonid′ium (μεγάλος, large ; + GONIDIUM) = MACROGONIDIUM.

Megaphan′erophytes, pl. (μέγας, large ; + PHANEROPHYTE), trees exceeding the height of 30 metres ; **Megaphyl′lidae** (φύλλον, a leaf), the Ferns, as possessing broad fronds ; **megaphyl′lous,** the leaves or leaf-like expansions large (Jeffrey) ; **Megaphyll′y** (φύλλον, a leaf), the possession of large leaves ; **Megaplank′ton** (+ PLANKTON), distinct from ordinary plankton by inclusion of megaphytes and Algae of special groups (Warming) ; **Megaplanogam′ete** (+ PLANOGAMETE), Brebner's term for a large planogamete, presumably female ; **Megaprothall′us** (+ PROTHALLUS), the prothallus producing archegonia ; **Megasporang′ium** (+ SPORANGIUM), the correct form of MACROSPORANGIUM ; **Megarchid′ium** (ἀρχίδιον, a rudiment), = NUCELLUS ;

megarhi′zous (ῥίζα, a root), large-rooted; **megascop′ic** (σκοπέω, I see), vision with the naked eye; **Megaso′rus** (+ Sorus), a sorus which gives rise to megasporangia in *Salvinia;* **Megasporan′ge** [four syll.] (σπορά, seed; ἀγγεῖον, a vessel), a sporangium which produces megaspores; **Meg′aspore**, the more correct form of Macrospore, (1) the larger spores of vascular Cryptogams; (2) used for Ovule; (3) = Embryo-sac; **pri′mary ~**, the megaspore mother-cell (Gibbs); **Megaspor′ocarp** (καρπὸς, fruit), the development of the megasporangium in *Azolla,* finally containing the single perfect megaspore; **Megaspor′ocyte** (κύτος, a hollow vessel), the early state of the embryo-sac; **Megasporogen′esis** (γένεσις, beginning), the development of a megaspore; **Megaspor′ophyll** (φύλλον, a leaf), (1) a carpel; (2) a sporophyll which bears megaspores; **Meg′atherm**, adj., **megather′mic**, the correct forms of Macrotherm, macrothermic, requiring much heat, as tropical plants; **Megazo′oids** (ζῶον, an animal; εἶδος, resemblance), large motile daughter-cells of certain unicellular Algae (Hazen); **Megazoosporan′ge** (σπορά, a seed; ἀγγεῖον, a vessel), in *Hydrodictyon,* the special sporangium which contains a swarm of megazoospores, the protoplasm of a cell giving rise to a large number, each provided with four cilia; **Megazo′ospore** (+ Zoospore), a motile spore, larger than those termed Microzoospores; **Meg′ecad** (+ Ecad), a group of several ecads of close affinity.

Megis′totherm (θέρμος, hot), a plant requiring high uniform temperature; adj. **megistotherm′ic.**

meiogy′rous (μείων, less; γυρὸς, round), rolled inwards a little; **mei′on**, prefixed to an organ, shows it is less than some other organ understood; **Meiophyl′ly** (φύλλον, a leaf), diminution in number of the leaves in a whorl, as compared with the preceding whorl.

Meio′sis (μείωσις, reduction), applied to reduction divisions of chromosomes (Farmer and Moore); adj. **meio′tic ; ~ Euapog′amy**, when the nuclei of the mother-cells of the sporophyte have the haploid number of chromosomes.

Meiosporan′ge (μείων, less ; + Sporangium), Sauvageau's name for the smaller plurilocular sporangia enclosing zoospores of *Ectocarpus virescens,* Thuret; **Mei′ostates** (στατὸς, a standing), the intermediate products of metabolism, comprising (*a*) Anastates, formed during anabolism, and (*b*) Katastates, during katabolism (Parker); **meioste′monous** (στήμων, a filament), with fewer stamens than petals; **Meiotax′y** (τάξις, order), the suppression of entire whorls; **Mei′otherm** (θέρμη, heat), a plant inhabiting cool temperate regions; all are hardy in England.

Melampy′rine, Melampy′rite, a substance occurring in *Melampyrum nemorosum,* Linn.; the same as Dulcite.

melangeoph′ilus (μέλας, black ; γῆ, earth ; φιλέω, I love), dwelling in loam ; **Melangeophy′ta** (φυτὸν, a plant), loam plants; **Melangeophyti′a**, loam or alluvium plant formations (Clements) ; **Mel′anin**, a black pigment of bacteria ; **Mel′anism**, a disease producing blackness; **melanochlor′us** (χλωρὸς, pale green), blackish green, atrovirens; **Mel′anophyll**, the chief colouring matter of Diatoms (Warming, Handbook, Engl. ed., p. 18); **melanophyl′lus** (φύλλον, a leaf), having leaves of a dark colour ; **melanosperm′ous** (σπέρμα, seed), having dark-coloured seeds or spores.

melasmat′ic (μέλασμα, black spot) **Tis′sue**, a group of large cells round the vascular bundles in the stems of *Calamites,* with dark brown or black contents.

melastoma′ceous, resembling or pertaining to those plants of which the genus *Melastoma* is the type.

Melez'itose (Fr., mélèze, larch), a
sugar from the larch.

Melib'iase (*mel*, honey), a synonym
of RAFFINASE.

me'linus (μήλινος, pertaining to
quinces), like quinces, or quince-
coloured.

Mel'itose (*mel*, honey), sugar from
Eucalyptus "Manna," produced in
Tasmania; also spelled **Mel'itoze**,
a synonym of RAFFINOSE; **Mel'i-
zitase**, an enzyme present in
Sterigmatocystis nigra, Sacc.; **Mel'i-
zitose**, a sugar existing in *Alhagi
Maurorum*, Linn.

Mellaro'se (Ital.), the name of a
variety of the orange in which the
carpellary whorl is multiplied, producing an appearance of prolification (Masters).

mel'leus (Lat., pertaining to honey),
(1) with the taste or smell of
honey; (2) honey-coloured.

Mel'ligo (Lat., honey-like juice), used
for "Honey-dew," the exudation
of Aphides.

mel'linus (*mel*, *mellis*, honey), the
colour of new honey.

Melittoph'ilae (μέλιττα, a bee; φιλέω,
I love), flowers which are adapted
for fertilization by the larger bees;
the colour and scent are attractive
to man also (H. Mueller); adj.
mellitoph'ilous.

Melon'ida ‡, **Melonid'ium** ‡ (μῆλον, an
apple; εἶδος, like), an inferior,
many-celled fruit, as an apple;
melo'niform (*forma*, shape), melon-
shaped; irregularly spherical with
projecting ribs as in *Melocactus*.

Mem'ber, any part of a plant regarded
with reference to its form and
position.

Mem'brane, *Membra'na* (Lat.), a delicate pellicle of homogeneous tissue;
Membra'na gongylif'era, the hymenium of Fungi; **membrana'ceous**,
-ceus (Lat.); **mem'branous**, thin and
semi-transparent, like a fine membrane, as the leaves of Mosses;
mem'branous Layer, ~ **Myce'lium**,
interwoven hyphae forming a layer;
membranogen'ic (γένος, race), produc-

tive of a membrane; **Membra'nula** ‡
the indusium of Ferns.

memnon'ius (Lat., from *Memnon*),
(1) brownish black, nearly as dark
as *piceus*; (2) = MATUTINUS.

Men'del's Law, the gametes of a
heterozygote bear the pure parental
allelomorphs completely separated
from one another, and the numerical
distribution of the separate allelomorphs in the gametes is such that
all possible combinations of them
are present in approximately equal
numbers (Lock); **men'delize**, to
work in accordance with **Men'delism**
as stated; **Mendel'ities**, pl., facts in
harmony with the foregoing.

Meneblaste'ma (μήνη, moon = a month;
βλάστημα, a sprout), Minks's term
for the soredia of Lichens.

menisca'tus (μηνίσκος, a crescent), "a
cylinder bent into half a circle"
(Lindley); **menis'coid**, *meniscoi'deus*
(εἶδος, like), thin and concavo-convex,
like a watch-glass; **Menis'cus**, pl.
Menis'ci, applied by H. H. Dixon to
crescentic bubbles in woody-tissues.

Menisperm'ine, an alkaloid from the
genus *Menispermum*.

menstrua'lis, **men'struus** (Lat.), lasting
for a month or so; *cf.* BIMESTRIS,
TRIMESTRIS.

Menta'gra (Lat., an eruption on the
chin) **parasit'ica** = SYCOSIS; **Menta'graphyte** (φυτόν, a plant), the
Fungus supposed to cause the
disease Mentagra or Sycosis.

Menthol'ogist (*Mentha*, λόγος, discourse) an expert or writer on
mints, the genus *Mentha*.

Men'tum (Lat., the chin), an extension
of the foot of the column in some
Orchids, in the shape of a projection
in front of the flower.

Merench'yma (μέρος, a part; ἔγχυμα,
an infusion), spherical cellular
tissue; ~ **Cells**, unpitted cells in
the pith of trees, with intercellular
spaces, and much elongated radially; *cf.* PALISADE CELLS;
merenchy'matous, belonging to or
like MERENCHYMA; **Mer'icarp**, *Meri-
car'pium* (καρπός, fruit), a portion

of a fruit which splits away as a perfect fruit ; as the two carpels in Umbelliferae ; **mericy´clic** (κύκλος, a circle), occupying a part only of the diameter, as spirally-arranged leaves (Čelakovský).

meridia´nus (Lat., belonging to noon), at mid-day or noon ; towards the south (in northern latitudes) ; **merid´ian**, applied by O. Mueller to the plane in Diatoms which contains the pervalvar axis.

Mer´idisk (μέρος, a part; δίσκος, a disc), term proposed by Clos for any process upon the receptacle apart from the floral organs, whether glandular or not (Crozier) ; **Mer´iphyte** (φυτὸν, a plant), employed by Lignier for the vascular tissue of the leaf ; **Mer´iplast** (πλαστὸς, moulded), a protoplast in a polyplast which remains distinct, and does not fuse with its fellows (Pirotta) ; **Mer´ism**, (1) Bateson's term for the repetition of parts to form a symmetry or pattern ; (2) division of cells, cellular structures, or dichotomous division of organs (Massart) ; **merismat´ic** (μέρισμα, a share), dividing into parts or similar portions ; ~ **Tis´sue**, formative tissue, cf. MERISTEM.

meris´moid (εἶδος, resemblance), having a likeness to the fungus-genus Merisma.

Mer´ispore (μέρος, a part; σπορὰ, seed), the segment of a sporidesm ; **Merispor´ocyst** (κύστις, a bag), the simple or branched SPOROCYST of Cephalideae, considered as a departure from the type of fructification of the Mucoraceae (Vuillemin) ; **Mer´istele** (στήλη, a pillar), a portion of the stele of a monostelic stem received by each leaf ; restricted by Brebner, by excluding ACTINOSTELE and HAPLOSTELE from it ; further particularized into DI-, EU-, HAPLO-, MONO-, TETRA-, TRI-MERISTELIC types ; **merist´ic Varia´tion**, see MERISM.

Mer´istem (μεριστὸς, divisible), nascent tissue, capable of being trans-

formed into special forms, as cambium, etc. ; **Pri´mary** ~, forms the whole tissue of very young organs ; **Sec´ondary** ~, occurs in organs along with permanent tissue, usually in thin layers ; **meristemat´ic**, pertaining to the Meristem ; **meristogenet´ic** (γενέτης, a begetter), produced by Meristem, actively dividing cell-tissue.

Mer´ithal, Merithal´lus (μέρος, a part ; θαλλὸς, a young shoot), an internode ; **meroblas´tic** (βλαστὸς, a bud) **Embryog´eny**, when only a part of the spore is concerned, cf. HOLOBLASTIC ; **Meroconid´ium**, pl. **Meroconid´ia** (+ CONIDIUM), conidia which arise from the simultaneous septation of a hypha in Zygomycetes, and mature together, while ACROCONIDIA mature in succession from the apex (A. Fisher) ; **Merog´amy** (γάμος, marriage), reduced autophagy, which does not require the participation of the whole of a second gamete, but only its cytoplasm or nucleus (Dangeard); **Merog´ony** (γονὴ, offspring), fertilization of the oogonia of Cystoseira, without nuclei (Winkler) ; **Meroplank´ton** (+ PLANKTON), that found only at certain seasons of the year (Forel) ; adj. **meroplankton´ic**.

meros- as a prefix, and its forms **-merous**, **-merus**, as suffixes, denote parts or numbers, as dimerous, etc.

Mer´otype (μέρος, part ; τύπος, a type), a specimen collected from the original type in cultivation, by means of vegetative reproduction (Swingle) ; **syn´chronous** ~, taken at the same time as the original (Swingle).

Mes´ad (μέσος, in the middle), a mesophyte (Clements) ; **mes´arch** (ἀρχὴ, beginning), applied by Solms-Laubach to those bundles in which the protoxylem lies in the interior of the primary strand of the wood, thus partly centripetal and partly centrifugal ; **mesendobiot´ic** (ἔνδον, within ; βίος, life), applied to a mesosaprophyte, as Pythium, etc. ; **Mesendozo´a** (ζῷον, an animal), animals resemb-

ling Fungi, as *Torubia;* **Mesenter'ica**
(εντερον, an intestine), "the mycelium of certain Fungals" (Lindley);
Mesid'ium, a strongly developed,
thickened portion of the mesochil in
the flower of certain orchids; **Mes'
istem,** contracted from **Mesomer'istem,** the thickening ring of Sanio,
a ring of tissue producing the bundle
system; **Mes'oblast** (βλαστὸς, a bud),
the nucleus; **Mesoblaste'sis,** medial
growth from Lichen hyphae (Minks);
Mes'ocarp, *Mesocar'pium* (καρπὸς,
fruit), the middle layer of a
pericarp; **Mesocauleorhi'za** (καυλὸς,
stem; ῥίζα, root), Gaudichaud's
term for "the line of demarcation
between the ascending and descending systems in his 'Phyta,'"
(Lindley); **Mes'ochil,** *Mesochil'ium*
(χεῖλος, lip), the intermediate part
of the lip of those Orchids which
have it separated into three distinct parts; **Mes'ochite** (χιτὼν, a
tunic), the middle layer surrounding the egg in Fucaceae, composed
of cellulose and attached at the
base (Farmer); **mesochthonoph'ilus**
(χθὼν, the ground; φιλέω, I love),
dwelling in midlands; **Mesochthonophy'ta** (φυτὸν, a plant), midland
plants; **Mesochthonophyti'a,** midland plant formations (Clements);
mesoclad'ous, -*dus* (κλάδος, a branch),
possessing branches of medium
length (Russow); **Mesocol'la** ‡
(κόλλα, glue), a supposed intermediate layer of the cuticle between
the upper and lower surfaces; **Mesocor'tex** (+ CORTEX), the middle
cortex (Groom); **Mescoot'yl** (+COTY
LEDON), an interpolated node in the
seedling of grasses, so that the sheath
and cotyledon are separated by it
(Čelakovský); **Mes'ocycle** (κύκλος,
a circle), a layer of parenchyma
between the phloem and xylem
of *Gleichenia* (Boodle); **Mes'ocyst**
(κύστις, a bag), the definite central
nucleus of the embryo-sac with
which the second antherozoid fuses
to form a TROPHIME (Van Tieghem);
Mesoder'mis (δέρμα, skin), the middle

layer of tissue in the theca of a
Moss; **Mes'odes,** pl., the two medium
cells of the embryo-sac of Angiosperms which contain the polar nuclei
(Dangeard); **Mesog'amy** (γάμος, marriage), a process of fertilization in
certain Urticaceae, intermediate between Basigamy and Acrogamy
(Pirotta and Longo); adj. **mesogam'ic; Mesogonid'ium** (+ GONI
DIUM), a gonidium which is partially
enveloped in new tissue; **mesogonim'icus** (γόνιμος, productive), having
the gonidial layer in the centre (Wallroth); **mesohydrophyt'ic,** intermediate between mesophytic and hydrophytic; plants which incline to a
damper habitat than the true MESO
PHYTE (Whitford); **mesohygromorph'ic** (μορφή, shape) = MESOPHY
TIC; **Mesomel'itae,** pl. (*mel,* honey),
Huxley's term for a series of Gentianeae which have honey-glands in
the central portion of the flower; *cf.*
PERIMELITAE; **Mesomer'istem** =
MESISTEM; **mesometatrop'ic** (+ ME
TATROPIC), when the "first ovary
receives pollen from an anther associated with a second ovary, but
the second ovary receiving pollen
from the anthers of the first plant
not associated with the first ovary"
(K. Pearson); **mesomor'phous** (μορφή,
shape), applied to plants not specially
protected against desiccating influences; **Mesomyce'tes** (μύκης, a mushroom), a group intermediate between
Phycomycetes and the higher Fungi
(Warming); **Mesopet'alum** (πέταλον,
a flower-leaf), Pfitzer's term for the
LABELLUM of Orchids; **Mesophan'erophyte** (+ PHANEROPHYTE), perennial plants from 8 to 30 metres
in height, with buds partially protected; **Mesophanerophyti'um,** a formation of mesophanerophytes (Vahl);
mesoph'ilus (φιλέω, I love), dwelling
in moist lands; **Mesophlo'ëm** (φλοιὸς,
bark), the middle, or green bark;
Mesophorbi'um (φορβή, pasture), alpine meadow formation (Diels);
Mes'ophyll, *Mesophyl'lum* (φύλλον, a
leaf), (1) the interior parenchyma

of a leaf, the whole interior ground
tissue of the blade ; (2) the demarcation between leaf and leaf-stalk;
mesophyl′lous, *-lus* (φύλλον, a leaf),
having leaves of medium length or
average size for the genus (Russow) ;
Mes′ophyte (φυτὸν, a plant) ; (1)
Warming's term for those plants
which are intermediate between Hydrophytes and Xerophytes ; avoiding both extremes of moisture and
drought ; (2) moist land plants.
Mesophyti′a, pl. moist land plant formations (Clements) ; **mesophyt′ic,**
relating to plants which require an
average amount of moisture only ;
Mesophy′tism, possessing the power
of withstanding a certain amount of
aridity ; **Mesophyti′um,** a mesophytic
formation (Clements) ; **Mesophy′tum,**
(1) a name given by Clarion to the
COLLAR or junction of stem and
root ; (2) by Lindley given as the
demarcation between the internode
and petiole ; **Mesopod′ium** (ποῦς,
ποδὸς, a foot), the intermediate part
of a leaf, the petiole or leaf-stalk ;
mesopro′teoid (*Protea,* εἶδος, resemblance), leaves which have sclerous
cells derived from the middle zone
of the mesophyll (Vesque) ; **Mesopte-
ride′tum** (*Pteris,* bracken), an association of *Pteris, Holcus lanatus* and
Scilla festalis (Woodhead) ; **Meso-
sapro′bia** (σαπρὸς, rotten ; βίος, life),
organisms requiring a medium
amount of impurity, as Algae in
contaminated waters ; **Mesosap′ro-
phyte** (+ SAPROPHYTE), used of
Fungi whose mycelium is wholly
within the host, but whose fruit-
bodies are produced externally;
Mes′osperm (σπέρμα, seed), the
second membrane or middle coat
of a seed, the sarcoderm ; **Mes′ospore**
(σπορὰ, seed), (1) Dietel's term for
an *Uredo*-spore which apparently will
only germinate after a resting period ;
(2) the middle portion of the spore
of *Isoëtes* (Fitting) ; **Mesosporin′ium,**
the middle coat of pollen in Angiosperms (Fitting) ; **mesostat′ic**
(στατικὸς, standing), completing the

succession under mesophytic conditions (Clements) ; **mesosty′lous**
(+ STYLUS), in trimorphic plants
those which possess flowers having styles of intermediate length ;
Mesothamni′um (θάμνος, a copse),
Diels's term for maquis, formed of
hard-leaved shrubs ; **Mesothe′cium**
(θήκη, a case), (1) the intermediate
layer of cells in the wall of the
anther ; in ripe anthers it often
occurs as the inner layer by disappearance of the endothecium proper ;
(2) the THECIUM of Lichens ; **Mes′o-
therm** (θέρμη, heat), a plant of the
sub-tropical or warm temperate zones,
in Britain needing protection against
frost ; adj. **mesotherm′ic** ; **meso-
thermoph′ilus** (φιλέω, I love), dwelling in the temperate zone ; **Meso-
thermophy′ta** (φυτὸν, a plant), pl. =
MESOTHERM ; **Mesothermophyti′a**
temperate plant formation (Clements) ; **mesotri′arch** (+ TRIARCH),
when in a triarch stele the two
principal xylem bundles are more
or less fused (Prantl) ; **mesotroph′ic**
(τροφή, food), applied to the peat
of transitional moors ; **mesot′ropic**
(τροπή, a turning), applied to successions which become mesophytic
(Clements) ; **mesoxerophyt′ic,** mid-
way between mesophytic and xerophytic ; *cf.* plants affecting a dryer
habitat than pure MESOPHYTES
(Whitford) ; **mesoxyl′ic** (ξύλον, wood),
a synonym of MESARCH.
Mess′mates, used by A. C. Jones for
SYMBIONTS.
Mes′tom or **Mes′tome** (μεστὸς, replete),
Schwendener's term for the ducts of
a bundle, those parts which do
not conduce to its strength ; *cf.*
STEREOME ; **Mes′tome-bun′dle,** a
fibro-vascular bundle ; ∼ **Sheath,**
bundle-sheath.
Metabio′sis (μετὰ, with ; βίος life),
symbiosis, with one of the organisms
preparing the way for the other ;
not synchronous ; **metabio′tic,** relating to METABIOSIS ; **Met′ablast**
(βλάστος, a bud), the NUCELLUS.
metabol′ic (μεταβολή, change), applied

230

to chemical changes in living organisms ; ~ *Equiseta*, those species whose fertile stems subsequently form branches and become green (Goebel) ; ~ **Force**, vital activity; **Metab′olism**, the sum of the chemical changes in a living cell, usually restricted to constructive change ; *cf*. ANABOLISM, KATABOLISM; **metab′-olize**, to change as described ; **Metab′olite**, a product of metabolism. **Metacel′lulose** (μετά, with ; + CELLU-LOSE), found in Lichens and Fungi ; it is the same as FUNGINE ; **Metachlamyd′eae** (χλαμύς, a cloak), (1) C. MacMillan′s proposed term for Compositae ; (2) Engler′s term for GAMOPETALAE ; **Age of** ~, C. Mac-Millan′s term for the present age, subsequent to the Glacial Epoch ; adj. **metachlamyd′eous ; Metachlorophyl′lin** (+ CHOROPHYLLIN), a class of chlorophyll derivatives, the crystallizable chlorophyll (Tsvett) ; **Metachro′matin**=VOLUTIN ; **Metachro′mosomes** (+ CHROMOSOMES), certain bodies found in the hyphae of Ascomycetes which appear to be of the nature of Chromatin ; **Metachro′my** (χρῶμα, colour), the changing from one colour to another ; adj. **metachromat′ic ; Metacollench′yma** (+ COLLENCHYMA), a result of secondary metamorphosis which has taken place at a late period (C. Mueller); **Met′acorm** (κορμός, a log), the plant body after the differentiation of its permanent members ; adj. **metacor′mal ; Metacra′sis** (κρᾶσις, a mixture), kinetic metabolism, transmutation of energy ; **Metader′ma** (δέρμα, a skin), a modified tissue which takes the place of cork in some structures, but does not possess the properties of cork (A. Meyer) ; **metad′romous** (δρόμος, a course), a form of venation in which in a single Fern-frond the first set of nerves in the segments are given off on the upper, or the lower (basal) side of the midrib (Prantl) ; **metagam′etal** (+ GAMETE) **Rejuvenes′cence**, a cell or mass of cells act-

ing as a gamete or zygote (Hartog) ; **Metagam′ophyte** (γάμος, marriage ; φυτόν, a plant), C. MacMillan′s proposed name for his highest group of Phanerogams ; a synonym of " Siphonogamia " ; **Metagen′esis** (γενέσις, a beginning), M'Nab′s term for true alternation of generations ; **Metagymnosper′mae** (+ GYMNO-SPERM), the higher Gymnosperms (Jeffrey) ; **Metag′yny** (γυνή, a woman), with male flowers sexually mature before female (Loew) ; protandry ; **Metakine′sis** (κίνησις, a moving), the separation of the threads in the metaphasis stage of nuclear division ; **Met′amer** (μέρος, a part), used by Sachs to denote a PHYTON, or one of a number of similar parts of a series ; **Metameriza′tion**, the multiplication of floral elements.
Metamorphogen′esis (μεταμόρφωσις, transformation; γένεσις, beginning), the process by which organs change from their normal to abnormal conditions, by means of transitional forms (Worsdell) ; **Metamorph′osis**, in botany the change of one organ into another, as stamens into petals ; syn. **Metamor′phy** ; adj. **metamor′-phosed**, changed.
Metanaphyto′sis (μετά, with ; + ANA-PHYTOSIS), the formation of the floral envelopes ; **Metan′dry** (ἀνήρ, ἀνδρός, a man), the female flowers ready before the male ; protogynous ; **Metane′ma** (νῆμα, a thread), C. Mac-Millan′s name for the second stage in the germination of Mosses which succeeds the protonema ; adj. **metane′mal ; Metanthe′sis** (ἄνθησις, flowering), retarded floral development, as opposed to PROANTHESIS (Wittrock) ; **Metaph′asis** (φάσις, a phase), in nuclear division the separation of the daughter chromosomes ; **Metaph′ery** (φορέο, I carry), the displacement of organs, as when alternate become opposite, etc. ; **Metaphlo′ëm** (+PHLOEM), Van Tieghem′s term for a simultaneous growth of bast-tissue with the

METAXYLEM ; **Metaphyll′a**, pl. (φύλλον, a leaf), the mature leaf, as opposed to the juvenile form (Goebel) ; **Metaphy′ta** (φυτὸν, a plant), (1) plants which manifest sexuality or indicate by accessory characters that in their ancestral lines sexually complete progenitors have occurred ; (2) plants with tissue differentiation ; *cf.* PROTOPHYTE, adj. **metaphy′tic** ; **Met′aplasm** (πλάσμα, moulded), Hanstein's term for the protoplasm which contains the formative or granular material ; **metaplast′ic** (πλαστὸς, moulded), formed of METAPLASM ; **Metaplas′tid**, used to designate the metaphytic organism (Moore) ; **Metaplas′y**, any progressive change of cells, other than by growth or division, such as by change of cell-contents (Küster) ; **Metar′abin** (μετὰ, with, beyond, sharing with ; + Arabin), a substance present in some varieties of gum arabic, possibly identical with the "Pectose" of sugar beet ; **Met′asperm** (σπέρμα, seed), (1) a sporophyte in which the egg-organ is aborted, and no purely vegetative cells are to be found in either male or female plants ; (2) a synonym for Angiosperms ; (3) applied by Boulger for the large-celled secondary prothallium in *Selaginella*, the secondary endosperm in Gymnosperms, and the endosperm, originally so-called, formed after fertilization by the division of the secondary nucleus of the embryo-sac in Angiosperms ; **metasper′mic, metasper′mous**, angiospermous ; **Metaspor′ophyte**, C. MacMillan's expression for **a** Cryptogam of the highest specialization, as *Selaginella*. **Metas′tasis** (μετάστασις, a removing), (1) the sum of the changes undergone by the products of assimilation in the cells ; metabolism ; (2) the shifting of an organ to some unusual position (Moquin-Tandon). **Metasynde′sis** (σύνδεσις, a binding together), when the chromosomes are paired end to end ; TELOSYNAPSIS. **metaton′ic** (μετὰ, with ; τόνος, a

strain), used of a stimulus which reverses action ; **metatop′ic** (τό′πος, a place), refers to imbricate bud-covering which has departed from the course of the normal genetic spiral, by secondary development (Pax) ; **metatrach′eal** (τραχεῖα, the windpipe), applied to wood-parenchyma when forming tangential bands (Solereder) ; **metatroph′ic** (τροφὴ, food), applied to bacteria restricted to substances fabricated by higher organisms (Jones) ; **Metatroph′ism**, the correlated catabolism of the reserves and anabolism of the living tissues (Hartog) ; **Met′atrophs**, applied to saprophytic Fungi, those which feed upon decaying matter ; **Met′atype** (τύπος, a type), a specimen from the original locality, recognized as authentic by the describer himself. **Metax′in** (μεταξὺ, between), a proteid, the material of the fibrils of plastids. **Metaxy′lem** (μετὰ, beyond ; + XYLEM), the central wood as distinguished from the peripheral xylem-strands (Scott). **meteor′ic** (Mod. μετέωρος, in mid air), applied to flowers whose expansion depends upon the weather. **metis′toid** (μετὰ, = sharing ; ἱστὸς, a web ; εἶδος, like), composed of differentiated cells, each cell being dependent on the other cells of the organism (Hartog). **metoe′cious** (μετὰ, beyond ; οἶκος, house), existing on different hosts, heteroecious ; **Met′onym** (ὄνυμα, name), a name rejected because an older valid name was based on another species of the same genus (O. F. Cook) ; **metox′enous** (ξένος, a host), the same as METOECIOUS. **Metrogonid′ium** (μήτηρ, mother ; + GONIDIUM) = HETEROCYST. **Mette′nian Glands**, organs peculiar to Plumbagineae which secrete mucilage and sometimes chalk. **Me′tuloids** (*metula*, a small pyramid ; εἶδος, like), modified cystidia, encrusted with lime, which project from the hymenium of *Peniophora*, giving it a velvety appearance.

Miasm′, Mias′ma (μίασμα, defilement), Naegeli's term for those diseases which are due to microbes.

Micel′la (L. Lat. from *mica*, a crumb), an aggregation of molecules in the manner of a pleon, but in larger numbers (Nägeli) ; **micel′lar Ag′gregate,** a combination of Micellae.

Micraërox′yl (μικρὸς, small ; ἀὴρ, air ; ξύλον, wood), dwarf woody plants, with one main axis, and branches free from the soil, as *Calluna*, or *Empetrum* (Lindman) ; **Micran′dre** (ἀνὴρ, ἀνδρὸς, a man) = DWARF-MALE ; **micro-aëroph′ilous** (ἀὴρ, air ; φιλέω, I love), Beijerinck's term for anaërobic, needing but little free oxygen ; **Microaplan′ospore** (+ APLANOSPORE), non-motile spores of small size, possibly due to unfavourable surroundings (Thaxter) ; **Microbacte′ria,** pl. (+ BACTERIUM), minute bacteria ; **Microb′asis** (βάσις, a base), a variety of the carcerule, as in Labiates ; **Mi′crobe,** pl. *Microʹbia* (βίος, life), Pasteur's term for such organisms as Schizomycetes, bacteria ; **Microbiol′ogy** (+ BIOLOGY), used by Duclaux for the biology of bacteria and enzymes ; **microbio′tic,** relating to microbes ; **Microcen′trum** (*centrum*, κέντρον, a sharp point), applied to the granular inclusions in the astrosphere of leucocytes ; probably the equivalent of Centrosome (Farmer) ; **Microchlor′oplast** (+ CHLOROPLAST), chlorophyll granules in *Tillandsia* of minute size, constituting MEGACHLOROPLASTS (Billings) ; **Micrococ′cus,** pl. **Micrococ′ci** (κόκκος, a kernel), a genus of bacteria, sometimes used to express microbiotic organisms ; **Microcon′id,** *Microconidʹium*, pl. *Microconidia* (+ CONIDIUM), the smaller conidia, when two sizes are produced ; **Mi′crocyst** (κύστις, a bag), an amoeboid cell which is surrounded by a membrane, the resting state of swarm-cells of Myxogastres ; **Mi′croderm** (δέρμα, skin) = MICROBE ; **Mi′cro-**

di′odange (+ DIODE ; ἀγγεῖον, a vessel), Van Tieghem's term for pollen-sac ; **Microdi′ode,** the same botanist's expression for pollen-grain ; **Microflor′a** (+ FLORA), (1) the alpine flora, especially when small and massed (Freshfield) ; (2) the microscopic flora of a given locality ; **Mi′croform** (*forma*, shape), used of a heteroecious Fungus with teleutospores only, which germinate only after a resting period ; **Microfun′gi** (+ FUNGUS), minute Fungi ; **Microgam′etes** (+ GAMETE), the smaller and male motile cells of Algae ; **Microgam′etophyte,** the individual bearing the male sexual organs of a dioecious species ; adj. **microgametophyt′ic ; Microge′oxyl** (γῆ, the earth ; ξύλον, wood), lowly woody plants, with numerous stems arising from a subterranean rootstock, as *Rosa* or *Vaccinium* (Lindman) ; **Mi′crogerm** (*germen*, offshoot) = MICROBE ; **Microgonid′ium** (+ GONIDIUM), (1) a small gonidium, as compared with others produced by the same species ; (2) small bodies in Cyanophyceae derived from the division of gonidia (Brand) ; **Microli′chens** (+ LICHEN), minute Lichens ; **Micromelittoph′ilae** (μέλιττα, a bee ; φιλέω, I love), applied to those flowers whose fertilization is effected by small bees and similar insects ; the attraction is incomprehensible by human sense ; **Microm′eter** (μέτρον, a measure), a device or apparatus to measure minute dimensions ; **Micromil′limeter,** the thousandth part of a millimeter, and the unit of microscopic measurement, denoted by the sign μ ; **Micromyioph′ilae** (μυῖα, a fly ; φιλέω, I love), flowers which are fertilized by small flies which are often imprisoned ; adj. **micromyioph′ilous ; Mi′cron,** a micromillimetre ; **micron′ic,** visible under the microscope ; **Micronu′cleus** (+ NUCLEUS), derivatives of the nucleolus by its breaking up ; **Micropar′asites** (+ PARASITE), minute organisms belonging to their respective categories; **Microphan′erophytes** (+ PHANEROPHYTES), trees and shrubs attaining the height of two to eight metres (Raunkiær); **microphyl′line** (φύλλον, a leaf), composed of small leaflets or scales; **microphyll′ous**, small leaved; **Mi′crophyte** (φυτὸν, a plant), (1) used of bacteria; (2) used by Schimper for the smallest Algae, as Diatoms; adj. **microphyt′ic**; ~ **Forma′tion**, a community exclusively composed of Lichens or Algae; **Microphytol′ogy** (+ PHYTOLOGY), used chiefly of bacteriology, but also applied to any branch which is entirely dependent on microscopic research; **Microprothall′us** (+ PROTHALLUS), the reduced prothallus due to the germination of a microspore in Pteridophyta and Gymnosperms; **Mi′cropteres** (πτερὸν, a wing), furrows in the stems of plants; **Micropuccin′ia,** having teleutospores only (Plowright); **Micropyc′nid** (πυκνὸς, dense) = PYCNO-CONIDIUM; **micropy′lar**, relating to the MICROPYLE; ~ **Fun′nel**, the lower part of the ~ TUBE where it expands to join the seed cavity; ~ **Mem′brane**, the integument lining the MICROPYLE; ~ **Scar**, the spot on the ripe seed occupied by the micropyle (Kerner); ~ **Tube**, the passage formed by the MICROPYLE; **Mi′cropyle** (πύλη, a gate), the aperture in the skin of the seed formerly the foramen of the ovule; it marks the position of the radicle; **micropylif′erous** (*fero*, I bear) Tube = EXOSTOME; **Microscle′rote** (σκληρὸς, hard), a sclerotium modified by unfavourable vital conditions; after a resting period it develops into a perithecium (Zukal); **Mi′crosome,** *Microso′ma*, pl. *Microso′mata* (σῶμα, a body), in the plural applied to small granules embedded in the protoplasm; **Microso′rus** (+ SORUS), the male sorus in *Azolla*; **Microspe′cies** (+ SPECIES), species founded on very minute differences, as those in *Erophila* by A. Jordan; **Microsporan′gium** (+ SPORANGIUM), a sporangium which produces microspores; **microsporan′giate Flow′er**, male, or staminate flower; **Mi′crospore** (σπορὰ, seed), (1) the smaller sized spore in heterosporous plants, as *Selaginella;* (2) of late years applied to the pollen-grain; adj. **microspor′ic, micros′porous** : **Microspo′rocarp** (καρπὸs, fruit), the growth from which the microsporangia of *Azolla* are produced; **Microspo′rocyte** (κύτος, a hollow), the mother-cell of a microspore or pollen-grain; **Microsporogen′esis** (γένεσις, beginning), the development of the pollen-grain, or microspore; **Microspor′ophore** (+ SPOROPHORE), an organ which bears MICROSPORES; **Microspor′ophyll** (φύλλον, a leaf), a leaf-like organ bearing microsporangia; **microsporophyl′lary Flow′er**, a male or staminate flower; **Mi′crostome** (στόμα, a mouth), a small orifice; **microst′omous**, applied to flowers having narrow apertures; **Microsty′lospore** (στῦλος, a column; σπορὰ, seed), stylospores of a small size, as in *Locularia*; **microsty′lous**, short-styled, as applied to dimorphic flowers; **Microsym′biont** (+ SYMBIONT), the smaller of the two associated organisms; **Mi′crotherm** (θέρμη, heat), used for plants characteristic of the arctic alpine zone, in England needing protection from drought and direct sunlight; adj. **microtherm′ic**; **microthermoph′ilus** (φιλέω, I love), dwelling in boreal regions; **Microthermophy′ta** (φυτὸν, a plant), boreal plants [note the distinction from MICROTHERMS]; **Microthermophyti′a**, boreal plant formations (Clements); **Mi′crotome** (τομὴ, a cutting), an instrument for section-cutting for microscopical purposes; **microtrich′al, microtrich′ous** (θρὶξ, τριχὸς, hair), used of pubescence when so minute as to be observable only under the microscope, but sometimes perceptible to the touch (Williams); **Mi′crotype** (τύπος,

234

a type), the type of a MICROSPECIES ;
Microzoogloe′a (ζῶον, an animal ;
γλοιὸς, a sticky substance), a stage
of Schizomycetes when they are
immersed in a gelatinous envelope ;
Microzoogonid′ium (+ GONIDIUM),
a motile form of microgonidium ;
microzooph′ilous (+ ZOOPHILOUS),
pollinated by insects and other
small animals (Hansgirg) ; **microzo-
oph′obous** (φόβος, fear), repelling
the visits of insects or other small
animals (Hansgirg) ; **Microzo′ospore**
(σπορὰ, seed), (1) a motile spore,
small in size compared with others
of the same species, (2) employed by
Dodel for Gametozoospore ; **Micro-
zo′oid** (εἶδος, resemblance), a small
motile reproductive cell in some
unicellular Algae, as *Sphaerella*
(Hazen) ; **Mi′crozyme** (ζύμη, yeast),
Béchamp's name for microbes and
small ferments.

Micti′um (μικτὸν, mixture), a mixed
formation (Clements).

mid, intermediate ; used by H. C.
Watson for ~ -agrar′ian, and ~
-arctic zones of vegetation ; ~ Er′ror,
see DEVIATION ; ~ Race, an intermediate capable of being improved
by artificial selection (de Vries).

Mid′body, a translation of the Germ.
"Zwischenkörper," probably the
homologue of the cell-plate in the
higher plants (Timberlake).

mid′dle, central ; ~ Lamel′la, the membrane or primary septum between
any two cells ; ~ Lam′ina, in a
lignified cell-wall, the portion between the ~ LAMELLA and inner
lamina ; ~ Lobe, see LOBE, Middle.

Mid′rib, the principal nerve in a leaf.

Mid′summer Growth, a second start
into growth after ceasing ; it does
not occur in all trees.

Mi′grant (*migrans*, wandering), a
plant that is migrating or invading
(Clements) ; **Migra′tion** (*migratio*,
change of habitation), (1) movement
of plants by invasion, becoming
denizens of places in which they
are not native ; (2) the passage of a
nucleus from a vegetative to a fertile

cell in *Phragmidium*, etc. ; ~ **Cir′cle**,
a circle employed to measure migration (Clements) ; **mi′gratory**, passing
or migrating.

mih′i (Dat. sing. of *ego*, I), as an
authority it means the particular
form accepted as the true one by
the author using it.

Mik′roflora = MICROFLORA.

Mil′dew, a disease in plants caused
by the attack of the conidial form
of Erysipheae ; frequently used in
a popular sense for any small
parasitic Fungus.

milia′rius (*milium*, millet), minute
glandular spots on the epiderm ;
Henslow spells it "miliaris" ; **Mil′i-
ary Glands** = STOMATA.

Milk, an opaque white juice ; the
latex ; ~ **Sac**, laticiferous vessels
in some species of *Acer ;* ~ **Sap** =
LATEX (Crozier) ~ **Ves′sels**, laticiferous vessels.

mill-sail shape, molendinaceous.

mimet′ic (μιμητικὸς, imitative), used
of organs or plants which resemble
each other in external appearance,
but not in characteristic structure ;
Mim′icry, resemblance to some
other species, usually serving as
protective.

Mi′motype (μῖμος, an imitator ; τύπος,
a type), forms distantly resembling
each other, fulfilling similar functions, and thus representing each
other in different floras.

min′iate, *minia′tus* (Lat., coloured
with cinnabar), the colour of red
lead ; more orange and duller than
vermilion.

min′imal (*minimus*, least), (1) in the
least degree ; (2) the lowest condition at which a phenomenon can
exist ; **Min′imum, Law of the**, growth
proportioned to the quantity of the
nutrient constituent present in least
amount, which regulates the total
assimilation.

Minus (−), used of spores whose nuclei
are presumably female (Blakeslee).

minu′te, *minu′tus* (Lat., small), very
small, inconspicuous.

Miophyl′ly = MEIOPHYLLY (Crozier).

mioste′monous = MEIOSTEMONOUS.

Mire, a north-country word for a marsh or boggy place.

Mischom′any (μίσχος, a pedicel; μανία, madness), increase in the number of pedicels, as in *Rhus Cotinus*, Linn., *Muscari comosum*, Mill., etc.

Mist′oform (*mistus*, mixed ; + FORM), a hybrid or cross from forms which themselves have varied from the original ; **Mistopro′liform** (*proles*, offspring), fertile hybrids of MISTO-FORMS (Kuntze).

mis′tus, mix′tus (Lat.), cross-bred.

Mitochon′dria, pl. (μίτος, a thread or web ; χόνδρος, a grain) = CHRO-MIDIA ; **Mitokinet′icism** (κίνησις, motion), kinesis which reveals itself by a thread structure (Hartog), adj. **mitokinet′ic; Mit′om**, Flemming's term for the network of threads of protoplasm ; **Mito′sis**, Flemming's term for nuclear division ; Karyo-kinesis of Schleicher ; adj. **mito′sic, mito′tic**.

Mi′tra (μίτρα, a head-dress), (1) the galea of a corolla ; (2) the thick rounded pileus of some Fungi ; **mi′triform**, *mitriform′is* (*forma*, shape), mitre-shaped ; ~ **Calyp′tra**, one which is entire at the base (W. J. Hooker).

mixed (*mixtus*) **For′est**, one composed of various kinds, growing inter-mingled ; ~ **Forma′tion**, caused by the intermingling of two or more neighbouring formations (Clements) ; ~ **Inflores′cence**, one in which partial inflorescence develop differ-ently from the main axis, as centri-fugal and centripetal together ; ~ **Ves′sels**, those having thickenings of more than one description, as annular and spiral (Crozier).

Mix′ie (μῖξις, a mingling), Maire's term for the fusion of two similar nuclei ; the product he terms **Mix′ote ; Mixochimae′ra** (+ CHI-MAERA, a monster), the artificial mingling of spore material, pro-ducing (+) (−) and neutral mycelia (Blakeslee) ; **Mix′otroph** (τροφὴ,

food), applied to any plant whose in-sufficient chlorophyll contents does not ensure a proper assimilation (Pfeffer) ; **Mix′tae**, applied to homo-sporous Ferns producing sporangia in succession in time but not in space (Bower) ; **mixotroph′ic**, half-sapro-phytic (Pfeffer) ; **mixtiner′vius** ‡ (Lat.), having veins of various sizes.

Mne′mon (μνήμων, unforgetting), Coutagne's term for the elemen-tary factors of heredity.

mni′oid, (1) resembling the Moss genus *Mnium* ; (2) used by E. New-man as resembling any kind of Moss.

mo′bile, *mo′bilis* (Lat.), (1) easily moved, movable or versatile ; (2) "modified for migration"(Clements); (3) as moving sands ; **Mobilideser′ta**, pl. (+ DESERT), include a variety of plant communities on unstable sub-stratum, as of shifting sand-dunes and screes ; **Mobil′ity**, power of movement ; *cf.* MOTILITY.

Mock-plums, abnormal growths known also as BAG-PLUMS.

Modifica′tion Forms, inconstant varia-tions due to alteration in external conditions (Hedlund).

modioliform′is `(*modiolus*, a small measure, nave of a wheel, etc. ; *forma*, shape), like the nave of a wheel, depressed, with narrow orifice, as the ripe fruit of *Gaul-theria*.

Mod′ulus (Lat., a measure) of elasticity = ELASTIC LIMIT.

Mol′ecule (*molecula*, a small mass), an aggregation of atoms, hence the ultimate particle of a chemical compound ; *cf.* PLEON, MICELLA ; adj. **molec′ular**.

molendina′ceous, *-ceus*, *-a′ris* (Lat., pertaining to a mill), furnished with large, wing-like expansions.

Moline′tum, a plant association com-posed of *Molinia caerulea*, Moench (Warming).

mol′lis (Lat.), soft ; usually meaning pubescent.

molyb′deus, molyb′dos (μόλυβδος, lead), lead-coloured ; sad, neutral grey.

Mon- (μόνος, one), in Greek compounds = one; **monac'mic** (ἀκμή, a point), applied to neritic Diatoms having but one maximum in the year; *cf.* DIACMIC; **Monacrorhi'zae** (ἄκρος, at the end; ῥίζα, a root), plants whose roots are derived from a single mother-cell, as most vascular cryptogams, except *Lycopodium* and *Isoëtes* (Van Tieghem); adj. **monac'rorhize**; **Mon'ad**, occasionally used for ZOO-SPORE; **Monadel'phia** (ἀδελφὸς, brother), a Linnean class in which the anthers are united by their filaments into a single brotherhood; adj. **monadel'phian, monadel'phous**; **monan'der**, Necker's term for **monan'drian, monan'drous** (ἀνὴρ, ἀνδρὸς, a man), with one stamen; **monan'dreous**, having but one perfect stamen, as most orchids (S. Moore); **Monan'dria**, a Linnean class, with one-stamened flowers; **Monan'dry**, the condition in question; **monan'gic** (ἀγγεῖον, a vessel), (1) Prantl's word for a sporangium when enclosed by a hood-like indusium; (2) used of a sorus containing one sporangium; **monan'gial** is a synonym; **monan'thous** (ἄνθος, a flower), one-flowered; **mon'arch** (ἀρχή, beginning), applied to a xylem-bundle which consists of one protoxylem-group; ~ **Bun'dle**, one in which there is only one strand; **monari'nus** (ἄρρην, male), Necker's expression for monandrous; **Monas'ter** (ἀστὴρ, a star), in nuclear division the mother-star, the chromosomes forming a ring round the central spindle; **monax'ial** (+ AXIAL), applied to a nuclear spindle of one axis, but not necessarily ending in fixed points (Hof); **Monax'on** (ἄξων, an axle), when the two transverse axes of an organ or organism are equal; **mone'cious** = MONOECIOUS; **Monem'bryony** (ἔμβρυον, an embryo), the production of one embryo only; adj. **monembryon'ic**; **moner'gic**, an abbreviation of **monergid'ic**, consisting of one

energid, that is, one unit or nucleus (Goebel).

mon'eroid, like the genus *Monera*, in which the protoplasm forms the whole structureless body of the fully developed organism, which is devoid of a nucleus; a presumed protistoid body.

Mon'grel, a cross or hybrid.

monil'iform, *moniliform'is* (*monile*, a necklace; *forma*, shape), necklace-shaped; like a string of beads.

Mon'ism (μόνος, one), employed by L. H. Bailey for "the doctrine of oneness; the supposition that all phenomena and all forms of life are derived from the unfolding or evolution of one single principle and substance."

Monob'asis (μόνος, one; βάσις, base), when the root is reduced to a small unbranched portion, as though it were only the base of the stem; adj. **monobas'ic**; **Monoblaste'sis**, used by Schneider for MESOBLASTESIS; **Monoblas'tus** (βλαστὸς, a shoot or bud), used of Lichen-spores when possessing a single cell; **Monocaro'tin** (+ CAROTIN), a lipochrome pigment allied to Carotin, the colouring of the root of the carrot; **Mon'ocarp** (καρπὸς, fruit), an annual or other plant that flowers but once (Crozier); **monocarp'ean** = MONOCARPIC; **monocarp'ellary**, composed of one carpel only; **monocar'pic, bien'nial-** ~, a biennial plant; **peren'nial-** ~, a plant which lives many years before fruiting and perishing; **monocar'pian**, *monocarpia'nus, monocar'picus*, **monocar'pous**, only fruiting once; **monocel'lular** (*cellula*, a little cell), cited by Crozier for UNICELLULAR; **monoceph'alous**, *-lus* (κεφαλή, a head), bearing a single head or capitulum; **monochas'ial** (χάσις, separation), a cyme with one main axis; **Monochas'ium, Monoch'asy**, a uniparous cyme, either pure, or resulting from the reduction of cymes (Urban); **Monochlamyd'eae** (χλαμὺς, a mantle), a large division of Phanerogams which have only one set of floral envelopes; **monochlamyd′eous,** *-deus,* having only one kind of perianth; **monochro′mic** ($\chi\rho\hat{\omega}\mu\alpha$, colour), of one tint, unicolorous; **monochron′ic** ($\chi\rho\acute{o}\nu os$, time), arising but once (Clements); **monocli′nous,** *-nus,* **monoclin′ian** ($\kappa\lambda\acute{\iota}\nu\eta$, a bed), (1) hermaphrodite, having both stamens and pistils in the same flower; (2) applied to the capitula of Composites which have only hermaphrodite florets; the condition is **Mon′ocliny; monocor′mic** ($\kappa o\rho\mu\grave{o}s$, a trunk), expressive of those trees which have one main axis bearing lateral branches of bilateral structure (A. H. Burtt); **Monocotyle′-don** ($\kappa o\tau v\lambda\eta\delta\grave{\omega}\nu$, a hollow), a plant having but one cotyledon or seed-lobe; **Monocot′ylae** was suggested by L. Ward as a shortened term; **monocotyle′donous,** with a single seed-lobe, as grasses and palms; **monocot′ylous** = MONOCOTYLEDON-OUS; **monocy′clic** ($\kappa\acute{v}\kappa\lambda os$, a circle), (1) when the members of a floral series are in one whorl, as the calyx, corolla, etc.; (2) annual plants; the state is **Monocy′cly; monocys′tic** ($\kappa\acute{v}\sigma\tau os$, a cavity), of one cell or cavity; **monodes′mic** ($\delta\epsilon\sigma\mu\grave{o}s$, a bond), possessing a single vascular bundle or meristele; used of petioles (Scott); **monodichlamyd′eous** ($\delta\iota$, twice; $\chi\lambda\alpha\mu\grave{v}s$, a mantle), having either one or both sets of floral envelopes; **monody′namous** ($\delta\acute{v}\nu\alpha\mu\iota s$, power), with one stamen much longer than the others; **Monoe′cia** ($o\hat{\iota}\kappa os$, a house), a Linnean class characterized by having flowers with the sexes separate, but on the same plant; **monoe′cious,** *-cius,* the stamens and pistils in separate flowers, but borne on the same individual; ~ **Homog′amy,** fertilization from another inflorescence of the same plant (Delpino); **monoec′-iously polyg′amous,** having hermaphrodite and unisexual flowers on the same specimen; **Monoe′cism,** the state of possessing monoecious flowers; **Monöepigyn′ia** ($\epsilon\pi\acute{\iota}$, upon;

$\gamma v\nu\acute{\eta}$, a woman), a class in Jussieu's system containing monocotyledons with epigynous stamens; **Monoen′-ergid** ($\acute{\epsilon}\nu\epsilon\rho\gamma\grave{o}s$, active), used of a protoplast possessing a single nucleus (Faull); **Mon′ogam** ($\gamma\acute{a}\mu os$, marriage), a plant with simple flowers, but united anthers; **Monogam′ia,** a Linnean order in the Composites with united anthers, but flowers free on the same receptacle; **monogam′-icus,** Necker's term for monogamous; **Monogen′esis** ($\gamma\acute{\epsilon}\nu\epsilon\sigma\iota s$, beginning), non-sexual reproduction; adj. **mono-genet′ic;** ~ **Reproduc′tion,** asexual reproduction; **monogenodiff′erent,** used of hybrids in which the gametes differ from each other in one single point (Johannsen); **monog′enous** ($\gamma\acute{\epsilon}\nu os$, race, offspring), = ENDOGEN-OUS; **monog′enus,** (1) monocotyledonous; (2) monotypic (Crozier, Dict. p. 18); **Monog′ony** ($\gamma\acute{o}\nu os$, offspring), means the same; **Mon′-ograph** ($\gamma\rho\acute{a}\phi\omega$, I write), a systematic account of a particular genus, order, or group; **Mon′ogyn** ($\gamma v\nu\acute{\eta}$, a woman), a plant having a single pistil in a flower; **Monogyn′ia,** a Linnean order, having a solitary pistil or style, though it may have many carpels; **monogyn′ian,** **monog′ynous,** *-nus,* possessing but one pistil; **monogynae′cial** ($\gamma v\nu\alpha\iota\kappa\epsilon\hat{\iota}o\nu$, women's quarters), simple fruits resulting from the pistil of one flower; **Monohy′brid** (+ HYBRID), a cross from parents which differ by one character only (De Vries); **Monohypogyn′ia** ($\acute{v}\pi\grave{o}$, under; $\gamma v\nu\acute{\eta}$, a woman), a class in Jussieu's system containing monocotyledons with hypogenous stamens; **monoicodimor′phic** (+ DIMORPHIC), cleistogamic; **monoi′oous** ($o\hat{\iota}\kappa os$, a house), used by bryologists for MONOECIOUS; **monokar′ic** ($\kappa\acute{a}\rho vo\nu$, a nut), having a single nucleus (Pirotta); **monolep′idus** ($\lambda\epsilon\pi\acute{\iota}s$, $\lambda\epsilon\pi\acute{\iota}\delta os$, a scale), one-scaled; **Monole′psis** ($\lambda\hat{\eta}\psi\iota s$, a receiving), false hybridism, where the characters of one parent only are transmitted (Bateson); **monol′-**

obus (λοβὸs, an ear-lobe), used by
Spruce for one-lobed ; **monoloc'-
ular**, *monolocula'ris* (*loculus*, a little
place), one-celled, unilocular, applied
to ovaries, etc.; **Monomer'istele** (+
MERISTELE), a single out-going leaf-
trace (Brebner); **monom'erous** (μέρος,
a part), formed of a single member, as
a fruit which may be of one carpel;
monomorph'ous (μορφὴ, shape), of
one form only, not polymorphic
(Bailey) ; **monopet'alous**, *-lus* (πέταλον, a flower-leaf), (1) literally one-
petalled ; (2) gamopetalous, where
the corolla is composed of several
petals laterally united ; **monoph'-
agous** (φάγος, a glutton), applied to
a Fungus confined to a single species
as its host ; **monophylet'ic** (φυλὴ, a
tribe), originally descended from one
tribe, as opposed to polyphyletic ;
monophyl'lus, *-lus* (φύλλον, a leaf),
(1) one-leaved, as an involucrum of
a single piece ; (2) used of a leaf-
bud where a single leaf is subtended
by an investing stipule ; (3) gamosepalous or gamopetalous ; **Mon'-
oplast** (πλαστὸς, moulded), the
organic form-element of protoplasm,
which group into polyplasts (Vogt);
adj. **monoplast'ic**; **Mon'opode, Monopod'ium** (ποῦς, ποδὸς, a foot), a stem
of a single and continuous axis ; adj.
monopod'ial; **monop'terous** (πτερὸν,
a wing), one-winged; **monopyre'nus**
(πυρὴν, a kernel), containing a single
stone or nutlet ; **monosep'alous**, *-lus*
(+ SEPALUM), gamosepalous, the
segments of the calyx being united;
monosiphon'ic (σίφων, a tube), applied to Algae consisting of a continuous tube, an algal filament of
a single row of cells ; **monosi'phon-
ous** (σίφων, a tube), consisting of a
single tube, as some Algae ; mono-
siphonic ; **Mono'sis**, the isolation of
an organ from the rest; **Mon'osomes**,
pl. (σῶμα, a body), used by Gates
for aberrant chromosomes which pass
undivided into one of the daughter-
nuclei; **Mon'osperm** (σπέρμα, seed),
a plant of one seed only ; **mono-
sperm'ous**, *-mus*, one-seeded ; **mono-**

spi'rous (σπεῖρα, a twisted cord),
Spruce's term for that condition of
the elater in Hepaticae, which consists of a single spiral ; **Monospi'rus**,
an elater of this kind ; **monospo-
ran'giate** (+ SPORANGIUM), (1)
unisexual ; (2) applied to a flower
with sporangia borne on separate
axes, as the beech and oak ; (3)
having one sporangium ; further
distinguished as **mac'ro-** or **mi'cro-
sporangiate**, as they bear sporangia
of the kind indicated ; **Monospo-
rang'ium**, used by Sauvageau for
the organ which produces mono-
spores ; **Mon'ospore**, a special spore
in *Ectocarpus*, by Sauvageau considered to be a GEMMA ; **monos'-
tachous** (στάχυς, a spike), arranged
in one spike ; **monoste'lic** (στήλη,
a pillar) ; **monoste'lous**, having but
one stele or central cylinder of vascular tissue ; **Monoste'ly**, the state
of having a single stele ; **monos'-
tichous**, *-chus* (στίχος, a row), (1) in
a single vertical row ; (2) applied to
bacteria arranged in one row or
chain (C. Jones) ; **monostromat'ic**
(στρῶμα, bed-covering), consisting of
a single layer ; applied to the leaves
of Mosses and the thallus of Algae
when so composed ; *cf.* DISTROMATIC;
monosty'lous, *-lus* (+ STYLUS), having a single style.

Mono'sy (μόνωσις, deserted), Morren's
term for the abnormal isolation of
parts due to (*a*) ADESMY or (*b*)
DIALYSIS.

monosymmet'rical (μόνος, one; σύμμετρος, proportionate), used of a
flower which can be bisected in one
plane only ; zygomorphic ; **mono-
thalam'ic, monothal'amous** (θάλαμος,
a bed-chamber), (1) applied to apothecia consisting of a single chamber ;
(2) when galls consist of only one
interior chamber ; **monothal'mic**,
derived from a single flower, as most
fruits (Crozier) ; **monothe'cal** (θήκη,
a case), having a single loculus or
cell ; **monot'ocous**, *-cus* (τόκος, child-
birth), fruiting once only, as annuals
and biennials, monocarpic ; **mono-**

top´ic (τόπος, a place), (1) originating once only (Clements), (2) arising from one centre (Drude); **monotrich´ous** (θρίξ, τριχὸς, hair), having one bristle or cilium, as certain Flagellata; **monotroph´ic** (τροφὴ, food), nutrition confined to one host-species; *cf.* POLYTROPHIC; **monotrop´ic** (τροπὴ, a turning), applied to bees which visit only one species of flower; **monotyp´ic** (τύπος, a type), having only one exponent, as a genus with but one species; **Monox´eny** (ξένος, a host), used of a parasite on one host only; autoecious; **monoxyl´ic** (ξύλον, wood), used of vascular bundles in which the centrifugal part is primary xylem.

Monsoon´ For´est, Schimper's term for tropical, deciduous high-forest, with heavy rainfall and long dry season.

Mon´ster, *Mon´strum* (Lat., an unnatural production), an abnormality; **Monstros´ity** *Monstro´sitas*, some conformation deviating from the usual and natural structure; adj. **mons´trous.**

mon´tane, *monta´nus* (Lat.), pertaining to mountains, as a plant which grows on them.

Moor´land, ranges from sea-level to the high hills in Britain, with peat, and ericaceous plants as chief vegetation; ∼ **Province,** an area in which climatic factors tend to produce moors (Crampton).

Mor´ia ‡ (μόρος, a share), parts of a flower in general, as *pentamorius*, all parts in fives.

Mor´in (*Morus*, mulberry), a principle derived from the yellow heartwood of fustic, *Maclura aurantiaca*, Nutt.; the name is derived from *Morus*, to which genus the plant was formerly referred; **mori´nus,** Hayne's term for mulberry black; the deep purple of the ripe fruit of *Morus nigra;* **Morozy´mase** (ζύμη, leaven), an assumed enzyme in the mulberry, now believed to be a mixture of diastase and zymase.

Morphaesthe´sia (μορφὴ, shape; αἴσθησις, perception by the senses),

Noll's term for the tendency to assume definite relations of symmetry.

Morph´ia, Morph´ine (*Morpheus*, the god of sleep), the best known of all the alkaloids contained in the opium poppy.

Morphogen´esis (μορφὴ, shape; γένεσις, beginning), the production of morphological characters; adj. **morphogenet´ic; morphog´enous Ir´ritants,** external factors requisite for inception of propagation (Herbst); **Morphog´eny** (γένος, offspring), the study of adaptations of the plant in its natural surroundings (Jaccard); **Morphog´raphy** (γράφω, I write), anatomy and descriptive histology (Vuillemin); **morpholog´ical,** relating to Morphology; ∼ **Spe´cies,** Parmentier's term for such specific forms as occur in *Rosa,* which are assumed to have departed from their ancestral form in consequence of varied environment; **Morphol´ogy** (λόγος, discourse), the study of form and its development.

Morpho´sis (μόρφωσις, a shaping), the manner of development; the order in which organs form from their earliest to their final condition.

mor´phus (μορφὴ, shape), in Greek compounds = appearance, as *rhizomorphus*, having the appearance of a root.

mor´ulose (*morulus*, dark-coloured), dark, almost black (Solereder); *cf.* MORINUS.

mosa´ic (Fr., mosaique, from late Lat. *musaicus*, tessellated work), (1) applied to hybrids which display patches of varying character (Bateson); (2) **Mosa´ic,** a disease ascribed to some physiological cause, showing patches on the leaves of tobacco and other plants.

mos´chate, *moscha´tus* (*moschus*, musk), musky.

Moss, (1) the common name for bryophyte; (2) a lowland moor; ∼ **Moor,** usually higher in the centre, with growth of *Sphagnum;* "Hochmoor" of the Germans; ∼ **Tun´dra** (Finnish), flat or undulating tract, devoid of forest, in the north of Russian Siberia ; **Moss′ing**, covering decorticated trunks with moss, to induce the production of renewed bark in *Cinchona* culture.

Moth′er, used in the sense of "parent"; ∼ **Cells**, those which divide to form other cells ; ∼ **Plant**, (1) the parent plant, from which vegetative portions have been derived ; (2) the female or seed-bearing parent of a hybrid ; ∼ **Skein**, a continuous ribbon-like figure of chromatin in the early stages of nuclear division, further divided into **close** ∼, **looped** ∼, and **loose** ∼ ; ∼ **Star** = MONASTER, a stage of nuclear division.

Moth′er-of-Vin′egar, the active agent in acetous fermentation, *Saccharomyces Mycoderma*, Reess.

Moth-flow′ers, adapted for moths as pollinating visitors: they are usually white flowers.

mo′tile (*motus*, a moving), moveable ; ∼ **Re′gion**, (1) the region of elongation in growing members ; (2) in mature members a distinct organ, such as the pulvinus in *Mimosa pudica*, Linn.

Motil′ity (Fr., motilité), the power of movement ; ∼ **of Pro′toplasm**, a suggested emendation of "contractility" of protoplasm.

Mo′tion-dicog′amy (+ DICOGAMY), when the sexual organs vary in length or position during flowering.

Mo′tor (Lat., a mover) ; ∼ **Re′flex**, negative chemotropism, a reactive motion ; ∼ **Zone**, another term for MOTILE REGION.

Mould, applied to microscopic saprophytic Fungi, such as *Mucor* and its allies.

Move′able, the same as MOTILE, (1) used of a versatile anther whose attachment is slight, therefore apt to be moved by wind or slight shock ; (2) with colours, "shot" or changeable (J. S. Henslow) ; (3) the annulus of an Agaric when it detaches itself from the stipes and remains free.

Move′ment, motion, continuous or

transient ; ∼ of **Varia′tion**, see ALLASOTONIC.

Mox′a (native name), the woolly leaves of *Artemisia Moxa*, DC.

Mu′cedin (*mucedus*, mouldy), a tough viscous body associated with gluten in vegetable gelatin (Goodale) ; **muce′dinous**, musty, mouldy.

mu′cic (*mucus*, nasal secretion), relating to gum ; **Mu′cilage** (Fr.), vegetable gelatine belonging to the amylose group of carbohydrates; ∼ **Canal′**; ∼ **Cav′ity**, space caused by the breaking down of the cell-wall of neighbouring cells ; ∼ **Cells**, cells whose contents are gum or similar secretions; ∼ **Slit**, an opening on the under surface of the thallus in Anthoceroteae, like a stoma without guard-cells, leading into a cavity filled with gum ; **mucilag′inous**, slimy, composed of mucilage ; **Mu′cine**, a constituent of wheat-gluten which is soluble in water; **Muco-cel′lulose** (+ CELLULOSE), alluded to under CELLULOSES ; **mu′coid** (εἶδος, resemblance), a secretion resembling that formed by the mucous membrane of animals.

Mu′corin, an albuminoid substance occurring in species of *Mucor* (De Bary) ; **mu′corine**, mucedinous, resembling the genus *Mucor;* **mucorin′eous**, resembling the Mucorineae ; **Mucormyco′sis** (+ MYCOSIS), any disease in animals due to mucorine Fungi (Barthelot).

mu′cous, *muco′sus* (Lat.), slimy ; *cf.* MUCUS.

Mu′cro (Lat., a sharp point), (1) a sharp terminal point ; (2) used by Arthur and Holway for MICROMILLIMETRE (= μ); *cf.* MICRON ; **Mucro′na** ‡ = MUCRO (Lindley) ; **mu′cronate**, *mucrona′tus*, possessing a short and straight point, as some leaves ; **Mucrona′tion** = MUCRO ; **mucronula′tus** (Lat.), dim. of mucronate.

Mu′cus (Lat., nasal secretion), gum-like matter soluble in water; **mu′cous**, mucilaginous.

Mu′darin, a substance occurring in the

bark of the "mudar," *Calotropis gigantea*, Dryand., and *C. procera*, Dryand.

Muel′ler's Bodies, ~ **Corpus′cles**, metamorphosed glands found in certain myrmecophilous plants, as *Cecropia adenopus*, Mart., which forms a velvety coating on the under side of the base of the petiole; they are utilized as food by ants.

Mule, in botany, means cross-bred, a hybrid.

Mul′ga Scrub, chiefly composed of thorny acacias, forming an impenetrable thicket (Warming).

multan′gular, *multangular′is*, *mulang′ulus* (*multus*, many; *angulus*, an angle), many-angled; **multicap′-sular** (*capsula*, a small box), having many capsules; **multicil′iate** (*cilium*, an eyelash), with many cilia; **mul′ti-ceps, multicip′ital** (*caput*, a head), with many heads; it refers to the crown of a single root; **multicos′-tate** (*costa*, a rib), many-ribbed; the ribs running from the base of a leaf towards its apex; **multiden′tate** (*dentatus*, toothed), with many teeth; **multidigita′to-pinna′tus**, having many secondary petioles with digitate-pinnate arrangement (J. S. Henslow).

multifa′riam (Lat., many-ranked),many ranked, as leaves in vertical ranks; **multifar′ious**, *multifar′ius*, (Lat., manifold).

multif′erous, *-rus* (*multifer*, bearing much), often bearing, fruitful.

multifid, *multif′idus* (Lat.), cleft into many lobes or segments.

multiflor′ous, *-rus* (*multus*, many; *flos, floris*, a flower), many-flowered; **multifolia′tus** (*folium*, a leaf), many-leaved; **multiju′gate**, *multijuga′tus*, **multiju′gous**, *-us* (*jugum*, a yoke), having many pairs or jugae; **multiju′gate Types**, phyllotaxis in which the parastichy ratios are divisible by a common factor (Church); **multilat′eral** (*latus*, a side), many-sided, having several flattened surfaces; ~ ′**Sym′metry**, radial disposition of parts; **mul-**

tiloc′ular, *multilocula′ris* (*loculus*, a little place), many-celled, as an ovary; ~ **Spore** = SPORIDESM; **Multilocula′res**, compound spores; **multino′dal** (*nodus*, a knot), used of a branch comprising one or more internodes (Shaw); **multinu′clear**, (+ NUCLEUS), multinucleate, having many nuclei; **multinu′cleate**, having more than one nucleus to a cell; **multip′arous** (*pario*, I bring forth), many-bearing, applied to a cyme which has many axes; **multipar′tite**, *multiparti′tus* (*partitus*, divided), many times divided, much cut.

mul′tiplex (Lat., with many folds), where many of the same parts occur together; **Mul′tiplex**, an individual resulting from multiple fusion of the product of a fertilized ovum (Worsdell); **mul′tiple Corol′la**, one that has more than one whorl of petals; ~ **Fruits**, the fruit of a flower-cluster when confluent into one mass; ~ **Pri′mary Root**, a root with several main divisions from the crown, as in *Dahlia* (Crozier); ~ **Spi′rals**, a system of more genetic spirals than one (Church).

multiplic′ate (*multus*, many; *plica*, a fold), folded often or repeatedly; ~ **Flow′er**, a double flower; **Multiplica′-tion**, *multiplica′tus* (Lat., increasing), augmentation, pleiotaxy, pleiophylly; adj. **multiplica′tus**; **multipo′lar** (*polus*, a pole), with more than two poles; ~ **di′arch**, a stage in spindle formation during nuclear division (Overton); ~ **Spin′dle**, Guignard's term for an achromatic spindle when extending in a star-shape between several nuclei; **Multipolar′ity**, the state in question; **multira′diate**, *multiradia′tus* (*radius*, a ray), with many rays; **multira′mose** (*ramus*, a branch), much branched; **multi-sep′tate**, *multisepta′tus* (*septum*, a hedge), with many partitions; **multi-se′rial**, *multiseria′lis*, **multise′riate**, *multiseria′lis* (*series*, a row), in several series; **multisil′iquous** (+ SILIQUA), having many pods or seedvessels; **multiste′lic** = POLYSTELIC.

Mummifica′tion of fruits, used by Tubeuf to express the fungal resting body or sclerotium.

Mumo′nian (*Momonia*, or *Mumonia*), relating to the province of Munster.

mu′niens (Lat.), fortifying; **munien′-tia Fo′lia**, protecting leaves which overhang or otherwise guard parts which need protection.

mu′ral, *mura′lis* (Lat., pertaining to a wall), growing on walls; **mura′rius** (Lat.) means the same; **mura′li-divi′ded** = MU′RIFORM.

mu′ricate, *murica′tus* (Lat., like *murex*), rough, with short and hard tubercular excrescences; **muric′ulate**, *muricula′tus*, diminutive of the preceding.

mu′riform, *muriform′is* (*murus*, a wall; *forma*, shape), (1) flattened cellular tissue, with cells resembling bricks in a wall; (2) Koerber applies the term to certain Lichen-spores.

muri′nus (Lat., of mice), mouse-coloured.

Mu′sa-form, gigantic tropical herbs with perennial, epigeous, evergreen stem of involute leaf-sheaths, such as *Musa* (Warming).

Muscardine′ (Fr.), a silkworm disease caused by *Botrytis Bassiana*, Bals.

muscar′ian (*musca*, a fly), Beccari's term when flowers attract flies by a putrid stench (Praeger).

muscar′iform, *muscariform′is* (*muscarium*, a fly-flap; *forma*, shape), (1) fly-brush shaped; (2) like the genus *Muscari* as to habit or inflorescence; **Mus′carine**, a poisonous alkaloid from *Amanita Muscaria*, P. Karst.; **Musca′rium** (Lat.), a loose and irregular corymb.

Mus′ci, sing. **Muscus** (Lat.), Mosses; **mus′ciform**, *musciform′is* (*forma*, shape), Moss-like in appearance; **mus′cicole**, **muscic′olous** (*colo*, I inhabit), growing on Mosses; **mus′-coid** (εἶδος, like), resembling or belonging to Moss; **Muscol′ogy** (λόγος, discourse), a hybrid term for BRYOLOGY; an account of Mosses.

mush′room-head′ed, a cylindric body topped by a convex head of larger diameter; fungiform.

mu′table, (1) = MUTABILIS; (2) able to produce mutants (Clements); **muta′bilis** (Lat.), changeable, either in form or colour.

Muta′tion (*mutatio*, a changing), De Vries's term for "species" derived by progressive or sudden changes in several generations of seedlings; ∼ **At′avism**, a tendency to revert; **degress′ive** ∼, when a change takes place in the partial latency of a character; **progress′ive** ∼, when an entirely new character appears; **retrogress′ive** ∼, when an active or present character becomes latent; **Mu′tant**, G. Henslow's name for a "species" so raised.

mu′ticous, *mu′ticus* (Lat., curtailed, docked), pointless, blunt, awnless.

Mu′tilate (*mutilus*, maimed); **mu′tilus** (Lat., maimed), applied to a flower nearly or wholly wanting the petals.

Mu′tualism (mutual + ism), the same as Commensalism; that is, an association of two organisms which is beneficial to both; also termed **Mu′-tual Par′asitism**; adj. **mutualis′tic**.

Mycelconid′ium (μύκης, a mushroom; ἧλος, excrescence; + CONIDIUM), A. Fischer's term for STYLOSPORE; **Mycele′** = MYCE′LIUM; **myce′lial**, relating to a mycelium; ∼ **Lay′er** = MEMBRANOUS MYCELIUM; ∼ **Strand**, fibrous mycelium; **Mycelia′tion**, taking on the aspect or form of MYCELIUM (A. S. Wilson); **myce′-lioid** (εἶδος, resemblance), resembling a mycelium (Archer); **Myce′litha** (λίθος, a stone), an old term for SCLEROTIUM; **Myce′lium**, the vegetative portion of the thallus of Fungi, composed of hyphae (Trattinick); **filamen′tous** ∼, the thread-like loose felting of hyphae; **mem′branous** ∼, the layer formed by the interweaving of the hyphae; **myce′loid** (εἶδος, like), resembling a mycelium; **mycetoge-net′ic** (γενέτης, a parent), producing Fungi; ∼ **Metamorph′osis**, deformation of parts by Fungi; **myce-tog′enous** (γένος, race, offspring),

producing Fungi; ~ **Chloran'thy,**
the development of green in organs
normally of some other colour, due
to a fungous parasite; ~ **Chlor'isis,**
where the chlorophyll is bleached
by the action of hyphae of some
Fungus (Tubeuf); **my'cetoid,** *myce-
toi'deus* (εἶδος, like), fungoid; with
the appearance of Fungi; **Myce-
tol'ogy,** *Mycetolo'gia* (λόγος, discourse), = MYCOLOGY; **Myce'tozoa**
(ζῶον, an animal), De Bary's term
for MYXOGASTRES; adj. **myceto-
zo'an.**

Mychogam'ia (μύχκιος, inmost), self or
direct fertilization, as opposed to
HERCOGAMY (Clements).

My'cina, in Lichens, a globular stipitate
apothecium.

Mycocecid'ium (μύκης, a mushroom;
κηκίς, κηκίδος, a gall-nut), a gall
produced by a Fungus; **Myco-
doma'tia** (δωμάτιον, a little house),
fungus-chambers, formations of
peculiar character found on the
roots of plants, regarded by Frank
as possessed of the power of attracting Fungi and digesting them;
Mycol'ogist (λόγος, discourse), one
skilled in the knowledge of Fungi;
Mycol'ogy, the science of Fungi;
My'coma, the body of a Fungus
(A. Braun); **Mycomyce'tes,** the
higher Fungi; **Mycomy'cophytes**
(φυτὸν, a plant), Marchand's term
to include Fungi and certain
Lichens; **mycoph'thorous** (φθόρος,
destruction), a Fungus parasitic on
another Fungus, as *Hypocrea fungi-
cola* (Rutland); **Mycophy'tophytes,**
Marchand's name for Lichens other
than MYCOMYCOPHYTES; **My'coplasm**
(πλάσμα, moulded), (1) Frank's term
for bacteroids, as the rhizobia on
leguminiferous roots; (2) an assumed property of the protoplasm
of parasitic Fungi of remaining
latent in the seed of the host, and
reawakening to complete its cycle,
on the return of favourable conditions; adj. **mycoplas'mic; Mycoplas'-
ma,** Eriksson's term for a latent
symbiotic form of *Puccinia* which

may exist in the seed and develop
into a mycelium when the host has
developed; **Mycopro'tein** (+ PRO-
TEIN), a gelatinous albuminoid
resembling protoplasm, of which
the putrefactive bacteria are composed; **Mycorhi'zome** (+ RHIZOME),
mycorrhiza-like structure in *Coral-
lorhiza* and *Epipogum* roots; **Mycorhi'za,** preferably **Mycorrhi'za**
(ῥίζα, a root), the symbiotic union
of Fungi and roots of plants; it
may be **ectotroph'ic,** feeding outside, or **endotroph'ic,** obtaining its
nourishment internally; farther as
ectotrop'ic, ~ entirely outside, or
endotrop'ic, ~ entirely within the
cells; adj. **mycorhy'zic; My'cose,
My'cosin,** the special nitrogenous
substance of the cell-wall in Fungi
corresponding to the animal substance chitin (Gilson); **Myco'sis,** a
disease in animal tissue caused by
species of *Eurotium;* **mycotroph'ic**
(τροφὴ, food), employed of plants
possessing mycorrhiza.

My'crocyst = MICROCYST.

Mycropro'tein = MYCOPROTEIN.

My'cropyle = MICROPYLE.

My'crozyme = MICROZYME.

Myioph'ilae (μυῖα, a fly; φιλέω, I
love), plants which are fertilized by
diptera; their flowers are dull in
colour and their odours are dis-
agreeable to man.

mykoklep'tic (μύκης, a mushroom;
κλεπτικὸς, thievish), applied to the
hairs on the rhizome of *Corallo-
rhiza innata,* R. Br., "which seize
the mycelium."

myoch'rous (μῦς, a mouse; χροῦς, of
the skin), mouse-coloured.

Myr, used in Norway and Iceland for
any kind of MOOR.

myr'cioid (εἶδος, resemblance), like
Myrcia or akin to it (F. v. Mueller).

myr'iaspored (μυριὰς, a myriad; +
SPORE), having innumerable spores.

myriophyll'oid (εἶδος, resemblance),
like *Myriophyllum* or having affinity
with it.

myrmecobro'mous (μύρμηξ, an ant;
βρώμη, food), applied to plants

affording food to ants (Hansgirg); **myrmecochor'ous** (χωρέω, I spread abroad), dispersed by means of ants; **Myrmecocho'ry** is the state itself; **Myrmecodoma'tia** (δωμάτιον, a little house), shelters formed by plants in which ants live; adj. **myrmecod'- omous**, affording shelter only; **myrmecoph'ilous** (φιλέω, I love), plants which are inhabited by ants and offer specialized shelters or food for them; **Myrmecoph'ilism**, the state described; **myrmecopho'bic**, **myrmecoph'obous** (φόβεω, I fear), shunning ants, used of plants which by hairs, or glands, repel ants; **Myrme'cophytes** (φυτὸν, a plant), ant-plants; **Myrmecosymbio'sis** (+ SYMBIOSIS), the mutual relations between the ants and their host-plants; adj. **myrmecosymbio'tic**; **myrmecotroph'ic** (τροφὴ, food), furnishing food; **myrmecox'enous** (ξένος, a host), supplying both food and shelter.

My'rosin (μύρον, sweet juice), a glucoside occurring in the seed of *Brassica sinapoides*, Roth, and other Crucifers.

Myrrh, an aromatic gum-resin yielded by *Commiphora Myrrha*, Engl.

myr'tiform, *myrtiform'is* (*myrtus*, the myrtle; *forma*, shape), resembling the myrtle; **myr'toid**, **myrtoi'deus** (εἶδος, like) is a synonym.

myrtilli'nus (Mod. Lat.), myrtle-green.

Mys'trin, a peculiar carbohydrate found in *Mystropetalon*, Harv. (H. Gibson).

myu'rus (μῦς, a mouse; οὐρὰ, a tail), long and tapering like a mouse's tail.

Myxamoe'bae or **Myxoamoe'bae**, pl. (μύξα, mucus; ἀμοιβὴ, interchange), the swarm-spores of Myxogastres; **Myxobacter'ia** (+ BACTERIA), applied to those bacteria which form colonies united by a gelatinous covering (Thaxter); **Myx'obia** (βίος, life), Schröter's term for Haeckel's Protista, *i. e.* Protophyta + Protozoa; **Myxogas'ters**, an Anglicized form of **Myxogas'tres** (γαστὴρ,

belly), Fries's term for the group of "Slime Fungi," otherwise known as **Myxomyce'tes** and MYCETOZOA; adj. **myxogas'trous**; **myxomyce'tous**, relating to the same group under its name of Myxomycetae; **Myxomon'ad** (μονὰς, a unit), a swarm-spore of Myxomycetes; **Myx'on**, a constituent of wheat-gluten precipitated by alcohol; **Myxophy'ceae** (φῦκος, seaweed) = SCHIZOPHYCEAE; **Myx'o-phyte** (φυτὸν, a plant), Wettstein's name for Rhizopoda regarded as plants; **Myx'opod** (πούς, ποδὸς, a foot), the amoeboid stage in contrast to the mastigopod; **Myx'ospore** (σπορὰ, a seed), a spore formed in the sporangia of Myxogastres; adj. **myxos'porous**; **Myxothallophy'tae** (+ THALLOPHYTE) = MYXOGASTRES; **myxotroph'ic** (τροφὴ, food), feeding by the ingestion of solid particles.

na'creous (Fr., nacre, mother-of-pearl), with pearly lustre (Heinig).

Nährlös'ung (Germ.), a nutrient solution for laboratory cultures; by mycologists usually restricted to a solution of horse-dung.

Nail, as a measure, about half an inch in length, the average length of a finger-nail; unguicularis.

Nail-head Rust, due to *Cladosporium herbariorum*, var. *citricola*.

na'ked, wanting its usual covering, as without pubescence, or flowers destitute of perianth, or buds without scales; ~ **seed'ed**, (1) gymnospermous; (2) formerly used of Labiates, from a false idea of the fruit.

Nama'tad (νᾶμα, νάματος, a stream; + AD), a brook plant; **Namati'um**, a brook formation; **namatoph'ilus** (φιλέω, I love), brook-loving; **Namatophy'ta** (φυτὸν, a plant), brook plants (Clements).

nanan'drous (νᾶνος or νάννος, a dwarf; ἀνὴρ, ανδρὸς, a man), used of certain Algae which produce DWARF-MALES; **Na'nism**, Chodat's term for becoming dwarf; **Nannan'der**, a dwarf-male (Wittrock); *cf.* NANNANDROUS; **Nann'oplankton** (+ PLANKTON), free

floating organisms of extremely small
size; **Nanophan'erophytes**, pl. (+
PHANEROPHYTES), shrubs not exceeding 2 metres in height (Raun-
skiær); **Nanophanerophyti'um**, a
formation of the shrubs in question;
na'nus (Lat.), dwarf, cf. PUMILUS.

napa'ceous (*napus*, a turnip; +
ACEUS); **na'piform** (*forma*, shape),
turnip-shaped or rooted.

nap'py, tomentose.

Nar'ceine (νάρκη, numbness), an opium
alkaloid forming silky, inodorous,
bitter crystals.

Nar'cotine (ναρκωτικὸς, making numb),
also an opium alkaloid, but of very
little narcotic power.

Narcot'ropism (ναρκάω, I grow stiff;
τροπή, a turning), movement due to
a narcotic cause.

Narde'tum, an association of *Nardus
stricta*.

Nar'dine, pertaining to Nard, *Nardo-
stachys Jatamansi*, DC.

nas'cent (*nascor*, to be born), in the
act of being formed; ~ **Tis'sue** =
MERISTEM.

Nas'tie (ναστὸς, pressed close), automatic curvature of a dorsiventral
organ influenced by continued
growth in length (De Vries); adj.
nas'tic.

na'tant, *na'tans* (Lat., swimming),
floating under water, that is, wholly
immersed.

na'tive, used by H. C. Watson for
undoubtedly indigenous.

nat'ural, produced or effected by
nature; ~ **Fam'ily**, a group of
genera formerly styled ORDER, but
since 1905 the latter has been restricted to a superior group; ~
Graft, when branches are naturally
united by "approach"; ~ **Or'der**,
an assemblage of FAMILIES, inferior
to CLASS; ~ **Sys'tem**, an arrangement according to the affinity of the
plants, and the sum of their characters, opposed to any artificial system,
based on one set of characters;
Naturaliza'tion, the act of becoming naturalized; **naturali'zed**,
of foreign origin, but established

and reproducing itself as though a
native.

Nau'cum, pl. **Nau'ca** (Lat., a trifle),
(1) the fleshy part of a drupe (Lindley); (2) seeds with a very large
hilum (J. S. Henslow); **Nau'cus**,
certain cruciferous fruits which have
no valves.

naut'iform (*nauticus*, pertaining to
ships or sailors; *forma*, shape) =
navicular (Crozier).

nau'tiloid (εἶδος, resemblance), spirally
formed, like the shell of a Nautilus
(Heinig).

nave-shaped, round and depressed,
with a small opening, modioliform.

Navic'ulae, pl. (*navicula*, a boat), free
frustules of Diatoms like those of
the genus *Navicula;* **navic'ulaeform**
(*forma*, shape) = naviculoid; **navic'ular**, *navicula'ris*, boat-shaped,
cymbiform; **navic'uloid** (εἶδος, like),
like the genus *Navicula*.

neb'ulose, *nebulo'sus* (Lat., vaporous),
(1) cloudy, misty, applied to such
finely divided inflorescences as of
Eragrostis; (2) used by Bischoff as
meaning smoke-coloured (= *fumeus*).

Necessa'ria (*necessarius*, unavoidable),
Linnaeus's term for a division of his
Syngenesia (= Compositae) in which
the ray florets are female and the
disk florets male.

Neck, (1) the collar or junction of stem
and root; (2) the point where the
limb separates from the sheath of
certain leaves; (3) the contracted
part of the corolla or calyx tube;
(4) the elongated portion of the
embryo sac or archegonium; (5) the
prolongation of the apex of the perithecium in Pyrenomycetes; ~ **Cells**
in the archegonium of Bryophytes,
the drawn-out portion, as distinct
from the venter.

neck'lace-shaped, moniliform.

Nec'rides, pl. (νεκρὸς, dead; εἶδος,
resemblance), certain cells in Cyanophyceae which become gelatinous
and disappear (Brand); **necroco-
leopteroph'ilous** (νεκρὸς, dead; +
Coleopteron; φιλέω, I love), when
fertilized by carrion beetles;

necrog′enous, *-us* (γένος, offspring), applied to certain fungoid parasites which hasten the decay of the plants on which they live; **necroph′agous** (φάγω, I eat), applied to saprophytes; **Nec′roplasm** (πλάσμα, moulded), the homologue of protoplasm in a dead seed; **Nec′roplast**, a protoplast whose organization has suffered irreparable injury and is dead; **Necro′sis**, (1) canker in plants; (2) used by Escombe as meaning the death of an organism; **Nec′rotype** (τύπος, a type), applied to forms formerly existing but now extinct; fossil.

Nec′tar (νέκταρ, the drink of the gods), a sweet fluid extruded from various parts of the plant; in the flower it is called honey; ~ **Flow′ers**, without coloured perianth or petals, producing sticky pollen, as *Salix*; ~ **Glands**, the secreting organs which produce the nectar; ~ **Guides**, lines of colour leading to the nectary; ~ **Marks** = ~ GUIDES (Crozier); ~ **Spots** = ~ GUIDES; **Necta′rium**, or **Nec′tary**, (1) the organ in which nectar is secreted, formerly applied to any anomalous part of a flower, as its spurred petals; (2) employed by Linnaeus for the utricle of *Carex*; **nectarif′erous**, *-us* (*fero*, I bear), nectar-bearing; **Nectarily′ma** (εἰλύω, I wrap round), any appendages to a nectary, as the long hairs in *Menyanthes*; **Nectari′nus** = NECTARY; **Nectarostig′ma** (στίγμα, a spot), some mark or depression indicating the presence of a nectariferous gland; **Nectarothe′ca** (θήκη, a case), the portion of a flower which immediately surrounds a nectariferous pore.

Nec′tism (νηκτός, swimming), swimming by means of cilia, as zoospores; **Nec′ton**, Haeckel's term for plankton in active movement; originally restricted to animals.

Nee′dle, the stiff linear leaf of Coniferae; **doub′le** ~, the specially metamorphosed leaf-organ of *Sciadopitys*; ~ **shaped**, acerose, acicular.

neg′ative (*negativus*, that denies), implying denial or absence of some quality or substance; ~ **Geot′ropism**, apogeotropism, the growing in a contrary direction to gravitation; ~ **Heliot′ropism**, apheliotropism, shunning light; ~ **Pres′sure**, when gases in plants are at a lower tension than air, in consequence of the withdrawal of water.

Neidioplank′ton (νηίς, a nymph; + PLANKTON), Forel's term for plankton organisms possessing swimming apparatus.

Ne′ism (νέος, new), the origin of an organ on a given place, as the formation of roots in a cutting.

Nek′ton = NECTON.

Ne′ma (νῆμα, a thread), a filament.

Nemati′um, water margin plant-formation (Ganong); *cf.* NAMATIUM.

Ne′mathece, **Nemathe′cium** (νῆμα, a thread; θήκη, a case), a wart-like elevation of the surface in some Algae containing antheridia and paraphyses or cystocarps; **Ne′matablast** (βλαστός, a bud), = NEMATOPLAST.

Ne′matodes (νηματώδης, thread-like), in botany, applied to Confervae.

Ne′matogone (νῆμα, a thread; γονή, offspring); Correns's term for an asexually produced gemma on the protonema of Mosses; adj. **nemato′genous**; **Ne′meae**, "Cryptogams whose sporules elongate into a thread-like form in germination" (J. S. Henslow); *cf.* NEMOBLASTUS; **ne′meous**, thread-like, filamentous (Crozier); **Nematomy′ces** (μύκης, a mushroom), a synonym of Hyphomycetous Fungi; **Ne′matoplast** (πλαστός, moulded), thread-shaped plastids observed in the cytoplasm of *Momordica Elaterium*; **Nemoblast′us** (βλαστός, a bud), used by Willdenow to include Mosses and Ferns.

nemora′lis (Lat., sylvan), inhabiting woods and groves; **nem′orose**, *nemoro′sus* (Lat., full of woods), used as if a synonym of *nemoralis*.

neogae′an, *neogae′us* (νέος, new; γῆ, earth), New World, that is, American or West Indian; *cf.* AMPHI-

GAEAN, GERONTOGAEAN; **neoge'ic**, migratory on recent geological formations (Crampton); **neomorphog'enous** (μορφή, shape; γένος, race), causing a new growth in contrast with that existing; **Ne'ophyte** (φυτόν, a plant), a newly introduced plant (Rikli); **Ne'oplast** (πλαστός, moulded), a new individual arising from one or more previously existing protoplasts, as the fertilized egg-cell (Hanstein); **neotrop'ic** (τροπή, a turning), South American, in plant distribution; **Ne'otype** (τύπος, a type), a specimen from the original locality whence the true type was obtained, which had been lost or destroyed.

Nepenth'in, a proteolytic enzyme occurring in the pitchers of *Nepenthes*.

neph'roid, *nephroi'deus* (νεφρός, the kidneys; εἶδος, like), reniform, kidney-shaped; **Nephros'ta**, Necker's term for the sporangia of *Lycopodium*.

nepion'ic (νήπιος, young), applied to the first leaves of seedlings developed immediately succeeding the embryonic stage of the cotyledons.

Ne'reid (*Nereis*, a sea nymph), a mythologic name used by Warming to designate water-loving plants which grow on rocks and stones; ~ **Forma'tion**, a community of Algae (Warming).

ner'itic (νηρίτης, son of Nereus), applied to plankton which is coastal; **Neroplan'kton** (+ PLANKTON), Haeckel's term for neritic plankton.

nerva'lis (Lat., pertaining to the nerves), (1) synonym of loculicidal, the dehiscence being along the midrib of the carpels; (2) relating to the midrib of a leaf, as a prolongation of it—as a tendril.

Nerva'tion, *Nerva'tio* (*nervus*, a nerve), venation, the manner in which the foliar nerves or veins are arranged; **ner'vate**, *nerva'tus* (Lat.), nerved or veined; **Nerve**, *Ner'vus*, in botany, a simple or unbranched vein or slender rib; **nerved**, *ner'viger* (*gero*, I bear), having nerves,

in a botanic sense; **ner'veless**, without apparent nerves; **Nervimotil'ity** (+ MOTILITY), used by Dutrochet to denote the stimulating effect of the substratum on a growing organ; **ner'vose**, *nervo'sus* (Lat., sinewy), full of nerves, or prominently nerved; **ner'vulose**, *nervulo'sus*, diminutive of NERVOUS; **Ner'vures**, the principal veins of a leaf.

Nest-ep'iphyte (+ EPIPHYTE), an epiphyte which accumulates humus around itself for its growth; ~ **Leaves**, pl., dimorphous-leaved ferns, those possessing heart-like bases acting as accumulators of humus (Goebel); ~ **Roots**, negatively geotropic roots of epiphytes which form nest-like masses within which humus accumulates (Goebel).

nest'ling, nidulant (Crozier).

Net-knot = KARYOSOME.

Net-plasmo'dium (+ PLASMODIUM), a state of Acrasieae, due either to fusion or merely contact (Olive).

net'ted, reticulated, net-veined with any system of irregularly anastomosing veins.

Neuramphipet'alae (νεύρον, a nerve or sinew; ἀμφί, around; πέταλον, a flower-leaf), Cassini's name for the Compositae; **Neura'tion** (+ ation) = NERVATION (Crozier).

neurop'terid, akin to or resembling *Neuropteris*.

neur'ose, *neuro'sus* = NERVOSE.

neu'ter (Lat., neither of two), sexless, as a flower which has neither stamens nor pistils; ~ **Flow'ers**, functionally asexual flowers; **neu'tral**, pertaining to neither sex; ~ **Axis**, that common to the several I-girders in stems (Haberlandt); ~ **Lam'ina**, the plane of zero-tension in a stem (or girder) when subjected to a bending force (Haberlandt); ~ **Zone**, in Characeae, that line or place where rotating streams of protoplasm flow beside each other in opposite directions, the "indifferent line" shown by the absence of chlorophyll granules; **neutriflor'us**

(*flos, floris,* a flower), used of the ray-florets of Compositae when neuter; **neu'trophile** ($\phi\iota\lambda\acute{\epsilon}\omega$, I love), a hybrid word for elements which do not take up either acid or basic stains, as hyalosomes.

new, the first publication of a genus, species, variety or form.

Newto'nian Curve, called also the binomial or Galtonian curve, a graphic representation of variations plotted geometrically in two dimensions; the **Half-Galtonian Curve** is a similar scheme, from the maximum to minimum, or *vice versa.*

Nex'us (Lat.), a connection.

nicked, emarginate or notched

nicotia'nus, tobacco-coloured, from the genus *Nicotiana;* it usually means a full brown; **Nic'otin**, an alkaloid found in tobacco-leaves.

nido'sus = **nidoro'sus** (Lat., reeking), having a foul smell, as of burnt meat or rotten eggs.

nid'ulant, *ni'dulans* (Lat., nesting), (1) partially encased or lying free in a cavity, as the gemmae of *Marchantia*; (2) embedded in pulp, as the seeds in a berry; **nidula'tus** (Lat.), nested, nestling; **Nidular'ium**, "the mycelium of certain Fungals" (Lindley). NOTE.—There is a genus of Fungi named *Nidularia,* Fries.

Ni'dus (Lat., a nest), a favourable place for a seed or spore to germinate.

Niederblät'ter (Germ.)=CATAPHYLLA.

ni'ger (Lat.), black.

Night-position, the position assumed by leaves during darkness, the edges usually being turned towards the zenith.

Nigre'do (Lat.), blackness; **nigres'cent**, *nigres'cens* (Lat.), turning black; **ni'gricant**, *ni'gricans* (Lat.), becoming black; this and the last are used for tints which turn black with age; **ni'gritus** (Lat.), blackened, clothed in black.

Nipe'tum, an association of *Nipa* palms.

ni'pho- ($\nu\acute{\iota}\phi\omega$, to snow), Drude's prefix for terms to denote snow.

Nip'ple, = PAPILLA.

niteli'nus (Lat., pertaining to a dormouse), dormouse-coloured.

nit'id (Crozier), = **nit'idous**, *nit'idus* (Lat., shining), smooth and clear, lustrous.

Nitrifica'tion (*nitrum,* nitre; + fication), the action of a nitric ferment resulting in the production of nitrates and nitrites; **Nitrobacte'ria** (+BACTERIA), bacteria which produce nitrification by their action; **Nitrocel'lulose** (+ CELLULOSE), see CELLULOSE.

nitroph'ilous ($\nu\acute{\iota}\tau\rho\sigma\nu$, potash or soda; $\phi\iota\lambda\acute{\epsilon}\omega$, I love), used of alkali-loving plants; **Ni'trophytes** ($\phi\upsilon\tau\grave{\sigma}\nu$, a plant), potash-loving plants, thriving best on soils affording most alkalies (Schimper).

Nit'schia-plank'ton (+ PLANKTON), floating masses of the Diatom-genus *Nitschia.*

Ni'valflora, the flora above the snow-line; **niva'lis** (Lat., snowy); (1) growing in or near the snow; (2) more correctly snow-white; **niv'eous**, *niv'eus* (Lat., snowy), snow-white; pure and lustrous.

Nix'us (Lat., an effort), affinity, as of one species to another of the same genus.

no'bis (dative pl. of *ego,* I), used as an authority in defining species, etc.

Nocona'mum (deriv. ?), Necker's term for the sporangium of *Selaginella* (?).

noctur'nal (*nocturnalis,* by night), occurring at night, or lasting one night only.

no'dal (*nodus,* a knot), relating to a NODE; ~ **Cell**, a cell at the base of the oogonium in *Chara* interposed between the egg-cell and the stalk-cell, with the "Wendungszelle"; ~ **Di'aphragm,** any septum which extends across the hollow of the stem at a node; ~ **Plex'us,** the net or transverse girdle of bundles which sometimes exists at a node;

~ **Wood**, *cf.* INFRANODAL, SUPRA-
NODAL.

nod'ding, hanging down, nutant.

Node, *No'dus* (Lat., a knot), that part
of a stem which normally has a leaf
or a whorl of leaves ; the "knot"
in a grass-stem ; Lindley gives the
following modifications : **closed** ~ ;
com'pound ~ ; **divi'ded** ~ ; **entire'**
~ ; **o'pen** ~; **sin'gle** ~ ; see his
Glossary (1849), p. lxii. ; **nodif'-
erous** (*fero*, I bear), bearing nodes ;
no'dose, *nodo'sus* (Lat., knotty),
knotty or knobby, chiefly used of
roots ; **Nodo'sity**, *Nodo'sitas* (Lat.,
knottiness), a woody swelling ; **Nod'-
ule**, *No'dulus* (Lat., a little knot),
(1) a small knot or rounded body ;
(2) = COAL-BALLS ; ~ of Diatoms
= STAUROS ; **no'dulose**, *nodulo'sus*,
the diminutive of NODOSE.

No'menclature (*nomenclatura*, a list
of names), the names of things in
any science ; in botany frequently
restricted to the correct usage of
scientific names in taxonomy.

Nom'ad (*νομὸs*, a pasture), a pasture
plant (Clements) [NOTE.—Not to
be confounded with the homonym
derived from *νομὰs, νομάδοs*, wandering ; *cf.* **nomad'ic**, used of certain
steppe plants, blown from their
original station] ; **Nomi'um**, pl. **Nomi'a**, pasture formation ; **nomoc'ola**
(*colo*, I inhabit), **nomoph'ilus** (*φιλέω*,
I love), dwelling in pastures ; **Nomo-
phy'ta** (*φυτὸν*, a plant), pasture
plants (Clements).

Nomolo'gia (*νόμοs*, custom ; *λόγοs*, discourse), relating to the laws which
govern the variations of organs ;
nomosper'mous (*σπέρμα*, seed), used
by Radlkofer to denote the seed
normally occurring in the order,
tribe, or genus.

non-anal'ogous = divergent (Osborn) ;
non-mari'time, inland (Kearney) ;
Non-occurrence, employed by Kearney to denote absence from a given
locality ; **non-saline**, shunning salt,
as plants of inland localities (Kearney) ; **non-undulate**, flat, not wavy
(Kearney).

no'nus (Lat.), ninth.

nor'mal, *norma'lis* (Lat.), according
to rule, usual as to structure.

Nosol'ogy (*νόσοs*, disease ; *λόγοs*, a discourse), see VEGETABLE NOSOLOGY.

Nos'toc-lay'er, in Lichens when the
Algal layer consists of *Nostoc* or
allied forms (De Bary) ; **nostocha'-
ceous**, resembling *Nostoc* or allied to it
(Archer) ; **nos'tocine** means the same.

notate', *nota'tus* (Lat., marked), marked
with spots or lines.

notched, emarginate, nicked.

noteroph'ilous (*νοτερὸs*, moist ; *φιλέω*,
I love), applied to plants which are
intermediate between hydrophytes
and xerophytes ; by Warming termed
mesophytes.

Nothog'amy (*νόθοs*, bastard ; *γάμοs*,
marriage), heteromorphic xenogamy,
crossing of various varieties in contradistinction to HYBRIDOGAMY ; **Notho-
gam'ia** has been proposed by Clements
for hybridization generally.

noth'us (Lat.), false or bastard, usually
applied to the false root of a parasite.

notorrhi'zal (*νῶτοs*, the back ; *ῥίζα*, a
root), used for incumbent ; the radicle
being on the back of the cotyledons
in certain Cruciferae ; **nototri'bal**
(*τρίβω*, I beat), pertaining to those
flowers described by Delpino as **no'to-
tribe**, whose stamens and styles turn
so as to strike their visitors on the
back ; syn. **nototri'bous**.

no'vem (Lat.), nine ; ~ **digita'tus**,
nine-fingered ; ~ **lo'bus**, nine-lobed ;
~ **ner'vius**, nine-nerved.

No'viform (*novus*, new), a CULTIFORM
of recent origin (Kuntze).

nu'bilus (Lat., dusky), greyish blue
(Hayne).

Nucamen'tum (Lat., a fir cone or
catkin), an amentum or catkin ;
nucamenta'ceous, *-ceus*, (1) having
the hardness of a nut ; (2) synonym
for indehiscent, monospermal fruit.

Nucel'la, = **Nucel'lus** (Lat., a small
kernel), (1) the kernel of an ovule ;
(2) the body of the ovule or macrosporangium containing the embryo
sac or macrospore ; **Nucel'lum**, Germain's form of NUCELLUS.

nucif'erous (*nux*, a nut; *fero*, I bear), bearing or producing nuts; **nu'ciform** (*forma*, shape), nut-like in shape.

nu'clear (*nucleus*, a kernel), pertaining to a nucleus; ~ **Associa'tion**, the fusion of protoplasts which contain them; ~ **Bar'rel**, a stage immediately preceding the nuclear spindle; ~ **Disc**, the mother-star stage; ~ **Divis'ion**, either direct by fragmentation, or indirect by karyokinesis, the entire history of the division of the cell-nucleus; ~ **Fi'brils**, chromosomes; *cf.* SPINDLE-FIBRES; ~ **Fil'ament**, the chromatin or chromatic filament; ~ **Fu'sion**, the union of two nuclei; *cf.* SYNGAMY; ~ **Osmo'sis**, the theory that the nucleus enlarges in the manner of a sap-vacuole (Lawson); ~ **Plate**, the demarcation of the daughter-cells in nuclear-division, see MOTHER-STAR; ~ **Reduc'tion**, when a smaller number of segments occur than at the previous divisions of the parent-cycle (Hartog); ~ **Ring**, the equatorial arrangement of chromosomes; *cf.* MOTHER-STAR; ~ **Sap**, the intermediate matrix (Schwarz); ~ **Spin'dle**, slender filaments from the poles, and crossing the equator, beginning in the skein stage, and completed in the mother-star; ~ **Star** = ASTER; ~ **Threads** = SPINDLE-FIBRES; **nu'cleated**, having a nucleus or nuclei.

Nu'clei; pl.: **Blad'der** ~, found in latex, which seem to increase by direct division (Molisch); **Giant** ~ of certain species of *Aloe*, remarkable for their size; **Thread** ~, long drawn out, in the mucilage of Amaryllideae (Molisch).

Nu'clein, Strasburger's term for CHROMATIN.

Nu'cleo-cen'trosomes (*nucleus*, a kernel), a term used by G. Karsten in describing the nuclear division of *Psilotum triquetrum*, Sw.; probably the same as Strasburger's "Secretion bodies"; ~ **Hy'aloplasm**, Strasburger's word for LININ; ~ **Id'loplasm**, the formative part of the

nuclear hyaloplasm; ~ **Mi'crosomes** (Strasburger) = CHROMATIN? **Nucleochyle'ma** (χυλὸς, juice), Strasburger's term for the fluid which fills the spaces in the LININ.

nu'cleolate, **nu'cleolated** (*nucleus*, a kernel), possessing a nucleolus; **Nu'cleole**, **Nucle'olus**, a sharply defined point in the cell-nucleus; **Nucle'olo-Nucle'olus**, = ENDONUCLEUS; **Nu'cleophy'ses** (φύω, I grow), tubular, septate projections in certain Fungi which correspond to the base of the perithecium, and ultimately become ascophyses; **Nu'cleoplasm** (πλάσμα, moulded), nuclear protoplasm, the nucleo-hyaloplasm of S. Vines; **nucleoplas'mic Ten'sion**, after cell-division when the increase of protoplasm and nucleus cannot proceed equally; this tension causes an increase of the nucleus and chromatin (R. Hertwig); **Nucleopro'teid** (+ PROTEID), any protein which is a characteristic constituent of the nucleus.

Nu'cleus (Lat., a kernel), (1) the kernel of an ovule or seed, the NUCELLUS; (2) an organized proteid body of complex substance; it contains one or more nucleoli, and divides either directly by FRAGMENTATION, or indirectly by KARYOKINESIS, otherwise called MITOSIS; (3) the hilum of a starch granule; (4) in Lichens, the disk of the apothecium, containing asci; (5) in Fungi, the centre of the perithecium; (6) a clove or young bulb; ~ **Bar'rel** = NUCLEAR BARREL; ~ of the **Em'bryo Sac**, the secondary nucleus; ~ of **O'osphere**, that in the oosphere (female pronucleus) with which a sperm-nucleus (male pronucleus) coalesces to form a germ nucleus; **closed** ~, that kind of nucleus which occurs in the higher plants, *cf.* OPEN ~; **gam'eto-** ~, the nucleus of a gamete; **gen'erative** ~, an active nucleus in karyokinesis; **Germ** ~, a nucleus resulting from the fusion of a male and female pronucleus; *cf.* PRONUCLEUS; **O'pen** ~, the central body of Phycochromaceae, of much looser structure than in higher plants, and destitute of true nuclear membrane (Hieronymus); **Rejec′tion ~**, sister-nuclei to the female nucleus which play no part in fertilization (Hartog); **~ Spin′dle** = NUCLEAR SPINDLE.

Nu′culane = **Nucula′nium** (*nucula,* a small nut), Richard's term for a drupaceous or baccate fruit containing more than one stone or seed, adopted by Lindley for a superior stony-seeded berry, such as a grape; **Nu′cule**, *Nuc′ula*, (1) a diminutive of NUTLET ; (2) the female sexual organ of *Chara*; **nuculo′sus** (Mod. Lat.), containing hard nut-like seeds.

nucumenta′ceous, an error for NUCAMENTACEOUS.

nude, *nu′dus* (naked), bare, naked, in various senses.

nudicau′lous, *nudicau′lis* (*nudus*, naked ; *caulis*, a stem), naked-stemmed, not leafy ; **nudius′culus** (Lat.), somewhat bare.

nulliner′vis (*nullus*, none ; *nervus*, a nerve), = ENERVIS.

nu′merous *numero′sus* (Lat., very many), in botany indefinite, not readily counted ; the sign is ∞.

Nuphare′tum, an association of *Nuphar* (Warming).

nup′tial (*nuptialis*), pertaining to marriage), employed to denote intra-floral nectaries.

Nursing-foot = HAUSTRUM.

Nut, *Nux* (Lat.), a hard and indehiscent one-seeded fruit, often vaguely applied to such fruits as those of the Labiatae and Cyperaceae; **spu′rious ~**, a fruit which owes its hardness to something other than the pericarp, **as** in *Mirabilis;* **Nux bacca′ta**, a nut enclosed in a pulpy covering, as in the Yew.

nu′tant, *nu′tans* (Lat.), nodding.

Nu′tation (*nutatio*, a nodding), the revolution of the growing tips of young organs ; **~ Chor′isis**, Fitting's term for a separation due to the growth of a tissue; **revol′ving ~** = CIRCUMNUTATION.

Nut′let, the diminutive of NUT ; *cf.*

NUCULE; variously applied to any dry independent fruit, as an achene, or part of a schizocarp.

Nu′tricism (*nutricius*, that nourishes), a form of symbiosis in which the Fungus becomes the nurse and feeder of the other symbiont, as in *Monotropa;* **Nutrit′ion**, the process of promoting the growth or repairing the waste caused by vital phenomena.

Nux (Lat., nut), see NUT.

nyctan′thous (νύξ, νυκτὸς, night ; ἄνθος, a flower), used of night-flowering plants ; **Nyctan′thy**, the condition of nocturnal flowering.

nyctig′amous (νυκτίγαμος, marrying by night), flowers which close by day, but open at night, often scented.

Nyctinas′tism, Nyctinas′ty (νύξ, νυκτὸς, night ; ναστὸς, pressed close), = NYCTITROPISM ; adj. **nyctinas′tic** ; **nyctipelag′ic** (+ PELAGIC), floating organisms which rise to the surface only at night (Forel) ; **nyctitrop′ic** (τροπὴ, a turning), placing the leaves as during the night ; **Nyctit′ropism**, assuming the sleep position.

nymphaea′ceous, resembling or akin to the waterlilies, Nymphaeaceae ; **Nymphaeë′tum**, an association of *Nymphæa* (Warming).

nymphaeform′is (*nympha*, a pupa; *forma*, shape); Koerber applies this to chrysalis-shaped spores of some Lichens.

Oak′wood Associa′tion, woods in which the oak is dominant.

Oan′gium (ὠὸν, an egg ; ἀγγεῖον, a vessel), an apocytial oogonium which forms oospores by free cell-formation, as in Saprolegnieae (Hartog).

ob, as a prefix, means inversely or oppositely ; as obovate, inversely ovate ; sometimes, but incorrectly, used for sub-.

obcla′vate (*ob*, inverse ; *clavatus*, club-shaped), attached at the thicker end ; **obcompres′sed**, *obcompres′sus* (*compres′sus*, pressed together), flattened the other way, antero-posteriorly instead of laterally ;

obcon′ic, obcon′ical, *obcon′icus* (*conus*, a cone), conical, but attached at the narrower end; **obcor′-date,** *obcorda′tus* (+ CORDATUS), inversely heart-shaped, the notch being apical; **obcor′diform,** *obcordiform′is,* are synonyms; **obcrena′-tus** (+ CRENATUS) ‡, denticulate; **obcur′rens** (*currens*, running ‡ running together and adhering at the point of contact; **obdiploste′mo-nous,** -*us* (διπλόος, double; στήμων, a thread), where the stamens are double the number of the petals to which the outer series are opposite; **Obdiploste′mony,** the condition itself; **Ob′forms,** in *Rosa* those forms with very glandular teeth and glands on margins of calyx (Almquist).

Ob′ices (pl. of *obex*, a barrier), Clements's term for hindrances to plant distribution; they may be **bio-log′ical** ~, as constitution of the plants, or **phys′ical** ~, as the shutting in, as by mountains.

obim′bricate, *obimbrica′tus* (*ob*, inverse, + IMBRICATUS), when the imbrication is from above, downward; **oblan′ceolate,** *oblanceola′tus* (+ LANCEOLATUS), strictly speaking this cannot occur, but the word is used for tapering towards the base more than towards the apex; **ob′late** (*latus*, broad), flattened at the poles, as an orange.

ob′ligate (*obligatus*, obliged), necessary, essential; the reverse of FACULTATIVE; ~ **Gam′ete,** a gamete which is incapable of further development without union with another gamete; ~ **Par′asite,** an organism in which parasitism is imperative in order to attain complete development; **ob′ligative, ob′ligatory,** as in OBLIGATE; ~ **Sym′biont,** an organism which is dependent upon another for its existence.

oblig′ulate, *obligula′tus* (*ob*, inverse, + LIGULATE), used of ligulate florets of Compositae extended on the inner side of the capitulum instead of the outside; **obliguliflor′ous** (*flos,*

floris, a flower), florets which are obligulate, as in *Zoëgea.*

oblique′, *obli′quus* (Lat., slanting), (1) slanting; (2) of unequal sides.

oblit′erated (*obliteratus,* erased), suppressed; **Oblitera′tion,** suppression.

ob′long, *oblon′gus* (Lat., rather long), much longer than broad, with nearly parallel sides.

obo′val, *obova′lis* (*ob*, inverse, + OVALIS), reversed ovate, the distal end the broader; **obo′vate,** *obova′-tus,* practically the same as the last; **obo′void** (εἶδος, like), an obovate solid; **obrin′gens** (+ RINGENS), ‡ a ringent floret of the Compositae, with an anterior lip one-fifth, and the posterior lip four-fifths of the whole, as though the lower lip were uppermost; **obro-tun′dus** (+ ROTUNDUS), ‡ somewhat round.

obscure′, *obscu′rus* (Lat., dark), (1) dark or dingy in tint; (2) uncertain in affinity or distinctiveness; (3) hidden.

ob′solete. *obsole′tus* (Lat., worn out), wanting or rudimentary; used of an organ which is scarcely apparent or has vanished; **obsoles′cent** (+ ESCENS), nearly obsolete.

obstruc′tus (Lat., blocked up), where hairs or other appendages partially close the throat of a tubular corolla.

obsubula′tus (*ob*, inverse, + SUBULATUS), very narrow, pointed at the base and widening a little towards the apex; **obsutura′lis** (*sutura*, a seam), ‡ applied to the suture of a pericarp; septifragal.

obtec′tus (Lat.), covered over by something; **obtec′to-veno′sus,** when the principal and longest veins are connected only by simple cross-veins; **ob′tegens** (Lat.), covering over.

Obtura′tor (*obturatus,* stopped up), (1) a small body accompanying the pollen-masses of Orchids and Asclepiads, closing the opening of the anther; (2) = CARUNCLE (J. D. Hooker), (3) a process of the wall of the ovary descending on the micropyle, in *Plumbago.*

obturbina′tus (*ob*, inverse, + TURBINA-
TUS), reverse top-shaped, swollen
at the bottom, narrowed at the
top.

obtuse′, *obtu′sus* (Lat.), blunt or
rounded at the end ; ~ **An′gled**
stem-angles rounded, as in *Salvia
pratensis*, Linn. ; **obtusius′culus**,
(Lat.), somewhat obtuse.

obval′late, *obvalla′tus* (*ob*, about ;
vallatus, walled round), apparently
walled up, guarded on all sides ;
obvalla′ris, surrounded as by a
wall, as in *Narcissus obvallaris*,
Salisb.

ob′verse, *cbver′sus* (Lat., turned towards) ; (1) the side facing, as
opposed to reverse ; (2) used when
the point of a radicle in a seed
approaches the hilum ; **ob′versely**,
in an obverse form.

ob′volute, *obvolu′tus* (Lat., wrapped
round), a modification of CONVO-
LUTE, when the margins of one
organ alternately overlap those of
an opposite organ, such as half-
equitant ; **obvolu′tive** is a synonym.

Occlu′sion (*occlusus*, shut up), the
process by which wounds in trees
are healed by the growth of callus,
then said to be **occlu′ded** (M. Ward).

occulta′tus (Lat.), hidden.

Occupa′tion, "possession of the ground
by plants" (Clements).

Oce′anad (*oceanus*, belonging to the
ocean, + AD), an ocean plant ;
ocean′ic, applied to organisms living
in the open sea ; **ocean′idus**, used of
a marine plant ; **Oceani′um**, an ocean
formation ; **oceanoph′ilus** (φιλέω, I
love), ocean-loving ; **Oceanophy′ta**
(φυτὸν, a plant), ocean plants (Clements) ; **oceanophyt′icus**, relating to
ocean plants.

ocel′late, *ocella′tus*, **ocella′ted** (*ocellus*,
a little eye), with a circular patch
of colour.

Ocel′lus (Lat., a little eye), (1) an eye-
spot as in *Halionyx*, a genus of
Diatoms ; (2) an epidermal cell of a
leaf which is sensitive to light
(Haberlandt).

Ocheti′um, or **Ocheti′on** (ὀχετὸς, a

conduit), a plant succession occasioned by drains or ditches (Clements).

ochra′ceous, **-ceus** (*ochra*, yellow earth),
ochre-coloured, yellow with a tinge
of red.

O′chrea=OCREA ; **o′chreate**=OCREATE.

ochroleu′cous, **-cus** (ὤχρα, yellow
earth ; λευκὸς, white), yellowish
white, buff.

Och′thad (ὄχθη, a bank, + AD), a bank
plant ; **Ochthi′um**, a bank formation ; **ochthoph′ilus** (φιλέω, I love),
bank loving ; **Ochthophy′ta** (φυτὸν,
a plant), plants of banks or dikes
(Clements).

O′crea (Lat., a greave), a tubular
stipule, or pair of opposite stipules
so combined ; **o′create**, *ocrea′tus*,
provided with ocreae.

Octagyn′ia (ὀκτὼ, eight ; γυνὴ, a
woman), a Linnean order of plants
with eight-styled flowers ; **octag′y-
nous**, *octagyn′icus*, having eight
styles : **octam′erous** (μέρος, a part),
in eights ; **octan′der** (ἀνὴρ, ἀνδρὸς,
a man), with eight stamens ; **Oc-
tan′dria**, a Linnean class of plants
with eight stamens ; **octan′drous**,
having eight stamens.

Oc′tant (*octans*, a half-quadrant), the
division of an oospore ; ~ **Wall**,
applied to the septum which cuts
the oospore into octants.

octan′therous (ὀκτὼ, eight ; ἀνθηρὸς,
flowery), having eight fertile stamens ; **octari′nus** (ἄρρην, a male),
Necker's term for OCTANDROUS ;
octinu′cleate (+ NUCLEUS), having
eight nuclei (Harper) ; **octodip′loid**
(+ DIPLOID), applied to a nucleus
formed by the fusion of eight diploid
nuclei (Němec).

octofa′rius (L. Lat.), in eight ranks or
rows.

octog′ynous = OCTAGYNOUS.

octoloc′ular (*octo*, eight ; *loculus*, a little
place), applied to an eight-celled
fruit or pericarp ; **octopet′alous**,
-lus (πέταλον, a flower-leaf), with
eight petals ; **octora′diate** (*radius*,
a ray), with eight rays, as some
Compositae ; **octosep′alous** (+ SEPA-

lum), with eight sepals; **octo-sper'mous** (σπέρμα, ṣeed), eight-seeded; **Oc'tospore** (σπορὰ, seed) = the CARPOSPORE of Porphyraceae; **octosp'orous**, eight spored; **octo-ste'monous** (στήμων, a thread), with eight fertile stamens; **octos'tichous**, -*us* (στίχος, a series), in eight rows; **octotrip'loid** (τριπλὸος, threefold), used of a nucleus, formed by division of syntriploid nuclei and subsequent fusion (Němec).

oc'ulate (*oculus*, an eye) = OCELLATE; **Oc'ulus**, (1) the first appearance of a bud, especially on a tuber; (2) the depression on the summit of some fruits, as the apple.

od'dly pin'nate, with a terminal leaf-let, imparipinnate.

-odes (εῖδος, resemblance), a suffix for similar to; as *phyllodes*, like a leaf.

odon'toid (ὀδοὺς, ὀδόντος, a tooth; εῖδος, resemblance), tooth-like dentate (Heinig).

odora'tus (Lat.), fragrant, usually restricted to sweet-smelling **O'dours**, which, in flowers, are sometimes due to essential oils which can be distilled off; at other times the scent cannot be collected by chemical means.

Oece'sis = ECESIS.

Oecol'ogy, and similar words derived from οἴκησις, dwelling, will be found under ECOLOGY, etc.

Oede'ma, pl. **Oede'mata** (οἴδημα, a swelling), (1) the tumid glands on woody tissues of Conifers; (2) proposed in place of "substitute Hydathodes"; (3) = INTUMESCENCES.

oedogonia'ceous, pertaining to *Oedogonium* or its allies.

Oek'iophytes (οἰκίον, a dwelling; φυτὸν, a plant), native cultivated plants for ornament or use (Naegeli and Thellung).

offici'nal, *officina'lis* (Lat., of the shops), used of medicinal or other plants procurable at shops.

Off'set, a lateral shoot used for propagating, as in the houseleek; **Off'-shoot**, an offset.

often-bear'ing, producing more than once in the season, multiferous.

-oides, -oideus, -odes, -ides, suffixes from εῖδος, resemblance; as *petal-oideus*, resembling a petal.

Oid'ium, pl. **Oid'ia** (ᾠὸν, an egg, + ίδιον, a diminutive), a term used to denote concatenate conidia (Cooke); not to be confounded with the form-genus *Oidium*, Link, the conidial stage of Erysipheae.

Oil, used for any fluid fat-bodies in plants, chiefly stearic, palmitic, or oleic acids; ~ **Cells**, gum-cells; ~ **Plas'tids**, ELAIOPLASTS; ~ **Tube**, a synonym of VITTA in the fruit of Umbelliferae.

oleag'inous, -*us* (*oleagineus*, pertaining to the olive), oily and succulent.

o'leic (*oleum*, olive oil) **Ac'id**, a glycer-ide or fat occurring in plants; **O'lein** or **O'leine**, one of the vegetable fats.

ol'ens (Lat.), smelling, especially sweetly odorous.

o'leoid (*Olea*, εῖδος, resemblance), used of plants whose leaves are traversed by fibres, as in the olive (Vesque).

Oleores'in (*oleum*, olive oil, + RESIN), the natural admixture of a resin and an essential oil, forming a vegetable balsam or turpentine.

oleo'so-loc'ular, applied to those Lichen-spores whose cells appear as drops of oil.

olera'ceous, *olera'ceus* (Lat., herb-like), (1) having the nature of a pot-herb, esculent; (2) ‡ growing in cultivated places (De Candolle).

Olib'anum (Arab., ol or al, the; Lubân, milk), a bitter and aromatic gum-resin from several species of *Boswellia*; the frankincense of commerce.

oligan'drous, -*rus* (ὀλίγος, few; ἀνὴρ, ἀνδρὸς, a man), with few stamens; **oligan'thous**, -*thus*, (ἄνθος, a flower), few-flowered; **ol'igarch** (ἀρχὴ, origin), (1) applied to a vascular cylinder containing but few bundles (Crozier); (2) when a stele possesses few protoxylem elements; **oligo-dynam'ic** (δύναμις, power), Naegeli's term for the poisonous condition of water containing minute traces of copper or brass ; it kills delicate cells of *Spirogyra ;* **oligom'erous** (μέρος, a part), parts consisting of few members ; **Oligom'ery,** of few parts ; **oligonitroph'ilous,** used of bacteria which occur in nutritive media wanting in nitrogenous compounds (Beyerinck) ; **oligope'lic** (πηλὸς, clay), applied to plants which prefer certain rocks which yield a small amount of clayey detritus (Thurmann) ; **Oligophyl'la** (φύλλον, a leaf), Necker's expression for a bract ; **oligophyl'lous,** having few leaves ; **oligopsam'mic** (ψάμμος, sand), for plants affecting certain granite and dolomite formations (Thurmann) ; both of these classes belong to the DYSGEOGENOUS series ; **Oligosapro'bia** (σαπρὸς, putrid ; βίος, life), organisms which flourish in waters but little contaminated ; **oligosperm'ous,** -*mus* (σπέρμα, a seed), few-seeded ; **oligoste'monous** (στήμων, a thread), with few stamens ; **Oligotax'y** (τάξις, order), the decrease in the number of whorls in a flower ; **oligotroph'ic** (τροφή, food), plants which grow on poor soil and compete for the nutritive salts in it (Warming) ; ~ **Peat,** moor peat (Weber) ; **oligotrop'ic** (τροπή, a turning), employed by Loew for bees which visit a restricted range of plants.

Olisthi'um, or **Olisthi'on** (ὄλισθος, slipperiness), a succession of plants on landslips (Clements).

oliva'ceous, -*ceus* (*oliva,* an olive, + ACEOUS, (1) olive-coloured ; (2) = **oli'veus** (Lat.), the colour of a ripe olive ; **olivas'cens** (Lat.), turning olive-coloured ; **olivaeform'is** (*forma,* shape), shaped like an olive, drupaceous ; **ol'ive-colour, ol'ive-green,** yellowish green darkened with black; **olivic'olor** (*color,* colour) = OLIVACEOUS.

olopetalar'ius (ὄλος, whole ; πέταλον, a flower-leaf), the floral envelopes changed partially or wholly, as stamens or pistils changed into petaloid organs ; the correct form would be **holopetalar'ius.**

Ombrom'eter (ὄμβρος, a storm of rain ; μέτρον, a measure), Clements's name for a rain-gauge ; **Om'brophile** (φιλέω, I love), Wiesner's term for a plant which likes rain ; **ombroph'ilous,** rain-loving ; **Ombroph'ily,** the condition described ; **Om'brophobe** (φόβος, fear), a similar term for a plant disliking rain ; **ombroph'obic,** hating rain ; **Ombroph'oby,** dislike or impatience of rain ; **Om'brophyte** (φυτὸν, a plant), a shade-loving plant (Hansgirg).

omniv'orous (*omnivorus,*all-devouring), applied to parasites which attack many species and are not confined to one host-plant.

Omoplephy'tum (ὁμοπλεκής, interlaced; φυτόν, a plant), applied to a monadelphous flower, the stamens being in one bundle.

Om'phalode, *Omphalo'dium* (ὀμφαλὸς, navel ; εἶδος, like), the mark in the hilum through which the vessels pass to the chalaza.

Omphalo'dium, Kerner's term for HILUM (1) ; **om'phaloid** (εἶδος, resemblance), navel-like, umbilicate (Heinig).

-on, suffix employed by Clements to denote " Family."

onagra'ceous, pertaining to *Oenothera,* a pre-Linnean name of which genus was *Onagra,* Tourn.

Onc'ospores, -*aè* (ὄγκος, a hook, + SPORE), plants having hooked seeds to aid in dispersion (Clements).

one-ribbed, having one prominent rib, as in the leaves of many grasses ; ~ **si'ded,** (1) turned to one side ; (2) the parts turned the same way ; (3) unequal sided.

onisciform'is (*oniscus,* a wood-louse ; *forma,* shape), Koerber's word for certain Lichen-spores resembling a wood-louse in shape ; **onis'cus** (Lat.), used for lead-coloured, from the tint of the same creature.

Onomatolo'gia (ὄνομα, a name ; λόγος, discourse), the rules to be observed in the construction of names.

Ontog′eny (ὄντα, things existing; γένος, race, offspring), the development of an individual in its various stages; adj. **ontogenet′ic**.

ooblas′tic (ᾠόν, an egg; βλαστὸς, a bud) **Fil′aments**, see next; **Ooblaste′ma** (βλάστημα, a sprout), **Fil′aments**, the FERTILIZING TUBES of Schmitz; **O′ocyst** (κύστις, a bag), (1) a female organ, an OOGONIUM; (2) Vuillemin's term for an envelope of the egg which is due to the cells composing that structure; **Ooga-m′ete** (+ GAMETE), a female gamete (Hartog); **oog′amous** (γάμος, marriage), conjugation in which the two coalescing gametes are of dissimilar form; **Oog′amy**, the reverse condition of ISOGAMY; the female gamete never active, the male a spermatozoon, and the product an OOSPERM (Hartog); **Oogem′ma** (gemma, a bud), Caruel's term for ARCHEGONIUM; **Oogen′esis** (γένεσις, beginning), (1) the formation of the OOSPHERE, the early stage of the ovule; (2) the differentiation of a large resting cell (oosphere) to fuse with a small motile cell (sperm) into a zygote (Hartog); **O′ogone**, *Oogo′nium*, pl. *Oogo′nia* (γονὴ, race, offspring), a female sexual organ, usually a spherical sac, containing one or more oospheres; **oogo′nial Tube** = NECK-CANAL; **ookinet′ic** (κινητικος, putting in motion), tending to produce the female element; **Col′ysis** (λύσις, a loosing), viridescence, especially in carpels and ovules (Penzig); **Oomyce′tes** (μύκης, a mushroom), those Fungi which reproduce sexually by antheridia and oogonia, the result being an oospore (Tubeuf).

O′ön (ᾠόν, an egg), proposed as an equivalent of EGG (P. F. Myles); **Oonang′ium**, the embryo sac (Radlkofer); **Oone′ion** (νηῖς, a nymph), Radlkofer's term for ARCHEGO-NIUM; **O′onyle** (ὕλη, raw material), the unfertilized female organ of any sort (Radlkofer); **Oonu′cleus** (+ NUCLEUS), the nucleus of an oosphere, cf. SPERM-NUCLEUS; **O′ophore** (φορέω, I carry), the OOPHYTE in Archegoniatae; **Oophoridan′gia** (ἀγγεῖον, a vessel), J. Smith's name for the macrosporangia of *Marsilea*, etc.; **Oophorid′ium**, a sporangium containing macrospores in *Selaginella*; **O′ophyte** (φυτὸν, a plant), that portion of the life-cycle of a plant during which it bears sexual organs; the same as OOPHORE; **O′oplasm** (πλάσμα, moulded), the protoplasm of the oosphere; **ooplasm′ic**, relating to the ooplasm; **O′oplast**, Kerner's term for OOSPHERE; **O′osperm** (σπέρμα, seed), the product of the fusion of a male and a female cell; **O′osphere** (σφαῖρα, a globe), a naked and nucleate mass of protoplasm, which, after coalescence with the sperm-nucleus, develops into an oosperm; the egg or ovum; **Com′pound ~**, one which contains several or many functional sexual nuclei, as in *Albugo* (Stevens); **oosphe′ric**, relating to the OOSPHERE; **Oospor-an′ge** = **Oosporan′gium**, pl. **Oosporan′gia** (σπορὰ, a seed; ἀγγεῖον, a vessel), the sacs or sporangia which produce oospores; **O′ospore**, the immediate product of fertilization in an oophore; **Oothe′ca** (θήκη, a case), the theca or sporangium of Ferns.

opa′cus (Lat., shady, giving shade), (1) not transparent; (2) dull, not shining; **opake** and **opaque** are anglicized forms of the word.

o′pen, (1) not closed; (2) expanded, the opposite of DIFFUSE; **~ Bun′dle**, one which retains a portion of cambium capable of further differentiation; opposed to closed bundle; **~ Forma′tion**, when the plants are scattered (Clements); **~ Nu′cleus**, the nucleus of Cyanophyceae (Hieronymus).

O′pening, expanding or becoming unclosed; **~ Cells**, those special cells by which the dehiscence of sporangia and pollen-sacs takes place (*a*) either by tangential contraction on drying, or (*b*) by a thickening which causes a hinge-like motion of the cells themselves (Schinz); *cf.* Lip-cells; ~ of **Flow'ers**, the expansion of the members at the period of maturity; anthesis.

oper'cular, oper'culate, *opercula'tus* (*operculum,* a lid), furnished with a lid, as in many Mosses and Myrtaceae; **Oper'cule,** (1) the lamina of the leaf of *Sarracenia* (Heckel); (2) the lid of the flower in *Eucalyptus;* (3) the Operculum of Mosses; **oper'-culiform** (*forma,* shape), shaped like a lid; **Oper'culum,** (1) a lid or cover which separates by a transverse line of division, as in the pyxis, and Moss capsules; (2) also in some pollen grains; (3) the cover of certain asci, which falls away at maturity (Traverso).

oper'tus (Lat., hidden), the same as *tectus.*

ophioglossa'ceous, akin to or resembling *Ophioglossum.*

oph'iure (ὄφις, a snake; οὐρά, a tail) **Cells,** used by Jönsson for Astro-sclereids of Tschirch; the name is from their resemblance to Echinoderms.

ophryd'eous, resembling or allied to the genus *Ophrys.*

opisthe'lial, an error for **opis'thial** (ὀπίσθιος, hinder) **Pore,** Tschirch's name for the posterior border of a stoma; **opis'thodal** is a synonym; *cf.* Eisodal; **opisthod'romous** (δρόμος, a course), a flower is so termed when the genetic spiral is assumed to pass on its shortest way from the bract to the first floral segment by the back of the flower, between it and the axis of the stem.

O'pium (Lat., dried poppy-juice), the concrete juice from the capsules of *Papaver somniferum,* Linn.; ~ **Al'kaloids** are numerous, the best known being Morphia.

Opi'um (ὄπιον, poppy juice), a parasitic plant formation; **opoph'ilus** (φιλέω, I love), sap-loving; **Opophy'ta** (φυτὸν, a plant), parasites (Clements).

Oplar'ium (ὁπλάρια, arms), Necker's word for Scyphus.

Opportu'nism (*opportunus,* convenient), the direction in metamorphosis due to the factors potent at the moment (Ganong).

op'posite, *opposi'tus* (Lat., standing in front); (1) set against, as leaves when two on one node; (2) one part before another, as a stamen in front of a petal; **opposi'te-pin'natus,** with leaflets on the same plane at right angles to the common petiole; **oppositiflor'us** (*flos, floris,* a flower), having opposite peduncles; **opposi-tifo'lious** (*folium,* a leaf), (1) with opposite leaves; (2) opposite a leaf, as a tendril; **oppositipet'-alous,** *-lus* (πέταλον, a flower-leaf), placed before a petal; **oppositisep'-alous** (+ Sepal), situated before a sepal; **oppositi'vus** (Lat.), when one part stands before another, the reverse of "alternate."

Opseosper'mata (ὄψις, ὄψεως, sight; σπέρμα, a seed), tubercles on the surface of some Algals containing spores (Lindley).

Opsig'ony (ὀψίγονος, posthumous), the production and development of proventitious buds (Wittrock); *cf.* Prolepsis.

-opsis (ὄψις, appearance), employed for those Fungi in which uredospores are rare or wanting, the aecidium giving rise to teleutospores, *e.g. Pucciniopsis.*

op'timal (*optimus,* best), the most advantageous for an organism or function; **Op'timum** refers to the degree of temperature, light, etc., which best conduces to the vital activities of a given organism.

Opulastera'num, a "layer" of *Opulaster* (Clements).

O'rae (*ora,* extremity) **Radi'cum** ‡ = Spongioles.

Or'ange, (1) the fruit of *Citrus Aurantium,* Linn.); (2) a secondary colour, red and yellow combined, taking its name from the tint of the fruit mentioned.

orbic'ular, *orbicula'ris* (Lat., circular), of a flat body with a circular outline; **orbic′ulate**, *orbicula′tus*, disk-shaped; **Orbic′ulus**, (1) the fleshy corona in the genus *Stapelia ;* (2) a round flat hymenium in Fungi.

Orbil′la (*orbis*, an orb), the shield of certain Lichens, as in *Usnea*.

Orchel′la, a general term for Lichens which yield dyes, as *Lecanora, Roccella*, etc.

orchida′ceous, *-eus*, (1) furnished with two tubers at the roots, as species of the genus *Orchis* and its allies; (2) pertaining to the order Orchideae; **orchid′ean, orchid′eous**, relating to the Orchideae; **Orchidol′ogy** (λόγος, discourse), the study of Orchids.

Or′chil, also known as CUDBEAR, and LITMUS, a valuable dye from *Lecanora tartarea*, Ach., and other Lichens.

Or′cin, the colouring principle from various tinctorial Lichens.

orculaeform′is (*orcula*, a small tun; *forma*, shape), used by Koerber for cask-shaped Lichen-spores.

Or′der, *Or′do* (Lat., methodical arrangement), in botany, a group between genus (tribe, suborder) and class; **or′dinal**, relating to an order, as ∼ **Char′acter**, that which marks it off from kindred orders.

Or′ead (ὀρειὰς, a mountain nymph), a sun-plant or heliophyte.

Orgadi′um (ὀργὰς, a meadow), an open woodland formation; **orgadoc′ola** (*colo*, I inhabit); and **orgadoph′ilus** (φιλέω, I love), dwelling in open woodland; **Orgadophy′ta** (φυτὸν, a plant), open woodland plants (Clements).

Or′gan (ὄργανον, an instrument), any definite part of a structure, as a cell, a fibre, a leaf, etc.; **Or′gans** of **Reproduc′tion**, those which are concerned in the production of seeds or spores; in Phanerogams the stamens and pistils are so termed; ∼ of **Vegeta′tion**, those connected with the growth simply, as roots and leaves; **organ′ic**, *organ′icus*,

relating to living organs; ∼ **Cen′tre**, the point or axis around which growth takes place, it may not be the structural centre; **Or′ganism**, a body possessing organic structure; **Organog′eny** (γένος, race, offspring), or **Organogen′esis** (γένεσις, beginning), the formation and development of organs from their primitive condition; adj. **organogenet′ic;** **Organog′raphy** (γράφω, I write); **Organol′ogy** (λόγος, discourse), the study of organs and their relations; **Org′anoid** (εἶδος, like), an organ of apparently unknown function(Swingle); **organoplas′tic** (πλαστικὸς, suitable for being wrought), with the power of producing organs; **Organophysiol′ogy**, the requisite modification in structure to enable a species to settle in a given place (Drude).

Orgy′a (ὀργυιὰ, a fathom), six feet in height; **orgya′lis**, a fathom long, the height of a man.

Orienta′tion (*oriens*, the east), (1) the correct placing with regard to the quarters of the compass; (2) generally means relative position, as applied to organs, etc.; **in′verse** ∼, applied to the inversion of the ovuliferous scale bundles in Coniferae.

Or′ifice, *Orific′ium* (Lat., an opening), an opening by which spores, etc., escape; ostiole.

Or′igin, employed by Hartog to express the German "Anlage"; *cf.* FUNDAMENT, INCEPT, INCEPTION, PRIMORDIUM, etc.

Orig′oma = ORYGOMA.

ornithog′amous (ὄρνις, ὀρνίθος, a bird; γάμος, marriage), fertilization effected by birds; **Ornithoph′ilae** (φιλέω, I love), plants habitually fertilized by pollen brought by birds; adj. **ornithoph′ilous**.

Or′mogon, cited by Crozier, = HORMOGONE.

oroph′ilus (ὄρος, a mountain; φιλέω, I love), dwelling in sub-alpine regions; **Orophy′ta** (φυτὸν, a plant), sub-alpine plants; **Orophyti′a**, sub-alpine plant formatio ns (Clements).

Or′thoblast (ὀρθὸς, upright ; βλαστὸς, a bud), used by Cramer for confervoid prothallia growing in an ascending direction ; **orthoclad′ous,** -*dus* (κλάδος, a branch), straight branched (Russow) ; **Orthen′chyma** (ἐγχέω, I pour in), Williamson's correction of **Orthosen′chyma,** Binney's term for parenchyma of vertically arranged cells ; adj. **orthen′chymous ; Orthogen′esis** (γένεσις, beginning), development along definite lines ; **orthoheliotrop′ic** (+ HELIOTROPIC), directed straight to the source of light, as linear leaves and grasses may do ; **orthomor′phous** (μορφή, shape), radial and erect (Wiesner) ; **Orthophototax′y** (φὼς, φωτὸς, light ; τάξις, order), the direct arrangement of such organisms as *Volvox* and *Spirogyra* assume under the stimulus of light (Oltmanns) ; **orthophototrop′ic** (τροπὴ, a turning), the direct influence of light shown in *Vaucheria, Phycomyces,* and shoots of flowering plants (Oltmanns) ; **Or′thophyte** (φυτὸν, a plant), Janet's term for a plant, the gametophyte + sporophyte ; **Orthoploc′eae** (πλοκή, a twining), those Cruciferae which have conduplicate cotyledons ; **orthoplo′ceous,** -*ceus,* when the incumbent cotyledons are folded round the radicle ; **Orthosper′meae** (σπέρμα, a seed), plants whose seeds have albumen flat on the inner face, neither involute nor convolute ; **orthosper′mous** (σπέρμα, a seed), having seeds with endosperm grooved on the ventral side, as in *Carum* ; **orthostich′ous,** straight ranked ; **Or′thostichy,** pl. **Or′thostichies** (στίχος, a row), a vertical row, as in phyllotaxis ; **orthos′tomous** (στόμα, a mouth), with a straight opening; **orthotac′tic** (ακτὸς, arranged), used by S. Moore in the sense of normal, applied to an interval in the PHOTRUM ; **orthot′ropal** ; **orthot′ropous** (τροπη, a turning), used of an ovule with a straight axis, the chalaza being at the insertion and the orifice or foramen at the opposite end, farthest from the hilum ;

orthotrop′ic, assuming a vertical position ; **Orthot′ropism** is the condition described ; **Or′thotype** (τύπος, a type), a genus provided with a type by original designation (O. F. Cook) ; adj. **orthotyp′ic.**

Oryg′oma (ὄρυγμα, a ditch or pit), Necker's term for the cup of a *Marchantia* containing gemmae.

Os, Or′is (Lat.), a mouth or orifice.

os′cillating = VERSATILE ; **oscilla′nus,** *oscillator′ius* (Lat., from *oscillo,* I swing), has the same meaning ; **Oscilla′tion,** the movement peculiar to Trichobacteria and Cyanophyceae (Jones).

oscillatoria′ceous, allied to the genus *Oscillatoria.*

Os′culum (Lat., a little mouth) = OSTIOLE.

Osmom′eter (ὠσμὸς, a thrusting; μέτρον, a measure), an instrument to measure OSMOSIS ; **Os′mose,** *Osmo′sis,* the diffusion of liquids through membranes ; **Nu′clear Osmo′sis,** the increased size of a nucleus, attributed to absorption of fluid through the nuclear membrane (Anstruther) ; adj. **osmo′tic.**

Os′mospores (ὀσμὴ, scent ; + SPORE), certain Uredineous spermagones, characterized by their having a scent (Vuillemin).

Osmotax′is (ὠσμὸς, a thrusting; τάξις, arrangement), rearrangement of moving organisms in response to the influence of fluids ; adj. **osmotac′tic ; Osmot′ropism** (τροπὴ, a turning), tropic stimulus due to osmotic action (Pfeffer) ; adj. **osmotrop′ic.**

os′seous, *os′seus* (Lat.), bony.

Ossic′ulus, *Ossic′ulum* (Lat., a little bone), the pyrene of a fruit, as a medlar.

os′sified (*os, ossis,* a bone ; *facio,* I make), becoming hard as bone, as the stones of drupes, such as the peach and plum.

Ostariphy′tum (ὀστάριον, a little bone ; φυτὸν, a plant), a plant which produces a drupe or drupe-like fruit.

Osteoscle′reids (ὀστέον, a bone; σκληρὸς,

hard), the "bone-shaped" sclereids of *Hakea*.

os′tiolate, *ostiola′tus* (*ostiolum*, a little door), furnished with an opening or mouth ; **Os′tiole**, *Os′tiolum*, (1) the opening of the conceptacle in some Algae ; (2) the aperture through which spores escape from the perithecium ; (3) a pore or opening in the prickles of *Victoria regia* (Trécul).

ostracodermat′inus (ὄστρακον, a hard shell ; δερμάτινος, leathern), resembling the shells of molluscs ; applied to certain Lichens.

-o′sus, a termination indicating augmentation, as *radio′sus*, large-rooted.

Oued or **Wed**, Arabic terms for valleys containing water in the rainy season.

out′er, exterior, abaxial ; ~ **Glumes**, one or more glumes at the base of a spikelet in grasses, enclosing one or more flowers ; ~ **Perid′ium** = PERIDIUM EXTERNUM.

Out′growth, (1) another name for EMERGENCE ; (2) a tuberous excrescence on roots.

Out′line, the continuous boundary-line of an organ, as of a leaf.

o′val, *ova′lis* (*ovum*, an egg), broadly elliptic.

Ovarioph′ylly (ὠάριον, a small egg ; φύλλον, a leaf), descending metamorphosis of a carpel into a leaf (Morren).

O′vary, *Ova′rium* (*ovum*, an egg), (1) that part of the pistil which contains the ovules, the immature fruit, formerly termed the GERMEN ; (2) = ARCHEGONIUM (H. Gibson).

o′vate, *ova′tus* (Lat., egg-shaped), (1) shaped like a longitudinal section of a hen's egg, the broader end basal ; (2) used for ovoid.

Ovel′lum, Dunal's term for a young carpel bearing the same relation to a mature carpel as an ovule to a seed.

Ovench′yma (*ovum*, an egg ; ἔγχυμα, an infusion), loose tissue of oval-shaped cells.

overhang′ing, projecting beyond the base.

overlap′ping, suggested to denote right or left, as right edge ~, = sinistrorse (*i.e.* dextrorse seen in front) ; left edge ~, = dextrorse (*i.e.* sinistrorse viewed from the front).

overly′ing, a suggested rendering of INCUBOUS (Potter).

overtop′ping, the gradual assertion of predominance of certain limbs of a branch system over the others (Potonié).

o′viform, *oviform′is* (*ovum*, an egg ; *forma*, shape), ovoid, egg-shaped ; **Ovocen′trum** (κέντρον, a sharp point), a central mass of fine-grained protoplasm surrounding the nucleus in the organism of *Achlya* (Trow) ; **o′void**, *ovoi′deus* (εἶδος, resemblance), an egg-shaped solid ; **ovoi′dal**, having the outline of an egg ; **ovula′ris** (Mod. Lat.) = OVOID ; **ov′ulate**, *ovula′tus*, (1) possessing ovules ; (2) somewhat ovoid (J. S. Henslow) ; **Ov′ule**, *Ov′ulum*, the young seed in the ovary, the organ which after fertilization develops into a seed ; ~ **Tube**, a thread-like extension of the amnios, rising beyond the foramen ; **ovulif′erous** (*fero*, I bear), bearing ovules; adj. **ov′ular** ; **O′vum**, (1) the ovule ; (2) = ZYGOTE ; (3) = OOSPHERE.

oxal′ic, pertaining to *Oxalis*, wood sorrel ; **oxalida′ceous**, referring to the genus *Oxalis*, or its allies ; ~ **Ac′id**, a vegetable acid of frequent occurrence, abundant in *Oxalis* ; **oxalif′erous** (*fero*, I bear), producing oxalic acid or its salts ; **Oxalileu′cite** (+ LEUCITE), Van Tieghem's name for a vacuole which contains oxalic acid.

Oxo′dad (ὀξώδης, sour), a plant of a humus marsh (Clements) ; **Oxodi′on**, an association on acid soil ; **Oxodi′um**, a humus marsh formation (Clements).

oxyacan′thous, *-thus* (ὀξὺς, sharp ; ἄκανθα, a thorn), furnished with many thorns or prickles ; **oxycar′pus** (καρπὸς, fruit), when fruit is sharp-pointed ; **Oxycel′luloses** +

CELLULOSE) constitute the main mass of the ground tissue of Phanerogams, and occur with lignin in the walls of wood-cells; **Oxychro'-matin** (+ CHROMATIN) granules in the linin thread, taking stain from acid tar-colours such as eosin (Heidenham); *cf.* BASICHROMATIN; **Ox'ydases**, a general term for oxydizing enzymes (J. R. Green); **Ox'ygenase**, a doubtful enzyme, considered to be a peroxydase.

Oxygenotax'is (ὀξὺς, sour; -γεν-, producing; τάξις, order), Pfeffer's term for **Oxygenot'ropism** (τροπὴ, a turning), movements induced by the presence of oxygen; ACROTROPISM; **oxygeoph'ilus** (γῆ, earth; φιλέω, I love), dwelling in humus; **Oxygeophy'ta** (φυτὸν, a plant), humus plants; **Oxygeophyti'a**, humus plant formations (Clements); **Oxyli'um** (ἰλὺς, mud), a humus marsh formation; **oxyloph'ilus** (φιλέω, I love), humus loving; **Oxylophy'ta** (φυτὸν, a plant), humus plants (Clements); adj. **oxylophyt'ic.**

Oxyrie'tum, an association of *Oxyria* plants (Clements).

Oxyt'ropism (ὀξὸς, sour; τροπὴ, a turning), movements caused by an excess of acid.

pachycar'pus (παχὺς, thick; καρπὸς, fruit), having a thick pericarp; **pachyclad'ous**, *-dus* (κλάδος, a branch), thick-branched (Russow); **pachyder'matous**;   **pachyder'mous** (δέρμα, skin or hide), applied to Mosses when the cells or capsules are firm and resistant; **Pachyne'ma** (νῆμα, a thread), in nuclear division, the period of the thick, unsplit spirem in late synapsis; **Pachyno'sis** (παχύνω, I make thick), plant-growth in thickness;   **pachyphyl'lous** (φύλλον, a leaf), thick-leaved; **pachystich'ous** (στίχος, a row), thick-sided, applied to cells only; **pach'y-tene** (ταινία, a ribband) **Loops**, when gamomites are in pairs during nuclear divisions, later on dividing longitudinally (Stevens).

Pack'et-form, the association of bacteria in such colonies as *Sarcina*; **Packing-cells**, Hillhouse's equivalent of Ger. Füllzellen; = COMPLEMENTARY-CELLS.

Pad, (1) a cushion-like growth; *cf.* SUBARCHESPORIAL PAD; (2) a popular name in the United States for the floating leaves of water-lilies; (3) the central portion of the lens or contracted tissue of the plinth of *Conostoma* (F. W. Oliver).

Paedog'amy (παῖς, παιδὸς, a child; γάμος, marriage), copulation of two gametes from the same gametangium (Hartmann); **paedog'amous Auto'gamy**, the copulation of the nuclei and gametes, in place of the complete gametes (Hartmann); **Paedogen'esis** (γένεσις, origin), applied by Costerus to cases of extreme precocity, as where the seedling of a tree flowers when only a few inches high.

Pa'gina (Lat., a leaf), the blade or surface of a leaf,

Pagi'um (πάγος, a peak), a succession of plants on glacial soils; **pagoph'ilus** (φιλέω, I love), dwelling on foothills; **Pagophy'ta** (φυτὸν, a plant), foothill plants; **Pagophyti'a**, foothill plant formations (Clements).

paint'ed, having coloured streaks of unequal density.

paired, (1) conjugated; (2) used of the teeth in the peristome of Mosses; **Pairing-cell**, an equivalent of GAMETE.

pala'ceous, *-ceus* (pala, a spade or shovel; + ACEOUS) when the edges of an organ, especially of a leaf, adhere to their support.

palaea'ceous = PALEACEOUS.

Palaeobiolog'ist (παλαιὸς, ancient; βίος, life; λόγος, discourse), a student of fossil plants; **Palaeobot'anist**, a student or expert in fossil botany; **Palaeobot'any** (βοτάνη, a herb), fossil botany, the study of plants in a fossil state; **palaeoge'ic** (γέα, earth), applied to soils derived from the older formations; **Palaeophytol'ogy** (φυτὸν, a plant; λόγος, discourse), the science of palaeobotany ; **palaeotrop′ic** (τροπὴ, a turning) **Flo′ra,** the tropical flora of the old world.

pa′lar, *pala′ris* (Lat., pertaining to a pale or stake), when the root is perfectly continuous with the stem ; **pala′ri-ramo′sus,** when a palar-root has many branches.

Pal′ate, *Pala′tum* (Lat., the palate), (1) the prominent lower lip of a ringent corolla ; (2) the projection in the throat of a personate gamopetalous corolla.

Pale, Pa′lea (Lat., chaff), (1) the chaffy scales on the receptacle of many Compositae ; (2) the inner bract or glume in grasses, called " Palet " by North American writers; (3) the ramenta or chaffy scales on the stipe of many Ferns ; *Pa′lea clathra′ta,* the latticed scale of Ferns (Luerssen) ; **palea′ceous** (+ ACEOUS), chaffy, furnished with paleae or chaff-like in texture ; **paleaeform′is** (*formis,* shape), resembling paleae ; **Pal′eola,** a diminutive of palea, or of secondary order, applied to the LODICULE of grasses ; **pal′eolate,** *paleola′tus,* furnished with a lodicule; **paleolif′erous** (*fero,* I bear), bearing paleae ; **pa′leous,** chaffy.

Paleophytol′ogy = PALAEOPHYTOLOGY.

Pal′et = PALEA.

Palingen′esis (πάλιν, again ; γένεσις, a beginning), Haeckel's term for the doctrine of simple descent ; also written **Palin′geny** ; adj. **palingenet′ic.**

Pal′isade Cells, perpendicular elongated parenchyma cells on the surface of most leaves ; ~ **Parench′yma,** ~ **Tis′sue,** tissue composed of the said cells ; **palisa′dic,** relating to the palisade cells.

pal′lens (Lat., wan), pale in colour; **palles′cent,** becoming light in tint ; **pal′lid,** *pal′lidus,* somewhat pallid ; **pallid′ulus,** slightly pallid.

Pal′lium (Lat., a covering or garment), a presumed gelatinous envelope of Diatoms.

Palm (*palma,* the palm of the hand),

three inches, the width of th hand ; ~ **veined** = PALMATELY VEINED ; **palmar′is** (Lat.), the breadth of the palm, about three inches ; **pal′mate,** *palma′tus,* lobed or divided, so that the sinuses point to the apex of the petiole ; **pal′mately,** in a palmate manner, as ~ **cleft** = PALMATIFID ; ~ **com′pound,** ~ **divided,** ~ **lobed** = PALMATILO- BATE ; ~ **nerved** = PALMATINERVIS ; ~ **part′ed** = PALMATIPARTITE ; ~ **veined** = PALMATINERVIS ; **palmat′- ifid,** *palmatif′idus* (*findo, fidi,* to cleave), cut in a palmate fashion nearly to the petiole ; **palmatiform′is** (*forma,* shape), the venation arranged in a palmate manner ; **palmatilo′bate** (*lobatus,* lobed), palmately lobed; **palmatiner′vis** (*nervus,* a nerve), palmately nerved ; **palma- tipart′ite** (*partitus,* divided), cut nearly to the base in a palmate manner; **palmat′isect,** *palmatisect′us* (*sectus,* cut), palmately cut.

Palmel′la (παλμὸs, palpitation), the zoogloea stage of Schizomycetes, etc., when embedded in a jelly-like mass; not to be confounded with the Algal genus, *Palmella,* Lyngb.

Palmel′lin, Phipson's name for the colouring-matter of *Palmella cru- enta,* Agh. ; **palmel′loid** (εἶδος, resemblance), characteristic of the genus named.

Pal′mid, J. Smith's term for Palms, Cycads and Tree-ferns of palm-like aspect.

palmif′erous (*palma,* a date palm ; *fero,* I bear), producing palms.

pal′miform (*palma,* palm of the hand ; *forma,* shape) = PALMATI- FORM ; **palminer′ved,** *palminer′vis* = PALMATINERVIS.

palmit′ic (*palma,* a palm), relating to palms, as ~ **Acid,** derived from **Pal′mitin,** a glyceride, a solid fat occurring in palm oil.

palmogloe′an, allied to *Palmogloea,* or resembling it (Archer).

Palmog′rapher (*palma,* a palm ; γράφω, I write), a describer or monographer of Palms.

Pal′mus (Lat., the palm of the hand), as a measure may denote a SPAN or a PALM, nine inches or three.

palu′dal (*palus*, a marsh), H. C. Watson's term for natives of marshes, wet all through the year; pal′udine, palu′dinous (Crozier) = pal′udose, *paludo′sus* (Lat., boggy), growing in marshy places.

palumbi′nus (Lat., of wood-pigeons), lead-coloured.

palus′ter (Lat., swampy); palus′trine, *palus′tris*, inhabiting boggy ground; the latter Latin form is more usual in botanic usage.

Pam′pas, the grass-steppes of South America, xerophilous in character, patchy, with taller grasses than meadows have; usually with two periods of rest, caused by drought in summer and cold in winter.

pam′piniform (*pampinus*, a tendril; *forma*, shape), resembling the tendril of a vine; Pampino′dy (εἶδος, resemblance), the change of foliar parts into tendrils (Worsdell).

Pan, a hard layer or substratum of earth impervious to plant-roots.

Pan-apos′pory (πᾶς, παντὸς, all; + APOSPORY), the condition of prothalli being developed aposporously over the entire surface of the frond.

pan′ary, *cf.* PANNARY.

pan′durate, *pandura′tus* (*pandura*, a musical instrument), fiddle-shaped, as the leaf of *Rumex pulcher*, Linn.; pandu′riform (*forma*, shape), fiddle-shaped, drawn in at the middle.

Pangen′esis (πᾶς, παντὸς, all; γένεσις, a beginning), a theory that each separate unit of a body throws off minute gemmules during all stages of development, which may develop at once, or remain dormant and be transmitted through the reproductive cells to later generations; Pan′gens, De Vries's term for the active particles assumed in Darwin's theory of Pangenesis; Pangen′osomes (σῶμα, a body), pl. Strasburger's term for a complex of pangens.

Pan′icle, *Panic′ula* (Lat., a tuft),

a loose flower-cluster, as a branched raceme or corymb; pan′icled, furnished with a panicle; panic′ulate, *panicula′tus* (Lat.), having an inflorescence of the kind described; panic′uliform (*forma*, shape), panicle-shaped (Crozier).

Panifica′tion (*panis*, bread; *facio*, I make), the fermentative changes by which dough is converted into bread.

Panmix′ia (πᾶς, παντὸς, all; μίξις, a mixing), Weismann's term to denote the agency of modification or evolution which results from the cessation of natural selection.

pan′nary (*panis*, bread), pertaining to bread, or suitable for making it (Crozier); more correctly pan′ary.

Pannexter′na (*pannus*, a cloth; *externus*, outside), = EPICARPIUM; pan′niform, *panneform′is* (*forma*, shape), having the appearance or texture of felt or woollen cloth; Panninter′na (*internus*, within) = ENDOCARPIUM; panno′sus (Lat., ragged), botanically, the same as panniform.

panphotomet′ric (πᾶς, παντὸς, all; φὼς, φωτὸς, light; μέτρον, a measure), used of leaves which adapt their position to both direct and diffused light (Wiesner); Pansperm′ism (σπέρμα, a seed), the universal diffusion of germs throughout the atmosphere.

pantachob′ryus ‡ (πανταχῇ, on every side; βρύω, I grow), growing in a circular manner.

pantog′enous (πᾶς, παντὸς, all; γένος, race, offspring), applied to those Fungi which grow everywhere, and are not confined to a single host; pantotac′tic (τακτὸς, arranged), used of the position of the sori in *Trichomanes reniforme*, where they may arise from any vein.

Papa′in, a peptic enzyme from *Carica Papaya*, Linn.

papavera′ceous, belonging to, or resembling the poppy, *Papaver;* papa′verous, resembling a poppy.

Papayo′tin, the dried leaves of *Carica Papaya*, containing a digestive enzyme.

pa′pery, having the texture of paper,
cf. CHARTACEOUS, PAPYRACEOUS.

papiliona′ceous (*papilio,* a butterfly;
+ ACEOUS), a butterfly-shaped corolla, as in the sub-order Papilion-
aceae of Leguminosae.

Papil′la (Lat., a nipple), pl. **Papil′lae,**
(1) soft superficial glands or protuberances; (2) "Also the aciculae
of certain Fungals" (Lindley);
papil′lar, *papilla′ris,* **papil′lary,**
resembling papillae; **pap′illate,** *pa-
pilla′tus* (Lat., bud-shaped), having
papillae; **papillif′erous,** *-rus* (*fero,*
I bear), producing papillae; **pa-
pil′liform** (*forma,* shape), shaped
like a papilla; **pap′illose,** *papillo′sus*
(Lat.), covered with papillae.

pappif′erous (*pappus,* plant-down; *fero,*
I bear), bearing pappus; **pap′piform,**
pappiform′is (*forma,* shape), resembling pappus; **Pap′po,** Blair's word
for the down of thistles; **pap′-
pose,** *pappo′sus,* **pap′pous,** having
pappus; **Pap′pus,** thistledown; the
various tufts of hairs on achenes or
fruits; the limb of the calyx of
Composite florets.

Pap′ula (Lat., a pimple), a pimple or
small pustule; **papulif′erous,** *-rus*
(*fero,* I bear), bearing pustules;
pap′ulose, *papulo′sus,* **pap′ulous,**
papillose.

papyra′ceous, *papyra′ceus* (Lat., made
of papyrus), (1) papery; (2) white as
paper; ~ **Ferns,** filmy Ferns.

parabol′ic, parabol′ical, *parabol′icus*
(παραβολή, a parabola), in botany,
ovate-oblong or ovate, obtuse and
contracted below the apex, used of a
leaf.

Parabux′ine (παρὰ, beside, +BUXINE),
and **Parabuxin′idine,** alkaloids occurring in *Buxus sempervirens,* Linn.;
Paracal′lus (+ CALLUS), a substance
resembling the callus of sieve-tubes,
but differing in reaction and chemical
constitution; **Paracarp′ium** (καρπὸς,
fruit), (1) an abortive pistil or carpel;
(2) the persistent portion of some
styles or stigmas; **paracar′pous,** used
to indicate ovaries whose carpels are
joined together by the margins only

(Goebel); **Paracel′lulose** (+ CELLU-
LOSE) forms the epidermal cells of
plants; **Parachro′matin** (+ CHRO-
MATIN), the same as LININ; **para-
chromatoph′orous,** having pigment
chiefly in the cell-wall (C. Jones);
parachromophor′ic (χρῶμα, colour;
φορέω, I carry), applied to bacteria
whose colouring is an excretory
product, but adheres to the organisms; **Paracorol′la** (+COROLLA), any
appendage to a corolla, the corona
of a flower.

Parachute′ (Fr.), sometimes applied to
fruits which are readily carried by
wind, by means of membranous expansions or pappus, recalling the
action of a parachute.

paracotyle′donary (παρὰ, beside, +
COTYLEDON), used of the axis, derived from the anterior inferior segment (quadrant) of the oosphere of
Marsilea (Vines); **Par′acyst** (κύστις,
a bag), (1) morphologically an antheridium, in *Pyronema*; (2) Tulasne's
term for gametes in *Peziza,* etc.;
Paradiphyl′lum (δὶς, twice; φύλλον,
a leaf), a double leaf resulting
from dichotomy of the lamina (Kronfeld).

par′affinoid (+ Paraffin, εἶδος, resemblance), Kerner's term for a group of
scents, such as those of the Rose,
Lime, and Elder.

Paragalac′tan (παρὰ, beside, + GALAC-
TIN), a reserve substance in the seeds
of lupins; **Parag′amy** (γάμος, marriage), vegetative or gametal nuclei
lying in a continuous mass of cytoplasm which fuse to form a zygote
nucleus; **apocyt′ial** ~, the vegetative nuclei of an apocytium which
fuse to form an "Oospore" in Saprolegnieae (Hartog); **Paragen′esis**
(γένεσις, beginning), all modes of
reproduction resulting in a body
which simulates a zygote in the
same or allied forms (Hartog);
Parahe′liode (ἥλιος, the sun), or
Par′asol, a peculiar set of spines in
Cacteae (Darbishire); **Paraheliot′ro-
pism** (+ HELIOTROPISM), diurnal
sleep, the movements of leaves to

avoid the effects of intense sunlight;
adj. **paraheliotrop′ic**; *cf.* PARATHER-
MOTROPIC; **Parali′nin** (+ LININ),
the substance composing the nucleo-
hyaloplasm (Schwarz).

par′allel (παράλληλος, parallel), extended in the same direction, bɳt
equally distant at every part; ~ **Chor′-
isis**, lateral separation into two or
more members; ~ **nerved**, ~ **-ner′vis**,
~ **veined**, *paralleliveno′sus*, straight
nerved or veined; (1) the lateral
ribs straight, as in *Alnus*; (2) the
entire system straight, as in the
leaves of grasses; ~ **Spires**, a former
term for spirals in phyllotaxy;
Parallelgeot′ropism(+ GEOTROPISM),
when an organ directs itself axially
towards the constraining force;
parallelod′romous, *-mus* (δρόμος, a
course), having parallel veins, as
in lilies (Ettingshausen); **Parallelo-
t′ropism** (τροπή, a turning), movement towards the source of light
parallel to its rays, as the leaves of
grasses placing themselves directly
toward the sun; ORTHO-HELIOTROP-
ISM; *adj.* **parallelot′ropic**; **Par′allel-
type** (τύπος, a type) = PARATYPE.

paramerid′ian (παρὰ, beside, + MERI-
DIAN), used of planes in a Diatom-
frustule which are parallel to the
meridian (O. Mueller); **Paramit′om**
+ MITOM), Flemming's term for the
more fluid portion of the cell-sub-
stance contained in the MITOM; the
paraplasma of Kupffer.

Para′mos, extensive fell-fields in South
America (Warming).

Paramu′tualism (παρὰ, beside + MU-
TUALISM), employed by Elenkin in
the case of facultative Lichens, *cf.*
PARASAPROPHYTISM; **Param′yl**, **Pa-
ramy′lum** (ἄμυλον, fine flour), a mucilaginous substance probably akin
to starch, in the cytoplasm of some
Algae, as Phaeophyceae and Rhodophyceae; **Paranas′ty** (ναστὸς, pressed
close), continued growth lengthwise
of lateral parts (De Vries); **Para-
ne′mata**, pl., νῆμα, a thread), the
paraphyses of Algae; **parane′matal
Fil′aments** = PARANEMATA; **Para-
nu′clein** = PARACHROMATIN; **Para-**

nu′cleolus (+ NUCLEOLUS), a secondary nucleolus when there are more
than one (Strasburger); **Paranu′cleus**
+ NUCLEUS), an apparently additional nucleus, generally near the
true nucleus, and sometimes budded
off from it; **parapec′tic** (+ PECTIC)
Ac′id, derived from pectin by the action of alkalies; **Parapec′tin**, hydrolysed pectin; **parapet′alous**, *-lus*
(πέταλον, a flower-leaf); **parapet′-
aloid** (εἶδος, likeness), (1) bearing a
parapetalum; (2) of stamens which
stand on each side of a petal; **Para-
pet′alum**, any appendage to a corolla,
consisting of several pieces (Moench);
Paraphotot′ropism (+ PHOTOTROP-
ISM), the same as DIAPHOTOTROPISM,
the act of placing at right angles to
incident light; adj. **paraphototro-
p′ic; Paraphyl′lia**, pl. (φύλλον, a leaf),
leaf-like bodies produced near the
leaves of Mosses, but not like stipules
at definite points; **Paraphyl′lium**
(φύλλον, a leaf), (1) ⇒ STIPULE; (2)
a foliaceous expansion in some
calyces; (3) a small interfoliar-
appendage on Moss-stems; **Paraph′-
ysagone** (γονή, offspring), the initial
elements giving rise to the branching terminated by the paraphyses;
Paraph′yses (φύσις, growth), (1) sterile filaments occurring in the fructification of Cryptogams; (2) the
rays of the corolla in *Passiflora*, the
parastades; (3) formerly used for
the cystidia of Fungi; ~ **En′velope**,
the peridium of Uredineae; adj.
paraph′ysate; Paraplas′ma (πλάσμα, moulded), the more liquid inter-
filar portions of protoplasm; **Para-
plectench′yma** (+ PLECTENCHYMA),
a modification of hyphal-tissue (Lindau); **Parasaprophyt′ism** (+ SAPRO-
PHYTISM), the same as ENDOSAPRO-
PHYTISM; **paraste′monal** (στήμων, a
filament = stamen), employed by
Huxley for structures which arise
from, or close to, the insertion of the
filaments with the corolla.

Par′asite (παράσιτος, one who lives at
another's expense), an organism subsisting on another (the host); ~
Sap′rophyte, a parasite which kills

its host and then continues to feed
on it; **parasit′ic**, deriving nourishment from some other organism ; ~
Castra′tion, sterility induced by the
effects of a parasite ; **parasiti′sed**,
infected by a parasite ; **Par′asitism**,
the state of preying upon another
organism ; **Parasi′tus spu′rius** =
EPIPHYTE ; **Parasperma′tia** (+
SPERMATIA), small reproductive
bodies resembling spores, found in
some Algals (Lindley).

Paras′tades (παραστὰς, a door-post),
the coronal rays of *Passiflora ; cf.*
PARAPETALA.

Parasta′men (παρὰ, beside, + STAMEN)
or **Paraste′mon** (στήμων, a filament),
an abortive stamen, a staminodium ;
Parast′ichy, *Parastich′ies* (στίχος, a
series), a secondary spiral in phyllotaxis; **Parastro′phe** (στροφὴ, turning), employed by Senn in place of
APOSTROPHE ; **Par′astyle** (+ STYLE),
an abortive style ; **Parasym′biont**
(συμβιόω, I live with), one of the
members constituting PARASYM-
BIOSIS ; **Parasymbio′sis** (+ SYM-
BIOSIS), (1) when the hyphae of a
parasite envelope the Algal constituents of a Lichen and inflict injury
(Zopf) ; (2) a synonym of PARASA-
PROPHYTISM, etc. (Elenkin) ; **Para-
synap′sis** (+ SYNAPSIS), the parallel
pairing of chromosomes; adj. **para-
synap′tic** ; **Parasynde′sis** (+SYNDE-
SIS) = PARASYNAPSIS ; **paratac′tic**
τακτὸς, arranged), used of the disposition of sori on the aborted vein,
which does not prolong the axis
(Prantl); **Paratag′ma** (τάγμα, an or-
dinance), Pfeffer's term for a mass of
MICELLAE ; **Parathe′cium** (θήκη, a
case), the circumscribing walls of
the Lichen thecium ; **parathermo-
trop′ic** (θερμὸς, warm ; τροπὴ, a turning), proposed by Macfarlane for
paraheliotrophic, in such cases as the
movements of leaves in *Drosera,
Oxalis* and *Mimosa* ; **paraton′ic**
(τόνος, tension), effect of light in
retarding growth ; **paratrach′eal**
(τραχεῖα, the windpipe), applied to
wood-elements arranged about the
vessels ; **paratransa′pical** (+ TRANS-

APICAL), sections parallel to the
straight transapical axis or plane in
Diatoms (O. Mueller) ; **paratransver′-
san** (*transversus*, lying across), used
of the planes parallel to the trans-
versan plane of a Diatom frustule
(O. Mueller) ; **Par′atroph** = PARA-
SITE ; **paratroph′ic** (τροφὴ, food),
able to exist only in animals or
plants, (C. Jones) ; **Parat′ropism**
(προπὴ, a turning), shortened from
PARALLELOTROPISM ; **Par′atype**
(τύπος, a type), (1) a specimen belonging to the original series, but
not the type selected by the author ;
(2) Schroeter's term for subordinate
groups, as "Curvuletum" or "Fir-
metum," from *Carex curva* and *C.
firma* ; **paraval′var** (+ VALVE), applied to those planes which are
parallel to the valvar plane of a
Diatom, either epithecal or hypothecal (O. Mueller).

parelli′nus (Mod. Lat., from *parellus ;*
Fr. parelle, dye-lichens, as *Lecanora
parella*), litmus violet (Hayne).

Parench′yma (παρεγχέω, I pour in beside), used by Grew, and since his
time for the tissue composed of cells
more or less isodiametric, especially
such tissue as the pith and mesophyll; ~ **Trach′eids**, short pithed
spiral ducts or vessels; **parenchy′-
matous**, consisting of parenchyma,
spongy, porous.

Parich′nos (παρὰ, beside; ἴχνος, a foot-
print), the two lateral prints on the
leaf-scar of Lepidodendreae.

Par′ies (Lat., a house wall), pl. **Par′-
ietes**, the wall of any organ; **pari′-
etal**, *parieta′lis*, borne on or belonging to a wall; ~ **U′tricle**, used by
Noll for the layer of protoplasm
next the cell-wall; **Pari′etin**, the
colouring-matter found in the
Lichen, *Physcia parietina*, De Not.

paripin′nate, *paripinna′tus* (Lat.), pinnate, with an equal number of leaflets, that is without a terminal
one.

parme′leine, parme′lioid (εἶδος, resemblance), like the genus *Parmelia,*
having shield-like apothecia.

paroe′cious (παρὰ, beside ; οἶκος, a

house), in Mosses, having the male and female organs in the same inflorescence, the male being naked in the axils of the lower bracts; **paroi'cous** is a synonym.

Paronychie'tum, an association of plants of *Paronychia* (Clements).

Parorthot'ropism (παρὰ, beside; ὀρθὸς, right; τροπὴ, a turning), Archangeli's term when leaves place themselves with the lamina vertical, but not necessarily meridional.

part'ed, part'ite, *parti'tus* (Lat.), cleft, but not quite to the base.

Parthemb'ryosperm (παρθένος, virgin, + EMBRYOSPERM), C. MacMillan's term for a PARTHENOSPERM, with parthenogenetic embryo, and endosperm resulting from fertilization; **Parthenapog'amy** (+ APOGAMY), the fusion of the nuclei of vegetative cells; adj. **parthenapog'amous; Parthend'osperm** (+ ENDOSPERM), a plant whose endosperm is parthenogenetic, and embryo the result of fertilization (C. MacMillan); **Parthenocar'py** (καρπὸς, fruit), Noll's term for the production of fruit without true fertilization; **Parthenogam'ete** (+ GAMETE), a gamete which develops without pairing (Hartog); **Parthenog'amy** (γάμος, marriage), the preliminary stage of fertilization exhibited by macrogamete or macrogametangium, presumably female (Hartmann); **Parthenogen'esis** (γένεσις, origin), a form of apogamy in which the oosphere develops into the normal product of fertilization without a preceding sexual act; **dip'loid** ~ = PARTHENAPOGAMY; **gen'erative** ~ = **hap'loid** ~ if the oosphere is provided with the reduced number of chromosomes; **somat'ic** ~ = PARTHENAPOGAMY; **parthenogenet'ic**, arising without fertilization; **Parthenog'eny** = PARTHENOGENESIS; **Parthenogonid'ia** (γονὸς, offspring), reproductive cells in a colony of *Volvox Globator*, Linn., acting asexually; **Parthenomix'is** (μῖξις, intercourse), Winkler's term for PAR-

THENOGAMY; **Par'thenosperm** (σπέρμα, a seed), (1) a body resembling a zygospore, but not resulting from the coalescence of the contents of two sexually different cells; (2) a plant having parthenogenetic embryos (C. MacMillan); **Par'thenospore** (σπορὰ, a seed), is the same thing.

par'tial, *partia'lis* (Lat.), in botany usually means secondary, as ~ **Involu'cre**, ~ **Ped'uncle**, ~ **Pet'iole**, ~ **Um'bel**; it is opposed to "general."

par'tible, *partib'ilis* (Lat., divisible), ultimately separating, or easily separable.

par'tim (Lat., partly); other expressions are *ex parte, pro parte*.

Partit'ion (*partitio*, a division into parts), (1) a wall or dissepiment; (2) a separated part or segment; (3) the deepest division into which a leaf can be cut without becoming compound (Lindley).

parti'tus (Lat.) = PARTED.

Par'tridge-wood, oak-wood destroyed by *Stereum* (Tubeuf).

parturi'tal (*parturio*, I bring forth), employed by C. A. White for SEXUAL.

parviflor'us (*parvus*, small; *flos, floris*, a flower), having smaller flowers than in its congeners; **parvifo'liate**, stem dominant, internodes long, leaves small, as in elm, wallflower, etc. (Worsdell); **parvifo'lius** (*folium*, a leaf), with smaller leaves than the allied species; **Parvo-carice'ta**, pl. associations of small species of *Carex* (Warming); **par'vus** (Lat.), small.

pas'cual (*pascuum*, a pasture), H. C. Watson's term for plants which grow in pastures and grassy commons, amongst less rank herbage than "pratal"; **pas'cuus** (Lat.), relating to pastures.

Pas'sage Cells, cells in the exodermis or endodermis of roots which retain thin unaltered walls, by which water can pass.

Pas'salus (πάσσαλος, a peg), a gamosepalous calyx.

Pasteuriza'tion, the preservation of

fermenting liquids by heating to about 140° Fahr., so as to germinate and then destroy, Fungi and their spores contained in the fluids treated (Crozier).

Pas′tids, an error for PLASTIDS (Zimmermann).

Pat′anas, pl., grass-lands in Ceylon derived from savannah woodland (Pearson).

Patel′la (Lat., a small dish), an orbicular sessile apothecium, with a marginal rim distinct from the thallus ; **patellar′oid** (εἶδος, likeness), resembling a patella ; **patel′liform**, *patelliform′is* (*forma*, shape), shaped like a small dish, circular and rimmed ; **Patel′lula**, a diminutive patella ; **patel′lulate**, possessing patellulae.

pa′tent, *pat′ens* (Lat.), spreading ; **patentis′simus** (Lat.), extremely spread out.

pat′eriform (*patera*, a dish or saucer, *forma*, shape), saucer-shaped.

Path-fi′nders = HONEY-GUIDES, lines of colour leading to nectaries ; ∼ **point′ers**, defensive protection, such as prickles, etc., against undesirable insect-visitors (Kerner).

pathogen′ic, **pathog′enous** (πάθος, suffering, disease ; γένος, race, offspring), producing disease ; **Pathogene′ity**, the quality of disease-giving ; **Pathol′ogy** (λόγος, discourse), the science of diseases ; **Veg′etable** ∼, that department of botany which treats of plant diseases.

patrocli′nous (πατήρ, father ; κλίνω, to slope), displaying the characters of the male parent (De Vries).

pat′ulous, *-lus* (Lat.), standing open, spreading.

pauciflor′ous, *-rus* (*paucus*, few ; *flos*, *floris*, a flower), few flowered ; **pauci-fo′lius** (*folium*, a leaf), having few leaves ; **paucijuga′tus** (*jugum*, a yoke), with only a few pairs of leaflets in a pinnate leaf.

Paul′ospore (παῦλα, a pause), Klebs's term for CHLAMYDOSPORE.

Pauper′culae, pl. (*pauperculus*, rather poor), depauperate generations, as the dwarf-males of *Oedogonium*, etc. (A. Braun).

pau′siacus (*pausia*, a kind of olive), olive-green.

pavoni′nus (Lat., pertaining to a peacock), peacock-blue.

pear-formed, ∼ **shaped**, obovoid or obconic with a tapering base.

Pearl-glands, structures in *Pterospermum javanicum*, etc., contained in cups serving as food-bodies for ants ; the cups are probably metamorphosed stipules (Raciborski).

pearl-grey, "pure grey, a little verging to blue" (Lindley).

Peat, the soil formed on moors ; **eutroph′ic** ∼, fen-peat ; **mesotroph′ic** ∼, from transitional moors ; **oligotroph′ic** ∼, moor-peat.

Pébrine′ (Fr.), a disease of silkworms caused by *Nosema Bombycis*, Naeg., a bacterial organism ; it is also named GATTINE.

pecop′teroid, resembling the fossil fern *Pecopteris ;* **pecopt′erid** means the same.

Pec′tase (πηκτὸς, coagulated), an enzyme which forms vegetable jelly from pectic substances occurring in the cell-wall.

Pec′ten (Lat., a comb) ‡ = STERIGMA.

pec′tic (πηκτὸς, coagulated), relating to pectin, as **pec′tic Ac′id**, supposed to form a large part of fruit-jelly ; **Pec′tin**, or **Pec′tine**, a jelly-like substance in fruits ; *cf.* PECTOSE ; **pectina′ceous** (+ ACEOUS) ; resembling pectin ; gelatinous ; **Pec′tinase**, a cytolytic enzyme.

pec′tinate, *pectina′tus* (Lat., like a comb), pinnatifid with narrow segments set close like the teeth of a comb ; **pec′tinatory**, applied by De Bary to two series ‑ of vascular bundles whose members alternate with each other as the teeth of two combs.

Pec′tines, pl. (*pecten*, a comb), fimbriae on the corolla of some Gentians, constituting the corona (Huxley).

pectinif′erous (*fero*, I bear), used of a characteristic brown coating of

269

the spores of *Albugo*, PECTIN being its constituent (F. L. Stevens).

Pec′tose (πηκτὸs, coagulated), a substance allied to mucilage which occurs in unripe fruits (Frémy); **pecto′sic Ac′id** is associated with pectic acid in fruit jelly ; **Pectocel′-luloses,** *cf.* CELLULOSE.

pedalin′eous, allied to the order *Pedalineae*.

peda′linerved, etc. = PEDATINERVED, probably a misprint in Henslow's Dictionary.

peda′lis (Lat.), a foot long or high.

ped′ate, *peda′tus* (Lat., footed), in botany, palmately divided or parted with the lateral divisions two-cleft ; **ped′ately cleft** = PEDATIFID ; ~ **veined** = PEDATINERVED ; **pedat′-ifid,** *pedatif′idus* (*findo, fidi,* cleft), divided in a pedate manner nearly to the base ; **pedatiform′is** (*forma,* shape) = PEDATIFID ; **pedatilo′bus, pedatiloba′tus, pedatilo′bed** (λοβὸs, earlap), palmate, with supplementary lobes at the base ; **peda′tinerved,** *peda′tinervis* (*nervus,* a nerve), when the midrib stops short, and two strong lateral nerves proceed from its base, giving rise to others which extend only to the apex ; **pedatipar′tite,** *pedatiparti′tus* (*partitus,* divided), with pedate venation, and the lobes nearly free ; **pedat′isect,** *pedatisec′tus* (*sectus,* cut), pedately veined, the divisions nearly reaching the midrib.

Ped′estal (Fr., from *pes, pedis,* a foot), the persistent base of a leaf which disarticulates from it, *cf.* PULVINUS.

Ped′icel, *Pedicel′lus* (Mod. Lat.), (1) an ultimate flower-stalk, the support of a single flower ; (2) in Hydropterideae the sporophore ; **pedicel′-late,** *pedicella′tus, pedicula′tus* ‡, borne on a pedicel ; **Ped′icle** = PEDICEL ; **Pedicel′lulus** (dim. of *pedicellus*), a filiform support to the ovary in certain Compositae ; **Pedic′ulus,** (1) = PEDICEL ; (2) the stalk of the apple and other fruits ; (3) the filament of an anther, as ~ **Anthe′rae.**

pedif′erus (*pes, pedis,* a foot ; *fero,* I bear), furnished with a stalk or support (J. S. Henslow) ; **Pedi′lis,** the contracted upper portions of the calyx tube in such florets of Compositae as have a stipitate pappus ; **pedila′tus,** furnished with a PEDILIS.

pedioph′ilus (πεδίον, level country ; φιλέω, I love), dwelling in uplands ; **Pediophy′ta** (φυτὸν, a plant), upland plants ; **Pediophyti′a,** upland plant formations (Clements).

Pedun′cle, *Pedunc′ulus,* the general term for the stalk of a flower, it may also bear a cluster of single flowers ; **peduncular′is,** relating to a peduncle or a modification, as *peduncular′es Cir′rhi,* tendrils proceeding from a peduncle ; **pedunc′u-late,** *peduncula′tus, pedunculo′sus,* furnished with a footstalk ; **peduncu-lea′nus,** with a modified state of the peduncle (J. S. Henslow).

Peel, the rind or skin of fruit ; Grew spells it " Pill."

Peg, an embryonic organ at the lower end of the hypocotyl of seedlings of *Cucumis, Gnetum,* etc., lasting till the cotyledons are withdrawn from the testa.

Pela′gad (πέλαγος, the sea, + AD), a plant of the sea surface ; **Pelagi′um,** a surface sea-formation ; **pela′gian** = **pelag′ic,** inhabiting the open ocean, as distinct from the shores ; **pela-goph′ilus** (φιλέω, I love), living at the sea surface ; **Pelagophy′ta** (φυτὸν, a plant), surface sea plants (Clements).

pel′ios (πελιὸs), black, livid.

Pel′licle, *Pellic′ula* (Lat., a small skin), a delicate superficial membrane, epidermis ; **pellicular′is,** having the character of a pellicle ; **pellic′ulose,** furnished with a skin (Stevenson).

pelli′tus (Lat., covered with skin), "skinned, deprived of skin or apparently so" (Lindley).

pellu′cid, *pellu′cidus* (Lat., transparent), wholly or partially transparent.

Pelochthi′um (πηλὸs, clay ; ὄχθη, a

bank), a mud bank formation; **pelochthoph'ilus** (φιλέω, I love), living on mud banks; **Pelochthophy'ta** (φυτὸν, a plant), plants of mud banks; **Pelochthophyti'a**, plant formations of mud-dwelling species (Clements; **Pelogen'ety** (γένος, offspring), amount of clay in soil, as affecting the plants growing on it; **pelog'enous**, applied by Thurmann to those rocks which yield a clayey detritus, and the plants which thrive thereon; **Peloph'ilae** (φιλέω, I love), clay-loving plants; **Pel'ophile**, a plant occurring on clay; **peloph'ilous** (φιλέω, I love), Warming's variation of PELOGENOUS; **pelopsam'mic** (ψάμμος, sand), yielding clay and sand; **pelopsammog'enous**, giving rise to clayey sand (Thurmann).

Pelo'ria (πελώριος, monstrous), an irregular flower become regular by an exceptional development of complementary irregularities; **irreg'ular** ~ by the symmetric multiplication of the irregular portions; **reg'ular** ~ by the suppression of the irregular parts; **pelo'ric**, relating to PELORIA (Potter); **Pelorisa'tion**, the process of conversion of a flower to a regular form, from its normal irregular form.

Pel'ta (Lat., a small shield), (1) the round shield-like apothecium of *Peltidea*, etc.; (2) a bract attached by its middle, as in Peppers; **pel'tafid** (*findo, fidi,* to cleave), when a peltate leaf is cut into segments; **pel'tate**, *pelta'tus*, target-shaped, as a leaf attached by its lower surface to a stalk, instead of by its margin; **pelta'to-digita'tus**, a digitate leaf with the petiole much enlarged at the insertion of the leaflets; **peltid'eus**, **pel'tiform** (*forma*, shape), orbicular or buckler-shaped, as the apothecia of many Lichens or the caps of Agarics; **peltiner'ved**, *peltiner'vis*, *-vius* (*nervus*, a nerve), with ribs arranged as in a peltate leaf; **peltoi'deus** (εἶδος, resemblance) = PELTIDEUS.

pel'viform, *pelviform'is* (*pelvis*, a basin; *forma*, shape), basin-shaped, formed like a shallow cup.

pen'cilled, marked with fine distinct lines.

pen'dent, *pen'dens* (Lat.), hanging down from its support; **Pend'ent**, used by Grew for ANTHER.

pen'dulous, *pen'dulus* (Lat.), hanging, pendent; **penduli'nus** (Lat.), having the habit of being pendulous (De Candolle); **Penduliflor'ae** (*flos, floris,* a flower), Delpino's term for wind-fertilized pendulous flowers.

penic'ellate, an error for the next.

penic'illate, *penicilla'tus* (*penicillus*, a little brush), pencil-shaped; **penicil'liform**, *penicilliform'is* (*forma*, shape), shaped like an artist's pencil; **Penicil'lium**, a tuft of hairs.

pen'nate, *penna'tus* (Lat., winged, = PINNATE; **pennaticis'sus** (*cissus*, cut), with incisions of a leaf in a pinnate manner; **pennat'ifid**, *pennatif'idus* = PINNATIFID; **pen'niform** (*forma*, shape), with ribs as in a pinnate leaf, but the upper segments confluent at the apex, as in the date palm; **penniner'ved**, *penniner'vis* (*nervus*, a nerve); **pennive'nius** (*vena*, a vein), pinnately veined.

pentacam'arus (πέντε, five; καμάρα, a vault), with five loculi; **pentacarpel'lary** (+ CARPELLARY), having five carpels; **Pentachae'nium** or **Pentake'nium** (+ ACHENIUM), having the structure of a cremocarp, but with five carpels instead of two; **pentacoc'cous**, *-cus* (+ COCCUS), with five cocci elastically splitting away from the main axis; **Pentacot'yl**, a seedling with cotyledons so divided as to appear to possess five seed-leaves (De Vries); **penta-cy'clic** (κύκλος, a circle), a flower with five whorls of members, *cf.* PENTAMEROUS; **pentadac'tylous** (δάκτυλον, a finger), five-fingered, or with five finger-like divisions; **pentadel'phous**, *-phus* (ἀδελφὸς, a brother), with five fraternities or

bundles of stamens; **pentag'onal**
(γωνία, an angle), with five angles;
Pentagyn'ia (γυνή, a woman), a
Linnean order of plants having five
pistils; **pentag'ynous**, with five
pistils or styles; **Pentake'nium** =
PENTACHAENIUM; **pentam'erous**,
-*rus* (μέρος, a part), with parts in
fives, as a corolla of five petals;
pentan'der (ἀνήρ, ἀνδρὸς, a man), of
five stamens; **Pentan'dria**, a Linnean class of plants possessing five
stamens, the largest in that system;
pentan'drous, five-stamened.

pentan'gular (πεντάγωνος, five-angles),
five-angled, pentagonal.

pentapet'alous, -*lus* (πέντε, five; πέταλον, a flower-leaf), with five petals;
pentaphylet'ic (φυλή, a tribe), used
of hybrids which are composed of
five strains, five species or forms
being represented in the hybrid;
pentaphyl'lous, -*lus* (φύλλον, a leaf),
with five leaves; **pentap'terous**,
-*rus* (πτέρον, a wing), five-winged;
pen'tarch (ἀρχή, beginning), with
five points of origin, applied to the
xylem strands in a stele; **pentar-
rhi'nus**, J. S. Henslow's emendation
of **pentari'nus** (ἄρρην, male), Necker's
term for PENTANDROUS; **pentasep'-
alous**, -*lus* (+ SEPALUM), having
five sepals; **pentasper'mous** (σπέρμα,
a seed), five-seeded; **pentastich'ous**
(στίχος, a row), in five vertical
ranks; **Pen'toses**, a name given to
compounds resembling glucose, but
having only five atoms of carbon in
the molecule.

Pep'o (Lat., a pumpkin), **Pepon'ida** ‡;
Peponid'ium ‡, a gourd fruit, a one-
celled, many-seeded, inferior fruit,
with parietal placentas and pulpy
interior.

Pep'sin (πέψις, cooking, digestion),
the digestive principle or peptic
enzyme.

Pep'tase (πεπτικὸς, promoting digestion), a fibrin-digesting enzyme
(Vines); **pep'tic**, digestive; ~ **Fer'-
ments**, those enzymes which convert
proteids into peptones.

Pep'tones (πεπτὸς, cooked), albumi-

noids after being acted on by ferments, as proteids, which are the
final result of their action; they
are present in germinating seeds;
peptoni'sing, applied to enzymes so
acting.

per-, in Latin compounds increases
their force as *per-similis*, very like.

Perano'sis (περαίνω, I penetrate), change
in the permeability of protoplasm.

Perapet'alum ‡ (περί, about + PETA-
LUM), any appendage to a petal, a
synonym of NECTARILYMA and PA-
RAPETALUM; **Peraphyl'lum** (φύλλον,
a leaf) = PARAPHYLLUM.

percur'rent (*percurrens*, running
through), extending throughout the
entire length.

Perem'bryo = PEREMBRYUM.

Perem'bryum (περί, about; ἔμβρυον,
an embryo), that part of a monocotyledonous embryo investing the
plumule and radicle, not externally
distinguishable.

Perench'yma (πήρα, a sack; ἔγχυμα,
an infusion), cellular tissue containing starchy matter (Stormonth).

Perenna'tion (*perennitas*, continuance),
lasting, a perennial state.

peren'nate, *peren'nans* (Lat.), **perenna'ting**, **peren'nial**, *peren'nis* (Lat.),
lasting the whole year through;
Peren'nial, is a plant which lasts
several years, not perishing normally after once flowering and
fruiting; ~ **Herb**, the above-ground
portion dies each year, the root
persisting; ~ **Mon'ocarp**, applied
by Möbius to such plants as *Agave
americana*, Linn., which live long,
but die after once flowering.

per'fect, *perfectus* (Lat., complete),
(1) applied to a flower which is
hermaphrodite; (2) of an organ
which has all its constituent members.

perfo'liate, *perfolia'tus* (*per*, through;
folium, a leaf), used when a stem
apparently passes through a leaf, as
in *Bupleurum perfoliatum*, Linn.

per'forate, *perfora'tus* (Lat., pierced),
pierced through, or having translucent dots which look like little

holes, as in *Hypericum perforatum*, Linn.

Per'forms, pl., in *Rosa*, those with doubly serrated leaves and glabrous calyxes (Almquist).

perfos'sus(Lat.,dug or pierced through), perfoliate.

perfu'sus (Lat., poured over), completely covered.

pergame'neous, *-neus* (*pergamena*, parchment), like parchment in texture; **pergamenta'ceous**, *-ceus* (+ ACEOUS), resembling parchment. **Per'iachene** (περὶ, about, + ACHENE), a term including EPIACHENE, for an Achene arising from a partially superior flower (Villari); **Perian'dra**, pl. (ἀνὴρ, ἀνδρὸς, a man), the bracts of the male inflorescence in Mosses; **perian'dricus** (ἀνδρικος, manly), used of a nectary when it is ranged round the stamens; **Per'ianth**, *Perian'thium* (ἄνθος, a flower), (1) the floral envelopes, calyx or corolla, or both; (2) in Hepaticae the inflated envelope surrounding the fertilized archegonium, the COLE-SULE or vaginule; **perian'theus**, **perian'thial**, relating to the PERI-ANTH; **perianthia'nus**, relating to or possessing a perianth; **Periantho-ma'nia** (μανία, madness), an abnormal multiplication of perianth segments; **periax'ial** (+ AXIAL) **Wood**, the so-called◊ outer wood, as in the stems of Bignoniaceae; **Per'iblast** (βλαστὸς, a bud), a misprint for PERIPLAST; **Periblaste'sis** (+ BLAS-TESIS), the envelopment of gonidia by surrounding tissue.

Per'iblem (περίβλημα, clothing), a layer of nascent cortex beneath the epidermis.

pericalyc'ius (περὶ, about + CALYX), = PERISTAMINEUS; **Pericam'bium** (+ CAMBIUM), thin walled cells of the central cylinder in contact with the inner face of the endodermis; the pericycle; adj. **pericam'bial**; ~ **Sheath**, a rhizogenous tissue within the endodermal sheath; **Per'icarp**, *Pericar'pium* (καρπὸς, fruit), (1) the wall of a fructified

ovary; (2) applied also to the wall of the capsule in Mosses; (3) improperly used of the protective husks surrounding certain fruits; adj. **pericar'pic**, **pericar'pial**, *pericar-pia'lis*; **Pericar'yoplasm** = PERI-KARYOPLASM; **Pericau'lome** (καυλὸς, stalk), the outer portion of the stem, including the leaf-trace bundles, derived theoretically from the fused bases of the leaves (Potonié); **pericen'tral** (κέντρον, a sharp point) **Cell** = AUXILIARY CELL; **pericen'tricus**, applied to perigynous stamens arranged concentrically with the calyx; **Per'ichaeth** (Crozier) = PERICHAETIUM; **Peri-chae'tium** (χαίτη, a mane), (1) the involucre around the base of the seta in Mosses; (2) W. J. Hooker's name for the perianth in Hepaticae; **perichae'tial** *perichaetia'lis*, relating to the same, as ~ **Bracts**, ~ **Leaves**, the organs composing the peri-chaetium itself in Mosses, and the involucre in Hepaticae; **Per'ichyle** (χυλὸς, juice), a plant whose water-storing tissue is between the epidermis and the chlorenchyma, as *Rhizophora;* **perichyl'ous**, employed of the aqueous tissue when between the epidermis and chlorenchyma (A. Schimper); **Periclad'ium** (κλάδος, a branch), the sheathing base of a leaf when it surrounds the supporting branch; **pericli'nal** (κλίνω, I bend down), curved in the same direction as the surface or circumference; ~ **Chimae'ra** = GRAFT-HYBRID; ~ **Planes**, planes which conform to the exterior; **Per'icline** = PERICLINIUM; **Per'iclines**, pl. periclinal walls; **Pericli'nium** (κλίνη, a bed), the involucre of the capitulum in Compositae; **Periclinoi'des**, ‡ a false involucre formed of the scales of the receptacle in Compositae, surrounding the sides of an elevated receptacle at its summit, as in *Evax;* **Pericoc'cium**, that portion of the protoplasm which envelopes the nucleus; in Germ. Kerntasche (Hanstein); **Pericol'ium** ‡ (κολεὸς,

273

a sheath) = PERICHAETIUM; **pericorolla'tus** (+ COROLLA), used of a dicotyledonous plant with a gamopetalous perigynous corolla; **Per'icycle** (*κύκλος*, a circle), the outermost zone of cells of the stele immediately within the endodermis; **inter'nal** ~, Flot's term for the procambium retained on the inner side of the vascular bundle; **pericy'clic Sec'tors**, interruptions of the pericycle of the root in certain Mosses, by tissues of cells whose walls are very slightly thickened (Campbell); **Per'iderm**, *Perider'ma*, *Perider'mis* (*δέρμα*, skin or hide), the outer bark or epiphloëm, at first restricted by Mohl to tough cork in distinction to the soft cork, now extended to the cork cambium and its products; phellogen; **Per'idesm** (*δέσμη*, a bundle), the layer of cells which surround each vascular bundle beneath the special endoderm in astelic stems (Van Tieghem); adj. **perides'mic.**

Perid'inin, one of the colouring-matters found in the Peridineae.

Perid'iole, *Perid'iolum*, pl. *Perid'iola* (dim. of PERIDIUM from *πηρίδιον*, a little pouch), (1) a chamber of the gleba forming a nest of spores, free or attached by a funicle within the peridium of the sporophore; (2) "a membrane by which the spores of some Algae are immediately covered" (Lindley); **Perid'ium**, a general expression for the outer enveloping coat of a sporophore upon which the spores develop within a cavity; ~ **exter'num**, the outer layer which opens in various ways and separates from the ~ **inter'num**, the inner layer directly enclosing the gleba; ~ **mitrifor'me**, "the receptacle of certain Fungals" (Lindley); adj. **perid'ial**; as ~ **Cells**, the outer cells of a peridium which are coherent.

Perid'roma (*περιδρομή*, a circuit), Necker's term for the rhachis of Ferns.

Perienchy'ma (*περί*, about; *ἔγχυμα*, an infusion), irregular cellular tissue, chiefly in glands and spheroidal masses (J. S. Henslow), *cf.* PERENCHYMA; **Perifor'ium** = PERIPHORIUM; **Perigam'ium** (*γάμος*, marriage), the portion of the fertile reduced branchlets of Mosses, which contain the archegonia; **Perigloe'a** (*γλοῖος*, glue), the entire gelatinous investment of a Diatom (Buffham); **Per'igone**, *Perigo'nium* (*γονή*, offspring), (1) a synonym of PERIANTH; (2) the same of PERICHAETIUM; (3) the involucre of the male inflorescence in Bryophytes; adj. **perigo'nial**, as ~ **Leaves**, the perichaetial leaves (excluding Bryophytes); **perigonia'rius**, (1) with the character of a perigone; (2) double flowers, resulting from transformation or multiplication of the floral organs taking on the character of perianth segments; **Perigynan'da**, **Perigynan'dra**, -*drum* (*γυνή*, a woman; *ἀνήρ*, *ἀνδρός*, a man), (1) the involucre of Compositae; ~ **commu'nis**, ~ **exte'rior**, the involucre, ~ **inte'rior**, the corolla of a composite floret; **Perigyn'ium**, (1) the hypogynous setae of sedges; (2) the flask or utricle of *Carex*; (3) any hypogynous disc; (4) the involucre of the female inflorescence in Bryophytes; **perig'ynous**, literally means round the ovary, used of organs adnate to the perianth, or adnate with the lower part of the pistil; **perihadromat'ic** (+ HADROME), surrounding the hadrome; **Perikar'yoplasm** (*κάρυον*, a nut; *πλάσμα*, moulded), a zone of granular protoplasm seen in *Cobaea scandens*, Cav., in the cytoplasm of the resting pollen mother-cell on its approaching division (A. A. Lawson); **perileptomat'ic** (+ LEPTOME), surrounding the leptome; **perimedul'lary** (+ MEDULLARY) **Zone**, the peripheral region of the inner tissue outwardly bounded by the protoxylem; *cf.* CIRCUMMEDULLARY;

Perimel′itae (*mel*, honey), having honey-glands placed in the lower portion of the perianth, as in certain Gentianaceae (Huxley) ; **Perimer′istem** (+ MERISTEM), consists of several layers of cells which at first divide in every direction, but subsequently divide tangentially in the external region (Guillaud) ; **perimicrop′ylar** (+ MICROPYLE), situated near or round the micropyle ; **Per′ine**, the outermost layer of sculpturing on pollen ; **perinectar′ial** (+ NECTARY), surrounding the nectarial area, as in certain Gentians (Huxley) ; **Perin′ium** (Mod. Lat.), the outermost of the three coats of a Fern spore ; the epispore.

perin′teger (Lat.), quite entire.

perinu′cleolar (περὶ, about, + NUCLEOLUS) ; **Vac′uole**, a clear zone surrounding each nucleolus in prophase of pollen-mother-cells (Stevens).

Per′iod, la′tent, see LATENT PERIOD.

Period′ic Movements, used to express the opening and closing of flowers, the nyctitropic movements of leaves, etc., when occurring habitually and with some regularity.

peripet′alous, *-us* (περὶ, about ; πέταλον, a flower-leaf), around the petals.

periphae′ricus (περιφέρεια, the circumference of a circle), peripheric, circumferential ; **periph′eral**, surrounding ; ∼ **Steles**, four long curved steles in *Psaronius* from which adventitious roots take their origin (Zeiller) ; ∼ **Tis′sue**, in roots, the piliferous layer furnished with root hairs ; **peripher′ic**, *peripher′icus*, pertaining to the circumference, as of an embryo coiled round the outside of the albumen ; **peripher′icotermina′lis**, belonging to the circumference and apex of a body, used of stems which grow both in length and breadth.

Periphlo′ëm (περὶ, about + PHLOEM), the phloëm-sheath or pericambium ; **periphloëmat′ic**, applied to concentric bundles in Ferns ; **Periphoran′thium** (φορέω, I carry ; ἄνθος, a

flower), the involucre of Compositae ; **Periphor′ium**, a fleshy and elongated support to the ovary, with the corolla and stamens attached to it ; J. S. Henslow spells it " Periforium " ; **Per′iphragm** (φράγμα, an enclosure), the pericycle of the stem (Dangeard) ; **Per′iphylls, Periphyl′lia** ‡ pl. (φύλλον, a leaf), the hypogynous scales or lodicules of grasses ; **Periphyllog′eny** (γένος, race, offspring), bearing numerous leaflets round the edge of a leaf-blade (Weismann) ; **Periph′yses**, pl. (φύσις, growth), hairs of like origin to PARAPHYSES but arising from the hymenium of Ascomycetes at places destitute of asci (Bennett and Murray) ; **Per′iplasm** (πλάσμα, moulded), protoplasm in the oogonium and the antheridium which does not share in the conjugation ; *cf.* GONOPLASM ; **Per′iplast** (πλάστος, moulded), a hyaline structure enveloping the cell-nucleus ; **Peripod′ium** (πούς, ποδὸς, a foot) = PERICHAETIUM ; **perip′terous, -rus** (πτερὸν, a wing), *periptera′tus*, surrounded by a wing or border ; **Periscy′phe** (σκύφος, a cup), Desvaux's word for PERICHAETIUM ; **Per′isperm**, *Perisper′mium* (σπέρμα, a seed), (1) the ordinary albumen of a seed, restricted to that which is formed outside the embryo sac ; (2) the pericarp or even the integuments of a seed ; **perisper′mic**, *perisper′micus*, **perisperma′tus**, (1) furnished with albumen ; (2) " when the perisperm is reduced to a single lamina, or when the seed is not furnished with a true perisperm " (J. S. Henslow) ; **Perisporan′gium** (σπορὰ, a seed ; ἀγγεῖον, a vessel), the indusium of Ferns, a membranous covering of the sorus ; **Per′ispore**, *Perispor′ium*, *-rum*, (1) the membrane or case surrounding a spore ; (2) the mother-cell of spores in Algae ; (3) = PERIGYNIUM ; (4) an incrustation containing much silica, outside the exospore of *Isoëtes* (Fitting) ; **Perisporin′ium**, the outermost membrane of pollen in

Angiosperms (Fitting); **Peristach′-yum** ‡ (στάχυς, a spike), the glume of grasses; **Peristamin′ia** (+ Stamen), **Periste′mones** (στήμων, a filament), pl., applied to petalous dicotyledons with perigynous stamens; **Per′istem** (abbrev. from Perimeristem), young cortex in a nascent condition; **Per′-istome,** *Perist′oma, Peristom′ium* (στόμα, a mouth), the fringe or its homologue round the orifice of a Moss-capsule; **perist′omate,** *peristoma′tus, perist′omus,* provided with a peristome; **peristomat′ic,** *peristomat′icus,* when perigynous stamens are attached round the mouth of the calyx tube; **peristy′licus** (+ Stylus), when epigynous stamens are inserted between the styles and limb of the calyx; **Perisy′phe,** more correctly Periscyphe; **Perithall′ium** (θαλλός, a twig), the upper layer of calcareous Algae (Rothpletz); **Per′i-thece = Perithe′cium,** pl. Perithe′-cia (θήκη, a case), (1) a case with a small opening containing asci, in Lichens; (2) in Fungi, a receptacle enclosing spores which are naked or in asci; **perithe′cioid** (εἶδος, like) **Glands,** those on the pitcher of *Nepenthes,* resembling the perithecium of a *Sphaeria* (Macfarlane); **perit′richous** (θρίξ, τρίχος, a hair), the whole surface beset with cilia (Jones); **perit′ropal, perit′ropous,** *-pus* (τροπή, a turning), used of a seed which is horizontal in the pericarp, or of a radicle which is directed to the side of a pericarp; **perixylemat′ic** (+ Xylem), said of concentric bundles in the roots of *Acorus,* Juncaceae and Cyperaceae (Laux); **perixy′lic,** Van Tieghem's expression for Mes-arch + Exarch; **Perizo′nium** (ζώνη, a belt), the thin non-silicious membrane of a young auxospore.

perlar′ius, perla′tus (Late Lat., *perla,* a pearl), (1) shining with a pearly lustre; (2) furnished with rounded tubercular appendages (J. S. Henslow). Note: not to be confounded with *perlatus,* carried through, derived from *perfero.*

perla′tent (*perlatens,* enduring), applied by De Vries to a permanently fixed character.

per′manent, *per′manens* (*permaneo,* I persist), persistent; ~ **Quad′rat,** a square of one metre each way, so marked as to permit of study from year to year (Clements); ~ **Tis′sue,** fully formed tissue, as distinct from merismatic or generative tissue.

Permeabil′ity (*permeabilis,* that can be passed through), applied to protoplasm, etc., and further distinguished as Extrameability, and Intrameability, the power of allowing the passage of certain substances out of or into its vacuoles respectively (Janse).

permo′bile (*per* = very; *mobilis,* easy to be moved), very easily moved, as many sand dunes.

Permuta′tion, *Permuta′tio* (Lat., a changing), enlargement of the floral envelopes with abortion of the sexual organs (Penzig).

permuta′tus (Lat.), completely changed.

Pernic′iasm (*pernicies,* destruction), Tubeuf's term for the killing of host-cells by a parasitic fungus.

Per′nio (Lat., a chilblain), a local affection resembling an ulcer, caused by cold.

Perocid′ium ‡ (περί, about; ὀγκίδιον, a tubercle), Necker's term for Perichaetium.

per′onate, *perona′tus* (Lat., leather booted), thickly covered with a woolly covering becoming mealy.

peronocar′pic, where occurring, probably a misprint for Pyrenocarpic.

Perovula′tae (*per,* much or very; *ovulatus,* ovuled), otherwise Semi-natae, Van Tieghem's terms for phanerogams furnished with true seeds.

Perox′ydase (*per,* very + Oxydase), an enzyme causing increased evolution of oxygen.

perpe′lic (*per,* much; πηλός, clay), Thurmann's term for rocks which yield clay, pure and abundant, also for the plants which thrive thereon.

perpendic'ular, *perpendicula'ris* (Lat.),
used of an organ with its direction
vertical, either (*a*) to the horizon,
or (*b*) to its attachment ; ~ **Sys'-
tem,** = FIBRO-VASCULAR SYSTEM
(Crozier).

perpsam'mic (*per*, much ; ψάμμos, sand),
yielding an abundance of sandy
detritus, with the flora thereon
growing.

perpusil'lus (Lat.), very small.

Per'quadrat, a quadrat of 16 square
metres or more.

persicic'olor (*persicum*, a peach ; *color*,
colour), **persici'nus** (Lat.), peach-
coloured, a rosy pink.

persis'tent, *persis'tens* (Lat., persevering), (1) remaining till the part
which bears it is wholly matured, as
the leaves of evergreens ; (2) in the
culture of Algae, when the supply
of prepared water keeps the culture
even ; **Persis'tence,** constancy, as
~ **of Varia'tion,** the variety or tendency to vary persisting.

per'sonate, *persona'tus* (Lat., masked),
used for a bilabiate corolla having
a prominent palate.

Perspira'tion (Crozier), see TRAN-
SPIRATION.

pertusar'ioid, resembling the Lichen-
genus *Pertusaria*.

pertu'sate, pertuse', *pertu'sus* (Lat.,
perforated), having slits or holes.

Pe'rula (Lat., a little wallet), (1) the
scale of a leaf-bud ; (2) Lindley also
gives it as a projection in the flower
of Orchids, the MENTUM ; (3) =
PERITHECIUM ; **per'ulate,** *perula'tus*,
furnished with protective scales.

perval'var (*per* = through ; *valva*, a
valve) **Ax'is,** the main longitudinal
axis of a Diatom frustule, the line
which forms the centre of the
dividing plane, penetrates the cell-
cavity in the epi- and hypothecal
directions at equal distances from
the enclosing walls, and unites
the centres of the valves (O.
Mueller).

Perver'sion (*perversio*, a turning
about), (1) turned aside ; (2) O.
Mueller's term for turned upside

down in the case of Diatoms ; **perver'ted,** so turned.

per'vious, *per'vius* (Lat., passable)
having an open passage-way.

Pes, Ped'is (Lat.), a foot, (1) used in
such compounds as *longipes*, long-
stalked ; (2) a foot of twelve inches
measurement ± 30·5 cm.; *cf.* FOOT.

Pet'al, *Pet'alum* (πέταλον, a flower-
leaf), (1) one of the leafy expansions
in the floral whorl styled the Corolla ; the word was taken by Blair
from Columna ; (2) of the Hop, the
scales of the strobile ; ~ **-like,**
~ **-shaped,** petaloid ; **petala'tus,**
possessing petals or a corolla ;
petalif'erous, bearing petals ; **Petali-
fica'tion** (*facio*, I make)=PETALODY;
pet'aliform, *petaliform'is* (*forma*,
shape), petal-shaped ; **pet'aline,**
petali'nus, petal-like, or relating to
petals ; **Pet'alode** (εῖδos, resemblance),
an organ simulating a petal ; **petalo'deus** (Lat.), (1) = PETALODY ;
(2) having petals ; **Petalo'dy,** the
metamorphosis of stamens or other
organs into petals ; **pet'aloid,** *pe-
taloi'deus*, like a petal, or having a
floral envelope resembling petals ;
~ **An'ther,** an anther borne on a
petal, the filament resembling a
petal ; **Petaloma'nia** (μανία, madness), an abnormal multiplication of
petals ; **Petaloste'mones** (στήμων, a
filament), plants with flowers whose
stamens are adherent to the corolla ;
pet'alous, Blair's term for having
petals ; **Pet'aly,** the condition of
possessing petals (J. M. Coulter).

Pet'asospores *-ae* (πέτασos, a broad
brimmed hat, + SPORE), plants
having seeds with parachute-like
appendages (Clements).

petiola'ceus (*petiolus*, a little foot or leg,
+ ACEUS) (Lat.), having reference
to the petiole by attachment, transformation, or appearance ; **petiola'-
neus** or **petiolea'nus** (Mod. Lat.),
consisting of the petiole or of some
modification of it ; **pet'iolans** (Lat.),
producing petioles ; used by Dr.
Burchell; **pet'iolar,** *petio'laris*, **pet'io-
lary,** borne on, or pertaining to a

petiole; **pet′iolate**, *petiola′tus*, having
a petiole ; **Pet′iole**, *Pet′iolus*, the foot-
stalk of a leaf ; ~ **Gut′ter**, the leaf-stalk
grooved and leading down to hairy
buds or grooves on the stem (S.
Elliot); ~ **Trace**, the strand of vascular
tissue, sectionally shaped as **H**, connecting the petiole and the stem
in *Diplolabis* (Gordon) ; **Pet′iolule**,
Petiol′ulus, (1) a small petiole ; (2)
the petiole of a leaflet ; **petiol′ulate**,
petiolula′tus, having a petiolule;
petiol′ular, *petiolula′ris*, belonging
to a petiolule.

Pet′rad (πέτρος, a rock, + AD), a rock
plant (Clements).

petrae′us (Lat.), growing amongst
rocks.

Pet′rifact (*petra*, rock ; *facio*, I make),
a fossil, due to petrification (Stopes) ;
Petrifac′tion, formerly applied to all
fossils, now restricted to those completely penetrated by silicic acid or
calcium carbonate, and so preserved
in a solid form.

Petri′um (πέτρος, a rock), a rock formation ; **Petrochthi′um**, pl. -*i′a* (ὄχθη,
a bank), a rock bank formation ;
petrochthoph′ilus (φιλέω, I love),
living on rock banks ; **Petroch-
thophy′ta** (φυτὸν, a plant), rock bank
plants (Clements).

Petro′dad (πετρώδης, stony, + AD), a
plant of a boulder field ; **Petrodi′um**,
a boulder field or stone formation ;
petrodoph′ilus (φιλέω, I love), dwelling in boulder fields ; **Petrodophy′ta**
(φυτὸν, a plant), boulder field plants
(Clements).

petroph′ilus (πέτρος, a rock ; φιλέω, I
love), rock dwelling ; **Petrophy′ta**
(φυτὸν, a plant), rock plants (Clements) ; **Pet′rophytes**, rock plants,
subdivided into LITHOPHYTES and
CHOMOPHYTES.

petro′sus (Lat., rocky), growing
amongst stones.

Pezizaxan′thine (+ XANTHIN), a special
orange colouring-matter, also termed
Pezi′zin, Rosoll's name for the same
pigment in *Peziza aurantia*, Pers.,
etc. ; **pezi′zoid** (εῖδος, resemblance),
peziza-, or cup-shaped.

phaenanth′erous (φαίνω, I appear; ἄνθος,
a flower), with stamens exserted ;
Phaenan′thery the condition described ; **phaenic′eus** = PHOENIC-
EUS ; **phaenobio′tic** (βίος, life),
Kuntze's term for that geologic
period when plants made their
appearance as evidenced by their
fossil remains ; **phaenocar′pous** -*pus*
(καρπὸς, fruit), having a distinct
fruit, with no adhesion to surrounding parts ; **phaenog′amous** (γάμος,
marriage), having manifest flowers,
phanerogamous ; **Phae′nogams** =
PHANEROGAMS ; **Phaenol′ogy** =
PHENOLOGY ; **Phae′notype** = PHENO-
TYPE.

Phae′ocyst (φαιὸς, brown and swarthy ;
κύστις, a bag), Decaisne's name for
the cell-nucleus ; **Phaeodict′yae** (δικτύον, a net), Dictyosporae with dark
or opaque spores (Traverso) ; **Phaeo-
did′ymae** (δίδυμος, double), Didymosporae with brown or dark-coloured
sporae (Traverso) ; **Phae′ophore**
(φορέω, I carry), Schmitz's term for
chlorophyll granule when dark
brown, as in Phaeophyceae ; **Phaeo-
phrag′mae** (φράγμα, a hedge), Fungi
having muriform spores of a dark
colour (Traverso) ; **phaeophy′cean**
(φῦκος, a sea weed), relating to the
Phaeosporeae, a group of olive or
brown marine Algae ; **Phae′ophyll**
(φύλλον, a leaf), the colouring-matter
in the living active chromatophores
of brown seaweeds (Reinke) ; **Phae′o-
phyte** (φυτὸν, a plant), the olive-
green seaweeds, or Phaeophyceae
(Wettstein) ; **Phae′oplast** (πλάστος,
moulded), the special name for
the chromatophores of Fucoideae
(Schimper); **Phaeospo′rae** (+SPORA),
Fungi having dark-coloured spores
as *Xylaria* (Traverso) ; **Phae′ospore**
(σπορὰ, a seed), a member of the
brown Algae ; adj. **phaeos′porous** ;
phae′us (Lat.), fuscous, swarthy.

Phai′ophyll (φαιὸς, brown ; φύλλον, a
leaf), a group of colouring-matters in
the leaves of plants of various tints
of brown.

Phalan′ges, sing. **Phal′anx** (φάλαγξ,

a band of soldiers), bundles of stamens in diadelphous and polyadelphous flowers; **phalarsiphy′tus** (ἄρρην = ἄρσην, male ; φυτὸν, a plant), Necker's term for polyadelphous.

Phal′line, a poisonous substance from various species of *Amanita;* **phall′oid** (εἶδος, resemblance), like the Fungus genus *Phallus,* or *Ithyphallus;* **Phal′lus,** "the peridium of certain Fungals" (Lindley) ; the name is immediately derived from *Phallus impudicus,* Linn., the Stinkhorn Fungus, now referred to *Ithyphallus.*

Phan′eri, pl. (φανερὸς, manifest), any organisms which are visible under the microscope without the use of reagents (Maggi) ; **phaneran′thus** (ἄνθος, a flower), where the flower is manifest ; **phaneranthe′rus** (ἀνθηρὸς, flowery), when the anthers protrude beyond the perianth ; **phanerogam′ic, phanerog′amous,** *phanerog′amus,* (γάμος, marriage), having manifest flowers ; **phanerogam′ic wood,** secondary or centrifugal wood ; **phanerogam′ian,** pertaining to **Phan′erogams,** plants with flowers in which stamens and pistils are distinctly developed ; **Phanerog′amy,** the condition of PHANEROGAMS ; **phanerop′orous** (πόρος, a way or passage), applied to stomata which lie in the same plane as the epidermis ; *cf.* CRYPTOPOROUS ; **Phan′erophytes** (φυτὸν, a plant), plants whose bulbs and tender extremities, which must pass the resting season, are on upright perennial stems, such as trees and shrubs (Raunkiær).

Pharmacogno′sy (φάρμακον, a drug ; γνῶσις, knowledge), the knowledge of the distinctive features of vegetable drugs (E. M. Holmes).

Phase′olin, a reserve proteid occurring in *Phaseolus* seeds, forming their main proteid store ; **Phaseolun′atin,** a glucoside in linseed and other Leguminosae.

Phel′lem (φέλλὸς, cork) = cork (Crozier) ; **Phelle′ma,** the outermost

layer of the periderm, consisting of true cork and phelloid (Hoehnel).

Phell′ad (φελλεὺς, stony soil + AD), "a rock field plant" (Clements) ; **Phell′i′um,** a "rock field formation."

Phel′loderm (φέλλος, cork; δέρμα, skin), the innermost layer of the periderm ; **Phel′logen** (γεννάω, I produce), the central layer of the three in the periderm, the active cork-producing tissue ; adj. **phellogenet′ic ; phel′loid** (εἶδος, resemblance), cork-like, as tissue which approaches cork in quality ; **Phel′loid,** non-suberized layers in the phellema (Hoehnel) ; **phelloph′ilous** (φιλέω, I love), dwelling in stony fields ; **Phellophy′ta** (φυτὸν, a plant), plants growing amongst loose stones (Clements).

phe′nicine, phenic′eous, (Heinig) = PHOENICEOUS.

Phenhy′brid (φαίνω, I appear, + HYBRID), Jeffrey's term for an obvious hybrid, as opposed to a CRYPTHYBRID.

Phe′nogam = PHANEROGAM ; adj. **phenogam′ian, phenogam′ic,** etc. = PHANEROGAMIAN, PHANEROGAMIC, etc.

Phenol′ogy, abbreviated from **Phenomenol′ogy** (φαινομενὸν, an appearance ; λόγος, a discourse), recording the periodical phenomena of plants, as leafing, flowering, etc. ; adj. **phenolog′ical,** as ∼ **Inver′sions,** an abnormal inversion of the relative blossoming of plants, caused by meteorologic conditions (Rahn) ; ∼ **Isola′tion,** by a time of flowering earlier or later than the other species of the same genus (Jeffery).

Phe′notype (φαίνω, I appear ; τύπος, a type), Johannsen's term for a biotype of mixed individuals having like external characters, but of unlike germinal composition ; adj. **phenotyp′ic.**

Phillile′sia, (φύλλον, a leaf ; ἐλίσσω, I wind), a name propounded by Re and adopted by Berkeley for "leaf-curl or blister" ; *cf.* PHYLLILESIA.

Phil′otherm (φιλέω, I love ; θέρμη, warmth), used by J. G. Baker for plants which need warmth to complete their life-cycle.

phleboi'dal (φλὲψ, φλεβὸs, a vein), has been applied to spiral annular, or porous moniliform vessels (Cooke) ; **Phlebomor'pha** (μορφὴ, form), the mycelium of some Fungi.

Phleume'tum, a plant-association consisting of *Phleum pratense*, etc. (Ganong).

Phlobaph'enes, pl. (φλοιὸs, bark ; βαφὴ, a dyeing), amorphous brown colouring-matters of the bark ; **phloeo'des** (εἶδοs, resemblance), bark-like in appearance ; **Phlo'ëm,** Naegeli's term for the bast elements of a vascular bundle ; it is separated in exogens from the wood (xylem) by the cambium ; ~ **Com'missure,** the apposition of phloëm elements as the beginning of a central strand (Brebner) ; ~ **I'slands,** groups of bast-strands surrounded by xylem (Chodat) ; ~ **-parench'yma,** *cf.* BAST-PARENCHYMA ; ~ **Ray,** a ray or plate of phloëm between two medullary rays ; ~ **Sheath,** a layer of thin-walled cells surrounding the vascular tissue next within the cortex, best seen in roots ; **Phloë-oter'ma** (τέρμα, a limit), the innermost layer of primary cortex ; **Phloeotrach'eides** (+ TRACHEID), the vascular elements of the haustorium of parasitic Santalaceae (Benson) ; **Phloe'um‡,** the cortical tissues ; **Phlorid'zin** (ῥίζα, a root), a white crystalline substance which gives the bitter astringency to the root-bark of the apple, pear, cherry, and plum-trees ; **Phloroglu'cin,** a body of frequent occurrence in the bark of trees, derived from glucosides.

Phlyktioplank'ton (φλυκτὶs, a blister, + PLANKTON), Forel's term for organisms supported by hydrostatic means.

pho'bic (φόβοs, fear), repulsive ; **Pho'b-ism,** Massart's term for repulsion of plants ; **phobochemotac'tic** (chem + τάξιs, arrangement), a chemical influence which is repellent, as in

swarm spores of Myxomycetes ; **Phobochemotax'is,** the condition described ; **Phobophotax'is** ; **Phobophotot'ropism** (φῶs, φωτὸs, light ; τροπὴ, a turning), movements induced by shunning light ; adj. **phobophotac'tic.**

phoenic'eous, *phoenic'eus* (Late Lat.), scarlet ; red with a little of yellow added.

phoeos'porous = PHAEOSPOROUS.

Pho'ma-stage, the perithecial stage of Beetroot Rot, *Phoma Betae ;* the ascigerous stage is that caused by *Sphaerella.*

Phoran'thium (φορὸs, bearing ; ἄνθοs, a flower), the receptacle of the capitulum in Compositae.

photeol'ic (φῶs, φωτὸs, light ; αἰόλοs, moving, motile), used of the sleep of plants ; **pho'tic,** influenced by, or adapted to, the action of light, well-illuminated, as the margins of pools, etc. ; **Pho'tism,** Massart's term for the emission of light under stimulus ; **Photo-aesthe'sia** (ἀἰσθησιs, perception), Csapek's term to express the power of an organ to respond to the stimulus of light ; **Photo'bia** (βίοs, life), pl., Tulasne's term for ectoparasitic Fungi ; **Pho'toblast** (βλασ-τὸs, a bud), used of a shoot developed above the soil, and adapted to live in light and air (Kirchner) ; **photocleistogam'ic** (+ CLEISTOGAMIC), used of flowers which do not open in consequence of the rapid growth of the outer side of the petals, due to PHOTOHYPONASTY (Hansgirg) ; **Photocleistog'amy** is the condition ; **Photocli'ny** (κλίνω, I bend), response due to the direction of the incident rays ; **Photoepinas'ty** (+ EPINASTY), epinasty induced by the action of light (Detmer) ; **photogen'ic** (-γεν-, producing), used of bacteria which are luminous ; **Photohar'mose** (ἀρμὸs, a joining), response to light stimuli (Clements) ; **Photohyponas'ty** (+ HYPONASTY), hyponasty caused by the effect of light (Vines) ; **Photokine'sis** (+ KINESIS), movement induced by light; **photokine′tic** (κίνητικός, having the power of movement), moving in consequence of the stimulus of light; **Photo-le′psy** (λῆψις, a seizing), catching the light; Wiesner's equivalent for the German "Lichtgenuss"; **Photol′ysis** (λύσις, a loosing), the arrangement of chlorophyll granules under the stimulus of light, including both apostrophe and epistrophe; **Photom′eter**, an instrument for measuring the amount of light; **photomet′ric** (μέτρον, a measure), (1) applied to organisms which turn either end to the direction of the light-rays; (2) leaves which assume a definite position in light, to obtain the most of it, or to screen themselves from too much (Wiesner); **Photom′etry**, the response to the amount of light (Oltmanns); **Photomorpho′sis** (μόρφωσις, configuration), that kind of mechanomorphosis which depends upon light as the cause; **Photonas′ty** (ναστὸς, pressed close), one-sided growth in length of an organ, due to the unrestricted action of light (De Vries); adj. **photonas′tic**; **Photop′athy** (πάθος, suffering) = PHOTOTAXIS; **photoph′ilic** = PHOTOPHILOUS; **photoph′ilous** (φιλέω, I love), sun-loving plants; **Photoph′obism** (φοβέω, I fear), avoidance of light; **photoph′ygous** (φυγὴ, flight), applied to shade plants; **Photoplagiot′ropy** (πλάγιος, placed sideways; τροπὴ, a turning), a tendency to arrangement obliquely towards incident light (Goebel); adj. **photoplagiotrop′ic**; **Photosyn′tax** (συντάξω, I put together), the formation of complex carbon compounds from simple ones under the influence of light (Barnes); **Photosyn′thesis** (σύνθεσις, a putting together), a proposed emendation of "photo-syntax"; **phototac′tic** (τακτικὸς, qualified to arrange in order), Strasburger's term for taking up a definite position with regard to the direction of light-rays; **Photo-tax′is** (τάξις, order), the definite

self-arrangement of organisms under the stimulus of light; **phototon′ic** (τόνος, tension), the increasing irritability by the influence of light; **Photot′onus**, (1) the normal mobile condition resulting from the alternation of day and night; (2) proposed by Nagel for botanic use instead of PHOTOKINESIS, which is considered more appropriate for zoologic use; **Photot′rophy** (τροφὴ, food), unequal increase on one side of an organ, due to the incidence of light in relation to the parent shoot (Oltmanns); **Photot′ropism** (τροπὴ, a turning), a synonym of HELIOTROPISM; **Pho′trum** (coined by analogy of Spectrum), S. L. Moore's term for the whole scale of illumination affecting PHOTOLYSIS; **Pho′to-type** (τύπος, a type), a photograph of a type specimen; an abbreviation of the word **Photograph′otype** (M. Kellerman).

Phrag′ma, pl. **Phrag′mata** (φράγμα, an enclosure), a spurious dissepiment in fruits; **Phrag′matospore** (σπορὰ, a seed), a multicellular spore, capable of germinating from more than one point (A. Braun); **phrag′-mifer** (fero, I bear), **phrag′miger**, phragmig′erus (gero, I bear), divided by partitions; **Phragmite′tum**, Warming's term for an association of reeds, Phragmites; **Phragmo-bas′id**, Phragmobasid′ia, pl. (+ BASID), septate basidia in Basidiomycetes (Van Tieghem); **Phrag′mo-plast** (πλαστὸς, moulded), Nemec's term for a connecting spindle between two nuclei in the same cell which is sometimes produced; **Phragmo-spo′reae** (+ SPORE) used of Fungi whose spores are multiseptate (Traverso).

Phreti′um (φρητίον, a water tank), a tank formation; **phretoph′ilus** (φιλέω, I love), dwelling in tanks; **Phretophy′ta** (φυτὸν, a plant), tank plants (Clements).

Phry′gana, pl. (φρύγανα, sticks for firewood), an old term for prickly and stiff under-shrubs.

Phthiria'sis (φθειρίασις, lousy disease), disease produced by aphides or plant-lice.

Phy'ad (φυὴ, form of growth, + AD), a vegetation form, as a tree, a shrub, etc. (Clements).

Phycobry'a (φῦκος, sea-weed ; βρύον, moss), a term proposed for Characeae ; **Phycobry'ophytes** (+ BRYO-PHYTES), Götz's term for Characeae ; **Phycocecid'ia** (κηκίς, a gall), galls due to the attack of Algae (Lundström) ; **phycochroma'ceous** (χρῶμα, colour, + ACEOUS), applied to gonidia which are not green (chlorophyllaceous) but blue-green ; **Phycochromace'tum**, a community of blue-green Algae and Diatoms (Warming) ; **Phy'cochrome**, the bluish-green colouring-matter of brown Algae (Bornet) ; **Phycochry'-sin** (χρύσος, gold), a constituent of the pigment PHYCOCHROME (Gaidu-kov) ; **Phycocy'anin** (κύανος, blue), the blue colouring-matter in Algae ; **Phycodoma'tia** (δωμάτιον, a little house), plant shelters inhabited by other plants (Lundström) ; **Phycoer'ythrine** (ἐρυθρὸς, red), the red pigment of Floridean Algae ; **Phycohae'matin** (αἷμα, blood), a special red colouring-matter in certain Algae, such as *Rhytiphloea tinctoria*, Agardh ; **Phycol'ogist** (λόγος, a discourse), a student or expert in the study of Algae ; **Phycol'ogy**, the department of botany which relates to Algae ; **Phy'coma**, the entire mass of an Alga ; the thallus and reproductive bodies ; **Phycoma'ter** (μάτηρ, Doric for mother), the hymeneal jelly in which some spores germinate ; **Phycomyce'tes** (μύκης, a fungus), a group of Fungi which approach the Algae in some characters ; **Phycophae'ine** (φαιὸς, brown), the brown colouring-matter of Algae ; **Phycophy'ta** (φυτὸν, a plant), Trevisan's name for Characeae ; **Phycoporph'yrin** (πορφύρα, purple), a purple pigment from several species of *Zygnema* (Lagerheim) ;

Phycopyr'rhine (πυρρὸς, dark red), a pigment occurring in the Peri-dineae ; **Phycoste'mones** ‡ (στήμων, a filament), "hypogynous or other scales adhering to the disk" (Lindley) ; **Phycoxan'thine** (+ XANTHIN), the yellowish-brown pigment of Algae.

Phygoblaste'ma (φυγὰς, a fugitive ; βλάστημα, a sprout), Minks's term for a modified form of soredia in Lichens.

Phykench'yma (φῦκος, sea-weed ; ἔγχυμα, an infusion), "the ele-mentary tissue of Algals" (Lindley); **Phy'kocyan** = PHYCOCYANIN ; **Phy-koer'ythrin** = PHYCOERYTHRINE.

Phy'la, pl. of **Phy'lum** (φῦλον, a tribe); a system of organisms arranged in the assumed succession of develop-ment ; adj. **phylet'ic** ; ~ **Mar'gin**, the true indusium of *Blechnum* (Bower).

Phyl'la, pl. (φύλλον, a leaf), the verticillate leaves which form the calyx ; used in composition as di-phyllous, two-leaved, etc. ; **Phyl'-lade**, a cataphyllary leaf ; **Phyl'-lary**, *Phylla'ris*, a member of the involucre of a Composite flower ; **Phyllid'ium**, term proposed by Bower for the homologue of the leaf in the gametophyte ; **Phyllile'sia**, the correct spelling of PHILLILESIA ; **Phyl'lite**, a fossilized leaf ; **Phyllo-biol'ogy** (+ BIOLOGY), the biology of the leaf, in its widest sense ; adj. **phyllobiolog'ic** ; **Phylloblas'tus** (βλάστος, a bud), Koerber's term for Lichens which have a flat leaf-like expansion of the thallus ; **Phyllobry'on** ‡ (βρύον, a moss), the contracted pedicel of an ovary, as in some peppers (Lindley) ; **Phyl'lo-clade**, *Phylloclad'ium* (κλάδος, a branch), (1) a flattened branch assuming the form and function of foliage ; (2) a thalline outgrowth of a Lichen (Lindsay) ; **Phyllocol'ly** (κόλλα, glue), the production of new leaflets from the leaf surface (Penzig) ; **Phyllocy'anin** (κύανος, blue), a blue pigment occurring in

282

chlorophyll, which when combined with phylloxanthin produces a green tint; *cf.* KYANOPHYLL; **Phyl'lode**, *Phyllo'dium*, a petiole taking on the form and functions of a leaf; **phyllodin'eous**, *-eus*, relating to phyllodes; **Phyllo'dy**, the metamorphosis of floral organs into leaves; **Phyl'logen** (γεννάω, I produce) = PHYLLOPHOR; **phyllogenet'ic**, leaf-producing; **phyllog'enous**, growing upon leaves; epiphyllous; **phyl'loid** (εἶδος, resemblance), leaf-like; ~ **Clad'ode** = PHYLLOCLADE; **Phyl'loid**, a leaf-like appendage to the stems of Algae; **phylloi'deus**, foliaceous; **Phyllolob'eae**, pl. (λοβὸς, a lobe), plants with cotyledons, green and leaf-like; **Phylloma'nia** (μανία, madness), an abnormal production of leaves; **Phyl'lome**, *Phyllo'ma*, (1) an assemblage of leaves, or of incipient leaves in a bud; (2) recently used for the leaf-organ in a generic sense, potentially that which answers to a leaf; *cf.* CAULOME; **epipel'tate** ~, when the base of the expansion results from the growth of the upper surface of the primordial leaf, as in *Cotyledon Umbilicus*, Linn., and *Tropaeolum majus*, Linn.; **hypopel'tate** ~, when the growth is from the under-surface, as in the sepals of *Viola* (C. de Candolle); **Phyllomor'phy** (μορφή, form) = PHYLLODY; **Phylloph'agist** (φάγω, I eat), term proposed by Boulger, for plants which derive their sustenance by their leaves; **Phyl'lophor, Phyl'lophore**, *Phylloph'orum* (φορέω, I carry), the budding summit of a stem on which leaves are developing, especially applied to palms; **phylloph'orous**, producing leaves; **Phyl'lophyte** (φυτὸν, a plant), (1) = CORMOPHYTE; (2) a plant which draws its nourishment chiefly from its leaves (Boulger); (3) a plant possessing leaves or leaf-like organs (Hansgirg); **Phyllop'odes**, pl. (ποῦς, ποδὸς, a foot), dead leaves in *Isoëtes*;

Phyllopod'ium, a leaf regarded morphologically as an axis, branched or unbranched; **phyllop'odous**, used of the genus *Hieracium* when the radical leaves are in full vigour at the period of flowering; **Phyllopor'phyrin** (πορφύρα, purple dye), a by-product of chlorophyll, in dark red-violet crystals; **Phyllopto'sis** (πτῶσις, fall), an unnatural fall of leaves; **Phyl'lorhize** (ῥίζα, a root), an organ intermediate between leaf and root, as the capillary leaves of many water plants (Clos); **phyllosipho'nic** (σίφων, a tube), having a tubular central cylinder in the higher plants, where leaf-gaps are constantly present (Jeffrey); the condition in **Phyllosi'phony**; **Phyllota'onin** (τάως, a peacock), Schunck's word for a product of chlorophyll, resembling phyllocyan, but dull green in tint; **Phyllotax'y**, *Phyllotax'is* (τάξις, arrangement), the mode in which the leaves are arranged with regard to the axis; **discontin'uous** ~ with a definite break of ratios; **fall'ing** ~, passing into a lower series; **ri'sing** ~, passing into a higher series (Church); adj. **phyllotac'tic**; **Phyl'lotype** (τύπος, a type), a type of leaf; **Phylloxan'thin** (+ XANTHIN); the yellow colouring-matter of leaves, xanthophyll; **Phyl'lula** (οὐλή, a scar) ‡, (1) the scar left on a branch by the fall of a leaf; (2) H. Gibson's term for that stage in the embryo of vascular plants at which the first leaf and root appear (Parker); **Phyl'lule**, used for the free portion of the pulvinus, in *Pinus* (Masters).

Phylog'eny (φῦλον, a tribe; γένος, lineage), ancestral history deduced from development; adj. **phylogenet'ic**.

phymato'deus (φῦμα, a growth or tumour; εἶδος, likeness), warted, verrucose.

phys'ical (φυσικὸς, natural) **Drought**, used of soil when it contains very little free water.

Physe'ma (φύσημα, an inflation), (1)

the frond of an aquatic Alga ; (2) a
branch of *Chara* (Lindley).

Physiogn'omy, botan'ic (φυσιογνωμονία,
science of judging by features), the
habit of a plant or plant commun-
ity; adj. **physiognom'ic**; **physiolog'ic**
(λόγος, discourse), relating to physiology ; ~ **Drought,** soil is thus
dry when containing a considerable
amount of water, which is, however,
scarcely available for plant-life ; ~
Ra'ces, ~ **Spe'cies,** forms differing
by internal habit of parasitism, and
not by morphologic difference ; also
styled **biolog'ic** ~ or **habita'tion** ~ ;
Physiol'ogy (veg'etable), the science
of the vital actions or functions of
plants and their parts.

Physo'des (φῦσα, a bladder ; εἶδος, likeness), vesicles in Algae filled with
liquid containing structures, formerly called "microsomes" (Crato).

Phytal'bumose (φύτον, a plant, +
ALBUMOSE), a proteid found in seeds,
as of *Abrus ;* **Phy'teris** (ἔρις, strife),
plant migration and competition
(Clements) ; **Phy'to-al'bumin,** see
ALBUMIN ; **Phytoben'thon** (βένθος,
depth), vegetation of the depths
(Forel) ; **Phytobiol'ogy** (βίος, life ;
λόγος, discourse), the study of the
vital functions in plants ; **Phy'toblast** (βλαστὸς, a bud or sprout),
Baillon's term for a cell in its first
stage of development ; **Phytocecid'ia**
(κηκὶς, or κηκίδιον, a gall), galls produced by other plants (Lundström) ;
Phy'tochemy (+ chem), the chemistry of vegetation and its products ;
Phy'tochlore (χλωρὸς, green) =
CHLOROPHYLL ; **Phy'tocyst** (κύστις,
a bag), Baillon's expression for a cell
with its walls, *cf.* PHYTOBLAST ;
Phytoder'ma (δέρμα, a skin), any
fungous parasite growing on the
skin ; **Phytoderm'ata,** pl., skin diseases caused by Fungi ; **Phytodoma'-
tia,** pl. (δωμάτιον, a little house),
shelters in which other plants live
(Lundström) ; **Phytodynam'ics** (δύναμις, power), relating to the movements of plants (Sachs) ; **Phytoë-
ro'sia,** a misprint of Lindley's for

PHYTOTEROSIA ; **Phytoflag'ellates,**
another name for FLAGELLATA ;
Phytogel'in (*gelo,* I congeal), the
gelatine of Algae ; **Phytog'amy**
(γάμος, marriage), cross-fertilization
of flowers (A. Gray) ; **Phy'togen**
(γένος, race), a vital centre (Fermond) ; **Phytogen'esis** (γένεσις, beginning), the origin and development
of the plant ; **Phytog'eny,** means the
same as the last ; **Phytogeogen'esis**
(γῆ, the earth ; γένεσις, beginning),
the origin of plants in geologic
time (Kuntze) ; **Phytogeog'rapher**
(γράφω, I write), an expert on plant-
distribution ; **Phytogeog'raphy,** *Phy-
togeograph'ia,* geographic botany,
the science of plant distribution ;
Phytogno'sis (γνῶσις, knowledge),
botany, phytology ; **Phytogonid'ium**
(+ GONIDIUM) ; an immobile gonidium, capable of independent germination (A. Braun) ; **Phytog'raphist**
(γραφὴ, a writing), a describing
botanist ; **Phytog'raphy,** the description and illustration of plants,
descriptive and systematic or taxi-
nomic botany ; **Phytohae'natins**
(ἁίμα, ἁίματος, blood), colourless
chromogens becoming pigments
under the action of oxygen in the
presence of oxydases (Palladin) ;
phy'toid (εἶδος, likeness), plant-like ;
Phy'tolite (λίθος, a stone) ; **Phy'to-
lith,** a plant in the fossil condition ;
Phytolithol'ogy (λόγος, discourse),
(1) the study of fossil plants, palaeobotany ; (2) the science of plant
distribution as affected by soil or
rock ; **Phytol'ogist,** a botanist ; **Phytol'ogy,** *Phytolo'gia,* botany, the
study of plants ; **Phytol'ysis** (λύσις,
a loosing), an error (?) for PHOTOLY-
SIS ; **Phy'tome, Phyto'ma,** pl. **Phyto'mata,** the vegetative body or
substance of all plants (A. Braun) ;
phytomastig'opod, see MASTIGOPOD ;
Phy'tomer, pl. **Phytom'era** (μέρος, a
part), the unit of a plant, an internode with its leaves ; an emendation
of **Phy'ton,** applied by Gaudichaud
to a plant-unit, out of a succession
of which plants are built up; adj.

phyton'ic ; **Phy'tomelane** (μέλας, black), a black structureless layer found in the pericarp of many Compositae (Hanausek) ; **Phytom'etry** (μέτρον, a measure or standard), a comparison between plants, or the different plans of their growth ; **Phytomorpho'sis** (μόρφωσις, a shaping), any change induced by plants ; by Appel used for galls caused by plant parasites ; **Phytomyxa'ceae** = MYXOMYCETES ; **Phyton'omy**, *Phytonom'ia* (νόμος, law), (1) botanic physiology ; (2) study of the organs of plants ; *cf.* PHYTOTOMY (Heinig) ; **Phytonym'ia** (ὄνομα, a name), plant organography ; **Phytopalaeontol'ogist** = PALAEOBOTANIST ; **Phytopathol'ogy** (παθολογικὸς, relating to diseases), vegetable pathology, the science of plant-diseases ; **Phytophenol'ogy** (+ PHENOLOGY), the observation and recording dates in leafing and flowering of plants ; **Phytoplank'ton** (+ PLANKTON), floating pelagic plant organisms ; **Phytopleu'ston** (+ PLEUSTON), plants which are lighter than the surrounding water, and consequently float on the surface ; **Phytopoli'tus** ‡ (πολίτης, a citizen), a plant which is or seems to be parasitic ; **Phytoptocecid'ia** (κῆκις, a gall), galls caused by Fungi (Loew) ; **Phytostat'ics** (στατικὸς, causing to stand), the various causes which tend to produce equilibrium in the energies of a plant ; **Phy'tostrotes** [trisyll.], *Phytostro'tae* (στρωτὸς, spread), distributed as surface plankton (Clements) ; **Phytotero'sia** (τέρας, a monster), Desvaux's term for plant pathology ; **Phytoteratol'ogy** (+ TERATOLOGY), the study of monstrous growths in plants ; **Phytot'omy** (τομὴ, a cutting), plant anatomy, or histology ; **Phytotroph'ia** (τροφὴ, nourishment), plant culture ; **phytotopograph'ical** (τόπος, a place ; γράφω, I write), relating to descriptive local botany ; the flora of a given locality ; **Phytozo'id** (ζῶον, an animal ; εἶδος, likeness) = ANTHEROZOID ; **Phytozo'a,**

pl. of **Phytozo'on**, antherozoids, mobile fertilizing bodies formed in antheridia.

pic'eus (Lat.), pitchy black.

Picnid'ium = PYCNIDIUM.

Pic'ro-er'ythrin (πικρὸς, bitter, + ERYTHRIN), a substance found in Lichens ; **Picrotox'in** (τοξικὸν, poison), a crystalline narcotic bitter ingredient in the berries of *Cocculus indicus*, the mediæval and trade name of *Anamirta paniculata*, Coleb. ; adj. **picrotox'ic.**

pic'tus (Lat., painted), adorned with colour, as though painted.

Pie'tra funga'ia (Ital.), "Mushroom-stone," the sclerotium of *Polyporus tuberaster*, Fr.

Piezot'ropism (πιέζω, I press hard ; τροπὴ, a turning), movement by compression acting as stimulus (Massart).

pila'ris ‡ (Lat., from *pilus*, a hair), composed of small hairs, pilose.

pi'leate, *pilea'tus* (Lat., wearing the *pileus*), having the form of a cap or PILEUS ; **pi'leiform**, *pileiform'is* (*forma*, shape), pileus shaped ; **Pi'leola**, *Pile'olus* (*pileolum*, a little cap), (1) a small cap or cap-like body ; defined by J. S. Henslow as a primordial leaf like an extinguisher, which encloses the bud ; (2) the diminutive of PILEUS ; (3) "the receptacle of certain Fungals" (Lindley) ; (4) the plumule in grasses (Van Tieghem).

Pileorhi'za (πίλεος, pileus, a cap ; ῥίζα, a root), the root-cap, a hood at the extremity of the root ; **Pi'leus,** (1) a convex expansion terminating the stipe of Agarics, and bearing the hymenium, now extended to all sporophores in which the hymenium faces the ground, the CAP ; (2) used by R. T. Lowe to express the habit of *Convolvulus Caput-Medusae*, Lowe.

Pi'li, pl. of **Pi'lus** (Lat., a hair), hairs.

Pilid'ium (πιλίδιον, a night-cap), an orbicular hemispherical shield in Lichens, the outside changing into a powdery substance, as in *Calicium*.

pilif'erous, *-rus* (*pilus*, a hair ; *fero*, I

bear), (1) bearing hairs, or tipped with them ; (2) hair-pointed (Lindley) ; ~ **Lay′er**, the young superficial tissue of roots, producing the root-hairs, when present ; **pi′liform**, (*forma*, shape), applied to the point of a nerve in Mosses, when like a long flexuose hair ; **pilig′erous** (*gero*, I bear), bearing hairs.

Pill, Grew's spelling of PEEL.

Pilocar′pine, the active principle of *Pilocarpus*, a genus of Rutaceae.

pil′o-glan′dulose (*pilus*, a hair), used by J. Smith for Ferns bearing glandular hairs ; **pi′lose**, *pilo′sus*, **pi′lous**, hairy, any kind of pilosity, usually meaning having soft and distinct hairs ; **Pilos′ity**, *Pilos′itas*, hairiness ; **pilosius′culus** (Lat.), slightly hairy ; **Pi′losism**, abnormal hairiness in plants ;—**deform′ing** ~, when in excess and completely disfiguring the species ; **physiolog′ical** ~, occasioned by circumstances, as growth in a dry soil ; **teratolcg′ical** ~, when it becomes a disease, *cf.* DEFORMING.

Pil′ula ‡ (Lat., a globule), (1) a cone like a galbulus ; (2) any spherical inflorescence.

Pi′lus (Lat.), a hair.

pimpinell′oid (εἶδος, resemblance), akin to or resembling the umbelliferous genus *Pimpinella*.

pim′pled, papillose.

pin-eyed, a florist's term for those flowers of dimorphic species, which have long styles, the stigma showing itself at the mouth of the corolla-tube.

Pinakench′yma (πίναξ, a table ; ἔγχυμα, an infusion), the muriform tissue of medullary rays, whose component cells are tabular ; **Pinench′yma** is a shortened form.

Pina′res, forests of *Pinus canariensis* with xerophytic undergrowth in the Canary Islands (Warming).

Pinch′ing-Bod′ies, the CORPUSCULA of Asclepiads ; the junction of the pollinia which cling to the leg of an insect visitor ; ~ **Traps**, another name for the same mechanism ; the German equivalents are Klemmkörper and Klemmenfallen ; **Pinchtrap** Flowers, those adapted for insect visitors able to draw out the pollinia.

Pine′tum (Lat., a pine-grove), (1) a work devoted to Coniferae ; (2) a collection of the same in a garden.

Pinheir′os, forests composed of *Araucaria brasiliensis* (Warming).

Pi′nite, a glucoside, sweet and crystalline, derived from *Pinus Lambertiana*, Dougl.

Pin′na, pl. **Pin′nae** (Lat., a feather), a primary division of a pinnate leaf, its leaflets, which sometimes themselves are pinnate, are restricted by Bower to the "branches of the first order borne upon the phyllopodium," the axis of the leaf ; ~ **Trace**, the vascular bundle connecting a pinna with the stem or principal petiole ; ~ **Trace Bar**, an arc of xylem formed by the fusion of two entering pinna traces of *Diplolabis* (Gordon) ; **pin′nate**, *pinna′tus*, with leaflets arranged each side of a common petiole ; ~ with an odd one = imparipinnate ; **pinna′tely**, in pinnate fashion, as ~ **com′pound**, ~ **cleft**, ~ **decom′pound**, ~ **divi′ded**, ~ **lo′bed**, ~ **par′ted**, ~ **ter′nate**, ~ **trifo′liolate**, ~ **veined** ; **pinnat′ifid**, *pinnatif′idus* (*findo*, *fidi*, to cut), pinnately cleft ; **pinnatilo′bate**, *pinnatiloba′tus*, *pinnatilo′bus* (*lobus*, a lobe), pinnately lobed ; **pinnatipar′tite**, *pinnatiparti′tus*, pinnately parted ; **pinnatiscis′sus** (*scissus*, cleft), pinnately divided or cut ; **pinnat′isect**, *pinnatisec′tus* (*sectus*, cut), pinnately divided down to the rhachis ; **pin′niform** (*forma*, shape), like a feather ; **pinniner′ved** (*nervus*, a nerve), pinnately veined, the veins running parallel towards the margin ; **pin′nulate**, with pinnules ; **Pin′nule** *Pin′nula*, pl. *Pinnulae*, (1) a secondary pinna ; (2) in Diatoms, thickened ribs on the valves, as in *Pinnularia*.

pi′noid (*pinus*, a pine ; εἶδος, resemblance), like a pine-needle.

Pinom′eter (πίνω, I drink; μέτρον, a measure), an instrument for observing the transpiration stream in plants.

Pip, (1) the popular name for the seeds of an apple or pear; (2) "small seeds or seed-like bodies including the bulbs of Lily of the Valley" (Crozier); (3) a florist's term for a single flower of a truss.

Pip′erin, the active principle of white and black pepper, *Piper nigrum*, Linn., a white crystalline body isomeric with morphine; **pip′eratus, piperi′tus** (Lat., peppered, peppery, having a hot, biting taste.

pisa′ceus (*pisum*, pea), pea-green, the colour of the unripe seeds (Hayne); **pi′siform,** *pisiform′is* (*forma*, shape), pea-shaped.

Pis′til, *Pistil′lum* (Lat., a pestle), (1) the female organ of a flower, consisting when complete of ovary, style and stigma; (2) the archegonium of the genus *Andreaea* (Hooker and Taylor), and of *Anthoceros* (Griffith); **pistilla′ceous** (+ACEOUS), growing on the pistil; **pistilla′ri-bac′illar** (*bacillum*, a staff), denotes spermatia which are oblong and slightly thicker at the ends; **pis′tillary,** relating to the pistil; ~ **Cord,** "a channel which passes from the stigma through the style into the ovary" (Lindley); **pis′tillate,** *pistilla′tus*, (1) having a pistil; (2) applied to a flower having pistils only, a female flower; **Pistillid′ium,** pl. **Pistillid′ia,** archegonia, organs analogous to pistils; **pistillif′erous,** -*rus* (*fero*, I bear); **pistillig′erous** (*gero*, I bear), bearing one or more pistils; **Pistillo′dy,** the change of floral organs into carpels; CARPELLODY suggested as more correct.

Pit, (1) a small hollow or depression, as in a cell-wall; (2) the endocarp of a drupe containing the kernel or seed-stone (Crozier); ~ **Cham′ber,** the cavity of a bordered pit on each side of a closing membrane; **primor′dial** ~, Sanio's term for oval patches in the wood of *Pinus* within which only bordered pits arise, a "primary pit area" (Groom).

Pitch, a resinous exudation from the spruce, *Picea alba*, Link, etc.

Pitch′er, a tubular or cup-shaped vessel, the terminal portion of a leaf-blade, usually containing a secreted digestive field; an ascidium; ~ **-shaped,** campanulate, but contracted at the orifice.

Pit′fall Flowers, transitional flowers, such as *Asarum*, which detain small Diptera.

Pith, the spongy centre of an exogenous stem, chiefly consisting of parenchyma; the medulla; ~ **Flecks,** dark marks in timber due to the cavities made by the larvae of insects in the cambium, but later filled up by cellular tissue (Hartig).

pit′ted, marked with small depressions, punctate; used in a restricted sense for pits in cell-walls; ~ **Ves′sels,** dotted ducts, vessels with secondary thickenings leaving thinner spots.

pitu′itous (*pituita*, phlegm), relating to mucus (Crozier).

Pityria′sis (πίτυρον, scurf) **versic′olor,** a skin disease caused by *Microsporon Furfur,* Rob.

Place-con′stant, an invariable factor of plant-life in a given locality; ~ **-condit′ion,** or ~ **-hab′it,** the sum of these under varying conditions; ~ **-mode,** the prevalent condition of size, number, colour, etc., of organs of a plant in a given locality (Shull).

Placen′ta (Lat., a cake), (1) the organ which bears the ovules in an ovary, often the margin of the carpellary leaves; (2) in Cryptogams, the tissue from which sporangia arise; ~ **-shaped,** placentiform; **Placenta′rium,** placenta; **Pla′centary‡,** a placenta which is long and narrow and bears many ovules; **placen′tary,** relating to the placenta; **Placenta′tion,** *Placenta′tio,* the disposition of the placentae; **placentif′erous** (*fero*, I bear), bearing placentae;

placen′tiform, *placentiform′is* (*forma*, shape), quoit-shaped or like a flat cake; **Placen′toid** (εἶδος, resemblance), organs described by Chatin as occurring in the anthers of certain Dicotyledons to assist in the dispersion of pollen.

placochromat′ic (πλάξ, πλάκος, a flat body; χρωματικὸς, relating to colour), used of Diatoms with endochrome in plates or discs; *cf.* COCCOCHROMATIC.

placo′des (πλακώδης, flat), used by Koerber for Lichens resembling a rounded plate in figure.

placo′dioid (εἶδος, resemblance), like the genus *Placodium*, with orbicular thallus, adpressed and lobed.

Placo′phytes (πλάξ, a flat body; φυτὸν, a plant), a term applied by Schuett to the Peridineae, Diatomaceae and Desmideae; *cf.* SACCOPHYTES; **Plac′oplast** (πλαστὸς, moulded), elaioplasts attached to the inner surface of the margin of the chromophores in certain Diatoms (Mereschkowsky).

Plad′oboles [trisyll.], *Pladob′olae* (πλάδος, moisture; βολὶς, thrown), plants distributed by the action of damp (Clements).

plagiod′romous (πλάγιος, oblique; δρόμος, a course), applied to tertiary leaf-veins when at right-angles to the secondary veins; **Plagio-heliot′ropism** (+ HELIOTROPIUM) = PLAGIOPHOTOTROPISM; **Plagiophototax′y** (φῶς, φωτὸς, light; τάξις, order), the oblique arrangement of chlorophyll granules with regard to incident light (Oltmanns); **plagiophototrop′ic** (τροπὴ, a turning), assuming an oblique position to the rays of light, as the leaflets of *Robinia, Tropaeolum*, etc. (Oltmanns); **Plagiophotot′ropism**, the condition itself; **plagiotrop′ic**, having the direction of growth oblique or horizontal; **Plagiot′ropism**, the condition described.

plain, applied to a margin which is not undulate, though it may be sinuate (Crozier).

plait′ed, plicate.

plane, *pla′nus* (Lat.), level, even, flat; **Plane of Inser′tion**, a plane which passes through the point of insertion of a lateral organ and coincides with the main axis and that of the organ; ~ **of Sym′metry**, that which divides an object into symmetrical halves;—**prin′cipal** ~, in a flattened seed, the plane of the longer axis in transverse section; **sec′ondary** ~, at right angles to the last, the shorter axis; **planius′culus** (Lat.), nearly flat.

Planktol′ogy (πλαγκτὸς, wandering; λόγος, a discourse), the department of pelagic botany, that is, of the floating organisms in the ocean; **Plank′ton**, free-swimming or floating oceanic life; **fresh′water** ~, that of lakes or rivers; **nerit′ic** ~, found near the coast; **ocean′ic** ~, pelagic, far from land; **tycholimnet′ic** ~, false plankton, Algae at first fixed, but afterwards buoyed up by gas, and floating; ~ **Form′ation**, a community of free, floating plants; **Planktonol′ogy** = PLANKTOLOGY; **Plank′tophyte** (φυτόν, a plant), a plant forming an integral part of the plankton (Forel).

Plan′ogamete (πλάνος, wandering; γαμέτης, a spouse), a mobile ciliated gamete or zoogamete, as in Chlorophyceae; **Plan′ospore** (σπορὰ, a seed), Sauvageau's term for a motile zoospore.

Plant, *Plan′ta*, a vegetable production nourished by gases or liquids and not ingesting solid particles of food (except in the plasmodial stage of Myxogastres); ~ **Bull′ions** = COALBALLS; ~ **Cane**, the first year's growth of the sugar-cane from seed; ~ **Cas′ein**, a substance akin to animal casein; ~ **Com′mune**, plants which are usually found in the same formation (Schimper); ~ **Forma′tion**, an assemblage of plants living together in a community under the same environment, as a moor or wood; ~ **Pathol′ogy**, the study of plant-diseases; ~ **-plankton** (+ PLANKTON), the same as PHYTO-

PLANKTON ; **Plan'tae tris'tes,** evening flowering plants, as *Matthiola bicornis*, DC., etc. ; **plan'tal,** pertaining to plants ; **Plan'ticle,** the embryo in a seed ; **Plan'tlet,** a little plant ; **Plant'ling,** a small plant, a product of recent germination (S. Moore) ; **Plan'tule,** *Plan'tula* = PLUMULE ; **Plantula'tio** = GERMINATION.

Plasm, Plas'ma (πλάσμα, that formed), used for PROTOPLASM ; **Plasm-sac** (+ SAC) of Diatoms, a colourless layer of protoplasm forming a lining to the frustule and enclosing the cell-contents (O'Meara) ; **Plas'mamem'brane,** an equivalent for the German "Hautschicht" (Mottier) ; **Plasmamoe'bae** (+ AMOEBA), amoebiform masses of protoplasm, the actinophrydia of Gobi ; **Plas'masome,** or **Plasmat'osome** (σῶμα, a body), a protoplasmic corpuscle, shortened to PLASOME ; **plasmat'ic,** ready, or serving for growth, plastic ; **plas'mative,** Beccari's term for period of creation of species ; **Plasmatogennyl'icae** (γεννάω, I beget ; ὕλη = *materia*), Radlkofer's term for Angiosperms and Gymnosperms ; **plasmatop'arous** (*pario*, I bring forth), in germination the whole of the protoplasm of a gonidium issues as a rounded mass, which at once becomes coated with a membrane, and puts out a germ-tube ; **Plas'mochym** (χύμα, that which is poured), the thick fluid albuminous substance of the cell-body (Strasburger) ; **Plas'mode** = PLASMODIUM; **Plasmoder'ma** (δέρμα, skin) = ECTOPLASM ; adj. **plasmoder'mal;** **Plasmodes'ma** (δεσμός, a bond), connecting threads of protoplasma passing through pores in the cell-walls ; adj. **plasmodes'mic ;** **Plasmo'diae,** Caruel's term for Myxogastres ; **plasmo'dial, plasmo'dic,** pertaining to a plasmodium ; ~ **Gran'ules,** minute, strongly refractive granules in certain Myxogastres ; **Plasmodia'tion,** the assumed softening of the outline of a spore on its germinating (A. S.

Wilson) ; **Plasmodie'resis** (διαίρεσις, division), the division of protoplasm, which may be (*a*) akinetic, or (*b*) karyokinetic ; **Plasmo'diocarp** (καρπός, fruit, an asymmetrical sporangium of Myxogastres (Rostafiński) ; **Plasmo'diogens** (γένος, race, offspring), C. MacMillan's word for the protoplasmic units of a plasmodium ; **plasmodioph'orus** (φορέω, I carry), producing a true plasmodium ; **Plasmo'dium,** a mass of naked much-nucleated protoplasm, showing amoeboid movements ; **aggrega'ted** ~, the myxamoebae congregated without fusion, each cell giving rise to a spore or foot-cell ; **fused** ~, union of myxamoebae and subsequent fructification (Van Tieghem) ; **Plas'molyte,** the substance causing plasmolysis ; **Plasmol'ysis** (λύσις, a loosing), a separation of the living protoplasm from the cell-wall by osmotic action ; **Plasmoliza'tion,** the same condition ; **plas'molysed,** subjected to plasmolysis ; adj. **plasmolyt'ic ; plasmoph'agous** (φάγω, I eat), absorbing the living organic matter of the host-plant without selection (Boulger) ; **Plasmop'tysis** (πτύω, I eject), the extrusion of protoplasm from bacteria, with subsequent envelopment by a membrane ; **Plas'masome** (σῶμα, a body) = (1) NUCLEOLUS ; (2) BIOBLAST ; **Plasmosyn'agy** (συνάγω, I collect), accumulation of the protoplasts of the polioplasm and of the plastids included in it, due to plasmolytic irritation (Tswett) ; **Plas'ome,** a living element of protoplasm, shortened from PLASMATOSOME (Wiesner) ; **plas'tic,** capable of being moulded or modified ; ~ **Equivalent,** of consumed carbon in a body is the amount contained in the substance of the organism (Waterman) ; *cf.* RESPIRATORY EQUIVALENT ; ~ **Prod'ucts** of katabolism, those which remain an integral part of the organism (Parker) ; ~ **Sub'stances,** those employed in building up, as cellulose, starch-grains, proteids, etc. ; **Plas-tic'ity**, (1) the quality of being plastic ; (2) the condition character-ized by ready response to stimuli (Clements); **Plas'tid**, *Plastid'ium*, a protoplasmic granule in active cells, differentiated as centres of chemical or vital activity, as CHLORO-, CHROMO-, and LEUCO-PLASTID ; ~ **-col'ours**, those due to plastids in the cells, as distinct from coloured sap (Wheeldale); **Plas'tid-plasm**, (+ PLASM), a supposititious substance differing from other forms of protoplasm by morphological characters (B. M. Davis); **Plas'tid-ule**, Elsberg's term for the smallest mass of protoplasm which can exist as such ; **Plas'tin**, an essential ele-ment of the entire protoplasmic cell-contents, including the nucleus and the chromatophores (Zacharias) ; **Plastog'amy** (γάμος, marriage), the fusion of cytoplasts into a plas-modium, the nuclei remaining dis-tinct (Hartog); adj. **plastogam'ic** ; **Plastog'eny** (γένος, race, offspring), when cytoplastic elements undergo a reorganization by fusion (Hartog) ; **Plas'toid** (εἶδος, likeness), a needle-shaped body found in the stalk-cells of the tentacles of *Drosera*, becoming rounded under stimulus ; a rhab-doid ; **Plas'tosome** (σῶμα, body) = CHONDRIOSOME ; **Plas'totype** (τύπος, a type), a cast from an original type, as of a fossil plant.

Plate, a flattened structure ; *cf.* NUCLEAR ~ , SIEVE ~ .

Plate-rings, the external concentric strands of vascular tissue in *Medul-losa* (Jeffrey).

Plateau' (Fr.), (1) the tubercular disk in a bulb which produces the scales upwards, and the roots downwards, *cf.* CORM (Crozier) ; (2) a similar structure in certain Compositae, interposed between the ovary and the other floral organs (Lecoq).

platycar'pic, **platycar'pous** (πλατὺς, broad ; καρπὸς, fruit), broad-fruited ; **Platygonid'ia**, pl. (+ GONIDIUM), gonidia in broadly spreading groups ;

Platylob'eae (λοβὸς, a lobe), used for certain Crucifers with flat coty-ledons ; **platylo'bate**, broad-lobed ; **platyphyl'lous** (φύλλον, a leaf), broad-leaved ; **Plat'ysperms** (σπέρμα, a seed), applied to certain fossil fruits, flattened in transverse sec-tion ; *cf.* RADIOSPERMS (F. W. Oliver) ; adj. **platysper'mic**.

Plecolep'is ‡, *Plecolep'idus* (πλέκω, I plait, λεπὶς, a scale), the involucre of Compositae when the bracts are united into a cup.

Plectench'yma (πλεκτὸς, woven ; ἔγχυμα, an infusion), a tissue of woven hyphae ; a pseudo-par-enchyma, further divided into PARAPLECTENCHYMA and PROSO-PLECTENCHYMA (Lindau).

Pleioblas'tus (πλεῖον, more ; βλαστὸς, a bud), used by Koerber for those Lichen spores which germinate at several points ; **Pleiochas'ium** (χάσις, separation), each relative main axis of a cyme producing more than two branches ; adj. **pleiochas'ial** ; **pleiocy'clic** (κύκλος, a circle), peren-nial as ~ **Herbs** ; **Pleiog'eny** (γένος, race), an increase from the parental unit, as by branching or interpola-tion of members ; **Pleiom'ery** (μέρος, a part), having more whorls than the normal number ; **Pleiomor'phism**, **Pleiomor'phy** (μορφὴ, change), the occurrence of more than one inde-pendent form in the life-cycle of a species ; adj. **pleiomor'phous** ; **Plei-ont'ism**, Delpino's term for POLY-MORPHY ; **Pleiopet'aly** (πέταλον, a leaf), doubleness in flowers (De Vries); adj. **pleiopet'alous** ; **pleiophyl'lous**, *-lus* (φύλλον, a leaf), with leaves having no apparent buds in their axils ; **Pleiophyl'ly**, having numerous leaves from the same point, or more than usual the number of leaflets in a compound leaf ; **Pleiopyre'nium** (+ PYRENIUM), small apothecia in one verruca, in Lichens ; **pleio-sper'mous** (σπέρμα, a seed), with an unusually large number of seeds ; **Pleiotax'is**, **Pleiotax'y** (ταξις, order), increase in the number of whorls in a flower ; **Pleiot′omy** (τόμος, a cut), multiple dichotomy or fission (Wordsell) ; **Pleiotrache′ae** (+ TRACHEA), "membranous tubes or tracheae containing a compound spiral fibre" (Cooke) ; **Pleiox′eny** (ξένος, a host or guest), where a parasite can invade several species of host-plants (De Bary).

ple′nus (Lat.), full, as *Flos plenus* = a double flower.

Pleochro′icism (πλέον, more ; χρόα, colour, complexion), with various colours in the cell-wall ; syn., **Pleochro′mism** (χρῶμα, colour), adj. **pleochro′ic, pleochrois′tic ; Pleog′amy** (γάμος, marriage), Loew's term for methods of pollination varying in respect of time, etc. ; **fe′male ~**, gynodioecism united with gynomonoecism ; **male ~**, androdioecism united with andromonoecism ; **Pleog′eny** (γένος, race), mutability of function ; adj. **pleogenet′ic ; Pleomor′phism** (μορφή, shape), mutability of shape ; adj. **pleomor′phic ; Pleomor′phy**, the same as PLEIOMORPHISM ; adj. **pleomor′phous =** PLEIOMORPHOUS.

Ple′on, Naegeli's term for an aggregate of molecules, but smaller than a MICELLA.

Ple′onasm (πλεόνασμα, a surplus), redundance in any part (Crozier).

pleoph′agous (πλέον, more ; φάγος, a glutton), not restricted to one host ; feeding on various species ; **Pleoph′agism** is the condition ; **pleophylet′ic** (φυλή, a tribe), descended from numerous lines, polyphyletic ; **pleor′ic**, an error for PELORIC ; **pleotroph′ic** (τροφή, food), feeding on various substances, not restricted to one (C. Jones).

Ple′rome (πλήρωμα, that which fills), the cylinder or shaft of a growing point enclosed and overarched by periblem ; **~ Sheath =** BUNDLESHEATH.

plesiomor′phous (πλησίος, near ; μορφή, shape), nearly of the same form (Crozier) ; **Ples′iotype** (τύπος, a type), a specimen compared with

a species, and newly described and figured.

Pleu′ra (πλευρὰ, a side or rib), the girdle or hoop of Diatoms (O. Mueller) ; **Pleurench′yma** (ἔγχυμα, an infusion), woody tissue ; **pleuroblas′tic** (βλαστὸς, a bud), (1) used of certain forms of Fungi, producing lateral outgrowths serving as haustoria ; (2) employed by Celakovský to denote the early stages of the monocotyledonous embryo ; *cf.* ACROBLASTIC ; **pleurocar′pous**, *-pus* (καρπὸς, fruit), applied to those Mosses which bear their fructification on lateral growths, *cf.* ACROCARPOUS.

pleurococca′ceous, **·pleurococc′oid** (εἶδος, resemblance), like the genus *Pleurococcus*, or its allies.

pleurodis′cous (πλευρὰ, a side or rib ; δίσκος, a quoit), when an appendage is attached to the sides of a disc ; **pleurogyn′ius, pleurogyn′us** (γυνή, a woman), used when a glandular or tubercular elevation rises close to or parallel with the ovary ; **pleurogy′rate,** *pleurogyra′tus* (γυρὸς, round), when Fern-sporangia have the annulus horizontal ; **pleuroplas′tic** (πλασ-τὸς, moulded), Prantl's term for a leaf in which the central portion first attains permanency, the meristem being marginal ; **pleurorhi′zal,** *-zus* (ῥίζα, a root), when an embryo has its radicle against one edge of the cotyledons, which are then accumbent ; **Pleur′osperms** (σπέρμα, a seed), Angiosperms which began with chalazogamy, but have become porogamous (Nawaschin) ; adj. **pleurosper′mic ; Pleurosporang′ium** (σπορά, a seed ; ἀγγεῖον, a vessel), a sporangium which produces pleurospores ; **Pleur′ospore**, a spore formed at the sides of a basidium in Basidiomycetes (Van Tieghem) ; **pleurotri′bal**, or **pleur′otribe** (τρίβω, I beat), used of flowers whose stamens are adapted to deposit their pollen upon the sides of insect-visitors.

Pleu′ston (πλευστικὸς, ready for sailing), (1) plants which float by reason

of their relative lightness (Forel);
(2) modified since to include rootless, free-floating, submerged spermophytes (Warming); ~ **-flora,**
practically PHYTOPLANKTON.

plexeoblas′tus ‡ (πλέξις, a knitting;
βλαστὸς, a bud), when cotyledons
rise above ground in germination,
but do not assume the appearance
of leaves; **plex′us** (Lat. ̣ ̣ ̣ining),
a network.

Pli′ca, pl. **Pli′cae** (*plico,* I fold or
plait), (1) a plait or folding; (2)
the lamella in Fungi; (3) a disease
of entangled twigs, the buds producing abnormally short shoots;
pli′cate, *plica′tus,* folded into plaits,
usually lengthwise; **plicat′ilis** (Lat.),
the property of folding together;
Plica′tion, a fold or folding; **plic′a-
tive,** *plicati′vus* = PLICATE; **Plic′a-
ture,** a fold or doubling; **plicat′u-
late,** the diminutive of plicate
(Crozier); **pli′ciform** (*forma,* shape),
plait-like.

Plinth, the tapering free end of the
nucellus of certain fossil seeds; ~
Jack′et, the epidermis of the soft
integument surrounding the plinth.

Plococar′pium (πλόκος, a chaplet;
καρπὸς, fruit), a fruit composed of
follicles ranged round an axis;
Plopocar′pium, an error for the last.

Plug, a growth of protoplasm which
closes the pore-openings in the cells
of certain Algae, homologous with
the STOPPER of *Ballia* (H.Gibson).

Plum-pock′ets = BAG-PLUMS.

pluma′tus (Lat.), feathered, pinnate.

Plumba′gine, a crystalline principle
in the roots of *Plumbago.*

plumb′eus (Lat., leaden), lead-coloured.

Plume (Lat., the down of a feather),
Grew's term for the PLUMULE; **plu′-
mose,** *plumo′sus* (Lat.), feathered, as
the pappus of thistles.

Plu′mule, *Plu′mula* (Lat., a little
feather), the primary leaf-bud of an
embryo; ~ **-bulb,** a bulb produced
directly from germination of the
seed; *cf.* RUNNER-BULB (Blodgett);
plu′mular, relating to the plumule;
~ **Ax′is,** the primary axis.

plur-, plu′ri (Lat.), used as a prefix
for many or several, as plurilocular,
many-celled, etc.

Plur-an′nual (+ ANNUAL), L. H.
Bailey's word for an annual plant,
which is so only by being killed by
the cold at the end of the season,
as *Reseda odorata,* Linn.; **pluri-
cel′lular** (+ CELLULAR), many-celled;
plu′riceps (*-ceps* from *caput,* a head),
with more than one head, as many
roots; **pluricil′iate** (+ CILIATE),
having many cilia; **plurifo′liate,**
plurifo′lious (*folium,* a leaf), having
several leaves; **plurifo′liolate,** with
several or many leaflets; **pluriflor′-
ous,** *-rus* (*flos, floris,* a flower), with
several flowers; **plurigamet′ic** (+
GAMETE), consisting of many gametes
or sexual units; **pluriloc′ular,** *pluri-
locula′ris* (*loculus,* a little place),
many-celled; **pluripar′tite,** *pluri-
parti′tus* (*partitus,* divided), deeply
divided into several nearly distinct
portions; **pluripet′alous** (πέταλον, a
flower-leaf), polypetalous; **pluri-
sep′tate** (*septum,* an enclosure), with
several partitions; **plurispor′ous**
(σπορὰ, a seed), having two or more
seeds; **pluriv′alent** (*valens,* strong),
used of nuclear divisions in which
each element is composed of two
normal elements (Haerker); **pluri-
val′vis** (+ VALVA), many-valved,
as opposed to uni-valved or follicu-
late; **pluriv′orous** (*voro,* I devour),
Dietel's term for those Fungi which
inhabit indifferently hosts belonging to widely different orders of
plants.

plus (Lat., more) or +, applied to
spores whose nuclei are presumably
male (Blakeslee).

Pluviifrutice′ta, pl. (*pluvia,* rain;
fruticetum, a thicket), rain-scrub;
Pluviiligno′sa, pl.(*lignosus,* woody),
rain-scrub and rain-forest combined;
Pluviisyl′vae, pl. (*sylva,* a wood),
rain-forest.

Pneu′machore, an error for PNEUMA-
TODE.

Pneumatho′dium (πνεῦμα, πνεύματος,
breath, air), (1) *cf.* PNEUMATODE;

(2) an AËRATING ROOT, as in *Taxodium*; **pneumat′ic Tis′sue**, open tissue containing much air (Kearney); **Pneu′mato - chymif′era [Va′sa]** ‡, spiral vessels (Lindley); **Pneu′-matode** (ὁδὸs, a way), any opening of the nature of a lenticel or stoma (Jost); **Pneu′matophore**, *Pneumatoph′orum* (φορέω, I carry), (1) used of air-vessels of any description, as tracheids; (2) intercellular spaces in Rhizophoreae (Karsten); (3) ‡ the membranous tube of a spiral vessel (Lindley); **pneumatotac′tic** (τακτικὸs, apt · for arrangement), applied to those zoospores whose irritability is dependent on the presence of dissolved gases, the products of respiration of the zoospores in the sporangium (Hartog); **Pneumatotax′y**, the condition described; **neg′ative** ∼, the irritability which determines the escape of certain spores, as in *Achlya*; **Pneumatof′erus** (*fero*, I bear), the external membranous tube of spiral vessels (J. S. Henslow).

Pnoi′um (πνοὴ, a blast), a succession of plants on æolian (drifting) soils, such as blown sand (Clements).

Po′ad (πόa, meadow, + AD), a meadow plant (Clements).

Pocil′lus, pl. **Pocil′li** (*pocillum*, a little cup), the scyphi of *Cladonia*, so termed by Nylander.

Pock′et, of *Lemna*, a hollow in the leaf, whence a new leaf arises (Potter); ∼ **-leaves**, specialized leaves which collect humus; MANTLE-LEAVES; ∼ **-plums** = BAGPLUMS; **Pock′eting**, applied to an intrusion of cortex (Lang).

poc′uliform, *poculiform′is* (*poculum*, a cup; *forma*, shape), shaped like a goblet or drinking-cup.

Pod, a dry and many-seeded dehiscent fruit, a legume or silique; ∼ **-like**, applied to such fruits as those of *Corydalis*, *Hypecoum*, and *Cleome*.

pode′tiiform (+ PODETIUM from ποῦs, ποδὸs, a foot; *forma*, shape), shaped like a podetium; **Pode′tium**, (1) a stalk-like elevation rising from the thallus and supporting an apothecium in some Lichens; (2) also applied to the support of the capitulum of *Marchantia*; and (3) the seta of Mosses; **Pode′ta** ‡ is given by Lindley as a synonym.

podicel′late, Leighton's term for stalked, as applied to Lichens.

Podicil′lum ‡, a very short podetium (Lindley); **Pod′ium**, **Pod′us**, a footstalk or similar support; **Pod′ocarp**, *Podocar′pus* (καρπὸs, fruit), a stipitate fruit, that is, when the ovary is borne by a gynophore; **podoceph′alous**, *-lus* (κεφαλὴ, a head), with a pedunculate head; **Podogyn′ium** (γυνὴ, a woman), an elevation in the centre of a flower which carries the ovary, a gynophore; adj. **podogyn′icus, podog′ynus**; **podop′terous** (πτερὸν, a wing), having winged peduncles (Crozier); **Pod′osperm**, *Podosper′mium*, *-ma* (σπέρμα, a seed), the stalk of a seed, the funicle.

poecilotherm′ic = POIKILOTHERMIC.

Po′gon (πώγων, a beard), used in composition to denote any collection of long hairs.

poikilodynam′ic (ποικίλοs, various; δύναμιs, power), in hybrids when the character of one parent is practically absent; **poikilother′mic** (θέρμη, heat), rising and falling in response to varying temperature (Jones).

Point′al, an old term for PISTIL; **point′less**, muticous; **point′letted**, apiculate.

Point′er Cell, an English equivalent for DEUTER ZELL.

Poi′um (πόa, meadow), (1) a plant association in which *Poa* is a predominant genus (Ganong); (2) a meadow formation (Clements).

Polache′na, Polacke′na, *Polake′nium* (πολὺs, many; a, without; χαίνω, I gape), Richard's term for a fruit like a cremocarp, but composed of five carpels, *cf.* PENTACHENIUM.

po′lar (πόλοs, a pivot), (1) relating to the poles of an organ; (2) derived from the smaller ends of a flattened rootlet (Lopriore) ;   ~ **biloc′ular**, applied to Lichen spores which have cells at the opposite apices ; **Bod′y, Bod′ies**, a portion of the protoplasm of a mother-cell thrown off as nucleated cells from the oospore before fertilisation ;   ~ **Cap**, an ill-defined region of kinoplasm, generally larger than a centrosphere, for insertion of spindle-fibres (B. M. Davis) ;   ~ **Cell**, = ~ Body ;   ~ **Corpus′cle**, the central mass in each Aster of a dividing nucleus ;   ~ **Glob′ule**, = ~ Body ;   ~ **Nu′cleus**, a fourth nucleus in each group at the two extremities of the embryo sac, which move towards the middle of the embryo sac and there coalesce to form the secondary nucleus ;   ~ **Plates**, the achromatic spheres at the poles of the spindle in mitosis ; ~ **Rays**, sometimes applied to the astral rays as opposed to the spindle-fibres ; **pola′ri- biloc′ular**, used of two-celled spores with a thick central wall traversed by a connecting tube, the lumen of the cell at the extreme end ; **Polar′ity**, (1) the condition of having distinct poles ; (2) the assumption of a direction pointing to the poles, as the compass-plant, *Silphium laciniatum*, Linn.

Polem′bryony = Polyembryony.

Polemonie′tum, a plant association of *Polemonium* (Clements).

po′leward [dissyl.], towards the poles, in nuclear division.

Polexosty′lus (πολύς, many ; ἔξω, out ; στύλος, style) = Carcerule.

Po′lioplasm (πολιός, grey ; πλάσμα, moulded), Tswett's term for the circulating portion of the cytoplasm.

Polit′ropism = Polytropism.

poli′tus (Lat.), polished.

pollacan′thic, preferably **pollachan′thic** ₐ(πολλαχῆ, often ; ἄνθος, a flower), applied to plants which flower more than once, as opposed to Hapaxanthic plants ; perennials (Kjellman) ; **pollachig′enus** (γεννάω, I bring forth) = Polycarpic.

Poll′ard, a tree dwarfed by frequent

cutting of its boughs a few feet from the ground, and subsequent thick growth of shoots from the place where cut ; **poll′arding**, cutting back to produce a mop-headed growth.

Pol′len (Lat., fine flour), (1) the fertilising dust-like powder produced by the anthers of Phanerogams, more or less globular in shape, sometimes spoken of as "Microspores" ; (2) the antherozoids of Mosses (Hooker and Taylor) ; ~ **Carr′ier**, the retinaculum of Asclepiads, the gland to which the pollen-masses are attached, either immediately or by caudicles ; ~ **Cells**, cavities of the anthers in which pollen is formed ; ~ **Cha′mber**, (1) a cavity at the apex of some ovules beneath the integuments in which the pollen-grains lie after pollination, as in *Cycas ;* (2) the extine of the pollen in some Coniferae dilated into two hollow expansions to facilitate dispersion by wind ; ~ **Flow′ers**, those which afford no nectar to insect visitors, but only pollen ; ~ **Grain, Gran′ule**, the small bodies which compose the entire mass ; the latter term is also used for the contents of the grain ; ~ **Mass**, pollen-grains cohering by a waxy texture or fine threads into a single body ; ~ **Prepo′tency**, when one kind of pollen is more effective in fertilisation than another ; ~ **Sac**, the micro-sporangium in Phanerogams ; ~ **Spore** = ~ Grain ; ~ **Tet′rad**, ~ **Tetrahed′ron**, the shape of certain groups consisting of four grains cohering in a pyramid, as in *Oenothera ;* ~ **Tube**, the tube emitted by a pollen-grain passing down from the stigma to the ovary and ovules ; ~ ~ **ectotrop′ic**, the course of the pollen-tube in acrogamy, proceeding along the conducting tissue of the style to the micropyle ; ~ ~ **endotrop′ic**, in basigamy, when their course is towards the base of the ovule (Pirotta and Longo). —The various markings of the pollen-grains in

Acanthaceae have received special names from L. Radlkofer and G. Lindau, which have been used in their original form in the "Flora of Tropical Africa"; the following account of them may be useful: **Dau'ben** ~ (Stave ~) a modification of Schalen- or Spalten ~, with broadened fissures having a stave-like insertion; **Do'sen** ~ (Box ~), elliptic, with three longitudinal stripes and a pore in each; **Facettier'ter** ~ (Facet ~), with facetted surface; **Fal'ten** ~ (Fold ~), with smooth surface and three deep longitudinal grooves; **glat'ter** ~ (smooth ~), destitute of prominent markings; **Gür'tel** ~ (Girdle ~), having a zone of varied marking; **Kam'mrad** ~ (Cogwheel ~), having regular projections on the equatorial region; **Knöt'chen** ~, an abbreviation for **Knötchendo'sen** ~ (Nodule ~), having a tuberculate surface; **Lin'sen** ~ (Lens ~), doubly convex in form; **Rah'men** ~ (Frame ~), with six small and three broad streaks between the poles; **Rip'pen** ~ (Rib ~), with longitudinal ribs having punctate markings on them; **run'der** ~ (round ~), spherical in form; **Scha'len** ~ (Shell ~), with three slits, which do not reach the poles, and without pores, the pollen-tubes emerging from the slits, _cf._ SPALTEN ~ ; **Spal'ten** ~ (Fissure ~), with three longitudinal fissures, sometimes with pores in them; _cf._ SCHALEN ~ ; **Span'gen** ~ (Clasp ~), main ribs three, smaller ribs six, with three pores in the equatorial region, one between each two of the smaller ribs: **Sta'chel** ~ (Spine ~), having a spiny surface, pores from three to many; **Wa'ben** ~ (Honeycomb ~), having an areolate surface; **pol'lenate**, to fertilise by pollen; **Pollena'tion** = POLLINATION; **pollenif'erous**, _-rus_ (_fero_, I bear), pollen-bearing; **Pol'lenine**, the contents of pollen-grains; **Polleno'dy**, the develop-

ment of sporogenous tissue of the nucellus into pollen, in place of an embryo-sac (Worsdell); **Pol'lenoid** = POLLINOID.

Pol'lex (Lat., a thumb), an inch in length, nearly 25·4 mm.

pollica'ris (Lat., pertaining to a thumb), an inch in length, about the length of the end joint of the thumb.

Pollina'rium, pl. **Pollina'ria** (_pollen_, fine flour), (1) = ANDROECIUM ; (2) = CYSTIDIUM.

pollina'rius (Lat.), pertaining to fine flour; **pollino'sus**, as though dusted with pollen.

poll'inate (_pollen_, fine flour), to apply pollen to the receptive surface of the female organ; **pol'linated**, _pollina'tus_, when a stigma is supplied with pollen; **Pollina'tion**, the placing of the pollen on the stigma or stigmatic surface; **lat'eral**, ~, _cf._ PLEUROTRIBAL ; **o'ver** ~ _cf._ NOTOTRIBAL ; **und'er** ~, _cf._ STERNOTRIBAL; **pollin'ic Chamb'er** = POLLEN-CHAMBER ; **pollin'icus**, composed of or bearing some relation to pollen; **Pol'linide**, a single antheridial corpuscle (Sirodot ; **Pollin'ium**, pl. **Pollin'ia**, a body composed of all the pollen-grains of an anther-loculus, a pollen-mass ; **Polliniza'tion** = POLLINATION ; **Pollino'dium**, in Ascomycetes, a male sexual organ which conjugates with a female organ, directly or by outgrowth ; **Pol'linoids** (εἶδος, resemblaance), naked motionless masses of protoplasm, spherical or elongated, sometimes beaked, acting in the place of antherozoids in Florideae.

Polot'ropism (πόλος, a pivot ; τροπή, a turning), the tendency to direct proximal or distal extremities to the same point or pole (Vöchting).

Pol'verine (Ital., polverino), calcined ash of a soda-yielding plant.

Polyadel'phia (πολὺς, many ; ἀδελφὸς, a brother), a Linnean artificial class with stamens grouped into several brotherhoods or bundles ; adj. **polyadelp'hous, polyadel'phian ; poly-**

ad′enous (ἀδήν, a gland), with many
glands ; **Pol′yam**, a phylogenetic
transition form (Correns) ; **Polyan′-
dria** (ἀνήρ, ἀνδρὸς, a man), a Linnean
class of plants possessing many
stamens in each flower ; **polyan′-
drian, polyan′drous**, having an indefinite number of stamens ; **Poly-
an′dry**, the state of having many
stamens ; **polyan′thous**, *-thus* (ἄνθος,
a flower), having many flowers, particularly if within the same involucre ; **poly′arch** (ἀρχή, beginning),
when a stele possesses many protoxylem groups ; **polyari′nus** (ἄρρην,
male), Necker's term for POLYAN-
DROUS ; **Polyas′ter** (+ ASTER), when
several centres exist in a cell, united
by spindles (Hartog) ; **poliax′ial** (+
AXIAL), used of an inflorescence in
which the flowers are borne on
secondary, tertiary, etc., branches ;
polyblas′tus (βλαστὸς, a bud), Koerber's term for those Lichens which
have polyseptate spores ; **polycam′-
arus** (καμάρα, a vault) = POLYCARP-
IC ; **polycarpel′lary** (CARPELLUM),
of many carpels, free or united ;
polycar′pic, polycar′picous (καρπὸς,
fruit), fruiting many times, indefinitely ; used by De Candolle to denote a perennial herb ; **polycar′pous**,
-pus, (1) = POLYCARPIC ; (2) of a
flower in which the gynaecium forms
two or more distinct ovaries ; *cf.*
MONOCARPIC ; **polyceph′alous**, *-lus*
(κεφαλή, a head), bearing many
heads or capitula ; *polycephali Pili*,
are hairs divided at the end into
several arms (Lindley); **polychlor′is**,
an error for POLYCHORIS ; **Polychor′-
ion ‡ Polychorion′ides ‡, Polichor′is**
(χόριον, foetal membrane), synonyms
for ETAERIO ; **Polychro′ite** (χρόα,
colour, complexion), the yellow
colouring matter of saffron ; **Poly-
chro′matism**(χρῶμα,colour),variation
of colour or tint in the same corolla
(Lindman) ; adj. **polychromat′ic**,
having various colours in the same
organ ; **Pol′ychrome**, a substance
occurring in the bark of the Horse-
chestnut which gives rise to varying

colours ; **polychron′ic** (χρόνος, time),
arising at two or more times
(Clements) ; **polycil′iate** (+CILIATE)
having numerous cilia ; **Polyclad′ia,
Polyclad′y** (κλάδος, a branch), plica,
a supernumerary development of
branches and leaves ; adj. **polycla-
d′ous**; **Polyclo′nus**, **Polyclo′ny**
(κλὼν, a branch), a synonym of
POLYCLADIA ; **polycoc′cous**, *-cus*
(κόκκος, a kernel), having many
cocci ; **polycorm′ic** (κορμὸς, a trunk),
expressive of such trees as the fasti-
giate Irish yew, which has a number
of erect radial axes (A. H. Burtt) ;
Polycotyle′don, pl. **Polycotyle′dones**
(+ COTYLEDON), a plant which has
several cotyledons, or when the seed
leaves are so divided as to appear
many; adj. **polycotyle′donous;Poly-
cotyle′dony**, an increased number of
the cotyledons, more than two;
polycy′clic (κύκλος, a circle), when
the members of a series, such as a
calyx, or corolla, are in several
circles ; **Polycy′cly**, the condition of
a stem which possesses accessory
vascular strands besides the principal cylinder (Tansley) ; **polycys′tic**
(κύστις, a bag), composed of several
cells (Baillon) ; **Polycyst′in**, pigment from *Polycystis Flos-aquæ*,
allied to carotin (Zopf) ; **polydel′-
phous** = POLYADELPHOUS (Crozier) ;
polyde′mic (δῆμος, district) occurring
in more than one formation or natural
district (Clements) ; **Pol′yderm**
(δέρμα, skin), a tissue composed of
endodermal and parenchymatous
cells, forming the endermous layers
of the central cylinders (Mylius);
polyem′bryonate (+ EMBRYO),
having more than one embryo in a
seed; **Polyem′bryony**, the production
of more than a single embryo in an
ovule ; adj. **polyembryon′ic** ; **poly-
er′gic**, from **polyergid′ic** (ἔργον,
work), used by Goebel of the Vasculares; **polyflor′ous**, *-rus* (*flos,
floris*, a flower), a barbarism for
MULTIFLOROUS or POLYANTHOUS ;
Polygam′ia, a Linnean class containing plants with polygamous flowers ;

296

polygam′ian = POLYGAMOUS; **polyg′-amous** (γάμος, marriage), with hermaphrodite and unisexual flowers on the same, or on different individuals of the same species; **Polyg′amy**, the condition described; **polygamodioe′cious**, dioeciously polygamous (Crozier); **Polygen′esis** (γένεσις, origin), Clement's term for POLYPHYLESIS, multiple origin; **Polyg′eny** (γένος, race), Huxley's term for POLYPHYLESIS.

polygona′ceous, allied to, or resembling the genus *Polygonum;* **Polygone′tum**, a plant association of that genus (Clements).

polygon′atus (πολὺς, many; γόνυ, a knee), where the stem has many knots; **polyg′onus** (γωνία, an angle), multangular; **polygynae′cial** (γυναικεῖον, the women's house), having multiple fruits formed by the united pistils of many flowers; **polygyn′ous**, **polygyn′icus** (γυνὴ, a woman), having many distinct styles; **Polygyn′ia**, a Linnean order of plants so constituted; **Polyg′yny** = POLYGAMY; **polygy′rus** (γῦρος, a circle), in several whorls or circles.

Polyhed′ron, pl. **Polyhed′ra** (πολύεδρον, a solid of many bases), a stage in the growth of *Hydrodictyon*, when the hypnosperm or resting spore breaks up into several megazoospores which put out horn-like appendages; these polyhedra break up into zoospores.

polykar′ic (πολὺς, many; κάρυον, a nut), multinucleate; **polylep′idus** (λεπίς, λεπίδος, a scale), having many scales; **pclymer′ic**, **polym′erous**, *-rus* (μέρος, a part), with numerous members to each series or cycle; **polymor′phic**, **polymor′phous**, *-phus* (μορφὴ, a change), with several or various forms; variable as to habit; **Polymor′phism**, displaying many diversities of form; **Polymor′phy**, the existence of more than one form of the same organ on a plant; **polyneur′is** (νευρίς, a sinew), where the veins of a leaf, especially the secondary veins, are

numerous; **polynu′cleate** (+ NUCLEATE), having many nuclei; **Polyoe′cism** (οἶκος, a house), the state of plants whose flowers differ in sex (Knuth); **polyoi′cous**, a combination of (*a*) AUTOICOUS, (*b*) HETEROICOUS, or (*c*) SYNOICOUS, with DIOICOUS Mosses; **polyovula′tus** (+ OVULUM), furnished with many ovules; **polypet′alous**, *-lus* (+ PETAL), having several distinct petals; **polyph′agous** (φάγος, a glutton), used of Fungi occurring on several or many species; **Pol′yphore**, *Polyphor′ium* (φορέω, I carry), a torus with many pistils, as of a strawberry; **Polyphyle′sis** (+ PHYLETIC), descent from more than one line of descent; adj. **polyphylet′ic**; **Pol′yphyll**, an increase in the normal number of organs in a whorl; **polyphyl′lous** (φύλλον, a leaf), having many leaves; **Polyphyll′y** = PHYLLOMANIA; **Polyphylog′eny** (+ PHYLOGENY), lineage through several lines; **Pol′yplast** (πλαστὸς, moulded), (1) a group of monoplasts which are the organic elements of protoplasm (Vogt); (2) the multicellular stage of the embryo, before the differentiation of cell-layers or organs in Mosses, Ferns, etc. (Parker); **polyplas′tic**, applied to septate spores.

polypodia′ceous, allied to or resembling the genus *Polypodium*.

polyp′oroid, **polyp′orous**, relating to the fungus genus *Polyporus*.

polyrhi′zal, **polyrhi′zous** (πολὺς, many; ρίζα, a root), (1) having numerous rootlets; (2) where parasites have many distinct rootlets apart from their haustoria; **Polysapro′bia**, pl. (σαπρὸς, rotten), organisms which are adapted to live in foul water (Kolkwitz); **Polysar′ca** (σάρξ, σαρκὸς, flesh), an unnatural growth due to excess of nutriment; **Polyse′cus** ‡ (σῆκος, a stall), Desvaux's term for an ETAERIO as in *Magnolia;* **polysep′alous**, *-lus*, (+ SEPAL), with many distinct sepals ; **polysi′phonous** (σίφων, a tube), applied to a filament of several coherent longitudinal rows of cells ; **pol′ysperm, polysper′mal, polysperm′atous, polysperm′ous,** -*mus,* (σπέρμα, a seed), when a pericarp has numerous seeds ; **polysporan′giate** (+ SPORANGIUM), having many sporangia ; **Pol′yspore** (σπορά, a seed), a multicellular spore composed of MERISPORES (Bennett and Murray) ; **pol′yspored** = POLYSPOROUS ; **polyspor′ous,** containing many spores, used of Cryptogams, as in asci when more than four or eight spores occur ; **polys′tachous** (Crozier) = **polystach′yous** (στάχυς, a spike), having many spikes ; **polyste′lic, polyste′lous** (+ STELE), with more than one plerome strand at the growing point, so that the stem has more than one stele, as in *Gunnera;* **Polyste′ly,** the condition specified ; adj. **polyste′lic ; polyste′monous,** -*nus* (στήμων, a filament), having many stamens, polyandrous).

polyst′ichous (πολύστιχος, in many lines), when leaves are borne in many series, as the leaf-scars in *Caulopteris.*

polystig′mus (πολὺς, many, + STIGMA), with many carpels, each originating a stigma ; **polys′tomous,** -*mus* (στόμα, a mouth), many-mouthed, with numerous suckers or haustoria ; **polystromat′ic** (+ STROMA), possessing many stromata ; **polysty′lous,** -*lus* (+ STYLE), with several styles ; **polysymmet′rical** (συμμετρία, apt proportion), having bilateral symmetry in more planes than one, actinomorphic ; **polytax′ic** (τάξις, order), a character varying in a discontinuous manner (Coutagne) ; **polythalam′ic** (θάλαμος, a bedchamber), (1) having more than one female flower within the involucre ; (2) derived from more than one flower, as a collective fruit ; **polythe′leus** (θηλή, a nipple), used of a flower which contains several distinct ovaries ; **polyt′ocous,** -*cus,* (τόκος, a birth), fruiting year after year, caulocarpous ; **polyt′omous,**

-*mus* (τομή, a cutting), apparently pinnate, but the pinnae not articulated to the common petiole ; **Polyt′omy,** (1) in an inflorescence, having more axes than in dichotomy ; (2) a false pinnation ; **polytop′ic** (τόπος, a place) applied to species supposed to be of independent origin in more than one place.

polytricha′ceous, resembling or akin to *Polytrichum;* **Polytriche′tum,** a formation of the genus *Polytrichum;* **polytricho′sus,** employed by Nilsson, when the ground under heather is carpeted with mosses.

polyt′richous (πολὺς, many ; θρίξ, τριχὸς, a hair), having many hairs ; **polytroph′ic** (τροφή, food), obtaining food from a wide area of selection (Jones) ; **polytrop′ic,** Loew's term for bees which visit a wide circle of flowers ; **Polyt′ropism** (τροπή, a twining), Archangeli's term when leaves place their lamina vertically and meridionally, the two surfaces facing east and west ; **polytyp′ic** (τύπος, a type), applied to a genus having several species ; **Polyx′eny** (ξένος, a guest), = PLEIOXENY ; **Polyzygo′sis** (ζυγὸς, a yoke), the conjugation of more than two gametes (Crozier).

poma′ceous (*pomum*), a fruit, + ACEOUS, relating to apples ; **poma′ceus,** (Lat.), apple-green (Hayne) ; **Pome,** *Po′mum,* an inferior fruit of several cells, of which the apple is the type.

pomeridia′nus (Lat.), in the afternoon.

pomif′erous *po′mifer* (*pomum,* a fruit ; *fero,* I bear), pome-bearing ; **po′miform,** *pomiform′is* (*forma,* shape), shaped like an apple ; **Pomol′ogy,** *Pomolo′gia* (λόγος, discourse), the science of edible cultivated fruits. **Pomo′na,** an account of the fruits cultivated in any given district or country ; the name is mythological.

pon′tic, belonging to the ancient Pontus, (1) the Black Sea ; (2) a north-eastern province of Asia Minor.

Ponti′um (πόντος, the sea), a deep sea formation; **pontoph′ilus** (φιλέω, I love), dwelling in the deep sea; **Pontophy′ta** (φυτὸν, a plant), deep-sea plants (Clements).

pooc′ola (πόα, grass, meadow; *colo*, I inhabit); **pooph′ilous, pooph′ilus** (φιλέω, I love), meadow-loving plants which consort with grasses (Pound and Clements); **Poophy′ta** (φυτὸν, a plant), meadow plants (Clements); **Po′ophyte**, a plant inhabiting meadows; adj. **poophyt′ic**, pratal.

popu′leus, the blackish-green of poplar leaves, *Populus nigra ;* **Po′-pulin**, a crystallisable substance from the bark of the aspen, *Populus tremula*, Linn.

poran′drous (πόρος, a passage; ἀνὴρ, ἀνδρὸς, a man), when the anthers open by pores.

porca′tus (*porca*, a ridge), ridged; employed by Lemaire.

Pore, *Po′rus* (πόρος, passage), (1) any small aperture, as in anthers, for the emission of pollen in the pollen grains themselves, in the epidermis as stomata or water-pores; (2) in *Polyporus*, any of the tube-like openings, forming the hymenium; (3) large pitted vessels or tracheids in wood; (4) an opening in the prickles of *Victoria regia* ; (5) cavities in soils not occupied by solid substances (Warming); **Pores, air** = (1) STOMATA; (2) PNEUMATHODES; **~, bor′dered,** in *Sphagnum*, the opening surrounded by a distinct thickened ring; **Pore Canal′**, the passage through a pit between neighbouring cells; **~ Cap′-sule**, a capsule dehiscing by pores, as in the poppy; **~ Cir′cle**, the zone in the annual rings of certain trees, such as an oak which displays numerous tracheids; **~ Cork**, cork-cells in lenticels with intercellular spaces between them (Klebahn); **~ Pas′sage**, the stomatic passage between the inner and outer cavities; **~ Space, ~ Vol′ume**, the sum of the spaces in soils not taken up by solid particles; **— a′pical ~**, *cf.*

HYDATHODES; **cor′tical ~**, = LENTICEL; **Porench′yma** (ἔγχυμα, an infusion), tissue of elongated cells, and apparently pierced by pores; pitted tissue; **porici′dal** (*cœdo, cecidi*, to cut), applied to anthers which open by pores, porandrous; **por′i-form** (*forma*, shape), like a pore (Leighton); **Por′ogams** (γάμος, marriage), phanerogamous plants which are fertilised by way of the chalaza instead of the micropyle (Treub); **Porog′amy**, the condition described; adj. **porog′amous ; Por′oids** (εἶδος, resemblance), small circular dots in the cell-wall of Diatoms resembling pores (O. Müller); **Porom′eter** (μέτρον, a measure), an instrument to measure the dimensions of stomata; **por′ose**, *poro′sus ;* **por′ous**, pierced with small holes; **~ Ves′sels**, pitted or dotted vessels.

porphyr′eus (πορφύρεος, purple), purple in colour, purpureus; **porphyroleu′-cus** (λευκὸς, white), light, purple.

porra′ceous, *porra′ceus* (Lat.), leek-green.

porrect′, *porrec′tus* (Lat., stretched out), directed outward and forward; *cf.* ARRECT.

por′ulus (Lat.), somewhat porous.

Por′us = PORE.

pos′itive, the absolute or effective condition, opposed to negative, and prefixed for emphasis to such terms as Geotropism, Heliotropism, Hydrotropism, etc.

postcarpotrop′ic (*post*, after, + CARPOTROPIC), curvature of the peduncle at the maturation of fruit to help in dissemination; **postcotyle′donary** (+ COTYLEDON), after the development of the seed-leaves.

Pos′teriform (*posterus*, last, + FORM), the late derivative of an ancestral form (Kuntze).

poste′rior (Lat., coming after), (1) next or towards the main axis, superior; the reverse of ANTERIOR; (2) in anthers = EXTRORSE.

Postfertiliza′tion (*post*, after, + FERTILIZATION), the processes from fertilization of the ovule to its maturation;

Postflora′tion (*flos*, flower), persistence of the floral envelopes after flowering (Lindman) ; **postgen′ital** (*genitalis*, pertaining to birth), refers to structures or characters which appear subsequent to birth, as contrasted with congenital (Worsdell).

posti′cal, posti′cous, *posti′cus* (Lat., that which is behind), on the posterior side, next the axis ; extrorse ; Spruce and others use "postical" for the ventral or rooting face of the stem of Hepaticae.

postmeio′tic (*post*, after, + MEIOTIC), after reducing divisions in karyokinesis (Farmer) ; **Post-phyl′lome** (φύλλον, a leaf), Potonié's term for leaves ; **Postreduc′tion** (+ REDUCTION), a reduction occurring in the metaphase of the second mitosis (Moreau) ; **Post-spor′ophyll** (+ SPOROPHYLL) ; **Postsynap′sis** (+ SYNAPSIS), the processes of nuclear division succeeding the contraction known as synapsis; adj. **postsynap′tic**; **Post-troph′ophyll** (+ TROPHOPHYLL) ; **Post-trophospor′ophyll** (+ SPOROPHYLL) ; these two and the last but one are similar refinements by the same author ; refer to SPOROPHYLL, etc. ; **postventit′ious,** *-tius* (*post*, after ; *venio*, I come), applied to growths which arise subsequent to their normal time ; *cf.* PREVENTITIOUS.

Pot′amad (ποταμὸς, a river, + AD), a river plant (Clements) ; **Potami′um,** a river formation.

Potamogetone′tum, a formation of species belonging to the genus *Potamogeton.*

potamoph′ilus (ποταμὸς, a river ; φιλέω, I love), river-loving (Clements) ; **Potamoplank′ton** (+ PLANKTON), the floating vegetation of inland waters; **Potamophy′ta** (φυτὸν, a plant), river plants (Clements).

poten′tial (*potentia*, force, existing in possibility, not in action ; used in opposition to KINETIC ; ~ **Gam′etophyte,** one which is functionally asexual; ~ **Par′asite,** a saprophyte which can live equally as

a parasite; ~ **Sap′rophyte,** a parasite capable of existing as a saprophyte.

Potetom′eter (ποτὴς, a drink ; μέτρον, a measure), apparatus for measuring the amount of water given off by the leaves of plants (Moll); **Potom′eter,** (1) a similar instrument for measuring the flow of liquids in tissues (F. Darwin); (2) for measuring absorption (Clements).

pottia′ceous, allied to the moss *Pottia ;* **pott′ioid** (εἶδος, likeness), resembling the genus *Pottia.*

Pouch = SILICLE; ~ **shaped,** hollow and bag-like, as the spur in many Orchids; **diges′tive ~** ; used by Van Tieghem and Douliot for the root-cap of the lateral roots of Leguminosae and Cucurbitaceae.

Powder-seed, minute seeds or spores (Ridley).

pow′dery, covered with a fine bloom, as the leaves of *Primula farinosa,* Linn. ; ~ **Mil′dew,** a destructive disease of the vine, due to *Uncinula spiralis ;* the conidial stage is known as *Oidium Tuckeri.*

prae-, or **pre-** (*prae*, before), expresses priority in time or place.

prae′cox (Lat., early ripe), appearing or developing early ; precocious.

Praeflora′tion (*praefloratio*, blossoming before time) = AESTIVATION.

Praefolia′tion (*prae*, before ; *folium*, a leaf = VERNATION; **Prae′form** (+ FORM), an early form, the original ancestral strain (Kuntze); **Prae′forms,** in *Rosa,* PERFORMS with glandular teeth (Almquist).

prae′morse, *praemor′sus* (Lat., bitten at the end), as though the end were bitten off.

Praemuta′tion (*prae*, before, + MUTATION); the inner preparation of a plant, for the outward manifestation ; MUTATION (De Vries).

praero′sus (Lat.), apparently gnawed off.

praeus′tus (Lat., burned at the end), looking as if scorched.

pras′inous, *pras′inus* (Lat.), grass-green, leek-green.

pra′tal (*pratum*, a meadow), H. C. Watson's term for those plants which grow in meadows or luxuriant herbage ; **praten′sis** (Lat.), growing in meadows, or pertaining thereto ; **Pra′tum** (Lat.), meadow, the dominant plants are herbaceous and the vegetation closed.

Preaecid′iospore (*pre*, before, + AECIDIOSPORE), the trichogyne of certain authors (Moreau) ; **Preaecid′ium** (+ AECIDIUM), young caeoma, a sorus which precedes the aecidium in Uredine Fungi (Moreau) ; **praeangiosper′mous** (+ ANGIOSPERM), existing before the Angiosperms came into being ; **Preang′iosperms**, early forms of plants previous to the evolution of plants with closed ovaries ; **preclepsy′droid** (+ CLEPSYDROID), the early state of the leaf trace in Ophioglossaceae (Lang).

Pre-bract′eole (*pre*, before, + BRACTEOLE), the sub-sporal bract in *Chara* ; it may be restricted to a single swollen cell (Allen).

precator′ius (Lat., relating to petitioning), used for a rosary, as the seeds of *Abrus* ; ~ **contex′tus**, necklace-shaped, moniliform.

pre′cius (Lat.), **preco′cious** = PRAECOX.

predom′inant, "very conspicuous" (Braithwaite) ; in excess (Leighton).

Prefertiliza′tion (*pre*, before, + FERTILIZATION), the early state of an ovule as far as completed pollination ; **Preflora′tion** = PRAEFLORATION ; **Prefolia′tion** = PRAEFOLIATION ; **Preforma′tion** (*formatio*, a shaping), the theory of the function of germ-plasm, a complex substance whose ultimate factors direct the vital activities of the cell, and resultant form of the plant ; **Prehaustor′ium** (+ HAUSTORIUM), papillate epidermal cells of *Cuscuta*, by which nutriment is obtained before the formation of haustoria (Peirce).

prehen′sile (*prehensio*, a seizing) **Type**, those flowers whose insect visitors grasp the style and stamens so as to cover their breasts with pollen and so effect crossing (Delpino).

premeiot′ic (*pre*, before, + MEIOTIC), previous to reducing divisions in karyokinesis.

premorse′ (Crozier) = PRAEMORSE.

Prepo′tency (*pre*, before ; *potentia*, power), the quality by which certain pollen fertilizes a given pistil, in preference to other pollen ; **Prereduc′tion** (+ REDUCTION), a reduction occurring in metaphase of first mitosis (Moreau).

Presenta′tion (*praesentatio*, a placing before) **Time**, the period required for an organ to take up perception (Macdougal).

Pres′sure (*pressura*, a pressing), stress or distributed force causing turgor or compression ; **root** ~, pressure existing in the root-tissues tending to cause the rise of liquid in the stem.

Presynap′sis (*pre*, before, + SYNAPSIS), the condition of nuclear division before the stage known as synapsis ; *adj.* **presynap′tic** ; **preventit′ious** (*venio*, I come) **Buds**, dormant eyes, present on any given portion of the stem, which produce epicormic branches (Hartig) ; **prever′nal** (*vernalis*, of the spring), early spring flowering.

Prick′le, outgrowths of the rind or bark, as those of the rose ; **prick′ly**, armed with prickles.

pri′mary, *prima′rius* (Lat., chief), (1) used of the part first developed ; (2) the main divisions of a leaf or umbel ; ~ **Ax′is**, the main stem ; ~ **Bast**, consists of sieve tissues and parenchyma ; ~ **Cor′tex**, the PERIBLEM ; ~ **Des′mogen**, = PROCAMBIUM ; ~ **Lamel′la**, of a spore, is the outermost layer of its coats, representing the original wall ; ~ **Lay′er**, see " tapetal cell " (*infra*) ; ~ **Leaves**, the primordial leaves ; ~ **Meg′aspore**, megaspore mother-cell, the early stage of the embryo-sac ; ~ **Mem′bers**, the primary shoot and root ; ~ **Mem′brane**, the first (?) cell-wall ; ~ **Mer′istem**, the embryonic tissue of a young organ ; ~ **Pet′iole**, the main rhachis of a compound leaf ; ~ **Phlo′em** = ~ BAST ;

~ **Root**, the main root developed from the radicle ; ~ **Shoot**, the main stem developed from the plumule ; ~ **Struc'ture**, a nascent organ, as of root or shoot ; ~ **Suspen'sor**, the filamentous row of cells preceding the actual embryological divisions, the early stage being the proembryo ; ~ **tape'tal Cell**, or **Lay'er**, the source whence the tapetum is formed by bipartition of a cell or layer of periblem ; the other part of the division becoming the archesporium ; **Tis'sue**, (*a*) that first formed or (*b*) formed during the first season's growth ; ~ **Wood**, the wood developed by the procambium.

prime'val (*primaevus*, youthful) **For'est**, virgin forest which has kept its original character undisturbed by man.

primigen'ius (Lat., first produced) = PRIMITIVUS.

Pri'mine, *Pri'mina* (*primus*, first), the outer integument of an ovule.

prim'itive, *primiti'vus* (Lat., first of its kind), applied to the part first developed ; specific types, in contrast to varieties and hybrids ; ~ **Wall**, a boundary between the ooplasm and periplasm of the oosphere in *Cystopus Bliti*, De Bary (Stevens).

Pri'mofilices, pl. (*primo*, at first, *filix*, a fern) a group of Fern-like plants, presumed to be the progenitors of the true Ferns (Arber).

Primor'dia, pl. of **Primor'dium** (Lat., the beginning), a member or organ in its earliest condition ; the German " Anlage " ; **primor'dial**, *primordia'lis*, first in order of appearance ; ~ **Cell**, a naked cell, one without a cell-wall ; ~ **Epider'mis**, the epidermis when the first formed ; ~ **Leaf**, an intermediate form between the cotyledon and those of the adult plant produced by growth from the plumule ; ~ **Tis'sue**, ground tissue ; ~ **U'tricle**, the outer layer of cell-protoplasm lining the inner surface of a vacuolated cell : by some considered the same as ECTOPLASM.

Pri'mospore (*primus*, first ; σπορά, a seed), term proposed by C. Mac-Millan for those cases in which the spore is but little differentiated from an ordinary cell of the parent organism.

Primule'tum, Clements's term for an association of *Primula*.

pri'or (Lat., earlier), cited by Clements for "earlier, used of alpine aspects."

prismat'ic, *prismat'icus* (Lat., like a prism) : ~ **Lay'er**, Farmer's term for a layer of cells in *Isoëtes* surrounding the xylem cylinder (Campbell) ; **prism-shaped**, with flat faces separated by angles ; **Prismench'-yma** (ἔγχυμα, an infusion), prismatic cellular tissue.

Pris'on Flow'ers, those which imprison their insect-visitors until fertilization is effected.

Proan'giosperms (*pro*, for, + ANGIOSPERM), an Angiosperm in the act of becoming so from some ancestral form (Saporta and Marion) ; **Proangiosper'my**, the state in question.

Proanthe'sis (πρὸ, early ; ἄνθησις, flowering), flowering in advance of the normal period, as some flowers appearing in autumn in advance of the ensuing spring (Pax) ; **Pro-antho-strob'ilus** (+ ANTHOSTROBILUS), the flower of the hypothetic ancestors of the Angiosperms (Arber and Parkin).

Prob'able Er'ror, see DEVIATION, PROBABLE.

Probas'id (*pro*, for, + BASIDIUM), Van Tieghem's term for an organ intermediate between a basidium and a sporophore in Basidiomycetes, bearing a teleutospore.

proboscid'eus (*proboscis*, a snout), having a large terminal horn, as the fruit of *Martynia*.

Procam'bium (*pro*, for, + CAMBIUM), the embryonic tissue, consisting of somewhat elongated cells, from which the vascular tissue is eventually formed) ; **Pro'carp**, *Procar'pium* (καρπὸς, fruit), an archicarp with a special receptive organ, the trichogyne.

proce′rus (Lat.), very tall, as a tree.
Pro′cess, *Proces′sus* (Lat., a prolongation), any projecting appendage,
Proces′sus Hyme′nii, "the aciculae
of certain Fungals" (Lindley); see
also BANDS, in fruit of *Zostera
minor*.
Prochosi′um (πρόχωσις, a deposition of
mud), a succession in an alluvial soil
(Clements, 1905).
Prochro′matin (*pro*, for, + CHROMA-
TIN), the substance of nucleoli
(Pfitzer); Prochro′mogen (+
CHROMOGEN), Palladin's name for
the form in which chromogens appear in the cell; in conjunction
with an enzyme it becomes a
chromogen; Prochro′mosome (+
CHROMOSOME), a definite collection
of chromatin granules in somatic
and germ cells, corresponding to,
but smaller than, chromosomes
(Overton).
procrastina′tus (Lat.), deferred; *cf.*
SEPTIO.
procum′bent, *procum′bens* (Lat., leaning forward), lying along the
ground.
Prodophyti′um (πρόοδος, a pioneer;
(φυτόν, a plant), an initial formation (Clements).
Prod′romus (Lat., a forerunner), frequently employed in botanic works,
which are intended should be
followed by more complete treatises.
Prod′ucts (*productus*, brought forth),
substances resulting from metabolism
or chemical changes in plants.
Produc′tum ‡ (*productus*, lengthened)
= CALCAR.
Pro-em′bryo (*pro*, for, + EMBRYO), (1)
in Characeae, the product of the
oospore, upon which the *Chara*-
plant develops as a lateral bud;
(2) in Archegoniatae the product of
the oospore before differentiation
of the embryo; (3) ‡ the youngest
thallus of a Lichen; proembryon′ic,
relating to a pro-embryo, as the
~ Branch in *Chara*, a propagative
body having the structure of a
pro-embryo arising from a node of
the stem.

proë′minens (Lat., projecting), used
of an unusually extended part.
Profer′ment (*pro*, for, *fermentum*,
leaven) = ZYMOGEN; Pro′file-lie, of
leaves, when turned edgewise to
strong light (Warming); progam′-
etal (+ GAMETE), of the nature of
a Progam′ete, a cell which divides
to form gametes, or occasionally
passes into a gamete (Hartog);
Progam′etange, *Progametan′gium*
(ἀγγεῖον, a vessel), resting bodies
in *Protomyces macrosporus*, Unger;
progam′ic (Hartog), pro′gamous,
in advance of fertilization; the sex
fixed before fertilization (Correns);
~ Cell, a cell formed in the pollen-
grain which has the sperm-nucleus
(Goebel); Progameta′tion, employed
by Maire to denote the act of
synkaryons becoming progametes;
Progamet′ophyte (φυτόν, a plant),
the plant which produces progametes
(Maire); Progemma′tion (+ GEM-
MATION), when stylospores are given
off from basidia, new terminal cells
being developed from older or basal
cells (Nylander); progeoesthet′ic
(γῆ, earth; αἰσθητικός, perceptible),
applied to the root-tip when tending
downwards.
progred′iens (Lat., advancing), extending at one part, and dying in
the rear.
Progress′ion (*progressus*, an advance),
the evolution of an inflorescence by
progressive expansion, in sequence
of development (Guillard); progres′-
sive, advancing; ~ Metamorph′osis,
the appearance of organs in an
ascending scale, as when petals are
replaced by stamens; opposed to
RETROGRESSIVE METAMORPHOSIS.
Progym′nosperms (*pro*, for, + Gymnosperm), prototypic Gymnosperms,
as *Bennettites* (Saporta and Marion);
Pro-Hepat′ic (+ HEPATIC), a hypothetic original thalloid state of the
higher plants (Lignier); Prohydro-
t′ropism (+ HYDROTROPISM), turning towards a source of moisture
(Macdougal); adj. prohydrotrop′ic;
Pro-Ly′copod (+ LYCOPOD), a hypo-

thetic ancestor of vascular plants, itself derived from the Pro-Hepatic form (Lignier).

Proios'pory = PROSPORY.

Projectu'ra (Lat., a jutting out), a small longitudinal projection on some stems where the leaf originates ;

Prokaryogam'ete (κάρυον, a nut, = nucleus ; γάμος, marriage), the nucleus of a primary progamete (Maire) ; **Prokaryogametisa'tion**, quantitative reduction (Maire).

Prokine'sis (πρὸ, before ; κίνησις, a moving), the early stage of nuclear division, up to the ASTER).

pro'late (*prolatus*, a bringing forward), drawn out towards the poles.

Prole (Crozier), = **Pro'les** (Lat., off-spring), (1) progeny ; (2) sometimes used for race ; (3) ‡ the species.

Prole'psis (πρόληψις, anticipation), (1) a foreshadowing, something of anticipation ; (2) "hurried development as in the disease known as 'peach-yellows' where axillary buds develop into branches the first year" (Crozier) ; **prolep'tic**, anticipatory ; **prole'pticus** (Lat.), used by Wimmer instead of PRAECOX.

Proleta'rian (*proletarius*, a citizen of the poorest class), a name suggested by M'Leod to denote plants having only a small reserve, and self-fertilized ; *cf.* CAPITALIST.

pro'lifer, *prolif'erus*, **prolif'erous** (*proles*, offspring ; *fero*, I bear), bearing progeny as offshoots ; **Prolifera'tion**, *Prolifera'tio*, development proliferously ; **prolif'ic**, *prolif'icus* (M. Lat., producing offspring), fruitful, fertile ; ~ **Cells**, reproductive cells (Wittrock) ; **prolifi'ed**, grown out into prolification, as a tuft of leaves from a cone ; **Prolifica'tion**, the production of terminal or lateral leaf-buds in a flower ; **prolig'erous**, *-rus* (*gero*, I bear), proliferous, in Lichens applied to the spore-bearing portion of the apothecium (J. S. Henslow) ; *cf.* LAMINA PROLIGERA.

prometatrop'ic (πρὸ, before ; μέτα, from ; τροπὴ, a turning), in crossing, when the interchange is between the plants, the pollen of one going to the other, but the pollen not from anthers associated with the ovaries fertilized (K. Pearson).

prom'inent, *prom'inens* (Lat., jutting out), standing out beyond some other part.

Promito'sis (πρὸ, before, + MITOSIS), simple or "dumb-bell" nuclear division in *Gymnodinium*.

Promycele' = **Promyce'lium** (*pro*, for, + MYCELIUM), the short-lived product of tube-germination of a spore, which abjoints a few spores unlike the mother-spore, and then perishes ; **promyce'lial**, relating to a promycelium ; ~ **Spores**, those generated in asci (Cooke) ; the Sporidia of continental mycologists (Plowright).

pro'nate, "inclined to grow prostrate" (Crozier).

prone, *pro'nus* (Lat., leaning forward), lying flat, especially the upper face downward.

Prong-cells, parenchymatous cells of a special form, containing silica bodies.

Pronu'cleus (*pro*, for, + NUCLEUS), the nucleus of a conjugating gamete, which on coalescing with another pronucleus forms the germ-nucleus.

Proodophyti'a (πρόοδος, in advance ; φυτὸν, a plant), initial plant formations (Clements).

Pro-Ophiogloss'um, an assumed ancestral form of *Ophioglossum* (Campbell).

Prop, used by Withering for STIPULE ; ~ **-roots**, the aërial roots of *Rhizophora*.

propaculif'erous ; Propaculum, errors for PROPAGULIFEROUS ; PROPAGULUM.

prop'agative (*propago*, a set or layer), tending to increase by asexually produced growths, as gemmae, soredia, etc.; **propagaculif'erous** (*fero*, I bear), bearing off-sets, as *Sempervivum*.

Propa'gulum (dim. of *propago*, a set or layer), (1) an off-set ; (2) in Lichens, the powdery organs which constitute the SOREDIA ; **Propa'go**, pl. **Propa'gines**, (1) a bulblet ; (2) the branch bent down for layering.

propen'dent, *propen'dens* (Lat.), ranging down.

prop'er, true, or correctly understood; ~ **Juice**, any characteristic "fluid" of a plant, as the "milk" of lettuce, etc.; ~ **Valves** = SPATHE-VALVES.

Properimer'istem (*pro*, for, + PERI-MERISTEM), a synonym of PERI-MERISTEM.

Proph'asis, pl. **Proph'ases** (πρὸ, before; φάσις, an appearance), the changes in the mother-nucleus previous to division, including the formation of the nuclear plate and the longitudinal division of the chromosomes; **Prophlo'ëm** (+ PHLOEM), (1) PROTŎ-PHLOEM; (2) the cylinder of elongated cells with thickened walls, occurring in the seta of some Mosses round the protoxylem; **prophototac'tic** (τακτικὸς, arranging), turning towards light (Macdougal); the condition itself is **Prophototax'is**; **Prophotot'ropism** (τροπή, turning), moving towards the centre of the radiating light (Macdougal); **Pro'-phyll**, bracteole, *cf.* PROPHYLLUM; **Pro'phyllum** (φύλλον, a leaf), the bracteole at the base of an individual flower, in German "Vorblatt"; **prophylla'tus**, provided with prophylla; **prophyl'loid** (εἶδος, resemblance), like prophylla.

Proph'ysis = PROSPHYSIS.

Prophy'togams (πρὸ, before; φυτὸν, a plant; γάμος, marriage), Focke's proposed name for vascular Cryptogams.

prop'rius (Lat, special, peculiar), partial.

pros- (πρὸς, towards), employed to denote positive phenomena by Rothert, as in the four following terms:— **Prosaërotax'is** (+ AEROTAXIS), the stimulus of oxygen on the movement of zoospores and other motile organisms; **proschairlimnet'ic** (χαίρω, I rejoice; λίμνη, a pool), occasionally belonging to Limno-plankton (Forel); **Proschemotax'is** + CHEMOTAXIS), attraction by certain substances, shown by bacteria, antherozoids, etc.; adj. **proschemo-**

tac'tic; **Proscol'la** ‡ (κόλλα, glue), a viscid gland on the upper side of the stigma of Orchids, to which the pollen-masses become attached, the RETINACULUM; **Prosem'bryum** (ἔμβρυον, an embryo), = PERI-SPERMIUM; **Prosench'yma** (ἔγχυμα, an infusion), tissue of lengthened cells with tapering ends which overlap; adj. **prosenchy'matous**; **Prosenth'esis** (ἔνθεσις, a putting in), when whorled flowers have a gap between two successive whorls; generally the divergence of this gap is greater than that of the whorl; if less, it is **negative** PROSENTHESIS (Eichler); **Prosgalvanotax'is** = GALVANOTAXIS; **prosgeotrop'ic** (+ GEOTROPIC), the positive influence of gravity on organs during growth; the condition is **Prosgeot'ropism**; **prosheliotrop'ic** (+ HELIOTROPIC), turning towards the source of light; the state is **Prosheliot'ropism**; **Pros-hydrotax'is** (+ HYDROTAXIS), negative osmotaxis; **Pros'oplasm** (πλάσμα, moulded), used of pathologic tissues caused by parasites as in galls (Trotter); adj. **prosoplast'ic**; **Pros'o-plasy** = HYPERTROPHY; **Prososmo-tax'is** (+ OSMOTAXIS), movement of motile organisms in consequence of the influence of fluids; **Prosphoto-tax'is** (+ PHOTOTAXIS), definite arrangement as the result of the action of light on organisms capable of response; **Pros'physes** (φύσις, growth), "abortive pistillidia of the muscal alliance" (Lindley); **Prosoplectench'yma** (+ PLECTEN-CHYMA), a modification of hyphal tissue (Lindau).

Prosporan'gium (πρὸ, for; σπορὰ, a seed; ἀγγεῖον, a vessel), (1) in Chy-tridieae, etc., a vesicular cell whose protoplasm passes into an outgrowth of itself, the sporangium, and then divides into swarm-spores; (2) in Phaeosporeae, an early formed sporangium, formed of a layer of the filament combined with an outgrowth (Kuckuck).

Pros'pory (πρώιος, precocious; σπορὰ,

a spore), abbreviated from PROIOS-
PORY), the precocious development
of spores in certain Algae ; **Pros′tady**
(στάδιος, steady), the early fruiting
stage described above.

proste′lic (πρὸ, for, + STELE), when
an axis consists of a single concentric
bundle (Jeffrey).

Prosthermotax′is (πρὸς, near, +
THERMOTAXIS), movement of bac-
teria or zoospores towards warmth ;
Prosthigmotax′is = THIGMOTAXIS.

pros′trate, *prostra′tus* (Lat., thrown to
the ground), lying flat.

Pros′typus (πρόστυπος, embossed) =
RAPHE.

Protal′bumose (πρῶτος, first, + ALBU-
MOSE) ; one of the primary albumoses, soluble in hot or cold water ;
protan′drous (ἀνὴρ , ἀνδρὸς, a man),
the anthers mature before the pistils
in the same flower ; **Protan′dry**,
the androecium ripening before the
gynaecium, the pollen being dispersed before the pistils are receptive ; **Protanthe′sis** (ἄνθησις, flowering), the normal first flower of an
inflorescence (Guillard).

protea′ceous, relating to or resembling
the order Proteaceae.

Pro′teases, pl., enzymes capable of
acting upon proteid substances,
both EREPHASES and PEPTASES
(Vines).

Protec′tive (*protectio*, a covering)
Lay′er, in leaf-fall, a layer of cells
becoming lignified, and then suberised, the whole of the protoplasm
being withdrawn ; this layer forms
the scar after the leaf has fallen
(Lee) ; **Protec′tive Sheath** = ENDO-
DERMIS.

Pro′teid, (1) a group of albuminoids,
more or less resembling albumen ;
with water, the group of proteids
constitute the bulk of protoplasm ;
(2) used also for ~ **Gran′ule** or ~
Plas′tid ; ~ **Ba′sis**, that portion of
protoplasm which is not composed
of granules, it is sometimes absent ;
~ **Crys′tal** = CRYSTALLOID ; ~ **Gran′-
ules**, reserve materials, or aleurone
granules ; ~ **Vac′uoles**, nuclei of

cells of the tapetal layer in Gymnosperms (Chamberlain).

Pro′tein, a group of complex nitrogenous
substances, as NUCLEIN, etc. ; adj.
pro′teinic ; ~ **Crys′tal** = CRYSTAL-
LOID ; ~ **Grain** = ALEURONE GRAIN ;
proteina′ceous (+ ACEOUS), pertaining to protein, or composed
of it.

Pro′teism (*Proteus*, a sea-god able to
assume various shapes), the faculty
of lower organisms of changing their
shape, as in Flagellates, Myxomycetes, etc. (Massart).

Pro′ten (Sachs) = PROTENCHYMA.

Protench′yma (πρῶτος, first ; ἔγχυμα,
an infusion), fundamental or ground
tissue ; **Protene′ma** = PROTONEMA,
the filamentous embryo in Mosses.

Pro′teo-bacte′ria (PROTEID + BAC-
TERIA), organisms capable of trans-
forming nitrogen compounds into
protein (Lipman) ; **Proteofica′tion**,
the process named ; **Proteohydrol′ysis**
(+ HYDROLYSIS), the decomposition
of proteids by hydrolysis ; adj.
proteohydrolyt′ic.

pro′teoïd (εἶδος, resemblance), applied
by Vesque to leaves provided with
sclerous cells, as in *Protea*.

Proteol′ysis (+ PROTEID, λύσις, a
loosing), the breaking up of proteids
by enzymes ; **proteolyt′ic** (λυτικὸς,
able to loose), decomposing proteids ;
~ **En′zyme**, an unorganized ferment
which is the active cause in breaking
up proteids ; **Pro′teose**, a soluble
albuminoid found in gluten ; **Pro′teo-
somes** (σῶμα, a body), granular pre-
cipitations in the cells caused by
the action of certain alkaloids, as
caffeine ; **Proteosynth′esis** (σύνθεσις,
composition), building up proteids.

proteran′drous (πρότερος, first ; ἀνὴρ,
ἀνδρὸς, a man), the anthers ripe before the pistils in the same flower ;
protandrous, one kind of dichogamy
(Delpino) ; **Proteran′dry**, the condition described ; **proteran′thous**,
-thus (ἄνθος, a flower), where flowering precedes leafing, hysteranthous ;
proterog′ynous, *-nus* (γυνὴ, a woman),

306

when the pistils are receptive before the anthers have ripe pollen (Delpino) ; **Proterog′yny**, the state described; **proteropet′alous** (πέταλον, a flower-leaf), the state of obdiplostemonous flowers, when the epipetalous whorl of stamens is the inner (Schumann) ; **proterosep′alous** (+ SEPALUM), as above, when the whorl in question is the outer ; **Pro′terotypes** (τύπος, a type), primary types ; all specimens which have served as the basis for descriptions and figures of organisms ; further divided into HOLOTYPE, COTYPE (or SYNTYPE), PARATYPE, LECTOTYPE, and CHIROTYPE.

Prothalla′tae (πρὸ, for ; θάλλος, a sprout), Haeckel's term for Mosses and vascular Cryptogams ; **Prothal′lial-cells**, in Cycads usually two, the second of which gives rise to the antheridial cell ; ~ **Tubes**, embryo sac tubes (Pearson) ; **prothal′liform** (*forma*, shape), resembling a prothallus ; **prothal′line, prothal′loid** (εἶδος, resemblance), pertaining to a prothallus, or resembling one ; **Prothal′lium**, pl. **Prothal′lia, Prothal′lus**, a thalloid oophyte or its homologue resulting from the germination of a spore, usually a flattened leafy expansion and bearing sexual organs ; **bul′bous** ~, a fleshy or tuberous form ; **expand′ed** ~, a filamentous or flattened form (Farmer and Digby); **Prothallogam′ia** (γάμος, marriage), Caruel's general term for the vascular Cryptogams ; **Prothal′logams**, vascular Cryptogams.

protis′toid (*Protista* = Protophyta + Protozoa, from πρώτιστος, the very first ; εἶδος, resemblance), in cell-division, not influenced by the cells forming part of a complex multicellular body (Hartog).

Pro′toblast (πρῶτος, first ; βλαστὸς, a bud), Baillon's term for the cell before the formation of a cell-wall, the naked mass of protoplasm ; **Protocaul′ome** (+ CAULOME), the first developed axis, frequently evanescent ; **Protochlor′ophyll** (+ CHLORO-

PHYLL), a pigment found in etiolated leaves with carotin and xanthophyll (Monteverde) ; **Protochlorophyl′line**, a product of reduction of the green principle of chlorophyll (Timiriazeff), *cf.* PROTOPHYLLINE ; **Protochro′mosome** (+ CHROMOSOME) in *Hygrocybe*, a variable number of chromatophile granulations which at the end of the prophase unite into two chromosomes (Maire).

protococ′coid (εἶδος, resemblance), resembling the algal genus *Protococcus*.

Protocollench′yma (πρῶτος, first. + COLLENCHYMA), the earliest formed elements of collenchyma ; **Pro′tocorm** (κορμὸς, a trunk), (1) the tuber of *Phylloglossum* and other Lycopods, the only branch which develops into next year's tuber ; (2) extended to cover the whole embryo before the primary differentiation is complete (Lyon), *cf.* METACORM ; adj. **protocor′mal** ; **Pro′toderm** (δέρμα, skin), the rudimentary dermal tissue derived from the primary meristem of the apical region ; **Protodoch′ae** (δοχὴ, reception), primary successions of plants (Clements) ; **Protoëp′iphyte** (+ EPIPHYTE), a plant which is primarily an epiphyte pure and simple ; *cf.* HEMIEPIPHYTE ; **Protogamophy′ta** (γάμος, marriage ; φυτὸν, a plant), a group of plants so named by C. MacMillan, without definition ; **Protog′amy**, when gametes combine without fusion of the nuclei (Dangeard) ; **Pro′togene** (γένος, descent). K. Pearson's term for the dominant or A element in inheritance ; *cf.* ALLOGENE ; **Protogen′esis** (γένεσις, a beginning), reproduction by budding ; **protogen′ic, protogenet′ic** (γένος, race, offspring), in development, structures formed when tissues begin to differentiate ; *cf.* HYPEROGENIC ; **Protogonid′ium** (+ GONIDIUM), the first generation of a succession of gonidia (A. Braun) ; **Pro′tograph** (γράφω, I write), the original figure of a species or variety

(Schuchert); **protog′ynous** (γυνὴ, a woman) = PROTEROGYNOUS; **Protog′yny** = PROTEROGYNY; **Protohad′rome** (+ HADROME) = PROTO-XYLEM; **Protohemicrypt′ophytes** (+ HEMICRYPTOPHYTES), plants whose aerial shoots have scales or undeveloped leaves at the base, and fully developed leaves towards the middle of the stem, as in *Veronica*, *Epilobium*, etc. (Raunkiaer); **Protolep′tome** (+ LEPTOME) = PROTO-PHLOEM; **Pro′tolog** (λόγος, a word), the original description of a genus, species, or variety (Schuchert); **Protol′ysis** (λύσις, a loosing), decomposition of chlorophyll with dissociation of CO_2 under the influence of light (Wager); **Protomer′istem** (+ MERISTEM), the meristem of the growing point forming the foundation of a member; **Protomyce′lium** (+ MYCELIUM), Eriksson's term for a plasmic mass formed between the cells of parasitic fungi as mycelial filaments or in the intercellular spaces; **Protone′ma** (νῆμα, a thread), the confervoid or plate-like growth in the Mosses on which the conspicuous plant is developed as a lateral or terminal shoot; adj. **protone′mal**, also **protone′matoid**; ~ **Em′bryo**, of *Cutleria multifida*, Grev., a form of embryo which reproduces the normal plant (Church); **Pro′toneme** = PROTONEMA; **Protophlo′ëm** (+ PHLOEM), the first-formed elements of bast in a vascular bundle; **Pro′tophyll**, *Protophyl′lum* (φύλλον, a leaf), a leaf borne by a PROTO-CORM; a cotyledon or primordial leaf, especially used of a Cryptogam; **Protophyl′line**, Timiriazeff's alternative name for PROTOCHLORO-PHYLLINE; **Pro′tophyt** (φυτόν, a plant), a plant of the sexual generation (Bower); **Pro′tophyte**, pl. *Protophy′ta*, the simplest plants, the lower unicellular Cryptogams; **Protophyti′a**, applied by Clements to initial stages of succession in plant growths; adj. **protophyt′ic**; **Protophytol′ogy** (λόγος, discourse) =

PALAEOBOTANY; **Pro′toplasm, Protoplas′ma** (πλάσμα, moulded), the viscous living substance in plants, into which all nourishment is taken, and from which all parts are formed; various modifications of it have special names; **Pro′toplast**, the unit of protoplasm capable of individual action, a cell either with or without a wall (Hanstein); **protoplas′tic**, used by Henfrey for PROTOPLASMIC; **Protoplas′tid**, an individual or presumable primitive type; **Protoplas′-tin**, Hanstein's term for a hypothetic substance, the ultimate source of vital movement and chemical combination; **Protopteridophy′ta** (+ PTERIDOPHYTA), a hypothetic primitive group of Pteridophytes, from which the known orders may be supposed to have been derived (Bower); **Protosclerench′yma** (+ SCLERENCHYMA), used for certain collenchyma which resemble true hard bast; the provisional collenchyma of Haberlandt; **protosiphonogam′ic** (+ SIPHONOGAMIC), used of the germination of pollen on the ligule or cone-scale in certain Gymnosperms, thence passing to the micropyle; **Pro′tospore** (σπορά, a seed), (1) a spore which develops a promycelium; (2) certain energids or uninucleate bodies in *Pilolobus*, etc., the ultimate product of cleavage (Harper); **Protospor′ophyte** (φυτόν, a plant) C. MacMillan's term for certain Cryptogams not otherwise defined; **Pro′tostele** (+ STELE), a simple and primitive form of stele; it has been applied to HAPLO- and ACTINO-STELES (Brebner); adj. **protoste′lic**; **Pro′tostrophes**, pl. (στροφή, a turning), secondary spirals in the development of leaves (Lindley); **Protothallog′amae**, pl. (+ THALLO-GAMAE), Ardissone's term to include Angiosperms, Gymnosperms, and vascular Cryptogams; **Protothal′lus** (θάλλος, a shoot) = HYPOTHALLUS, the first-formed stratum of a Lichen; **Pro′totroph** (τροφή, nourishment), a "lodger" in *Lecidia intumescens*,

Nyl., which eventually gets its nourishment by means of another lodger, a different Lichen (Minks); **prototroph'ic** (τροφὴ, food), requiring no organic compounds for nourishment (C. Jones); **Prototroph'ism**, or **Protot'rophy**, is the state itself; the peculiar commensalism also styled "Wet-nurse relationship"; also spelled **Pro'trophy**; **Pro'totype** (τύπος, a type), the assumed ancestral form, from which the descendants have become modified; adj. **prototyp'ic**; **Protoxy'lem** (+ XYLEM), the first-formed elements of wood in a vascular bundle; **protozooph'ilous** (ζῷον, an animal; φιλέω, I love), used of certain water-plants which are fertilized by small animals, or protozoa; **Protozy'gote** (+ ZYGOTE), K. Pearson's term for a homozygote possessing the dominant AA elements in inheritance; cf. ALLOZYGOTE; **Pro'trophy** = PROTOTROPHY; **protrop'ic** (πρὸ, in front of, + TROPIC), movement towards the exciting cause (Rothert).

protru'ding (protrudo, I thrust out), exserted.

protu'berans (Lat.), bulging out, *Protuberan'tia elonga'ta*, "the aciculae of certain Fuugals" (Lindley).

provect'us (Lat.), carried forward.

Prov'ince (*provincia*, a government), an area in which climate tends to dominance, as of woodland or moorland (Crampton).

provine' (Fr., provigner), to layer a vine.

prox'imal (*proximus*, next, nearest), the part nearest the axis, as opposed to DISTAL.

proxy'lar ‡ (πρὸ, ready for; ξύλον, wood), capable of forming wood; **Proxyle**, **Proxy'lem** = PROTOXYLEM; **Prozy'mogen** (+ ZYMOGEN), a material formed of the chromatin of the nucleus which is extruded into the cytoplasm, there becoming zymogen (Macullum).

Prui'na (Lat., hoar-frost) **semina'lis**, "the spores of certain Fungals" (Lindley); **pru'inate**, *pruina'tus*,

pru'inose, *pruino'sus*, **pru'inous**, having a waxy powdery secretion on the surface, a "bloom."

Pru'nase, an enzyme found in many species of *Prunus*; **Pru'nasin**, a glucoside associated with it.

prunif'erous (*prunum*, a plum; *fero*, I bear), bearing plums; **pru'niform**, *pruniform'is* (*forma*, shape), plum-shaped; **pruni'nus** (Mod. Lat., from *prunum*, a plum), plum-colour (Hayne); **Pru'nus** ‡ = DRUPE.

pru'rient, *pru'riens* (Lat., itching), causing an itching sensation.

Psam'athad (ψάμαθος, sea-sand, + AD), a strand formation (Clements); **Psamathi'um**, a strand formation; **psamathoph'ilus** (φιλέω, I love), strand - loving; **Psamathophy'ta** (φυτὸν, a plant), strand-plants (Clements).

Psamme'tum, an association of *Psamma arenaria* on sand dunes.

Psammogen'ity (ψάμμος, sand; γένος, offspring), amount of sand in the soil, as affecting the plants growing thereon; **psammog'enous**, producing a sandy soil (Clements); **Psam'mophile** (φιλέω, I love), a plant affecting light sandy soils (F. A. Lees); **psammoph'ilous** (φιλέω, I love), sand-loving, as the vegetation of dunes; **Psam'mophyte** (φυτὸν, a plant), a sand-plant, confined to sandy habitats, as dunes; **Psammophyti'a**, used by Clements for sand or sandstone plant formations.

Pseudacran'thic (ψευδής, false, + ACRANTHIC), applied to flowers from dichasial shoots which are apparently terminal (K. Schumann); **Pseudan'nual** (+ ANNUAL), an herbaceous plant which hibernates as a tuber or bulb (L. H. Bailey); **Pseudan'nulus** (+ ANNULUS), an apparent annulus of specialized cells, exterior to the peristome in Mosses; **pseudan'thic** (ἄνθος, a flower), a flower which simulates a simple flower, but is composed of more than a single axis, with subsidiary flowers (Delpino); **Pseudan'this**, the state in question; **Pseudapog'amy** (+ APOGAMY), the

309

fusion of gametophytic nuclei, morphologically but not sexually differentiated (Farmer and Digby); **faculta'-tive** ~, of occasional occurrence; **ob'ligate** ~, essential; **Pseudax'is** (+ Axis) = Sympodium; **Pseudem'-bryo** (+ Embryo), a group of cells cut off in the endosperm of *Balanophora* (Gates); **pseudhomonym'ic** (+ Homonym), used by F. N. Williams for a partial homonomy, as in *Gastrolychnis* and *Gastrosilene;* **Pseudin'ulin** (+ Inulin), a subordinate constituent of inulin (Tancret); **pseu'do-adven'tive** (+ Adventive) **Buds,** young branches of Lycopods which have been arrested at a very early stage (Bruchmann); **pseudo-autoi'cous** (+ Autoicous), a dioicous Moss when occasionally autoicous; **pseudobiator'ine,** falsely biatorine, having an apothecium without a conspicuous thalline margin; **Pseu'do-bulb** (+ Bulb), a thickened and bulb-like internode in Orchids; a corm; **Pseudo-bul'bil** (+ Bulbil), (1) a growth from the roots of *Acriopsis javanica,* Reinw., composed of two internodes, and bearing leaves at the apex; (2) a structure replacing a sporangium in apospory of certain Ferns; **pseu'do-calca'reous,** used by F. A. Lees for plants growing on clay-slate, etc.; **Pseudocamb'ium** (+ Cambium), Williamson's term for a meristematic tissue resembling cambium; **Pseudo-capillit'ium** (+ Capillitium), Lister's term for a structure in *Enteridium,* consisting of the perforated walls of the component sporangia; **Pseu'docarp,** *Pseudocar'pium, Pseudocar'pus* (καρπὸς, fruit), (1) a fruit with its accompanying parts, as a strawberry; (2) = Galbulus (J. S. Henslow); **Pseudocel'lulose** (+ Cellulose), see Cellulose; **Pseudocephalo'dium** (+ Cephalodium), a growth formed in the protothallus by a germinating hypha investing an algal colony of some other type than the normal gonidia of the Lichen (Forsell); **Pseudochro'-matin** (+ Chromatin) = Prochro-

matin; **Pseudochro'mosomes** (+ Chromosome), amalgamated filaments of chromatin, passing into the spireme stage and then segmenting into chromosomes (Berghs); **Pseudo-cil'ium** (*cilium,* an eyelash), a motionless whip-like body, proceeding in pairs from each cell of *Apiocystis Brauniana,* Naeg. (Correns); **Pseudocleistog'amy** (+ Cleistogamy), when flowers remain closed, but the genitalia are quite normal in size and function (Hansgirg); **Pseudocolumell'a** (+ Columella), in certain Myxomycetes, a mass of lime-knots confluent in the centre of the sporangium, resembling a columella but remaining free from the stalk; **Pseudocor'tex** (+ Cortex), in certain Algae a tissue of secondary branches appressed to the stem, or cells in the same position (Bennett and Murray); **pseudocos'tate,** *pseudo-costa'tus* (*costatus,* ribbed), false-ribbed, as where a marginal vein is formed by confluence of the true veins; **Pseudocotyle'don** (+ Cotyledon) = Proembryo; **Pseu'docysts,** pl. (κύστις, a bag), green protoplasmic bodies destitute of definite cellwall in Protococcoideae; **Pseudodys'-tropy** (δυσ- = bad; τροπὴ, a turning), when eutropous insects gain access to honey by secondary means, as when certain bees bore through to the nectaries, instead of entering by the opening of the flower (Loew); **Pseudoela'ters** (+ Elater), sterile cells in the spore-capsule of *Anthoceros,* which form a netted tissue and later break up into a more or less connected chain; **Pseudoëphe'mer** (+ Ephemer), a flower which lasts a little over a day expanded and then finally closes (Hansgirg); **Pseudo-ëpinas'ty** (+ Epinasty) = Geotropism; **Pseudoëp'iphyte** (+ Epiphyte), a plant whose stems die away at the base, and the upper part derives its nourishment from its own aërial roots, as Aroids (Went); **Pseu'do-fecunda'tion** (+ Fecundation), two nuclei of four combine to form the egg, the other two form the albumen (Guignard); **Pseudogam'etange** (+ GAMETANGE), certain swellings in Ascomycetes which give rise to gametophores (Dangeard); **Pseudog'amy** (γάμος, marriage), (1) parthenogenetic fruiting, as pollination without impregnation of ovules; (2) the fusion of two vegetative nuclei (Fraser and Chambers); (3) a pseudosexual copulation of two cells not specially differentiated for reproduction (Hartmann); **Pseu'do-gen'us** (+ GENUS), Lindsay's term for a FORM-GENUS; a condition, not an independent genus; **pseudogeog'enous** (γῆ, the earth; γεννάω, I bring forth), intermediate between dys- and eugeogenous rocks, such as Yoredale Limestones (F. A. Lees); **pseudogran'ular** (+ GRANULAR), a state resembling granulation, but not truly so; **pseudogyra'tus** (γυρὸς, curved), falsely ringed, as when the annulus is confined to the vertex of the sporangium in Ferns; **Pseudohaustor'ium** (+ HAUSTORIUM), an immature or rudimentary organ observed in seedlings of *Cuscuta* (Kinzel); **pseu'do-hermaph'rodite** (+ HERMAPHRODITE), Kerner's term for flowers which have become functionally unisexual by the suppression of either stamens or pistils; **Pseudohermaphrodi'tism** (*hermaphroditus*, having the characters of both sexes), the occurrence of spermatogenous filaments within the oogonium of *Nitella* (Ernst); **Pseudohybrida'tion** (*hybrida*, a mongrel), Millardet's term when the resultant hybrids are practically the same as either parent, showing no signs of crossing; **Pseudohyme'nium** (+ HYMENIUM), a covering of sporidia, resembling the hymenium of Fungi; **Pseudoimpregna'tion** (+ IMPREGNATION), the coalescence of the two nuclei of the cells of a teleutospore (Dangeard and Sapin-Trouffy); **Pseudola'tex** (+ LATEX), Heckel's term for an abundant gummy juice, white or colourless, in certain species of *Vanilla*;

Pseudoli'ber (+ LIBER), Guillaud's term for libriform tissue, derived from secondary meristem without genetic affinity with the cambium or vascular bundles; **Pseudoli'chen** (+ Lichen), a Lichen which does not possess an algal layer of its own, but is parasitic on another Lichenthallus; **Pseud'o-ma'qui**, a xerophytic evergreen bush-formation, capable of withstanding a severer winter than MAQUI; **Pseudomeio'sis** (+ MEIOSIS) = PSEUDO-REDUCTION; **Pseudomito'sis** (+ MITOSIS), nuclear division intermediate between mitosis and amitosis in the teleutospores of *Coleosporium Tussilaginis*; after the spireme the chromatin becomes granular and no chromosomes are formed (Blackman); **Pseudomix'is** (μῖξις, a mingling) = PSEUDAPOGAMY; adj. **pseudomic'tic**; **Pseudomonocotyle'don** (+ MONOCOTYLEDON), in Dicotyledons the early abortion of one of the cotyledons, as in *Capsella* (Pax); **pseudo-monocotyle'donous** (+ MONOCOTYLEDON), having two or more cotyledons consolidated into a single mass, as in the Horse-Chestnut; ~ **Em'bryo**, having one cotyledon only developed, although two were originally indicated; **Pseu'domorph** (μορφή, a form), an unusual or altered form, a term borrowed from mineralogy; **Pseudomorph'ism**, the condition of a PSEUDOMORPH; **pseudomorphy'tus** (φυτὸν, a plant), when a capitate inflorescence affects the form of a capitulum of Compositae; **Pseudonemathe'cium** (+ NEMATHECIUM), a thread-like body in certain Algae, which is now stated to be a parasitic Alga, *Actinococcus subcutaneus*, K. Rosenv. (Darbishire); **Pseudonod'ule** (+ NODULE), a space on a Diatom valve devoid of markings resembling a nodule, but not thickened; **Pseudonu'cleole** (+ NUCLEOLE), described by Rosen as a cyanophilous nucleole; **Pseudonucle'olus** (+ NUCLEOLUS), pl. **Pseudonucle'oli**, structures which form part of the chromatic network, and are used up in the formation of the chromosomes (Wager); **Pseudonu'cleus** (+ NUCLEUS), name given by Gates to a cavity containing chromatin masses surrounded by a definite membrane during the process of cytomixis; **Pseudoparaph'yses** pl. (+ PARAPHYSIS), organs growing in company with paraphyses but of much greater development (Traverso); **Pseudopar'asite** (+ PARASITE), a false parasite, either (a) a SAPROPHYTE, or (b) an EPIPHYTE; **Pseudoparench'yma** (+ PARENCHYMA), a tissue resembling parenchyma, but the cells not organically related; **pseudoparenchy'matous**, possessing symphyogenetic cellular tissue; **Pseudoper'ianth** (+ PERIANTH), the cup-shaped envelope of the archegonium which develops after fertilization in certain Hepaticae; **Pseudoperid'ium** (+ PERIDIUM), employed by Maire for the exterior of the sporophore in *Endophyllum;* the peridium of the aecidium of the Uredineae generally; adj. **pseudoperid'ial**; **Pseudoperithe'cium** (+ PERITHECIUM), a covering of sporidia resembling a perithecium; **Pseudophel'loid**, cork-like tissue in *Angiopteris* (Hannig); **pseudophotomet'ric** (+ PHOTOMETRIC), used of leaves which do not conform to the action of light, as in *Sedum* (Wiesner); **pseudophyllop'odous** (+ PHYLLOPODOUS), in *Hieracium* when the lower leaves of a normally aphyllopodous species are more or less appressed to the ground (Zahn); **Pseudoplank'ton** (+ PLANKTON), organisms accidentally found floating (Forel); **Pseudoplasmo'dium** (+ PLASMODIUM), myxamoebae aggregating into colonies, the first stage of fructification in Acrasieae (Olive); **Pseu'dopode** = PSEUDOPODIUM; **Pseudopleus'ton**(+ PLEUSTON), the pollen of Conifers floating in quantity (Schroeter); **pseudo'podal** (πούς, ποδὸς, a foot), resembling a pseudopodium (Archer); **Pseudopod'ium** (+ PODIUM), (1) a temporary changeable foot-like pro-

trusion of protoplasm in the plasmodium of Myxogastres; (2) the stalk-like extremity of the oophyte bearing a sporogonium or gemmae in Mosses, etc. ; **Pseudo-polyemb'ryony** (+ POLYEMBRYONY), the occurrence of either (a) coalescence of ovules, (b) division of the nucellus, or (c) development of several embryo-sacs in one nucellus (A. Ernst); **Pseud'opore** (+ PORE), in *Sphagnum* leaves, thickened rings without perforations (Russow); **Pseudopyre'nium** (+ PYRENIUM), the perithecium of "certain Fungals" (Lindley); **Pseudora'mulus** (+ RAMULUS), a spurious branch in certain species of *Nostoc*, a young filament adherent to an older one for part of its length; **Pseudora'phe** (+ RAPHE), an apparent raphe in Diatoms, a transitional form towards its entire disappearance; **Pseudoreduc'tion** (+ REDUCTION), (1) the period of tetrad formation in nuclear division (Rueckert); (2) an association in prophase of somatic chromosomes in pairs (Gregoire); **Pseu'dorhize** (ῥίζα, a root), (1) a root shaped like a turnip or carrot in bulbous Monocotyledons (Royer); (2) a root-like mycelial structure which develops at the base of a carpophore from its cells (Fayod); **Pseud'o-shrub**, produced by the growth of suckers after cutting back of *Ulmus*, etc. ; **Pseud'osperm**, *Pseudosper'mium* (σπέρμα, a seed), (1) any fruit which is indehiscent and resembles a seed, as the "nuts" or carpels of Labiatae; (2) C. MacMillan's term for plants possessing facultative seeds; e. g. *Selaginella; cf.* EUSPERM ; adj. **pseudosper'mic**, *pseudosper'micus*, **pseudosper'mous** ; **Pseudosporan'ge**, **Pseudosporan'gium** (+ SPORANGIUM), an organ producing gemmae or propagula, a simulated - sporangium (Davis); **Pseud'ospore** (σπορὰ, a seed), (1) a gemma or asexual vegetative bud; (2) Olive's term for MICROCYST, the resting stage of Acrasieae; **Pseudostau'ros** (+ STAUROS), a broadening of the stauros in some Diatoms; **Pseud'ostele** (+ STELE), when a petiole assumes the conditions of a stem, with similar arrangement of tissues (Tansley); adj. **pseudoste'lic**; **pseudoster'eus** ‡ (στερεὸς, solid), partly grown together, as the bud-scales of the crown-imperial; **Pseudostip'ules** (+ STIPULE), lowermost leaflets in *Crataegus, Cineraria*, etc., the true stipules being parts of the leaf-sheath (Worsdell); **Pseudostro'-ma** (+ STROMA), the perithecium of certain Fungi; **Pseudostroph'iole** (+ STROPHIOLE), Sernander's term for a part of the floral axis which remains attached to the nutlets in Labiatae; **pseudosynap'tic** (+ SYN-APSIS), shrunk together, as in synapsis of the nuclear filament in mitosis; **pseudoter'minal** (*terminalis*, pertaining to boundaries), intercalary inflorescence ceases and a false terminal flower appears (Parkin); **Pseudoty'pe** (τύπος, a type), an erroneous indication of a type (O. F. Cook); adj. **pseudotyp'ic**; **Pseudosyn'carp** (+ SYNCARP), a collective fruit; *cf.* SYNCARP; **Pseudothal'lus** ‡ (+ THALLUS), the axis of a crowded inflorescence as a Glomerule or Umbel; **Pseudotrich'ophore** (+ TRI-CHOPHORE), a vegetative filament of Algae, which simulates a trichophore; **pseu'do-unicel'lular** (+ UNI-CELLULAR), apocytial, as *Caulerpa*; **pseudovas'cular** (+ VASCULAR), apparently composed of vessels (Williamson); **Pseudo-vess'els**, the components of such tissue; **Pseudo-vivip'ary** (+ VIVIPARY), the production of leafy rooting shoots in the floral region, side by side with the flowers, as in *Juncus bufonius*, Linn. (Potonié); **pseu'do-xeroph'-ilous** (+ XEROPHILOUS), a subxerophilous condition, the plants exhibiting less sensitiveness to moisture (F. A. Lees); **Pseu'do-yeast** (+ YEAST), any yeast which does not produce fermentation; **Pseudozy'-gospore** (+ ZYGOSPORE) = AZYGO-SPORE.

psilo- (ψιλὸς), a Greek prefix, usually meaning slender, but more correctly used for bare or naked. **Psi'lad** (ψιλὸς, bare, + AD), a prairie plant (Clements); **Psili'um**, a prairie formation; **psiloc'ola** (*colo*, I inhabit), and **psiloph'ilus** (φιλέω, I love), inhabiting treeless prairies; **Psilophy'ta, Psi'lophytes** (φυτὸν, a plant), prairie plants (Clements); **psilostach'ys**, which is cited by A. Gray as bare-spiked, under the form *psilostach'yus*.

psilota'ceous, resembling *Psilotum*. **Psychoph'ilae** (*Psyche*, φιλέω, I love), plants which are fertilized by diurnal lepidoptera, possessing brightly coloured flowers, with honey in the flower tube.

psychro- (ψυχρὸς, cold), Drude's prefix for "frost."

Psychrocleistog'amy (ψυχρὸς, cold, + CLEISTOGAMY), cleistogamy induced by want of warmth (Hansgirg); **Psy'chrograph** (γράφω, I write), a psychrometer which records automatically; **Psychrokli'ny** (κλίνω, I incline), Voechting's term for the behaviour of growing parts under the influence of low temperatures; **Psychrom'eter** (μέτρον, a measure), an instrument for measuring humidity by the fall of temperature; **psychromet'ric**, applied by Pfeffer to the hygrometric movements of plants (Voechting); **Psy'chrophytes** (φυτὸν, a plant), alpine plants, on soil which hinders root-action by its low temperature.

psydomorphy'tus=PSEUDOMORPHYTUS. **Ptenophylli'um** ("πτηνόφυλλos [late Greek], with deciduous leaves"), a deciduous forest formation; **ptenophylloph'ilus** (φιλέω, I love), dwelling in deciduous forests; **Ptenophyllophy'ta** (φυτὸν, a plant), deciduous forest plants.

Ptenophyti'a (πτηνὸς, winged; φυτὸν, a plant), intermediate plant formation (Clements). **Ptenothali'um** ("πτηνοθαλὴs, deciduous"), a deciduous thicket formation; **ptenothaloph'ilus** (φιλέω, I love), dwelling in deciduous thickets; **Ptenothalophy′ta** (φυτὸν, a plant), deciduous thicket plants (Clements).

Pteram′pelid (πτέρις, a fern ; ἄμπελος, a vine), any climbing Fern (J. Smith).

ptera′tus (πτερὸν, a wing), winged ; Pterid′um, Pterid′es = SAMARA.

Pteridograph′ia (πτερὶς, πτερίδος, a fern ; γραφὴ, a writing), a treatise on Ferns, or the science of Ferns ; shortened by J. Smith to **Pterigraph′ia; Pterig′raphist,** and **Pterigraph′ilist** (φιλέω, I love), a writer on Ferns ; pter′idoid (εἶδος, resemblance), used by E. Newman for Fern-like, as ~ **Ac′rogens ; Pterido′ma**, the body or substance of a Fern ; **Pter′idophyte** (φυτὸν, a plant), a Fern, or closely allied plant ; **pteridophyt′ic,** Fern-like; **Pter′idosperm** (σπέρμα, a seed), MacMillan's term for plants with obligatory and pteridophytic seeds, and monomorphic embryos, as *Lepidostrobus;* adj. **pteridosperm′ic, pteridosperm′ous ; Pteridospermaphy′ta** (φυτὸν, a plant), pteridophytic seed-bearing plants (L. Ward).

pterig′ynus (πτερύγινος = πτέρινος, winged = PTERYGNUS).

pterocar′pous, *-pus* (πτερὸν, a wing ; καρπὸς, fruit), wing-fruited ; **pterocau′lous,** *-lis* (καυλὸς, a stem), wing-stemmed ; **Ptero′dium,** = SAMARA ; **pterogo′nus** (γωνία, an angle), **pter′oid,** *pteroi′dous* (εἶδος, resemblance), (1) having an elevation of surface assuming a wing-like appearance ; (2) J. Smith uses "pteroid" for Fern-like ; **pterop′odous** (ποῦς, ποδὸς, a foot), wing-footed, the petiole being marginally winged.

Pterop′sida (πτέρις, a fern ; ὄψις, sight), the group of Filicales, Gymnosperms, and Angiosperms, with ample leaves ; phyllosiphonic Vasculares (Jeffrey) ; adj. pterop′sid.

pterosper′mous *-mus* (πτερὸν, a wing ; σπέρμα, a seed), with the seeds winged; **Pter′ospores,** *-ae* (+SPORE), plants having winged seeds (Clements).

Pteryg′ium (πτερύγιον, a little wing), a wing.

pteryg′opous, *-pus* (πτέρυξ, a wing ; ποῦς, ποδὸς, a foot), having the peduncle winged ; **pterygosperm′ous** *-mus* (σπέρμα, a seed), = pterospermous.

pteryg′ynus (πτέρινος, winged), wing-seeded.

Pto′maïne (πτῶμα, calamity, corpse), used of any alkaloid due to the activity of pathogenous bacteria.

Pty′alin (πτύαλον, saliva), a ferment contained in saliva which transforms starch into a sugar capable of fermenting.

Pty′chode *Ptycho′des* (πτὺξ, πτυχὸς, a fold), the primordial utricle ; **Ptychoi′des** (εἶδος, resemblance), the outer surface of the same (Hartig).

Ptyx′is (πτύξις, a folding), vernation.

pu′bens (Lat., arrived at puberty) = pubescent ; **Pu′ber** (Lat.), maturity, as of flower or fruit; **pu′bera [Ae′tas]**, the period in a fruit succeeding the fertilization of the ovules ; **Pu′berty,** *Pu′bertas*, the transition from a young state to maturity of function ; **puber′ulus** (dim. of Lat. *puber*, downy, ripe), slightly hairy ; **Pu′bes** (Lat.), **Pubes′cence,** the hairiness of plants ; **pubes′cent,** *pubes′cens*, clothed with soft hair or down ; **pubig′erous** (*gero*, I bear), pubescent.

Puccin′ia, a genus of Uredineous Fungi ; for its divisions, see AUTOEU-, BRACHY-, EU-, HEMI-, HETEROEU-, LEPTO-, MICRO-, and OPSIS-, FORMS.

Puf′fing, the emission of spores in a cloud ; the equivalent of the German "Stäuben."

Puffs, Sir J. E. Smith's equivalent for PILIDIA in Lichens.

pugio′niform, *pugioniform′is* (*pugio*, a dagger; *forma*, shape), daggershaped.

Pull-root, a special form whose function is to contract, and so draw the plant deeper into the soil (Goebel).

pulla′tus (Lat.), clothed in black.

pulley-shaped, compressed and usually grooved in its circumference.

pul′lulate (*pullulo*, I bud), to bud,

314

as in spring; **Pullula'tion**, sprouting; especially characteristic of the yeast-plant.

pul'lus (Lat., dusky), black or nearly black.

pulp, *Pul'pa* (Lat., the flesh of fruit), the juicy or fleshy tissue of a fruit; **pul'pose**, *pulpo'sus*, pulpy.

Pulsa'tion (*pulsatio*, a beating), of vacuoles, the rhythmic increase and decrease of size in naked zoospores and plasmodia.

Pulsel'lum (*pulso*, I beat), a posterior flagellum of a zoospore (Lankester).

pulvera'ceous, *-ceus*, **pulver'eus** (Lat.), powdery; **pulvera'ceo-delites'cent** (*delitesco*, to lurk), covered with a layer of powdery granules; **pulver'-ulent**, *pulverulen'tus* (Lat., dusty), powdered, as if dusted over.

Pulvil'lum (Lat.), in botanic gardens, a hot-bed.

pul'vinate, *pulvina'tus* (Lat.), cushion-shaped; **pulvi'niform**, *pulvini-form'is*, having the shape of a cushion or pad; **pul'vinoid** (εἶδος, resemblance), cushion-shaped; **Pul'-vinoid**, a portion of a petiole, usually swollen, resembling a Pulvinus, but frequently non-mobile (Bose); **Pulvi'nulus**, pl. **Pulvi'nuli**, simple or branched excrescences on the surface of some Lichens, soredia; **Pulvi'nus** (Lat., a cushion), an enlargement close under the insertion of a leaf, the swollen base of the petiole, as in *Mimosa pudica*, Linn.

Pul'vis (Lat.), dust, powder, etc.

Pulvis'culus (Lat., small dust), "the powder contained in the spore-cases of some Fungi" (Henslow).

pu'milus (Lat., dwarfish), low or little.

Pump-form, applied to Papilionaceous flowers, with concealed anthers, as *Lotus*, *Coronilla*, and *Ononis*.

Pun'as, pl., Andine fell-fields, most of the plants having stout tap-roots (Warming).

Punc'ta, pl. of **Punc'tum** (Lat., a point), the marking on the valves of Diatoms; **punc'tate**, *puncta'tus* (Lat.), marked with dots, depressions or translucent glands;

puncta'ta Va'sa = dotted vessels; **punctiflor'us** (*flos, floris*, a flower), having dotted flowers; **punc'tiform** (*forma*, shape), in the form of a point or dot, reduced to a mere point; **punctic'ulate**, *puncticula'-tus*, **puncticulo'sus**, minutely punctate; **Punc'tum Vegetatio'nis**, the growing point.

pun'gent, *pun'gens* (Lat., piercing), ending in a rigid and sharp point, as in a holly-leaf.

punic'eous, *-ceus*, crimson.

pure, applied to forests, means unmixed, the growth being confined to one form; ~ **Cul'tures**, uncontaminated by admixture of any other form than that under observation; *e.g.* a race of yeast-plants obtained from a single individual; ~ **For'est**, restricted to a single form; ~ **Line**, the descendants from a single plant by self-fertilization.

pur'ple, a secondary tint, a mixture of red and blue in varying proportions.

purpurar'ius (Lat.), pertaining to purple; **purpuras'cens** (Lat.), becoming or turning purple; **pur-pura'tus** (Lat.), empurpled; **pur-purel'lus** (Lat.), purplish; **purpu'-reus** (Lat.), purple; **Pur'purine**, a colouring principle in madder, *Rubia tinctoria*, Linn.; **purpuri'nus** (Lat.), somewhat purplish.

purse-shaped, pouch-shaped.

pusil'lus, (Lat., petty), very small, or weak and slender.

pus'tular (*pustula*, a pimple), having slight elevations like blisters; **pus'tulate**, *pustula'tus*, as though blistered; **Pus'tule**, (1) a pimple or blister; (2) used by Sir J. E. Smith for Variola; **pus'tulose**, *pustulo'-sus* (Lat.), blistery or pimply.

Pu'sula (Lat., a bubble), the contractile vesicle in Peridiniae (Schütt).

Pusz'tas, pl., Hungarian steppes, closely resembling those of southern Russia (Warming).

Puta'men (Lat., shells, rind), (1) the shell of a nut; (2) the hardened endocarp of stone fruit; **putamina'-**

ceus ($+$ ACEOUS), having the texture of the stone of a drupe.

Pyc′nid, Pyc′nide, Pycnid′ium, pl. **Pycnid′ia** (πυκνὸς, dense), a cavity resembling a pyrenocarp in Lichens, etc., containing gonidia (pycnoconidia or stylospores) ; **Pycnid′iophore** (φορέω, I carry), a compound sporophore bearing pycnidia ; **Pycnid′iospore** (σπορά, a spore), a spore produced in a pycnidium ; **Pyc′nium**, a sorus of Uredineae in the initial stage (Arthur) ; adj. pyc′nial ; the spores are termed **Pyc′nospores** ; **pycnoceph′alous** (κεφαλή, a head), thick-headed, as when Composite flower-heads are clustered closely ; **Pycnoconid′ium** ($+$ CONIDIUM), a conidium produced in a pycnidium ; a stylospore ; **Pycnogonid′ium** ($+$ GONIDIUM) $=$ PYCNOCONIDIUM ; **Pycnophyti′a** (φυτὸν, a plant), "closed formations" (Clements) ; **Pyc′nospore** (σπορά, a seed), $=$ PYCNOCONIDIUM ; **pycnos′tachous** (στάχυς, a spike), in compact spikes.

Pycno′sis (πύκνωσις, condensation), used by Maire to express atrophy by becoming dense and thickened.

pygmae′us (Lat.), dwarf, pygmy.

Pyocy′anase, the enzyme of *Bacillus pyocyanus*.

pyogenet′ic (πῦον, pus ; γένεσις, beginning), pus-forming, the function of certain bacteria ; **pyogen′ic** $=$ PYO-GENETIC.

pyracan′thus (πῦρ, fire ; ἄκανθα, a thorn), with red or yellow spines.

pyram′idal, *pyramida′lis* (Lat.), pyramid-shaped.

Py′rene, *Pyre′na* (πυρὴν, kernel or stone), (1) a nucule or nutlet ; (2) a small stone of a drupe, or similar fruit ; **Pyrenar′ium**, a pear-fruit, pome-like, but tapering ; **Pyren-a′rius**, a drupaceous pome, as in *Crataegus* ; **Pyre′nin**, Schwarz's term for the constituent of the body of the nucleus ; *cf.* AMPHIPYRENIN ; **Pyre′nium**, an old name for the receptacle of Sphaeriaceous Fungi ; **Pyre′nocarp** (καρπὸς, fruit), (1) $=$

PERITHECIUM ; (2) $=$ DRUPE ; **pyrenocar′pic** ; **pyrenocar′pous**, relating to a pyrenocarp, or perithecium ; **pyreno′deous** (εἶδος, resemblance), like a pyrenoid, wart-like ; **pyreno′dine**, "globular and nuclear" (Leighton) ; **Py′renoid**, minute rounded granular colourless bodies, embedded in the chromatophores, amylum-centres (Schmitz) ; **Pyreno-li′chenes** ($+$ Lichen), Wainio's term for a series of Lichens analogous to **Pyrenomy′cetes**, that is, Fungi possessing perithecia.

pyrenopsid′ian, similar to the genus *Pyrenopsis*.

Pyrid′ion (*pyrus*, or *pirus*, a pear), used by Linnaeus for the pear-fruit, a tapering pome, ; **pyrif′erous** (*fero*, I bear), pear-shaped ; **py′riform** *pyriformis* (*forma*, shape), resem' bling a pear in shape.

Pyri′um (πῦρ, πυρὸς, fire), "a burn succession" (Clements) ; **pyroph′ilous** (φιλέω, I love), growing by preference on burnt earth.

Pyr′rhophyll (πυρρὸς, flame-coloured ; (φύλλον, a leaf), the colouring-matter contained in the Peridineae (Warming).

pyx′idate, *pyxida′tus* (Lat., box-like), furnished with a lid, as some capsules ; **Pyxid′ula** ‡ $=$ **Pyxid′ium**, Moench's term for the fruit of *Amaranthus*, a dehiscent capsule, sometimes used for the following : **Pyx′is**, (1) a capsule with circumscissile dehiscence, the upper portion acting as a lid ; (2) ‡ the theca of a Moss ; (3) "the same as Scyphus" (Lindley).

quadran′gular, *quadrangular′is*, (Lat.), four-cornered ; **quadran′gulus, quadrangula′tus**, (Lat.), having four angles, which are usually right angles.

Quad′rant (*quadrans*, a fourth part), the quarter of an oospore, which is so divided by the $\sim$ **Wall** ; **Quad′-rat**, a square marked out for study of the vegetation therein contained, usually one metre square $=$ 1·0936 of an English yard (Clements); **Chart** ~, with the position of each plant marked; **denu'ded** ~, the original plants cleared away; **ma'jor** ~, a square of four units, each side being two metres; **Per'quadrat,** one of sixteen metres; **per'manent** ~, intended for study from year to year; **quadricap'sular** (+ CAPSULA), having four capsules; **quadricotyle-do'neus** (+ COTYLEDON), apparently with four cotyledons, each normal cotyledon being divided to the base; **quadricru'ral,** *quadricru'ris* (*crus, cruris,* a leg), with four supports; **quadriden'tate,** (*dentatus,* toothed), having four teeth; **quadridigita'to-pinna'tus** (*digitus,* a finger), with four digitate divisions, each of which is pinnate; **quadridigita'tus,** divided into four divisions; **Quadriere'mus** (+ EREMUS) = COENOBIUM; **quad-rifar'ious,** *-rius* (Lat., fourfold), in four ranks, as leaves; **quad'rifid,** *quadrif'idus* (Lat.), four-cleft, to about the middle or below; **quad'-rifoil** (*folium,* a leaf) = **quadrifo'li-ate,** when the petiole bears four leaflets at the same point; **quadri-fo'liolate,** strictly, with four sub-ordinate leaflets, but sometimes used as an equivalent of quadrifoliate; **quadrifur'cate** (*furcatus,* forked), dividing into four branches; **quad-rigem'inate** (*geminus,* a twin), growing in fours; **quadrihila'tus** (+ HILUM), having four apertures, as in some pollen-grains; **quadriju'-gate,** *quadrijuga'tus,* **quadriju'gous,** *-gus* (*jugum,* a yoke), having four pairs of leaflets; **quadrilo'bate** (*lobus,* a lobe), with four lobes; **quadriloc'-ular** (*loculus,* a little space), having four cells, as some anthers; **quad'-rinate,** *quadrina'tus,* **quadri'nus,** with four leaflets at the end of a petiole, in a digitate arrangement; **quadrinu'cleate** (+ NUCLEUS), used of a cell with four nuclei, from the division of a binucleate cell; **quad-ripar'tite,** *quadriparti'tus,* (*partitus,* divided), four-cleft, nearly to the base; **quadriphyl'lous** (φύλλον, a

leaf) = quadrifoliate; **quadripo'lar** (*polus,* a pole), in nuclear division, when four daughter nuclei arise at the same time; **quadriv'alent** (*valeo,* to be effective), (1) applied to a cell which divides into four daughter cells; (2) ~ **Chro'mosomes,** having four chromosomes in one, theoreti-cally; *cf.* BIVALENT; **quad'rivalve, quadrivalv'ular** (*valva,* a door-leaf), four-valved.

quaquaver'sal (*quaqua,* wheresoever; *verso,* I turn round), directed or bending in every direction.

Quar'tospore (*quartus,* fourth; σπορà, a seed), C. MacMillan's term for a spore enclosing protective and more or less vegetative cells as in *Riccia;* **Quar'tine,** a fourth integument of some ovules, "in reality a mere layer of either the secundine or" nucellus (Lindley).

quasiradia'tus ‡ (*quasi,* as though; *radiatus,* spoked), slightly radiant, as where the florets of the ray in some Compositae are small and in-conspicuous.

Quas'sine, a bitter principle in quassia wood.

quater'nary, quater'nate, *quaterna'tus* (*quaternarius,* consisting of four), an arrangement in fours); **quater'-ni** (Lat., by fours), growing four together.

Querce'tum, an association of oaks, *Quercus;* ~ *Ro'buri* = consisting of *Q. Robur,* etc.; **Quer'cite,** a gluco-side derived from acorns, sweet like sugar, but not fermenting with yeast.

Quer'citrin, a glucoside in quercitron bark; its colouring matter, and a commercial dye-stuff.

Quetelet'-Gal'ton Curve. See NEWTO-NIAN CURVE.

quilled, normally ligulate florets which have become tubular.

qui'nary (*quini,* five each), in fives; **qui'nate,** *quina'tus,* growing to-gether in fives, as leaflets from the same point.

quincun'cial (*quincuncialis,* contain-ing five-twelfths), (1) arranged in a quincunx; (2) in aestivation partially imbricated of five parts, two being exterior, two interior, and the fifth having one margin exterior, the other interior, as in the calyx of the rose ; **Quin′cunx** (Lat., the fraction $\frac{5}{12}$), (1) an arrangement like the five on dice, four at the corners, and one in the centre ; (2) in five ranks, quinquefarious ; (3) "the disposition of objects so that the intervening spaces are all hexagons" (Crozier).

Quin′ia, Quinin′, or **Quinine′,** an alkaloid occurring in the bark of species of *Cinchona, Remija,* etc.

Quin′icine and **Quin′idine,** alkaloids from *Cinchona* bark.

Quinin′, see QUINIA.

quinquan′gular, *quinquangular′is* (*quinquangulus,* five-cornered), five-angled ; **quinquecap′sular** (+ CAP-SULA), with five capsules ; **quinquecos′tate** (*costatus,* ribbed), having five ribs ; **quinqueden′tate** (*dentatus,* toothed), with five teeth ; **quinquefar′ious,**-*rius* (*fariam,* suffix=rank), in five ranks ; **quin′quefid** (*fid,* the root of *findo,* I cleave), five-cleft ; **quinquefo′liate,** *quinquefolia′tus* (*quinquefolius,* five-leaved), with five leaves ; **quinquefo′liolate,** *quinque-foliola′tus,* with five leaflets ; **quinqueju′gate** (*jugum,* a yoke), in five pairs, as of leaflets ; **quinquelo′bate,** *quinqueloba′tus* (*lobus,* a lobe), five-lobed ; **quinqueloc′ular,** *quinque-locular′is* (*loculus,* a little space), five-celled ; **quinquener′ved,** *quin-quener′vis,* -*vius* (*nervus,* a nerve), the midrib dividing into five, that is, the main rib, and a pair on each side ; **quinquepar′tite,** *quinquepar-ti′tus* (*partitus,* divided), deeply divided into five parts ; **Quinquere′-mus** (+ EREMUS), a five-celled gyno-basic fruit, as *Gomphia ;* **quinque-val′vate, quin′quevalve,** *quinque-val′vis* (*valva,* a door-leaf), five-valved ; **quinquevein′ed,** "the same as quinquenerved" (Crozier).

Quin′tine, *Quinti′na* (*quintus,* the fifth), a supposed integument of an ovule, the fifth from the outside, "in reality the skin of the" nucellus (LINDLEY) ; **Quin′tospore** (σπορὰ, a seed), C. MacMillan's term for a spore which has attained sexual potentiality, as in vascular Crypto-gams and Phanerogams.

quin′tuple, quin′tupled (*quintuplex,* five-fold), multiplied by five ; ~ -nerved, quinquenerved ; ~ ribbed, quinquecostate ; when of five ribs the four lateral arise from about the base of the mid-rib ; **quintupli-ner′ved, quintuplivein′ed,** quinque-nerved, five-veined.

Rab′doid (ραβδος, a rod) = RHABDOID.

Race, (1) a variety of such fixity as to be reproduced from seed ; (2) used also in a loose sense for related individuals without regard to rank ; **Adap′tive** ~ or **Biolog′ical** ~, a RACE distinguished by its physiological characters, not by its morphology ; **Between′-** ~, consisting of (1) **Half-** ~, showing a small number of plants with racial characters, the majority being of the original specific type ; (2) **Mid-** ~, showing racial characters in about half the seedlings produced, or various combinations ; **Habit′ation** ~, or **Physiolog′ical** ~, those not differing morphologically, but showing great difference in vital function, as in parasitism.

Racema′tion (*racematio,* the gleaning of a vineyard), a cluster, as of grapes ; **Raceme′,** *Race′mus* (Lat., a bunch of grapes), an indeterminate or centripetal inflorescence with lengthened axis, and equally pedi-cellate flowers ; **racemif′erous** (*fero,* I bear), bearing racemes ; **racemi-flor′us** (*flos, floris,* a flower), flowers borne in a raceme ; **race′miform,** *racemiform′is* (*forma,* shape), in the form of a raceme ; **rac′emose,** *race-mo′sus,* rac′emous, having racemes, or raceme-like ; **race′mulose,** *race-mulo′sus,* a diminutive of the last, somewhat racemose ; **Rac′emule,** a small raceme.

rachemor′phus (Lindley) = RACHI-MORPHUS.

Rachil′la = RHACHILLA.

rachimor′phus (ῥάχις, the backbone; μορφή, shape), the small zigzag flowering axis of some grasses, as *Rottboellia;* preferably **rhachimor′-phous.**

Ra′chis = RHACHIS; **Ra′cheae,** used by J. Smith as the plural of Rachis; **ra′chiform** = RHACHIDIFORM; **Rachi′-tis,** in botany, a disease producing abortion in the flower or seed.

ra′dial, *radia′lis* (*radius*, the spoke of a wheel), (1) radiating, as from a centre; (2) belonging to the ray, as in the flowers of Composites; (3) = ACTINOMORPHIC; ~ **Bun′dle,** a bundle or stele which has strands of bast and wood in different radii, a frequent occurrence in roots; ~ **Plane,** any plane which passes through the axis of growth, and cuts the surface at right angles; ~ **Strand,** large cells forming with the hypodermal strand in the stem of Bryophytes, wedge-shaped masses of tissue (Tansley); ~ **Sym′metry,** cf. RADIOSYMMETRIC; **ra′dio-ac′tive,** applied to substances which give off emanations of radium; **Radiat′rop-ism,** the influence of radioactive minerals upon plants, **neg′ative** or **pos′itive,** inhibiting growth or favouring it; adj. **radiatrop′ic;** **ra′diant,** *rad′ians,* radiating as from a centre; ~ **Um′bel,** when flowers on the outside are conspicuously larger than those which form the rest of the umbel; **ra′diar,** a system of branching uniformly on all sides (Goebel); **ra′diate,** *radia′tus,* (1) spreading from or arranged round a common centre, as the circumference of a circle; (2) bearing rays, or ray-florets; ~ **-veined** = palmately veined; **ra′diating,** passing in a straight line from the centre; **radia′tiform,** *radiatiform′is* (*forma,* shape), when the ligulate florets of Compositae increase in length outwards; **radia′tim** (Lat.), in a radiate manner; **Radia′tion,** used in a special sense as the emanation of radio-active agents upon plants.

rad′ical, *radica′lis* (*radix, radicis,* a root), arising from the root, or its crown; **rad′icant,** *radi′cans* (Lat., striking root), rooting, usually applied to stems or leaves; **rad′i-cated,** having a root or roots (Crozier); **rad′icating,** rooting; **Radica′tion,** *Radica′tio,* the root-system of a plant, its disposition and branching; **radica′tus** (Lat.), possessing roots, especially a tap-root; **Rad′icel,** *Radicel′la,* = RADI-CULA; **Radicella′tio** (Lat.) = RADI-CATION; **radicic′olous,** *-la* (*colo,* I inhabit), (1) when the flower is seated immediately upon the crown of the root; (2) dwelling in the root as a parasite; **radicif′erous** (*fero,* I bear), root-bearing, or rooting, as prostrate stems; **radi-ciflor′ous,** *-rus* (*flos, floris,* a flower), flowering apparently from the root; **radic′iform** (*forma,* shape); **radi-ci′nus** (Lat.), of the nature or appearance of a root; **Rad′icle,** *Radi′cula,* the hypocotyledonary and primal internode, the rudimentary root of the embryo; **Radi′cula byssoi′dea,** the mycelium of Fungi; **rad′icose,** *radico′sus* (Lat., having many roots), having large or abundant roots; **radic′ular,** pertaining to the radicle; **radiculiform′is** (*forma,* shape), shaped like a radicle; **Radi-culo′da, radiculo′dium,** the apex of the radicle in grasses; **radic′ulose,** *radiculo′sus,* bearing rootlets.

Ra′diosperms (*radius,* spoke of a wheel; σπέρμα, a seed), certain fossil fruits, circular in transverse section (F. W. Oliver); *cf.* PLATYSPERMS, adj. **radio-sper′mic; radiosymmet′ric,** displaying symmetry from the centre, as opposed to a bilateral symmetral.

Ra′dius, pl. **Ra′dii** (Lat., a ray), (1) the ray of Compositae, the outermost florets when distinct in form from those composing the disk; (2) a partial umbel in Umbelliferae; (3) the structures known as medullary rays; ~ **medulla′ris** = MEDULLARY RAY.

Ra′dix, pl. **Radi′ces** (Lat., a root),

the root or descending axis, the developed radicle.

rad′ulan, akin to *Rubus Radula.*

Raf′fia, Raph′ia, or **Rof′fia,** the native Malagasy names for the fibre-like material obtained from the leaves of *Raphia pedunculata,* Beauv., and *R. vinifera,* Beauv.

Raf′finase (Fr. *raffiner,* to refine), an enzyme which decomposes **Raf′finose,** a sugar occurring in beet, and germinating cereals.

Rain For′est, due to sufficient precipitation, as **High** ∼, having over 72 inches rainfall annually; **Hot** ∼, equatorial evergreen forest-zones of the Amazon and Congo basins; **Trop′ical** ∼, corresponding to the last; **Subtrop′ical,** practically the same as **High** ∼ ; **Rain-leaves,** those which are adapted to shed the rain from their surfaces, and generally are acuminate, *cf.* DRIP-TIP.

ra′mal (*ramus,* a branch), belonging to branch; **Ramas′trum** ‡ (*-astrum,* a suffix = likeness), a secondary petiole or petiolules of compound leaves; **ra′meal,** *ramea′lis,* pertaining to a branch; **ramear′ius,** restricted to aërial roots, which arise from branches (J. S. Henslow).

Ramen′ta, pl. of **Ramen′tum** (Lat., scrapings, shavings, thin chaffy scales of the epidermis, as the scales of many Ferns; **Ra′ments** = RAMENTA ; **ramenta′ceous,** *-ceus* (+ ACEOUS), possessing ramenta, clothed with them.

ra′meous, *ra′meus* (Lat.), belonging to a branch.

Ramie′ (Fr.), the fibre of Rhea, *Boehmeria tenacissima,* Hook. et Arn.

ramif′erous, *-rus* (*ramus,* a branch ; *fero,* I bear), bearing branches, ramose; **Ramifica′tion,** *-tio* (*facio,* I make), the scheme of branching or separation into branches; **ramifica′tus** (Lat.), branched; **ramiflor′ous,** *-rus,* (*flos, floris,* a flower), flowering on the branches; **ra′miform,** *ramiform′is* (*forma,* shape), shaped like a branch; **Ra′miform** (+ FORM), an extreme modification

of GREGIFORM, usually of mono-phyletic origin (Kuntze); **ra′millary,** term employed by Massart for those buds of climbers which develop into short branches, fruit or leaves, *cf.* SARMENTARY ; **ramip′-arous** (*pario,* I bring forth), producing branches, ramose; **ra′mose,** *ramo′sus,* **ra′mous,** branching, having many branches; **ramosis′simus,** very much branched; **ram′ify,** to branch; **ram′ular,** pertaining to a branchlet; **Ra′mulet,** used by Grew for the vascular strands in the shell of a nut; **ram′uline,** applied to leaves on the branches of Mosses; **ra′mulose,** *ramulo′sus,* having many branchlets; **Ra′mulus** (Lat.), a branchlet; **Ramun′culus,** a twig, the ultimate division of a branch; **Ra′mus** (Lat.), a branch; **Ramus′-culum** (Lat.), *-lus,* (1) the same as ramulus, a branchlet; (2) ‡ "the mycelium of certain Fungals" (Lindley).

Rand, the latest formed layer of a starch-grain (Salter).

Range, the region over which a given form grows spontaneously.

Rank, a row, especially a vertical row.

ranuncula′ceous, (1) buttercup yellow (Hayne); (2) allied to the genus *Ranunculus* ; **Ranuncule′tum,** an association of *Ranunculus* ; **ranunc′u-loid,** resembling that genus.

rapa′ceus (*rapum,* a turnip), fusiform or turnip-shaped.

ra′phal (ῥαφή, a seam), relating to the RAPHE ; **Raph′e** (pr. raph′y), *Raph′a* (1) in a more or less ana-tropous ovule a cord or ridge of fibro-vascular tissue connecting the base of the nucellus with the placenta, the adherent funicle; it may occur on the side of the ovule turned to the axis (ventral), or on the external face of the ovule, that in dorsal ; (2) in Diatoms, the median line or rib of a valve, and may be heteropolar or isopolar (O. Mueller); (3) the suture between the carpels in Umbelliferae (Crozier).

Raph'ia = RAFFIA.

Raph'id, pl. **Raph'ides**, *Raph'ida*, or **Rhaph'ides** (ῥαφίς, ῥαφίδος, a needle), needle-shaped crystals in the cells of plants ; **raphid'ian**, pertaining to raphides ; ~ **Cell**, one which contains raphides ; **Raph'idines**, Radlkofer's term for free, needle-shaped cells, with partly lignified cellulose-walls, occurring amongst phloëm-islands in certain Acanthaceae ; **Raphidoplank'ton** (+ PLANKTON), floating organism of a needle- or spindle-shape (Forel) ; **raph'ioid** (εἶδος, resemblance) **Fi'bres**, Roulet and Chodat's term for RAPHIDINES.

rare-ripe, early ripe, precocious ; **rath-ripe** (Crozier) means the same.

Ra'roform (*rarus*, infrequent, + FORM), a new form having imperfect connections with its surroundings (Kuntze).

ra'rus (Lat., not close or thick), thinly placed, not congested.

Ratoon', a shoot from the root of a plant which has been cut down (Crozier).

Raumpar'asit (Germ.) = AULOPHYTE.

ra'ven-black, Lat. *pullus, coracinus*.

ra'vidus, ra'vus (Lat.), grey or tawny, applied to doubtful tints.

Ray, *Ra'dius*, (1) the marginal portion of a Composite flower, when distinct from the disk ; (2) a branch of an umbel, a partial umbel ; ~ **Flo'ret, Flow'er**, an outer floret, ligulate or tubular, of Compositae ; ~ **Paren-ch'yma**, thick-walled cells elongated radially ; ~ **Trach'eids,** pithed cells ; **medull'ary** ~, the primary rays in the tissue between the different bundles, passing radially outwards, the secondary rays are derived from the fascicular cambium, their extremities being the bast and the wood ; subsidiary are :—**agg'regate** ~, **com'pound** ~, **fo'liar** ~, **multi-se'riate** = SECONDARY ~ ; **unise'-riate** ~ = PRIMARY ~ ; **wood** ~ = MEDULLARY ~ ; **Rays, disten'ded**, lines of ray-tracheids, of peculiar shape ; **fusi'form** ~, are walled by a flattened epithelium, and further

surrounded by thin-walled paren-chyma arranged radially ; **unise'ri-ate** ~ or ray-parenchyma, the cells being vertical and singly placed over one another.

Reac'tion (*re* = back ; *actio*, a perform-ing), (1) term used to denote any alteration in organization or form consequent upon STIMULATION ; (2) the effect of the formation upon the habitat (Clements) ; ~ **Time**, the period needed for an organ to show response to stimulus (Macdougal).

Recapitula'tion (*recapitulo*, to go over the points again) **Hypoth'esis**, that every organism in its individual life-history recapitulates the various stages through which its ancestors have passed in the course of evolution.

Recaules'cence (*re*, back, + CAULES-CENT), the adnation of leaves on their stalks to the stem (C. Schimper).

Recep'tacle, *Recepta'culum* (Lat., a reservoir), (1) that part of the axis which bears one or more organs, the torus ; (2) in Fungi, variously applied, usually a hollow or cup-like body containing other bodies, as (*a*) Léveillé's term for a sporophore ; (*b*) = STROMA ; (*c*) an apothecium in Ascomycetes ; (*d*) a pycnidium ; (*e*) the inner portion of the sporo-phore supporting the gleba in Phal-loideae ; (*f*) a cup of the Lichen-thallus, which contains soredia ; (3) the placenta ; ~ **of a Flow'er**, the axile part of the blossom which supports the sepals, petals, stamens and pistils ; ~ **of In-flores'cence**, the rhachis or axis of the head, spike, or other dense cluster ; ~ **of Oil**, a cyst containing an oily secretion, as in the rind of an orange ; ~ **of Secre'tion**, any cavities of the interior containing special pro-ducts ; **Recepta'cula accidenta'lia**, indeterminate passages filled with secretion ; ~ **caeciform'ia**, ‡ the vittae of the fruit of Umbelliferae ; ~ **Suc'ci prop'rii** ; ~ **tubulo'sa**, ━ CINENCHYMA, of laticiferous vessels ;

~ **vesiculo′sa,** receptacles of oil; **receptac′ular,** *receptacular′is*, pertaining to the receptacle, or attached to the receptacle; ~ **Tube,** the calyx-tube.

recep′tive (N. Lat., *receptivus*), having the quality of receiving; ~ **Spot,** (1) the point in the oosphere of Ferns, etc., where the antherozoids enter; (2) that hyaline spot on a large planogamete where it will coalesce with a small (male) planogamete.

Recess′ = Sinus.

recip′rocal (*reciprocus*, going backward and forward), mutual; ~ **Autoph′agy**, sexuality in primitive forms of Algae; the gametes acting mutually (Dangeard); ~ **Hy′brids,** hybrids between the same parents, each being fertilized by the other.

rec′linate, *reclina′tus* (Lat., bent back), turned or bent downward; **re-cli′ned, recli′ning,** having its base on the ground, also one plant pressed on another.

reclu′sus (Lat., laid open), improperly used for *inclusus*.

recon′ditus (Lat., concealed), hidden, not readily seen.

Recrudes′cence (*recrudesco*, to open afresh), the production of a young shoot from a ripened infructescence.

rectiflo′rus (*rectus*, straight; *flos, floris*, a flower), where the axes of the florets are parallel to the main axis of the inflorescence, as in some Compositae; **Rectigrada′tion** (*gradatio*, a structure of steps), a qualitative change, the genesis of a new character (H. E. Osborn), *cf.* Allometron ; **rectiner′ved,** *rectiner′vis, -vius* (*nervus*, a nerve); **rec-tive′nius** (*vena*, a vein), straight-veined, parallel-veined, as in grasses; **Rectipetal′ity** (*peto*, I seek), Voechting's term to express the tendency of organs to grow in a straight line; **rectip′etive** (*peto*, I seek), applied to certain stimuli which continue a formative impulse; **rectise′rial** (*series*, a row), in straight ranks; **rec′tus,** in a right line, straight, not curved.

Recur′rence (*recurro*, I run back), the repetition of the same type in an influorescence (Guillard); **recur′rent** (*recurrens*, running back), in venation, when the veinlets return towards the main rib.

recur′vate, recur′ved, *recur′vus* (Lat., bent back), curved backward or downward.

recuti′tus (Lat., skinned), apparently bare of epidermis.

red, a general term for the most vivid of the primary colours, in Latin *ruber;* ~ **-brown,** *porphyreus,* according to Lindley; ~ **Mould,** due to species of *Fusisporium ;* ~ **Rust,** attacking the tea plant is *Cepha′eurus mycoidea*, P. Karst; ~ **Snow,** discolouration of snow by *Haematococcus nivalis,* Agardh, etc.

red′ivive (*redivivus*, renewed), of herbaceous perennials, the plant dying down each year, and growing the following year from an underground bed.

Redu′ced Ves′sels, a term used by Rothert for (*a*) replacement of bordered pits by simple pits, (*b*) an incomplete development of the thickening bands and their looser arrangement; ~ **Fertiliza′tion,** in the absence of spermatia (normal male cells) the female cell fuses with a vegetative or another female cell; ~ **Mem′bers,** those which having ceased to act normally, have retrograded, as the tubers of potatoes were originally shoots.

Reduc′tion (*reductio*, a leading back), (1) when the development of the mature organism falls short of its ancestry; (2) diminution, as of the number of chromosomes in nuclear division; ~ **Divis′ion** = Nuclear Reduction ; ~ **Se′ries,** changes brought about by arrest.

redu′plicate, *reduplica′tus* (Lat., doubled) = **redu′plicative,** *reduplicati′vus,* doubled back, a term of aestivation when the edges are valvate and reflexed; **Reduplica′-tion,** an increase of parts by the insertion of additions on the same plan, as of whorls, etc.

Reed-swamp, a formation of tall, usually monocotyledonous plants growing in standing water.

reflec′ted (*reflecto*, I bend back), reflexed.

Re′flex (*reflex′us*, bent back) **Cent′rum**, a term suggested by Czapek for a potential link between the organ of perception and that of response ; ~ **Move′ments**, a term employed by Massart for certain responses to stimuli, usually classed under RE-ACTION ; **reflexed′**, abruptly bent or turned downward or backward ; **Reflex′ion**, a teratological change in position.

Reflores′cence (*refloresco*, I blossom anew), flowering again, a second blossoming.

refract′ed, *refrac′tus* (Lat., broken), bent sharply from the base backward.

Reg, applied in Algeria to alluvial desert.

Regenera′tion (*regeneratio*, a reproduction), vegetative growth after a wound or amputation and the drying of the surface.

Regermina′tion (*regermino*, I sprout again), resumption of germination after it has been completely interrupted (L. H. Bailey).

Re′gion, the area occupied by given forms ; ~ **of Distribu′tion**, H. C. Watson's term for the British regions defined by him ; adj. **re′gional** ; ~ **Succes′sions**, cycles due to secular change (Cowles) ; **Re′gions, aust′ral** ~, southern parts of the globe ; **bor′eal** ~, northern portions ; **trop′-ical** ~, within the tropics.

Re′gma (ῥῆγμα, a fracture), a fruit with elastically opening segments or cocci, as in *Euphorbia*, a form of schizocarp ; **Re′gmacarp**, *Regma-car′pium* (καρπòς, fruit), a general name for a dry and dehiscent fruit.

Regres′sion (*regressio*, a retreat), Galton's term for REVERSION ; **regres′-sus** (Lat., gone back), (1) the same as REFLEXUS ; (2) the change from one organ into that which preceded it, as of petals into sepals ; **regres′sive**,

in hybrids, applied to those characters which become more or less dormant ; *cf.* DOMINANT.

reg′ular, *regula′ris* (Lat., according to rule), uniform or symmetrical in shape or structure ; of a flower, actinomorphic ; ~ **Pelo′ria**, peloria which have not produced their normal irregular parts ; **regulariflor′ous** (*flos, floris*, a flower), when a disk or head of Compositae contains only tubular florets ; **regulariform′is** (*forma*, shape), approximating regularity ; **Regular′ity**, symmetry ; **Regula′tion**, the ability to preserve the normal state and function in spite of unfavourable circumstances ; **Auto′- ~** or **Self- ~**, the inherent power of an organism to adjust itself.

Rejec′tion-nu′clei, pl., certain nuclei which do not become part of the functional oospheres, the nuclei of abortive oospheres (Hartog).

Rejuvenes′cence (*re*, back ; *juvenesco*, I grow young), the formation of a new cell from the protoplasm of a cell already existing ; **meta-gam′etal** ~, see METAGAMETAL REJUVENESCENCE.

Rel′ic (*relictus*, left) or **retrogress′ive**, applied to stable plant formations due to past climatic factors (Crampton) ; **Rel′ict**, a species properly belonging to an earlier type than that in which it is found (Clements).

Reliq′uiae (Lat., leavings) = INDUVIAE.

remote′, *remo′tus* (Lat., distant), scattered, not close together, the same as *rarus*.

renar′ius (*renes*, the kidneys), reniform.

renas′cent (*renascor*, I revive) = RE-DIVIVE.

Renew′al, the act of forming anew ; ~ **of Cells** = REJUVENESCENCE.

re′niform, *reniform′is* (*renes*, the kidneys ; *forma*, shape), kidney-shaped ; *reniform′i-corda′tus*, combined heart and kidney shape, as the leaves of *Asarum europaeum*, Linn.

Ren′net, veg′etable, an enzyme which curdles milk, found in the flowers of *Galium verum*, Linn., and other plants.

Reorienta′tion (+ ORIENTATION-), alteration of relative position of organs.

Repair′, making good, as ~ of **Waste**, restoring the spent material.

repand′, *repan′dus*, repan′dous (Lat., bent backwards), with slightly uneven margin, less so than "sinuous."

repar′ative (*reparo*, I repair) **Steles**, four bands corresponding to the four orthostichies of leaves, in *Psaronius* (Scott).

re′pent, *re′pens* (Lat., creeping), prostrate and rooting.

Repi′um [? Rhepi′um] (ῥέπω, I sink), succession of plants on soils which have subsided (Clements).

Repla′cement, a theory of fertilization which assumes that the female cell gets rid of certain elements which leaves it an imperfect cell until fusion with the male cell replaces them.

Reple′tum (*repletus*, filled), a fruit with the valves connected by threads, persistent after dehiscence, such as in Orchids, *Aristolochia*, and some Papaveraceae.

rep′licate, *replica′tus* (Lat., folded back), (1) doubled down, so that the upper part comes against the lower; (2) employed by writers on Asclepiads, in the sense of REDUPLICATE; rep′licative, *replicati′vus*=replicate.

Re′plum (Lat., door-case), (1) a frame-like placenta from which the valves fall away in dehiscence; (2) frequently used so as to include the septum of Cruciferae in the term.

Reproduc′tion, increase (*a*) asexually from one individual, (*b*) sexually from two individuals or organs; reproduc′tive, applied to parts which share in reproduction; ~ **Cells**, cells which have no power of further vegetative development, but by coalescence give rise to a product which forms the starting point of a new plant; ~ Or′gans, the parts especially concerned in the production of seeds, spores, and analogous bodies; in Phænogams, the stamens and pistils.

Reprogress′ion (*re*, back; *progressus*, advanced), when in an inflorescence, the primordial flower at the summit opens first, followed in succession from the bottom upwards (Guillard).

rep′tant, *rep′tans* (Lat., crawling), REPENT; creeping on the ground and rooting.

Repuls′ion (*repulsus*, a driving back), the opposite to COUPLING; a mutual avoidance by organisms or allelomorphs.

Res herba′ria, (Lat.), the science of plants; botany.

Reserve′ (*reservus*, laid up), a storage; ~ Cel′lulose, a special thickening in the cells of seeds, such as the date, which can be turned to account in germination as food material; ~ Mate′rial, the plastic products of metabolism, assimilated food material in a resting condition, as starch and other carbohydrates; ~ Pro′teid, nitrogenous substances stored in the plant, as proteids, amides, etc.; ~ Tra′cheids, tracheid-like cells from the parenchyma sheath, for the storage of water (Heinricher).

resil′ient (*resiliens*, springing back), springing or bending back, as some stamens.

Res′in (*resina*, resin), a term applied to a group of oxydised hydrocarbons, solidified or hardened turpentine, and insoluble in water; ~ Cell, a cell which secretes resin; ~ Ducts, canals which contain fluid resin; ~ Flux, an unnatural and abundant flow of resin caused by the attack of *Armillaria mellea*, Sacc. on Conifers; ~ Gland, a group of cells which form resin; ~ Glut = RESIN-FLUX; ~ Pas′sage; ~ Plates, found in conifers most frequently in contact with the medullary rays (Groom); ~ Tube, an intercellular passage containing resin, a resin-duct; resinif′erous, -*rus* (*fero*, I bear), secreting resin; Res′inocysts (κύστις, a bag), hemispheric structures in the cell-wall of the hairs of the stem and leaf of *Begonia* (Schoennett); **Resino′sis** = RESIN-FLUX.

Respira′tion (*respiratio*, breathing),
the gaseous interchange between
the plant and the air in which the
plant absorbs oxygen, and gives off
carbon dioxide ; **aero′bic** ~, carried
out by an enzyme in the presence of
oxygen ; **anaero′bic** ~, performed
by a catalytic enzyme in the absence
of free oxygen; **ferment′ative** ~,
due to enzyme action, possibly an
exaggerated anaerobic function
(Barnes) ; **Insula′tion** ~, the plant
gives off oxygen in the decomposition
of vegetable acids; **Inter′nal** ~,
gives off carbon dioxide, but does
not absorb free oxygen, as in yeast-
fermentation; **Nor′mal** ~, as defined;
Vincula′tion ~, oxygen is absorbed,
but no carbon dioxide is given off ;
it occurs in the early stages of germination of oily seeds (Detmer) ;
adj. **respi′ratory**, as ~ **Cav′ity**, ~
Cham′ber = STOMATIC CHAMBER ;
~ **Equiv′alent**, the percentage of
carbon which has re-appeared in a
given body as carbon dioxide (Water-
mann) ; *cf.* PLASTIC EQUIVALENT ;
Respirom′eter (μέτρον, a measure),
an instrument to measure gaseous
exchange in respiring material as
germinating seeds (Ganong).

Rest, induced in cold climates by low-
ness of temperature, in hot climates
by want of moisture ; **res′ting**, in a
dormant state; ~ **Cell**, an isolated
cell which has passed into a quiescent
state ; ~ **Nu′cleus**, a nucleus not in
the act of division ; ~ **Pe′riod**, the
time during which dormancy is
maintained, the involution period; ~
Spor′ange, in *Saprolegnia* occasionally formed on old mycelia, their
contents being zoospores ; ~ **Spo-
ran′gium**, dormant gonidia of such
Fungi as *Saprolegnia*, which ultimately give rise to swarmspores ; ~
Spore, a spore with a thick integument, needing time before germinating, usually passing the winter or
dry season in a dormant state ; ~
Stage, the resting period ; ~ **State**,
quiescence, as of winter spores, or
dormant bulbs ; ~ **Swarm-Cell,**

naked masses of protoplasm with
amoeboid motion, in Confervaceae.
res′tant (Crozier) ; **res′tans** (Lat.,
standing still), persistent.
restib′ilis (Lat., restored), perennial.
Resolu′tion (*resolutio*, an untying), the
division of a coenocyte into uninucleate cells (Hartog).
Resting′a, a Brazilian forest, forming
a transition from the littoral to the
xerophytic forests (Warming).
resu′pinate, *resupina′tus* (Lat., bent
back), upside down, or apparently
so, as when the hymenium of a
Fungus is uppermost.
Resurrec′tion Plants, those which
after being dried, when placed in
water assume their living position,
as *Anastatica* and *Selaginella lepi-
dophylla*, Spring.
Reta′ma Bushland, in the South of
Spain, may be regarded as allied to
shrub steppe : the name is Spanish
for *Genista* and similar shrubs.
Retarda′tion, the influence of light on
growth in certain structures.
Re′te (Lat., a net), network ; **retic′-
ulate**, *reticula′tus*, netted like network, as in certain cell-thickening ;
~ **veined**, netted veined ; **reticu-
la′ted Ves′sel**, one with netted
thickenings (Crozier) ; **Reticula′tion,**
network, the regular crossings of
threads ; **Retic′uloplasm** (+PLASMA)
= ALVEOLARPLASM ; **Retic′ulum**
(Lat., a little net), (1) a membrane
of cross-fibres found in Palms at the
base of the petiole ; (2) applied to
the network of linin in the nucleus ;
retif′erus ‡ (*fero*, I bear), **re′tiform**,
retiform′is (*forma*, shape), apparently netted.
retina′culate, possessing RETINACULA.
retinac′ulatus (Lat.), hooked ; **Re-
tina′culum** (Lat., a tether), (1) the
gland to which one or more pollinia
are attached in Orchids ; (2) in
Asclepiads, a horny elastic body to
which the pollen-masses are fixed,
the Corpusculum of Bentham, Pol-
len-carrier of N. E. Brown, Trans-
lator of the Germans ; (3) the funicle
in most Acanthaceae, which is curved

like a hook, and retains the seed till mature.

retiner′ved, *retiner′vis*, *retiner′vius* (*rete*, a net ; *nervus*, a nerve), net-veined.

Retort′ Cells, special enlarged cuticular cells with an apex more or less recurved in *Sphagnum*.

retrac′tus (Lat., drawn back), when cotyledons are so far prolonged at their base as completely to hide the radicle.

retrocur′ved, *retrocur′vus*, *retrocurva′tus* (*retro*, backward ; *curvus*, curved), recurved, bent back ; **retroflex′ed**, *retroflex′us* (Lat.), bent back, reflexed ; **retrofrac′ted**, *retrofrac′tus* (Lat.), refracted.

Retrogres′sion (*retrogressus*, a movement backward), reversion or development towards simpler organization ; **retrogres′sive**, (1) decadent in structure, (2) when a stable plant-formation is due to past climatic factors (Crampton) ; ~ **Metamorph′osis**, in teratology the occurrence of organs of lower grade in place of the normal structures, as pistils converted into stamens or petals ; ~ **Muta′tion**, when an active character becomes latent (De Vries) ; *cf.* REGRESSIVE.

retrorse′, *retror′sum* (Lat.), directed backward or downward ; **retror′sely acu′leate**, with prickles turned back or down, as in *Galium Aparine*, Linn.

retroser′rate (*retro*, backward ; *serratus*, sawed) = RUNCINATE ; **retrover′ted**, *retrover′sus*, inverted ; **Retrover′sio** (Lat.), an inversion.

Ret′ting, the steeping of flax or hemp in water to obtain the fibro-vascular portion freed from the cellular.

retuse′, *retu′sus* (Lat., blunted), with a shallow notch at a rounded apex.

revect′us (Lat.), carried back ; *cf.* SEPTUM.

reversed′, *rever′sus* (Lat., turned back), upside down, resupinate ; **Rever′sion**, *Rever′sio*, a change backward, as to an earlier condition ; ~ **Shoots**, exhibiting the young or larval form of foliage.

revolu′bilis (Lat.), capable of being rolled back ; **rev′olute**, *revolu′tus* (Lat.), rolled back from the margin or apex ; **revoluti′vus** (Lat.), in aestivation when the edges roll back spirally on each side, as in Rosemary.

Revol′ver Flow′ers, Kerner's term for those flowers "which exhibit within their outer portals a number of fine tubes resembling the barrels of a revolver."

revol′ving Nuta′tion (Sachs), = CIRCUMNUTATION.

Rhabarb′arin, a proximate principle of rhubarb ; **rhabarbari′nus**, rhubarb-coloured, the colour of the officinal root, orange brown.

rhabdocar′pous (ῥάβδος, a staff ; καρπὸς, fruit), long-fruited ; fruits shaped like a rod ; **Rhab′doid** (εἶδος resemblance), a rod-shaped body found in the cells of the tentacles of *Drosera*, and in the mesophyll cells of *Dionaea*, becoming more spherical on stimulation ; **Rhab′dolith** (λίθος, a stone), a detached portion of a **Rhab′dosphere** (σφαῖρα, a sphere), applied to certain pelagic Algae, *Rhabdosphaera tubifer* and *R. claviger*, G. Murr. and Blackm.

Rhab′dus ‡, the stipe of some Fungi (Lindley).

Rhache′ola (ῥάχις, a backbone), = **Rhachil′la**, a secondary axis in the inflorescence of grasses ; **Rha′chis**, *Rach′is*, the axis of an inflorescence or compound leaf or frond.

rhacimor′phous, see RACIMORPHOUS.

rhag′adiose (ῥαγάς, a chink), cracked or fissured.

rhamna′ceous, resembling or belonging to Rhamnaceae ; **Rham′nase**, an enzyme acting upon glucosides which occurs in the berries of *Rhamnus infectoria*, Linn. ; **Rham′nin**, the colouring matter of the same fruit.

Rhaph′e (ῥαφή, a seam), usually spelled RAPHE.

Rhaph′is, pl. **Rhaph′ides** (ῥαφίς, a needle), more usually occurring as RAPHIS and RAPHIDES.

Rhe′gma, = REGMA.

Rhe'ine, a proximate principle of the officinal rhubarb, *Rheum.*

rheotac'tic, adj. of **Rheotax'is** (τάξις, order), a synonym of RHEOTROPISM.

Rheot'ropism (ῥέω, I flow ; τροπὴ, a turning), the phenomena in a growing organism produced by the influence of a current of water (Jönsson) ; adj. **rheotrop'ic.**

Rhepi'um, *cf.* REPIUM.

rhexigenet'ic (ῥῆξις, a rending ; γένος, offspring), the origin of tissues when formed by mechanical rupture (De Bary) ; also written **rhexig'enous ; rhexolyt'ic** (λυτικὸς, able to loose), when gemmae are detached by the rupture of a cell and the disorganization of its contents (Correns).

Rhipid'ium (ῥιπὶς, ῥιπίδος, a fan), a fan-shaped cyme, the lateral branches being developed alternately in two opposite directions.

rhizamor'phoid, = RHIZOMORPHOUS.

rhizan'thous, *-thus* (ῥίζα, a root ; ἄνθος, a flower), root-flowered, flowering from the root or seeming to do so ; *cf.* RADICALIS : **Rhi'zanths,** plants so characterized, RHIZOGENS ; **rhizauto'icous,** in Mosses when the male inflorescence is on a short branch, cohering to the female by a rhizoid ; **Rhi'zel,** Van Tieghem's term for the "base" of the root, that is, the root apart from its radicles ; **Rhizid'ium,** term suggested for RHIZOID in the oophore condition (Bower) ; **Rhizi'na,** pl. **Rhizi'nae,** or **Rhiz'ines,** the root hairs of Mosses, etc., RHIZOIDS ; **Rhizinophyl'la** or **Rhizophyl'la,** pl. (φύλλον, a leaf), the postical bracts of Hepaticae, which bear the rhizoids (Spruce) ; **Rhizioph'ysis** ‡ (φύσις, a natural production), an expansion of the radicle, as in *Nelumbium ;* **Rhizo'bia** (βίος, life), the organisms which cause root-tubercles in Leguminosae ; **Rhizoblas'tus** ‡ (βλαστὸς, a bud), an embryo which emits roots ; **Rhi'zocarp** (καρπὸς, fruit), used of Marsileaceae, which produce sporangia on root-like processes ; **rhizocar'pous, rhizocar'pic,** *-picus,* (1) root-fruited, used

by De Candolle to denote a perennial herb ; (2) producing subterranean flowers and fruit, in addition to aërial, as *Cynometra cauliflora,* Linn., and *Anona rhizantha,* Eichl. (Huth) ; **Rhizocol'lesy** (κόλλησις, a gluing), the union of the axes of two individuals of the same species solely by the roots (Morren) ; **Rhi'zocorm** (+ CORM), J. Smith's term for the fleshy rhizomes of *Iris, Acorus,* etc. ; **Rhizocton'iose,** disease caused by the attack of *Rhizoctonia ;* **Rhizocton'ia** (κτόνος, murder), hyphae twisted into strands like twine which fasten on the roots of trees ; **Rhizoder'mis** (δέρμα, a skin), the outermost of the cortical layers (A. Meyer) ; **Rhi'zogen** (γένος, race, offspring), (1) a plant which produces a root and flower only, as *Rafflesia ;* (2) parasitic on the roots of other plants ; (3) any organ which gives rise to roots or rhizoids ; **rhizogenet'ic, rhizogen'ic,** producing roots ; **~ Cells, ~ Tis'sue,** the mother-cells of the peripheral layer of the central cylinder which frequently give rise to all the tissues of the rootlet ; **Rhizog'enum,** the dilated base of the frond in some Algae, from which proceed holdfasts (J. S. Henslow) ; **Rhi'zoid** (εἶδος, resemblance), a hair, frequently branched, serving as a root in Mosses and Hepaticae, not morphologically distinct from the protonema, the same as RHIZINE ; **rhi'zoid,** *rhizoid'eus,* root-like ; **rhizoi'dal Cell,** a small cell in the antheridium of *Isoëtes* (Belajeff) ; **rhizoma'tiform** (*forma,* shape), resembling a rhizome in shape ; **Rhi'zome.** *Rhizo'ma,* pl. *Rhizo'mata,* (1) the rootstock or dorsiventral stem, of root-like appearance, prostrate on or under ground, sending off rootlets, the apex progressively sending up stems or leaves ; (2) = CAUDEX (J. S. Henslow) ; (3) = RADICLE (Henslow) ; **~ Ge'ophytes,** perennial herbs with horizontal underground shoots, which give rise to leaves and flowers (Warming) ;

rhizomat'ic, -cus, rhizo'matose, having the character of a rhizome; rhizo'mic is used by Harvey for the same thing; Rhi'zomorph (μορφὴ, shape), a root-like branched strand of mycelial hyphae; rhizomor'phic, -phoid, -phous, (1) root-like; (2) resembling a rhizomorph; Rhizoph'agist (φαγεῖν, to eat), Boulger's term for a plant which is nourished by its own roots, an autophyte or rhizophyte; rhizoph'ilous (φιλέω, I love), growing attached to roots; Rhi'zophore (φορέω, I carry), a leafless branch in *Selaginella*, which eventually emits true roots.

Rhizophore'tum, an association of *Rhizophore*, such as the mangroves on the margin of salt-water lagoons.

rhizoph'orous (ρίζα, a root; φορέω, I bear), giving rise to roots; Rhi'zophyll (φύλλον, a leaf), Schuett's name for a compound pigment in Algae, consisting of Phycoerythrin and Floridean Green; Rhizophyll'aceae (φύλλον, a leaf, + *aceus*), a division of Ferns proposed by E. Newman for those in which the fronds are attached to the rhizome or root; rhizophylla'ceous, resembling such Ferns; rhizophyl'lous, when roots proceed from the leaves; Rhizoph'ysis = RHIZIOPHYSIS; Rhi'zophyte (φυτὸν, a plant), (1) = RHIZOPHAGIST; (2) Van Tieghem's term for Vasculares; Rhi'zoplast (πλαστὸς, moulded), (1) a chromatic thread which starts from the blepharoplast towards the interior of the cell (Dangeard); (2) the intermediate fibril of *Gymnodinium* (Pavillard); Rhizopod'ium ‡ (πούς, ποδὸς, a foot), the mycelium or "spawn" of Fungi; rhizop'odous, used in the sense of amoeboid; Rhizotax'is, Rhizotax'y (τάξις, order), the system of arrangement of the roots; Rhi'zula ‡, the protonema of Mosses, etc.

Rho'ad (ῥόος, a stream, + AD), "a creek plant" (Clements).

rhodel'lus (ῥόδον, a rose), rosy pink; rhodoch'rous (χρόα, colour), rose-coloured, pink.

Rhododendre'tum, an association of *Rhododendron*.

Rhod'ogen (ῥόδον, a rose; γένος, offspring), an easily oxidizable body in the beet (Reinke); rhodoleu'cus (λευκός, white), reddish-white; Rhodol'ogist (λογός, discourse), a student of Rhodol'ogy, that part of botany which treats of roses; Rhod'ophyll (φύλλον, a leaf), a name for the compound pigment of the Red Algae (Reinke), *cf.* RHIZOPHYLL; Rhodophy'ta (φυτὸν, a plant), the Red Algae (Wettstein); Rhodoplas'tid, the chromatophore of Rhodophyceae (Darbishire); Rhodosperm'in (σπέρμα, a seed), rose-coloured granules arising from the effects of reagents in cell-contents.

Rhoi'um, trisyll. (ῥόος, a stream), "a creek formation"; rhooph'ilus (φιλέω, I love), creek-dwelling; Rhoophy'ta (φυτὸν, a plant), creek plants (Clements).

rhom'beus, rhom'bic, *rhom'bicus* (ῥόμβος, a top), shaped like a rhomb, an equilateral oblique-angled figure; rhombifo'lius (*folium*, a leaf), rhomboidal-leafed; rhombiform'is (*forma*, shape), rhomb-shaped; rhom'boid,*rhomboi'deus*,rhomboi'dal, *rhomboida'lis* (εἶδος, resemblance), approaching a rhombic outline, quadrangular, with the lateral angles obtuse.

Rhoptom'eter (ῥοπτὸν, something absorbed), an instrument to measure absorption of water by the soil (Clements).

Rhya'cad (ῥύαξ, a mountain torrent, + AD), a torrent plant (Clements); Rhyaci'um, a torrent formation; rhyacoph'ilus (φιλέω, I love), torrent-loving; Rhyacophy'ta (φυτὸν, a plant), torrent plants (Clements).

Rhynchospore'tum, an association of *Rhynchospora*; rhynchos'porous (ῥύγχος, a beak; σπορὰ, a seed), when the fruit ends in a beak.

Rhysi'um, or Rhysi'on (ῥύσις, a flowing), a plant succession on volcanic soil (Clements).

Rhytido'ma (ῥυτίδωμα, a wrinkle), the

formation of plates of cellular tissue within the liber.

Rib, a primary vein, especially the central longitudinal or midrib ; **ribbed,** furnished with prominent ribs.

Ricino'lein, the glyceride of Ricinoleic Acid, present in the seeds of *Ricinus.*

Ric'tus (Lat., the opened mouth), the mouth or gorge of a bilabiate corolla.

Ridge, an elevated line on the fruit of Umbelliferae ; either primary or secondary.

rig'ens (Lat.), stiff, rigid ; **riges'cent,** *riges'cens,* having a stiff consistence.

right-hand'ed = DEXTRORSE ; *cf.* Appendix C.

rig'id, *rig'idus* (Lat.), stiff, inflexible ; **rigid'ulous,** somewhat rigid.

Ri'ma (Lat., a cleft), (1) a chink or cleft ; (2) the ostiole of certain Fungi (Lindley) ; **rima'tus,** ‡ (Mod. (Lat.), rimose ; **ri'miform** *(forma,* shape), shaped like a cleft ; **ri'mose,** *rimo-us,* **ri'mous,** with chinks or cracks, as old bark ; **rimulo'sus** ‡ (Mod. Lat.), a diminutive of RIMOSE.

Rims of Sanio, *cf.* SANIO'S RIMS.

Rind, (1) the outer bark of a tree, all the tissue outside the cambium ; (2) sometimes restricted to the tissues exterior to the active phloëm ; (3) the outer layer or cortex of Fungi ; (4) in Lichens the *Stra'tum cortica'le,* also styled **Rind-lay'er.**

Ring, see ANNULUS for the various senses in which it is used ; ~ **Bark,** the outer bark when disengaged in strips or layers (Hartig) ; ~ **Fascia'tion,** the apical division of a stem or flower by the formation of a central, circular, inversely-orientated set of tissues corresponding to the external normal set (Worsdell) ; ~ **Pores,** vessels in wood when arranged in the annual rings as seen in transverse section ; ~ **Scale,** disease caused by *Trametes Pini,* Fr. ; ~ **Type,** an appearance in nuclear division ; ~ **Wood,** the innermost

part of the wood (Solereder); **Ring'worm,** a disease of the skin due to *Trichophyton tonsurans,* Malmsten.

rin'gent, *rin'gens* (Lat., gaping), wide open, gaping, as the mouth of a labiate corolla ; **ringentiflo'rus** *(flos,* a flower), the receptacle of such Compositae as bear ringent florets (J. S. Henslow); **ringenti'-form'is** *(forma,* shape), apparently gaping.

ripa'rian, ripa'rious, *ripa'rius* (Lat., frequenting river-banks), growing by rivers or streams.

Ripe, mature, the completion of an organ or organism for its allotted function; **ri'pening,** maturing.

riva'lis (Lat., pertaining to a brook), growing by a brook-side.

ri'vose, *rivo'sus* (*Lat.* well-watered), having sinuate channels (Crozier).

rivularia'ceous, resembling the genus *Rivularia* ; **rivula'rioid** (εἶδος, resemblance), means the same.

rivula'ris (*rivulus,* a rill), growing by watercourses ; **riv'ulose,** (1) having small sinuate channels (Crozier); (2) marked with lines like a rivulet (Stevenson).

rizo'mic, an error for RHIZOMATIC.

robori'nus (Mod. Lat., from *robur, roboris,* oak), the grey colour of last year's oak twigs (Hayne).

Rod-fructifica'tion, special simple gonidiophores in Basidiomycetes ; **Rod'lets,** straight rigid bacteria.

Roff'ia = **Raffia.**

Rogue, a gardener's name for a plant which does not come true from seed ; a variation from the type.

Root, the descending axis, growing in the opposite direction from the stem, enodose, mostly developing underground, and absorbing moisture from the soil ; ~ **Bacil'lus,** a bacillus which has its station on roots, as the nitrifying bacteria ; ~ **Cap,** large cells which form a cap-like covering for the smaller cells in rear (growing point) ; ~ **Cli'mbers,** plants which clamber up tree trunks by their root-like holdfasts ; ~

329

Hairs, slender outgrowths from the cells of the piliferous layer of the newly formed portions of roots ; ~ **Knot,** a disease of cucumbers and tomatoes, due to eelworms ; ~ **Leaf,** a leaf springing from the base of the stem ; ~ **Parasit′ism,** when plants are partially parasitic and their roots penetrate others, as in *Rhinanthus* ; ~ **Poc′ket,** the false "Cap" in *Lemna* roots ; ~ **Pole,** the seat of new growth when the root is detached ; ~ **Pres′sure,** (1) the forcing of fluids into the xylem by osmotic force in the roots ; (2) see EXUDATION PRESSURE ; ~ **Rot,** diseases due to fungi ; **White** ~ ~, caused by *Rosellinia necatrix,* and **Black** ~ ~, by *Thielavia basicola* ; ~ **Sheath** = COLEORHIZA.

Root′stalk, the primary unbranched root in a young plant ; **Root′stock** = RHIZOME ; ~ **Tu′bercles,** the result of attack by Fungi or bacteria, a case of symbiosis, and source of nitrogenous nourishment to the host.

Root, adventit′ious, any not developed as a branch of the primary root, but from other members ; **aërial** ~, used of those which are developed above ground, as of epiphytes ; **pri′mary** ~, that developed at the opposite pole of the embryo to the shoot, the main descending axis.

root′ing, radicant.
Root′let, (1) a very slender root, or (2) the branch of a root ; (3) appendages of *Stigmaria* in quincuncial order on its surface ; **Root′stock,** a rhizome.
rope-shaped, funicular.
ror′idus (Lat., bedewed), dewy, covered with particles which resemble dew-drops.
rosa′cean, used by batologists to indicate an affinity or likeness to *Rubus rosaceus.*
rosa′ceous, *-ceus* (*rosa,* + ACEOUS), (1) arranged like the five petals of a normal rose ; (2) belonging to the order of which *Rosa* is the type ; (3) rose-colour, pink.

rosela′tus = (1) ROSULATUS, or (2) ROSACEOUS.
Rosel′la (dim. of *rosa*) = **Rosette′,** a cluster of leaves or other organs in a circular form, as *Plantago major,* Linn. ; ~ **Plants,** those with short internodes and closely-set leaves, usually epigeous and evergreen (Warming) ; ~ **Shoot,** a cluster of leaves on a branch from the same point ;—double ~, = DYASTER ; **Peach** ~, a disease attacking peach-trees, shown by short rosette-like growths in spring ; the **Umbili′cal** ~ of Diatoms is a central star-shaped projection or depression of a few larger cells, as in *Coscinodiscus.*
ros′eolus (Mod. Lat.), pink or pinkish.
Rose′tum (Lat.), a rose-garden.
ros′eus (Lat.), rosy, pale-red. pink.
Ro′sile, a "society" of *Rosa* (Clements).
Ros′in, crude RESIN ; **ros′inous** (Grew) = RESINOUS.
Ros′tel = ROSTELLUM.
rostell′ate, *rostella′tus* (*rostellum,* a little beak), the diminutive of rostrate, somewhat beaked ; **Rostel′lum,** (1) a small beak ; (2) applied by Linnaeus to the caudicle or radicle ; (3) a narrow extension of the upper edge of the stigma of certain Orchids, the abortive anterior lobe ; (4) the projecting free ends of perithecia in certain Fungi (Travers) ; **ros′trate,** *rostra′tus,* with a beak, narrowed into a slender tip or point ; **ros′triform** (*forma,* shape), beak-shaped ; **Ros′trum** (Lat., a beak), (1) any beak-like extension ; (2) the inner segment of the coronal lobes in Asclepiads.
Ros′ula (dim. of *rosa*), (1) a small rose ; (2) = ROSETTE ; a collection of clustered leaves, as the Houseleek ; **ros′ular,** *rosular′is,* **ros′ulate,** *rosula′tus,* collected into a rosette.
Rot, applied to various diseases of fungous or bacterial origin.
rota′ceus ‡ (*rota,* a wheel, + *aceus*) = **rotate′,** *rota′tus,* wheel-shaped,

330

circular and flat, applied to a
gamopetalous corolla with a short
tube ; **ro'tate-plane**, wheel-shaped
and flat, gamopetalous and without a tube; **Rota'tion**, *Rota'tio*,
the internal circulation of the
protoplasmic contents of a cell
cyclosis ; ~ **of Gyra'tion**, the
peculiar rotation in Characeae ;
~ **of Pro'toplasm**, the movement
round and within the cell ; **rota'to-
plane** = ROTATE-PLANE ; **ro'tiform**,
rotiform'is ‡ (*forma*, shape), wheel-
shaped, as of a gamopetalous
corolla with spreading limb and
a short tube.

rotund', *rotund'us* (Lat., round),
rounded in outline, somewhat
orbicular, but a little inclined
towards oblong ; **rotunda'tus** (Lat.),
rounded ; **rotundifo'lious**, *-lius*
(*folium*, a leaf), round-leaved.

rough, (1), scabrous ; (2) also of
surfaces covered with stiff coarse
hairs ; ~ **Leaves**, a gardener's name
for the first true leaves of a
seedling; **rough'ish**, scabrous.

Rube'do = RUBOR.

rubel'lus (Lat.), reddish.

rub'ens (Lat.), blush-red.

rub'eolus (N. Lat.), somewhat red,
ruddy.

rub'er (Lat., red), red in a general
sense ; **rubes'cent**, *rubes'cens*, turning red.

rubia'ceous, belonging to Rubiaceae.

rubic'olous (*rubus*, a bramble; *colo*, I
inhabit), parasitic on brambles, or
attached to them ; J. S. Henslow
spells it *rubic'olus*.

rubicun'dus (Lat., red, ruddy), blush-
red.

rub'idus (Lat.), reddish; **rubid'eus**
(Mod. Lat.) means about the same.

rubig'inose, *rubigino'sus*, **rubig'inous**,
rubigin'eus (*robiga* or *rubigo*, rust),
rust-coloured, usually implying it
is due to glandular hairs.

Rubol'ogist (*Rubus*, a bramble ; λόγος,
a discourse), a mongrel term for
BATOLOGIST, a student of brambles.

Ru'bor, **Rube'do** (Lat.), redness of any
kind.

ru'deral, *rudera'lis* (from *rudus*, old
rubbish), growing in waste places,
or among rubbish ; ~ **Plants**, those
which are characteristic of rubbish
heaps, etc. ; **Ru'derals**, plants growing on rubbish heaps or waste lands
(Thornber).

Ru'diment (*rudimentum*, a first attempt), (1) an imperfectly developed
and functionally useless organ, a
vestige ; (2) has been suggested as
an equivalent of the German term
" Anlage "; *cf.* INCEPT, PRIM-
ORDIUM ; **rudimen'tal**, **rudimen'-
tary**, arrested in an early stage
of development ; ~ **Or'gans**, those
whose development has been
arrested at an early stage.

rufes'cent, *rufes'cens* (Lat.), becoming
reddish.

Ruf'fle, used by Withering for the
VOLVA of Fungi ; **ruf'fled**, with a
strongly waved margin (Crozier).

rufid'ulus (N. Lat.), somewhat red.

ru'fous, *ru'fus* (Lat.), reddish, of all
shades.

Ru'ga, pl. **Ru'gae** (Lat.), a wrinkle or
fold ; **ru'gate**, wrinkled.

rug'ged, scabrous (Crozier).

ru'gose, *rugo'sus*, **ru'gous**, covered
with, or thrown into wrinkles ;
ru'gulose, *rugulo'sus*, somewhat
wrinkled.

ru'minate, *rumina'tus* (Lat., chewed),
looking as though chewed, as the
albumen of the nutmeg ; ~ **En'dosperm**, mottled in appearance, due
to the infolding of a dark inner
layer of the seed-coat into the
lighter coloured endosperm ; **Rumina'tion**, the condition described.

run'cinate, *runcina'tus* (*runcina*, a
large saw), saw-toothed or sharply
incised, the teeth retrorse.

Run'dle, used by Withering for UMBEL;
and **Run'dlet**, for a partial or
secondary umbel.

Run'ner, (1) a stolon, an elongated
lateral shoot, rooting at intervals,
the intermediate part apt to perish,
and thus new individuals arise ; (2)
in Fungi, mycelial stolons, as in
Rhizopus ; ~ **-bulb**, a bulb formed by

a stolon, as distinct from one formed direct from the main axis; **run′ning**, repent, reptant.

rupes′tral (*rupes,* a rock), H. C. Watson's term for plants of walls and rocks; **rupes′trine** (Crozier), *rupes′tris,* growing among rocks, or as Lichens, on rocks; some write it *rupes′ter;* **Rupic′ola** (*colo,* I inhabit), a plant which dwells among rocks; adj. **rupic′olous.**

rup′tile, *rup′tilis* (*ruptus,* broken), dehiscing in an irregular manner; **ruptiner′vis, ruptiner′vius** (N. Lat.), when a straight-ribbed leaf has its ribs interrupted and swollen at intervals; **rup′turing,** bursting irregularly.

rura′lis (Lat., rustic), growing in peculiarly rural places, as the thatch of a cottage.

rus′ciform (*Ruscus, forma,* shape), with leaflets recalling the shape of the phyllodes of *Ruscus aculeatus,* Linn.

rus′sus (Lat.), red; russet, when meaning reddish-brown.

Rust, a fungous disease in cereals caused by *Puccinia graminis,* Pers.; it is also applied to other diseases of plants from similar attacks; **rusty,** rubiginose, ferruginous, the colour of iron rust.

ruta′ceous, having affinity with the Rutaceae.

ru′tilant, *rut′ilans, rut′ilus* (Lat., red, glowing), used for plants having glowing flowers: red, orange, yellow, or an admixture of these.

rytidocar′pus (ῥυτὶς, ῥυτίδος, a wrinkle; καρπὸς, fruit), when the surface of the fruit is covered with wrinkles.

Sabulic′ola (*sabulum,* sand; *colo,* I inhabit); a plant growing on sandy places; **sab′ulose,** *sabulo′sus,* grow-in .sandy places; J. S. Henslow prints the former word *sabuli′colus;* **sab′uline** (Crozier) is a synonym.

Sac (*saccus,* a bag), a pouch, as **Air ~,** an empty cavity in the pollen of *Pinus;*—**Em′bryo ~,** see EMBRYO SAC; **Tan′nin ~,** a cell secreting or

containing tannin; **Sacs, water,** peculiar bowl-shaped leaflike organs in Hepaticae (Warming); **sac′cal,** relating to a sac, as the EMBRYO SAC; **sac′cate,** *sac′catus,* bag-shaped; **Sac′-cospores,** *-ae* (+ SPORE), Clements's term for plants having fruit enveloped by a membrane.

sacchara′tus (*saccharum,* sugar), sugary, or yielding sugar, as the sap of some species of maple; **Saccharifica′tion,** the conversion of starch into sugar; **saccharif′erous** (*fero,* I bear), sugar-bearing; **sacchari′nus** (Lat.), sugary; **Sac′charose,** cane-sugar; **Saccharophyl′ly** (φύλλον, a leaf), the production of "Sugar" leaves, *cf.* AMYLOPHYLLY.

sac′ciform, *sacciform′is* (*saccus,* a bag; *forma,* shape), bag-shaped; **Sac′-culus** (Lat., a little bag), the peridium of Fungi; **Sac′cus,** sometimes applied to the coronet of *Stapelia,* etc.

Sac′cophytes (σάκκος, a sack; φυτὸν, a plant), Schuett's term for all plants which are not PLACOPHYTES.

Sacel′lus (Lat., a little bag), (1) a one-seeded indehiscent pericarp, inclosed within a hardened calyx, as the Marvel of Peru; (2) applied to such fruits as those of *Chenopodium,* which burst irregularly.

Sachs's Cur′vature, a curved growth of the root, due to a difference in the rate of growth of the two sides of the organ (Wiesner).

Sack = SAC.

sad′dle-shaped, applied to such valves of Diatoms as those of *Coscinodiscus.*

Saf′fron, the dried stigmas of *Crocus sativus,* Linn., which yield a yellow dye; **~ col′oured,** = *crocatus.*

sagit′tal (*sagitta,* an arrow), applied to a section; the median line in plane of division of bilateral symmetry; introduced into botany from zoology.

sag′ittate, *sagitta′tus,* enlarged at the base into two acute straight lobes, like the barbed head of an arrow; **sagit′tiform,** *sagittiform′is* (*forma,* shape), arrow-shaped.

Sa´go, granulated starch obtained from the pith of certain palms, especially from species of *Sagus*.

Sainī´-Valery´ Ap´ple, a monstrosity in which the petals are sepaloid, the stamens absent, and a double row of carpels present.

Sal´ep, the dried tubercles of some species of *Orchis*, also spelled **Sal´op**, **Saloop´**.

Salice´tum, (1) a collection of willows; (2) a volume so entitled devoted to the genus; (3) recently applied to a plant association of *Salix;* **Sal´icin**, a glucoside occurring in the bark of willows, species of *Salix;* **Salicol´- ogist**, (1) an expert or student of the genus *Salix;* or (2) of willow-barks only.

Salicorne´tum, Ganong's term for a plant association consisting of *Salicornia;* a salt marsh; **salicor´nioid** (εἶδος, resembling), akin to or resembling *Salicornia*.

Salicyl´ous Ac´id occurs in many flowers, especially of *Spiraea*, probably by oxidation of its corresponding alcohol, SALIGENIN.

sa´lient (*saliens*, springing forward), projecting forward.

Salig´enin, an aromatic substance formed by the decomposition of SALICIN, etc.

saline´, *sali´nus* (*sal, salis*, salt), (1) consisting or partaking of the qualities of salt; (2) growing in salt-marshes; ~ **Mat´ters**, chemical salts occurring in plants, the union of acids with bases.

Salitra´les, Argentine salt-steppes.

salmo´neus (*salmo*, a salmon); **salmonic´olor** (*color*, colour), salmon-coloured, pink with a dash of yellow.

Sal´op, Saloop´ = SALEP.

Salpigan´thy (σάλπιγξ, a trumpet; ἄνθος, a flower), the transformation of ligulate or disk-florets of Compositae into conspicuous tubular florets (Morren).

Salsole´tum, an association of *Salsola*.

salsu´ginous, *salsugino´sus* (*salsugo*, saltness), growing in places inundated by salt or brackish water, as saltings; **sal´sus** (Lat., salted), is used in the same sense.

Salt-bush´land, of the Mediterranean region consists of *Salicornia fruticosa*, with *Atriplex portulacoides* and *Statice;* **Salt- des´ert** in Persia, is destitute of a single plant or grass; ~ **-glands**, excreting salts in leaves; ~ **-steppe**, incompletely furnished with plants, which are usually grey with scales or hairs, or with wax (Warming); ~ **Swamp**, found in still maritime inlets, with *Phragmites* and *Scirpus* (Warming).

Salt´atory (*saltatorius*, pertaining to dancing) **Evolu´tion**, showing discontinuous advance with long strides.

Salt´ings, salt-marshes, the grass being overflowed at high-water, leaving numerous muddy channels.

sal´ver-form, ~ **shaped**, hypocrateri-morphous (A. Gray).

Sama´ra (or *Same´ra*, Lat., the fruit of the elm), an indehiscent winged fruit, as that of the sycamore; **samarid´eous, sam´aroid**, *samaroi´deus* (εἶδος, resemblance), used of a fruit resembling a samara.

Sam´bucene, a terpene derived from *Sambucus nigra*, Linn.

san´guine, *sanguin´eus* (Lat., blood-red), the colour of blood, crimson.

Sa´nio's Bars, rods stretching across from one tracheid to another in coniferous wood; ~ **Law**, the order of cell-division of the cambium, as set forth in Pringsheim, Jahrb. ix. 60; ~ **Rims**, markings on the radial walls of tracheids, especially the springwood of *Pinus* (Groom).

San´talin, a resinous substance from red sandal-wood, *Pterocarpus santalinus*, Linn. f., whence its name.

San´tonin, a bitter principle from wormwood, *Artemisia Santonicum*, Linn.

Sap (*sapa*, new wine boiled thick), the juice of a plant; the fluid contents of cells and young vessels consisting of water and salts absorbed by the roots and distributed through the tissues; ~ **Cav´ities**, vacuoles; ~ **col´our**, flower-tints due to coloration of the sap, and not to plastids (Wheeldale); ~ -part'icles, vesicular bodies present in cell-sap (Price); ~ Per'iderm, distinguished from ordinary periderm by its cell-wall and contents being in a living condition, serving as absorption tissue (Wiesner); ~ Pres'sure, the force exerted on passing upwards through the tissues; ~ Rot, *Poly-porus adustus* attacking the sap-wood of *Liquidambar*; ~ Ve'sicle, a vacuole surrounded by a thin skin of protoplasm; ~ Ves'sel, a duct or continuous vessel; ~ Wart'ing, ruptures and corky outgrowths in the bark of stems and branches when grown under glass; ~ Wood, the new wood in an exogenous tree, so long as it is pervious to the flow of water, the alburnum; the sap of oak is Grew's term for the alburnum of that tree; Sap'a = SAP; sap'less, dry, destitute of sap; Sap'ling, a young tree.

sap'id, *sap'idus* (Lat., savoury), having a pleasant taste.

sapona'ceous (*sapo*, soap, + ACEOUS), soapy, slippery to the touch; sapona'rius (N. Lat.), having scouring qualities like soap; Sap'onin, a soap-like principle from *Saponaria officinalis*, Linn., and other plants.

Sap'or (Lat., flavour), the taste which a plant offers.

sapota'ceous, relating to or resembling Sapotaceae.

Sapri'um (σαπρὸς, rotten), a saprophytic plant formation (Clements); Sapro'bia (βίος, life), a general term for organisms growing in polluted water; saprogen'ic, saprog'enous (γένος, offspring), growing on decaying substances.

saprolegnia'ceous, saproleg'nious, allied to or resembling *Saprolegnia*.

Sapromyioph'ilae (σαπρὸς, rotten; μυῖα, a fly; φιλέω, I love), plants which are fertilized by carrion- or dung-flies; the flowers are putrid-smelling; adj. sapromyioph'ilous; Sap'rophile, a plant growing on humus; sapro-ph'ilous (φιλέω, I love), humus-

loving; Sap'rophyte (φυτὸν, a plant), a plant which lives upon dead organic matter; adj. saprophy'tal, saprophyt'ic; Sap'rophytism, the state of subsisting on humus or similar material;—symbio'tic ~, a phanerogam which subsists by means of a mycorrhiza, or felting of hyphal tissue on the roots; Saproplank'ton (+ PLANKTON), foul-water plankton, such Flagellates as *Euglena*, etc.

Sarcob'asis (σάρξ, σαρκὸς, flesh; βάσις, base), a carcerule, used for gynobasis when very fleshy; Sarc'ocarp *Sarcocar'pium* (καρπὸς, fruit), (1) the succulent and fleshy part of a drupe; (2) a general name for a baccate fruit; Sar'cocaul (καυλὸς, a stem), a fleshy stemmed plant, as the Cacti and many Euphorbias (J. Smith).

Sar'code (σαρκώδης, flesh-like), Dujardin's term for protoplasm; Sar'-cody, the acquirement of a fleshy consistency (Wordsell).

Sar'coderm, *Sarcoder'ma, Sarcoder'mis* (σάρξ, flesh; δέρμα, skin), a fleshy layer in seed-coats between the exopleura and the endopleura; sarcoi'des (εἶδος, resemblance), having the appearance of flesh.

Sarcoll'in, a glucoside from sarcocolla gum, itself an exudation from *Astragalus fasciculifolia*, Borzi.

Sar'coma ‡, a fleshy disk.

Sar'cospores, *-ae* (+ SPORE), Clements's name for plants having fleshy fruits; Sarcotes'ta (+ TESTA), the fleshy outer seed coat, as of *Cycas* (F. W. Oliver); adv. sarcotes'tal.

Sar'ment, *Sarmen'tum* (Lat., twigs, brush-wood), a long slender runner, or stolon, as in the strawberry; sarmenta'ceous, *-ceus* (+ ACEOUS), sarmentif'erous, *-rus* (*fero*, I bear), sarmentose; sar'mentary, applied by Massart to the buds of climbing plants which develop into long slender branches and tendrils; Sarmentid'ium ‡, a group of cymes or spikes arranged centrifugally as those in the cyme itself (Lindley); sarmentit'ius, belonging to twigs

(Henslow) ; **sar′mentose**, *sarmento′-sus*, **sarmen′tous** (Lat., full of twigs), producing long and lithe runners ; **Sarmen′tum**, a runner, *cf.* SARMENT.

Sar′nian, H. C. Watson's term for plants confined to the Channel Islands ; *Sarnia* = Jersey.

sathroph′ilous (σαθρòς, decayed; φιλέω, I love), applied by Pound and Clements to those Fungi which feed on " offal " ; **Sathrophy′ta** (φυτòν, a plant), humus plants; **Sathrophyt′ia**, saprophytic formations (Clements).

Sat′iform (+ FORM), a NOVIFORM which is reproduced by seed (Kuntze).

sati′vus (Lat.), that which is sown or planted, as opposed to spontaneous or native.

satura′te-vi′rens (Lat.), green as grass ; a full deep green.

Satura′tion, Relative = RELATIVE SATURATION.

Sat′us (Lat., a sowing), arising from seed sown.

Saur′ochore (σαύρος, a lizard ; χώρεω, I spread abroad), a plant disseminated by lizards or snakes (Borzi) ; **Saurocho′ry** (χωρìs, asunder) is the condition ; **sauroph′ilous** (φιλέω, I love), the adj. of **Sauroph′ily**, used of fruits adapted for this mode of dispersion.

sau′sage-shaped, allantoid.

Sautel′lus (Fr. sautelle, a vine shoot), a bulbil, such as those of *Lilium tigrinum*, Ker ; misprinted by J. S. Henslow as "Santellus" with an erroneous derivation.

Savan′nah, xerophilous grassland containing isolated trees (Schimper).

saw-toothed, or **sawed**, serrate.

sax′atile (Crozier), *saxa′tilis* (Lat.), dwelling or growing among rocks ; **sax′icole, saxic′oline, saxic′olous** (*colo*, I inhabit), growing on rocks, as do many Lichens ; **Saxic′ola**, a dweller among rocks, printed by J. S. Henslow as "saxi′colus"; **saxif′ragous** (*frag*, the root of *frango*, I break), rock-breaking, as plants which grow in crevices seem to be ; **saxo′sus** (Lat.), stony.

Scab, a disease due to various Fungi,

causing roughness of the cortex ; in the potato it is ascribed to *Sorosporium scabies*, Fisch. de Waldh., in the United States attributed to *Oospora scabies*, Thaxter.

scab′er (Lat.), rough, scurvy ; **scab′rate**, *scabra′tus*, made rough or roughened ; **scab′rid**, *scab′ridus;* **scab′ridous** (Lat., rough), somewhat rough ; **scabrid′ulous** and **scabridius′culus**, slightly rough ; **Scabrit′ies** (Lat.), roughness of surface ; **scab′rous**, = SCABER, rough to the touch.

scalar′iform, *scalariform′is* (*scalaris*, pertaining to a ladder; *forma*, shape), having markings suggestive of a ladder ; ∼ **Conjuga′tion**, when the entire algal filament is concerned in the act of conjugation (A. W. Bennett); ∼ **Duct**, ∼ **Ves′sel**, a vessel having scalariform markings, as in many Ferns; ∼ **Mark′ing**, an elongated pit of a scalariform vessel (Crozier).

Scale, (1) any thin scarious body, usually a degenerate leaf, sometimes of epidermal origin ; (2) a trichome, if disc-like ; (3) sometimes used for GLUME ; ∼ **Bark**, outer bark which is thrown off in scale-like portions, as in the plane-tree ; ∼ **-formed**, shaped like a scale ; ∼ **-hairs** of Ferns, clothing the stipes, often resembling a leaf; ∼ **Leaves**, cataphyllary leaves, usually on underground shoots, but sometimes on the above-ground portions; ∼ **-trace**, the strand connecting scale with stem in Bryophytes; **Scales, intersem′inal**, the scales of a cone-like fruit which are between successive seeds or ovules.

scall′oped, crenate.

scalpel′liform, *scalpelliform′is* (*scalpellum*, a lancet ; *forma*, shape), shaped like the blade of a penknife ; often set vertically.

sca′ly, squamose, scarious ; ∼ **Bark**, that which is thrown off in patches, as in the plane-tree ; ∼ **Buds**, leaf-buds of a strong character, that is, well protected by scales ; ∼ **Bulb**, one having separate scales, as in lilies.

scan'dent, *scan'dens* (Lat., climbing), climbing, in whatever manner.

Scape, *sca'pus* (Lat., a stem, (1) a leafless floral axis or peduncle arising from the ground, as in *Cyclamen;* (2) the stipe of Fungi; Scapel'lus ‡, the neck or caulicle of a germinating embryo (Lindley); sca'peless, destitute of a scape.

Scaphid'ium (*scaphium*, a hollow vessel), the sporangium of Algae; Scaph'ium‡, the keel of a papilionaceous corolla; Scaph'obrya (βρύω, I sprout), a term applied to the Marattiaceae, an order of Ferns in which the frond rises from between two stipular appendages forming a socket.

scaph'oid (σκάφη, a boat; εἶδος, resemblance), boat-shaped; scaph'y- form (*forma*, shape), used by J. Smith for boat-shaped.

scapiflo'rous, *-rus* (*scapus*, a stem; *flos, floris*, a flower), having flowers borne on a scape; sca'piform, *scapiform'is* (*forma*, shape), resembling a scape, a stem wanting leaves; scapig'erous (*gero*, I bear), scape-bearing; sca'- poid (εἶδος, resemblance), scapiform (Crozier); sca'pose, *scapo'sus*, having scapes; Sca'pus (Lat.) = SCAPE.

Scar, a mark left on a stem by the separation of a leaf, or on a seed by its detachment, a cicatrix.

sca'riose, *scario'sus*, sca'rious (*scaria*, Late Lat., a thorny shrub), thin, dry and membranous, not green.

scar'let, vivid red, having some yellow in its composition, coccineus.

scarred, marked by scars.

scar'rose ‡, a variant spelling of squarrose.

scat'tered, without apparent order.

Schimp'er-Braun, *cf.* FIBONACCI series.

schista'ceous, *-ceus* (*schistos*, a stone easily split, *e. g.*, slate, + *aceus*), slate-coloured, a deep-toned grey; schis'tose, *schisto'sus*, slaty, as to tint.

Schistog'amae (σχιστός, cleft; γάμος, a marriage), used by Ardissone to designate the Characeae; Schist'o- gams, *Schistogam'ia*, Caruel's terms for the same.

Schizob'olites (σχίζω, I split; βολίς,

a missile), a product of catabolism, due to decomposition of a body of definite composition (Beyerinck); Schi'zocarp (καρπὸς, fruit), a pericarp which splits into one-seeded portions, mericarps or "split-fruits"; Schizo- cot'yly (κοτύλη, a small vessel), division of a cotyledon, either by forking or complete separation into two (Worsdell); schizogenet'ic (γένος, offspring), formed by splitting; ~ intercel'lular Spaces are formed by the separation of tissue elements owing to the splitting of the common wall of the cells; schizo- gen'ic Devel'opment, development arising from division; schizog'enous = schizogenetic; schizo-lysig'enous (λύσις, a loosing), arising from splitting or tearing of the tissues, applied by Tschirch to those cavities which arise at first from splitting of the cell-wall, but are enlarged by the breaking down of surrounding tissues; schizo- lyt'ic (λυτικὸς, able to loose), applied to those gemmae which are detached by splitting through the middle-lamellae of the cells (Correns); schi- zog'onous = schizo-ögonous; schizo- m'erous (μερὸς, a part), splitting into portions; Schizomyce'tes (μύκης, a fungus), Naegeli's term for bacteria (Cohn); Schizont' (ὄν, ὄντος, being), employed when nuclei divide or split in a distinctive manner; schizo- ö'genous (γόνος, race), Correns's term for the same phenomenon as that called ISOGONOUS by De Vries; not breeding true; Schizophy'tae (φυτὸν, a plant) was also used by Cohn for SCHI- ZOMYCETES; Schi'zophytes, plants which increase by fission; Schizo- spor'eae (σπορὰ, a seed), a name proposed by Cohn for the Schizo- mycetes; Schizoste'ly (στήλη, a column), when the single primitive stele breaks up into as many distinct strands as there are vascular bundles; adj. schizoste'lous; schizotra'cheal, tracheae dividing.

Sci'ad (σκιά, shade, + AD), a sciophyte; Sc'ias, a shade form of any plant (Clements).

scimitar-shaped, acinaciform.

Sci′on, a young shoot, a twig used for grafting.

scioph′ilous (σκιὰ, shade; φιλέω, I love), shade-loving; **Sci′ophyll** (φύλλον, a leaf), the leaf of a shade plant ; **Sciophy′ta** (φυτὸν, a plant), plants of the shade ; **Sciophyti′a**, shade plant-formations (Clements).

Scirpe′tum, Warming's term for an association of *Scirpus* plants.

scis′sile (*scis′silis*, easily split), separating.

Scis′sion (*scissio*, a cleaving) **Lay′er** = ABSCISS - LAYER ; **scissip′arous** (*pario*, I bring forth), used for FISSIPAROUS, as bacteria.

scitamin′eous, referring to the Scitamineae.

sci′uroid, *sciuroi′des*, *sciuroi′deus* (σκίουρος, a squirrel ; εἶδος, resemblance), curved and bushy, like a squirrel's tail.

Scleran′thium (σκληρὸς, hard ; ἄνθος, a flower), an achene enclosed in an indurated portion of the calyx-tube, as in *Mirabilis ;* **Sclerench′-yma** (ἔγχυμα, an infusion), (1) formerly applied to stone-cells, SCLEREIDS ; (2) afterwards proposed for bast or liber cells, which are immensely thickened, with their protoplasm usually lost : ~ **Cells**, all thick-walled cells which retain their protoplasm (Tschirch); adj. **sclerenchy′matous;** as ~ **Tis′sue**, composed of thick-walled cells ; **Scle′reid**, a sclerotic or stone-cell, a strongly thickened or lignified cell; it is sometimes spelled **Scle′-rid; scle′rified**, hardened; **scle′rised**, sclerosed ; **Scle′rites**, pl., large, thick-walled ideoblasts with the walls of their numerous arms thickly set with small crystals (Seward) ; **Scleriza′tion**, the process of becoming hardened ; **Scle′roblast** (βλαστὸς, a bud), a stone-cell, or sclereid ; **Sclerocau′ly** (καυλὸς, stem), the possession of dry hard stems, as in *Ephedra* (Schimper) ; **Sclerocypera′-ceae**, a division of that family characterized by sclerotic elements

in place of assimilatory mechanism (Plowman) ; **Scle′rogen** (γένος, offspring), the hard lignified deposits in such cells as those which compose the shell of the walnut, or grit-cells of the pear ; **Sclerogen′ia**, Berkeley's term for induration of parts amounting to a disease ; **Sclerogonid′ia**, pl. (+ GONIDIUM), loose, yellowish or colourless gonidia, of uncertain function ; **scle′roid**, *scleroi′dus* (εἶδος, resemblance), having a hard texture ; **Scleromyce′tes**, pl. (μύκης, a mushroom), an obsolete name for the Sphaeriaceae ; **sclerophyll′ous**, *sclerophyl′lus* (φύλλον, a leaf), having hard and stiff leaves ; **Sclerophyl′ly**, the condition itself; **Scle′rophytes**, pl. (φυτὸν, a plant), a shrub or bush having sclerophyllous leaves, usually evergreen and resistant to summer-drought; **sclerop′odous** (πούς, ποδὸς, a foot), when persistent peduncles become hard and horny ; **sclero′sed**, hardened, lignified ; **Sclero′sis**, the hardening of a tissue or cell-wall by lignification of a membrane or intercellular deposits; **Sclerotes′ta** (+ TESTA), the hard bony seed-coat, as the middle coat of *Cycas ;* **Sclerote′**, a proposed emendation of SCLERO-TIUM ; **sclero′tic**, hardened, stony in texture; ~ **Cells**, grit-cells or sclereids; ~ **Nests**, characteristic groups of dark-coloured tissue of uncertain origin seen in sections of *Lyginodendron ;* ~ **Parench′yma**, grit-cells or stone-cells in pears, etc. ; **Sclero′tiet**, A. S. Wilson's name for a small SCLEROTIUM ; small concretions of lime have been also so termed, in error ; **Sclerotin′iose**, a disease of lettuce caused by *Sclerotinia Libertiana ;* **sclero′tioid, sclero′toid** (εἶδος, resemblance), like a sclerotium ; **Sclero′tium**, pl. **Sclero′-tia**, (1) a compact mass of hyphae in a dormant state, occurring in several groups of Fungi ; (2) also applied by some to the resting stage of the plasmodium of the Myxogastres.

scobic′ular (*scobis*, sawdust) = SCOBI

FORM (Crozier); **scobicula′tus**, in
fine grains like sawdust ; **scob′iform**;
scobiform′is (*forma*, shape), having
the appearance of sawdust.

Scobi′na (Lat., a rasp), the zigzag
rhachis of the spikelet in some
grasses ; **scobi′nate**, *scobina′tus*,
when the surface feels rough as
though rasped.

εcole′cite (σκώληξ, a worm), Tulasne's
term for the vermiform archicarp
of *Ascobolus pulcherrimus*, the
" Vermiform Body" of Woronin ;
Scolecospo′rae (+ SPORA), spores
having a long, worm-like shape
(Traverso).

scor′pioid, scorpioi′dal, *scorpioi′des,*
scorpioida′lis (σκορπίων, a scorpion ;
εἶδος, resemblance), when the main
axis (pseudaxis) of inflorescence is
coiled like the tail of a scorpion,
more strictly with flowers two-
ranked, these being alternately
thrown to opposite sides ; ~ **Cyme,**
or CINCINNUS, the lateral branches
developed on opposite sides alternately as in Boragineae ; in some
English text-books erroneously given
as " helicoid " ; ~ **Dichot′omy,** when
alternate branches develop dicho-
tomously ; ~ **unip′arous Cyme.** a
cymose branching when the right
and left forks are alternately the
larger.

Scoticaplank′ton, floating masses of
Ceratium.

scotoph′ilus (σκότος, darkness ; φιλέω,
I love), dwelling in darkness ;
Scotophy′ta (φυτὸν, a plant), " darkness plants"; **Scotophyti′a,** darkness plant formations (Clements).

Scotot′ropism = SKOTOTROPISM.

Scot′tish Type of Distribution, used
by H. C. Watson for those plants
in Great Britain whose headquarters are in Scotland.

Screw-lines, spirals in phyllotaxis
(Solms-Laubach).

Scri′nium (Lat., a case), Necker's term
for the fruit of Myrtaceae, as of
Lecythis ; adj. **scrina′ceus.**

scrobic′ulate, *scrobicula′tus* (*scrobi-
culus,* a little trench), marked by

minute or shallow depressions,
pitted ; **Scrobicula′tion,** employed
by algologists for the minute depressed markings in Desmidiae ;
scrobiculo′sus, pitted or punctiform.

Scroll-gall, Kerner's term for malformations caused by insects on
leaves, which curl up on the side
attacked.

scro′tiform, *scrotiform′is* (*scrotum,* a
pouch ; *forma,* shape), pouch-shaped ;
Scro′tum, the pouch or volva of
some Fungi.

Scrub, stunted growth, due to want of
water, with strong transpiration.

Scurf, small bran-like scales on the
epidermis ; **Scur′finess,** the appearance produced by membranous
scales ; **scurf′y,** lepidote, scaly.

scu′tate, *scuta′tus* (*scutum,* an oblong
shield), buckler-shaped ; *scuta′ti Pi′li*
= scales.

Scu′tel (*scutella,* a salver) = SCUTEL-
LUM ; **scutella′ris, scu′tellate,** *scutel-
la′tus,* shaped like a small platter ;
scutel′liform *scutelliform′is* (*forma,*
shape), patelliform, but oval and
round (Lindley) ; platter-shaped (A.
Gray) ; **Scutel′lum,** pl. **Scutel′la,**
(1) a second and anterior cotyledon in grasses, as in wheat
(Scribner) ; (2) the conical cap
of the endosperm in Cycadeae ;
(3) in Lichens, such an apothecium
as in *Parmelia,* with an elevated
rim derived from the thallus.

scu′tiform, *scutiform′is* (*scutum,* a
shield ; *forma,* shape), buckler-
shaped ; ~ **Leaf,** the first formed
leaf in *Salvinia,* the protophyll
which differs in shape from those
which succeed it.

Scu′tum (Lat., a shield), (1) used by
Jacquin to denote the outer corona
in *Duvalia,* Haw. ; (2) the broad
dilated apex of the style in Asclepiads.

scym′itar-shaped (A. Gray) = SCIMI-
TAR-SHAPED.

Scyph′a or **Scyph′us** (σκύφος, a cup or
goblet), (1) a cup-like dilatation of
the podetium in Lichens, having
shields on its edge ; **Scy′phi,** pl.

"open cups" (Leighton) ; (2) ‡ the corona of *Narcissus* (Lindley) ; **scyph'iform** (*forma*, shape), cup-like ; **scyphiph'orous** (φορέω, I carry), bearing cups ; **Scyphog'eny** (γεννάω, I produce), Morren's term for the production of ascidia ; **scyph'ose**, possessing scyphi ; **Scyph'ulus**, the colesule or VAGINULE of Hepaticae.

Scy'tinum (σκύτινος, leathern), used by Necker to denote an indehiscent pulpy pod, as of the Tamarind.

scytone'matous, allied to the genus *Scytonema* (Archer) ; **Scytone'min**, a brown pigment peculiar to that group of Algae.

sea-green, glaucous.

Seam, see TRACHEID-SEAM ; ~ **Cells**, flat cells with thickened walls, which direct the line of rupture in the stomium of Fern-sporangia (Goebel) ; ~ **Nod'ules** = COAL-BALLS.

Seas'onal Amphichro'matism (+ AMPHICHROMATISM), the production of two differently coloured flowers on the same stock, due to the season (Lindman) ; ~ **Heterochro'matism** (+ HETEROCHROMATISM), different colours in the flowers of the same inflorescence due to season (Lindman).

seba'ceous, *seba'ceus* (Lat., a tallow candle), like lumps of tallow.

sebif'erous (*sebum*, tallow ; *fero*, I bear), bearing vegetable wax or tallow.

sec'ondary, *secundar'ius*, not primary, subordinate ; ~ **Bast**, the result of the continued activity of the cambium, a formation of bast of the same essential character as the primary bast, but not forming a part of the original bundle ; ~ **Bud**, additional to the usual bud, when more than one occurs in or near the axil ; ~ **Cor'tex**, successive formations of liber or bast within the cortical sheath and primary cortex, exclusive of the secondary cork, phelloderm ; ~ **Des'mogen**, formed from the cambium and destined to become

secondary permanent tissue ; ~ **Emb'ryo-sac**, the central utricles of *Welwitschia*, which correspond to the corpuscula of Coniferae (J. D. Hooker) ; ~ **Forma'tions**, those formations which have arisen through human interference ; the "Substitute Associations" of W. G. Smith (Warming) ; ~ **Fun'gus**, a parasite or saprophyte which attacks a plant after it has been injured or killed by some other Fungus ; ~ **Growth**, additional or subsequent to primary growth ; ~ **Hy'brid**, a hybrid one or both of whose parents were also hybrids ; ~ **Li'ber**, = ~ BAST ; ~ **Medul'-lary Rays**, those which are intermediate between the primary rays, and do not extend to the pith ; ~ **Mem'-bers**, all those which are developed from the primary members, if borne directly, they are said to be of the first order, if on the latter, of the second order, and so on ; ~ **Mer'istem**, a cambium which arises in an organ after its first development, by means of which further growth is possible ; ~ **Myce'lium**, rhizoid attachments to the base of the sporophore resembling the normal mycelium ; ~ **Nu'cleus**, the nucleus of the embryo-sac, resulting from the union of the two polar nuclei ; ~ **Pedun'cle**, a branch of a many-flowered inflorescence ; ~ **Pet'iole**, the footstalk of a leaflet ; ~ **Root**, a lateral root, or a branch from the primary root ; ~ **Scleren-ch'yma** consists of elongated prosenchymatous cells having lignified walls marked with narrow oblique bordered pits ; ~ **Spore**, a spore borne on a promycelium or derived from another spore ; ~ **Struc'ture**, (1) any structure not primary, or (2) after it has grown beyond its early condition ; ~ **Tis'sue**, refer to DESMOGEN, VASCULAR TISSUE, etc. ; ~ **Wood**, derived from the cambium but not in the original bundle as first formed, it differs from the primary wood by not having spiral or annular vessels like those on the protoxylem (Vines).

Sec'ondine = SECUNDINE (Crozier).

Secre'tion (*secretio*, a dividing), a substance formed from the fluids of the plant by the agency of glandular cells ; ~ **Bod'ies**, secretory sacs ; **secre'tory**, producing a secretion ; ~ **Sac**, a unicellular or aggregated sac containing excreta as gum, resin, oil ; ~ **Space**, an intercellular space containing similar products of secretion ; ~ **Tis'sue**, as above, it forms a storehouse for the waste products of the plant.

sec'tile, *sect'ilis* (Lat., cut or cleft), as though cut up into portions, as the pollen of some Orchids.

Sec'tion (*sectio*, a cutting), (1) a thin slice taken usually for microscopic inspection, in a given direction ; (2) an important division of a genus.

Sec'tor (Lat., one who cuts), the term **pericy'clic** ~, is used by Bastit for interruptions of the continuity of the central cylinder of the subterranean portion of *Polytrichum*, as viewed in cross-section ; **Sec'tors**, *cf.* PERICYCLIC SECTORS.

sec'tus (Lat., cut), parted, completely divided to the base ; in composition it forms the suffix -SECT.

secund', *secun'dus* (Lat., following or second), parts or organs directed to one side only, usually by torsion ; **secunda'tus** (Lat., second in rank) is given by J. S. Henslow as synonymous ; **secundiflo'rus** (*flos, floris*, a flower), the flowers all turned in the same direction ; **sec'undine**, the second, that is, the inner coat of an ovule ; *Secundi'nae inter'nae*, an old term for ALBUMEN of a seed ; **Secun'do-spore** (+ SPORE), C. MacMillan's term for a spore which can also act as a gamete, as in *Ulothrix*.

Se'des Flor'is (Lat.) ‡, the torus of a flower.

Se'dile, Clements's term for a society of *Sedum*.

sedimen'tary Yeast, bottom-yeast.

Seed, (1) the fertilized and matured ovule of a phenerogamous plant ; (2) provisionally used in fossil botany, for certain seed-like fruits ; ~ **Bed**, Blair's word for PLACENTA ; ~ **Bud**, in Milne's Dictionary is cited for OVARY ; ~ **Coat** = TESTA ; ~ -**gen'us**, any fossil genus of which the seed or fruit is the only portion known ; ~ **Leaf**, ~ **Lobe** = COTYLEDON ; ~ -**ped'icels**, of *Bennettites*, the strand supporting each seed ; ~ **Sport**, a seminal variation ; ~ **Stalk**, the FUNICLE or podosperm ; ~ -**stems**, the seminiferous spadix of *Bennettites* ; ~ **Varia'tion**, a variation arising from a seed, and not bud ; ~ **Vari'ety**, a variety produced from a seed-sport, or one which comes true from seed ; ~ **Ves'sel** = PERICARP ; **Seed'age**, proposed by L. H. Bailey for the state or condition of being reproduced by seed ; **Seed'ling**, (1) a plant produced from seed, in distinction to a plant propagated artificially ; (2) a young plant so produced.

segeta'lis (Lat., pertaining to standing crops), growing in fields of grain.

Seg'ment, *Segmen'tum* (Lat., a piece cut off), (1) one of the divisions into which a plant organ, as a leaf, may be cleft ; (2) each portion of meristem which originates from a single SEGMENT CELL ; ~ **Cell**, the basal portion which is successively cut off from the apical cell in growth ; ~ **Halves**, in Hepaticae the two external cells in apical-cell division, the remaining cell being internal ; **Segmenta'tion**, (1) division into members ; (*a*) similar, as in a thallophyte, or (*b*) dissimilar, as in a cormophyte ; (2) the division of the apical cell ; the primitive cell-divisions of the embryo.

se'gregate, *segrega'tus* (Lat., separated), kept apart ; a **Se'gregate** is a species separated from a super-species.

Segrega'tion (*segregatio*, a parting), the dissociation of characters from each other in the formation of the germs (Bateson).

seirolyt'ic (σειρὰ, a rope; λυτικὸς, able to loose), separation of hereditary characters; **Sei'rospore** (σπορὰ, a seed), a spore produced in a branched row resulting from the division of terminal cells of particular branches in certain Ceramiaceae; adj. **seirospor'ic**.

seismonast'ic, seismon'ic (σεισμὸς, a shaking), sensible to vibration; **Seismot'ropism** (τροπὴ, a turning), the power of appreciating and responding to vibration (Pfeffer).

seju'gous, *se'jugus* (*sex*, six; *jugum*, a yoke), having six pairs of leaflets, as some pinnate leaves.

Sela'go Type the presence of alternate fertile and sterile zones, as in *Lycopodium Selago* (Bower).

Sel'agraph (σέλας, a flash; γράφω, I write), an instrument for the automatic recording of light values (Clements).

Selec'tion, Nat'ural, Darwin's expression for that which Herbert Spencer has termed the "survival of the fittest."

Selenot'ropism (σελήνη, the moon; τροπὴ, a turning), movements of plants caused by the light of the moon (Musset).

Self, a florist's term for having the same tint throughout, without markings of other colours or tints; ~ **-bred,** the offspring of self-fertilized flowers (F. Darwin); ~ **-col'oured,** uniform in tint; ~ **-fertil'ity,** producing fruit from its own pollen; ~ **Fertiliza'tion,** fertilized by its own pollen; ~ **Par'asitism,** parasitic on its own species, as sometimes happens with *Viscum* ; ~ **Pollina'tion,** the pollen of the same flower brought into close contact with its own stigma; ~ **Steril'ity,** when pollen though ripe is inoperative on the stigma of its own flower; **selfed,** [monosyll.], fertilized by its own pollen.

sellaeform'is (*sella,* a saddle; *forma,* shape), saddle-shaped.

Se'men (Lat., seed), the seed of flowering plants; ~ **cornicula'tum,** the receptacle of certain Fungals (Lindley); ~ **mul'tiplex** = SPORIDESM.

Semes'ter (*semestris,* half-yearly) **Ring,** the ring produced in the wood of many tropical trees, in consequence two periods of growth and rest in the year.

Se'met (*semen,* seed), a term used by Grew and others for ANTHER, *cf.* SEMINE.

sem'i (Lat.), half; **sem'i-adhe'rent,** *sem'i-adhe'rens* (*adherens,* sticking), half-adherent, that is, the lower part or half; **sem'i-amplec'tens,** ~ **amplec'tus** (Lat., wound about), equitant; ~ **amplecti'vus** is also cited for the same; **sem'i-amplex'i-caul,** *sem'i-amplexicau'lis* (*amplexus,* embracing; *caulis,* the stem), applied to leaves whose lower portion half embraces the stem; **sem'i-amplex'us,** half-embracing; **sem'i-anat'ropal, sem'i-anat'ropous** (+ ANATROPOUS)=amphitropous; **sem'i-aquat'ic** (+ AQUATIC), term for those water-plants which root in the soil, but produce aquatic leaves, otherwise living as land-plants; **sem'i-automat'ic** (+ AUTOMATIC), nearly automatic in response to a stimulus, **Sem'i-autom'atism** is the state (Bose); **sem'i-calyc'iform** (+ CALYCIFORM), half cup-shaped (J. Smith); **Sem'i-cap'sula** (+ CAPSULA) = CUPULE ; **Sem'icell,** one half of a Desmid; **semicolum'nar,** *semicolumna'ris* (+ COLUMNAR), semiterete; **semicon'-nate** (+ CONNATE), applied to such structures as the half-united filaments of certain willows (Wimmer); **semi-cor'date,** *semicorda'tus* (+ CORDATE), heart-shaped on one side only; **semicordiform'is** (*forma,* shape), somewhat cordate; **semicylindra'ceus,** ~ *cylin'dricus* (+ CYLINDRICUS), semiterete; **Sem'i-des'ert,** a transition between desert and wood- or grass- land

(Schimper); **semidi′gynus** (+ DIGY-
NUS), when two carpels cohere
near the base only; **semidoub′le**,
semidu′plex, when the inner stamens continue perfect, and the
outer are petaloid, half changed
into a double flower; **semiellip′tic**
(+ ELLIPTIC), half-elliptic, the division being longitudinal; **semieq′ui-
tant** (+ EQUITANT), half-equitant;
Semiflor′et (+ FLORET), a ligulate
floret; **semiflos′cular, semiflos′cu-
lous**, *semifloscu′sis* (+ FLOSCULAR),
having the corolla split and turned
to one side as in ligulate florets of
Compositae; **Semiflos′cule**, a semi-
floret (Crozier); **Semifru′tex** (*frutex*,
a shrub), an under-shrub; **semi-
hasta′tus** (+ HASTATUS), hastate on
one side only; **semilan′ceolate** (+
LANCEOLATE), half-lanceolate, longitudinally divided; **semila′tent** (*lateo*,
I lie hid), when the progeny of an
abnormal individual repeats that
marked departure in only a few
individuals (De Vries); **semilentic′-
ular** (+ LENTICULAR), sublenticular
(Crozier); **Semilia′nes** (+ LIANES),
applied to scrambling plants in
hedges and margins of forests
(Warming); **Semili′chen** (+LICHEN),
Zukal's term for forms which when
destitute of their appropriate Alga
can subsist as saprophytes, or
Fungi which can combine with
some Alga to form a Lichen; **semi-
loc′ular**, *semilocula′ris, semiloc′ulus*
(+ LOCULAR), with incomplete dissepiment, practically unilocular; **se-
milu′nar, semilu′nate**, *semiluna′tus*
(+ LUNATE), lunate, shaped like a
half-moon, or crescent-shaped; **semi-
mesophyt′ic** (+ MESOPHYTIC), intermediate between xerophytic and
mesophytic.

se′minal, *semina′lis* (Lat., pertaining
to seed), relating to the seed; ~
Leaf, a cotyledon; ~ **Sport**, =
SEED-SPORT; **Se′minase**, an enzyme
occurring in *Trigonella* and *Medicago*.

Semina′tae (*semen*, a seed), Van Tieghem's term for plants furnished

with true seed-coats; **Semina′tio**,
the act of natural dispersion of
seeds; **Se′mine**, used by Grew to
include both his Semet and Chive,
the genitalia; **seminif′erous**, *-rus*
(*fero*, I bear), (1) seed-bearing; (2)
used for the special portion of the
pericarp bearing the seeds; (3)
= Dicotyledons; ~ **Scale**, in Coniferae, that scale above the bract-
scale on which the ovules are placed
and the seed borne; **seminif′ic**
(*facio*, I make), forming or producing seed; **Seminifica′tion**, propagation from seed; **seminiform′is**
(*forma*, shape), applied to reproductive bodies in Cryptogams which
are not part of the fructification;
Se′menin, a sinistrorse carbohydrate
occurring in reserve-cellulose in the
endosperm of some seeds (Reiss);
Se′minose, a dextrose form from
ordinary cellulose belonging to the
group of grape-sugars (Reiss); **Se′mi-
nule**, *Semin′ulum*, = SPORE; **Semi-
nulif′erus** (*fero*, I bear), (1) that
part of Cryptogams which bears the
spores, a sporophore; (2) the cavity
of the ovary while the ovules are
yet unfertilized.

semiorbic′ular, *semiorbicula′tus* (*semi*,
half, + ORBICULAR), half-round or
hemispherical; **semio′val**, *semiova′-
lis*, **semio′vate**, *semiova′tus* (+ OVAL,
half-oval, one side only, or ovate in
longitudinal halves; **semipetaloi′-
deus** (+ PETALOID), petaloid; of
the shape or texture of a petal;
semi-pollica′ris (*pollex*, a thumb-
breadth; about half an inch in
length; **semira′dians, semira′diate**,
semiradia′tus (*radians*, emitting
beams), when only a portion of the
outer florets of a Composite are
radiant and different from those of
the disk; **semire′niform**, *semireni-
formis* (*renes*, the kidneys; *forma*,
shape), kidney-shaped on one side
only; **semireticula′tus** (*reticulatus*,
netted), when one of several layers
is netted, the others membranous;
semirevect′us (*revectus*, carried back),
cf. SEPTUM; **semisagitt′ate**, *semi-*

sagitta'tus (*sagitta*, an arrow), arrow-shaped on one side of the longitudinal axis ; **semisamaroi'deus** (+ SAMAROIDEUS), partially samaroid, used of the fruit known as samara ; **semisep'tate**, *semisepta'tus* (+ SEPTATUS), half partitioned, the dissepiment not projecting far enough to divide it into two cells ; **semistam'inate**, *semistaminar'ius*, *-ris* (+ STAMEN), when part of the stamens are changed into petals ; **semisymphioste'monis** (+ συμφύω, I unite ; στήμων, a stamen), when some of the stamens cohere, the rest remaining free (J. S. Henslow) ; **sem'iterete**, *semiter'es* (*teres*, round and tapering), half-terete ; **semitrig'ynus** (τρὶς, three ; γυνή, a woman), when of three styles two are united half way, the third being free on the ovary (Meissner) ; **semival'vate**, *semivalva'tus* (+ VALVATE), when the valves of a fruit are only partially dehiscent ; **semivertic'illate** (+ VERTICILLATE), subverticillate (Crozier) ; **semi-xerophyt'ic** (+ XEROPHYTIC), showing a strong tendency to xerophytic conditions.

sempervi'rent, *sempervi'rens* (Lat.), evergreen, retaining its leaves during the winter ; **Sempervirentipra'ta**, pl. (*pratum*, a meadow), meadow associations dominated by species mostly evergreen, in temperate climates, where frequent rain enables them to grow during most of the year.

se'nary, *sena'rius* (Lat.), belonging to, or containing, six.

Senes'cence (*senesco*, I grow old), the ageing of protoplasm ; a term used by Maupas for the condition of the offspring of a long-continued series, which, after continued fission, ultimately degenerate, and lose first the power of conjugating, and finally that of fission ; **senes'cent**, growing old or effete.

sensib'ilis (Lat.), sensitive, manifesting irritability ; **sen'sitive**, *sensiti'vus*, responsive to stimulus, as the leaves of *Mimosa pudica*, Linn. ; ~ **Tis'sues**, those in which the

sensibility resides ; **Sen'sitiveness**, irritability ; **sen'sory**, sensitive.

Sep'al, *Sep'alum* (σκέπη, a covering), Necker's convenient term in universal use for each segment composing a calyx ; **sep'aline**, *sepali'nus*, **sep'alous**, relating to sepals ; **sep'aloid**, *sepaloi'deus* (εἶδος, resemblance), resembling a sepal ; **Sepalo'dy**, the metamorphosis of petals into sepals or sepaloid organs ; **Sepal'ulum**, Necker's diminutive for a small sepal.

sep'arate (*separatus*, put apart) **Flow'ers**, those of distinct sexes, diclinous ; **sep'arating Lay'er**, the ABSCISS-LAYER, as in leaf-fall ; **Separa'tion**, multiplication by naturally detachable portions, such as gemmae, bulbils, etc. ; ~ (or **frac'tional**) **Cul'tures**, a method of obtaining a pure culture by repeated inoculation in successive media ; selecting the surviving species or form ; ~ **Lay'er**, the absciss layer in defoliation, whence the leaf is ultimately detached.

sepia'ceus (*sepia*, a cuttle fish), sepia-coloured, a dark clear brown.

Sepic'ola (*sepes*, a hedge ; *colo*, I inhabit), an inhabitant of hedges, J. S. Henslow prints it *sepi'colus*.

Sep'ta, pl. of **Sep'tum** (Lat., a hedge or enclosure), any kind of partition, whether a true dissepiment or not ; **septa'lis** (Lat.), belonging to a septum ; **sep'tal**, H. C. Watson's term for plants growing in hedgerows ; **sep'tate**, *septa'tus*, divided by a partition ; ~ **Spore** = SPORIDESM.

septem'fid (*septem*, seven ; *fid*, the root of *findo*, I cleave), cut into seven divisions ; **septempar'tite** (*partitus*, cut), divided into seven lobes ; **sept'enate**, *septena'tus*, *septe'nus*, having parts in sevens, as in a compound leaf, with seven leaflets arising from the same point ; **septena'tal-pin'nate**, used by Babington for those brambles which have seven pinnules in each leaf.

septici'dal, **sep'ticide**, *septicida'lis* (*septum*, a hedge or enclosure ; *caedo*, I cut), when a capsule dehisces through the dissepiments or lines of junction; **septif'erous** (*fero*, I bear), bearing the partition or dissepiment.

septifo'lious (*septem*, seven; *folium*, a leaf), seven-leaved.

sep'tiform, *septiform'is* (*septum*, a hedge; *forma*, shape), having an appearance of a dissepiment, as the placenta of *Plantago;* **septif'ragal**, *septif'ragus* (*frag*, the root of *frango*, I break), when in dehiscence the valves break away from the dissepiments; **sept'ilis**, of or belonging to dissepiments; **Septio** (Lat.), a fencing in; ~ **prae'cox**, a cell-wall formed early in development; ~ **procrastina'ta**, a cell-wall delayed in progress (Brand); **sep'tulate**, having spurious transverse dissepiments, (*a*) sparsely septate, (*b*) indistinctly septate, its true sense; **Sep'tulum**, a little partition of any kind; **Sep'tum**, a partition or dissepiment; ~ **provect'um**, applied by Brand to a cell-wall advanced into a branch of *Cladophora;* ~ **revect'um**, a cell-wall formed across the stem of the same; ~ **semirevect'um**, when the cell-wall forms an angle of 45° (Brand).

septupliner'vis, *-vius* (*septuplum*, in sevens; *nervus*, a nerve), seven-nerved, applied to a leaf.

Se'reh, a disease of sugar-cane, probably due to *Hypocrea Sacchari*, Went.

se'rial, *seria'lis*, **se'riate**, *seria'tus* (*series*, a row), disposed in series of rows, either transverse or longitudinal.

seric'eous, *seric'eus* (Lat.), silky, clothed with close-pressed soft and straight pubescence.

Se'ries (Lat.), (1) a row; (2) by A. Gray used as equivalent to subkingdom, by others used for various groups.

sero'tinal, **sero'tinous**, *-nus* (Lat.), that comes late), produced late in the season, or the year, as in autumn.

Ser'ra (Lat., a saw), the tooth of a serrate leaf; **serraefo'lius**, prefer-

ably **serratifo'lius** (*folium*, a leaf), having serrate leaves; **ser'rate**, *serra'tus*, beset with antrorse teeth on the margin; **ser'rate-cil'iate**, toothed, and with a marginal series of hairs; **serra'tulus**, slightly toothed, denticulate; **Ser'rature**, *Serratu'ra*, the toothing of a serrate leaf; **ser'rulate**, *serrula'tus*, serrate, but the teeth minute; **Serrula'tion**, (1) being serrulate; (2) a serrulate tooth.

ser'ried, close together in rows (Crozier).

Ser'tulum (*sertum*, a garland), (1) ‡ a simple umbel; (2) a selection of plants described or figured; **Ser'tum**, used for an account of a collection of plants.

se'samoid (*Sesamum*, + εἶδος, resemblance), granular, like the seeds of sesamum.

ses'qui (Lat.), a prefix meaning one and a half; **sesquial'ter**, (1) when the stamens are half as many again as the petals or sepals; (2) when a fertile flower is accompanied by a neuter flower, as in some grasses; **sesquipeda'lis** (Lat.), a foot and a half in length; **sesquirecip'rocal** (*reciprocatio*, alternation), applied to hybrids between an F_1 individual and one of its parents (De Vries).

ses'sile, *ses'silis* (Lat., sitting, as though sitting close, destitute of a stalk.

Se'ston (σηστὸς, sifted), plankton material retained by very fine meshed sieves; **Sestonol'ogy**, the science in question.

Se'ta (Lat., a bristle), (1) a bristle or bristle-shaped body; (2) the sporophore of a Moss, the stalk which supports its capsule; (3) the arista or awn of grasses, when terminal; (4) a peculiar stalked gland in *Rubus;* (5) by cyperologists used for the bristle within the utricle of certain species of *Carex;* it represents the continuation of the floral axis (C. B. Clarke); **seta'ceous**, *-ceus* (+ ACEOUS), bristle-like; applied to a stem it means slender, less than

subulate ; **seta′ceo-serra′tus**, having
the serratures ending in a bristle-
like point ; **setife′rous** (*fero*, I bear),
bristle-bearing ; **se′tiform** (*forma*,
shape), in the shape of a bristle ;
setig′erous (*gero*, I bear), bristle-
bearing ; **se′tose**, *seto′sus* (Lat.),
bristly, beset with bristles ; (2)
having setae usually ending in
glands (Babington) ; **Se′tula**, (1) the
stipe of certain Fungi (Lindley) ;
(2) a minute bristle ; **se′tuliform**
(*forma*, shape), thread-like ; **se′tu-
lose**, *setulo′sus*, resembling a fine
bristle.

Sex, *Sex′us* (Lat.), in botany, male or
female functions in plants.

sexan′gular, *sexangula′ris*, *sexan′gulus*
(Lat.), six-angled.

sexfar′ious, *-us* (*sex*, six ; *fariam*,
suffix = in rows), presenting six
rows, extending longitudinally
round an axis ; **sex′ifid** (*fid* = cleft),
six-cleft (Crozier) ; **sexloc′ular** (*loculus*, a small cell), six-celled.

sexpar′tite, *sexparti′tus* (Lat.), cut into
six segments.

Sex′tant (*sextans*, a sixth part), a
radial cell division of segments in
three series, a sixth part of the
original (De Bary).

sex′tuplex (Lat.), six-fold or six-times.

sex′ual, *sexua′lis* (Lat., pertaining to
sex), (1) the distinction of sex ;
(2) applied to the phenomena of
conjugation generally ; ~ **Gener-
a′tion**, the stage which bears the
sexual organs ; in Ferns the prothallus ; ~ **Sys′tem**, Linnaeus's artificial arrangement by the number
and position of the sexual organs.

Shade-leaves, those adapted to modified light ; ombrophile ; ~ **-plants**,
(1) quick-growing plants, employed
to protect permanent trees, and removed when that result is attained ;
(2) used by Clements as shade-loving
plants.

Shaft, Withering's word for STYLE.

Shag-ha′irs, = VILLI, in German
"Zotten" ; **shag′gy**, villous.

Shake, defect in timber due to the
attacks of *Trametes Pini*, Fr. ; also

known as **Bark-**, **Heart-**, or **Ring-
shake**.

sharp-pointed, acute.

shear′ing, displacement of the particles
of a body by lateral strain ; **Shear-
resis′tance**, the property inherent in
a body which resists shearing.

Sheath, (1) a tubular or enrolled part
or organ, as the lower part of the
leaf in grasses ; (2) a limiting layer
of surrounding cellular tissue, as
the BUNDLE-SHEATH ; (3) the lower,
longer portion of the cell-wall in
division in *Oedogonium* (Potter);
sheath′ing, enclosing as though by
a sheath.

Shelf, **conduct′ing**, Dickson's term for
a ledge within the ascidium of
Cephalotus follicularis, Labill.

Shell, (1) the hard envelope of a nut ;
(2) a mass of layers in the cell-wall.

Shel′ter-par′asite, see DOMATIA.

Shield, (1) an apothecium or disk arising
from a Lichen-thallus, containing
asci ; (2) in Characeae, one of the
eight cells forming the globule ;
(3) the staminode of *Cypripedium*
(S. Moore) ; (4) in Coniferae, the
thick rhomboid extremity of the
cone-scales (Potter) ; ~ **shaped**, in
the form of a buckler ; clypeate,
peltate, or scutate.

Shift′ing, the same as GLIDING
GROWTH ; in Germ. Verschiebung.

Shing′le-banks, accumulations of rolled
pebbles, due to tides or sea-currents.

shi′ning, lucid, a clear and polished
surface.

Shoot, (1) a young growing branch or
twig ; (2) the ascending axis ; when
segmented into dissimilar members
it becomes a STEM ; ~ **Pole**, that
point where new shoot growth begins,
cf. ROOT-POLE ; **leaf′y** ~, a branched
shoot ; **thal′loid** ~, an unsegmented
shoot.

Short-rods, short bacteria.

Shos′hungraph (Sanscrit, *shoshun*,
suction ; γραφὴ, writing), apparatus
to record suctional response in plants
(Bose).

Shot, or **Chott**, a hollow which in Algeria accumulates water with salts ;

a " salt spot " ; **Shot-hole,** an attack on plum trees and their allies, due to to the fungus *Cercospora circumscissa,* small holes being formed in the leaves.

Shoul'der, in *Lagenostoma* that part which curves inwards towards the apex of the seed.

Shrub, a woody perennial of smaller structure than a tree, wanting the bole ; ~ **Lay'er,** chiefly formed of hazel, with sallow and dogwood ; ~ **Stra'tum,** in mixed woodland from about 3 to 15 feet in height ; ~ **Wood,** when shrubs form the chief feature ; **shrub'by,** like a shrub ; **Shrub'let,** an undershrub.

Sib'ling (Sib, bird fanciers' term for in-bred), applied to a pair of plants from the ovaries or the pollen of the same plant (Pearson) ; **Sib'ship,** the relationship in question.

Siccideser'ta, pl. (*siccus,* dry, + *desertum,* a desert), steppe formations ; **Siccissimideser'ta,** pl., deserts on which less than half of the substratum is covered with vegetation ; **sic'cus** (Lat.), dry, juiceless, containing little or no watery juice ; **siccita'te** (Lat., abl. absol.), in the dry state, that is, herbarium specimens.

Sic'kle, = DREPANIUM (Potter).

Sick'le-stage, of nuclear division, Zimmerman's term for the PARANUCLEUS of Strasburger, a crescent-shaped body at one margin of the nucleus, supposed to represent a stage in the disappearance of the nucleolus.

Sieve-cells, the individual cells which constitute the SIEVE TUBES ; ~ **Disk,** ~ **Field,** ~ **Plate,** the pierced plate on the transverse or lateral walls of vessels covered on both sides by callus ; ~ **Pores,** the openings in a sieveplate ; ~ **Tis'sue,** long articulated tubes, whose segments communicate by means of the sieveplates ; ~ **Tubes,** the tubes composing the tissue described ; ~ **Xy'lem,** applied by Chodat to groups of sieve-cells in the wood of *Dicella.*

Sieverse'tum, a plant association in which *Sieversia* is the predominant factor (Clements).

sigilla'rian, resembling or allied to *Sigillaria,* a genus of fossil plants whose surface is marked with numerous scars ; **sig'illate,** *sigilla'tus* (Lat., sealed), as if marked with impressions of a seal, as the rhizome of *Polygonatum.*

sig'matoid (σῖγμα, the Greek *s* ; εἶδος, resemblance), or **sig'moid,** *sigmoi'deus,* doubly curved in opposite directions, like the Greek *s.*

Signs, arbitrary symbols for shortly stating certain facts ; a selection of those more generally used, is given in Appendix A.

Silene'tum, an association of *Silene* (Clements).

silic'eous (*silex, silicis,* a flint), pertaining to silica, as ~ **-grasslands,** or **silic'icole,** showing a preference for siliceous soils ; **silicic'olous,** *colo,* I inhabit), used of Lichens which grow on flints ; **Silicifica'tion,** the deposition of silica in tissues ; **Silic'ion,** denoting the prevalence of silica in the soil ; **Sil'ico-cel'lulose** (+ CELLULOSE), the condition of tissue when silex is intimately blended with it is as in *Equisetum hyemale,* Linn. (Tschirch).

Sil'icle, *Silic'ula,* **Sil'icule** (Lat., a little husk or pod), (1) a short siliqua, not much longer than wide ; (2) ‡ = CARPOCLONIUM of Algae ; **silic'ulose,** having silicles as fruits, or resembling a silicle.

Sil'iqua (Lat.), **Silique'** (pr. Si-leek'), (1) the peculiar pod of the Cruciferae, two valves falling away from a frame, the REPLUM, on which the seeds grow, and across which a false partition is formed ; (2) ‡ by Blair employed for Legume ; **Siliquel'la,** a subordinate part of a fruit such as the poppy, consisting of a carpel with two extended placentas ; **siliq'uiform** (*forma,* shape), shaped like a silique ; **sil'iquose,** *siliquo'sus,* when the fruit is a silique, or resembles one.

sil'ky, sericeous.

Sil′va = SYLVA.

Sil′ver-grain, the appearance in radial longitudinal section of exogenous wood, especially of oak, due to shining plates of the medullary rays; ~ -leaf, a disease of plum-leaves, ascribed to *Stereum purpureum*.

sil′very, having a lustre like silver.

sim′ilary Parts ‡, elementary organs or tissues (Lindley).

similiflo′rous (*similis*, like; *flos, floris*, a flower), applied to an umbel when its flowers are all alike; **Simili-sym′metry** (+ SYMMETRY), when the two halves of a Diatom valve are similar (Schuett); consimilarity.

sim′ple, *sim′plex*, of one piece or series, opposed to compound; ~ **Fruits**, those which result from the ripening of a single pistil; ~ **Gland**, a single cell containing a special secretion; ~ **Gonid′iophore** (+GONIDIOPHORE), a single hypha as in *Pencillium*; ~ **Hairs**, not compound or branched, the prolongation of a single epidermal cell; ~ **Inflores′cence**, a flower cluster with one axis, as a spike, spadix, or catkin; ~ **Leaf**, of one blade, with incomplete segmentation; ~ **Nuta′tion**, nutation in one direction only; ~ **Pis′til**, consisting of one carpel; ~ **Pit**, ~ **Pore**, with only a slight enlargement at the centre, where it meets the neighbouring cell; ~ **pri′mary Root**, a tap-root; ~ **Spor′ophore**, a single hypha or its branch; in German, Fruchtfaden; ~ **Stem**, a stem which is unbranched.

simplicis′simus (Lat.), entirely simple.

simulta′neous (*simultaneus*, Late Lat., at the same time) **Whorls**, when the members are of the same age and developed at the same time.

Sina′grin, or **Sin′igrin**, a glucoside occurring in the seeds of *Brassica sinapoides*, Roth, formerly termed *Sinapis nigra*, Linn., the origin of the name.

Sinal′bin, mustard oil from *Brassica alba*, Boiss., formerly termed *Sinapis alba*, Linn., whence the name.

Sina′pin or **Sina′pisin**, an alkaloid from *Brassica alba*, Boiss. (Hanbury and Flückiger).

sin′gle, used of a flower which has only one set of petals, as opposed to double or any approach to doubling.

Sing′uliform (*singulus*, separate, + FORM), a plant in which one organ varies independently of another (Kuntze).

sinis′trad = SINISTRAL.

sinis′tral, **sinis′trorse**, *sinistror′sus*, turned to the left; *cf.* DEXTRORSE, and Appendix C.

Sin′istrin (*sinister*, the left), a carbohydrate from *Urginea* and other bulbs, formerly regarded as a gum; **Sinistrosty′ly** (+ STYLE) in enantiostylous flowers when the styles are bent to the left (Knuth).

Sin′ker, (1) the secondary roots of Mistletoe, *Viscum album*, Linn., forming laterals which strike perpendicularly downward into the wood of the host; (2) similar growths in *Pilostyles Ulei* (Solms).

sin′uate, *sinua′tus* (Lat., curved), with a deep wavy margin; **sin′uated**, deeply waved; **sin′uolate**, *sinuola′tus*, repand, faintly or minutely sin′uate; **sin′uose**, **sin′uous**, sinuate.

Sin′us (Lat., a curve, a fold), (1) a recess or re-entering angle; (2) a pore in some Fungi (Lindley); (3) the recess between the half-cells of Desmidiae; (4) in *Lagenostoma* the space between the free portion and the nucellus and the integumental lining; (5) in the same genus, the gaps in a fimbriated micropyle (Oliver).

Siot′ropism (σείω, I shake; τροπή, a turning), stimulus by shaking, as with *Mimosa pudica* Linn.

Si′phon (σίφον, a tube), a pericentral elongated tube in the frond of *Polysiphonia* and allied Algae; **sipho′neous**, relating to Algae, possessing tubular structure; **sipho′nic**, tubular, as applied to a DICTYOSTELE; **Siphoniphy′ton** (φυτὸν, a plant), a Composite with all its florets tubular; **Si′phonogam** (γάμος, marriage), plants fertilized by means of pollen-tubes ; all Phanerogams ; adj. **siphonogam′ic, siphonog′amous**, the condition being **Siphonog′amy** ; **siphonoste′lic** (στήλη, a column), having a tubular stele (Jeffrey) ; **Si′-phonostele** (+ STELE), the central vascular cylinder when complete as a tube.

Siraplank′ton (+ PLANKTON), floating marine vegetation mainly composed of *Thalassosira*.

sirosi′phoid (εἶδος, resemblance), like the genus *Sirosiphon*, in which the cells occur in two or more rows ; **sirosiphona′ceous**, allied to *Sirosiphon* (Archer).

Sis′ter-cells, cells of the same generation produced by the division of a single (mother) cell, as the pollen-grains of a tetrad.

Sit′us (Lat., situate), (1) the position occupied by an organ ; (2) ‡ the mycelium of some Fungi (Lindley).

Skaphoplank′ton (σκάφη, a skiff, + PLANKTON), boat-shaped organisms floating as a mass (Forel).

Skein, a condition of the chromatin of the nucleus in the initial and final stages of division ; **daugh′ter** ~ or **moth′er** ~, according to their development.

Skel′eton (σκελετός, mummy), any framework which persists after the destruction of the organ by fire or corrosion, as the remainder of the cell-wall in ash, or the starch grain after partial solution by an enzyme.

Skin, a thin external covering, the cuticle or epidermis.

Ski′ophyte (σκιά, shade ; φυτόν, a plant), a plant which is not adapted to full exposure, but prefers shade.

Skoliotrop′ic (σκολιός, bent ; τροπή, a turning), curved, *cf.* CAMPYLOTROPOUS.

skotoph′ilous (σκότος, darkness; φιλέω, I love), = GEOPHILOUS ; **Skotot′ropism** (τροπή, a turning), seeking darkness ; apheliotropic.

Slacks, pl., Yorkshire name for shallow valleys, due to glacier lakes in the Ice-age.

slashed, laciniate.

slate-grey, the colour of slate, schistaceous.

Slean, the smut of oats due to *Ustilago Avenae*.

Sleep, the repose of plants, with changes in position of organs such as leaves, due to absence of light ; ~ **Move′ments**, positions taken by leaves during the night, nyctitropic movements.

Slee′ping (or **Slee′py**) disease of Tomato plants, the result of *Fusarium Lycopersici*.

slen′der, long and thin.

Sli′ding Growth, a gradual change in the relative position of vessels, fibres, etc., due to their development in a longitudinal direction.

Slime-flux, a flow of liquid from diseased fruit and forest trees, due to the attacks of various Fungi, producing a fermentation of the cortical elements down to the cambium zone (Massee) ; ~ **Fun′gi** = MYXOGASTRES ; ~ **Moulds**, a popular term for MYXOGASTRES, otherwise called Myxomycetes and Mycetozoa ; ~ **Strings**, metabolized material in a state of flux, which passes by the pores of the sieve-plates from one sieve-tube to another (A. W. Hill).

sli′my, mucous.

Sling-fruit, applied to any fruit which by possessing contractile tissue projects its seeds to a distance.

Slip, (1) described by Loudon as a shoot from the collar or lower part of the stem of a plant, used for propagation, stem-suckers ; (2) a popular name for CUTTING, but not used by cultivators.

smarag′dine, *smarag′dinus* (σμάραγδος, an emerald), emerald green.

Smi′lacine, a crystalline body occurring in the roots of the officinal sarsaparilla, *Smilax*.

smo′ky, smoke-coloured, fumosus.

smooth, (1) not rough, opposed to scabrous, free from hairs ; (2) glabrous, as opposed to pubescent.

Smut, disease in grain produced by

various species of *Ustilago* ; ∼
Spores, reproductive bodies of
Ustilagineae.

Snail-plants, those which are supposed
to be fertilized by snails and slugs,
malacophilous plants.

snow-white, white of absolute purity,
niveus.

Snow-flushes, pl. (Germ. Schneetäl-
chen), dark patches of soil, due to
accumulated deposit from melting
snow, the vegetation is known as
as ANTHELIETUM ; ∼ -leaves, Jung-
ner's name for certain leaves which
are thin or leathery, folded in the
bud, and with no pulvinus; winter-
leaves; ∼-patch-flor′a = ∼ -FLUSHES.

Sob′ole, *Sob′oles* (Lat., a sprout), a
shoot, especially from the ground ;
sobolif′erous (*fero,* I bear), bearing
vigorous shoots.

Sobri′niform (*sobrinus,* a cousin, +
FORM), a VERSIFORM which belongs
to a SUBGREGIFORM, as *Rubus
moluccanus,* Linn. (Kuntze).

so′cial (*socialis,* pertaining to companionship), (1) when individuals of
the same species usually grow in
company, and occupy a considerable extent of ground ; (2) dominant
species which give the main character
to the vegetation (Drude); (3) completely grouped ;—(*a*) **compet′itive**
∼, when the roots of the competing
plants are at the same level ; (*b*)
complement′ary ∼, when the component plants root at different
levels; (*c*) **exclu′sive** ∼, a pure
growth ; (*d*) **inclu′sive** ∼, permitting
the entrance of other forms (Clements) ; ∼ **Flow′ers,** Knuth's term
for Compositae, the flowers being
grouped into heads.

Soci′ety (Plant), (1) see ASSOCIATION ;
(2) an area characterized by a principal species; it is shown by addition
of *ile-*, as Androsacile for a society
of *Androsace* (Clements).

soft, applied to tissue which readily
yields to the touch ; ∼ **Bast,** the
tissue of sieve-tubes and parenchyma, opposed to the HARD BAST
of layers of fibres.

Sola′nin, a poisonous crystallizable
alkaloid in many species of *Solanum,* especially in *S. nigrum,* Linn.,
the potato, and the tomato.

So′lar (*sol, solis,* the sun) **Plants,** Grew's
name for those which twine with the
sun, that is dextrorse ; **Sola′rium,** in
botanic gardens a spot for exposing
plants to the full rays of the sun.

sold′ered [dissyll.], united together.

sole, applied to a carpel to denote the
end furthest from the apex (Goebel).

sol′eaeform,*soleaeform′is* (*solea,*a sandal;
forma, shape), slipper-shaped, almost
resembling an hour-glass.

Solena′idy (σωλήν, a tube ; αἰδοῖα,
genitals), the conversion of the
genitals into barren tubes (Morren).

Soleniaplank′ton (+ PLANKTON), floating neritic vegetation characterized
by abundance of *Rhizosolenia* (Warming).

Sole′nostele (σωλήν, a tube, + STELE),
an amphiphloic vascular tube with
widely separated leaf-gaps; **per′-
forated** ∼, in which gaps other than
leaf-gaps occur (Tansley); **Soleno-
ste′ly** is the condition ; **solenoste′lic**
(στήλη, a pillar), having a tubular
stele with internal and external
phloëm (Van Tieghem).

Solfatar′as, pl. (It., *solfo,* sulphur),
hot sulphur springs, round which
grows a special xerophilous vegetation (A. F. W. Schimper).

sol′id, *sol′idus* (Lat.), not hollow, free
from cavities ; ∼ **Bulb** = CORM.

sol′itary, *solita′rius* (Lat., lonely),
(1) single, only one from the same
place ; (2) Stokes used this for
monotypic genera ; (3) species of
which the individuals occur in extreme isolation ; ∼ **gregar′ious,** a
single clump of one species.

solu′bilis (Lat., that may be loosed),
separating into portions or pieces ;
Solubil′ity, *Solubil′itas,* the condition
of being readily loosed.

solute′, *solu′tas* (Lat. unbound), free,
not adherent, becoming separate ;
Solu′tion, the detachment of various whorls normally adherent ; the
opposite of ADHESION.

So′ma (σῶμα, a body), the body as distinguished from the germ or reproductive portion (L. H. Bailey), pl. So′mata, granules of any kind; So′ma-plasm (πλάσμα, moulded), Weissmann's term for the protoplasm of the body or vegetative portion, in opposition to the germplasm; somatar′chous (ἀρχή, beginning), that kind of cell-division in which one portion continues the reproductive function and the other transmits the somatic function (De Vries); Somat′ia, starch-like structures in the fovilla of pollen-grains (Saccardo); somat′ic Apog′amy, when the cell which gives rise to the sporophyte possesses the haploid chromosomes; = EUAPOGAMY; ~ Cell, (1) cell not specially modified, the opposite of a reproductive cell; (2) a cell with unreduced number of chromosomes (Benson); somatogen′ic (γένος, offspring), Weismann's word for "acquired characters"; Somat′ophytes (φυτὸν, a plant), the higher plants, possessing adult parts and organs; adj. somatophyt′ic; Somatot′ropism (τροπή, a turning), Van Tieghem's term for the directive influence of the substratum on the growth of an organism; frequently shortened to Somat′ropism; adj. somatrop′ic.

soot′y, fuliginous; ~ Mould, on *Citrus*, caused by various species of *Meliola* which cause sooty patches on the fruit and leaves.

sor′al, relating to a SORUS.

Sor′bin, a glucose occurring in *Pyrus*, some species of which were formerly ranked under *Sorbus*.

sor′did, sor′didus (Lat., fouled), dirty in tint, chiefly applied to pappus when of an impure white; sordidis′simus, very dirty coloured, grey.

Sorede′ (σωρὸς, a heap), a proposed emendation of Sore′dium, pl. Sore′-dia, in Lichens a single algal cell or group of them, enveloped in hyphal tissue, which is able to grow at once into a thallus when detached; a brood-bud; sore′dial, pertaining to a soredium; ~ Branch, a branch produced by development of a soredium into a new thallus, while still attached to the mother-thallus; sore′diate, soredia′tus, bearing small surface patches; sorediif′erous (*fero*, I bear), bearing soredia.

Sore′ma (σώρευμα, what is heaped), a heap of carpels belonging to one flower; Soreu′ma = SOREDIUM (J. S. Henslow).

Sor′ghin, Passerini's term for the product of transformation of Sorghoru′bin, the natural pigment of *Sorghum vulgare*, Pers.

Sorid′ium, Hicks's variant of SOREDIUM.

sorif′erous (σωρὸς, a heap; *fero*, I bear), bearing sori; Sor′ophore (φορέω, I bear), a gelatinous cushion on the ventral edge of the sporocarp of *Marsilea*, and Ferns; Sor′osphaeres (σφαῖρα, a ball), globular groups of wedge-shaped spores in *Sorosphaera*.

Soror′es (Lat., sisters), used of physiological species (Schröter).

Soro′se, Soro′sis, Soro′sus (σωρὸς, a heap), a fleshy multiple fruit, as a mulberry or pine-apple; adj. sor′ose.

Sor′rowful Flow′ers, "those which exhale their odours only at certain hours of the day, as *Pelargonium triste*," Soland. (Crozier); *cf.* PLANTAE TRISTAE.

So′rus, pl. So′ri (σωρὸς, a heap), (1) a cluster of sporangia in Ferns; (2) in Synchitrieae, a group of sporangia from a single swarm-cell; (3) a heap of soredia forming a powdery mass on the surface of a thallus; ~ Canals′, cavities in the young sporangia of certain Pteridophytes (Campbell); ~ Gametang′ium, reproductive bodies in *Giraudia* on the assimilating cells (Kjellman); ~ Sporang′ium, reproductive bodies crowded into groups on the branches of *Kjellmania*; — Fu′sion ~, several sori which have run into one, without apparent distinction.

spadic′eous, *spadi′ceus* (σπάδιξ, a palm-branch), (1) as to colour, date-brown ; (2) having the nature of, or bearing a spadix ; **spa′dicose,** resembling a spadix ; **Spa′dix,** a spike with a fleshy axis, as in Aroids.

Span, usually about nine inches, between the extremities of the thumb and little finger, DODRANS ; sometimes the small span of seven inches is intended, the space between the thumb and middle finger when stretched out.

Spanand′ry (σπανὸς, scarce ; ἀνήρ, ἀνδρὸς, a man), Marchal's term for disappearance or extreme rarity of males in normal bisexual lines of descent ; **spanan′thus** (ἄνθος, a flower), having few flowers.

Spang′les, used by J. E. Smith for PATELLULAE.

Sparga′nium-cor′tex (the genus *Sparganium,* + CORTEX), applied to fossil stems with a vertical system of fibrous strands which do not anastomose, as *Medullosa* ; ~ **Type,** the cortex having short, radiating bands of fibrous sclerenchyma running vertically without anastomoses (Kidston).

sparse, *spar′sus* (Lat., spread open), scattered ; **sparsiflo′rus** (*flos, floris,* a flower), with scattered flowers ; **sparsifo′lius** (*folium,* a leaf), with scattered leaves.

Spar′sioplasts (πλαστὸς, moulded), ELAIOPLASTS, variable in position and numbers (Mereschkowsky).

Spartine′tum, a plant association made up of *Spartina* (Ganong).

spart′oid (σπάρτος, esparto grass ; εἶδος, resemblance), used by Fayod for persistent mycelium which is corticated.

Spathe, *Spath′a* (σπάθη, a spatula), a large bract enclosing a flower cluster, usually a spadix ; ~ **Valves,** the bract-like envelopes beneath the flowers in certain Monocotyledons, as *Allium* and *Narcissus ;* **spatha′ceous,** *-ceus* (+ *aceus*), spathe-bearing, or of the nature

of a spathe ; **spathae′us ‡,** having a very large spathe (Lindley) ; **spa′thal, spa′thate, spathed,** furnished with a spathe ; **Spathel′la,** an old name for the glumes of grasses, sometimes also the paleae were included ; **Spathel′lula,** a palea of a grass ; **Spathil′la ‡,** a secondary spathe, as in the inflorescence of Palms ; **spa′those,** spathe-like ; **spath′ulate,** *spathula′tus,* **spat′ulate,** oblong, with the basal (proximal) end attenuated like a druggist's spatula.

Spawn, mycelium.

Spec′ialized Form, Erikson's term for BIOLOGICAL RACE.

Spe′cies (Lat., a shape, kind, or sort), the particular kind, the unit in classification, the aggregate of all those individuals which have the same constant and distinctive characters ; they may be distinguished as **biolog′ic** ~, **morpholog′ic** ~, or **physiolog′ic** ~, according to the basis of discrimination ; **element′ary** ~, a true unit, not a collective species ; ~ **Hy′brid,** a hybrid between two species of the same genus ; ~ **Soror′es,** Schröter's term for any two species of Uredineae which inhabit two distinct hosts, but show no morphological difference, as in *Puccinia ;* **specif′ic** ~, relating to a species ; ~ **Cen′tre,** the particular spot where the species is supposed to have originated ; ~ **Char′acter,** the diagnosis which separates one species from another ; ~ **Name,** the Latin appellative appropriated to a given species, usually an adjective, but sometimes a substantive used in apposition.

Spec′imen (Lat., an example), a plant, or portion of one, prepared for botanic study.

spec′tans (Lat., looking), "se invicem *spectantia* folia," = opposite-leaved.

Spec′trophore (*spectrum,* an appearance ; φορέω, I carry), apparatus designed by Reinke to determine

351

the action of the different rays of light in the elimination of oxygen by plaɴts.

Speir′anthy (σπεῖρα, a twist ; ἄνθος, a flower), when a flower assumes a twisted form.

Speire′ma (σπείρημα, a fold or coil), in Lichens, a gonidium.

Speirogonim′ia (σπεῖρα, a twist, + GONIMIA), gonimia single or scattered ; **Speirostich′ies** (στίχος, a row), a spiral series (Hance).

Sper′gulin, a fluorescent substance occurring in the seeds of *Spergula*.

Sperm (σπέρμα, a seed) **Cell**, a male reproductive cell, as (*a*) an antherozoid, (*b*) a pollen-graiɴ ; usually a minute, active cell, whose function is that of fusion with a large resting cell (oosphere), to form a zygote ; ∼ **-cell**, sometimes restricted to the spermatozoid mothercell ; ∼ **Chro′matin**, that portion of the male nucleus which is receptive of staining ; ∼ **Nu′cleus**, the nucleus of a male gamete (male pronucleus) which coalesces with the nucleus of an oosphere (female pronucleus) to form a germ-nucleus ; **Sperm′agone**, *Spermagon′ium* (γόνος, offspring) = SPERMOGONE, etc. ; **Spermamoe′bae** (+ AMOEBAE), Pringsheim's term for certain specialized portions of the antheridial protoplasm of Saprolegniae, which fertilize the oosphere ; **Sperman′gium** (ἀγγεῖον, a vessel), the sporangium of an Alga (Lindley) ; **Sperm′aphore**, *Spermaphor′ium* (φορέω, I carry), (1) the placenta ; (2) the funicle ; **Sperm′aphytes** (φυτὸν, a plant), used to include both Angiosperms and Gymnosperms ; all plants except Cryptogams (Sachs) ; adj. **spermaphyt′ic** ; **Spermapod′ium** or **Spermapodoph′orum** (πούς, ποδὸς, a foot), a branched gynophore in Umbelliferae ; **Sperma′rium**, H. Gibson's term for ANTHERIDIUM ; **Sperm′ary**, = (1) POLLENTUBE ; (2) employed by T. J. Parker for a male organ of reproduction, as a gamete ; **Sperm′atange**, *Sperma-*

tan′gium (ἀγγεῖον, a vessel), (1) the antheridium of Bangiaceae (T. Johnson) ; (2) by A. Braun employed for spermogonia and antheridia generally ; **Spermat′ia**, pl. of **Sperma′tium**, male non-motile gamete-cell ; **Sperm′atid**, *Spermatid′ium* (εἶδος, resemblance), (1) the mother-cell of antherozoids ; (2) formerly used for an Algal spore ; **spermatif′erous** (*fero*, I bear) ; **spermatig′erous** (*gero*, I bear), bearing spermatia ; **Spermatoconid′ium** (+ CONIDIUM), A. Braun's term for SPERMATIUM ; **Spermato′cyst**, *Spermatocystid′ium* (κύστις, a bag), the mother-cell of antheridia, especially of Mosses ; **Sperm′atocyte** (κύτος, a hollow), (1) Goebel's term for the preceding ; (2) used by Shaw for four primary organs, each containing a pair of blepharoplastoids, the eight secondary or spermatid mother-cells each contains two blepharoplasts (Coult., Bot. Gaz. xxvi., Dec. 1898, p. 449) ; **Spermatocy′tium** (κύτος, a hollow vessel), a simple sporangium containing spermatozoids (A. Braun) ; **Spermatogam′ete**, Hartog's term for a male gamete ; **Spermatogen′esis** (γένεσις, a beginning), the development of the male elements, antherozoids, pollen-grains, and analogous bodies ; **spermatog′enous** (γεννάω, I beget), (1) productive of the male element ;· (2) producing seed ; **Spermatogonid′ium** (+ GONIDIUM), A. Braun's term for SPERMATOZOID ; **Spermatogon′ium** (γόνος, offspring), the male gametogonium, a cell which divides to form gametes, or itself passes into the state of one (Hartog) ; **Spermatoid′ium**, one of "small cells containing gonidia in Algae" (Lindley) ; **Spermatokal′ium** (καλιά, a cabin), name given by Gibelli to the perithecium of *Verrucaria ;* **spermatokine′tic** (κινητικὸς, having the power of movement), tending to produce the male element in plants ; **Sperm′atophore** (φορέω, I carry), a structure bearing a spermatium ; **spermatophyt′ic**, relating to seed-bearing plants ; **Sperm′atophyte** (φυτὸν, a plant), a Phanerogam, a plant with true seeds ; **Sperm′atoplasm** (πλάσμα, moulded), the protoplasm of a male cell ; **Sperm′atoplast** (πλαστὸς, moulded), a male sexual cell ; **spermatoplas′mic**, relating to the SPERMATOPLASM ; **Spermatosphae′ria**, pl. (σφαῖρα, a ball), Itzigsohn's term for a presumed male body in *Spirogyra*, declared by Pringsheim to be an undoubted error ; **Spermat′ostrotes**, *-ae* (στρωτὸς, spread), plants distributed by seeds (Clements) ; **Spermatotham′nia** (θάμνος, a bush), the antheridial filaments of Rhodophyceae (A. Braun) ; **Spermatozo′id** (ζῷον, a living creature ; εἶδος, resemblance), a male ciliated motile gamete produced within an antheridium ; **Spermatozo′on**, by Shaw taken as the product of a blepharoplast ; **sperm′ic**, relating to a seed (Crozier) ; **spermid′eus**, producing seed ; **Spermid′ium**=ACHENE ; **Sper′mocarp** (καρπὸς, fruit), the fruit of Characeae (Bennett and Murray) ; **spermocar′pous** has been used as a synonym of PHANEROGAMOUS ; **Sperm′oderm**, *Spermoder′mis* (δέρμα, a skin), the covering of a seed, the seedcoat ; **Spermodoph′orum** (ὁδὸς, a way ; φορέω, I carry), the gynophore in Umbelliferae ; **Spermogem′ma** (*gemma*, a bud), Caruel's term for ARCHEGONIUM ; **Sperm′ogone**, *Spermogon′ium* (γόνος, offspring), a cup-shaped receptacle in which spermatia are abjointed, differing from a pycnidium by its smaller spores ; **Sperm′o-nu′cleus** = SPERMNUCLEUS ; **Sperm′ophore**, *Spermoph′orum* ‡ (φορέω, I carry), (1) the gynophore in Umbelliferae ; (2) the placenta ; (3) the modified shoot of the thallus of certain Algae, producing male organs (Darbishire) ; **Sperm′ophyte** (φυτὸν, a plant), cited by Crozier for a Phanerogam or flowering plant ; **Spermothe′ca** ‡ (θήκη, a case) = PERICARP ; **sperm′**-

ous = SPERMIC ; **Sper′motype** (τύπος, a type), Swingle's term for a specimen cut from a seedling raised from the original type ; **Sperm′um**, a seed or its analogue.

sphac′elate (σφάκελος, gangrene), dark and withered as though dead ; **Sphacel′ia**, formerly a genus, now known to be the conidial stage of ergot, *Claviceps purpurea*, Tul. ; **Sphac′elic Ac′id** is derived from ergot (Tubeuf).

Sphaeraph′ides (σφαῖρα, a sphere ; ῥαφὶς, a needle), clusters of crystals in plant-cells of a more or less spherical form ; **Sphaeraplank′ton** (+ PLANKTON), floating vegetation chiefly composed of *Halosphaera viridis ;* **Sphaerench′yma** (ἔγχυμα, an infusion), spherical cells composing cellular tissue, as the pulp of fruits.

sphaeria′ceous, sphae′rioid (εἶδος, resemblance), resembling or allied to the Fungus genus *Sphaeria*.

Sphaer′ites (σφαῖρα, a sphere), starch grains which have been asserted to be crystallized bodies ; **Sphaerobacte′ria** (+ BACTERIA), bacteria with extremely small rounded cells which become detached ; **Sphaeroblas′tus** ‡ (βλαστὸς, a bud), a cotyledon which rises above ground, bearing at its apex a rounded tumour (Lindley) ; **sphaerocar′pous** (καρπὸς, fruit), when a fruit is globular ; **sphaeroceph′alus** (κεφαλὴ, a head), having flowers in a close globular head ; *cf.* SOROSIS ; **Sphaerochor′isis** (+ CHORISIS), the division of an axis in all directions, as in "witches-broom," etc. (Fermond) ; **Sphae′ro-crys′tals** = SPHAERAPHIDES ; **sphae′roid** (εἶδος, resemblance), globular, any solid figure approaching that of a sphere ; **~ Cell**, a reserve-receptacle in some calcareous Lichens (Zukal) ; syn., **spheroi′dal** ; **Sphaerophy′tum** (φυτὸν, a plant), a Fern, its sporangia being globular ; **Sphae′rospore**, *Sphaerospor′a* (σπορά, a seed), a name proposed in substitution for TETRASPORE ; **Sphaer′ula**, a globose peridium emitting sporidia buried in pulp (Lindley); ~ **ascig′era**, the receptacle of certain Fungi (Lindley).

Sphagne′tum, a plant society of *Sphagnum* moss ; **Sphagni′on**, a *Sphagnum* moor ; **Sphagniopra′tum** (*pratum*, a meadow), moss-moor, dependent upon rain rather than underground water ; examples, SPHAGNION, ERIOPHORETUM ; **Sphagnol′ogy** (λόγος, discourse), the study of the genus *Sphagnum;* **sphagnoph′ilous** (φιλέω, I love), applied to **Sphag′nophytes**, pl. (φυτὸν, a plant), those plants which prefer to grow on sphagnum cushions ; **sphagno′sus**, used by Nilsson to denote a *Sphagnum* undergrowth to a heath ; **sphag′nous**, resembling or allied to the genus *Sphagnum*.

Sphalerocar′pum, -pium (σφαλερὸς, unsteady ; καρπὸς, fruit), an accessory fruit, as an achene in a baccate calyx-tube.

sphe′noid (σφὴν, a wedge), wedge-shaped, cuneate (Heinig).

sphenophylla′ceous, resembling or allied to the extinct family of Sphenophyllaceae.

Sphenop′sida (ὄψις, appearance), Scott's name for a group of plants allied to Lycopsida, consisting of Equisetales and other articulate vascular cryptogams.

sphenop′teroid (εἶδος, resemblance), like the fossil genus *Sphenopteris*.

Sphere - crys′tals and **Sphe′ro-crys′-tals** (σφαῖρα, a sphere) are synonyms of SPHAERAPHIDES ; **Sphere-yeast**, a growth form of *Mucor* which resembles yeast ; **spher′ical**, *sphe′ricus*, relating to a sphere ; *sphe′ricus Li′mes* = ORBICULAR ; **Sphe′roblast** (βλαστὸς, a bud or shoot), a wood-ball on the beech and other trees, from a dormant eye, disconnected from its vascular bundles (Ward) ; **spherogen′ic** (γένος, race), the self-rounding of amoeboid organisms (Pfeffer) ; **Sphe′rules**, rounded bodies occurring in the sporangioles of *Selaginella* (Janse).

sphinct′riform (*forma*, shape), having the apothecia almost sessile, as in *Sphinctrina*.

Sphingoph′ilae (σφίγξ = Hawkmoth ; φιλέω, I love), flowers fertilized by hawkmoths and nocturnal lepidoptera ; they have a strong, sweet smell, and honey in the flower-tube (H. Mueller) ; adj. **sphingoph′ilous**.

Sphrigo′sis (σφριγάω, to be full of sap), rankness (Berkeley).

Sphyg′mism (σφυγμὸς, the pulse), the formation of contractile vacuoles through some stimulus (Massart).

Sphyri′um, or **Sphyri′on** (σφύρον, ankle), a plant succession on "colluvial" soils (Clements) = talus or scree.

Spi′ca (Lat.) = SPIKE.

spi′cate *spica′tus* (Lat., spiked), like a spike, or disposed in a spike ; **spicif′erous**, *-rus* (*fero*, I bear) ; **spiciflor′us** (*flos, floris*, a flower) ; **spi′ciform**, *spiciform′is* (*forma*, shape), spike-like ; **spicig′erous**, *-rus* (*gero*, I bear), bearing flower spikes ; **spi′cose**, and **spi′cous** (Crozier) = SPICATE ; **Spic′ule**, *Spi′cula* (*spiculum*, a small needle), (1) a diminutive or secondary spike ; (2) the point of a basidium in Fungi ; also (3) their aciculae ; (4) a fine, fleshy, erect point (Lindley) ; **spic′ular**, spiky ; **spic′ulate**, *spicula′tus*, with a surface covered with fine points ; **Spicula′tion**, Nylander's term for a hyphal constriction in spore-formation, the extremity being left as a spicule.

Spike, *Spi′ca* (Lat., an ear of corn), (1) an indeterminate inflorescence, with flowers sessile on a common elongated axis ; (2) an aggregation of sporophylls at the apex of the shoot ; **com′pound ~**, an inflorescence consisting of spikes.

Spi′kelet, *Spic′ula*, a secondary spike, a cluster of one or more flowers subtended by a common pair of glumes, as in grasses.

spiladoph′ilus (σπιλὰς, σπιλάδος, a crag, occasionally clay ; φιλέω, I love), "dwelling in clay" ; **Spiladophy′ta** (φυτὸν, a plant), "clay plants"; **Spiladophyti′a**, "clay plant formations."

Spil′us ‡ (σπίλος, a stain), the hilum in grasses.

Spi′na (Lat.) = SPINE.

Spin′dle, any structure which in shape suggests a thread-spindle; ~ **Fi′bres**, the achromatic filaments which make up the nuclear spindle; ~ **Pole**, an extremity of the nuclear spindle; ~ **Hairs**, resembling malpighiaceous hairs, attached centrally, with the ends hooked (De Bary); ~ **shaped** = FUSIFORM; **Achromat′ic** ~, or **Nu′clear** ~, the thread-like protoplasmic figures in nuclear division between the poles.

Spine, *Spi′na* (Lat., a thorn), a sharp-pointed woody or hardened body, usually a branch, sometimes a petiole, stipule, or other part; **Spine-arm**, in the genus *Najas*, the representative of a barren stigma (Rendle); ~ **Cell**, (1) a transitional ~ ARM (Rendle); (2) in *Chara*, certain cells of the cortex on the internodes, ending in a spine; **Spines** of the leaves, as of Holly, hardened extremities of the lobes, or spiny elevations; **Spinel′la** (dim. of *spina*), a prickle; **spinello′sus**, armed with small spines or hairs; **spines′cent**, *spines′cens*, ending in a spine or sharp point; **spinicar′pous** (καρπὸs, fruit), with spiny fruit; **spinif′-erous**, *-rus* (*fero*, I bear), bearing thorns; **spinifo′lius** (*folium*, a leaf), having spiny leaves; **spi′niform** (*forma*, shape), thorn-like; **spi′niger, spinig′erous** (*gero*, I bear), bearing or producing thorns; **spi′nose**, *spino′sus*, **spi′nous**, spiny, having spines; **Spi′nula** (Lat.), **Spi′nule**, a diminutive spine; **Spinula′tion**, a minute spine or prickle; **spinules′cent**, slightly spiny, or having spinules; **spinulif′erous**, *-rus* (*fero*, I bear), having small spines; **spi′nulose**, *spinulo′sus*, with small spines or spinules; **spi′ny**, beset with spines, or resembling a spine.

spi′ral, *spira′lis* (*spira*, a coil), as though wound round an axis; ~

Duct, a spiral vessel; ~ **Flow′er**, when the members are arranged in spirals and not in whorls; ~ **Mark′-ings**, secondary deposits in tracheids; ~ **Phyllotax′y**, see PHYLLOTAXY; ~ **Tor′sion** = TORSION; ~ **Ves′sels**, ducts having markings in a spiral form; **Spi′ralism**, monstrosity of a flower due to torsion. ⸱

Spire (σπεῖρα, a twist), (1) a young leaf or shoot of grass; (2) "the continuation of the trunk in ex-current trees like pines" (Crozier); (3) one turn of a coil or twist; (4) when spiral curves become vertical spiral rows (Church).

Spi′rem, or **Spi′reme** (σπείρημα, a coil), a preliminary stage of nuclear division as in *Lilium*, the nucleus assuming an involved filamentous condition or "ribbon" from which the chromosomes are formed.

Spi′ricle (σπεῖρα, a twist), a delicate coiled thread in the surface cells of certain seeds and achenes which uncoils when moistened, as in *Collomia;* **Spiril′lum**, pl. **Spiril′la**, (1) a term for ANTHEROZOID; (2) also see next; **Spirobacter′ia**, pl. (+ BACTERIUM), bacteria which form spirally curved filaments, as the genus *Spirillum*, Cohn; **Spirofi-bril′lae**, pl. (*cf.* FIBRIL), Fayod's term for the spirally twisted hollow threads which he asserts constitute all living protoplasm; **Spi′roid**, a delicate thickening in the cells of the tentacles of *Drosera* (Kerner); **Spi′roism**, the coiling of an organ in development (Morren); **Spirolo′beae** (λοβὸs, a lobe), Cruciferae which have cotyledons folded transversely and the radicle dorsal; **spirolo′bous**, with the cotyledons spirally rolled up, shown thus o ‖‖‖; **spirophotot′ropous** (φὼs, φωτὸs, light; τροπὴ, a turn), the majority of plants, those whose leaves so surround the axis, that the light in turn falls upon all (Drude); **Spi′rospart** (σπαρτὸs, sown, scattered), hypothetically the finest spirals of hyaloplasm, which constitute the SPIROFIBRILLAE (Fayod).

Spith'ama (σπιθαμή, a span), a span of seven inches, from the tip of the thumb to that of the forefinger ; **spithamae'us** (Mod. Lat.), measuring a short span.

splen'dens (Lat., gleaming), glittering or shining.

Splint, a forester's term for ALBURNUM or Sapwood.

split, cleft or divided, parted ; ~ **Fruit** = CREMOCARP ; ~ **Lay'er**, a loose felt of hyphae in *Geaster*, connected with the inner peridium, and torn into flakes at maturity.

split'ting, employed of hybrids, to denote division of characters from the parents.

spodoch'rous (σποδὸς, ashes ; χρόα, colour), of a grey tint.

Spong'elet = SPONGIOLE ; **Spong'iole** (*spongia*, a sponge), a name given to the root-tip, formerly thought to be a special absorbing organ, the Epiblema of Schleiden ; *Spong'iola radica'lis*, De Candolle's name for the root-cap ; ~ *pistilla'ris*, the extremity of the pistil, the stigma ; ~ *semina'lis*, the caruncle of certain seeds ; **Spong'ioplasm** (πλάσμα, moulded), the assumed spongy basis of protoplasm ; **spongio'sus** (Lat.), spongy, soft ; **Spong'ophyll** (φύλλον, a leaf),a shade leaf (Clements); **spong'y**, having the texture of a sponge, cellular and containing air, as in many seed coats ; ~ **Cor'tex**, cortical tissue with air-bearing intercellular spaces, frequent in waterplants ; ~ **Parench'yma**, loosely aggregated tissue, or having conspicuous intercellular spaces.

Sponsa'lia (Lat., espousals), **Planta'rum ‡** = ANTHESIS ; the fertilization period.

sponta'neous (*spontaneus*, voluntary) **Genera'tion**, the assumed origin of living organisms from non-living matter.

spoon'form, "having the inner surface of a leaf concave or dish-shaped, as the outer leaves of a cabbage-head" (Crozier).

Spor'a (σπορά, a seed), = SPORE ; ~

cellulo'sa, ~ **compos'ita**, ~ **multilocula'ris** = SPORIDESM ; **spor'al**, relating to a spore ; ~ **Arrest'**, partial or complete arrest of the development of the spores themselves, and consequent loss of reproductive function (Bower).

sporad'ic (σποραδικὸς, dispersed), widely dispersed or scattered.

Sporadophyti'um (σπορὰς, σπορὰδος, scattered ; φυτὸν, a plant), open plant formation (Clements).

Spor'ange, Sporan'gium (σπορὰ, a seed ; ἀγγεῖον, a vessel), (1) a sac endogenously producing SPORES ; (2) ‡ "sometimes applied to the volva among Fungals" (Lindley) ; **Sporangid'ium**, (1) the columella of Mosses ; (2) "the spore-case of certain Fungals" (Lindley) ; (3) C. Mueller's term for the Moss-capsule; **Sporangio'dy**, the change of sterile tissue into sporangia, as in *Botrychium* ; **sporangiogen'ic** (γένος, race, offspring), giving rise to sporangia ; **Sporang'iole**, *Sporan'giola*, or *Sporan'giolum*, (1) a small sporangium in Mucorini produced in addition to the larger sporangia ; (2) formerly used for ASCUS ; (3) organs of an endophyte in *Selaginella*, composed of filaments rolled into the shape of a ball (Janse) ; (4) *Sporangiolum* is used in a double sense by Lindley : (*a*) for spore, (*b*) a case containing sporidia ; **Sporangiolif'erum** (*fero*, I bear), the axis on which the thecae of Ferns are borne (Lindley) ; **sporangif'erous**, bearing sporangia ; **Sporan'giophore**, *Sporangioph'orum* (φορέω, I carry), a sporophore bearing a sporangium, such as the sporophyll in *Equisetum*, or the columella in Ferns ; **sporangioph'orous**, bearing sporangiophores ; **Sporan'giospore** (σπορὰ, a seed), a term proposed for the spores of Myxogastres ; **Sporan'gism**, the condition of producing sporangia; **Sporan'gium**, *cf.* SPORANGE.

Spore, *Spor'a* (σπορὰ, a seed), a cell which becomes free and capable of direct development into a new

bion; in Cryptogams the analogue
of seed in Phanerogams, understood
by Saccardo as a BASIDIOSPORE;
further particularized by C. Mac-
Millan into **Pri′mo-**, **Secun′do**, **Ter′-
tio-**, **Quar′to-**, and **Quin′to-spores**,
according to their assumed development; *cf.* CARPOSPORE, KINOSPORE,
PAULOSPORE, etc.; ~ **-bed**, applied
to a layer of cells parallel to the
surface in Uredineous Fungi (Grove);
~ **Bul′bils**, abortive apothecia in
certain Lichens; ~ **Case**, = SPOR-
ANGIUM; ~ **Cell**, a spore, or a cell
which gives rise to a spore (Crozier);
~ **Forms**, the divisions of a genus
according to the characters of the
spores, as, for example, in *Puccinia*
(Arthur); ~ **Group**, = SPORIDESM;
~ **Hy′brid**, a hybrid arising in the
gametophytic stage; ~ **Init′ials**,
small processes borne by the fertile
hyphae of *Graphiola*, which produce spores by one or more bi-
partitions of their contents (E.
Fischer); ~ **Lay′er**, a layer of mother-
cells of the spores of *Phascum;* ~
-sac = Moss-capsule (Berkeley); ~
Sport, a variation arising from a
sexual reproductive act; *cf.* ~ **Hy′-
brid**; **Spor′eling**, a young plant
from a germinated spore; **Spor′e-
plasm** (πλάσμα, moulded), the protoplasm in a sporangium destined
to produce spores; **Spore′tia**, pl.,
generative chromidia (Goldschmidt);
Spor′id, see SPORIDIUM; **Spor′idesm**
(δεσμὸς, a bond), a pluricellular
body, becoming free like a spore, in
which each cell is an independent
spore with power of separate germination; **sporid′eus**, bearing spores;
acotyledonous (Henslow); **sporidif′-
erus** (+ SPORIDIUM, *fero*, I bear),
bearing sporidia; **sporidiform′is**
(*forma*, shape), shaped like a sporidium; **sporidig′erus** (*gero*, I bear),
sporidifer′us; **Sporid′iole**, *Sporidi′-
olum*, pl. *Sporid′iola*, formerly used
for spores in the lower Cryptogams;
Sporid′ium, (1) a synonym or diminutive of SPORE, or a granule
which resembles a spore (Fries); (2)

a spore abjointed from a promycelium; (3) by Saccardo the term
is used as equivalent to ASCOSPORE;
it should be restricted to spores
generated in asci, *i. e.* promycelial
spores (Plowright); **Sporidoch′ia**,
Sporidoch′ium (δοχεῖον, a holder),
" the receptacle or even the stipe of
certain Fungals" (Lindley); **spor-
if′erous** (*fero*, I bear), spore-bearing;
Sporifica′tion, the process of producing spores (Ganong); **spor′o-
antherid′ic**, Brebner's term for that
condition of *Haplospora* when spores
and antheridia are borne by distinct
individuals; ~ **-hermaph′rodite**,
when some are hermaphrodite and
others bear asexually produced
spores; ~ **-oogonous**, bearing spores
in one individual and oogonia in
another; **Spor′oblast** (βλαστὸς, a
bud), (1) Koerber's word for MERI-
SPORE; (2) applied to secondary
cysts in *Gymnodinium;* **Sporo′carp**,
Sporocar′pium (καρπὸς, fruit), (1)
a many-celled body resulting from
a sexual act as from an archicarp,
serving for the formation of spores;
(2) the indusium or body enclosing
the sporangia in Hydropterideae;
Spor′ocide (*cido*, stem of *caedo*, I
cut or kill), a germicide, any agent
which destroys the vitality of spores
or germs; **Sporoclad′ium** (κλάδος, a
branch), a branch on which the
reproductive bodies of some Algae
are found; **Sporoconid′ium** (+ CON-
IDIUM), used by A. Braun for ACRO-
SPORE; **Spor′ocyst** (κύστις, a bag),
a unicellular structure, producing
asexual spores (Davis); **Sporocys′ta**,
the sporangium of an Alga; **Spor′-
ocyte** (κύτος, a hollow), Goebel's
term for the mother-cell of a spore;
Sporocy′tium, a simple sporangium
containing spores (A. Braun);
Spor′oderm, *Sporoderm′is* (δέρμα, a
skin), the integument of a spore;
Sporodoch′ium, pl. **Sporodoch′ia**
(δοχεῖον, a holder), the sporiferous
apparatus in Fungi belonging to
Tuberculariae, *cf.* SPORIDOCHIA;
Sporogam′ia (γάμος, marriage), a

term which has been suggested for the heterosporous Cryptogams; **Sporogem'ma** (*gemma*, a bud), A. Braun's term for the oogonium (nucule) of *Chara*; **Spor'ogen** (γένος, offspring), a plant which bears spores, a Cryptogam; **Sporogen'esis** (γένεσις, origin), the origin and development of seeds or spores; **sporog'enous** (γεννάω, I beget), producing spores; ~ **Fil'aments**, Oltmann's term for certain outgrowths of the fertilized carpogonium of *Dudresnaya*; the ooblastema-filaments of Schmitz; ~ **Lay'er** = HYMENIUM; ~ **Nu'cleus**, the nucleus resulting from the fusion of the nuclei of the spermatium and the carpogonium of Florideae (Oltmanns); **Spor'ogone, Sporogon'ium** (γονή, progeny), the sporocarp in Muscineae, the whole product of a sexual act remaining attached to the oophyte or plant bearing the sexual organs; **spor'oid** (εἶδος, resemblance), spore-like (Crozier); **Sporomyce'tes** (μύκης, a mushroom), Marchand's term for a group to comprise Myco-, Sipho-, Theca-, and Basidio-mycetes; **Sporont'** (ὄντα, things in being), the sporogenous stage of *Plasmodiophora* (Schwarz); **Spor'ophore, Sporoph'orum** (φορέω, I carry), (1) ‡ the PLACENTA; (2) a branch or portion of a thallus which bears one or more spores; (3) in Ferns and Mosses, the SPOROPHYTE; (4) a spore-containing capsule (Lyon); **Spor'ophase** (φάσις = appearance), the production of a fruit-body giving rise to spores (Tansley); **Sporophy'as**, A. Braun's term, the same as **Sporophyd'ium** (dimin. of φυάς, a shoot), T. F. Allen's term for the nucule of Characeae while still unfertilized; **Spor'ophyll, Sporophyl'lum** (φύλλον, a leaf), (1) a leaf which bears spores; (2) a leaf-like division of the thallus of an Alga bearing fruit, as in *Carpoclonium*; adj. **sporophyl'lary**; ~ **Leaves**, stamens and pistils; **Sporophyllo'dy**, the change of vegetative leaves into sporangiferous organs

(Worsdell); **Spor'ophyte** (φυτὸν, a plant), in Ferns and Mosses, the plant in the life-cycle of alternation which produces spores; **sporophyt'ic**, belonging to SPOROPHYTES: **Spor'osome** (σῶμα, the body), the body which actually serves for reproduction (Potonié); **Sporosteg'ium** (στέγος, a covering), the cellular envelope of the nucule in *Chara* (Allen); **Spor'ostrotes**, -*ae* (στρωτὸς, spread), plants distributed by means of spores (Clements); **Sporotami'um‡** (ταμεῖον, a storehouse), the cellular layer immediately beneath the disk of the shield of a Lichen; **Sporothalam'ia** (θάλαμος, a bed-chamber), compound or branched sporophores, as of fruticose Lichens or Agarics (A. Braun); **Spor'ozoid** (ζῷον, a living creature; εἶδος, resemblance), a ZOOSPORE.

Sport, variation starting from a bud or seed.

Spor'ula, Spor'ule (dim. of SPORA), (1) a small spore; (2) a spore produced in a perithecium, but not in an ascus (Ellis and Everhart), (3) formerly used vaguely for spore; **sporulif'erous**, -*rus* (*fero*, I bear), **sporulig'enous** (γένος, offspring), producing sporules; **sporulig'erous** (*gero*, I bear), bearing sporules; **Sporula'tion**, the production of spores (Crozier).

Spor'us, Lindberg's emendation of SPORA.

Spot, a disease of orchids, apparently caused by chill.

Spot-bound, stationary, sedentary.

spot'ted, when colour is disposed in spots on a ground of a different colour.

spread'ing, having a gradually outward direction, as petals from the ovary.

Spring-wood, the wood produced early in the year, characterized by larger ducts and cells than the later growths.

Sprout, a shoot or germinated seed; ~ **Cell**, one produced by sprouting, or vegetative growth; ~ **Chain**, a chain of cells so produced; ~ **Gem'ma,**

= CHAIN-GEMMA; ~ **Germina'tion,**
the germination of a spore in which
a small process, or germ-cell, pro-
trudes from the surface, becomes
cylindric, and finally abjoints as a
SPROUT-CELL.

sprout'ing, the form of an excrescence
in a cell, becoming cut off by a
transverse wall; ~ **Fun'gus,** growth-
form in which the thallus consists of
sprout-cell or chain.

spumes'cent, *spumes'cens* (*spumesco,* I
become foamy), froth-like in appearance; **spu'mose,** *spumo'sus,* frothy.

Spur, (1) a hollow and slender extension of some part of the flower,
usually nectariferous, as the calyx of
Larkspur or the corolla of the Violet;
(2) sometimes a solid spur-like process; (3) a contracted lateral bearing
shoot, sometimes, as in forests, with
a few foliage leaves in a tuft, and
a terminal bud; (4) a buttress-like
projection of a tree-trunk; (5) see
ERGOT; **fo'liar** ~, a short branch,
bearing leaves only; **fruit** ~, a
short branch which bears blossom
buds, as in the Peach; **spurred,**
calcarate, producing a spur.

spu'rious, *spur'ius* (Lat., illegitimate),
counterfeit, false; ~ **Branch =**
PSEUDORAMULUS; ~ **Dissep'iment,**
a partition in fruit but not from the
primary infolding of the margins of
a carpel or upward growth of the
torus; ~ **Fruit =** PSEUDOCARP; ~
Tis'sue, cell-aggregation of felted
hyphae in Agarics, or of coenocytes
in certain Algae; ~ **Whorl,** organs
developed at different times, which,
by some displacement, appear at
the same level.

Squa'ma (Lat., a scale), a scale of any
sort, usually the homologue of a
leaf; ~ **fructif'era,** a seminiferous
scale; **squama'ceous** (+ ACEOUS),
scaly; **squa'mate,** *squama'tus,* furnished with scales; **Squama'tio,** the
unnatural formation of rosettes of
scale-like leaves as in the Rose-
Willow; **Squamel'la,** (1) diminutive
of SQUAMA, a scale of the second
order, or reduced in size, as in the

disk of Composites; pl. **Squamel'lae**
(2) = LODICULES.

squamellif'erous, *-us* (*fero,* I bear),
scale-bearing; **squamel'liform** (*forma,*
shape), shaped like a scale; **Squamel'lula,** (1) a sub-division of the
pappus-limb in Compositae; (2) a
scale-like appendage within the tube
of certain corollas; **squamif'erous,**
-rus (*fero,* I bear), bearing scales;
squamiflo'rous (*flos, floris,* a flower),
having a perianth of scale-like bracts,
but not disposed round an axis as in
Coniferae; **squa'miform,** *squamiform'is* (*forma,* shape), scale-like;
squamig'erous (*gero,* I bear), scale-
bearing; **Squamo'dy** (ὁδὸς, a way),
the change of foliar organs into
scale-leaves (Worsdell); **squa'moid**
(εἶδος, resemblance), squamiform
(Crozier); **squa'mose,** *squamo'sus,*
squa'mous, scaly or scale-like; ~
Bulb = SCALY BULB (Crozier);
Squamo'sis, a disease of the orange-
tree, the bark scaling off, believed
to be a form of GUMMOSIS (Butler);
squa'mulate=SQUAMULOSE(Crozier);
Squa'mule, *Squa'mula,* (1) the hypogynous scale of grasses, the lodicule;
(2) **Squa'mulae intervagina'les,** the
axillary scales of *Halophila;* **squa'-
muliform,** *squamuliform'is* (*forma,*
shape), resembling a small scale;
squa'mulose, *sqaumulo'sus,* beset
with small scales.

squar'rose, *squarro'sus,* **squar'rous**
(Lat., rough, scurfy), rough or
scurfy with spreading and out-
standing processes, as the tips of
bracts; **squarro'so-denta'tus,** having
teeth which do not lie in the plane
of the leaf, but at an angle; ~
squar'rulose, *squarrulo'sus,* diminutive of squarrose.

Sta'ble (*stabilis,* able to stand), fixed,
not changeable; ~ **Forma'tion,**
opposed to migratory formations,
occurring on palaeogeic or past
geological processes (Crampton);
Stabiliza'tion, the tendency of succession in which each stage becomes
more stable (Clements); **stab'ilized,**
settled; **Stabil'ity,** (1) the condition

of fixedness; (2) when the plant makes little or no response (Clements); **Stab'iloplasts** ($\pi\lambda\alpha\sigma\tau\grave{o}s$, moulded), elaioplasts which are fixed in number and position.

stag-head'ed, a forester's term for a tree which is bare of leaves at the top.

stair'case Response', when successive stimuli by increasing molecular mobility greatly enhance responses (Bose).

stale, botanically when growth ceases in cultures; **Stale'ness** (dissyl.), the condition itself; **sta'ling**, becoming stale (Balls).

Stalk, any lengthened support of an organ, as the seta of a Moss; ~ -cell, the cell arising from division of the antheridial cell in *Pinus*, which does not become the generative cell; **stalked**, borne on a stalk; ~ **Gland**, a glandular hair; **Stalk'et**, a secondary petiole, the stalk of leaflets.

Sta'men, pl. *Sta'mina*, or **Sta'mens** (*stamen*, a filament), a male sporophyll in a flower, one of the elements of an androecium consisting of anther and filament; **ster'ile** ~, a body belonging to the series of stamens, but without pollen; **sta'minal**, *stamina'lis, stamina'ris*, **stamin'eal**, *staminea'lis*, relating to stamens, or consisting of stamens; **sta'minal Col'umn**=ANDROPHORE; ~ **Leaves**, the stamens regarded as metamorphosed leaves; **Sta'minalpode** ($\pi o \hat{v}s$, $\pi o\delta\grave{o}s$, a foot), Goethart's name for the organs in the androecium of Malvaceae which produce the stamens on their margins; **sta'-minate**, applied to flowers which are wholly male; **stamin'eous, -neus** (Lat., consisting of threads), relating to stamens; **Staminid'ium**, pl. **Staminid'ia** = ANTHERIDIA; **staminif'erous, -rus** (*fero*, I bear), **staminig'erous** (*gero*, I bear), stamen-bearing; **Sta'minode**, *Stamino'dium*, (1) a sterile or abortive stamen, or its homologue, without an anther; (2) = ANTHERIDIUM (Gray's Manual, ed. I, p. xxxvi); **Sta'minody**, the conversion of other floral organs into stamens; **sta'minose**, *stamino'sus*, when the stamens form a marked feature of the flower.

Stand (Germ.), a pure association, as a beech-wood.

Stan'dard, (1) the fifth or posterior petal of a papilionaceous corolla; (2) a tree or bush with a clear stem; **Stand'els**, old expression for the standards in a coppice.

stans (Lat., standing), supporting itself in an erect position.

Star-rings, small central steles in the fossil Medulloseae.

Starch, a carbohydrate of the same percentage composition as cellulose; an amylose which occurs abundantly in grains as a reserve material in plants; ~ **Buil'der**, a plastid which forms the starch-grain; ~ **Cel'lulose**, the framework of starch-grains, remaining after the soluble parts have been removed; ~ **Genera'tors** = LEUCO-PLASTIDS; ~ **Grain**, ~ **Gran'ule**, a body of definite shape, varying according to the plant which produces it, having the appearance of parallel layers around a hilum; ~ **Lay'er**, a form of Bundle Sheath, consisting of a single layer of cells filled with small grains of starch; ~ **Produ'cer** = LEUCOPLASTID; ~ **Sheath**, the innermost layer of the primary cortex; ~ **Star**, of *Chara stelligera*, Bauer, stellate nodules or internodes on the roots, filled with starch; ~ **Sub'stance**, A. Meyer's term for the pure starch material, apart from any associated or transformed matters which may be also present.

star'ry, stellate.

starved, when a plant or part is less developed than the normal condition, by want of nourishment.

Stas'ad ($\sigma\tau\acute{a}\sigma\iota s$, a standing or pause, + AD), a plant of stagnant water (Clements); **Stas'imorphy** ($\mu o\rho\phi\acute{\eta}$, a shape), a deviation from the normal, arising from arrest of development; **Stas'is**, used to denote retardation especially of longitudinal growth;

Stasi´um, a stagnant water formation; **stasoph´ilus** (φιλέω, I love), dwelling in stagnant water; **Stasophy´ta** (φυτὸν, a plant), stagnant water plants (Clements).

State, the most trivial variation from the type.

Statice´tum, an association of *Statice*, Linn.

Sta´tion (*statio*, a standing still), botanically means a particular locality for a given plant.

Sta´tocysts (στάτος, standing still; κύστις, a bag), gravitational sense organs, sensory cells containing free starch-grains and ectoplast, sensitive to the pressure of these grains (Haberlandt); **Sta´tocytes** = STATOCYSTS; **Sta´tolith** (λίθος, stone), starch grains regarded as causing curvature by their weight; **Sta´toplasts** (πλαστὸς, moulded), movable starch grains; **Statosper´mus** (σπέρμα, a seed), when a seed is straight or erect within the pericarp; **Sta´tospore** (σπορὰ, a seed), a resting spore.

Staurogam´ia (σταυρὸς, a stake or cross; γάμος, marriage), Delpino's term for cross-fertilization; adj. **staurogam´ic**.

stauromat´ic, resembling the genus *Stauroma*; isidioid.

Stau´ros (σταυρὸς, a stake or cross), in Diatoms, (1) the central nodule of the valve; (2) a transverse band without markings; **Staur´ophyll** (φύλλον, a leaf), Clements's term for a leaf consisting of palisade cells; **staurophyl´lus**, cruciate.

Ste´arin (στέαρ, suet), an abundant ingredient of animal and vegetable fats; **Stearop´tene** (πτηνὸς, winged = volatile), a solid crystallizable matter allied to camphor, present in many essential oils.

Steganochamaephyti´um (στεγανὸς, roofed over, + CHAMAEPHYTIUM), dwarf-shrub association under trees (Vahl); **Steganocryptophyti´um** (+ CRYPTOPHYTIUM), an association of hemicryptophytes and geophytes under an upper layer (Vahl).

Stegi´um (στέγη, a roof or covering), term proposed by Miers for the thread-like appendages sometimes found covering the style of Asclepiads; **Steg´mata**, pl., flat, tabular cells in certain Ferns, etc., containing a mass of silica in contact with their inner wall (Mettenius); also termed Covering-plate; **stegocar´pic**, **stegocar´pous** (καρπὸς, fruit), applied to those Mosses whose capsules have a distinct operculum.

ste´lar (στήλη, a pillar), possessing a stele; **Stele**, an axial cylinder of tissue passing from the plerome into the older tissues, in which the vascular tissue is developed; sometimes more than one, *cf.* POLYSTELY, SCHIZOSTELY; *also* PERIPHERAL ~ ; REPARATIVE ~ ; **ste´lic**, relating to a stele or its tissues.

Stelid´ium, pl. **Stelid´ia** (στηλίδιον, a small pillar), Ridley's term for the teeth of the column in *Bulbophyllum*.

stel´late, *stella´tus* (Lat., starry), star-shaped or radiating like the points of a star; ~ **Hairs**, hairs of a star-like form; ~ **Scales**, trichomes, discs borne by their edge or centre; **stellif´erous** (*fero*, I bear), star-bearing; **stelliform´is** (*forma*, shape), star-shaped; **stellig´erus** (*gero*, I bear), star-bearing or producing; **stella´to-pilo´sus**, covered with stellate hairs; **stelliner´vius** (*nervus*, a nerve), star-ribbed, as the leaves of *Hydrocotyle vulgaris*, Linn.; **Stel´lula** (Lat., a little star), (1) a whorl of perigonial leaves in Mosses; (2) a small rosette; **stel´lular**, **stel´lulate**, *stellula´tus*, diminutive of stellate.

Stelolem´ma (στήλη, a pillar; λέμμα, bark or skin), a sheath of thickened peridesmic or stelar tissue in angiospermous petioles (Strasburger).

Stem, the main ascending axis; ~ **Bud**, the plumule; ~ **clasp´ing**, amplexicaul; ~ **-form**, in Germ. Stammform, the ancestral form (Kuntze); ~ **Leaf**, a leaf given off from the stem, as opposed to a radical leaf; ~ **Par´asite**, a parasitic plant which lives on the stem of its host, as Loranthaceae; ~ **Ten´dril**, a tendril which is morphologically a stem structure; **subter-**

ra'nean ~, a rhizome ; stem'less,
having no visible stem, acaulous ;
Stem'let, a small stem, such as the
plumule.

stenocar'pus (στένος, narrow ; καρπὸς,
fruit), narrow fruited ; stenocho'ric
(χωρέω, I spread abroad), applied to
a family, genus or species, with a
range of distribution over a narrow
area of constant climate, and confined to one, or very few, plant-
formations (Drude) ; Stenocho'ry is
the state in question ; stenohal'ine
(ἅλς, ἁλὸς, salt), applied to organisms which can endure only 3 or
4 per cent of salt in solution (Forel) ;
stenopet'alous (πέταλον, a flower-
leaf), narrow-petalled ; stenopho'tic
(φὼς, φωτὸς, light), requiring a constant amount of light, within
narrow variation ; stenophyl'lous,
-lus (φύλλον, a leaf), (1) narrow
leaved ; (2) Beccari's term for plants
on river banks, etc., with linear or
very narrow leaves; Stenoph'yllism is
the state in question ; Steno'sis, (1)
cell-formation with constriction of
the original cell-wall ; (2) the contraction of a passage ; stenother'mic
(θέρμη, heat), needing a uniform
temperature.

stephanocar'pus (στεφανώδης, wreath-
ing ; καρπὸς, fruit), with fruit arranged so as to resemble a crown ;
Stephanodophy'tum (φυτὸν, a plant),
a plant producing an inferior achene,
as Compositae.

stephanokon'tan, relating to Stepha-
nokontae, a class of green Algae,
whose zoospores are characterised
by a crown of cilia round the
anterior end.

Steph'anoum (στέφανος, a crown), a
synonym of CREMOCARP and CYP-
SELA.

Steppe, a wide, treeless plain of grass-
land (Schimper) ; cf. PRAIRIE,
PAMPAS ; ~ -pe'riod, a time following the TUNDRA-PERIOD in
Switzerland, when steppe plants
were dominant.

Ster'eid (στερεὸς, solid), a lignified
cell from the stereome.

stereodonta'ceous, allied to the genus
Stereodon.

Stereogen'nylae (στερεὸς, solid ; γένος,
race ; ὕλη = materia), Radlkofer's
term for BRYOPHYTES ; Ster'eom or
Ster'eome, the elements of a bundle
which impart strength to it, the
fibres, or strengthening tissue
generally (Schwendener) ; stereo-
mat'ic, resembling or composed of
STEREOME ; Stereone'ma, pl. Stereone'mata, solid threads which make
up the capillitium in Fuligo (Zopf) ;
Ster'eoplasm (πλάσμα, moulded), the
solid part of protoplasm (Naegeli) ;
stereosperm'ous (σπέρμα, a seed),
with solid seed (Heinig) ; Stereo-
tax'is (τάξις, order) = THIGMOTAXIS ;
Stereot'ropism (τροπὴ, a turning),
a definite direction towards the
substratum (Loeb).

Sterig'ma, pl. Sterig'mata (στήριγμα,
a prop), (1) in Fungi, a stalk from
which a spore is abjointed ; (2)
any leafy prolongation or elevated
line from the blade of a leaf down
the stem by decurrence ; (3)
Desvaux's name for CARCERULE ;
Sterig'mum is a synonym of the
last definition.

ster'ile, ster'ilis (Lat.), (1) barren, as
a flower destitute of pistil, or a
stamen wanting the anther ; (2)
used for a male or staminate
flower ; (3) free from living organisms, such as bacteria ; ~ Basid'ium,
a body in the hymenium of Agarics
like a basidium, but not producing
spores, possibly a paraphysis ; ~
Cells, cells of unknown function in
the pollen-grains of Cycas and
microspores of Isoëtes and Selaginella ; Steril'ity, Steril'itas (Lat.),
barrenness, incapacity of producing
seeds ; Self ~, when the pollen is
inactive on the stigmas of the same
flower (Knuth) ; Steriliza'tion, the
act of sterilizing ; ster'ilize, to make
free from living organisms or their
germs.

sternotri'bal (στέρνον, the breast ;
τρίβω, I beat), Delpino's term for
those flowers whose anthers are so

arranged as to dust their pollen on the under part of the thorax of their insect visitors; **stern′otribe, sternotri′bous,** are synonyms.

Ster′om = STEREOME (Crozier).

Ster′rhad(στερρὸς, rugged—of countries, +AD), a moor plant (Clements); **Sterrhi′um,** a moor formation; **sterroph′ilus** (φιλέω, I love), moorloving; **Sterrophy′ta** (φυτὸν, a plant), moor plants (Clements).

Ste′somy (στήσομαι, fut. med. of ἵστημι, to stop), Morren's term for an arrest of metamorphosis.

Stich′id = STICHIDIUM.

Stichid′ium (στιχίδιον, a little row or rank), (1) in Rhodophyceae, a special branch of the thallus with embedded tetragonidia; (2) = CARPOCLONIUM.

stichocar′pus, stichocar′picus (στίχος, a row; καρπὸς, fruit), when fruit is disposed along a spiral line; **stich′us,** in Greek compounds = row or rank, usually vertical.

stictopet′alus (στικτὸς, punctured; πέταλον, a flower-leaf), when petals are covered with glandular points.

Stig′ma, pl. _Stig′mata,_ or **Stig′mas** (στίγμα, a point), (1) that part of the pistil or style which receives the pollen; (2) a point on the spores of _Equisetum;_ (3) a caducous point on the apex of the columella in Mosses; (4) an old name for STERIGMA; (5) a coloured spot in unicellular Algae; ~ **Disk,** a disk forming the stigmatic surface as in Asclepiads; ~ of Mosses (Hook. Musc. ed. 2), the mouth of the archegonium.

stigmar′ian, resembling _Stigmaria_ in structure or affinities; **Stigm′aria,** roots of fossil plants having regular dotted or pitted markings; **Stig′marhize** (ρίζα, a root), a form of _Stigmaria,_ regarded by Renault as a root; **Stigmarhi′zome** (+ RHIZOME), Renault's term for a form of _Stigmaria_ which he considered a rhizome.

Stig′matae (στίγμα, a point), Van Tieghem's term for Phanerogams having stigmata; **Stigmataste′mon** ‡ (στήμων, a filament), a body formed by the union of anthers to the

stigma (De Candolle); **stigmat′ic,** _stigmat′icus,_ relating to the stigma; ~ **Cells,** of archegonia, = LID-CELLS; ~ **Cham′ber,** that part of the rostellum in Orchids in which the retinaculum is developed; ~ **Flu′id,** ~ **Secre′tion,** the viscid fluid secreted by the stigma at maturity, securing the adhesion of pollen grains and their subsequent germination; **Stigmat′icae,** Knuth's term for wind-fertilized flowers with conspicuous stigmas; **stigmatif′erous** (_fero,_ I bear), stigma-bearing; **stigmatiform′is** (_forma,_ shape), shaped like a stigma, or having the appearance of one; **stigmatoi′deus** (εἶδος, resemblance) = stigmatiformis; **Stigmatoph′orus** ‡ (φορέω, I carry), that part of the style of Compositae which bears the stigmas; **stig′matose,** _stigmato′sus,_ provided with stigmas, or having them conspicuous; **Stig′matospore** (+ SPORE) = OSMOSPORE; **Stig′mula,** a division of a stigma, when present.

Stilid′ium (στυλὶς, a small post), a canal-like portion of the archegonium of a Moss.

Stiliplank′ton (+ PLANKTON), floating marine vegetation, chiefly consisting of _Rhizosolenia styliformis._

still, dormant; ~ **Spore,** a resting spore.

Stilogonid′ia = STYLOGONIDIA.

Stilt-roots, the oblique adventitious roots of the Mangrove and similar forms (Kerner).

Stimula′tion (_stimulatio,_ incitement), the act of being roused by some exciting cause, such as heat or light; _cf._ REACTION; **Stimula′tors,** pl., tactile hairs or bristles which transmit stimuli to the sensitive mortissue (Haberlandt); **Stim′uli,** pl. of **Stim′ulus** (Lat., a goad) = (1) STING; (2) the particular active agent which produces definite changes in the organism, as moisture, light, etc.; **stim′ulose,** _stimulo′sus,_ covered with stinging hairs; **stim′ulous** (Lat.), stinging.

Sting, a hollow hair seated on a gland

which secretes an acid lymph, as in nettles.

Sting′ing-hair = STING.

Stink′ing-smut, of wheat, is *Tilletia Tritici* (Winter).

sti′pate (*stipatus*, surrounded), pressed together, crowded; **Stipa′tion**, an accumulation in the tissues or cavities.

Stipe, *Sti′pes* (Lat., a stock or trunk), a support such as (1) the stalk which bears the pileus of Agarics; (2) the "leafstalk" of a Fern; (3) the support of a gynaecium or carpel.

Stip′el, suggested by F. v. Mueller for STIPELLA.

Stipel′la, Stipel′lum (dim. of STIPULA), a minute stipule on a partial petiole of compound leaves; **stipel′late,** *stipella′tus*, furnished with Stipellae.

Stipel′lus (*dim.* of STIPES), a synonym of the FILAMENT of an anther.

stipif′erus ‡ (*stipes*, a stock; *fero*, I bear), bearing small flower-stalks, as the receptacle of some Composites; **sti′piform,** *stipiform′is* (*forma*, shape), having the appearance of the trunk of an endogenous tree, as the Papaw; **stip′itate,** *stipita′tus*, having a stipe or special stalk; **stip′-itiform,** *stipitiform′is*. = STIPIFORM.

stip′ticus = STYPTICUS, astringent.

stipula′ceous, *-ceus* (STIPULA+ACEUS), (1) belonging to a stipule; (2) with large stipules; **stip′ular,** having stipules, or relating to them; **stip′ulary,** (1) occupying the place of stipules, as some tendrils; (2) formed of stipules (Crozier).

stip′ulate, *stipula′tus, stipular′is*, (1) having stipules, or conspicuously provided with them; (2) with scales which are degenerate stipules; **stip′ulaeform, stip′uliform** (*forma*, shape), shaped as though a stipule; **Stipula′tion,** *Stipula′tio*, the arrangement of the stipules; **Stip′ule,** *Stip′ula* (Lat., stubble), an appendage of a leaf on each side of the leaf-insertion of those plants which possess them; **stipulea′nus,** resulting from the transformation of a stipule; *cf.* PSEUDO-STIPULE; **stip-ulif′erous,** *-rus* (*fero*, I bear), bear-

ing stipules; **Stip′ulode,** a stipular organ of one cell, in one or more rows subtending the branchlets in *Chara*; **stip′ulose,** *stipulo′sus*, having very large stipules.

stirpa′lis ‡ (*stirps*, a trunk, a plant), growing upon a stem; **Stirps,** pl. **Stir′pes,** (1) a race or permanent variety, as the Red Cabbage; (2) formerly equivalent to species; (3) a stem (Kerner), as **Stirps cirrho′sa,** a tendril-bearing stem; ~ **clath′rans,** a lattice-forming stem; ~ **fluctu′ans,** a floating stem; ~ **humifu′sa,** a prostrate stem; ~ **palar′is,** an erect, unbranched stem; ~ **plec′tens,** a weaving stem; ~ **radi′cans,** a stem which climbs by means of roots; ~ **volu′bilis,** a climbing stem.

Stock, (1) a synonym of RACE; (2) the stem which receives the scion in grafting; (3) a caudex or rhizome which emits roots.

Stole, Sto′lon, *Stol′o* (Lat., a shoot), a sucker, runner, or any basal branch which is disposed to root; **stolonif′erous** *-rus* (*fero*, I bear), sending out or propagating itself by stolons; **stolon′iform** (*forma*, shape) **Stem,** "a slender creeping stem with minute leaves" (Dixon and Jameson).

Stom′a, pl. **Stom′ata** (στόμα, a mouth) or **Sto′mate,** (1) a breathing pore or aperture in the epidermis, surrounded by two guard-cells, leading into an intercellular space communicating with internal tissue; according to Tschirch of four types; **angiosper′mal** ~, **archego′nial,** ~ **eiso′dial** ~, and **opisthe′lial** ~; (2) the ostiole of certain Fungi, *cf.* EPIPHRAGMA; **sto′matal, stomat′ic,** pertaining to stomata; **stomat′ic Cells** = GUARD-CELLS; ~ **Cleft,** an actual stoma without the guard-cells; **stomatif′erous,** *-rus* (*fero*, I bear), bearing stomata; **Stomat′ium** = STOMA; **Stomat′ograph** (γράφω, I write), an instrument for measuring stomatal variation; **stom′atose,** in Mosses, possessing stomata; **Stom′-ium,** an opening on the side of Fern-sporangia, between the lip-cells, through which dehiscence takes place.

Stone, the 'hard endocarp of a drupe; ~ **Cells**, the individual cells which have become hardened by secondary deposit, the components of sclerogen; ~ **Fruit**, a drupe such as a plum or peach.

Stool, (1) a plant from which offsets or layers are taken; (2) when several stems rise from the same root, as in wheat.

Stop'per, a word applied by Archer to the callus-plates in Algae; ~ **of Pol'len**, hyaline protoplasmic deposits in pollen-tubes (Degaguy).

Stop'ples, the projection or lids in pollen-grains which fall away to admit of the passage of the pollen-tube.

Stor'ax = STYRAX.

Stor'ey, the same as LAYER.

strag'gling, divaricate.

Stra'gulum ‡ (Lat., a covering), the paleae of grasses.

straight, in a right line, not curved; ~ **ribbed**, ~ **veined**, when the ribs run in a straight line, as in the leaves of many Monocotyledons.

Strain, (1) in atavism, the influence of some ancestor; (2) a slight variety of race.

Stra'men (Lat.), straw; **straminel'lus** (N. Lat.), somewhat straw-coloured; **stramin'eous**, *-neus*, straw-like or straw-coloured.

Strand, (1) a bundle of vascular tissue, resembling a cord; (2) shore, as ~ **-plants**, used by C. MacMillan for shore plants; ~ **Myce'lium** = mycelial strand.

stran'gulated (*strangulatus*, choked), contracted and expanded in an irregular manner.

Strap, the ligule of a ray floret in Compositae (Crozier); ~ **shaped**, ligulate or lorate.

Stra'ta, pl. (*stratum*, a layer), layers of tissue; **Stratifica'tion** (*facio*, I make), (1) the successive deposition of layers on the cell-wall, and the arrangement of the said layers;

(2) the differences in vegetation at different vertical levels; the various stages may be called strata or layers (Yapp); **strat'ified**, disposed in layers; ~ **Thal'lus**, a Lichen thallus in which the gonidial layer or layers are evident; **stra'tose**, in distinct layers (Crozier); **Stra'tum**, a layer of tissue; ~ **cellulo'sum**, the bark layer next within the epidermis; ~ **cortica'le**, any bast layer; ~ **gonidia'le**, ~ **gon'imon**, the Algal layer in Lichens; ~ **lig'-neum**, a layer of wood; ~ **medulla're**, the medulla or pith; ~ **sporidiif'erum**, the flesh of Agarics; ~ **sporoph'orum**, the hymenium of Fungi. For ecological purposes there are:—Ground- ~ immediately above the soil; Field- ~ formed by grass and herbs; Shrub- ~ of the taller shrubs; Tree- ~, composed of trees.

Straw, the jointed hollow culm of grasses.

Streak, a disease in *Lathyrus odoratus*, ascribed to *Thielavia basicola*, Zopf.

Stream'ing, the flow of protoplasm as in Myxogastres.

strephotrich'ial, belonging to the genus *Strephothrix*.

Strepsine'ma (στρέψω, I will twist; νῆμα, a thread), delicate parallel threads twisted about each other in the nucleus in a stage of synapsis; adj. **strep'sitene**.

streptocar'pus (στρεπτὸς, twisted; καρπὸς, fruit), when fruit is marked spirally.

Stri'ae, pl. (*stria*, a furrow), markings on the valves of Diatoms which present the appearance of lines; **stri'ate**, *stria'tus*, marked with fine longitudinal parallel lines, as grooves or ridges; **Stria'tion**, of cell-wall, markings believed to be due to the manner of formation in bands by the protoplasm.

strict, *stric'tus* (Lat., drawn together), close or narrow and upright, very straight.

Strig'a (Lat., a swathe), "a small straight hair-like scale" (J. S. Henslow).

strig'illose (*strigilis*, a currycomb) = STRIGOSE (Henslow).

stri'gose, *strigo'sus* (Lat., lank, meagre), beset with sharp-pointed appressed straight and stiff hairs or bristles; hispid.

strike, to emit roots as from a cutting.

String, any fibre or strand (Hillhouse).

Stri'olae, pl. (*stria*, a groove), lines of minute pustules on the outer surface of cells of *Sphagnum* (Spruce); **stri'olate**, finely striate.

striped, marked with longitudinal stripes of colour.

Strob'il = STROBILE; **strobila'ceous**, *-ceus* (στρόβιλος, a cone, + ACEOUS), relating to or resembling a cone; **strob'ilate** means the same; **Strob'ile**, *Strob'ilus*, (1) an inflorescence largely made up of imbricated scales, as the Hop or Fir-cone; (2) *cf.* STROBILOID; (3) the special form of the assumed type of the angiospermous flower (Arber and Parkin); **strobilif'erous**, *-rus* (*fero*, I bear), cone-bearing; **strobili'nus**, cone-like; **strobil'iform**, *strobiliform'is* (*forma*, shape), cone-shaped; **strob'iloid** (εἶδος, resemblance), cone-like; ~ **The'ory**, the assumed origin of Pteridophytes, in those forms whose sporophytes are the most primitive, as *Lycopodium* and *Equisetum* (Bower).

Stro'ma (στρῶμα, a mattress), a cushion-like body, on or in which the perithecia are immersed, a compound Fungus-body; ~ **Starch**, in certain Algae, as in *Hydrodictyon*, the fine starch deposited throughout the chlorophyll-body; **stro'matoid** (εἶδος, resemblance), having the nature or seeming of a stroma; **stro'matous**, producing stroma (Crozier).

strombulif'erous, *-rus* (*strombus*, a spiral shell; *fero*, I bear), **stromb'uliform**, *strombuliform'is* (*forma*, shape), when the fruit is spirally twisted; **Strom'bus**, a spirally coiled legume, as in *Medicago*; **strom'bus-shaped**, like a snail-shell.

Strophan'thine, a poisonous alkaloid from *Strophanthus hispidus*, DC.

Stroph'es, pl. (στροφή, a turning), any spirals shown in phyllotaxy; **stroph'ic**, applied by Rothert to a twisting movement in Chemotaxis and Phototaxis, as contrasted with APOBATIC or repulsive movements; **Stroph'iole**, **Stroph'iola** (*strophiolum*, a small chaplet), an appendage to the hilum of some seeds, a caruncle; **stroph'iolate**, possessing such appendages.

Stroph'ism (στροφή, a turning), tendency to twist in response to some external stimulus (Czapek); **Strophogen'esis** (γένεσις, origin), differentiation of a single original generation into the phases regarded as alternation of generations (Strasburger); **Strophoma'nia** (μάνια, madness), special torsion, as in the stems of certain monstrosities; **Strophotax'is** (τάξις, order), arrangement due to the twisting movement; **Stroph'y** = STROPHISM.

Struc'ture, *Structu'ra* (Lat., fitting together), the peculiar organization of plants, with special modifications; adj. **struc'tural**; ~ **Bot'any**, includes Organography, Morphology, Anatomy, and Histology of plants.

Stru'ma (Lat., a scrofulous tumour), a wen or cushion-like swelling on an organ; **strumif'erous** (*fero*, I bear), having a strumous or goitre-like swelling; **stru'miform**, *strumiform'is* (*forma*, shape), with the appearance of a wen; **stru'mulose**, *strumulo'sus*, somewhat strumous, or having a small struma; **stru'mose**, *strumo'sus*; **stru'mous**, as though scrofulous; **stru'mosely**, with cushion-like swellings.

Strych'nia, **Strych'nin**, a powerfully poisonous alkaloid from *Strychnos Nux-vomica*, Linn.

strychni'nus (Mod. Lat.), the colour of the seeds of *Strychnos Nux-vomica* (Hayne).

Stud'y-set, the principal set of a collector's plants, enriched by notes.

stuffed, solid, farctate (Crozier).

Stu'pa or **Stup'pa** (Lat., the coarse

part of flax), a tuft or mass of hair or filaments matted together ; **stu'peous**, *stu'peus* or *stup'peus*, woolly.; **stu'pose**, *stupo'sus*, towlike, with tufts of long hairs.

styg'ius (*Styx*, *Stygis*, an infernal river), used of plants which grow in foul waters.

sty'lar (*stylus*, from στῦλος, a column), relating to the style, as ~ **Brush**, the collecting hairs of flowers, *cf.* COLLECTORS ; ~ **Canal'**, the tube or loose tissue through which the pollen-tubes pass ; ~ **Col'umn**, the column of Orchids ; ~ **Foot** = STYLOPODIUM ; **sty'lans** (+ STYLE), used by Burchell for a gradual enlargement of the style into the ovary ; **styla'tus** (Lat.) = STYLOSUS ; **Style**, *Sty'lus*, (1) the usually attenuated part of a pistil or carpel between the ovary and the stigma ; ~ of Hepaticae, = INTERLOBULE ; ~ of Mosses, (1) an old term for the neck of the archegonium ; (2) the ostiole of certain Fungi (Lindley) ; **Styleta'ble**, used by Haworth for the flattened apex of the style in Asclepiads ; **sty'liform**, *styliform'is* (*forma*, shape), style-shaped, drawn out ; **stylif'erous** (*fero*, I bear), bearing a style ; **styli'nus** (Lat.), belonging to the style ; **Styliplank'ton** (+ PLANKTON), floating neritic vegetation composed of *Rhizosolenia styliformis*; **Stylis'cus** = STYLAR CANAL.

stylo'deus (Lat.), furnished with a style ; **Stylod'ium**, Mod. Lat. from *Stylus*, (1) a style-like stigma, as in grasses, and Compositae ; (2) a false style, as the appendages to the anthers of *Cynomorium*.

Stylogonid'ium (στῦλος, a column, + GONIDIUM), a gonidium formed by abstriction from special hyphae in such Fungi as Aecidiomycetes and Basidiomycetes, that is, uredo-, teleuto-, and basidio-spores ; **Sty'-loids**, pl. (εἶδος, resemblance), columnar crystals occurring in plant-cells (Solereder) ; **Sty'lopod**, *Stylopod'ium* (πούς, ποδός, a foot), the enlargement at the base of the styles in Umbelli-

ferae ; **sty'lose**, *stylo'sus*, having styles of a remarkable length or persistence ; **Sty'lospore** (σπορά, a seed), a spore borne on a filament ; adj. **stylosp'orous** ; **Stylosteg'ium** (στέγη, a roof), a peculiar hood surrounding the style, as in Asclepiads ; **Styloste'-mon** ‡ (στήμων, a filament), an epigynous stamen ; **styloste'mus**, hermaphrodite ; **Styloteg'ium** (τέγος, a covering) = STYLOSTEGIUM ; **Sty'lus** = STYLE.

styp'ticus (Lat. from στυπτικὸς, astringent) ; usually implies use to stanch a wound.

Sty'rax, or **Stor'ax**, (1) a solid resin from *Styrax officinale*, Linn. ; (2) at the present day a similar balsamic resin from *Liquidambar styraciflua*, Linn.

styrido'phytus (σταυρὸς, a cross ; φυτὸν, a plant), with cruciform petals (J. S. Henslow).

suav'eolent, *suav'eolens* (Lat.), sweet-smelling, fragrant.

sub (Lat.), under or below, in compounds usually implies an approach to the condition designated, somewhat, or slightly ; **subacau'lis** (+ ACAULIS), with the stem hardly apparent : **sub'acute** (+ ACUTE), somewhat acute ; **subarc'tic** (+ ARCTIC), northern plants above the limit of cultivation ; *cf.* INFER-ARCTIC ; **subaë'rial** (*aërius*, airy), situated almost on the ground level, as a rhizome which is covered with leaves, etc., but above the soil ; **subal'pine** (+ ALPINE), applied to vegetation above the general limit of vegetation but below the uppermost series or alpine ; **subapicula'ris** (+ APICULARIS), when the stem is prolonged beyond an inflorescence without branch or leaf ; **subapic'ulate**, with an ill-defined point ; **subarbores'cent** (+ ARBORESCENT), with a tendency to become somewhat tree-like ; **subarchespor'ial** (+ ARCHESPORIAL) **Pad**, Bower's term for a cushion-like group of cells below the archesporium in *Lycopodium* ; **subax'ile** (+AXILE), nearly **subaxil'lary**, below the axil ;

sub-ba'sal (+ BASAL) Cell, the cell next below the BASAL CELL in Angiosperms (Wiegand); **sub-Bellar'dian,** slightly resembling *Rubus Bellardi* (Rogers); **subbiator'ine** (+ BIATORINE), somewhat as in the Lichen genus *Biatora*; **subbif'ido-rum'pens‡** (+ BIFIDUS), "bursting into somewhat two divisions" (Lindley); **subbilocula'ris** (+ BILOCULARIS), with partitions which do not quite join, but leave a small interval; **subbys'soid** (+ BYSSOID), somewhat cobwebby; **subcaules'cent** (+ CAULESCENT), with a very short stem, a trifle more developed than acaulescent; **subces'pitose** (+ CAESPITOSE), somewhat tufted (Crozier); **Sub'class** (+ CLASS), a group of Orders or Cohorts next in rank to a Class, or intermediate between Class and Cohort; **subconcat'enate** (+ CONCATENATE), growing in imperfect chains or connections; **subcon'ical** (+ CONICAL), slightly conical; **subcontin'uous** (*continuus*, unbroken), rarely or imperfectly septate (Crozier); **subcon'volute,** *subconvolu'tus* (+ CONVOLUTE), partially convolute; **subco'pious** (*copiosus*, plentifully), "scattered somewhat loosely" (Clements); **subcor'date** (+ CORDATE); **subcordifor'mis** (+ CORDIFORM), somewhat heart-shaped; **subcre'nate** (+ CRENATE), obscurely crenate; **subcul'trate** (+CULTRATE), slightly cultrate; **subden'droid** (+ DENDROID), somewhat tree-like; **subden'tate** (+ DENTATE), imperfectly dentate; **subdentic'ulate** (+ DENTICULATE), with small or imperfect marginal teeth; **subdifform'is** (+ DIFFORMIS), having some amount of irregularity; **Subdioe'cism** (+ DIOECISM), a tendency to be dioecious; **subdom'inant** (+ DOMINANT), less than dominant, but present in some force; **sub'effuse** (+ EFFUSE), slightly spreading; **sub'entire** (+ ENTIRE), having very slight marginal incisions; **subeph'edroid** (εἶδος, resemblance), like the genus *Ephedra*; **subepiderm'al** (+ EPIDERMAL), below the epidermis; ∼ **Tis'sue,** = HYPODERMA.

Su'ber (Lat., the cork-oak), cork or phellogen; **suber'eous,** = suberose; **Suber'ification** (*facio,* I make) = SUBERIZATION; **Su'berin,** the substance of cork, nearly the same as cutin; ∼ **Mem'brane,** with cell-walls turned into cork; **Suberinlamel'la** (+ LAMELLA), a thin layer of cork-like tissue in the cortex (Höhnel); **Suberiza'tion,** conversion into cork, cutinization; **su'berized,** converted into cork; **su'berose,** *subero'sus,* **su'berous,** corky in texture.

sub'erect, *suberect'us* (*sub,* somewhat, + ERECT), nearly erect, but nodding at the top (Babington); **suberose'** (+ EROSE), slightly gnawed in appearance.

Su'bex (Lat., support, underlayer), that part of the axis which bears cataphyllary leaves (Kerner).

Subfam'ily (*sub,* below), a group of genera within a family; **subflex'uose** (+ FLEXUOSE), somewhat wavy; **Subforma'tion** (+ FORMATION), a plant-formation of lesser grade; **Subforms,** pl. (+ FORM), in *Rosa,* with irregular serration and glandular calyx-segments (Almquist); **subgenic'ulate** (+ GENICULATE), slightly bent or kneed; **Subgen'us** (+ GENUS), a group, ranking as a section, or possibly a true genus held doubtful; **subglobose'** (+ GLOBOSE), nearly globular; **subgluma'ceous** (+GLUMACEOUS), somewhat glumaceous; **subgrega'rious** (*gregarius,* belonging to a herd), "arranged in loose groups" (Clements); **Subgreg'iform** (*grex, gregis,* a flock; + FORM), a VERSIFORM which has varied in different localities or countries (Kuntze); **subhyme'nial** (+ HYMENIAL), below the hymenium; ∼ **Lay'er** or **Subhyme'nium** = HYPOTHECIUM.

Subic'ulum (Lat., an underlayer), a felted or byssoid stratum of hyphae, bearing perithecia.

subim'bricate, *subimbrica'tus* (*sub,* somewhat, + IMBRICATE), somewhat overlapping.

subinsip′idus (*sub*, below ; *insipidus*, tasteless), almost devoid of flavour ; **subja′cent** (*jacens*, lying), lying just below (Dixon and Jameson) ; **Subking′dom**, the main division of a kingdom, a primary botanic division, as Phanerogams and Cryptogams ; **sub-Koeler′ian**, somewhat resembling *Rubus Koeleri* (Rogers).

subla′tus (Lat., lifted up), when the ovary has a support, real or apparent. **sublentic′ular** (*sub*, somewhat, + LENTICULAR), more or less doubly convex ; **sublit′toral** (+ LITTORAL), employed by H. C. Watson for those plants which have a tendency to grow near the sea, but not actually shore-plants ; **submar′ginal** (+ MARGINAL), near the margin ; **submar′itime** plants characteristic of the sea, but also occurring inland, as *Armeria maritima*.

submerged′, submersed′, *submer′sus* (Lat., dipped or plunged under), growing under water ; **submersi′bilis** (Mod. Lat.), capable of existing when submersed ; **Submersipra′ta,** pl. (*pratum*, a meadow), formations of macrophytic aquatic plants, with submerged or floating leafy shoots.

submicron′ic (*sub*, below ; μίκρος, small), used of objects visible only under the ultra-microscope.

subnas′cent (*subnascor*, I grow up under), growing or arising from below some object.

subni′ger (Lat., somewhat black) = NIGRICANS ; **sub′nude** (*nudus*, naked), nearly destitute of covering, as leaves or hairs ; **sub′obtuse** (+ OBTUSE), slightly obtuse or blunt ; **suborbic′ular** (+ ORBICULAR), nearly circular ; **Subor′der,** *Subordo,* a group of genera lower than an order ; **sub′o′vate** (+ OVATE), somewhat ovate ; **subpedunc′ulate** (+ PEDUNCULATE), supported on a very short stem ; **subperiphaer′icus** (+ PERIPHERIC), nearly peripheric, used of an embryo, such as in *Atriplex* (S. F. Gray) ; **subpet′iolar,** *subpetiola′ris,* **subpet′iolate** (+ PETIOLATE), under

the petioles, as the buds of *Platanus ;* **Subquad′rat** (+ QUADRAT), a quadrat of 1 to 8 decimetres (Clements) ; **subramea′lis** (+ RAMEAL), growing on a branch below a leaf ; **subra′mose,** *subramo′sus,* **subra′mous** (+ RAMOSE), (1) having a slight tendency to branch ; (2) with few branches ; **subrig′id** (+ RIGID), slightly rigid ; **subro′seus** (+ ROSEUS), somewhat rose-coloured, pinkish ; **subrotund′** (+ ROTUND), roundish ; **subscyph′iform** (+ SCYPHIFORM), somewhat boat-shaped ; **Subsec′tion** (+ SECTION), the division of a genus below a section, a small section ; **subser′rate,** *subserra′tus* (+ SERRATE), vaguely serrate ; **subses′sile** (+ SESSILE), nearly sessile, almost devoid of a stalk ; **Sub′shrub,** an under-shrub, or small shrub which may have partially herbaceous stems.

subsid′iary (*subsidiarius*, serving for support) **Cells,** certain epidermal cells which are less thickened or situated lower than the guard-cells which they surround (Strasburger).

subsigillar′ian (*sub,* somewhat), *Sigillaria* stems without ribs (Arber and Parkin) ; **subsim′ple** (+ SIMPLE), with few divisions ; **Subspe′cies,** a group of forms ambiguous in rank, between a variety and a species, usually marked by an asterisk(*) ; **subspor′al** (σπορά, a seed) **Cells,** applied to certain colourless cells in *Pithophora,* found in spore-bearing individuals (Wittrock).

sub′stantive (*substantivus,* self-existent) **Varia′tion,** used by Bateson to denote change in actual composition.

sub′stitute (*substitutus,* put in place of) **Associa′tion** = SECONDARY FORMATION ; ~ **Fi′bres,** like libriform fibres, but a much reduced form of prosenchyma, the "Ersatzfasern" of Sanio ; **Substitu′tion,** Lopriore's term for healing processes by formation of new growth from secondary meristem.

substomat′ic (*sub,* below, + STOMATIC)

Cham'ber = STOMATIC CHAMBER ; **substo'mal** has the same meaning ; **substra'tose** (+STRATOSE),somewhat stratified, or in layers.

subtend' (*subtendo*, I stretch underneath), to extend under, or be opposite to ; **subten'ding Leaf**, that leaf whose axil gives rise to a bud or peduncle.

subterete' (*sub*, somewhat, + TERETE), somewhat terete.

subterra'neous, *subterra'neus* (Lat.), underground.

Subtrac'tion (*subtractus*, drawn off) **Stage**, employed by Bateson for the loss of a factor.

subtremell'oid (*sub*, under ; ϵἶδos, resemblance), gelatinous, somewhat resembling *Tremella* ; **Sub'tribe** (+ TRIBE), a division between a tribe and a genus ; **subtrop'ic** (+ TROPIC), applied to half-hardy plants which in temperate climates can thrive in summer only.

Su'bula (Lat., a small weapon), a fine sharp point ; **Su'bule**, Duval-Jouve's term for the terminal, non-twisted portion of the awn of grasses ; **su'bulate**, *subula'tus*, awl-shaped ; **Su'buli**, pl., "the aciculae or sharp processes formed by some Fungals" (Lindley); **su'bulifer, subulif'erous** (*fero*, I bear), bearing sharp points ; **su'buliform**, *subuliform'is* (*forma*, shape), awl-shaped.

subum'bellate (*sub*, somewhat, + UMBELLATE), somewhat umbellate, as the inflorescence of some Rosaceae ; **Subvari'ety**, *Subvar'ietas* (+ VARIETY), a trifling variety or form ; **subven'tricose** (+VENTRICOSE),somewhat inflated ; **subvertic'illate**, in imperfect or irregular whorls; **subxeroph'ilous** (+ XEROPHILOUS), preferring dry situations, but not confined to them.

Succeda'neum (*succedaneus*, substituted), a substitute.

Succes'sion (*successio*, a following), appearing in successive intervals, on soils of differing character.

succes'sive (*successivus*, following) **Whorl**, one whose members did not originate simultaneously, but in succession.

succif'erous (*succus*, sap ; *fero*, I bear), producing or conveying sap.

succinc'tus (Lat., ready) = CIRCINATUS.

succin'eus or *sucin'eus* (Lat., of amber), amber-coloured ; **Suc'cinite**, the commonest and best known form of amber, resin exuded by *Pinus succinifera*, Goepp., ‡ ; **Succino'sis**, Conwentz's term for an abnormal occurrence of resin in fossil amber-trees.

succise', *succi'sus* (Lat., cut off), as if abruptly cut or broken off at the lower end.

suc'cose, *succo'sus* (Lat., juicy), succulent, sappy.

suc'cubous, -*bus* (Lat., lying under), the oblique insertion of distichous leaves of Hepaticae, so that the upper overlaps the lower on the dorsal side of the stem, as in *Plagiochila*.

suc'culent, *succulen'tus* (Lat., sappy), juicy.

Suc'cus (Lat., sap), any juice which can be expressed from a plant.

Suc'ker, (1) a shoot of subterranean origin ; (2) an haustorium, sometimes restricted to the penetrating organ or papilla.

Su'crase (Fr., *sucre*, sugar, + ase) = INVERTASE ; **Su'crose** (+ ose), a group of sugars, such as cane-sugar and maltose.

Suc'tor (*suctus*, sucked), J. S. Henslow's term for the haustoria of *Bartsia* and other root-parasites.

Suda'tion (*sudatus*, sweated out), exudation of water containing a small amount of substances in solution ; as opposed to Secretion.

suffrutes'cent, *suffrutes'cens* (*sub*, somewhat ; *frutex*, a shrub), obscurely shrubby ; **Suffru'tex**, an undershrub ; **suffru'ticose**, *suffrutico'sus*, **suffrutic'ulose**, somewhat shrubby.

suffful'tus, (1) supported or propped ; (2) **Sufful'tus**, a plate or disc forming the basis of a bulb ; when much lengthened gives rise to the term *Bul'bus suffultus* (Endlicher).

Su'gar, a group of sweet, crystalline substances and soluble in water (sucroses and glucoses); **Beet ~,** extracted from specially selected strains of *Beta vulgaris,* Linn.; **Cane ~,** or saccharose, from *Saccharum officinarum,* Linn.; **Fruit ~** = LAEVULOSE; **Grape ~** = GLUCOSE or DEXTROSE; **Inver'ted ~,** occurs in some ripe fruits and honeydew; **Ma'ple ~,** from *Acer saccharinum,* Wangenh.; **Palm ~,** from species of *Arenga,* etc.

sul'cate, *sulca'tus* (Lat., furrowed), grooved or furrowed.

Sul'ci, pl. of **Sul'cus,** (1) small grooves or FOSSULAE in some Diatom valves; (2) lamellae of certain Fungi (Lindley); **sul'ciform** (*forma,* shape) = SULCATE.

sulfu'reous, etc., see SULPHUREOUS, etc.

Sulphobacter'ia (*sulphur,* brimstone, + BACTERIA), those microbes which reduce sulphur out of its solutions; **Sulphofica'tion,** the production of sulphur by bacteria (Lipman); **sul'phur-col'oured** = SULPHUREOUS; **~ Rain,** pollen from pines brought by currents of air; **Sulphurar'ia,** Planchard's name for Algae which reduce sulphates from waters containing those salts; **sulphurel'lus,** slightly sulphur-coloured; **sulphu'reous,** *-reus,* the colour of brimstone, a very pale yellow; **sulphures'cens,** becoming sulphur-coloured; **sulphuri'nus,** sulphury in tint.

Sum'mer-spore, any spore which germinates quickly, and retains its vitality a short time only, as conidia and uredospores, in contrast to winter- or resting-spores; **~ -wood,** that formed during the middle of the growing season.

Sum'mit, used by Grew and his successors for ANTHER.

Sun-leaves, leaves adapted to develop in full exposure to the sun; **~ -plants,** plants which prefer full sun-light; their stems are often

short, and their leaves have the palisade cells well-developed (Willis).

su'per (Lat.), above; often modified into *supra-*; **superagrar'ian** (+ AGRARIAN), a name applied to a zone which includes the region of vegetation in Great Britain above the limits of cultivation; **superarc'tic,** those plants which are confined to the highest zone in Great Britain, the most alpine of the flora in our islands; **superaxil'lary,** *superaxilla'ris* (+ AXILLARY), growing above an axil; **supercompos'itus** = SUPRACOMPOSITUS; **Supercres'cence** (*cresco,* I grow), the state of a parasite (Crozier); **supercres'cent,** growing above or on another body; **superdecom'pound** = SUPRADECOMPOUND; **Superfecunda'tion** (+ FECUNDATION), the union of more than two gametes.

Superficia'les, pl. (*superficialis,* on the surface), applied to leptosporangiate Ferns, with sori arising from the surface of the frond (Bower); *cf.* MARGINALES.

Superficiar'ius (Lat., on another's land), on the surface of an organ.

Superfic'ies (Lat., the surface), **Cor'poris, ~ Placenta'ris,** "the hymenium of certain Fungals" (Lindley).

Super'flua, pl. of **Super'fluum** (*superfluus,* overflowing), a Linnean order of Syngenesia (Compositae), containing plants with the florets of the disk hermaphrodite, and those of the ray female.

Superfoeta'tion (*super,* above; *fetus,* pregnant), the fertilization of an ovary by more than one kind of pollen; **superfolia'ceous** = SUPRAFOLIACEOUS; **superfo'lius** = SUPRAFOLIUS; **Su'performs,** in *Rosa,* those with doubly serrated leaves and glandular calyx-segments (Almquist).

supe'rior (Lat., higher), (1) growing or placed above; (2) also in a lateral flower on the side next the axis: the posterior or upper lip of a corolla is the superior; **~ O'vary,** when all the floral envelopes are

inserted below it, on the torus ; *cf.*
HALF-SUPERIOR.

superna′tant (*supernatans*, swimming
above), floating on the surface.

supernu′merary (*supernumerarius*,
over and above), additional ; ~
Buds, are either ADVENTITIOUS ~,
or POSTVENTITIOUS ~.

Superpar′asite (*super*, above, +
PARASITE), a parasite of a parasite ;
Su′per-plant, a plant which grows
upon another, either as an epiphyte
or parasite.

superpo′sed, *superpos′itus* (Lat., placed
over), vertically over some other
part ; **Superposit′ion**, placed vertically, or in parts of the flower,
opposite.

Superspe′cies (*super*, above, +SPECIES),
a group of sub-species or new species
regarded as an entity ; **Supertubera′-
tion** (+ TUBER), the production of
secondary tubers upon the normal
primary tubers.

supervac′uus (Lat.), redundant.

supervolute′, *supervolu′tus*, rolled
over, when applied to plants, the
same as CONVOLUTE ; **supervolu′tive**,
supervoluti′vus, convolute aestivation.

supine′, *supi′nus* (Lat., lying on the
back), prostrate, with face turned
upward.

suppor′ting (*supporto*, I carry or bring
up) **Fi′bres**, in nuclear division those
fibres which run from pole to pole of
the spindle ; ~ **Plant**, a plant upon
or in which another grows ; a host
plant (Crozier).

Suppres′sion (*suppressio*, a keeping
back), complete abortion.

su′pra = above, in compounds from
Latin ; **su′pra-axil′lary** (+ AXIL-
LARY), growing above an axil ;
supracomp′osite, *supracompos′itus*,
supradecompos′itus (*compositus*, composed), excessively subdivided ;
supracuta′neous (*cutis*, skin), above
the epidermis ; **suprano′dal** (+
NODAL), above a node ; **suprafolia′-
ceous**, -*ceus* (+FOLIACEOUS), inserted
above the petiole, growing above a
leaf ; **suprafo′lius** (*folium*, a leaf),

growing on a leaf ; **su′pra-litt′oral**
(*litoralis*, pertaining to the seashore),
a coast region above high-water
mark (Warming) ; **supraterra′neous**
(+ TERRANEUS), used by Spruce as
the opposite of subterraneous, as
~ **Perianth** ; *cf.* Spruce, *Cephalozia*,
p. 92.

supreme′ (*supremus*, highest), as the
top or highest point.

surculig′erous, -*rus* (*surculus*, a young
branch ; *gero*, I bear), bearing
suckers ; **sur′culose**, *surculo′sus*,
producing suckers ; **Sur′culus**, (1)
a sucker, a shoot rising from an
underground base, as from the root ;
(2) the leafy stem of Bryophytes
and Lycopods (Bischoff) ; **Sur′culum**
is used by J. Smith for the rhizome
of a Fern.

surcur′rent (Fr., sur = upon, + current = running), having winged
expansions from the base of the
leaf prolonged up the stem.

Sur′face-yeast, the same as HIGH-
YEAST.

Sur′foyl, Grew's word for outer scales.

sur′sum (Lat., upwards), directed upward and forward ; ~ **hamulo′sus**,
bordered with hooks pointing to the
apex.

survi′val (Fr., *survivre*, to outlive)
Char′acters, those which do not
become merged or lost in transmission
(Lotsy).

suspend′ed, *suspen′sus* (Lat., hung up),
hanging directly downward, or from
the apex of a cell ; **Suspen′sor** (1) of
the embryo, a thread of cells at the
extremity of a developed embryo ;
(2) the cell which supports the conjugating cell in Mucorini ; **pri′mary**
~, the whole of the row of cells
preceding the actual embryological
divisions.

su′tural, *sutura′lis* (*sutura*, a seam),
relating to a suture ; **Su′ture**, (1) a
junction or seam of union ; (2) a line
of opening or dehiscence ; **sutura′rius**,
possessing a suture.

Swang, local Yorkshire term for moorland bogs, particularly those in
hollows.

372

Swarm, a number of spores or unicellular Algae of similar origin, which remain in company without being united ; *cf.* ADELPHOTAXY ; ~ **Cell,** ~ **Spore,** a motile naked protoplasmic body, a zoospore ; **Swarm′ers,** zoospores ; **swarm′ing,** moving by means of cilia, applied to zoospores.

swim′ming, used vaguely for aquatics which float or have floating leaves ; also restricted to those wholly immersed and free ; ~ **Appara′tus,** in *Azolla,* three apical episporic spongy masses of tissue, surrounding a central conical body with an array of fine filaments (Campbell).

Switch-plants, plants whose leaves are wanting or reduced, with green shoots acting in place of leaves.

sword-shaped, ensiform.

sychnocar′pous, *-pus* (συχνὸς, frequent ; καρπὸς, fruit), able to produce fruit many times without perishing, as trees and herbaceous perennials.

Sy′con = Sycon′ium, or **Sy′conus** (σῦκον, fruit of the fig-tree), a multiple hollow fruit, as that of the fig.

Syco′sis (σύκωσις), a skin disease ascribed to species of *Microsporon.*

Sygolli′phytum, Necker's name for **Syncolliphy′tum** (σύγκολλος, glued together ; φυτὸν, a plant), a plant in which the perianth becomes combined with the pericarp.

Syke, (1) Yorkshire vernacular for a rivulet, which drains out of a bog ; (2) the bog itself.

Syl′va, or **Sil′va** (Lat., a wood), applied to an account of the trees of a district, or a discourse on trees ; **syl′van,** relating to woods ; **sylvat′-icus** or *silvat′icus,* growing amongst trees ; **sylves′tral,** used by H. C. Watson for plants which grow in woods and shady places ; **sylves′tris** or *silves′tris,* growing in woods ; **sylves′trine** (Crozier), growing in woods ; **Syl′vula,** (1) a plantation ; (2) a small SYLVA.

sym, a modification of *syn* (σὺν), with ; **symbas′ic** (βάσις, a pedestal), based on several types ; **Symbas′is,** the condition of having several independent types ; **Sym′bion** (βίος, life), an organ which lives in a state of SYMBIOSIS ; **Sym′biont (Symbio′tes,** of Tubeuf), an individual existing in **Symbio′sis,** the living together of dissimilar organisms, with benefit to one only, or to both ; also styled commensalism, consortism, individualism, mutualism, nutricism, prototrophy and syntrophism ; **antagonis′tic** ~ is a struggle between the two organisms ; **conjunc′tive** ~, where the symbionts are intimately blended so as to form an apparently single body ; **contin′gent** ~, when one plant lives in the interior of another for shelter, not parasitism, in Germ. Raumparasitismus ; **disjunc′tive** ~, when the association is only temporary (Frank) ; **mutualis′tic** ~, when of reciprocal advantage ; **symbio′tic,** relating to symbiosis ; ~ **Sap′rophytism,** the condition of a higher plant, as a Phanerogam, in symbiosis with a Fungus (Macdougal) ; **symbiotroph′ic** (τροφὴ, food), deriving nourishment by symbiotic relationship (Kirchner).

symmetran′thus (σύμμετρος, commensurate ; ἄνθος, a flower), when a perianth is divisible into equal parts by several planes of division ; **symmet′ric, symmet′rical,** (1) actinomorphic ; (2) similar in the number of members in calyx, corolla, and androecium ; **symmetricar′pus** (καρπὸς, fruit), a fruit which is symmetric, as first defined ; **Sym′metry,** *Symmet′ria,* (1) capable of division into similar halves ; (2) "used of topography when it shows uniform changes" (Clements) ; **bilat′eral** ~, (1) capable of equal division in one plane only ; (2) "where the areas occur in two similar rows (Clements) ; **ma′jor** ~, that of an organism, as a whole ; **mi′nor** ~, that of part of an organism, as of a flower ; **multilat′eral** ~ = RADIAL ~ ; **ra′dial** ~, (1) capable of equal division in more than one direction through the centre ; (2) "a condition in which

the different areas are concentric "
(Clements).

Symmix′is ($\sigma \grave{v} \nu = \sigma \grave{v} \mu$, with ; $\mu \hat{\iota} \xi \iota s$, a
mingling), chromosome pairing in
which there is an actual interchange
of chromosome parts (Haecker).

Sym′pathy ($\sigma \upsilon \mu \pi \acute{a} \theta \epsilon \iota a$, fellow-feeling),
(1) the faculty of ready union in
grafting ; (2) readiness to hybridize,
or receive foreign pollen ; adj.
sympathet′ic.

Sym′peda ($\sigma \grave{v} \nu$, with ; $\pi \acute{\epsilon} \delta \eta$, a fetter),
symmetry by an intersecting plane ;
Sym′pedae, pl., applied by O. Mueller
to those Diatoms having superficial
symmetry ; **Sympet′alae** ($\pi \acute{\epsilon} \tau a \lambda o \nu$,
a flower leaf) = GAMOPETALAE ;
sympetal′icus ‡, the cohesion of the
stamens to the petals, as in *Malva ;*
sympet′alous, *-lus*, with united
petals, gamopetalous.

symphianthe′rous, *-rus* ($\sigma \upsilon \mu \phi \acute{v} \omega$, I
cause to grow together ; $\breve{a} \nu \theta \eta \rho o s$,
flowery), a synonym of Synantherus
and Syngenesius (J. S. Henslow) ;
symphicar′pous ($\kappa a \rho \pi \grave{o} s$, fruit), with
confluent fruits ; **symphiogenet′ic**
($\gamma \acute{\epsilon} \nu o s$, a race), formed by union of
previously separate elements ; **sym-
phyanthe′rous** ‡ = symphiantherous ;
sym′phycarpous = SYMPHICARPOUS.

Symphyl′lode ($\sigma \grave{v} \nu$, with ; $\phi \upsilon \lambda \lambda \acute{\omega} \delta \eta s$,
leaflike), cone scales of Abietineae
(Celakovský) ; **Symphyllo′dium**, the
combined ovuliferous scales in the
flower of certain Coniferae (Warming) ; **symphyl′lous**, gamophyllous ;
symphyogenet′ic = symphiogenetic ;
symphyoste′monous ($\sigma \tau \acute{\eta} \mu \omega \nu$, a stamen), having the stamens united.

Sym′physis ($\sigma \acute{\upsilon} \mu \phi \upsilon \sigma \iota s$, growing together), (1) coalescence ; (2) fusion
of parts (Bessey) ; **Symphys′ia** is a
synonym

symphyste′monous = symphyoste-
monous.

symphytan′therus = symphiantherus.

symphyt′ic ($\sigma \acute{\upsilon} \mu \phi \upsilon \tau o s$, innate), formed
by fusion of several nuclei, as a
gameto-nucleus (oogamete) of Peronosporeae or (isogamete) of *Dasycladus*
(Hartog) ; **symphytog′ynus** ($\gamma \upsilon \nu \grave{\eta}$, a
woman), the calyx and pistil more

or less adherent, the ovary being
inferior ; **symphytothe′lus** ($\theta \eta \lambda \grave{\eta}$, a
nipple) = SYMPHYTOGYNUS.

Sym′plast ($\sigma \grave{v} \nu$, with ; $\pi \lambda a \sigma \tau \grave{o} s$, formed),
an assemblage of energids, as in
Caulerpa prolifera, Lamour. ; **Sym-
plo′cium**. or **Symplo′kium** ($\pi \lambda \acute{\epsilon} \kappa \omega$, I
plait), old names for the sporangium
of a Fern ; **Sym′pode**, *Sympod′ium*
($\pi o \hat{v} s$, $\pi o \delta \grave{o} s$, a foot), a stem made up
of a series of superposed branches, so
as to imitate a simple axis ; adj. ;
sympod′ial ; ~ **Dichot′omy**, where at
each forking, one branch continues
to develop and the other aborts ;
Sympolymor′phism (+ POLYMOR-
PHISM), the occurrence of various
forms in a given organ in the same
individual (Lindman).

syn ($\sigma \grave{v} \nu$, with), adhesion or growing
together ; *cf.* SYM ; **synac′mic** ($\acute{a} \kappa \mu \grave{\eta}$,
a point = prime of life), adj., of
Synac′my, the stamens and pistils
mature together, being the opposite
of HETERACMY ; **Synan′drium** ($\acute{a} \nu \grave{\eta} \rho$,
$\acute{a} \nu \delta \rho o s$, a man), the cohesion of the
anthers of each male flower in certain
Aroideae ; **Synan′dry**, Morren's term
where stamens normally separated
are soldered or united ; **Synan′gia**,
pl. of **Synan′gium** ($\acute{a} \gamma \gamma \epsilon \hat{\iota} o \nu$, a vessel),
(1) an aggregated exannulate Fern
sporangium forming a series of loculi,
as in *Marattia* (J. Smith) ; (2) the
anthers in *Ephedra ;* adj. **synan′gial;**
synan′gic, relating to a SYNANGIUM ;
synanthe′ricus ($\breve{a} \nu \theta \eta \rho o s$, flowery), the
growing together of anthers, as in
Composites, syngenesious ; **Synan′-
therae**, a name for Compositae ;
adj.**synan′therous:Synantherol′ogist**
($\lambda \acute{o} \gamma o s$, discourse), an expert in the
study of Compositae ; **Synanthe′rus**,
a flower with coalesced anthers ;
Synanthe′sis ($\breve{a} \nu \theta \eta \sigma \iota s$, flowering),
simultaneous anthesis,. stamens and
pistils ripe at the same time, synacmy ;
Synantho′dy ($\epsilon \hat{\iota} \delta o s$, resemblance), the
lateral adhesion of two flower-buds
on the same stalk, or on two peduncles which have become fasciated ;
Synan′thy ($\breve{a} \nu \theta o s$, a flower), (1) C.
Morren's term for the adhesion of

two or more flowers; (2) fruit resulting from pollen from the same flower
(Pearson); adj. **synan'thic**, **synan'thous**; **Synanthrophy'tum** (σὺν,
with; ἀθρόος, crowded; φυτὸν, a plant),
whose fruit is compounded of many
carpels [the word as cited by J. S.
Henslow seems to be an error for
Necker's group Synathrophytum];
Synan'throse, a sugar found in the
roots and tubercles of certain Compositae.

Synapho'sis (συναφίστημι, I join in
revolt), change in the cohesion of
plasma.

Synap'sis (συνάπτω, I join), the condensation of the nuclear filament to
one side of the nucleus previous to
heterotypic mitosis; adj. **synap'tic**;
~ **Knot** = SYNAPSIS; ~ **Pe'riod**,
the time during which synapsis takes
place.

Synap'tase (συναπτὸς, joined), the same
substance as EMULSIN.

Syn'arch (σὺν, with; ἀρχή, beginning), the fusion of two sexual cells
(Meyer).

Synarmophy'tus (σύναρμος, joined;
φυτὸν, a plant), gynandrous.

Syn'carp, *Syncar'pium* (σὺν, with;
καρπὸς, fruit), a multiple or fleshy
aggregate fruit, as the mulberry, or
Magnolia; **syncar'pous**, *-pus,* composed of two or more united carpels;
Syncar'py, the accidental adhesion of
several fruits; **Syncar'yocyte** (κάρυον,
a nut; κυτὸs a vessel), the egg (Maire);
Syncar'yon, a nucleus formed by
fusion of two nuclei (Maire); **Syncar'yophyte** (φυτὸν, a plant) =
SPOROPHYTE; **Synchor'ion** ‡ (χόριον,
foetal membrane, Mirbel's name for
CARCERULE; **synchorolog'ic** (χωρέω,
I scatter; λόγος, discourse), relating
to the distribution of plant associations and their conditioning factors
(Schröter); **Synchronog'amy** (χρόνος,
time; γάμος, marriage), the simultaneous maturity of male and
female flowers on the same stock
(Kirchner); **synclad'ous** (κλάδος, a
branch), used when branchlets grow
in tufts from the same point; **syn-**

cotyle'donous, *-do'neus* (+ COTYLE-
DON), with coalesced cotyledons;
Syncotyle'dons, seedlings in which
the cotyledons are united (De Vries);
Syncot'yly, the state of cohesion of
cotyledons by one margin only;
Syn'cyte, *Syncyt'ium* (κυτὶs, a small
box), a structure derived from the
more or less complete absorption of
the cell-walls, which places their
lumina in direct contact.

Syn'desis (συνδέω, I bind together), the
pairing of homologous chromosomes
during synapsis.

Syndimor'phism (σὺν, with, + DIMOR-
PHISM), the different forms of a
given organ on the same individual
(Lindman); adj. **syndimor'phic**;
syndip'loid (+ DIPLOID), the fusion
of two or more diploid nuclei
(Němec); **Synecol'ogy** (+ ECOLOGY),
the study of plant-communities; adj.
synecolog'ic.

syned'ral, **syned'rous**, *-drus* (σύνεδρος,
of the same seat), growing on the
angles.

Syne'ma (σὺν, with; νῆμα, a thread),
(1) the column of monadelphous stamens, as in Malvaceae; (2) ‡ that
part of the column of an Orchid
which represents the filament of
the stamens (Lindley); **Syner'gids**,
Syner'gidae (συνεργὸς, an assistant),
the two nuclei of the upper end
of the embryo-sac, which with the
third (the oosphere) constitute the
egg-apparatus; **Syn'gamete** (+
GAMETE), C. MacMillan's expression
for the cell which arises from the
fusion of two gametes; *cf.* OOSPERM,
ZYGOTE; **syn'game**, sex determined
by fertilization (Correns); **Syn'gamy**
(γάμος, marriage), fertilization in
modern restricted sense, fusion of
a male and female cell producing
a zygote; **bi'nary** ~, when sex is
present (Hartog); adj. **syn'gamous**,
syngam'ic.

Syngenes'ia (συγγενὴs, connate), a
Linnean class, with flowers having
united anthers, Compositae; **syngenes'icus** = **syngenes'ious**, *syngenes'us*, (1) with anthers cohering

375

in a ring; (2) belonging to the order
Compositae.

Syngonim′ia (σὺν, with, + GONIMIA),
gonimia united in clumps; **Syn′-
grammae** (γράμμα,‿ an outline),
Diatoms with linear symmetry (O.
Mueller; **synhap′loid** (+ HAPLOID),
the union of two or more haploid
nuclei (Němec).

Synize′sis (συνίζω, to sit together)
= SYNAPSIS.

Synkar′ion (σὺν, with; κάρυον, a nut)
= SYNCARYON; **synoc′reate** (+
OCREA), having opposite united
stipules which enclose the stem in a
sheath; **synoe′cious** (οἶκος, a house),
(1) having antheridia and archegonia
in one inflorescence; bryologists
seem to prefer the form **synoi′cous**;
(2) the occurrence of flowers of
different sexes in the same inflorescence (Kirchner); **Synne′ma** (νῆμα, a
thread), a columnar bundle of closely
united conidiophores (Traverso and
Saccardo).

Syn′onym (συνώνυμος, having the same
name), a superseded or unused
name; **Synon′ymy**, all that relates
to synonyms.

Synop′sis (σύνοψις, a glance), a condensed description of a genus or
other group of plants.

synpet′alous (σὺν, with; πέταλον, a
flower leaf) = gamopetalous;
Synphyllo′dium (φύλλον, a leaf),
Celakovský's name for CONE-SCALE;
Synoph′thy, the corrected abbreviation of **Synophthal′my** (ὀφθαλμός,
an eye), see next;— Moquin-
Tandon's term for adhesion of
(1) embryos; (2) buds; **Synoph′ty**
(deriv., see last); **Synoph′yty**
(Crozier) = SYNOPHTHY; **Syn′plast**
= SYMPLAST; **synorhi′zus** (ῥίζα, a
root), having a radicle whose point
is united to the albumen; **synsep′-
alous**, -*lus* (+ SEPALUM), gamosepalous, the sepals coalescent;
synsper′mous, adj. of **Synsper′my**
(σπέρμα, a seed), the union of
several seeds; **Syn′sperms** (σπέρμα,
a seed), plants with "seeds integrated with placenta" (C. MacMil-

lan); **synspor′ous** (σπορά, a seed),
propagating by conjugations of cells,
as in Algae " (Stormonth); **Synstig′-
ma** (στίγμα, a point), when symmetry
is based upon a point; **synstig-
mat′icus** (στίγμα, a point), when a
pollen-mass is furnished with a
retinaculum by which it adheres
to the stigma, as in Orchids.

syntac′tic (συντακτικὸς, putting together), used of irregularity which
is zygomorphic (Pax).

Syntag′ma, pl. **Syntag′mata** (σὺν,
with; τάγμα, an array), Pfeffer's
term for bodies built up of TAG-
MATA, themselves aggregations of
MOLECULES; **syntep′alous** (+ TEP-
ALUM), the tepals united; **Synth′-
ease**, a soluble enzyme effecting the
union of sugar and phosphates
(Ivanoff); **syntrip′loid** (+ TRIP-
LOID), the union of triploid nuclei
(Němec); **syntroph′icus** (τροφὴ,
food), epiphytic; **Syntroph′ism** and
Syn′trophy, the antagonistic symbiosis of Lichen with Lichen; **Syn′-
trophs**, "Lodgers" in Lichens;
Syn′type (τύπος, a type) = COTYPE;
synzo′ic (ζῷον, an animal), used of
intentional dispersal by means of
animals (Sernander); **Synzoocho′ry**
(χωρέω, I spread abroad), dispersed
by animals; **Synzyg′ia** ‡ (ζυγὸς, a
yoke), the point of contact of
opposite cotyledons.

Sy′phon, = SIPHON.

Syring′in, a substance occurring in
Syringa, the Lilac; **syringi′nus**,
lilac-coloured, a light purple.

Syringoden′dron, used by palaeo-
botanists for old or partially decorticated sigillarian stems; the
name was formerly generic.

Syr′tidad (σύρτις, σύρτιδος, a sand-
bank, + AD), a plant of a dry
sandbar (Clements); **Syrtidi′um**, "a
dry sandbar formation"; **syrtidoph′-
ilus** (φιλέω, I love), "dwelling
on dry sandbars"; **Syrtidophy′ta**
(φυτὸν, a plant), "dry sandbar
plants" (Clements).

Systellophy′tum (συστέλλω, I wrap
closely; φυτὸν, a plant), when a

persistent calyx appears to form part of the fruit.

Sys'tem (σύστημα, a composition), a scheme of classification; **systemat'ic**, *systemat'icus*, relating to system; ~ **Bot'any**, the study of plants in their mutual relationships and taxonomic arrangement.

Syst'ole (συστολὴ, a contraction), the contraction of the contractile vesicles in certain Algae, plasmodia, and zoospores.

Syst'rophe (συστοφὴ, rolling up), when strong light causes chlorophyll grains to congregate into a few masses (A. F. W. Schimper); adj. **systroph'ic**, as ~ **In'terval**, or **Systroph'ion**, that portion of the PHOTRUM in which systrophe can take place (S. Moore).

systy'lius (σὺν, with; στῦλος, a column), the lid fixed to the columella in Mosses, and elevated above the capsule when it dries; **systy'lous** (Berkeley) = SYSTYLIUS; **systy'lus**, when styles coalesce into one body, as in *Rosa systyla*, Bast.

tabaci'nus, pale brown, "tobacco-coloured;" the name is from *Nicotiana Tabacum*, Linn.

Tabasheer', a siliceous concretion occurring in the joints of bamboo.

Ta'bes (Lat., a wasting away), a disease, the loss of the power of growth and consequent wasting away; **tabes'cent**, *tabes'cens*, wasting or shrivelling.

Tab'let (*tabula*, a board or plank), (1) the frustule of Diatoms when quadrangular; (2) the rectangular colony of *Gonium;* **Tab'ula**, the pileus of certain Fungi; **tab'ular**, *tabula'ris*, flattened horizontally; ~ **Roots**, buttress-like roots of certain tropical trees (Kerner).

tabula'tus ‡ (Lat., boarded or floored), layer on layer.

Tach'yspore (ταχὺς, quick; σπείρω, I sow), applied to plants which quickly disperse their seeds (Ulbrich); adj. **tachyspor'ous**.

tac'tic (τακτικὸς, fit for order), reacting to a stimulus by internal change (Wager).

tac'tile (*tactilis*, that may be touched), sensitive to touch; ~ **Hairs** or ~ **Bris'tles**=STIMULATORS; ~ **Papill'a**, a mechanical sense-organ such as a projecting cell on a tendril; ~ **Pit**, an unthickened area on the outer wall of a superficial sensory cell.

taemop'terid, a Fern resembling *Taemopteris*, in structure.

taenia'nus ‡ (*taenia*, a band), long, cylindric and contracted in various places; **taeniop'teroid**, in fossil botany, resembling the genus *Taeniopteris*.

Tag'ma, pl. **Tag'mata** (τάγμα, an array), Pfeffer's term for all aggregations of molecules; **tagmat'ic Com'plex**, a higher molecular system.

Tail, any long and slender prolongation; ~ **point'ed**, excessively acuminate, caudate; **tailed**, said of anthers which have a prolongation from the loculus, which part is destitute of pollen-grains.

Take-all, an Australian name for the ravages of *Ophiobolus graminis* on wheat; termed "Straw Blight" in England.

Tala'ra ‡ (*talaria*, the winged shoes of Mercury), the wing or ala of a papilionaceous corolla.

Ta'lea (Lat.), a cutting, a small branch for propagating.

tall, exceeding the normal height.

Ta'lus (Fr., slope), an accumulation of loose fragments at the base of rocks (Warming).

tangen'tial (*tangens*, touching), at right angles to the radial or medullary rays.

Tan'ghin, the poison occurring in the ordeal poison plant of Madagascar, *Cerbera Tanghin*, Hook.

Tan'gle, the same as SKEIN (Crozier).

Tank-ep'iphyte (+ EPIPHYTE), epiphytes in which the roots are reduced to anchoring appendages (Schimper).

tan'kard-shaped, thickened and gradually enlarged downward, then suddenly contracted or ended, as some varieties of turnip (Crozier).

Tan′nase, an enzyme occurring in *Aspergillus;* **Tan′nin** or **Tan′nic Ac′id,** an important group of astringents, especially abundant in some barks, as that of the oak; **Tan′nin-sacs,** ~ **-ve′sicles,** strongly refractive globular bodies in cells, which contain tannin; **aplas′tic** ~, probably an excretion, as in the germinating date; **plas′tic** ~, presumably connected with nutrition; capable of being modified; **physiolog′ical** ~, believed in this state to be a waste product.

Tap-root, the primary descending root, forming a direct continuation from the radicle; **tap-root′ed,** possessed of a tap-root.

ta′per, cylindric but angular, and gradually diminishing towards the end; ~ **point′ed,** acuminate, as the leaf of *Salix alba,* Linn.; **ta′pering,** regularly diminishing in diameter.

Tape′sium (τάπης, a carpet), dense and wefted superficial mycelium, having ascophores seated on it; **tape′tal,** relating to the tapetum; ~ **Cell,** cell of a tapetum; ~ **Lay′er** = TAPETUM; ~ **Sept′um,** the wall between the megaspore cavity and the nucellus in Palæozoic seeds (F. W. Oliver); **Tapete′,** a suggested emendation of **Tape′tum,** a membrane of granular cells investing the sporogenous cells in the archesporium, absorbed as the spores mature.

Taphrench′yma (τάφρος, a ditch; ἔγχυμα, an infusion), = BOTHRENCHYMA.

Taph′rad (τάφρος, a ditch, + AD), a ditch plant (Clements); **Taphri′um,** a ditch formation; **taphroph′ilus** (φιλέω, I love), ditch-dwelling; **Taphrophy′ta** (φυτὸν, a plant), ditch plants (Clements).

Tapio′ca, prepared starch of the roots of several species of *Manihot.*

Tarax′acine, a bitter crystalline principle found in dandelion, *Taraxacum officinale,* Weber.

Tar′gets, Smith's term for PELTAE.

tartar′eous, -eus (Mid. Lat., *tartrum,* wine tartar), having a rough crumbling surface, like some Lichens.

taw′ny, fulvous, a dull brownish-yellow.

taxa′ceous, taxin′eous, relating to the Taxineae.

Taxe′tum, an association of yew trees, *Taxus baccata.*

taxiform′is (*taxus,* the yew; *forma,* shape), arranged distichously like the leaves of yew.

taxigno′mic (τάξις, order; γνώμη, judgment, Vesque's term for anatomical characters.

taxinom′ic = TAXONOMIC.

Tax′is (τάξις, order), used by Czapek to express reaction of free organisms in response to external stimuli by movement; **Tax′ism,** the tendency of unicellular organisms to arrange themselves according to lines of force or stimulation; **Taxit′ery** (τέρας, a monster), a modification which is so slight as to admit of comparison with the normal form; **Taxol′ogy** (λόγος, discourse) or **Taxon′omy** (νόμος, law), classification; **Taxon′omist,** one skilled in classification; adj. **taxonom′ic; Tax′y,** the constituent of a variation (Coutagne), a modality "clearly disjoint."

Tear, a drop of gum or resin in its native state; **tear-shaped,** like the pip of an apple, lachrymiform.

Tectopar′atype (τέκτων, a craftsman, + PARATYPE), a specimen selected to show the microscopic structure of the original type of a species or genus (Chapman); **Tectoples′iotype** (+ PLESIOTYPE), the same, but with subsequently described specimens; **Tec′totype,** a fragment or otherwise for microscopic investigation.

Teeth, (1) any small marginal lobes; (2) in Mosses, the divisions of the peristome.

Teg′men (Lat., a covering), (1) the inner coat of a seed, previously the secundine of an ovule; (2) the glume of a grass; pl. **Tegmen′-ta,** the scales of a leaf-bud; ~

378

folia'cea, *fulcra'cea*, *petiola'cea*, *stipula'cea*, modifications of leaves, stipules and petioles, petioles and stipules only (Lindley); **tegmina'-tus** (Lat.), when the nucellus is invested by a covering.

tegument'ary (*tegumen*, a cover), relating to some covering; **Tegumen'tum**, (1) the indusium of a Fern; (2) the spermoderm.

Teich'osome (τεῖχος, a wall; σῶμα, a body), droplets or spherules composing the cell-wall (Gardiner).

Tek'nospore (τεκνόω, I bear children, + SPORE), a spore produced directly from male or female organs of Equisetaceae and many Ferns (Radlkofer).

Te'la (Lat., a web), elementary tissue, as meristem; ~ **contex'ta**, a weft of distinct hyphae, felted tissue; Ger. "Filzgewebe."

Teleb'olites (τῆλε, afar; βολίς, a missile), the products of enzyme action (Beyerinck); **Teleomito'sis** (+ MITOSIS) = KARYOKINESIS.

teleian'thus (τέλειος, perfect; ἄνθος, a flower), hermaphrodite.

Teleol'ogy (τέλεος, gen. of τέλος, completion; λόγος, discourse), the doctrine of final causes, or theory of tendency to an end; adj. **teleolog'ic**; **Teleomito'sis** (μίτος, a thread), an indirect division of the nucleus, when the chromosomes divide to rejoin the daughter-nuclei (Dangeard).

Teleutoconid'ium = **Teleutogonid'ium** (τελευτή, an end, + GONIDIUM) = TELEUTOSPORE; **Teleutosor'us** (+ SORUS), an aggregation of teleutospores (Arthur and Holway); **Teleu'tospore** (σπορά, a seed), a resting bilocular spore of Uredineae, on germination producing a promycelium; **teleutospor'ic**, relating to a TELEUTOSPORE; **teleutosporif'erous** (*fero*, I bear), producing teleutospores (Cooke).

Teli'um (τέλος, completion), Arthur's term for TELEUTOSORUS; adj. **tel'ial**; **Tel'iospores** (+ SPORE) = TELEUTOSPORE.

tellu'ric (*tellus*, the earth), applied to ground water, as distinct from rain.

Tel'matad (τέλμα, a pool, + AD), a wet meadow plant (Clements); **Telmati'um**, (1) Ganong's expression for a wet marsh; (2) Clements's expression for a wet meadow formation; **Telmatol'ogy** (λόγος, discourse), account of the origin of moors (Dörfler); **telmatoph'ilus** (φιλέω, I love), dwelling in wet meadows (Clements); **Telmatophy'ta** (φυτὸν, a plant), wet meadow plants (Clements).

Telog'amae (τέλος, an end; γάμος, marriage), Ardissone's term for Florideae; **Telogonid'ium** (+ GONIDIUM), a gonidium arising from successive generations in the same cell (A. Braun); **Tel'ophase** (φάσις, an appearance), the last phase of nuclear division; adj. **telopha'sic**; **Telosynap'sis** (+ SYNAPSIS, that form of nuclear contraction in which the chromosomes are paired end to end; adj. **telosynap'tic**.

Tem'peratures, the sum of, used to mark a given period in the life-cycle of a plant.

temulen'tous (*temulentus*, drunken), nodding in a jerky irregular manner; *cf.* NUTANS (Heinig).

Tem'ulin, an active principle occurring in *Lolium temulentum*, Linn.

Tena'culum, pl. **Tena'cula** (Lat., a holder), haptera or holdfasts of Algae; adj. **tenac'ular**.

Ten'dril, a filiform production, cauline or foliar, by which a plant may secure itself in its position; **ten'drillous**, possessed of tendrils.

Ten'sion (*tensio*, a stretching), due to turgidity in cells, and manifested by movements of parts; ~ **Form**, Delpino's term for papilionaceous flowers, with concealed anthers, such as *Genista* and *Ulex*.

Tent-pole, a raised central portion of the apex of the prothallus (F. W. Oliver).

Ten'tacle (*tentaculum*, Mod. Lat., a feeler), a sensitive glandular hair, as those on the leaf of *Drosera*; **Tentac'uloid** (εἶδος, resemblance), applied to long processes which pass through mammiform protuberances of the perigloea of Diatoms (Buffham).

tenuifo′lious, -*lius* (*folium*, a leaf), thin or fine-leaved ; **Tenuinucella′tae** (*tenuis*, narrow,+ Nucellus), Van Tieghem's term for those plants with true seeds, in which the nucellus is reduced to a layer of cells or wholly absorbed by the endosperm ; **ten′uis** (Lat.), thin.

Tep′al, *Tep′alum* (anagram of *petalum*), a division of the perianth, sepal or petal ; restricted by H. G. Reichenbach to the two unchanged petals of Orchids.

teph′reus, teph′rus (τεφρὸς, ashy), ash-coloured ; **tephro′sius**, ashy-grey.

Tepida′rium (Lat., a tepid bath-room), in botanic gardens a "Cape House."

Teratog′eny (τέρας, τέρατος, a sign or prodigy ; γένος, offspring), the production of monsters ; **Teratol′ogy** (λόγος, discourse), the study of malformations and monstrosities ; adj. **teratolog′ic**.

Ter′cine, *Terci′na* (*ter*, thrice), a supposed third integument of an ovule, really a layer of the primine or secundine.

Ter′ebene, a terpene which holds resin in solution, as turpentine ; the name is from *Pistacia Terebinthus*, Linn. ; **terebin′thine**, pertaining to, or consisting of, turpentine.

ter′ebrate (*terebra*, a borer), having scattered perforations ; **Terebra′tor**, Lindau's name for the so-called trichogyne in *Gyrophora*; **Terebratorhy′pha** (+ Hypha) means the same.

Tere′do (Lat., a boring beetle), disease caused by the boring of insects.

terete′, *te′res* (Lat., rounded), circular in transverse section, cylindric and usually tapering.

tergem′inal = **tergem′inate**, *tergemina′tus, tergem′inus* (three at a birth), "thrice-twin" (Lindley).

tergif′erous (*tergum*, a back ; *fero*, I bear), **tergisperm′ous**, -*us* (σπέρμα, a seed), bearing dorsal sporangia, as Ferns ; **Ter′gum**, back, dorsum.

ter′minal, *termina′lis* (Lat., relating to boundaries), proceeding from or belonging to the end or apex ; ~ **Bud**, a bud which is apical.

Terminol′ogy (*terminus*, a limit=term ; λόγος, discourse), glossology, definition of technical terms ; **Ter′minus** (Lat.), a term, a technical word.

ter′nary, *terna′rius* (Lat., consisting of three), (1) in threes, trimerous ; (2) the result of a third axial order, as derived from the primary ; ~ **Hy′brid**, the result of crossing a hybrid with a species different from either of its parents.

ter′nate, *terna′tus* (*terni*, by threes), in threes, as three in a whorl or cluster ; **ter′nate-pin′nate**, when the secondary petioles proceed in threes from the summit of the main petiole ; **terna′tely trifo′liolate**, with three leaflets attached at one point, as in clover (Crozier); **ter′nus** = Ternate.

Ter′pene (modif. of Turpentine), a group of hydrocarbons present in turpentine, liquid resin, or essential oils ; **terp′enoid** (εἶδος, resemblance), Kerner's name for that group of flower-scents produced by terpenes, as Orange-flowers, *Gardenia*, Thyme, etc.

terpin′nate (*ter*, thrice, + Pinnate) = Tripinnate.

terra′neus ‡ (*terra*, earth), growing on dry land.

terres′trial, *terres′tris* (Lat., pertaining to the earth), used of plants of the dry ground; the Latin *terres′ter* is also employed.

ter′reus (Lat., earthen), "earth coloured" ; **ter′ricole, terric′olous** (*terra*, the earth ; *colo*, I inhabit), living on the ground, as some Lichens.

terrig′enous (*terrigena*, earth-born) = Terrestrial, a hybrid word used by A. Cunningham.

Terripra′ta (*terra*, earth ; *pratum*, a meadow), a class of plant-formations developed upon substrata not influenced by ground water, and consisting of grasses, herbs and bryophytes.

Ter'siforms (*tersus*, neat), in *Rosa*, those forms which have all the ribs of their leaves hairy (Almquist).

Ter'tiospore (*tertius*, third ; σπορὰ, a seed), C. MacMillan's term for a fertilized egg which undergoes rejuvenescence and segments into usually four spores, motile and similar to the spores of a gametophyte generation ; the result of sporophytic segmentation, as in *Oedogonium*.

tes'sellate, *tessella'tus* (Lat., of squared stones), chequer-work, as in *Fritillaria Meleagris*, Linn.

tessula'ris (*tesserula*, a small square stone), of cubic dimensions, all sides equal.

Tes'ta (Lat., a brick or tile), the outer coat of the seed, usually hard and brittle.

testa'ceous, *testa'ceus* (Lat., of bricks or tiles), brick-red.

testic'ular, testic'ulate, *testicula'tus* (Lat.), shaped like the tubers of *Orchis*, and fruit of *Mercurialis;* Testic'ulus ‡, Tes'tis ‡ (Lat.) = ANTHER.

Tes'tule (*testula*, a dim. of TESTA), an old name for FRUSTULE.

te'ter (Lat., offensive), having a foul smell.

Tetrablas'tus (τέτρας, four ; βλαστὸς, a bud), Koerber's term for those Lichen-spores which consist of four cells ; tetracam'arous, *-rus* (+ CAMARUS), of four closed carpels ; tetracarpel'lary (καρπὸς, fruit), of four carpels ; Tetracaro'tin (+ CAROTIN), a lipochrome pigment resembling carotin.

Tetrachae'nium ‡ (τετράς, four, + ACHAENIUM), a fruit of four adherent achenes, as in Labiatae ; Tetrachocar'pium (τέτραχα, fourfold ; καρπὸς, fruit) = TETRASPORE ; tetrachot'omous, *tetrachot'omus* (τέμνω, I cut), when a cyme, in its restricted sense of fascicle, bears four lateral peduncles about the terminal flower ; Tetrachot'omy, the fission of a stem into four branches of equal rank (Worsdell).

tetracoc'cous, *-cus* (τετράς; four, κόκκος,

a berry), (1) consisting of four closed carpels ; (2) applied to bacteria when in four segments ; Tetracot'yl (+ COTYLEDON), a seedling with both cotyledons deeply bifid (De Vries) ; tetracy'clic (κύκλος, a circle), when a flower is composed of four whorls of organs.

Tet'rad (τετράδιον, a set or group of four), (1) a body formed of four cells, as in the formation of pollen in the pollen-mother-cells ; (2) = TETRASPORE ; (3) in heterotypic nuclear division, one division of a chromosome into four parts, forming a set ; tetradip'loid (+ DIPLOID), the fusion of four nuclei (Němec) ; Tetradogen'esis (γένεσις, origin), the formation of a tetrad of spores, thus including all the phenomena of Meiosis.

tetrad'ymous (τετράδυμος, fourfold), (1) having four cells or cases ; (2) when the lamellae of an Agaric are arranged so that alternate lamellae are shorter than the intermediates, and one complete lamella terminates a set of four pairs, short and long.

Tetradynam'ia (τετράς, four ; δύναμις, power), a Linnean class which is characterized by possessing tetradynamous stamens ; tetrady'namous, *-mus*, having four long stamens and two short, as in Cruciferae ; tetrafolia'tus, tetrafo'lius (*folium*, a leaf), four-leaved, more correctly tetraphyllous ; tetrag'onal (γωνία, an angle), four-angled ; Tetragonidan'gium (+ GONIDANGIUM), a sexual reproductive organ in Floridean Algae, producing tetragonidia ; Tetragonid'ium (+ GONIDIUM), asexually produced spores of Florideae, etc., usually in groups of four ; tetrag'onous (γωνία, an angle), four-angled ; Tetragyn'ia (γυνὴ, a woman), a Linnean artificial order, the members having flowers with four pistils ; tetrag'ynous, of four carpels or styles ; tetrameriste'lic (+ MERISTELE), used of leaf-traces when composed of four meristeles (Brebner) ; tetram'erous, *-rus* (μέρος,

part), of four members; **tetramor′-
phic** (μορφή, shape), having flowers
of four forms, varying as to length
of style, anthers and stigmas, as in
Epigaea repens, Linn. ; **tetran′der,
tetran′drous** (ἀνήρ, ἀνδρὸς, a man),
with four stamens ; **Tetran′dria,** a
Linnean class of tetrandrous plants ;
tetranu′cleate (+ Nucleus), having
four nuclei (Brebner) ; **tetra-pet′-
alous,** -*lus* (πέταλον, a flower leaf),
having four petals ; **tetraphylet′ic**
(φυλή, a tribe), applied to hybrids
with four strains in their descent ;
tetraphyl′lous, -*lus* (φύλλον, a leaf),
four-leaved.

tetraplocau′lous (τετραπλόος, fourfold,
+ Caulis), having quaternary axes
(Pax) ; **tetrap′loid** (εἶδος, resemblance), used of a nucleus due to
the fusion of four (Němec) ; **Te-
trap′loidy,** the condition itself.

tetrap′terous τετρὰς, four ; πτερὸν, a
wing), four-winged, four produced
angles ; **tetrapyre′nus** (πυρὴν, a
kernel), with four stones or seeds
in the fruit ; **tetraque′ter, tetra-
que′trous** (*quadra*, a square), with
four sharp angles ; **tet′rarch** (ἀρχή,
beginning), with four vascular
strands in a fibrovascular cylinder
or stele ; **tetrari′nus** (ἄρρην, male),
Necker's version of Tetrandrous ;
tetraschis′tic (σχιστὸς, split), dividing into four ; **tetrasep′alous,** -*lus*
(+ Sepalum), having four sepals ;
tetrasperm′ous (σπέρμα, a seed), with
four seeds ; **tetraspora′ceous, tetra-
spor′ic, tetraspor′ine,** connected with
the production of Tetraspores ;
Tetrasporan′gium (+ Sporangium),
a unicellular sporangium containing
tetraspores ; **Tet′raspore** (σπορὰ, a
seed), a spore formed by division of
the spore-mother-cell into four parts ;
tetraspor′ic, tetraspor′ous, bearing
tetraspores ; **Tetras′ter** (+ Aster),
in nuclear division, a spindle of
four centres (Hartog) ; **tetras′tichous,**
-*chus* (στίχος, a row), in four vertical
ranks ; **tetratrip′loid** (+ Triploid),
concerning the fusion of the ditri-
ploid nuclei (Němec).

tex′tile, *tex′tilis* (Lat., woven), used
for weaving.

Tex′ture, *Tex′tura* (Lat., a web),
applied by Starbäck to hyphal
structures in Discomycetes, thus :
~ **epidermoi′dea,** the walls of
hyphae more or less confluent ; ~
globo′sa, when the cells are nearly
isodiametric, the separate hyphae
not distinguishable ; ~ **intrica′ta,**
the hyphae running in various directions, with walls not coalescent ; ~
ob′lita, hyphae nearly parallel, and
having small cavities with thickened walls ; ~ **porrec′ta,** hyphae
with large cavities and no thickened
walls ; ~ **prismat′ica,** cells not isodiametric, hyphae not distinguishable.

thalamiflor′al, thalamiflor′ous, (θάλαμος, a bed-chamber ; *flos, floris,* a
flower), when the parts of the
flowers are hypogynous, separately
inserted on the thalamus ; **Thala-
miflor′ae,** a group of Phanerogams
so distinguished ; **Thala′mium,** (1)
" a hollow case containing spores in
Algals " ; (2) " the disk or *Lamina
prolifera* in Lichens " ; (3) " a form
of the hymenium in Fungals " (all
from Lindley) ; **Thal′amus,** the receptacle of the flower, the torus.

Thalas′sad (θάλασσα, the sea, + Ad), a
sea-plant (Clements) ; **thalas′sinus,
thalas′sicus** (Lat.), sea-green ; **Thal-
assi′um,** "a particular sea formation" ; **thalassoph′ilus** (φιλέω, I
love), sea-loving ; **Thalassophy′ta**
(φυτὸν, a plant), sea-plants
(Clements); **Thalas′sophyte,** a marine Alga ; **Thalassoplank′ton** (+
Plankton), oceanic plankton (Forel).

Thallid′ium (θαλλὸς, a sprout), (1) a
vegetative reproductive body, especially amongst Thallophytes and
Muscineae (Kerner) ; (2) the medullary layer in Lichens in a young
state ; **thal′line,** *thalli′nus,* **thallo′-
dal, thallo′dic,** *thallo′des,* **thal′lose,**
pertaining to a thallus ; **Thallog′-
amae** (γάμος, marriage), Ardissone's
term for Algae ; **Thal′logams,** term
used by Focke for Vascular Cryp-

togams ; **Thal′logen** (γένος, race, offspring), a synonym of THALLOPHYTE ; **thal′loid** (εἶδος, resemblance), having the nature or form of a thallus ; applied to Hepaticae in which the vegetative body is not a leafy stem as *Marchantia ;* **thalloi′dal** (Crozier), is a synonym ; **Thal′lome,** a thallus-like growth ; *cf.* CAULOME ; **Thal′lophyte** (φυτὸν, a plant), a plant whose growth is thalloid, no clear distinction of leaf or axis ; **Thall′ostrote** (στρώτος, strown), a species migrating by means of offshoots (Clements) ; **Thal′lus,** pl. **Thal′li,** (1) a vegetative body without differentiation into stem and leaf ; in Fungi the whole of the body which does not serve for reproduction ; (2) Goebel's term for the organ of attachment in *Terniola,* a genus of Podostomaceae, composed of coalesced dorsiventral branches ; ~ **Gonid′ia,** the gonidia in the thallus of a Lichen ; the Lichen thallus is subdivided into ~ **lepo′des,** crustaceous ; ~ **pla′codes,** foliaceous ; ~ **thamno′des,** fruticose.

Tham′nium ‡ (θάμνος, a shrub), the bushy thallus of such Lichens as *Cladonia rangiferina,* Hoffm. ; **thamnoblas′tus** (βλαστὸς, a bud), used by Koerber for a fruticose Lichen.

Theba′ine (from Thebes, where opium was much employed), one of the crystallized alkaloids occurring in the opium poppy.

The′ca (θήκη, a case), (1) the sporangium of a Fern ; (2) the capsule of a Moss ; (3) ‡ an anther ; (4) ‡ used by Necker for the fruit of Myrtaceae ; (5) ‡ "a cell of any sort" (Lindley) ; (6) = ASCUS ; (7) used by Vines for the loculus of an anther ; (8) "a hollow space in the pericarp formed by the doubling of the endocarp" (Gray) ; **The′caphore** (φορέω, I carry), the stipe of a carpel, homologous with the petiole ; **The′caspore** (σπορὰ, a seed) = ASCOSPORE ; **Thecaspo′rae** (Traverso) = SPORIDIA ; **thecaspor′ous,** used of Fungi which have

the spores in asci (Stormonth) ; **theca′tus,** bearing a theca ; **the′cial,** possessing thecae or pertaining to them ; ~ **Al′gae,** the hymenial gonidia of Lichens ; **Thecid′ion,** *Thecid′ium* ‡, = ACHENE ; **thecif′erous** (*fero,* I bear), bearing thecae or asci ; **the′ciger,** *thecig′erus* (*gero,* I bear), theca-bearing, applied to the hymenium of Fungi, and branches of Mosses which bear setae ; **The′cium,** a layer of tissue below the epithecium, which contains the sporangia in Lichens (Minks), *cf.* EPITHECIUM, HYPOTHECIUM.

The′in, an alkaloid in the leaves of *Thea,* the tea-plant.

The′ke, sometimes used for the theca (ascus) of Lichens.

thelephor′oid (*Thelephorus,* εἶδος, resemblance), like the genus *Thelephorus.*

thele′phorus (θηλἠ, a nipple ; φορέω, I carry), covered with nipple-like prominences.

thelotre′moid, having tubercular apothecia like those of *Thelotrema.*

thelyg′enous (θῆλυς, female ; γένος, race, offspring), inducing the female element, as ~ **Castra′tion,** the production of pistils in the male-flowers of a host by *Ustilago.*

Theobro′mine, the active principle of the cacao-bean, *Theobroma Cacao,* Linn. ; **theobro′minus,** the deep chocolate brown of the seed of the same plant.

theoret′ic (θεωρητικὸς, speculative), pertaining to theory as distinct from practice ; ~ **Di′agram,** a floral diagram of the theoretic components, not necessarily the same as seen on inspection.

Theri′um, or **Theri′on** (θήρ, a wild beast), a plant succession due to animal agency (Clements).

Ther′mad (θέρμη, heat, + AD), a hot spring plant (Clements) ; **ther′mic,** warm ; ~ **Con′stant,** the sun of the mean temperatures of the days of active vegetation, up to some definite phase in the plant's life, minus a certain initial temperature determined by several years' observations, and varying for the species (Oettinger) ; **Thermi'um**, a hot spring formation ; **Ther'mo-cleistog'amy** (+ CLEISTOGAMY), when flowers do not expand as a consequence of insufficient warmth (Knuth); **thermonast'ic** (ναστὸς, pressed), close appression of an organ due to heat; **Thermonas'ty**, the condition described ; **thermoph'ilic** (φιλέω, I love), applied to those bacteria which thrive in high temperatures ; **Thermo'sis**, change due to warmth upon an organism; **Thermotax'is** (τάξις, order), movement induced by heat, moving towards its source ; **Thermotox'y** (τοξικὸν, poison), death caused by excess of heat, especially if the plant is short of water (Balls) ; **Thermot'onus** (τόνος, strain), the relation between temperature and the manifestation of irritability ; **thermotrop'ic** (τροπὴ, a turning), relating to **Thermot'ropism**, curvature dependent upon temperature (Wortmann).

Therodrymi'um (θέρος, summer ; δρυμὸς, a coppice), leafy-forest formation (Diels); **Theromeg'atherm** + MEGATHERM), having the high summer temperature of 20° C. = 68° F. and above ; **Theromes'otherm** (+ MESOTHERM), with summer heat of 12° — 20° C. = 54° — 68° F. ; **therophyll'ous** (φύλλον, a leaf), producing leaves in summer, deciduous leaved plants ; **Ther'ophyte** (φυτὸν, a plant), a plant which completes its development in one season, its seeds remaining latent during the hot season.

Thick'ening Lay'er, an apparent layer of cellulose on the inner face of a cell-wall ; ~ **Ring**, Sanio's term for a ring of meristem in which the first fibro-vascular bundles originate.

Thigmomorpho'sis (θιγγάνω, I touch,+ MORPHOSIS), change in the original structure due to contact, as the adhering discs of *Ampelopsis* ; **Thigmotax'is** (+ TAXIS), the result of mechanical stimulus ; adj. **thigmo-**

tac'tic ; **Thigmot'ropism** (τροπὴ, a turning), curvature induced in climbing plants by the stimulus of a rough surface (Czapek).

Thin'ad (θὶς, θινὸς, a sand heap, + AD), a dune plant; **Thini'um**, a dune formation ; **thinoph'ilus** (φιλέω, I love), dune-loving ; **Thinophy'ta** (φυτὸν, a plant), dune plants (Clements).

Thorn, usually an aborted branch, simple or branched ; ~ **Fo'rest**, the CAA-TINGA forests of Brazil.

Thread, used by Blair for the FILAMENT ~ **-blicht**, the destructive Fungus on tea-plants, *Stilbum nanum;* **Thread-ind'icator**, a form of apparatus for measuring the rate of growth ; **thread-shaped**, filiform.

three-an'gled, trigonous ; ~ **cleft**, trifid ; ~ **cor'nered**, ~ **edged**, with three sides, plain or incurved, and three acute angles, triquetrous ; ~ **leav'ed**, trifoliate ; ~ **lobed**, trilobed ; ~ **nerved**, with three principal veins ; ~ **parted**, tripartite ; ~ **ranked**, with three vertical rows on a stem ; ~ **ribbed**, the midrib and one rib on each side more prominent than the rest ; ~ **valved**, trivalvate.

thrice-digita'to-pin'nate = TRITERNATE.

Throat, the orifice of a gamopetalous corolla or calyx, the fauces.

Thrum (Grew), **Thrumb** (Blair), (1) the filament of a stamen ; (2) in Composite florets, the anthers; **thrum-eyed**, applied to a short-styled dimorphic flower, such as a primrose, the stamens alone being visible in the throat of the corolla.

Thrush-fun'gus, the disease ascribed to *Dermatium albicans*, Laurens.

Thun'der-broom = WITCHES' BROOM.

Thyll, Thyl'la, Thy'lose, Thy'llose (Germ. Thylle), *cf.* TYLOSE.

Thy'mol, a crystallized product chiefly obtained from the seeds of *Carum copticum*, but found in many plants, as *Thymus Serpyllum*, whence its name.

thy'roid (θυρεὸς, a shield ; εἶδος,

resemblance), shield-like, peltiform (Heinig).

Thyrse, *Thyr'sus* (Lat., the Bacchic staff), a mixed inflorescence, a contracted or ovate panicle, the main axis indeterminate, but the secondary and ultimate axes cymose ; **thyrsif'erous,** *-rus,* (*fero,* I bear), bearing a thyrse ; **thyrsiflor'us** (*flos, floris,* a flower), the flowers in a thyrse ; **thyr'siform** (*forma,* shape), shaped like a thyrse ; **thyr'soid** (εἶδος, resemblance), like a thyrsus ; **Thyr'sula,** the little cyme which is borne by most Labiates in the axil of the leaves.

Tige, pr. teej (Fr., *tige*), stem ; **Tig'el = Tigelle',** *Tigel'la,* **Tigel'lum,** *Tigel'lus,* a miniature or initial stem, used for (*a*) caulicle or hypocotyl, (*b*) plumule ; **tigella'tus‡,** (1) having a short stalk, as the plumule of the bean ; (2) when the stalk is well marked ; **Tigel'lula ‡,** a short filament or stalk observed in the truffle ; **tigellula'ris,** vascular.

Tig'line, the acrid principle in the seeds of *Croton Tiglium,* Linn.

Til'ler, a sucker or branch from the bottom of the stem ; **til'lering,** throwing out stems from the base of the stem ; **Til'low** (Crozier) = TILLER.

Tim'ber-line, the upper limit of tree vegetation on the mountains.

Time, *cf.* **Exposit'ion ~, Presenta'tion ~, Reac'tion ~.**

tinctor'ious, *-rius,* **tinctor'ial** (Lat., pertaining to dyeing), used for dyeing, imprinting colour.

Tin'der-fung'us, *Polyporus fomentarius* Fr.

Tinoleu'cite (τείνω, I extend, + LEUCITE), Van Tieghem's term for directing spheres, the centrosomes.

Tip, used by Withering for ANTHER.

Tiph'ad (τῖφος, pool, + AD), a pond plant ; **Tiphi'um,** a pond formation ; **tiphoph'ilus** (φιλέω, I love), pondloving ; **Tiphophy'ta** (φυτὸν, a plant), pond plants (Clements).

Ti'rad (τείρω, I rub away, + AD), "a

bad land plant " ; **Tiri'um,** a bad land formation (Clements).

Tis'sue, the texture or material formed by the union of cells of similar origin and character, and mutually dependent ; tissues united form systems, these again form organs ; **~ Cord,** central cord (Crozier) ; **aq'ueous ~,** a form of hypoderma, consisting of thin-walled parenchyma wanting chloroplastids, but containing much watery sap ; **Conjun'ctive ~,** ground tissue arising from the plerome or young stele ; **cutic'ularized ~,** modified cell-walls, as epidermis and periderm ; **embryon'ic ~ =** MERISTEM ; **ex'tra-ste'lar ~,** see GROUND TISSUE ; **false ~ =** SPURIOUS **~ ; glan'dular ~,** composed of secreting cells or glands ; **Ground ~,** fundamental tissue, neither vascular nor epidermal, either within or without the stele ; **heteroge'neous ~,** consisting of various kinds of cells ; **homoge'neous ~,** when the cells are uniform; **intra-ste'lar ~ =** CONJUNCTIVE-TISSUE; **lim'itary ~,** epidermal tissue ; **parenchy'matous ~,** (*a*) thinwalled, as pith cells ; (*b*) thickwalled, as collenchyma ; **per'manent ~,** adult tissue ; **pri'mary ~,** first formed tissue ; **prosenchy'matous ~,** woody tissue ; **sclerenchy'matous ~,** thickened or hardened, as fibres or sclereids ; **sec'ondary ~,** resulting from growth from continuous meristematic activity ; **sieve ~,** of long articulated tubes, communicating by means of their sieve-plates in their walls ; **spu'rious ~,** an approach to a tissue, by hyphae massing into a felt, or their apices forming a collective apical growing point ; **tegumen'tary ~,** the external epidermal layer ; **tra'cheal ~,** composed of tracheids, especially adapted for the conveyance of liquids; **vas'cular ~,** the components of the vascular system of a plant.

Tjemo'ro-for'est, or aphyllous-forest ; formed by *Casuarina* in Eastern Java and the Sunda Isles.

Tme'ma (τμῆμα, section), a cell rup-

tured in setting free a Moss-gemma
(Correns).

tofa´ceus (Lat., formed of tufa), (1)
tufa-coloured, buffy drab ; (2) gritty.

Toise (Fr., a fathom), a measure formerly used in France, 6·395 feet,
1·9492 metre, 6 French feet.

Tolu´, a resinous exudation from
Myroxylon toluiferum, H. B. K.

to´mentose, *tomento´sus*, **tomen´tous**,
densely pubescent with matted wool,
or short hairs ; **tomen´tulose**, slightly
tomentose ; **Tomen´tum** (Lat., cush-
ioning), (1) pubescence ; (2) ‡ mycelium.

Tomillar´es, a sclerophyllous vegetation
with small rainfall and dry air.

tomip´arous (τόμη, a cutting ; *pario*,
I produce), Bory applies the term
to all plants which reproduce themselves by fission ; **Tom´iange** (ἀγγεῖον,
a vessel), the organ which produces
TOMIES ; **Tom´ie**, pl. **Tom´ies**, Van
Tieghem's name for asexual reproductive bodies which are neither
SPORES nor DIODES, living cells
which do not arise from an adult
stage, but produce an adult individual direct ; **Tom´iogone** (γόνος,
offspring), the organ which produces
TOMIES.

Tongue = LIGULE ; **tongue-shaped**,
long, nearly flat, fleshy and rounded
at the tip, as the leaves of some
Aloes.

Tone´sis (τόνος, strain), Massart's term
to express the ability of an organism
to exhibit a strain ; **Ton´ie**, or **Ton´y**,
the unit of pressure expressed by
the action of the DYNE on a square
centimetre (Errera) ; **Ton´oboles**, *-ae*
(βολή, a throw), plants distributing
the seeds by tension of the carpels
(Clements) ; **Tono´sis**, changes in
turgescence due to intercellular osmotic force ; **Ton´oplast** (πλαστὸς,
moulded), De Vries's term for a
vacuolar living membrane, controlling the pressure of the cell-sap ;
Tonotax´is (τάξις, order), sensitiveness to osmotic variation (Beyerinck);
Tonot´ropism (τροπή, a turning), response to osmotic stimulus.

Tooth, see TEETH ; **toothed**, dentate ;
Tooth´let, a small or secondary
tooth ; **tooth´letted**, finely denticulate (Lindley).

top-shaped, inversely conical.

Topia´ria, pl. (Lat.), ornamental gardening ; **topia´rian**, **top´iary**, relating to the same, especially used of
trees and shrubs clipped into formal
shapes.

top´ical (τοπικὸς, local), local, confined
to a limited area.

topha´ceous, = TOFACEUS (2).

Topochemotax´is (τόπος, a place, +
CHEMOTAXIS) ; = STROPHIC CHEMO-
TAXIS ; adj. **topochemotact´ic** ; **Topo-
galvanotax´is** (+ GALVANOTAXIS),
attraction towards the stimulus by
galvanic action; **Topograph´ic**(γράφω,
I write), (1) place-changes due to
water, wind, gravity, etc. ; (2) used
of stable plant-formations where the
prevailing factors are physiographic
and edaphic (Crampton); **Topophoto-
tax´is** (+ PHOTOTAXIS), movement
towards the place whence the light
comes ; **Topotax´is** (τάξις, order),
attraction to some stimulus and
movement towards it ; adj. **topo-
tact´ic** ; **Topot´ropism** (τροπή, a turning), turning towards a place whence
a stimulus proceeds ; **Top´otype**
(τύπος, a type), a specimen of a
named species from the original
locality.

Tor´als (*torus*, a bed), Bessey's proposed name for THALAMIFLORAE.

torfa´ceus, *turfo´sus* (Henslow), growing in bogs.

tor´iloid, resembling *Torilis* in habit.

torn, when marginal incisions are deep
and irregular.

tor´ose, *toro´sus* (Lat., fleshy, brawny),
cylindric, with contractions or swellings at intervals ; the diminutive
is **torulo´sus**.

Tor´sion, a spiral twisting or bending ;
ap´ical ~, lateral displacement of
the apical cell in certain Mosses,
resulting in the twisting of the
resultant stem (Correns) ; **antid´-
romous ~**, against the direction of
twining, as may be caused by fric-

tion of support; **homod'romous** ~, in the same direction as twining, the internode gyrating in the same way; **Tor'sion-sym'metry** (+ SYM-METRY), Schuett's term for those Diatoms whose valves are twisted; **tor'sional**, in a twisting manner; ~ **Response'**, when stimulus is applied laterally to an organ (Bose); **torsi'vus** 'Mod. Lat., squeezed out), spirally twisted, not quite as in contortea, there being no obliquity in the insertion, as in the petals of *Orchis;* **tor'tilis** (Lat., twisted), susceptible of twisting; **Tort'ism**, Schwendener's term for TROPISM; **tor'tus**, twisted; **tor'tuous**, *tortuo'-sus*, bent or twisted in different directions.

torula'ceous (+ ACEOUS); **tor'uloid**, resembling the genus *Torula*, Pers.

tor'ulose, *torulo'sus* (*torulus*, muscular part), cylindric, with swollen portions at intervals, somewhat moniliform; ~ **Bud'ding**, increasing by budding as yeast.

Tor'us (Lat., a bed), the receptacle of a flower, that portion of the axis on which the parts of the flower are inserted; when elongated it becomes the GONOPHORE and GYNOPHORE; ~ **of Pits**, the thickening of the closing membrane in bordered pits.

Touch'wood, decayed wood due to Fungus-mycelium, formerly used as tinder.

Tox'in (τοξικὸν = poison), in botany, a poisonous secretion by certain Fungi, which kills the cells of the host-plant and facilitates parasitism.

Trabec'ula, pl. **Trabec'ulae** (Lat., a little beam), a cross-bar, (1) the transverse bars of the teeth of the peristome in Mosses; (2) plates of tissue forming partial septa in the microsporangium of *Isoëtes*; (3) the lacunar tissue in *Selaginella*, between the cortex and the central bundle; **trabec'ular**, like a cross-bar; ~ **Duct**, ~ **Ves'sel**, a vessel with cross-bar markings; **trabec'u-late**, *trabecula'tus*, cross-barred; **Trab'ecule** = TRABECULA; **trabec'u-**

lose, used of reticulating fibrils in Lichens.

Trace, a strand of vascular tissue connecting a leaf with the stem, etc.; ~ **-gap**, the gap in the wood caused by the passage of a leaf-trace bundle in the stele.

Tra'chea (Lat., the windpipe), a spiral duct or water-conducting vessel arising by cell-fusion; used by De Bary to include TRACHEID also; **tra'cheal**, belonging to or resembling tracheae; ~ **Cells**, tracheids; ~ of the vascular bundles, the woody portion, the cribrose part associated with bast; **tra'cheary** = TRACHEAL; **Tra'cheid** (εἶδος, resemblance), an elongated closed cell of the wood having secondary thickening and conducting water; the vasiform wood-cell of Goodale; ~ **Seam**, a group of peculiarly thickened cells found in the leaves of Conifers on both sides of the vascular bundle, and formerly regarded as part of the transfusion tissue; **aut'umn** ~, having thicker walls and smaller lumina than **spring** ~, produced early in annual growth; **trache'idal**, pertaining to tracheids; **Trachen-ch'yma** (ἔγχυμα, an infusion), tissue composed of tracheids or spiral vessels; **Tra'cheome**, stated by Potonié not to be the tracheal, but the hydral system of the bundle, he therefore names it HYDROME.

trachycar'pous, *-pus* (τραχὺς, rough to the touch; καρπὸς, fruit), rough-fruited; **trachysper'mous**, *-mus*, (σπέρμα, a seed), rough-seeded.

Tractel'lum (*tractus*, dragged), the anterior flagellum of the zoospore of Saprolegnieae (Hartog).

Trac'tion (*tractus*, a dragging) **Fi'bres**, certain fibres in the mitotic spindle attached to the chromosomes.

Trag'acanth, a gum which flows from *Astragalus Tragacantha*, Linn.; **Tra-gacan'thin**, the same as BASSORIN.

trail'ing, prostrate but not rooting.

trajec'tile, *trajec'tilis* (*trajectus*, a passing over), when the connective completely separates the anther-cells.

Tra′ma (Lat., weft), a mass of hyphae in the lamellae of some Fungi, from which the hymenium springs; Fayod subdivides it thus: ~ **contex′ta,** the hyphae usually parallel, or slightly oblique; ~ **inver′sa,** when they are derived from the sub-hymenium; ~ **permix′ta,** when without apparent order.

transa′pical (*trans,* across or beyond, + APICAL), used by O. Mueller for ~ **Ax′is,** at right angles to the apical axis, passing through the centre of the pervalvar (main longitudinal) axis of a Diatom; ~ **Plane,** the plane at right angles to both valvar and apical planes, passing through the pervalvar and transapical axis (O. Mueller); **Trans′ect** "a cross-section of vegetation" (Clements); **belt** ~, a band varying in width from a decimetre (= nearly four inches) to a meter; **line** ~, an enumeration of species found in a direct line between two points; **Transec′tion** (*sectio,* a cutting), a term proposed by C. MacMillan for "transverse section."

Trans′fer (*transfero,* I bring over), of water, the passage of water by ducts or cells.

Trans′formation (*transformatio,* a change of shape), (1) metamorphosis; (2) morphologic changes in an organ during its existence; adj. **transformed′;** as ~ **Branch,** may be a tendril, thorn, or similarly changed organ; ~ **Cell,** the final shape of the cell, as a fibre, tracheid, etc.

Transfu′sion (*transfusio,* a pouring out); **Tis′sue,** the network of tracheidal cells accompanying the vascular bundle in the leaves of conifers of two kinds: (*a*) unpitted, with abundant protoplasmic contents; or (*b*) tracheidal cells, with similar contents; ~ **Strand,** consisting of parenchymatous or slightly thickened cells at the junction of phloëm and xylem bundle elements, when a ring of sclerenchyma is formed.

Transit′ion (*transitio,* a passing over), the area where change takes place; ~ **Cells,** cells which are continuations of sieve-tubes, the longitudinal division into sieve-tubes and companion cells stops, and **Transit′ion-tissue** is formed; **Lev′el** of ~; in seedlings where the root and stem systems meet; **high** ~, much of the hypocotyl structure hardly distinguishable from the root; **interme′diate** ~, in the region of the collet up to the hypocotyl; **low** ~, begins below the collet and is complete in that region (Compton); **transitor′ius** (Lat., adapted for passing through), temporary, soon passing away (S. F. Gray); **trans′itory,** applied to starch formed of other carbohydrates and not from assimilation direct; the grains are usually small.

Transla′tor (Lat., a transferrer), employed for the RETINACULUM of Asclepiads.

Transloca′tion (*trans,* across; *locatio,* a placing), the transference of reserve material from one part to another.

Transmis′sion (*transmissio,* a sending across), used for the conveyance of stimulus as in *Drosera* and *Mimosa pudica,* Linn., other leaves acting in sympathy; ~ **Cells** = TRANSFUSION-TISSUE.

Transmuta′tion (*transmuto,* I shift), chemical change by addition or alteration of composition without complete resolution into its elements; ~ **of Host,** = LIPOXENY.

Transovula′tae (*trans,* across, + OVULUM), Van Tieghem's term for Phanerogams furnished with transitory ovules; **Transpira′tion** (*spiratio,* a breathing), the exhalation of watery vapour from the stomata of plants, not mere evaporation; **cutic′ular** ~, the small amount passed through the cuticle (Brown and Escombe); **sto′matal** ~, the normal and chief means of transpiring; **Transpirom′eter** (μέτρον, a measure), apparatus for measuring the amount of transpiration.

Trans′port (*transporto*, I carry across), the conveyance of assimilated substance from one part to another; translocation.

Transvect′ion (*transvectus*, carried across), when in *Cladophora* the basis of the initial branch-cell is partly in contact with the mother-cell and partly against the succeeding cell (Brand); *cf.* EVECTION.

transver′sal (*transversus*, athwart), lying crosswise; ~ **Ax′is** of Diatoms, that axis which lies in the transversal plane, cutting the pervalvar (main longitudinal) axis (O. Mueller); ~ **Wall**, that which divides the basal and median walls of the proëmbryo of Archegoniatae, at right angles into upper and lower halves; **transver′san Plane**, that which passes through the centre of a Diatom frustule vertically to the pervalvar axis (O. Mueller); **tran′sverse**, *transver′sus*, *transversa′lis*, across, right and left as to bract and axis, collateral; Lindley gives "broader than long" as the definition of *transversus*; ~ **Cho′risis**, when two or more organs instead of one appear above or within another; ~ **Geot′ropism** = DIAGEOTROPISM; ~ **Heliot′ropism** = DIAHELIOTROPISM; ~ **Planes**, those which cut the axis of growth and surface at right angles.

trape′ziform, *trapeziform′is* (τραπέζιον, a figure of four unequal sides; *forma*, shape), an unsymmetrical four-sided figure, as a trapezium, almost the same as rhomboid; **trap′ezoid**, *-deus* (εἶδος, resemblance), like a trapezium.

Trap-hairs, the special hairs which confine insects in certain flowers till pollination is effected; *cf.* WICKER-HAIRS.

Traps, pl., Prison-flowers, such as *Aristolochia*, which confine insect visitors until pollination has taken place.

Traube′s Cells, artificial cells formed by various solutions of gelatine and other colloids, which have been used to explain the phenomena of intussusception.

traumat′ic (τραῦμα, a wound), due to a wound; **Trau′matism**, abnormal growth in consequence of injury; **Traumat′otax′is** (τάξις, order), or **Traumatotax′y**, response due to a wound; adj. **traumatotac′tic**; **traumatrop′ic** (τροπή, a turning); showing the influence of wounded root-tips; ~ **Cur′vature**, the bending of roots in consequence of injury to their tips; **Traumat′ropism** (τροπή, a turning), Pfeiffer's term for the phenomena consequent on the infliction of wounds on the tip of a growing root.

Trechom′eter (τρέχω, I run; μέτρον, a measure), an instrument to measure loss of water by surface flow.

Tree, a perennial woody plant with an evident trunk; **tree-like**, resembling a tree, but smaller; dendroid; ~ **Stra′tum**, in woodlands, the highest layer, composed of developed trees; **Trees**, pl.; **Can′opy** ~, having well-branched crowns; **Tuft** ~, trunks usually unbranched, as palms, cycads, and arborescent Liliaceae.

Tre′halase, an enzyme which hydrolizes **Tre′halose**, a sugar found in many Fungi and stated to be identical with the "Trehala" (Persian Manna), a waxy excretion produced by a coleopterous larva to form its cocoon.

tremel′loid (*Tremella*, εἶδος, resemblance), jelly-like in substance or appearance, like the genus *Tremella*.

tri, in compounds, from Greek (τρεῖς) or Latin (*tres*) = three or triple.

Triachae′nium (*tri*, from *tres*, three + ACHAENIUM), like a cremocarp, but of three carpels; **Triacrorhi′zae** (ἄκρος, at the end; ῥίζα, a root), plants whose roots arise from three initial cells or groups at the apex, as the Phanerogams (Van Tieghem); adj. **triac′rorhize**; **Triadel′phia** (ἀδελφός, a brother), a Linnean order of plants with their stamens in three sets; **triadel′phous**, filaments in three brotherhoods; **Triake′nium** = TRIACHAENIUM; **trian′der** = trian′drous, **trian′drian** (ἀνήρ, ἀνδρὸς, a man), having three stamens;

Trian′dria, a Linnean class of three-stamened plants ; **trian′gular,** *triangula′ris* (*angulus,* an angle), with three angles ; **triangula′tus** (Lat.), three-angled ; **trian′thous** (ἄνθος, a flower), three-flowered, as a peduncle; **tri′arch** (ἀρχὴ, beginning), a fibro-vascular cylinder with three ligneous groups ; **triari′nus** (ἄρρην, male), Necker's term for TRIANDROUS ; **Trias′ter** (+ ASTER), in nuclear division when three asters are formed.

Tribe, *Tri′bus* (Lat., a division of the people), a group superior to a genus, but less than an order.

Tribi′um (τριβὴ, a grinding down), a succession of plants on eroded soils (Clements).

triblas′tus (τρι-, three ; βλαστὸς, a bud), Koerber's term for a Lichen-spore, which is trilocular and able to germinate from each loculus.

trib′uloid (εἶδος, resemblance), like the fruit of *Tribulus,* beset with sharp bristles, echinate (Heinig).

Tri′ca (deriv. ?), the button-like apothecium of the genus *Gyrophora.*

tricam′arus (*tri,* three, + CAMARUS), when a fruit is composed of three loculi ; **tricar′inate** (*carinatus,* keel-formed), with three keels or angles, as certain Diatoms; **tricarpel′lary, tricar′pellate, tricar′pous,** *-pus* (καρπὸς, fruit), of three carpels ; **tricel′lular** (+ CELLULAR), consisting of three cells (A. Braun) ; **triceph′alous,** *-lus* (κεφαλὴ, a head), triple-headed, with three heads of flowers ; **Tricha′sium** (+ [DI]CHASIUM), a cymose inflorescence with three branches (Parkin).

Trichid′ium (θρὶξ, τριχὸς, a hair or bristle) = STERIGMA ; **trichif′erous** (*fero,* I bear), producing or bearing hairs ; **trich′iform** (*forma,* shape), bristle-shaped (J. Smith); **Trich′ite,** a needle-shaped crystal of amylose in starch grains, stated to form the latter by aggregation (A. Meyer) ; **Trichobacte′ria** (+ BACTERIA), those bacteria which possess cilia ; **Trich′oblast** (βλαστὸς, a bud), (1) used by

Sachs for such IDIOBLASTS as are especially distinguished by their size or branching ; (2) employed by Leavitt for specialized cells which give rise to root-hairs ; **trichocar′pus** (καρπὸς, fruit), when fruit is covered with hair-like pubescence ; **tricheceph′alus** (κεφαλὴ, a head), when flowers are collected into heads, and surrounded by hair-like appendages ; **tricho′des** (εἶδος, resemblance), resembling hair ; **Trichogo′nium** (γονὴ, race, offspring), a proposed emendation of TRICHOGYNE ; **Trich′ogyne** (γυνὴ, a woman), (1) the receptive filament of the procarp in certain Algae, by which fertilization is effected ; (2) in the Lichen genus *Gyrophora,* by Lindau termed TEREBRATOR ; **trichogyn′ial,** relating to a trichogyne ; **Tricholo′ma** (λῶμα, a fringe), when an edge or border is furnished with hairs.

Trich′oma, pl. **Trichom′ata** (τρίχωμα, a growth of hair), (1) the filamentous thallus of such Algae as *Conferva* (Lindley) ; (2) the filaments in *Nostoc.*

trichom′anoid (*Trichomanes,* εἶδος, resemblance), like the genus *Trichomanes* in habit.

Trich′ome, *Tricho′ma* (τρίχωμα, a growth of hair), any hair-like outgrowth of the epidermis, as a hair or bristle; adj. **tricho′mic ; Trich′-ophore** (φορέω, I carry), a row of cells of a procarp bearing the trichogyne in Florideae ; adj. **trichophor′ic , ~ Cell,** the central cell in the procarp of *Laboulbenia,* becoming fused with the carpogenic cell ; **Trichoph′orum,** the stipe of Fungi when formed of "filaments" (J. S. Henslow) ; **trichophyl′lus** (φύλλον, a leaf), hair-like leaves, that is, finely cut ; **Trichoplank′ton** (+ PLANKTON), floating marine vegetation chiefly composed of *Thalassiothrix* (Cleve); **Trichosporan′ge = Trichosporan′gium** (+ SPORANGIUM), Thuret's term for the multilocular sporangium of the Phaeosporeae, apparently of jointed hairs ; **tricho-**

thal′lic (θαλλὸs, a sprout), when the shoot ends in one or more multicellular hairs or tuft of such ; ~ **Gemma′tion**, the origin of young plants from the hairs scattered on the thallus of *Asperococcus* ; ~ **Growth**, with filiform thallus, the tips bearing tufts of hairs.

trichot′omous, -*mus* (τρίχα, in a three-fold manner; τομή, a cutting), three-forked, branching into three divisions ; adv. **trichot′omously** ; **Trichot′omy**, division into threes.

tricoc′cous, -*cus* (*tri*, three, + Coccus), consisting of three cocci ; **tri′color** (*color*, colour), having three colours ; **tricos′tate** (*costatus*, with ribs), having three ribs ; **tricotyle′donous** (+ Cotyledon), when three cotyledons are present, or when one of two is so deeply divided as to seem double ; **Tricotyle′dony** is the condition.

tricus′pid, tricus′pidate, *tricuspida′tus* (*tricuspis*, having three points or tines), tipped with three cusps or pointed tips.

tricus′sate (*tri*, three, + cussate), used for whorls of three leaves each, the leaves of each whorl alternating with those above and below ; *cf.* decussate (G. Henslow).

tricy′clic (τρι-, from τρεῖs, three; κύκλοs, a circle), when the members of a series are in three whorls ; **Tricy′cly** is the state in question.

triden′tate, *tridenta′tus* (*tridens*, three-pronged), three-toothed, trident-pointed.

tridig′itate, *tridigita′tus* (*tri*, three ; *digitus*, a finger), thrice digitate, ternate.

tri′duus (*triduum*, the space of three days), lasting three days.

trid′ymus (τρίδυμοs, triple), when of three laminae in Agarics, the middle is the larger.

tridy′namous (τρι-, three ; δύναμιs, power), when three stamens out of six are longer than the rest ; **trie′der** (ἕδρα, a seat), triangular.

trien′nis, triennia′lis (*triennium*, the space of three years), lasting three years.

trifar′iam (Lat., triply), **trifar′ious**, -*ius*, facing three ways ; in three vertical ranks.

trif′id, *trif′idus* (Lat.), three cleft.

triflo′rous (*tri*, three ; *flos*, *floris*, a flower), three-flowered ; **trifo′liate**, *trifolia′tus*, *trifo′lius* (*folium*, a leaf), three-leaved ; **trifo′liolate**, *trifoliola′tus* (+ foliolate), with three leaflets.

triform′is ‡ (Lat., having three forms), bearing flowers of three different kinds, as certain Composites ; trimorphic.

trifur′cate (*trifurcus*, with three prongs), having three forks or branches.

trig′amous (τρι, three ; γάμοs, marriage), bearing three kinds of flowers ; trimorphic.

trigem′inous (*trigeminus*, triplets), tergeminate, trijugate.

tri′glans (*tri*, three ; *glans*, an acorn), containing three nuts within an involucre, as *Castanea sativa*, Mill.

trig′onal (τρίγωνοs, three-cornered), three - angled ; **Trig′ones**, pl., Spruce's term for the thickening in the angles of the cells of the leaves in certain Hepatics, or as in collenchyma ; **trigonocar′pus** (καρπὸs, fruit), fruit having three evident angles ; **trig′onous**, -*nus*, three-angled, with plane faces.

Trigyn′ia (τρι, three ; γυνὴ, a woman), a Linnean order of plants with three styles; **trig′ynous**, -*nus*, with three pistils or styles.

trihila′tus (*tri*, three, + Hilum), having three apertures, as in some grains of pollen ; **tri′jugate**, *triju-ga′tus*, **tri′jugous**, *tri′jugus* (*jugum*, a yoke), with three pairs of pinnae ; **trilam′ellar** (*tri*, three ; *lamella*, a plate of metal), applied to a compound stigma having three divisions flattened like bands ; **trilat′eral**, *trilatera′lis* (*latus*, *lateris*, a side), prismatic, with three sides ; **trilo′bate**, *trilo′bus* (*lobus*, a lobe), three-lobed ; **triloc′ular**, *trilocula′ris* (*loculus*, a little cell), three-celled ; **Trimer′i-**

stele (+ MERISTELE), a stele formed of three members (Brebner) ; adj. **trimeriste'lic** ; **tri'merous**, *-rus* (μέρος, a part), in threes, three membered parts.

trimes'tris (Lat., of three months), lasting three months, or maturing in that time, as *Lavatera trimestris,* Linn.

Trimonoe'cism (τρι, three + MONOE-CISM), having male, female, and perfect flowers on the same plant ; monoecious, but existing in trimorphous condition ; **trimor'phic, trimor'phous** (μορφή, shape), occurring under three forms, of stamens and styles, long, short, and intermediate ; **Trimor'phism,** heterogony, with long-, short-,and mid-styled flowers.

tri'mus (Lat.), lasting three years.

triner'vate, *trinerva'tus,* **trinerved'**, *triner'vis, triner'vius* (*tri*, three ; *nervus,* a nerve), three-nerved ; **trinervula'tus** (Lat.), with three nerve-like strands in the placenta ; **trino'dal** (*nodus,* a knot), with three nodes or joints ; **Trioe'cia** (οἶκος, a house), a Linnean order of plants with trioecious flowers ; **trioe'cious,** with staminate, pistillate, and hermaphrodite flowers on three distinct plants ; **Trioe'cism,** or **trioe'cious Polyg'amy,** some individuals hermaphrodite, others male, and still others female, as in the ash, *Fraxinus ;* **trioe'ciously hermaph'rodite** = TRIMORPHIC ; **trioi'cous,** *·-cus,* the mode of spelling preferred by bryologists for trioecious ; **trioper'culate,** *trioopercula'tus* (+ OPERCULUM), having three lids; **triov'ulate,** *triovula'tus*(+OVULUM), with three ovules ; **tripaleola'-tus** (+ PALEA), consisting of three paleae, as the flowers of bamboo ; **tripar'ted** (*partitus,* cleft), parted to the base in three divisions ; **tripar'tible** (*partibilis,* divisible), tending to split into three parts.

tripar'tite (*triparti'tus,* three-fold), divided into three parts.

tripen'nate, *tripenna'tus* (*tri,* three; *penna,* a feather), = tripinnate ;

tripet'aloid, *tripetaloi'deus* (πέταλον, a flower-leaf ; εἶδος, resemblance), as if three-petalled ; **tripet'alous,** *-lus,* having three petals.

triphylet'ic (τρι-, three ; φυλετικὸς, tribal), used of hybrids containing the blended strains of three species ; **Triphyl'lome** (φύλλον, a leaf), hypothetically three segments to form a carpel, two hypophylls. superior and fertile, the third sterile and inferior (Pasquale) ; **triphyl'-lous,** *-lus,* three-leaved ; **tripin'nate,** *tripinna'tus* (+ PINNA), thrice pinnate ; **tripinnat'ifid,** *tripinnatif'idus* (*fid,* from *findo,* I cleave), thrice pinnatifid ; **tripinnat'isect** (*sectus,* cut), thrice pinnatisect.

Trip'lasy (*triplasius,* threefold), the division of an organ into three analogous structures (Fermond).

Trip'le Fu'sion, a suggested emendation of the term DOUBLE FERTILIZATION ; ~ **nerved,** ~ **ribbed,** ~ **veined** (*triplex,* threefold), with a midrib dividing into three, or sending off a strong branch on each side above the base of the blade ; **trip'lex,** triple ; **trip'licate, triplica'tus** (Lat.), in a triple manner, as **triplica'to-gemina'tus,** tergeminate ; ~ -nerva'tus, triplinerved; ~ -pinna'-tus, tripinnate ; **trip'licate-ter'nate,** triternate (Crozier) ; **trip'liciter** (Lat.), thrice repeated ; **triplicos'tate** (*costatus,* ribbed), having three ribs, triple-ribbed ; **tripliform'is** (*forma,* shape),as*tripliform'ia Fo'lia,* "leaves resembling the triple-leaved form" (Lindley) ; **triplinerved',** *tripliner'vis, -vius* (*nervus,* a nerve), see TRIPLE-NERVED, etc.

trip'lo-caules'cent (*triplus,* triple ~ CAULESCENT), when a plant has a third (tertiary) system of axes ; **triplocau'lous** (+ CAULIS) possessing ternary axes (Pax) ; **trip'loid** (εἶδος, resemblance), applied to a nucleus having half·as many again chromosomes as a diploid nucleus ; as by the union of a haploid and a diploid germ ; **Triploi'dity,** the condition described.

trip′lus (Lat.), threefold ; tripo′lar (+ POLAR), having three poles.

Triposplank′ton (+ PLANKTON), floating marine vegetation made up chiefly of *Ceratium Tripos* (Cleve).

trip′terous, -*rus* (τρι-, three ; πτερὸν, a wing), three-winged.

triq′ueter (Lat., three-cornered), trique′trous, *triq′uetrus*, three-edged, with three salient angles.

triqui′nate, *triquina′tus* (*tri*, three, + QUINATUS), divided into three, then into five ; tri-ridged, having three ridges or projecting ribs ; tri′sect, trisec′ted, *trisec′tus* (*sectus*, cut), divided into three, three-cleft to the base; trisep′alous, *trisep′alus* (+ SEPALUM), having three sepals; trisep′tate (+ SEPTUM), with three septa or partitions, as in many spores ; trise′rial, *triseria′lis ;* trise′-riate, *triseria′tus* (*series*, a row), in three horizontal ranks or series, trifarious ; trisperm′ous (σπέρμα, a seed), three-seeded ; tristach′yus (στάχυς, a spike of corn), three-spiked ; tris′tichous, -*chus* (στίχος, a series), in three vertical ranks ; tristigmat′ic, *tristigmat′icus* (+ STIGMA), having three stigmas.

tris′tis (Lat., sad), (1) of a dull or unattractive colour, as the flowers of *Matthiola tristis*, R. Br. ; (2) flowering only at night (Heinig).

tristy′lous, -*lus* (*tri*, three, + STYLUS), with three styles; trisyncotyle′-donous (De Vries), = TRICOTYLE-DONOUS.

trisul′cate, *trisulca′tus* (*trisulcus*, having three furrows), with three grooves or furrows.

triter′nate (*tri*, three, + TERNATE), thrice ternate.

Tritice′tum, an association of *Triticum junceum ;* Tri′ticin, the proteid of wheat, *Triticum vulgare*, Vill., present in its gluten.

triun′dulate (*tri*, three, + UNDULATE), used for Diatoms having three undulations on the dorsal side of the valve.

trival′vular (*tri*, three, + VALVULAR), three-valved.

triver′ted, O. Müller's term for asymmetric as applied to Diatoms.

triv′ial (*trivialis*, common-place), ordinary, common ; ~ Names, the common name of a plant, the adjective, or more rarely, the second substantive appended to a generic name to connote a species.

Trix′eny (τρι, three ; ξένος, a guest or host), De Bary's term for the condition of a parasite which passes its career in three host-plants.

troch′lear, *trochlea′ris* (*trochlea*, a pulley) ; trochlea′riform (*forma*, shape), pulley-shaped.

Tropax′is (τροπὴ, a turning, + AXIS), a theoretic plane between the epicotyl and hypocotyl, whence growth proceeds in opposite directions (White) ; *cf.* TRANSITION.

troph′ic (τροφὴ, nourishment), relating to increase in thickness, *cf.* TROPHY; trophileg′ic (λέγω, I collect), collecting food-material for the plant, as the shell-like barren fronds of *Platycerium* are supposed to do (Archangeli) ; Troph′ime (τρόφιμος, a nursling), the result of the fusion of the central nucleus of the embryo sac, the mesocyst, with the second antherozoid (Van Tieghem) ; Trophochromid′ia (+ CHROMIDIA), Mesnil's term for vegetative chromidia ; Troph′ogone (γόνος, offspring), a growth in Ascomycetes similar to those which produce gametophores, but having a nutritive function (Dangeard) ; Troph′ophyll (φύλλον, a leaf), a vegetative leaf or frond, as distinct from one which produces fructification ; Troph′ophyte (φυτὸν, a plant), (1) an error for TROPOPHYTE ; (2) the fusion-product in *Welwitschia* and angiosperms, to distinguish it from the prothallus of the lower Cryptogams ; it has been mistakenly applied to the endosperm of Cycads (Pearson) ; Troph′oplasm (πλάσμα, that formed), the ALVEO-LAR-PLASMA of Strasburger ; trophoplas′mic, adj. of TROPHOPLASM ; Troph′oplast (πλαστὸς, moulded), A. Meyer's term for the essential

granules in protoplasm, *cf.* PLASTID;
Troph′opollen ‡ (+ POLLEN), the
partition of an anther-loculus or
its remains (Lindley); **Troph′osome**
(σῶμα, a body), any organ which is
concerned with supplying nourishment only ; **Troph′osperm,** *Tropho-
sperm′ium, Trophosper′mum* (σπέρμα,
a seed), = PLACENTA ; **Troph′ospore**
(+ SPORE), applied to the spores of
Diatoms, Desmids, *Bulbochaete* and
Coleochaete(Radlkofer); **Trophospor′o-
some,** applied to organs which are
engaged in nourishing and also in
reproducing the plant (Potonié) ;
Trophotax′is (τάξις, order), Stahl's
term for **Trophot′ropism** (τροπή, a
turning), phenomena induced in a
growing organ by the chemical nature
of its environment; **Troph′y,** pl.
Troph′ies, Wiesner's term for an
unequal lateral growth of tissue or
organ, depending on its relation to
the horizon and the mother-shoot.
trop′ic (τροπή, a turning), reacting to
a stimulus by internal change in an
organism (Wager), it may be **neg′a-
tive,** or **pos′itive ; trop′ical,** *trop′icus*
(Lat., pertaining to a turning), (1)
growing within the tropics ; (2) used
for flowers which expand in the
morning and close at night during
several successive days.
Trop′is (τρόπις, the keel of a vessel), in
composition used for the keel of a
papilionaceous flower, or resembling
the same.
Trop′ism(τροπή, a turning), a curvature
which results from a response to
some stimulus; the disposition to
respond by turning or bending
(Copeland) ; **tropis′tic,** movement in
response to stimulus (Czapek).
trop′o-, employed as a prefix by Drude,
to denote climates alternating between torrential rain and sunny
drought ; **Tropodrymi′um** (δρυμὸς, a
coppice), savanna forest formation
(Diels); **tropoph′ilous** (φιλέω, l love),
loving change of condition as
TROPOPHYTES ; **Trop′ophyll** (φύλλον,
a leaf), leaves of shrubs and trees
(Potonié) ; **Trop′ophyte** (φυτὸν, a

plant), applied to the large majority
of plants, which are xerophilous and
hygrophilous according to season
(A. F. W. Schimper).
True-par′asite = OBLIGATE-PARASITE.
trul′lifer, trullifor′mis (Lat.), shaped
like a bricklayer's trowel.
Trum′pet-hy′phae, tubes in Laminarieae
having swollen portions with transverse septa (F. W. Oliver) ; **trum′pet-
shaped,** tubular, with dilated orifice.
trun′cate, *trunca′tus* (Lat., shortened),
as though cut off at the end.
Trun′cus (Lat., tree-stem), (1) the
main-stem or **Trunk** of a tree ; (2)
in Lichens, the thallus.
Truss, a florist's term for a flower-
cluster.
Try′ma (τρῦμα, a hole or opening),
Necker's term for a drupaceous nut
with dehiscent exocarp, as the
walnut.
Tryp′sin (θρύπτω, I break in pieces),
a group of proteolytic enzymes analogous to the pancreatic ferment in
animals, such as Bromelin and
Papaïn ; **Trypt′ases,** pl., enzymes of
the trypsin group (Vines) ; **trypt′ic,**
relating to TRYPSIN, or a similar
enzyme.
tubaeform′is (*tuba,* a trumpet ; *forma,*
shape), trumpet-shaped ; **tuba′tus**
(Mod. Lat.) is a synonym.
Tube, *Tu′bus* (Lat., a pipe), (1) any
hollow elongated body or part of
an organ ; (2) the united portion
of a gamopetalous corolla or gamosepalous calyx, etc.; ∼ -**cell,** the cell
which gives rise to the pollen-tube ;
∼ **Germina′tion,** the germination of
a spore in which the first product is
a germ - tube ; **tube - form, tube-
shaped,** tubular or trumpet-shaped
(Crozier) ; **Tubes, prothall′ine** = EM-
BRYO-SAC TUBES.
Tu′ber (Lat., a tumour), a thickened
and short subterranean branch, beset with buds or "eyes" ; **Tu′ber-
cle,** *Tuber′culum* (Lat.), (1) a little
tuber ; (2) a wart-like apothecium
in *Verrucaria* ; (3) any similar excrescence, as on roots, ascribed to
the action of symbiotic organisms ;

(4) a tuberous root, as of the *Dahlia*
(Crozier); **tu′bercled**, covered with
warty excrescences, as the seeds of
Silene; **Pri′mary Tu′bercle**, is used by
Treub to denote an ovoid body formed
by the germination of the spore of
Lycopodium; **Tu′bercorm** (+CORM),
J Smith's name for such fleshy
roots as the beet, yam, and turnip;
tuber′cular, having tubercles or like
a tubercle; **tuber′culate**, *tubercula′-
tus*, beset with knobby projections
or excrescences; **Tuberculiza′tion**,
the formation of tubers, assumed to
be due to the attack of a Fungus
(Bernard); **tuber′culose, tuber′culous**,
consisting of or having tubercules;
tuberif′erous (*fero*, I bear), tuber-
bearing; **Tuberogem′ma** (+GEMMA),
a budlike tuber, occurring in the axil
of the leaves, or as a root-tubercle,
which asexually propagates the
plant, as in *Ranunculus Ficaria*,
Linn.: **tu′berose**, *tubero′sus*, **tu′-
berous** (Lat., full of humps), (1)
producing tubers; (2) resembling a
tuber.

Tub′i, pl. of **Tub′us** (Lat., a pipe), the
hymenial tubes of such Fungi as
Polyporus; **tubiflo′rous**, *-rus* (*flos,
floris*, a flower), when the florets are
tubular, as in many Compositae: **tu′bi-
form,** *tubiform′is* (*forma*, shape), tube-
shaped; **Tubil′lus**, (1) an elongated
cell of cellular tissue; (2) the tube
of the filaments in Compositae; **tu′-
bular**, *tubula′tus*, apparently a cylindrical figure and hollow; ∼ **Flo′ret**,
in Compositae a disk or regular
floret.

Tub′ulus, pl. **Tub′uli** (Lat., a small
pipe), (1) the pores or hymeneal
tubes of some Hymenomycetous
Fungi, as *Polyporus;* (2) in Pyrenomycetes, the prolonged apex of
perithecium pierced by a canal, the
same as NECK (5); **tubuliflo′rous**,
-rus (*flos, floris*, a flower) = tubiflo-
rous; **tubuliform′is** (*forma*, shape),
= tubiform.

Tuft, used by Withering for CYME;
tuft′ed, caespitose; ∼ **Hairs**, a modification of stellate hairs, but

branched from the base upwards
(Weiss); ∼ **Trees**, those having
unbranched stems, such as palms
and arborescent Liliaceae as *Yucca*
and *Cordyline*.

tu′itans (*tueor*, I defend), when leaves
assume the sleep-position, appearing
to guard the stem.

Tülle (Ger.) = TYLOSE.

Tum′ble-weeds, a name applied to
certain weeds which break adrift
when dry, and are blown to a distance, scattering their seeds by the
way.

tumes′cent (*tumescens*, swelling up),
somewhat tumid.

tu′mid, *tu′midus* (Lat., swollen), inflated, swollen.

Tun′dra, an extensive flat or undulating tract without trees, but having moorlike plant-communities;
∼ **Pe′riod**, succeeded the Ice-age in
Switzerland (Früh and Schroeter).

Tu′nic, *Tun′ica* (Lat., an under-gar-
ment), (1) the skin of a seed, the
spermoderm; (2) any loose membranous skin not formed from the
epidermis (Lindley); (3) the coat
of a bulb; (4) the peridium of certain Fungi; (5) employed by Smith
for UTRICLE of *Carex*); ∼ **Gras′ses**,
employed by Hackel for those whose
leaf-sheaths remain attached after
their upper parts have died; **tu′ni-
cate**, *tunica′tus* (Lat.), having coats
or tunics; **tu′nicated** is a synonym;
∼ **Bulb**, one covered with complete
enveloping coats, as an onion; *cf.*
IMBRICATE BULB.

turbar′ian (*turbaria*, Late Lat., peat
pit), a stage in the formation of
peat, characterized by the presence
of dwarf willows.

tur′binate, *turbina′tus* (Lat., cone-
shaped); **turbiniform′is** (*forma*,
shape), shaped like a top.

turfa′ceus, **turfo′sus**, = TORFACEUS,
growing in bogs; **Turfoph′ilae**, pl.
(φιλέω, I love), bog-plants.

Turges′cence (*turgesco*, I swell), the
distension of a cell or cellular
tissue by water or other liquid;
turges′cent, becoming turgid.

395

tur'gid, *tur'gidus* (Lat., inflated), swollen, but not with air; **Tur'gor** (Lat.), turgidity, turgescence.

Tu'rion, *Tu'rio* (Lat., a shoot), a scaly sucker, or shoot from the ground, as *Asparagus;* **turionif'erous**, -*rus* (*fero*, I bear), throwing up turions.

Turm'eric (said to be from *terra merita*, valuable earth), the powdered rhizome of *Curcuma longa*, Linn., which yields a yellow dye.

turned, in botany, directed towards; as ~ **in'wards** = introrse; ~ **out'-wards** = extrorse.

tur'nip-shaped, also termed napiform.

Tur'pentine (*terebinthus*, turpentine tree), the solution of resins in terebene; ~ **Ves'sels**, tubes in the wood in which the turpentine collects during growth, common in Conifers.

Tus'sock, a tuft of grass or grass-like plants; ~ **Forma'tion**, occurring in New Zealand and the Falkland Islands, composed of thick tufts of certain grasses.

Twig, a small shoot or branch of a tree; ~ **Cli'mbers**, Schenck's term for certain Brazilian lianes, the young leafy lateral branches being sensitive where in contact with their supports; ~ **Gall**, a morbid growth ascribed to the action of bacteria; ~ **-like**, long, flexible and wandlike.

Twin, in pairs, geminate, didymous; ~ **-bund'le**, the double leaf-trace of *Lyginodendron;* ~ **Crys'tals**, double styloids.

Twi'ners, plants which twine or climb by winding their stems round their support; **twi'ning**, winding spirally.

twist'ed, contorted.

two-armed, used of Malpighiaceous hairs; ~ **cleft**, bifid; ~ **edged**, ancipital, laterally compressed with two sharp angles parallel with the axis; **-forked**, dichotomous; ~ **lipped**, bilabiate; ~ **-part'ed**, bipartite; ~ **-ranked**, distichous; ~ **-toothed**, bidentate.

tycholimnet'ic (τύχη, chance, + LIM-NETIC), **tychopelag'ic** (πέλαγος, the open sea), used of that floating vegetation which at times is at the surface, and at others is attached to plants or rocks at the bottom; **tychopot'amic** (ποταμὸς, a river) **Plank'ton**, the floating organisms of pools and river overflows (Zimmer).

tylic'olor (Mod. Lat.), the colour of a woodlouse, slate or dark grey.

Ty'lose, *Tylo'sis* (τύλος, a callosity), a cell intruding into a duct.

tym'paniform (*tympanum*, a drum; *forma*, shape), drum-shaped, as the membrane covering a Moss-capsule; **tymp'anoid**, Berkeley's term for "resembling the head of a drum;" **Tym'panum**, the membrane across the mouth of the capsule of a Moss, the epiphragm.

Type (*typus*, a type), the ideal representative of a group, genus, species; ~ **Spec'imen**, the original specimen from which a description was drawn up;—**pri'mary** ~ = PROTEROTYPE; **sec'ondary** ~ or **supplemen'tary** ~ = PLESIOTYPE, NEOTYPE; **typ'ical**, *typ'icus* (Lat.), representing the plan or type; ~ **Cells**, fundamental cells; ~ **Di'agram**, the resultant form from several empiric diagrams; ~ **Spec'imens** = ICOTYPES.

Typhe'tum, Warming's term for an association of *Typha* plants.

Ty'piform (+ FORM), a constant form arising either by natural selection or by animal adaptations; its existence is frequently dependent on animals (Kuntze).

Ty'ponym (ὄνομα, a name), a name rejected because an older name was based upon the same type (O. F. Cook); adj. **typonym'ic**.

Ty'rosin (τυρὸς, cheese), an amide, similar to Asparagin; **Ty'rosinase**, an oxidizing enzyme which attacks the chromogen of certain Fungi (Bertrand); probably a compound.

Ubi'quist (*ubique*, everywhere), used by Thurmann and adopted by Warming for a plant which occurs on any kind of geological formation.

ulig'inose, *uligino'sus*, **ulig'inous**, *uliginar'ius* (Lat., marshy), growing in swamps; **ulig′inal**, occasionally used for the foregoing.

Ul′na (Lat., the elbow), a measure of about twenty-four inches; **ulna′ris**, the length of the forearm.

uloden′droid (εἶδος, resemblance), like the former fossil genus *Ulodendron*, Rhode, applied to branches of *Lepidodendron* and *Sigillaria*, bearing two opposite rows of large, cup-shaped scars (Scott).

ulotricha′ceous, resembling or allied to the algal genus *Ulothrix* (Kütz.).

u′lothrix (οὖλος, shaggy; θρίξ, hair), (1) in hair-like crisp linear divisions (J. S. Henslow); (2) *Ulothrix* is a genus of chlorophyllaceous Algae.

ulter′ior (Lat., farther) **Pith**, cellular structure formed in the axis of the root after the separation of the stele (Frémont).

Ult′imate (*ultime*, to the last degree) **Strength**, the minimum load on a tissue which causes its rupture (Drummond).

Ulto′nian (*Ultonia*, Ulster), relating to the province of Ulster (Praeger).

ul′tra-seta′ceous (*ultra*, beyond; *seta*, a bristle, + ACEOUS), very long-drawn-out.

Um′bel, *Umbel′la* (Lat., a sunshade), (1) an inflorescence, properly indeterminate, in which a cluster of pedicels spring from the same point, like the ribs of an umbrella; (2) ‡ the pileus of certain Fungi (Lindley); **com′pound ~**, when each ray itself bears an umbel; **cy′mose ~**, an apparent umbel, but with the flowers opening centrifugally; a cyme which simulates an umbel; **par′tial ~**, **sim′ple ~**, an umbel each of whose rays bears a single flower only; **um′bellate**, *umbella′tus*, having the inflorescence in umbels; **Um′bellet**, a small umbel or a simple one; **Umbel′lifer** (*fero*, I bear), a plant which bears umbels; **umbellif′erous**, *-rus*, bearing umbels; **umbelliflo′rus** (*flos, floris*, a flower), umbellate; **umbel′liform**, *umbelliform′is* (*forma*, shape), umbrella-shaped; **Um′bellule**, *Umbel′lula*, an ultimate umbel in a com-

pound one; **umbel′lulate**, *umbellula′tus*, having partial or secondary umbels; **umbellulif′erous**, *-rus* (*fero*, I bear), bearing simple umbels.

um′ber, a cool brown; *cf.* UMBRINUS.

umbili′cal (pertaining to the *umbilicus*, the navel) **Cord**, a vascular strand by which seeds are sometimes attached to the placenta, the funicle; **umbili′cally**, as a Lichen thallus centrically affixed to its matrix, or an epithecium which is navel-like; **umbili′cate**, *umbilica′tus*, (1) navel-like, depressed in the centre; (2) ‡ = PELTATE; **Umbili′cus**, (1) the hilum of a seed; (2) the ostiole of certain Fungi (Lindley); (3) a much-branched rhizoid in some Lichens, as in *Umbilicaria;* (4) the boss on the valves of some Diatoms.

Um′bo (Lat., any convex elevation), a boss, as the centre of the apophysis of the cone-scales in *Pinus Pinaster*, Soland.; **um′bonate**, *umbona′tus*, bearing an umbo or boss in the centre; **umbo′nulate**, *umbonula′tus*, having or ending in a very small boss or nipple.

umbraculif′erous (*umbraculum*, a sunshade; *fero*, I bear), having the shape of an expanded umbrella; **umbra′culiform**, *umbraculiform′is* (*forma*, shape), having the general form of a parasol, as the stigmas of *Sarracenia;* **Umbra′culum**, the stalked capitulum of the sporophore in *Marchantia*, bearing the reproductive organs on the underside.

umbratic′olous (*umbraticus*, shady, *colo*, I inhabit), growing in shady places.

umbrel′la-shaped, umbraculiform.

um′brine, **umbri′nus** (Mod. Lat.), the colour of raw umber, a cool but turbid brown; burnt umber is deeper and warmer.

umbro′sus (Lat., shady), growing in shady places.

unangula′tus (*unus*, one; *angulus*, a corner), one-angled, as applied to a stem or similar organ.

unarmed′, destitute of prickles or

other armature ; sometimes it means pointless, muticous.

un′cate, *unca′tus* (Lat.), hooked, bent at the tip in the form of a hook ; **Un′ci**, pl. of **Un′cus** (Lat., a hook), hooks, uncinate hairs.

uncer′tain, indeterminate.

Un′cia (Lat.), an inch ; **uncia′lis** (Lat.), one inch in length ; about 25·4 mm.

un′ciform, *uncifor′mis* (*uncus*, a hook ; *forma*, shape), hook-shaped ; **un′cinate**, *uncina′tus*, hooked.

uncortica′ted (*corticatus*, covered with bark), destitute or deprived of cortex.

uncov′ered, naked.

unc′tuous, *unctuo′sus* (*unctus*, anointment), having a surface which feels greasy.

Unc′us (Lat.), a hook, or hooked hair.

un′date, *unda′tus* (*unda*, a wave), waved, undulate ; Crozier also gives **un′dated**.

Un′derleaves, stipules in Hepatics.

underly′ing, used for succubous leaves of Hepaticae (Potter).

Un′dershrub, (1) any low shrub ; (2) ‡ partially herbaceous, the ends of the branches perishing during the winter.

undo′sus (Lat., billowy), undulate, wavy.

un′dulate, *undula′tus* (Lat.), wavy.

une′qual (*un* = not, + EQUAL), (1) dissimilar ; (2) applied to stamens of diverse lengths, ~ **si′ded**, irregular ; **une′qually pin′nate**, imparipinnate.

unguic′ular, *unguicular′is*, (1) furnished with a claw ; (2) the length of the middle finger-nail, about 15 mm. or a little over half an inch ; **Unguic′ulus**, the length of the nail of the little finger ; **unguic′ulate**, *unguicula′tus*, contracted at the base into a claw ; **un′guiform** (*forma*, shape), like the claw of a petal (Crozier) ; **Un′guis** (Lat., a nail or claw), a claw-like base of a petal, as in *Dianthus ;* (2) the length of a finger-nail, roughly half an inch.

un′gulate, *ungula′tus* (Lat., having claws or hoofs), clawed.

uni (from *unus,* one), in composition, one, or single ; **uniala′tus** (+ ALATUS), having one wing or decurrent ridge ; **uniax′ial** (+ AXIAL), when a primary stem does not branch, though it may innovate, but ends in a flower ; **unicalcara′tus** (+ CALCARATUS), one-spurred ; **unicap′sular**, *unicapsula′ris* (+ CAPSULAR), with all the carpels united into one capsule ; **unicar′inated** (*carina,* a keel), one-keeled (Crozier) ; **unicarpel′late** (καρπὸs, fruit), the fruit consisting of a single carpel ; **U′nicell** (+ CELL), a plant which consists of a single cell ; **unicel′lular**, *unicellular′is* (+ CELLULAR), formed of one cell ; **unicolor′ous**, *unic′olor* (*color,* colour), of one colour or uniform in tint ; **unicos′tate** (+ COSTATE), having a single rib or costa, with a mid-rib ; **unicotyle′donous** = MONOCOTYLEDONOUS.

u′nicus (Lat., one only), single or solitary.

uniembryona′tus (*uni* from *unus,* one, + EMBRYONATUS), having one embryo ; **unifa′rious** (+ *farius,* as in *bifarius*), one-ranked (Crozier) ; **unif′erus** (*fero,* I bear), bearing once a year (S. F. Gray) ; **uniflor′ous**, *-rus* (*flos, floris,* a flower), one-flowered ; **unifo′liate**, *unifolia′tus* (*folium,* a leaf), with one leaf ; **unifo′liolate**, *unifoliola′tus,* with one leaflet only ; **unifo′lius**, single-leafed ; **unifora′tus** (*foratus,* pierced), opening by one aperture.

uniform′is (Lat., having one shape), used when the receptacle of Compositae bears only one kind of florets, as all ligulate or all tubular.

unigem′mius (*uni* = one, *gemma,* a bud), giving rise to a single bud ; **unig′enus** (*gen,* the root of *gigno,* I produce), leafing annually (J. S. Henslow) ; **uniju′gate**, *unijuga′tus, unij′ugus* (*jugum,* a yoke), with one pair of leaflets ; **unila′biate**, *unilabia′tus* (*labium,* a lip), one-lipped, as the corolla of *Acanthus,* the upper lip being obsolete, or the lingulate florets of Composites ; **unilat′eral**, either *unilatera'lis* (*latus*, a side), one-sided, either originating or, usually, all turned to one side ; **uniloc'ular** (*loculus*, a small compartment), one-celled; **uniner'viate**, *uninervia'tus*, *uniner'-vis*, *uniner'vius* (*nervus*, a nerve), one-veined or ribbed ; **unino'dal** (*nodus*, a knot), having a single node.

uninterrup'ted, continuous.

uninu'clear, **uninu'cleate**, **uninu'cleated**, *uninuclea'tus* (*uni* = one, + NUCLEUS), having a single nucleus ; **uniocula'tus** (*oculatus*, furnished with eyes), having only one vegetating point.

U'nion (*unio*, oneness) of gametes, generally termed FERTILIZATION.

uni'onized (*un* = not, + ION), when the molecules are undivided (J. F. Clark).

uniov'ulate (*uni* = one, + OVULE), with a solitary ovule ; **u'nipared** = **unip'arous** (*pario*, I bring forth), bearing one, as a cyme giving forth one axis at each branching ; **unipet'alous** (+ PETALUM), (1) having a corolla of only one petal, the others not being developed ; (2) erroneously used for GAMOPETALOUS ; **unipo'lar** (+ POLAR), with only one pole ; **uniprophylla'tus** (+ PRO-PHYLLA), with only one prophyllum (Buchenau) ; **unisep'tate** (+ SEP-TATE), having only one septum, as in most teleutospores ; **unise'rial**, *uniseria'lis*, **unise'riate**, *uniseria'tus* (*series*, a row), in one horizontal row or series) ; **unisex'ual**, *unisexua'lis*, *unisex'us* (*sexus*, sex), (1) of one sex ; stamens or pistils only, or their representatives ; (2) in hybrids, when the characters of one parent only are reproduced ; ~ **Hered'ity**, the property of transmitting the qualities of one parent only (Macfarlane) ; **uniso'rous** (+ SORUS), consisting of one sorus ; **unistra'tose** (*stratum*, a layer), of one layer of cells.

U'nit (*unitus*, joined), the male synangium or anther of Gnetaceae ; ~ **Char'acters**, or ~ **Fac'tors**, definite factors in the gamete which in heredity behave as indivisible entities.

Unitegmina'tae (*uni* = one, *tegmen*, a covering), Van Tieghem's term for those Phanerogams which possess only one covering to their ovules ; **uniteg'minous**, having one coat to the ovule ; **Uniteg'miny**, the state itself ; **unityp'ic** (τύπος, a type) = MONOTYPIC ; **univ'alent** (*valens*, strong), applied to chromosomes of simple character ; a pair may contract and thus form a BIVALENT chromosome ; **u'nivalved**, *u'nivalvis*, **univalv'ular** (*valva*, a door-leaf), of one valve or piece, dehiscing by one valve.

univer'sal, *universa'lis* (Lat., pertaining to the whole), general, as ~ **Involu'cre**, a general involucre ; ~ **Um'bel**, a general or compound umbel.

univert'ed (*uni*, one ; *verto*, I turn), O. Müller's term for mirror-like symmetry ; **univesicula'ris** (+ VESICULAR) = UNICELLULAR ; **univ'-orous** (*voro*, I devour), used of a Fungus restricted to a single host ; monophagous (Salmon).

Unli'ning (*un* = not, + line), the separation of parts originally united ; chorisis ; adj. **unlined'** (Lindley) ; **unor'ganized** (+ ORGAN), without structure or organs ; ~ **Fer'ment** = ENZYME ; **unsep'tate** + SEPTATE), applied to a plant which has not partitioning divisions, as plasmodia or certain unicellular Fungi and Algae ; ~ **Fi'bres**, libriform cells ; **unstrat'ified** (*stratum*, a layer), used of those Lichens which do not show distinct layers of hyphae and gonidia ; **unsymmet'rical** (+ SYM-METRY), irregular.

Uo'voli, pl. of **Uovolo** (Ital.), gnaurs of the olive-trees, used for propagation.

ur'ceolar, **ur'ceolate**, *urceola'tus* (*urceolaris*, relating to pitchers), pitcher-like, hollow and contracted at the mouth like an urn or pitcher ; **Ur'ceolus** (Lat.), (1) a pitcher-shaped organ, as an ascidium ; (2) the two confluent bracts of *Carex*, the utricle ; (3) any flask-shaped anomalous organ.

U′rease, an enzyme from the soy bean, *Glycine Soja,* which acts on urea.

urea′ceus (Mod. Lat.), of a charred black colour (Hayne).

Uredinol′ogist (*Uredo,* a blight, from *uro,* I burn ; λόγος, discourse), one skilled in the knowledge of parasitic Fungi, as *Uredo* and its allies; **Uredino′sis,** disease produced by "Rust" Fungi ; **Uredin′ium,** proposed by Arthur in place of Uredosorus ; adj. **uredin′ial** ; **Uredin′iospore** (Arthur) = Uredospore ; **Ure′do,** a form genus, the hymenium producing uredospores exclusively ; adj. **uredin′ial, uredin′eous, ure′dinous; Ure′do-conid′ium** (+ Conidium = Uredospore ; **ure′doform** (*forma,* shape), resembling *Uredo* in appearance; **Uredo-fruit,** a group of uredospores ; **Uredogonid′ium** (+ Gonidium) = Uredospore; **Uredosor′us** (+ Sorus), a group of uredospores ; **Ure′dospore** (σπορά, a seed), a spore formed by acrogenous abjunction from a sterigma, germinating immediately and producing a mycelium which bears other uredospores alone, or with teleutospores ; **uredospor′ic** (+ Spora), bearing Uredospores ; **uredosporif′erous** (*fero,* I bear), bearing uredospores ; **Ure′do-stage,** the summer stage of Uredineae, when uredospores only are produced.

u′rens (Lat., burning), stinging, as nettles.

Urn, *Ur′na* (Lat., a water-pot), (1) the capsule of a Moss ; (2 the base of a pyxidium ; **urn-shaped,** urceolate.

u′rophile (οὖρον, urine ; φιλέω, I love), expressive of Algae growing on soil containing much ammonia (Chodat).

urtica′ceous (*urtica,* a nettle, + aceous), pertaining to the order Urticaceae, of which the nettle is the type.

usta′lis (Mod. Lat., from *ustus,* burnt), charred, brownish black ; **Ust′erophyte** (φυτὸν, a plant), Berkeley's name for one of the Ustilagineous Fungi ; **Ustilagino′sis,** disease caused by *Ustilago,* a genus of Fungi which produces "Smut" in corn, the contents of each cariopsis being replaced by a black powdery mass of spores ; **ustilag′inous,** like *Ustilago,* or allied to it ; **us′tulate,** *ustula′tus,* blackened, as though burned or charred.

U′terus (Lat., the womb), the volva, or receptacle of the Phalloideae.

U′tricle, *Utric′ulus* (Lat., a small skin, or husk), (1) a small bladdery pericarp, as in *Atriplex;* (2) a membranous sac surrounding the fruit proper in *Carex;* (3) any bladder-shaped appendage ; (4) a synonym of a parenchymatous cell ; *Utric′uli semina′les,* the spores of certain Fungi (Lindley) ; **utric′ular,** *utricular′is,* **utric′ulate,** *utricula′tus,* **utric′uliform,** *utriculiform′is* (*forma,* shape), **utric′ulose,** *utriculo′sus,* having bladders, or bladder-like in appearance, inflated.

u′triform, *utriform′is* (*uter,* a skin bottle ; *forma,* shape), bag-shaped, utricular ; **utrig′erus** (*gero,* I bear), bearing utricles.

uva′rius (*uva,* a bunch of grapes) ; **u′veous,** composed of rounded parts connected by a support, like a bunch of grapes ; **uvif′erus** (*fero,* I bear), grape-bearing ; **uviform′is** (*forma,* shape), grape-like.

u′vidus (Lat.), moist, damp.

Vaccinie′tum, an association of *Vaccinium,* such as *V. Myrtillus.*

vacci′nus (Lat., relating to cows), the colour of a dun cow ; bay.

vacil′lans (Lat., swaying), swinging freely, as the anthers of grasses.

vac′uolar, vac′uolate (dim. of *vacuus,* empty), possessing vacuoles ; ~ -wall, the condensed plasmatic boundary of a vacuole (De Vries) ; **Vac′uole,** a cavity in the protoplasm of cells which contains a watery liquid, the cell-sap ; **Vac′uoles,** see Proteid-Vacuoles ; **Vacuoliza′tion,** the formation of vacuoles ; **vac′uus** (Lat.), empty or void of the proper contents.

vagiform′is (*vagus,* inconstant ; *forma,* shape), having no certain figure.

Vagi′na (Lat., a sheath), (1) a sheath,
as of a leaf ; (2) a part which in-
vests another ; **vag′inant,** *vagi′nans*,
sheathing or wrapping round ; **vag′i-
nate,** *vagina′tus*, sheathed ; **Vagi-
nel′la,** (1) a small vagina ; (2) in the
plural = Ramenta (Lindley).

vaginer′vis, *vaginer′vius*, **vaginer′vose**
(*vagus*, inconstant ; *nervus*, a nerve),
when the veins are arranged without apparent order.

vaginif′erus (*vagina*, a sheath ; *fero*,
I bear), furnished with a sheath ;
Vag′inule, *Vagi′nula* (Lat., a little
sheath), (1) a sheath surrounding
the base of the seta in Bryophytes ;
(2) ‡ a tubular floret in Compositae ;
vaginulif′eri Flor′es, the tubular
florets of an anthodium (Lindley).

vague, *va′gus* (Lat., unsettled), having no particular direction.

Vail = Veil.

Vallec′ula or **Vallic ula** (dim. of *vallis*,
a valley), applied to the grooves in
the intervals between the ridges in
the fruit of Umbelliferae ; **vallec′u-
lar,** pertaining to such grooves ; ∼
Canal′, in *Equisetum*, an intercellular canal in the cortical parenchyma,
opposite a groove on the surface
(Goebel).

valva′ceus ‡ (*valva*, the leaf of a
door, + *aceus*), furnished with visible
valves ; **valvar′is** (Lat.) = **val′vate,**
valva′tus (Lat.), (1) opening by doors
or valves, as in most dehiscent fruits
and some anthers ; (2) when parts of
a flower-bud meet exactly without
overlapping ; **Valve,** *Val′va* (Lat.,
the leaf of a door), (1) a piece into
which a capsule naturally separates
at maturity ; (2) the segment of a
calyx meeting in vernation without
overlapping ; (3) in Diatoms, each
half of the silicified membrane in
side view ; (4) the lid of an ascidium
(Crozier) ; (5) the flowering glume
of grasses (Stapf) ; (6) a partially
detached flap of an anther ; *Val′vae
Se′minum* = Cotyledons ; **valve-
view,** the Diatom frustule seen from
the side, the girdle being then
marginal ; **val′var Plane,** that plane

which passes through the apical
and transapical axes of a Diatom
(O. Mueller) ; **valvea′nus,** when a
partition arises from the expansion
of the inner substance of a valve ;
valved = **val′vate,** hence three-
valved, five-valved, etc. **; Val′velet,**
Val′vula = **Val′vule,** (1) a diminutive valve ; (2) a flowering glume of
grasses ; (3) a bract in Cyperaceae ;
val′vular = valvate ; **valvula′tus**
(Mod. Lat.), articulate, jointed.

Vanil′lin (*Vanilla*, an orchid genus)
is deposited in the cell-wall on
lignification ; with coniferin it gives
wood-reactions.

Vapora′rium (Lat., a steam-pipe), in
botanic gardens, a stove or formerly
a " Bark-stove."

Variabil′ity, tendency to vary; **var′i-
able,** *varia′bilis* (Lat., changeable),
not constant in appearance ; **var′ians**
(Lat.), varying ; **Var′iant,** a form
arising from a variation ; **Var′iate,**
one of the separate numerical values
from which a curve of variability
can be made ; **Varia′tion** (*variatio*,
a difference), (1) a slight variety ;
(2) a tendency to vary or depart
from the type ; **acqui′red** ∼, arising
during the development of an individual : **correla′ted** ∼, change in
one organ causing change in another,
though seemingly not connected ;
discontin′uous ∼, arising by distinct steps ; **genet′ic** ∼, having its
origin in the germ cells ; **meris′tic**
∼, change in symmetry and number
of part ; **sub′stantive** ∼, change in
the actual constitution or substance
of the parts themselves.

var′icose (*varicosus*, full of dilated
veins), abnormally enlarged in
places, used of filamentous organs.

var′iegated, *variega′tus* (Lat., party-
coloured), irregularly coloured in
patches, blotched.

Vari′ety, *Var′ietas* (Lat., difference),
a sort or modification subordinate to
species ; ∼ **Hy′brid,** so called, a cross
between varieties of the same species.

variifol′ius (*varius*, variegated), possessing leaves of different forms.

Var′iola (Mod. Lat., the pustule of small-pox), a pustular shield occurring on the thallus of the Lichen genus *Variolaria*; **var′iolate**, *variola′tus*, *variola′ris* (Mod. Lat.), marked as though pitted.

variolar′ioid (εἶδος, resemblance), with granular tubercles like the fructification of the old genus *Variolaria*; **variolose′** has the same meaning.

var′ius (Lat., variegated), liable to change or modification.

Var′nish = BLASTOCOLLA; **var′nished** = VERNICOSE (Crozier).

Var′zea, in Brazil, means the partially submerged forest.

Vas, pl. **Va′sa** (Lat.), vessels, ducts. [Lindley (Glossary, p. 98), gives nineteen names for modifications of these.] *Va′sa exhalan′tia* = stomates; ~ *pro′pria*, sieve-tubes or thin-walled tubular cells of the phloëm; **va′sal** = **vas′cular**; ~ **Bun′dle** = VASCULAR-BUNDLE.

vas′cular, *vascular′is* (*vasculum*, a small vessel), relating to or furnished with vessels; ~ **Bun′dle**, a strand of specialized tissue; ~ **Bun′dle-sheath**, the enveloping cylinder of closely united parenchyma; ~ **Cyl′inder**, the central cord of vascular tissue; ~ **Plants, Vascula′res**, those which possess vessels, as Phanerogams and Filicales; ~ **Sys′tem**, the interior parts in which the vessels occur; ~ **Tis′sue**, consists chiefly of vessels, in contradistinction to cellular tissue; **vasculif′erous** (*fero*, I bear), producing vessels; **vas′culose**, a component of the vegetable skeleton of the cellulose group; **Vas′culum** (1) = ASCIDIUM; (2) a collecting-box for botanic specimens.

vase-shaped, "shaped like a flowerpot" (Lindley).

vasicen′tric (*vas*, *vasis*, a vessel; *centrum*, a centre), with parenchyma round the vessel); **Vasiduc′tus** (*ductus*, led) = RAPHE; **va′siform**, *rasiform′is* (*forma*, shape), in the shape of a vessel or duct; ~ **El′ements**, ~ **Tis′sue**, ducts or tubes

with spiral markings; ~ **Wood-cell** = TRACHEID; **vascula′ris** = vase-shaped.

Vaucher′ia-gall, an hypertrophied formation on *Vaucheria*, due to some animal attack, as of Rotifers.

vault′ed, fornicate.

veg′etable (*vegetabilis*, animating), belonging to or consisting of plants; [**Veg′etable**, in a restricted sense is a kitchen garden plant, anything cultivated for culinary purposes]; ~ **Ac′ids**, the most frequent and abundant are **cit′ric**, **ma′lic**, **oxal′ic**, and **tartar′ic**; ~ **Al′bumen**, a substance resembling animal albumen [NOTE, not to be confounded with the ALBUMEN of seeds]; ~ **Anat′omy**, the structure of plants; ~ **Ca′sein**, the same as LEGUMIN; *cf.* PLANT-CASEIN; ~ **Cell**, see CELL; ~ **Fi′brin** = GLUTEN; ~ **Glob′ulin**, see GLOBULIN; ~ **I′vory**, the seed of *Phytelephas macrocarpa*, Ruiz and Pav.; ~ **Mu′cus**, **Mu′cilage**, see MUCILAGE; ~ **Nosol′ogy**, the classification and diagnosis of plant-diseases; ~ **Parch′ment**, paper after treatment with acids; ~ **Pathol′ogy**, the science of the diseases of plants, and remedial treatment; ~ **Taxon′omy**, the classification of plants in systematic order; ~ **Wax**, a substance resembling animal wax, occurring as BLOOM on the surface, or in bulk in certain fruits; **veg′etal**, (1) having power to produce growth; (2) an abbreviation of "vegetable"; **veg′etate**, to sprout or grow as plants; **Vegeta′tion**, (1) the process of plant-growth; (2) plants in general; ~ **Form**, a characteristic plant form, as a tree, shrub, etc.; ~ **Types**, primary divisions of the ecologists; **Lines of** ~, the boundary lines of the distribution of a given species (Kerner); **veg′etative**, growing or causing to grow; ~ **Apog′amy** = APOGAMY; ~ **Cell**, (1) the larger of the two cells in a pollen granule, which causes the growth of the pollen-tube; (2) in *Selaginella*, a portion of the apical end of the microspore cut off by a septum on germination ; ~ **Cone**, the apex of the shoot, a conical protuberance ; ~ **Divis'ion**, heterotypic nuclear division ; ~ **Nu'cleus**, any pollen-tube nucleus which does not take an active part in fertilization ; ~ **Or'gans**, those concerned with the growth of the plant, not the reproduction ; ~ **prop'agative Cells**, in German "Brutzellen" = GONIDIA ; ~ **Reproduc'tion**, asexual increase, as by detached buds, gemmae, bulbils, etc. ; **vegetist'ic**, relating to plants ; **ve'getive**, having the nature of plants ; **Vegetom'eter** (μέτρον, a measure) ; **electro-** ~, apparatus for applying electric currents to growing crops.

Vehic'ulum (Lat., a conveyance), Necker's term for the stigmatic secretion.

Veil = (1) VELUM ; (2) CALYPTRA of Mosses.

Vein (as distinct from a NERVE), a strand of vascular tissue in a flat organ, as a leaf ; **cos'tal** ~, or **pri'mary** ~, such as spring from the midrib ; **exter'nal** ~, a vein close to the margin ; **veined**, furnished with or traversed by fibrovascular bundles, especially if divided or reticulated ; **Vein'ing**, the general arrangement of the veins ; **vein'less**, destitute of veins ; **Vein'let**, a small vein, the ultimate division of a vein ; **Vein'ulet**, a branch of a veinlet (Crozier).

Vela'men (Lat., a covering), or ~ **Radi'cum**, a parchment-like sheath or layer of spiral-coated air-cells on the roots of some tropical epiphytic Orchids and Aroids ; **velamina'ris**, when an anther dehisces by rolling up one side of a cell from base to apex ; **ve'late**, *vela'tus* (Lat.), veiled; **velo'sus**, applied to Agarics ; not Latin, and presumably a blunder for *velatus*, veiled.

Veld, or **Veldt**, the tree-steppe or African savannah in South Africa.

Vel'lus (Lat., a fleece), the stipe of some Fungi.

Ve'lum (Lat., an awning), (1) a special envelope in Agarics within which the growth of the sporophore takes place ; (2) by Persoon applied to the CORTINA ; (3) the membranous indusium in *Isoëtes* (A. Braun) ; ~ **partia'le**, marginal veil ; ~ **universa'le** = VOLVA.

Ve'lumen (Lat., a fleece), close, short, soft hairs.

velu'tinous, *velu'tinus*, *velutino'sus* (Mod. Lat.), velvety, due to a coating of fine soft hairs ; **vel'vety**, an equivalent of the same.

Ve'na (Lat., a vein), a vein ; **Ve'nae exter'nae**, white veins seen in some Gasteromycetes and Tuberaceae in sections of the sporophore, produced by air tissue in the sporiferous chambers ; ~ **inter'nae**, ~ **lymphat'icae**, dark-coloured veins, in the same group of Fungi, denoting the walls of the sporiferous chambers, but destitute of air ; **Vena'tion**, the mode of veining.

venena'tus (Lat.), poisonous, venomous.

venenif'erous (*venenifer*, containing poison), bearing poison.

vene'nose, *veneno'sus* (Lat.), very poisonous.

ve'nose, *veno'sus* (Lat., veiny), having veins ; **veno'so-nervo'sus** ‡ when the primary veins branch and unite irregularly.

Ven'ter (Lat., the belly), (1) the expanded basal portion of an archegonium in which the oosphere is formed ; (2) by T. J. Parker applied to the OVARY.

ventila'ting (*ventilo*, I fan) **Pits**, in certain Ferns, resembling lenticels, and probably pneumathodes (Haberlandt) ; ~ **Tiss'ue**, used for the spongy parenchyma of the leaf.

ventilato'rious (*ventilator*, a winnower), flabellate, fan-shaped.

ven'tral, *ventra'lis* (Lat., pertaining to the belly), (1) the anterior or inner face of a carpel, opposed to dorsal ; (2) relating to the VENTER ; ~ **Canal'-cell**, a small cell in the archegonium cut off from the apex of the mother-cell of the oosphere next the neck ; ~ **Su′ture,** the ventral seam or line of dehiscence in a carpel ; **ven′tricose,** *ventrico′sus,* **ven′tricous,** swelling or inflated on one side, as the corolla of some Labiates and Scrophularineae ; **ventric′ulose,** *ventriculo′sus* (Lat., pertaining to the belly), slightly ventricose.

ventricum′bent (*venter,* belly ; *cumbens,* lying down), face downward, prone (Crozier) ; **ven′tri-dor′sal,** the reversed position of DORSI-VENTRAL (G. Henslow).

Ve′nulae, pl. of **Ve′nula** (Lat., a small vein), veinlets ; ~ **commu′nes** ‡, veinlets which proceed from anastomoses of the ~ **pro′priae** ‡, those which first leave the costal or primary veins ; **Ve′nule,** employed by J. Smith for veins of secondary importance ; **ve′nulose,** *venulo′sus,* profusely veined ; **venulo′so-hinoi′deus,** having equally curved parallel veins originating in the midrib and not losing themselves in the passage ; ~ **nervo′sus,** with straight parallel veins connected by cross-veinlets.

Ver-spe′cies, Syme's name for a true species, neither super-, nor sub-species ; the epithet is derived from *verus.*

Vera′trine, an alkaloid derived from *Veratrum.*

verbena′ceous, allied to or resembling *Verbena.*

Ver′digris (Fr., Vert-de-gris), the sea-green "rust" of brass ; ~ **Green,** the bluish-green colour of the same.

vermic′ular, *vermicular′is,* **vermic′ulate,** *vermicula′tus* (*vermiculus,* a little worm), worm-shaped, thickened and bent in places, as the root of *Polygonum Bistorta,* Linn.

ver′miform (*vermis,* a worm ; *forma,* shape), worm-shaped ; ~ **Bod′y =** SCOLECITE.

Vermil′ion (Old Fr., Vermillon, the Kermes insect) **col′oured,** scarlet, brilliant red approaching orange.

Ver′muth-steppe, extensive plains on

which the dominant plants are species of *Artemisia* (Warming).

ver′nal, *verna′lis,* *ver′nus* (Lat., pertaining to spring), appearing in spring ; **Verna′tion,** *Verna′tio* (Lat., casting off a slough), the order of unfolding from leaf-buds, prefoliation.

ver′nicose, *vernico′sus* (Mod. Lat., varnished), shiny, as though varnished.

Verru′ca (Lat., a wart), (1) a wart or elevation sometimes of a glandular nature ; (2) a sessile apothecium, as in *Verrucaria ;* (3) the perithecium of some Fungi.

verruca′rioid, resembling *Verrucaria* as to the verrucae or apothecia.

verru′ciform (*verruca,* a wart ; *forma,* shape), wart-shaped.

ver′rucose, *verruco′sus* (Lat., full of warts) ; **ver′rucous,** warty.

verru′culose, *verruculo′sus* (*verrucula,* a small wart), very warty, much covered with warts.

ver′satile, *versa′tilis* (Lat., movable), turning freely on its support, as many anthers on their filaments.

versic′olor (Lat., of changeable colour), **versicolor′ous,** changing colour, or one colour passing into another.

ver′siform (*versiformis,* changing shape), altering in shape as it ages.

Ver′siform (*versus,* turned towards), a form which varies from the STEM-FORM in several particulars (Kuntze).

versipal′mus (*versus,* turned ; *palma,* a palm), a palmate arrangement, the divisions not all in the same plane.

ver′tebrate (*vertebratus,* jointed), contracted at intervals, like the backbone of animals.

Ver′tex (Lat., that which revolves about itself), (1) the apex of an organ ; (2) ‡, the pileus of Agarics ; **ver′tical,** *vertica′lis,* (1) perpendicular to the horizon ; or (2) to the support, usually longitudinal ; ~ **An′ther,** an innate anther ; ~ **Chor′isis,** transverse chorisis ; ~ **Leaves,** those which stand erect like *Iris* leaves, with no obviously

dorsal or ventral surfaces; ~
Sys'tem, the fibro-vascular system
(Crozier); **ver'tically compres'sed**
= DEPRESSED (Crozier).

Ver'ticil, *Verticil'lus* (Lat., the whirl
of a spindle), a whorl, or circular
arrangement of similar parts round
an axis; **Verticil'lus spu'rius**, =
VERTICILLASTER; **Verticillas'ter**
(*-aster*, a suffix = small), a false
whorl, composed of a pair of opposed cymes, as in Labiates; **verticillas'trate**, possessing false whorls;
vertic'illate, *verticilla'tus*, whorled;
verticilliflor'us (*flos, floris*, a flower),
when whorls have a spicate arrange-
ment.

verucula'tus (Lat., furnished with a
small pike), cylindric and somewhat
pointed.

vesicato'rius (*vesica*, a blister), blister-
ing, as from caustic sap.

Ve'sicle, *Vesi'cula* (Lat., a little bladder), (1) a small bladder or cavity;
(2) Grew's term for CELL; **multinu'-
cleated** ~, peculiar bodies found in
the hyphae of the endophytic Fungus of the prothallus of *Lycopodium
clavatum*, Linn. (Lang); **Vesi'cula
Am'nios**, ~ **Colliquamen'ti**, the
embryo-sac (Lindley); ~ **sporoph'ora**, the sporophore of a Fungus;
vesiculaeform'is (*forma*, shape),
bladder-shaped; **vesic'ular**, *vesicular'is*, *vesicula'tus*, composed of
vessels; ~ **Ves'sels**, laticiferous
cells; **vesic'ulose**, *vesiculo'sus*, **vesi-
c'ulous**, as if composed of little
bladders.

ves'pertine, *vesperti'nus* (Lat., pertaining to the evening), appearing or
expanding in the evening.

Ves'sel, a duct or articulated tube
rendered continuous by the more or
less complete absorption of the
intervening transverse walls.

Ves'tibule (*vestibulum*, a fore court),
a chamber above the stoma formed
by the depression of the guard-cells,
and growth of the cells round them,
as in *Cycas*; **vestib'ular**, applied to
stomata, *cf.* VESTIBULE.

Ves'tige (*vestigium*, a footstep), the

remaining trace of an organ which
was fully developed in some ancestral form; adj. **vestig'ial**.

Vex'il (Crozier) = VEXILLUM; **vex'-
illar**, *vexillar'is* (*vexillum*, a
standard), pertaining to the VEX-
ILLUM; **vexil'lary**, (1) a form of
inflorescence in which the vexillum
is folded over the other petals; (2)
employed by Plateau to denote the
giving an attractive signal to insects;
~ **Aestiva'tion**, peculiar to papilionaceous flowers; **vexil'late**, *vexilla'-
tus*, bearing a standard or vexillum;
Vexil'lum, the standard or large
posterior petal of a papilionaceous
flower.

vi'able (Fr., viable, likely to live),
used of seed which is capable of
germinating; **Viabil'ity**, the possibility of growth.

viat'ical (*viaticus*, pertaining to a
road), applied to those plants
which grow by the roadside or
path.

vi'bratile (Fr., vibratile), capable of
vibration, motion to and fro.

Vib'rio, pl. **Vib'riones** (*vibro*, I quiver),
minute thread-like bacteria;
vib'rioid (*eἶδος*, resemblance), like
a vibrio; ~ **Bod'ies**, special structures, slender, cylindric, and of
sharply definite outlines in the
superficial layer of cytoplasm of
some Algae (Swingle); **Vib'rogen**,
(*gen-*, root of *gigno*, I produce),
subepidermal tissue of thin-walled
parenchymatous cells with a large
amount of chlorophyll, which seems
to play an important part in the
movements of tendrils (Penhallow).

Vibris'sae, pl. (Lat., hairs of the
nostrils), the sensitive hairs of
Dionaea (Boulger).

vica'rious (*vicarius*, substituted), supplying the place or function of some
other organ (Crozier).

vice'ni (Lat., twenty each), in
twenties.

vi'cine (*vicinus*, near), used by
Clements for species derived from
adjacent regions; **Vi'cinism**, variation due to growth of other plants

405

in close proximity (De Vries);
Vi′cinist, a plant derived from such
ancestry (De Vries).

Vic′inin (*vicia*, a vetch), a principle
from *Lathyrus sativus*, Linn.

Vigil′ia (Lat., keeping watch) or
Vigil′iae Flor′um, periods during
which certain plants open and close
their flowers.

Vil′li, pl. of **Vil′lus** (Lat., a shaggy
hair), long weak hairs; **villif′erus**
(*fero*, I bear), bearing villi; **vil′li-
form** (*forma*, shape), resembling
villi (Crozier); **vil′lose**, *villo′sus*,
vil′lous, bearing villi; **Villos′ity**,
shagginess, a coating of long weak
hairs.

Vi′men (Lat., a switch), a long flexible
shoot; **vi′minal**, *vimina′lis*, consisting of twigs; **vimin′eous**, -*neus*,
bearing long and flexible twigs.

vina′ceous, *vina′ceus* (*vinum*, wine, +
aceus), wine-colour, purplish red.

Vine, (1) the plant which bears grapes,
Vitis vinifera, Linn.; (2) in the
United States applied to any trailing or climbing stem, or runner;
vinea′lis (Lat.), growing in vine-
yards.

Vin′egar-plant, or mother-of-vinegar,
Mycoderma Aceti, Desmaz.

vinic′olor (*vinum*, wine ; *color*, colour),
the colour of wine, dark or purple
red; **vino′sus** (Lat.), in botany
means the same.

viola′ceous, -*ceus* (*Viola*, + ACEOUS),
violet-coloured, ianthinus; **violas′-
cens** (+ ascens), becoming violet;
vi′olet, *viol′eus*, the colour of
violets, a cold purple; **Vi′oline**,
a poisonous principle existing in
Viola odorata, Linn.

virel′lus (dim. of *virens*), somewhat
green or greenish.

vir′ent, *vir′ens* (Lat., green), (1) green
in colour; (2) evergreen; **vires′cent**,
virescens, turning green; **Vires′-
cence**, the development of chlorophyll in place of the normal colouring; *cf.* FRONDESCENCE.

vir′gate, *virga′tus* (Lat., made of
twigs), (1) wand-shaped, twiggy;
(2) with radiating lines in pileus

of Agarics ; either ribs or streaks
of colour (Fries), as in *Tricholoma
virgata*, P. Karst.

virgin′eus (Lat., maidenly), (1) the
purest white ; (2) having arrived
at the flowering period (Endlicher,
fide Lindley).

vir′gulate, "diminutive of VIRGATE,
shaped like a little twig or wand "
(Crozier), but *virgulatus* also means
striped.

Virgul′tum (Lat., a copse), a vigorous
twig or shoot.

vir′idans (Mod. Lat.), **virides′cent**,
virides′cens, becoming green; **Vir-
idi′na** = CHLOROPHYLL; **vir′idis**
(Lat.), green ; **virid′ulus**, greenish ;
Vir′or (Lat.), greenness, verdure.

viro′sus (Lat., fetid), "venomous" (A.
Gray): having an unpleasant smell.

vis′cid, *vis′cidus* (Lat., clammy),
sticky from a tenacious coating or
secretion ; ~ **Disk**, the retinaculum
of an Orchid.

Vis′cin (*viscum*, birdlime), (1) a substance intermediate between resin
and caoutchouc (Weinling); (2) the
sticky substance forming threads
uniting pollen-grains (Kerner);
Viscosac′charose (+SACCHAROSE),an
enzyme producing a viscous mass
from cane-sugar (Beijerinck); **vis′c-
ous**, *visco′sus* (Lat., sticky), glutin-
ous, clammy.

Vi′talism (*vitalis*, pertaining to life),
a directive tendency through the
organism alone, and peculiar to
life ; **Vi′talist The′ory**, Pasteur's
theory of fermentation as an effect,
with vegetation as a cause ; **Vital′ity**,
in seeds the period during which
the seeds retain their power of
germination, varying according to
the species.

Vitel′lin, *vitelli′nus* (*vitellus*, the yolk
of an egg), the colour of the yolk
of an egg; **veg′etable Vitel′lin**,
Weyl's term for a reserve proteid
found as crystals in potato-tubers ;
Vitel′lus, (1) an old name for
peculiar albumen which in some
cases is deposited within the embryo-sac; *cf.* SCUTELLUM (2) ; (2)

an oily substance adhering to the spores of *Lycopodium*.

vitic'olous (*Vitis*, a vine ; *colo*, I inhabit), living on or within the vine ; **Vitic'ola**, a parasite of the vine ; J. S. Henslow prints the word *viti'colus*.

Vitic'ula (Lat., a vine tendril), also printed **Vitic'ulus** = SURCULUS; **vitic'ulose**, *viticulo'sus*, sarmentose, producing viticulae.

vit'reous, *vit'reus* (Lat., of glass), transparent, hyaline ; formerly used for the light green of glass; **vit'ricole** (*colo*, I inhabit), applied to Lichens which are found growing on glass bottles, etc.; **vit'ricus**, "having a glassy appearance" (Lindley).

Vit'ta, pl. **Vit'tae** (Lat., a fillet), the aromatic oil tubes of the pericarp of most Umbelliferae ; ~ of Diatoms, are longitudinal ribs; **vit'tate**, *vitta'tus*, bearing vittae; longitudinally striped ; **Vit'tin**, a substance found in the more watery vittae of Umbelliferae.

Vivip'arism = VIVIPARY.

vivip'arous (*viviparus*, producing young alive), germinating or sprouting from seed or bud, while attached to the parent plant ; ~ **Germina'tion** = **Vivip'ary**, the phenomenon in question.

vixgregar'ious (*vix*, hardly ; *gregarius*, belonging to a flock), "arranged in small or indistinct groups" (Clements).

void, empty.

vol'uble, **volu'bile**, *volu'bilis* (Lat., twining), twining round a support.

volute', *volu'tus* (Lat., a rolling), rolled up in any way ; **Volu'tion**, a spiral turn or wreath.

Volu'tin, or metachromatin, granules in the yeast-cell occurring in the nuclear vacuole; possibly a reserve substance (Wager and Peniston).

Vol'va (Lat., a wrapper), a covering or external wrapper, especially the sac enclosing the sporophore of Agarics, ruptured at its apex by the growth of the unfolding pileus.

volvoca'ceous, **vol'vocine**, constituted like the genus *Volvox* (F. Blackman) ; **volvocina'ceous**, of the nature of the genus *Volvox*.

Vul'va [from *Volva*] **Vegetabil'ium**, a Linnean name for the STIGMA ; **vul'viform** (*forma*, shape), like a cleft with projecting edges.

Wa'dy, Arabic term denoting a valley containing water only in the wet season ; *cf.* OUED, WED.

Wart, a hard or firm excrescence ; **wart'y**, covered with warts or verrucae.

Wasp-flow'ers, flowers adapted for wasp-visitors, but may also be visited by other insects and be pollinated by them.

Wat'er-bal'ance, the depletion and repletion of moisture in a plant ; ~ -blad'ders, hairs acting as water-reservoirs (Warming) ; ~ **Bloom**, a sudden development of certain algae in lakes, also known as the "Breaking of the Meres"; ~ **Capac'ity**, the power of a soil to take up and retain liquid ; ~ **Cells**, large suberized cells in the palisade-tissue of succulent plants (Brebner) ; ~ **Con'tent**, the water in the soil ; either **phys'ical** ~, the total amount of soil water ; or **physiolog'ical** ~, the amount available to plant-life ; ~ **Cult'ure**, growth of plants in compound solution of salts ; ~ **Gland**, a group of cells beneath a water-pore, which help to excrete water ; ~ -in'take, the amount absorbed under given conditions ; ~ **Leaf**, in *Salvinia*, a submersed and finely divided leaf, which simulates a root; -loss, the sum transpired ; ~ **Par'asite**, when the host serves only as a root, and provides absorption, conduction and mechanical support, as in Mistletoe, whose haustoria contain no sieve-tubes ; ~ **Plants**, those growing in water, immersed wholly or in part ; ~ -pol-lina'ted, by means of water; under water as *Zostera*, or on the surface as *Vallisneria:* hydrophily ;

~ **Pore,** ~ **Stom'a,** a stoma devoid
of guard-cells, discharging water ;
~ **Sacs,** in Hepaticae, lobes of the
leaves which retain moisture; ~
Stor'ing-tis'sue, a form of water-
tissue adapted for storing water,
especially in dry climates ; ~
Ta'ble, the level of saturation of
soil by ground water ; ~ **Tis'sue,**
parenchyma filled with clear sap
and some mucilage.

waved, wa'vy, undulate, or sinuate.

Wax, veg'etable, a fatty body occurring as a waste product, either
superficially as BLOOM on leaves,
or in quantity in fruits and stems
as in *Myrica cerifera,* Linn., and
Ceroxylon Klopstockia, Mart.; **wax'y,**
resembling beeswax in consistence
or appearance ; ~ **Coat'ing,** a thin
epidermal layer of rods or grains,
forming a glaucous bloom on fruits
and leaves ; ~ **yel'low** an impure
yellow, *cf.* cereus, melleus.

Wed = WADY or OUED.

wedge-form, ~ shape, cuneate.

Weed, any useless or troublesome
plant which occurs without intentional cultivation.

Weel, a term borrowed from a wicker
eel-trap, for an arrangement of hairs
which keeps out unbidden insect
guests from flowers (Ogle).

Weep'ing, excessive loss of sap from
wounds, as in the vine or birch;
bleeding ; adj. = pendulous in habit.

Welt, a raised stripe on fruit such as
the lemon (Crozier); **welt'ed** is given
by Crozier as "flaccid, drooping";
it is probably an error for WILTED.

Wendungszel'len (Ger.), a disc-shaped
group of hyaline cells (or a single
cell) at the base of the oosphere in
Characeae.

wett'able, capable of being wetted;
Wettabil'ity, the condition described
(modern ecological terms).

Wheat-ear Carnation, an abnormal
increase or pleiotaxy of bracts.

wheel-shaped, rotate.

whip-shaped, flagelliform.

Whirl (S. F. Gray) = WHORL.

white, when positive colour is absent ;

(*albus* is white generally, *niveus,* as
pure as snow, *candidus,* radiantly
white, etc.) ; ~ **Chlor'ophyll,** Gautier's
term for chlorophyll which is rich in
hydrogen and colourless ; the normal
green type is stated to be poorer in
that gas ; ~ -**heads,** = TAKE-ALL disease in wheat ; ~ **Root-rot,** a Fungus
scourge in parts of Europe caused
by *Dematophora necatrix;* **whi'tened,**
dealbate, with a darker ground tint ;
whi'tish, albidus, albulus, etc.

Whorl (pr. hwurl), the arrangement of
organs in a circle round an axis ;
false- ~ , **spu'rious** ~ , = VERTICIL-
LASTER ; **whorled** (pr. hwurld), disposed in one or more whorls.

Wick'er-hairs, an awkward and inex-
pressive rendering of the German
"Reusenhaare"; *cf.* TRAP-HAIRS ;
WEEL.

wild, spontaneous, growing without
cultivation or introduction.

Wild'ering (Crozier) = **Wi'lding,** (1)
any wild plant ; (2) an escape from
cultivation.

Wilt-disease, attributed to *Fusarium
vasinfectum* or *F. Lini,* on different
plants ; **wilt'ed,** become flaccid, the
opposite of turgid ; **wilt'ing,** drooping, having lost the quality of fresh-
ness ; **Wilt'ing Coeffic'ient,** the
amount of water in the soil when a
plant droops.

wind-pollina'ted, the pollen conveyed
by the agency of the air; anemophily.

Win'dows, employed for openings when
the flowers do not expand, remaining
united at base and apex of perianth,
as in *Cryptophoranthus* (Rolfe) ;
win'dow-bear'ing, the condition
described.

Wing, (1) = ALA, any membranous expansion attached to an organ ; (2)
a lateral petal of a papilionaceous
corolla ; ~ **Bract,** the attached subtending bract of *Tilia;* **winged,**
alate.

Win'ter-an'nual, a plant which germinates in autumn, and living through
the winter, fruits and dies; *cf.*
BIENNIAL ; ~ -**kil'ling,** destruction
by exposure to variations of weather

and temperature; ~ **Rot**, a disease of stored potato-tubers, due to *Nectria Solani*; ~ **spore**, a resting spore.

Witches' Brooms, a disease shown by tufts of shoots, due to attack by Fungi or mites; in German "Hexenbesen"; **Steppe-wit′ches**, or **Wind-** ~, ball-like felted masses of plants in steppe regions, which have become detached from their roots and are blown about by the wind.

with′ering, marcescent. ￢

With′er-tip, of *Citrus*, due to *Colletotrichum gloeosporoides*.

With′y, a willow twig, a pliable wand.

Woad, = ISATIN, the blue colouring matter of *Isatis tinctoria*, Linn.

Wood, the lignified portion of plants, included within the cambium layer, but exclusive of the pith; the xylem elements of the united vascular bundles; ~ **Ball**, = SPHEROBLAST; ~ **Cells**, are lengthened and thickened, combined into threads, fascicles, or bundles, forming prosenchyma; ~ **El′ements**, the fibres which make up the xylem; ~ **Fi′bre**, the fibro-vascular tissue; ~ **Gum**, contained in the wood of Dicotyledons, said to consist chiefly of xylan; ~ **Parench′yma**, tissue of thick-walled cells; ~ **Ray** = MEDULLARY RAY; ~ **Rot**, due to *Stereum hirsutum*, Fr.; **Au′tumn** ~, the outer portion of each annual ring of growth, having smaller ducts and wood cells, with walls much thickened; **cryptogam′ic** ~, the centripetal portion of the xylem in the stem of Cycadoxyleae; **Spring** ~, the inner portion of each annual increment, consisting of larger, thinner-walled cells and ducts.

Wood′land, woody plants dominating the vegetation.

wood′y, approaching the nature of wood, ligneous; ~ **Fi′bre**, wood-tissue; ~ **Rings**, the annulations seen on cross section, which usually denote one year's growth; ~ **Tis′sue**, xylem; ~ **Wedg′es**, Williamson's expression for the fibro-vascular bundles in *Calamites* (W. R. M′Nab).

Wool, long, dense, curled hairs (Crozier); **wool′ly**, lanate, tomentose, clothed with long and tortuous or matted hairs.

worm-shaped, more or less cylindric, and contorted.

Woro′nin′s Hy′pha, a coiled hypha in some forms of Ascomycetes, occurring in the centre of the future sporocarp, and probably homologous with an archicarp.

Wort (pr. wurt), (1) a plant, especially a cabbage; (2) the sweet infusion of malt, or unfermented beer

Wound, any injury caused by abrasion or incision in the cortical layers of a tree; ~ **Cam′bium**, a layer of phellogen resulting from the tangential division of epidermal cells, or from cortical cells beneath the epidermis; ~ **Cork**, the non-conducting tissue which shuts off fungus-diseased portions of bast from the sound parts; ~ **Gum**, a substance abundantly secreted in the vessels by the surrounding starch-cells, closing the wound-cavities (Temme); ~ **Par′asite**, a Fungus which attacks the surface of a wound, and so effects an entrance into the tissues of the host; ~ **Rot**, various forms of decay not accounted for by parasitic Fungi; ~ **Wood**, abnormal growth, distinguished by its short cells and absence or scarcity of vessels (De Vries).

Wrap′per = VOLVA.

Wrin′kle, a fold or crease; **wrin′kled**, rugose, creased.

X-**Genera′tion** (Lotsy) = GAMETO-PHYTE.

Xan′theïn (ξανθὸs, yellow), a yellow-colouring of plants, the same as ANTHOCHLORIN, *cf.* XANTHINE; **xanthel′lus**, somewhat yellow; **xan′thic**, tending to yellow; ~ **Flow′ers**, those which display yellow in their tints, opposed to cyanic flowers; **Xan′thin**, (1) a pure yellow substance from chlorophyll (Kraus); (2) a solid insoluble pigment; also **Xan′thine**, (1) found in seedlings of

Cicer arietinum, Linn. ; (2) a mixture of colouring matters described by Kuhlmann as a single body (Green) ; **Xantholeu′cite** (+ LEU-CITE), a leucite of an etiolated plant (Van Tieghem) ; **Xan′thones**, pl., a series of yellow colouring principles in plants ; *cf.* FLAVONES ; **Xan′thophyll** (φύλλον, a leaf), a constituent of chlorophyll, a yellow colouring matter insoluble in water ; **Xanthophyl′lidrine**, a yellow crystallizable pigment, like the last, but soluble in water ; **Xanthophyl′lins**, yellow constituents of Chlorophyll, as Carotin, Erythrophyll, and Chrysophyll (Tswett) ; *cf.* CHLOROPHYL-LINS ; **Xanthopic′rine** (πικρὸς, bitter), a yellow bitter principle from the bark of *Zanthoxylon caribaeum*, Lam. ; **Xanthorham′nin**, the yellow colouring matter of the ripe fruits of *Rhamnus*; **Xanthotra′metin** (+ TRAMA), a colour resin in Fungi, as *Polyporus cinnabarinus*, Fr.

Xenemb′ryosperm (ξένος, a stranger, + EMBRYO ; σπέρμα, a seed), MacMillan's term for a PARTHEN-EMBRYOSPERM with endosperm arising from fecundation, and the pollen derived from a flower of another stock.

Xen′ia (ξένιος, belonging to a guest), Focke's term for the direct influence of foreign pollen on the parts of the mother-plant (Stift).

Xenocar′py (ξένος, a stranger ; καρπὸς, fruit), producing fruit as the result of xenogamy ; **Xenodoch′ae** (δοχὴ, reception), employed by Clements to denote anomalous successions of plants; **Xenochro′ma** (χρῶμα, colour), Focke's term for the effect of foreign pollen producing a change in the colour of the fruit ; **Xenoënd′osperm**, a plant with embryo the result of fecundation, with endosperm parthenogenetic, and the pollen derived from another individual (MacMillan); **Xenog′amy** (γάμος, marriage), cross-fertilization between sexual elements borne by different individuals (Loew) ; *cf.* GEITONOGAMY ; **Xeno-**

morpho′sis (+ MORPHOSIS) = ACTI-NOMORPHOSIS ; **Xenopar′asite** (+ PARASITE), (1) a specialized form of a parasitic fungus when growing on injured parts of a strange host, or on injured parts of its normal host which are immune previous to injury (Salmon) ; the condition is **Xenopar′asitism**, also (2) artificial parasitism ; *cf.* ECOPARASITE ; **Xenoplas′ma** (πλάσμα, moulded), employed by Focke to denote change in shape of fruit produced by the action of foreign pollen.

Xe′rad (ξηρὸς, dry, + AD), a xerophyte (Clements).

xerampel′inus (Lat.), the dull red or purple of dead vine leaves.

Xe′ras (ξηρὸς, dry), a dry form of a plant (Clements).

Xerasi′um (ξηρασία, drought), a succession due to drainage or drought (Clements).

Xeriob′oles, -ae (ξηρὸς, dry ; βολὴ, a throw), plants dispersing their seeds by the drying up of their carpels (Clements); **xerochas′tic** (χασμάω, I gape), applied by Ascherson to plants whose fruits burst by desiccation and their seeds or spores are scattered; **Xeroch′asy**, the condition ; **Xerocleistog′amy** (+ CLEIS-TOGAMY), when flowers remain closed by reason of insufficient moisture (Hansgirg) ; **Xerodrymi′um** (δρυμὸς, a coppice), xerophyte-forest formation (Diels) ; **Xerohy′lad** (ὕλη, forest, + AD), a dry forest plant ; **Xerohyli′um**, a dry forest formation ; **xerohyloph′ilus** (φιλέω, I love), dwelling in dry forests; **Xerohylophy′ta** (φυτὸν, a plant), dry forest plants ; **xeromorph′ic** (μορφὴ, change), pertaining to **Xeromorph′y**, protected from desiccation by special devices, as hair, wax, thick cuticle, etc. ; **Xeromorpho′sis** (+ MORPH-OSIS), changes induced by the action of increased temperature as the thickening of the epidermis (Herbst); **Xe′rophile** (φιλέω, I love), a plant which grows in a dry situation ; **xeroph′ilous**, growing in arid places ;

Xeroph'ily, the state ; **xeroph'obous** (φόβος, fear), shunning drought ; **Xerophorbi'um** (φορβή, pasture) = GARIDE (Diels) ; **Xe'rophyte** (φυτὸν, a plant), a plant which can subsist with a small amount of moisture, as a desert plant ; adj. **xerophyt'ic** ; **Xerophyti'a**, dry forest formations (Clements) ; **Xeropo'ad** (ποὰ, grass, + AD), a heath plant ; **Xeropoï'um**, a heath formation ; Diels's term for STEPPE formation ; **xeropoöph'ilus** (φιλέω, I love), heath-loving ; **Xeropoöphy'ta** (φυτὸν, a plant), heath plants (Clements) ; **Xe'ro-pteride'tum** (πτέρις, a fern), an association of bracken with heath plants ; **Xe'rosere**, cf. Additions ; **Xerosi'um**, or **Xerosi'on**, a plant succession on drained and dried up soil (Clements) ; **xerostat'ic** (στατικὸς, causing to stand), used of successions completed under xerophytic conditions (Clements) ; **Xerothamni'um** (θάμνος, a copse), spiny shrub formation (Diels) ; **Xe'rotherm** (θέρμος, heat), capable of withstanding drought and heat ; adj. **xerotherm'ic** ; ~ **Period**, Briquet's term for the post-glacial period ; **xeroth'erous** (θέρος, summer), adapted to a dry summer, a rainless period ; **Xerot'ropism** (τροπή, a turning), the tendency of plants or parts thereof to alter their position to protect themselves from desiccation (Borzi) ; adj. **xero'tropic**.

xiph'ioid (ξίφος, a sword ; εἶδος, resemblance), sword-like, ensiform ; **xiphophyl'lous**, -lus (φύλλον, a leaf), with ensiform leaves, as *Iris*.

Xy'lan (ξύλον, wood), the chief constituent of WOOD-GUM) ; **Xy'lem**, the wood elements of a vascular bundle, possessing tracheal tissue ; ~ **Bridg'es**, connections surrounding phloëm-islands ; ~ **I'slands**, detached strands of xylem in certain species of *Thunbergia* (Roulet) ; ~ **Parench'yma**, oblong cells which retain their protoplasm, with thick and lignified walls, occurring in longitudinal bands ; ~ **Plate**, ~

Ray, a radial plate of xylem between two medullary rays ; cf. PHLOËM RAY ; **xyl'inus**, woody, pertaining to wood ; **Xyli'um**, a wood formation ; **xylocar'pous**, -pus (καρπὸς, fruit), the fruit becoming hard and woody ; **Xyl'ochrome** (χρῶμα, colour), (1) wood-dyes, chiefly tannins ; (2) the dark coloured contents of the vessels of the duramen (Hartig) ; **Xylo'dia**, **Xylo'dium** (εἶδος, like), (1) the woody fruit of *Anacardium ;* cf. XYLOPODIUM ; (2) an old name for ACHENE ; **Xyl'ogen** (γένος, offspring), used by Sachs for woodsubstance ; **Xylo'ma**, a sclerotioid body which does not produce branched sporophores, but sporogenous structures within itself ; **Xylomy'ces** (μύκης, a mushroom), a Fungus which grows on wood or bark ; **Xy'lonite**, cellulose manufactured in plastic masses ; **xyloph'ilous**, -lus (φιλέω, I love), woodloving ; applied to Fungi which attack woody tissue ; **Xylophy'ta** (φυτὸν, a plant), wood-plants (Clements) ; **Xylopod'ium** (πούς, ποδὸς, a foot), a fruit like a nucule, but wanting a cupule, and borne upon a fleshy support, as in *Anacardium ;* **Xy'lose**, a pentose occurring in wood ; **Xylostro'ma**, the leathery felted mycelium of certain Fungi which destroy timber ; **Xylot'omy** (τομὸς, a cut), the anatomy of wood, and woody tissues ; adj. **xylotom'ic**.

yearly, annual, of a year's growth.

Yeast (pr. yeest), the minute unicellular organisms which effect alcoholic fermentation in sugary liquids ; ~ **Bud'ding**, giving rise to similar yeast-gonidia : ~ **Fun'gus**, *Saccharomyces Cerevisiae*, J. Meyer ; sometimes termed SPROUTING FUNGUS :— **Bot'tom** ~, **Low** ~, that which forms at the bottom of the vats, "Unterhefe" of the Germans ; **Up'per** ~, or Barm, that which floats on the surface, the German "Oberhefe" wild ~, some undesired form, which gives a bitter taste to the wort without fermentation.

Ygapò, a Brazilian term for a forest wholly submersed during two months (Trail).

Ypomne'ma (ὑπὸ, under; μένω, I remain), Necker's term for an inferior calyx.

Yuc'cal, the resin from *Yucca angustifolia.*

Zan'thophyll = XANTHOPHYLL.

Ze'in, a proteid existing in maize, *Zea Mays*, Linn.

zelotyp'ic (ζηλοτυπία, rivalry), asexual (Radlkofer); the condition is Zelot'ypy.

Zenot'ropism (zenith; τροπὴ, a twining), negative geotropism (Fayod); adj. zenotrop'ic.

ze'orine, zeori'nus, resembling the Lichen genus *Zeora*, Fr., the apothecium having a double margin.

Ze'ro-points, the extremes of high and low temperatures which plants can endure without being killed (Schimper); zerozy'gous (ζυγὸς, a yoke), when a special factor is wholly absent (Hurst).

Zeu'gite (ζευγίτης, yoked together), a Fungus spore derived from the fusion of two nuclei; as a teleutospore (Raciborski).

zig'zag, having short bends or angles from side to side.

Zi'mome = ZYMOME.

Zoadu'la, pl. Zoadu'lae (Fr. zoadule), Gaillon's term for ZOOSPORE.

Zoal'lospore (ζῷον, an animal, + ALLOSPORE), Radlkofer's term for the zoospore of *Bulbochaete* and *Coleochaete;* Zoan'drospore (+ ANDROSPORE), a motile androspore or antherozoid of *Oedogonium* (Radlkofer).

zodioph'ilous (ζῴδιον, a little animal; φιλέω, I love) = ZOIDIOPHILOUS.

Zoidog'amae (ζῷον, an animal; γάμος, marriage), plants in which pollination is effected by animal agency (Kirchner); zoidiog'amus, Engler and Prantl's term when an archegoniate plant has ciliated antherozoids; Zoidoph'ily (φιλέω, I love), means the same; zoidioph'ilous, pollinated by the agency of animals; Zoidioph'ilae, plants which are so fertilized.

zo'nal (ζώνη, a belt or girdle), applied to those "plant-formations" by C. MacMillan, which exhibit well marked radial symmetry as though spreading from one centre; zonar'ic, relating to the intermediate depths, the Mesoplankton of some authors (Forel); zo'nate, marked circularly, as the leaves of *Pelargonium zonale*, L'Hérit.; ~ Tetragonid'ia, those formed by transverse divisions; *cf.* CRUCIATE; ~ View, the side- or girdle-view of a diatom frustule; Zone (1) of temperature, with its influence on distribution; (2) a belt of more or less uniform vegetation; (3) the connection between two valves of a Diatom; the hoop or girdle; ~ of Distribu'tion, in Great Britain, altitudes of plant growth as defined by H. C. Watson; divided into in'fer-, mid-, and su'per-; *cf.* REGION; zoned, coloured in rings or circles, as the cap of some Agarics (Stevenson); Zona'tion, (1) the formation of a hollow sphere by the nucleus in metaphasis, with a film of granulated protoplasm which marks the boundary of the compound oosphere in *Cystopus Bliti*, De Bary (F. L. Stevens); (2) the gradual spreading outward from a centre, shown by many plants; Zo'ning, the arrangement of plants according to favourable condition, as Algae by depth of water.

Zoobiot'ic (ζῷον, a Fungus; βίος, life), applied to a Fungus whose host is an animal; Zo'ocarp (καρπὸς, fruit) = ZOOSPORE; Zoocecid'ia (κηκὶς, a gall), plant-galls produced by animals (Tubeuf); Zo'ochore, a plant distributed by animals (Clements); zoochor'ic (χωρὶς, asunder), employed for those fruits which are separated by animal agency (Sernander); Zoo-chor'y, the state of distribution by animal agency; Zoocoe'nocyte

(+ Coenocyte), a free-swimming coenocyte ; **Zo′ocyst** (κύστις, a bag), a cyst, which, in Monadineae, gives rise to ciliated or amoeboid zoogonidia ; **Zoodomat′ia** (δωμάτιον, a small house), shelters formed by a plant for those animals which are of benefit to it ; **Zoog′amae** (γάμος, marriage), plants with motile reproductive elements, Cryptogams ; **Zo′ogamete** (γαμέτης, a spouse) = Planogamete ; **Zoog′amy**, applied to plants having motile sexual elements, as most Cryptogams ; **Zoogloe′a** (γλοιòς, viscous, clammy), a stage of Schizomycetes when they are embedded in a jelly-like substance ; **Zoogonan′gia** (γόνος, offspring ; ἀγγεῖον, a vessel), certain cells in *Ctenocladus*, which enlarge, become pear-shaped, and hibernate, afterwards producing planogametes (Borzì) ; **Zoogonidan′gium** (+ Gonidangium), employed by W. West for an organ in certain Algae which produces zoospores ; **Zoogonid′ium** (+ Gonidium) = Zoospore ; **Zo′oid** (εἶδος, resemblance), a motile spore or gamete (Hazen); **zooidiog′amous** (γάμος, marriage), used of gametes when at least one is actively motile, flagellate, ciliate, or amoeboid (Hartog); **Zoomorpho′sis** (μόρφωσις, a shaping), changes produced in plants from the action of animals ; used by Appel for galls when caused by animal parasites ; **Zo′on**, an affix or suffix, in botany denoting antherozoid ; **Zooph′ilae**, plants pollinated by animals ; **zooph′ilous** (φιλέω, I love), pollinated by the agency of animals ; **zooph′obous** (φοβέω, I fear), used of plants which protect themselves against animals, such as ants, by hairs, secretions, etc. ; **Zo′osphere** (σφαῖρα, a sphere), a biciliated swarmcell of Algae, afterwards an oosphere; **Zo′osperm**, *Zoosper′ma* (σπέρμα, a seed), pl. **Zoosper′mata**, = Zoospore ; **Zoosporang′iophore** (+ Sporangiospore), club-shaped or cylindric structures in Peronosporeae, which bear the Zoosporangia; **Zoosporan′gium**

(+ Sporangium), a sporangium which produces zoospores or planogametes ; adj. **zoosporan′gial** ; **Zo′ospore** (σπορὰ, a seed), a free-moving spore, an asexual reproductive cell with cilia, sometimes a planogamete; adj. **zoospor′ic, zoospor′ous**, relating to Zoospores ; **Zoospor′ocyst** (+ Spore; κύστις, a bag), the zoosporangia of Saprolegniaceae (Vuillemin) ; **Zoozy′gosphere** (ζυγὸς, a yoke ; σφαῖρα, a sphere) = Planogamete ; **Zoozy′gospore**, a motile zygospore.

Zostere′tum, an association of *Zostera*; **zost′eroid** (εἶδος, resemblance), resembling or akin to *Zostera*.

Zygog′amae (ζυγὸς, a yoke ; γάμος, marriage), Ardissone's term for Algae, excluding the Florideae ; **Zygogon′ium** (γόνος, offspring), the female conjugating cell in Conjugatae ; **zygolyt′ic** (λυτικὸς, able to loose), the separation of allelomorphic pairs of unit-characters; **Zy′gomites**, pl. (μίτος, a thread), pairs of conjugated filaments ; **zygomorph′ic, zygomor′phous** (μορφὴ, shape), used of flowers which are divisible into equal halves in one plane only, usually the antero-posterior, *cf.* Actinomorphic ; Sachs extends the meaning to such flowers as may be equally bisected in any one plane, as *Dicentra;* **Zygomorph′ism**, or **Zygomor′phy**, the state just described ; it may be **diag′onal** ~, as in Solanaceae, or **trans′verse** ~ as in Papaveraceae ; **Zygomyce′tes** (μύκης, a mushroom), a division of Phycomycetes possessing zygospores (Tubeuf) ; **zygomy′cetous**, relating to the Zygomycetes, a division of the Phycomycetes possessing zoopores ; **Zygone′ma** (ζυγὸς, a yoke ; νῆμα, a thread), a pair of filaments believed to be formed by the approximation of single thread ; **Zy′gophyte** (φυτὸν, a plant), a plant which is reproduced by zygotes, the conjugation of two gametes; applied to Algae which conjugate ; adj. **zygophyt′ic**.

zygopt'eroid (εἶδος, resemblance) ; **zygopteride'an**, resembling or allied to *Zygopteris*.

Zygo'sis (ζυγὸς, a yoke), M'Nab's term for the union of gametes to form a zygote ; **Zy'gosperm** (σπέρμα, a seed), a proposed emendation of ZYGOSPORE ; **Zy'gosphere** (σφαῖρα, a sphere) = GAMETE ; **Zy'gospore** (σπορά, a seed), a body produced by the coalescence of two similar gametes ; **Zygospor'ophore** (+SPOROPHORE), the suspensor in Mucorini ; **Zygoso'ma, Zygosom'es**, pl. (σῶμα, a body), bodies formed by the union of gamosomes in pairs, becoming bivalent chromosomes ; **Zygotact'ism**, the mutual attraction of sexual hyphae for each other ; **Zygotax'is** (τάξις, order), arrangement by sexual pairs ; the pairing attraction ; **zy'gotene**, applied to a nucleus containing a ZYGONEMA.

Zy'gote (ζυγωτὸς, yoked), (1) a body produced by fertilization or conjugation of two gametes ; (2) by Bateson extended to denote the individual which develops by somatic divisions from the cell resulting from the gametic union ; adj. **zygo'tic** ;

Zy'gotoid (εἶδος, like), the result of the union of two gametoids, that is, apocytial structures, as in *Mucor* (Hartog).

Zygozo'ospore (ζυγὸς, a yoke, + ZooSPORE), a motile zygospore.

Zy'mase (ζύμη, leaven), (1) formerly applied to the whole group of ferments ; (2) an enzyme occurring in yeast ; cf. ANTHOZYMASE, and ZYTHOZYMASE ; **zy'mic**, relating to fermentation ; **Zy'mogen** (γεννάω, I produce), the "mother of fermentation," an antecedent body of an enzyme ; **zymogen'ic**, applied to a peptonizing enzyme ; **Zymohydrol'ysis** (ὕδωρ, water ; λύσις, a loosing), fermentation induced by the absorption of water ; **Zymol'ysis**, decomposition by the action of ferments ; **Zy'mom** or **Zy'mome**, one of the proximate principles of wheat-gluten, cf. GLIAN ; **Zymo'sis**, fermentation ; **zymo'tic**, (1) relating to fermentation ; (2) applied to diseases due to infection by germs, with their rapid increase.

Zythozy'mase (ζῦθος, beer, + ZYMASE), an enzyme in yeast, also found in certain Fungi.

SUPPLEMENT

OF ADDITIONAL TERMS SINCE THE PREVIOUS EDITION.

SUPPLEMENT

OF ADDITIONAL TERMS SINCE THE PREVIOUS EDITION.

The derivations are strictly supplemental to those in the main alphabet.

abiet'iform (*abies*, a fir-tree; *form*, shape), used of hairs when shaped like a fir-tree.

Abs'ciss-mech'anism, proposed to replace ABSCISS-LAYER (Yapp).

Abund'ance, a synonym for FREQUENCY; Clements uses these modifications : co′pious ~ or cop.[1], 100–50 in a meter quadrat; cop.[1], 50–25; cop.[3], 25–10; gregar′ious ~, subco′pious; subgregar′ious ~, sparse ~; vixgregar′ious.

Abys′sal Associa′tion, peculiar to marine depths.

Acarophy′ta, used by Macfarlane for the lowest algae and fungi, "primitive plants."

acentron′ic (κέντρον, a sharp point), wanting a geometric or definite axis.

Aciculisil′vae, pl. (*silva*, a wood), forests containing needle-leaved trees, coniferous woods.

Ac′olytes (ἀκόλουθος, attending), employed by Blakeslee for VARIETIES.

acranth′ous, applied to a sympodium with a main axis of annual portions of successive axes, each beginning with scale leaves, and ending with an inflorescence.

acrog′enous, *add* (2), borne at the tips of hyphae.

Acrog′onel (ἄκρος, apex; γονή, birth), a concentration of parts making a monocentric axis (Vuillemin).

acrost′ichoid, resembling *Acrostichum* Linn., a genus of ferns.

acroton′ic = ACROTONOUS

Actinom′eter (μέτρον, measure), a light-measuring instrument for actinic rays; Actinomyce′tes (μύκης, fungus), delicate branching threads which break up into spore-like bodies (Conn).

Activa′tors, pl. (*activus*, active), enzymes which stimulate; opposed to PARALYZERS; ac′tive Pro′toplasm, the ANDROPLASM of male gametes (N. Jones).

Ac′us (Lat., needle), the needle-like leaf of such conifers as *Pinus* (Henry).

Adapta′tion, *cf.* MORPHOGENY, p. 240.

Addit′ion (*additio*, an adding) Stage, the gain of a factor (Bateson).

adiabat′ic (ἀδιάβατος, not to be crossed), not transferable, as a product which cannot be transferred to another tissue or part; cannot be translocated.

Ad′sere (*ad*, to, + SERE), that portion of a sere which precedes its convergence into another at any time before the climax stage (Clements).

Adynamogy′ny (ἀδύνατος, to want power; γυνή, a woman), loss of function in the female organs of a flower (Loew).

aecid′ioid (εἶδος, resemblance), like tne genus *Aecidium* Pers.; Ae′ciotel′iospore, with the aspect of an aeciospore, and the nature of a teliospore (Harshberger).

aequichromoso′mal (*aeque*, equally, CHROMOSOMAL), the exchange of chromosomes or of their quality (Lotsy); aequipotent′ial (+ POTEN-

417

TIAL), of equal power, applied to theory of phyllotaxis (Church).

Aër'ial Wat'er, rain or dew, as distinguished from terrestrial or underground supply; **Aëromorpho'sis** (μόρφωσις, form), change due to greater exposure to air or wind (Turesson); **aëroper'meable,** the permeable part of the root to the passage of gases and liquids (S. Baker); **Aërophi'lae** (φιλέω, I love), algae living fully exposed to the air, and not on the ground (Ivanoff); **Aerox'yl** (ξύλον, wood), applied by Lindman to trees and woody plants with an evident bole, and branches above ground; *cf.* GEOXYL.

Aestatifrutice'ta (*aestas*, summer; *fruticetum*, a thicket), summer coppices; **Aestatisil'vae** (*silva*, a wood), woods with leafage in summer.

aetiogen'ic, = AITIOGENIC.

Afforesta'tion (late Lat. *afforestare*), bringing land under the conditions of forest; the act of conversion into forest or woodland.

Agame'tospore, Janet's form of AGAMOSPORE; **Agamog'ony** (γόνος, offspring) = SCHIZOGONY; **Ag'ametes** [trisyl.] pl.; reproductive bodies capable of growth to adult form without syngamy; **Agamohyp'nospore** (+ HYPNOSPORE), a large resting spore (Wittrock); **Ag'amont** (ὄντα, things existing), the individual which produces AGAMETES.

Age and Area, Willis's theory that the older a species is within a given country, the greater its area.

Agglutina'tion, when bacteria draw together in masses (Conn).

Agi'um, afterwards altered by the author to AIGIALIUM.

Agrol'ogy (λόγος, discourse), the science of soils, and their support of special vegetation; **Agron'omy** (νομός, custom), agriculture.

Agrostide'tum, an association of *Agrostis.*

aigic'olous (*colo,* I dwell), a tenant of stony strand, also applied to an association of such plants.

Air-bags, Withering's term for FOL-

LICLE; ~-pits, well-developed pits in thick cell-walls for aeration (Jeffrey); ~-spaces, carinal cavities in the fibrovascular strands of *Equisetum* Linn. (Jeffrey).

albinot'ic, affected with albinism; ~ Cells, ~ Lay'ers, or Tis'sue, those parts when destitute of chlorophyll.

albopellicula'tus (*pelliculatus,* skinned), having a layer of colourless cells below the epidermis, with a green core, as in *Mesembrianthemum,* Dill. (Correns); **albotunica'tus** (*tunicatus,* wearing a tunic), a similar phenomenon in *Pelargonium* L'Hérit.

Albu'min-cells, groups of 6–12 small cells, with granular contents and large nuclei on outer flanks of phloem of each bundle in stems of Gymnosperms (Church).

Alchemille'tum, an association of *Alchemilla* Linn.

-ale, suffix for COLONY; *cf.* Hordeale, etc. (Clements).

allocho'ric (χῶρος, a place), used of a species inhabiting two or more closely related formations in the same region, as adjoining forest and grassland (Drude). **allochth'onous** (χθών, χθονός, earth), applied to peat due to gradual accumulation of drifted material in still water (Forsaith); **alomerist'ic** (μεριστικός, fit for division), groups which differ meristically from the majority of related groups, as *Veronica* Linn. with a 4-lobed corolla, when most Scrophulariaceae have 5 (Riley); **Allomet'ron** (μέτρον, a measure), "quantitative and intensive characters" (Osborn). **All'osomes** (σῶμα, a body), a general term for aberrant chromosomes.

Allu'vial Associa'tion, a boundary zone between water and dry land, such as favours the growth of *Tamarix* Linn. and *Hippophäe* Linn.

Alne'tum, an association of *Alnus* Linn.

Alpi'no-arc'tic   Forma'tion = AN-
THELIETUM.

Alterna'tion, applied by Clements to
a mixed succession; **Alter'nes,** two
alternations of dominancy over
the same area (Clements).

Al'var, term to denote dwarf growth
of perennial shrubs in parts of
Sweden (Warming).

Alve'olar Spheres, pl. certain bodies
in the cytoplasm of the microsporangia of *Cupressus* Linn. which
do not take stain (Nichols) :
Alveola'tion The'ory, chromosomes
in telophase becoming honey-
combed with numerous vacuoles;
Al'veoles, pl. vacuoles which split
chromosomes into network of chromatin (Grégoire).

Amae'bula pl. -ae, a swarm-spore
which creeps like an *Amaeba*
(Minchin).

amara'lioid, like the genus *Amaralia*
Benth. and Hook. f.

amathic'olous (ἄμαθος, sandy soil;
colo, I dwell), growing in sandy
plains.

ambilat'eral (*ambo,* both; *lateralis,*
pertaining to the side); ∼ **Segrega'tion,** unrestricted to either sex
(Bateson); *cf.* UNILATERAL.

Amblystegie'tum, an association
formed of the moss *Amblystegium*
Bruch et Schimp.

Amen'ta, pl. *add* (2) employed by
Parlatore for male flowers.

Ammophile'tum, an association of
dune-grass, *Ammophila* Host.

amnic'olous (*amnis,* river; *colo,* I
dwell), growing on the sandy
banks of rivers.

Amphich'romy (χρῶμα, colour), a
plant displaying two distinct colours
when in flower (Lindman); **Am-
phicli'nous** (κλίνη, a bed) **Hy'brids,**
when in F₁ hybrid progeny, some
resemble one parent, the remainder
the other (De Vries); **Amphicrypt'-
ophytes,** helophytes having their
vegetative organs amphibious
(Gams); **Amphig'onel** (+ GONEL),
the reproductive apparatus having
polycentric axes (Vuillemin); **am-**

phigy'nous (γυνή, woman), when
the oogonium of *Phytophthora*
De Bary projects from the top of
the antheridium, the male surrounding the female element (Murphy);
Amphilep'sis, *add* (2) when in
hybrids the influence of both
parents is shown (Bateson); *cf.*
MONOLEPSIS; **Amphine'reids** (+
NEREID), amphibious plants; **Amph'iphytes,** pl. (φύτον, a plant),
Gadeceau's term for the same as
the last : **Amph'itene** (ταινία, a
ribbon), the early stage of synapsis
(H. J. Müller); **amphitrich'ous**
(θρίξ, τριχός, the hair), having a
flagellum at each pole as of a
flagellate; **Amphitrisyncot'yl,**
Bexon's term for a tricotyledonary
seedling with special development;
Amphitact'ism (τακτός, arranged),
the mutual attraction of several
hyphae for each other, as in *Mucor*
Linn. : zygotactism.

Amy'loplasts (πλάσμα, that formed),
the colourless starch-forming plastids of plant cells (Errera); **Amylo-
stat'oliths** pl. (+ STATOLITHS),
starch-grains simple or compound.

Anabase'tum, an association of *Ana-
basis* Linn.

Anaphylax'is (ἀνά, up; φύλαξ, cau-
tion), sensitive condition from use
of antitoxin serum (Conn); **ana-
poret'ic** (πορευτός, going), Martius's
term for botanic skill in the closet,
as opposed to PERIPATETIC; **An-
arhi'zophyte** (ρίζα, a root, φύτον, a
plant), a plant able to root in soil
which covers its original spot, as
Suaeda Moq. (F. W. Oliver);
anarthrodacty'lous (ἄρθρον, a joint,
+ DACTYL), with ultimate rays
each of a single cell, in Characeae;
anatropist'ic = anatropous.

Androe'cy (οἶκος, a house), occurrence
of purely male individuals in a
species (Uexküll); **Androgyno-
cladogonid'ium,** an hermaphrodite
merid (Janet). **Androgy'ny,** the
monoecious or androgynal state.
And'rophile (φιλέω, I love), a plant

partial to the neighbourhood of man; nitrophilous (Woodhead); **And'rophore**, add, (3) the support of antheridia (West); in'ner ~, torus bearing inner stamens in *Couroupita* Aubl.; ou'ter ~, ligulate hooded structure in same, bearing outer stamens (Thompson); **And'roplasm** (πλάσμα, that formed), active protoplasm, as in male gametes (N. Jones); adj. **androplas'mic**, sperm-producing; **Andropleog'amy** (+ PLEOGAMY), one individual with staminate, perfect, and andromonoecious flowers (Robinson); **Androzoogonid'ia**, pl. (+ ZOOGONIDIUM), male filaments derived from zoogonidia in *Oedogonium* Link., cf. GYNOGONIDIA.

Anectar'ia, pl. (+ NECTARIUM), flowers lacking spurs (Gates); **anemocho'rous** (χῶρος, a place), distributed by wind; **Anemog'amae** (γάμος, marriage), plants fertilized by the wind (Kirchner); **anemog'amous**, wind-fertilized (Sernander).

anemo'neous, allied to *Anemone* Linn. **Anemoph'obae** (φόβος, fear), plants fearing wind; adj. **anemoph'obous**, (1) the same; (2) plans against wind damage (Hansgirg); **Anemospor'ae**, pl. (+ SPORA), plants disseminated by wind.

aneup'loid (ἄνευ, without), destitute of chromosomes (Hurst); **Aneup'loidy**, the condition stated.

An'geosere, cf. CENEOSERE, the climax of Angiosperms; **Ang'iospermy**, the state of angiospermous plants.

An'gle-cells, on the edges of the leaves of gymnosperms forming small teeth (Church).

An'ion, an ion charged with electricity which moves towards the anode or position pole; it may be **univ'alent, biv'alent, triv'alent** or **tetrav'alent** (Raber).

anisog'amous, cf. ANISOGAMY; **Anisog'eny** (γένος, race), variety in offspring; **anis'okont** (κοντός, a pole), having two unequal flagella; **anisost'ichous** (στίχος, a row),

having unequal rows in the stem-cortex of *Chara* Linn.; **Anisosty'ly** (στῦλος, a column), short and long styled flowers in the same species, without change in sexual properties (Loew).

anoclad'ous (κλάδος, a branch), branches curving outwards (Russow).

anomoph'yllous (ἄνομος, without law), leaves abnormal for its genus (Radlkofer); **anomosper'mous** (σπέρμα, a seed), seeds abnormal in its genus.

anta'pical (+ APICAL), Kofoid's term for "posterior" in Dinoflagellates; ~ **Plate**, that part of the hypovalve—the posterior extremity of the cell—of Peridineae, which is not postcingular (West).

Anten'nae, pl. add, (2) the poles of a vascular trace extended into arms, two or four in number (Bower).

anthecolog'ical (+ ECOLOGICAL), relating to one flower and its surroundings, such as insect visitors; **Anthecol'ogist**, an observer of such phenomena; **Anthecol'ogy**, the study in question.

anthemid'eous, pertaining to *Anthemis* Linn.

Anthe'ra, add, (4) used by Parlatore for the loculi in Coniferae.

Antherid'ium, add, (2) afterwards used for the mother-cell of antheridia, cf. SORUS; **anth'erine**, like an anther (Forbes); **Anth'eroblast** (βλαστός, shoot), a term for ANDROCYTE.

anthocarpolog'ic, cf. CARPOLOGY, the relation of flower and fruit; **Anthog'onel** (+ GONEL), with developed corolla, the popular idea of a "flower" (Vuillemin); **antholog'ic**, -**cal** (λόγος, discourse), (1) pertaining to flowers; (2) flower gathering; **Anthoplank'ton** (+ PLANKTON), algae which produce the "breaking" of the meres.

Anthracrin'y (κρίνω, I separate), decomposition into humus (Falck); **Anthrag'eny** (γένος, race), the formation of peat by decomposition (Falck).

anthropocho′rous (χῶρος, a place)′ distributed by the action of man (Rübel); **anthropoph′ilous** (φιλέω, I love), applied to plants that follow man (Thellung).

antibacte′rial, *cf.* BACTERIA; of substances protective against poisonous bacteria; lysins (Conn); **Antibod′ies**, protective substances as antitoxins (Conn); **Anticonsimili′tude** (*consimilis*, entirely similar), when the plane of a diatom divides the frustule into two similar parts which are doubly inverted (O. Mueller); **Antien′zymes**, substances antagonistic to soluble ferments; **Antiplei′on** (πλεῖος, full), a lean year or cycle of scarcity (Arctowski); **Antisym′metry** (+ SYMMETRY), a synonym of ANTICONSIMILITUDE; it may be **invert′ed** ~, having a part turned upside down; **pervert′ed** ~, a part turned round, or **triverted** ~, a part inverted and perverted at the same time (O. Mueller); **antithet′ic**, p. 27, INTERPOLATION THEORY suggested as its substitute (Church); **Antit′ropy** (τροπή, a turning), applied to secondary roots which arise from the main axis in regular outward direction (Lopriore).

ant′ler-like, ~-**sha′ped**, applied to branched trichomes.

apet′aloid (εἶδος, resemblance), Herbert's term for apetalous.

A′pex Time, when a leaf moves down after a shock; the period between the latent period to its recovery (Bose).

Aphan′imere (*a*, privative; φαίνω, I appear; μέρος, a part), Delle Valle's expression for AMITOSIS; **Aphercot′ropism** (τροπή, a turning), the turning away from an obstruction (G. Henslow); **Aphle′bioids**, pl. (εἶδος, resemblance), pinnules serving as bud protectors in fronds of *Gleichenia* Sm.; **aphotomet′ric**, *add*, (2) Wiesner's term for leaves not affected by light; **aphototrop′ic**, turning away from light; **Aphyll′ous For′est**, formed of *Casuarina*

Linn. in Java and Sunda; Tjemoro Forest (Warming).

a′pical, *add*, (2) Kofoid's term for anterior in Dinoflagellates; ~ **Cap,** striations at the upper end of cells in *Oedogonium* Link, due to repeated cell-divisions (West); ~ **Plate,** part of the epivalve in Peridineae (West).

aplanoplast′id, Janet's term for non-flagellate cells; *cf.* PLANOPLASTID; **Aplanosporan′gia** (+ SPORANGIA), organs giving rise to APLANOSPORES (West); **apogam′ic**, asexual (Turesson); **apomict′ial**, -t′ical, relating to APOMIXIS; **Aposporog′ony**, suppression of sporogamy; the production of spores after gametic fusion.

appendic′ular, used by M. J. Benson for ovules derived from foliar origins, as capillary leaf-traces.

Approxima′tion (L. Digby) = ASSOCIATION.

Aquipra′ta, damp meadows.

arach′noideus, *add*, (2), seedlings not webbed but resembling spiders.

araucar′ian, **araucar′ioid**, resembling the structure of *Araucaria* Juss.; **Araucarie′tum**, an association of *Araucaria*.

Arb′uscules (*arbuscula*, a shrub, a peacock's tuft), tufts of hyphae within cells; endotrophic mycorrhiza (Gallaud).

Archebio′sis (βίωσις, living), early development of life (Troland); adj. **archebiot′ic**; **Archen′teron** (ἔντερον, intestine), a sac in *Volvox*; communicating with outside by a blastopore (Janet); **Archiproct′um**, an early formed exit for spent material in the same genus; **Archisto′ma** (στόμα, mouth), a previous formation in the same alga (Janet); **Arch′esphera**, the archesperm before fertilization (Bennett and Murray); **Archian′giosperms**, pl. (+ ANGIOSPERMS), primitive angiosperms; **archchlamyd′eous** (χλαμύς, a cloak), term to include Polypetalae and Incompletae (Engler); **Archid′ium**, Chodat's term for the structure in

higher plants which bears the
sporangia ; **Archigon'iophore** (γόνος,
offspring ; φορέω, I bear), a gametophore in cryptogams borne on a
specialized branch with a terminal
receptacle having female organs ;
cf. ANTHERIDIOPHORE ; **Archili'chens**,
lichens in which the gonidia are
bright green ; **Archigym'nosperms**,
gymnosperms fertilized by antherozoids (Jeffrey) ; **Arch'iplast** (πλαστός,
formed), the protoplasmic unit of
Cyanophyceae (Nadson) ; **Archi-
sto'ma** (στόμα, a mouth), a primitive
oral opening (Janet).

arched, bow-shaped.

arctalp'ine, Clements's term for alpine
plants in the arctic zone.

Arctostaphyle'tum, an association of
Arctostaphylus Adans.

-are, p. 33, now restricted to the
CLAN (Clements).

A'rea, *add,* (5) ground occupied by a
formation or association (Waterman) ; **attachment ~,** the junction
on the anterior schizont of Peridineae
(Kofoid) ; **ax'ial ~,** the smooth
surface between the margins of
diatoms ; **cent'ral ~,** hyaline space
round the nodule of a diatom valve ;
lat'eral ~, occasional blank marginal
spaces of a diatom (West) ; **opt'imal
~,** that best adapted for the
growth of a species (Warming) ;
cf. AGE and AREA ; **a'real,** belonging
to the areas enclosed by the reticulate vessels of leaves (Barton).

are'coid (εἶδος, resemblance), like
the *Areca* palm.

Areg, (1), sand-desert ; (2) dunes in
Algeria.

ar'illated, provided with an ARIL.

Ari'zophytes (a privative ; ῥίζα, a
root ; φύτον, a plant), term to include Bryophytes and Thallophytes.

Aroideol'ogy (λόγος, discourse), a
treatise on Aroids.

Arrhe'noplasm (ἄρρην, male ; πλάσμα,
formed), male protoplasm ; *cf.*
THELYPLASM.

Arroy'o (Span.), a watercourse,
especially when dry.

Artemisie'tum, an association of
Artemisia Linn.

arthoniomorph'ic (μορφή, form),
arthonioid.

arthrodact'ylous (ἄρθρον, a joint ;
δάκτυλος, a finger), the ultimate
rays of *Nitella* Ag., composed of
more than one cell apiece.

art'ioploid, applied to "even multiples of the gametophytic number"
(Jeffrey) ; **Artioploi'dy** is the state :
cf. PERISSOPLOID.

-as, patronymic suffix, as "Erio-
gonas" (Clements).

Ascoli'chenes, *add,* defined as in
symbiosis with algae.

Asco'mata, pl. of ASCOMA.

Asexual'ity (a, privative ; + SEXUAL),
destitute of sex.

Asincronog'onism (σύγχρονος, coeval ;
γόνος, offspring), Delpino's term for
DICHOGAMY.

Assim'ilates, *cf.* ASSIMILATA, perfected
products of the plant's vital
functions.

Associa'tion, *add,* (2), or approximation, the pairing of two threads or
half-univalent spiremes to form
a univalent chromosome (Digby) ;
compliment'ary ~, where two or more
avoid competition by developing
at different times or at different
depths, as *Holcus, Pteris* and *Scilla*
(Woodhead) ; **~ Com'plex,** a union
of associations to a phytogeo-
graphical unit ; **~ Frag'ments,**
varied aspects from normal or
optimal (Braun-Blanquet) ; **~
Types,** formed from the series of
associations which inhabit them
(Nichols).

Assoc'ies (*associo,* I join with),
developmental units of consocies
(Clements) ; transitory units (Tansley).

Asterice'tum, an association of *Aster*
Tourn.

At'avism, false, VICINISM.

Atelio'sis (ἀτελής, imperfect), a zoo-
logical term used by Gates for
dwarfs of normal proportions but
reduced size ; adj. ateliot'ic.

athiorhoda'ceous (a, primitive ; θίς,

θίνος, deposit from rivers), relating to a group of purple sulphur bacteria.

Atmom´eter (ἀτμός, vapour; μέτρον, a measure), an instrument for measuring loss of moisture by evaporation.

atrich´ous (a, privative; θρίξ, τριχός, hair), destitute of cilia on flagella, therefore non-motile.

Atriplice´tum, an association of *Atriplex, Sueda*, etc.

Atryg´ia (ἀτρύγετος, unfruitful), Ludwig's term for self-sterility.

Attach´ment-a´rea, the place of junction on the anterior schizont of Peridineae (Kofoid).

atyp´ic, *add*, (2) in mitosis, indirect nuclear division, which does not proceed normally.

aulacanth´ous (αὖλαξ, αὐλακος, a furrow), stem-cortex of Characeae having secondary grooves more prominent than the primary, and spine-cells apparently seated in the furrow.

Autallog´amy (αὐτός, self; ἄλλος, another; γάμος, marriage) = Homodichogamy; **Autatryg´ia** (+ Atrygia), self-sterility, its own pollen not ensuring fertilization; **Autamphine´reids**, pl. (ἀμφί, around, + Nereids), autotrophic amphibious plants; **Autecol´ogy** (+ Ecology), ecology of the individual organism (Turesson); **Autephaptom´enon** (ἐφάπτομαι, I am grasped); autotrophic type of plants, including those which are half-parasitic (Gams); **Autobasidiomyce´tes** (+ Basidiomycetes) consist of the subordinate groups;—Hymenomycetes and Gasteromycetes: basidiospores definite in numbers, usually four; **Autobiol´ogy** (βίος, life; λόγος, discourse), special biology, as opposed to association (Gams); **Autocatal´ysis** (κατά, down; λύσις, a loosing), ferment action which generates further quantities of the same substance; adj. **autocatalyt´ic**; **autochorolog´ic** (χωρέω, I spread abroad; λόγος, discourse), applied to self-distri-

bution of plants as systematic units —species, genus, family; local botany; **autochronolog´ic** (χρόνος, time), self-timed, applied chiefly to fossils (Rübel); **Autochrenol´ogy** is the condition; **Aut´oclave** (*clavis*, a key), a sterilizer acting by steam pressure; **autocla´ved** [trisyll.], subjected to the operation cited; **Autocol´ony** (*colonia*, as plants living beyond usual range), in coenobic algae, the product of a mother-cell (West); **Autoëcol´ogy** (+ Ecology), the environment and adaptation of a species, confined to its habitat by local conditions; adj. **autoëcolog´ic**; *cf.* Synecology; **Autogenet´ics** (+ Genetics), changes in floras effected by the conditions of the district and constitution of the plants themselves; **autogenotyp´ic** (+ genotypic), isogenotypic; **Autohybridiza´tion**, naturally effected crossing; **Autoirriga´tion** (*irrigatio*, a watering), the automatic supply of water to a culture; **Auto-irriga´tor**, the apparatus employed; **Autol´ysis**, *add*, (2), Němec's term for Analysis; **aut´olysed** = autolyt´ic; **auton´omous** (νέμω, I possess), used of such shoots as independently place themselves in most favourable conditions (Kirchner); **autonyctonast´ic** (νύξ, νυκτός, night; ναστός, close-pressed) = autonyctotropic; **Autone´reids**, pl. (+ Nerei s), autotrophic water-plants (Gams); **autoörthot´ropous** (+ orthotropous), the tendency of an organ to grow in a straight line forward (Czapek).

Autopar´asitism (+ Parasitism), a parasite growing upon a parasite, as mistletoe upon mistletoe; **autoph´ilous** (φιλέω, I love), self-pollinated (Moss); **Autoregula´tion**, *cf.* Regulation; **autoscoliot´ropous** (σκολιός, bent; τροπή, a turning), the tendency to grow in a curved line (Czapek); **Aut´osome** (σῶμα, a body), normal chromosomes (Bridges), *cf.* Intersex, Supersex;

Aut'ospore (+ Spore), (1) protoplast division into spore-like bodies usually assuming the character of mother-cells before being liberated (West); (2), in lichens, daughtergonidia (Paulson); **autotroph'ic,** applied to those bacteria which act directly upon mineral matter (Conn).

Autop'ta (αὐτόπης, an eye-witness), used by Linné and Jacquin for an observer who makes an autopsy.

Aux'imones, pl. (αὐξιμος, promoting growth), plant-food accessories, essential to growth, only differing from vitamines in withstanding 150 C., while the latter are largely destroyed by boiling (Bottomley); adj. **auximon'ic.**

Avicennie'tum, a mangrove association.

Ax'ial Ar'ea, a hyaline area sometimes occurring on diatom valves on each side of the raphe (West); **axill'ary shoot,** ~ **Strand,** a bundle in *Zygopteris* Corda, the state of the main stem (Scott).

Azoospor'ia (a, = not, ζῶον, an animal), motionless reproductive cells in certain fresh-water algae.

Azy'gospore (+ Spore) = Parthenospore.

Back-cross, a hybrid of reversed parentage, the male and female parents being interchanged.

Bacte'riad, Hillhouse's term for any bacterium; **bacte'rial,** pertaining to bacteria.

Baha'da (Span. descent), app ied to accumulations of débris on slopes in Central America; adj. **baja'dal.**

Bambuse'tum, a bamboo forest association.

Barotax'is (βάρυς, heavy; τάξις, order), reaction to mechanical stimulus.

Ba'sal Cell, add, (2) sister-cell below antheridial mother-cell.

basiton'ic = basitonous.

Batrachie'tum, an association of batrachian *Ranunculus* Linn.

bead'ed, old term for granulate.

Beggiatoe'tum, an association of *Beggiatoa* Trev.

Beha'viour, dynam'ic, the part played by the species in the development of the community.

bennettit'ean, pertaining to the fossil genus, *Bennettites* Carruth.

benth'ic, relating to Benthos.

Bertill'onage, a combination of figures by measurement of many characters from a person *n,* applied to botany by J. MacLeod.

Bestand' (Germ.), durable form (Schroeter).

biator'ine, add, apothecia soft or waxy, and often brightly coloured.

Bif'erae, pl. (*bifer,* twice-fruiting), flowering twice in each year; **biflor'us,** biflorous, add, (2), old writers meant flowering in autumn as well as in spring; **bi-indu'siate,** having a double indusium, as *Pteris* Linn.

Bill, an antique term for Beak.

Biocat'alysts, pl. (+ Catalysis), a synonym of Enzymes; **Biochar'acter** (χαρακτήρ, to engrave), characters found separable as units in heredity, evolution or individual development (Osborn); **Biocoenol'ogy, Biocoeno'sium** (κοινός, common vegetation of a unitary habitat; social life; ecology (Gams); adj. **biocoenolog'ic; Biocoll'oid** (+ Colloid), a mixture of a base and an inert carbohydrate as agar and albumen; **Bio-commu'nity,** ecology is its science (Clements); **Bi'omes,** evidences of past human communities and climates (Clements); **Bi'ont** (ὄντα, things existing), a living being; *cf.* Metabiont; Protabiont; **biophor'ic** (φορέω, to bear), having vital and heritable properties (Adami); **Biosociol'ogy,** the life of organisms in communities (Du Rietz); adj. **biosociolog'ic; Bi'osphere** (σφαῖρα, a globe), the intermediate part between the atmosphere and the geosphere where life is lived; vegetation is the controlling influence (Clements);

adj. **biospher'ic**, agency of plants in migration of peoples (Adams).

bird-foot'ed, pedate.

Bi'sect, a vertical section of a quadrat to show the layers of soil and roots in normal position; also styled LAYER TRANSECT (Clements); **bispor'ous**, having two spores; **bi'- strate** (*stratum*, a layer), used when indumentum is in two layers, the outermost falling off and disclosing the inner, as in *Rhododendron fictolactum* Balf. f. (Balfour).

Blast'ea, a spherical shell formed of a single layer of cells, developed from a coenobium; adj. **blast'ean**; ~ **Chlor'ophytes** (CHLOROPHYTES), Volvocineae; **Blaste'nio-spore** (+ SPORE), a plurilocular spore; **blastocoe'lian** (κοῖλος, hollow), applied to the central cavity of *Volvox* (Janet); **Blast'ogen** (γένος, race), Poulton's term for Bateson's use of "Mutation," *cf.* (3), that is, **blastogen'ic Varia'tion**; `Blast'opore` (πόρος, passage), an opening from the ARCHENTERON or cyst in the same alga (Janet); **Blast'ula**, the mother-cell in *Volvox* of the sexual elements (Janet).

blech'noid (εἶδος, resemblance), like the fern *Blechnum* Linn.

Blemato'gen (βλῆμα, βλήματος, coverlet; γένος, offspring), the universal veil in *Pholiota* Fr. (G. F. Atkinson).

Blend Hy'brid (+ HYBRID), allelomorphic factor pains blend in an intermediate form (Atkinson).

Bleph'aroplast, *add*, (2), by zoologists applied to a centrosome, the centre of the kinetic activity of the nucleus (Hertwig).

blist'ered, old term for "bullate."

Blos'som, *add*, (2), corolla.

Bod'ies, suspens'ory, = PSEUDOVACUOLES.

Bod'y, cen'tral, incipient nucleus.

-bole, "combining term for propulsion" (Clements).

Bord'ered-pores of *Sphagnum* Dill., openings surrounded by a distinct flattened ring (Russow).

borragin'eous, pertaining to *Borago* Linn.

botryopt'erid, allied to the fern *Botryopteris* Presl.

botryt'ic, Worsdell's term for botryoid, like a bunch of grapes.

Bot'ulism (*botulus*, a sausage), a disease due to a spore-forming anaerobic bacterium (Conn).

brachybioste'monous (στήμων, stamen), having non-persistent stamens (Delpino); **brachyclad'ous** (κλάδυς, a branch), having short branches; **brachydact'ylous** (+ DACTYL), the short ultimate rays of *Nitella* Ag.; **Brachyne'ma** (νῆμα, a thread), the condition in meiosis derived from STREPSINEMA (Chodat); **Brach'ysteles**, pl., short upper branchlets in Characeae; **Brach'ymeiosis** (μείωσις, réduction), a second meiotic reduction; **Brach'ysomes** (σῶμα, a body) = TETRADS.

Bracte, R. A. Salisbury's spelling of BRACT.

Bractea, *add*, (2) Parlatore's term for connective in conifers; **bract'eoid** (εἶδος, resemblance), bract-like or bracteate.

bradycarp'ic (βραδύς, slow; καρπός, fruit), fruiting after the winter, in the second season after flowering (Wittrock); **Bradyspore** (σπείρα, I sow), applied to a plant which disperses its seeds slowly (Ulrich); adj. **bradyspor'ous**; *cf.* ANEMOCHOROUS.

Branch-leaf of *Sphagnum* Dill, a highly developed leaf from the middle or lower part of a sterile spreading branch (Horrell); ~ **-gaps**, in a fern stele, openings in the central cylinder where a branch is given off (Jeffrey).

Breech Fertiliza'tion (Jeffrey) = CHALAZOGAMY.

brevifurca'tus, applied to shortly forked branchlets of Nitelleae; **brevischist'ostyle** (σχίζω, I split, + STYLE), a floral type, with short style, "stigma badly formed, and style folded some distance down" (Gates).

Brig'alow Scrub, formed chiefly of *Acacia harpophylla* F. Muell.

Brochone'ma (βρόχος, a loop; νῆμα, a thread), the stage of nuclear division in which the spireme is regularly looped in number corresponding to those of the chromosome pairs (Gates).

Brome'tum, an association of *Bromus* Linn.

Bronz'ing, a form of sun-scorch, due to want of moisture in the soil, or defect in root-action during hot, dry periods (Harshberger).

Bul'bil, *add*, (c), spore-balls of *Urocystis*, Rab. etc. (Hobson).

Bulbo-gemma, bulbil (Bischoff).

bul'ging, in old writers for gibbous.

Bulk-ra'tio, " the ratio of the diameter of the axis to that of the primordium arising on it " (Church).

Bunch, Withering's term for raceme.

But'tresses, plank-like growths at the base of certain trees.

Buxe'tum, an association of *Buxus* Linn.

By-fruit, an unusual form of fruit (Van de Walk).

Ca'ble Type, " consolidated filamentous soma " (Church).

Cakile'tum, an association of *Cakile* Linn.

Calamagrostide'tum, the same of *Calamagrostis* Adans., shortened by Clements to Calamagroste'tum.

cal'amoid, long slender elastic stems as in *Calamus* Linn.

cal'cipete (*peto*, I seek), seeking chalky soils (Druce).

callolyt'ic (+ CALLUS, λύσις, a loosing), S. Moore's term for a ferment which dissolves callus from sieveplates.

Cal'lus, *add*, (2) definitive ~ or fi'nal ~, shows dissolution of the functional elements of the phloem; sea'sonal ~, temporary callus. Cal'lus Pads, that deposited on the sieve-plates of algae (Sykes); ~ Rods, that which passes through the apertures of sieve-tubes (Sykes afterw. Thoday); Harshberger

divides the various kinds, as ~ heteroplas'ia, heteroplastic tissue formed; ~ homooplas'ia, from wound-stimuli; ~ hypert'rophy, abnormal growth with voluminous vesicles; ~ metaplas'ia, from metaplastic change of the cells affected.

cal'ycled, having a whorl of bracts exterior to the true calyx.

campanula'ceous, belonging to *Campanula* Linn.

Cam'pine, African Congo savannah (Warming).

Cañ'on (Span. a hollow), or Can'yon, a deep gorge worn by water, between high and steep banks.

Carbohydra'ses, carbohydrate-splitting enzymes.

Cardamine'tum, an association of *Cardamine* Linn.

Carice'tum, pl. -ta associations of *Carex* Linn. as ~ infla'tae, of *Carex inflata* Huds., ~ semperviren'tis, of *Carex sempervirens* Vill., *cf.* STRICTETUM; other sections are Mag'no-~, and Par'vo-~, of large or small species (Warming).

cari'nal (*carina*, a keel) Air Spa'ces, cavities in the fibro-vascular strands of *Equisetum* by the ridges (Jeffrey).

Car'pel, *add*, (2) a component only of a megasporophyll (H. H. Thomas); (7) pseu'do-valve (or semi-sol'id ~), with placentae displaced from edges to centre, and double central strand splitting there at maturity (Saunders); sol'id ~, of a fibro-vascular cord, with a few lateral veins or reticulations (*id.*); valve (or hollow ~), midrib inconspicuous, with reticulate venation, more or less of leafshape (*id.*).

carposporif'erous (+ CARPOSPORE, *fero*, I bear), producing spores in Floridean algae (Phillips); Carpospor'ophyte (+ SPOROPHYTE), a plant which bears carpospores.

Caryomer'ites, pl. (μέρος, a part) = IDIOMERES; they may be monochromosomic or polychromosomic (Chodat); Caryophy'ta (φύτον, a plant), nucleated plants (Macfarlane).

Caspar'ian Strip, a band of peculiar cellular tissue in the endodermis of certain water-plants, first investigated by R. Caspary.

casuar'inoid (εἶδος, resemblance), like the genus *Casuarina* Linn.

Catabrose'tum, an association of *Catabrosa* Beauv.

Catacorol'la (+ COROLLA), the production of a corolla in a tubular flower, with inverted surface; **Catal'ysis,** *cf.* AUTOCATALYSIS, HETEROCATALYSIS. **Cataplas'ia** (πλάσσω, I form), functional decline of the cell; **Cat'aplasm,** a diseased abnormal growth; adj. **cataplast'ic**; **Cat'aplasy,** degeneration of tissue combined with increased size; **catoclad'ous** (κλάδος, a slip or twig), deflexed, bent outwards or downwards.

Caudic'ula (*caudex*, plant-axis), used by Engler for ROOTSTOCK.

Caul, sometimes used for STEM; **Caulesc'ence,** development of the stem; **Caul'oid** (εἶδος, resemblance), the branch of the ancestral plant (Signier); pl. **Caul'oids.**

Cells, pl. **Erect,** in the phloem of the pine, vertically placed cells in contact with the rays (Jeffrey); **hel'icoid** ∼, apical coenocytes in *Pithophora* Wittr. (Wittrock); **prolif'ic** ∼, disjointed parts of the thallus in *Cladophora* Kütz. (West).

Cembre'tum, an association of *Pinus Cembra* Linn.; **Ce'neosere** (+ SERE), the geologic period marked by the change of plant-dominance, from gymnosperms to angiosperms (Clements); **Ce'neostrate,** a cenophytic eostrate (Clements); **cenogenet'ic** (+ GENETIC), a bisexual individual when dedoubled into a male and female being (Janet); **cenophyt'ic** (φύτον, a plant), relating to the most recent era of plant life.

Cent'imorgan (+ MORGAN), one hundred times the length of a morgan.

Cent'rad, centripetal wood (Jeffrey); **Cen'tral A'rea,** a hyaline portion of a diatom valve, sometimes surrounding the central nodule (West); ∼ **Bod'y,** an incipient nucleus (West); ∼ **Fi'bres,** pl. a band between bundles, and especially over phloem regions with thick walls and tannin contents, characteristic of *Pinus*; ∼ **Gran'ules,** pl. occur in Cyanophyceae in the meshwork of the incipient nucleus (West); **Centrodes'mose** (δεσμός, a band), the central spindle or axis of achromatinic spindle (Minchin).

Ceratophylle'tum, an association of *Ceratophyllum* Linn.

Cerebro'sides (*cerebrum,* the brain), a group of lipases containing fatty acids, nitrogen and a sugar, but no phosphorus.

Cervix, *add,* (2), elongated neck of a bulb, now obsolete.

C_H, *see* pH; hydrogen-ion concentration in soil (Atkins).

chaetomall'us (χαίτη, flowing hair; μαλλός, fleece), thick-maned (Balfour).

Chain Chan'nel, a depression round the anterior schizont of Peridineae (Kofoid); ∼ **Forma'tion,** diatoms and Peridineae in attached trains (West).

Chalici'um, a gravel slide formation; originally " **Chalicodi'um** " (Clements).

Chalicospor'ae (+ SPORE), plants disseminated by movement of earth or soil (Clements).

Chamaephy'tion, an association of chamaephytes (Moss); **chamaesipho'neous,** pertaining to dwarf algae (Macfarlane).

Chan'nel, *cf.* CHAIN CHANNEL.

Char'ads, charophytes; **Chare'tum,** a variation of *Charace'tum*; **Charophytes** (φύτον, a plant), plants allied to the genus *Chara* Linn.

Chasmocleistog'amy, some flowers being chasmogamic, the others cleistogamic (Errard and Gevaert); **chasmoph'ilous** (φιλέω, I love),

427

loving crannies or chinks in rocks;
Chasmoph'ily, the condition of
cranny-loving plants.
cheilanth'oid (εἶδος, resemblance),
allied to or resembling the fern
genus *Cheilanthes* Sw.
Cheilocystid'ia, pl. (+ CYSTIDIUM,
bodies of unknown function, from
the face of the lower edges of gills
in Agarics (Buller); *cf.* PLEURO-
CYSTIDIA.
chemosynthet'ic (σύνθησις, composition), responsive to chemical
action; *cf.* PHOTOSYNTHETIC.
Cher'nogens, continental soils
developed under a small range of
rainfall, permanently grass-covered,
as the Russian black soils.
Chias'ma (χίασμα, two lines crossed),
of four chromosome strands, two
fuse at crossing, one strand uniting
endwise with the other (Janssens);
Chias'motype (+ TYPE), the basis
of " crossing-over " (Chodat).
Chil'ling, exposure of perennial plants
to wintry cold, as necessary for
early growth in the following spring
(Coville).
Chimae'ras : hyper ~, is due to similar
fusion producing abnormal fruits
(Harshberger); **nu'clear ~,** pl.
exchange of chromosomes (Lotsy);
perichaetial ~, having a skin of
different quality from the core (Bateson); **sectional ~,** a mutant
arising from mixed cells; **sector'ial
~,** due to bud-variation in a
branch; Correns adds: **albopellicula'tus, albotunica'tus, chlorotiderm'is, leucoderm'is, pseudoleuco-
derm'is.**
Chlamydobacte'ria (+ BACTERIA), bacteria having strong affinities with
algae (Conn); **Chlamydomone'ta,**
pl. communities of *Chlamydomonas*
and diatoms (Warming).
Chloralbi'no (+ ALBINO), variegated
with green and white in the leaves
(Shull); **Chloren'chym,** *see* CHLOREN-
CHYMA; **chlorococ'cine** refers to
algae without vegetative cell-
division, but only by zoogonia or
motile gametes; formerly termed

" endospherine " (West); **chlorococ'coid,** resembling in habit the
genus *Chlorococcum* Fr. ; **Chlorophyl-
l'in,** *cf.* CHLOROPHYLLAN ; **Chlorophyll'oplast** (φύλλον, a leaf; πλαστός,
formed), a chromoplast containing
chlorophyll as colouring matter
(Janet); **Chlorophy'ta,** green
algae; **Chlorosta'toliths,** pl.
(+ STATOLITH), starch-containing
chloroplasts; **chlorotiderm'is**
(δέρμα, skin), with greenish-yellow
subepidermal layer and a green
core, in *Arabis* Linn. (Correns).
Chol'ine (χολή, bile), a base derived
from lecithin.
chomophyt'ic, adj. *cf.* CHOMOPHYTE.
Chondriocon'tes (κοντός, a pole),
elongated forms of misochondria
from which chromoplasts are derived (Guillermand).
Chorisep'aly (+ SEPAL), having the
sepals free; **chorolog'ic** (λόγος,
discourse), topographic (Rübel);
Chorol'ogy, the study of migration
or area of distribution (Jaccard).
Chott, a salt-spot in the Algerian
desert.
Chromid'iosome (σῶμα, a body), the
ultimate individual particle of
chromatin, either inside or outside
a nucleus (Minchin); **Chromogen'esis**
(γένεσις, origin), colour produced
by bacteria (Conn); **Chromolip'oids,**
pl. (λίπος, grease; εἶδος, resemblance), a fatty colour allied to
carotin (Czapek); **Chromone'ma**
(νῆμα, a thread), a ripe chromosome
of an achromatic core round which
is wound a chromatic fibre, as in
Paris Linn. (Vejdovsky); **chromo-
ph'ilous** (φιλέω, I love), readily
taking stain; **Chro'moplast,** *add,*
(2), used by Janet for a granule
containing chlorophyll as a colouring matter; **chromosomat'ic,** relating to chromosomes.
Chronol'ogy (κρόνος, time; λόγος,
discourse), the appearance of plants
in the history of the earth (Rübel).
chroolepoid'ly = CHROOLEPOID.
Chrysoherm'idin (+ HERMIDIN), a labile
chromogen in *Mercurialis* Linn.

Chrysophy'ta, a group of algae including Chrysophyceae and diatoms.

cichora'ceous, related to *Cichorium* Linn.

cil'iolate, adj. from CILIOLA; **Cil'iospore** (+ SPORE), a swarm-spore with a coat of cilia (Minchin).

Cing'ulum, *add,* (2) the girdle in Peridineae which separates the epivalve from the hypovalve (West).

Cir'rhoids, pl. (εἶδος, resemblance), balls of *Cladophora* Kütz, which are formed of coiled shoots which do not change their shape.

Cladie'tum, an association of *Cladium* P. Br.

Clad'ina Heaths or **Tun'dra,** barren peaty lands with plenty of the lichen *Cladina* Nyl.

Cla'do-androgonid'ium (+ANDROGO-NIDIUM), a male androspore or merid, terminal or intercalated (Janet); **cla'dofied,** becoming branched (Benson); **Cla'do-gonid'ium** (+ GONIDIUM), the gonidium which gives rise to a merid, either intercalated or subterminal (Janet); **Cla'do-gynogonid'ium,** a female merid (Janet); **Cladoph'ora Balls,** rounded accumulations of shoots of that alga; **cladophora'ceous,** allied to *Cladophora*; **Cladophyll'um,** *add,* (3) the special bract in *Schoenoxiphium* Nees and *Kobresia* Willd., the utricles being free at the edges; it may be ὁ'creaform, horn-shaped and more or less attached, or utric'uliform, approaching the guise of the normal utricle (Kükenthal).

Clan, the next group below a society, usually local and restricted (Clements).

Clas'totype (κλαστός, broken; τύπος, a type), a fragment from the original type (Swingle).

clath'roid, resembling the fungus genus *Clathrus* Mich.; latticed.

clau'sus (Lat. shut), used of closely placed verticils.

Cla'vis (Lat. a key), an artificial key to a genus or other group of plants, by contrasted characters leading to speedy determination of the units.

cleistocarp'ous, *add,* (2) used of the perithecium of a fungus which has no opening (Harshberger).

Cle'ma (κλῆμα, a twig), employed for "branchlet."

clepsyd'roid, *add,* (2) applied to pinna-traces in fossils when in two rows (Scott); **Clepsydrop'sis** is the state.

Cli'max, the full perfection and development of an association (Clements); adj. **climat'ic** [= climact'ic]; **edaph'ic** ∼, due to soil; **temp'orary** ∼, balanced growth for a period: ∼ **Commu'nities,** stable type, no further change unless surroundings alter (Tansley and Chipp): ∼ **U'nits,** association, consociation, society, clan (Clements, 1916); ∼ **Zones,** changes due to amount of controlling factors (*id.*); **Cli'sere** (+ SERE), a successional development from one climax to another (*id.*); adj. **cli'seral**; **Cli'stase** (+ STASE), when the climax layer of each stase differs from the preceding or succeeding stase (*id.*); **Cli'strate** (+STRATE), change from one climax to another (*id.*).

Clistog'amy = CLEISTOGAMY.

clo'nal, relating to a bud; **Clone,** *add,* (2) the group of plants descended asexually from a single ancestor (Shull); **Clo'notype** (τύπος, a type), a specimen propagated from the original type by a bud or cutting (Swingle).

Coagula'tion (*coagulatio,* a curdling), the change from liquid to thick consistence by chemical action, as the formation of a GEL; **Coag'ulum,** hard jelly.

Coal, Moth'er of, charred wood found in the seams (Jeffrey).

Co-dom'inants, pl. used of competing plants; **Co-effic'ient Genet'ic,** defined as "dynamic behaviour" (Fuller).

coeno'bic, relating to a COENOBIUM as *Volvox* (West); **Coenospe'cies** (+ SPECIES), the total sum of possible combinations in a genotype compound (Holmberg).

Coe′nosium (κοινός, common), a community of plants, further subdivided as BIOCOENOSIUM, ISOCOENOSIUM, PERMANENT ∼ and TEMPORARY ∼ (Gams).

Coleoph′ylly (φύλλον, a leaf), leaf-sheathing (Druce); **Coleop′tile,** an English form of COLEOPTILUM.

Col′ony, an initial community of two or more species, the sign is -ale, as " Hordeale " (Clements). **Col′ony, Mo′tile,** an associated group of algae, not fixed to one place; **Palmelloid** ∼, in form recalling *Palmella* Lyngb. **Col′onies,** pl. *add,* (2) of bacteria grown in plate culture from a single bacterium (Conn).

-colus, Clements's suffix for habitat forms, classically—cola.

Columel′la, *add,* (6) the central column in the pollen-chamber of the apex of the megasporangium of a cycad (Jeffrey).

coma′lius (Mod. Lat.) having comal tufts (Dixon).

Commu′nities, pl. grouping of plants, they may be fi′nal ∼, init′ial ∼, or transit′ional ∼ (Warming); *cf.* CLAN.

Compatibil′ity (L. Lat. *compatibilis*), botanically means capable of self-fertilisation; adj. **compat′ible,** fertile.

Compensa′tion-strand (*compensatio,* weighing), in *Saccoloma* Kaulf., strands given off by the inner ring of the stele, connecting with outer ring (Bower).

Complementa′tion (*complementum,* filling up), division of a phyllome, each portion acting as a complete whole (Penzig): **Complement′ary Associa′tion,** where competition is avoided by the various species rooting at different depths, and coming to the surface at various times of the year (Woodhead).

Com′plex (*complexus,* comprise), or **Forma′tion** ∼, a higher grade than formation in respect of plants

(Waterman); ∼ **Muta′tion,** one with simultaneous changes in several factors in one region of a chromosome (Nilsson-Ehle).

Conduct′ive Hy′phae, those which in dry-rot convey moisture.

Con′dyle, *add,* (3) the basal granule of Gymnodiniaceae (Dangeard).

Cone-scale, the peculiar cone of *Cheirostrobus* Scott (Benson).

Conif′erophyte, a coniferous plant, or one akin to Coniferae.

conioph′ilous (κόνις, dust; φιλέω, I love), applied to lichens which benefit by dust (Sernander); **Conid′iospores** pl. (+ SPORE), non-sexual spores in Peronosporeae.

Con′jugant (*conjugo,* I unite), a sexual individual of two conjugating, partial karyogamy; **Conjuga′tion,** total karyogamy.

Conjunc′tion (*conjunctio,* union), the pairing of two univalent spiremes to become the heterotype chromosome (Digby); **conjunc′tus** when antheridia and oogonia of Characeae are at the same nodes.

Connect′ive Flaps, vestigial imbricating laminae in gymnospermic cones (Church).

conni′ving, Herbert's term for CONNIVENT.

Conodrym′ium (δρυμός, a wood); **Conophor′ium** (φορέω, I bear), synonyms of CONISILVAE.

Con′sere, *cf.* COSERE.

conspecif′ic, -cus (Mod. Lat.) belonging to the same species; **Con′stancy,** drawn from the number of times met with in the association in which the plant grows.

Con′tour, *cf.* DOUBLE CONTOUR; **Cont′rary Cross,** a hybrid with reversed parentage (H. J. Müller). **Conver′gence** (*vergo,* I turn), similar results obtained by different methods (Church).

coprophyt′ic (φυτόν, a plant); **coprozo′ic** (ζῷον, an animal), terms for flagellates growing in faecal matter or the alimentary canal.

Cor′alline, applied to the roots of cycads, due to root-nodules.

cord′iate, Wieland's term for any species of *Cordaites* Unger.

cordiller′an, belonging to the Cordilleras (Clements).

Corid′iospores, misprint for CONIDIOSPORES.

Cormophytast′ers (*aster,* suffix of inferiority), mosses (Trelease); *cf.* PSEUDOCORMOPHYTES.

Corne′tum, an association of *Cornus* Linn.

Correla′tion (*cor* for *con, relatio,* carrying back), the inhibiting power of growing buds of *Bryophyllum* Salisb. have upon the growth of other buds on the same leaf (J. Loeb).

Coryle′tum, an association of hazels, *Corylus* Linn.

Cory′phad, an alpine meadow plant (Clements).

coryphae′us (κορυφαῖος, leading), notable in its genus.

Co′sere or **Con′sere** (Co + SERE), a series of unit succession in the same spot; an organic unity (Clements); **Co′stase** (+ STASE), two or more stases, the record of a cosere (*id.*); **Co′strate** (+ STRATE), a layer of inorganic matter between stases (*id.*); **Co′type** (+ TYPE), one of several specimens originally described, without specification of one as the HOLOTYPE; SYNTYPE is a synonym.

Cream′ing, in plant-cells, the ascent of protein particles in the cytoplasm, as fat globules cream to the surface of milk (Small).

crenic′olous, dwelling in brooks fed by springs.

Crest: dor′sal ∼, dorsal scale in fan-leaved palms (Arber); ven′tral ∼, ligule in the same (*id.*); **crest′ing,** the graded forking of an organ.

Cre′tin (F. idiot), a monstrous *Lathyrus* flower with straight stigma protruded from a cleft in the keel (Bateson).

Cribel′lum (Lat. a small sieve), applied to the network of canals connecting the cells of *Volvox* (Janet).

Crisp′ing, the copious marginal incision of a leaf.

Crist′a (Lat. a tuft), used by Druce for the ligule of palm-leaves.

Cross′over or **Crossing-o′ver,** the interchange of factors in chromosomes, opposed to LINKAGE; **cross-fert′ile,** a fertile hybrid: **double** ∼, parents mutually crossed; **Cross-frag′ment,** applied to chromosomes which have parted and crossed over (R. T. Hance); ∼ **ster′ile,** a sterile hybrid.

Crotone′tum, an association of *Croton* Linn.

Crymi′on = CRYMIUM; **Cryoplank′ton** (+ PLANKTON), the plankton of perpetual ice and snow, polar and glacial.

Crypthy′brid (+ HYBRID), a hidden hybrid, apparently a good species, but its nature shown by its reproductive cells being more or less abortive (Jeffrey); **Cryptocotyledo′neae** = MONOCOTYLEDONS.

crystallog′enous, forming crystals, as ∼ **Cells** (Hillhouse).

Cul′tivar, a botanical variety, originated under cultivation (L. H. Bailey); **Cul′tiform,** a variety risen from culture (Sprague); **Cul′tigen,** (1), a plant, group or series, only known in cultivation, opposed to INDIGENE; (2) **Cultig′ena,** T. A. Sprague's suggested Latinized form for CULTIGEN; **Cul′tispecies** (+ SPECIES), one which has arisen under cultivation (Sprague).

cu′mulate (*cumulatus,* piled up), " heaped on one another " (Herbert).

Cupel′lea (*cupella,* a small cask), a curved colony of merids (Janet).

cupressin′eous, allied to or resembling *Cupressus* Tourn.

Curvule′tum, an association of *Carex curvula* All.

Cu′tin, recently defined as a substance present as a continuous external lamella on the outer wall of the epidermis of leaf or stem; **cu′tinized,** transformed into CUTIN.

Cyanoherm′idin, *cf.* HERMIDIN.

cyath'eoid, like the fern *Cyathea* Sm.

cyca'deid, resembling *Cycas* Linn.; cycada'ceous and cyca'deous, akin to that genus; Cy'cadophyte (φυτόν, a plant), applied to the whole group of cycad-like plants (Wieland).

cyclop'teroid, used for pinnules like those of *Cyclopteris* Brongn.

cymbal'iform, the shape of the corolla in *Convolvulus* Linn.

cymbomor'phus (κύμβος, a cup; μορφή, shape), cup-shaped (I. B. Balfour).

Cynodactyle'tum, an association of *Cynodon Dactylon* Pers.

Cyst'ospores, *add*, (2) encysted zoospores of *Thraustotheca* Humph.

Cyte = CELL; Cy'tea, a monoplast flagellate (Janet); Cytec'dysis = ECDYSIS; Cy'tioplasm, anglicized form of CYTIOPLASMA; Cytokine'sis, (1) form suggested for all terms of KINESIS and MITOSIS; (2) division of cytoplasm (E. B. Wilson); Cytolip'oids, pl. (λίπος, grease), the fat-particles contained in the plant-cells (Czapek); Cytomi'crosome (+ MICROSOME) = CHONDRIOSOME.

Dac'tyl, the ultimate ray of a branchlet of *Nitella*.

Darwinizing, fractional culture (Conn).

daval'lioid, like the fern *Davallia* Sm.

Day Plants, long day plants; if exposure to light is unduly shortened, flowering is prevented or delayed; short day plants, shortened light period hastens blooming.

Da'ya, a poorly drained area in Algeria, slightly undulating, but not salt.

dec'aploid, having five double sets of chromosomes (Hurst).

decomposed', applied to cortex of gelatinous, indistinct, or amorphous hyphae (A. L. Smith).

dec'uple, ten sets of chromosomes (Blakeslee).

Decurta'tion (*decurto*, I mutilate), the spontaneous fall of branches (Heckel).

decur'ved (*decurvus*, Mod. Lat.), bent downwards, deflexed.

Dedifferentia'tion (*de*, not; *differens*, distinct), loss of DIFFERENTIATION; an apparent approach to the embryonic condition (Child); De-fertiliza'tion (+ FERTILIZATION), when insects clear away the pollen (N. E. Brown); Deforma'tion (+ FORMATION), changes of surface, rapid or slow, due to flood or earthquakes (Clements); adj. deforma'tional; Degenera'tion, *add*, (2) when chromosomatic, due to inheritance from parents (Gussow).

dek'asome, = decaploid.

deliques'cent (*liquescere*, to melt), branching so that the stem is lost in the branches; opposed to excurrent; Demineraliza'tion (*minerale*, Mod. Lat.), by action of hydrofluoric acid to free fossils from extraneous matter (Jeffrey).

dendroc'ola, dwelling on trees, epiphytic; dendrolog'ic, relating to trees.

dennstaedt'ioid, like the fern *Dennstaedtia* Bernh.

Denuda'tion, *add*, (2) area may be bared by a parasitic plant as *Cuscuta salina* Engelm.

Dep'ea (δέπας, a beaker), a cell with a cap capable of taking in nourishment (Janet).

Depollina'tion (+ POLLINATION), caused by insects eating pollen from anthers or stigmata (N. E. Brown).

Deposit'ion (*depositio*, placing), fresh soil added as by floods; progres'sive ~, the process continuing; retrogres'sive ~, when the fresh earth is gradually removed.

Dermatoplas'm, the living protoplasm asserted as forming a part of the cell-membrane in plants (Wiesner).

Deschampsie'tum, an association of *Deschampsia* Beauv.

Determ'iner (*determino*, I limit), a unit producing a visible effect independently of other units of inheritance (Coulter); they may be du'plicate, or plu'ral (Shull), reinforcing each other.

deter'sile (*detersilis*, can be wiped), referring to the wool on young branches which readily falls or is cleaned off (I. B. Balfour).

deutoplas′mic (πλάσμα, that formed), metaplasmic granules of reserve food material stored in protoplasmic substance (Minchin).

dexiotrop′ic (δεξιός, right-hand; τροπή, turning), (1) the movement of *Volvox* in normal rotation; (2) the direction of spiral cleavages; **dex′tral**, used of respective daughter-cells resulting from spiral cleavage (Treadwell).

diage′ic, *add*, (2) used for plants whose shoots protrude through the soil; *cf.* EPIGEIC (M. Vahl).

Diagno′sis (διάγνωσις, discrimination), shortly-drawn characters to define a species, genus or family (Bischoff, supplementing A. Gray's definition).

di′allel (διάλληλος, crossing), of lines which cross (Schmidt).

diarthrodact′ylous (+ ARTHRODACTYL-OUS), in Characeae each dactyl consisting of two cells; **Diate′siae**, pl. (ἐτήσιος, annual), above-ground shoots lasting the entire year (Krause); **Dicar′yon** (κάρυον, a nut), a binucleate cell of secondary hyphae in *Coprinus fimetarius* (Bensande); **Dicli′nery** (Church) = DI-CLINISM; **Dicotyle′dony**, the condition of being dicotyledonous (Jeffrey).

dickso′nioid (εἶδος, resemblance) like the fern *Dicksonia* L'Hérit.

Dictyoste′ly, having a DICTYOSTELE.

Diëcodichog′amy (+ DICHOGAMY), some flowers having male flowers in advance of the female, and in others the reverse (Delpino); **Di-Hy′brid** (+ HYBRID), *cf.* DIHYBRIDISM; ～ **Ra′tio**, the Mendelian proportions of 9 : 3 : 3 : 1; **di′merous** (μέρος, part), seedlings which have two cotyledons and two primordial leaves; **Dim′ery**, the condition just described (Church).

dineur′oid, used of pinna-traces in Zygopteridae, fossil ferns, when in four rows as in *Dineuron* Scott (Scott); **dioe′cious**, ～ **macran′drous**

in *Oedogonium*, where the antheridia are little less in size than the female filaments, and ～ **nannan′drous**, male plants very small (West); **dipho′tic** (φῶς, light), leaves set on stem at an angle to get more light on the upper surface than on the lower (Clements).

Dinoflagella′ta (δῖνος, rotation, + FLAGELLATA), infusoria possessing more than two flagella for their propulsion.

Dip′lasy (διπλάσιος, double), the division of an axial organ into two parts.

Diplobi′ont (διπλόος, twofold; βίος, life), a plant flowering or fruiting twice in each season; adj. **diplobion′tic**; **dip′loid**, *add*, (2) the result of two gametes (Lotsy); **diplosteph′anous**, (στέφανος, a crown), a double circle of stipulodes at the base of each whorl of branchlets in Characeae.

dip′terid, resembling the genus *Dipteris* Reinw.

Dirup′tion (*dirumpo*, I break), division.

disbud′ded, the nascent buds removed; ～**mu′tant**, *cf.* MUTANT.

Disc′olith (λίθος, stone), a coccolith shaped like a disc (Lohmann).

dis′color, *add*, (2) " also any green colour altered by a mixture of purple " (Lindley).

discontig′uous (*dis* = not; *contiguus*, touching), used by I. B. Balfour for rhododendron leaves having gaps between them.

Discs or **Disks**, pl. (*discus*, a quoit); ～-**fil′aments**, tubular prolongation of thallus-cells in *Ulva* Linn. (West); *cf.* SEPARATION-DISCS.

Disjunc′tion (*dis* = not; *junctio*, joining), (1) separation of a bivalent spireme into two univalent spiremes; (2) separation of a bivalent or heterotype chromosome into two entire chromosomes (Digby).

di′some or **dis′some**, diploid.

Dissociation, *add*, (2) fission (Digby).

disterigmat′ic, having two spores abjointed from each of the basidia of certain fungi (Buller).

Distribu′tion (*distributio*, division), the partition of plants over the world according to their needs of growth, temperature, soils, and aspects.

Distroph′ophytes, pl. (+ TROPHO- PHYTES), plants of firm soil with full proportion of moisture (Gadeceau); **ditrip′loid** (+ TRIPLOID), applied to *Rumex Acetosella* Linn., with a single pair of sex chromosomes and another pair transitional between sex-chromosomes and autosomes (Gates).

Divul′sion (*divulsus*, torn asunder), diruption.

dizy′gous, (ζυγός, a yoke) dependent on two rows of chromosomes (Frost).

dodek′asome = dodecaploid (Blakeslee).

Dom′inance, preponderance in surface occupied; **Dom′inants**, *add*, (4) genera which have persisted through geologic times to the present (Clements).

Doub′le Recip′rocal, hybrid obtained from reciprocally crossing two previously crossed hybrids (De Vries); *cf.* RECIPROCAL HYBRID; ~ **Roots**, when lateral roots of mono-cotyledone occur in the intennal between two protoxylem bundles (Jeffrey).

dros′ophile (δρόσος, dew; φιλέω, I love), fertilized by dew (Errera).

Dryade′tum, an association of *Dryas* Linn.

Dry′mophytes (δρυμός, coppice; φύτον, a plant), bushes and small trees, chaparral and woodland (Clements); **Dry′on**, scrub climax (*id.*).

Dryophant′in (φανσάζω, to appear), a pathologic colouring-matter from galls produced by *Dryophante divisa* Adler, on leaves of British oaks.

dryop′terid, like the fern *Dryopteris* Adans.

duodec′uple, twelve sets of chromosomes affected (Blakeslee).

du′plex, two dominant factors (Blakeslee).

Durifrutice′ta, pl. associations of MACCHIA and GARRIGUES; **Duriligno′sa**, pl. (*lignosus*, woody), hard-wood plants; **Duripra′ta**, pl. (*pratum*, a meadow), pasturage; **Durisil′vae**, woods of firm-leaved trees.

Dynam′ic Beha′viour, the part played by the species in the development of the community.

dys′ploid, non-multiploid variatioñ in the number of chromosomes, as *Carex* Linn.; **Dysploi′dy** is the condition (Jeffrey); **Dysteleolog′ue**, H. Mueller's term for DYSTELEO- LOGIST; **dystrop′ic**, Loew = dystropous.

ece′sic, relating to ECESIS; **ec′ize**, to colonize.

eclec′teus (ἐκλεκτέος, to be chosen out), selected.

Ecodichog′amy (+ DICHOGAMY), monoecious asynchronism in fertilization; **Ec′ograph** (γράφω, I write), an instrument to measure the physical factors of a station or habitat (Clements); **Ecol′ogy**, the modern spelling for the original OECOLOGY; regulated by biot′ic, climat′ic, edaph′ic, and orograph′ic factors; **Ec′ophene** (φαίνω, I appear), the reaction of ECOTYPE to extreme habitat factor (Turesson); **Ecoproteran′dry** (+ PRO- TERANDRY), staminal flowers maturing before the pistillate (Delpino); **Ecoproterog′yny** (+ PRO- TEROGYNY), pistillate flowers maturing before the staminate (Delpino); **Ecospe′cies** (+SPECIES), a species modified to fit its locality (Turesson); **Ec′otype** (τύπος, type), a habitat type of plant, a sub-unit of the ECOSPECIES resulting to conditions of environment; adj. **ecotyp′ical**.

ectendotroph′ic (EC-, ENDOTROPHIC), combined type of parasitism, inward and outward (Melin); intermediate intercellular infection in cortical tissues of mycorrhiza (Rayner).

ectocarp′oid, resembling the alga *Ectocarpus* Lyngb.

ectokinet′ic (κίνησις, movement), applied to a sporangium which dehisces by epidermal mechanism; cf. ENDOKINETIC (Jeffrey); **Ec′toplasts** (πλαστός, moulded), cyanophycin granules in blue-green algae (Fritch); **Ect′otroph** (τροφή, food), a parasite feeding from outside its host; **Ectothiobacter′ia** (θεῖον, sulphur, + BACTERIA), which form sulphur outside the cells; **Ectothioleuka′ceae,** colourless sulphur bacteria with the sulphur outside the cells.

Edaph′ic Cli′max or ~ **Forma′tion,** "an association complex which is related to a specific physiographic area" (Nichols); **Edaph′on,** the qualities of the soil as regards plant-growth (Francé).

effig′urate, *add,* (3) having a thallus like the lichen *Placodium* DC.

Electr′olyte (λυτήρ, a release), (1) a compound decomposable by an electric current; (2) the current of electricity evoked by irritation in the pulvinus of *Mimosa* Linn. (Blackman).

El′eoplast, Jeffrey's term for ELAIOPLAST.

elep′idote, destitute of scurfy scales, non-lepidote.

Eluvia′tion (*eluvio,* washing away), elutriation, decanting the finer particles from the heavier by a stream of water; adj. **eluvia′ted.**

Emargina′tion (*e,* from; *margo,* edge), notching of the leaf-apex.

Emersipra′ta (*emersus,* emerged; *pratum,* a meadow), upper portions of moist meadows.

E′mophytes, pl. (ἠμύα, I sink; φυτόν, a plant), entire plant submerged, no functional stomata (Clements).

-en for **-anum,** layer societies (Clements).

encap′suled, certain protophytes with a firm envelope (Fritch).

Encyoneme′tum, an association of fresh-water algae, inclusive of *Encyonema* Kütz.

endobasid′ial, cf. ENDOBASIDIUM; **endoconid′ial,** relating to endoconidia; **Endoconideoph′ora** (φορέω, I bear), the organ producing endoconidia in *Thielavia* Zopf; **End′oderm,** cf. ENDODERMIS; **endokinet′ic** (κίνησις, movement), a fruit opening by mechanism of internal origin; cf. ECTOKINETIC; **Endolith′ophytes,** pl. (λίθος, stone), lichens which penetrate into rock, adj. **endolith′ic; End′ome,** the inner layer of Van Tieghem's PACHYTE, the phelloderma; cf. EXOME; **Endomix′is** (μῖξις, a mingling), the intermingling of nuclear and cytoplasmic substances within the cell; reorganization without conjugation (Woodruff); **Endopet′rion,** growing in the interstices of rock (Gams); **endophlo′ic** (φλοιός, bark), of the inner bark; **En′doplasts** (πλαστός, moulded), certain bodies in the centroplasm of the blue-green algae (Fritch); **Entorhiz′oid** (ῥίζα, a root; εἶδος, resemblance), a rhizoid from the foot of the seta of a moss and growing down within the tissue of the gametophyte; the root of the sporophyte; **endoscop′ic** (σκοπέω, I see), the apical pole of a plant-embryo when turned towards the base of the archegonium, as in seed-plants (Bower); **End′osome,** a vesicle at or near its centre, containing chromatin; **Endosphaerosi′ra,** a small form of male plant in *Volvox* (Janet); **End′otroph** (τροφή, food), a parasitic fungus feeding internally on its host; **Endothiobacter′ia** (θεῖον, sulphur, + BACTERIA), bacteria which temporarily store sulphur within their cells; **Endothioleuka′ceae,** colourless sulphur bacteria: **Endothiorhoda′ceae,** purple sulphur bacteria; **En′gram** (γράμμα, a letter), the tendency in the nucleus of a somatic cell to be transferred to a sexual cell so as to transmit the special structure or function (Semon).

enne′asome, enne′aploid with nine chromosomes (Blakeslee).

Ensporula′tion (+ Sporulation), applied to the reproduction of bacteria (Hort).

Entel′echy (ἐντελέχια, an actuality), (1) actuality, (2) the condition of " intensive manifoldness " with suspension of certain vital functions by a non-spatial, non-perceptual, hypothetical agent (Driesch); adj. **entelech′ian.**

entomorph′ilous, add, (2) fungi living on insects (Clements and Pounds).

En′zyme; **genet′ic** ～, a formative substançe; **heterolyt′ic,** splitting other substances into more than one; **homolyt′ic,** turning the subject into more of the same nature; **enzymat′ically,** caused by enzyme action.

Eophyt′ic (φυτόν, a plant), used regarding the earliest vegetable life (Saporta); **E′oplasm** (πλάσμα, that formed), an assumed primitive substance antedating protoplasm (Troland); **E′osere** (+ Sere), a climax of vegetation during an eon or era (Clements); adj. **eose′ral; E′ostase** (+ Stase), a series of layers resulting in part from an eosere (id.); **Eo′strate** (+ Strate), the sum-total of all the strates in the same great vegetative era; a succession after a stase when the inorganic matter exceeds the organic (id.); divided into **ceno-phyt′ic** ～, **mesophyt′ic** ～, **paleo-phyt′ic** ～, according to age, as denoted by the terms; all taken together constitute a geostrate.

epeirogen′ic (ἤπειρος, the mainland; γένος, race), movement raising continents; cf. Orogenic.

Ephaptomenon (ἐφάπτομαι, to be fastened on), the adnate type of plants (Gams).

epharmon′ic, add, (2) ～-adapta′tion or ～-varia′tion, " change in the form or physiological behaviour, beneficial to an organism, evoked by the operation of some environmental stimulant " (Cockayne); **Epibiot′ica,** pl. (βίος, life), survivors of a lost flora (Ridley);

Epicotyle′donary Node, the place of the normal emission of leaves above the seed-leaves; **epige′ic** (γῆ, the earth), applied to plants whose shoots do not protrude from the soil, but rest upon it; cf. Diageic (M. Vahl); **epig′ynous,** add, (2) when the antheridia are upon or above the oogonia, as in Phyto-phthora De Bary (Murphy); **epi-lith′ic,** add, (2) of plants as **Epili-thoph′ytes,** those growing on stone or rock, as do many lichens (Wetter).

epilose (e = without, + pilose), destitute of hairs.

epiontolog′ic (ὄντα, things existing; λόγος, discourse), relating to the origin of individuals; the condition is **Epiontol′ogy; Epiphy-to′tisms** (πτωτός, fallen), epidemic plant diseases; adj. **epiphyto′tic** (Harshberger); **Ep′iplasts** (πλαστός, moulded), spherical bodies within the cytoplasmic lamellae and the blue-green algae (Fritch); **Epi-pod′ium,** Bower's term for the apical part of the leaf; **epistat′ic** (στατικός, caused to stand), Bateson's term for Dominant (Hurst); cf. Hypo-static; **epiterra′nean** (terra, the earth), in amphicarpic plants the above-ground fruiting portion, as opposed to the subterranean, as in Sieglingia decumbens Bernh.; **Epi-xy′loneae** (ξύλον, wood), plants growing on timber, as lichens and fungi (Mirbel).

Equisete′tum, an association of Equi-setum Linn.; **equise′toid** (εἶδος, resemblance), hairs on stem and leaf of Botryopteris forensis Ren., recalling a miniature Equisetum; **Equiseto′sis,** poisoning from equi-setum as fodder (Pammel).

Erect′ Cells, cf. Cells, Erect.

Eremi′on (ἔρημος, desert), originally **Eremi′um;** a desert formation (Clements); **Ere′mophytes,** pl. (φυτόν, a plant), desert and steppe plants (Warming).

Ergol′ogy (λόγος, discourse), Delpino's equivalent for Biology.

erileuc′us (ἐρίλευκος, white on the surface), lustrous white (Balfour).

Erin′eum, pl. Erin′ea, *Phytoptus* mites producing galls on the surface of leaves, resembling fungi.

Eripleog′amy (ἔρις, strife, + PLEO-GAMY), Loew's term for flowers, one each with stamens and pistils, perfect, · ·so andromonoecious and gynomonœcious.

Ero′sion, waste by water in various forms; **progres′sive** ∼, deposits; retrogres′sive, removal (Cowles).

Er′rera's Law, " a cellular membrane at the moment of its formation, tends to assume the form which would be assumed, under the same conditions, by a liquid film destitute of weight."

ese′tulose (+ SETULOSE), destitute of bristles.

Esparte′tum, an association of esparto grass, *Stipa tenacissima* Linn.

Es′ters, pl. (invented by L. Gmelin), ethereal salts or compound ethers; many are fragrant and are used for artificial fruit essences; **Es′t′erases,** fat-splitting enzymes like LIPASES.

Etheogen′esis (ἔθος, custom, + GENESIS), parthenogenesis of a male individual (Prowasek).

Ethnobot′any, popular as folk-botany.

E′thomere (ἔθος, custom; μέρος a part), when the normal number of chromosomes are present (Della Valle).

-eto′sum, group name denoting the chief species of a subassociation, as "Cistelosum," concerning *Cistus* Linn.

Euaposp′ory (+ APOSPORY), no sexual act of fertilization; **Eubacter′ia** (+ BACTERIA), or **Haplobacteria,** true bacteria (Conn); **Euchro′mosome** (+ CHROMOSOME), an autosome; **Eucy′clic Type,** used of flowers which are diplostemonous or pentacyclic, as *Geranium* Linn. (Church); **Euge′ophytes** (+GEOPHYTES), their resting period due to want of warmth or light (Massart).

eugle′noid (εἶδος, resemblance), resembling the algae genus *Euglena* Ehrenb. (Minchin).

Eumyce′tes (μύκης, a mushroom), true fungi (Conn); **Eunu′cleus** (+ NUCLEUS), a nucleus containing red corpuscles (Auerbach); **Euphyl′lode** (+ PHYLLODE), the flattened primary axis of a bipinnate leaf, which has lost its pinnae (Fletcher).

eurycoe′nose (+ COENOSE), widely distributed, common (Gams); *cf.* STENOCOENOSE; **Eu′rycysts,** pl. Morin's term for POINTER CELLS, the DEUTER CELLS of Limpricht; *cf.* STENOCYSTS; **eurysynu′sic,** widely distributed groups of plants (Gams); *cf.* STENOSYNUSIC; ∼ **Spe′cies,** "due to constant and solid grouping" (Rübel); **euryther′mal,** applied to a species of wide distribution, able to withstand diverse temperatures (Setchell); the condition is **Euryther′my; eurytrop′ic,** wide adaptation of species of varied condition (Solms); *cf.* STENOTROPIC; **eusporang′iate,** for ferns possessing special sporangia and of primitive type (Bower); *cf.* LEPTOSPORANGIATE; **eutroph′ic,** applied to a swamp rich in nutrients (Clements).

Evaporim′eter, having the same use as an ATMOMETER.

Exclu′siveness, closeness of definition or fidelity to its characters of any species in question.

exobasid′ial (+ BASIDIAL), when a sporophore is without a secondary sporiferous branch (A. L. Smith); **exocort′ical,** belonging to the EXO-CORTEX; **Ex′oderm,** the vernacular equivalent of EXODERMIS; **exog′amous** = exogamic; **Exolith′ophytes** (+ LITHOPHYTES), mosses and lichens, from their seat of growth (Wetter); **Ex′ome,** secondary liber (Van Tieghem); **exoscop′ic** (σκοπέω, I see), Bower's term for the apical pole of an embryo when turned towards the neck of the archegonium, as in mosses, *cf.* ENDOSCOPIC; **Exothio-**

P

bacter′iaceae, *cf.* ECTOTHIOBACTERI-
ACEAE; **Expansiv′ity,** diruption, di-
vulsion (St. Pierre); **Exten′sion,**
final lengthening of the filament
of the stamen-filaments due to
water-press ire (Thompson); **Exu-
da′ses,** any exudations from tissues
(Priestley).

F₁, F₂, (1) hybrids of the first or
second generation; (2) Chauvaud's
terms for successive leaf-like organs.
F₀, pure parental type (Engledow).
Fac′tors, pl. elements which con-
tribute to produce a result; they
may be divided thus :—**biot′ic ∼,**
vital functions; **climat′ic ∼,**
depending on the temperatures;
edaph′ic ∼, depending on the
character of the soil; **geodynam′ic
∼,** the latent forces of the earth;
le′thal ∼, fatal or at least injurious;
physiograph′ic ∼, the earth's combined forces.
Fam′ile, for FAMILY (Clements).
Fat′uoid, a mutation from *Avena
sativa* Linn., resembling *A. fatua*
Linn. (Huskins).
fauc′ial (*fauces*, the throat), situated
in the throat or mouth of the
perianth (Herbert).
Fell-field, (1) **Al′pine ∼,** in the Euro-
pean mountains; (2) **Arc′tic ∼,**
round the North Pole.
Fertiliza′tion, Breech (Jeffrey), =
CHALAZOGAMY.
Fibonac′ci An′gle = 137·5° (Church).
Fi′bres, Cen′tral, *cf.* CENTRAL FIBRES;
Fibro′sis, exaggerated development
of the fibrous strands in *Iris*
Tourn. (Arber).
Fidel′ity, *cf.* EXCLUSIVENESS.
Fil′ament, *add,* (3) an entire univalent
spireme (Digby); *cf.* DISC-FILA-
MENTS.
Fis′sion, *add,* (2) longitudinal separa-
tion, (1) of the entire univalent
spireme into two threads, and (2)
that of a univalent chromosome into
two daughter-chromosomes (Digby).
Fis′tula, *add,* (2) **medul′lary ∼,** the
central cavity in the stem of
Equisetum Linn. (Jeffrey).

Fix′ity, the condition of little or
no response to stimuli (Clements).
Flagel′lar Pore, an aperture in the
cell-wall of Peridiniae, through
which the two flagella pass as they
leave the protoplast (West);
Flagel′lidae, flagellates in the strict
sense (Calkins); **Flagel′lispore** or
Flagel′lula, a swarm-spore provided with one or more flagella
(Minchin); **Flagello′sis,** an invasion
by flagellate organisms causing
disease; **Flagel′lulae,** *cf.* FLAGEL-
LATES (Church).
Flap, an old term for the pileus of an
agaric; **Flaps,** *see* CONNECTIVE
FLAPS.
Flask-cell, the stalk-cell of the
antheridium in Characeae.
Floccula′tion (*floccus,* a flock of wool),
the aggregation of precipitated
particles into large soft masses
remaining suspended in the medium
(Addams).
florist′ic, relating either to (1) flowers
or floral emblems, or (2) local
botany; *cf.* ∼ GEOBOTANY, ∼
PHYTOSOCIOLOGY; **Flos** ♂, Parlatore's term for anther in Coniferae.
Fluctua′tion (*fluctus,* a wave), change
due to direct effect of the environment during lifetime; opposed
to MUTATION, due to the presence
of specific factors in the organism
(Punnett).
Fo′liar Base, Bower's term in place
of Eichler's "Blattgrund"; ∼
Ray, *see* RAY, FOLIAR.
Fo′lioid, a hypothetical conception
of a leaf-like organ.
Forb (φορβή, fodder), herb (Clements).
Fore′dune [dissyll.], the surface of a
dune exposed to the prevalent wind
(Cockayne).
Fos′sula, *add,* (2) a space between
the ridges of an oospore of Charads;
sulcus.
fragariform′is (*fraga,* strawberries;
forma, shape), a fruit shaped like
a strawberry.
Frag′ment, portion of a chromosome;
Fragmenta′tion, *add,* (2) the con-

dition of breaking up before crossing over (R. T. Hance).

Fre'quency, the degree of common occurrence of a species; adj. **fre'quent.**

Frigorideser'ta, *add,* tundra.

Fron'dome, the abstract entity of a FROND, corresponding to the allied CAULOME and PHYLLOME (Vuillemin).

Fu'cin, a special substance in the cell-wall of *Fucus* Linn. (Czapek).

Ful'crum (Lat. bed-post), in lichens the SPOROPHORE (A. L. Smith).

Fun'goid, *add,* (2) phanerogamous parasites whose autotrophic mother-group is unknown, but distinguish themselves by their fungus-like habit (Johow).

Fu'ture Genera'tions, an expression employed by Buller to denote successive generations of BASIDIA.

Gallorubro'nes, pl. (*galla,* oak-apple; *rubor,* redness), red pigments from plant-galls (Mierenstein).

Game'tocyte (κύτος, a hollow vessel), a mother-cell of gametes (Minchin); **Gametogen'esis,** *add,* (2) restricted to mere fusion of gametes (West); **Gametogonid'ium** (+ GONIDIUM), the initial plastids of gametes in *Volvox* (Janet).

Gam'o-gem'mie (sic), the " intimate association of two or several floral rudiments " (Worsdell); **Gamog'ony** (γόνος, race) = SPOROGONY; **Gam'ont,** a gamete-producing form; *cf.* SPORONT; **Gamom'ery** (μέρος, part), when normally distinct petals are joined into a gamopetalous corolla (Engelmann).

ga'ping, ringent : **Gaps,** *add,* (2), branch ∼, fo'liar ∼, or leaf ∼, when openings exist in the siphonosteles to permit the passage of vascular tissue to form branch or leaf (Jeffrey).

gashed [monosyll.], lobed.

Gastre'a (γαστήρ, the belly), consists of a DEPEA with feeding area, surrounded by a sac with communi-

cation outside by a blastopore (Janet).

Gel, a solid formed from a jelly by heat or chemical reagents and irreversible by the addition of water (Addams); **gel'ate,** to become coagulated.

Gem'ini (Lat. twins), applied to pairs or bivalent chromosomes (Fisk).

Gemmipar'ity, used of leaves arising from adventitious buds (Penzig).

Genecol'ogy, ecology concerned chiefly with species; adj. **genecolog'ical; Genet'ic Coeffic'ient,** or dynamic behaviour, the part played by the species in the development of the community; *cf.* GEOBOTANY; **Genet'ics,** the study of heredity and variation (Bateson); **Genet'-icist,** a student of genetics.

Genera'tions, pl. *add,* (2) of basidia ranked as com'ing ∼, fu'ture ∼, past ∼, pres'ent ∼, according to their state of growth (Buller).

gen'ic, relating to genes; **Gen'ophene** (φαίνω, I appear), a reaction type of a genotype; **Genospe'cies** (+ SPECIES), embodies the facts of the genotypical construction of the ecospecies; (1) a homozygotic biotype (Raunkiaer); (2) a genotypical construction of a Linnean species (Turesson); **Gen'otype** (τύπος, a type), Mendelian sub-units of the genospecies, as the ecotypes are to the ecospecies, *i.e.* local species (Turesson); ∼ **Comp'ounds,** products of recombined Mendelian factors (Turesson); adj. **genotyp'ical.**

-gen'ous, Clements's suffix for " producing."

Gentiacau'line, a glucoside from *Gentiana acaulis* Linn.

Geobi'ont (βίος, life; ὄντα, things existing), an inhabitant of the soil, as an alga or moss, in a *wider* sense, all soil-nurtured plants; **Geobot'any** (βοτάνη, pasture, grass), phyto-geography; plant distribution (Grisebach); (1) divided by J. Pavillard into (*a*) ecolog'ic ∼,

(b) florist′ic ~, local botany; (c)
genet′ic ~, changes, and PHYTO-
SOCIOLOGY, q.v.; geodynam′ic
(δύναμις, power), the influence of
soils as agents; Geogen′esis (γένεσις,
origin), botanic origins; adj. geo-
genet′ic; geognost′ic (γνῶσις, wisdom), that knowledge of the structure of the earth informatory of
distribution; Geoph′ilae (φιλέω, I
love), algae growing on bare earth,
or mossy ground (Ivanoff); Ge′o-
sere (+ SERE), the total plant succession of the geological past
(Clements); Ge′osphere (σφαῖρα, a
globe), the earth itself as a whole
(Clements); Ge′ostrate (+STRATE),
the entire series of strates, subdivided as Ce′neostrate, the strate
corresponding to the Cainozoic or
Tertiary period in geology; the
Me′seostrate to Mesozoic ~ and
Pal′eostrate to Palaeozoic periods;
Geox′yl (ξύλον, wood), having a
woody stem, partly hypogeic,
partly epigeic; cf. Aeroxyl (Lindman); Ge′otome (τόμος, a cut), an
instrument to cut sods or soil
(Clements).

Germ′ules, pl. (germen, a germ), small
seeds or other means of distribution
(Clements).

Gi′antism, of gigantic size, giganticism.

gink′goid, like the genus Ginkgo Linn.;
Gink′gophyte (φυτόν, a plant), a
plant resembling the modern
Ginkgo (Wieland).

Gitonog′amy, an American form of
GEITONOGAMY.

gloeocar′pous, when the fruits are
immersed in mucus.

Glucostact′y (+ GLUCOSE, tactio,
touch), maize seedlings which
sweat a sugary fluid; glucose
(Eyster); adj. glucostact′ous.

glu′moid, glume-like.

Gneta′leans = Gnetaceae (Wieland);
gneta′lian, belonging to Gnetum
Linn. or Gnetaceae.

Gon′el (γονή, offspring), floral repro-
ductive apparatus subdivided into
AMPHIG′ONEL, ACROG′ONEL, and
ANTHOG′ONEL; Gon′elet, part of a

Gonel, built up of Gon′oclines, pl.,
units of Amphigonel receptacles
(Vuillemin).

Grada′tae (gradatus, furnished with
steps), definite succession in time
and space in the production of sori
in homosporous ferns; the dominant ferns of the present time
(Bower); gradate′, the intermediate
condition of a fern-sorus (Bower);
Grada′tion, the variation of a given
character along a given axis (Mac-
Leod); ~ Curve represents observed
values of a character (MacLeod).

-graph, suffix for " a recording instrument " (Clements).

Grass′veld, the predominant feature
of South African vegetation.

gregarin′iform applied to spores which
glide along (Minchin); Gregarin′-
ulae, the spores mentioned.

gregar′ious (gregarius, belonging to a
herd), applied in varying degrees
to the frequency of a species
(Clements).

Gubernac′ulum (Lat. a rudder), the
" trailer " of two flagella (Church).

Gym′neosere (+ SERE), a mesosere or
sere of prevalent gymnosperms
(Clements); gymnophyl′lous(φύλλον,
a leaf), having branchlets destitute
of cortex.

Gynan′dromorph (ἀνήρ, ἀνδρός, a man;
μορφή, shape), a female plant
assuming the appearance of a male
plant; gynecogen′ic (γένος, race),
parthenogenic (Janet); Gyneco-
l′ogy, ecology of species (Turesson);
Gynoe′cium, formed from γυνή and
οἶκος, which give the corrected
spelling [cf. Roeper in Linnaea, i.
(1826) 438 in textu]; Gynoe′cy, the
occurrence of purely female individuals in a plant (Uexküll); Gyno-
gonid′ium (+ GONIDIUM), Janet's
term for OOSPORE; Gy′noplasm
(πλάσμα, that formed), passive
protoplasm as in female gametes
(N. Jones); adj. gynoplas′mic;
Gynopleog′amy (+ PLEOGAMY), one
individual with pistillate flowers,
another with perfect flowers, and a
third gynomonoecious (Schutz);

Gyno-zoogonidi'um (+ Zoogonidium), female filaments derived
from zoogonidia in *Oedogonium*
Link (West).

Gyp'sophiles (*gypsum*, plaster of Paris),
plants loving chalk.

Gyrog'onites, pl. (γύρος, round; γόνος,
offspring; + ite), fossil fruits of
Chara Linn., at first taken to be
shells, " Gyroliths."

H +, see pH; **H-i'on** [hydrogen ion]
(ἴον, pt. of verb to go), a physical
term for acid-alkali equilibrium
(Duggar). H-ions are acid and
bear a positive electric charge;
pH-ions are basic, with a negative
electric charge; **H-pieces**, the
halves of neighbouring cells of
Tribonema Derb. et Sol.

Hab'itat-Com'plex, *cf.* Edaphic Formation; ~ **Types** formed from
parallel series of habitats (G. E.
Nichols).

Hairs: **Muc'ilage** ~, possessed by
certain algae; **sheathed** ~, of
Sphacelariaceae, the apical cell
dies and the cell below proliferates
through the cavity, leaving a basal
sheath (Church).

hal'arch (ἀρχή, origin), saline conditions prevailing in this succession.

Half-sta'men (+ Stamen), in *Cucumis* Linn., that stamen of the
three which has only one loculus
(Heimlich).

Hali'on, saline scrub climax (Clements);
Halone'reid (+ Nereid), marine
association of algae (Warming);
haloph'il'ic = halophilous; ~ **Bac-
ter'ia**, bacteria seated on marine
fishes; **Hal'osere** (+ Sere), a hydrosere with salt contents (Clements).

Hama'da, a stony desert.

Haplobacter'ia, true bacteria (Conn);
haplo-biot'ic, applied to certain
Red Algae, as *Scinaia* Bivona;
Haplochro'mosomes, single chromosomes, which combine into a pair
of myxochromosomes (Chodat);
hap'loid, *add*, (2) the result of a
single gamete such as the moss-
plant (Lotsy); **Haploi'dy** the state

in question; **Hap'lophyll** (φύλλον,
a leaf), the primitive universal leaf
as in *Tmesipteris* Bernh. and lycopods (Benson); **haplosteph'anous**
(στεφάνη, diadem), having a single
circle of stipulodes at the base of
each whorl of branchlets; **haplo-
stich'ous** (στιχός, rank), the cortex
with one row of cells to each
branchlet or bract-cell of Charads;
hap'teral, adj. from Hapteron.

Hard'pan, a hard substratum under
the cultivated soil, which requires
to be broken up for the penetration
of roots.

Har'tig Net, an intercellular growth
associated with a fungus mantle
on the roots of conifers (Frank).

Hat, an old term for Pileus.

Head-cells, (1) cells at the distal end
of the manubrium of Characeae,
bearing the filaments containing
the antherozoids; (2) cells on
exterior of node-cells of the stem-
cortex bearing spine-cells in certain
Charads.

Heleochare'tum, shortened from
Heleocharite'tum, an association
of *Heleocharis* R.Br.

Helichryse'tum, association of *Heli-
chrysum* Vaill.

Heli'on, changed from **Heli'um**,
swamp scrub climax (Clements).

heliotac'tic (*tactio*, touch), light per-
ceptivity.

hemerodiaph'orous (ἥμερος, cultivated;
διάφορος, different); varied under
cultivation (Linkola); **hemero-
ph'ilous** (φιλέω, I love), readily
cultivated (*id.*); **hemeropho'bous**
(φόβος, fear), hard to cultivate (*id.*).

Hemiang'iosperms, *cf.* Proangiosperms; **Hemibasidiomyce'tes** (+
Basidiomycetes) consist of the
Ustilaginales with an indefinite
number of basidiospores; **Hemi-
cryptophytosynu'sia**, life-forms such
as perennial plants with buds
on the level of the soil, but not
related to each other (Gams);
Hemicycada'les, plants akin to
Cycas, but more or less distinct,
bisexual (Wieland); **Hemihetero-**

thall'ism, semi-dioecism; **Hemi-homothal'lism,** semi-monoecism; **hemitrim'erous** (μέρος, a part), applied to seedlings with a whorl of three cotyledons, but with a normal pair of primordial leaves (Harris); **hemitrop'ic,** half-inverted **hemizeu'xis** (+ ZEUXIS), half-yoking; **hemizy'gous** (ζυγός, a yoke), half-yoked (Frost).

hendec'aploid = hendek'asome, having eleven sets of chromosomes.

Hep'edochae (ἕπω, I follow; δοχή, succession), a secondary succession, a subsere (Clements).

Heptan'dra (ἀνήρ, ἀνδρός, a man), a monstrosity in *Digitalis* Linn., where three divisions of the corolla are transformed into stamens, making seven in all; **hept'aploid, hept'asome,** with seven sets of chromosomes; **heptasterigmat'ic** (στιγμή, a point), applied to basidia with seven sterigmata (Buller).

Herb'alism, herbs when used in magic or medicine (Church).

Hered'ity, *add,* (2), *cf.* MENDEL'S LAW.

hermaphrodit'ic = hermaphrodite.

Her'midin (ἑρμῆς, Hermes, the Latin *Mercurius*), a colourless extract from *Mercurialis* Linn., by oxygenation yielding a blue compound, CYANOHERMIDIN, and a yellow one, CHRYSOHERMIDIN (Haas and Hill).

Heterephaptom'enon (ἐφάπτομαι, grasped), Gams's life-form of more or less parasitic plants; **heterop'loid,** used of chromosomes varying in number, as of 21,.5 short, 6 medium, 1C long (De Mol); **Het'erism,** normal diversity; **Heterocaryo'sis** (κάρυον, a nut), when mycelium is formed from + and − elements containing two kinds of nuclei (Burgeff); adj. **heterocaryot'ic**; *cf.* HOMOCARYOSIS; **Heteroca'ry** is used for a strain of pure line from a single spore (Brierley); **Heterocatal'ysis** (+ CATALYSIS), chemical change without the agent itself suffering loss; *cf.* AUTOCATALYSIS; **Heterochro'mosomes pl.** (+ CHROMOSOMES), aberrant chromosomes, or allosomes;

Heterochro'my, colour differences between individuals of the same species (Lindman); **heterocle'ma** (κλῆμα, a shoot), heterophyllous; **Heterodist'yly,** with short stamens and long styles in the same plant (Errera); **Heterogame'tism** (+ GAMETE), having gametes of different functions, as male or female; **Heteroge'ophytes,** saprophytic or parasitic cryptogams (Gams): **Heterolyt'ic En'zymes,** the power of chemical change not restricted to one way (Armstrong); **heteromas'tigote** (μάστιξ, a whip), with one or more anterior flagella, and a trailing one behind (Minchin); **heteromerist'ic** (μέρος, part), where floral formulas differ, as in the same group of Rubiaceae, where corolla-lobes vary from four to ten (Riley); **Heterom'ery** is the condition; **heteromorph'ous** (μορφή, shape), differing in shape as sterile and fertile whorls in Charads may be unlike.

Heterophylle'tum, an association of *Potamogeton heterophyllus* Schreb.

Heteroplas'ia (πλαστός, moulded), abnormal tissues differing from normal, and cells also abnormal (Harshberger); adj. **heteroplas'tic**; **Het'eroplasm,** in single spore or pure-line strains, which may occur (Brierley); adj. **heteroplas'mic**; **het'eroploid,** other than diploid; **Heteroplo'idy** is the condition (De Mol); **Hetero'sis,** a shortened form of **Heterozygo'sis,** the diverse effects following a cross between heterozygous elements; **Heterostyl'ism,** *add,* (2) used by Darwin to replace HETEROMORPHISM; **Heterosty'ly** is a synonym; **Heterothal'lism** (θαλλός, young twig), dioecism; adj. **heterothal'lic**; **heterotop'ic** (τόπος, a place), changing locality (Dahl); **Heterotri'styly,** having styles of three lengths, as long, short, and medium; **heterozygot'ic,** referring to plants derived from heterozygotes.

hex'aploid, used of a nucleus due to

the fusion of six times the normal haploid number of chromosomes; **hexaso'mic** = hexaploid; **hexasterigmat'ic**, basidia having six sterigmata (Buller).

Hiemefrutice'ta, scrub which sheds its leaves in dry seasons.

Hiera'ciarch (αρχός, chief), an expert in the genus *Hieracium* Journ.; **Hieraciol'ogy** (λόγος, discourse), the special study of the same genus.

high'er, Hurst's term in place of "dominant."

Hippophaë'tum, an association of *Hippophaë* Linn.

Hippuride'tum, a similar one of *Hippuris* Linn.

Hofpor'en, of *Sphagnum*, cell-membranes within the thickened ring round the pore (Warnstorf).

Holobi'ont (βίος, life; όντα, existing things) = holophyte; **holodactylous** (+ DACTYL), ultimate rays of a Charad each of a single cell; **holog'amous**, *adj.* of HOLOG'AMY; **Hologen'esis** (γένεσις, beginning), theory of descent by species developing and then dividing, the mother species disappearing (Rosa); **holopetalar'ious**, defined under OLOPETALARIOUS; **Ho'lophyte** (φυτόν, a plant), growth maintained by its own organs, neither a saprophyte nor a parasite; *adj.* holophyt'ic; **holozo'ic** (ζῷον, an animal), feeding as an animal (West).

Hometerost'yly, shortened from HOMOHETEROSTYLY; **Homobi'um** (βίος, life), an interdependent association of alga and fungus (A. L. Smith); **Homocaryo'sis** (κάρυον, a nut), when mycelium is of + or − nuclei only; unisexual (Burgeff); **homoeophyl'lous** (φύλλον, a leaf), having only one form of branchlet; **homoemorph'ous**, sterile and fertile whorls in Charads similar; **Homog'eny** (γένος, race), inheritance of a common part; *adj.* homogen'ic, homogenet'ic; homol'ogous, *cf.* TRANSFORMATION THEORY (Bower); ~ **Varia'tion**, parallel variations; similar variations in allied species

(Vavilov); **Homolytic En'zymes**, the chemical action confined to one way (Armstrong); **homomer'ic** (μέρος, a part), having the same number of parts; **Homom'ery** is the condition; a gene singly can produce as much as many genes in POLYMERY (Lang); **homomerist'ic**, where subordinate groups have the same floral formula (Riley); **homomor'phic**, *adj.* of HOMOMORPHY; **Homoplas'ia** (πλαστός, formed), abnormal tissue formed by increase of the normal elements (Harshberger); *adj.* homoplast'ic; **homothal'lic** (θαλλός, young twig), monoecious; **Homothal'lism**, monoecism; **Homoty'py** (τύπος, mark), development of a structure or organ in the place where another normally originates; **Homozygos'ity**, plants derived from the same group; *adj.* homozygot'ic, (1) plants originally from the same strain, (2) of pure line (Turesson).

Hor'mocysts (όρμος, a chain; κύστις, a cavity), short hormogonia enclosed in thick sheaths (Borzi); **Hor'mon**, used by A. H. Church for "anchored somata" in the sea, without absorptive roots; **Hor'mones**, enzymes serving as digestive agents; **hormoph'orous** (φορέω, I bear), necklaced (Balfour); **Hormoph'orus**, anchorage (Church).

Huk'win, a white ring in the corolla of *Ipomoea hederacea* Jacq., in Japan (Miyazawa).

Hull, the outer shell of grain; **hulled** [monosyll.], deprived of husks; **hull'less**, without husks; **Hull'lessness**, of *Avena nuda* Linn. (Love).

Humusnec'ron (νεκρός, dead), decayed vegetable matter, as leaves (Sernander).

hunched, old word for GIBBOUS.

Hybridog'amy (γάμος, marriage), fertilization between various species.

Hy'drarch (ἀρχή, beginning), a succession arising in a moist area (Cooper); HYDROSERE (Clements);

443

Hydri'on (+ Ion), hydrogen-ion concentration (Herklots); **Hydrocleistog'amy,** cleistogamous flowers pollinated by submersion; **Hydrocrypt'ophytes,** pl. vegetative parts permanently in water (Gams).

Hydrochare'tum, an association of *Hydrocharis* Linn. (Gadeceau).

hy'droid (εἶδος, resemblance), used by Clements for watery; ~ **Ar'eas,** of algae climaxes in pre-Devonian times (*id.*); **Hydromorpho'sis,** *add,* (2) change due to watery situation (Massart).

Hydronarde'tum, an association of *Nardus stricta* Linn.

hydroperm'eable (*permeabilis,* that may be passed through), parts of roots specialized for water absorption (S. Baker); **Hy'drose,** the internal moisture of tissues (Devaux); **Hy'drosere** (+ Sere), succession in a wet habitat to a climax (Clements); **hydrospher'ic** (σφαῖρα, a globe), the agency of water in migration (Adams); **Hydrospor'ae,** pl. (σπορά, a seed), plants whose seeds are distributed by water (Clements); **hydrotrop'ic** (τροπή, a turn), changing to a greater water-content of a succession (*id.*); **hydrostat'ic** (στάσις, a standing), a succession less prone to change towards greater moisture (*id.*); **Hydrox'yl I'ons** (ὀξύς, sharp, + Ion) water-ions negatively charged with electricity; OH-; opposed to hydrogen-ions.

Hygrodry'mium (δρυμός, a wood), rain-forest (Diels); **Hygrophor'bium** (φορβή, pasture), moist pasture or fen-lands (*id.*); **Hygropoi'um** (πόα, grass), evergreen meadows (*id.*); **Hygrosphag'nium,** high moor, *cf.* Sphagniopratum.

Hyli'on, originally **Hyli'um,** forest climax (Clements); **hyloc'ola,** forest dwelling; **Hy'lophyte** (φυτόν, a plant), a dry woodland plant; *cf.* Hylodophyte.

hymenomyce'te, fructification resembling that of Hymenomycetes (Rayner).

Hyperchro'masy (χρῶμα, colour), an increase of the nuclear substance relatively to the cytoplasm (Minchin); **Hyperplas'ia** (πλαστός, formed), an abortive quantitative increase produced by cell-division (Virchow); **hyperton'ic** (τόνος, strain), having a greater osmotic concentration than the cell-sap (Stiles); **Hyper'trophy** (τροφή, food), abnormal growth with voluminous callus (Harshberger).

Hy'poderm, *add,* (2) Kraus's term for the outer cortex immediately below the epidermis, as in *Begonia* Linn. and fossil plants; **hypog'ynous,** *add,* (2) when the antheridia are below the oogonia, as in *Phytophthora* De Bary (Murphy); **Hy'ponym** (ὄνομα, a name), a generic name not supported by a type-specimen.

hypophae'us (ὑπόφαιος, somewhat grey), grey in tint.

Hypopod'ium, Bower's term for the basal part of the leaf.

Hy'postase, *add,* (2) tissue containing chromatic substance in the chalazal region (Ishikawo); **hypostat'ic,** Bateson's equivalent for recessive; lower, of Hurst; *cf.* Epistatic; **hypostom'atal** = hypostomatous; **hypoton'ic,** having a lower osmotic concentration than the cell-sap (Stiles); **hypotrip'loid** (+ Triploid), having fewer chromosomes than the triploid number (De Mol).

I₁. Symbol for parent of self-fertile plant, amidst incompatibles (Heribert Nilsson); his $I_2 = F_1,$ $I_3 = F_2,$ etc.

Idiobiol'ogy, proposed in place of Autobiology (Gams); pertaining to individual organism (Turesson); **Idiochorol'ogy,** for Autochorology, applied to self-distribution of plants as distinct and separate units (Gams); **Idiochro'matin** (+ Chromatin), chromatin temporarily dormant (Minchin); **Idiochromid'ia,** pl., chromidia of a generative character; **Idiochro'mosomes** pl. (+

CHROMOSOME), used by Church for a pair of x and y chromosomes; cf. HETEROCHROMOSOMES; **Idioecol'ogy** (Schroeter), cf. AUTOECOLOGY; **Id'iopher** ($\phi o \rho \epsilon \omega$, I hear), Siemens's term for GENE.

-i'es, proposed to denote CONSOCIES, as "Scirpies" (Clements).

-i'le, locative suffix for SOCIETAS (id.).

imbibit'ional, cf. IMBIBITION.

immune' (*immunis*, exempt), power of an organism to resist invasion by a microscopic parasite (Conn).

Imp'otence (*impotentia*, inability), sterile, including floral abortion and arrested development (Stout).

impu'bes (Lat. *immature*), not mature.

Incept', *add*, **oogo'nial** ~, an early stage of the oogonium (Pethybridge); cf. MANOCYST.

inchoate' (*inchoatus*, unfinished), not complete.

Incip'ient Nu'cleus, formerly termed "Central Body," "an achromatic ground substance occupying the alveoli of a reticulum in which are located minute granules" (West).

incompat'ible, Stout's term for sterile; **Incompatibil'ity**, the condition mentioned; **anatom'ical** ~, due to structural differences, as hercogamy; **cross** ~, hybridism barred; **physiolog'ical** ~, due to some functional disability; **self** ~, self-sterile.

Indica'tor (Lat. one that points out), (1) a colour-test for pH or hydrogen-ion test; (2) Clements's term for climax and successional communities as showing " factors, processes and practice "; cf. PLANT INDICATORS; (3) plants which show no condition of the soil (Tansley and Chipp).

Indumen'tum, *add*, (2) **bi'strate** ~, of two layers, the outer layer, caducous; **u'nistrate** ~, of one layer, persistent (I. B. Balfour).

Inhib'itor (*inhibitus*, curbed), cf. LOEB EFFECT.

Initia'tion (*initiatio*, admission to rites), the early stages of staminal

growth, succeeded by the later EXTENSION (Thompson).

in'ner, *add*, (2) the morphologic upper surface of a *Sphagnum* leaf (Horrell).

Inoc'ulum (*inoculo*, I graft), spores employed for infection.

inor'dinate (*inordinatus*, irregular), when spores in an ascus show no regular arrangement.

interc'alary, *add*, ~ **Bands**, in diatoms; ~ **Plates**, either anterior or posterior in Peridineae; ~ **Valves**, in diatoms those with bands having longitudinal septa (West); **interchromoso'mal** (+ CHROMOSOME), between the chromosomes (De Vries); **Int'erphase** ($\phi \acute{a} \sigma \iota \varsigma$, an appearance) = INTERKINESIS (Wilson); **interplast'idic**, between the plastids and uniting them (Janet); **Interpola'tion The'ory**, suggested in place of ANTITHETIC; **Intersex'es**, individuals which display more of a male or female type than is normal; also styled SUPERSEXES and POLYGAMOUS; **Intersex'ualism**, in plants showing alternative development of either sex-organs (Stout); **Interspecif'ic Hy'brids**, between two given species in characters; **intraclo'nal** (+CLONE), within the limits of bud-variation; **in'tra-fer'tile**, two species fertile between themselves; **in'tra-ster'ile**, two species barren between themselves.

in'tus (Lat. within), the modern term EXTUS is based on this.

intyba'ceous, akin to or part of *Cichorium Intybaceum* Linn.

Inva'sion, *add*, Clements defines eight variations of this.

invi'able (+ VIABLE), short-lived (H. J. Müller).

-i'on, *add*, (2) the lower group to one of the principal associations.

-is, suffix for ASSOCIES.

isochi'menal ($\chi \epsilon \hat{\iota} \mu a$, winter weather), applied to lines of winter temperatures; isothermal, is the more generally used term; **Isoc'ies**, synusia showing resemblances, but of various affinities (Gams); habitat-groups (Pound and Clements);

P*

Isocoeno′sium, pl. **-ia,** an association composed of Isocies; **Isoc′ryma** (κρυμός, frost), winter isotherm (Setchell); **Isoelec′tric Point** (ἤλεκτρον, amber), the point of absolute neutrality as regards hydrogen-ion concentration; **Isohy′et** (ὑετός, heavy rain), term for rainfall in climatic observation on plants; lines of equal rainfall; **Isoho′lotype** (+ HOLOTYPE), specimen taken in after years from the type bush or tree (Wilmott); **i′sokont** (κοντός, a pole), both flagella equal (Church); **Isolateral′ity** (+ LATERALITY), having both sides exposed to light; **Isolect′otype** (+LECTOTYPE), specimen taken from a chosen type long after publication (Wilmott); **Isomast′igote** (μάστιξ, μάστιγος, a whip), having two or four flagella of equal length; **isomeris′tic** (μέρος, a part), agreeing in number of parts; **Isom′ery** is the state; **Isophene′** (φαίνω, I show), applied to districts of equivalent phenologic date with their area; **I′sopore,** add, (2) a swarm spore or gamete; **isosmo′tic** (+ OSMOTIC), having the same osmotic pressure (Stiles); **isost′ichous** (στικός, a row), when the rows in the stem-cortex of *Chara* are equal; **isosty′led** (στῦλος, a column), equal styled (Errera); **isoton′ic,** having the same osmotic concentration as the cell-sap (Stiles).

-ite, -ites (-ίτης, belonging to), suffixes denoting like or nature of, used in forming names of fossil plants and animals.

it′erative (*iteratio*, a repeating), repeating when applied to crosses (B. M. Davies); **-itis,** inflammation.

Jacket-cells, cells surrounding the nucellus in *Thuya* Linn. (Land).

Jor′danon (Jordan, ὄντα, things existing), " a form which breeds true to type but may not be termed a species " (Lotsy); Alexis Jordan (1814–97) published many microspecies; *cf.* LINNEANON.

Junce′tum, an association of *Juncus*, Linn.

Junipere′tum, a similar group of Junipers.

Kalahar′i Re′gion, in South Africa between the Orange River and Bechuanaland (Bews).

kar′roid, Karroo-like (Schönland); **Kar′roo,** a region in South Africa, dry and continental in character (Bews).

Karyomer′ites, *cf.* CARYOMERITES.

Kat′ion, *cf.* CATHION.

Khor, a waste of stony desert.

Kin′ase, a complex organic body which incites to enzymic energy.

Knobs, add, (2) the tubers of terrestrial orchids (J. E. Smith).

Label′lum-pel′ory, when an orchidflower becomes symmetrical (Worsdell).

Lag Phase, the initial phase in the growth of the yeast plant.

Lamel′lae, add, (2) layers of membrane in the oospore of Charads.

lancea′te, somewhat lanceolate, but wider at the base than at the middle.

Larice′tum, an association of *Larix*, Tourn.

La′tent Per′iod, the time between the incidence of stimulus and the beginning of the responsive movement (Bose).

Lat′eral Ar′ea, a smooth place in a diatom valve, sometimes parallel to the axis, but nearer the margin (West).

Lat′erites (*later*, a brick), tropical argillaceous soils, under a heavy rainfall of at least 50 inches annually (Tansley and Chipp).

Lat′tices, abortive and lateral sieveplates in Angiosperms (Jeffrey).

Laurifrutice′ta, thickets with predominance of evergreens (Rübel).

Lay′er Soci′eties, growths in layers, as of standards with bushes lower down, and herbs beneath all; ~ **Trans′ect,** *cf.* BISECT; **Lay′ering,** add, (2) R. C. Rose's term for sowing on a large scale(!) ; this is opposed to the accepted meaning of the word.

leached [monosyll.], soil washed of its plant-nutriment.

Leaf, Branch, of *Sphagnum*, *cf.* BRANCH-LEAF ; ~ **Gaps,** *cf.* FOLIAR GAPS ; **Up'per** ~, Bower's equivalent for Eichler's " Oberblatt."

Leaf-skin Theory ; the superficial layers of the shoot formed by downward growth of leaf rudiments (Saunders).

Lec'ithin, see under LIPINS.

leimic'olous (λειμών, a meadow), inhabiting moist grass-land.

leiotrop'ic (λεῖος, smooth ; τροπή, turning), the direction of spiral cleavages.

Lemne'tum, an association of *Lemna* Linn.

len'diger *(lens, lentis,* a nit), applied to such inflorescences as of *Gastridium lendigerum* Gaud.

lenit'ic *(lenis,* smooth), used of " still-water societies " (Needham and Lloyd).

lepidoden'drid, Jeffrey's variant for LEPIDODENDROID fossils.

Lep'idophyte (λεπίς, λεπίδος, a scale ; φυτόν, a plant), occasionally used to denote a petrified fossil plant.

Lep'idotes (λεπίς, a scale), scale-like structures on the shoots of *Tillandsia* Linn. ; **Lepid'ium,** employed by Parlatore for the ovuliferous lamina in Coniferae.

leptocle'ma (κλῆμα, a twig), slender branched ; **Lep'tophyll** (φύλλον, a leaf), Raunkiaer's term for his smallest leaf catalogued.

Leptomia'sis, a flagellate disease chiefly attacking Euphorbiaceae.

Lep'to-zygcne'ma (+ ZYGONEMA), the transition of the meiotic nucleus between the leptonene and zygotene stages by parallel fusion of thin threads.

Lep'to-zygo'tene (+ ZYGOTENE), applied to a nucleus containing a ZYGONEMA.

le'thal, *add,* (2) **Fac'tor,** applied to a mutation ending fatally ; ~

Gam'ete, ~ **Zy'gote,** each being fatal to a normal blend.

Leucoder'mis, a " variegated periclinal chimaera," with white markings through the green epidermis of *Arabis* Linn., and *Aubrietia* Adans. (Correns) ; **Leuc'osin,** a substance in algae of unknown composition, the result of photosynthesis (Fritch).

Licop'oli Glands = CHALK-GLANDS.

Life-forms, living forms of the present day (Clements).

Lig'ule, *add* to (6), sealing growth in cones between the angles of the primary scales in *Dammara* Lam. (Church).

Lime-cell, a hard shell round the oospore, due to a secretion of lime in the spirals of the oogonium in Charads.

limnic'olous (λίμνη, a pool), lake-dwelling ; **Lim'naen,** submersed plants forming associations (Rübel). **Limni'um,** submersed wet meadows (Diels).

Li'mosphere (λιμός, famine ; σφαῖρα, a globe), a hollow sphere enclosing a vacuole in the spermatid of a bryophyte (Farmer).

Limosequise'tum, an association of *Equisetum limosum* Linn.

lind'sayoid, like *Lindsaya* Dryand. (Bower).

Link'age, a later term for COUPLING ; **linked'** characters are found in cross-breeding ; the tendency of factors to stay together, opposed to crossing over (Lotsy).

Linne'on (Linné ; ὄντα, things existing), " the group of individuals which resemble one another more than they do any others " (Lotsy) ; a Linnean, or superspecies.

lipal'ian (λείπα, left ; ἅλς, the sea), an era of marine deposit, when pelagic life was adapted to littoral conditions, and the appearance of the species of the Lower Cambrian formation (Walcott).

Lip'ins, fatty acids in combination, divisible into (*a*) **Creb'rosides,** with nitrogen and sugar, and (*b*) **Phos'-**

447

phatides, with phosphorus and nitrogen; Lec′ithin is one of the three known (Priestley).

Liriog′amae (λείριον, the white lily; γάμος, marriage), monocotyledons with a perianth never glumaceous.

Lith′arch (ἀρχή, beginning), a succession or adsere on hard rock (Clements); **Lith′ophyte** (φυτόν, a plant), plants growing on rock or stones; adj. **lithophyt′ic; Lith′osere** (+ SERE), a rocky ADSERE (Clements); beginning on bare rock (Tansley and Chipp); **lithospher′ic** (σφαῖρα, a globe), earth or rock agency in migration (C. C. Adams).

Littorelle′tum, an association of *Littorella* Berg.

Local′ity, *add,* (2) the ground occupied by an individual association (Waterman).

Loc′ule for **Loc′ulus, Loc′uli spu′rii** are certain cavities in the seeds of *Bertholletia* Humb. et Bonpl., the brazil-nut of commerce.

"Lo′cus" Change, restricted to one of a pair of chromosomes, without affecting its allelomorphic mate; the change first appears in the heterozygous condition.

Loeb Effect′, the action of an inhibitor, probably a single active substance in early bud, before the later growth.

Logarith′mic Phase, the second stage in the growth of the yeast plant.

Loiseleurie′tum, an association of *Loiseleuria procumbens* Desv.

Long shoot = LEADER; **long-styled,** when the styles exceed the stamens in length; *cf.* SHORT-STYLED.

lopped′ [monosyll.], old term for truncate.

lorantha′ceous, akin to or resembling Loranthaceae.

lo′tic (*lotus,* washed), used of associations in rapidly flowing streams (Needham and Lloyd).

low′er, suggested by Hurst to supersede Bateson's "hypostatic," as a substitute for "recessive."

Luzule′tum, an association of *Luzula* DC.

Lychne′tum, abbreviation for **Lychnide′tum,** an association of *Lychnis* Linn.

lycopodin′eous, relating to *Lycopodium* Linn. (Jeffrey).

Mac′chia (Ital.), shrubby growth, mainly evergreen, in Mediterranean regions.

macran′drous, *add,* (2) used of antheridia developed in male filaments of *Oedogonium* Link, nearly as large as the filaments themselves (West); **macrobioste′monous, -ic,** (βίος, life; στήμων, a thread), having persistent stamens (Delpino); **macrocle′ma** (κλῆμα, a twig), with long branchlets; **macrodac′tylous,** the ultimate rays of *Nitella* Ag., long; **Macrog′amy** (γάμος, marriage) = HOLOGAMY; **Macronu′cleus** (+ NUCLEUS), in diatoms the nucleus as commonly received (West); **Macrophan′erophytes** (+ PHANEROPHYTES), trees; **Mac′rophyll** (φύλλον, a leaf), Raunkiaer's term for a long leaf, but less than a megaphyll; **Macrophytoplank′ton,** floating Angiosperms, large algae, etc.; **macropt′ilus** (πτίλον, a feather), longibracteate; **Macropycnid′ia** (+ PYCNIDIA), large conidiospores in pycnidia; **Macropyc′nospores,** the long spores of certain fungi; **Mac′roscope** (σκοπέω, I see), a hand microscope, magnifying about 10 diameters, for field-work.

Magmaph′ilae, pl. (φιλέω, I love), algae which prefer warm and well lit waters, forming a coloured mixture (Ivanoff).

Mag′nigrade (*gradus,* a step), applied to a large variation, as ∼ **Transil′ient,** or ∼ **Salta′tion;** ∼ **Evolution** = discontinuous; *cf.* PARVIGRADE; **Magnocarice′tum,** an association of large species of *Carex* Linn.

mala′ceous (μαλακός, delicate), used

by Thurston when referring to
Rosaceae, etc.

man'ifest (*manifestus*, palpable),
anthers visible at the mouth of the
corolla-tube, but neither inserted
nor exserted.

Man'ocyst (μανός, rare; κύστις,
pouch), the receptive papilla protruding from the oogonium of
Phytophthora De Bary (Murphy);
manoxyl'ic (ξύλον, wood), the
cycadean type of wood (Seward);
cf. PYCNOXLIC.

Mantle, Trache'ary, of *Stephano-
spermum* Brongn. in the wall of
the nucellus ending in the pollen-
chamber (Jeffrey).

Maqui' (Fr.), *cf.* MACCHIA.

mastigoclad'ous (κλάδος, a branch),
flagellate, having runners (Russow).

Mates, synap'tic, leptotene-threads
(Hurst).

matroclin'ic, -ous (κλίνη, a bed), in
hybrids, a quality derived from
the ovular or female parent; *cf.*
PATROCLINIC; **Mat'rocliny** is the
condition.

Mat'tae, pl. (Mod. Lat.), mats or
plants which form matted growths
(Clements).

matteuc'coid, like the fern genus
Matteuccia Todaro (Bower).

me'dian, *add,* ~ **anter'ior,** in phyllotaxis, the first sepal; ~ **poster'ior,**
the second sepal in the quincuncial
calyx (Church).

Medul'lary Fis'tula, *cf.* FISTULA,
MEDULLARY.

Megalophyl'la (φύλλον, a leaf), leaves of
extreme size; **Megalophyl'ly,** bipin-
nation of fern frond (Church); **Meg'-
aphyll** (1) Raunkiaer's term for
his largest leaves; (2) Benson's
MEIOPHYLL and MERIPHYLL taken
together; adj. **megaphyl'lous;
Megaplank'ton** (+ PLANKTON); *cf.*
PLEUSTON; **Meg'aphytes** (φυτόν,
a plant), spermophytes; **Mega-
soro'ma** (σώρευμα, a heap), the
sporangial apparatus of the vascular plant, with its receptacle
or stalk (Benson); **Megaspor'ophyll**
(+ SPOROPHYLL), the female cone

of cycads; **Megastrob'ilus** (+
STROBILUS), the female flower and
cone of *Cycas* Linn. and its allies;
Meg'atherms (θέρμη, heat), plants
which need high temperature for
active growth; **Megazo'id** (ζῷον,
an animal), a female gamete of
algae (Sauvageau).

Meiocyc'lic (κύκλος, a circle), "an
isostemonous bicarpellate construction, tetracyclic or more conveni-
ently mesocyclic" (Church) = a
smaller circle; **Meio'phyll** (φύλλον,
a leaf), a simply elaborated leaf,
as in *Pseudobornia* Nath. (Benson);
Mei'ospore [or **Me'ospore**] (+
SPORE), the product of a MEIO-
SPORANGE; arising through an
ontogenetic reduction (Janet).

Me'matea, a misprint for NEMATEA.

Men'del, fifty units distance of gene
from chromosome, a measure of
length equivalent to fifty per cent.
of crossing over (D. F. Jones),
name derived from Grigor Mendel.

Menyanthe'tum, an association of
Menyanthes Linn.

Mer'id (μερίς, μερίδος, a part), an assemblage of plastids formed by successive divisions from one original; it
may be solitary or colonial (Janet);
Mer'iphyll (φύλλον, a leaf), "the
complex meriphytic leaf of the ferns,
leading to Angiosperms" (Benson);
meriphyt'ic, divided, as many plants
are; **Mer'ism,** a primordial assemblage of cells (Janet).

merogon'ically (μέρος, a part; γόνος,
race), monopolizing the sexual
portion; **Merog'ony,** the condition
itself.

Mesench'ym (ἐγχέω, I pour in), tissue
which separates xylem and phloem
elements in root-bundles (Clements);
Mes'eosere (+ SERE), a mesophytic
eosere; it corresponds to the Eozoic
Period of geology; also termed
GYMNEOSERE (*id.*); **Mes'eostrate** (+
STRATE), a mesophytic eostrate
(*id.*); **Mes'ocline,** a moist, cool,
slope (*id.*); **Mesomito'sis** (+ MI-
TOSIS), mitosis within the nuclear
membrane, without co-operation

of cytoplasmic elements (Chatton);
Mesophor'bium, pl. -ia, evergreen
meadows (Diels); **Mesophyl'lum**,
add, (3) Raunkiaer's term for a
medium-sized leaf; **mesophyt'ic**,
add, (2) relating to the vegetation
era of the Mesozoic Age (Clements);
Mesopod'ium (πούς, ποδός, a foot),
the petiole of a leaf (Bower); **Meso-
po'ium** (πόα, grass), Diels's term for
steppe; **Mesotham'nium**, partly
LAURIFRUTICETA and partly DURI-
FRUTICETA (Diels); **Mes'otherms**
(θερμός, heat), plants which need
temperate conditions of heat for
active growth; **mesotrop'ic** (τροπή,
a turning), a medium succession
changed from xerotropic to hydro-
tropic (Clements); **mesostat'ic**, a
medium succession due to water-
content (*id.*); **mesotroph'ic**, used of
a swamp moderately provided with
nutrients (*id.*).
Metabi'ont (+ BIONT), a polyplastid,
a many-celled individual (Janet);
metachromat'ic (+ CHROMATIC)
gran'ules, bodies in bacteria which
take a deep stain (Conn);
metachromatin'ic (Minchin) is a
synonym; **Metachro'my**, changing
or losing colour in the same flower,
usually from age; **metaclin'ic**,
a reversed cross in hybridizing;
Metacli'ny is the state; **meta-
genet'ic** (+ GENETIC), truly alternate in generations (McNab);
Metagymnosper'mae, pl., Coniferae
fertilized by means of pollen-tubes
(Jeffrey); **Metamito'sis**, mitosis
of an advanced type in which both
cytoplasmic and nuclear elements
take part (Minchin); **Met'anym**
(ὄνομα, a name), an older, valid
name, based on another member
of the same group; **Met'aphyte**
(φυτόν, a plant), a many-celled—
polyplastid—individual (Janet);
Met'aplast, -ia, tissue which has
taken on a changed appearance
due to upward or downward metabolism; **metaplast'ic** is an adjec-
tival form; **Metasyn'desis** (+
SYNDESIS), reduction in which

chromosomes are united end to
end (Agar).
-me'ter, "suffix for instrument"
(Clements).
Methodol'ogy (μέθοδος, system; λόγος,
discourse), the science of arrangement.
microclad'ous (κλάδος, a branch),
having small branches; **micro-
cle'ma** (κλῆμα, a twig), with small
branchlets; **Mi'crocyst** (κύστις, a
cavity), an encysted form of a
MYXOFLAGELLATE; **Mi'crocyte**(κύτος,
a hollow vessel), a detached chromosome (Belling and Blakeslee);
Mi'croform, *add*, (2) used by I. B.
Balfour, for an elementary or
Jordanian species; **Microg'amy**
(γάμος, marriage), cf. MEROGAMY;
Mi'crogene (+ GENE), a form of
micro-species or variety; **Mi'cro-
morph** (μορφή, a form), also employed to describe a species of low
grade; **Micronu'cleus** (+ NU-
CLEUS), the centrosome of diatoms
(Lauterborn); **Mi'crophyll** (φύλλον,
a leaf), a small leaf, as defined by
Raunkiaer; **micropt'ilus**, brevi-
bracteate; **Micropycnid'ia** (+
PYCNIDIA), receptacles containing
small conidiospores; **Micropyc'no-
spores**, the spores borne on micro-
pycnidia; **Microsoro'ma** (+ So-
ROMA), the pollen-bearing apparatus
(Benson); **Microstrob'ilus** (+
STROBILUS), a small cone in cycads;
in all genera aggregated into cones
which resemble those producing
seed; **Mi'crotherms** (θερμός, heat),
plants capable of growth at low
temperatures; **Microzo'id** (ζῷον,
an animal), a male gamete in algae
(Sauvageau); **Microzy'ma** (ζύμη,
leaven), small bodies considered
by Galippe the living part of protoplasm; **Microzy'me**, a substance
found in tissues strongly antagonistic to, and destructive of, bacteria
(A. Fleming).
Mi'grarc (*migratio*, migration; *arcus*,
a bow), Clements's term for migration circle; **Mi'grules**, units of
migration (*id.*).

mimosa′ceous, resembling or akin to *Mimosa* Linn.

Min′imal Ar′eas, the tendency for an organism to be compressed into the least bulk (Berthold).

Mitochon′drium, a chondriosome; now reserved for smaller structures which do not form plastids; **Mitoplast′**, a band appressed to the nuclear membrane of *Selaginella* Spring, which divides just before cell-division; successive divisions of this band give rise to several chloroplasts (Dangeard).

Mixochro′mosome (+Chromosome), a hypothetical complete fusion of synaptic mates to form a new chromosome; **mixotroph′ic**, fed by holophytic and saprophytic nutrition (Minchin).

Mode Spores, due to **Mo′dal Varia′tion**, variation in size and shape due to the substratum on which the fungus is growing (Brierley).

Molinie′tum, an association of *Molinia* Schrank.

monarthrodacty′lous (ἄρθρον, a joint, + Dactyl), with the ultimate branches of a single cell in *Nitella* Ag.; **monochromoso′mic** (+ Chromosome), an idiomere having only one chromosome (Chodat); **monoclin′ic** (κλίνη, a bed), having one oblique intersection, applied to crystals; **monoclo′nal** (κλών, a little branch), succession derived asexually from a common ancestor, a single Clone (Agar); **monofa′cial** (+ facial), a leaf equitant as that of *Iris* (Archer); **Monogen′esis**, *add*, (2) origin of a new form at a single place or time (Clements); **Monocotyle′dony**, the state of possessing a single cotyledon (Jeffrey); **Monokar′yon**, a nucleus with a single centriole, a centrosome (Minchin); **mon′okont** (κοντός, a pole), having a single flagellum (Church); **Monole′psis**, *add*, maternal or paternal; **monomas′tigote** = monokont; **Monophyle′sis** (φυλή, a clan), origin from a single ancestral type (Clements); **mon′o-**

some = haploid; **monomer′ic**, *cf.* monomerous; **monosp′orous**, having only one spore; **monosterigmat′ic**, with a single sterigma, applied to fungi (Buller); **monotrich′ic**, *cf.* monotrichous; **Monotype**, a genus having but one species; **monozy′gous** (ζυγός, a yoke), used by Frost for linked.

Mon′te Forma′tion, bush-land of thorny growth (Lorentz).

morchel′loid, resembling *Morchella* Linn., as regards the hymenium.

Mor′ea (μόρον, the black mulberry), a hypothetic and non-existent stage of *Volvox*, as a **Mor′ula** (Janet).

Mor′es, pl. of **Mos** (Lat. custom), groups of organisms agreeing in habit, reproduction and reaction; Consocies are groups of Mores (Shelford).

Mor′gan, unit of distance in a chromosome; *cf.* Centimorgan, name derived from T. H. Morgan.

morphocytolog′ical, evidence drawn from systematic and genetic sources (Jeffrey).

Mosaic, *add*, (3) used by Church as a pattern characteristic of each species, e.g. leaf-mosaic; (4) ~ **Variabil′ity**, due to conditions within the habitat (Vestal).

Mother-of-Coal, charred wood found in coal (Jeffrey).

Mu′cilage, *add*, ~ **Ducts**, *cf.* Mucilage-canal; ~ **Glands**, secreting organs at the back of the leaf-sheaths and axils in Plumbagineae (Wilson and de Fraine); ~ **Hairs**, "trichome growths" in certain Phaeophyceaen algae (Church); **Mu′cus**, *add*, (2) used for the gelatinous envelope of the nucule in Characeae.

Mul′tiple Fac′tors, a series of similar factors which produce F, as 3 : 1, 15 : 1, 63 : 1 (1, 5, 21) (Nilsson-Ehle); **Mul′tiplets**, *cf.* Multiplex (Worsdell); **mul′tiploid**, occurring in even multiples; applied to genera differing in number of chromosomes; *cf.* dysploid, perissoploid (Jeffrey).

mun'dus (Lat.) neat, elegant.

Mu'tant, *add,* (2) a total suppression of all lateral buds, giving rise to an unbranched stem, the "disbudded ~." (Church); **Mu'tants,** may be **aequichromoso'mal** ~, with an exchange of chromosomes, or **plurichromoso'mal** ~, ~-ic, when one of the chromosome complexes takes one or more chromosomes of the other in the reduction divisions (Lotsy); **Muta'tion,** *add,* (1) a simultaneous and probably gradual change, in a majority or the whole of a species (Waagan); (2) used by De Vries = SALTATION, TRANSILIENT; (3), used by Bateson = BLASTOGEN, *i.e.* BLASTOGENIC VARIATIONS.

Mycocle'na (χλαῖνα, a cloak), the fungus-mantle in mycorrhiza (Peyronel); **Mycoc'riny** (κρίνω, I separate), humus reduction by fungi (Falck); **mycophyt'ic** (φυτόν, a plant), belonging to the **My'cophytes,** or fungi.

My'onemes (μῦς, muscle; νῆμα, a thread), contractile mechanism of ectoplasm of flagellates (Minchin).

Myricarie'tum, an association of *Myricaria germanica* Desv.

Myrice'tum, a similar group of *Myrica* Linn.

Myr'iomere (μέρος, a part), a transition from mitosis to amitosis (Della Valle); *cf.* PSEUDOMITOSIS.

Myriophylle'tum, an association of *Myriophyllum* Ponted.

Myrmecophy'tism, the condition of being ant-plants.

Myrtille'tum, an association of *Vaccinium Myrtillus* Linn. (Warming).

Myxamoe'bae (ἀμοιβή, change), uninucleate organisms passing into **Myxoflagel'lates,** having developed flagella.

Myxophy'cin, a form of carotin occurring in Myxophyceae (Chodat); **Myxochimae'ra** (+CHIMAERA), the plasma of *Mucor* Mich., when parasitized by *Chaetocladium* Fres. (Burgeff); **Myxochromoso'mes** (+ CHROMOSOMES), paired chromo-

somes; **Myxopod'ia,** pl. (+PODIUM), *cf.* PSEUDOPODIUM; **Myxoso'mes,** = DYADS (Chodat).

n generation has the nucleus with haploid number of chromosomes; 2*n* generation has diploid number.

N and P i'ons, nitrogen and phosphorus in plankton (Church).

nannan'drous, *add,* (2) used of antheridia from small male plants attached to the female filaments near the oogonia of *Oedogonium* Link (West); **Nanan'drium** = NANNANDER; **Nannoplank'tonts** (+ PLANKTON, ὄντα, things existing), items comprising the nannoplankton; **Nan'ophyll,** Raunkiaer's term for a small leaf, 9×25 sq. millim.

Narde'tum, an association of *Nardus* Linn.

Necrid'ia (νεκρός, dead), dead cells in algae (West); **Nec'ron,** dead plants, not yet turned into humus; adj. **necroni'sed** (Sernander); **Nec'ton,** *cf.* NECRON.

Nectar'ia, pl. (+ NECTARIUM), used to denote peloria with every petal or sepal spurred; **Nectarose'ma** (σῆμα, a mark), Errera's term for NECTAROSTIGMA.

Ne'matea (νῆμα, νήματος, a thread), a flagellate consisting of a linear series of plastids (Janet); **nemathe'cioid** (εἶδος, form), resembling a nemathecium; **Nemathecium,** *add,* (2) **cor'tical** ~, occurring in cortical cells; **medul'lary** ~, consisting of loosely packed thread in the interior of an algal thallus (Phillips).

Neog'amous, precocious syngamy in early stage of gametocyte (Minchin); **Ne'o-Men'delism,** modern developments of Mendelian doctrine; **neophyt'ic** (φυτόν, a plant), applied to fossil Tertiary plants (Clements); **neotrop'ic,** pertaining to the tropics of America (Campbell); *cf.* PALAEOTROPIC.

nephro'dioid, resembling or akin to *Nephrodium* Rich.

Nereid'ion, an association of waterplants (Moss).

Net, loose tissue of pseudoparenchyma; *cf.* HARTIG NET.

Neu'ston (νευστάς, swimming), floating vegetation (Sernander).

New Place effect, seed from a distant locality producing changed results (Collins).

Nipe'tum, association of *Nipa* Thumb.

Nitelle'tum, a similar one of *Nitella* Ag.

Ni'trogen Fixa'tion, non-symbiotic by anaerobic bacteria, symbiotic by means of bacteroids (Conn); **nitroph'ilous,** *add,* nitrogen-loving, applied to lichens (Sernander).

nomoph'yllous (φύλλον, a leaf), leaves normal for genus or other group (Radlkofer).

non'tuple, nine sets of chromosomes affected; Blakeslee has it as **non'uple.**

Nu'cleolar Bo'dy, at the periphery of the nucleolus of *Lathyrus* Tourn. is a darkly staining thread; **Nucle'oli,** Erikson's term for fungus-protoplasm which separates itself from that of the host into " special corpuscles "; **Nucleosta'toliths** (+ STATOLITH), nuclei more or less united to starch grains or starch-containing chloroplasts to form a gravitational unit (Prankerd); **Nu'cleus, Incip'ient,** of myxophycean cell, formerly termed "Central Body " (West); ~ of diatoms, (*a*) **Macronu'cleus,** the nucleus; (*b*) **Micronu'cleus,** the centrosome (West).

Nuda'tion (*nudatio,* nakedness), the occurrence of bare areas due to various causes, termed by Clements " Denudation " (Gams).

nul'liplex, no dominant genes, but one dominant factor (Blakeslee).

Nuphare'tum, association of *Nuphar* Sibth. et Sm.

Nymphaee'tum, the like of *Nymphaea* Linn.

Oc'tad, with eight nuclei; **oc'tosome,** with eight sets of chromosomes (Blakeslee); **octosterigmat'ic,** having eight sterigmata (Buller); **oc'tokont** (κοντός, a pole), possess-
G 2

ing eight equal flagella (Church); **oc'tuple,** eight sets of chromosomes affected (Blakeslee); **oc'toploid,** with somatic chromosomes 56 in number, *i.e.* eight times the normal seven in *Rosa* Linn.

oecolog'ic, *cf.* ECOLOGIC

Oec'otype, *cf.* ECOTYPE.

OH, *cf.* H-IONS.

oid'ial, *add,* adj. of *Oidium* Link; **Oid'iospores** (+SPORE), arise from hyphae in a chain in close order.

Old Wood, also termed "Cryptogamic" or " Primary " wood (Jeffrey); *cf.* WOOD.

oligorhi'zous (ρίζα, a root), used of marsh plants forming few roots (Clements); **oligotroph'ic** (τροφή, nourishment), applied to swamps poor in plant nutrients (Clements).

Ologen'esis, *cf.* HOLOGENESIS.

Ombrocleistog'amy (ὄμβρος, rain, + CLEISTOGAMY), flowers self-fertile whilst unexpanded, due to rainy weather (Kerner).

omnic'olous (*omnis,* all; *colo,* I inhabit), used of lichens indifferent to their substrata.

Ontogen'esis (γένεσις, beginning), *cf.* ONTOGENY; **Ontoplas'tids** (πλαστός, moulded), cells in process of division; *cf.* PROPLASTID.

ooapog'amous (ὠόν, an egg, + APOGAMOUS), producing partheno-genetically (Juel); **O'ocarp** (καρπός, fruit) = OOSPORE; **O'ocyte** (κύτος, a cavity), a gametocyte or spermatocyte (Minchin); **Oogo'nial In'cept,** the early stage of the ooganium of certain fungi; **O'ophyte** (φυτόν, a plant) = GAMETOPHYTE.

Oper'cle, the persistent base of a style, forming a prominent point to an ovary in an epigynous flower (Herbert).

Opt'imal Ar'ea, the most favourable quarters for the development of a species or variety (Warming).

orcu'liform (*orcula,* a little cask), polarilocular, as a spore.

Or'gadad (ὀργάς, ὀργάδος, a well-wooded meadow), **an open woodland plant (Clements).**

Or′ganel, cf. PLASMORGAN.

Or′gans, Conser′vative, the root, stem, leaf and sporange (Jeffrey).

ornithocoproph′ilous (κόπρος, dung; φιλέω, I love), applied to lichens, which benefit by the excreta of birds (Sernander).

orobancha′ceous, akin to *Orobanche* Linn.

orogen′ic (γένος, race), "mountain-making" (Clements); **Orohyli′on** (+ HYLION), an alpine forest of *Picea* Link and *Abies* Linn. (*id.*)

Orthid′ium (ὀρθός, straight; ἴδιος, personal), a supposed fructification in lichens, but actually a parasitic lichen (A. L. Smith); **Orthobi′ont** (ὄντα, things existing), a being of direct succession from one zygote to a new one (Janet); adj. **ortho-biont′ic**; **orthocle′ma** (κλῆμα, a twig), straight branched or leaved; **orthogenet′ic,** cf. ORTHOGENESIS; **Orthog′amy** (γάμος, marriage), the normal relations of male and female; **or′thoploid** (probably an error for OCTOPLOID); **Or′thophyte** (φυτόν, a plant), a plant from egg to egg; sporophyte + gameto-phyte (Janet).

osmunda′ceous, akin to *Osmunda* Linn.

Ostruthie′tum, an association of *Peucedanum Ostruthium* Koch.

out′er, add, (2) morphologically the lower surface of the leaf of *Sphagnum* Dill. (Horrell).

Ox′arch (ἀρχή, beginning), the character of an OXYSERE (Clements); **oxygy′rus,** sharply twisted; **oxyly-ᵇh′ilus** (Clements) = OXYLOPH′ILUS (Warming); **Oxylyphy′ta** (Clements) = OXYLOPHYTA; **Oxy′on,** a heath climax (*id.*); **Ox′yphytes,** plants which show a want of oxygen in the soil, with low chresard (*id.*); **Ox′ysere** (+ SERE), a hydrosere with acid land contents (*id.*).

P i′ons, = phosphorus ions; cf. pH, hydrogen-ion concentration of soil to plant distribution; neutrality is pH7.

P₁, pure line.

pachycle′ma (κλῆμα, a twig), with stout branches; **pachygy′rus,** coiled in thick whorls.

Pach′yte (παχύτης, thickness), the secondary region of the stem, composed of secondary phloem and xylem with liber (Van Tieghem); cf. ENDOME, EXOME.

palaeotrop′ic, cf. PALEOTROPIC.

Pal′ecology (Seward), cf. PALEO-ECOLOGY (Clements); **pale′ic,** past or fossil; **Paleobot′any** (+ BOTANY), fossil plants as a study; **Paleo-ecol′ogy** (+ ECOLOGY), the ecology of geological periods; **paleophyt′ic** (φυτόν, a plant), relating to the vegetation of Paleozoic times characterized by pteridophytes (Clements); **Pal′eosere** (+ SERE) or **Pter′osere,** the EOSERE or plant succession in the Paleozoic Age (*id.*); **Pale′ostrate** (+ STRATE), a definite paleophytic EOSTRATE (*id.*); **paleotrop′ic,** belonging to the tropics of the Old World, Asia, Africa and N. Australia, cf. NEOTROPIC (Campbell); **Paleozo′ic** (ζῷον, an animal), a geological term used to specify formations in which the oldest fossils occur.

Paludoph′ilae (φιλέω, I love), algae with thin filaments, or unicellular green algae (Ivanoff).

Panaschier′ing, an enzyme-produced variation of leaf-coloration marking (Küsten).

panmict′ic, adj. from PANMIXIA.

Papil′la, Recep′tive, of *Phytophthora* De Bary, cf. MANOCYST.

Paracycada′les, Wieland's term for PROANGIOSPERMS.

parag′ynous (γυνή, a woman), applied to such antheridia or male organs as grow up the side of the oogonium of a fungus and pierce it there (Murphy).

Par′alysers (παράλυσις, palsy), enzymes which inhibit action; cf. ACTIVATORS.

Paramas′tigote (μάστιξ, μάστιγος, a whip), a flagellate having one principal flagellum and one short and accessory; **Paramy′lum** (+

AMYLUM), special starch in flagellates, not reacting to iodine (Minchin); **Parasynapt'ist** (+SYNAPSIS), one who regards the parallel threads of the heterotype prophase as the pairing of entire chromosomes; *cf.* TELOSYNAPTIST; **Parasyn'desis** (+ SYNDESIS), reduction by chromosomes are paired in parallel positions (Häcker); **Parich'ni**, plural of PARICHNOS.

Parmelie'tum, an association of *Parmelia* Ach.

Parthenocarp'y, *add*, **aitionom'ic** ~, stimulative (Fitting); **autonom'ic** ~, vegetative (*id.*); **parthenogen'ic** ~, preferably **parthenogenet'ic**.

Par'vigrade (*gradus*, a step), applied to a small variation or transilient; ~ **Evolu'tion** is continuous (Poulton); *cf.* MAGNIGRADE.

Pas'sive Pro'toplasm, in a female gamete = GYNOPLASM.

patroclin'ic, (*κλίνη*, a bed), in hybrids where the influence of the male or pollen parent is manifest; **Patrocli'ny** is the condition; *cf.* MATROCLINIC; **Patrogen'esis** (*γένεσις*, beginning), development from male nucleus only breeding true, the female nucleus being dispossessed (Collins).

Pedol'ogy (*πέδον*, land; *λόγος*, discourse), soil-science, the quality and ability of the various soils.

Pe'lophytes (*πηλός*, mud; *φυτόν*, a plant), plants growing in clayey or marshy places (Gadeceau).

Pel'ory, Worsdell's adaptation of PELORIA.

pent'aploid, five times as many chromosomes as in the haploid condition; **pent'asome** is a synonym; **Pentaploi'dy** is the state; **pentasterigmat'ic**, with basidia having five sterigmata (Buller).

pen'tasome = pentaploid.

pento'san, referring to PENTOSES.

Percnoso'mes (*πρεκνός*, dusky; *σῶμα*, a body), small granules in androcytes of bryophytes (Wilson).

peren'niate, variation of PERENNATE; **Perennia'tion** = PERENNATION.

Perfora'tion, an actual aperture in the wall of a vessel (Jeffrey).

Perig'yny, being PERIGYNOUS.

perinu'clear, surrounding the nucleus; **peripatet'ic** (*πατέω*, I walk), applied to field botany; *cf.* ANAPORETIC; **periph'eral** (*φέρω*, I bear), centrifugal or outward growth (Jeffrey); **periphialop'orous**, round the PHIALOPORE (Janet); **Periplast'id**, *cf.* PERIPLAST; **peritrich'ic, -ous** (*θρίξ*, *τριχός*, hair), flagella completely surrounding an organism, as *Bacillus* Cohn (Conn); **periva'sal** (*vasa*, Lat. pl. vessels) = VASICENTRIC.

Periodic'ity, the seasonal duration of a species (Pavillard).

peris'soploid (*περισσός*, odd), uneven multiples (Jeffrey); *cf.* ARTIOPLOID.

per'oid (*πηρός*, maimed; *εἶδος*, like), defective in fruiting, as *Polypori*, annual or perennial (Harshberger).

Per'ule, *cf.* PERULA.

petalod'ic, having a tendency to double flowers; *cf.* PETALODY.

petiola'ted (+ PETIOLE), having leaf-stalks (Salisbury).

pet'ran (*πέτρα*, a rock), applied to Rocky Mountain vegetation (Clements).

Pe'tri Dish'es, two shallow circular glass dishes, one slightly smaller than the other, for cultures free from dust.

Peucedane'tum, an association of *Peucedanum Ostruthium* Koch.

Ph, introduced by Sörenson (also occurs as PH. pH) to show the negative logarithm of the hydrogen-ion concentration in soil; *cf.* CH, and H+.

Phae'no- oecol'ogy, diagram displaying the range of the species enumerated (Gams); **Phaen'otype** (*τύπος*, a type), a type resulting from hybridizing, inclusive of the different genophenes of a genotype, then becomes the phaenotype (Johannsen); **phaenotyp'ically, in** the manner noted.

Phagocyto'sis (*φαγεῖν*, to eat; *κύτος*, a hollow), intercellular digestion

(Bernard); **Pha'gocytes,** the cells in question; **Phagoplank'ton** (+ PLANKTON), autotrophic algae (Gams); an individual member has been named **Pha'gont** (*id.*).

Phanerophyti'on (φυτόν, a plant, + ion), a main Isocies of phanerogamous plants (Moss); **Phanerocotyledo'neae** = DICOTYLEDONS.

Phe'nhybrid (+ HYBRID), an obvious hybrid (Jeffrey); **Phenosper'my** (σπέρμα, a seed), used to denote an abortive seed-condition (Goodspeed); **Phe'notype,** *cf.* PHAENOTYPE; adv. **phenotyp'ical,** "reaction type," Turesson.

Phiale'a (φιάλη, a bowl), a hollow sphere as *Volvox* (Janet); **Phi'alocoele** (κοίλη, a hollow), the young internal buds of *Volvox*; adj. **phialoce'lian** (Janet); **Phi'aloderm** (δέρμα, skin), the coat of the young buds of *Volvox* (*id.*); **Phi'alopore** (πόρος, a passage), an outlet from the cenobial *Volvox* (*id.*); *cf.* PHYTOBLASTEA; adj. **phialopor'ic**; **Phialu'la,** stage of sixteen plastids formed by successive bipartition into a hollow sphere (*id.*).

-philous (φιλέω, I love), attractive (Clements).

Phlocoter'ma (φλοιός, bark; τέρμα, boundary), Strasburger's term for ENDODERMIS.

-pho'tic, pertaining to light (Clements); **Photocleistog'amy** (+ CLEISTOGAMY), flowers remain closed in consequence of deficient light (Hansgirg); **Photol'ysis,** *add,* (2) breaking up by the action of light; **Photom'eter** (μετρέω, I measure), an instrument to record the intensity of light; **photoperiod'ic,** reaction due to relative length of day; **photosynthet'ic,** *cf.* PHOTOSYNTHESIS.

Phrag'mosphere (σφαῖρα, a globe), spindle-fibres and associated cytoplasm becoming transformed into a large hollow sphere.

Phre'tad (φρεατία, a tank), a tank plant (Clements); **Phreat'ophytes** (φυτόν, a plant), "well-plants," *i.e.* desert plants which can send

roots down to the water-table, 8–50 feet down (Meinzer).

Phycoli'chenes (+ LICHEN), lichens with blue-green gonidia; **Phycomyce'tes,** fungi resembling algae; **phy'comycete,** a form of fungus attack characterized in the host by vesicles and arbuscules, the latter changing into sporangioles (Peyronel); **Phy'coscope** (σκοπέω, I see), tube to view sea weeds *in situ* under water (Tansley and Chipp).

Phyle'sis, the assumed succession of development (Bower); adv. **phylet'ically**; **Phyll,** Chauveaud's term for primitive leaf; **phyllocarp'ic, -ous,** carpotropic movements of the peduncle by which the young fruit is hidden under the leaves: **phyllo'dic,** *cf.* PHYLLODINEOUS; **Phyl'lomorph** (μορφή, shape), "dorsiventral frondose systems resembling compound leaves and deciduous by cladoptosis in three or four years" (Church); adj. **phyllomor'phic**; **Phyllonecro'sis** (+ NECROSIS), decay or death in leaves or leaflike organs; **Phyl'lorhize,** *add,* (2) Chauveaud's term for the fundamental plant-unit, the entire primitive plant; **Phyl'losperms** (σπέρμα, a seed), leaf-borne seeds as in Cycadales and Pteridosperms (Pilger); *cf.* STACHYSPERMS.

Phylogen'esis (γένεσις, origin) = PHYLOGENY; adj. **phylogenet'ic,** referring to the history of floras; successional (Rübel).

-phyte, suffix for "plant" (Clements); **Phytent'oscope** (ἐντός, inside; σκοπέω, I see), an instrument to ascertain how far light rays penetrate into plant-tissues (Wager); **Phyti'um** (φυτεῖον, place covered with plants), combining term for FORMATION (Clements); **Phytoblast'ea** (βλαστός, forme) a spherical coenogenetic alga, as *Volvox* (Janet); **Phytocoeno'sium,** vegetation of a unitary habitat (Schroeter); an association (Clements); **Phytochem'istry,** *cf.* PHYTOCHEMY; **Phytodichog'amy, cf.**

456

Dichogamy; **Phytoëcol′ogy** (+
Ecology), the relation of a plant
to its environment; **Phytoflagella′ta**
(+ Flagellata), the initial plant;
a unicellular ciliate alga (Jameson);
Phytoflagel′lida, Delage's name for
flagellates; **Phytogeograph′ical
Forma′tion,** Grisebach's early term,
changed to Vegetative Formation
by Warming; **Phyt′oid,** the individual unit in a plant-colony
(Child): **Phytom′eter,** plants counted
as single or in groups (Clements);
adj. **phytomet′ric**; **Phytom′etry,**
the process in question; **Phyto-
monad′ina** (Minchin) = Phyto-
flagellata; **Phytomorphol′ogy,** the
science of plant-form and structure
(Ball); **Phytopathol′ogist** (πάθος,
suffering; λόγος, discourse), a
student of plant diseases; **Phyto-
pathol′ogy** is the study; **Phyto-
physiol′ogy,** cf. Physiology; **Phyto-
proteran′dry** (+ Proterandry),
the stamens ripe before the styles
are receptive; **Phytoproterog′yny,**
the styles mature before the
stamens have ripe pollen; **Phyto-
sociolog′ical** (socius, a companion),
plant-sociology, a branch of ecology
devoted to consideration of vegetation rather than the habitat
factors, this being Geobotany;
Phytosociol′ogy, the condition under
review may be divided into (a)
Autecology, the relation between
the individual and its habitat;
(b) Autochorology, local botany;
(c) Autogenetics, the change of
floras; further, (d) Synecology,
the relations between the plant
association and the habitat; (e)
Synechorol′ogy, the distribution
of plant associations, and (f) Syn-
genetics, change of plant associations (Rübel); **Phytost′erol**
(στέαρ, fat), derived from plants,
resembling cholesterol, which is
formed by animals; **Phytotaxo-
n′omy** (τάξις, order), systematics
of plants, described in terms of
arrangement; **Phytothal′lea** (θαλλός,
a young twig), the origin of the

vegetable phylum (Janet); **phyto-
tom′ic,** adj. of Phytotomy; **Phyto-
zo′a,** add, (2)= Flagellata; **Phy′to-
zo′o-flag′ellate,** the initial organism (Janet).
Pig′ment-spot, in the motile algae,
a red spot, commonly called the
" Eye-spot."
Pil′lar, an old term for Stipe (2).
Pine′tum, an association of Pinus
Linn.; ~ **cladino′sum,** with the
soil covered with Cladonia Hill;
~ **herb′idum,** grasses clothing the
soil; ~ **hylocomio′sum,** with
masses of mosses Hylocomium
Bruch et Schimp. and Dicranum
Hedw. (Warming).
Pin′na-bar, cf. Pinna Trace Bar.
Pi′noid (εἶδος, form), a conifer with
characteristic dry cones and wind-
dispersed seeds (Church).
Pi′oneer Stage, towards a climax,
" the extreme condition of a
primary area," as lichens for rock
seres and submerged plants for
water seres (Clements).
pionno′tal, a continuous spore layer,
as in the fungal genus Pionnotes Fr.
Pistie′tum, an association of Pistia
Linn.
Pis′tillode, Pistillo′dium (+ Pistil),
a rudimentary pistil in the male
flowers of such genera as Elatostema
Forst.; cf. Staminode.
Pit′ting, the presence of pits in the
tracheids of conifers, further characterized as **alterna′ting** ~; **op′po-
site** ~; **ra′dial** ~, or **tangen′tial** ~;
Pits, locally thin parts in cell-walls,
corresponding with similar places
in neighbouring cells; **Air** ~,
have no counterpart on the side
of the air space (Jeffrey).
Placo′diomorph (μορφή, shape), used
of a polarilocular spore, as in the
lichen Placodium DC.
Pla′cula (πλακοῦς, a flat cake), a stage
of Volvox with four plastids in a
plane; adj. **plac′ular** (Janet).
Plagiot′ropy, cf. Plagiotropism.
Plak′ea (πλάξ, flat), a tabular colony
of phytoflagellates in a single
layer (Janet).

Plana'tion, employed by Clements to denote stream-erosion.

plane'tous, plane'tus (πλανητός, wandering), applied by I. B. Balfour to a migratory species.

Plank-butt'resses, the flat roots given off from the base of certain trees, as *Bombax* Linn.

Plank'tont, a constituent of plankton.

Planom'enon, wandering plankton; **Plan'ont,** a wandering organism.

Pla'no-plast'id, a flagellate cell; *cf.* APLANO-PLASTID.

Plant-sociol'ogy, *cf.* PHYTOSOCIOLOGY.

Plasmog'amy (γάμος, marriage), the fusion of cytoplasm, not of nuclei (Minchin); **Plasmogen'esis** (γένεσις, origin), the origin of protoplasm (Herrera); **plasmomet'ric** (μέτρον, a measure), measurement of the osmotic pressure of individual cells (Höpler); **Plasmone'ma** (νῆμα, a thread), the conducting thr ls of protoplasm, communicating with plastids (Janet); **Plasmop'tyse** (πτύσις, spitting), mycorrhiza infection of Asclepiads and Apocynaceae in the exodermis of the root (Demeter); **Plasmor'gan** (+ORGAN), a rudimentary organ (Janet); **Plasmot'omy** (τόμος, a cut), cleavage of a plasmodium into two or more nucleated parts (Minchin); **Plast'id Primor'dia,** large microchondria-like structures which produce leucoplastids (Mottier); **Plastids,** *add,* (2) granules which take a deeper stain than the cytoplasmic matrix in which they are imbedded (Collins); **Plast'idome** (δόμος, a house, or chamber), the sum-total of plastid contents in a cell (Wilson).

Plates, the exterior parts of Peridinaceae, enumerated by West, as a'pical ~; ant'apical ~; interc'alary ~; postcin'gular ~, precin'gular ~, and ventral ~.

Platyopun'tia, any *Opuntia* or succulent plant with flattened stems (MacDouglas).

Play'a (Span.), sea-coast or beach.

plectenchym'atous (πλεκτός, woven),

hyphae matted in growth; *cf.* PLECTENCHYMA, PSEUDOPARENCHYMA, PSEUDO-PYCNIDIAL: **Plectomyce'tes,** a group of fungi in which the richly septate types are never reached and detached spermatia are unknown, as Erysiphaceae (Gwynne-Vaughan).

Plei'omere (μέρος, a part), when mitoses have a higher number of chromosomes, and therefore smaller in size (Della Valle); **Plei'on,** a cycle of abundant corn-crops with excess of temperature (Arctowski); **pleiozy'gous** (ζυγός, a yoke), Frost's term for unlinked.

Pleist'omere (πλεῖστος, most; μέρος, a part), when the chromatin is divided only by granules (Della Valle).

Pleog'amy (γάμος, marriage), having flowers of various degrees of maturity, as ANDROPLEOGAMY, ERIPLEOGAMY and GYNOPLEOGAMY.

Plesias'my (πλησιασμός, an approach), abnormal shortening of the stem, so that the leaves arise from nearly the same point (Fermond).

Ple'thea (πλῆθος, a crowd), Janet's term for MERISM, of a sporadic swarm with its later transformations, adj. ple'thean; **Ple'theoblas'teas,** alternations of plethea and blastea resulting in the formation of plano-spores (Janet).

pleuran'thous (ἄνθος, a flower), when in a sympodium the inflorescences are borne on lateral axes, the main axis not ending in an inflorescence, but simply stopping in growth; **Pleurocystid'ia** (+CYSTIDIA), the cystidia being lateral (Buller); **pleurog'enous** (γένος, offspring), borne laterally on hyphal cells (A. L. Smith).

Plo'tophytes (πλωτός, floating; φυτόν, a plant), floating plants, their functional stomata on the upper surface of their leaves (Clements).

plurichromoso'mal, when one chromosome complex takes one or more chromosomes of the other in the reduction division (Lotsy); **plur'i-**

458

ploid, having multiple chromosomes (Němec); **plurisporang'iate,** with many sporangia; **pluriv'orous,** applied to parasitic fungi not confined to one species (Thurston); the condition is **Pluriv'ory.**

Pneu'matocyst (κύστις, a pouch), an air-cavity for flotation, as in *Fucus vesiculosus* Linn. (Church).

podocarpin'eous, resembling or allied to *Podocarpus* L'Hérit. (Jeffrey).

Podosyncar'py, when a double moss-capsule has one half fully developed, the other abortive (Worsdell).

Pod'sols, soils of a few inches of light powder below the humus layer (M. Vahl).

Poe'tum, an association of *Poa* Linn.

Poн, hydroxyl-ion concentration; alkalinity obtained by subtracting pH value.

Poi'on, or **Poi'um,** a meadow association (Clements).

polaribiloc'ular, applied to two-celled spores with thick median wall traversed by a connecting tube; **polariloc'ular** is a shortened form.

Poles, of embryo; the **anter'ior** ~, in vascular plants the apex of the axis; the **poster'ior** ~, in bryophytes the base of the sporogonium, in vascular bryophytes, the tip of the suspensor (Bower).

Pol'laplasy (πλάσσω, I form), division of a normally simple organ into several of the like shape (Fermond).

Pol'len, *add,* **Fur'chen** ~ (Furrow-pollen); **Pollina'tion;** **Self** ~, (*a*) in the strictly botanical sense, from the same flower; (*b*) in the cultivator's sense, where it may be effected by any flower of the same variety in its vicinity; ~ **Presenta'tion,** the sensitive action of the styles in Compositae during pollination (Small).

poloic'ous (πολύς, many; οἶκος, a house), having both fertile and barren flowers on the same and on different plants (Lindberg); **polyarthrodac'tylous** (ἄρθρον, a joint; δάκτυλος, a finger), with ultimate rays or dáctyls each of more than

two cells, as in some species of *Nitella* Ag.; **Polycar'yon** (κάρυον, a nut), when a nucleus has many centrioles or centrosomes; **polychromoso'mic** (+ CHROMOSOME), an idiomere having many chromosomes (Chodat); **Polychro'my** (Lindman) = POLYCHROMATISM; **polyclo'nal** (+ CLONE), used of a population of many clones, each descended from an original ancestor not asexually associated with the original ancestors of the others (Agar); **polyclad'ous,** employed for "descended from two male clones," as *Sphaerocarpus* Bull.; **Pol'ycots,** an abbreviation of POLYCOTYLEDONES; **polycoty'lous,** with many cotyledons, actual or apparent; **Polyde'mics** (δῆμιος, belonging to the people), Clements's term for sun and shade form of the same species.

Polygone'tum, an association of *Polygonum* Linn.

pol'ykont (κοντός, a pole), a flagellate with many flagella (Church).

Polylepide'tum, an association in which *Polylepis* Ruiz et Pav. is predominant (Herzog).

Polymast'igote (μάστιξ, a whip), having a tuft of flagella (Minchin); **Polym'ery** (μέρος, a part), the production of a given character by the action of two or more independent factors or genes, each of which when separate is able to produce the same character (Lang); it may be, **cu'mulative** ~, when the action of several genes accumulates, or, **non-cu'mulative** ~, one single gene can produce as much as the many, HOMOMERY (Lang); **Polyphylla'dea** (φυλλόν, a leaf), a polymeric individual, with each component merid having produced a leaf (Janet); **pol'yploid,** when consisting of more than double the number of chromosomes in the haploid generation; **Pol'yploidy** is the condition.

polypod'ioid, like the fern *Polypodium* Linn.

459

Polysac'charid (σάκχαρ, sugar) =
Callus (Church); **polyso'ma** (σῶμα,
a body) = polyploid; **polysapro'bic**
(σαπρός, rotten), putrid material
abundant (Lauterborn); **Pol'y-
stele** = Polystely; **Polythal'lea**
(+Thallus), a thallus of several
merids (Janet); **polythal'mic,** a
misprint for **polythalam'ic**; **Polytop'ism,** the condition of being
polytop'ic, of multiple origin;
Polygenesis is a synonym
(Clements).

pomolog'ic, relating to Pomology;
Pomol'ogist, a student of fruit
culture.

Pontederie'tum, an association of
Pontederia Linn.

pontohalic'olous (ἅλς, ἁλός, the sea),
inhabiting a salt-marsh.

por'al, relating to a Pore; ~ **Ax'is,**
the long axis; ~ **Ring,** four to
six epidermal cells surrounding
the pore in fossil species of *Sequoia*
Endl. (Bandulska); **Pore,** *add,* (6)
minute canals in certain diatom-
valves, which pass through the
cell-wall (West); ~ **Flagel'lar,** *cf.*
Flagellar Pore; ~ **Or'gans,** part
of cell-wall in desmids, each pore
being surrounded by a cylindrical
tube-like structure, but not of
cellulose (West); **Sphagnum** ~ ;
cf. Sphagnum Pores; **Pore'cork**
[dissyll.], strips of a few layers of
compact brownish cells in lenticels;
Por'oids, minute circular dots in
diatoms, more than 0·6μ in diameter, tiny cavities resembling
pores, but not actual perforations
(O. Müller).

postcing'ular (+Cingulum), plates in
the hypovalve of Peridiniae, behind
the girdle, fewer, and sometimes
larger, than the precingular plates
(West); **Postcli'max** (+Climax),
when change of climate increases
the water-content, and vegetation
alters thereby; the passing of a
climax; *cf.* Preclimax (Clements);
Postcli'sere (+Clisere), proceeds
from lower to higher climaxes,
succeeding a clisere (*id.*); **post-**

synapt'ic (+Synapsis), after synapsis; **Postsynezis,** following that
stage (Gates); **post-synize'tic,** after
synizesis.

potamic'olous, river-dwelling.

Potent'iometer (*potentia* power +
Meter), an instrument to determine the hydrogen–ion concentration in soils.

Prair'ies, grass-steppes in North
America.

precing'ular (+Cingulum), applied
to a plate in the epivalve of Peridiniae, behind the apical plates
and usually larger (West).

Precli'max (+Climax), the vegetation preceding the full development
of a climax (Clements); **Precli'sere**
(+Clisere), one which proceeds
from higher to lower climaxes, preceding a clisere (*id.*); **Pregameto-
spore,** an early stage of *Volvox*
(Janet).

Presenta'tion, *cf.* Pollen-presenta-
tion.

presynapt'ic (+Synapsis), previous
to synapsis; **pre-synize'tic,** preceding synizesis.

Prim'itive Spin'dle, an embryo with
polarity (Bower).

Primor'dia, *add,* analogous to Men-
delian unit characters (MacLeod);
Pri'sere (+Sere), primary sere
(Clements).

Proang'iosperms, fossil plants in
structure approaching the present
Angiosperms (Saporta); **Prochon'-
driomes** (+Chondriome), chromatic
granules more or less globular,
probably derived from the nucleolus; **Prochro'matin,** *add,* (2) chromatic substance in diffused and
modified condition (Latter); **Pro-
cormophy'ta** (+Cormophyte), the
flora of the Devonian period (Arber).

Pro'files (Ital. *profilo,* shape), dia-
grammatic records of the vertical
relation of the local vegetation
(Tansley and Chipp).

Progen'ies (Lat. descent), special
progeny for genetic investigation.

progna'thous (γνάθος, the jaw), when
anthers project forward at the base.

proli'fic, Cells, applied to disjointed cells of the thallus of *Pithophora* Wittr., serving for vegetative propagation (Wittrock); **Promer'-istem** (+ MERISTEM), in seedlings, the apex of the stem of undifferentiated parenchymatous cells in active division in all directions (Randolph); adj. **promeristemat'ic**; **Promito'sis** (+ MITOSIS), a simple form of nuclear division, seen in nuclei of the protokaryon type (Nägler).

Propag'ule (*propago*, a slip or shoot), a bud, gemmule or bulb capable of continuing its kind.

propha'sic, adj. of PROPHASIS.

Prophylax'is (προφυλακτικός, precautionary), prevention of disease, adj. **prophylac'tic.**

Proplas'tid (πλαστός, formed), (1) Janet's term for mother-cell of ONTOPLASTID; (2) a minute granule in cytoplasm, definitely concerned with the formation of chloroplasts (Randolph); **Propteridophy'ta,** pl. (+ PTERIDOPHYTE), Arber's term for PROCORMOPHYTA.

Pro'soplasy (πρός, in addition; πλάσσω, I mould), new histological characteristics and functional activities associated with hyperplasia; adj. **prosoplast'ic**; **Pro'soplasm,** the state in question.

Prosor'us (+ SORUS), body developed from a zoospore in a cell of *Synchitrium* De Bary, into nucleus, cytoplasm and outer membrane (K. M. Curtis); adj. **prosor'al.**

Prosper'ity, the extent a species completes its cycle of development in a given population.

Pro'tase, hypothetical first enzyme of archebiotic process (Troland).

proteochemotrop'ic (*cf.* CHEMOTROPISM), applied to pollen-tubes attracted by protease, *cf.* SACCHAROCHEMOTROPIC; **Pro'teosere** (+ SERE), *cf.* THALLOSERE; **Protobasidiomyce'tes** (+ BASIDIOMYCETES), with septate basidia, four basidiospores on each, such as Uredinales and Tremellales; **Protoben'thon**

(+ BENTHON), not defined by the author, but probably the earliest bottom vegetation (Church); **Protobi'ont** (+ BIONT), a primitive being; a protophyte (Janet); **Protobot'anist** (+ BOTANIST), Greene's term for Theophrastus Eresios (B.C. 372?— 287).

protococca'ceous, belonging to *Protococcus* Ag.

Protodoch'ae (δοχή, reception), *cf.* PRISERES; **Protokar'yon** (κάρυον, a nut), a simple nucleus of chromatin, suspended in the nuclear sap (Minchin); **proteroclad'ous** (κλάδος, a branch), disposed to a rudimentary branch division (Janet); **Protoderm'-a-state,** a culture state of *Protococcus* Ag. resembling *Protoderma* Kütz.; **protomorph'ic** (μορφή, shape), Masters's term for primordial leaves; **Proton'ta** (ὄντα, things existing), ultra-microscopic organisms, differing fundamentally from bacteria (Gates); **Pro'toplasm,** add, **ac'tive** ~, as in male gametes, androplasm; **pas'sive** ~, as in female gametes, gynoplasm (N. Jones); **Protoste'ly,** *cf.* PROTOSTELE; **protosynthet'ic** (σύνθετος, compound), early or simply-formed (Church); **protozo'al** (ζῷον, an animal), related to the simplest animals (K. M. Smith).

Prune'tum, scrub formed of various shrubby forms of *Prunus spinosa* Linn.

Psam'march (ἀρχή, beginning), the condition of an adsere starting on sand (Clements).

Psamme'tum, an association of *Psamma* Beauv. = *Ammophila* Host; on high dunes (Warming); **Psam'mophiles** (φιλέω, I love), plants preferring sandy soil for their growth (Druce); **Psam'mosere** (+ SERE), a loose, sandy adsere (Clements).

Pseudamito'sis (+ AMITOSIS), having been forced to the simpler method of nuclear division, by outward circumstances (Tischler); **pseudocon'choid** (κόγχη, *concha*, a shell), a curve in phyllotaxis enunciated by Schoute; **Pseudocormophy'tes** (+ CORMOPHYTES), Trelease's term for mosses; **Pseudocotyledo'neae** pl. (+ COTYLEDON), Agardh's expression for vascular cryptogams; **Pseudocyphel'lae**, pl. (+CYPHELLA), pulverulent, sparingly sorediate, excavated points in the under surface of lichens (A. L. Smith); **Pseudodichot'omy** (+ DICHOTOMY), "monopodial production of lateral axes from the segments of a dominant 3-sided apical cell" (Church); **Pseudofertil'ity**, in self-sterile plants "a mere environmental fluctuation having nothing to do with heredity" (East); **Pseudog'amy** (γάμος, marriage), the fusion of two hyphal cells of different thalli (Bensaude); **Pseudogym'nosperms** (+ GYMNOSPERMS), cycadeoid plants (Wieland); **Pseudoid'ia** (+OIDIA), disarticulated hyphal cells which may germinate (Bensaude); **Pseudoi'on** (+ION), acid combined with colloid dissociating into the named substance (Lloyd); **Pseu'dolam'ina** (+ LAMINA), the leaf-blade of the monocotyledons, as a palm-leaf regarded as a petiolar phyllome (Arber); **Pseudoleucoder'mis**, a periclinal chimaera in *Arabis* Linn., and *Glechoma* Linn.; the seedling inherits a white subepidermal layer; **Pseudolo'bes**, segments of palm-leaves, from having been torn in development (Arber); **Pseudomac'chia**, xerophilous evergreen scrub-juniper and evergreen oak predominating; *cf.* LAURIFRUTICETA; **Pseu'do-Ma'qui**, xerophytic evergreen bush, as the foregoing; **Pseu'do-mito'sis** (+ MITOSIS), the action of a pair of bivalent chromosomes (Tischler); **pseudomonocarp'ous**, adj. of **Pseudomonocar'py** (+ MONOCARP), in cycads the occurrence of mature cones imbedded in the trunk, the seeds not being shed until the death of the tree, conserved as in the leaf-bases until set free (Wieland);

Pseudomycorrhi'za (+ MYCORRHIZA), false-mycorrhiza in which the fungus is a one-sided parasite (Melin); **Pseu'do-nemathe'cia, pl.** (+ NEMATHECIUM), parasitic algae assuming the guise of nemathecia; **Pseudonu'cleus** (+ NUCLEUS), a nucleus containing blue corpuscles (Auerbach); **Pseudoparenchy'matous,** to be shortened to **parenchy'matous;** *add*, (2) the pycnidial wall of certain fungi, of more or less hexagonal cells (W. B. Grove); **Pseudopet'al,** one of the numerous petal-like constituents of the corolla in *Mesembryanthemum* Dill.; **Pseu'dophyll** (φύλλον, a leaf), the sheathing bracts of certain bamboos which fall off when the leaves develop; **pseu'do-phyllo'dic,** the peculiar semi-equitant leaf of *Phormium* Forst.; **Pseudoplasmo'dium** (+ PLASMODIUM), constituent amoebulae remaining distinct and not fusing into a true plasmodium (Minchin); **Pseudopod'ium, pl. -ia** (+ PODIUM), portions of moving protoplasm in Myxogastres, myxopodia; **Pseudopod'iospore** (+ SPORE), = AMOEBULA (Minchin); **pseudopycnid'ial** (*cf.* PYCNID), Potebnia's term for plectenchymatous hyphae; **Pseudovac'uoles** (+ VACUOLE), dark-reddish granules in the cytoplasm of certain Cyanophyceae, "suspensory bodies" of Molisch (West); **Pseudo-valve,** a semi-solid carpel splitting at maturity between the two vascular bundles of the midrib (Saunders).

psilic'olous (ψιλός, bare), prairie-dwelling.

Pter'eosere (+ SERE), characterised by fossil pteridophytes, a paleophytic eosere; = PALEOSERE (Clements); **pter'id,** allied to *Pteris* Linn. (Bower); **Pteride'tum,** an association of ferns.

Pul'vinoid (εἶδος, form), a petiole acting in a degree as the pulvinus (Bose).

Pusillaejunce'tum (*pusillus*, petty),

an association of small species of *Carex* Linn.

Pu'sule, *add,* ~ **appara'tus,** peculiar vacuoles in the protoplast of certain Peridineae (Schütt); **collect'-ing** ~, a small specimen with a duct leading to the flagellar pore (*id.*); ~ **Sack,** a large bilobed example in *P. Steinii* Jörg. (West).

pycnoxyl'ic (ξύλον, wood), the coniferous type of wood (Seward); *cf.* MANOXYLIC.

pyrenomyce'te, relating to PYRENO-MYCETES.

Py'rophobe (πῦρ, πυρός, fire), a plant liable to destruction in forest fires, and incapable of being replaced under the altered condition (Gates); **Py'rophyte** (φυτόν, a plant), a tree having a thick, fire-resisting bark, thus escaping permanent damage from forest fires (*id.*).

Quad'rifid Or'gan, in the bladders of *Utricularia* Linn., four long, terminal cells arising from a collar-cell at the apex of a pear-shaped cell; believed to be absorptive (Clarke and Gurney); **quadri-cilia'ted** (+ CILIATE), having four cilia (West); **quad'ruple,** four sets of chromosomes affected (Blakeslee); **Quad'ruple Hy'brids,** hybrids which in the first generation split into four types (Atkinson).

Qua'si-cir'cle (Lat. as though, + CIRCLE), Church's term thus defined, the "ovoid curve in a Log-spiral quasi-square mesh" in phyllotaxis.

Querci'on, an association of *Quercus Ilex* Linn.

quint'uple, five sets of chromosomes affected (Blakeslee).

R₁, R₂, etc., Chauveau's signs for successive root-like organs.

Ra'ches, suggested in place of RHACHIDES, as plural of RHACHIS (Sahni); **Ra'chitism,** hypertrophy of floral envelopes, especially in grasses and sedges (Touchy).

Rachil'la-flaps, *cf.* RHACHILLA.

Rad'ical, *add,* (2) Vanilov's term in place of Lotsy's LINNEON, or super-species.

Rama'lia, pl. (Lat. sticks), "Ramuli to carry out the greater part of metabolic activity" (Church); **cor'tical** ~, near the cortex.

Ramel'lus (Mod. Lat.), side branch in algae (Agardh).

rana'lian, resembling or akin to Ranales, a group including Ranun-culaceae (Jeffrey).

ranuncula'ceous, having affinity with *Ranunculus* Linn.; **Ranuncule'tum,** an association of aquatic species of Ranunculus, *i.e.* § *Batrachium,* DC.

Ray, *add,* **diffuse'** or **diver'ging** ~, scattered in the woody tissue; **medul'lary** ~; (2), limb of a branchlet in *Nitella* Ag.; **ul'timate** ~, = DACTYL.

Reac'tion, *add,* ~ **Lev'el,** bisected by the surface, a few inches above or below (Clements); ~ **Type** (Johannsen) = PHENOTYPE.

Recept', an abbreviation for RECEP-TACLE, as in Euphorbiaceae; **Re-cep'tive Papil'la,** *cf.* MANOCYST.

reces'sive (*recessus,* a going back), a character which tends to disappear in hybrids; the opposite to DOMI-NANT.

Recip'rocal Hy'brids, *add,* they are divided into **Blend** ~, **Dou'ble** ~, **Itera'tive** ~, **Quad'ruple** ~, **Selec'-tive** ~, **Ses'qui-** ~.

Rectigrada'tion (*recte,* straight; *gradatio,* gradation), adaptive evolutionary tendency from the beginning (Osborn); **rectiser'ial,** *add,* (2) the orthostichy spiral when the axis is conical or circular (Church).

Reduplica'tion, *add,* (2) used for former expressions COUPLING and REPULSION, *i.e.* LINKAGE (Punnett).

Reg, alluvial desert in Algeria.

Regenera'tion, *add,* (2) of woodland or forest, its renewal; of grassland, growth after burning (Tansley and Chipp).

Re′gion, *add,* (2) that occupied by a
formation complex (Waterman).

Rejuvenesc′ence, *add,* (2) also a
synonym of REGENERATION.

Rel′ic, *add,* (2) what is left of former,
but now suppressed, vegetation
(Warming).

Reliquefac′tion (*re* = back; *lique-
facio,* I melt), the resumption
of its normal state by protoplasm, after temporary hardening
(Szücs).

Restitu′tion (*restitutio,* restoring),
stimulated to renewal of lost parts
or organs (Harshberger).

Retain′er, a double sheet of thin
paper containing a specimen
throughout the drying process
(Tansley and Chipp).

Retard′ed Phase, the third in the
growth of yeast.

Rever′sion, to recall ancestral features
of organization as an effect of
injury (Jeffrey); adj. **rever′sionary.**

Rhachil′la-flaps, upward outgrowths
from internodes of the spikelet axis
of grasses (Arber).

Rhacomitrie′tum, an association of
Rhacomitrium lanuginosum Brid.
(Moss).

Rheoph′ilae (φιλέω, I love), algae in
running water (Ivanoff).

Rhize (monosyll.), Chauveaud's term
for the root element in succession,
R₁, R₂, etc.; as primary, secondary,
etc.; **Rhi′zoïd,** *add,* (2) the end-
cell of a shoot of *Cladophora* Kütz.,
which adapts itself to neighbouring
structures and interlocks into
AEGAGROPILAE; **Rhizolith′ophytes**
(+LITHOPHYTE), lichens (Wetter);
rhizomast′igoid (μάστιξ, a whip;
εἶδος, form), whip-like flagellum
or pseudopodium (Church); **Rhizo-
mat′icae,** pl. root-stalk plants.

Rhizophore′tum, an association of
mangroves, *Rhizophora* Linn.

rhizopod′ial, resembling rhizopods in
habit (Fritch); **Rhizotham′nion,**
Miehe's term for tubercles on roots
of *Casuarina* Linn.

Rhizu′menon (ὄντα, existing things),
of a rooting type (Gams).

Rhodore′tum, an association of *Rhododendron Rhodora* J. F. Gmel.

Rhyncospore′tum, an association of
Ryncospora alba Vahl.

ring′porous, when the vessels in the
spring growth of wood are larger
than those of later growth (Jeffrey).

Roeste′lia-Stage, a form in rust-fungi
in which the peridium is elongated
and fimbriate, recalling the genus
Roestelia Rebent.

Root′knobs, Syme's term for orchid
tubers; **Roots,** "double," lateral
roots in monocotyledons in the
interval between two protoxylem
clusters (Jeffrey).

rose′form [dissyll.], the shape of
the rose when in flower (Greene);
rosula′ceous, pertaining to a **Ros′ule,**
a rose-like tuft of leaves, having
the form of an ∙umbel (Herbert).

rudiment′ary, *add,* (2) (*a*) vestig′ial,
(*b*) formerly applied to an organ
disappearing in evolution.

Ru′gula, a longitudinal groove in
the upper lip of the flower, which
encloses the style of *Justicia* Houst.
(Lindau).

saccharochemotrop′ic (+ CHEMO-
TROPISM), applied to pollen-tubes
attracted to sugar (Tokugawa);
cf. PROTEOCHEMOTROPIC; **Saccharo-
myce′tes,** fermenting fungi such
as beer-yeast, *Saccharomyces cerevisiae* Meyen.

Sac′cospores (+ SPORE), plants having sack-like envelopes as dissemin-
ules (Clements).

Sachs's Rule, "a cell-wall always
tends to set itself at right angles
to another cell-wall" (Thompson).

Sadd, or **Sudd,** floating and matted
vegetation on the upper Nile,
blocking navigation.

Salic′inase, an enzyme from almonds,
which decomposes SALICIN.

Salicornie′tum, *cf.* SALICORNETUM.

Sal′itrates, salt-steppes of Argentina.

Sal′tant (*saltus,* a leap), a variable
form or mutant from the normal;
salta′ted, varied; **Salta′tion,** a mutation or large transilient (Poulton).

Sa′nio, Trabec′ulae of, ligneous processes crossing the cavity of the
tracheid, possibly due to parasitic
fungi (Jeffrey).

Sap′ropel (πηλός, clay), sedimental
remains of plants in water (Sernander); saprope′lic, applied to
algae in colonies on decaying vegetation at the bottom of ponds or
lakes (Lauterborn); Saproge′o-
phytes (+ GEOPHYTES), saprophytic
flowering plants, as Epipogum
S. G. Gmel., and many fungal
mycelia (Gams); Saproplank′ton
(+ PLANKTON) consists of autotrophic flagellates (Gams).

scapa′ceous, Herbert's expression for
"having a scape."

Scenedesme′tum, an association of
Scenedesmus Meyen.

Schine′tum, a similar group in which
Schinus Linn. is predominant.

Schinopside′tum, a like group of
Schinopsis Engl.

schizae′oid, like the fern Schizaea
Sm.; schizae′ous is a synonym
(Jeffrey).

Schizocot′yly (cf. COTYLEDON), the
forking and multiplying of cotyledons (Worsdell); Schizog′ony
(γόνος, offspring), splitting off
without a sexual process (Minchin);
Schi′zosomes (σῶμα, a body),
reduced chromosomes (Chodat).

Schizotriche′tum, an association of
Schizothrix Kütz.

scim′itar, used of leaves presenting
an edge to incident light, as
Eucalyptus L'Hérit. (Church).

Sciophy′ta, add, Sci′ophytes.

sclerophel′loid (σκληρός, hard; φελλός,
cork; εἶδος, form), used for lens-
shaped groups of compact cells
in lenticels (Neger); Sclerophyl′lous
For′est, ~Scrub, cf. DURIFRUTICETA.

Screef′ing, weeding or thinning a
forest (A. S. Watt).

Scrub, stunted or densely packed
bushes.

Scu′tum, add, (3) pl. Scu′ta, name applied to the eight shield-like plates
which unite to form the outside of
the antheridium of Chara Linn.

Se′bakh, a depression holding salt
water in the rainy season, dry in
summer.

Sector′ial Chimae′ra, bud variation
resulting in mixed tissue in branch
of tree or shrub (Harshberger).

secundifo′lius (folium, a leaf), the
leaves all turned towards one side
(Herbert).

Sede′tum, an association of Sedum
Tourn.

Seed-stage, in Gymnosperms, the
formation of cones (Church).

seep, to ooze; Seep′age, oozing;
slow flow from ill-drained land.

seismonast′ic, add, (2) Blackman's
term for the movements of Mimosa
pudica Linn.

sejunc′tus (Lat.), separated.

Selec′tive Hy′brid, certain factors
selected from the parents which
are fully developed later (Atkinson).

self-compat′ible, self-fertile (Stout);
~ incompat′ible, infertile by its own
pollen.

sem′i-apog′amy (+ APOGAMY), a reduced form of fertilization, as in
Phragmidium Link (Blackman);
sem′i-ectotroph′ic (+ECTOTROPHIC),
an intermediate type of mycorrhiza
infection in certain conifers (Laing).

Sempervire′tum, an association of
Carex sempervirens Vill.

Senecione′tum, a like group of
Senecio Cineraria DC.

Separa′tion Discs in Myxophyceae,
of a substance secreted by two
adjoining cells, appearing like a
ring (West).

Sep′tet, applied to the sets of chromosomes in Rosa Tourn., in sevens
or a multiple of seven (Hurst);
sep′tuple, seven sets of chromosomes affected (Blakeslee).

se′ral (+ SERE) U′nits; thus Asso-
CIES, COLONY, CONSOCIES, FAMILY,
SOCIES (Clements); Sere (sero, I
put in a row), the unit of succession
in Clements's scheme; a concrete
developmental · series which can
be traced (Tansley and Chipp);
adj. se′ral, opposed to climax.

Se'ries, *add*, (3) applied to a group of sister-plants from the same parent, or same cross, in any one season (Stout); (4) used by Vavilov for the phenomena of variation; cycles, one or more.

serolog'ical (*sero*, I sow; λόγος, discourse), concerning raising seedlings of Leguminosae and grasses (Zade) [Note.—not to be confounded with the medical usage of this word.]

Seslerie'tum, an association of *Sesleria* Scop.

Sex Int'ergrades = polygamous (Yampolsky); ~ Intergrada'tion, polygamy; ~ lim'ited, inheritance restricted; ~ linked, needful for inheritance of certain factors.

sex'tuple, six sets of chromosomes involved (Blakeslee).

Shift, segregation of one factor causing variation (Engledow); shift'ed, varied in form.

Shoot, *add*, (3) long ~ = LEADER; short ~ = SPUR (3).

Short-shoot, (1) spur; dwarfed, fertile branch; (2) in conifers, special leaf-spurs (Jeffrey); ~ styled, flowers with styles shorter than the anthers.

Sib'ljak, bush-land; a transition from grass-steppe to forest, of light and warmth-loving shrubs (Adamović).

Sib'ship (sib, old term for related), relationship.

Si'derophiles (σιδηρίτης, a magnet; φιλέω, I love), iron-loving plants; Si'derophobes (φόβος, fear), iron-hating plants; Si'deroplasts (πλαστός, formed), plants taking their shape from the iron in the soil (Naumann).

sier'ran (Sierra, Span.), applied to the vegetation of the Pacific coast and Rocky Mountains.

sikyot'ic (σικύα, a cupping-glass), parasitic, as by fusion of plasma in fungi, as *Chaetocladium* Fres. on *Mucor* Mich. (Burgeff).

Si'lage, corn or hay preserved in a Si'lo, a tall, airtight compartment, for fermentation of its contents.

silic'icole, *cf.* SILICOLOUS; Silici'on, sand-flinty soils (Moss).

Silks, stigmas of maize, in United States of America.

Simp'lices, homosporous ferns, whose sporangia are produced simultaneously, especially those occurring in primary rocks, as the Marattiaceae (Bower).

Sing'ular-becom'ing, Driesh; explained by Worsdell as mechanical causality.

sinist'ral, *add*, (2) applied to respective daughter-cells resulting from spiral cleavage (Treadwell).

Sipho'nea (σίφων, a tube), a stage in *Volvox* when the blastopore is drawn out and the archenteron has become tubular (Janet).

skin'ny, W. Wilson's term for SCARIOSE.

smila'ceous, like *Smilax* Tourn. or *Ruscus* Tourn. (Drude).

snipt, old term for INCISED.

Sociabil'ity, the disposition of individuals in the interior of an association; so'cial exclu'sive, with no other species; ~ inclu'sive, admitting other species; Sociol'ogy, Plant: economic botany.

Sol, abbreviated from Solu'tion; stiffens into GEL.

solana'ceous, akin to *Solanum* Tourn.

Somat'ogen, somatogenic variation (Poulton).

sonor'an, the vegetation of Sonora in the Gulf of California, a very dry region.

Sora'lium, a group of soredia surrounded by a definite margin (A. L. Smith).

Sor'i, *add*, (4) antheridia so arranged on male fronds of *Rhodymenia palmata* Grev.

So'roma (σώρευμα, a heap), pl. Soro'-mata, the sporangial apparatus of the vascular plant, with its receptacle or stalk (Benson).

So'rosphere (σφαῖρα, a ball), a hollow sphere of cells, each cell becoming a spore, as in *Sorosphaera* Schroet. (Minchin).

Sor′us, *add*, (2) used for grouped antheridia in male fronds of marine algae; (3) a cluster of spores in certain Gasteromycetes (Minchin).

spargania′ceous, akin to *Sparganium* Tourn.; **Spargenie′tum**, an association of the same genus.

Spar′ganum (σπάργανον, swaddling band), founded by Unger as a genus, and now regarded as a type of cortex of parenchymatous tissue with vertical groups of thick-walled fibres (Seward).

Specia′tion, (1) a specific quality (Hurst); (2) evolution of species (U.S.); **Speciol′ogy** (λόγος, discourse), a discourse on species (Turesson).

spermatial, adj. of SPERMATIUM.

Spermat′ocyte (κύτος, hollow vessel) = ANDROCYTE (Allen); GAMETOCYTE (Minchin); **Sperm′ocarp**, *add*, (2) a body arising in *Coleochaete* Bréb., after fertilization remaining dormant through the winter (West).

Sphac′ela, apical cell mechanism (Church); **sphac′elate**, *add*, (2) applied to the colour of the interior of coniferous scales, as though charred (Henry).

Sphaer′ome, composed of microsomes, alone or in chains, not enclosed in a vacuole (Dangeard); **Sphaer′oplast** = BIOBLAST; CYTOMICROSOME; **Sphaerosir′ian**, the usual state of a male *Volvox* (Janet).

Sphagnum-pores, *cf.* PORES.

Sphe′rule, in *Padina Pavonia* Lamour., a small chromophilous body persisting until the formation of chromosomes (J. L. Williams).

Spike-stalk, an old name for RHACHIS.

Spin′dle, prim′itive, Bower's term for an embryo with polarity; *cf.* ENDOSCOPIC, EXOSCOPIC.

Spi′ral Cells, five cylindrical cells which clasp the egg-cell in Characeae.

Spirogyre′tum, an association of species of *Spirogyra* Link.

Spi′rophase, a stage in synapsis (Hogben).

Splint-wood, *add*, (2) soft-wooded.

Spokes, old term for pedicels of Umbelliferae, *cf.* RADIUS (2).

Sporang′iospore, *add*, (2) a non-motile spore in *Thraustotheca* Humph. (Weston).

-Spore, "migration contrivance" suffix (Clements); **Spore-balls**, *cf.* BULBIL (c); **Spore′tia**, pl., *cf.* CHROMIDIA, IDIOCHROMIDIA; **Spor′oblast** (βλαστός, a shoot), a spore mother-cell; **Sporob′ola** (βολή, a throw), the trajectory of a spore shot out horizontally (Buller); **Spor′ocyst** (κύστις, a bag), ′a tough, resistant envelope, enclosing a spore; a spore mother-cell (Minchin); **sporodoch′ial**, adj. of SPORODOCHIUM; **Spor′ont**, *cf.* GAMONT, giving rise to Gametes; **Spor′ophore**, *add*, (2) plasmodium growing out into anther-like processes in Myxomycetes; **Sporog′amy** (γάμος, marriage), the production of spores after gametic fusion.

Spur-pel′ory, when a flower is symmetrical by all the sepals or petals becoming spurred (Worsdell).

Stabiliza′tion (*stabilis*, stable), equilibrium in plant growth, the final adult stage of development (Clements).

Stach′yosperms (στάχυς, ear of corn; σπέρμα, seed), plants which bear seeds on their stems, as *Cordaites* Unger, Ginkgoales and Coniferales (Pilger).

Stad′dles, old term for standards in coppice.

Stade (*stadium*, a racecourse), used by Janet for PHASE.

Stagnoplank′ton (*stagnum*, a still pool + PLANKTON), floating vegetation of stagnant water (Ivanoff).

Sta′ling, the state in cultures when growth is hindered by the condition of the medium (Pratt).

Stalk-cell, *add*, the cell between the antheridial mother-cell and the vegetative cell (Yamanouchi); **Stalk-nu′cleus**, delimited from male prothallus of *Pinus* Linn. (Church).

Sta′men-lod′icules, organs partaking of the characters of both stamen and lodicule (Arber).

467

Start′ers, cultures used to start ripening or fermentation (Conn).

Stase, fossil deposit when in stagnant water (Clements); **Sta′sis,** an arrest of growth; at a standstill (*id.*); **Statench′yma,** tissue formed of STATOCYSTS.

Stauroso′mes = TETRADS (3) (Chodat).

Stearinolip′oids (στέαρ, tallow; λίπος, grease), fatty compounds occurring in plants (Czapek).

stenocoe′nose (κοινός, common), restricted in distribution (Gams); **Sten′ocysts** (κύστις, a cavity), auxiliary cells in the leaves of certain mosses (Morin); **Sten′omorph** (μορφή, shape), a diminutive form due to a cramped habitat (Bartsch); **stenother′mal** (θέρμη, heat), applied to species restricted to limited areas and temperatures (Setchell); **Stenother′my** is the condition; **stenosynu′sic** (+ SYN-USIA), groups of plants restricted in distribution (Gams); *cf.* EURY-SYNUSIC; **stenotrop′ic** (τρόπος, a turn), with narrow limits of adaptation to varied conditions (Solms).

Stigmatomyco′sis (+ MYCOSIS), fruits apparently sound, but unsound within, due to punctures by plant-feeding bugs.

Stipe′tum, an association of *Stipa tenacissima* Linn.

Stokes′s Law, the fall of spherical particles in a medium varies directly as the square of their radius (Buller).

sto′mal, Clements's expression for STOMATAL; **Stomat′ograph** (γράφω, I write), a self-recording instrument of the stomatal apertures of a leaf (Balls).

Stone-cork, "of units with thick, sclerosed and pitted walls," in Conifers (Church).

Strands, *add,* (3) very fine strands of linin in mitoses (Digby).

Stra′ta pl., *add,* (2) groups of CON-SOCIES (Shelford); **Strates,** scattered fossil deposits, opposed to STASES (Clements).

Stream′way, the bed of a watercourse or dry channel.

Stri′ae, pl., *add,* (2) the spiral ridges of the oospore in Charads (Groves).

Stricte′tum, an association of *Carex stricta* Good.

Strig ("origin obscure," Oxf. Dict.), applied to petiole, peduncle or pedicel.

-strote, "means of migration" (Clements).

sty′led, in dimorphic flowers, long or short.

Suaede′tum, an association of *Suaeda* Forsk.

Subassocia′tion (+ ASSOCIATION), a minor association; **Sub-bacter′ia,** filter-passing bacteria or ultramicroscopical germs (Cheshire); **Sub-cli′max,** an edaphic minor climax (Tansley and Chipp); **subco′pious,** few (Clements); **subdom′inant** (+ DOMINANT), applied to a prominent character which falls short of dominant.

Su′berin, *add,* recently defined as a substance present in median lamella of periderm cells, between the middle lamella outside and the cellulose layer within (Priestley); **suberogen′ic** (γένος, offspring), forming suberin.

subgregar′ious, somewhat gregarious (Clements); **sublit′oral,** near the sea-shore; **Subpalisa′de** (+ PALISADE), tissue lying below the palisade tissue; **Sub′sere** (+ SERE), partial development of a climax of vegetation (Clements); a secondary sere (Tansley and Chipp); **Subsucces′sion,** used for seres beginning on rock surfaces or crevices and ending in mat-growth (Clements); **subxeroph′ilous** (+ XEROPHILOUS), growing on fairly dry soil.

Succes′sion, *add,* defined by Clements as abrupt′ ~, contin′uous ~, imper′fect ~, intermit′tent ~, inter′-polated ~; by Cowles as biot′ic ~, phytogener′ic ~, re′gional ~, topograph′ic ~; by Gams as catastroph′ic ~, lo′cal ~, and sec′ular ~, with yet finer distinctions.

Sul'ci, *add*, (3) = FOSSULAE.

Sulphure'tum, a natural, ecological community of sulphur bacteria.

Sum'mit, an old term for STIGMA.

Sun'scald, injury due to too brilliant sunlight; **Sun'scorch**, the burning of foliage when the soil is parched.

Su'persex, ratio of chromosomes, $2x:2$ = female, $x:2$ = male; $2x:3$, an intermediate, the intersex or supersex (Bridges).

suprava'sal (+ VASAL), when situated opposite the xylem-groups in the wood (Solereder).

Suspen'sory Bod'ies (Molisch) = PSEUDOVACUOLES.

Symbas'is, *add*, free intercrossing lines of descent (O. F. Cook).

Sym'biophiles, pl. (φιλέω, I love), free mycorrhiza of hymenomycetous fungi, neither parasites nor saprophytes (Rayner).

Symbio'sis, *add*, defined by Mc-Dougall as I. **conjunc'tive** ~; and II. **disjunc'tive** ~, with further divisions of each, as **nu'tritive** ~, with **antagonis'tic** ~ and **recip'rocal** ~ as forms; **Sym'pode, Sympod'-ium**, *add*, it may be ACRANTHOUS ~ or PLEURANTHOUS.

Symptomatol'ogy (σύμπτωμα, mischance; λόγος, discourse), the science of the signs of disease; **Symphys'iology** (+ PHYSIOLOGY), the science of correlation (Gams).

Synandrod'ium, applied to the imperfect flower of the aroid *Mangonia* Schott.

Synanth'ody, side-growth of two flower-heads on the same stalk, or on two long-drawn-out stalks (Penzig).

Synap'sis, *add*, by recent observers used for the entire period from the contraction of the nucleus until the spireme segments into chromosomes (Gates); **Synaptosper'my** (σπέρμα, a seed), plants with seeds germinating close at home, instead of being dispersed at maturity (Murbeck); **Synchorol'ogy** (χωρέω, I spread abroad; λόγος, discourse), distribution of plant associations

(Rübel); adj. **synchorolog'ic**, as ~ **Geobot'any**, or ecology in a wide sense; **Synchronol'ogy** (χρόνος = time), plant distribution in time, that is, fossil species and their duration during geological periods (Gams); **Syncot'yls** = SYNCOTYLEDONS.

Syndin'ial Mito'sis, in the peridinial genus *Syndin'ium*, taking place without an achromatic spindle being formed, the chromosomes breaking apart (Chatton).

Synecol'ogy (+ ECOLOGY), (1) the relation between the plant association and its habitat (Rübel); (2) the ecology of communities (Turesson); **dynam'ic** or **genet'ic** ~, the study of plant communities as the result of biotic factors; **geograph'ic** ~, distribution of plant communities influenced by factors of environment; **morpholog'ical** and **physiolog'ical** ~, physiognomy, ecologic structure and floristic composition of plant communities as related to factors of environment (Waterman); adj. **synecolog'ic**; **Syngam'eons** (γάμος, marriage), pairing communities, frequently taken for superspecies, formerly styled LINNEONS.

Syngen'esis (συγγενής, of same descent), (1) formation of the embryo in sexual reproduction of male and female elements; (2) the origin of a species in mass (Stephanos); **Syngenet'ics**, change of plant associations (Rübel); **syngenet'ic Geobot'any** = Synecol'ogy, the ecologic investigation of plant communities (Schroeter).

syn'gynous, epigynous; **Syn'gyny**, epigyny.

Synize'sis *add*, (συνίζησις, collapse), distinguished by Gates from SYNAPSIS for its tightly contracted phase of the nucleus.

Synkar'yon (κάρυον, a nut), the fusion of pronuclei in the zygote (Minchin).

Synu'sia, pl. -ae, sometimes printed as **Synu'sium**, pl. -ia (συνουσία, a gathering), life-forms associated in growth and habitat, but distinct as to affinity (Gams); further distinguished as (1) composed of the same species; (2) of different species but the same class of life-forms; (3) different life-forms but an ecological unit by fixed correlation, *i.e.* an association; **synusiolog'ic** = ECOLOGIC.

Synzo'ospores (+ ZOOSPORE), large, solitary zoogonidia in *Vaucheria* DC. (West).

Syste'maty, classification by academic systems (Church) = systematic or taxonomic botany.

T, used by Church for terminal; **T′,** second series (?).

tab'ular, *add,* (2) placular (Janet).

Tachygen'esis (γένεσις, origin), embryonic acceleration.

Tai'ga, Siberian primeval forest (Warming).

Tamarice'tum, an association of *Tamarix* Linn.

tanninif'erous (*fero,* I bear), yielding tannin.

Tap'estry (τάπης, a carpet), applied to forest growth on steep slopes, forming an unbroken arboreous mantle.

Taut'onym (ταυτό, the same; ὄνομα, a name), a name in which the specific name merely repeats the generic, as *Linaria Linaria* Karst. (Sprague).

taxadin'eous, related to *Taxodium* Rich.

tax'oid, resembling or allied to *Taxus* Tourn.; **Tax'oids,** seeds of conifers, more or less succulent, solitary, and dispersed by birds (Church).

Tectone'tum, an association of *Tectona* Thunb.

tegulic'olous (*tegula,* a tile; *colo,* I inhabit), used for lichens living upon tiles (A. L. Smith).

Teleplast'ids (τέλος, an end, + PLASTID) reproductive cells (Janet); **Tel'eplasts,** products of division forming a merism (*id.*); **Teliosor'us**

(+ SORUS), Harshberger's term for TELEUTOSORUS.

telmic'olous (*colo,* I dwell), dwelling in fresh-water marshes.

Telosyn'desis (+ SYNDESIS), *cf.* TELO-SYNAPSIS; **Telosynap'sis** (+ SYNAP-SIS), **Telosynap'tist,** one who regards each parallel thread of the heterotype prophase as half of a somatic chromosome which separated in the preceding telophase; *cf.* PARASYNAPTIST (Digby); **Tela-syn'desis** (+ SYNDESIS), *cf. supra.*

Terato'ma, an abnormal growth of leaf-tissue in crown-galls, due to bacteria.

terrip'etal (*petere,* to seek), Bronn's term for gravitation shown by plants; **Terripra'ta** (*pratum,* a meadow), the covering of meadows, grasses.

Tetradsporang'ium (+ SPORANGIUM), a tetrad mother-cell (Church); **tet'rakont** (κοντός, a pole), having four equal flagella (Church); **tetra-so'mic** (σῶμα, a body), tetra-ploid; **tetrasporif'erous** (*fero,* I bear), producing tetraspores; **Tetraspor'ophyte** (+ SPOROPHYTE), a plant which bears tetraspores; **tetrasterigmat'ic** (+ STERIGMA), having four sterigmata to each basidium (Buller); **tetrav'alent** (*valens,* strong), having hypothetically four chromosomes in each apparent single one, in nuclear reduction divisions (Marchal).

Thal'lea, a mass formed of several layers of plastids, but a single merid (Janet); **Thal'leosere** (+ SERE) = PROTEOSERE (Clements); **Thal'lochlore** (χλωρός, pale green), the green colouring matter of lichens (Paulson); **Thal'loid Cli'-maxes,** in the pre-Devonian period, consisting of bryophytes (Clements).

thelyton'ic (τόνος, strain), gyneco-genic, *i.e.* parthenogenetic (Janet).

Thermocleistog'amy (+ CLEISTO-GAMY), fertilization of unex-panded flowers, due to want of heat (Knuth); **thermogen'ic** (γένος, offspring), heat-producing, as in the case of certain bacteria; **thermotac'tic** (τακτικός, apt for tactics), heat perceptive as shown by growth.

thinic'olous (*colo*, I dwell), dwelling on shifting sand dunes (Warming).

Thiobacter'ia (θεῖον, sulphur, + BACTERIA), sulphur-oxidizing bacteria; **thiogen'ic** (γένος, offspring), sulphur-producing; **thiorhoda'ceous**, belonging to Thiorhodaceae, a family of bacteria; **thiox'idans**, bacteria oxidizing sulphur compounds to sulphates.

Thlaspie'tum, an association of *Thlaspi* Dill.

Thread, the longitudinal half of an entire univalent spireme or chromosome (Digby); **Thread-ring**, spireme halves in karyokinesis (Balls).

Thyme'tum, an association of *Thymus* Linn.

Tier, a stage or layer.

tiled [monosyll.], Withering's term for imbricate overlapping.

Till, the product of glaciation, ground moraine; **Till'ite**, the same when fossil (Clements).

tiphic'olous (*colo*, I dwell), ponddwelling.

Tjemo'ro, an aphyllous forest, formed chiefly of *Casvarina* Linn., in Java (Warming).

Tolypotriche'tum, an association of *Tolypothrix* Kütz.

Trabec'ulae of Sanio, *cf.* SANIO.

Trans'ect, it may be **Belt** ∼; (denu'ded or per'manent) **Lay'er** ∼, or **Li'ne** ∼ (Clements).

Transil'ients (*transilio*, I leap across), Galton's term for MUTATIONS (I).

Tre'malith (τρῆμα, a hole), having a hole through the structure (Lohmann).

Tri'chome Hy'dathodes (+ HYDATHODE), hair-like organs secreting moisture in Agaricineae (Knoll).

Trichophore'tum, an association of *Trichophorus* Desv.

trichromoso'mal, concerned with three chromosomes (Frost).

Tricot'yl (+COTYLEDON), *cf.* TRICOTYLEDONY; adj. **tricot'ylous**; **Trigen'er** (*genus*, kind), the product from three genera (Hurst); **Trihy'brid**, Church's term for a hypothetical working of three factors at once; **Trihy'bridism** is the condition; **trim'erous**, *add*, (2) seedlings with three cotyledons, and as many primordial leaves; **Trim'ery**, the possession of trimerous members (Salisbury); **trimo'dal**, three forms or modes; **Trimodal'ity** is the state (Engledow); **trimonoe'cious**, *cf.* TRIMONOECISM; **trip'lex**, three dominant factors (Blakeslee); **trip'loid**, *add*, used loosely for hybrids between forms one of which has twice as many chromosomes as the other; **Triploi'dy**, the state in question; **triplost'ichous** (στίχός, a row), three rows of cortical cells to each branchlet or bract-cell in Charads; **triso'me**, **triso'mic** (σῶμα, a body), triploid (Blakeslee); **tristerigmat'ic**, having three sterigmata to each basidium (Buller); **Trisyncot'yls**, having three cotyledons fused for half their length (Bexon); **trizy'gous** (ζυγός, a yoke), dependent on three pairs of chromosomes.

Tritice'tum, an association of *Triticum junceum* Linn., and other congeneric species.

triv'alent (*valens*, power), having apparently three chromosomes in each single one, in nuclear reductions.

Trophochro'matin (+ CHROMATIN), vegetative chromidia (Minchin); **Troph'ocyte** (κύτος, a hollow vessel), a zygote, or fusion cell (Phillips); **Trophone'ma** (νῆμα, a thread), a synonym of PLASMONEMA, as conveying nutriment (Janet).

Tu'ba or **Tube**, *add*, (3) = STYLE, used by Vaillant, and Haller; **Tubenu'cleus**, named by Church as delimited from the male prothallus of *Pinus* Linn.

Tu'bercle, *add*, (5) the bulbil of Charads; **Tuberid'ium**, pl. -ia, the pseudo-bulb of an orchid (Reichenbach); **tuber'iform** (*forma*, shape), tuber-like.

Tu'mor-strands, conveying infection into healthy tissue and inducing the growth of galls.

Tur'gor Pres'sure, the pressure of protoplasm on the cell-wall (Salisbury).

Tur'io, Tur'ion, *add*, (2) used by Mrs. Arber for winter-buds, such as those of *Hydrocharis* Linn.

Turn'ing Cells, three small cells at the base of the oogonium of *Nitella*, derived from one at the base of the oosphere.

ty'phaceous, akin to or resembling *Typha* Tourn.

Ty'ponym (ὄνομα, a name), an older name than the current one, based on the same type (U.S. rule).

-ule, for SOCIES, as Sedule, Silenule, etc. (Clements).

Ulice'tum, an association of *Ulex* Linn.

ulna'ceous, pertaining to *Ulna* Linn.

ultra-microscop'ic (σκοπέω, I see), beyond visibility by modern microscopic means.

um'belloid, somewhat umbellate.

undec'uple, eleven sets of chromosomes (Blakeslee).

unifa'cial, reduction to one surface from bifacial; " suppression of adaxial surface " (Adamson); **u'ni-indu'siate,** having only one indusium, as *Cheilanthes* Sw. (Bower); **unilat'eral,** *add*, (2) ~ **Segrega'tion,** when confined to one sex (Bateson); **unimo'dal,** confined to one shape or make (Engledow); **Unimodal'ity,** the state in question; **uni'strate** (*stratum*, a layer), when leaf-indumentum is of one kind and persistent (Balfour).

Urcaul'ome (Ur, Germ. = first, + CAULOME), the primitive stem (Potonié).

urti'cal, urticaceous.

Vaccine'tum, Vaccinie'tum, an association of *Vaccinium* Linn.

Vac'uome, composed of metachromatic

corpuscles in vacuoles of *Selaginella* Spring (Dangeard).

Vag'in, a brown colouring substance in certain ferns, " a form of phlebotannin " (Bäseke); **Vag'inule,** the withered basal portion of an archegonium enclosing the base of the sporogonium (Worsdell).

Varia'tion, *add,* **anal'ogous** ~ or **par'allel** ~, similar variations in allied species; **homol'ogous** ~, in distinct species from a morphological point of view, colour, shape, etc. (Vavilow).

Varie'tum, an association of various species of *Festuca* Linn.

Vegeta'tion Forms, usually divided as monocarpic and polycarpic (Warming), or woody plants, perennial and annual herbs.

velam'inous, used of roots possessing velamen (Moss).

Veld (Dutch), used for all native vegetation from rich forest on the south-east coast of South Africa to desert in interior Karroo (Pole Evans).

Ven'tral Plate, cover of the ventral area in Peridineae (Kofoid).

vexil'lar (Worsdell), vexillary.

Vicar'ial Spe'cies, applied to elementary or micro-species (Turesson).

Vid'uae, pl. (*viduus*, bereft), used by Crantz for unisexual plants or flowers.

Vina'cea, pl. (Lat.), grape stones.

vi'oletiform, Greene's expression for violaceous.

Viride'tum, an association of *Alnus viridis* DC.

Vi'tamines, accessory food-factors in plants, of catalytic nature; also termed food-hormones, sitacoids, vitellites, advitants; A is fat-soluble, in green leaves; B, water-soluble, abundant in legumes; C, anti-scorbutic; the others, D and E, are but little known as yet.

vixgregar'ious, Clements's term for sparse vegetation.

volvo'cean, belonging to *Volvox* (Janet).

Volu'tin, a reserve material in grains for the nucleo-proteids of the

472

chromatin substance in *Spirillum volutans* Ehrenb. (Minchin).

Wa′ter-con′tent, the amount held in tissue or soil; ~ **Loss,** amount removed by some natural event or artificial operation.

Welwitschie′tum, an association of *Welwitschia* Hook f.

Wiesner′s Law, refers to leaf-position with regard to light for maximum illumination.

wor′king, an expression for " breaking of the meres," as of *Oscillatoria prolifica* Gomont in a lake in New York Botanic Garden.

x chromosome, one which conveys the quality of sex.

Xenautog′amy (+ AUTOGAMY), with homogamous flowers, favouring cross-pollination, but self-fertile under adverse conditions (Robertson); **Xe′niophyte** (φυτόν, a plant), the endosperm of Angiosperms, constituting a third generation hitherto overlooked, now sporophyte, gametophyte and xenophyte (Trelease); **Xenodoch′ae** pl. (δοχή, succession), COSERES and CLISERES; anomalous successions (Gams).

Xer′arch (ἀρχή, beginning), succession originating in a dry area (Cooper); **Xerocleistog′amy** (+CLEISTOGAMY), pollination in closed flowers on account of dryness (Hansgirg); **Xer′ocline** (κλίνω, to recline), a dry, warm slope (Clements); **Xerodry′mium** (δρυμός, coppice), dry thicket; *cf.* DURISILVAE; **Xeroge′ophytes** (+GEOPHYTE), plants whose rest period is in dry periods (Massart); **Xer′oid Ar′eas,** pre-Devonian algal climax (Clements); **Xerophor′bium** (φορβάς, feeding), tundra, dunes (Diels); **Xeropoi′um** (+ POIUM), steppes (Diels); in a dry area (Cooper); **Xer′osere** (+ SERE), a succession with reference to the scanty water-content of the bare area; its subsidiary seres are LITHOSERES and PSAMMOSERES (Gams); **xerotrop′ic** (τροπή, a turning), reaction towards a dry

succession (Clements); **xerotac′tic** (τακτικός, fit for order), applied to successions not greatly changing (*id.*); **Xylopod′ium** ~, pl. -ia, *add,* (2) more or less stony, hard, tuberous thickening of the roots and underground parts of shrubs in Brazil in the steppe regions (Lindman).

Zeu′xis (ζεῦξις, a joining), Frost′s expression for chromosomal heredity.

Zo′ïd, applied also to a zoospore or swarm-spore (Church); **zoïdogam′ic** (γάμος, marriage), fertilized by zoïds (Wieland); **Zoïdog′amy** (γάμος, marriage), fertilization by antherozoïds; **Zoïd′iospore** (+ SPORE), plants whose seeds are dispersed by animals (Clements); **Zona′tion,** *add,* (3) separation of the ooplasm from the periplasm in *Phytophthora* De Bary (Murphy); **Zoochlorel′lae,** pl., a symbiotic form of *Chlorella* Beyer., associated with infusoria (West); **zooch′orous** (χωρέω, I retire), distributed · by animals (Rübel); **Zoogonidang′ium** (+GONIDANGIUM), an organ containing zoogonidia, said to be (*a*) **fun′nel** ~, always terminal; (*b*) **ses′sile** ~, discharging from side or terminal; (*c*) **stalked** ~, from side or end; (*d*) **ter′minal** ~, from its apical cell (Brand); **Zooxanthel′lae,** pl., holophytic flagellates containing a yellow pigment.

Zygneme′tum, an association of *Zygnema* Ag.

Zygogen′esis (γένεσις, origin), derived from sexual union; adj. **zygogen′ic**; **Zygone′ma** (νῆμα, a thread), when at the role of a nucleus the leptotene threads fuse in pairs (Agar); *adj.* **zy′gotene**; **Zygo-pachyne′ma** (+ PACHYNEMA), the transitional condition of the meiotic nucleus in which heavy pachytene threads are fusing side by side to form a zygoma.

zygop′terid, zygopteride′an, relating to the fossil genus *Zygopteris* Corda.

Zymol′ogist, a student of the course of fermentation (Harshberger).

APPENDIX A

SIGNS AND ABBREVIATIONS

⊙ annual, usually monocarpic; (also = therophytes).

① strictly annual.

② or ☉ biennial.

♃ perennial; (also = hemicryptophytes).

♄ a tree, or with a woody trunk; (also = chamaephytes).

♂ male; ♀ female; ♀ or ☿ hermaphrodite (used when it is exceptional). ♂ also used for antheridia. ♀ also used for oogamia.

∞ indefinite, employed when the number is too great to be easily counted, as stamens or ovules.

× hybrid; when placed between the names of species, to be read as "fertilized with - pollen from"; also used to denote the magnifying power in figures or plates.

! seen by the author: thus *Aotus villosa*, Sm. !, means that the type specimen, or a specimen ticketed by Smith, has been verified by inspection; if appended to a collector's number, that is verified, as Burchell 3641 !

* employed in divers senses, as (1) by Linnaeus, De Candolle and others to indicate that a good description or figure will be found at the place cited; (2) when between the specific name and a third appended name, denotes a subspecies; (3) in an index, shows that the genus, species, or variety, was ostensibly first published at the place indexed.

† an obscure or doubtful species.

§ section, the division of a genus.

= equals, the sign of a synonym.

± more or less.

> greater than, < less than.

+ for spores whose nuclei are presumably male; — for spores whose nuclei are presumably female; cf. PLUS, MINUS.

⊕ tetrasporangia; ø o, used by Phillips for cystocarp.

° ′ ″ or ′ ″ ‴ have been used for feet, inches, and lines respectively.

μ micromillimetre, the one-thousandth of a millimetre.

The positions of the cotyledons of Cruciferae in the seed are denoted thus: o=, accumbent; o||, incumbent; <<o, conduplicate; o || ||, spirolobous; o || || || for those of the Diplecolobeae.

Dates of flowering are sometimes shown in floras by the numbers of the months, either in Roman or Arabic numerals, as IV–VI, or 4–6.

A   (1) in plan of flower, for Androecium; (2) by H. Mueller, used to denote a flower with free honey; (3) in Mendelian formulae = dominant.

a   = recessive, as in formula 1A : 2A*a* : 1*a* in a monohybrid cross.

AB   for a flower with concealed honey (H. Mueller).

B   flower with wholly concealed nectar (H. Mueller).

char.   character.

cm.   centimetre.

D.V.   dorsiventral (Church).

fem.   *feminea*, female.

F_0 pure parental type.

F_1 first filial generation; F_2, second filial generation, etc.

fl.	*flos* or floret.	pH.	hydrogen ion concentration in soils.
fr.	*fructus* or fruit.		
G	in plan of flower for Gynoecium.	Po.	pollen-flowers (H. Mueller).
		p.p.	*pro parte*, partly ; on the title-page of a thesis it stands for *publice proponit*.
gen.	genus.		
H	hymenopterous flowers (H. Mueller).		
H+.	*see* pH, H-ion.	ppm.	parts per millions.
Hab.	*Habitatio, habitat.*	R_1, R_2.	roots, primary and secondary.
Hb., Herb.	Herbarium, as *Herb. Lugd. Bat.*, the Herbarium of the Leyden University.		
		s.s.	*sensu stricto.*
		T.	terminal (Church).
		T'.	terminal second series (?)
I	symbol of self-fertile plant.	sp.	*species ;* spp., two or more species.
I_1	= F_1.		
I_2	= F_2.	t. or tab.	*tabula*, plate; t. sometimes, but rarely, means *tomus*, volume.
Ic.	*Icon*, pl. *Icones*, figures; *Ic. xyl.*, a woodcut.		
ined.	*ineditus*, unpublished; it either remains in manuscript or is about to be published.	T.S.	transverse section.
		U.V.	forms assumed by chromosomes during nuclear division.
l.c.	*loco citato*, in the place mentioned; ll. cc. *locis citatis*, in the places mentioned; to avoid repetition of titles.	V.B.	vascular bundle.
		v.s.c.	*vidi siccam cultam*, I have seen a dried cultivated specimen.
		v.s.s.	*vidi siccam spontaneam*, I have seen a dried wild specimen.
J	Geophytes.		
L.S.	longitudinal section.		
Lin.	a line in measurement, *linea*, the twelfth of an inch: 2·116665 mm.	v.v.c.	*vidi vivam cultam*, I have seen a living cultivated specimen.
m.	metre : 39·370113 ins.	v.v.s.	*vidi vivam spontaneam*, I have seen a living wild specimen.
masc.	*masculus*, male.		
mm.	millimetre, the one-thousandth of a metre; ·039370 in.	v.	shrub.
		x-generation, the gametophyte, as the prothallus of a Fern.	
M.R.	medullary ray.		
M.R.P.	med. ray parenchyma.		
M.R.T.	medullary ray tracheids (Church).	$2x$-generation, the sporophyte, as a developed Fern.	
n.	*numerus*, number.	x and y.	chromosomes conveying the quality of sex.
n.	haploid generation.		
2*n.*	diploid generation.	*y*.	trees.
N ions.	phosphorus in plankton (Church).	α	= female, as a gamete.
		β	= male, as a gamete.
Nat. Ord.	Natural Order, *Ordo naturalis.*	φ	= (1) form ; (2) ratio.
o.	ornithopterous flowers (H. Mueller).	Names of authors when long are properly abbreviated by giving the first syllable and the first consonant of the second, as *Lam.* for *Lamarck ;* when there are more of the same name, an initial or other sign is	
p.	*pagina*, page.		
P.	original parent generation.		
P ions.	*cf.* pH.		

added. The latest list is to be found in Gray's *Botanical Text-book*, ed. 6, pp. 385–390.

Parentheses are sometimes used to show synonymy in a compact form, as *Mycena tenella* (Fr.) Sacc., which, if expanded, would read *Mycena tenella*, Saccardo; syn. *Agaricus tenellus*, Fries. (Parentheses if misapplied lead to grave error.)

Special signs will be found in many works, but their use is usually explained, as in Eichler's " Blüthendiagramme," or Pfeffer's signs for diatropism, etc. For longer lists refer to Candolle (A. P. de), "Systema Vegetabilium," i. pp. 12, 13; Trattinick (L.), " Synodus," i. pp. 13, 14; Loudon (J. C.), " Hortus Britannicus," " En-cyclopaedia of Plants," and " Arboretum "; Lindley (J.), " Introduction to Botany," ed. 1, pp. 422–431.

The meaning of chemical signs, such as CO_2 for carbon dioxide, H_2O, water, and the like, must be obtained from a text-book of chemistry.

Lichenologists employ certain signs when chemically testing Lichens, as CaCl —, no reaction by hypochlorite of lime, or K—, none by hydrate of potash; the latter reagent is noted also by K=, K±, K‡, etc. *Cf.* Leighton's " Lichen-flora of Great Britain," ed. 3, 1879, p. xv.

Floral Clock, *see* Linn., " Phil. Bot." (1751), pp. 272–275; Kerner, " Nat. Hist. Pl.," Engl. ed., ii. pp. 215–218.

SPECIAL SYMBOLS FOR UREDINOUS FUNGI

O = Spermagones : I. Aecidia; II. Uredospores; III. Teleutospores, with ensuing Basidiospores.

O. I, II, III. a Eu-form :—
Auteu-form, if all four are on one plant. Hetereu-form, if O.I on one plant, and II, III on another.

O. I, III.   an Opsis-form.
O. II, III.   a Brachy-form.
II, III.   a Hemiform (sometimes half of a Hetereu-form.

[O] III.   a Micro-form (spermagones sometimes absent).

APPENDIX B

THE PRONUNCIATION OF LATIN AND LATINIZED WORDS

The old or traditional method is as follows :—

a short, as in fat.			a long, as in gave.		
e	,,	pet.	e	,,	evil.
i	,,	thin.	i	,,	ice.
o	,,	not.	o	,,	note.
u	,,	tub.	u	,,	tube.
y	,,	cygnet.	y	,,	cypress.

ae, oe, as in feet, ei as in eye, au as in bawl.
and g hard before a, o, u; soft before e, i, y; ch as k.

The modern or continental method :—

a	short, as in	apart.	a long, as in	psalm.
e	„	lend.	e	„	vein.
i	„	thin.	i	„	seen.
o	„	not.	o	„	note.
u	„	full.	u	„	rule.

y short, like German ü, and French u.
ae, oe, ei, practically as in pain.
au   as in house.
c and g   always hard, as in cut and good.
ch   as in Christian.

APPENDIX C

THE USE OF THE TERMS "RIGHT" AND "LEFT"

These terms are but seldom required in botanic descriptions, being only used to denote the direction of a twist or spiral. Unfortunately they have been employed in opposite senses, so that the meaning of one author may be completely perverted by his misuse of the correct method. In zoology, where bilateral symmetry is common, these terms are always applied to the limbs or organs of an animal with regard to its axis, and the majority of botanists have carried out the same idea with regard to plants. A spiral may be considered as turning to the right or the left, that is, two spirals may run in contrary directions, but the same spiral may be differently designated according to the position of the observer. The orthodox way regards the observer as being placed within while noting the direction of the twist, as if he were looking south, and recording the apparent passage of the sun from his left towards his right; this, *dextrorse*, is the common acceptance of " with the sun " or " like the clock hands "; it is also the motion of driving home a screw, which receives its name of " right-handed " from the motion, and not from the aspect of the pitch of its threads.

A few observers have disregarded these considerations, and have placed their point of view outside the spiral. The result of this is to reverse the terms, for a dextrorse climbing plant then seems to pass from right to left, which they then term *sinistrorse*. If we ascend a spiral staircase constantly bearing to our right, we are describing a right-handed spiral, and the staircase is also dextrorse. Many climbing plants, as the Hop and the Honeysuckle, take this course, others, as the White Convolvulus and Scarlet Runner, take the opposite.

Torsion of the corolla is sometimes highly characteristic, as in some genera of Apocyneae and Myrsineae. It has been recommended that a few words should be added to define the position of the observer, as *e centro visum*, or *externe visum*, as the case may be. For a fuller discussion of these points reference should be made to Alphonse de Candolle, " La Phytographie," pp. 201–208, O. B. Clarke in the *Journal of the Linnean Society*, xviii. (1881), 468–473, and R.. H. Compton, in the *Journal of Genetics*, ii. (1912), 53–70. Short notices will also be found in *Journ. Bot.* ix. (1871), 216, 333,; *Gard. Chron.*, N.S. vii. (1877), 48, 147, 280, 630; *id.* Ser. III. lxii. (1917), 125; *Beitr. z. Bot. Centralb.*, Orig. Arb. xli. (1925), 51–81, Taf. 1–4; *Bot. Zeit.* lix. (1901), 379—381.

APPENDICES

The botanists who have used DEXTRORSE and SINISTRORSE in the sense defined in this Glossary are A. P. de Candolle and his son Alphonse de Candolle, Alexander Braun, G. W. Bischoff, J. C. Doell, W. P. Hiern, J. S. Henslow, H. von Mohl, C. Naegeli, A. F. Schlotthauber, and L. H. Palm; those in the contrary sense are G. Bentham, Asa Gray, A. W. Eichler, C. R. Darwin, and Sir J. D. Hooker. Linnaeus's definition is confused by examples, most of which contradict his words, while a correction in his " Errata " nullifies the text; see " Philosophia botanica " (1751), 39, 103 note, 310.

APPENDIX D

BIBLIOGRAPHY

FUCHS (LEONARD). Explicatio quarundam vocum toto hoc opere passim occurrentium in quibus assequendis non admodum peritus lector haerere posset. De hist. stirpium comm. Basil. 1542. Sig. β3–β4 verso.

KYBER (DAVID). Lexicon rei herbariae trilingue . . . item Tabulae . . . per XII menses in usum conscriptae per Conradum GESNERUM. Argentorati, 1553, pp. 548, praef. Sm. 8vo.
    The author died of the plague during the printing of the book, and Gesner saw it through the press from *Elate* onwards. The prefatory matter is addressed to LUKE KYBER, the author's father.
    The early phenology of the " Tabulae," pp. 467–548, is worth notice.

RAY (JOHN), *latinized* RAIUS. Terminorum quorundam et vocum generaliorum interpretatio et explicatio brevis.
    Forms pp. 84–99 of Part II. of his anonymous " Catalogus plantarum circa Cantabrigiam nascentium," *etc.*, 1660; reprinted with some alterations in his " Historia plantarum," 1686. He embodies several of Jung's terms from a MS. list, which he acknowledges.

JUNG (JOACHIM), *latinized* JUNGIUS. Isagoge phytoscopica, ut ab ipso privatis in collegiis solita fuit tradi . . . recensente Jo. VAGETIO. Hamburgi [1678]. 4to.
    Posthumous; the author died in 1657.

LINNÉ (CARL VON), *latinized* LINNAEUS. Termini botanici, *Resp.* JOHAN ELMGREN. Upsaliae, 1762. 4to. Reprinted in Amoenitates Academicae, vi. 217–246.
    A succinct statement of terms which were previously set out at greater length in his " Philosophia botanica," etc.

BERKENHOUT (JOHN). Clavis anglica linguae botanicae; or a botanical Lexicon in which the terms of botany . . . are applied, derived, explained, contrasted, and exemplified.
    London, 1764. Sm. 8vo.—2nd ed. ib. 1789. 8vo.

LEE (JAMES). A glossary; explaining the technical terms in botany : in alphabetical order. (Forms pp. 449–479 of Lee's " Introduction," ed. 2. London, 1765; believed to be drawn up by SAMUEL GRAY, from Berkenhout's " Clavis.")

MILNE (COLIN). A Botanical Dictionary. London, 1770. 8vo.—Ed. 2, ib. 1778.—Ed. 3, ib. 1805.

LEERS (JOHANN DAVID). Nomenclator Linnaeanus seu explicatio terminorum technicorum in hoc opusculo occurrentium ordine alphabetico exhibita. Forms pp. i.–lix. of his "Flora herbornensis," Herbornae Nassoviorum, 1775. 8vo.—Ed. altera [a WILLDENOW]. Berolini, 1789. 8vo.; in this edition the "Nomenclator" is paged xxv.–lxxviii.

BULLIARD (JEAN BAPTISTE FRANÇOIS PIERRE). Dictionnaire élémentaire de botanique ou exposition alphabétique des préceptes de la botanique. Paris, 1783, fol. Ib. 1797, fol. Ed. revue . . . par L. C. RICHARD, Paris an VII [1798], 8vo. "Ed. II." ib. 1802, 8vo.; Ed. III. ib. 1812, fol.

MARTYN (THOMAS). The Language of Botany : being a dictionary of the terms made use of in that science, principally by Linnaeus, etc. London, 1793.—Ed. 2, 1796.—Ed. 3, 1807. 8vo.

HAYNE (FRIEDRICH GOTTLOB). Termini botanici iconibus illustrati, oder botanische Kunstsprache durch Abbildungen erläutert. Berlin, 1807. 8vo.

THÉIS (ALEXANDRE DE). Glossaire de botanique, ou dictionnaire étymologique de tous les noms et termes relatifs à cette science. Paris, 1810. 8vo.

DUPPA (RICHARD). A Dictionary of Botanical Terms [in Latin]. *In :* Classes and Orders of the Linnean System. London, 1816. 8vo. [79 unnumbered pages in the third volume.]

GERARDIN, DE MIRECOURT (SÉBASTIEN). Dictionnaire raisonné de botanique . . . publié, revu et augmenté . . . par Mr. N. A. DESVAUX, etc. A Paris, 1817. 8vo.

GRAY (SAMUEL FREDERICK). A Natural Arrangement of British Plants . . . with an introduction to botany, in which the terms newly introduced are explained, etc. London, 1821. 2 vols. 8vo.
    Contains :—Explanation of the terms used in botany, i. 36–227; Index of terms, i. 799, 800.

LLOYD (GEORGE N.). Botanical Terminology, or a dictionary explaining the terms most generally employed in systematic botany. Edinburgh, 1826. 8vo.

LECOQ (HENRI) et J. JUILLET. Dictionnaire raisonné des termes de botanique et des familles naturelles. Paris, 1831. 8vo.
    Special attention is given in this work to the derivations, especially those from the Greek.

JOURDON (ANTOINE JACQUES LOUIS). Dictionnaire raisonné . . . des termes usités dans les sciences naturelles, comprenant . . . la botanique, etc. Paris, 1834. 2 vols. 8vo.

BISCHOFF (GOTTLIEB WILHELM). Handbuch der botanischen Terminologie und Systemkunde. Nürnberg, 1833–44. 3 vols. 4to.

LINDLEY (JOHN). An introduction to Botany. Ed. 2. London, 1835. 8vo.
    Contains :—Book III. Glossology; or, of the Terms used in Botany, pp. 370–432; Index I. Substantives, 563–570. II. Adjectives, 570–580.— Ed. 3, 1839.—Ed. 4, 1848. 2 vols.—The Glossary separate, 1848.

KEITH (REV. PATRICK). A Botanical Lexicon, or Expositor of the Terms, Facts, and Doctrines of the Vegetable Physiology, brought down to the present time. London, 1837. 8vo.

BISCHOFF (GOTTLIEB WILHELM). Wörterbuch der beschreibenden Botanik oder die Kunstausdrücke . . . Lateinisch-deutsch . . . alphabetisch geordnet und erklärt. Stuttgart, 1839. 8vo.—Ed. 2. von J. A. SCHMIDT, ib. 1857. 8vo.

LINDLEY (JOHN). The Elements of Botany . . . being a sixth edition of the " Outline " . . . and a Glossary of Technical Terms. London, 1849. 8vo.
   The Glossary of Technical Terms forms Part II., pp. 1–100; it has been in constant use for the present work, and is cited as " Glossary "; 443 woodcuts; no derivation or key to pronunciation given.

HENSLOW (REV. JOHN STEVENS). A Dictionary of Botanical Terms. London [1849–56 ?]. 8vo.
   Constantly used for this volume; it was partly issued with Maund's " Botanic Garden," but completed by itself : there are 190 small woodcuts in the text. Derivations and accents marked throughout. Re-issued with new, undated, title-page in 1858, 1875, and 1882.

HOEFER (FERDINAND). Dictionnaire de botanique pratique. Paris, 1850. 8vo.

COOKE (MORDECAI CUBITT). Manual of Botanic Terms. London [1862]. 8vo. With 293 figures.—Ed. 2, slightly enlarged, ib. [1871]. 8vo. With 307 figures.

GERMAIN DE ST. PIERRE (ERNEST). Guide du botaniste, etc. Paris, 1852. 2 vols. 8vo.
   Contains :—Seconde partie, Livre cinquième.—Dictionnaire raisonne des mots techniques, français et latin, employés dans les ouvrages de botanique.—Ed. 2. Nouveau dictionnaire de botanique, comprenant la description des familles naturelles, etc. Paris, 1870. 8vo.
   I am indebted to this excellent work for the plan of denoting a substantive by a capital letter (previously so employed by A. P. de Candolle), and the use of italic type for Latin words.

GRAY (ASA). The Botanical Text-book. (Sixth edition.) Part I. Structural Botany . . . and a Glossary of Botanical Terms. New York and Chicago, 1879. 8vo.
   The Glossary occurs at pp. 393–442, and may be described as the basis of the present work as regards the definition of terms used in descriptive botany.

STORMONTH (REV. JAMES). A Manual of Scientific Terms . . . chiefly comprising terms in botany, etc. Edinburgh, 1879. 8vo.—Ed. 2. ib. 1885. 8vo.
   The arrangement in paragraphs and the style of type have been adapted in the present volume from the " Manual."

DU PORT (REV. JAMES MOURANT). On the Colours of the Fungi as indicated by the Latin words used by FRIES. Trans. Woolhope Club, 1883, 113.

CROZIER (ARTHUR ALGER). A Dictionary of Botanical Terms. New York, 1892. 8vo.
   Confined chiefly to modern terms, of which about 5600 are given, with the pronunciation marked, but no derivations.

HEINIG (ROBERT LAWRENCE). Glossary of the Botanic Terms used in describing Flowering Plants. Calcutta, 1899. 8vo.

An enumeration of about the same extent as the last, but including the names of many orders, and medical terms relating to the action of plants, as anti-dysenteric, dysentery, etc.

JACKSON (BENJAMIN DAYDON). A review of the Latin terms used in botany to denote colour. *Journ. Bot.* xxxvii. (1899) 97–106.

—— A glossary of botanic terms with their derivation and accent. London (Duckworth), 1900. 8vo.—Second edition, revised and enlarged, ib. 1905.—Third edition, again revised and enlarged, ib. 1916.

CLEMENTS (FREDERIC EDWARD). A system of nomenclature for phytogeography [with a note by Prof. A. Engler]. *Engl. Bot. Jahrb.* xxxi. (1902), Beibl. n. 70, pp. 1–20.

—— Glossary [of phytogeographic terms] consists of pp. 314–323 of his "Research Method in Ecology." Lincoln, Nebraska (University Publishing Co.), 1905. 8vo.

SCHNEIDER (CAMILLO KARL). Illustriertes Handwörterbuch der Botanik. Leipzig, 1905. 8vo.

BILANCIONI (GUGLIELMO). Dizionario di botanica generale. Milano, 1906. Sm. 8vo.

This and the previous volume are more like encyclopaedias than dictionaries, many articles being given at great length.

SHULL (GEORGE HARRISON). Genetic Definitions in the New Standard Dictionary. Amer. Natur. xlix. (1915), 52–59.

A critical redefinition of about thirty terms.

CLEMENTS (FREDERIC EDWARD). Plant Succession : an analysis of the development of vegetation. Washington, 1916. 8vo.

—— Plant Indicators : the relation of plant communities to process and practice. Washington, 1920. 8vo.

ARTSCHWAGER (ERNST) and EDWINIA W. SMILEY. A Dictionary of Botanical Equivalents (Fr.-Engl., Germ.-Engl.). Baltimore, 1920. 16mo.